PETERSON'S

PROFESSIONAL DEGREE PROGRAMS IN THE VISUAL AND PERFORMING ARTS 1996

Peterson's
Princeton, New Jersey

Editorial inquiries concerning this book should be addressed to the editor at Peterson's, P.O. Box 2123, Princeton, New Jersey 08543-2123.

ISSN 1073-2020
ISBN 1-56079-536-0

Design by Greg Wuttke for Peterson's and Carlisle Communications, Ltd.

Printed in the United States of America

10 9 8 7 6 5 4 3 2 1

Visit Peterson's Education Center on the Internet (World Wide Web) at http://www.petersons.com

CONTENTS

INTRODUCTION

Whether you're still in high school, have just graduated, or are already in college, you've opened this book because you are thinking about a career in the arts. Maybe you've *always* dreamed of performing on Broadway or playing in a symphony orchestra. Perhaps you've taken dance lessons since you were five years old. Or it could be that you feel you'd be a good art teacher but aren't very confident about your artistic talent. How can you begin to sort out your priorities and turn your dreams into reality?

This book, designed especially to help arts students identify the right college program to get them on their way toward achieving their professional goals, will help you answer questions like:

- Should you go to college? To what kind of school? A music conservatory? A large state university?
- Should you enroll in a Bachelor of Arts program or pursue the Bachelor of Fine Arts degree?
- What are your chances of getting into an arts program?
- How realistic are your worries that there are already enough "starving artists" in the world (whose ranks you certainly *don't* want to join)? Are your parents concerned too?

Peterson's Professional Degree Programs in the Visual and Performing Arts offers guidance from admissions counselors at top music, art, theater, and dance programs as well as detailed information on professional programs in each field offered at U.S. and Canadian institutions. At the end of the guide you'll also find an additional listing of *all* U.S. and Canadian schools that offer bachelor's-level degrees in the arts, most within a liberal arts context. The guide should be used as a *first step* when identifying potential programs; students are encouraged to consult with their school counselors and arts teachers for additional guidance.

The Professional Degree Versus the Liberal Arts Degree

Perhaps one of the largest difficulties you face as an arts student is deciding which kind of degree to pursue and at what type of school—the options may seem a little overwhelming.

Although the details vary from program to program and among art, dance, music, and theater, "professional" degrees—such as the Bachelor of Fine Arts or the Bachelor of Music—generally differ greatly from "liberal arts" degrees—the Bachelor of Arts and Bachelor of Science, for example. Professional degree programs are more likely to require that a much higher percentage of course work be in the chosen arts field—say, 75 percent. The remaining academic course work to be taken will most likely also incorporate the arts into its curriculum.

A student in a professional degree program will generally have a particular focus—an individual musical instrument or style, for example. A liberal arts degree student's studies will be more general, covering a wider range of subject areas, with less emphasis on performance or studio work. This is not to say that a liberal arts degree cannot prepare you for a career in your chosen field—these degrees may be especially appropriate for you if you are unsure of what specialty you want to pursue or if you do not yet want to close any other doors.

You may be unsure whether you want to pursue a degree at an institute that focuses solely on the arts or at a liberal arts college or university that provides a greater diversity in course offerings. Again, one choice is not necessarily better than the other—it depends on your goals. Many professional programs will be more competitive in the particular field you want to enter—your audition or portfolio review is then all-important. A liberal arts college or university may be more difficult academically; there your SAT scores, for example, will play a bigger role in the admissions decision. Perhaps you want to be around other artists all day, every day, surrounded by music practice rooms and other musicians or in the company of future sculptors and painters. Then a professional program may be appropriate for you. Perhaps you would like to focus on one of the arts but also have the opportunity to study history; then a liberal arts program may be more suitable than a professional degree program.

Remember, there is no "best" school, only the best school *for you*. Start examining your goals, your interests, your personality, and your talents. Read the articles of guidance that open each of the Program Descriptions sections in this book. Most importantly, talk to your teachers and guidance counselors.

Performing Arts College Fairs

The National Association of College Admission Counselors sponsors Performing Arts College Fairs each fall. These events are for college and college-bound students interested in pursuing undergraduate and graduate programs of study in the areas of music, dance, and theater. Attendees learn about educational and career opportunities, admission and financial aid, audition and entrance requirements, and other information by meeting with representatives from colleges, universities, conservatories, festivals, and other educational institutions. The fairs are scheduled in cities across the country.

For information about the 1996 Performing Arts College Fair schedule, call the Information Line at 703-836-2222.

How Is This Book Organized?

This book is divided into four main parts:

- Quick-Reference Chart of Programs
- Program Descriptions (divided into Art, Dance, Music, and Theater sections)
- Appendix of Bachelor's-Level Arts Programs
- Index of Schools

Quick-Reference Chart of Programs

If you want to find out quickly which professional degrees are offered by a specific school, turn to the **Quick-Reference Chart** on pages 11–36. Organized geographically, this chart provides the most basic information about each school in the guide:

- Institution name and location
- Professional degrees offered in music, art, theater, and dance
- Total school enrollment
- Tuition and fees

Program Descriptions

The **Program Descriptions** are divided into four sections: Art (beginning on page 39), Dance (beginning on page 199), Music (beginning on page 239), and Theater (beginning on page 471).

At the beginning of each the four sections you'll find invaluable information about the different types of programs available, what the admissions process entails (including auditions and portfolios), how to evaluate your own educational goals and needs, and what to look for in a program.

Program Descriptions appear following these articles. Listed in alphabetical order by institution name, these descriptions present the following facts about each school:

- school type and enrollment
- degrees offered and majors within each degree
- profile of arts students
- faculty
- student life, including student groups and special arts housing
- expenses (tuition and fees) and financial aid designated exclusively for arts students
- application information (including auditions or portfolio preparation)
- complete contact information

In addition, many schools have chosen to provide more detailed information about their program's facilities; faculty, resident artists, and alumni; student performance opportunities; and special programs. You'll find these Expanded Descriptions immediately following the school's short program description.

Program Descriptions profile "professional" programs that meet the following criteria:

- Colleges and universities offering programs are accredited baccalaureate degree–granting institutions in the United States and Canada. (Accreditation is through an organization recognized by the U.S. Department of Education or Canadian province.)
- The profiled institution grants one or more of the following undergraduate professional degrees in studio art, dance, music, or theater:

B.F.A.	Bachelor of Fine Arts
B.A./B.F.A.	Bachelor of Arts/Bachelor of Fine Arts dual degree
B.I.D.	Bachelor of Industrial Design
B.M.	Bachelor of Music
B.M.A.	Bachelor of Musical Arts

B.M.Ed. or B.M.E.	Bachelor of Music Education
B.S.M.	Bachelor of Sacred Music
B.M.T.	Bachelor of Music Therapy

Many of these institutions additionally offer advanced degrees at the master's or doctoral level:

M.F.A.	Master of Fine Arts
M.M.	Master of Music
M.M.A.	Master of Musical Arts
M.M.E. or M.M.Ed.	Master of Music Education
M.S.M.	Master of Sacred Music
M.M.T.	Master of Music Therapy
M.A.M.	Master of Arts Management
D.M.A.	Doctor of Musical Arts
D.A.	Doctor of Arts

Peterson's obtained program information through a questionnaire completed by music, art, theater, and dance program directors in the spring and summer of 1995. While the editors believe that the information in this book is accurate and up to date, Peterson's does not assume responsibility for the quality of the programs or the practices of the institutions. Students are encouraged to obtain as much information as possible from the schools themselves.

Appendix of Bachelor's-Level Arts Degree Programs

Many schools offer the Bachelor of Arts or Bachelor of Science degrees in art, dance, music, or theater either *in addition to* or *instead of* the professional degrees featured in the Program Descriptions sections. Such schools are listed alphabetically by institution name in the Appendix that begins on page 531. Information included after each institution name tells you if the school offers a degree in music, art, dance, or theater and provides complete contact information for each school.

Index

The index, which begins on page 609, lists every professional degree-granting institution in the guide and gives the page number(s) on which its Program Description(s) can be found.

Acknowledgments

The editors thank the many arts education professionals who generously gave their advice and encouragement throughout the planning stages of this guide, especially:

Teresa Bedoya, Maryland Institute, College of Art
Nadine Bourgeois, Parsons School of Design
Steven Estrella, Temple University
James Gandre, Manhattan School of Music
Bonita Matthews, University of Southern California
Judy McCumber, Syracuse University
Peter Sander, Hofstra University
Carol Walker, Purchase College, State University of New York

NATIONAL PORTFOLIO DAYS

Each year members of the National Portfolio Day Association sponsor National Portfolio Days in 35 cities across the nation and in Canada. These events provide an opportunity for the students interested in pursuing undergraduate or graduate study in the visual arts to meet with representatives from some of the most outstanding colleges, universities, and independent schools that teach art and design. Attendees have their portfolio of artwork reviewed and gain guidance about their future artistic development. Participating institutions also provide information about programs of study, careers in art, admission requirements, financial aid, and scholarships.

Posters announcing dates and locations are mailed in September to high school art departments, or call 1-800-639-4808 for more information.

COVERING YOUR COLLEGE COSTS: FINANCIAL AID BASICS

5

A college education is expensive: upwards of $100,000 for four years at some of the high-priced colleges and universities, and more than $50,000 even at lower-cost, state-supported colleges. Figuring out how you and your family will come up with the necessary funds to pay for your education in the arts requires planning, perseverance, and learning as much as you can about the options available.

For most families, paying the total cost of a student's college education out of savings is not possible. Obviously, the more the family has saved, the better off you will be, and the less you will need to earn and borrow. But paying for college should not be looked at merely as a four-year financial commitment. While some of the money you will need will likely come from funds that you and your parents have managed to save, some will come from a portion of your—or your parents'—current income. The rest will come from future earnings, through loans you or your parents will pay off later.

So if your family has not saved the total amount or does not earn enough, you can still attend college and, hopefully, the college of your choice. That's where financial aid comes in. The amount you and your family will have to contribute toward your college expenses will be based upon how much you and your family already have and how much you earn. But if this is not enough, the rest of the expenses will be met through financial aid programs.

How Financial Aid Is Awarded

When you apply for aid, an analysis is done of your family's financial situation based upon a government-approved formula. The result of this is the amount you and your family are expected to contribute toward your college expenses, called your Family Contribution, or FC. If this is equal to or more than the cost at a particular college, then, of course, you have no financial need for additional funds. However, even if you don't have financial need, it's possible you will still qualify for aid since there are many grants and scholarships that do not consider financial need, and you will certainly want to explore this possibility.

If the cost of education is greater than your FC, then you will likely qualify for assistance, hopefully enough to meet the full costs.

Total Cost of Attendance
– Calculated Family Contribution
= Financial Need

The total aid you are awarded by any one college will likely differ from the amount offered by other colleges you may be applying to because, among other things, the costs of attendance are different. But, in theory, the amount you are expected to contribute (your FC) should remain about the same regardless of which college you attend.

Sources of Financial Aid

The largest single source of aid is the federal government, which awards some $31 billion to over 7 million students each year. Eligibility for federal aid is based on the federal Family Contribution, which is calculated using a federally approved formula, the Federal Methodology.

But the federal government is not the only source of financial aid. The next largest sources of financial aid are colleges and universities themselves. Institutions award an estimated $8 billion to students each year. Some of this aid is awarded to students who have a demonstrated need based on either the Federal Methodology or on another formula, the Institutional Methodology. Some is not based on need and is referred to as merit aid. Merit aid is usually awarded based on a student's academic performance or specific talent or ability in the arts or to students the institution most wants to attract. A college may also use merit-based aid to help the institution meet its enrollment goals.

Another large source of financial aid is state government. All fifty states offer grant aid, most of which is need-based, but some that is merit-based. Most state programs award aid only to students attending a college in their home state.

Other sources of financial aid include private agencies, foundations, corporations, clubs, fraternal and service organizations, civic associations, unions, and religious groups that award grants, scholarships, and low-interest loans, as well as employers that provide tuition reimbursement benefits for employees and their dependents. More information about these different sources of aid is available from high school guidance offices, public libraries, college financial aid offices, and directly from the sponsoring organization. In addition, Peterson's offers a personalized computer search that includes its entire private aid database—over 2,000 sources—as well as college-administered financial aid and government aid that might be available to you. For more information about this service, call a Peterson's Software Representative at 1-800-338-3282.

Applying for Financial Aid

Some students applying for 1996–97 will go through a new application process and will use a new application. Whether you use this new process depends on which college(s) you are applying to, since it is up to the college to decide whether it will use only the Free Application for Federal Student Aid (FAFSA) or a supplemental application, the Financial Aid PROFILE. You must use the FAFSA to apply for federal aid, while the PROFILE asks additional questions that some colleges and awarding agencies use to award their own funds.

The first thing you will have to do is determine whether you will need to fill out only the FAFSA or whether you will also have to complete the PROFILE.

If Every School You're Applying to in 1996–97 Requires Just the FAFSA

. . . then it's pretty simple: Complete the FAFSA sometime after January 1, 1996, being certain to send it in before any college-imposed deadlines. You are not permitted to send in the 1996–97 FAFSA before January 1, 1996, and most college deadlines fall later on. It's best if you wait until you have all your financial records for the previous year available, but if you don't and a deadline is approaching, you can use estimated numbers.

After you send in your FAFSA, you'll receive a Student Aid Report (SAR) in the mail that reviews the information you reported and contains your Federal Family Contribution (FC). If you used estimated numbers to complete the FAFSA, you may have to resubmit the SAR with any corrections to the data. The college(s) you have designated on the FAFSA will receive the information you reported and will use that data to award you financial aid. In many instances, the colleges you've applied to will ask you to send copies of your and your parents' income tax returns for 1995 plus any other documents needed to verify the information you reported.

Institutions award an estimated $8 billion to students each year.

If at least one or more of the colleges you've applied to for admission requires the Financial Aid PROFILE, you will most likely need to start the process earlier.

Step 1: Complete the PROFILE Registration

The PROFILE registration is a one-page form that begins the financial aid process. These forms are available in most high school guidance offices and are available electronically using either Peterson's admission application service or the College Board's ExPAN admission application service.

There is a fee for using this application, and the amount is based on the number of colleges you designate (approximately $19.50 for the first college and $14.50 for each additional college).

On your PROFILE Registration Form, you must fill in basic demographic information about your family and list all the colleges you've applied to that require the Financial Aid PROFILE (list only those colleges that use the PROFILE, even if you've applied to other colleges that don't use it). You must then send this registration form to the College Scholarship Service along with the payment required.

You can also call in the information or fax the form, using a credit card to pay the required fee. (You can request overnight delivery service for an additional charge if a financial aid deadline is approaching.)

Step 2: The Financial Aid PROFILE

A few weeks later, unless you've requested overnight delivery, you'll receive in the mail a customized financial aid application that you can use to apply for institutional aid at the colleges you've designated, as well as from some private scholarship programs like the National Merit Scholarship. This form will contain all the questions necessary to estimate your family contribution based on the federal formula plus the questions that the colleges and organizations you've designated want answered. Your individualized packet will also contain codes to tell you which colleges wanted which additional questions, a customized cover letter instructing you what to do and informing you about deadlines and requirements for the colleges and programs you designated on the PROFILE Registration, and supplemental forms if they relate to you and if any of the colleges you're applying to require them (such as the Business/Farm Supplement if your parents own their own business or the Divorced/Separated Parent's Statement).

Make sure you submit your PROFILE by the earliest deadline listed. Two to four weeks after you do so, you will receive an acknowledgment and a report that will contain an estimated Federal Family Contribution (remember, only the FAFSA can be used to get an official FC) and another calculated family contribution using a second formula—the Institutional Methodology—that uses the additional data elements you provided. Colleges that require the PROFILE use this methodology to award their own funds in conjunction with federal aid.

If at least one college you're applying to requires the PROFILE, and at least one does not, then you'll have to complete both the PROFILE and the FAFSA. Do not list on the PROFILE any college that does not require it, but do list all colleges you are applying to on the FAFSA.

Financial Aid Awards

After you've submitted your financial aid application, either the FAFSA, PROFILE, or both, and usually after you've been accepted for admission, each college will send you a letter containing your financial aid award. Most award letters show you the college budget, how much you and your family are expected to contribute, and the amount and types of aid awarded. Most students who are eligible are awarded aid from a combination of sources and programs, hence your award is often called a "package." For first-year students, award letters are often sent with, or soon after, the letter of admission.

Most students who are eligible for aid are awarded aid from a combination of sources and programs.

Financial Aid Programs

There are three types of financial aid: scholarships (also known as grants or gift aid), loans, and student employment. Scholarships and grants are outright gifts and do not have to be repaid. Loans are borrowed money that must be repaid (usually after graduation); the amount you have to pay back is the total you've borrowed plus an interest charge. Student employment is a job arranged for you during the academic year. Loans and student employment programs are generally referred to as self-help aid.

The federal government has two large grant programs—the Federal Pell Grant and the Federal Supplemental Educational Opportunity Grant; a student employment program called Federal Work-Study; and several loan programs, including two for parents of undergraduate students.

The Subsidized Federal Direct Loan, the Federal Perkins Loan, and the Subsidized Federal Stafford Loan are all need-based, government-subsidized loans. Students who borrow under these programs do not have to pay interest on the money they borrow until after they graduate or leave school. The Unsubsidized Federal Direct Loan, Unsubsidized Federal Stafford Loan, and the parent loan programs are not awarded based on need, and borrowers are responsible for interest even when the student is in school.

If You Don't Qualify for Need-Based Aid

If you are not eligible for need-based aid, you and your college should try to put together an aid package that will lessen the burden on your parents.

There are basically three sources to look into. First is the search for merit scholarships that you can start at the initial stages of the aid application process. Merit-based awards are becoming an increasingly important part of college financing plans.

Second is employment, both during the summer and the academic year. The student employment office at your college should be able to help most students locate a school-year job. Many colleges and local businesses have vacancies remaining after they have placed aid students in their work-study jobs. Third is borrowing through the Unsubsidized Federal Stafford Loan or Unsubsidized Federal Direct Loan, both of which are open to all students. The terms and conditions are similar to the subsidized loans. The biggest difference is that the borrower is responsible for the interest while still in college, although most lenders permit students to delay paying the interest right away and add the accrued interest to the total amount owed.

After you've contributed what you can through scholarships, working, and borrowing, your parents will have to figure out how they will meet their share of the college bill, that is, the "family contribution." Many colleges offer monthly payment plans that spread the cost over the academic year rather than at the beginning of each term. For many parents, the monthly payments turn out to be more than they can afford, so they borrow their share either through the Federal Parent Loan for Undergraduate Students (PLUS loan), through one of the many private education loan programs available, or through home equity loans and lines of credit. Families seeking assistance in financing college expenses might seek the advice of professional financial advisers and tax consultants.

Students and parents who are interested in more information about financing a college education and in learning more about the new financial aid application process for 1996–97 should read Peterson's 1996 edition of *Paying Less for College*.

QUICK-REFERENCE CHART OF PROGRAMS

	Art	Dance	Music	Theater	Enroll-ment	Tuition and Fees	Page
Alabama							
Auburn University	BFA, MFA		BM, BMEd	BFA	21,226	$2100*	A55, M250, T479
Birmingham-Southern College			BM, BMEd		1,583	$12,524	M257
Jacksonville State University	BFA		BM, BMEd, MM, MMEd		7,553	$1840	A91, M313
Samford University			BM, BMEd, MM	BFA	4,571	$8648	M373, T504
Troy State University			BMEd		5,480	$2007	M396
University of Alabama	BFA, MFA		BM, MM, DMA		19,366	$2374	A157, M397
University of Alabama at Birmingham	BFA				16,252	$2604	A157
University of Montevallo	BFA		BM, BMEd, MM		3,282	$2407*	A172, M423
University of North Alabama	BFA		BM, BMEd		5,221	$1892	A173, M426
University of South Alabama	BFA		BM, BMEd		12,386	$2541	A177, M435
University of West Alabama			BMEd		2,320	$2003*	M446
Alaska							
University of Alaska Anchorage	BFA		BM, BMEd		15,113	$2228	A157, M398
University of Alaska Fairbanks			BM		7,807	$2400	M398
Arizona							
Arizona State University	BFA, MFA	BFA, MFA	BM, MM, MMEd, DMA	BFA, MFA	42,189	$1894*	A50, D204, M248, T478
Northern Arizona University			BM, BMEd, MM		19,242	$1914	M347
University of Arizona	BFA, MFA	BFA, MFA	BM, MM, DMA	BFA, MFA	35,306	$1950	A158, D223, M399, T511
Arkansas							
Arkansas State University	BFA		BM, BMEd, MM, MMEd	BFA	9,631	$1950	A50, M249, T479
Harding University	BFA		BMEd		3,817	$6450**	A86, M301
Henderson State University			BM, BMEd		3,796	$1942	M302
Ouachita Baptist University			BM, BMEd		1,440	$7070	M359
Southern Arkansas University–Magnolia			BMEd		2,957	$1728	M380
University of Arkansas	BFA, MFA		BM, MM		14,655	$2330	A158, M399
University of Arkansas at Monticello			BMEd		2,398	$1786	M400

	Art	Dance	Music	Theater	Enroll-ment	Tuition and Fees	Page
Arkansas *continued*							
University of Central Arkansas			BM, BMEd, MM, MMEd		9,192	$2010	M402
University of the Ozarks			BMEd		577	$6540	M443
Williams Baptist College	BFA				607	$4550	A194
California							
Academy of Art College	BFA, MFA				3,621	$12,555	A44
American Academy of Dramatic Arts/West				AA, Cert	147	$8875	T478
American College	BFA				517	$10,080	A47
Art Center College of Design	BFA, BS, MFA, MS				1,164	$14,400	A51
Art Institute of Southern California	BFA				164	$10,200	A53
Biola University			BM		2,961	$12,652	M257
California College of Arts and Crafts	BFA, MFA				1,135	$14,400	A62
California Institute of the Arts	BFA, MFA	BFA, MFA	BFA, MFA	BFA, MFA	1,051	$15,525	A63, D207, M265,T484
California State University, Chico	BFA				14,232	$2006*	A64
California State University, Fullerton	BFA, MFA		BM, MM		22,097	$1800*	A64, M265
California State University, Long Beach	BFA, MFA	BFA, MFA	BM, BMEd, MM, MMEd		26,227	$1751	A64, D208, M265
California State University, Los Angeles			BM, MM		18,224	$1749	M266
California State University, Northridge			BM, BMEd, MM		24,310	$1916*	M266
California State University, Sacramento			BM, MM		22,726	$1860*	M266
Chapman University		BFA	BM, BMEd	BFA	3,285	$17,916**	D208, M273,T485
College of Notre Dame	BFA		BM, MM		1,707	$13,482	A70, M277
Dominican College of San Rafael	BFA				1,249	$13,890	A78
Holy Names College			BM, MM		975	$12,700	M303
La Sierra University	BFA				1,456	$12,975	A98
Louise Salinger Academy of Fashion	BFA				200	$12,180*	A101
Mount St. Mary's College			BM		1,621	$12,914*	M337
Otis College of Art and Design	BFA, MFA				714	$14,670	A126
Pacific Union College			BM		1,597	$12,360	M360

* Expenses for 1994–95. ** Estimated expenses for 1995–96. *** Data not available.

	Art	Dance	Music	Theater	Enroll-ment	Tuition and Fees	Page
California *continued*							
San Diego State University		BA/BFA	BA/BFA, BM, MM, MMA		27,787	$1902*	D219, M373
San Francisco Art Institute	BFA, MFA				664	$15,486	A139
San Francisco Conservatory of Music			BM, MM		273	$14,750	M373
San Francisco State University			BM, MM		26,552	$1982	M375
San Jose State University	BFA, MFA		BM		26,299	$1976	A140, M375
Sonoma State University	BFA				6,610	$2070*	A146
University of California, Santa Barbara		BFA	BM, MM, DMA	BFA	17,834	$4098	D223, M401, T511
University of Redlands			BM, MM		3,950	$17,335	M432
University of Southern California	BFA, MFA		BM, MM, MMEd, DMA	BFA, MFA	27,864	$19,550	A178, M437, T520
University of the Pacific	BFA		BM, MM		4,140	$17,550	A183, M444
Colorado							
Colorado Christian University			BCM, BM, BME		2,568	$7600	M279
Colorado State University			BM, MM		21,461	$2709*	M279
Metropolitan State College of Denver	BFA				16,296	$1849	A109
Rocky Mountain College of Art & Design	BFA				366	$6210*	A137
University of Colorado at Boulder	BFA, MFA	BFA, MFA	BM, BMEd, MM, MMEd, DMA	BFA	24,548	$2757	A160, D224, M405, T512
University of Colorado at Denver	BFA				9,537	$2129	A161
University of Denver	BFA, MFA		BA/BFA, BM, MM, MMEd		8,522	$15,300*	A162, M407
University of Northern Colorado			BM, BMEd, MM, MMEd, DA, DME		10,426	$2408	M429
Connecticut							
Albertus Magnus College	BFA			BFA	600	$12,545	A45, T476
Paier College of Art, Inc.	BFA				292	$10,100	A128
University of Bridgeport	BFA		BM		1,939	$13,124*	A159, M400
University of Connecticut	BFA, MFA		BM, MM, DMA	BFA, MFA	15,626	$4849	A161, M405, T512

	Art	Dance	Music	Theater	Enrollment	Tuition and Fees	Page
Connecticut *continued*							
University of Hartford	BFA, MFA	BFA	BM, MM, MMEd, DMA		7,253	$15,610	A164, D225, M409
Delaware							
University of Delaware	BFA, MFA		BM, BMEd, MM		18,080	$4286	A162, M406
District of Columbia							
American University	BFA, MFA		BM, MM		11,708	$17,110	A48, M245
Catholic University of America			BM, MLM, MM, DMA		6,128	$15,052	M270
Corcoran School of Art	BFA				315	$11,550	A74
George Washington University			BM		19,298	$18,170*	M298
Howard University	BFA, MFA		BM, BMEd, MM, MMEd	BFA	10,961	$7531*	A87, M304, T491
Florida							
Florida Atlantic University	BFA		BM	BFA, MFA	17,484	$1791*	A83, M295, T489
Florida Baptist Theological College			BM		491	$2784	M296
Florida International University	BFA				22,052	$1775*	A83
Florida Southern College			BM, BMEd, BSM		1,820	$9400	M296
Florida State University	BFA, MFA	BFA, MFA	BM, BMEd, MM, MMEd, DMA, DME	BFA, MFA	29,630	$1798	A83, D210, M296, T490
International Academy of Merchandising & Design, Ltd.	BFA				415	$8100*	A90
Jacksonville University	BFA	BFA	BFA, BM, BMEd	BFA	2,480	$10,580	A92, D211, M314, T493
Palm Beach Atlantic College			BM		1,894	$8600	M360
Ringling School of Art and Design	BFA				805	$11,700	A135
Stetson University			BM, BMEd		2,883	$13,700	M389
University of Central Florida	BFA		BM, BMEd, MMEd	BFA	25,363	$1937	A160, M402, T511
University of Florida	BFA, MFA		BM, MM	BFA, MFA	38,277	$1820	A163, M408, T513
University of Miami	BFA, MFA		BM, MM, DMA	BFA	13,410	$17,700**	A168, M417, T515
University of North Florida	BFA		BM		10,064	$1820**	A175, M428
University of South Florida			BM, MM		36,058	$1877	M436
University of Tampa			BM		2,388	$13,612	M439

* Expenses for 1994–95. ** Estimated expenses for 1995–96. *** Data not available.

	Art	Dance	Music	Theater	Enroll-ment	Tuition and Fees	Page
Florida *continued*							
University of West Florida	BFA				7,816	$1711	A184
Georgia							
American College	BFA				831	$9690	A47
Armstrong State College			BMEd		5,040	$1719	M249
Atlanta College of Art	BFA				424	$10,500	A54
Augusta College	BFA		BM, BMEd		5,673	$1632*	A55, M251
Berry College			BM		1,876	$9216	M256
Brenau University	BFA	BFA	BM	BFA	2,241	$9855**	A60, D205, M261, T482
Brewton-Parker College			BM		2,250	$4881	M261
Clayton State College			BM		4,760	$1566**	M275
Columbus College			BM, MM		5,534	$2031	M280
Covenant College			BM		707	$10,920	M283
Georgia College			BM, BMEd, BMT		5,655	$1820	M299
Georgia Southern University	BFA, MFA				14,138	$1797**	A84
Georgia Southwestern College	BFA				2,533	$2442	A85
Georgia State University	BFA, MFA				23,776	$2249	A85
Kennesaw State College			BM, BMEd		11,915	$1776	M317
Mercer University			BM, BMEd		6,823	$12,987	M330
Savannah College of Art and Design	BFA, MFA				2,488	$10,800	A140
School of Visual Arts/Savannah	BFA				30	$9620	A145
Shorter College			BCM, BFA, BM, BMEd		1,455	$7610	M377
University of Georgia	BFA, MFA		BM, BMEd, MM, MMEd, DMA		29,469	$2508	A163, M409
Valdosta State University	BFA		BM, MMEd	BFA	9,160	$1887	A187, M451, T523
West Georgia College	BFA		BM, BMEd, MM, MMEd		8,310	$1884	A191, M459
Hawaii							
University of Hawaii at Manoa	BFA, MFA	BFA, MFA	BM, MM		19,983	$1631	A164, D225, M410

	Art	Dance	Music	Theater	Enroll-ment	Tuition and Fees	Page
Idaho							
Boise State University			BM, BMEd, MM, MMEd		14,647	$1876*	M258
Idaho State University			BM, BMEd		11,877	$1820	M305
University of Idaho			BM, BMEd, MM		11,730	$1620	M411
Illinois							
American Conservatory of Music			BM, MM, DMA		117	$7075	M245
Barat College		BFA			729	$11,300	D204
Bradley University	BFA, MFA		BM		5,882	$11,490	A60, M261
DePaul University			BM, MM	BFA, MFA	16,747	$11,886	M285, T487
Eastern Illinois University			BM, MM		11,301	$2776	M291
Elmhurst College			BM		2,775	$10,264**	M292
Harrington Institute of Interior Design	BFA				293	$9424	A86
Illinois State University	BFA, MFA		BM, BMEd, MM, MMEd		19,166	$3572	A87, M306
Illinois Wesleyan University	BFA		BFA, BM, BMEd	BA/BFA	1,855	$15,510	A88, M306, T491
International Academy of Merchandising & Design, Ltd.	BFA				662	$8550*	A90
Millikin University	BFA		BM, BMEd	BFA	1,863	$12,687	A111, M332, T496
Moody Bible Institute			BM		1,532	$1209	M335
Northern Illinois University	BFA, MFA		BM, MM	BFA, MFA	22,881	$3707	A121, M348, T498
North Park College			BM, BMEd		1,647	$13,280	M346
Northwestern University			BM, MM, MMEd, DMA		12,179	$16,404*	M350
Quincy University	BFA				1,164	$10,910	A133
Ray College of Design	BFA				610	$8930	A133
Roosevelt University			BM, MM	BFA, MFA	6,709	$9535	M369, T504
Saint Xavier University			BM		4,060	$11,600	M371
School of the Art Institute of Chicago	BFA, MFA				2,891	$15,900	A141
Southern Illinois University at Carbondale	BFA, MFA		BM, MM		23,162	$3336	A147, M381
Southern Illinois University at Edwardsville	BFA, MFA		BM, MM		10,938	$2330	A147, M381
University of Illinois at Chicago	BFA, MFA				24,865	$3628*	A165

* Expenses for 1994–95. ** Estimated expenses for 1995–96. *** Data not available.

	Art	Dance	Music	Theater	Enrollment	Tuition and Fees	Page
Illinois *continued*							
University of Illinois at Urbana-Champaign	BFA, MFA, DA	BFA, MFA	BM, BME, MM, MMEd, DMA	BFA, MFA	36,191	$3680*	A165, D225, M411, T514
VanderCook College of Music			BME, MMEd		149	$9320**	M452
Western Illinois University	BFA				12,599	$2702	A192
Wheaton College			BM, BMEd		2,642	$12,300	M462
Indiana							
Ball State University	BFA		BM, MM, DA		19,515	$3048	A56, M253
Butler University		BFA	BM, BMEd, MM, MMEd		3,758	$13,990	D206, M264
DePauw University			BA/BFA, BM		2,042	$15,475	M286
Grace College			BM		680	$9230	M300
Huntington College			BM		638	$10,200*	M305
Indiana State University	BFA, MFA		BM, BME, MM, MME		11,641	$2928	A88, M307
Indiana University Bloomington	BFA, MFA		BM, BMEd, MM, MMEd, DMA		35,594	$3582	A89, M308
Indiana University–Purdue University Fort Wayne	BFA		BM, BMEd, BMT		11,513	$2495*	A89, M310
Indiana University–Purdue University Indianapolis	BFA				26,766	$3029*	A89
Indiana University South Bend	BFA		BM, BMEd, MM, MMEd		7,936	$2664	A90, M309
Oakland City University			BMEd		983	$7666	M352
Saint Mary's College	BA/BFA		BM		1,545	$14,234	A138, M371
Taylor University			BM, BMEd		1,831	$11,914	M392
University of Evansville	BFA		BM	BFA	3,162	$12,400	A162, M408, T513
University of Notre Dame	BFA, MFA				10,000	$17,967	A176
Valparaiso University			BM, BMEd, MM		3,480	$12,860	M452
Iowa							
Coe College			BM		1,343	$14,875	M277
Cornell College			BM, BMEd		1,133	$16,440	M281
Drake University	BFA, MFA		BM, BMEd, MM, MMEd	BFA	5,954	$14,100	A78, M287, T488
Iowa State University of Science and Technology	BFA, MFA		BM, BMEd		24,728	$2574**	A91, M310

	Art	Dance	Music	Theater	Enroll-ment	Tuition and Fees	Page
Iowa *continued*							
Iowa Wesleyan College			BMEd		887	$10,920	M311
Maharishi International University	BFA, MFA				624	$13,976	A102
Morningside College			BM, BMEd		1,214	$11,226	M336
Simpson College			BM		1,613	$12,275	M378
Teikyo Westmar University			BMEd		566	$10,276	M392
University of Iowa	BFA, MFA	BFA, MFA	BFA, BM, MFA, MM, DMA		26,932	$2558	A166, D226, M413
University of Northern Iowa	BFA		BM, MM		12,572	$2562	A176, M429
Wartburg College			BM, BME/MT, BMEd		1,405	$12,370	M455
Kansas							
Baker University			BM, BMEd		1,997	$9870	M251
Benedictine College			BMEd		843	$10,020	M255
Emporia State University	BFA		BM, BMEd, MM, MMEd	BFA	6,075	$1782	A81, M293, T489
Fort Hays State University	BFA, MFA		BM		5,496	$1902**	A84, M297
Friends University		BFA	BM, BMEd, MM		2,326	$8746	D210, M297
Kansas State University	BFA, MFA		BM, BMEd, MM		20,664	$2199	A94, M316
Pittsburg State University	BFA		BM, BME, MM, MMEd		6,377	$1806	A130, M363
Southwestern College			BM		752	$7850	M384
University of Kansas	BFA, MFA		BM, BMEd, MM, MMEd, DMA		28,046	$2182	A166, M413
Washburn University of Topeka	BFA		BM, BMEd		6,439	$2822	A189, M455
Wichita State University	BFA, MFA	BFA	BM, BMEd, MM, MMEd	BFA	14,558	$2116*	A193, D234, M462, T527
Kentucky							
Campbellsville College			BM		1,260	$6420	M268
Cumberland College			BM		1,550	$7130**	M284
Eastern Kentucky University			BM, BMEd, MM, MMEd		16,060	$1900	M291
Georgetown College			BM, BMEd		1,405	$8890	M298
Kentucky State University			BM, BMEd		2,564	$1860	M318

* Expenses for 1994–95. ** Estimated expenses for 1995–96. *** Data not available.

	Art	Dance	Music	Theater	Enroll-ment	Tuition and Fees	Page
Kentucky *continued*							
Kentucky Wesleyan College			BM, BMEd		740	$9100	M318
Morehead State University			BM, BMEd, MM		8,697	$1900**	M336
Murray State University	BFA		BM, BMEd, MMEd		7,960	$1940	A116, M338
Northern Kentucky University	BFA		BM, BMEd	BFA	11,978	$1960	A121, M348, T499
Union College			BM, BMEd		1,003	$8200	M396
University of Kentucky			BM, MM, DMA	BFA	23,622	$2590	M414, T515
University of Louisville	BFA		BM, BMEd, MM, MMEd		21,377	$2670**	A166, M414
Western Kentucky University		BFA	BM, BMEd	BFA	14,765	$2035	D233, M458, T526
Louisiana							
Centenary College of Louisiana			BM, BMEd		1,014	$10,122	M271
Louisiana College			BM		1,013	$6118	M323
Louisiana State University and Agricultural and Mechanical College	BFA, MFA		BM, BMEd, MM, DMA		25,317	$2648	A101, M324
Louisiana Tech University	BFA, MFA		BFA		10,023	$2262*	A101, M324
Loyola University, New Orleans	BFA		BM, BMEd, BMT, MM, MMEd, MMT		5,634	$12,016	A102, M325
McNeese State University			BM, BMEd, MMEd		8,729	$1966	M329
Nicholls State University			BMEd		7,205	$1990*	M344
Northeast Louisiana University			BM, BMEd, MM		11,379	$1926*	M347
Northwestern State University of Louisiana			BM, BMEd, MM		8,762	$2254	M350
Southeastern Louisiana University			BM, BMEd, MM		13,912	$2030	M380
Southern University and Agricultural and Mechanical College			BM, BMEd		9,800	$2028**	M382
University of Southwestern Louisiana			BM, BMEd, MM		16,789	$1898*	M438
Xavier University of Louisiana			BM		3,486	$7015*	M466
Maine							
Maine College of Art	BFA				281	$12,350	A103
University of Maine			BM, BMEd, MM, MMEd		10,001	$3920	M414

	Art	Dance	Music	Theater	Enroll-ment	Tuition and Fees	Page
Maine *continued*							
University of Southern Maine	BFA		BM, BMEd		9,628	$3470	A179, M437
Maryland							
Johns Hopkins University			BM, MM, DMA		4,812	$19,700**	M315
Maryland Institute, College of Art	BFA, MFA				906	$13,990	A105
Towson State University		BFA			14,551	$3530	D223
University of Maryland College Park			BM, BMA, MM		32,493	$3794	M415
Massachusetts							
Anna Maria College	BFA		BM		1,797	$11,780	A49, M247
Art Institute of Boston	BFA				388	$10,660	A52
Atlantic Union College			BM		704	$11,750	M250
Berklee College of Music			BM, MM		2,686	$12,390	M255
Boston Conservatory		BFA, MFA	BM, BMEd, MM	BFA, MM	414	$13,850	D204, M258, T480
Boston University	BFA, MFA		BM, MM, DMA	BFA, MFA	28,664	$19,700	A59, M260, T481
Emmanuel College	BFA				1,528	$13,450	A81
Gordon College			BM		1,178	$13,950	M299
Massachusetts College of Art	BFA, MFA				1,367	$3983	A108
Montserrat College of Art	BFA				292	$9730	A114
New England Conservatory of Music			BM, MM, MMEd, DMA		774	$15,400*	M339
New England School of Art and Design	BFA				118	$11,050	A117
School of the Museum of Fine Arts	BA/BFA, MFA				705	$14,315	A143
University of Massachusetts Amherst		BFA	BM, MM		22,332	$5575	D226, M415
University of Massachusetts Dartmouth	BFA, MFA		BM		5,6245	$6298	A167, M416
University of Massachusetts Lowell	BFA		BM, MM		12,731	$4602*	A168, M416
Michigan							
Adrian College	BFA				1,059	$11,840	A44
Albion College	BFA				1,641	$15,334	A46
Andrews University	BFA		BM, MM		2,952	$10,623	A48, M246

* Expenses for 1994–95. ** Estimated expenses for 1995–96. *** Data not available.

	Art	Dance	Music	Theater	Enroll-ment	Tuition and Fees	Page
Michigan *continued*							
Aquinas College	BFA		BM		2,443	$11,852	A49, M248
Center for Creative Studies—College of Art and Design	BFA				835	$12,550	A66
Central Michigan University	BFA, MFA		BM, BMEd, MM		16,126	$3037*	A67, M272
Cornerstone College			BM, BMEd		791	$7516	M282
Eastern Michigan University			BM, BMEd, BMT		23,321	$3130	M291
Grand Valley State University	BFA		BM, BMEd		13,553	$3140	A85, M300
Hope College			BM, BMEd		2,825	$13,318	M303
Kendall College of Art and Design	BFA				574	$10,050*	A94
Marygrove College			BM		1,218	$8716	M328
Michigan State University	BFA, MFA		BM, MM, DMA		40,254	$4626*	A110, M331
Northern Michigan University			BMEd		7,898	$2998**	M349
Oakland University			BM, MM		13,165	$3396	M352
Siena Heights College	BFA				1,141	$9810	A146
University of Michigan	BFA, MFA	BFA, MFA	BFA, BM, BMA, BMEd, MM, MMEd, DMA	BFA, MFA	36,543	$5215*	A169, D227, M418, T516
University of Michigan–Flint	BFA		BM, BMEd		6,236	$3304	A170, M419
Wayne State University	BFA, MFA		BM, MM	BFA, MFA, DA	32,906	$3130*	A190, M456, T524
Western Michigan University	BFA, MFA	BFA	BM	BFA	26,673	$3160*	A192, D233, M458, T526
Minnesota							
Augsburg College			BM, BMEd		2,958	$12,602	M250
Bethel College			BM, BMEd		2,208	$12,260	M256
College of Visual Arts	BFA				210	$8500	A71
Concordia College			BM		2,970	$10,720	M281
Crown College			BCM, BMEd		620	$8086	M283
Mankato State University	BFA		BM, MM		12,624	$2695**	A104, M327
Minneapolis College of Art and Design	BFA, MFA				543	$13,938	A112
Moorhead State University	BFA		BM, BMEd, MM, MMEd		7,037	$2710**	A116, M335
St. Cloud State University	BFA		BM, MM		14,673	$2841	A149, M385

	Art	Dance	Music	Theater	Enroll-ment	Tuition and Fees	Page
Minnesota *continued*							
St. Olaf College			BM		2,958	$15,080	M386
University of Minnesota, Duluth	BFA		BM, MM	BFA	7,497	$3305*	A170, M420, T516
University of Minnesota, Twin Cities Campus	BFA, MFA	BFA	BM, MM, DMA		36,699	$3826*	A171, D227, M420
Mississippi							
Alcorn State University			BM, BMEd		2,742	$2589	M244
Belhaven College			BM		1,109	$7620**	M253
Delta State University	BFA		BMEd, MMEd		3,775	$2294	A77, M286
Jackson State University			BM, BMEd, MMEd		6,224	$2380	M313
Mississippi College			BM, BMEd, MM, MMEd		3,781	$6350	M333
Mississippi State University	BFA				13,371	$2561*	A113
Mississippi University for Women	BFA		BM		3,020	$2749	A114, M333
Mississippi Valley State University			BMEd		2,182	$2278*	M334
University of Mississippi	BFA, MFA		BM, MM, DA		10,075	$3096*	A171, M421
University of Southern Mississippi	BFA, MFA	BFA	BM, BME, MM, MME, DMA	BA/BFA, BFA, MFA	11,587	$2428*	A179, D230, M438, T520
William Carey College			BM	BFA	2,139	$4650*	M464, T527
Missouri							
Avila College				BFA	1,429	$9600	T480
Calvary Bible College and Theological Seminary			BMEd		272	$3840	M267
Central Methodist College			BM, BMEd		1,134	$9430	M271
Central Missouri State University	BFA		BM, BMEd		10,805	$2460	A68, M272
Columbia College	BFA				817	$8546	A72
Culver-Stockton College	BFA		BMEd	BFA	1,057	$8400	A76, M283, T487
Evangel College	BFA		BM		1,541	$7300	A81, M293
Fontbonne College	BFA, MFA				1,681	$9040	A84
Kansas City Art Institute	BFA				559	$14,785	A93
Lincoln University			BMEd		3,512	$2016	M323
Lindenwood College	BFA				3,375	$9850	A99
Maryville University of Saint Louis	BFA				3,425	$9800	A107

* Expenses for 1994–95. ** Estimated expenses for 1995–96. *** Data not available.

	Art	Dance	Music	Theater	Enroll-ment	Tuition and Fees	Page
Missouri *continued*							
Northeast Missouri State University	BFA		BM		6,317	$2890	A121, M347
Southeast Missouri State University			BM, BME, MME		7,921	$2760	M379
Southwest Baptist University			BM, BMEd		3,202	$7481	M383
Southwest Missouri State University	BFA	BFA	BM, MM	BFA	17,310	$2546	A148, D220, M383, T506
Stephens College	BFA	BFA		BFA	600	$14,400	A151, D221, T508
University of Missouri–Columbia			BM, BME, MM		22,136	$3765**	M421
University of Missouri–Kansas City		BFA	BM, BMEd, MM, MMEd, DMA		9,962	$3799	D228, M422
University of Missouri–St. Louis			BM		12,045	$3062	M422
Washington University	BFA, MFA				11,655	$18,800*	A190
Webster University	BFA	BFA	BFA, BM, BMEd, MM	BFA	10,834	$9160*	A191, D232, M457, T525
Montana							
Montana State University–Bozeman			BMEd		10,962	$2378	M334
University of Montana–Missoula	BFA, MFA	BFA	BM, BMEd, MM, MMEd	BFA, MFA	11,067	$2251*	A171, D228, M422, T517
Nebraska							
Bellevue University	BFA				2,159	$3350	A58
Concordia College	BFA				953	$9480	A73
Hastings College			BM		1,064	$10,164	M301
Nebraska Wesleyan University			BM	BFA	1,610	$10,316	M339, T497
University of Nebraska at Kearney			BFA		7,584	$2084	M423
University of Nebraska at Omaha			BM, MM		15,570	$2188**	M423
University of Nebraska–Lincoln	BFA, MFA	BFA	BM, BMEd, MM, DMA	BFA, MFA, DA	23,854	$2775*	A172, D228, M424, T517
Nevada							
University of Nevada, Las Vegas	BFA, MFA		BM, MM		20,239	$1850**	A173, M424
University of Nevada, Reno			BM, MM		11,746	$1740*	M425
New Hampshire							
Keene State College			BM		3,931	$3604	M316
Rivier College	BFA				2,759	$11,150	A136
University of New Hampshire	BFA		BM		12,518	$4559*	A173, M425

	Art	Dance	Music	Theater	Enroll-ment	Tuition and Fees	Page
New Jersey							
Caldwell College	BFA				1,688	$9500	A62
Centenary College	BFA				917	$12,100	A66
Jersey City State College	BFA				7,199	$3158	A93
Montclair State University	BFA	BFA	BM	BFA	12,675	$3000*	A114, D213, M334, T496
Rider University			BM, MM		5,026	$13,940	M368
Rowan College of New Jersey			BM		8,936	$3095*	M370
Rutgers, The State University of New Jersey	BFA, MFA	BFA	BM, MM, DMA	BFA, MFA	647	$4840	A137, D218, M370, T504
Seton Hall University			BM, BMEd		8,400	$13,030	M375
Trenton State College	BFA		BM		6,981	$4240	A156, M395
William Paterson College of New Jersey			BM, BMEd		9,699	$3072**	M464
New Mexico							
College of Santa Fe	BFA		BFA	BFA	1,365	$11,796	A70, M278, T486
Eastern New Mexico University	BFA		BM, BMEd, MM	BFA	3,853	$2258	A79, M292, T489
New Mexico Highlands University	BFA				2,797	$1506	A117
New Mexico State University	BFA, MFA		BM, BMEd, MM		15,645	$2028*	A117, M339
University of New Mexico	BFA, MFA		BM, BMEd, MM, MMEd	BFA	24,344	$2080	A173, M426, T517
New York							
Adelphi University				BFA	8,012	$13,070*	T476
Alfred University	BFA, MFA				2,326	$16,972*	A46
American Academy of Dramatic Arts				AOS, Cert	224	$9150	T477
Brooklyn College of the City University of New York	BFA, MFA		BM, MM	BFA, MFA	13,045	$2631	A61, M263, T483
City College of the City University of New York			BFA		14,885	$3304	M274
College of New Rochelle	BFA				2,383	$12,300**	A69
Concordia College			BM		614	***	M280
Cooper Union for the Advancement of Science and Art	BFA				1,064	$400	A73
Cornell University	BFA, MFA				18,811	$19,066	A75
Daemen College	BFA				1,884	$9780	A76
Fashion Institute of Technology	BFA				8,422	$2310*	A82

* Expenses for 1994–95. ** Estimated expenses for 1995–96. *** Data not available.

	Art	Dance	Music	Theater	Enroll-ment	Tuition and Fees	Page
New York *continued*							
Five Towns College			BM, BMEd		732	$8400	M294
Hofstra University				BFA	11,545	$11,710*	T490
Houghton College			BM		1,332	$10,300*	M303
Hunter College of the City University of New York			BM		18,390	$2557*	M305
Ithaca College	BFA, BFA		BM, MM	BFA	5,556	$15,250	A91, M311, T491
Juilliard School		BFA	BM, MM, DMA	BFA	825	$13,600	D211, M316, T494
Lehman College of the City University of New York	BFA, MFA				8,921	$2564**	A98
Long Island University, C.W. Post Campus	BFA, MFA			BFA	7,919	$12,990	A99, T494
Long Island University, Southampton Campus	BFA				1,441	$13,030	A100
Manhattan School of Music			BM, MM, DMA		921	$14,880	A100, M325
Manhattanville College	BFA		BM		909	$16,000	A104, M326
Marymount Manhattan College		BFA			1,973	$11,450	D213
Nazareth College of Rochester			BM		2,723	$11,582	M338
New School for Social Research (Mannes College of Music)			BM, MM		267	$12,975*	M341
New School for Social Research (Parsons School of Design)	BFA, MFA				1,912	$15,180*	A118
New School for Social Research (New School/Mannes Jazz and Contemporary Music Program)			BFA		***	$15,180*	M340
New York Institute of Technology	BFA				10,221	$10,040**	A119
New York School of Interior Design	BFA				399	$11,570	A119
New York University	BFA	BFA, MFA	BM, MM, MMT, DA	BFA, BFA, BFA, MFA, MFA	33,428	$18,739*	A120, D213, M342, T497
Nyack College			BM, BSM		790	$9450	M351
Pace University				BFA	12,312	$11,400*	T501
Pratt Institute	BFA, BID, MFA, MID				2,979	$15,214	A130
Purchase College, State University of New York	BFA, MFA	BFA	BFA, MFA	BFA, MFA	2,498	$3799	A131, D216, M364, T503
Queens College of the City University of New York			BM		17,958	$2637*	M365
Rochester Institute of Technology	BFA, MFA				12,250	$14,937	A137
St. John's University	BFA				17,820	$10,450	A150

	Art	Dance	Music	Theater	Enrollment	Tuition and Fees	Page
New York *continued*							
School of Visual Arts	BFA, MFA				3,049	$12,600	A144
State University of New York at Binghamton			BM, MM		12,088	$2961*	M388
State University of New York at Buffalo	BFA, MFA		BMus, MM		24,943	$3244**	A150, M388
State University of New York College at Brockport		BFA, MFA			7,910	$3795	D221
State University of New York College at Fredonia			BFA, BM, MM	BFA	4,892	$3919	M386, T507
State University of New York at New Paltz	BFA, MFA			BFA	7,897	$3751	A150, T507
State University of New York College at Potsdam			BM, MM		4,293	$2961*	M387
Syracuse University	BFA, BID, MFA, MID		BM, MM	BFA, MFA	14,550	$16,280	A152, M390, T509
University of Rochester			BM, MM, DMA		8,336	$17,818	M434
North Carolina							
Appalachian State University	BFA		BM, MM		11,866	$1670**	A49, M248
Barton College	BFA				1,465	$8395	A56
East Carolina University	BFA, MFA	BFA	BM, MM	BFA	16,373	$1557*	A79, D210, M288, T489
Guilford College	BFA				1,187	$14,390	A86
Lenoir-Rhyne College			BMEd		1,418	$10,886	M322
Mars Hill College			BFA, BM	BFA	1,056	$8400	M328, T495
Meredith College			BM, MM		2,336	$7100	M330
Methodist College			BM		1,612	$9950	M331
North Carolina Agricultural and Technical State University				BFA	8,050	$1431*	T498
North Carolina Central University			BM		5,634	$1518*	M345
North Carolina School of the Arts		BFA	BM, MM	BFA, MFA	613	$1999*	D214, M345, T498
Pembroke State University			BM		3,017	$1146*	M361
Queens College			BM		1,572	$11,520	M365
Salem College			BM		901	$11,245	M372
University of North Carolina at Chapel Hill			BMEd, MM		24,463	$1569*	M426
University of North Carolina at Charlotte	BFA		BM		15,513	$1459*	A174, M427
University of North Carolina at Greensboro	BFA, MFA	BFA, MFA	BM, MM, DMA	BFA, MFA	12,094	$1765*	A174, D229, M427, T518

* Expenses for 1994–95. ** Estimated expenses for 1995–96. *** Data not available.

	Art	Dance	Music	Theater	Enrollment	Tuition and Fees	Page
North Carolina *continued*							
Western Carolina University	BFA			BFA	6,619	$1551*	A192, T526
Wingate University			BM, BMEd		1,383	$8800	M465
North Dakota							
University of North Dakota	BFA, MFA		BM, MM	BFA	11,521	$3196	A175, M428, T519
Ohio							
Art Academy of Cincinnati	BFA				187	$10,420	A50
Ashland University			BM		5,826	$12,422	M249
Baldwin-Wallace College			BM, BMEd		4,716	$11,580*	M251
Bowling Green State University	BFA, MFA		BM, MM		17,564	$3954	A60, M260
Capital University	BFA		BM		3,924	$13,700	A65, M268
Cedarville College			BMEd		2,278	$8004	M271
Central State University			BM		3,068	***	M272
Cincinnati Bible College and Seminary			BM		922	$5445	M274
Cleveland Institute of Art	BFA				520	$11,700*	A68
Cleveland Institute of Music			BM, MM, DMA		335	$15,911	M275
Cleveland State University			BM, MM		16,504	$3231*	M277
College of Wooster			BM, BMEd		1,644	$17,600	M278
Columbus College of Art and Design	BFA				1,726	$10,540	A72
Denison University	BFA				1,834	$18,630	A78
Heidelberg College			BM, BMEd		1,372	$14,606	M302
Kent State University	BFA, MFA		BM, MM		21,413	$4084	A95, M317
Lake Erie College	BFA	BFA	BFA	BFA	732	$12,320	A98, D212, M318, T494
Marietta College	BFA				1,319	$14,850	A104
Miami University	BFA, MFA		BM, MM		15,882	$4884	A110, M331
Mount Union College			BM, BMEd		1,481	$13,480	M338
Oberlin College			BM, MM, MMEd		2,744	$20,746	M353
Ohio Northern University	BFA		BM	BFA	2,872	$16,950	A122, M354, T499
Ohio State University	BFA, MFA	BFA, MFA	BM, BME, MM, DMA		49,542	$3273	A122, D215, M354
Ohio University	BFA, MFA	BFA	BM, MM		18,855	$3666	A123, D215, M355

	Art	Dance	Music	Theater	Enroll-ment	Tuition and Fees	Page
Ohio *continued*							
Ohio Wesleyan University	BFA		BM		1,732	$17,569	A123, M355
Otterbein College			BFA, BMEd	BFA	2,599	$13,611	M359, T500
University of Akron	BFA	BFA	BM		26,009	$3572	A156, D223, M397
University of Cincinnati	BFA, MFA	BFA	BM, MM, DMA, DME	BFA, MFA	18,473	$3898*	A160, D224, M403, T512
University of Dayton	BFA		BM, BMEd		10,204	$11,830*	A161, M406
University of Toledo			BM, MM, MMEd		23,107	$3398*	M444
Wittenberg University			BM, BMEd		2,160	$17,696	M465
Wright State University		BFA	BM, MMEd	BFA	16,823	$3429	D234, M466, T528
Xavier University	BFA				6,180	$12,270	A194
Youngstown State University	BFA		BM, MM		13,979	$2910*	A195, M467
Oklahoma							
Cameron University			BM		5,927	$1665*	M267
East Central University			BM		4,538	$1529*	M289
Northwestern Oklahoma State University			BM, BMEd		1,861	$1586*	M349
Oklahoma Baptist University	BFA		BM, BMEd		2,440	$6524	A123, M355
Oklahoma Christian University of Science and Arts			BMEd		1,508	$7160	M356
Oklahoma City University			BM, BMEd, MM		4,571	$7435	M356
Oklahoma Panhandle State University			BMEd		1,259	$1656	M357
Oklahoma State University	BFA		BM		18,561	$1850	A124, M357
Oral Roberts University			BM, BMEd		3,318	$8730	M358
Phillips University			BME, BMT		905	$6550	M362
Southeastern Oklahoma State University			BM, BMEd		4,104	$1559	M380
Southwestern Oklahoma State University			BM, BMEd, MMEd		4,737	$1431*	M384
University of Central Oklahoma			BM, BMEd, MMEd		16,039	$1716	M403
University of Oklahoma	BFA, MFA	BFA, MFA	BFA, BM, BMA, BMEd, MM, MMEd, DMA		19,683	$1870*	A176, D229, M430
University of Tulsa			BM, BMEd, MM, MMEd		4,573	$12,300	M445

* Expenses for 1994–95. ** Estimated expenses for 1995–96. *** Data not available.

	Art	Dance	Music	Theater	Enroll-ment	Tuition and Fees	Page
Oregon							
Bassist College	BID				134	$8600	A57
Marylhurst College	BFA		BM		1,183	$8547*	A107, M329
Oregon School of Arts and Crafts	BFA				27	$9490	A125
Oregon State University	BFA				14,336	$3048**	A125
Pacific Northwest College of Art	BFA				269	$9103	A127
Pacific University			BM		1,837	$15,140	M360
Portland State University			BM		14,426	$3060*	M363
Southern Oregon State College	BFA			BFA	4,554	$2835*	A148, T506
University of Oregon	BFA, MFA		BM, MM, DMA		16,681	$3380**	A177, M430
University of Portland			BMEd, MFA		2,600	$13,250	M431
Willamette University			BM		2,519	$16,490	M463
Pennsylvania							
Beaver College	BFA				2,387	$13,970	A57
Bucknell University			BM		3,528	$19,470	M264
Carnegie Mellon University	BFA, MFA		BFA, MM	BFA, MAM, MFA	7,141	$18,760	A65, M269, T485
Clarion University of Pennsylvania	BFA		BM	BFA	5,567	$3878*	A68, M275, T485
Curtis Institute of Music			BM, MM		156	$600*	M284
Duquesne University			BM, MM, MMEd		9,001	$12,578	M287
Grove City College			BM		2,280	$6174	M300
Immaculata College			BM, BMEd, MM		2,088	$10,880	M307
Indiana University of Pennsylvania			BFA		13,814	$3863	M310
Kutztown University of Pennsylvania	BFA, BFA, BFA				7,916	$3699*	A97
Lebanon Valley College			BM		1,754	$14,785	M321
Lock Haven University of Pennsylvania			BFA		3,687	$3662*	M323
Lycoming College	BFA				1,507	$14,860	A102
Mansfield University of Pennsylvania			BM, MM		2,992	$3624*	M327
Marywood College	BFA, MFA		BM		3,068	$12,240	A107, M329
Moore College of Art and Design	BFA				365	$14,422**	A115
Moravian College			BM		1,353	$16,060	M336

	Art	Dance	Music	Theater	Enroll-ment	Tuition and Fees	Page
Pennsylvania *continued*							
Pennsylvania Academy of the Fine Arts	BFA, MFA				325	***	A129
Pennsylvania State University University Park Campus	BFA, MFA		BM, BMA, MM, MMEd	BFA, MFA	38,294	$5036*	A130, M362, T501
Philadelphia College of Bible			BM		1,050	$8060	M362
Point Park College		BFA		BFA	2,397	$10,552	D215, T502
Saint Vincent College	BFA		BM		1,077	$12,000	A138, M371
Seton Hill College	BFA		BM		923	$11,340*	A145, M376
Slippery Rock University of Pennsylvania			BM		7,563	$3837*	M378
Susquehanna University			BM		1,512	$17,080	M390
Temple University	BFA, MFA	BFA, MFA	BM, MM, DMA		26,952	$5514	A153, D222, M392
University of the Arts	BFA, MFA, MID	BFA	BM, MM	BFA	1,298	$13,670	A182, D231, M443, T521
West Chester University of Pennsylvania			BM, MM		11,168	$3646*	M457
Westminster College			BM		1,620	$13,515	M459
Rhode Island							
Rhode Island College	BFA		BM, MMEd		9,900	$2970**	A134, M367
Rhode Island School of Design	BFA, MFA, MID				2,011	$17,600	A134
University of Rhode Island			BM, MM		12,110	$4404	M433
South Carolina							
Anderson College			BME		932	$8888**	M246
Columbia College		BFA	BM		1,229	$10,995	D208, M280
Converse College	BFA		BM, MM		1,160	$13,150	A73, M281
Furman University			BM		2,663	$14,576	M297
Lander University			BMEd		2,779	$3450	M320
Newberry College			BM, BMEd		624	$10,950	M344
University of South Carolina	BFA, MFA		BM, MM, MME, DMA	BA/BFA, MFA	26,754	$3280	A178, M436, T519
Winthrop University	BFA, MFA		BM, BMEd, MM, MMEd		5,164	$3821**	A194, M465

* Expenses for 1994–95. ** Estimated expenses for 1995–96. *** Data not available.

	Art	Dance	Music	Theater	Enroll-ment	Tuition and Fees	Page
South Dakota							
Northern State University			BMEd		3,078	$2340	M349
South Dakota State University			BMEd		9,140	$2695	M379
University of South Dakota	BFA, MFA		BM, BMEd, MM	BFA, MFA	7,739	$2753	A178, M436, T519
Tennessee							
Austin Peay State University	BFA				8,207	$2140	A56
Belmont University	BFA		BM, BMEd, MMEd		2,961	$8750	A59, M254
Carson-Newman College			BM		2,163	$9000	M269
East Tennessee State University	BFA, MFA		BM		11,512	$1870	A80, M289
Fisk University			BM		872	$7055	M294
Lambuth University			BM		1,209	$5600	M319
Lee College			BMEd		2,197	$5362	M322
Maryville College			BM		843	$12,248	M329
Memphis College of Art	BFA, MFA				216	$9500**	A108
Middle Tennessee State University	BFA		BM		17,120	$1972	A110, M332
Southern College of Seventh-day Adventists			BMEd		1,652	$8880	M381
Tennessee Wesleyan College			BMEd		633	$6200	M394
Union University			BM		2,036	$6430	M397
University of Memphis	BFA, MFA	BFA	BM, MM, DMA	BFA, MFA	19,848	$2094	A168, D226, M417, T515
University of Tennessee at Chattanooga	BFA		BM, MM		8,281	$1850*	A179, M439
University of Tennessee at Martin	BFA	BFA	BM, BMEd	BFA	5,627	$1900*	A180, D230, M440, T521
University of Tennessee, Knoxville	BFA, MFA		BM, BMEd, MM		25,890	$2052*	A180, M440
Vanderbilt University			BM		10,088	$19,422	M452
Texas							
Abilene Christian University	BFA		BM		4,207	$8520	A44, M244
Angelo State University			BM		6,276	$1784	M246
Baylor University	BFA		BM, BMEd, MM	BFA, MFA	12,240	$8394	A57, M253, T480
Dallas Baptist University			BM		2,989	$7140	M285
East Texas Baptist University			BM, BSM		1,333	$5960	M289

	Art	Dance	Music	Theater	Enroll-ment	Tuition and Fees	Page
Texas *continued*							
East Texas State University	BFA, MFA		BM, BMEd, MM, MMEd		7,952	$1754*	A80, M290
Hardin-Simmons University			BM, MM		2,133	$7080	M301
Howard Payne University			BM		1,488	$6240	M304
Incarnate Word College			BM, BME, BMT		2,801	$9635	M307
Lamar University–Beaumont			BM, MM, MMEd		8,356	$1736	M319
Midwestern State University	BFA		BM	BFA	5,819	$1646	A111, M332, T496
Prairie View A&M University			BM		5,849	$1900	M364
Rice University			BMus, MMus, DMA		4,073	$10,775*	M367
Sam Houston State University	BFA, MFA	BFA, MFA	BM, BMEd, MM, MMEd		12,906	$1602*	A139, D218, M372
Southern Methodist University	BFA, MFA	BFA, MFA	BM, MM, MMT	BFA, MFA	9,014	$14,396*	A147, D220, M382, T505
Southwestern University			BM	BFA	1,238	$12,700	M385, T507
Southwest Texas State University	BFA		BM, MM		20,899	$1806**	A149, M383
Stephen F. Austin State University	BFA, MFA		BM, MM	BFA	12,206	$1728*	A151, M389, T508
Sul Ross State University	BFA				3,145	$1572	A151
Tarleton State University			BM		6,460	$1634*	M391
Texas A&M University–Corpus Christi			BM		5,152	$1588**	M394
Texas A&M University–Kingsville			BM, MM		6,548	$1712	M394
Texas Christian University	BFA, MFA	BFA, MFA	BM, BMEd, MM, MMEd	BFA	6,706	$10,000	A154, D222, M394, T510
Texas Southern University	BFA				10,872	$1470	A155
Texas Tech University	BFA, MFA, DA		BM, MM, MMEd		24,083	$1770**	A155, M395
Texas Woman's University	BFA, MFA				10,090	$1538*	A155
Trinity University			BM		2,479	$13,044	M396
University of Houston	BFA, MFA		BM, MM, DMA		31,298	$1594*	A164, M410
University of Mary Hardin-Baylor	BFA				2,244	$5862	A167
University of North Texas	BFA, MFA		BM, MM, DMA		25,605	$1713	A175, M428
University of Texas at Arlington	BFA		BM		23,280	$1636	A180, M441

* Expenses for 1994–95. ** Estimated expenses for 1995–96. *** Data not available.

	Art	Dance	Music	Theater	Enroll-ment	Tuition and Fees	Page
Texas *continued*							
University of Texas at Austin	BFA, MFA	BFA	BM, MM, DMA	BFA, MFA	47,957	$2208	A181, D230, M441, T521
University of Texas at El Paso			BM, BMEd, MM, MMEd		17,188	$1621	M442
University of Texas at San Antonio	BFA, MFA		BM, MM		17,579	$2068	A181, M443
University of Texas–Pan American	BFA				13,298	$1593**	A182
Wayland Baptist University			BM		897	$5750	M456
West Texas A&M University		BFA, MFA	BM, BMEd, MM		6,738	$1534	D233, M460
Utah							
Brigham Young University	BFA, BFA, MFA		BM, MM	BFA, MFA	30,413	$2450	A61, M262, T482
University of Utah	BFA, MFA	BFA, BFA, MFA, MFA	BM, BMEd, MM, MMEd	BFA, MFA	25,226	$2298*	A183, D231, M445, T522
Utah State University	BFA, MFA		BM, MMEd		20,371	$2373	A187, M451
Vermont							
Green Mountain College	BFA				518	$12,900**	A85
University of Vermont			BM		9,072	$6909	M445
Virginia							
Christopher Newport University			BM		4,705	$3350	M274
George Mason University			BM		21,774	$4212	M298
James Madison University	BFA, MFA		BM, MM		11,539	$4014	A92, M314
Liberty University			BM		4,879	$7350	M322
Longwood College	BFA		BM	BFA	3,277	$4370	A101, M323, T495
Norfolk State University			BM, MM		8,667	$2865	M344
Old Dominion University	BFA, MFA		BM, BMEd		16,500	$4086	A124, M358
Radford University	BFA, MFA	BFA	BM, BMT		9,105	$3114	A133, D218, M366
Shenandoah University		BFA	BM, BMT, MM, MMEd	BFA	1,652	$11,470	D219, M376, T505
University of Richmond			BM		4,315	$15,500	M433
Virginia Commonwealth University	BFA, MFA, DA	BFA	BM, MM	BFA, MFA	21,523	$3914**	A187, D232, M453, T524
Virginia Intermont College	BFA	BFA	BFA	BFA	682	$9600	A189, D232, M454, T524
Virginia State University	BFA		BM, BMEd		4,007	$3256	A189, M454

	Art	Dance	Music	Theater	Enroll-ment	Tuition and Fees	Page
Washington							
Central Washington University			BM, MM		8,468	$2421	M273
Cornish College of the Arts	BFA, BFA	BFA	BM	BFA, BFA	623	$10,540	A75, D209, M282, T486
Eastern Washington University			BM		8,360	$2463	M292
Pacific Lutheran University	BFA		BM, BMA, BMEd		3,257	$13,312*	A127, M359
University of Puget Sound			BM		3,163	$17,450	M432
University of Washington	BFA, MFA		BM, MM, DMA		33,719	$3021	A184, M446
Walla Walla College			BM, BMEd		1,725	$11,475	M454
Washington State University	BFA, MFA		BM, BMEd		19,314	$3153*	A189, M455
Western Washington University			BM, MM		10,598	$2556**	M458
West Virginia							
Marshall University	BFA		BFA	BFA	12,659	$2050	A105, M328, T495
Shepherd College	BFA				3,648	$2064	A145
West Virginia University	BFA, MFA		BM, BMEd, MM, MMEd, DMA	BFA, MFA	22,500	$2192	A193, M460, T527
West Virginia Wesleyan College			BM, BMEd		1,680	$14,750	M460
Wisconsin							
Alverno College			BM		1,876	$8928	M244
Cardinal Stritch College	BFA				5,654	$8357	A65
Lawrence University			BMus		1,161	$18,057	M320
Milwaukee Institute of Art and Design	BFA				511	$13,100	A111
Mount Senario College			BM, BMEd		475	$8277	M337
St. Norbert College			BM		2,092	$13,015	M386
Silver Lake College			BM		990	$8950	M377
University of Wisconsin–Eau Claire	BFA		BM, BMEd, MM		10,331	$2312*	A185, M447
University of Wisconsin–Green Bay			BM		5,630	$2286*	M447
University of Wisconsin–Madison	BFA, MFA		BM, MMA, MMEd, DMA		38,139	$2737*	A185, M447
University of Wisconsin–Milwaukee	BFA, MFA	BFA	BM, MM	BFA, MFA	22,984	$2772*	A,185 D231, M448, T522
University of Wisconsin–Oshkosh	BFA		BM, BMEd		10,567	$2162*	A186, M449
University of Wisconsin–River Falls			BMEd		6,432	$2304*	M449

* Expenses for 1994–95. ** Estimated expenses for 1995–96. *** Data not available.

	Art	Dance	Music	Theater	Enroll-ment	Tuition and Fees	Page
Wisconsin *continued*							
University of Wisconsin–Stevens Point	BFA	BFA	BM, MMEd	BFA	8,424	$2395**	A186, D231, M449, T523
University of Wisconsin–Stout	BFA				7,413	$2316*	A186
University of Wisconsin–Superior			BM, BMEd	BFA	2,420	$2182*	M449, T523
University of Wisconsin–Whitewater	BFA		BM, MMEd		10,438	$2327*	A187, M450
Viterbo College			BM		1,701	$9850	M454
Wyoming							
University of Wyoming			BM, BMEd, MM, MMEd		12,020	$2005	M450
Canada							
Acadia University			BM		4,115	***	M244
Alberta College of Art and Design	BFA				750	***	A45
Brock University			BM		11,324	$2696	M263
Carleton University			BM		22,412	$2577*	M268
Dalhousie University			BM, BMEd		10,910	$3124*	M284
Lakehead University	BFA		BM		7,918	$2561*	A98, M318
Mount Allison University	BFA		BM		2,376	$3268*	A116, M337
Nova Scotia College of Art and Design	BFA, MFA				601	$3052*	A122
Queen's University at Kingston	BFA				18,656	$2730*	A132
St. Francis Xavier University			BM		3,160	$3048*	M385
Simon Fraser University	BFA, MFA	BFA, MFA	BFA, MFA	BFA, MFA	18,252	$2368*	A146, D220, M377, T505
University of Alberta			BM, MM, DMus		30,494	$2600*	M399
University of British Columbia	BFA, MFA		BM, MM, DMA		31,118	$2500	A159, M400
University of Calgary	BFA, MFA		BM, MM		21,885	$3008**	A159, M401
University of Manitoba	BFA				25,462	$2346*	A167
University of Prince Edward Island			BM		3,156	$2920*	M431
University of Regina	BFA, MFA		BM, BMEd, MM		11,537	$2540*	A177, M433
Wilfrid Laurier University			BM, BMT		8,068	$2543*	M463
York University	BFA, MFA	BFA	BFA	BFA, MFA	38,313	$2860*	A195, D234, M466, T528

ART PROGRAMS

ART PROGRAMS

Undergraduate Degrees: Visual Arts

Students can choose between a Bachelor of Fine Arts (B.F.A.) degree, which is the professional degree for artists, and a Bachelor of Arts (B.A.) or Bachelor of Science (B.S.) degree, which are liberal arts degrees.

Enrolling in a B.F.A. degree program typically means that 65 to 70 percent of your course work will be focused in art and design, and 30 to 35 percent will be focused in liberal arts. A B.F.A. program allows you not only to major in art but often offers specialization in a field of interest, such as painting or graphic design. The B.F.A. is offered by four-year independent art colleges such as Pratt, The California College of Arts and Crafts, and The Maryland Institute, as well as by universities like Syracuse and Carnegie Mellon.

The B.A. or B.S. degree places greater emphasis on liberal arts and is usually offered by comprehensive colleges and universities. Your art major will be more generalized and will comprise about 30 to 45 percent of your studies; 55 to 70 percent of your course work will be in liberal arts courses.

B.F.A. Programs: Independent Art College or University

There is a common misperception that B.F.A. students complete more liberal arts course work at universities than they do at art colleges. Actually, B.F.A. candidates, whether studying at a professional art school or at a comprehensive university, normally take the same credit-hour requirements in the liberal arts. The major difference between B.F.A. programs can be found in the overall educational environment provided by the art college or university.

At an independent art college, all the resources of the institution—faculty, facilities, student services, and educational programs—focus on the needs of the developing professional artist. The size of art colleges tend to be comparatively small, providing an intimate and supportive atmosphere. There is a strong sense of community, shared by both students and faculty members, that grows out of common commitment and mutual respect. The creation and study of art is central to the educational experience. It is clearly understood that students have selected this environment because they want to become practicing artists. Therefore, art colleges usually offer extensive and in-depth course work in art and design as well as areas of specialization. There is also emphasis on career counseling and development specific to the visual arts.

The liberal arts programs at professional art colleges, while they do not offer the broad choices found at universities, are usually designed to integrate the study of studio art and liberal arts. For example, a physics course might focus on light and color—the content might then be integrated with concepts that are addressed in a studio course. Students majoring in graphic design might be encouraged to take psychology because this field involves marketing and management. Frequently, the liberal arts programs at art colleges emphasize courses related to creative expression—visual, verbal, and written—as well as art history, criticism, and other areas of the humanities.

The diversity of career choices for artists has never been greater. Media and technology have opened many doors for creative expression.

A university, on the other hand, offers other benefits. Students who wish to merge their ability in art with other interests and want to interact with students engaged in the study of many different disciplines might choose a university. Although not developed to support the specific needs of artists, the university can offer resources such as sports facilities, a comprehensive library, or a computer center. There are social clubs (such as fraternities and sororities), theater groups, and student government organizations, all of which provide opportunities for students to participate in the larger life of the university and meet students with other interests and talents.

Usually offered outside the department or school of art, liberal arts programs offer a wide range of electives from many disciplines, including business, biology, languages, and literature. Art students interested in developing in-depth study in a liberal arts subject can often do so through the options of minors or dual majors. The university B.F.A. program in the visual arts will be rigorous and professional, typically offering a broad range of courses and electives. Universities will vary, though, as to whether or not areas for specialization are available.

The University B.A./B.S. Programs

Because B.A. and B.S. degrees are liberal arts degrees, students who are interested in art but want to focus on academic course work should choose one of these programs. This is also a good choice for students who are unsure whether they want to major in art, who have had less artistic training, or who are less prepared for the competitive atmosphere of B.F.A. programs.

Specialization

For students at an art school, art is the central specialization. Most colleges that offer a B.F.A. have what's called a "foundation year," a first-year program that all students take before they choose a major. Usually, this curriculum is designed to expose students to new concepts and media while helping them build on existing skills, so they can then decide on an area of specialization.

Options for Non-Studio Artists

The diversity of career choices for artists has never been greater. For one thing, media and technology have opened many doors for creative expression. Many students consider

> ### *Student Self-Evaluation*
>
> **Questions to Ask Yourself Before Applying to a Visual Arts Program**
>
> *How seriously am I committed to pursuing a career in art?* Most students have known for many years that they want to be artists. They may not know if they want to be an illustrator or a painter, but they do know that they want to study art. Determining how central art is to your career goals will help you decide what kind of college you want to attend.
>
> *If I choose a B.F.A. program, do I want the very focused professional training an arts college would give me, or do I want to study art within a broader liberal arts context at a university?* Do I want to go to an arts college with a group of peers who share a strong sense of community and support or to a university where I can get more of a diverse "college experience" with students interested in other subjects besides art?
>
> *What are my strengths and weaknesses?* Students should have their portfolios reviewed, usually in their junior year in high school, either by an art college or university they are interested in or at a National Portfolio Day.
>
> *What size school do I want?* Will I be most comfortable in a smaller, more intimate setting, or do I want the anonymity and diversity of a large school?
>
> *What geographic area do I want to be in?* A major urban cultural center? Near a specific artist, gallery, or museum with which I would like to work?

careers in the film industry, doing animation or special effects or even screen writing, because of its visual language. In television, there is production and video graphics. Newspapers and magazines need artists to create information graphics and do electronic imaging. The game industry has become a big employer of artists to design computer and board games.

An artist might become an art consultant and connect artists with people who want art in their homes or corporations. There are art designers, gallery owners, event planners, and model makers for industrial products. There are many types of work in museums, from assisting conservators to designing traveling exhibits to archeological illustration.

If you follow your B.F.A. with a master's degree, there is art therapy, which combines art and psychology, and medical illustration, which combines art and biology. You can go into arts administration and work for a college or a nonprofit or government organization. Then there are art history and art criticism. Additionally, art education is offered at many universities and independent art colleges. In general, to teach at the elementary or secondary school level you need a bachelor's degree and teaching certification. To teach at the college level you need an M.F.A. or Ph.D. A new degree being offered by many colleges is a five-year dual degree that allows students to earn a B.F.A. in art as well as a Master of Arts in Teaching. For students who have a B.F.A. but no certification, there are growing opportunities to develop art programs for special populations in alternative educational settings.

Faculty

Check the faculty biographies in the college catalog to see what degrees they have and from which institutions they received them. Look for a high percentage of M.F.A.s or equivalent degrees. Also look at their professional experience in terms of awards and exhibitions. Whether faculty members are exhibiting in a top gallery in New York or at a regional gallery in Pennsylvania is not as important as the fact that they've continued to be active professionally, because they bring that back to the classroom. Look at the liberal arts faculty as well, because liberal arts are part of the B.F.A. Do they have Ph.D.s? From what universities?

The Application Process

It is important to note that there is a difference between art colleges and universities in terms of the timing and the steps you take. Most universities have hard application deadlines. You send all of your materials together—transcripts, essays, teacher recommendations, SAT or ACT scores, letters of recommendation, the whole package. B.F.A.

Program Evaluation

Questions to Ask About a Visual Arts Program to Determine if It Is the Right One for You

What depth of study is available in the area I am interested in? Look at how many and what kinds of courses are offered. Say you want to study package design. One program may offer one course a year, and another may have an entire major with 10 courses and 5 faculty members.

How large is the art college or university school of art? How many people are majoring in the program I am interested in? What is the student-faculty ratio in my area of study?

Where do the students in the program come from? Is this a regional school of commuting students, or does it attract students from all over the country or at least from a broad region? What is the age group? At some art colleges you will have a high percentage of adult students. It does make a difference in terms of environment.

Does the school's location suit my needs and preferences?

What kinds of facilities are available to me to practice my craft? The kind of working space and equipment a visual artist has is critical. Sometimes it is hard to tell that from a catalog, and a visit to a school can really make a difference. Is there independent studio space for painting majors? Is there a foundry for sculptors? What kind of computer equipment does the school have?

What level of professional exposure is available? Are there exhibition opportunities on campus? Off campus? Do you have to wait until your senior year, or can you exhibit as a freshman? Are there student memberships in professional organizations? Are there opportunities while in school for reality-based course work, such as designing a poster for a community group?

Does the program feature visiting artists or critics so I can meet practicing professionals and learn the latest theories and techniques? Who are they? How many come each semester? How long do they stay on campus? Do they lecture in an auditorium, or do they come into the studios and talk and work with students? Do they teach a master class, or do they work with beginning students as well?

Does the program arrange job internships? What kind? With whom? For credit?

Who is on the faculty? How many teach in my area of interest? What degrees do they hold? What about their experience and professional activities? Have they published recently? In what publications?

Are alumni of the program working in their chosen field? Ask especially about recent grads. What kind of entry-level jobs did they get? Did networking help them? What internships helped them? What aspects of their college curriculum helped them?

What kind of networking opportunities are available with faculty, visiting artists, and alumni? Networking is really important to artists. This is how students make connections for exhibition opportunities and jobs.

What kind of career development help does the school offer? A good B.F.A. program should have a career development center that helps students in both placement and assessment. Does the center have listings for both jobs and internships? Are the opportunities local and/or national? Does the center help students assess their abilities, skills, and interests early on and assist them in putting together their programs of study?

Does the program or school offer opportunities to study abroad?

Does the school offer financial aid and merit scholarships?

programs require a portfolio of artwork, but the B.A. and B.S. programs probably won't.

Art colleges are more inclined to have rolling admissions, partly because the portfolio plays such an important part in their evaluation and they want to give students the time and opportunity to build the best portfolio. Some art colleges send faculty or admission staff members to high schools to do presentations and evaluate portfolios. More often, students send their portfolio—usually on slides or videotape—with the rest of their admission materials. Many art colleges and universities encourage students to visit for a personal interview and portfolio review, but few require it.

Admission Criteria

The portfolio will weigh heaviest in the admission decision for art colleges, followed by the academic record. Most art colleges will place more weight on humanities courses than on math and the sciences in their evaluation of transcripts, except in the case of architecture candidates. When reviewing course work, art colleges look at what kind of high school students attend. Is it a vocational school or a private prep school? Are the courses Advanced Placement or standard? Test scores are generally used more for placement than for admission. You find many people applying to art schools who are extremely bright and very visual but who aren't good test takers.

It can be different at universities, since art students are applying for admission to the university itself. Universities generally evaluate test scores and grades first, then portfolios—or at least place equal weight on art and academics.

Portfolio Evaluation

Universities usually use faculty from the department or school of art. Art colleges use trained admission staff members, who are usually artists themselves, as well as faculty members. Portfolio evaluators at the more selective art colleges and universities are looking for more than raw talent. They are looking for a particular level of competency and technical skill as well as conceptual ability. The emphasis placed on concept versus skill will vary from college to college because each has a different philosophy of education and programmatic thrust and will look for students who are a good match for that institution. Every college, however, is looking for students who demonstrate through their artwork that they are creative, intellectually curious, and seriously invested and committed—even compelled—to make art.

The Admission Process

Students should take advantage of opportunities for early counseling and review of their work. As juniors, they should visit the school or send in their slide portfolio for feedback and advice. They can also attend one of the two dozen National Portfolio Days sponsored each year across the country by the National Portfolio Day Association of major art colleges and universities. Students have their portfolios reviewed by representatives from a number of colleges, and they can give advice on how to build on existing strengths.

Attending summer programs in art is also recommended. It is looked upon very favorably by admission committees as demonstrating an additional level of commitment to art and can be invaluable in developing a portfolio.

The Importance of Location

For artists, the location—the city you are in—is an extension of your campus. If you are not in or near a major city, you lose many opportunities for exposure to art, for exhibiting your work, for internships, and for jobs.

Internships

Internships are a practical way to bridge the world of the classroom with the world of work. There are internships available in government, in industry, in museums, even with individual artists. They provide students with the opportunity to learn new skills, explore career options, and make valuable contacts for future employment. Many colleges arrange internships and carry listings in their career center.

Abilene Christian University

Abilene, Texas

Independent-religious, coed. Urban campus. Total enrollment: 4,207.

Degrees Bachelor of Fine Arts. Majors: ceramic art and design, graphic design, jewelry and metalsmithing, painting/drawing, sculpture. Cross-registration with Hardin–Simmons University, McMurry University.

Art Student Profile Fall 1994: 65 total; all matriculated undergraduate.

Art Faculty Total: 6; 5 full-time, 1 part-time; 100% of full-time faculty have terminal degrees. Graduate students do not teach undergraduate courses. Undergraduate student–faculty ratio: 10:1.

Expenses for 1995–96 Application fee: $10. Comprehensive fee of $12,150 includes full-time tuition ($8320), mandatory fees ($200), and college room and board ($3630). College room only: $1600. Part-time tuition: $260 per semester hour. Special program-related fees: $25–$125 for supplies.

Financial Aid Program-specific awards for Fall of 1994: Juanita Tittle Pollard Scholarship for program majors ($125–$1000), Whitefield Scholarship for program majors.

Application Procedures Deadline—freshmen and transfers: continuous. Required: high school transcript, college transcript(s) for transfer students, letter of recommendation, ACT test score only. Recommended: interview, portfolio. Portfolio reviews held as needed on campus; the submission of slides may be substituted for portfolios.

Undergraduate Contact Department of Art, Abilene Christian University, ACU Station, P.O. Box 7987, Abilene, Texas 76999; 915-674-2085, fax: 915-674-6966.

Academy of Art College

San Francisco, California

Proprietary, coed. Urban campus. Total enrollment: 3,621.

Degrees Bachelor of Fine Arts in the areas of advertising design, computer arts, fashion, graphic design, illustration, interior design, photography, product and industrial design, motion pictures/video, digital media. Majors: 3-dimensional studies, advertising design, computer graphics, fashion design and technology, graphic design, illustration, industrial design, interior design, painting/drawing, photography, printmaking, production/design, sculpture. Graduate degrees offered: Master of Fine Arts in the areas of advertising design, computer arts, fashion, graphic design, illustration, interior design, photography, product and industrial design, motion pictures/video. Cross-registration with University of San Francisco.

Art Student Profile Fall 1994: 4,000 total; 3,200 matriculated undergraduate, 800 matriculated graduate.

Art Faculty Graduate students do not teach undergraduate courses. Undergraduate student–faculty ratio: 20:1.

Student Life Student groups include American Society of Interior Designers, Western Art Directors Club.

Expenses for 1995–96 Application fee: $50. Comprehensive fee of $19,055 includes full-time tuition ($12,375), mandatory fees ($180), and college room and board ($6500). College room only: $4950 (minimum). Part-time tuition: $375 per unit. Part-time mandatory fees: $100 per semester. Special program-related fees: $45–$150 for studio lab fee.

Application Procedures Deadline—freshmen and transfers: continuous. Required: high school transcript or GED.

Contact Community Outreach Office, Academy of Art College, 79 New Montgomery Street, San Francisco, California 94105; 415-274-2222, fax: 415-546-9737.

More about the Academy

Program Facilities The Academy is composed of twelve buildings in downtown San Francisco, including four student art galleries. The newly acquired Sculpture Building houses extensive studio space, including a large metal-welding space and neon sculpture facility. The Computer Center has well over 120 units, including more than twenty-five silicon graphics workstations for multimedia and film/video special effects. New major degree programs are offered in computer arts and digital media. The Academy offers an extensive photography center, including twenty-five black-and-white and eight color enlargers. The newly expanded Film Department has the latest in creative technology, including Arriflex SR-1 cameras and Sony S-VHS master editing suites.

Faculty, Resident Artists, and Alumni Nearly all of the Academy's instructors are professional artists. The school aggressively pursues artists and designers from the top firms on the West Coast. Notable faculty include Ruth Asawa (fine art), Ken Light (photo), Howard Brodie (illustration), and Ning Hou (fine art).

Student Exhibit Opportunities Over seventy student shows are given per year, including a campuswide Spring Show each May. The yearly AAC Fashion Show presents outstanding student designers. Ongoing student exhibitions take place in all buildings.

Special Programs The Academy's outstanding ESL program, equipped with a state-of-the-art Tannberg multimedia language lab and highly motivated instructors, allows all international students, even those with low English proficiency, to begin art classes immediately. International Student Office offers immigration and cultural assistance. Other features include the Career Placement Office, extensive art supply store, shuttle bus service, and free drawing seminars. A Western Art Director's Club office is on campus, as well as one of the largest ASID (American Society of Interior Designers) student chapters in the country.

Adrian College

Adrian, Michigan

Independent-religious, coed. Small-town campus. Total enrollment: 1,059.

Degrees Bachelor of Fine Arts in the areas of art, interior design, fashion design. Majors: art education, art/fine arts, arts administration, fashion design and technology, interior design. Cross-registration with Siena Heights College, Fashion Institute of Technology, Center for Creative Studies–College of Art and Design.

Art Student Profile Fall 1994: 75 total; all matriculated undergraduate; 10% minorities, 66% females, 4% international.

Art Faculty Total: 10; 4 full-time, 6 part-time; 100% of full-time faculty have terminal degrees. Graduate students do not teach undergraduate courses. Undergraduate student–faculty ratio: 14:1.

Student Life Student groups include American Society of Interior Designers, Fashion Club, Art Club.

Expenses for 1995–96 Application fee: $15. Comprehensive fee of $15,530 includes full-time tuition ($11,740), mandatory fees ($100), and college room and board ($3690). College room only: $1640. Part-time tuition: $270 per credit hour.

Financial Aid Program-specific awards for Fall of 1994: 3–10 Studio Art Scholarships for program majors ($3000–$6000).

Application Procedures Deadline—freshmen and transfers: August 15. Required: high school transcript, college transcript(s) for transfer students, minimum 2.0 high school GPA, SAT I or ACT test scores, minimum combined SAT I score of 800, minimum composite ACT score of 16. Recommended: essay, minimum 3.0 high school GPA, 2 letters of recommendation. Portfolio reviews held 1 time on campus and off campus in Fort Wayne, IN; the submission of slides may be substituted for portfolios.

Undergraduate Contact George Wolf, Director of Admissions, Adrian College, 110 South Madison Street, Adrian, Michigan 49221; 800-877-2246, fax: 517-264-3331.

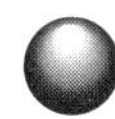

Alberta College of Art and Design

Calgary, Alberta, Canada

Independent. Urban campus. Total enrollment: 750.

Degrees Bachelor of Fine Arts in the areas of ceramics, drawing, glass, jewelry and metals, painting, printmaking, sculpture, textiles, photographic arts, visual communications, interdisciplinary studies. Majors: art/fine arts, ceramic art and design, commercial art, computer graphics, glass, graphic arts, illustration, jewelry and metalsmithing, painting/drawing, photography, printmaking, sculpture, studio art, textile arts.

Art Student Profile Fall 1994: 750 total; 725 matriculated undergraduate, 25 nondegree; 55% females, 2% international.

Art Faculty Total: 92; 42 full-time, 50 part-time; 25% of full-time faculty have terminal degrees. Undergraduate student–faculty ratio: 16:1.

Financial Aid Program-specific awards for Fall of 1994: 1 Entrance Scholarship for incoming students ($4000), 100 General Scholarships for program students ($700).

Application Procedures Deadline—freshmen and transfers: April 15. Notification date—freshmen and transfers: June 15. Required: essay, high school transcript, college transcript(s) for transfer students, portfolio, 60% average GPA on 4 grade 12 subjects. Auditions held on campus and off campus. Portfolio reviews held 4 times on campus and off campus; the submission of slides may be substituted for portfolios for large works of art, 3-dimensional pieces or when distance is prohibitive.

Undergraduate Contact Kevin Bird, Admissions Officer, Registrar's Office, Alberta College of Art and Design, 1407-14 Avenue NW, Calgary, Alberta T2N 4R3; 800-251-8290, fax: 403-289-6682.

More about the College

Program Facilities The Alberta College of Art and Design is a public college that offers four-year diploma programs and a Bachelor of Fine Arts degree in visual arts and design including: ceramics, drawing, glass, jewelry and metals, painting, printmaking, sculpture, textiles, interdisciplinary studies, photographic arts, and visual communications. The College is located in Calgary, Alberta, Canada in a 245,000-square-foot building designed specifically as an art college. ACAD studios are spacious and well-equipped. The College is the home of two contemporary art galleries, a well-stocked art supply/bookstore, a tool bank, a wood shop, an audio/visual resource center, several computer labs, a library, and a cafeteria.

Faculty, Resident Artists, and Alumni All ACAD instructors are professional artists whose own work is exhibited locally, nationally, and internationally. Practicing professional artists from across the country and around the world come to ACAD to give workshops and lectures. Recent visiting artists have included New York performance artist Karen Finley and environmental artist Alan Sonfist.

Student Performance/Exhibit Opportunities Ongoing student exhibitions take place in the student gallery and throughout the building. There are over 64 exhibiting galleries and artist run centers in the city that support and encourage emerging artists.

Special Programs ACAD has an active student exchange program which allows students to spend their third year studying at other art colleges and institutes across North America, in Great Britain, France, Germany, Norway, Sweden, and Australia.

Albertus Magnus College

New Haven, Connecticut

Independent-religious, coed. Urban campus. Total enrollment: 600.

Degrees Bachelor of Fine Arts in the area of art. Majors: graphic design, studio art. Cross-registration with Paier College of Art, Inc., University of New Haven, Quinnipiac College.

Art Student Profile Fall 1994: 20 total; all matriculated undergraduate.

Albertus Magnus College *(continued)*

Art Faculty Total: 5; 2 full-time, 3 part-time; 100% of full-time faculty have terminal degrees. Graduate students do not teach undergraduate courses. Undergraduate student–faculty ratio: 11:1.

Expenses for 1995–96 Application fee: $35. Comprehensive fee of $18,209 includes full-time tuition ($12,350), mandatory fees ($195), and college room and board ($5664). Part-time tuition: $412 per credit. Special program-related fees: $25–$40 for material fees for some studio classes.

Application Procedures Deadline—freshmen and transfers: continuous. Required: high school transcript, minimum 2.0 high school GPA, 2 letters of recommendation. Recommended: interview.

Undergraduate Contact Richard Lolatte, Dean of Admissions, Albertus Magnus College, 700 Prospect Street, New Haven, Connecticut 06511; 203-773-8501, fax: 203-773-9539.

More about the College

Program Facilities Studio facilities include a ceramics studio, a printmaking studio, a weaving room, painting and drawing studios, a computer lab, a photography studio and dark rooms, and an art gallery.

Faculty Members Notable members include Beverly Brann Chieffo, painter, printmaker; Jerome Nevins, photographer; Peter Ziou, painter; Robert Day, architect; and Lisa Wolko, ceramist.

Exhibition Opportunities The Gallery, on campus, offers ongoing shows of professional artists and also provides exhibition space for student work. All seniors present degree exhibitions in the Gallery. At least one student show is scheduled each semester.

Special Programs The Fine Arts Series brings major artists from various fields of art to the campus on a regular basis. With proximity to Yale University, students have access to many Yale facilities, such as the Yale Art Library, the Yale Art Gallery, the British Art Center, and Peabody Museum. Internships and practica at Yale or with established artists in and around New Haven offer students additional practical experience. Technical courses in illustration, interior design, and graphic design are available to students at Paier College of Art as a supplement to the program. Study-abroad opportunities are available and encouraged. An ELS Center, an intensive English Language program, is housed on campus. Students at Albertus also have the opportunity to enroll in the College's Tri-Session Plan, which enables them to earn a Bachelor of Arts or a Bachelor of Fine Arts degree in three years. During three years, the academic calendar runs from September to the end of June. Students carry 15 credits each session. Students enrolled in the Tri-Session Plan not only save valuable time but also reduce tuition costs. Art education and art therapy specializations are available. The Art Therapy program combines the two fields of art and psychology.

Albion College

Albion, Michigan

Independent-religious, coed. Small-town campus. Total enrollment: 1,641.

Degrees Bachelor of Fine Arts in the area of visual arts. Majors: art/fine arts.

Art Student Profile Fall 1994: 48 total; all matriculated undergraduate; 8% minorities, 49% females, 2% international.

Art Faculty Total: 5; 5 full-time; 100% of full-time faculty have terminal degrees. Graduate students do not teach undergraduate courses. Undergraduate student–faculty ratio: 11:1.

Student Life Student groups include Art Club.

Expenses for 1995–96 Application fee: $20. Comprehensive fee of $20,184 includes full-time tuition ($15,334) and college room and board ($4850). College room only: $2400. Part-time tuition: $2608 per unit. Special program-related fees: $25–$50 for lab fees.

Financial Aid Program-specific awards for Fall of 1994: 7 Fine Arts Scholarships for freshmen ($1000), 1 Janson Scholarship for program majors ($750).

Application Procedures Deadline—freshmen and transfers: continuous. Required: high school transcript, college transcript(s) for transfer students, letter of recommendation, portfolio, SAT I or ACT test scores. Recommended: essay, minimum 2.0 high school GPA, interview.

Undergraduate Contact Director of Admissions, Albion College, 616 East Michigan, Albion, Michigan 49224; 517-629-0321, fax: 517-629-0509.

Alfred University

Alfred, New York

Independent, coed. Rural campus. Total enrollment: 2,326.

Degrees Bachelor of Fine Arts in the areas of ceramics, graphic design, 2–dimensional studies, 3–dimensional studies. Majors: art education, art history, art/fine arts, ceramic art and design, ceramics, electronic imaging, glass, graphic design, painting/drawing, photography, printmaking, sculpture, video art, wood. Graduate degrees offered: Master of Fine Arts in the areas of ceramics, glass, sculpture. Cross-registration with State University of New York, College of Technology at Alfred.

Art Student Profile Fall 1994: 412 total; 380 matriculated undergraduate, 25 matriculated graduate, 7 nondegree; 11% minorities, 61% females, 3% international.

Art Faculty Total: 35; 25 full-time, 10 part-time; 96% of full-time faculty have terminal degrees. Graduate students do not teach undergraduate courses. Undergraduate student–faculty ratio: 13:1.

Student Life Student groups include Student Gallery exhibitions, Alternative Cinema, The Student Gallery.

Expenses for 1994–95 Application fee: $25. Comprehensive fee of $22,378 includes full-time tuition ($16,548), mandatory fees ($424), and college room and board ($5406). College room only: $2808. Part-time tuition: $375 per credit. Part-time mandatory fees: $212 per semester. Special program-related fees: $300–$700 for lab fees.

Financial Aid Program-specific awards for Fall of 1994: 6 Portfolio Scholarship for students with 5 or 6 portfolio scores ($2500–$3500), 300 Art and Design Grants for program majors demonstrating need ($500–$4200).

Application Procedures Deadline—freshmen: February 1; transfers: March 1. Notification date—freshmen: March 15; transfers: April 1. Required: essay, high school transcript, college transcript(s) for transfer students, letter of recommendation, portfolio, SAT I or ACT test scores, slides. Recommended: minimum 3.0 high school GPA, interview. Portfolio reviews held 21 times on campus.

Contact Laurie Richer, Director, Admissions Office, Alfred University, 26 North Main Street, Alfred, New York 14802; 800-541-9229, fax: 607-871-2198.

More about the University

Program Facilities Extensive facility includes state-of-the-art printmaking studio, expansive painting studios, new photography and video labs, ceramics studios equipped with 36 indoor and outdoor kilns, hot and cold glass shop and neon fabrication studio, sculpture (foundry and fabrication shop), excellent wood shop, comprehensive computer facility for graphic design, and other specialized areas. Facilities provide an optimum working environment. The Fosdick-Nelson Gallery presents exhibitions of national or international scope. Scholes Library of Ceramics houses an extensive collection of books on the arts and art history, including a rich collection of all facets of glass and ceramic art. Museum of Ceramic Art provides students with the opportunity for hands-on study of ceramic art objects.

Faculty, Resident Artist, and Alumni Faculty members are practicing artists, national and internationally renowned. They exhibit in major cities and as far as Spain, China, and Mexico. Students are well exposed to contemporary art through faculty and active visiting artists' program. The 1993–94 series on Confronting Taboos featured artists Andres Serrano, writer Susie Bright, and sculptor Mark Prent. The 1994–1995 program on The Narrative Object/The Narrative Image included artists' residences. Renowned alumni include Joel Philip Myers, glass; Ken Price, ceramics; and Michael Lax, industrial design.

Special Programs Freshman Foundation is a unique team-taught interdisciplinary course. The four-year program culminates in the all-school celebration of the Senior Show. Art Education and Pre-Art Therapy programs offer strong career opportunities. Internships are encouraged. A junior-year study abroad program is provided through exchange with England, Italy and the Czech Republic (for glass art only).

Allen R. Hite Art Institute

See University of Louisville, Allen R. Hite Art Institute

American College

Atlanta, Georgia

Proprietary, coed. Urban campus. Total enrollment: 831.

Degrees Bachelor of Fine Arts in the areas of interior design, fashion design, commercial art, video production. Majors: commercial art, fashion design and technology, graphic arts, interior design, photography, video production.

Art Student Profile Fall 1994: 612 total; all matriculated undergraduate; 21% minorities, 76% females, 22% international.

Art Faculty Total: 49; 9 full-time, 40 part-time; 100% of full-time faculty have terminal degrees. Graduate students do not teach undergraduate courses. Undergraduate student–faculty ratio: 12:1.

Student Life Student groups include American Society of Interior Designers, Portfolio Club, Dressers Club.

Expenses for 1995–96 Application fee: $35. Tuition: $9210 full-time, $975 per course part-time. Full-time mandatory fees: $480. College room only: $3750. Special program-related fees: $50 for computer lab fee.

Financial Aid Program-specific awards for Fall of 1994: 1 Travilla Scholarship for fashion design majors ($9360), 1 High School Scholarship Competition for incoming freshmen ($9360), 1 Emilio Pucci Scholarship for incoming freshmen ($1800).

Application Procedures Deadline—freshmen and transfers: continuous. Required: essay, high school transcript, college transcript(s) for transfer students, 2 letters of recommendation. Auditions held on campus and off campus. Portfolio reviews held on campus and off campus.

Undergraduate Contact Suzanne McBride, Vice President for Admissions, American College, 3330 Peachtree Road, Atlanta, Georgia 30326; 404-231-9000, fax: 404-231-1062.

American College

Los Angeles, California

Proprietary, coed. Urban campus. Total enrollment: 517.

Degrees Bachelor of Fine Arts in the areas of interior design, fashion design, commercial art, video production. Majors: commercial art, fashion design and technology, graphic arts, interior design, photography, video production.

Art Student Profile Fall 1994: 462 total; all matriculated undergraduate; 12% minorities, 68% females, 63% international.

Art Faculty Total: 54; 6 full-time, 48 part-time; 100% of full-time faculty have terminal degrees. Graduate stu-

American College *(continued)*

dents do not teach undergraduate courses. Undergraduate student–faculty ratio: 10:1.

Student Life Student groups include American Society of Interior Designers, Comma Club, Dressers Club.

Expenses for 1995–96 Tuition: $9525 full-time, $215 per credit hour part-time. Full-time mandatory fees: $555. College room only: $3825. Special program-related fees: $50 for computer lab fee.

Financial Aid Program-specific awards for Fall of 1994: 1 Travilla Scholarship for fashion design majors ($9360), 1 High School Scholarship Competition for incoming freshmen ($9360), 1 Emilio Pucci Scholarship for incoming freshmen ($1800).

Application Procedures Deadline—freshmen and transfers: continuous. Required: essay, high school transcript, college transcript(s) for transfer students, 2 letters of recommendation. Recommended: interview. Auditions held on campus and off campus. Portfolio reviews held on campus and off campus.

Undergraduate Contact Laurie Nalepa, Director of Admissions, American College, 1651 Westwood Boulevard, Los Angeles, California 90024; 310-470-2000, fax: 310-477-8640.

American University

Washington, District of Columbia

Independent-religious, coed. Suburban campus. Total enrollment: 11,708.

Degrees Bachelor of Fine Arts in the area of studio art. Majors: art/fine arts, arts administration, graphic arts, painting/drawing, printmaking, sculpture, studio art. Graduate degrees offered: Master of Fine Arts in the areas of painting, printmaking, sculpture. Cross-registration with consortium of Washington universities.

Art Student Profile Fall 1994: 126 total; 100 matriculated undergraduate, 26 matriculated graduate; 8% minorities, 55% females, 20% international.

Art Faculty Total: 20; 10 full-time, 10 part-time; 100% of full-time faculty have terminal degrees. Graduate students do not teach undergraduate courses. Undergraduate student–faculty ratio: 12:1.

Student Life Student groups include Thursday Night Artist on Art Lecture Series, Visiting Artists Programs.

Expenses for 1995–96 Application fee: $45. Comprehensive fee of $23,808 includes full-time tuition ($16,890), mandatory fees ($220), and college room and board ($6698). College room only: $4160. Part-time tuition: $563 per semester hour. Part-time mandatory fees: $220 per year.

Application Procedures Deadline—freshmen: February 1; transfers: July 1. Notification date—freshmen: April 1; transfers: continuous. Required: high school transcript. Recommended: minimum 3.0 high school GPA, letter of recommendation, interview, portfolio, slides of portfolio preferred. Portfolio reviews held continuously on campus.

Contact Glenna Haynie, Administrator, Art Department, American University, 4400 Massachusetts Avenue, NW, Washington, District of Columbia 20016; 202-885-1670, fax: 202-885-1132.

More about the University

The Department of Art is housed in the Watkins Art Building on the University's main campus. The building contains studios for painting, printmaking, sculpture, and drawing as well as the Watkins Gallery for rotating exhibitions. Individual studio space is provided for all graduate students. The proximity of the University to such institutions as the National Gallery of Art, the Hirshhorn Museum, the Phillips Collection, the Corcoran Gallery of Art, the National Museum of American Art, the National Museum of African Art, the National Museum of Women in the Arts, the Sackler Museum, the Freer Museum, and many other major museums and collections (including the department's own Watkins Collection), most of which offer free admission, makes many of the most important art works in the world a firsthand, integral component of an art student's resources and experience.

The University designated the studio program of the Department of Art a Center of Excellence, resulting in support for numerous components of the graduate program. For instance, there are two nationally recognized visiting artists in residence each semester. Rather than a one-time critique, these artists critique work two days each month for a full semester. Recent visiting artists in residence have included Gregory Amenoff, Vija Calmins, John Walker, Judy Pfaff, Sam Gilliam, George McNeil, Katherine Porter, Nathan Oliveira, Wayne Thiebaud, Joan Snyder, and Jake Berthot, to mention only some of those participating in the past few years. In addition, there is a vigorous short-term visiting artist program bringing in one-day visitors.

Andrews University

Berrien Springs, Michigan

Independent-religious, coed. Small-town campus. Total enrollment: 2,952.

Degrees Bachelor of Fine Arts in the areas of graphic design, fine arts. Majors: art history, ceramic art and design, graphic design, painting, photography, printmaking, sculpture. Cross-registration with Newbold College, United Kingdom.

Art Student Profile Fall 1994: 30 total; all matriculated undergraduate; 23% minorities, 50% females, 17% international.

Art Faculty Total: 5; 4 full-time, 1 part-time; 100% of full-time faculty have terminal degrees.

Student Life Special housing available for art students.

Expenses for 1995–96 Application fee: $30. Comprehensive fee of $13,833 includes full-time tuition ($10,476), mandatory fees ($147), and college room and board ($3210). College room only: $1890. Part-time tuition: $262 per quarter hour. Special program-related fees: $25–$100 for material fees.

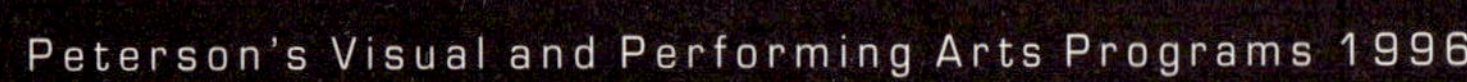

Application Procedures Deadline—freshmen and transfers: continuous. Required: high school transcript, college transcript(s) for transfer students, 2 letters of recommendation, portfolio, SAT I or ACT test scores, minimum 2.5 high school GPA. Portfolio reviews held by appointment at student's convenience on campus; the submission of slides may be substituted for portfolios for transfer applicants.

Undergraduate Contact Dr. Cheryl J. Jetter, Chair, Department of Art, Art History, and Design, Andrews University, Berrien Springs, Michigan 49104; 616-471-3529, E-mail address: cjetter@orion.cc.andrews.edu.

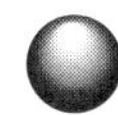

Anna Maria College

Paxton, Massachusetts

Independent-religious, coed. Small-town campus. Total enrollment: 1,797.

Degrees Bachelor of Fine Arts in the areas of art therapy, studio art, art and business. Majors: art and business, art education, art therapy, art/fine arts, studio art. Cross-registration with Worcester Consortium.

Art Student Profile Fall 1994: 10 total; all matriculated undergraduate; 1% minorities, 42% females, 1% international.

Art Faculty Total: 6; 1 full-time, 5 part-time; 50% of full-time faculty have terminal degrees. Graduate students do not teach undergraduate courses. Undergraduate student–faculty ratio: 3:1.

Student Life Student groups include senior art exhibit. Special housing available for art students.

Expenses for 1995–96 Application fee: $30. Comprehensive fee of $16,808 includes full-time tuition ($11,280), mandatory fees ($500), and college room and board ($5028). Part-time tuition: $151 per credit hour. Special program-related fees: $25 for model fees, $40 for studio fee, $130 for art practicum internship.

Application Procedures Deadline—freshmen and transfers: continuous. Required: essay, high school transcript, college transcript(s) for transfer students, minimum 2.0 high school GPA, 3 letters of recommendation, portfolio, SAT I or ACT test scores. Recommended: interview. Portfolio reviews held 18 times on campus; the submission of slides may be substituted for portfolios when distance is prohibitive.

Undergraduate Contact David Pirani, Director of Admissions, Anna Maria College, Box 78, Paxton, Massachusetts 01612-1198; 508-849-3360, fax: 508-849-3362.

Appalachian State University

Boone, North Carolina

State-supported, coed. Small-town campus. Total enrollment: 11,866.

Degrees Bachelor of Fine Arts in the areas of art, graphic design. Majors: art education, art/fine arts, arts administration, ceramic art and design, fibers, graphic design, jewelry and metalsmithing, painting/drawing, photography, printmaking, sculpture, studio art.

Art Student Profile Fall 1994: 360 total; 300 matriculated undergraduate, 60 nondegree; 2% minorities, 50% females, 2% international.

Art Faculty Total: 25; 19 full-time, 6 part-time; 100% of full-time faculty have terminal degrees. Graduate students do not teach undergraduate courses. Undergraduate student–faculty ratio: 16:1.

Student Life Student groups include Student Art League, National Art Education Association Student Chapter, American Institute of Graphic Arts Student Chapter.

Estimated Expenses for 1995–96 Application fee: $25. State resident tuition: $800 full-time. Nonresident tuition: $7600 full-time. Full-time mandatory fees: $870. College room and board: $2630. College room only: $1470.

Financial Aid Program-specific awards for Fall of 1994: 5 Fine Arts Scholarships for freshmen ($1000), 8 Talent Awards for program majors ($1800), 8 Work Study Awards for program majors ($1200–$1600).

Application Procedures Deadline—freshmen: April 1. Required: high school transcript, slides for portfolios. Recommended: minimum 3.0 high school GPA. Portfolio reviews held 3 times on campus.

Undergraduate Contact Judy Humphrey, Director of Portfolio Reviews, Art Department, Appalachian State University, 233 Wey Hall, Boone, North Carolina 28608; 704-262-2220, fax: 704-262-6312.

Aquinas College

Grand Rapids, Michigan

Independent-religious, coed. Suburban campus. Total enrollment: 2,443.

Degrees Bachelor of Fine Arts in the areas of drawing, painting, printmaking, photography, sculpture. Majors: art/fine arts.

Art Student Profile Fall 1994: 173 total; 140 matriculated undergraduate, 33 nondegree; 4% minorities, 75% females, 1% international.

Art Faculty Total: 8; 5 full-time, 3 part-time; 100% of full-time faculty have terminal degrees. Graduate students do not teach undergraduate courses. Undergraduate student–faculty ratio: 12:1.

Expenses for 1995–96 Application fee: $25. Comprehensive fee of $15,976 includes full-time tuition ($11,852 minimum) and college room and board ($4124). College room only: $1864. Part-time tuition per credit: $240 for the first 6 credits, $350 for the next 5 credits.

Application Procedures Deadline—freshmen and transfers: continuous. Required: high school transcript, minimum 2.5 high school GPA. Recommended: letter of recommendation, interview.

Aquinas College *(continued)*

Undergraduate Contact Tom Mikowski, Director of Admissions, Aquinas College, 1607 Robinson Road, SE, Grand Rapids, Michigan 49506-1799; 616-459-8281 ext. 5150, fax: 616-732-4487.

Arizona State University

Tempe, Arizona

State-supported, coed. Suburban campus. Total enrollment: 42,189.

Degrees Bachelor of Fine Arts in the area of art. Majors: art education, ceramics, drawing, fibers, graphic design, intermedia, jewelry and metalsmithing, painting, photography, printmaking, sculpture. Graduate degrees offered: Master of Fine Arts in the area of art.

Art Student Profile Fall 1994: 950 total; 800 matriculated undergraduate, 150 matriculated graduate; 15% minorities, 50% females, 10% international.

Art Faculty Total: 58; 53 full-time, 5 part-time; 94% of full-time faculty have terminal degrees. Graduate students teach a few undergraduate courses. Undergraduate student–faculty ratio: 16:1.

Expenses for 1994–95 State resident tuition: $1894 full-time. Nonresident tuition: $7500 full-time, $310 per credit part-time. State resident part-time tuition per semester ranges from $96 to $576. Part-time mandatory fees: $32 per year. College room and board: $4690. College room only: $3090. Special program-related fees: $15–$40 for lab fees.

Application Procedures Deadline—freshmen and transfers: continuous. Required: high school transcript, SAT I or ACT test scores, portfolio for graphic design applicants, minimum 2.5 college GPA for nonresident transfer students. Portfolio reviews held 1 time for graphic design applicants on campus.

Undergraduate Contact Dolores Hauptman, Undergraduate Advisor, School of Art, Arizona State University, Tempe, Arizona 85287-1505; 602-965-6296, fax: 602-965-8338.

Graduate Contact Mary Ivasutyn, Graduate Secretary, School of Art, Arizona State University, Tempe, Arizona 85287-1505; 602-965-6303, fax: 602-965-8338.

Arkansas State University

State University, Arkansas

State-supported, coed. Urban campus. Total enrollment: 9,631.

Degrees Bachelor of Fine Arts in the areas of studio art, art education, graphic design. Majors: art education, ceramics, graphic design, painting/drawing, printmaking, sculpture, studio art.

Art Faculty Total: 13; 11 full-time, 2 part-time; 100% of full-time faculty have terminal degrees. Graduate students do not teach undergraduate courses. Undergraduate student–faculty ratio: 10:1.

Expenses for 1995–96 Application fee: $25. State resident tuition: $1950 full-time, $82 per credit hour part-time. Nonresident tuition: $3600 full-time, $150 per credit hour part-time. College room and board: $2590.

Application Procedures Deadline—freshmen and transfers: continuous. Required: high school transcript, portfolio, SAT I or ACT test scores, minimum 2.0 college GPA for transfer students. Portfolio reviews held at end of college sophomore year for entrance into BFA program on campus.

Undergraduate Contact Curtis Steele, Chair, Art Department, Arkansas State University, P.O. Box 1920, State University, Arkansas 72467; 501-972-3050, fax: 501-972-3932.

Art Academy of Cincinnati

Cincinnati, Ohio

Independent, coed. Urban campus. Total enrollment: 187.

Degrees Bachelor of Fine Arts in the areas of fine art, communication design. Majors: art history, art/fine arts, commercial art, computer graphics, illustration, painting/drawing, photography, printmaking, sculpture. Cross-registration with University of Cincinnati, Xavier University, Northern Kentucky University, Miami University.

Art Student Profile Fall 1994: 187 total; all matriculated undergraduate; 5% minorities, 45% females, 1% international.

Art Faculty Total: 41; 16 full-time, 25 part-time; 98% of full-time faculty have terminal degrees. Graduate students do not teach undergraduate courses. Undergraduate student–faculty ratio: 10:1.

Expenses for 1995–96 Application fee: $25. Tuition: $9990 full-time, $350 per credit hour part-time. Part-time mandatory fees: $430 per year. Full-time mandatory fees: $430.

Financial Aid Program-specific awards for Fall of 1994: 10–15 Entrance Scholarships for incoming students ($2000–$6000).

Application Procedures Deadline—freshmen and transfers: March 15. Required: essay, high school transcript, college transcript(s) for transfer students, minimum 2.0 high school GPA, interview, portfolio, SAT I or ACT test scores. Recommended: 2 letters of recommendation. Portfolio reviews held continuously on campus; the submission of slides may be substituted for portfolios when distance is prohibitive.

Undergraduate Contact Douglas Dobbins, Director of Admissions, Art Academy of Cincinnati, 1125 Saint Gregory Street, Cincinnati, Ohio 45202; 800-323-5692, fax: 513-562-8778.

Art Center College of Design

Pasadena, California

Independent, coed. Suburban campus. Total enrollment: 1,164.

Degrees Bachelor of Fine Arts in the areas of advertising, illustration, graphic and packaging design, photography, fine arts, film; Bachelor of Science in the areas of environmental design, product transportation. Majors: advertising design and communication, art/fine arts, commercial art, computer graphics, graphic arts, illustration, industrial design, painting/drawing, photography, transportation design. Graduate degrees offered: Master of Fine Arts in the areas of advertising, illustration, graphic and packaging design, photography, fine arts, film, computer graphics; Master of Science in the areas of environmental design, transportation design, product design. Cross-registration with California Institute of Technology, Occidental College.

Art Student Profile Fall 1994: 1,859 total; 1,207 matriculated undergraduate, 72 matriculated graduate, 580 nondegree; 33% minorities, 38% females, 22% international.

Art Faculty Total: 294; 60 full-time, 234 part-time; 95% of full-time faculty have terminal degrees. Graduate students do not teach undergraduate courses. Undergraduate student–faculty ratio: 10:1.

Student Life Student groups include Asian Artists Network, Art Center.

Expenses for 1995–96 Application fee: $45. Tuition: $14,400 full-time.

Financial Aid Program-specific awards for Fall of 1994: 300 Art Center Scholarships for program majors ($7200), 30 Entering Grants for program majors ($5000), 10 Irvine Scholar Grants for Hispanic, African American, Native American students ($7200), 6 Ford Minority Scholarships for Hispanic, African-American, or female transportation designers ($7200).

Application Procedures Deadline—freshmen and transfers: continuous. Required: essay, high school transcript, college transcript(s) for transfer students, portfolio, SAT I or ACT test scores, minimum TOEFL score of 550 for international students. Recommended: minimum 3.0 high school GPA, interview. Portfolio reviews held continuously on campus.

Contact Kit Baron, Vice President, Student Services, Art Center College of Design, 1700 Lida Street, Pasadena, California 91103; 818-396-2373, fax: 818-405-9104.

Art Center was founded in 1930 in downtown Los Angeles with a single purpose—to educate students for careers of achievement in the visual arts professions. The founder, Tink Adams, vowed to work closely with the leaders of industry to prepare professionals for meaningful careers. This tradition of close industry relationships continues today at the Pasadena campus and at the European campus in Switzerland.

Recognized by *U.S. News and World Report* in 1992 and 1993 as the leading visual arts college in the country in "The Best Specialty Schools" category, Art Center attracts attention from firms throughout the world. Companies such as Ford, Nike, Honda, Sony, Hallmark, and Kodak have decided to sponsor special student research projects at the College. Students have the opportunity to work with real clients on futuristic and conceptual projects.

In addition to visiting industry guests, the College features a faculty of practicing professionals who reinforce this tradition of real-world influence. Most are part-time faculty who maintain their own distinctive client lists.

Fine arts students have an opportunity to work with some of the most provocative artists and painters working today, such as Mike Kelley, Steve Prina, and Jeremy Gilbert Rolfe.

David Jacobs

Maryland Institute, College of Art—Writer, Creator, and Producer, NBC Productions, and director and teacher of screenwriting at the American Film Institute

I achieved my professional success as a writer, but my art education enabled me to take that success as far as it could go. Being trained in fine arts is the best training in problem solving. You learn to communicate in many "languages"—words, images, or sound. In my work I must draw on these communication skills a hundred times a day. I also learned to take risks and to think boldly in ways I think are unique to an artist's education. I can't think of any pressurized field where one doesn't paint oneself into corners. At the Maryland Institute you're encouraged to paint yourself into corners, than paint yourself out. That's learning to be truly creative, and creativity is welcome in any field.

Art Center College of Design *(continued)*

Art Center acknowledges and encourages the dissolution of boundaries between disciplines, and, although students apply to and study within specific majors, there are opportunities for new kinds of art-making based on digital and other technologies. A common link among students in all majors has become the computer. The College's mission is to lead the way for the industry in exploring new roles for design, photography, and film.

The average freshman at Art Center is 23 years old; all students must declare a major before entering the College. This has resulted in a mature and focused student body. Campus life, too, is influenced by the maturity of the students. There is no on-campus housing. Students choose from an abundance of housing within the Pasadena and Los Angeles area.

Facilities Art Center is an acknowledged leader in providing new technologies and state-of-the-art facilities to its students. Features include a distinctive contemporary campus in the hills overlooking Pasadena's Rose Bowl; 215,000-square-foot glass and steel building designed by Craig Ellwood; 11,000-square-foot computer graphics lab with seventy-eight Macintosh stations, thirty-one Silicon Graphic platforms, and one of the world's largest computer-aided industrial design (CAID) networks as well as a vast array of software to introduce students to the newest digital technologies; photography areas with black-and-white labs with seventy-five enlargers, color lab with 20″ fully automated E-6 processor, 20″ fully automated cibachrome processor, and 20″ RA4 fully automated processor; two 4,600-square-foot shooting stages providing twenty-six shooting states equipped with seamless background colors, including one 15 x 30 flying flat; and digital imaging facilities including Kodak XL 7700 thermal printer, RFS 2035 film scanners, H-P Paint Jet printer, Quadra 700 workstations, 840 AV workstation, and a Microtech 4 x 5 film scanner and Agfa flatbed transparency scanner.

Special Programs Art Center has a sister campus in Vevey, Switzerland, on Lake Geneva, which offers degree programs in communications design, product, and transportation design. Students may study in Europe full-time or make take advantage of an exchange program from Pasadena. Classes are conducted in English. The College encourages a global and international approach to design education. The Art Center encourages a wide variety of internship opportunities with major corporations and firms such as Ford, General Motors, Walt Disney Pictures, Reebok, Microsoft, Frogdesign, and Weiden and Kennedy. Students may also accept paid mentorship positions or enroll in a mentorship class to assist local Pasadena high school students.

Art Center's graduates have made significant marks in the world of art and design, and alumni return to the campus to recruit for their own employment needs. The high demand for Art Center graduates is attributable to the degree of specialization and professionalism required of the students. In excess of 200 firms visit the College to interview graduating students each year, and job listings are printed regularly for the use of students and alumni. Some of the firms that recruited on campus in 1993–94 included: Harcourt Brace & Co.; Warner Brothers Records; The Walt Disney Company; Ford Motor Company; General Motors Corporation; Mattel Toys; Ogilvy and Mather; Goodby, Berlin, and Silverstein; Virgin Records; Landor Associates; Honda; Texas Instruments; L.A. Gear; Young and Rubicam; Nike; Hal Riney and Partners; Mercedes-Benz; MCA-Universal Studios; Motorola; Hallmark Cards; Neiman Marcus Direct; and CALTY Design Research.

Located on an idyllic campus in suburban Pasadena, Art Center offers a contemplative environment juxtaposed with the internationalism of Los Angeles and the Pacific Rim. Art Center encourages a diverse student population of students and faculty. In bringing together a community of students from throughout the United States and the world, the goal is to develop new solutions to design issues and to promote the importance of design within the world communities. It is within this context that students receive highly individualized and rigorous programs of study. Critical thinking as well as development of technical skills are emphasized.

Art Institute of Boston

Boston, Massachusetts

Independent, coed. Urban campus. Total enrollment: 388.

Degrees Bachelor of Fine Arts in the areas of fine arts, illustration, design, fine arts/illustration, illustration/design, photography. Majors: advertising design, animation, art/fine arts, drafting and design, graphic arts, graphic design, illustration, painting/drawing, photography, printmaking, sculpture, studio art. Cross-registration with The Boston Architectural Center, Pine Manor College, The Association of Independent Colleges of Art and Design, Parson's School of Design, Berklee College of Music.

Art Student Profile Fall 1994: 548 total; 397 matriculated undergraduate, 151 nondegree; 8% minorities, 51% females, 10% international.

Art Faculty Total: 88; 15 full-time, 73 part-time; 99% of full-time faculty have terminal degrees. Graduate students do not teach undergraduate courses. Undergraduate student–faculty ratio: 12:1.

Student Life Student groups include Peer Advisors, student exhibitions in galleries and sites around Boston.

Expenses for 1995–96 Application fee: $30. Comprehensive fee of $17,360 includes full-time tuition ($9990), mandatory fees ($670 minimum), and college room and board ($6700). Part-time tuition: $400 per credit. Mandatory fees for photography and design students: $650. Special program-related fees: $650 for photography department fees, $650 for design department fees, $530 for other departments' fees.

Financial Aid Program-specific awards for Fall of 1994: 16 Merit Scholarships for incoming students ($1000–$4000), 1 Presidential Scholarship for incoming students ($9450), 111 Art Institute of Boston Grants for those demonstrating need ($500–$2000), 18 Portfolio Scholarships for enrolled students ($500–$4500).

Application Procedures Deadline—freshmen and transfers: continuous. Required: essay, high school transcript, college transcript(s) for transfer students, interview, portfolio. Recommended: minimum 2.0 high school GPA, letter of recommendation, SAT I test score only. Portfolio reviews held as needed on campus and off campus on National Portfolio Days; the submission of slides may be substituted for portfolios if a campus visit is impossible.

Undergraduate Contact Diana Arcadipone, Dean of Admissions, Art Institute of Boston, 700 Beacon Street, Boston, Massachusetts 02215; 617-262-1223, fax: 617-437-1226.

More about the Institute

Program Facilities The Art Institute of Boston's (AIB) facilities include a 1,500-square foot Exhibition Gallery; painting/drawing studios; a Macintosh computer laboratory; a production room containing stat cameras and production facilities; three private and gang photography labs with color and black-and-white systems, a nonsilver facility, several studios, and yearlong photo gallery exhibiting student work; a wood shop; a printmaking lab with etching press and lithography press; and a clay lab with kilns. The library collection contains over 7,000 books; 55 serial titles; 26,000 slides; a video viewing room; and a picture reference file of 10,000 photographs and illustrations. The library is the Boston conservator of the National Gallery of Art's American Art Collection on videodisc, a visual reference of more than 26,000 images that span three centuries. Students and faculty have full access to the library at Suffolk University, Boston.

Special Programs The DuPont Visiting Artist Fellowship program (annual grant of $15,000) supporting the work of an accomplished minority photographer; a collaboration with The Boston Film and Video Foundation; a work-study and internship program with leading advertising and design firms; study abroad programs in Paris, France, and Florence and Tuscany, Italy, among others; full- and part-time job listings; freelance and placement listings through the Artists Resources Services, and a Counseling and Guidance Center.

The Art Institute of Boston is an independent college of art founded in 1912. Its programs are studio intensive, integrating liberal arts courses specifically designed to broaden students' intellectual and artistic perceptions. The Institute of Boston provides an environment for students dedicated to achieving success in their careers—the atmosphere is both challenging and nurturing, helping to maximize personal and intellectual growth and artistic potential.

The school is small and intimate, and most students and faculty know each other by the end of the first semester. The Art Institute of Boston has an exceptional faculty, many of whom are well-known practicing artists, designers, illustrators, and photographers. Some of AIB's faculty include Professor and Chair of the Foundation Department, Nathan Goldstein, a leading author of art education textbooks, lecturer, and artist; Christopher James, Professor and Chair of the Photography Department, an internationally recognized photographer who has won numerous awards and fellowships and whose work is in museum collections around the world; Jane Tuckerman, Associate Professor of Photography, a widely exhibited photographer and recipient of an NEA fellowship and other prestigious grants and fellowships; and Anthony Apesos, Associate Professor and Chair of the Fine Arts Department, who is an accomplished painter, lecturer, and art critic.

The faculty members at The Art Institute of Boston serve as mentors to their students and are very accessible to them. Students at AIB benefit from lectures, exhibitions, and from the visiting artists who bring the classroom to life. Activities and opportunities for growth and learning at AIB include exhibition exchanges, art auctions, student exhibitions both on and off-campus, lectures, a visiting artist program, and special events. Acclaimed artists such as Chuck Close, Duane Michals, and Norman Laliberté have recently been guest lecturers at the college.

Education at AIB is not confined to the rooms and galleries of The Art Institute of Boston. Students benefit from the talent and experience of the faculty as well as the extensive connections to the art and business communities that the school has nurtured over the past several decades. In addition to year-long exhibitions of student work in AIB's Gallery South and throughout the Institute, students exhibit at numerous galleries around Boston. Students are encouraged to show their work long before graduation, gaining valuable life experience outside the classroom.

The practical aspect of developing a career in art is part of the formal curriculum at AIB. By the time students graduate, they are well prepared for their profession through courses exclusively devoted to career-related skills, such as presentation and portfolio building as well as learning to make contacts in their field. AIB graduates cite the practical skills and the encouragement they received as key factors in building the confidence and skills needed to succeed in their careers.

The city of Boston is a thriving and vibrant center for the arts, education, and business. Home to countless museums and galleries, symphonies, theaters, libraries, and sports events, students find themselves immersed in exciting and stimulating surroundings. Boston has more than seventy colleges or universities in the area, which offer constant opportunities for exploration and learning.

Art Institute of Southern California

Laguna Beach, California

Independent, coed. Small-town campus. Total enrollment: 164.

Degrees Bachelor of Fine Arts in the areas of drawing/painting, graphic design, illustration. Majors: art/fine arts, graphic arts, graphic design, illustration.

Art Student Profile Fall 1994: 160 total; all matriculated undergraduate; 25% minorities, 55% females, 15% international.

Art Faculty Total: 28; 8 full-time, 20 part-time; 80% of full-time faculty have terminal degrees. Graduate students do not teach undergraduate courses. Undergraduate student–faculty ratio: 8:1.

Student Life Student groups include Student Government.

Expenses for 1995–96 Application fee: $35. Tuition: $10,200 full-time, $425 per unit part-time. Tuition guaranteed not to increase for student's term of enrollment.

Art Institute of Southern California *(continued)*

Financial Aid Program-specific awards for Fall of 1994: Competitive Scholarships for enrolled students ($700–$1200).

Application Procedures Deadline—freshmen and transfers: continuous. Required: essay, high school transcript, college transcript(s) for transfer students, minimum 2.0 high school GPA, letter of recommendation, portfolio for transfer applicants. Recommended: interview, portfolio. Auditions held on campus and off campus. Portfolio reviews held 8-10 on campus and off campus in various locations; the submission of slides may be substituted for portfolios.

Undergraduate Contact John Walker, Director of Admissions, Art Institute of Southern California, 2222 Laguna Canyon Road, Laguna Beach, California 92651-1136; 714-497-3309, fax: 714-494-4399.

More about the Institute

The Art Institute of Southern California, located in Orange County's Laguna Beach, is a small, specialized school for students interested in becoming artists or designers. The college combines personal attention with the best in faculty members and facilities to attain this goal. AISC's sole purpose is to help train students to become professional artists or designers.

Program Facilities At the Art Institute, students pursue four-year Bachelor of Fine Arts degrees in drawing and painting, graphic design, or illustration, where the work in the studio will be complemented by a diverse liberal arts course of study. All classes needed for the degree are taught on AISC's 5-acre campus.

AISC offers students excellent facilities; the recently redesigned Barbara Auerbach Computer Facility exclusively features Macintosh Power PCs for student use, as well as two scanners, color, and laser printers. Drawing, painting, three dimensional, and photographic studios are designed to fit the needs of students in the visual arts. All studios are accessible to students for their use when classes are not in session.

Faculty AISC's faculty members have been selected for their professional experience and teaching abilities. All studio instructors are practicing artists or designers, and most hold terminal degrees in their field of study.

Special Programs Students enjoy small class sizes and individual attention. In addition, AISC's administration realizes the high cost of college educations, and has worked to keep tuition costs less than 75% of all other accredited colleges offering similar programs.

Atlanta College of Art

Atlanta, Georgia

Independent, coed. Urban campus. Total enrollment: 424.

Degrees Bachelor of Fine Arts. Majors: advertising design, art/fine arts, communication design, computer art, computer graphics, electronic arts, graphic design, illustration, interior design, painting/drawing, photography, printmaking, sculpture, video art. Cross-registration with University of Georgia System.

Art Student Profile Fall 1994: 424 total; all matriculated undergraduate; 24% minorities, 50% females, 6% international.

Art Faculty Total: 73; 24 full-time, 49 part-time; 100% of full-time faculty have terminal degrees. Undergraduate student–faculty ratio: 12:1.

Student Life Student groups include Visions of Color, Icon Club. Special housing available for art students.

Expenses for 1995–96 Application fee: $25. Tuition: $10,500 full-time. College room only: $3350.

Financial Aid Program-specific awards for Fall of 1994: 50–75 President's Scholarships for incoming students ($500–$1000), 20–25 Dean's Scholarships for incoming students ($1000), School of Excellence Awards for incoming students ($1000), Undergraduate Awards for continuing students.

Application Procedures Deadline—freshmen and transfers: continuous. Required: essay, high school transcript, college transcript(s) for transfer students, minimum 2.0 high school GPA, portfolio, SAT I or ACT test scores. Recommended: minimum 3.0 high school GPA, letter of recommendation, interview. Portfolio reviews held continuously on campus and off campus on National Portfolio Days and in various high schools in U.S. and abroad; the submission of slides may be substituted for portfolios.

Undergraduate Contact John A. Farkas, Director of Enrollment Management, Atlanta College of Art, 1280 Peachtree Street, NE, Atlanta, Georgia 30309; 800-832-2104, fax: 404-733-5107.

More about the College

Program Facilities Studios: Black-and-white color, nonsilver and cibachrome photography darkrooms, drawing and painting, video shooting and editing, computer graphics and animation, woodworking, metal, foundry, ceramics, blacksmithing, lithography, intaglio, screen print, paper and book-making, individual student workspace in design, senior painting, and sculpture. Gallery: Student exhibition space, ACA Gallery of Contemporary Art and Design. Library; 30,000 volumes primarily dedicated to contemporary art, 70,000 slides, 250 journals, and 1,000 artists' books.

The Atlanta College of Art is a thriving artistic community that offers the student an opportunity to engage creative people unified through the search for artistic excellence. Students from all over the globe form the ACA community. ACA offers majors in drawing, electronic arts (computer art, computer graphics, video or experimental sound), painting, photography, printmaking, sculpture, interior design, or communication design (advertising design, graphic design, or illustration). One of the great strengths of the ACA curriculum is that the student may build an individualized major from several studio disciplines.

The first-year curriculum, considered to be somewhat unique among art colleges, combines a comprehensive training in the art skills and media with the conceptual rigor needed to be a successful artist and designer today. The student encounters the role of the artist in the diverse cultures of our world. The Artist and World Cultures course, which is the foundation of the general education requirement, prepares the student for the intensive study of the relationship between art and culture.

The faculty at ACA is committed to the education of the student and designer. The faculty comprises award-winning artists, designers, and scholars. In addition to full-time faculty, well-known artists and designers regularly invigorate the life of the College through lectures and workshops. An international artist and designer residency program was established in 1993 to bring global issues in art design directly into the community.

Professional skills are reinforced through courses such as "The Artist as Professional" and through student internships at regional art and design institutions such as the High Museum of Art, Sandler Hudson Gallery, Art Papers, and notable companies such as IBM, CNN, and Coca-Cola. Many of these internships result in full-time employment after graduation.

Extensive renovations to the Woodruff Arts Center will be completed in time for the 1996 Olympic Games. This $15 million makeover will include new professional and student galleries, a greatly expanded two-story library, additional studio space, and renovations to Lombardy Hall, the college residence hall. The Electronic Media Center is well-known in the region for its computer, sound, and video technology. Advanced painting, sculpture, and design students have their own studio spaces, and most work areas are available 24 hours a day. The library houses a fine regional collection of contemporary art references, including an outstanding collection of artist-made books. The ACA gallery is well-known in Atlanta for its collection of nationally and internationally known contemporary art.

The ACA campus is part of the Woodruff Arts Center which includes the High Museum of Art, The Alliance and Studio Theaters, and the Atlanta Symphony Orchestra. The Atlanta College of Art is one of the founding members of the University Center in Georgia. Students at ACA have access to libraries, lectures, and exhibitions at all of the thirteen member institutions. Cross-registration with institutions such as Georgia Institute of Technology, Emory University, Spelman College, and Agnes Scott College make it easy for students to expand their education beyond the ACA campus.

Auburn University

Auburn University, Alabama

State-supported, coed. Small-town campus. Total enrollment: 21,226.

Degrees Bachelor of Fine Arts in the areas of applied art, graphic arts. Majors: ceramics, commercial art, graphic arts, graphic design, illustration, painting/drawing, printmaking, sculpture, studio art. Graduate degrees offered: Master of Fine Arts in the areas of applied art, graphic arts.

Art Student Profile Fall 1994: 1,036 total; 230 matriculated undergraduate, 6 matriculated graduate, 800 nondegree; 2% minorities, 53% females, 1% international.

Art Faculty Total: 25; 25 full-time; 100% of full-time faculty have terminal degrees. Graduate students teach a few undergraduate courses. Undergraduate student–faculty ratio: 10:1.

Student Life Student groups include Auburn Students in Graphic Design, Association of Visual Artists.

Expenses for 1994–95 Application fee: $25. State resident tuition: $2100 full-time. Nonresident tuition: $6300 full-time. Part-time tuition per quarter ranges from $178 to $758 for state residents, $534 to $2274 for nonresidents. College room only: $1410 (minimum). Special program-related fees: $20–$65 for material fees.

Application Procedures Deadline—freshmen and transfers: September 1. Notification date—freshmen and transfers: continuous. Required: high school transcript, college transcript(s) for transfer students, SAT I or ACT test scores. Recommended: portfolio. Portfolio reviews held 4 times on campus; the submission of slides may be substituted for portfolios when distance is prohibitive.

Undergraduate Contact Ross Heck, Academic Advisor, Department of Art, Auburn University, 101 Biggin Hall, Auburn University, Alabama 36849-5125; 334-844-4373, fax: 334-844-4024, E-mail address: heckdon@mail.auburn.edu.

Graduate Contact Nancy Hartsfield, Graduate Program Officer, Department of Art, Auburn University, 101 Biggin Hall, Auburn University, Alabama 36849-5125; 334-844-3383, fax: 334-844-4024.

Augusta College

Augusta, Georgia

State-supported, coed. Urban campus. Total enrollment: 5,673.

Degrees Bachelor of Fine Arts in the area of art. Majors: applied art, studio art.

Art Student Profile Fall 1994: 70 total; all matriculated undergraduate.

Art Faculty Total: 6; 6 full-time; 100% of full-time faculty have terminal degrees. Graduate students do not teach undergraduate courses. Undergraduate student–faculty ratio: 10:1.

Expenses for 1994–95 Application fee: $10. State resident tuition: $1632 full-time. Nonresident tuition: $4476 full-time. Part-time tuition per quarter ranges from $270 to $470 for state residents, $670 to $1270 for nonresidents.

Financial Aid Program-specific awards for Fall of 1994: 1 Department Scholarship for program majors ($500), 1 Mary Byrd Scholarship for graduates of local Georgia high schools ($1000), 1 Nathan Bindler Award for artistically talented program majors ($500).

Application Procedures Deadline—freshmen and transfers: August 15. Required: high school transcript, minimum 2.0 high school GPA, 2 letters of recommendation. Recommended: portfolio. Portfolio reviews held 1 time on campus; the submission of slides may be substituted for portfolios when distance is prohibitive.

Augusta College *(continued)*

Undergraduate Contact Dr. Clayton Shotwell, Chairman, Fine Arts Department, Augusta College, 2500 Walton Way, Augusta, Georgia 30904-2200; 706-737-1453.

Austin Peay State University

Clarksville, Tennessee

State-supported, coed. Suburban campus. Total enrollment: 8,207.

Degrees Bachelor of Fine Arts in the area of studio arts. Majors: ceramic art and design, graphic design, painting/drawing, photography, printmaking, sculpture.

Art Student Profile Fall 1994: 145 total; all matriculated undergraduate.

Art Faculty Total: 19; 10 full-time, 9 part-time; 100% of full-time faculty have terminal degrees. Graduate students do not teach undergraduate courses.

Student Life Student groups include Student Art League.

Expenses for 1995–96 Application fee: $5. State resident tuition: $1878 full-time, $72 per semester hour part-time. Nonresident tuition: $5812 full-time, $244 per semester hour part-time. Part-time mandatory fees: $68 per semester. Full-time mandatory fees: $262. College room and board: $2930. College room only: $1460.

Financial Aid Program-specific awards for Fall of 1994: 2 Center for the Creative Arts Scholarships for program majors.

Application Procedures Deadline—freshmen and transfers: July 1. Required: ACT test score only, minimum composite ACT score of 19. Recommended: portfolio. Portfolio reviews held on campus; the submission of slides may be substituted for portfolios for 3-dimensional work.

Undergraduate Contact Susan Bryant, Acting Chair, Department of Art, Austin Peay State University, P.O. Box 4677, Clarksville, Tennessee 37044; 615-648-7333, fax: 615-648-5997.

Ball State University

Muncie, Indiana

State-supported, coed. Urban campus. Total enrollment: 19,515.

Degrees Bachelor of Fine Arts in the area of art. Majors: ceramic art and design, commercial art, drawing, jewelry and metalsmithing, painting, photography, printmaking, sculpture.

Art Student Profile Fall 1994: 365 total; 347 matriculated undergraduate, 18 matriculated graduate; 5% minorities, 53% females, 2% international.

Art Faculty Total: 31; 21 full-time, 10 part-time; 90% of full-time faculty have terminal degrees. Graduate students do not teach undergraduate courses. Undergraduate student–faculty ratio: 13:1.

Student Life Student groups include National Art Education Association Student Chapter, Fine Arts League, Crafts Guild.

Expenses for 1995–96 Application fee: $25. State resident tuition: $3048 full-time. Nonresident tuition: $7824 full-time. Part-time tuition per semester ranges from $458 to $1224 for state residents, $1260 to $2955 for nonresidents. College room and board: $3768.

Financial Aid Program-specific awards for Fall of 1994: 3 Freshmen Scholarship Awards for freshmen ($1500).

Application Procedures Deadline—freshmen: April 1; transfers: continuous. Notification date—freshmen: May 1. Required: high school transcript, college transcript(s) for transfer students, SAT I or ACT test scores, minimum combined SAT I score of 800, minimum composite ACT score of 19, slides of portfolio. Recommended: minimum 2.0 high school GPA. Portfolio reviews held continuously on campus.

Undergraduate Contact Barbara Giorgio-Booher, Primary Department Advisor, Department of Art, Ball State University, Muncie, Indiana 47306-0405; 317-285-5841, fax: 317-285-3790, E-mail address: 00bjgiorgio@bsuvc.bsu.edu.

Graduate Contact Dr. Marilynn Price-Richard, Coordinator- Graduate Program in Art, Department of Art, Ball State University, Muncie, Indiana 47306-0405; 317-285-5807, fax: 317-285-3790, E-mail address: 01mjprice@bsuvc.bsu.edu.

Barton College

Wilson, North Carolina

Independent-religious, coed. Small-town campus. Total enrollment: 1,465.

Degrees Bachelor of Fine Arts in the areas of commercial design, ceramics, painting, photography. Majors: ceramic art and design, commercial art, painting/drawing, photography.

Art Student Profile Fall 1994: 60 total; all matriculated undergraduate.

Art Faculty Total: 6; 5 full-time, 1 part-time; 90% of full-time faculty have terminal degrees. Graduate students do not teach undergraduate courses. Undergraduate student–faculty ratio: 12:1.

Expenses for 1995–96 Application fee: $20. Comprehensive fee of $11,995 includes full-time tuition ($7795), mandatory fees ($600), and college room and board ($3600). College room only: $1800. Part-time tuition: $332 per semester hour.

Financial Aid Program-specific awards for Fall of 1994: 1 Bessie Massengill Award for sophomores and juniors ($1000), 1 TEAM Award for sophomores and juniors ($1000), 2 National Scholastic for freshmen ($1000).

Application Procedures Deadline—freshmen and transfers: continuous. Required: high school transcript, letter of recommendation, SAT I or ACT test scores. Recommended: minimum 2.0 high school GPA.

Undergraduate Contact Thomas Marshall, Coordinator of Visual Arts, Barton College, College Station, Wilson, North Carolina 27893; 919-399-6479, fax: 919-237-4957.

Bassist College

Portland, Oregon

Proprietary, coed. Urban campus. Total enrollment: 134.

Degrees Bachelor of Industrial Design in the area of industrial design. Majors: apparel design, industrial design, interior design, textiles and clothing.

Art Student Profile Fall 1994: 106 total; all matriculated undergraduate; 13% minorities, 86% females, 8% international.

Art Faculty Total: 20; 9 full-time, 11 part-time; 33% of full-time faculty have terminal degrees. Graduate students do not teach undergraduate courses. Undergraduate student–faculty ratio: 12:1.

Student Life Student groups include American Society of Interior Designers Student Chapter.

Expenses for 1995–96 Application fee: $100. Tuition: $8600 full-time, $150 per credit part-time. College room only: $2775. Tuition guaranteed not to increase for student's term of enrollment. Special program-related fees: $85–$120 for laboratory fees.

Financial Aid Program-specific awards for Fall of 1994: 1 Industrial Design Scholarship for program majors ($500), 1 Fashion Group Scholarship for artistically talented ($500), 1 Make it Yourself With Wool Scholarship for artistically talented ($500).

Application Procedures Deadline—freshmen and transfers: September 10. Notification date—freshmen and transfers: September 20. Required: high school transcript, college transcript(s) for transfer students, minimum 2.0 high school GPA, 2 letters of recommendation. Recommended: essay, minimum 3.0 high school GPA, interview, portfolio. Portfolio reviews held continuously on campus.

Undergraduate Contact Matthew Bassist, Director of Admissions, Bassist College, 2000 Southwest Fifth Avenue, Portland, Oregon 97201; 503-228-6528, fax: 503-228-4227.

Baylor University

Waco, Texas

Independent-religious, coed. Urban campus. Total enrollment: 12,240.

Degrees Bachelor of Fine Arts in the areas of painting, printmaking, graphic design, ceramics, jewelry/metalsmithing, art education. Majors: art education, ceramic art and design, commercial art, jewelry and metalsmithing, painting/drawing, printmaking, studio art.

Art Student Profile Fall 1994: 800 total; all matriculated undergraduate; 3% minorities, 75% females, 7% international.

Art Faculty Total: 13; 13 full-time; 100% of full-time faculty have terminal degrees. Undergraduate student–faculty ratio: 14:1.

Student Life Student groups include Art Club, Advertising Club of Baylor.

Expenses for 1995–96 Application fee: $25. Comprehensive fee of $12,533 includes full-time tuition ($7740), mandatory fees ($654), and college room and board ($4139). College room only: $1790. Part-time tuition: $258 per semester hour. Part-time mandatory fees: $21 per semester hour. Special program-related fees: $30 for studio lab fees.

Financial Aid Program-specific awards for Fall of 1994: 1 Friends of Baylor Fine Arts Award for continuing students ($1600), 12–14 Patricia Johnston Scholarships for continuing students ($500–$900), 1 C. C. and Helen Reid Scholarship for continuing students ($250), 2 Freshmen Art Scholarships for freshmen ($2500).

Application Procedures Deadline—freshmen and transfers: April 15. Required: high school transcript, minimum 2.0 high school GPA. Recommended: minimum 3.0 high school GPA, letter of recommendation.

Undergraduate Contact John D. McClanahan, Chair, Art Department, Baylor University, P.O. Box 97263, Waco, Texas 76798-7263; 817-755-1867, fax: 817-755-1765, E-mail address: martha_voyles@baylor.edu.

Beaver College

Glenside, Pennsylvania

Independent-religious, coed. Suburban campus. Total enrollment: 2,387.

Degrees Bachelor of Fine Arts in the areas of graphic design, interior design, painting, printmaking, ceramics, metals and jewelry, photography, art education. Majors: art education, art history, art/fine arts, ceramic art and design, commercial art, graphic design, interior design, jewelry and metalsmithing, painting/drawing, photography, printmaking, studio art. Cross-registration with London Guildhall University.

Art Student Profile Fall 1994: 158 total; 148 matriculated undergraduate, 10 matriculated graduate; 15% minorities, 65% females, 3% international.

Art Faculty Total: 16; 6 full-time, 10 part-time; 83% of full-time faculty have terminal degrees. Graduate students do not teach undergraduate courses. Undergraduate student–faculty ratio: 13:1.

Student Life Student groups include Matrix (graphic design club), Beaver Association of Fine Arts.

Expenses for 1995–96 Application fee: $30. Comprehensive fee of $19,720 includes full-time tuition ($13,690),

Beaver College *(continued)*

mandatory fees ($280), and college room and board ($5750). Part-time tuition: $260 per credit. Part-time mandatory fees: $30 per semester. Special program-related fees: $25–$75 for lab supplies.

Financial Aid Program-specific awards for Fall of 1994: 5–10 Achievement Awards ($1000–$5000).

Application Procedures Deadline—freshmen and transfers: continuous. Required: essay, high school transcript, college transcript(s) for transfer students, minimum 2.0 high school GPA, letter of recommendation, portfolio. Recommended: minimum 3.0 high school GPA, interview. Portfolio reviews held 6 times and by appointment on campus and off campus in Philadelphia, PA; Baltimore, MD; New York, NY; the submission of slides may be substituted for portfolios.

Undergraduate Contact Office of Undergraduate Admissions, Beaver College, 450 South Easton Road, Glenside, Pennsylvania 19038-3295; 800-776-2328, fax: 215-572-4049.

Graduate Contact Richard Polis, Dean, Graduate Studies, Beaver College, 450 South Easton Road, Glenside, Pennsylvania 19038; 215-572-2900, fax: 215-572-0240, E-mail address: polis@turret.beaver.edu.

More about the College

Everybody has to do something. Why not something great? Beaver College is where you can start sketching your future in the art world. With Philadelphia's seven renowned museums and numerous galleries, and with New York, Baltimore, and Washington D.C. within easy access by train or car, Beaver College students enjoy a distinct advantage. Students can discover first-hand what's hot in the current art world through trips, internships and co-ops.

At Beaver College, students learn the principles of design as well as the principles of problem solving. By supplementing art courses with courses in the natural sciences, social sciences and humanities, students gain an understanding of the world around them from which they can draw ideas for creative expression.

Beaver College offers several programs to help students fulfill their artistic and career goals: The Bachelor of Fine Arts in Studio Art offers courses in basic design principles concentrating in one specific area such as ceramics, graphic design, interior design, metals and jewelry, painting, photography, or printmaking. The Bachelor of Arts in Art allows students to concentrate in art, while taking a wider selection of courses outside the Fine Arts Department. Students may double major, for example, combining art with business, English, or a foreign language. The Bachelor of Arts in Art with a concentration in art history combines liberal arts with studio courses that demonstrate creative procedures and basic techniques. Graduates often work in galleries, museums, publishing or merchandising. The Bachelor of Fine Arts and Certification in Art Education prepares students to teach art in grades K through 12. The Bachelor of Arts in Scientific Illustration obtained in cooperation with the Biology Department prepares students for a career in scientific illustration, publication, laboratory research, or graduate work in medical illustration. The concentration in art therapy, in cooperation with the Psychology Department, combines studio art with psychology, sociology, anthropology, and art therapy. It follows guidelines approved by the National Association of Schools of Art and Design in cooperation with the American Art Therapy Association.

Faculty Our fine arts faculty are practicing artists as well as gifted, caring teachers whose work is regularly exhibited and honored. Their work has been lauded in national art magazines and has been exhibited in the Philadelphia Museum of Art, The Whitney Museum, and The American Craft Museum.

Student Exhibition Opportunities Prominent in the Philadelphia area for exhibiting cutting edge artists, the Beaver College Art Gallery offers many shows and lectures. Senior art majors participate in a culminating exhibit at the Gallery.

Program Facilities The college includes ample studio space; kilns and sand blasters; welders; drills; band saws and grinders for ceramics, metals, and jewelry; photography darkrooms; enlargers; process camera; blueprint processor; etching, lithography, and silkscreen equipment; and presses for printmaking. Desktop publishing facilities include Macintosh computers and IBM computer imaging equipment. Interior design students can utilize computer-aided design.

Special Programs Through Beaver's Center for Education Abroad, students can study overseas in one of our programs in Australia, Austria, England, Germany, Greece, Ireland, Hungary, Mexico, Scotland, or Wales for about the same cost as studying on the Glenside campus.

Bellevue University

Bellevue, Nebraska

Independent, coed. Urban campus. Total enrollment: 2,159.

Degrees Bachelor of Fine Arts in the area of studio art. Majors: ceramic art and design, drawing, painting/drawing, photography, printmaking, sculpture, watercolors.

Art Student Profile Fall 1994: 22 total; all matriculated undergraduate; 10% minorities, 45% females, 10% international.

Art Faculty Total: 7; 5 full-time, 2 part-time; 100% of full-time faculty have terminal degrees. Graduate students do not teach undergraduate courses. Undergraduate student–faculty ratio: 5:1.

Expenses for 1995–96 Application fee: $10. Tuition: $3300 full-time, $110 per credit hour part-time. Full-time mandatory fees: $50. Special program-related fees: $30 for studio fee, supplies.

Financial Aid Program-specific awards for Fall of 1994: 3 CLASS Scholarships for high school seniors ($1500).

Application Procedures Deadline—freshmen and transfers: continuous. Required: high school transcript, college transcript(s) for transfer students, minimum 2.0 high school GPA, SAT I or ACT test scores. Recommended: 3 letters of recommendation, interview, portfolio. Portfolio reviews held 2 times on campus; the submission of slides may be substituted for portfolios when distance is prohibitive.

Undergraduate Contact Admissions Office, Bellevue University, 1000 Galvin Road South, Bellevue, Nebraska 68005; 402-293-3767, fax: 402-293-2020.

Belmont University

Nashville, Tennessee

Independent-religious, coed. Urban campus. Total enrollment: 2,961.

Degrees Bachelor of Fine Arts in the areas of studio, graphic design, art education. Majors: art education, graphic design, studio art.

Art Student Profile Fall 1994: 103 total; 38 matriculated undergraduate, 65 nondegree; 67% females, 5% international.

Art Faculty Total: 6; 3 full-time, 3 part-time; 100% of full-time faculty have terminal degrees. Graduate students do not teach undergraduate courses. Undergraduate student–faculty ratio: 12:1.

Student Life Student groups include Art Association.

Expenses for 1995–96 Application fee: $25. Comprehensive fee of $12,482 includes full-time tuition ($8500), mandatory fees ($250), and college room and board ($3732 minimum). Part-time tuition: $354 per semester hour. Part-time mandatory fees: $90 per semester. Special program-related fees: $25 for lab fees, model fees.

Application Procedures Deadline—freshmen: continuous. Required: high school transcript, college transcript(s) for transfer students, letter of recommendation, SAT I or ACT test scores. Recommended: minimum 2.0 high school GPA, interview, portfolio.

Undergraduate Contact James M. Meaders, Chair, Department of Art, Belmont University, 1900 Belmont Boulevard, Nashville, Tennessee 37212-3757; 615-386-4578, fax: 615-385-5084, E-mail address: meadersj@belmont.edu.

Boston University

Boston, Massachusetts

Independent, coed. Urban campus. Total enrollment: 28,664.

Degrees Bachelor of Fine Arts in the areas of painting, sculpture, graphic design, art education. Majors: art education, graphic design, painting/drawing, sculpture. Graduate degrees offered: Master of Fine Arts in the areas of painting, sculpture, graphic design, art education, studio teaching. Cross-registration with Boston College, Brandeis University, Tufts University.

Art Student Profile Fall 1994: 281 total; 213 matriculated undergraduate, 57 matriculated graduate, 11 nondegree; 10% minorities, 65% females, 9% international.

Art Faculty Total: 31; 18 full-time, 13 part-time; 100% of full-time faculty have terminal degrees. Graduate students do not teach undergraduate courses. Undergraduate student–faculty ratio: 16:1.

Student Life Special housing available for art students.

Expenses for 1995–96 Application fee: $50. Comprehensive fee of $26,800 includes full-time tuition ($19,420), mandatory fees ($280), and college room and board ($7100). College room only: $4110. Part-time tuition: $607 per credit. Part-time mandatory fees: $40 per semester.

Financial Aid Program-specific awards for Fall of 1994: 109 Grants–Need/Performance Awards for enrolled students ($9698), 49 Grants–Performance Awards for enrolled students ($6766).

Application Procedures Deadline—freshmen and transfers: April 1. Notification date—freshmen: April 15; transfers: May 30. Required: essay, high school transcript, college transcript(s) for transfer students, video, portfolio. Recommended: minimum 3.0 high school GPA, 3 letters of recommendation, SAT I or ACT test scores. Portfolio reviews held continuously on campus and off campus in Washington, DC; Chicago, IL; Los Angeles, CA; New York, NY; Miami, FL; San Diego, CA; San Francisco, CA; Baltimore, MD; Louisville, KY; the submission of slides may be substituted for portfolios.

Undergraduate Contact Stuart Baron, Director, Visual Arts Division, School for the Arts, Boston University, 855 Commonwealth Avenue, Boston, Massachusetts 02215; 617-353-3371, fax: 617-353-5331.

More about the University

Program Facilities Painting, drawing, studios, sculpture, welding and wood shop, graphic design and computer labs; book and slide library.

Faculty, Visiting Artists, and Alumni Faculty: John Walker, painter; Alfred Leslie, painter; John Moore, painter; Joseph Ablow, painter; Stuart Baron, painter; Harold Reddicliffe, painter; Richard Raiselis, painter; Margaret McCann, painter; Paul Sattler, painter; Peter Hoss, painter, Isabel McIlvain, sculptor; Nick Edmonds, sculptor; Carol Keller, sculptor; Alston Purvis, graphic designer; Bryce Ambo, graphic designer; Robert Burns, graphic designer, Stephen Frank, photographer; Janet Olson, art educator; Margaret Clark, art educator. Visiting Artists (1994–95): Tom Doyle, sculptor; John Elderfield, curator; Clifford Ackley, curator; Richard Baker, painter; Dimitri Hadzi, sculptor; James Hennessey, painter; Diana Horowitz, painter; Sharon Horvath, painter, John Jacobsmeyer, painter; Lisa Janelle, Painter; Bill Jensen, painter; Margrit Lewczuk, painter; Annette Morris, painter; Kathryn Myers, painter; Jennifer Nuss, painter; Harvey Quaytman, painter; Ira Yoffe, graphic designer. Alumni: Brice Marden, painter; Nicole Hollander, cartoonist; Rick Meyerowitz, illustrator; Howardena Pindell, painter; Ira Yoffe, graphic designer.

Exhibition Opportunities Three scheduled student exhibitions each year.

Special Programs Summer program at Tanglewood Institute, Lenox, Massachusetts; Program Abroad in Venice, Italy (beginning September 1, 1995); Graphic design internships.

Bowling Green State University

Bowling Green, Ohio

State-supported, coed. Small-town campus. Total enrollment: 17,564.

Degrees Bachelor of Fine Arts in the areas of ceramics, computer art, drawing/painting, fibers, glassworking, graphic design, jewelry/metalsmithing, photography, printmaking, sculpture. Majors: ceramic art and design, computer art, fibers, glassworking, graphic design, jewelry and metalsmithing, painting/drawing, photography, printmaking, sculpture, studio art. Graduate degrees offered: Master of Fine Arts in the areas of ceramics, painting/drawing, fibers, glassworking, graphic design, jewelry/metalsmithing, photography, printmaking, sculpture. Cross-registration with University of Toledo.

Art Student Profile Fall 1994: 600 total; all matriculated undergraduate.

Art Faculty Total: 28; 28 full-time. Graduate students teach a few undergraduate courses.

Student Life Student groups include Student Art Education Association, Student Art Therapy Association.

Expenses for 1995–96 Application fee: $30. State resident tuition: $3954 full-time, $197 per credit hour part-time. Nonresident tuition: $8512 full-time, $414 per credit hour part-time. College room and board: $3522. College room only: $2068. Special program-related fees: .

Financial Aid Program-specific awards for Fall of 1994: 20–25 Art Scholarships for outstanding studio art majors.

Application Procedures Required: high school transcript, college transcript(s) for transfer students, SAT I or ACT test scores. Auditions held on campus and off campus. Portfolio reviews held on campus and off campus.

Undergraduate Contact Director of Admissions, Bowling Green State University, Bowling Green State University, Bowling Green, Ohio 43403; 419-372-2086, fax: 419-372-6955.

Graduate Contact Pat Evans, Graduate College, Bowling Green State University, Bowling Green State University, Bowling Green, Ohio 43403; 419-372-7709, fax: 419-372-8569.

Bradley University

Peoria, Illinois

Independent, coed. Urban campus. Total enrollment: 5,882.

Degrees Bachelor of Fine Arts in the area of art. Majors: art/fine arts, ceramic art and design, graphic arts, painting/drawing, photography, printmaking, sculpture. Graduate degrees offered: Master of Fine Arts in the area of art.

Art Student Profile Fall 1994: 868 total; 157 matriculated undergraduate, 9 matriculated graduate, 702 nondegree; 52% females, 1% international.

Art Faculty Total: 26; 19 full-time, 7 part-time; 91% of full-time faculty have terminal degrees. Graduate students do not teach undergraduate courses. Undergraduate student–faculty ratio: 15:1.

Student Life Student groups include "Spectrum" art club, "Broadside" (student literary/art publication).

Expenses for 1995–96 Application fee: $35. Comprehensive fee of $16,110 includes full-time tuition ($11,410), mandatory fees ($80), and college room and board ($4620). Part-time tuition per credit: $295 for the first 7 credits, $368 for the next 4 credits. Special program-related fees: $14 for supplies.

Financial Aid Program-specific awards for Fall of 1994: 1 Kottemann Scholarship for senior sculpture majors ($2100), 1 Dow Mitchell Award for printmaking majors ($660), 10–15 Scholastic Art Award Scholarships for program majors ($650–$2500), 1 Linder Scholarship for art/music majors ($500).

Application Procedures Deadline—freshmen and transfers: continuous. Required: high school transcript, college transcript(s) for transfer students, minimum 2.0 high school GPA, letter of recommendation, interview, SAT I or ACT test scores. Portfolio reviews held off campus in Chicago, IL; St. Louis, MO.

Contact James Ludwig, Acting Chairperson, Art Department, Bradley University, 1501 West Bradley Avenue, Peoria, Illinois 61625; 309-677-2967, fax: 309-677-2330, E-mail address: ludwig@bradley.edu.

Brenau University

Gainesville, Georgia

Independent, primarily women. Small-town campus. Total enrollment: 2,241.

Degrees Bachelor of Fine Arts in the areas of arts management, interior design, commercial art, studio art. Majors: ceramics, painting/drawing, sculpture.

Art Student Profile Fall 1994: 80 total; all matriculated undergraduate; 10% minorities, 99% females, 3% international.

Art Faculty Total: 18; 5 full-time, 13 part-time; 100% of full-time faculty have terminal degrees. Graduate students do not teach undergraduate courses. Undergraduate student–faculty ratio: 10:1.

Estimated Expenses for 1995–96 Application fee: $30. Comprehensive fee of $16,040 includes full-time tuition ($9855) and college room and board ($6185). Part-time tuition: $205 per semester hour.

Financial Aid Program-specific awards for Fall of 1994: 12 Art Scholarships for program majors ($2225).

Application Procedures Deadline—freshmen and transfers: continuous. Required: high school transcript, letter of recommendation. Recommended: interview. Portfolio reviews held as needed on campus; the submission of slides may be substituted for portfolios.

Undergraduate Contact Dr. John D. Upchurch, Dean of Admissions, Brenau University, One Centennial Circle, Gainesville, Georgia 30501; 800-252-5119, fax: 404-534-6114.

Brigham Young University

Provo, Utah

Independent-religious, coed. Suburban campus. Total enrollment: 30,413.

Degrees Bachelor of Fine Arts in the areas of ceramics, painting, printmaking, sculpture. Majors: art education, art/fine arts, ceramic art and design, painting/drawing, printmaking, sculpture, studio art. Graduate degrees offered: Master of Fine Arts in the areas of studio art (ceramics, painting, drawing, printmaking, drawing, sculpture).

Art Student Profile Fall 1994: 355 total; 312 matriculated undergraduate, 43 matriculated graduate.

Art Faculty Total: 40; 20 full-time, 20 part-time; 100% of full-time faculty have terminal degrees. Graduate students do not teach undergraduate courses. Undergraduate student–faculty ratio: 12:1.

Expenses for 1995–96 Application fee: $25. Comprehensive fee of $6190 includes full-time tuition ($2450 minimum) and college room and board ($3740 minimum). Part-time tuition: $125 per credit (minimum). Tuition for non-church members: $3510 full-time, $180 per credit part-time.

Financial Aid Program-specific awards for Fall of 1994: 18 Talent Awards for program majors ($600), 1 Printmaker Scholarship for printmaking majors ($1000), 1 Demerey Scholarship for program majors ($1000), 3 BFA Awards for BFA students ($1100), 1 Art Education Award for art education majors ($1100).

Application Procedures Deadline—freshmen: February 15; transfers: March 15. Required: essay, high school transcript, minimum 3.0 high school GPA, letter of recommendation, ACT test score only, slides of portfolio. Portfolio reviews held for studio applicants at end of sophomore year for entrance into BFA program on campus.

Undergraduate Contact Academic Advisement Center, Brigham Young University, D-444 HFAZ, Provo, Utah 84602; 801-378-3777.

Graduate Contact Wayne Kimball, Graduate Coordinator, Art Department, Brigham Young University, B-481-C HFAC, Provo, Utah 84602; 801-378-3033.

Brigham Young University

Provo, Utah

Independent-religious, coed. Suburban campus. Total enrollment: 30,413.

Degrees Bachelor of Fine Arts in the areas of ceramics, painting, printmaking, sculpture. Majors: art education, art/fine arts, ceramic art and design, painting/drawing, printmaking, sculpture, studio art. Graduate degrees offered: Master of Fine Arts in the areas of studio art (ceramics, painting, drawing, printmaking, drawing, sculpture).

Art Student Profile Fall 1994: 355 total; 312 matriculated undergraduate, 43 matriculated graduate.

Art Faculty Total: 40; 20 full-time, 20 part-time; 100% of full-time faculty have terminal degrees. Graduate students do not teach undergraduate courses. Undergraduate student–faculty ratio: 12:1.

Expenses for 1995–96 Application fee: $25. Comprehensive fee of $6190 includes full-time tuition ($2450 minimum) and college room and board ($3740 minimum). Part-time tuition: $125 per credit (minimum). Tuition for non-church members: $3510 full-time, $180 per credit part-time.

Financial Aid Program-specific awards for Fall of 1994: 18 Talent Awards for program majors ($600), 1 Printmaker Scholarship for printmaking majors ($1000), 1 Demerey Scholarship for program majors ($1000), 3 BFA Awards for BFA students ($1100), 1 Art Education Award for art education majors ($1100).

Application Procedures Deadline—freshmen: February 15; transfers: March 15. Required: essay, high school transcript, minimum 3.0 high school GPA, letter of recommendation, ACT test score only, slides of portfolio. Portfolio reviews held for studio applicants at end of sophomore year for entrance into BFA program on campus.

Undergraduate Contact Academic Advisement Center, Brigham Young University, D-444 HFAZ, Provo, Utah 84602; 801-378-3777.

Graduate Contact Wayne Kimball, Graduate Coordinator, Art Department, Brigham Young University, B-481-C HFAC, Provo, Utah 84602; 801-378-3033.

Brooklyn College of the City University of New York

Brooklyn, New York

State and locally supported, coed. Urban campus. Total enrollment: 13,045.

Degrees Bachelor of Fine Arts in the area of art. Majors: painting/drawing, photography, printmaking, sculpture, studio art. Graduate degrees offered: Master of Fine Arts in the area of art. Cross-registration with City University of New York System.

Art Student Profile Fall 1994: 90 total; 40 matriculated undergraduate, 35 matriculated graduate, 15 nondegree; 20% minorities, 50% females, 15% international.

Art Faculty Total: 24; 14 full-time, 10 part-time; 100% of full-time faculty have terminal degrees. Graduate students do not teach undergraduate courses. Undergraduate student–faculty ratio: 10:1.

Brooklyn College of the City University of New York *(continued)*

Student Life Student groups include Art Group.

Expenses for 1995–96 State resident tuition: $2450 full-time, $100 per credit part-time. Nonresident tuition: $5050 full-time, $210 per credit part-time. Part-time mandatory fees: $53.35 per semester. Full-time mandatory fees: $181. Special program-related fees: $15–$20 for supplies and model fees.

Financial Aid Program-specific awards for Fall of 1994: 10–15 Charles G. Shaw Memorial Awards for painting students ($250–$1000), 2 Bernard Horlick Awards for program majors ($750), 2 Jerome J. Viola Memorial Awards for program majors ($350), 2 Bernard Cole Memorial Scholarships for photography students ($150), 1 Stuart Hall Zidenberg Memorial Award for program majors ($100).

Application Procedures Deadline—freshmen and transfers: March 1. Notification date—freshmen and transfers: June 1. Required: high school transcript, college transcript(s) for transfer students, slides of portfolio. Recommended: SAT I or ACT test scores.

Contact Michael Mallory, Chair, Art Department, Brooklyn College of the City University of New York, 2900 Bedford Avenue, Brooklyn, New York 11210-2889; 718-951-5181.

Caldwell College

Caldwell, New Jersey

Independent-religious, coed. Small-town campus. Total enrollment: 1,688.

Degrees Bachelor of Fine Arts in the areas of fine arts, visual communications. Majors: art education, art/fine arts, painting/drawing, sculpture, studio art.

Art Student Profile Fall 1994: 52 total; all matriculated undergraduate; 21% minorities, 63% females, 12% international.

Art Faculty Total: 11; 3 full-time, 8 part-time; 100% of full-time faculty have terminal degrees. Graduate students teach a few undergraduate courses. Undergraduate student–faculty ratio: 10:1.

Student Life Student groups include Art Club.

Expenses for 1995–96 Application fee: $25. Comprehensive fee of $14,400 includes full-time tuition ($9500) and college room and board ($4900). Part-time tuition: $240 per credit. Special program-related fees: $40 for photography lab fees, $10–$40 for consumable supplies for studio classes.

Financial Aid Program-specific awards for Fall of 1994: 4 Art Scholarships for above-average students with exceptional artistic ability ($3000).

Application Procedures Deadline—freshmen and transfers: August 15. Required: high school transcript, college transcript(s) for transfer students, minimum 2.0 high school GPA, letter of recommendation, SAT I or ACT test scores. Recommended: portfolio. Portfolio reviews held on a case-by-case basis on campus; the submission of slides may be substituted for portfolios by prior arrangement.

Undergraduate Contact Admissions Office, Caldwell College, 9 Ryerson Avenue, Caldwell, New Jersey 07006; 201-228-4424.

California College of Arts and Crafts

Oakland, California

Independent, coed. Urban campus. Total enrollment: 1,135.

Degrees Bachelor of Fine Arts in the areas of furniture, glass, ceramics, sculpture, painting, drawing, printmaking, photography, textiles, jewelry/metal arts, graphic design, illustration, industrial design, interior architecture, fashion design. Majors: architecture, ceramic art and design, fashion design, furniture design, glass, graphic arts, illustration, industrial design, interior architecture, jewelry and metalsmithing, painting/drawing, photography, sculpture, textile arts. Graduate degrees offered: Master of Fine Arts in the areas of glass, ceramics, textiles, sculpture, jewelry/metal arts, painting, printmaking, drawing, photography. Cross-registration with Mills College, Holy Names College.

Art Student Profile Fall 1994: 1,135 total; 996 matriculated undergraduate, 83 matriculated graduate, 56 nondegree; 20% minorities, 58% females, 10% international.

Art Faculty Total: 263; 35 full-time, 228 part-time; 51% of full-time faculty have terminal degrees. Graduate students do not teach undergraduate courses. Undergraduate student–faculty ratio: 12:1.

Student Life Student groups include American Institute of Graphic Artists, American Institute of Architects, American Society of Interior Designers. Special housing available for art students.

Expenses for 1995–96 Application fee: $30. Comprehensive fee of $19,700 includes full-time tuition ($14,300), mandatory fees ($100), and college room and board ($5300). College room only: $2150. Part-time tuition: $596 per unit. Part-time mandatory fees: $50 per semester. Special program-related fees: $25–$250 for lab fees.

Financial Aid Program-specific awards for Fall of 1994: 50 Creative Achievement Awards for freshmen ($1000–$6000), 50 Faculty Honors Awards for transfer students ($1000–$6000), 30 Alumni Honors Awards for continuing students ($2000–$5000).

Application Procedures Deadline—freshmen and transfers: continuous. Required: essay, high school transcript, college transcript(s) for transfer students, minimum 2.0 high school GPA, letter of recommendation, portfolio. Recommended: interview, SAT I or ACT test scores, slides of portfolio. Portfolio reviews held continuously on campus.

Undergraduate Contact Sheri McKenzie, Director, Office of Enrollment Services, California College of Arts and Crafts, 5212 Broadway, Oakland, California 94618; 510-653-6522 ext. 312, fax: 510-547-5379.

Graduate Contact Phoebe Brookbank, Graduate Studies Program Coordinator, Graduate Office, California College of Arts and Crafts, 5212 Broadway, Oakland, California 94618; 510-653-8118, fax: 510-655-3541.

More about the College

Program Facilities CCAC's specially designed facilities at the Oakland Campus include the Noni Eccles Treadwell Ceramics Arts Center and the Shaklee Building, which houses a metal foundry, extensive glass facilities, and studios for jewelry/metal arts and sculpture. The Barclay Simpson Sculpture Studio accommodates large-scale sculpture. Other workspaces include drawing and painting studios and fully equipped film/video, textile, wood, printmaking, and photo facilities. The San Francisco campus, located in the heart of the design community, is devoted to CCAC's architecture and design schools. The facility features spacious, well-lit studios organized around a common atrium space. Computer facilities at both campuses include four different computer labs. These labs contain the latest in Apple computer technology. CCAC's professional galleries include the Oliver Art Center's Tecoah Bruce Gallery, which shows works by contemporary artists, and the Design Gallery, which features design and architecture.

Faculty, Resident Artists, and Alumni Faculty work resides in the Museum of Modern Art, New York; the Whitney Museum, the Hirshhorn Museum; the Smithsonian Institution; and other major institutions. Architecture and Design faculty members are recognized internationally. Noted alumni include painters Raymond Saunders, Manuel Neri, and Squeak Carnwath; ceramicists Robert Arneson and Peter Voulkos; filmmaker Wayne Wang; and designer Michael Vanderbyl. Acclaimed artists, designers, and architects visit CCAC each semester to enhance the studio experience.

Student Exhibitions Ongoing exhibitions show student work in the Irwin Student Center, Isabelle Percy West Gallery, Door 3 Gallery, and CCAC's Architecture and Design Gallery.

Special Programs CCAC students may enrich their studies abroad or through the AICAD Mobility Program. Internships may be arranged in many majors and are required in Graphic Design and Architecture.

Since 1907, California College of Arts and Crafts has educated young artists to take a leadership role in the work of art and design. Today, after completing a diversified program in the arts and the humanities, CCAC students graduate fully prepared to enter the professions of architecture and design or to begin the practice of the fine arts. The College provides in-depth training and an awareness of the broader role artists play in the shaping of culture.

Students at CCAC have an unusual opportunity to work closely in the studio with accomplished artists and designers, many of whom have attained international recognition. CCAC has strong connections to the professional arts community and helps students make the transition from school to career by offering internships in many majors. Students develop professional contacts while still in school and learn to function like working designers, architects, and artists as interns in offices, studios, museums, and arts organizations.

One of the most creatively vital areas in America surrounds CCAC. The Bay Area offers exposure to the arts through world-class museums, galleries, theaters, film festivals, and diverse exhibition and performance spaces. In addition, visiting artists, designers, and writers bring a fresh perspective to the CCAC campus. Stimulating lectures, symposiums, studio visits, and other programs are offered throughout the year. Students also work side by side with creative, serious students from around the world who contribute to the atmosphere of camaraderie that exists at the College.

At CCAC, students tend to spend significantly more time in the studio than their counterparts at a liberal arts college or university. The flexible curriculum is designed to meet the individual needs of students preparing to become working architects, designers, and artists. Core courses introduce basic concepts and skills, enabling students to become conversant with several visual languages. Each program allows in-depth exploration of a chosen discipline, while grounding that work in the larger context of the humanities and sciences and art history, theory, and criticism. Educational technology is integrated into the studio curriculum. The College encourages students to find their own expressive voice to explore various media and to consider how theories of art and the practice of art converge.

Students find CCAC's range of interdisciplinary classes to be especially relevant and challenging. Interdisciplinary exploration is reflected through the practice of art in the real world and benefits all those involved. There are collaborations between architecture students and those majoring in glass, between filmmakers and performance artists, and between industrial designers and sculptors. Students also find that CCAC's Ethnic Studies program offers provocative discussion and an appreciation of the cultural milieu in which artists work.

Students who choose CCAC have an opportunity to work with well-known artists and designers to find support for personal goals and to prepare for professional achievement. The small size of the College allows for individual attention in the studio. At the same time, a wide range of approaches seeks to ensure a lively exchange of ideas in an environment where excellence is the standard.

California Institute of the Arts

Valencia, California

Independent, coed. Suburban campus. Total enrollment: 1,051.

Degrees Bachelor of Fine Arts in the areas of art, graphic design, photography. Majors: art/fine arts, computer graphics, graphic arts, painting/drawing, photography, printmaking, sculpture, studio art. Graduate degrees offered: Master of Fine Arts in the areas of art, graphic design, photography.

Art Student Profile Fall 1994: 255 total; 146 matriculated undergraduate, 99 matriculated graduate, 10 nondegree; 37% minorities, 30% international.

Art Faculty Total: 34; 22 full-time, 12 part-time; 90% of full-time faculty have terminal degrees. Graduate stu-

California Institute of the Arts *(continued)*

dents do not teach undergraduate courses. Undergraduate student–faculty ratio: 8:1.

Student Life Special housing available for art students.

Expenses for 1995–96 Comprehensive fee of $21,225 includes full-time tuition ($15,450), mandatory fees ($75), and college room and board ($5700). College room only: $2550 (minimum). Special program-related fees: $50 for photo lab fee, $55 for computer lab fee.

Financial Aid Program-specific awards for Fall of 1994: 1–5 Irvine Foundation Awards for minority students ($1000–$5000), 1–5 Herb Albert Scholarships for Hispanic/Latino students ($5000), 6 Philip Morris Foundation Awards for minority students ($10,000).

Application Procedures Deadline—freshmen and transfers: continuous. Required: portfolio. Recommended: essay, interview. Portfolio reviews held continuously on campus; the submission of slides may be substituted for portfolios.

Contact Dee McMillan, Admissions Department, California Institute of the Arts, 24700 McBean Parkway, Valencia, California 91355; 805-255-1050, fax: 805-254-8352.

California State University, Chico

Chico, California

State-supported, coed. Small-town campus. Total enrollment: 14,232.

Degrees Bachelor of Fine Arts in the areas of studio art, interior design. Majors: ceramic art and design, glass, interior design, painting/drawing, printmaking, sculpture, studio art, weaving and fibers. Cross-registration with California State University System.

Art Student Profile Fall 1994: 25 total; all matriculated undergraduate; 50% females.

Art Faculty Total: 23; 18 full-time, 5 part-time. Graduate students do not teach undergraduate courses.

Student Life Student groups include General Student Art Club, Ceramics Student Art Club, Printmaking Club.

Expenses for 1994–95 Application fee: $55. State resident tuition: $0 full-time. Nonresident tuition: $7380 full-time, $246 per unit part-time. Part-time mandatory fees: $670 per semester. Full-time mandatory fees: $2006. College room and board: $4632.

Application Procedures Deadline—freshmen: continuous. Notification date—freshmen: continuous. Required: high school transcript, college transcript(s) for transfer students, portfolio, SAT I or ACT test scores. Auditions held on campus and off campus. Portfolio reviews held 2 times on campus and off campus; the submission of slides may be substituted for portfolios.

Undergraduate Contact Chairman, Department of Art and Art History, California State University, Chico, Chico, California 95929-0820; 916-898-5331.

California State University, Fullerton

Fullerton, California

State-supported, coed. Suburban campus. Total enrollment: 22,097.

Degrees Bachelor of Fine Arts in the areas of drawing/painting, printmaking, sculpture, crafts, ceramics, graphic design, illustration, creative photography, environmental design. Majors: art education, ceramic art and design, craft design, graphic design, illustration, jewelry and metalsmithing, painting/drawing, photography, printmaking, sculpture. Graduate degrees offered: Master of Fine Arts in the areas of drawing/painting, printmaking, sculpture, ceramics and glass, crafts, design, creative photography, environmental design, illustration. Cross-registration with California State University System.

Art Student Profile Fall 1994: 846 total; 694 matriculated undergraduate, 152 matriculated graduate; 6% minorities, 57% females, 1% international.

Art Faculty Total: 57; 26 full-time, 31 part-time; 61% of full-time faculty have terminal degrees. Graduate students teach a few undergraduate courses. Undergraduate student–faculty ratio: 19:1.

Student Life Student groups include Orange County AIDS Project, The Art Network, Graphic Design Club.

Expenses for 1994–95 Application fee: $55. State resident tuition: $0 full-time. Nonresident tuition: $7380 full-time, $246 per unit part-time. Part-time mandatory fees: $567 per semester. Full-time mandatory fees: $1800. College room only: $3476. Special program-related fees: $10–$16 for lab fees, $10 for ceramic glaze fee.

Financial Aid Program-specific awards for Fall of 1994: 2 Mert Purkiss Awards for incoming freshmen ($1000), 2 Florence Arnold Awards for continuing students ($500), 1 John Olson Award for design/crafts majors ($700), 2 Tribute Fund Awards for transfer students ($750).

Application Procedures Deadline—freshmen and transfers: continuous. Required: high school transcript, minimum 2.0 high school GPA, SAT I test score only.

Undergraduate Contact Karen Bell, Department Secretary, Department of Art, California State University, Fullerton, Fullerton, California 92634; 714-773-3471, fax: 714-773-3005.

Graduate Contact Jackie Reynolds, Graduate Secretary, Department of Art, California State University, Fullerton, Fullerton, California 92634; 714-773-3471, fax: 714-773-3005.

California State University, Long Beach

Long Beach, California

State-supported, coed. Suburban campus. Total enrollment: 26,227.

Degrees Bachelor of Fine Arts in the areas of art, design. Majors: 3-dimensional studies, ceramic art and design, drafting and design, graphic arts, illustration, painting/drawing, photography, printmaking, sculpture.

Graduate degrees offered: Master of Fine Arts in the areas of art, design. Cross-registration with California State University System.

Student Life Student groups include Student Art Association.

Expenses for 1995–96 State resident tuition: $0 full-time. Nonresident tuition: $7626 full-time, $246 per unit part-time. Part-time mandatory fees: $542.50 per semester. Full-time mandatory fees: $1751. College room and board: $5300.

Financial Aid Program-specific awards for Fall of 1994: Art Scholarships for program majors.

Application Procedures Deadline—freshmen and transfers: continuous. Required: high school transcript, college transcript(s) for transfer students, minimum 2.0 high school GPA, portfolio, SAT I or ACT test scores. Auditions held on campus and off campus. Portfolio reviews held 2 times and as needed on campus and off campus; the submission of slides may be substituted for portfolios.

Undergraduate Contact Art Department, California State University, Long Beach, Long Beach, California 90840-0119; 310-985-4111.

Capital University

Columbus, Ohio

Independent-religious, coed. Suburban campus. Total enrollment: 3,924.

Degrees Bachelor of Fine Arts in the areas of studio art, commercial art. Majors: art/fine arts.

Expenses for 1995–96 Application fee: $15. Comprehensive fee of $17,700 includes full-time tuition ($13,700) and college room and board ($4000). Part-time tuition: $457 per semester hour.

Application Procedures Deadline—freshmen and transfers: continuous. Required: high school transcript, letter of recommendation, SAT I or ACT test scores, minimum 2.5 high school GPA. Recommended: interview, portfolio. Portfolio reviews held as needed on campus; the submission of slides may be substituted for portfolios for large works of art.

Undergraduate Contact Gary Ross, Chairman, Art Department, Capital University, 2199 East Main Street, Columbus, Ohio 43209; 614-236-6332.

Cardinal Stritch College

Milwaukee, Wisconsin

Independent-religious, coed. Suburban campus. Total enrollment: 5,654.

Degrees Bachelor of Fine Arts. Majors: ceramics, graphic design, interdisciplinary studies, metals, painting/drawing, photography, printmaking, sculpture.

Art Faculty Total: 10; 5 full-time, 5 part-time. Graduate students do not teach undergraduate courses.

Student Life Student groups include Student Art Club.

Expenses for 1995–96 Application fee: $20. Comprehensive fee of $12,022 includes full-time tuition ($8320), mandatory fees ($37), and college room and board ($3665 minimum). Part-time tuition: $260 per credit. Part-time mandatory fees: $31 per year. Part-time tuition per credit for nursing program: $275. Special program-related fees: $15–$40 for lab fees.

Financial Aid Program-specific awards for Fall of 1994: 5 Art Scholarships for those demonstrating talent and academic achievement ($1000).

Application Procedures Deadline—freshmen and transfers: continuous. Required: essay, high school transcript, minimum 2.0 high school GPA, portfolio, SAT I or ACT test scores. Recommended: interview. Portfolio reviews held as needed on campus; the submission of slides may be substituted for portfolios if a campus visit is impossible.

Undergraduate Contact Admissions Department, Cardinal Stritch College, Milwaukee, Wisconsin 53217; 414-352-5400 ext. 331.

Carnegie Mellon University

Pittsburgh, Pennsylvania

Independent, coed. Urban campus. Total enrollment: 7,141.

Degrees Bachelor of Fine Arts in the area of art. Majors: art/fine arts. Graduate degrees offered: Master of Fine Arts in the area of art. Cross-registration with Chatham College, University of Pittsburgh, Duquesne University, Carlow College, Pittsburgh Filmmakers.

Art Student Profile Fall 1994: 199 total; 181 matriculated undergraduate, 18 matriculated graduate; 16% minorities, 58% females, 1% international.

Art Faculty Total: 27; 23 full-time, 4 part-time; 100% of full-time faculty have terminal degrees. Graduate students do not teach undergraduate courses. Undergraduate student–faculty ratio: 10:1.

Expenses for 1995–96 Application fee: $45. Comprehensive fee of $24,610 includes full-time tuition ($18,600), mandatory fees ($160), and college room and board ($5850). College room only: $3610. Special program-related fees: $10 for material fees.

Application Procedures Deadline—freshmen and transfers: January 1. Notification date—freshmen and transfers: continuous. Required: high school transcript, college transcript(s) for transfer students, 3 letters of recommendation, portfolio, SAT I or ACT test scores. Recommended: minimum 3.0 high school GPA, interview. Portfolio reviews held 8 times on campus and off campus in New York, NY; the submission of slides may be substituted for portfolios if a campus visit is impossible.

Undergraduate Contact Admissions Office, Carnegie Mellon University, 5000 Forbes Avenue, Pittsburgh, Pennsylvania 15213-3890; 412-268-2082.

Carnegie Mellon University *(continued)*

Graduate Contact Laurel Quigley, Graduate Program and Special Projects Coordinator, Art Department, Carnegie Mellon University, College of Fine Arts, 5000 Forbes Avenue, Room 312, Pittsburgh, Pennsylvania 15213-3890; 412-268-2409, fax: 412-268-7817, E-mail address: lq03@andrew.cmu.edu.

More about the University

Program Facilities The department maintains over 50,000 square feet of space, including well-equipped studios for two-dimensional work (painting, drawing, printmaking), three-dimensional work (sculpture, installation, site-work), and electronic and time-based work (computer, video, performance, kinetics). The Carnegie Mellon library maintains extensive contemporary art holdings. The Pittsburgh community offers a variety of exhibition venues, including the Carnegie Museum of Art, the Frick Museum of Art, the Pittsburgh Center for the Arts, and the Andy Warhol Museum.

Faculty, Resident Artists, and Alumni The full-time faculty members are all nationally and internationally recognized practicing artists and/or scholars. In addition, a visiting faculty program adds 5 prominent artists and scholars to the full-time faculty each year. Alumni contribute throughout the United States and the world in a variety of roles, from freelance artist and educator to museum curator and media industry professional. A list of prominent alumni includes Jonathan Borofsky, Joyce Kozloff, Philip Pearlstein, and Andy Warhol.

Student Exhibition Opportunities Students exhibit their work regularly in a variety of campus venues. The student-operated Forbes Gallery presents weekly-changing student exhibitions that engage both the campus and the Pittsburgh community.

Special Programs All art majors participate in art-in-context courses through which they affiliate themselves with organizations in the Pittsburgh community and make art within the context of these organizations. The department strongly encourages international study by all art majors and has established a growing list of exchange programs with art schools and universities outside of the United States. Students in exchange programs remain officially enrolled at Carnegie Mellon and retain their financial aid packages.

Centenary College

Hackettstown, New Jersey

Independent-religious, coed. Small-town campus. Total enrollment: 917.

Degrees Bachelor of Fine Arts in the areas of commercial art, graphic arts, interior design. Majors: art and design, interior design.

Art Student Profile Fall 1994: 48 total; all matriculated undergraduate; 35% minorities, 68% females.

Art Faculty Total: 10; 4 full-time, 6 part-time; 50% of full-time faculty have terminal degrees. Graduate students do not teach undergraduate courses. Undergraduate student–faculty ratio: 12:1.

Student Life Student groups include American Society of Interior Designers, Art Guild, Performing Arts Guild.

Expenses for 1995–96 Application fee: $25. Comprehensive fee of $17,600 includes full-time tuition ($11,900), mandatory fees ($200), and college room and board ($5500). Part-time tuition: $225 per credit. Part-time mandatory fees: $10 per semester.

Application Procedures Deadline—freshmen and transfers: continuous. Required: essay, high school transcript, college transcript(s) for transfer students, portfolio, SAT I or ACT test scores. Recommended: minimum 2.0 high school GPA, letter of recommendation, interview. Portfolio reviews held as needed on campus; the submission of slides may be substituted for portfolios when distance is prohibitive.

Undergraduate Contact Dennis Kelly, Dean of Admissions, Centenary College, 400 Jefferson Street, Hackettstown, New Jersey 07840; 800-236-8679, fax: 908-852-3454.

Center for Creative Studies—College of Art and Design

Detroit, Michigan

Independent, coed. Urban campus. Total enrollment: 835.

Degrees Bachelor of Fine Arts in the areas of fine arts, crafts, photography, graphic communications, industrial design. Majors: applied art, art direction, art/fine arts, ceramic art and design, commercial art, furniture design, glass, graphic arts, illustration, interior design, jewelry and metalsmithing, painting/drawing, photography, printmaking, production/design, sculpture, studio art, textile arts, transportation design. Cross-registration with Association of Independent Colleges of Art and Design.

Art Student Profile Fall 1994: 780 total; all matriculated undergraduate; 16% minorities, 39% females, 3% international.

Art Faculty Total: 166; 48 full-time, 118 part-time; 59% of full-time faculty have terminal degrees. Undergraduate student–faculty ratio: 13:1.

Student Life Student groups include Student Council, Black Artists Researching Trends, Industrial Design Society of America.

Expenses for 1995–96 Application fee: $35. Comprehensive fee of $18,050 includes full-time tuition ($12,420), mandatory fees ($130), and college room and board ($5500). College room only: $2550 (minimum). Part-time tuition: $414 per credit hour.

Application Procedures Deadline—freshmen and transfers: continuous. Notification date—freshmen and transfers: continuous. Required: high school transcript, interview, portfolio, minimum 2.5 high school GPA. Recommended: essay, letter of recommendation. Portfolio reviews held throughout the year on campus.

Graduate Contact Admissions, Center for Creative Studies—College of Art and Design, 201 East Kirby Street, Detroit, Michigan 48202; 313-872-3118, fax: 313-872-8377.

More about the College

As a complete college of visual arts with an extensive and diverse curriculum, the Center for Creative Studies offers students a broad, yet focused arts education. Upon arrival at CCS, students enter their chosen major, giving them the opportunity for a concentrated program of study in one area. They become immersed very early on in all facets of their intended field of study. Students are strongly encouraged, however, to take classes outside of their majors to broaden their understanding of art and design in general and enhance their individual approach to their own specialty. Industrial design majors can augment their exploration of products and interiors with a glass-blowing class, for example. Graphic communication students may find a fine arts printmaking or watercolor class useful to their approach to design.

Generous access is available to the many instructional resources at CCS, including extensive computing facilities with Macintosh, IBM, and Silicon Graphics workstations; a central shop with work space and woodworking and metalsmithing tools for student use under the supervision of skilled shop technicians; a visual arts library with an extensive collection of art and design publications, periodicals, and slides; graphic arts services, including computerized typesetting, color laser printing, and stat cameras; and photography facilities, including darkrooms, photo studios, film-editing equipment, and animation equipment.

Exhibiting is an important part of the life of an artist, and CCS provides many opportunities for students to show their work to the public. Student artwork is displayed at events such as Open House, Detroit Festival of the Arts, and others. The annual Student Exhibition, held in conjunction with commencement each year, is a major public event that draws literally thousands of people who view and purchase student artwork.

The Center for Creative Studies–College of Art and Design is among the nation's leading schools of art and design. Students can pursue a Bachelor of Fine Arts in seventeen different majors through the Departments of Crafts, Fine Arts, Graphic Communication, Industrial Design, and Photography.

Through a combination of studio classes, academic studies, one-on-one instruction, and internship opportunities, each department emphasizes four distinct components of a visual arts education: technical skills, aesthetic sensibility, conceptual abilities, and practical experience. This educational approach leaves CCS students very well prepared to succeed in their postgraduation pursuits, whether that means a career as a professional artist or designer, graduate school, working in a graphics or photography studio, or other creative endeavors.

The faculty at CCS consists of professional artists, designers, and photographers, all working or exhibiting in their fields. This immediate connection to the real world has a significant impact on the education of the students. These faculty members bring new trends, practical insights, and networking opportunities to the school, shedding some realistic light on theoretical classroom exercises.

Studies at CCS are fully supported by its instructional resources. The computer facility is one of the fastest growing on campus and features twenty Macintoshes running Quark XPress, Pagemaker, Illustrator, Free Hand, and Photo Shop software; twenty IBM workstations running CAD programs; and fifteen SGI workstations running Alias programs. Computer-aided design, desktop publishing, illustration, multimedia, and animation are among the courses taught.

Private and semiprivate studio space is made available to many advanced students, where they can develop a serious body of work and explore their own vision and style. Though left on their own to develop their techniques, the students are regularly visited by faculty for input and guidance.

As a unique aspect of their visual arts education, students may earn elective credit through the Institute of Music and Dance, a non-degree-granting arm of the Center for Creative Studies. Dance classes include ballet, tap, and modern; music instruction ranges from private lessons to group classes.

CCS's location is a valuable resource in itself. The campus is situated in Detroit's University Cultural Center, within walking distance of a number of educational and cultural institutions, including the Detroit Institute of Arts, one of the nation's finest art museums; the Museum of African American History; the Detroit Public Library; and Wayne State University, a major urban institution of higher education.

The surrounding metropolitan area provides much from which an art student can draw inspiration. Eclectic neighborhoods with their own distinct characters, galleries displaying the work of emerging and established artists, coffeehouses and cafés, spectacular natural resources, sports, and other entertainment are all a thriving part of what Detroit has to offer.

Along with the cultural resources, professional opportunities abound in the Detroit metropolitan area. The automotive manufacturing and supplier industries have a regular need for creative industrial designers. They support a thriving advertising industry where creative professionals from many disciplines are in constant demand.

For a visual arts education that stresses the personal development of style and vision and practical experience needed to succeed in the real world, the Center for Creative Studies is an excellent educational option.

Central Michigan University

Mount Pleasant, Michigan

State-supported, coed. Small-town campus. Total enrollment: 16,126.

Degrees Bachelor of Fine Arts in the areas of 2–dimensional studies; 3–dimensional studies, design/graphic design. Majors: ceramic art and design, fibers, graphic design, jewelry and metalsmithing, painting/drawing, photography, printmaking, sculpture. Graduate degrees offered: Master of Fine Arts in the area of studio art.

Art Faculty Graduate students teach a few undergraduate courses.

Student Life Student groups include Graphic Design Club, Graphic Design Club, North Arts Students League, Photography Club.

Expenses for 1994–95 State resident tuition: $2767 full-time, $89.25 per credit part-time. Nonresident tuition:

Central Michigan University *(continued)*

$6882 full-time, $231.75 per credit part-time. Full-time mandatory fees: $270. College room and board: $3900. Special program-related fees.

Financial Aid Program-specific awards for Fall of 1994 available.

Application Procedures

Contact Dr. Lee Ann Wilson, Chair, Art Department, Central Michigan University, 132 Wightman Hall, Mount Pleasant, Michigan 48859; 517-774-3025.

Central Missouri State University

Warrensburg, Missouri

State-supported, coed. Small-town campus. Total enrollment: 10,805.

Degrees Bachelor of Fine Arts in the areas of commercial art, interior design, studio art. Majors: commercial art, graphic design, illustration, interior design, studio art.

Art Student Profile Fall 1994: 340 total; 325 matriculated undergraduate, 15 matriculated graduate; 5% minorities, 60% females, 5% international.

Art Faculty Total: 15; 12 full-time, 3 part-time; 92% of full-time faculty have terminal degrees. Graduate students teach a few undergraduate courses. Undergraduate student–faculty ratio: 20:1.

Expenses for 1995–96 State resident tuition: $2460 full-time, $82 per credit hour part-time. Nonresident tuition: $4920 full-time, $164 per credit hour part-time. College room and board: $3578 (minimum). College room only: $2328 (minimum). Special program-related fees: $5–$25 for consumable supplies.

Financial Aid Program-specific awards for Fall of 1994: 20–30 Art Achievement Awards for incoming freshmen ($200–$600).

Application Procedures Deadline—freshmen and transfers: continuous. Required: high school transcript, college transcript(s) for transfer students, ACT test score only.

Undergraduate Contact Delores Hudson, Director of Admissions, Central Missouri State University, Administration Building 104, Warrensburg, Missouri 64093; 816-543-4290, fax: 816-543-8517.

Clarion University of Pennsylvania

Clarion, Pennsylvania

State-supported, coed. Rural campus. Total enrollment: 5,367.

Degrees Bachelor of Fine Arts in the areas of painting, drawing, sculpture, fiber/fabric, ceramics, graphic arts, printmaking. Majors: art/fine arts, ceramics, drawing, fabric styling, fibers, graphic arts, painting, printmaking, sculpture.

Art Faculty Total: 9; 9 full-time; 100% of full-time faculty have terminal degrees. Graduate students do not teach undergraduate courses. Undergraduate student–faculty ratio: 7:1.

Student Life Student groups include Visual Arts Association.

Expenses for 1994–95 State resident tuition: $3086 full-time, $129 per credit part-time. Nonresident tuition: $7844 full-time, $327 per credit part-time. Part-time mandatory fees: $46.45 per credit. Full-time mandatory fees: $792. College room and board: $2924. College room only: $1710. Special program-related fees: $100–$400 for supplies.

Financial Aid Program-specific awards for Fall of 1994: 1–4 Lesser Scholarships for undergraduates ($500).

Application Procedures Deadline—freshmen and transfers: continuous. Required: high school transcript, minimum 2.0 high school GPA. Recommended: letter of recommendation.

Undergraduate Contact Catherine Joslyn, Chair, Art Department, Clarion University of Pennsylvania, 114 Marwick-Boyd, Clarion, Pennsylvania 16214; 814-226-2291, fax: 814-226-2039, E-mail address: joslyn@vaxb.clarion.edu.

Cleveland Institute of Art

Cleveland, Ohio

Independent, coed. Urban campus. Total enrollment: 520.

Degrees Bachelor of Fine Arts in the areas of ceramics, drawing, enameling, fiber, glass, industrial design, interior design, graphic design, illustration, medical illustration, painting, photography, printmaking, metals, sculpture. Majors: ceramic art and design, enameling, fibers, glass, graphic arts, illustration, industrial design, jewelry and metalsmithing, medical illustration, painting/drawing, photography, printmaking, sculpture. Cross-registration with members of Cleveland Commission on Higher Education.

Art Student Profile Fall 1994: 520 total; 510 matriculated undergraduate, 10 nondegree; 16% minorities, 48% females, 3% international.

Art Faculty Total: 72; 30 full-time, 42 part-time; 99% of full-time faculty have terminal degrees. Graduate students do not teach undergraduate courses. Undergraduate student–faculty ratio: 17:1.

Student Life Student groups include Industrial Design Society of America. Special housing available for art students.

Expenses for 1994–95 Application fee: $30. Comprehensive fee of $16,470 includes full-time tuition ($11,400), mandatory fees ($300), and college room and board ($4770). College room only: $2650. Part-time tuition: $1200 per course.

Financial Aid Program-specific awards for Fall of 1994: 15–40 Portfolio Scholarships for freshmen ($1000–$8000).

Application Procedures Deadline—freshmen and transfers: continuous. Required: essay, high school transcript, college transcript(s) for transfer students, minimum 2.0 high school GPA, 2 letters of recommendation, portfolio, SAT I or ACT test scores. Recommended: interview. Portfolio reviews held bi-monthly on campus; the submission of slides may be substituted for portfolios slides preferred.

Undergraduate Contact Tom Steffen, Director of Admissions, Cleveland Institute of Art, 11141 East Boulevard, Cleveland, Ohio 44106; 216-421-7422, fax: 216-421-7438.

More about the Institute

Program Facilities Individual studio spaces for all students in a major; four computer labs for use in liberal arts and studio classes; two-story shooting studio for photography students; multimedia laboratory for photo/video production; foundry for sculpture; interdisciplinary studio space adjacent to majors' space.

Student Performance/Exhibit Opportunities Generous student gallery space for group shows; "Coffeehouse" gallery space for majors' shows; Jessica R. Gund Memorial Library gallery space for individual and group shows; annual Student Independent Show in the Reinberger Galleries; "Parade the Circle" festival in University Circle; various local restaurants, coffeehouses, and gallery connections. **Special Programs** New York Studio program; LaCoste School of the Arts (France)—summer and fall semesters; extensive internship potential (students develop their own with faculty guidance or choose from a wide array of internships on file); cross-registration with fourteen other colleges and universities in and around Cleveland; nationally known artists for intensive summer workshops; wide range of tutoring possibilities in liberal arts courses and studio courses; art education major in conjunction with Case Western Reserve University for undergraduates and opportunities for graduate work through Case Western; medical illustration students work with the Medical and Dental Schools of Case Western Reserve University, University Hospitals, Cleveland Clinic Foundation, and Mt. Sinai Hospital.

The Cleveland Institute of Art (CIA) is not about numbers but about individual students learning and developing as artists. In its mission statement, the Institute states its aim "to provide a quality education" to those "who seek professional art careers . . . to demonstrate leadership in education in the visual arts, putting consideration of quality before quantity." This goal is evident throughout the Institute.

The faculty is a strong teaching group. Since CIA is exclusively undergraduate, professors—not graduate assistants—teach. But while they are teachers, faculty members are all working professionals. This shows in the awards they have received—from Emmys and IDSA Awards to the Outstanding American Educator award and the Ohio Designer Craftsman Award for Excellence. Faculty members have lectured everywhere from Alfred University to Yale University, teaching at locations ranging from Aichi University in Japan to San Diego State University to the Glasgow School of Art. Faculty artwork can be seen in collections ranging from those at the Art Institute of Chicago to the Library of Congress. Clients like the Cleveland Indians, Black & Decker, and Sherwin-Williams are well served by this high-caliber assembly.

The University Circle area surrounding the Institute is a rich resource for students. The Cleveland Museum of Art, Severance Hall for the Cleveland Orchestra, and Case Western Reserve University are just a few of the educational and cultural organizations located "in the Circle." Originally the University Circle was developed in a parklike setting away from manufacturing as a center for the cultural institutions of Cleveland. Now, with a rebirth of Cleveland, the "Circle" and the Institute are minutes away by rapid transit or car from the "Flats," Jacobs Field, and the Rock and Roll Hall of Fame.

Career Services offers a monthly Jobline, which highlights potential offerings from a national and international pool of part-time, freelance, and full-time jobs. Opportunities are gleaned from many sources and also include competitions and possibilities for student and alumni shows. The Career Services office is not only for soon-to-be-graduates or recent alumni; students use the services throughout their careers at the Institute. Coordinating internships and assistance in finding the right part-time job to pay for school are just a part of a multifaceted operation. There is also a computer database of potential employers.

Sometimes, student concern about concentrating solely in the visual arts surfaces. Such students may choose to focus on particular liberal arts minors such as art and film history, literature/criticism/creative writing, multicultural studies, and art therapy. Opting for Honors in all of the liberal arts courses is also possible. If these offerings do not match the students' needs, cross-registration may be undertaken with fourteen different colleges and universities in and around Cleveland at no additional cost. Students can create a program that rivals most comprehensive universities and still includes emphasis on art.

"Quality before quantity" for those seeking professional art careers permeates the Cleveland Institute of Art.

College of New Rochelle

New Rochelle, New York

Independent, primarily women. Suburban campus. Total enrollment: 2,383.

Degrees Bachelor of Fine Arts in the areas of studio art, art therapy, art education. Majors: art education, art history, art therapy, art/fine arts, studio art. Cross-registration with Iona College.

Art Student Profile Fall 1994: 75 total; all matriculated undergraduate; 100% females.

Art Faculty Total: 9; 5 full-time, 4 part-time; 100% of full-time faculty have terminal degrees. Graduate students do not teach undergraduate courses. Undergraduate student–faculty ratio: 10:1.

Estimated Expenses for 1995–96 Application fee: $20. Comprehensive fee of $17,900 includes full-time tuition ($12,200 minimum), mandatory fees ($100), and

College of New Rochelle *(continued)*

college room and board ($5600). Part-time mandatory fees: $50 per year. Part-time tuition per credit ranges from $353 to $380 according to class level.

Financial Aid Program-specific awards for Fall of 1994: Art Scholarships for program majors ($2000).

Application Procedures Deadline—freshmen and transfers: continuous. Required: essay, high school transcript, college transcript(s) for transfer students, minimum 2.0 high school GPA, interview, portfolio, SAT I test score only. Portfolio reviews held 10 times on campus; the submission of slides may be substituted for portfolios if a campus visit is impossible.

Undergraduate Contact Susan M. Canning, Chair, Art Department, School of Arts and Sciences, College of New Rochelle, 29 Castle Place, New Rochelle, New York 10805; 914-654-5275, fax: 914-654-5290.

College of Notre Dame

Belmont, California

Independent-religious, coed. Suburban campus. Total enrollment: 1,707.

Degrees Bachelor of Fine Arts in the areas of drawing, painting, photography, sculpture, advertising design, printmaking. Majors: advertising design, art/fine arts, interior design, painting/drawing, photography, printmaking, sculpture, studio art. Cross-registration with Trinity College, Emmanuel College.

Art Student Profile Fall 1994: 45 total; all matriculated undergraduate; 52% minorities, 66% females, 45% international.

Art Faculty Total: 8; 3 full-time, 5 part-time; 100% of full-time faculty have terminal degrees. Graduate students do not teach undergraduate courses. Undergraduate student–faculty ratio: 10:1.

Student Life Student groups include American Society of Interior Designers Student Chapter.

Expenses for 1995–96 Application fee: $35. Comprehensive fee of $19,582 includes full-time tuition ($13,482) and college room and board ($6100). Part-time tuition: $500 per unit.

Application Procedures Deadline—freshmen: July 1; transfers: August 1. Notification date—freshmen: August 1; transfers: September 1. Required: essay, high school transcript, minimum 3.0 high school GPA, letter of recommendation.

Undergraduate Contact Undergraduate Admissions, College of Notre Dame, 1500 Ralston Avenue, Belmont, California 94002-1997; 415-508-3589, fax: 415-637-0493.

College of Santa Fe

Santa Fe, New Mexico

Independent, coed. Small-town campus. Total enrollment: 1,365.

Degrees Bachelor of Fine Arts in the area of studio art. Majors: painting/drawing, photography, printmaking, sculpture.

Art Student Profile Fall 1994: 110 total; all matriculated undergraduate.

Art Faculty Total: 7; 5 full-time, 2 part-time.

Expenses for 1995–96 Application fee: $25. Comprehensive fee of $16,006 includes full-time tuition ($11,796) and college room and board ($4210). College room only: $2036. Part-time tuition: $371 per semester hour. Part-time mandatory fees: $50 per year.

Application Procedures Deadline—freshmen and transfers: March 1. Required: high school transcript, minimum 2.0 high school GPA. Recommended: minimum 3.0 high school GPA, interview, portfolio. Portfolio reviews held 2 times on campus and off campus in various high schools in U.S.; the submission of slides may be substituted for portfolios.

Undergraduate Contact Admissions Office, College of Santa Fe, 1600 Saint Michael's Drive, Santa Fe, New Mexico 87505; 505-473-6131, fax: 505-473-6127.

More about the College

The art program at the College of Santa Fe is an extraordinary blend of theory and application. Because of the school's location in Santa Fe—the arts center of the Southwest—CSF is able to offer students a tremendous variety of hands-on experiences as well as a fine liberal arts education. Santa Fe holds a special attraction for artists. There's something about the light, colors, and intensity of nature that captures the creativity in artists and allows this creativity to flow freely. CSF wants students to be caught up in the magic that is Santa Fe and in the art that makes this community so unique. Students are encouraged to develop their talents under the direction of some of the finest artists this area has to offer. Upper-level art students are often placed in internships with local studios, galleries, foundries, museums or printmaking shops. The curriculum is challenging, with high expectations for student performance, and the student-faculty ratio low. Developing the talents of its students is CSF's primary concern.

CSF offers either a Bachelor of Arts or a Bachelor of Fine Arts degree and concentrated studies in drawing, painting, photography, sculpture, or printmaking. The B.A. degree is the choice for those wishing a broad-based education with serious study in the visual arts. The B.F.A. is a focused, professional degree with primary emphasis on the development of artistic skills and art history awareness.

The CSF Fine Arts Gallery provides students, faculty, and the public the opportunity to study and view a wide range of original art on campus and offer students experience in gallery practices. Studios for painting, drawing, and sculpture are available. Facilities and equipment for the study of film, video, and art history are shared with the Moving Image Arts Department.

Advanced studio majors are usually provided individual space in which to work, and all art students have access to studios anytime of day.

Groundbreaking for a new arts building is scheduled for fall 1995. The building will house the college's new Center for Photographic Arts, a state-of-the-art facility where students can explore studio photography as well as the history of photography and conservation of works on paper and museum studies. The college is also home to the Beaumont Newhall Photographic Library.

College of Visual Arts

St. Paul, Minnesota

Independent, coed. Urban campus. Total enrollment: 210.

Degrees Bachelor of Fine Arts in the areas of visual communication, fine arts. Majors: applied art, art/fine arts, commercial art, computer graphics, drawing, graphic arts, graphic design, illustration, painting, photography, printmaking, sculpture, studio art, visual communication.

Art Student Profile Fall 1994: 220 total; 210 matriculated undergraduate, 10 nondegree; 7% minorities, 50% females, 2% international.

Art Faculty Total: 38; 10 full-time, 28 part-time; 70% of full-time faculty have terminal degrees. Graduate students do not teach undergraduate courses. Undergraduate student–faculty ratio: 6:1.

Expenses for 1995–96 Application fee: $25. Tuition: $8500 full-time, $354 per credit part-time.

Financial Aid Program-specific awards for Fall of 1994: 4 Merit Scholarships for continuing students ($3000), College of Visual Arts Grants for those demonstrating need ($1200–$1500).

Application Procedures Deadline—freshmen and transfers: continuous. Notification date—freshmen and transfers: continuous. Required: essay, high school transcript, college transcript(s) for transfer students, interview, portfolio, ACT scores for first-time freshmen. Recommended: minimum 3.0 high school GPA, 2 letters of recommendation. Portfolio reviews held continuously on campus; the submission of slides may be substituted for portfolios.

Undergraduate Contact Sherry A. Essen, Director of Admissions, College of Visual Arts, 344 Summit Avenue, St. Paul, Minnesota 55102-2124; 612-224-3416, fax: 612-224-8854.

More about the College

Founded in 1924, the College of Visual Arts (CVA) is a nonprofit, four-year college of art and design, offering Bachelor of Fine Arts programs in visual communication (design, illustration, photography) and fine arts (painting, sculpture, printmaking, drawing), with 40% of the BFA program consisting of general education coursework. With a 1995 enrollment of 220 students and a faculty of 38, CAA blends a rigorous curriculum and individualized attention allowing students to realize their full creative and intellectual potential in a challenging, yet supportive, educational environment.

A CVA education begins with a structured Foundation Program during which students develop and practice the skills on which the rest of their education will be built. During this year they draw, learn basic design and color theory, and experiment with computers, photography, and three-dimensionality. Students learn the fundamentals of visual language by engaging in artistic dialogue with their peers and faculty, and they explore issues relating to their own unique creative and aesthetic processes. Students learn how to communicate both visually and verbally while developing critical thinking skills, problem-solving abilities, and a general aesthetic awareness. At the end of their Foundation year, students engage in an intensive portfolio review during which they have an opportunity to show their work to a panel of faculty, to reflect on their first year experience, and to receive advice and guidance about their potential in a particular major area.

Following the Foundation year, the aim of each of CVA's programs is to offer a curriculum that combines structured elements with the freedom to experiment in electives outside the major area. Students benefit from a dynamic faculty of professionals who challenge them to find new means of expression and to discover a personal artistic vision. In addition, internship opportunities, business and portfolio development classes, and contact with various visiting professionals prepares students to apply their artistic skills and conceptual knowledge to a profession. They leave with a genuine understanding of the connections between concept and practice, and a readiness to take their places as artists at work in society.

College of Visual Arts graduates have established themselves in numerous companies and nonprofit organizations across the nation, pursuing careers in graphic and advertising design, children's book illustration, art direction, package design and photography. They are creating art at Nike headquarters in Oregon, Walt Disney Studios in Los Angeles, *Minneapolis/Saint Paul* Magazine in the Twin Cities, WCCO television studio in Minneapolis, and the Museum of Fine Arts in Boston. Other graduates have had the initiative and confidence to launch their own design, illustration, and fine arts businesses, while others have gone on to attend graduate school.

College of Visual Art's location is a remarkable place for artists, and the Twin Cities of Minneapolis/Saint Paul are home to countless theaters, restaurants, and galleries, including the nationally renowned Walker Art Center, the Minneapolis Institute of Arts, and the Weisman Art Museum at the University of Minnesota. The Twin Cities community is an accepting, sophisticated place for artists and designers, and is one that supports the arts handsomely.

Program Facilities College of Visual Arts students enjoy access to the following facilities: the College's library, which offers both print and audio/visual resources, art-related books and periodicals, and a slide library; the sculpture studio, which is furnished with a full metal shop equipped for cutting, drilling and welding all types of metal, equipment for ceramic work, a complete line of woodworking tools and equipment, and full facilities to cast bronze, aluminum, and iron; a printmaking studio equipped with presses for monotype, intaglio, relief and woodblock printing, and a complete

College of Visual Arts *(continued)*

line of screenprinting equipment; a fully equipped photography studio and copy camera room for production of color slides, and darkrooms for processing both color and black-and-white film; outdoor courtyard space for exhibiting large scale sculptures; and a permanent gallery for regular student, faculty and visiting artist exhibitions. CVA's efficient and technologically advanced computer labs are outfitted with current Macintosh hardware and the latest computer software.

Faculty College of Visual Arts views its faculty as its single greatest resource, and the strong mentoring relationships built between faculty and students have long been primary to the success of a CVA education. In addition to teaching, CVA faculty are working artists, illustrators, and designers in the Twin Cities, and their ability to bring the "outside inside" lends relevancy and currency to the curriculum.

Special Programs CVA offers an internship program and career placement services, personal counseling, and individual tutoring.

Columbia College

Columbia, Missouri

Independent-religious, coed. Small-town campus. Total enrollment: 817.

Degrees Bachelor of Fine Arts in the areas of art, fashion design. Majors: art education, art/fine arts, ceramic art and design, computer graphics, fashion design and technology, graphic arts, illustration, jewelry and metalsmithing, painting/drawing, photography, printmaking, sculpture. Cross-registration with University of Missouri, Stephens College, William Woods College, Lincoln University, Westminster College.

Art Faculty Total: 6; 5 full-time, 1 part-time; 100% of full-time faculty have terminal degrees. Graduate students do not teach undergraduate courses. Undergraduate student–faculty ratio: 10:1.

Expenses for 1995–96 Application fee: $25. Comprehensive fee of $12,376 includes full-time tuition ($8546) and college room and board ($3830). College room only: $2410. Part-time tuition: $175 per semester hour.

Financial Aid Program-specific awards for Fall of 1994: 10 Talent Awards for program majors ($500–$1000).

Application Procedures Deadline—freshmen and transfers: continuous. Required: high school transcript, minimum 2.0 high school GPA.

Undergraduate Contact Admissions Office, Columbia College, 1001 Rogers Street, Columbia, Missouri 65216; 314-875-7352, fax: 314-875-8765.

Columbus College of Art and Design

Columbus, Ohio

Independent, coed. Urban campus. Total enrollment: 1,726.

Degrees Bachelor of Fine Arts in the areas of fine art, advertising design, interior design, industrial design, photography, illustration. Majors: art/fine arts, commercial art, fashion design and technology, graphic arts, illustration, industrial design, interior design, photography. Cross-registration with Higher Education Council of Columbus.

Art Student Profile Fall 1994: 1,726 total; all matriculated undergraduate; 15% minorities, 45% females, 4% international.

Art Faculty Total: 130; 67 full-time, 63 part-time; 60% of full-time faculty have terminal degrees. Graduate students do not teach undergraduate courses. Undergraduate student–faculty ratio: 13:1.

Student Life Special housing available for art students.

Expenses for 1995–96 Application fee: $25. Comprehensive fee of $16,240 includes full-time tuition ($10,300), mandatory fees ($240), and college room and board ($5700). Part-time tuition: $350 per semester hour. Special program-related fees: $40–$150 for lab fees.

Financial Aid Program-specific awards for Fall of 1994: 150 Honor Scholarships for those demonstrating talent and academic achievement ($100–$2500), 133 National Scholarship Competition for incoming freshmen ($8000).

Application Procedures Deadline—freshmen and transfers: continuous. Required: high school transcript, college transcript(s) for transfer students, minimum 2.0 high school GPA, letter of recommendation, portfolio. Recommended: interview, SAT I or ACT test scores. Portfolio reviews held continuously by appointment on campus; the submission of slides may be substituted for portfolios.

Undergraduate Contact Thomas E. Green, Director of Admissions, Columbus College of Art and Design, 107 North Ninth Street, Columbus, Ohio 43215; 614-224-9101, fax: 614-222-4040.

Founded in 1879, the Columbus College of Art and Design is one of the oldest, continuously operating art schools in the country. With a total enrollment of nearly 1700 students, CCAD is also one of the largest private colleges of art.

The educational goal of CCAD is professionalism. The curriculum is carefully structured so that courses taken at the same time complement each other, and courses taken in sequence progress logically from the first year to the time of graduation. Emphasis is placed on skill-building, resourcefulness, versatility, and creativity to help students realize their full aesthetic potential. The College stresses the actual work methods used in today's art studio, agency, business, or industry, but the curriculum provides a thorough foundation in the methods and concepts of the finer realms of art expression. Students are encouraged to seek the ideal by experiencing the practical.

The Bachelor of Fine Arts degree requires the completion of 145 semester credit hours (approximately 100 credit hours in art courses and 45 credit hours in general studies). During the first year of study, all students are required to take a sequence of core courses in anatomy, color concept, design, drawing, painting, and perspective. In the second year, students choose a major area of concentration and receive instruction in the fundamentals within a specific area. In the third and fourth years, students develop as professionals within their respective fields.

CCAC participates in the Federal Perkins Loan Program, the Federal Work-Study Program, the Federal Supplemental Educational Opportunity Grant Program, the Ohio Instructional Grant Program for Ohio residents, and the Federal PLUS Loan Program. For priority consideration, students should submit applications for these programs before May 1 for the following fall semester and by October 31 for the spring semester.

The College also conducts a scholarship competition open to high school seniors, with portfolios of artwork due March 1. Other entering student scholarship opportunities include the Scholastic Art Awards, Battelle Scholars Program (for Central Ohio students), National Art Honor Society, Art Recognition Talent Search Scholarship, and the Ohio Governor's Youth Art Exhibition. Applicants should contact the CCAD Admissions Office for additional information regarding these programs.

Concordia College

Seward, Nebraska

Independent-religious, coed. Small-town campus. Total enrollment: 953.

Degrees Bachelor of Fine Arts in the area of commercial art. Majors: commercial art.

Art Faculty Total: 7; 5 full-time, 2 part-time; 80% of full-time faculty have terminal degrees. Graduate students do not teach undergraduate courses. Undergraduate student–faculty ratio: 10:1.

Expenses for 1995–96 Application fee: $15. Comprehensive fee of $12,950 includes full-time tuition ($9480) and college room and board ($3470). Part-time tuition: $134 per credit hour. Part-time mandatory fees per term range from $75 to $125.

Application Procedures Deadline—freshmen and transfers: continuous. Notification date—freshmen and transfers: continuous. Required: high school transcript, college transcript(s) for transfer students, minimum 2.0 high school GPA, SAT I or ACT test scores, health form. Recommended: interview.

Undergraduate Contact William R. Wolfram, Chair, Art Department, Concordia College, 800 North Columbia Avenue, Seward, Nebraska 68434; 402-643-7499.

Converse College

Spartanburg, South Carolina

Independent, women only. Urban campus. Total enrollment: 1,160.

Degrees Bachelor of Fine Arts in the areas of studio art, interior design. Majors: applied art, ceramic art and design, interior design, painting/drawing, photography, printmaking, sculpture, studio art. Cross-registration with Wofford College.

Art Student Profile Fall 1994: 85 total; 75 matriculated undergraduate, 10 nondegree; 5% minorities, 100% females, 5% international.

Art Faculty Total: 12; 7 full-time, 5 part-time; 100% of full-time faculty have terminal degrees. Graduate students do not teach undergraduate courses. Undergraduate student–faculty ratio: 12:1.

Student Life Student groups include Student Art Club, American Society of Interior Designers. Special housing available for art students.

Expenses for 1995–96 Application fee: $35. Comprehensive fee of $16,975 includes full-time tuition ($13,150) and college room and board ($3825). Special program-related fees: $20 for drawing courses, $30–$40 for lab fees, .

Application Procedures Deadline—freshmen and transfers: continuous. Required: high school transcript, minimum 2.0 high school GPA, letter of recommendation. Recommended: interview.

Undergraduate Contact John Fluke, Vice President for Enrollment Management/Dean of Admissions, Converse College, 580 East Main Street, Spartanburg, South Carolina 29302; 803-596-9040.

The Cooper Union School of Art

Cooper Union for the Advancement of Science and Art

New York, New York

Independent, coed. Urban campus. Total enrollment: 1,064.

Degrees Bachelor of Fine Arts in the areas of drawing, graphic design, photography, printmaking, painting, sculpture. Majors: art/fine arts, drawing, graphic arts, graphic design, painting/drawing, photography, printmaking, sculpture, studio art. Cross-registration with Parsons School of Design&–New School for Social Research.

Art Student Profile Fall 1994: 254 total; all matriculated undergraduate.

Expenses for 1995–96 Application fee: $25. Tuition: $0 full-time. Living expenses are subsidized by college-administered financial aid. Full-time mandatory fees: $400. College room only: $4900.

Application Procedures Deadline—freshmen and transfers: January 10. Notification date—freshmen and trans-

Cooper Union for the Advancement of Science and Art *(continued)*

fers: April 1. Required: high school transcript, SAT I test score only. Recommended: letter of recommendation. Portfolio reviews held 4 times during fall semester on campus and off campus.

Undergraduate Contact Richard Bory, Dean of Admissions and Records, Cooper Union for the Advancement of Science and Art, 30 Cooper Square, Suite 300, New York, New York 10003; 212-353-4120, fax: 212-353-4343.

The Cooper Union School of Art offers a four-year program leading to the Bachelor of Fine Arts degree. The curriculum has been planned to provide an intensive general visual arts education that will provide artists/designers with the intellectual ability as well as specific professional skills to prepare them for their future endeavors.

The Foundation program consists of a series of prerequisite courses taken during the freshman year. The Foundation program is designed to be an indispensable base for the entire educational program of the School of Art and is not intended to prepare students exclusively for any one particular discipline. Through exposure to varied 2-D and 3-D projects subject to intense critique by faculty and students, the students are given a rigorous introduction to the peculiarities of visual and spatial phenomena as well as to concepts, principles, and techniques of visual literacy.

Beyond the Foundation year, students select advanced course work in the disciplines of drawing, graphic design, painting, photography, printmaking, and sculpture. Courses are also available in film, video, and calligraphy. An area of specialization is not required. On the upper levels, a more individual direction is established in the selection of courses within the area of concentration. The resulting flexibility is a fundamental strength of the program.

The development of the educational program is an ongoing process undergoing continued review, fine tuning, and coordination. The faculty represents varied philosophies, aesthetic viewpoints, and technical expertise echoing the multifaceted and pluralistic nature of the contemporary visual arts.

The location of the School of Art in New York City—the world art center—provides access to an outstanding pool of highly qualified exhibiting artists, faculty members, and lecturers to enrich the core faculty.

The facilities provide dedicated home space for all sophomores, juniors, and seniors as well as rooms assigned for foundation projects. The availability of equipment, from bronze casting to computer animation, is wide ranging and reflects the move to the future while including the past.

Candidates for the Bachelor of Arts degree are expected to complete 128 credits within eight semesters of study.

The School of Art offers a number of exchange opportunities with schools abroad in countries such as Japan, Israel, England, France, Italy, the Netherlands, and Switzerland, among others.

The Cooper Union School of Art is a member of AICAD (Association of Independent Colleges of Art and Design) and the East Coast Consortium and participates in an active mobility program with these schools. The School of Art is accredited by NASAD and Middle States Association of Colleges and Schools.

Corcoran School of Art

Washington, District of Columbia

Independent, coed. Urban campus. Total enrollment: 315.

Degrees Bachelor of Fine Arts in the areas of fine arts, graphic design, photography. Majors: art/fine arts, graphic arts, photography.

Art Student Profile Fall 1994: 325 total; all matriculated undergraduate; 10% minorities, 51% females, 12% international.

Art Faculty Total: 80; 45 full-time, 35 part-time; 60% of full-time faculty have terminal degrees. Graduate students do not teach undergraduate courses. Undergraduate student–faculty ratio: 7:1.

Student Life Student groups include Visual Arts Community Outreach Program. Special housing available for art students.

Expenses for 1995–96 Application fee: $30. Tuition: $11,550 full-time. College room only: $4360.

Financial Aid Program-specific awards for Fall of 1994: 40–60 Dean's Merit Scholarships for freshmen ($500–$2500), 20 Departmental Scholarships for undergraduates ($1000–$2500).

Application Procedures Deadline—freshmen and transfers: continuous. Required: high school transcript, college transcript(s) for transfer students, minimum 2.0 high school GPA, portfolio, SAT I or ACT test scores. Recommended: interview. Portfolio reviews held continuously by appointment on campus and off campus on National Portfolio Days; the submission of slides may be substituted for portfolios when distance is prohibitive.

Undergraduate Contact Mark Sistek, Director of Admissions, Corcoran School of Art, 500 17th Street, NW, Washington, District of Columbia 20006; 202-628-9484, fax: 202-628-3186, E-mail address: admofc@aol.com.

More about the School

Program Facilities Art & Design: The Corcoran's location, at the heart of Washington's cultural center, provides students with unsurpassed resources for artistic inspiration. Just one block from the White House, The Corcoran School of Art is within walking distance of the National Gallery of Art, the Library of Congress, and the Smithsonian Institution. Offering the B.F.A. degree in three disciplines, fine arts, graphic design, and photography, the college enrolls 325 full-time degree candidates, maintaining an intimate community of students and faculty. Its immediate environment is dedicated to the arts in their every aspect and is totally interrelated to the cultural infrastructure of the surrounding city.

Faculty The Corcoran faculty, active practitioners of art and design, is drawn from the vital and active professional community of the Washington metropolitan area. With 80 faculty members, The Corcoran School of Art has a favorable student-faculty ratio of less than 7:1, ensuring personal attention and a close working relationship within the school community.

Special Programs Seniors exhibit their thesis work in the Corcoran Museum's Hemicycle Gallery. Senior exhibitions highlight each student's accomplishments to visitors from all over the world. Internships are available at organizations throughout the Washington, D.C., area, such as the Goddard Space Flight Center and the National Gallery of Art. The aspiring young professionals who study today at The Corcoran School of Art will join a long tradition of involvement in the development of American art and design.

Cornell University

Ithaca, New York

Independent, coed. Small-town campus. Total enrollment: 18,811.

Degrees Bachelor of Fine Arts. Majors: art/fine arts, painting/drawing, photography, printmaking, sculpture, studio art. Graduate degrees offered: Master of Fine Arts.

Art Student Profile Fall 1994: 150 total; 140 matriculated undergraduate, 10 matriculated graduate; 34% minorities, 68% females, 1% international.

Art Faculty Total: 16; 13 full-time, 3 part-time; 85% of full-time faculty have terminal degrees. Graduate students do not teach undergraduate courses. Undergraduate student–faculty ratio: 16:1.

Student Life Student groups include Images Unseen, Minority Organization of Architecture, Art and Planning. Special housing available for art students.

Expenses for 1995–96 Application fee: $60. Comprehensive fee of $26,616 includes endowed full-time tuition ($19,066) and college room and board ($6550). Tuition for state-supported programs: $8556 full-time, part-time for state residents; $16,526 full-time, part-time for nonresidents. Special program-related fees: $50–$150 for departmental fees.

Application Procedures Deadline—freshmen: January 1; transfers: March 15. Notification date—freshmen: April 1; transfers: May 1. Required: essay, high school transcript, college transcript(s) for transfer students, minimum 3.0 high school GPA, 2 letters of recommendation, SAT I or ACT test scores, slides of portfolio. Recommended: interview. Portfolio reviews held by appointment on campus.

Undergraduate Contact Elizabeth Cutter, Director of Admissions, College of Architecture, Art and Planning, Cornell University, 135 East Sibley Hall, Ithaca, New York 14853; 607-255-4376, fax: 607-255-1900.

Graduate Contact Barry Perlus, Graduate Field Representative, Department of Art, Cornell University, 100 Olive Tjaden Hall, Ithaca, New York 14853; 607-255-4376, fax: 607-255-3462.

More about the University

Program Facilities Studios for painting and drawing, intaglio, lithography, and silkscreen; sculpture with bronze casting capability; multimedia labs and photography darkrooms for black-and-white, color, and alternative processes; digital imaging facilities under development. All facilities will be expanded with upcoming building renovation. Fine arts library contains over 146,000 volumes. Slide library contains about 400,000 slides.

Faculty, Resident Artists, and Alumni Faculty members are practicing artists, exhibiting nationally. An art faculty exhibition is held annually in Herbert F. Johnson Museum of Art, located on campus, adjacent to the school's facilities. The Visiting Artist Lecture Series includes artists such as Gregory Amenoff, Tina Barney, Rafael Ferrer, Helen Frankenthaler, Richard Hunt, Barbara Kasten, Barbara Kruger, Michael Mazur, Philip Pearlstein, Martin Puryear, Joyce Scott, Jaune Quick-to-See Smith, William Wegman, and Jacqueline Winsor.

Student Exhibit Opportunities Opportunities for student exhibits on campus in Olive Tjaden, John Hartell, and Willard Straight galleries. A Senior Thesis Exhibit is required. Grants up to $500 available to students from Council for the Arts at Cornell encourage artists to work on projects not primarily concerned with course work.

Special Programs Access to Cornell University courses, resources, facilities, activities, etc.; dual-degree program (B.F.A., B.A.) with College of Arts and Sciences; junior year program in Rome to study art, architecture, urban issues; visits to artists' studios and museums in other cities. Career services available: alumni forum to discuss careers, apprenticeships with artists, internships, externships, summer employment, and portfolio development.

Cornish College of the Arts

Seattle, Washington

Independent, coed. Urban campus. Total enrollment: 623.

Degrees Bachelor of Fine Arts in the areas of fine art, painting, photography, print art, sculpture, video art. Majors: art/fine arts, painting/drawing, photography, printmaking, sculpture, video art.

Art Student Profile Fall 1994: 175 total; 160 matriculated undergraduate, 15 nondegree; 11% minorities.

Art Faculty Total: 19; 6 full-time, 13 part-time; 99% of full-time faculty have terminal degrees. Graduate students do not teach undergraduate courses. Undergraduate student–faculty ratio: 8:1.

Expenses for 1995–96 Application fee: $30. Tuition: $10,540 full-time, $405 per credit part-time. Special program-related fees: $25–$75 for lab fees.

Financial Aid Program-specific awards for Fall of 1994: Merit Awards for continuing students ($1000), Endowed/Restricted Awards for continuing students ($1000), Trustee Grants for all students ($800–$1500), Cornish Scholarships for new students ($1000), 2–5 Kreielsheimer Scholarships for new students from Washington, Oregon, or Alaska ($15,000).

Application Procedures Deadline—freshmen and transfers: August 15. Required: essay, high school transcript, college transcript(s) for transfer students, minimum 2.0

Cornish College of the Arts *(continued)*

high school GPA, portfolio. Recommended: letter of recommendation, interview. Auditions held on campus. Portfolio reviews held 8 times and by appointment on campus and off campus on National Portfolio Days; the submission of slides may be substituted for portfolios when distance is prohibitive.

Undergraduate Contact Jane Buckman, Director, Admissions Office, Cornish College of the Arts, 710 East Roy Street, Seattle, Washington 98102; 206-323-1400, fax: 206-720-1011.

More about the College

Cornish College of the Arts provides students aspiring to become practicing artists with an exclusively arts-oriented environment that nurtures creativity and intellectual curiosity, and prepares them to contribute to society as artists, citizens, and innovators. Founded in 1914 as the Cornish School of Music, Cornish College of the Arts became accredited in 1977 and now offers the Bachelor of Fine Arts degree in art, dance, design, acting and performance production, and the Bachelor of Music degree. Classes are kept small so that students receive individualized attention. Cornish College instructors are practicing artists, many of national and international renown. They provide students with exposure to the professional arts arena on a daily basis. An active program of visiting artists and guest speakers, including curators, architects, composers, choreographers, and historians enriches the curriculum. Classes in the humanities and sciences develop critical thinking and provide valuable perspective.

Cornish College of the Arts is located in Seattle, Washington. Seattle's abundant resource of professional theaters, musical groups, dance companies, galleries, and museums offers many opportunities to participate in the vibrant local arts community.

The Cornish community consists of over 600 students. The average age of the students is 26. Students are expected to be self-motivated and will be encouraged to test the limits of their creativity. Cornish's staff and faculty provide a supportive environment for students to realize their potential as artists.

The Cornish College Art Department curriculum leads to a B.F.A. degree in five major areas of study: painting, photography, print art, sculpture, and video art. The curriculum emphasizes contemporary intellectual and expressive art processes based on the understanding of formal skills. Through work with practicing professional artists, students discover the visual language of historical works and current elements of contemporary art. The faculty helps students develop a vision unique to each individual.

The Art Department encourages students to examine both traditional and contemporary thought and processes within the five major areas of study offered. After experiencing the introductory courses, students select two areas of concentration and pursue art-making in longer, more intensive studio classes as juniors and seniors, where classes are generally no larger than 12 students. Seniors work in individual studios on campus.

The Design Department offers a B.F.A. degree in design, with an emphasis on graphic, furniture or interior design, or illustration. Students learn the skills of their art as well as its business practices, trends, and history. A faculty of professional designers and visiting artists provide the training.

During the first year, students gain a broad foundation of skill and knowledge in classes such as drawing, color theory, drafting, and perspective. Students refine their conceptualization skills in the second year and begin learning the techniques specific to their area of interest. In the third and fourth years, students apply their skills to the planning and execution of design projects, which are professionally oriented and provide students with commercially viable design solutions.

Culver-Stockton College

Canton, Missouri

Independent-religious, coed. Small-town campus. Total enrollment: 1,057.

Degrees Bachelor of Fine Arts in the areas of studio art, graphic design. Majors: applied art.

Art Student Profile Fall 1994: 30 total; all matriculated undergraduate; 8% minorities, 60% females, 4% international.

Art Faculty Total: 4; 2 full-time, 2 part-time; 100% of full-time faculty have terminal degrees. Graduate students do not teach undergraduate courses. Undergraduate student–faculty ratio: 15:1.

Student Life Student groups include Images Unlimited (art club).

Expenses for 1995–96 Comprehensive fee of $12,200 includes full-time tuition ($8400) and college room and board ($3800). College room only: $1700. Part-time tuition: $350 per hour. Special program-related fees.

Financial Aid Program-specific awards for Fall of 1994: Art Awards for program majors ($1000–$2000), Interest Awards for program minors ($500).

Application Procedures Deadline—freshmen and transfers: August 31. Required: high school transcript. Recommended: interview, portfolio. Portfolio reviews held as needed on campus; the submission of slides may be substituted for portfolios.

Undergraduate Contact Betty Smith, Director of Admissions, Culver-Stockton College, College Hill, Canton, Missouri 63435-1299; 314-288-5221 ext. 461, fax: 314-288-3984.

Daemen College

Amherst, New York

Independent, coed. Suburban campus. Total enrollment: 1,884.

Degrees Bachelor of Fine Arts in the areas of applied design, graphic design, drawing, illustration, painting, sculpture. Majors: art education, art/fine arts, drawing, graphic design, illustration, painting, printmaking, sculpture. Cross-registration with area universities.

Art Student Profile Fall 1994: 58 total; all matriculated undergraduate; 17% minorities, 60% females, 3% international.

Art Faculty Total: 10; 6 full-time, 4 part-time; 80% of full-time faculty have terminal degrees. Graduate students do not teach undergraduate courses. Undergraduate student–faculty ratio: 15:1.

Student Life Student groups include Student Art Organization.

Expenses for 1995–96 Application fee: $15. Comprehensive fee of $14,680 includes full-time tuition ($9400), mandatory fees ($380), and college room and board ($4900). Part-time tuition: $315 per credit. Part-time mandatory fees per semester (6 to 11 credits): $68.

Application Procedures Deadline—freshmen and transfers: continuous. Required: high school transcript, portfolio. Recommended: letter of recommendation, interview. Portfolio reviews held continuously on campus; the submission of slides may be substituted for portfolios.

Undergraduate Contact Admissions Office, Daemen College, 4380 Main Street, Amherst, New York 14226; 716-839-8225, fax: 716-839-8516.

More about the College

At Daemen, art is seen as both a lifestyle and a lifework. It calls for intense dedication, strong personal initiative and discipline, and, of course, talent. Art students at Daemen are continually challenged to find the creative solution; their understanding of the history and tradition of art-making will expand through studies and experiences at the college.

Large, well-equipped studios provide the backdrop for in-depth study in the chosen degree area. The small class size is ideal for the sharing of ideas and techniques, and for the critique of the students' works. It also ensures careful attention to the individual artistic needs because it leads to the opportunity for optimum interchange with faculty, all of whom are professionally active artists and designers.

Starting in their freshman year, students work with a team of faculty in the foundation program, where they develop their artistic and perceptual skills in the areas of 2- and 3-D design and drawing. Upon completion of the foundation courses, students spend their sophomore, junior, and senior years of study focusing on specific areas of interest in art and design. They take courses in their major studio area along with other studio courses in the department that will expand their vision as young artists. Daemen offers fully equipped studios in drawing, design, painting, sculpture, photography, fibers, ceramics, metalcraft, and a media studio for graphic design.

Careers in the arts are numerous and diverse. Possible career opportunities include: working in an art gallery or as an art consultant; self-employment in graphic design and production; and jobs in research, art conservation, publishing, or advertising. In addition, art education students can be certified to teach at the elementary or secondary levels.

Daemen offers three degree options: the Bachelor of Fine Arts prepares students for careers as professional artists. specialization in art (painting, sculpture, or drawing and illustration) and in applied design (printmaking) prepare you for professional studio work or for acceptance into graduate programs. The Bachelor of Fine Arts in graphic design integrates a solid background in basic art disciplines with the skills necessary for your success in business and industry. The Bachelor of Science in Art is planned to encourage your artistic growth through exposure to a variety of art experiences. The Bachelor of Science in Art Education is based upon the philosophy that competent art teachers are also practicing artists. Upon successful completion of the degree requirements, students receive provisional New York State certification to teach at the elementary and secondary levels.

Program Facilities Daemen College has a great deal to offer any student pursuing a degree in the arts. The Art and Graphic Design Department has twelve large and well-equipped studios that may be utilized for any of the College's various fine Art programs. Senior art students are given individual studio space according to their major area of study. Daemen offers instruction in many areas, including graphic design, foundation drawing and design, watercolor and illustration, painting, figure drawing, photography, sculpture, printmaking, and ceramics.

Faculty James Allen, M.F.A., Wayne State University; Dennis Barraclough, M.F.A., University of Michigan; Donald Bied, M.A., California State University; Jeanne File, OSF, Ph.D., Catholic University; Donna M. Stanton, M.F.A., SUNY at Buffalo.

Student Exhibit Opportunities On-campus exhibits are continuous in Daemen's Fanette Goldman and Carolyn Greenfield Art Gallery. There are annual student exhibits, and senior art majors are required to hold a Senior Thesis Exhibit in the gallery for graduation. Students' current artwork is always on display in the halls of the Art Department. The gallery holds a full schedule of exhibits each year featuring professional artists and designers from the area.

Special Programs The Art and Graphic Design Department sponsors a student art organization that allows students in the program to visit major art centers, travel to special exhibits, and bring in speakers. There are ample opportunities for students to take part in co-op arrangements in which they work in their field of interest for college credit.

Delta State University

Cleveland, Mississippi

State-supported, coed. Small-town campus. Total enrollment: 3,775.

Degrees Bachelor of Fine Arts in the areas of graphic design, painting, interior design, crafts, sculpture, photography. Majors: art education, graphic arts, interior design, painting/drawing, sculpture.

Art Student Profile Fall 1994: 110 total; all matriculated undergraduate; 11% minorities, 57% females.

Art Faculty Total: 12; 11 full-time, 1 part-time; 88% of full-time faculty have terminal degrees. Graduate stu-

Delta State University *(continued)*

dents do not teach undergraduate courses. Undergraduate student–faculty ratio: 10:1.

Expenses for 1995–96 State resident tuition: $2294 full-time, $83 per semester hour part-time. Nonresident tuition: $4888 full-time, $176 per semester hour part-time. College room and board: $2180.

Financial Aid Program-specific awards for Fall of 1994: 10–15 Art Scholarships for incoming freshmen ($1000).

Application Procedures Deadline—freshmen and transfers: August 2. Required: college transcript(s) for transfer students, minimum 2.0 high school GPA, SAT I or ACT test scores. Recommended: portfolio. Portfolio reviews held 1 time on campus.

Undergraduate Contact Frances Short, Coordinator of Admissions, Delta State University, Kethley 107, Cleveland, Mississippi 38733; 601-846-4018, fax: 601-846-4016.

Denison University

Granville, Ohio

Independent, coed. Small-town campus. Total enrollment: 1,834.

Degrees Bachelor of Fine Arts in the area of studio art. Majors: art/fine arts, photography, printmaking, sculpture. Cross-registration with Great Lakes Colleges Association.

Art Student Profile Fall 1994: 427 total; 99 matriculated undergraduate, 328 nondegree; 10% minorities, 52% females, 3% international.

Art Faculty Total: 8; 6 full-time, 2 part-time; 98% of full-time faculty have terminal degrees. Graduate students do not teach undergraduate courses. Undergraduate student–faculty ratio: 11:1.

Expenses for 1995–96 Application fee: $35. Comprehensive fee of $23,570 includes full-time tuition ($17,770), mandatory fees ($860), and college room and board ($4940). College room only: $2720. Part-time tuition: $554 per credit hour. Part-time mandatory fees per semester (6 to 8 credit hours): $410. One-time mandatory fee: $300.

Financial Aid Program-specific awards for Fall of 1994: 2 Marimac Scholarships for those demonstrating talent ($500–$2000).

Application Procedures Deadline—freshmen and transfers: February 1. Notification date—freshmen and transfers: May 1. Required: essay, high school transcript, college transcript(s) for transfer students, minimum 2.0 high school GPA, 2 letters of recommendation, SAT I or ACT test scores. Recommended: minimum 3.0 high school GPA, interview, video, portfolio. Portfolio reviews held by request on campus; the submission of slides may be substituted for portfolios on a case-by-case basis.

Undergraduate Contact Joy Sperling, Chair, Art Department, Denison University, Granville, Ohio 43023; 614-587-6704, fax: 614-587-6417, E-mail address: sperling@denisoncc.edu.

Dominican College of San Rafael

San Rafael, California

Independent-religious, coed. Suburban campus. Total enrollment: 1,249.

Degrees Bachelor of Fine Arts in the areas of photography, ceramics, painting, drawing, printmaking, ceramic sculpture. Majors: ceramic art and design, painting/drawing, photography, printmaking, sculpture.

Art Faculty Total: 7; 2 full-time, 5 part-time; 100% of full-time faculty have terminal degrees. Graduate students do not teach undergraduate courses.

Expenses for 1995–96 Application fee: $35. Comprehensive fee of $19,860 includes full-time tuition ($13,620), mandatory fees ($270), and college room and board ($5970 minimum). Part-time tuition: $568 per unit. Part-time mandatory fees: $270 per year.

Application Procedures Deadline—freshmen and transfers: August 29. Required: essay, high school transcript, 2 letters of recommendation, SAT I or ACT test scores, minimum 2.5 high school GPA or 2.0 college GPA for transfer students.

Undergraduate Contact Edythe Bresnehan, Chairperson, Art Department, Dominican College of San Rafael, 50 Acacia Avenue, San Rafael, California 94901; 415-485-3269, fax: 415-485-3205.

Drake University

Des Moines, Iowa

Independent, coed. Suburban campus. Total enrollment: 5,954.

Degrees Bachelor of Fine Arts in the areas of painting, drawing, sculpture, printmaking, graphic design, interior design. Majors: art/fine arts, drawing, graphic arts, illustration, interior design, painting, painting/drawing, printmaking, sculpture. Graduate degrees offered: Master of Fine Arts in the areas of painting, printmaking.

Art Student Profile Fall 1994: 144 total; 140 matriculated undergraduate, 4 matriculated graduate.

Art Faculty Total: 17; 10 full-time, 7 part-time; 70% of full-time faculty have terminal degrees. Graduate students do not teach undergraduate courses. Undergraduate student–faculty ratio: 12:1.

Student Life Student groups include Art Student Club.

Expenses for 1995–96 Application fee: $25. Comprehensive fee of $18,830 includes full-time tuition ($14,100) and college room and board ($4730 minimum). College room only: $2500. Part-time tuition per semester hour: $325 for daytime classes, $210 for evening classes.

Financial Aid Program-specific awards for Fall of 1994: 15–25 Art Scholarships for freshmen ($500–$4000).

Application Procedures Deadline—freshmen and transfers: continuous. Required: essay, high school transcript.

Contact Jules Kirschenbaum, Chair, Art Department, Drake University, 25th and University Avenue, Des Moines, Iowa 50311; 515-271-3831, fax: 515-271-2558.

East Carolina University

Greenville, North Carolina

State-supported, coed. Urban campus. Total enrollment: 16,373.

Degrees Bachelor of Fine Arts in the areas of art, art education. Majors: art education, ceramic art and design, graphic design, illustration, jewelry and metalsmithing, painting/drawing, printmaking, sculpture, surface design, textile arts, weaving, woodworking design. Graduate degrees offered: Master of Fine Arts in the area of art.

Art Student Profile Fall 1994: 610 total; 573 matriculated undergraduate, 37 matriculated graduate; 48% females.

Art Faculty Total: 48; 48 full-time; 90% of full-time faculty have terminal degrees. Graduate students teach a few undergraduate courses. Undergraduate student–faculty ratio: 17:1.

Student Life Student groups include Visual Art Forum, North Carolina Art Education Association Student Chapter, American Institute of Architectural Students.

Expenses for 1994–95 Application fee: $35. State resident tuition: $764 full-time. Nonresident tuition: $7248 full-time. Part-time tuition per semester ranges from $96 to $287 for state residents, $906 to $2718 for nonresidents. Part-time mandatory fees per semester range from $99 to $298. Full-time mandatory fees: $793. College room and board: $3030. College room only: $1590 (minimum).

Financial Aid Program-specific awards for Fall of 1994: 2 Gravely Scholarships for program majors ($500), 1 Jenni K. Jewelry Scholarship for metal design majors ($1000), 2 University Book Exchange Scholarships for program majors ($500), 1 Richard Bean Scholarship for communication arts majors ($600), 1 Della Wade Willis Scholarship for textiles majors ($500), 1 Art Enthusiasts Scholarship for program majors ($500), 1 Tran and Marilyn Gordley Scholarship for painting majors ($500), 1 K Eastern Carolina Advertising Federation Scholarship for communication arts majors ($500).

Application Procedures Deadline—freshmen: May 15; transfers: April 15. Required: high school transcript, college transcript(s) for transfer students, SAT I or ACT test scores, minimum 2.5 high school GPA.

Undergraduate Contact Art Haney, Assistant Dean, School of Art, East Carolina University, Jenkins Fine Arts Center, East Fifth Street, Greenville, North Carolina 27858-4353; 919-328-6563, fax: 919-328-6441.

Graduate Contact Roxanne Reep, Director of Graduate Studies, School of Art, East Carolina University, Jenkins Fine Arts Center, East Fifth Street, Greenville, North Carolina 27858-4353; 919-328-6563, fax: 919-328-6441.

More about the University

Program Facilities The Leo Jenkins Fine Arts Center is the home facility for the School of Art. All art courses are taught in this building, which has 142,000 square feet. Besides containing studios, labs, classrooms, and faculty and administrative offices, the Jenkins Building also houses a media center, two computer labs, a 250-seat auditorium, and three galleries. The exhibition facilities are some of the best in the country. They include the Wellington B. Gray Gallery (6,000 square feet), the Burroughs Wellcome Senior Gallery (1,100 square feet), and the Foundations Gallery (1,350 square feet).

Faculty and Visiting Artists In order to augment the teaching of its nationally and internationally known faculty, the School of Art hosts as many as two dozen visiting artists, lecturers, and critics each year. These visiting scholars present slide lectures, workshops, demonstrations, and critiques. Their presentations are also videotaped and placed into the School's extensive collection, which is kept in the Media Center. Visiting artists during the past two years have included such noted artists as Anne Matlock (fibers); Sydney Scherr (metals); John Clark (wood); Nick Joerling (clay); Rob Levin (glass/clay); Ken Botnick (book arts); Norman Keller (sculpture); Donna Nichols (ceramics); Bob Trotman (wood design); Yrjo and Marja Turkka (environmental design); Jill Dacey (textiles); Stefany Blyn (painting); Gregory Amenoff (photography); Angela Bourdimos (photography); Adrian Piper (video concept art); Patsy Allen (fibers); Jackie Peters (textile design and watercolor); David Steel (curator); Val Cushing (ceramics); Karin Weckstrom (ceramics); Paulus Berensohn (clay); Tom Muir (metals); Lucy Lippard (art critic and author); Vladimir Gorislavstev (ceramics); Ron Meyers (ceramics); Yves Paquette (ceramics); Darcy Nicholas (Maori artist); Lisa Sotilis (metals); Jaak Kangilaski (Estonian artist); Emily DuBois (textiles); Charles Hinmall (painting); Joel Fuller (communication arts); Bo Nilsson (curator); Anders Knutssun (painting); Pat Flynn (metals); Sherman Lee (art historian); Ms. Maxine Relton (printmaking); Ken Bloom (curator); Dr. Hilterd Westermann-Angerhausen (Director of the Schnutgen-Museum, Cologne, Germany); Dr. Lesa Mason (art historian); Martha Enzmann (interdisciplinary artist); Gunter Minas (curator); James Lankton (art collector) and many others. The School of Art also hires several visiting faculty persons to teach in the painting and drawing area for one year. This ensures an infusion of new ideas in teaching each and every year.

Eastern New Mexico University

Portales, New Mexico

State-supported, coed. Small-town campus. Total enrollment: 3,853.

Degrees Bachelor of Fine Arts in the areas of 2–dimensional art, 3–dimensional art, photography, graphic design. Majors: applied art, art/fine arts, ceramic art and design, graphic arts, jewelry and metalsmithing, painting/drawing, photography, sculpture, studio art.

Art Faculty Total: 9; 7 full-time, 2 part-time; 100% of full-time faculty have terminal degrees. Graduate students do not teach undergraduate courses.

Student Life Student groups include Clayhounds.

Eastern New Mexico University *(continued)*

Expenses for 1995–96 Application fee: $15. State resident tuition: $2258 full-time, $94 per credit hour part-time. Nonresident tuition: $6500 full-time, $270.80 per credit hour part-time. College room and board: $2728. College room only: $1268. Special program-related fees: $90 for ceramic lab fee, $60 for graphic design lab fee, $35 for photography lab fee.

Financial Aid Program-specific awards for Fall of 1994: 1 Metcalf Award for program majors ($1000), 4 Talent Day Awards for freshmen program majors ($400), 15 Participation Grants for freshmen program majors ($200).

Application Procedures Deadline—freshmen and transfers: July 23. Required: high school transcript, minimum 2.0 high school GPA, portfolio. Portfolio reviews held continuously on campus; the submission of slides may be substituted for portfolios when distance is prohibitive.

Undergraduate Contact Greg Erf, Chair, Art Department, Eastern New Mexico University, Station #19, Portales, New Mexico 88130; 505-562-2778.

East Tennessee State University

Johnson City, Tennessee

State-supported, coed. Small-town campus. Total enrollment: 11,512.

Degrees Bachelor of Fine Arts in the areas of drawing, painting, sculpture, ceramics, metals, fibers, graphic design, photography, printmaking. Majors: art education, art/fine arts, ceramic art and design, commercial art, computer graphics, interior design, jewelry and metalsmithing, painting/drawing, photography, printmaking, sculpture, textile arts. Graduate degrees offered: Master of Fine Arts in the areas of drawing, painting, sculpture, ceramics, metals, fibers, graphic design, photography, printmaking. Cross-registration with Penland School of Crafts.

Art Student Profile Fall 1994: 493 total; 175 matriculated undergraduate, 18 matriculated graduate, 300 nondegree; 5% minorities, 52% females, 1% international.

Art Faculty Total: 25; 13 full-time, 12 part-time; 100% of full-time faculty have terminal degrees. Graduate students teach a few undergraduate courses. Undergraduate student–faculty ratio: 10:1.

Student Life Student groups include Art Students League, Student Photographers Association, Student Ceramics Association.

Expenses for 1995–96 Application fee: $5. State resident tuition: $1870 full-time, $87 per semester hour part-time. Nonresident tuition: $6000 full-time, $268 per semester hour part-time. College room and board: $2550 (minimum). College room only: $1450 (minimum).

Financial Aid Program-specific awards for Fall of 1994: 1 Hays Scholarship for entering freshmen ($1000), 1 Adams Scholarship for rising sophomores ($1000), 1 Adams Scholarship for rising juniors ($300–$500).

Application Procedures Deadline—freshmen and transfers: continuous. Required: high school transcript, college transcript(s) for transfer students, SAT I or ACT test scores, minimum composite ACT score of 18.

Contact David G. Logan, Chairperson, Art Department, East Tennessee State University, P.O. Box 70708, Johnson City, Tennessee 37614-0708; 615-929-4247, fax: 615-929-4393.

East Texas State University

Commerce, Texas

State-supported, coed. Small-town campus. Total enrollment: 7,952.

Degrees Bachelor of Fine Arts in the areas of sculpture and metals, painting, ceramics, photography, printmaking, illustration, experimental studies. Majors: art education, art/fine arts, ceramic art and design, commercial art, experimental studies, graphic arts, illustration, jewelry and metalsmithing, painting/drawing, photography, printmaking, sculpture, studio art. Graduate degrees offered: Master of Fine Arts in the areas of sculpture and metals, painting, ceramics, printmaking, illustration, experimental studies, photography. Cross-registration with University of North Texas, Texas Woman's University.

Art Student Profile Fall 1994: 60% females, 2% international.

Art Faculty Total: 18; 10 full-time, 8 part-time. Graduate students teach a few undergraduate courses. Undergraduate student–faculty ratio: 14:1.

Student Life Student groups include Students Arts Association, Photo Society.

Expenses for 1994–95 State resident tuition: $840 full-time. Nonresident tuition: $5130 full-time, $171 per semester hour part-time. State resident part-time tuition per semester ranges from $100 to $308. Part-time mandatory fees per semester range from $57 to $376. Full-time mandatory fees: $914. College room and board: $3600 (minimum).

Financial Aid Program specific awards for Fall of 1994: 7–12 Endowed Scholarships for program majors ($200–$500).

Application Procedures Deadline—freshmen and transfers: August 8. Required: high school transcript, college transcript(s) for transfer students, SAT I or ACT test scores, minimum combined SAT I score of 920, minimum composite ACT score of 20.

Undergraduate Contact Dr. William Wadley, Head, Art Department, East Texas State University, East Texas Station, Commerce, Texas 75429-3011; 903-886-5203, fax: 903-886-5987.

Graduate Contact Jerry Dodd, Graduate Coordinator, Art Department, East Texas State University, East Texas Station, Commerce, Texas 75429-3011; 903-886-5207, fax: 903-886-5415.

Emmanuel College

Boston, Massachusetts

Independent-religious, primarily women. Urban campus. Total enrollment: 1,528.

Degrees Bachelor of Fine Arts in the areas of painting and printmaking, visual communications and graphic design. Majors: art education, art history, graphic arts, painting/drawing, printmaking, studio art. Cross-registration with Simmons College.

Art Student Profile Fall 1994: 80 total; all matriculated undergraduate; 99% females, 10% international.

Art Faculty Total: 9; 4 full-time, 5 part-time; 100% of full-time faculty have terminal degrees. Graduate students do not teach undergraduate courses. Undergraduate student–faculty ratio: 15:1.

Student Life Student groups include professional gallery on campus, membership in Boston Museum of Fine Arts and Gardner Museum, Art Club and First Expressions (student gallery in Boston).

Expenses for 1995–96 Application fee: $30. Comprehensive fee of $19,725 includes full-time tuition ($13,150), mandatory fees ($300), and college room and board ($6275). Part-time tuition: $391 per credit. Special program-related fees.

Financial Aid Program-specific awards for Fall of 1994: 2 Sr. Vincent Scholarships for freshmen ($4500).

Application Procedures Deadline—freshmen and transfers: September 1. Notification date—freshmen and transfers: September 16. Required: essay, high school transcript, college transcript(s) for transfer students, minimum 2.0 high school GPA, 2 letters of recommendation, interview. Recommended: portfolio. Portfolio reviews held 2 times on campus.

Undergraduate Contact Maureen Ferrari, Director of Admissions, Emmanuel College, 400 The Fenway, Boston, Massachusetts 02115; 617-735-9715, fax: 617-735-9877.

Emporia State University

Emporia, Kansas

State-supported, coed. Small-town campus. Total enrollment: 6,075.

Degrees Bachelor of Fine Arts in the areas of ceramics, commercial art, painting, photography, printmaking, sculpture and glassforming, weaving. Majors: ceramic art and design, commercial art, glassworking, painting/drawing, photography, printmaking, sculpture, weaving.

Art Student Profile Fall 1994: 128 total; 103 matriculated undergraduate, 25 nondegree; 5% minorities, 57% females, 3% international.

Art Faculty Total: 13; 8 full-time, 5 part-time; 70% of full-time faculty have terminal degrees. Graduate students do not teach undergraduate courses. Undergraduate student–faculty ratio: 15:1.

Student Life Student groups include Alpha Rho Theta, Glass Guild.

Expenses for 1995–96 Application fee: $15. State resident tuition: $1782 full-time, $65 per credit hour part-time. Nonresident tuition: $5764 full-time, $198 per credit hour part-time. College room and board: $3220.

Financial Aid Program-specific awards for Fall of 1994: 6 Jerry Ely Awards for art majors ($400), 1 Hazelrigg Memorial Award for metalry majors ($250), 3 Art Faculty Awards for art majors ($250), 4 Beulah Holton Memorial Awards for art education majors ($400).

Application Procedures Deadline—freshmen and transfers: continuous. Required: high school transcript, college transcript(s) for transfer students, ACT test score only. Auditions held on campus and off campus. Portfolio reviews held on campus and off campus.

Undergraduate Contact Donald Perry, Chair, Division of Art, Emporia State University, Box 15, Emporia, Kansas 66801; 316-341-5246, fax: 316-341-5073.

Evangel College

Springfield, Missouri

Independent-religious, coed. Urban campus. Total enrollment: 1,541.

Degrees Bachelor of Fine Arts. Majors: art/fine arts, graphic arts. Cross-registration with Drury College, Southwest Missouri State University.

Art Student Profile Fall 1994: 43 total; all matriculated undergraduate; 5% minorities, 50% females, 10% international.

Art Faculty Total: 6; 2 full-time, 4 part-time; 100% of full-time faculty have terminal degrees. Graduate students do not teach undergraduate courses. Undergraduate student–faculty ratio: 10:1.

Expenses for 1995–96 Application fee: $25. Comprehensive fee of $10,470 includes full-time tuition ($7120), mandatory fees ($180), and college room and board ($3170). College room only: $1550. Part-time tuition: $277 per credit hour. Part-time mandatory fees per semester range from $40 to $50. Special program-related fees: $30–$80 for supplies.

Financial Aid Program-specific awards for Fall of 1994: 4 Humanities Awards for undergraduates ($715), 1 Ben Messick Scholarship for undergraduates ($1000), 1 Riepma Scholarship for undergraduates ($685), 2 Seed Scholarships for incoming freshmen ($500), 2 Young Christian Leadership Awards for incoming freshmen ($500), Academic Scholarships for incoming freshmen ($1000–$2000).

Application Procedures Deadline—freshmen and transfers: continuous. Required: high school transcript, minimum 2.0 high school GPA. Recommended: 2 letters of recommendation, interview, portfolio. Portfolio reviews held 2 times on campus; the submission of slides may be substituted for portfolios for large works of art.

Undergraduate Contact Stan Maples, Professor, Art Department, Evangel College, 1111 North Glenstone, Springfield, Missouri 65802; 417-865-2811 ext. 7395.

Fashion Institute of Technology

New York, New York

State and locally supported, coed. Urban campus. Total enrollment: 8,422.

Degrees Bachelor of Fine Arts in the areas of advertising design, fabric styling, fashion design, illustration, interior design, packaging, restoration, textile surface design, toy design. Majors: advertising design, fabric styling, fashion design and technology, graphic design, illustration, interior design, packaging design, restoration, textile arts, toy design. Cross-registration with State University of New York colleges.

Art Student Profile Fall 1994: 12,703 total; 5,059 matriculated undergraduate, 60 matriculated graduate, 7,584 nondegree; 50% minorities, 11% international.

Art Faculty Total: 931; 181 full-time, 750 part-time. Graduate students do not teach undergraduate courses. Undergraduate student–faculty ratio: 14:1.

Expenses for 1994–95 Application fee: $25. Part-time mandatory fees: $5 per term. Full-time tuition for associate degree program: $2100 per year for state residents, $5050 per year for nonresidents. Full-time tuition for bachelor's degree program: $2585 per year for state residents, $6000 per year for nonresidents. Part-time tuition for associate degree program: $50 per credit for state residents, $130 per credit for nonresidents. Part-time tuition for bachelor's degree program: $58 per credit for state residents, $145 per credit for nonresidents. Full-time mandatory fees: $210. College room and board: $4800. College room only: $3900.

Financial Aid Program-specific awards for Fall of 1994 available.

Application Procedures Deadline—freshmen and transfers: continuous. Required: essay, high school transcript, college transcript(s) for transfer students, minimum 2.0 high school GPA, portfolio. Recommended: letter of recommendation, interview, SAT I or ACT test scores. Portfolio reviews held several times on campus; the submission of slides may be substituted for portfolios with permission of the chair.

Undergraduate Contact Office of Admissions, Fashion Institute of Technology, Seventh Avenue at 27th Street, New York, New York 10001-5992; 212-760-7675.

More about the College

Today, to know the Fashion Institute of Technology only by name is not to know it very well at all. The name reflects back 50 years to the college's origins when it was devoted exclusively to educating students for careers in the apparel industry. But the name no longer tells the whole story.

A "fashion college" that offers programs in interior design, advertising design, marketing, and even toy design; a community college that offers bachelor's and master's degree programs in addition to the traditional two-year associate degree, F.I.T. is an educational institution like no other.

The campus leaves behind the rolling green lawns of the more traditional college campus in favor of the challenges and excitement of "unique New York." F.I.T.'s location in the heart of Manhattan—where the worlds of fashion, art, design, communications, and manufacturing converge—permits an exceptional two-way flow between the college and the industries and professions it serves.

F.I.T. is rooted in industry and the world of work. Industry visits by students and lectures by many different leaders in the field provide a cooperative and creative bridge between the classroom and the actual world of work. And though the college is now associated with many industries and professions, not just one, F.I.T.'s commitment to career education is still its hallmark, and a source of pride to an institution whose industry connection is an integral part of its history.

F.I.T. serves more than 4,000 full-time and 8,000 part-time students yearly, who come not only from within commuting distances, but from all 50 states and as many foreign countries.

Founded in 1944, F.I.T. today is a college of art and design, business and technology of the State University of New York. More than 15 majors in art and design and 9 in business and technology lead to the A.A.S., B.F.A., or B.S. degree (in addition to the M.A. degree).

F.I.T. is an accredited institutional member of the Middle States Association of Colleges and Schools, the National Association of Schools of Art and Design, and the Foundation for Interior Design Education Research.

The eight-building campus includes classrooms, studios, and labs that reflect the most advanced educational and industrial practices. Facilities include photography studios and darkrooms, painting rooms, sculpture studio, toy design workshop, a graphics laboratory, model-making workshop, printmaking room, life-sketching rooms, restoration lab, television studios, display and exhibit design rooms, and textile labs for floor, hand, and computer-aided looms. Also of importance and located on three floors is the Gladys Marcus Library, which houses more than 110,000 titles including books, periodicals and nonprint materials. Three dormitories serve approximately 1,230 students and offer various accommodations.

At F.I.T., placement is the bottom line; with a consistent job placement rate of 86%, F.I.T. graduates are well prepared to meet employers' needs. Working with both undergraduates and graduates, placement counselors develop job opportunities for full-time, part-time, freelance, and summer employment.

Student participation is encouraged through more than 60 campus clubs, organizations, and athletic teams.

Program Facilities The Computer-Aided Design and Communications facility provides art and design students with the opportunity to explore technology and its integration in the design of textiles, toys, interiors, fashion, and advertising as well as photography and computer graphics. Also located on campus is the design/research lighting laboratory, an educational and professional development facility for interior design and other academic disciplines.

The Museum at F.I.T. is the repository for the world's largest collection of costumes, textiles, and accessories of dress (with an emphasis on 20th century apparel), and is used by students, designers, and historians for research and inspiration.

Student Opportunities The museum's galleries provide a showcase for a wide spectrum of exhibitions relevant to fashion and its satellite industries. The annual student art and design exhibition is shown here as are other student projects during the year. Student work is also displayed throughout the campus. Fashion shows of menswear, womenswear, and accessories occur each academic year.

Faculty and Alumni Those who do, teach at F.I.T. Members of the F.I.T. community have considerable experience and are on the cutting edge of their various fields and industries. The F.I.T. counts among its alumni such superstars as Calvin Klein and Norma Kamali, as well as successful and talented professionals in advertising, marketing, packaging, television, the design fields, merchandising, manufacturing, public relations, advertising, and retailing.

Special Programs F.I.T. offers semester abroad programs and a number of international short study courses, including its own international fashion design program in New York and Florence, Italy. Internships are also offered in most majors.

Saturday Live programs are available during fall, spring, and summer. These 25 programs offer high school students the chance to learn in a studio environment, to explore the business and technology side of the fashion industry, and to discover natural talents and creative abilities. Classes are taught by a faculty of artists, designers, and other professionals. High school credit may be earned at the discretion of each student's school.

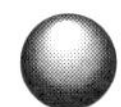

Schmidt College of Arts and Humanities

Florida Atlantic University

Boca Raton, Florida

State-supported, coed. Suburban campus. Total enrollment: 17,484.

Degrees Bachelor of Fine Arts in the area of art. Majors: ceramics, graphic design, painting/drawing, photography, printmaking, sculpture.

Art Student Profile Fall 1994: 272 total; all matriculated undergraduate; 13% minorities, 67% females, 12% international.

Art Faculty Total: 15; 9 full-time, 6 part-time; 100% of full-time faculty have terminal degrees. Graduate students do not teach undergraduate courses. Undergraduate student–faculty ratio: 30:1.

Student Life Student groups include Potters Guild, Juried Student Show, Bachelor of Fine Arts Show.

Expenses for 1994–95 Application fee: $20. State resident tuition: $1791 full-time, $59.69 per semester hour part-time. Nonresident tuition: $6693 full-time, $223.10 per semester hour part-time. College room and board: $3930. Special program-related fees: $15 for studio lab fee.

Application Procedures Deadline—freshmen and transfers: May 27. Required: high school transcript, college transcript(s) for transfer students, minimum 2.0 high school GPA, SAT I or ACT test scores, minimum 2.0 college GPA for transfer students.

Undergraduate Contact Dr. Kathleen Russo, Chair, Art Department, Florida Atlantic University, 777 Glades Road, Boca Raton, Florida 33431; 407-367-3870, fax: 407-367-3870.

Florida International University

Miami, Florida

State-supported, coed. Urban campus. Total enrollment: 22,052.

Degrees Bachelor of Fine Arts in the area of fine arts. Majors: art/fine arts.

Expenses for 1994–95 Application fee: $20. State resident tuition: $1695 full-time, $56.49 per credit hour part-time. Nonresident tuition: $6597 full-time, $219.90 per credit hour part-time. Part-time mandatory fees: $40 per semester. Full-time mandatory fees: $80. College room and board: $3716.

Application Procedures Deadline—freshmen and transfers: May 31.

Undergraduate Contact William Maguire, Head Advisor, Department of Visual Arts, Florida International University, University Park, Miami, Florida 33199; 305-348-2897, fax: 305-348-3561.

Florida State University

Tallahassee, Florida

State-supported, coed. Suburban campus. Total enrollment: 29,630.

Degrees Bachelor of Fine Arts in the area of studio art. Majors: studio art. Graduate degrees offered: Master of Fine Arts in the area of studio art.

Art Student Profile Fall 1994: 375 total; 250 matriculated undergraduate, 25 matriculated graduate, 100 nondegree; 5% minorities, 50% females, 1% international.

Art Faculty Total: 30; 15 full-time, 15 part-time; 100% of full-time faculty have terminal degrees. Graduate students teach a few undergraduate courses. Undergraduate student–faculty ratio: 16:1.

Student Life Student groups include Art Students League.

Expenses for 1995–96 Application fee: $20. State resident tuition: $1798 full-time, $59.93 per semester hour part-time. Nonresident tuition: $6700 full-time, $223.34 per semester hour part-time. College room and board: $4500. College room only: $2360.

Application Procedures Deadline—freshmen and transfers: continuous. Required: essay, high school transcript, college transcript(s) for transfer students, minimum 2.0 high school GPA, SAT I test score only. Recommended: minimum 3.0 high school GPA, letter of recommenda-

Florida State University *(continued)*

tion. Auditions held on campus and off campus. Portfolio reviews held on campus and off campus.

Undergraduate Contact Undergraduate Admissions Coordinator, Department of Art, Florida State University, 220 FAB-2037, Tallahassee, Florida 32306-2037; 904-644-6474, fax: 904-644-8977.

Graduate Contact Robert Fichter, Director of the Graduate Program, Studio Art Department, Florida State University, 220 FAB-2037, Tallahassee, Florida 32306-2037; 904-644-6474, fax: 904-644-8977, E-mail address: rficht@mailer.fsu.edu.

Fontbonne College

St. Louis, Missouri

Independent-religious, coed. Suburban campus. Total enrollment: 1,681.

Degrees Bachelor of Fine Arts in the areas of sculpture, painting, drawing, ceramics, studio art. Majors: ceramics, painting/drawing, sculpture, studio art. Graduate degrees offered: Master of Fine Arts in the areas of sculpture, painting, drawing, ceramics, studio art.

Art Student Profile Fall 1994: 72 total; 39 matriculated undergraduate, 33 matriculated graduate.

Art Faculty Total: 9; 4 full-time, 5 part-time; 100% of full-time faculty have terminal degrees. Graduate students do not teach undergraduate courses. Undergraduate student–faculty ratio: 14:1.

Expenses for 1995–96 Application fee: $20. Comprehensive fee of $13,980 includes full-time tuition ($8890), mandatory fees ($150), and college room and board ($4940). Part-time mandatory fees: $6 per semester (minimum). Part-time tuition per credit: $270 for daytime classes, $215 for evening classes. Special program-related fees: $25–$45 for studio lab fee.

Application Procedures Deadline—freshmen and transfers: continuous. Required: essay, high school transcript, college transcript(s) for transfer students, minimum 2.0 high school GPA, portfolio, SAT I or ACT test scores, minimum 2.0 college GPA for transfer students. Recommended: interview. Portfolio reviews held at end of sophomore year for entrance into BFA program on campus.

Undergraduate Contact Admissions Office, Fontbonne College, 6800 Wydown Boulevard, St. Louis, Missouri 63105; 314-889-1400, fax: 314-889-1451.

Graduate Contact Hank Knickmeyer, Graduate Advisor, Art Department, Fontbonne College, 6800 Wydown Boulevard, St. Louis, Missouri 63105; 314-889-1431.

Fort Hays State University

Hays, Kansas

State-supported, coed. Small-town campus. Total enrollment: 5,496.

Degrees Bachelor of Fine Arts in the areas of design, graphic design, interior design, drawing, painting, printmaking, sculpture, ceramics, jewelry. Majors: art education, art/fine arts, ceramic art and design, commercial art, computer graphics, graphic arts, illustration, interior design, jewelry and metalsmithing, painting/drawing, photography, printmaking, sculpture, studio art. Graduate degrees offered: Master of Fine Arts in the areas of design, graphic design, drawing, painting, printmaking, sculpture, ceramics, jewelry.

Art Student Profile Fall 1994: 243 total; 217 matriculated undergraduate, 20 matriculated graduate, 6 nondegree.

Art Faculty Total: 13; 12 full-time, 1 part-time; 83% of full-time faculty have terminal degrees. Graduate students do not teach undergraduate courses. Undergraduate student–faculty ratio: 18:1.

Student Life Student groups include Creative Arts Society, American Art Therapy Association.

Estimated Expenses for 1995–96 Application fee: $15. State resident tuition: $1902 full-time, $61.15 per credit hour part-time. Nonresident tuition: $6169 full-time, $193.85 per credit hour part-time. College room and board: $3172. College room only: $1600. Special program-related fees: $15–$50 for supplies.

Financial Aid Program-specific awards for Fall of 1994: 40 Awards of Excellence for freshmen ($400), 20 Art Scholarships for upperclassmen ($200).

Application Procedures Deadline—freshmen and transfers: continuous. Required: high school transcript. Recommended: minimum 2.0 high school GPA, portfolio. Portfolio reviews held 2 times on campus and off campus in various Kansas cities; the submission of slides may be substituted for portfolios.

Undergraduate Contact Leland Powers, Assistant Professor, Art Department, Fort Hays State University, 600 Park Street, Hays, Kansas 67601-4099; 913-628-4247, fax: 913-628-4087.

Graduate Contact Graduate School, Fort Hays State University, 600 Park Street, Hays, Kansas 67601-4099; 913-628-4236.

Georgia Southern University

Statesboro, Georgia

State-supported, coed. Small-town campus. Total enrollment: 14,138.

Degrees Bachelor of Fine Arts in the area of art. Majors: art/fine arts. Graduate degrees offered: Master of Fine Arts in the area of art.

Art Student Profile Fall 1994: 280 total; 125 matriculated undergraduate, 15 matriculated graduate, 140 nondegree.

Art Faculty Total: 16; 15 full-time, 1 part-time; 100% of full-time faculty have terminal degrees. Graduate students do not teach undergraduate courses. Undergraduate student–faculty ratio: 12:1.

Student Life Student groups include Club MUD.

Estimated Expenses for 1995–96 Application fee: $10. State resident tuition: $1341 full-time, $40 per quarter hour part-time. Nonresident tuition: $4185 full-time, $120 per quarter hour part-time. Part-time mandatory fees per quarter (6 to 11 quarter hours): $152. Full-time mandatory fees: $456. College room and board: $3285.

Application Procedures Deadline—freshmen and transfers: continuous. Required: high school transcript, SAT I or ACT test scores.

Contact Richard Tichich, Chair, Art Department, Georgia Southern University, Landrum Box 8032, Statesboro, Georgia 30460; 912-681-5358, fax: 912-681-5104.

Georgia Southwestern College

Americus, Georgia

State-supported, coed. Small-town campus. Total enrollment: 2,533.

Degrees Bachelor of Fine Arts in the area of art. Majors: ceramic art and design, commercial art, glass, painting/drawing, photography, sculpture.

Art Student Profile Fall 1994: 140 total; 64 matriculated undergraduate, 76 nondegree; 21% minorities, 44% females, 14% international.

Art Faculty Total: 4; 4 full-time; 75% of full-time faculty have terminal degrees. Graduate students do not teach undergraduate courses. Undergraduate student–faculty ratio: 15:1.

Expenses for 1995–96 Application fee: $10. State resident tuition: $1926 full-time, $42 per quarter hour part-time. Nonresident tuition: $5136 full-time, $132 per quarter hour part-time. Part-time mandatory fees per quarter range from $11 to $121. Full-time mandatory fees: $516. College room and board: $2940. College room only: $1380.

Application Procedures Deadline—freshmen and transfers: August 24. Required: high school transcript, college transcript(s) for transfer students, minimum 2.0 high school GPA, interview, portfolio, SAT I or ACT test scores, minimum combined SAT I score of 800.

Undergraduate Contact Jack Lewis, Coordinator, Visual Arts Program, Department of Fine Arts, Georgia Southwestern College, 800 Wheatley Street, Americus, Georgia 31709-4693; 912-931-2204.

Georgia State University

Atlanta, Georgia

State-supported, coed. Urban campus. Total enrollment: 23,776.

Degrees Bachelor of Fine Arts in the areas of studio art, art education. Majors: ceramic art and design, graphic arts, interior design, jewelry and metalsmithing, painting/drawing, photography, printmaking, sculpture, textile arts. Graduate degrees offered: Master of Fine Arts in the area of studio art.

Art Faculty Total: 30; 25 full-time, 5 part-time.

Expenses for 1995–96 Application fee: $10. State resident tuition: $2003 full-time, $44.50 per quarter hour part-time. Nonresident tuition: $7178 full-time, $159.50 per quarter hour part-time. Part-time mandatory fees: $82 per quarter. Full-time mandatory fees: $246.

Application Procedures Deadline—freshmen and transfers: July 15. Required: high school transcript, college transcript(s) for transfer students, minimum 2.0 high school GPA, SAT I or ACT test scores, minimum combined SAT I score of 800. Auditions held on campus and off campus. Portfolio reviews held on campus and off campus.

Undergraduate Contact Office of Admissions, Georgia State University, P.O. Box 4009, Atlanta, Georgia 30303; 404-651-2365.

Grand Valley State University

Allendale, Michigan

State-supported, coed. Small-town campus. Total enrollment: 13,553.

Degrees Bachelor of Fine Arts in the areas of printmaking, painting, ceramics, graphic design, metalsmithing, sculpture. Majors: ceramic art and design, graphic arts, jewelry and metalsmithing, painting/drawing, printmaking, sculpture.

Expenses for 1995–96 State resident tuition: $2780 full-time, $124 per semester hour part-time. Nonresident tuition: $6462 full-time, $279 per semester hour part-time. Part-time mandatory fees per semester range from $48 to $128. Full-time mandatory fees: $360. College room and board: $4181.

Application Procedures Deadline—freshmen and transfers: continuous.

Undergraduate Contact Dr. J. David McGee, Chairman, Art and Design Department, Grand Valley State University, 1 College Landing, Allendale, Michigan 49401; 616-895-2575.

Green Mountain College

Poultney, Vermont

Independent, coed. Small-town campus. Total enrollment: 518.

Degrees Bachelor of Fine Arts in the areas of studio arts, pre–architecture. Majors: art/fine arts.

Green Mountain College *(continued)*

Art Student Profile Fall 1994: 52 total; all matriculated undergraduate; 7% minorities, 50% females, 6% international.

Art Faculty Total: 5; 3 full-time, 2 part-time; 100% of full-time faculty have terminal degrees. Graduate students do not teach undergraduate courses. Undergraduate student–faculty ratio: 14:1.

Estimated Expenses for 1995–96 Application fee: $20. Comprehensive fee of $15,900 includes full-time tuition ($12,700), mandatory fees ($200), and college room and board ($3000). Part-time tuition: $395 per credit. Special program-related fees: $10–$60 for studio fees.

Financial Aid Program-specific awards for Fall of 1994: 1 Vargish Award for incoming freshmen ($3000).

Application Procedures Deadline—freshmen and transfers: continuous. Required: essay, high school transcript, minimum 2.0 high school GPA. Recommended: letter of recommendation, interview, portfolio. Auditions held on campus. Portfolio reviews held as needed on campus; the submission of slides may be substituted for portfolios.

Undergraduate Contact Louise Field, Associate Dean, Admissions Department, Green Mountain College, 16 College Street, Poultney, Vermont 05764; 802-287-9313, fax: 802-287-9313.

Guilford College

Greensboro, North Carolina

Independent-religious, coed. Suburban campus. Total enrollment: 1,187.

Degrees Bachelor of Fine Arts in the area of studio art. Majors: ceramics, painting/drawing, photography, printmaking, sculpture. Cross-registration with University of North Carolina at Greensboro.

Art Student Profile Fall 1994: 52 total; all matriculated undergraduate; 2% minorities, 60% females, 2% international.

Art Faculty Total: 6; 3 full-time, 3 part-time; 100% of full-time faculty have terminal degrees. Graduate students do not teach undergraduate courses. Undergraduate student–faculty ratio: 12:1.

Student Life Student groups include Annual Student Art Exhibition, senior thesis exhibition.

Expenses for 1995–96 Application fee: $25. Comprehensive fee of $19,660 includes full-time tuition ($14,180), mandatory fees ($210), and college room and board ($5270). College room only: $2786. Part-time tuition: $443 per credit. Part-time mandatory fees: $15 per semester.

Financial Aid Program-specific awards for Fall of 1994: 1–2 J. S. Laing Scholarships for program majors ($200–$400).

Application Procedures Deadline—freshmen: February 1; transfers: May 1. Notification date—freshmen: March 15; transfers: June 1. Required: essay, high school transcript, college transcript(s) for transfer students, minimum 2.0 high school GPA, SAT I test score only. Recommended: letter of recommendation, interview, portfolio. Portfolio reviews held (once at end of junior year) on campus.

Undergraduate Contact Adele Wayman, Hege Professor of Art, Guilford College, 5800 West Friendly Avenue, Greensboro, North Carolina 27410; 910-316-2337.

Harding University

Searcy, Arkansas

Independent-religious, coed. Small-town campus. Total enrollment: 3,817.

Degrees Bachelor of Fine Arts in the areas of graphic design, painting, 3–dimensional design. Majors: applied art, art education.

Art Student Profile Fall 1994: 115 total; all matriculated undergraduate; 5% minorities, 67% females, 2% international.

Art Faculty Total: 7; 6 full-time, 1 part-time; 60% of full-time faculty have terminal degrees. Graduate students do not teach undergraduate courses. Undergraduate student–faculty ratio: 18:1.

Estimated Expenses for 1995–96 Application fee: $25. Comprehensive fee of $10,200 includes full-time tuition ($5450), mandatory fees ($1000), and college room and board ($3750). College room only: $1800. Part-time tuition: $180 per semester hour. Part-time mandatory fees: $33 per semester hour. Special program-related fees: $8–$60 for supplies.

Financial Aid Program-specific awards for Fall of 1994: 15 Art Scholarships for program majors ($250–$500).

Application Procedures Deadline—freshmen and transfers: continuous. Required: high school transcript, 2 letters of recommendation, interview, SAT I or ACT test scores.

Undergraduate Contact Chairman, Art Department, Harding University, Box 2253, Searcy, Arkansas 72149; 501-279-4426.

Graduate Contact Dr. Wyatt Jones, Director of Graduate Studies, Harding University, Box 2261, Searcy, Arkansas 72149.

Harrington Institute of Interior Design

Chicago, Illinois

Proprietary, coed. Urban campus. Total enrollment: 293.

Degrees Bachelor of Fine Arts in the area of interior design. Majors: interior design.

Art Student Profile Fall 1994: 347 total; 175 matriculated undergraduate, 172 nondegree; 9% minorities, 66% females, 9% international.

Art Faculty Total: 31; 12 full-time, 19 part-time; 24% of full-time faculty have terminal degrees. Graduate students do not teach undergraduate courses. Undergraduate student–faculty ratio: 16:1.

Student Life Student groups include American Society of Interior Designers, International Society of Interior Designers.

Expenses for 1995–96 Tuition: $9424 full-time.

Financial Aid Program-specific awards for Fall of 1994: 2 Manhoff Scholarships for incoming students ($500), 2 Mallin Scholarships for incoming students ($250).

Application Procedures Deadline—freshmen and transfers: continuous. Required: high school transcript, college transcript(s) for transfer students, interview. Recommended: minimum 2.0 high school GPA, SAT I or ACT test scores. Auditions held on campus and off campus. Portfolio reviews held on campus and off campus.

Undergraduate Contact Robert C. Marks, Dean, Harrington Institute of Interior Design, 410 South Michigan Avenue, Chicago, Illinois 60605-1496; 312-939-4975, fax: 312-939-8005.

More about the Institute

Program Facilities The Harrington Institute of Interior Design has a completely equipped CAD Lab, and a highly specialized Interior Design Library. The school's studios and classrooms offer views of Lake Michigan and Grant Park. The historic Fine Arts Building is an inspiring location for the study of design.

Faculty, Resident Artists, and Alumni The faculty consists of highly experienced, practicing designers and architects. Alumni of the Harrington Institute of Interior Design teach at and head numerous interior design programs.

Student Performance and Exhibit Opportunities Harrington students regularly enter and win regional and national design competitions.

Special Programs Harrington Institute of Interior Design is the only college in the Midwest exclusively devoted to interior design. It is also the only college in the Chicago area with institutional accreditation by the National Association of Schools of Art and Design (NASAD), and full six-year accreditation by the Foundation for Interior Design Education Research (FIDER) for its Bachelor of Fine Arts in Interior Design program.

In addition, it is the only interior design college to offer all courses every semester. Its curriculum is designed as a unified whole, and its faculty is unsurpassed in its unity of purpose, professionalism, knowledge, and teaching accomplishment. Harrington Institute offers an exchange program with the Rotterdam College of Design in the Netherlands.

The Hartford Art School

See University of Hartford, The Hartford Art School

Herron School of Art

See Indiana University–Purdue University Indianapolis, Herron School of Art

Hope School of Fine Arts

See Indiana University Bloomington, Hope School of Fine Arts

Howard University

Washington, District of Columbia

Independent, coed. Urban campus. Total enrollment: 10,961.

Degrees Bachelor of Fine Arts in the areas of painting, design, printmaking, photography, ceramics, sculpture, electronic studio, experimental studio. Majors: ceramic art and design, design, electronic arts, experimental studies, painting/drawing, photography, printmaking, sculpture. Graduate degrees offered: Master of Fine Arts in the areas of painting, ceramics, printmaking, design, electronic studio, experimental studio, sculpture.

Art Student Profile Fall 1994: 225 total; 194 matriculated undergraduate, 31 matriculated graduate.

Art Faculty Total: 33; 15 full-time, 18 part-time; 95% of full-time faculty have terminal degrees. Graduate students teach a few undergraduate courses. Undergraduate student–faculty ratio: 10:1.

Expenses for 1994–95 Comprehensive fee of $11,676 includes full-time tuition ($7130), mandatory fees ($401), and college room and board ($4145). Part-time tuition: $275 per credit hour. Part-time mandatory fees: $401 per year.

Application Procedures Deadline—freshmen and transfers: April 1. Required: essay, high school transcript, minimum 2.0 high school GPA, letter of recommendation, interview, portfolio, SAT I test score only. Auditions held on campus and off campus. Portfolio reviews held continuously on campus and off campus; the submission of slides may be substituted for portfolios.

Undergraduate Contact Undergraduate Admissions, Howard University, Washington, District of Columbia 20059-0002; 202-806-2763.

Graduate Contact Graduate Admissions, Howard University, Washington, District of Columbia 20059-0002; 202-806-2755.

Illinois State University

Normal, Illinois

State-supported, coed. Urban campus. Total enrollment: 19,166.

Degrees Bachelor of Fine Arts in the area of art. Majors: art/fine arts, ceramics, fibers, graphic design, intaglio, jewelry and metalsmithing, lithography, painting/drawing, photography, printmaking, sculpture, studio art. Graduate degrees offered: Master of Fine Arts in the area of fine arts.

Art Student Profile Fall 1994: 550 total; 500 matriculated undergraduate, 50 matriculated graduate.

Illinois State University *(continued)*

Art Faculty Graduate students teach a few undergraduate courses.

Expenses for 1995–96 State resident tuition: $3572 full-time, $119.05 per credit part-time. Nonresident tuition: $8954 full-time, $298.45 per credit part-time. College room and board: $3782. College room only: $1984. Special program-related fees: $10–$50 for studio lab fee.

Application Procedures Deadline—freshmen and transfers: continuous. Required: high school transcript, portfolio, SAT I or ACT test scores. Portfolio reviews held at end of sophomore year for entrance into BFA program on campus.

Undergraduate Contact Dr. Ron Mottram, Chair, Art Department, Illinois State University, Campus Box 5620, Normal, Illinois 61790-5620; 309-438-5623.

Graduate Contact Ken Holder, Graduate Director, Art Department, Illinois State University, Campus Box 5620, Normal, Illinois 61790-5620; 309-438-5623.

Illinois Wesleyan University

Bloomington, Illinois

Independent, coed. Suburban campus. Total enrollment: 1,855.

Degrees Bachelor of Fine Arts in the area of art and design. Majors: art/fine arts, ceramic art and design, commercial art, computer graphics, drawing, graphic arts, painting, photography, printmaking, sculpture, studio art. Cross-registration with Institute for European and Asian Studies.

Art Student Profile Fall 1994: 632 total; 65 matriculated undergraduate, 567 nondegree; 8% minorities, 52% females, 3% international.

Art Faculty Total: 7; 6 full-time, 1 part-time; 100% of full-time faculty have terminal degrees. Graduate students do not teach undergraduate courses. Undergraduate student–faculty ratio: 11:1.

Gareth Hinds

Parsons School of Design—Artist, Looking Glass Technologies, Boston

Gareth is creating artwork for three-dimensional first-person immersive computer games like FLIGHT Unlimited, an aerobatic flight simulator. He says that in his last year at Parsons he experienced a fundamental change in his perception of drawing and its role in identity as an artist. "I developed the computer skills that I am using today, the sketchbooks which convinced the Art Director of my ability, and the awareness of this and other job markets I had not considered before."

Expenses for 1995–96 Comprehensive fee of $19,800 includes full-time tuition ($15,410), mandatory fees ($100), and college room and board ($4290). College room only: $2450. Part-time tuition: $1925 per course. Special program-related fees: $100 for departmental fee.

Financial Aid Program-specific awards for Fall of 1994: 60 Art Talent Awards for freshmen ($2500–$6500).

Application Procedures Deadline—freshmen and transfers: continuous. Required: essay, high school transcript, college transcript(s) for transfer students, minimum 3.0 high school GPA, portfolio, SAT I or ACT test scores. Recommended: interview. Portfolio reviews held by appointment on campus; the submission of slides may be substituted for portfolios when distance is prohibitive.

Undergraduate Contact James Routi, Director of Admissions, Illinois Wesleyan University, P.O. Box 2900, Bloomington, Illinois 61702-2900; 309-556-3031.

Indiana State University

Terre Haute, Indiana

State-supported, coed. Urban campus. Total enrollment: 11,641.

Degrees Bachelor of Fine Arts in the area of studio art. Majors: ceramic art and design, furniture design, graphic design, jewelry and metalsmithing, painting/drawing, photography, printmaking, sculpture, studio art, wood. Graduate degrees offered: Master of Fine Arts in the area of studio art.

Art Student Profile Fall 1994: 250 total; 200 matriculated undergraduate, 50 matriculated graduate.

Art Faculty Total: 20; 19 full-time, 1 part-time; 79% of full-time faculty have terminal degrees. Graduate students teach a few undergraduate courses. Undergraduate student–faculty ratio: 15:1.

Student Life Student groups include Undergraduate Gallery Organization.

Expenses for 1995–96 Application fee: $20. State resident tuition: $2928 full-time, $104.50 per credit hour part-time. Nonresident tuition: $7224 full-time, $252.50 per credit hour part-time. College room and board: $3859. Special program-related fees: $12 for studio lab fee.

Financial Aid Program-specific awards for Fall of 1994: 6–7 Creative and Performing Arts Scholarships for freshmen ($1200), 1 Indiana Artist–Craftsmen/Talbot Street Art Fair Scholarship for program majors ($350), 1 Violet Helen Rich Scholarship for painting majors ($1500).

Application Procedures Deadline—freshmen and transfers: August 15. Notification date—freshmen and transfers: continuous. Required: high school transcript, minimum 3.0 high school GPA, 3 letters of recommendation.

Contact Chairperson, Art Department, Indiana State University, Fine Arts 108, Terre Haute, Indiana 47809; 812-237-3697, fax: 812-237-4369.

Hope School of Fine Arts

Indiana University Bloomington

Bloomington, Indiana

State-supported, coed. Small-town campus. Total enrollment: 35,594.

Degrees Bachelor of Fine Arts in the areas of ceramics, graphic design, jewelry and metalsmithing, painting, photography, printmaking, sculpture, textiles. Majors: ceramic art and design, graphic arts, jewelry and metalsmithing, painting/drawing, photography, printmaking, sculpture, textile arts. Graduate degrees offered: Master of Fine Arts in the areas of ceramics, graphic design, jewelry and metalsmithing, painting, photography, printmaking, sculpture, textiles.

Art Student Profile Fall 1994: 469 total; 391 matriculated undergraduate, 78 matriculated graduate; 7% minorities, 60% females, 2% international.

Art Faculty Total: 26; 23 full-time, 3 part-time; 92% of full-time faculty have terminal degrees. Graduate students teach about a quarter undergraduate courses. Undergraduate student–faculty ratio: 15:1.

Student Life Student groups include Fine Arts Students Association.

Expenses for 1995–96 Application fee: $35. State resident tuition: $3582 full-time, $98.65 per credit hour part-time. Nonresident tuition: $10,770 full-time, $323.50 per credit hour part-time. College room and board: $4148. Special program-related fees: $20–$55 for material fees.

Financial Aid Program-specific awards for Fall of 1994: 10–15 Hope School of Fine Arts Student Awards for program majors ($100–$800).

Application Procedures Deadline—freshmen: February 15; transfers: July 15. Notification date—freshmen and transfers: August 29. Required: high school transcript, letter of recommendation, portfolio, SAT I or ACT test scores. Portfolio reviews held 1–2 times on campus.

Undergraduate Contact Office of Admissions, Indiana University Bloomington, 300 North Jordan, Bloomington, Indiana 47405; 812-855-0661.

Graduate Contact Patricia Crouch, Graduate Services Coordinator, Hope School of Fine Arts, Indiana University Bloomington, Fine Arts 123, Bloomington, Indiana 47405; 812-855-0188, fax: 812-855-7498, E-mail address: pcrouch@indiana.edu.

Indiana University–Purdue University Fort Wayne

Fort Wayne, Indiana

State-supported, coed. Urban campus. Total enrollment: 11,513.

Degrees Bachelor of Fine Arts in the areas of computer design, crafts, drawing, graphic design, painting, photography, printmaking, sculpture. Majors: art/fine arts, ceramic art and design, commercial art, computer graphics, graphic arts, jewelry and metalsmithing, painting/drawing, photography, printmaking, sculpture.

Art Student Profile Fall 1994: 224 total; 219 matriculated undergraduate, 5 nondegree.

Art Faculty Total: 19; 10 full-time, 9 part-time; 90% of full-time faculty have terminal degrees. Graduate students do not teach undergraduate courses. Undergraduate student–faculty ratio: 12:1.

Expenses for 1994–95 Application fee: $30. State resident tuition: $2408 full-time, $80.25 per semester hour part-time. Nonresident tuition: $5966 full-time, $198.85 per semester hour part-time. Part-time mandatory fees: $2.90 per semester hour. Full-time mandatory fees: $87. Special program-related fees: $27 for material fees.

Financial Aid Program-specific awards for Fall of 1994: 6 Departmental Scholarships for incoming students ($800–$1500), 8 Departmental Scholarships for continuing students ($800–$1500).

Application Procedures Deadline—freshmen and transfers: August 1. Notification date—freshmen and transfers: continuous. Required: high school transcript, college transcript(s) for transfer students, minimum 2.0 high school GPA, 3 letters of recommendation, SAT I or ACT test scores. Recommended: portfolio. Portfolio reviews held as needed on campus; the submission of slides may be substituted for portfolios for large works of art.

Undergraduate Contact Leslie P. Motz, Chair, Fine Art Department, Indiana University–Purdue University Fort Wayne, 2101 Coliseum Boulevard East, Fort Wayne, Indiana 46805; 219-481-6705.

Herron School of Art

Indiana University–Purdue University Indianapolis

Indianapolis, Indiana

State-supported, coed. Urban campus. Total enrollment: 26,766.

Degrees Bachelor of Fine Arts in the areas of painting, printmaking, ceramics, woodworking, sculpture, visual communication, photography and fine arts. Majors: art/fine arts, ceramic art and design, commercial art, computer graphics, graphic arts, painting/drawing, photography, printmaking, sculpture, woodworking design.

Indiana University–Purdue University Indianapolis *(continued)*

Art Student Profile Fall 1994: 1,025 total; 500 matriculated undergraduate, 525 nondegree; 10% minorities, 52% females, 5% international.

Art Faculty Total: 46; 31 full-time, 15 part-time; 98% of full-time faculty have terminal degrees. Graduate students do not teach undergraduate courses. Undergraduate student–faculty ratio: 14:1.

Student Life Student groups include Herron Student Senate.

Expenses for 1994–95 Application fee: $25. State resident tuition: $2766 full-time, $92.20 per credit hour part-time. Nonresident tuition: $8490 full-time, $283 per credit hour part-time. Part-time mandatory fees: $131.25 per semester. Full-time mandatory fees: $263. College room and board: $3260. Special program-related fees: $150 for technology fee.

Financial Aid Program-specific awards for Fall of 1994: 20 New Student Awards for program majors ($1500), 20 New Student Awards for program majors ($1500).

Application Procedures Deadline—freshmen and transfers: June 1. Notification date—freshmen and transfers: July 15. Required: high school transcript, college transcript(s) for transfer students, portfolio, SAT I or ACT test scores, minimum combined SAT I score of 850. Portfolio reviews held 8 times on campus; the submission of slides may be substituted for portfolios.

Undergraduate Contact John D. Werenko, Assistant Dean and Director of Student Services, Admissions Department, Indiana University–Purdue University Indianapolis, 1701 North Pennsylvania Street, Indianapolis, Indiana 46202; 317-920-2416, fax: 317-920-2401.

Indiana University South Bend

South Bend, Indiana

State-supported, coed. Suburban campus. Total enrollment: 7,936.

Degrees Bachelor of Fine Arts in the area of visual arts. Majors: applied art, art/fine arts, computer graphics, drafting and design, graphic arts, guitar, painting/drawing, photography, printmaking, sculpture, studio art. Cross-registration with Indiana University System.

Art Student Profile Fall 1994: 10 total; all matriculated undergraduate; 10% minorities, 60% females, 5% international.

Art Faculty Total: 6; 3 full-time, 3 part-time; 100% of full-time faculty have terminal degrees. Graduate students do not teach undergraduate courses. Undergraduate student–faculty ratio: 15:1.

Student Life Student groups include Student Art Show.

Expenses for 1995–96 State resident tuition: $2544 full-time, $84.80 per credit hour part-time. Nonresident tuition: $6957 full-time, $231.90 per credit hour part-time. Part-time mandatory fees: $2.00 per credit hour. Full-time mandatory fees range. Full-time mandatory fees range from $120 to $150.

Application Procedures Deadline—freshmen and transfers: August 15. Notification date—freshmen and transfers: September 1. Required: high school transcript, minimum 2.0 high school GPA. Recommended: interview, video, portfolio. Portfolio reviews held 2 times on campus; the submission of slides may be substituted for portfolios for international applicants.

Undergraduate Contact Christine Seitz, Academic Coordinator, Division of the Arts, Indiana University South Bend, 1700 Mishawaka Avenue, P.O. Box 7111, South Bend, Indiana 46634; 219-237-4306.

International Academy of Merchandising & Design, Ltd.

Chicago, Illinois

Proprietary, coed. Urban campus. Total enrollment: 662.

Degrees Bachelor of Fine Arts in the areas of interior design, fashion design, advertising and design. Majors: advertising design, fashion design, interior design.

Art Student Profile Fall 1994: 662 total; all matriculated undergraduate; 44% minorities, 86% females, 5% international.

Art Faculty Total: 75; 5 full-time, 70 part-time. Graduate students do not teach undergraduate courses. Undergraduate student–faculty ratio: 14:1.

Student Life Student groups include American Society of Interior Designers, Fashion Group International, Inc..

Expenses for 1994–95 Tuition: $8550 (minimum) full-time. Tuition ranges up to $8910 full-time, and from $570 to $594 per course part-time, according to program.

Application Procedures Deadline—freshmen and transfers: continuous. Required: high school transcript, minimum 2.0 high school GPA, interview.

Undergraduate Contact Admissions Department, International Academy of Merchandising & Design, Ltd., One North State Street, Chicago, Illinois 60602-3300; 800-222-3369, fax: 312-541-3929.

International Academy of Merchandising & Design, Ltd.

Tampa, Florida

Proprietary, coed. Urban campus. Total enrollment: 415.

Degrees Bachelor of Fine Arts in the areas of fashion design, interior design. Majors: fashion design, interior design.

Art Student Profile Fall 1994: 465 total; all matriculated undergraduate.

Art Faculty Total: 90; 5 full-time, 85 part-time. Graduate students do not teach undergraduate courses. Undergraduate student–faculty ratio: 8:1.

Expenses for 1994–95 Tuition: $8100 full-time, $540 per course part-time.

Application Procedures Deadline—freshmen and transfers: continuous. Required: college transcript(s) for transfer students, minimum 2.0 high school GPA, interview, high school transcript or GED.

Undergraduate Contact Pam James, Director of Admissions, International Academy of Merchandising & Design, Ltd., 5225 Memorial Highway, Tampa, Florida 33634; 813-881-0007, fax: 813-881-0008.

Iowa State University of Science and Technology

Ames, Iowa

State-supported, coed. Suburban campus. Total enrollment: 24,728.

Degrees Bachelor of Fine Arts in the areas of graphic design, interior design, art and design. Majors: art/fine arts, craft design, graphic design, interior design, painting/drawing, printmaking, visual studies. Graduate degrees offered: Master of Fine Arts in the areas of graphic design, interior design.

Art Student Profile Fall 1994: 891 total; 850 matriculated undergraduate, 41 matriculated graduate; 1% minorities, 60% females, 1% international.

Art Faculty Total: 55; 41 full-time, 14 part-time; 80% of full-time faculty have terminal degrees. Graduate students teach a few undergraduate courses. Undergraduate student–faculty ratio: 18:1.

Student Life Student groups include Interior Design Student Association, Graphic Design Student Association, Art Appreciation Club.

Estimated Expenses for 1995–96 Application fee: $20. State resident tuition: $2386 full-time, $100 per semester hour part-time. Nonresident tuition: $8004 full-time, $334 per semester hour part-time. Full-time mandatory fees: $188. College room and board: $3386. Special program-related fees: $5–$100 for in-studio expenses.

Financial Aid Program-specific awards for Fall of 1994: 1 Beresford/Seeds Award for incoming freshmen ($3000), 10–12 Art and Design Excellence Awards for program majors ($500–$1500), 2 Garfield/Boody Awards for program majors ($1000), 3 Pickett/Kiser Awards for interior design majors ($500).

Application Procedures Deadline—freshmen and transfers: continuous. Required: high school transcript, college transcript(s) for transfer students, SAT I or ACT test scores, standing in top half of graduating class, TOEFL scores. Recommended: minimum 2.0 high school GPA.

Undergraduate Contact Director of Admissions, Iowa State University of Science and Technology, 100 Alumni Hall, Ames, Iowa 50011-2010; 515-294-5836, fax: 515-294-6106.

Graduate Contact Nancy Polster, Chair, Art and Design Department, Iowa State University of Science and Technology, 158 College of Design, Ames, Iowa 50011-3092; 515-294-6724, fax: 515-294-9755, E-mail address: npolster@iastate.edu.

Ithaca College

Ithaca, New York

Independent, coed. Small-town campus. Total enrollment: 5,556.

Degrees Bachelor of Fine Arts in the area of art. Majors: art/fine arts. Cross-registration with Cornell University.

Art Student Profile Fall 1994: 3 total; all matriculated undergraduate; 33% minorities, 67% females, 67% international.

Art Faculty Total: 6; 5 full-time, 1 part-time; 100% of full-time faculty have terminal degrees. Graduate students do not teach undergraduate courses. Undergraduate student–faculty ratio: 5:1.

Student Life Student groups include Ithaca College Art Club.

Expenses for 1995–96 Application fee: $40. Comprehensive fee of $21,844 includes full-time tuition ($15,250) and college room and board ($6594). Part-time tuition: $477 per credit hour.

Financial Aid Program-specific awards for Fall of 1994: Donald and Martha Negus Scholarships for program majors ($500–$1000).

Application Procedures Deadline—freshmen: March 1; transfers: July 15. Notification date—freshmen: April 15. Required: essay, high school transcript, college transcript(s) for transfer students, minimum 2.0 high school GPA, letter of recommendation, SAT I or ACT test scores. Recommended: interview, slides of portfolio.

Undergraduate Contact Paula J. Mitchell, Director, Admissions, Ithaca College, 100 Job Hall, Ithaca, New York 14850-7020; 800-429-4274, fax: 607-274-1900.

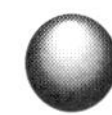

J. William Fulbright College of Arts and Sciences

See University of Arkansas, J. William Fulbright College of Arts and Sciences

Jacksonville State University

Jacksonville, Alabama

State-supported, coed. Small-town campus. Total enrollment: 7,553.

Degrees Bachelor of Fine Arts in the area of studio art. Majors: commercial art, painting/drawing, photography, printmaking, studio art.

Jacksonville State University *(continued)*

Art Student Profile Fall 1994: 130 total; all matriculated undergraduate; 16% minorities.

Art Faculty Total: 9; 7 full-time, 2 part-time; 100% of full-time faculty have terminal degrees. Graduate students do not teach undergraduate courses. Undergraduate student–faculty ratio: 18:1.

Student Life Student groups include Student Art Alliance.

Expenses for 1995–96 Application fee: $20. State resident tuition: $1840 full-time, $77 per semester hour part-time. Nonresident tuition: $2760 full-time, $116 per semester hour part-time. Residents of Georgia counties contiguous to Alabama pay state resident tuition. College room and board: $2320.

Financial Aid Program-specific awards for Fall of 1994: 1 Art Department Award for incoming freshmen ($1400), 2 Art Department Awards for upperclassmen ($2800), 1 Art Scholarship for undergraduates ($1700).

Application Procedures Deadline—freshmen and transfers: continuous. Required: high school transcript, college transcript(s) for transfer students, portfolio, SAT I or ACT test scores. Recommended: minimum 2.0 high school GPA. Portfolio reviews held 2 times on campus.

Undergraduate Contact Charles Groover, Head, Art Department, Jacksonville State University, 700 Pelham Road North, Jacksonville, Alabama 36265; 205-782-5626, fax: 205-782-5645.

Jacksonville University

Jacksonville, Florida

Independent, coed. Suburban campus. Total enrollment: 2,480.

Degrees Bachelor of Fine Arts in the areas of studio art, visual communications, computer art. Majors: art education, commercial art, computer graphics.

Art Student Profile Fall 1994: 101 total; all matriculated undergraduate; 14% minorities, 42% females, 3% international.

Art Faculty Total: 19; 4 full-time, 15 part-time; 100% of full-time faculty have terminal degrees. Graduate students do not teach undergraduate courses. Undergraduate student–faculty ratio: 15:1.

Expenses for 1995–96 Application fee: $25. Comprehensive fee of $15,178 includes full-time tuition ($10,080), mandatory fees ($500), and college room and board ($4598). Part-time tuition: $336 per semester hour. Part-time mandatory fees: $80 per semester. Special program-related fees: $30–$135 for materials and departmental fees.

Financial Aid Program-specific awards for Fall of 1994: 10 Art Department Awards for program majors ($1000–$3000).

Application Procedures Deadline—freshmen and transfers: continuous. Required: high school transcript, portfolio. Portfolio reviews held as needed on campus and off campus in various high schools in Duval County; the submission of slides may be substituted for portfolios if a campus visit is impossible.

Undergraduate Contact Jack Turnock, Chair, Deoartment of Art, Jacksonville University, 2800 University Boulevard North, Jacksonville, Florida 32211; 904-744-3950, fax: 904-744-0101.

More about the University

Program Facilities Classes are held in the Phillips Fine Arts Building and in special purpose art buildings. Special purpose studio facilities are available for printmaking, ceramics, glassblowing, photography, painting, drawing, jewelry and metal, sculpture, graphic design, computer art, and airbrush. The Alexander Brest Museum houses a permanent collection of art and presents monthly exhibits of contemporary art.

Faculty, Resident Artists, and Alumni The Art Department has 4 full-time faculty members and up to 15 adjunct instructors, all of whom are exhibiting professional artists of local and regional note. The department presents a series of workshops each year highlighting visiting artists of regional and national reputation.

Student Exhibition Opportunities Exhibition opportunities are available each year in the Alexander Brest Museum in the annual juried student art exhibition and in the senior art exhibition. Additional opportunities are arranged each semester in alternative exhibition spaces both on and off campus in the metropolitan Jacksonville area.

Special Programs The curriculum at Jacksonville University is based on the guidelines of the National Association of Schools of Art and Design. Students may choose to pursue a B.F.A. in studio art, visual communications, or computer art; a B.A.E. in art education, or a B.S. or B.A. in art and art history. Internships are required in visual communications and computer art and are also available in art history and studio art.

James Madison University

Harrisonburg, Virginia

State-supported, coed. Small-town campus. Total enrollment: 11,539.

Degrees Bachelor of Fine Arts in the areas of graphic design, interior design, general fine arts. Majors: ceramic art and design, graphic design, interior design, jewelry and metalsmithing, painting/drawing, papermaking, photography, printmaking, sculpture, stained glass, weaving and fibers. Graduate degrees offered: Master of Fine Arts in the area of fine arts.

Art Student Profile Fall 1994: 255 total; 241 matriculated undergraduate, 14 matriculated graduate.

Art Faculty Total: 30; 24 full-time, 6 part-time; 96% of full-time faculty have terminal degrees. Graduate students teach a few undergraduate courses. Undergraduate student–faculty ratio: 17:1.

Student Life Student groups include National Art Education Association Student Chapter, American Society of Interior Designers Student Chapter, Kappa Pi.

Expenses for 1995–96 Application fee: $25. State resident tuition: $4014 full-time. Nonresident tuition: $8294 full-time. Part-time tuition per semester ranges from $264 to $1660 for state residents, $689 to $3238 for nonresidents. College room and board: $4576. College room only: $2474.

Application Procedures Deadline—freshmen: January 15; transfers: February 2. Notification date—freshmen: April 7; transfers: April 15. Required: essay, high school transcript, SAT I test score only. Recommended: 2 letters of recommendation, interview, portfolio. Portfolio reviews held 7 times on campus and off campus in Washington, DC; Hampton Roads, VA; the submission of slides may be substituted for portfolios.

Undergraduate Contact Dr. Cole Welter, Director, School of Art and Art History, James Madison University, Harrisonburg, Virginia 22807; 703-568-6216, fax: 703-568-6598, E-mail address: dovefj@jmu.edu.

Graduate Contact Kenneth Szmagaj, Professor, School of Art and Art History, James Madison University, Harrisonburg, Virginia 22807; 703-568-6216, fax: 703-568-6598, E-mail address: dovefj@jmu.edu.

Jersey City State College

Jersey City, New Jersey

State-supported, coed. Urban campus. Total enrollment: 7,199.

Degrees Bachelor of Fine Arts in the areas of fine arts, design and crafts, photography, communication design and technology. Majors: art history, art therapy, art/fine arts, ceramic art and design, commercial art, communication design, computer graphics, graphic arts, illustration, jewelry and metalsmithing, painting/drawing, photography, printmaking, sculpture.

Art Student Profile Fall 1994: 307 total; 289 matriculated undergraduate, 18 nondegree; 49% minorities, 58% females, 15% international.

Art Faculty Total: 41; 18 full-time, 23 part-time; 100% of full-time faculty have terminal degrees. Graduate students do not teach undergraduate courses. Undergraduate student–faculty ratio: 15:1.

Student Life Student groups include Art Association.

Expenses for 1995–96 Application fee: $20. State resident tuition: $3158 full-time, $104.50 per credit part-time. Nonresident tuition: $4448 full-time, $147.50 per credit part-time. College room and board: $4800. College room only: $2800. Special program-related fees: $15–$25 for lab fees.

Application Procedures Deadline—freshmen and transfers: June 1. Required: high school transcript, college transcript(s) for transfer students, minimum 2.0 high school GPA, SAT I test score only. Recommended: essay, letter of recommendation, interview, portfolio. Auditions held on campus and off campus. Portfolio reviews held continuously on campus and off campus; the submission of slides may be substituted for portfolios.

Undergraduate Contact Denise Mullen, Chair, Art Department, Jersey City State College, 2039 Kennedy Boulevard, Jersey City, New Jersey 07305; 201-200-3241, fax: 201-200-3238.

Kansas City Art Institute

Kansas City, Missouri

Independent, coed. Urban campus. Total enrollment: 559.

Degrees Bachelor of Fine Arts in the areas of ceramics, design, illustration, fiber, painting, printmaking, photography, sculpture. Majors: art/fine arts, ceramic art and design, computer graphics, drafting and design, graphic arts, illustration, painting/drawing, photography, printmaking, sculpture, studio art, textile arts. Cross-registration with Kansas City Regional Council for Higher Education.

Art Student Profile Fall 1994: 559 total; all matriculated undergraduate; 11% minorities, 43% females, 2% international.

Art Faculty Total: 77; 52 full-time, 25 part-time; 98% of full-time faculty have terminal degrees. Graduate students do not teach undergraduate courses. Undergraduate student–faculty ratio: 12:1.

Student Life Student groups include Student Gallery Committee, Ethnic Student Association, Student Film Series Committee.

Expenses for 1995–96 Application fee: $25. Comprehensive fee of $19,125 includes full-time tuition ($14,785) and college room and board ($4340). Part-time tuition: $588 per credit hour. Special program-related fees: $170 for ceramics materials.

Financial Aid Program-specific awards for Fall of 1994: 300–350 Need-based Scholarships for program majors ($2000–$8000), 100–125 Merit-based Scholarships for program majors ($2000–$8000).

Application Procedures Deadline—freshmen and transfers: continuous. Required: essay, high school transcript, college transcript(s) for transfer students, minimum 2.0 high school GPA, 2 letters of recommendation, portfolio, SAT I or ACT test scores, minimum combined SAT I score of 900, minimum composite ACT score of 18. Recommended: interview. Portfolio reviews held continuously on campus and off campus on National Portfolio Days; the submission of slides may be substituted for portfolios.

Undergraduate Contact Larry E. Stone, Vice President for Enrollment Management, Kansas City Art Institute, 4415 Warwick Boulevard, Kansas City, Missouri 64111; 800-522-5224, fax: 816-531-6296.

More about the Institute

Program Facilities Kansas City Art Institute, located on a 15-acre campus, offers the Bachelor of Fine Arts degree in design, illustration, sculpture, ceramics, fiber, photo/video, painting, or printmaking. Among the buildings on campus is the newly opened Kemper Museum of Contemporary Art and Design. The Computer Center contains software for digital illustration, 3-D modeling/

Kansas City Art Institute *(continued)*

animation, graphic design/layout, digital video/ multimedia, computer-aided design, and special hardware and computing platforms. The Photo/Video Department contains an electronic imaging lab with an integrated universal digital lab that incorporates silicon graphic workstations, Macintosh multimedia workstations, PC's running Sense-8's world tool kit virtual reality/cyberspace software, and an Agfa Matrix digital film recorder with 35mm, 4 x 5, and 8 x 10 backs. The lab is fully Ether-netted with a slip connection to an Internet node and the World Wide Web. In addition to being linked to the computer graphic center, this web is also linked to the video studio and the AVID digital, nonlinear video and sound editing system.

Faculty, Resident Artists, and Alumni Among KCAI's faculty are Stefan Lindfors, Design Department Chair, one of Finlands's most interesting designers; Ken Ferguson, Ceramics Department Chair, one of the world's 12 greatest potters; and Warren Rosser, Painting Department Chair, who is widely exhibited throughout the United States, the United Kingdom, and Europe. Successful alumni include Walt Disney, computer graphics designer April Greiman, painter Keith Jacobshagen, and ceramicist Akio Takamori.

Student Exhibit Opportunities Over 30 student shows are presented each year, including a campuswide spring show each May.

Special Programs Visiting artist programming brings distinguished artists and scholars from around the world to KCAI. Overseas study opportunities are available for students who wish to augment their KCAI experiences.

Kansas State University

Manhattan, Kansas

State-supported, coed. Suburban campus. Total enrollment: 20,664.

Degrees Bachelor of Fine Arts. Majors: ceramic art and design, graphic design, jewelry and metalsmithing, painting/drawing, printmaking, sculpture. Graduate degrees offered: Master of Fine Arts. Cross-registration with Norfolk School of Art and Design.

Art Student Profile Fall 1994: 400 total; 375 matriculated undergraduate, 25 matriculated graduate.

Art Faculty Total: 28; 25 full-time, 3 part-time; 90% of full-time faculty have terminal degrees. Graduate students teach about a quarter undergraduate courses. Undergraduate student–faculty ratio: 11:1.

Expenses for 1995–96 Application fee: $15. State resident tuition: $1766 full-time, $59 per semester hour part-time. Nonresident tuition: $7484 full-time, $249 per semester hour part-time. Full-time mandatory fees: $433. College room and board: $3370.

Application Procedures Deadline—freshmen and transfers: continuous. Required: high school transcript, college transcript(s) for transfer students, ACT test score only. Recommended: interview. Portfolio reviews held on campus.

Undergraduate Contact Anna Holcombe, Head, Department of Art, Kansas State University, Willard Hall 322, Manhattan, Kansas 66506; 913-532-6605.

Graduate Contact Dr. Lou Ann Culley, Director of Graduate Studies, Department of Art, Kansas State University, Willard Hall 322, Manhattan, Kansas 66506; 913-532-6605.

Kendall College of Art and Design

Grand Rapids, Michigan

Independent, coed. Urban campus. Total enrollment: 574.

Degrees Bachelor of Fine Arts in the areas of furniture design, industrial design, interior design, illustration, visual communications, fine arts. Majors: art/fine arts, commercial art, computer graphics, furniture design, graphic arts, illustration, industrial design, interior design, painting/drawing, printmaking, sculpture, studio art.

Art Student Profile Fall 1994: 574 total; all matriculated undergraduate; 14% minorities, 54% females, 4% international.

Art Faculty Total: 59; 33 full-time, 26 part-time; 66% of full-time faculty have terminal degrees. Graduate students do not teach undergraduate courses. Undergraduate student–faculty ratio: 11:1.

Student Life Student groups include Industrial Design Society of America, American Society of Interior Designers, Grand Rapids Area Furniture Designers.

Expenses for 1994–95 Application fee: $35. Tuition: $9990 full-time, $333 per credit part-time. Full-time mandatory fees: $60. Special program-related fees: $15–$25 for computer lab use, $10–$25 for studio lab fee.

Financial Aid Program-specific awards for Fall of 1994: 180 Scholarships of Merit for undergraduates ($2000).

Application Procedures Deadline—freshmen and transfers: continuous. Required: essay, high school transcript, college transcript(s) for transfer students, minimum 2.0 high school GPA, portfolio, SAT I or ACT test scores. Recommended: letter of recommendation. Portfolio reviews held continuously on campus and off campus on National Portfolio Days; the submission of slides may be substituted for portfolios.

Undergraduate Contact Amy Packard, Director of Admissions, Kendall College of Art and Design, 111 Division Avenue North, Grand Rapids, Michigan 49503; 616-451-2787, fax: 616-451-9867.

More about the College

Facilities A library with a comprehensive collection of books, periodicals, slides, and videotapes; large, fully equipped model and wood shop with on-site coordinator; computer labs; printmaking lab; photography studio and darkroom; Student Gallery; and Kendall Gallery, which features a full schedule of national traveling exhibitions and faculty and student exhibits; large, roomy classrooms and studios; and individual studios for junior and senior fine arts majors.

Faculty and Alumni The KCAD faculty members are highly regarded artists, designers, and scholars, with an impressive professional record of national and international exhibitions, noted clients, and scholarly writings and activities. Alumni, most employed successfully in their chosen fields throughout the world, regularly return to give workshops and lectures.

Student Organizations and Exhibits Student chapters of professional organizations—Grand Rapids Furniture Designers Association, Industrial Designers Society of America, American Society of Interior Designers, American Center for Design—are available. The Student Gallery and the Kendall Gallery offer numerous formal exhibit opportunities, and there is an annual public Student Exhibit the first week in May. In addition, student work is exhibited throughout the building all year.

Lectures and Guest Artists Over the past several years, several artists, designers and educators have visited Kendall's campus giving lectures, critiques and demonstrations, often meeting with students in the classroom. Among the artists are Siah Armajani, Miriam Shapiro, Ed Paschke, Tom Friedman, Jeanne Dunning, Julia Fish, Margo Mensing, Gilda Snowden, Lyman Kipp, Jerry Peart; Designers P. Scott Makela, Massimo and Lella Vignelli, Katherine McCoy, Steve Frykholm, Eva Maddox, Clodagh, Martha Burns, Elizabeth McClintock, Margaret McCurry, and Carol Groh. Illustrators include Greg Spalenka, Murray Tinkelman, Ken Dallison, David Small, and Steve Brodner. Others who have visited include Rudolph Arnheim, author and theorist; Vince Carducci, critic and Michigan regional editor of *New Art Examiner*; Lambert Zuidervaart, author and philosopher; Joan Truckenbrod, author and computer artist; Kathryn Hixson, critic and associate editor of the *New Art Examiner*); Marianne Deson, gallery owner; Greg Landahl, architect; Beverly Russell, writer and editor; and Rachel Fletcher, mathematician and theatre designer.

Special Programs KCAD offers Mobility Programs, a New York Studio Program, and opportunities for foreign study. Contact the Admissions Office for more information.

Scholarships and Financial Aid Kendall's Scholarship of Merit program awards more than $430,000 annually based on the creative potential and academic achievement of freshman, transfer, and currently enrolled students. Financial need is not a requirement. The college's experienced financial aid officers have helped up to 85 percent of the students receive some form of financial assistance. In addition to nearly a dozen different financial aid programs, the College offers federal and state college work-study programs and is approved for veteran's benefits.

Kendall College of Art and Design, founded in 1928, offers an art and design education to a select group of students who are serious about refining their talent and who seek in-depth preparation for significant careers. Some choose Kendall for its favorable faculty-student ratio of 1:11, others for its programs' national reputation, and others because they want to be around people who share their interests.

Kendall is located in the heart of downtown Grand Rapids, Michigan, a rapidly growing metropolitan area of 750,000 people. KCAD is across the street from the Grand Rapids Art Museum and only blocks away from theaters, galleries, and music halls, where the work of leading regional and international artists is exhibited or performed.

The faculty consists of working artists, designers, and scholars dedicated to providing students with the necessary tools to explore and pursue their own creative journey. Their experience and background create an innovative and diverse force of instructors dedicated to sharing their knowledge. The faculty continually weighs changing methods and technology, striving to provide students with meaningful, real-world experiences while maintaining a solid and proven art and design education. They are a valuable resource, and through their guidance students can take risks, based on history, that will create work that is both fresh and relevant. That rare blend of professional artists and practiced professors makes the faculty highly qualified to help students define their vision as an artist or designer.

Kendall provides individual attention for all its students. This personalized approach to education not only helps students learn the principles of visual thinking but also provides the skills necessary to achieve career success.

The College's individual majors are based on a strong Foundation program that includes intense classical training while also allowing some freedom and variety. A wide range of special lectures, exhibits, and seminars by noted artists and designers enhance the academic environment. In addition to the required courses, elective courses related to the majors can be taken in photography, computer arts, CAD/CAP and CAD/CAM, and video arts.

Of particular note is Kendall's Furniture Design program, which is recognized throughout the world and can claim nearly 90 percent of this nation's residential furniture designers as its alumni. Also, students of the Kendall Illustration program consistently place among the top winners in the Society of Illustrators' annual national scholarship competition, not only winning scholarship awards for themselves, but raising money for the College as well. The quality of Kendall's programs, combined with individual attention from its professional faculty, establishes this institution among the finest colleges of art and design.

Shannon Rodgers/Jerry Silverman School of Fashion Design and Merchandising

Kent State University

Kent, Ohio

State-supported, coed. Small-town campus. Total enrollment: 21,413.

Degrees Bachelor of Fine Arts in the area of art. Majors: art education, art history, ceramic art and design, glass, illustration, jewelry and metalsmithing, painting/drawing, printmaking, sculpture, textile arts, visual communication. Graduate degrees offered: Master of Fine Arts in the area of art.

Kent State University *(continued)*

Art Student Profile Fall 1994: 965 total; 850 matriculated undergraduate, 115 matriculated graduate; 7% minorities, 60% females, 1% international.

Art Faculty Total: 54; 29 full-time, 25 part-time; 76% of full-time faculty have terminal degrees. Graduate students teach a few undergraduate courses.

Student Life Student groups include Art Education Council, Art Students Association, Art History Club. Special housing available for art students.

Expenses for 1995–96 State resident tuition: $4084 full-time, $185.75 per semester hour part-time. Nonresident tuition: $8168 full-time, $371.50 per semester hour part-time. College room and board: $3834. College room only: $2242. Special program-related fees: $10–$45 for consumable supplies.

Financial Aid Program-specific awards for Fall of 1994: 16 Art Scholarships for program majors ($500), 10–20 Creative Art Awards for incoming freshmen demonstrating academic achievement ($1000–$2000).

Application Procedures Deadline—freshmen and transfers: continuous. Required: high school transcript, college transcript(s) for transfer students, SAT I or ACT test scores. Recommended: minimum 2.0 high school GPA.

Undergraduate Contact Joseph Fry, Assistant to the Director, School of Art, Kent State University, 211 Art Building, Kent, Ohio 44242-0001; 216-672-2192, fax: 216-672-4729.

Graduate Contact Dr. Frank D. Susi, Graduate Coordinator, School of Art, Kent State University, 211 Art Building, Kent, Ohio 44242-0001; 216-672-2192, fax: 216-672-4729.

College of Visual and Performing Arts

Kutztown University of Pennsylvania

Kutztown, Pennsylvania

State-supported, coed. Small-town campus. Total enrollment: 7,916.

Degrees Bachelor of Fine Arts in the areas of painting, drawing, printmaking, sculpture, photography. Majors: painting/drawing, photography, printmaking, sculpture.

Art Student Profile Fall 1994: 213 total; all matriculated undergraduate.

Art Faculty Total: 17; 16 full-time, 1 part-time; 89% of full-time faculty have terminal degrees. Graduate students teach a few undergraduate courses. Undergraduate student–faculty ratio: 13:1.

Student Life Special housing available for art students.

Expenses for 1994–95 Application fee: $25. State resident tuition: $3086 full-time, $129 per credit part-time. Nonresident tuition: $7844 full-time, $327 per credit part-time. Full-time mandatory fees range from $613 to $691. College room and board: $2990. College room only: $2000.

Application Procedures Deadline—freshmen and transfers: October 31. Required: high school transcript, portfolio, SAT I or ACT test scores. Portfolio reviews held 2 times on campus.

Undergraduate Contact George McKinley, Director of Admission, Kutztown University of Pennsylvania, College Hill, Kutztown, Pennsylvania 19530; 610-683-4472.

More about the University

Program Facilities Visual arts: the Sharadin Building, a major university facility devoted entirely to the visual arts; art studios open 7 days a week; 45-station computer design laboratory and classrooms open 6 days a week; continuous exhibitions in the art gallery. Theater: Schaeffer Auditorium, housing a 780-seat proscenium theater and a 75-seat black box theater; Rickenbach Theatre, a 200-seat proscenium theater. Music: Schaeffer Auditorium for larger concerts; Georgian Room for smaller ensembles; music practice rooms; piano labs; extensive disc and audiovisual library.

Faculty, Resident Artists, and Alumni Faculty members are practicing professionals with regional, national, and international recognition, including artists whose works are in major museums and who exhibit in galleries around the country; musicians who perform in chamber ensembles and symphony orchestras and who lead performance workshops; professionals who conduct national art education workshops; and theater directors who lead regional and national festival performances. Visiting artists, lecturers, and alumni come to campus regularly, work with students in studios, and present master classes.

Student Performance/Exhibit Opportunities All students in the visual arts participate in gallery exhibitions; communication design students have portfolios professionally reviewed during their fourth year; senior art show, a highlight of the University cultural calendar; workshops in elementary and secondary schools conducted by art education students; curricular instrument and voice instruction for music students; numerous student concerts and recitals; faculty performance of student compositions; numerous theater performances and production opportunities; participation in college theater festivals; theater student opportunities to direct their own plays; readers' theater and children's theater.

Special Programs Students in Related Arts major work in three art forms simultaneously; visiting/touring art exhibitions; Performing Artists Series brings world-celebrated music, theater, and dance to campus.

The College of Visual and Performing Arts offers exceptional opportunities for students seeking training and experience in the arts in addition to a well-rounded university education. Students benefit from dedicated faculty members who are experts in music, theater, speech, public relations, drawing, painting, sculpture, printmaking, ceramics, woodworking, metalworking, graphic design, advertising design, illustration, photography, art education, and related arts. Typically, classes in the arts are small, and students receive personal attention.

Because nearly all faculty members teach full-time in the College, they are regularly available to students. In addition, all courses are taught by faculty members—not by graduate students. Even full professors may be found teaching freshman- and sophomore-year courses. Alumni who have distinguished themselves in the visual and performing arts often return to the campus to share their ideas and experiences with students. In the past two years these have included painter Mark Innevst, scene designer David Mitchell, graphic designer Steve Frederick, jewelry designer Lisa Sorrelli, sculptor James Clarke, and Metropolitan Museum of Art photographer Robert Coscia.

Students have the advantage of receiving intensive instruction in arts disciplines in a small college as well as being part of a larger university. Outside of their major, they have the broadening experience of relating with students in the liberal arts and sciences, business, and education. In addition to the specialized facilities and equipment in the arts, they have access to the total academic, extracurricular, and career services resources of a modern regional university. Students may choose to live in campus residence halls. In addition, beginning in 1994, one of the University's special interest living houses is designated for students in the communication design program.

Students have access to excellent equipment and facilities, such as well-equipped sculpture, ceramics, serigraphy, and printmaking studios; a photography lab; a computer design lab; campus theaters with well-equipped carpentry, costume, and lighting shops; music practice rooms; piano labs; and a state-of-the-art Yamaha electronic piano lab with thirty stations.

There are sixteen student clubs serving various interests in music, art, theater, and dance. In addition, there are more than fifty other student clubs and organizations as well as a complete student activities program at Kutztown University.

Opportunities extend beyond the campus to internships for communication design students, field work and student teaching for art education students, and study-abroad opportunities for students in all arts majors. In 1994, there were an environmental illustration course in England; landscape painting, Renaissance art, and organ and opera courses in Italy; and an art tour of the American and Canadian Pacific Northwest.

Kutztown University has often been described as having the ideal college campus—traditional and modern buildings in a spacious, quiet setting, nestled in beautiful Pennsylvania Dutch country—yet the major arts centers in the eastern United States are within easy driving distance: Philadelphia, 1½ hours; New York City, 2½ hours; Baltimore, 3 hours; and Washington, D.C., 3½ hours. Throughout the year, classes or student-faculty groups visit museums, art galleries, theaters, and concert halls in these locations and in nearby Allentown and Reading, Pennsylvania.

Communication Design Department

Kutztown University of Pennsylvania

Kutztown, Pennsylvania

State-supported, coed. Small-town campus. Total enrollment: 7,916.

Degrees Bachelor of Fine Arts in the area of communication design. Majors: advertising design, graphic design, illustration.

Art Student Profile Fall 1994: 250 total; all matriculated undergraduate; 7% minorities, 46% females, 1% international.

Art Faculty Total: 11; 10 full-time, 1 part-time; 90% of full-time faculty have terminal degrees. Graduate students do not teach undergraduate courses. Undergraduate student–faculty ratio: 17:1.

Student Life Special housing available for art students.

Expenses for 1994–95 Application fee: $25. State resident tuition: $3086 full-time, $129 per credit part-time. Nonresident tuition: $7844 full-time, $327 per credit part-time. Full-time mandatory fees range from $613 to $691. College room and board: $2990. College room only: $2000.

Financial Aid (Fall 1994) Program-specific awards: 1 Morning Call Scholarship for minority students ($800), 1 Karen Anderson Scholarship for those demonstrating need ($500).

Application Procedures Deadline—freshmen and transfers: January 19. Required: high school transcript, SAT I or ACT test scores, minimum combined SAT I score of 900, art test.

Undergraduate Contact George McKinley, Director of Admission, Kutztown University of Pennsylvania, College Hill, Kutztown, Pennsylvania 19530; 610-683-4472.

Related Arts Program

Kutztown University of Pennsylvania

Kutztown, Pennsylvania

State-supported, coed. Small-town campus. Total enrollment: 7,916.

Degrees Bachelor of Fine Arts in the area of related arts. Majors: art/fine arts, dance, music, theater arts/drama.

Art Student Profile Fall 1994: 104 total; all matriculated undergraduate; 62% females.

Student Life Student groups include Art Students Association, Sunshine Players, Reader's Theater. Special Housing available for art students.

Expenses for 1994–95 Application fee: $25. State resident tuition: $3086 full-time, $129 per credit part-time. Nonresident tuition: $7844 full-time, $327 per credit part-time. Full-time mandatory fees range from $613 to $691. College room and board: $2990. College room only: $2000.

Application Procedures Deadline—freshmen: January 1. Required: high school transcript, college transcript(s) for transfer students, SAT I or ACT test scores, minimum 2.0 college GPA for transfer students. Recommended: interview. Portfolio reviews held on campus and off campus.

Undergraduate Contact George McKinley, Director of Admission, Kutztown University of Pennsylvania, College Hill, Kutztown, Pennsylvania 19530; 610-683-4472.

La Sierra University

Riverside, California

Independent-religious, coed. Suburban campus. Total enrollment: 1,456.

Degrees Bachelor of Fine Arts in the areas of art, 2–dimensional studies, 3–dimensional studies. Majors: art education, art/fine arts, computer graphics, illustration, studio art.

Art Student Profile Fall 1994: 42 total; all matriculated undergraduate; 50% minorities, 34% females, 20% international.

Art Faculty Total: 7; 4 full-time, 3 part-time; 100% of full-time faculty have terminal degrees. Graduate students do not teach undergraduate courses. Undergraduate student–faculty ratio: 8:1.

Expenses for 1995–96 Application fee: $30. Comprehensive fee of $16,860 includes full-time tuition ($12,750), mandatory fees ($225), and college room and board ($3885). College room only: $2190. Part-time tuition: $354 per unit. Part-time mandatory fees: $105 per year. Special program-related fees: $20–$50 for materials fee, $25 for model fees, , , .

Financial Aid Program-specific awards for Fall of 1994: 23 Katchamakoff Scholarships for program majors ($500).

Application Procedures Deadline—freshmen and transfers: continuous. Required: high school transcript, college transcript(s) for transfer students, minimum 2.0 high school GPA, letter of recommendation, portfolio. Recommended: minimum 3.0 high school GPA, SAT I or ACT test scores. Portfolio reviews held 2 times on campus; the submission of slides may be substituted for portfolios.

Undergraduate Contact University Admissions, La Sierra University, 4700 Pierce Street, Riverside, California 92515-8247; 909-785-2176.

Lake Erie College

Painesville, Ohio

Independent, coed. Small-town campus. Total enrollment: 732.

Degrees Bachelor of Fine Arts in the area of art. Majors: visual arts.

Art Student Profile Fall 1994: 5 total; all matriculated undergraduate.

Art Faculty Total: 2; 2 part-time.

Expenses for 1995–96 Application fee: $20. Comprehensive fee of $17,226 includes full-time tuition ($11,840), mandatory fees ($480), and college room and board ($4906). Part-time tuition: $356 per semester hour. Part-time mandatory fees: $15 per semester.

Application Procedures Deadline—freshmen: July 1; transfers: August 20. Required: essay, high school transcript, minimum 2.0 high school GPA, 2 letters of recommendation, SAT I or ACT test scores. Recommended: interview.

Undergraduate Contact Paul Gothard, Director, Fine Arts Department, Lake Erie College, 391 West Washington Street, Painesville, Ohio 44077; 216-639-7856.

Graduate Contact Chris DiCello, Visiting Artist, Dance, Fine Arts Department, Lake Erie College, 391 West Washington Street, Painesville, Ohio 44077; 216-639-7856.

Lakehead University

Thunder Bay, Ontario

Province-supported, coed. Suburban campus. Total enrollment: 7,918.

Degrees Bachelor of Fine Arts in the area of studio art. Majors: ceramic art and design, painting/drawing, printmaking, studio art. Cross-registration with Confederation College.

Art Student Profile Fall 1994: 58 total; all matriculated undergraduate.

Art Faculty Total: 10; 4 full-time, 6 part-time.

Expenses for 1994–95 Application fee: $50. Canadian resident tuition: $2228 (minimum) full-time, $460 per course part-time. Nonresident tuition: $8402 (minimum) full-time, $1736 per course part-time. Part-time mandatory fees: $40.40 per course. (All figures are in Canadian dollars.). Full-time mandatory fees: $333. College room and board: $4325. College room only: $3338.

Application Procedures Deadline—freshmen and transfers: continuous. Required: high school transcript, portfolio. Portfolio reviews held 3 times on campus; the submission of slides may be substituted for portfolios when distance is prohibitive.

Undergraduate Contact Mark Nisenholt, Chair, Department of Visual Arts, Lakehead University, Thunder Bay, Ontario P7B 5E1, Canada; 807-343-8787.

Lehman College of the City University of New York

Bronx, New York

State and locally supported, coed. Urban campus. Total enrollment: 8,921.

Degrees Bachelor of Fine Arts in the areas of printmaking, painting, sculpture, ceramics, photography. Majors: art/fine arts, ceramic art and design, computer graphics, graphic arts, painting/drawing, photography, printmaking, sculpture, studio art. Graduate degrees offered: Master of Fine Arts in the areas of painting, graphics, sculpture. Cross-registration with City University of New York system.

Art Student Profile Fall 1994: 575 total; 50 matriculated undergraduate, 25 matriculated graduate, 500 nondegree; 75% minorities, 60% females, 15% international.

Art Faculty Total: 12; 8 full-time, 4 part-time; 100% of full-time faculty have terminal degrees. Graduate students do not teach undergraduate courses. Undergraduate student–faculty ratio: 8:1.

Estimated Expenses for 1995–96 Application fee: $35. State resident tuition: $2450 full-time, $100 per credit part-time. Nonresident tuition: $5050 full-time, $210 per credit part-time. Part-time mandatory fees: $57 per semester. Full-time mandatory fees: $114.

Application Procedures Deadline—freshmen and transfers: continuous. Required: high school transcript, minimum 3.0 high school GPA, standing in top third of high school graduating class.

Undergraduate Contact Clarence Wilkes, Director of Admissions, 155 Shuster Hall, Lehman College of the City University of New York, 250 Bedford Park Boulevard West, Bronx, New York 10468; 718-960-8256.

Graduate Contact Kathleen Morgan, Graduate Admissions, Lehman College of the City University of New York, 250 Bedford Park Boulevard West, Bronx, New York 10468.

Lindenwood College

St. Charles, Missouri

Independent-religious, coed. Suburban campus. Total enrollment: 3,375.

Degrees Bachelor of Fine Arts in the area of art. Majors: art education, art history, art/fine arts, ceramic art and design, commercial art, computer graphics, graphic arts, painting/drawing, photography, printmaking, sculpture, studio art. Cross-registration with Maryville University of Saint Louis, Fontbonne College, Missouri Baptist College, Webster University.

Art Student Profile Fall 1994: 75 total; 71 matriculated undergraduate, 4 nondegree; 2% minorities, 7% international.

Art Faculty Total: 7; 4 full-time, 3 part-time; 100% of full-time faculty have terminal degrees. Graduate students do not teach undergraduate courses. Undergraduate student–faculty ratio: 15:1.

Student Life Student groups include Student Art Association.

Expenses for 1995–96 Application fee: $25. Comprehensive fee of $14,650 includes full-time tuition ($9600), mandatory fees ($250), and college room and board ($4800). College room only: $2400. Part-time tuition: $250 per credit hour. Special program-related fees: $65–$80 for lab fees.

Financial Aid Program-specific awards for Fall of 1994: Art Scholarships for upperclassmen and transfers ($1500–$4500).

Application Procedures Deadline—freshmen and transfers: continuous. Required: essay, high school transcript, college transcript(s) for transfer students, minimum 2.0 high school GPA, interview, portfolio, SAT I or ACT test scores. Recommended: letter of recommendation. Portfolio reviews held continuously on campus; the submission of slides may be substituted for portfolios.

Undergraduate Contact Elaine C. Tillinger, Chair, Department of Art, Lindenwood College, 209 South Kings Highway, St. Charles, Missouri 63301; 314-664-8713, fax: 314-949-4910.

Long Island University, C.W. Post Campus

Brookville, New York

Independent, coed. Small-town campus. Total enrollment: 7,919.

Degrees Bachelor of Fine Arts in the areas of graphic design, ceramics, painting/drawing, sculpture, photography, printmaking. Majors: art education, art history, art therapy, art/fine arts, ceramic art and design, computer graphics, graphic design, photography. Graduate degrees offered: Master of Fine Arts in the areas of graphic design, ceramics, painting/drawing, sculpture, photography, printmaking.

Art Student Profile Fall 1994: 175 total; 135 matriculated undergraduate, 40 matriculated graduate; 40% females, 12% international.

Art Faculty Total: 52; 14 full-time, 38 part-time; 90% of full-time faculty have terminal degrees. Graduate students do not teach undergraduate courses.

Student Life Special housing available for art students.

Expenses for 1995–96 Application fee: $30. Comprehensive fee of $18,735 includes full-time tuition ($12,430), mandatory fees ($560), and college room and board ($5745). College room only: $3500. Part-time tuition: $387 per credit. Part-time mandatory fees: $130 per semester.

Application Procedures Deadline—freshmen and transfers: continuous. Required: high school transcript, college transcript(s) for transfer students, portfolio, SAT I or ACT test scores. Recommended: 2 letters of recommendation, interview. Portfolio reviews held as needed for transfer applicants on campus; the submission of slides may be substituted for portfolios for large works of art.

Undergraduate Contact Undergraduate Admissions, Art Department, Long Island University, C.W. Post Campus, Northern Boulevard, Brookville, New York 11548; 516-299-2435.

Graduate Contact Graduate Admissions, Art Department, Long Island University, C.W. Post Campus, Northern Boulevard, Brookville, New York 11548; 516-299-2435.

More about the University

Program Facilities Tilles Center for the Performing Arts (2,200 seats); Hillwood Recital Hall (500 seats); Little Theatre MainStage (200 seats); Hillwood Cinema (330 seats); Music Rehearsal Building (100–150 seats); Great Hall (75–100 seats); Rifle Range Theatre (50 seats). The campus has two art galleries; ceramic and wood workshops; photography labs; welding, sculpture, jewelry, and graphic design studios; a dance studio; rehearsal, costume, and scene shops; drafting room; and Long Island's largest computer graphics laboratory. The

Long Island University C.W. Post Campus *(continued)*

film area includes a 50-seat movie theater/classroom, professional 16mm film, sound editing, and video equipment. The Broadcasting program offers a state-of-the-art television video production center, campus radio stations, and several student publications.

Faculty and Students Ninety percent of the full-time faculty hold a doctorate or the highest degree in their field. Several are international performers, working professionals in the entertainment industry, theater, music, and the media, as well as journalists and experts in their fields. Students have danced at Lincoln Center, interned at NBC television, sung across Europe, and displayed their artwork in Manhattan galleries.

Student Organizations Merriweather Consort, Madrigal and Chamber Singers, Long Island Sound/Vocal Jazz, C. W. Post Orchestra, Symphonic Winds, Jazz and Percussion Ensembles, Post Theatre Company, WCWP-FM Radio, Broadcasters of Tomorrow.

The School of Visual and Performing Arts, one of six prestigious schools at Long Island University's C. W. Post Campus, provides a solid liberal arts education with professional training essential to a successful career in the arts. The University's suburban campus is widely recognized as one of the most beautiful college campuses in the nation. Located on 305 wooded acres, the campus is just 40 minutes from New York City.

Long Island University, Southampton Campus

Southampton, New York

Independent, coed. Rural campus. Total enrollment: 1,441.

Degrees Bachelor of Fine Arts in the areas of art, graphic design, communication arts. Majors: art history, art/fine arts, ceramics, graphic arts, museum studies, painting/drawing, photography, printmaking, studio art.

Art Student Profile Fall 1994: 170 total; all matriculated undergraduate; 60% females.

Art Faculty Total: 26; 9 full-time, 17 part-time; 90% of full-time faculty have terminal degrees. Graduate students do not teach undergraduate courses. Undergraduate student–faculty ratio: 17:1.

Expenses for 1995–96 Application fee: $30. Comprehensive fee of $19,260 includes full-time tuition ($12,430), mandatory fees ($600), and college room and board ($6230). College room only: $3480. Part-time tuition: $387 per credit hour. Part-time mandatory fees per year range from $130 to $600. Special program-related fees: $15–$75 for lab fees.

Financial Aid Program-specific awards for Fall of 1994: 6 Continuing Student Awards for upperclassmen ($2000).

Application Procedures Deadline—freshmen and transfers: continuous. Required: high school transcript, SAT I test score only. Recommended: interview.

Undergraduate Contact Admissions Department, Long Island University, Southampton Campus, 239 Montauk Highway, Southampton, New York 11968; 516-283-4000.

More about the University

It is hard to imagine a more beautiful or creatively stimulating environment for the study and production of art than the East End of Long Island. With its quiet farm fields and ocean vistas, Southampton offers solitude and time for contemplation. But it also reflects the excitement and culture of New York City, only 90 miles away. As many have found, Southampton is a special place for artists to work and live. The area has one of the most famous art communities in the country. Current residents include Robert Dash, Willem de Kooning, Jane Freilicher, Roy Lichtenstein, and Larry Rivers. The Southampton Campus art faculty, also well known, includes Yoshi Higa, and Roy Nicholson. Two museums, several art societies and foundations, and more than thirty galleries are located in the Hamptons. Many art dealers, critics, and reviewers also have homes here. Students are linked with the cultural resources of the area in a variety of ways. Local artists participate in many of the college's programs and show their work in the Fine Arts Gallery. Some courses include visits to studios of local artists as well as trips to galleries and museums. Formal and informal contact is made with artists who are Southampton Campus alumni. Graduates are willing to share their experiences and describe how they did it.

The Art Department offers a B.F.A. in fine arts, graphic design, and arts management and a B.A. in art. A program leading to certification in art education is also available. These programs offer courses in the basic techniques of art, including drawing, two- and three-dimensional design, color theory, and art history. The B.F.A. student's course work culminates in a major Directed Study Project. Students may spend a term preparing for their own exhibition in the gallery. Those interested in commercial art and graphics may choose to work for a semester at an advertising firm, design studio, or newspaper. Internships are also available at printing or graphic firms, galleries, and museums.

Facilities at the campus include studios and equipment for drawing, painting, photography, ceramics, printmaking, graphics, and sculpture.

Southampton offers thirty to forty art scholarships every year to students whose art portfolios show talent and promise. A competition is held annually at the campus on the first Saturday in March. Students are expected to present their artwork in person on that day. Students can win scholarships of $1000 to $3000 per year; scholarships are renewable annually if students maintain a 3.0 cumulative average. Both freshmen and transfer students may compete. Scholarships are based solely on the portfolio. Financial need and age of applicant are not considered. Students must apply for admission prior to the competition in March, and they must plan to major in art at Southampton.

Longwood College

Farmville, Virginia

State-supported, coed. Small-town campus. Total enrollment: 3,277.

Degrees Bachelor of Fine Arts. Majors: architectural design, art history, ceramic art and design, craft design, graphic design, jewelry and metalsmithing, painting/drawing, photography, printmaking.

Art Student Profile Fall 1994: 100 total; all matriculated undergraduate.

Art Faculty Total: 8; 7 full-time, 1 part-time.

Expenses for 1995–96 Application fee: $25. State resident tuition: $2684 full-time, $112 per credit hour part-time. Nonresident tuition: $8156 full-time, $340 per credit hour part-time. Part-time mandatory fees: $25 per credit hour. Full-time mandatory fees: $1686. College room and board: $3934. College room only: $2352.

Application Procedures Deadline—freshmen: February 15; transfers: continuous. Required: essay, high school transcript, SAT I or ACT test scores. Recommended: letter of recommendation.

Undergraduate Contact Randy Edmonson, Chair, Department of Art, Longwood College, 201 High Street, Farmville, Virginia 23909; 804-395-2286, fax: 804-395-2775.

Louise Salinger Academy of Fashion

San Francisco, California

Independent, coed. Urban campus. Total enrollment: 200.

Degrees Bachelor of Fine Arts in the area of fashion design. Majors: fashion design and technology, textiles and clothing.

Expenses for 1994–95 Application fee: $150. Tuition: $11,880 full-time, $330 per unit part-time. Full-time mandatory fees: $300.

Application Procedures

Undergraduate Contact Admissions Office, Louise Salinger Academy of Fashion, 101 Jessie Street, San Francisco, California 94105; 415-974-6666.

Louisiana State University and Agricultural and Mechanical College

Baton Rouge, Louisiana

State-supported, coed. Urban campus. Total enrollment: 25,317.

Degrees Bachelor of Fine Arts in the area of studio art. Majors: ceramics, graphic design, jewelry and metalsmithing, painting/drawing, photography, printmaking, sculpture. Graduate degrees offered: Master of Fine Arts in the area of studio art.

Art Student Profile Fall 1994: 343 total; 275 matriculated undergraduate, 68 matriculated graduate.

Art Faculty Total: 31; 30 full-time, 1 part-time.

Expenses for 1995–96 Application fee: $25. State resident tuition: $2648 full-time. Nonresident tuition: $5948 full-time. Part-time tuition per semester ranges from $285 to $860 for state residents, $435 to $2215 for nonresidents. College room and board: $3310. College room only: $1500 (minimum).

Application Procedures Deadline—freshmen and transfers: June 1. Required: high school transcript, minimum 2.0 high school GPA, SAT I or ACT test scores. Recommended: portfolio. Portfolio reviews held 2 times for graphic design applicants on campus.

Contact Michael Crespo, Director, School of Art, Louisiana State University and Agricultural and Mechanical College, 123 Art Building, Baton Rouge, Louisiana 70803; 504-388-5411.

Louisiana Tech University

Ruston, Louisiana

State-supported, coed. Small-town campus. Total enrollment: 10,023.

Degrees Bachelor of Fine Arts in the areas of studio art, photography, interior design, graphic design. Majors: art/fine arts, ceramic art and design, commercial art, computer graphics, graphic arts, illustration, painting/drawing, photography, printmaking, sculpture, studio art. Graduate degrees offered: Master of Fine Arts in the areas of studio art, photography, interior design, graphic design.

Art Student Profile Fall 1994: 194 total; 183 matriculated undergraduate, 6 matriculated graduate, 5 nondegree; 5% minorities, 50% females, 2% international.

Art Faculty Total: 15; 13 full-time, 2 part-time; 100% of full-time faculty have terminal degrees. Graduate students teach a few undergraduate courses. Undergraduate student–faculty ratio: 18:1.

Student Life Student groups include Dark Horse (Graphic Design), American Society of Interior Designers, Art and Architecture Student Association. Special housing available for art students.

Expenses for 1994–95 Application fee: $20. State resident tuition: $2262 full-time. Nonresident tuition: $3957 full-time. Part-time tuition per quarter ranges from $218 to $634 for state residents, $218 to $1124 for nonresidents. College room and board: $2325. College room only: $1245. Special program-related fees: $30 for art and architecture fee.

Financial Aid Program-specific awards for Fall of 1994: Departmental Scholarships.

Application Procedures Deadline—freshmen and transfers: continuous. Required: high school transcript, college transcript(s) for transfer students, minimum 2.0 high

Louisiana Tech University *(continued)*

school GPA, ACT test score only, minimum composite ACT score of 22. Recommended: interview, portfolio.

Undergraduate Contact Dr. Joseph W. Strother, Director, School of Art and Architecture, Louisiana Tech University, P.O. Box 3186, Ruston, Louisiana 71272; 318-257-3909, fax: 318-257-4890.

Graduate Contact Edwin Pinkston, Graduate Coordinator, School of Art and Architecture, Louisiana Tech University, P.O. Box 3186, Ruston, Louisiana 71272; 318-257-3909, fax: 318-257-4890.

Loyola University, New Orleans

New Orleans, Louisiana

Independent-religious, coed. Urban campus. Total enrollment: 5,634.

Degrees Bachelor of Fine Arts in the areas of sculpture, painting, printmaking, ceramics. Majors: arts administration, ceramic art and design, graphic arts, painting/drawing, photography, printmaking, sculpture.

Art Student Profile Fall 1994: 75 total; all matriculated undergraduate; 2% minorities, 65% females, 33% international.

Art Faculty Total: 21; 7 full-time, 14 part-time; 100% of full-time faculty have terminal degrees. Undergraduate student–faculty ratio: 5:1.

Expenses for 1995–96 Comprehensive fee of $17,316 includes full-time tuition ($11,766), mandatory fees ($250), and college room and board ($5300). Part-time mandatory fees: $126.50 per year. Part-time tuition per credit hour: $390 for daytime classes, $180 for evening classes. Special program-related fees: $50 for lab fees.

Financial Aid Program-specific awards for Fall of 1994: 1 Scully Scholarship for upperclassmen ($500–$1000), 1–3 Visual Arts Scholarships for freshmen ($6000–$8000).

Application Procedures Deadline—freshmen and transfers: February 1. Notification date—freshmen and transfers: March 15. Required: high school transcript, minimum 2.0 high school GPA, letter of recommendation, portfolio. Portfolio reviews held 2 times on campus; the submission of slides may be substituted for portfolios.

Undergraduate Contact Admissions Office, Loyola University, New Orleans, 6363 St. Charles Avenue, New Orleans, Louisiana 70118; 504-865-3240, fax: 504-865-2110.

Lycoming College

Williamsport, Pennsylvania

Independent-religious, coed. Small-town campus. Total enrollment: 1,507.

Degrees Bachelor of Fine Arts in the area of sculpture. Majors: sculpture. Cross-registration with Johnson Atelier Institute of Technical Sculpture.

Art Student Profile Fall 1994: 65 total; all matriculated undergraduate; 1% minorities, 50% females, 1% international.

Art Faculty Total: 5; 4 full-time, 1 part-time; 100% of full-time faculty have terminal degrees. Graduate students do not teach undergraduate courses. Undergraduate student–faculty ratio: 15:1.

Student Life Special housing available for art students.

Expenses for 1995–96 Application fee: $25. Comprehensive fee of $19,260 includes full-time tuition ($14,700), mandatory fees ($160), and college room and board ($4400). Part-time tuition: $460 per credit.

Financial Aid Program-specific awards for Fall of 1994: 10 Art Scholarships for program majors ($1500).

Application Procedures Deadline—freshmen and transfers: continuous. Required: high school transcript, letter of recommendation. Recommended: essay, portfolio. Portfolio reviews held by request on campus; the submission of slides may be substituted for portfolios.

Undergraduate Contact James Spencer, Dean of Admissions, Lycoming College, 700 College Place, Williamsport, Pennsylvania 17701-5192; 800-345-3920, fax: 717-321-4337.

Maharishi International University

Fairfield, Iowa

Independent, coed. Small-town campus. Total enrollment: 624.

Degrees Bachelor of Fine Arts in the area of visual arts. Majors: art/fine arts, ceramic art and design, painting/drawing, photography, sculpture, studio art, visual technology. Graduate degrees offered: Master of Fine Arts in the area of visual arts.

Art Student Profile Fall 1994: 52 total; 30 matriculated undergraduate, 12 matriculated graduate, 10 nondegree; 10% minorities, 50% females, 60% international.

Art Faculty Total: 12; 7 full-time, 5 part-time; 75% of full-time faculty have terminal degrees. Graduate students teach a few undergraduate courses. Undergraduate student–faculty ratio: 5:1.

Student Life Student groups include Iowa wide exhibits.

Expenses for 1995–96 Application fee: $25. Comprehensive fee of $17,704 includes full-time tuition ($13,760), mandatory fees ($216), and college room and board ($3728). College room only: $1440. Part-time tuition: $345 per unit. Part-time mandatory fees: $108 per semester.

Application Procedures Deadline—freshmen: continuous. Notification date—freshmen: September 15. Required: essay, high school transcript, 2 letters of recommendation, portfolio, SAT I or ACT test scores, minimum 2.5 high school GPA. Portfolio reviews held 2 times on campus; the submission of slides may be substituted for portfolios for transfer applicants.

Contact Brad Mylett, Director, Office of Admissions, Maharishi International University, 1000 North 4th Street DB 1155, Fairfield, Iowa 52557; 515-472-1166.

Maine College of Art

Portland, Maine

Independent, coed. Urban campus. Total enrollment: 281.

Degrees Bachelor of Fine Arts in the areas of ceramics, graphic design, painting, printmaking, photography, sculpture, metalsmithing and jewelry. Majors: art history, ceramic art and design, drawing, graphic arts, jewelry and metalsmithing, photography, printmaking, sculpture. Cross-registration with Bowdoin College, Greater Portland Alliance of Colleges and Universities.

Art Student Profile Fall 1994: 281 total; all matriculated undergraduate; 1% minorities, 61% females, 3% international.

Art Faculty Total: 41; 18 full-time, 23 part-time; 95% of full-time faculty have terminal degrees. Graduate students do not teach undergraduate courses. Undergraduate student–faculty ratio: 10:1.

Student Life Student groups include Art in Service. Special housing available for art students.

Expenses for 1995–96 Application fee: $30. Comprehensive fee of $17,266 includes full-time tuition ($12,300), mandatory fees ($50), and college room and board ($4916 minimum). Part-time tuition: $512 per credit hour.

Financial Aid Program-specific awards for Fall of 1994: 10 Half-Tuition Scholarships for incoming freshmen ($5600), 3 Half-Tuition Scholarships for transfer students ($5600), 15–20 ARTS Scholarships for ARTS registrants ($1000), 250 Maine College of Art Grants for those demonstrating need ($1900).

Application Procedures Deadline—freshmen and transfers: continuous. Notification date—freshmen and transfers: continuous. Required: essay, high school transcript, college transcript(s) for transfer students, minimum 2.0 high school GPA, 2 letters of recommendation, portfolio, SAT I or ACT test scores. Recommended: interview. Portfolio reviews held continuously on campus and off campus on National Portfolio Days; the submission of slides may be substituted for portfolios when distance is prohibitive.

Undergraduate Contact Elizabeth Shea, Director of Admissions, Maine College of Art, 97 Spring Street, Portland, Maine 04101; 207-775-3052, fax: 207-772-5069.

More about the College

Program Facilities Departmental studios: well-equipped studios for each of the following majors: ceramics, graphic design, jewelry and metalsmithing, painting, photography, printmaking, and sculpture. Private studio space: Individual studio space is provided for all third- and fourth-year students. All MECA students are granted 24-hour studio access. Galleries: The College hosts exhibitions in three of its gallery spaces—the Baxter, Clapp, and Photography galleries. Works by MECA students as well as regional, national, and international artists are exhibited in these professional gallery spaces. In addition, students have opportunities to exhibit work in galleries and businesses throughout the community. Library: MECA has the largest open-to-public art library in northern New England. The library's collections number 18,000 volumes, 112 periodicals, and 42,000 slides.

Special Programs The Association of Independent Colleges of Art and Design (AICAD) is a consortium of thirty-two internationally recognized colleges of art and design. The association provides opportunities such as a student mobility program, access to international study, and internships in New York City. Bowdoin College Exchange is an arrangement that allows cross-registration between the two schools. Internships are credit-bearing employment opportunities that give students professional, hands-on experience in a business, museum, gallery, or studio environment. Visiting Artist Lecture Series: Each year, MECA hosts 10–20 well-known artists, designers, writers, and other scholars who lecture on their work and contemporary issues in the arts. In addition, the artists often meet with classes and individual students.

Maine College of Art (MECA) is an independent professional art institution located in northern New England. Through a structured, four-year curriculum of studio and liberal arts courses, students grow as artists and human beings. The College fosters an environment that nurtures individual development and successfully prepares students to work in every area of the visual arts, from painting and sculpture to ceramics and jewelry, from furniture and textile design to art education and photojournalism, from video graphics and publication design to advertising and curatorial work. Graduates enter the professional world with one of the finest visual arts educations available.

One of the great attractions of MECA is its location in Portland, Maine. Portland is a small, cosmopolitan city of 65,000 situated on the Atlantic Ocean's Casco Bay. Portland consistently ranks as one of the safest and most livable cities in the United States. The city offers many of the cultural advantages of a large urban center but in a more relaxed setting. The city is home to the Portland Museum of Art, Portland Symphony Orchestra, Portland Stage Company, and numerous other cultural resources. Jazz, blues, reggae, rock, and folk music are featured in a variety of clubs in the historic Old Port district.

The state of Maine is well known for its extraordinary beauty, high quality of life, and rich artistic heritage. Over the past two centuries Maine has played a vital role in American art. Such renowned artists as Winslow Homer, Bernice Abbot, Edward Hopper, and Andrew Wyeth have all drawn inspiration from the Maine landscape and people.

In 1996, MECA will be moving the majority of its facilities into a recently purchased major landmark building. Renovations are currently under way in this five-story Beaux Arts–style building located in the downtown arts district. The renovation project has been nationally recognized as an "Energy Star Showcase" by the Environmental Protection Agency—one of only twenty-four projects in the country chosen as an outstanding model of energy efficiency and environmental sensitivity. This state-of-the-art facility will more than double the College's existing space and will allow for future expansion.

Maine College of Art *(continued)*

The professional excellence of the MECA faculty is well established, and the College seeks to ensure that students receive personal attention. All MECA instructors are accomplished, practicing artists. One example of such recognition is the prestigious Guggenheim Fellowship granted to Paul D'Amato, Associate Professor of Photography. The John Simon Guggenheim Memorial Foundation appoints Guggenheim Fellows on the basis of unusually distinguished achievement in the past and exceptional promise for future accomplishments.

Tim McCreight, Chair of the Metals and Jewelry Department, is currently putting the finishing touches on his new book about the design process entitled *Design Spirit*. The book is the culmination of more than five years of research, with publication set for 1995. *Design Spirit* will undoubtedly follow the precedent set by McCreight's 1982 textbook publication *The Complete Metalsmith,* which is considered by many to be the definitive work on the subject of metals and jewelry.

Because of its excellent reputation, Maine College of Art draws students not only from New England but also from states across the country. In addition, MECA is home to a growing number of international students. Students come from a variety of ethnic and cultural backgrounds, but all share in common the desire to study in one of the most challenging and respected art colleges in the United States.

Manhattanville College

Purchase, New York

Independent, coed. Suburban campus. Total enrollment: 909.

Degrees Bachelor of Fine Arts in the area of studio art. Majors: art history, studio art. Cross-registration with Purchase College, State University of New York.

Art Student Profile Fall 1994: 70 total; all matriculated undergraduate.

Art Faculty Total: 16; 4 full-time, 12 part-time. Graduate students do not teach undergraduate courses. Undergraduate student–faculty ratio: 10:1.

Expenses for 1995–96 Application fee: $35. Comprehensive fee of $23,370 includes full-time tuition ($15,500), mandatory fees ($500), and college room and board ($7370). Part-time tuition: $345 per credit.

Application Procedures Deadline—freshmen: March 1; transfers: continuous. Required: essay, high school transcript, college transcript(s) for transfer students, minimum 2.0 high school GPA, 2 letters of recommendation, SAT I or ACT test scores. Recommended: minimum 3.0 high school GPA, interview, portfolio. Portfolio reviews held as needed; the submission of slides may be substituted for portfolios when distance is prohibitive.

Undergraduate Contact Robin Beth Askins, Admissions Counselor, Manhattanville College, 2900 Purchase Street, Purchase, New York 10577; 914-694-2200 ext. 649, fax: 914-694-1732.

Mankato State University

Mankato, Minnesota

State-supported, coed. Small-town campus. Total enrollment: 12,624.

Degrees Bachelor of Fine Arts in the area of art. Majors: art education, ceramic art and design, drawing, graphic arts, painting, photography, printmaking, sculpture, textile arts.

Art Student Profile Fall 1994: 241 total; 229 matriculated undergraduate, 12 nondegree; 2% minorities, 5% international.

Art Faculty Total: 17; 13 full-time, 4 part-time; 92% of full-time faculty have terminal degrees. Graduate students teach a few undergraduate courses. Undergraduate student–faculty ratio: 17:1.

Student Life Student groups include Art League.

Estimated Expenses for 1995–96 Application fee: $15. State resident tuition: $2355 full-time, $58.45 per quarter hour part-time. Nonresident tuition: $4893 full-time, $115.90 per quarter hour part-time. Full-time mandatory fees: $340. College room and board: $2905. Special program-related fees: $10–$50 for departmental fees.

Financial Aid Program-specific awards for Fall of 1994: 6 Faculty Nominated Awards for program majors.

Application Procedures Deadline—freshmen and transfers: continuous. Notification date—freshmen and transfers: continuous. Required: high school transcript, SAT I or ACT test scores. Recommended: college transcript(s) for transfer students.

Undergraduate Contact Robert Finkler, Chairperson, Art Department, Mankato State University, Mankato, Minnesota 56002-8400; 507-389-6412, fax: 507-389-5887, E-mail address: roberter@msl.mankato.msus.edu.

Marietta College

Marietta, Ohio

Independent, coed. Suburban campus. Total enrollment: 1,319.

Degrees Bachelor of Fine Arts in the area of art. Majors: art education, art/fine arts, commercial art, studio art.

Art Student Profile Fall 1994: 40 total; 30 matriculated undergraduate, 10 nondegree; 60% females.

Art Faculty Total: 6; 2 full-time, 4 part-time; 100% of full-time faculty have terminal degrees. Graduate stu-

dents do not teach undergraduate courses. Undergraduate student–faculty ratio: 10:1.

Student Life Student groups include Art Club.

Expenses for 1995–96 Comprehensive fee of $18,880 includes full-time tuition ($14,450), mandatory fees ($400), and college room and board ($4030). College room only: $2070. Part-time tuition: $480 per credit hour. Part-time mandatory fees: $40 per semester.

Financial Aid Program-specific awards for Fall of 1994 available.

Application Procedures Deadline—freshmen and transfers: continuous. Required: essay, high school transcript, letter of recommendation. Recommended: interview, minimum 2.5 high school GPA.

Undergraduate Contact Admission Office, Marietta College, 215 Fifth Street, Marietta, Ohio 45750-4000; 614-376-4600.

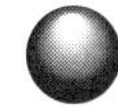

Marshall University

Huntington, West Virginia

State-supported, coed. Urban campus. Total enrollment: 12,659.

Degrees Bachelor of Fine Arts in the area of art. Majors: craft design, graphic design, painting/drawing, photography, printmaking, sculpture, visual arts.

Art Student Profile Fall 1994: 5% minorities, 52% females, 1% international.

Art Faculty Total: 15; 10 full-time, 5 part-time; 100% of full-time faculty have terminal degrees. Graduate students teach a few undergraduate courses. Undergraduate student–faculty ratio: 17:1.

Student Life Student groups include Art Opportunities Program (teaching elementary students in enrichment program), Keramos (Ceramics Club), Graphic Design Club.

Expenses for 1995–96 Application fee: $10. State resident tuition: $2050 full-time, $85.75 per semester hour part-time. Nonresident tuition: $5696 full-time, $237.50 per semester hour part-time. Tuition for Kentucky residents. College room and board: $4050.

Financial Aid Program-specific awards for Fall of 1994: 4–5 Art Scholarships for program majors ($400), 5 Tuition Waivers for program majors ($520–$1882).

Application Procedures Deadline—freshmen and transfers: August 15. Notification date—freshmen and transfers: continuous. Required: high school transcript, minimum 2.0 high school GPA, SAT I or ACT test scores, minimum combined SAT I score of 810, minimum composite ACT score of 17. Recommended: letter of recommendation, portfolio. Portfolio reviews held by appointment on campus; the submission of slides may be substituted for portfolios if a campus visit is impossible.

Undergraduate Contact Michael Cornfeld, Chairman, Department of Art, Marshall University, 400 Hal Greer Boulevard, Huntington, West Virginia 25755; 304-696-6760, fax: 304-696-6658, E-mail address: dfa003@marshall.wvnet.edu.

Maryland Institute, College of Art

Baltimore, Maryland

Independent, coed. Urban campus. Total enrollment: 906.

Degrees Bachelor of Fine Arts in the areas of drawing, painting, sculpture, printmaking, general fine arts, ceramics, fibers, photography, illustration, interior architecture and design. Majors: art/fine arts, ceramic art and design, fibers, graphic arts, illustration, interior design, painting/drawing, photography, printmaking, sculpture. Graduate degrees offered: Master of Fine Arts in the areas of painting, sculpture, art education, photography, mixed media. Cross-registration with Johns Hopkins University, University of Baltimore, Goucher College, Loyola College.

Art Student Profile Fall 1994: 906 total; 814 matriculated undergraduate, 92 matriculated graduate; 18% minorities, 56% females, 6% international.

Art Faculty Total: 156; 73 full-time, 83 part-time; 74% of full-time faculty have terminal degrees. Graduate students do not teach undergraduate courses. Undergraduate student–faculty ratio: 11:1.

Student Life Student groups include Student Exhibitions Committee, Programming Arts Committee, American Institute of Graphic Arts. Special housing available for art students.

Expenses for 1995–96 Application fee: $40. Comprehensive fee of $19,430 includes full-time tuition ($13,850), mandatory fees ($140), and college room and board ($5440). College room only: $4000. Part-time tuition: $540 per credit. Part-time mandatory fees: $140 per year.

Financial Aid Program-specific awards for Fall of 1994: 26 Thalheimer Scholarships for freshmen ($10,000–$25,000), 5 Academic Excellence Scholarships for freshmen ($8000), 5 National Art Honor Society Scholarships for freshmen ($4000), Competitive Scholarships for transfers ($4000–$20,000), 1 Morris Lewis Scholarship for upperclassmen ($18,000).

Application Procedures Deadline—freshmen: March 1; transfers: April 1. Notification date—freshmen: April 1; transfers: June 1. Required: essay, high school transcript, college transcript(s) for transfer students, portfolio, SAT I or ACT test scores. Recommended: interview. Portfolio reviews held continuously on campus and off campus on National Portfolio Days.

Undergraduate Contact Theresa Lynch Bedoya, Vice President, Admissions, Admissions and Financial Aid Office, Maryland Institute, College of Art, 1300 Mt. Royal Avenue, Baltimore, Maryland 21217; 410-225-2222, fax: 410-669-9206.

Graduate Contact Dr. Leslie King-Hammond, Graduate Dean, Graduate Office, Maryland Institute, College of Art, 1300 Mt. Royal Avenue, Baltimore, Maryland 21217; 410-225-2255.

Maryland Institute, College of Art *(continued)*

More about the Institute

Program Facilities Campus of nineteen buildings; 135,000 square feet of instructional facilities designated to departments of painting, ceramics, drawing, sculpture, photography, printmaking, fibers, interior architecture, graphic design/illustration, and liberal arts; independent studio space for seniors; seven art galleries; art-oriented library: 50,000 volumes, 200 periodicals, 60,000 slides of contemporary and historical art; computer facilities include 3 computer classrooms outfitted with 42 Power Macintosh 7100AV; a computer classroom with 16 Quadra 660AV; a computer writing and tutoring lab consisting of 23 486 PCs; individual workstations for each interior architecture student; 3 Avid digital video suites; computer workstations in the sculpture department; and internet access stations in the College Center and Library; equipment includes flatbed scanners, high resolution color printers, digital cameras, video capture capability, slide scanners, digital slide markers, and CD writing capability; communications capabilities include e-mail addresses for each student, student e-mail access workstations, and classroom access to the World Wide Web; intimate liberal arts classrooms; 250-seat auditorium for performance art, theater, poetry readings, and lectures; 24-hour access to studios.

Visiting Artists and Lecturers: Each year over 175 visiting artists, designers, critics, poets, writers, historians, and filmmakers take part in classroom/studio instruction. During the past two years, resident artists from Asia, Eastern Europe, and Latin America were included.

Faculty One hundred thirty-six professional artists, designers, and scholars; represented in public and private collections from MOMA to the Stedelijk; nationally recognized recipients of Fulbright, Guggenheim, MacArthur, Louis Comfort Tiffany, Prix de Rome, and National Foundation for the Arts and for the Humanities; published authors of articles, books, poetry, plays, and critical reviews: over fifty publications published in two years; exhibit in national, regional, and international museums and galleries from Leo Castelli Galleries in New York to Galleria Tucci-Russo in Italy.

Special Programs A five-year dual degree (B.F.A/M.A.T.) combines an undergraduate degree in studio art with teaching certification at the master's level; study abroad opportunities in Canada, England, Scotland, France, Greece, Italy, Mexico, Japan, and the Netherlands; New York Studio program for juniors; career development programs include job internship opportunities in corporations, cultural institutions, design and architectural firms, photography studios. Other reality-based programs and courses are offered in topics ranging from promoting oneself as an artist to developing business skills. Job listings are national.

For over 160 years, the Maryland Institute, College of Art, has brought together some of the most talented and committed students and faculty from across the nation and around the world to create art in a highly energized and intellectual environment.

The Institute offers a strong foundation in the fine arts and design, complemented by a challenging liberal arts component. Students can choose from twelve different studio majors as well as minors in art history, literature, and writing. Visual communication and interior architecture and design programs are computer based. Once students choose a major, they may opt to take electives in an array of subjects outside their major area of study in order to further develop their individual voice. The dialogue between departments and disciplines is constant. Faculty and visiting artists from all disciplines, including liberal arts, are regularly invited to take part in critiques and make studio visits to lend their diverse perspectives to the creative process.

Located in a beautiful residential neighborhood in Baltimore and surrounded by other cultural institutions, the Institute offers students the best of urban and town life. Baltimore is home to a vibrant visual and performing arts community. Its world-class museums and galleries present traditional art as well as work by contemporary and emerging artists. Additionally, Baltimore is located in the middle of the New York–Washington, D.C., arts corridor and is home to many colleges (including the Johns Hopkins University and the Peabody Conservatory of Music) that offer cooperative academic exchange programs for Institute students.

As the Maryland Institute looks toward the future, the College is planning for the influences that advances in technology and a more global society will have on the education of artists. In 1996, it will open a new facility that includes a multimedia center, an expanded library, and a new home for all design, liberal arts, and humanities programs. Additionally, the Institute offers excellent mobility programs and extensive opportunities for students to study abroad during the summer or during their junior or senior years.

The Institute's campus includes the Commons, a housing complex designed especially for student artists. There, students live in apartment-style housing, complete with access to 24-hour project rooms and gallery space on site. The College Center houses the career center, dining hall, and meeting rooms for student organizations and is located next door to the art supply/bookstore.

The Institute provides an array of career services for its students. The professional career center staff prepares students for a myriad of art-related professional positions. The center helps place upperclassmen in art-related internships for academic credit and job experience as well as in part-time and freelance positions while they are in school. The career center also assists students in graduate school preparation and provides national job listings for graduating seniors.

The Institute hosts over sixty exhibitions a year by international, regional, and local artists as well as students and faculty; an extensive program of visiting artists, critics, and lecturers; an annual poetry and film series; and many special interest clubs, ranging from a multicultural club and a student exhibitions committee to several student publications and a variety of social and political organizations.

Marylhurst College

Marylhurst, Oregon

Independent-religious, coed. Suburban campus. Total enrollment: 1,183.

Degrees Bachelor of Fine Arts in the area of art. Majors: art/fine arts, interior design, painting/drawing, photography, printmaking, sculpture.

Art Student Profile Fall 1994: 180 total; 150 matriculated undergraduate, 30 nondegree; 5% minorities, 80% females, 1% international.

Art Faculty Total: 25; 1 full-time, 24 part-time; 100% of full-time faculty have terminal degrees. Graduate students do not teach undergraduate courses. Undergraduate student–faculty ratio: 7:1.

Student Life Student groups include American Society of Interior Designers Student Chapter.

Expenses for 1994–95 Application fee: $73. Tuition: $8505 full-time, $189 per quarter hour part-time. Part-time mandatory fees: $14 per quarter. Full-time mandatory fees: $42.

Financial Aid Program-specific awards for Fall of 1994: 20 Mayer Scholarships for program majors ($100).

Application Procedures Deadline—freshmen and transfers: continuous. Required: high school transcript.

Undergraduate Contact Paul Sutinen, Assistant Chair, Art Department, Marylhurst College, P.O. Box 261, Marylhurst, Oregon 97036; 503-636-8141 ext. 414, fax: 503-636-9526.

Maryville University of Saint Louis

St. Louis, Missouri

Independent, coed. Suburban campus. Total enrollment: 3,425.

Degrees Bachelor of Fine Arts in the areas of interior design, studio art. Majors: drawing, interior design, studio art. Cross-registration with Webster University, Fontbonne College, Missouri Baptist College, Lindenwood College.

Art Student Profile Fall 1994: 109 total; 84 matriculated undergraduate, 25 nondegree; 3% minorities, 72% females, 6% international.

Art Faculty Total: 25; 6 full-time, 19 part-time; 83% of full-time faculty have terminal degrees. Graduate students do not teach undergraduate courses. Undergraduate student–faculty ratio: 12:1.

Student Life Student groups include Maryville Chapter of American Society of Interior Designers, It's Visual.

Expenses for 1995–96 Application fee: $20. Comprehensive fee of $14,550 includes full-time tuition ($9800) and college room and board ($4750). Part-time tuition: $280 per credit hour. Part-time tuition per credit hour for Weekend College students: $190. Special program-related fees: $5–$40 for supplies, $5 for audiovisual teaching resources.

Financial Aid Program-specific awards for Fall of 1994: 5 Art and Design Scholarships for undergraduates, first time freshmen and outstanding transfer students ($4000).

Application Procedures Deadline—freshmen and transfers: continuous. Required: high school transcript, college transcript(s) for transfer students, minimum 2.0 high school GPA, portfolio, SAT I or ACT test scores. Recommended: letter of recommendation, interview. Portfolio reviews held continuously on campus and off campus in St. Louis, MO; Kansas City, MO; Memphis, TN; Indianapolis, IN on National Portfolio Days; the submission of slides may be substituted for portfolios if original work is unavailable or for large works of art.

Undergraduate Contact Dr. Martha G. Wade, Dean, Admissions and Enrollment Management, Maryville University of Saint Louis, 13550 Conway Road, St. Louis, Missouri 63141-7299; 314-529-9350, fax: 314-529-9927, E-mail address: wade@maryville.edu.

Marywood College

Scranton, Pennsylvania

Independent-religious, coed. Suburban campus. Total enrollment: 3,068.

Degrees Bachelor of Fine Arts in the areas of studio art, design. Majors: ceramic art and design, graphic arts, illustration, interior design, painting/drawing, photography, sculpture. Graduate degrees offered: Master of Fine Arts in the areas of painting, fibers, ceramics.

Art Student Profile Fall 1994: 293 total; 200 matriculated undergraduate, 85 matriculated graduate, 8 nondegree; 2% minorities, 76% females, 1% international.

Art Faculty Total: 33; 13 full-time, 20 part-time; 100% of full-time faculty have terminal degrees. Graduate students do not teach undergraduate courses. Undergraduate student–faculty ratio: 14:1.

Student Life Student groups include St. Luke Art Society, Zeta Omicron Chapter of Kappa Pi, Pennsylvania Art Education Association.

Expenses for 1995–96 Application fee: $20. Comprehensive fee of $17,040 includes full-time tuition ($11,840), mandatory fees ($400), and college room and board ($4800). Part-time tuition: $370 per credit.

Financial Aid Program-specific awards for Fall of 1994: 21 Art Talent Awards for artistically talented students ($2600).

Application Procedures Deadline—freshmen and transfers: continuous. Required: high school transcript, college transcript(s) for transfer students, minimum 2.0 high school GPA, 2 letters of recommendation, portfolio. Recommended: interview. Portfolio reviews held continuously on campus and off campus on National Portfolio Days; the submission of slides may be substituted for portfolios when distance is prohibitive.

Contact Mathew Povse, Chairperson, Art Department, Marywood College, 2300 Adams Avenue, Scranton, Pennsylvania 18509; 717-348-6278, fax: 717-348-1817.

Mason Gross School of Arts

See Rutgers, The State University of New Jersey, Mason Gross School of Arts

Massachusetts College of Art

Boston, Massachusetts

State-supported, coed. Urban campus. Total enrollment: 1,367.

Degrees Bachelor of Fine Arts in the areas of art education, art history, fine arts, design, media and performing arts. Majors: applied art, architectural design, art education, art/fine arts, ceramic art and design, commercial art, computer graphics, fashion design and technology, glass, graphic arts, illustration, industrial design, jewelry and metalsmithing, painting/drawing, photography, printmaking, sculpture, studio art, textile arts. Graduate degrees offered: Master of Fine Arts in the areas of design, fine arts, media and performing arts. Cross-registration with ProArts Consortium, College Academic Program Sharing, Public College Exchange Program.

Art Student Profile Fall 1994: 2,145 total; 1,328 matriculated undergraduate, 70 matriculated graduate, 747 nondegree; 12% minorities, 60% females, 4% international.

Art Faculty Total: 156; 66 full-time, 90 part-time; 100% of full-time faculty have terminal degrees. Graduate students teach a few undergraduate courses. Undergraduate student–faculty ratio: 14:1.

Student Life Student groups include All School Show, Annual Program of Working Environmentally at Haystack School in Maine, Visiting Artists and Professional Exhibitions, Christmas Art Sale. Special housing available for art students.

Expenses for 1995–96 Application fee: $10. State resident tuition: $1463 full-time. Nonresident tuition: $6422 full-time. Part-time tuition per course ranges from $182.88 to $548.63 for state residents, $802.75 to $2408 for nonresidents. Part-time mandatory fees per semester range from $761 to $1202. Tuition for nonresidents who are eligible for the New England Regional Student Program: $2195 full-time, $274.31 to $822.94 per course part-time. Full-time mandatory fees: $2520. College room and board: $5412 (minimum).

Financial Aid Program-specific awards for Fall of 1994 available.

Application Procedures Deadline—freshmen: March 15; transfers: April 1. Notification date—freshmen and transfers: May 15. Required: essay, high school transcript, college transcript(s) for transfer students, portfolio, SAT I test score only. Recommended: minimum 3.0 high school GPA, letter of recommendation, interview. Portfolio reviews held continuously on campus; the submission of slides may be substituted for portfolios.

Contact Kay Ransdell, Associate Dean for Admissions and Retention, Massachusetts College of Art, 621 Huntington Avenue, Boston, Massachusetts 02115-5882; 617-232-1555 ext. 235, fax: 617-566-4034.

Meadows School of the Arts

See Southern Methodist University, Meadows School of the Arts

Memphis College of Art

Memphis, Tennessee

Independent, coed. Urban campus. Total enrollment: 216.

Degrees Bachelor of Fine Arts in the areas of fine arts, design arts. Majors: applied art, book arts, ceramic art and design, commercial art, computer graphics, graphic arts, illustration, jewelry and metalsmithing, painting/drawing, papermaking, printmaking, sculpture, studio art, textile arts. Graduate degrees offered: Master of Fine Arts in the areas of studio art, computer arts. Cross-registration with Rhodes College, Christian Brothers University.

Art Student Profile Fall 1994: 249 total; 198 matriculated undergraduate, 28 matriculated graduate, 23 nondegree; 17% minorities, 43% females, 7% international.

Art Faculty Total: 41; 18 full-time, 23 part-time; 70% of full-time faculty have terminal degrees. Graduate students teach a few undergraduate courses. Undergraduate student–faculty ratio: 10:1.

Student Life Student groups include Student Government, Arteli (Arts in the Schools), Children's Community Art Classes. Special housing available for art students.

Estimated Expenses for 1995–96 Application fee: $25. Comprehensive fee of $13,850 includes full-time tuition ($9450), mandatory fees ($50), and college room and board ($4350). College room only: $2990. Part-time tuition: $395 per semester hour.

Financial Aid Program-specific awards for Fall of 1994: Portfolio Scholarships for program majors ($2500), Work Study Awards for program majors ($1000).

Application Procedures Deadline—freshmen and transfers: continuous. Required: essay, high school transcript, college transcript(s) for transfer students, letter of recommendation, portfolio, SAT I or ACT test scores. Recommended: interview. Portfolio reviews held weekly on campus; the submission of slides may be substituted for portfolios.

Contact Susan S. Miller, Director of Admissions, Memphis College of Art, 1930 Poplar Avenue, Overton Park, Memphis, Tennessee 38104; 800-727-1088 ext. 30, fax: 901-726-9371.

More about the College

Program Facilities Computer labs have Macintosh and Amiga color workstations, LaserWriter printers, grayscale and color scanners, high-resolution film recorder, and high-end multimedia facilities. MCA's shop has 4,400 square feet, with machines for woodworking, metalworking, plastic molding, glass cutting, shrink wrapping, and stretcher and frame construction. The library has 14,000 volumes, 100 art journals and periodicals, 32,000 slides, an extensive reproduction collection, audiovisual equipment, a computer writing lab, and an image file. Students have studio spaces. Conference rooms allow for slide viewing, critiques, and lectures. Sculpture, small metals, and clay have studios with foundry/welding areas for casting and metal work. Clay has nine wheels, handbuilding and glazing space, and a semi-enclosed firing room. Fiber/surface design has three studios, a dye room, manual and computerized looms, washer/dryer, range tops, refrigerators, and sewing machines. Printmaking, papermaking, and book arts studios provide interaction between these media. Printmaking has facilities for lithography, etching, serigraphy, and other processes. Book arts include letter presses and bindery. Papermaking has beaters, 36-square-foot vacuum table, hydrolic press, and pulper. Airbrush equipment, computerized stat cameras, darkrooms, light tables, and lucigraphs are also available.

Special Programs The New York Studio Program offers students an exciting semester in New York City with artists and students from across the country. The Mobility Program can place a student at another art college for a semester of study. Internships offer experience in fine and design arts fields, such as museum work, art therapy, set design, and advertising. Consortiums with local colleges provide a greater variety of course selection.

Since 1936, Memphis College of Art has been a special community of artists. The MCA experience is organized around small classes, independent work, and one-on-one attention and guidance not usually found at a larger institution. Currently students from twenty-six states and eleven other countries attend MCA, providing a diversity often associated with larger schools.

MCA is located in a 342-acre park in midtown Memphis adjacent to the Memphis Brooks Museum of Art and the Memphis Zoo. A nearby student residence provides living space for new and returning students. Two roommates share a furnished apartment with hardwood floors, a sun porch, a kitchen, and studio space. A large variety of affordable housing is also available off-campus to suit all lifestyles and budgets.

Memphis is a great place for an aspiring artist. Known for blues, barbecue, and Elvis, Memphis is also home to Fortune 500 companies, a symphony, an opera, a theater, other colleges and universities, museums, galleries, and almost 1 million residents. Annual festivals on Beale Street and the Mississippi River are popular with students.

MCA is a close-knit community where it's easy to make friends. There are plenty of organized activities to keep students busy, such as Friday night movies, exhibition receptions, and an annual Hike and Bike and Halloween Costume Ball. Not-so-organized activities include tunnel ball and volleyball.

Tobey Exhibition Hall hosts numerous shows that expose students to a wide range of contemporary art; the Lower Gallery is a large space dedicated to student art. Students also have the opportunity to learn from visiting artists who provide a constant flow of new creative and intellectual energy. MCA organizes study trips to cities around the world renowned for their culture. In early May, a weeklong workshop is held on Horn Island off the Mississippi coast.

The Student Life Office offers job placement assistance for graduating students and part-time job placement for current students. Informative sessions are held to prepare students for career choices and for the job search/interview process. The Job Fair brings regional and national companies to MCA each spring for interviews. Internships and the student-run design agency provide students with professional experience while in school.

Faculty members have been selected for their understanding of the relationship between art and teaching. MCA's Fine Arts faculty members are professional artists who exhibit frequently and regularly execute commissions. The Design Arts faculty stays on top of the industry through continuing professional design projects. With their knowledge of the job market and galleries at the regional and national levels, faculty members are well qualified to guide students on their career paths. Liberal Studies faculty members are chosen for their impressive credentials and their understanding of the unique nature of MCA students.

MCA is concerned about students whose financial resources are limited. Over 80 percent of the College's students receive some type of financial assistance. Financial aid programs include scholarships, loans, grants, and work-study awards. More than $350,000 is awarded by MCA in scholarship and grants each year.

Metropolitan State College of Denver

Denver, Colorado

State-supported, coed. Urban campus. Total enrollment: 16,296.

Degrees Bachelor of Fine Arts in the areas of fine arts, design, crafts, art history. Majors: advertising design, applied art, art education, art/fine arts, ceramic art and design, computer graphics, jewelry and metalsmithing, painting/drawing, photography, printmaking, sculpture. Cross-registration with University of Colorado at Denver, Community College of Denver.

Art Faculty Total: 38; 14 full-time, 24 part-time; 100% of full-time faculty have terminal degrees. Graduate students do not teach undergraduate courses. Undergraduate student–faculty ratio: 20:1.

Student Life Student groups include Art Club, Clay Club, Printmaking Club.

Expenses for 1995–96 Application fee: $25. State resident tuition: $1849 full-time. Nonresident tuition: $6483 full-time. Part-time tuition per semester ranges from $140.41 to $784.51 for state residents, $341.41 to $2916 for nonresidents. Special program-related fees: $5–$45 for expendable materials.

Application Procedures Deadline—freshmen and transfers: continuous. Notification date—freshmen and transfers: continuous. Required: high school transcript, college transcript(s) for transfer students, SAT I or ACT test scores, minimum 2.5 high school GPA. Recommended: letter of recommendation. Auditions held on campus and off campus. Portfolio reviews held on campus and off campus.

Undergraduate Contact Dr. Susan Josepher, Chairperson, Art Department, Metropolitan State College of

Metropolitan State College of Denver *(continued)*

Denver, P.O. Box 173362, Denver, Colorado 80217-3362; 303-556-3090, fax: 303-556-4094.

Miami University

Oxford, Ohio

State-related, coed. Small-town campus. Total enrollment: 15,882.

Degrees Bachelor of Fine Arts in the areas of painting/drawing, jewelry and metalsmithing, printmaking, sculpture, ceramic art and design, graphic arts, photography. Majors: ceramic art and design, computer graphics, jewelry and metalsmithing, painting/drawing, photography, printmaking, sculpture. Graduate degrees offered: Master of Fine Arts in the areas of painting, ceramics, sculpture, jewelry and metalsmithing. Cross-registration with John E. Dolibois European Center (Luxembourg).

Art Student Profile Fall 1994: 347 total; 332 matriculated undergraduate, 15 matriculated graduate; 3% minorities.

Art Faculty Total: 27; 19 full-time, 8 part-time; 81% of full-time faculty have terminal degrees. Graduate students teach about a quarter undergraduate courses. Undergraduate student–faculty ratio: 15:1.

Student Life Student groups include Art History Association, National Art Education Association Student Chapter, Designers Ink.

Expenses for 1995–96 Application fee: $30. State resident tuition: $3964 full-time, $166 per credit hour part-time. Nonresident tuition: $9394 full-time, $393 per credit hour part-time. Part-time mandatory fees: $45.50 per credit hour. Full-time mandatory fees: $920. College room and board: $4210. College room only: $1950. Special program-related fees: $50–$60 for studio courses.

Financial Aid Program-specific awards for Fall of 1994: 1 Miami University Scholarship for program majors ($4300), 1 American Greetings Award for program majors ($1000), 1 Arthur Damon Art Award for program majors ($1500), 1 School of Fine Arts Award for program majors ($2000), 1 Marston D. Hodgin Award for program majors ($1000), 1 George R. and Galen Glasgow Hoxie Award ($890), 2 Fred and Molly Pye Awards for sophomores and juniors ($475).

Application Procedures Deadline—freshmen: January 30; transfers: continuous. Notification date—freshmen: March 15. Required: high school transcript, portfolio, SAT I or ACT test scores. Portfolio reviews held 2 times on campus; the submission of slides may be substituted for portfolios with approval from the department.

Undergraduate Contact Lon Beck, Professor, Department of Art, Miami University, Art Building, Oxford, Ohio 45056; 513-529-2900, fax: 513-529-3841.

Graduate Contact Ed Montgomery, Associate Professor, Department of Art, Miami University, Art Building, Oxford, Ohio 45056; 513-529-2900, fax: 513-529-3841.

Michigan State University

East Lansing, Michigan

State-supported, coed. Small-town campus. Total enrollment: 40,254.

Degrees Bachelor of Fine Arts in the areas of studio art, art education. Majors: art education, ceramics, graphic design, painting/drawing, photography, printmaking, sculpture. Graduate degrees offered: Master of Fine Arts in the area of studio art.

Art Student Profile Fall 1994: 282 total; 239 matriculated undergraduate, 43 matriculated graduate; 11% minorities, 66% females, 4% international.

Art Faculty Total: 27; 26 full-time, 1 part-time; 100% of full-time faculty have terminal degrees. Graduate students teach a few undergraduate courses. Undergraduate student–faculty ratio: 18:1.

Student Life Student groups include Annual Undergraduate Exhibit at Kresge Art Museum, Saturday Art Program.

Expenses for 1994–95 Application fee: $30. State resident tuition: $4102 full-time. Nonresident tuition: $10,658 full-time. Part-time tuition per semester hour ranges from $129.50 to $144 for state residents, $349 to $361.50 for nonresidents, according to class level. Full-time mandatory fees: $524. College room and board: $3764.

Financial Aid Program-specific awards for Fall of 1994: 1–4 Creative Arts Scholarships for studio art majors ($500–$2000).

Application Procedures Deadline—freshmen and transfers: continuous. Required: high school transcript, college transcript(s) for transfer students, minimum 2.0 high school GPA, portfolio, SAT I or ACT test scores. Recommended: minimum 3.0 high school GPA. Portfolio reviews held on campus.

Contact Studio Art Undergraduate Program, Michigan State University, 113 Kresge Art Center, East Lansing, Michigan 48824-1119; 517-355-7611, fax: 517-432-3938.

Middle Tennessee State University

Murfreesboro, Tennessee

State-supported, coed. Suburban campus. Total enrollment: 17,120.

Degrees Bachelor of Fine Arts in the areas of studio art, graphic design. Majors: ceramic art and design, graphic design, jewelry and metalsmithing, painting/drawing, printmaking, sculpture.

Art Student Profile Fall 1994: 284 total; all matriculated undergraduate.

Art Faculty Total: 27; 15 full-time, 12 part-time; 90% of full-time faculty have terminal degrees. Graduate students do not teach undergraduate courses.

Expenses for 1995–96 Application fee: $5. State resident tuition: $1972 full-time, $74 per semester hour

part-time. Nonresident tuition: $6102 full-time, $255 per semester hour part-time. College room and board: $2438. College room only: $1376.

Application Procedures Deadline—freshmen and transfers: continuous. Required: high school transcript, minimum 2.0 high school GPA, portfolio, SAT I or ACT test scores. Portfolio reviews held 1 time at end of sophomore year on campus; the submission of slides may be substituted for portfolios for transfer students or continuing education applicants.

Undergraduate Contact Carlyle Johnson, Chair, Art Department, Middle Tennessee State University, P.O. Box 25, Murfreesboro, Tennessee 37132; 615-898-2455, fax: 615-898-2254.

Midge Karr Fine Art Department

See New York Institute of Technology, Midge Karr Fine Art Department

Midwestern State University

Wichita Falls, Texas

State-supported, coed. Small-town campus. Total enrollment: 5,819.

Degrees Bachelor of Fine Arts in the area of art. Majors: jewelry and metalsmithing, painting/drawing, printmaking, sculpture.

Art Faculty Total: 5; 4 full-time, 1 part-time. Graduate students do not teach undergraduate courses.

Expenses for 1995–96 State resident tuition: $1646 full-time. Nonresident tuition: $7406 full-time. Part-time tuition per semester ranges from $184.05 to $822.75 for state residents, $286.05 to $3703 for nonresidents. College room and board: $3430 (minimum). College room only: $1830. Special program-related fees: $9 for course fees.

Financial Aid Program-specific awards for Fall of 1994 available.

Application Procedures Deadline—freshmen and transfers: August 7. Required: high school transcript, SAT I or ACT test scores. Recommended: portfolio. Portfolio reviews held continuously on campus; the submission of slides may be substituted for portfolios.

Undergraduate Contact Richard Ash, Coordinator of Art Program, Midwestern State University, Fain Fine Arts Center, Wichita Falls, Texas 76308; 817-689-4386.

Millikin University

Decatur, Illinois

Independent-religious, coed. Suburban campus. Total enrollment: 1,863.

Degrees Bachelor of Fine Arts in the areas of art education, studio art, graphic design/commercial art, art therapy, art management. Majors: applied art, art education, art therapy, art/fine arts, arts administration, ceramic art and design, commercial art, computer graphics, graphic arts, painting/drawing, photography, printmaking, sculpture, studio art.

Art Student Profile Fall 1994: 100 total; all matriculated undergraduate; 4% minorities, 50% females.

Art Faculty Total: 6; 5 full-time, 1 part-time; 100% of full-time faculty have terminal degrees. Graduate students do not teach undergraduate courses. Undergraduate student–faculty ratio: 16:1.

Student Life Student groups include Computer Imaging Alliance.

Expenses for 1995–96 Application fee: $25. Comprehensive fee of $17,283 includes full-time tuition ($12,596), mandatory fees ($91), and college room and board ($4596). College room only: $2392. Part-time tuition: $364 per credit. Special program-related fees: $10–$50 for lab fees.

Financial Aid Program-specific awards for Fall of 1994: 20–30 Talent Awards for incoming students ($500–$3000).

Application Procedures Deadline—freshmen and transfers: continuous. Required: high school transcript, college transcript(s) for transfer students, letter of recommendation, interview, SAT I or ACT test scores. Recommended: portfolio. Portfolio reviews held by appointment on campus and off campus in St. Louis, MO; Indianapolis, IN; the submission of slides may be substituted for portfolios for large works of art.

Undergraduate Contact James Schietinger, Chairman, Art Department, Millikin University, 1184 West Main Street, Decatur, Illinois 62522; 217-424-6227, fax: 217-424-3993, E-mail address: jschietinger@mail.millikin.edu.

Milwaukee Institute of Art and Design

Milwaukee, Wisconsin

Independent, coed. Urban campus. Total enrollment: 511.

Degrees Bachelor of Fine Arts in the areas of illustration, interior design, painting, photography, printmaking, sculpture, graphic design, industrial design, drawing. Majors: drawing, graphic design, illustration, industrial design, interior design, painting/drawing, photography, printmaking, sculpture. Cross-registration with Marquette University.

Art Student Profile Fall 1994: 505 total; all matriculated undergraduate; 14% minorities, 42% females, 58% international.

Art Faculty Total: 74; 22 full-time, 52 part-time; 55% of full-time faculty have terminal degrees. Graduate students do not teach undergraduate courses. Undergraduate student–faculty ratio: 10:1.

Student Life Special housing available for art students.

Expenses for 1995–96 Application fee: $25. Comprehensive fee of $18,815 includes full-time tuition ($12,600), mandatory fees ($500), and college room and board

Milwaukee Institute of Art and Design *(continued)*

($5715). Part-time tuition: $420 per credit. Special program-related fees: $5–$95 for supplies.

Financial Aid Program-specific awards for Fall of 1994: 1 Milwaukee Institute of Art and Design Scholarship for incoming freshmen ($11,200), 7 Milwaukee Institute of Art and Design Admissions Scholarships for incoming freshmen ($5600), 5 Layton Scholarships for sophomores ($2200), 22 Milwaukee Institute of Art and Design Scholarships for continuing students ($2000).

Application Procedures Deadline—freshmen and transfers: continuous. Required: high school transcript, interview, portfolio. Recommended: essay, minimum 3.0 high school GPA, letter of recommendation. Portfolio reviews held continuously on campus and off campus on National Portfolio Days; the submission of slides may be substituted for portfolios.

Undergraduate Contact Mary Strupp, Executive Director of Enrollment Services, Milwaukee Institute of Art and Design, 273 East Erie Street, Milwaukee, Wisconsin 53202; 414-276-7889, fax: 414-291-8077.

More about the Institute

Program Facilities MIAD is located in a newly renovated state-of-the-art design and fine art facility in the historic Third Ward area of Milwaukee. The facility features large, light-rich studio classrooms; artist-in-residence studios; a writing center with word processors and computers; a state-of-the-art computer graphics laboratory; and personal studios/workspaces for all junior and senior students. MIAD has a technologically advanced ventilation system designed specifically to ensure safety.

Faculty, Resident Artists, and Alumni MIAD's faculty members are all practicing artists, designers, writers, or scholars. The range of their professional activity extends from artists who have active exhibition records to those who work as designers, illustrators, industrial or interior designers, and writers of fiction, poetry, and nonfiction.

Student Performance Opportunities MIAD students have a wide range of exhibition and internship opportunities each year. These include an ongoing series of shows in the MIAD Student Gallery, the annual All Student Show, the annual Senior Exhibition, the Scholarship Exhibition, and internships with many of Milwaukee's most prestigious design, architectural, and photographic studios and several of the city's professional performing art troupes, such as Theatre X. Also, MIAD students are regularly invited by local galleries to submit work for local and regional exhibitions.

Special Programs MIAD offers a New York Studio Program, during which qualified students spend a semester or entire academic year working and studying in New York; a mobility program, which allows students to spend a semester or year at one of MIAD's sister AICAD schools; special programs for second-language students and students with learning disabilities; and peer tutoring in writing and reading.

Minneapolis College of Art and Design

Minneapolis, Minnesota

Independent, coed. Urban campus. Total enrollment: 543.

Degrees Bachelor of Fine Arts in the areas of design, fine arts, media arts. Majors: advertising design, art/fine arts, furniture design, graphic design, illustration, painting/drawing, photography, printmaking, sculpture, video art. Graduate degrees offered: Master of Fine Arts in the area of visual studies. Cross-registration with Macalester College.

Art Student Profile Fall 1994: 543 total; 486 matriculated undergraduate, 29 matriculated graduate, 28 nondegree; 12% minorities, 48% females, 3% international.

Art Faculty Total: 60; 43 full-time, 17 part-time; 65% of full-time faculty have terminal degrees. Graduate students teach a few undergraduate courses. Undergraduate student–faculty ratio: 12:1.

Student Life Student groups include Friday Film Series, Open Mic (poetry readings), International Association of Graphic Artists Student Chapter. Special housing available for art students.

Expenses for 1995–96 Application fee: $35. Tuition: $13,870 full-time, $462 per credit part-time. Part-time mandatory fees: $34 per semester. Full-time mandatory fees: $68. College room only: $1920 (minimum). Special program-related fees: $60 for computer lab fee, $20–$60 for lab fees, $50–$60 for design fees, $50 for foundation studies fees.

Financial Aid Program-specific awards for Fall of 1994: 1 Abby Weed Grey Award for transfer students ($6000), 1 Minneapolis College of Art and Design Portfolio Award for freshmen ($6000), 1–20 Minneapolis College of Art and Design Admissions Awards for freshmen ($2000).

Application Procedures Deadline—freshmen and transfers: continuous. Required: essay, high school transcript, college transcript(s) for transfer students, letter of recommendation, portfolio, SAT I or ACT test scores. Recommended: minimum 2.0 high school GPA, interview. Portfolio reviews held as needed on campus and off campus on National Portfolio Days; the submission of slides may be substituted for portfolios.

Contact Admissions Department, Minneapolis College of Art and Design, 2501 Stevens Avenue South, Minneapolis, Minnesota 55404; 612-874-3760, fax: 612-874-3704, E-mail address: admissions@mn.mcad.edu.

More about the College

Program Facilities Computer Center: seven labs and a campus network (120 seats), graphics design, digital media, 3-D animation, and Internet and E-mail access; Media Center: black-and-white and color photography facilities (more than 50 enlargers), two production lighting studios, super-8mm and 16mm synchronous sound films, film/video animation, video production—Hi8 or ¾-inch formats, tapeless digital suite, B-track tape suite, and computer facilities for image capturing and manipulation. 3-D Shop: fabrication facility; metals, plastic, and wood facilities: metals area—gas and arc welding; foundry for metals casting; and a gas-fired forge for blacksmithing projects. Library: 60,000 books and bound periodicals, 200 current magazine subscriptions, picture files, 100,000 slides, videos, films, laser disks, compact disks, and audiocassettes. Also featured are painting studios (collective and individual spaces); and printmaking shop for intaglio, lithography, relief, serigraphy, and book arts; a papermaking studio; individual student work spaces; on-campus housing; an on-campus bookstore; and an Apple computer store.

Student Exhibition Opportunities Seven dedicated exhibition spaces; policy that permits the use of the walls, halls, and grounds of both classroom buildings for installations and exhibiting art work and design projects; Calhoun Square Gallery; an off-campus student exhibition program; and auditoriums equipped to present media work in film and video.

Special Programs Florence Honors Program: MCAD is the only college in the United States to have an exchange with three colleges in Florence, Italy. Designs Work Center offers an on-campus design internship. The Language Center gives advice and feedback on writing, research, and study skills.

The Minneapolis College of Art and Design is a private college that focuses exclusively on the education of undergraduate and graduate students in visual art and design. Founded in 1886 in a modest studio above a library, MCAD's campus shares a city block with the Minneapolis Institute of Arts and the Children's Theater Company and is located in a vibrant city that is known for its support of the arts.

MCAD offers the Bachelor of Fine Arts and the Master of Fine Arts degrees. The curriculum is based on the belief that to become a professional artist or designer, one must study theory and skill as well as form and content.

MCAD's Bachelor of Fine Arts program offers majors in design, fine arts, media arts, and interdisciplinary studies. Areas of study include painting, drawing, printmaking, sculpture, advertising design, graphic design, furniture design, illustration, photography, video, film, computer graphics, and sound. All majors include elective courses. The electives may be taken in the student's major area of study, which provides an opportunity for in-depth, concentrated study, or used to explore the rich diversity of courses in any of the major areas of study.

No matter what the major area of concentration, the flexibility of the program provides endless potential for exciting and stimulating advanced study. At MCAD, students take responsibility for their own educational experiences. They devise independent study projects, take courses through the Mobility program at other select colleges such as Macalester College in St. Paul, and earn tuition-free credits in MCAD's Continuing Studies program.

Students can study off-campus through the College's special programs in New York City; Florence, Italy; or Osaka, Japan. And, with special approval, students can spend a semester off-campus working with a specific artist or designer at another college or on the road. In the past, students have spent a semester in the Far East, where they studied with a Balinese mask maker, or traveled to Paris or throughout Africa making videos and shooting photographs. Another student worked in a design firm in London. Other students prefer to remain on campus and create independent studies that are either interdisciplinary or incorporate multimedia.

MCAD prepares students for the future. The Career Development office provides assistance with résumé writing and interview skills. Internships as well as job placement are available. Visiting artists, designers, and alumni are brought on campus to meet with students to share their experience and expertise.

MCAD has many advantages—a curriculum that encourages exploration, spacious studios, and state-of-the art equipment. At MCAD's core are an experienced and talented faculty, motivated and curious students, classes in which students receive much personal attention, and a rigorous liberal studies program that prepares students for their future as visual artists. The College's programs teach students how to think conceptually, to analyze and theorize, to solve problems, and to make art.

Mississippi State University

Mississippi State, Mississippi

State-supported, coed. Small-town campus. Total enrollment: 13,371.

Degrees Bachelor of Fine Arts in the areas of fine arts, graphic design. Majors: art/fine arts, ceramic art and design, commercial art, computer animation, computer graphics, graphic arts, painting/drawing, photography, printmaking, sculpture, studio art.

Art Student Profile Fall 1994: 165 total; all matriculated undergraduate; 8% minorities, 1% international.

Art Faculty Total: 14; 10 full-time, 4 part-time; 99% of full-time faculty have terminal degrees. Graduate students do not teach undergraduate courses. Undergraduate student–faculty ratio: 12:1.

Expenses for 1994–95 Application fee: $15. State resident tuition: $2561 full-time, $83 per credit hour part-time. Nonresident tuition: $5021 full-time, $186 per credit hour part-time. Part-time mandatory fees: $23.54 per credit hour. College room and board: $3084. College room only: $1400. Special program-related fees: $40–$60 for supplies.

Financial Aid Program-specific awards for Fall of 1994: 3 Gulman Scholarships for freshmen ($1000), 3 Johnston Awards for sophomores ($500), 3 Clifford Awards for sophomores ($500).

Application Procedures Deadline—freshmen and transfers: July 26. Required: high school transcript, college transcript(s) for transfer students, minimum 2.0 high school GPA, SAT I or ACT test scores. Recommended: essay, letter of recommendation, interview, video, portfolio. Portfolio reviews held 2 times on campus; the submission of slides may be substituted for portfolios.

Undergraduate Contact Linda Hightower, Head, Art Department, Mississippi State University, P.O. Box 5182, Starkville, Mississippi 39762; 601-325-2970, fax: 601-325-3850, E-mail address: da@ra.msstate.edu.

Mississippi University for Women

Columbus, Mississippi

State-supported, primarily women. Small-town campus. Total enrollment: 3,020.

Degrees Bachelor of Fine Arts in the area of fine arts. Majors: art education, art/fine arts, ceramic art and design, graphic arts, interior design, painting/drawing, printmaking.

Art Student Profile Fall 1994: 68 total; 65 matriculated undergraduate, 1 matriculated graduate, 2 nondegree; 20% minorities, 80% females, 1% international.

Art Faculty Total: 9; 6 full-time, 3 part-time; 100% of full-time faculty have terminal degrees. Graduate students do not teach undergraduate courses. Undergraduate student–faculty ratio: 12:1.

Student Life Student groups include Art Students League, American Society of Interior Designers, Kappa Pi.

Expenses for 1995–96 State resident tuition: $2244 full-time, $93.50 per semester hour part-time. Nonresident tuition: $4746 full-time, $197.66 per semester hour part-time. Full-time mandatory fees: $505. College room and board: $2450. College room only: $1160.

Financial Aid Program-specific awards for Fall of 1994: 5–7 Specified Scholarships for program majors ($250–$500), 10–12 Division Scholarships for program majors ($250–$500).

Application Procedures Deadline—freshmen and transfers: continuous. Required: high school transcript, college transcript(s) for transfer students, minimum 2.0 high school GPA, portfolio, SAT I test score only. Recommended: interview. Portfolio reviews held 1 time on campus.

Undergraduate Contact Dr. Sue S. Coates, Head, Division of Fine and Performing Arts, Mississippi University for Women, Box W-70, Columbus, Mississippi 39701; 601-329-7341, fax: 601-329-7348.

Montclair State University

Upper Montclair, New Jersey

State-supported, coed. Suburban campus. Total enrollment: 12,675.

Degrees Bachelor of Fine Arts in the areas of studio art, painting, drawing, sculpture, ceramics, fibers, graphic design, illustration, printmaking, photography. Majors: art education, ceramic art and design, fibers, graphic design, illustration, painting/drawing, photography, printmaking, sculpture, studio art.

Art Student Profile Fall 1994: 290 total; all matriculated undergraduate; 13% minorities, 83% females, 5% international.

Art Faculty Total: 43; 19 full-time, 24 part-time; 90% of full-time faculty have terminal degrees. Graduate students do not teach undergraduate courses. Undergraduate student–faculty ratio: 16:1.

Expenses for 1994–95 Application fee: $35. State resident tuition: $3000 full-time, $94.50 per semester hour part-time. Nonresident tuition: $4248 full-time, $133.50 per semester hour part-time. College room and board: $4834. College room only: $3160. Special program-related fees: $15–$50 for studio lab fee.

Financial Aid Program-specific awards for Fall of 1994: 1–2 Anne Chapman Memorial Awards for artistically talented ($200), 1 Ellen Mohammed Scholarship for minority student art majors ($500), 1–10 Art Directors Club Scholarships for sophomore, junior and senior graphic design and illustration majors ($1000), 3 Montclair Craft Guild Awards for competition winners ($200), 1 Ruth Lewin Award for art education majors ($1000).

Application Procedures Deadline—freshmen: March 1; transfers: May 1. Notification date—freshmen and transfers: continuous. Required: high school transcript, interview, portfolio. Portfolio reviews held 4–6 times on campus and off campus in New York, NY; Philadelphia, PA; the submission of slides may be substituted for portfolios when distance is prohibitive.

Undergraduate Contact Klaus Schnitzer, BFA Advisor, Fine Arts Department, Montclair State University, 1 Normal Avenue, Upper Montclair, New Jersey 07043; 201-655-4750, fax: 201-655-5279.

Montserrat College of Art

Beverly, Massachusetts

Independent, coed. Suburban campus. Total enrollment: 292.

Degrees Bachelor of Fine Arts in the areas of painting, drawing, printmaking, photography, graphic design, illustration, sculpture, art teacher certification. Majors: art education, art/fine arts, graphic design, illustration, photography, printmaking, sculpture. Cross-registration with Northeast Consortium of Colleges and Universities in Massachusetts, Association of Independent Colleges of Art and Design.

Art Student Profile Fall 1994: 291 total; all matriculated undergraduate; 10% minorities, 45% females, 10% international.

Art Faculty Total: 51; 14 full-time, 37 part-time; 90% of full-time faculty have terminal degrees. Graduate students do not teach undergraduate courses. Undergraduate student–faculty ratio: 11:1.

Student Life Special housing available for art students.

Expenses for 1995–96 Application fee: $30. Tuition: $9730 full-time, $397 per credit part-time. College room only: $2780. Special program-related fees: $250 for model fees, material fees, equipment fees.

Financial Aid Program-specific awards for Fall of 1994: 104 Montserrat Grants for those demonstrating need ($1670), 13 Merit Awards for program majors ($1000), 2 Dean's Merit Awards for program majors demonstrating need ($3000), 1 Presidential Award for program majors demonstrating need ($6000–$8000).

Application Procedures Deadline—freshmen and transfers: August 1. Notification date—freshmen and transfers: August 15. Required: essay, high school transcript, college transcript(s) for transfer students, minimum 2.0 high school GPA, interview, portfolio, SAT I or ACT test scores, minimum combined SAT I score of 950, minimum composite ACT score of 17. Recommended: 2 letters of recommendation. Portfolio reviews held continuously on campus and off campus on National Portfolio Days; the submission of slides may be substituted for portfolios if a campus visit is impossible.

Undergraduate Contact Lena Hill, Admissions Secretary, Montserrat College of Art, Box 26, Beverly, Massachusetts 01915; 508-921-2350, fax: 508-922-4268.

More about the School

Additional Educational Opportunities A variety of programs provide cocurricular opportunities for Montserrat students to study abroad, or at other colleges, or to take advantage of special internship experiences tailored to individual needs. Montserrat has a number of programs that bring visiting artists and other professionals to the college to present their work and ideas to the Montserrat community. A weekly lecture series provides a diverse schedule of slide lectures, performance pieces, panel discussions, and other events. In addition, the Montserrat gallery offers gallery talks and other opportunities for discussion with artists, curators, and scholars. Academic credit may be awarded for internships completed outside the college in an approved setting. Students intern in galleries, design firms, and other art-related areas. Montserrat is a member of the Northeast Consortium of Colleges and Universities in Massachusetts (NECCUM), which allows students attending any member college to take two classes per semester and to use the library facilities at any other NECCUM institution at no additional charge. In addition, Montserrat is a member of the Association of Independent Colleges of Art and Design (AICAD). An association of internationally recognized colleges of art and design, AICAD provides numerous benefits to students, which include a student mobility program and access to international study opportunities. Montserrat also has a sister school, the Niigata Design College in Niigata City, Japan, and offers two summer programs in Italy with La Scuola del Vedere. The Italian summer program focuses on painting, drawing, and photography and allows for an intensive five-week studio experience in another culture.

Montserrat College of Art is a vital learning community of both student and faculty artists and scholars. Because members of this community share intense involvement in the arts and commitment to education, the atmosphere is one in which students find both support for the rigorous exploration of art and opportunity for additional study in the liberal arts. The major areas of study at Montserrat are painting and drawing, illustration, graphic design, printmaking, photography, sculpture, and teacher certification. Student interaction within the studio and the classroom is central to this experience, but the whole of student life outside of formal classes is also shaped by this passion for art.

Montserrat is located in Beverly, Massachusetts, a pleasant residential city convenient to Boston. The city has a harbor and several parks and beaches on the ocean. A number of other picturesque fishing harbors are nearby in Gloucester, Marblehead, and Rockport. The historic town of Salem, with its noted Peabody Essex Museum, is immediately adjacent to Beverly. In just 30 minutes by train or car, one can be in the center of Boston, with its many galleries, museums, and libraries, and with the shopping, sports, and entertainment facilities of a great city. Students find it easy to live and work in Beverly, while enjoying convenient access to a major metropolitan area.

Montserrat provides an intensive visual arts education that enables students to sustain a lifelong involvement in art and design. After graduation, Montserrat students have the opportunity to enter a professional world that offers many possible roles. Depending upon the abilities and interests of the individual, one may work with an agency or as a freelance artist, designer, or illustrator; sell art work through a gallery; work as a designer within a business, government agency, or institution; work in a museum or gallery; operate any of a number of art-related businesses; teach visual arts; or pursue art as a personal interest for its own sake rather than as a specific career. Whatever the individual's goals or specific interest, students remark about how much they learn from Montserrat's faculty of professional artists and designers and how the advantage of being in a close-knit community has helped them define their unique role within the visual arts.

Moore College of Art and Design

Philadelphia, Pennsylvania

Independent, women only. Urban campus. Total enrollment: 365.

Degrees Bachelor of Fine Arts in the areas of graphic design, illustration, fashion design, interior design, textile design, two dimensional fine arts, three dimensional fine arts. Majors: 2-dimensional studies, 3-dimensional studies, fashion design and technology, graphic arts, illustration, interior design, textile arts.

Art Student Profile Fall 1994: 533 total; 329 matriculated undergraduate, 204 nondegree; 20% minorities, 100% females, 6% international.

Art Faculty Total: 70; 36 full-time, 34 part-time; 65% of full-time faculty have terminal degrees. Graduate students do not teach undergraduate courses. Undergraduate student–faculty ratio: 8:1.

Student Life Special housing available for art students.

Estimated Expenses for 1995–96 Application fee: $35. Comprehensive fee of $19,565 includes full-time tuition ($14,097), mandatory fees ($325), and college room and board ($5143). Part-time tuition: $600 per credit. Special program-related fees: .

Financial Aid Program-specific awards for Fall of 1994: 2 National Art Honor Society Awards for talented students ($3500), 1 Evelyn A. Whittaker Award for those demonstrating need and talent ($14,100), 100 Moore College of Art and Design Presidential and Merit Awards for academically and artistically talented students ($500–$5500), 10 W. W. Smith Awards for those demonstrating talent and academic achievement ($2000), 1 Moore College of Art and Design Partnership Award for Philadelphia public school applicants demonstrating need ($14,100).

Moore College of Art and Design *(continued)*

Application Procedures Deadline—freshmen and transfers: continuous. Required: high school transcript, college transcript(s) for transfer students, minimum 2.0 high school GPA, portfolio, SAT I or ACT test scores, minimum combined SAT I score of 650, minimum composite ACT score of 16. Recommended: essay, interview. Portfolio reviews held continuously on campus and off campus on National Portfolio Days; the submission of slides may be substituted for portfolios when distance is prohibitive.

Undergraduate Contact Karina Dayich, Associate Director of Admissions, Moore College of Art and Design, 20th and The Parkway, Philadelphia, Pennsylvania 19103-1179; 215-568-4515, fax: 215-568-8017.

Roland Dille Center for the Arts

Moorhead State University

Moorhead, Minnesota

State-supported, coed. Urban campus. Total enrollment: 7,037.

Degrees Bachelor of Fine Arts in the areas of ceramics, graphic design, painting, pictorial illustration, art education, photography, printmaking, sculpture. Majors: art education, art/fine arts, graphic arts. Cross-registration with Concordia College, North Dakota State University.

Art Student Profile Fall 1994: 233 total; all matriculated undergraduate; 4% minorities, 60% females, 2% international.

Art Faculty Total: 17; 10 full-time, 7 part-time; 100% of full-time faculty have terminal degrees. Graduate students do not teach undergraduate courses. Undergraduate student–faculty ratio: 18:1.

Student Life Student groups include Students Involved in Visual Arts, Straw Hat Summer Theatre, Academic Year Theatre.

Estimated Expenses for 1995–96 Application fee: $15. State resident tuition: $2332 full-time, $72.85 per credit part-time. Nonresident tuition: $5060 full-time, $101.40 per credit part-time. Part-time mandatory fees: $15.75 per credit. Wisconsin and South Dakota residents pay tuition at the rate they would pay if attending a comparable state-supported institution in their home state. North Dakota residents pay approximately 25% above Minnesota state tuition. Full-time mandatory fees: $378. College room and board: $2912. College room only: $1695.

Financial Aid Program-specific awards for Fall of 1994: 10 Talent Awards for freshmen program majors ($300), 7 Talent Awards for upperclass program majors ($500).

Application Procedures Deadline—freshmen and transfers: August 7. Notification date—freshmen and transfers: continuous. Required: high school transcript, college transcript(s) for transfer students, minimum 2.0 high school GPA, SAT I or ACT test scores, minimum composite ACT score of 21. Recommended: portfolio. Auditions held on campus. Portfolio reviews held continuously on campus; the submission of slides may be substituted for portfolios with permission of the chair.

Undergraduate Contact Jean Lange, Admissions Director, Moorhead State University, 1104 7th Avenue South, Moorhead, Minnesota 56563; 218-236-2161, fax: 218-236-2168.

Mount Allison University

Sackville, New Brunswick

Province-supported, coed. Small-town campus. Total enrollment: 2,376.

Degrees Bachelor of Fine Arts in the areas of painting, photography, printmaking, sculpture. Majors: art/fine arts, painting/drawing, photography, printmaking, sculpture, studio art. Cross-registration with Université de Strasbourg, France; Universitat Tubingen, Germany.

Art Student Profile Fall 1994: 99 total; all matriculated undergraduate; 70% females, 4% international.

Art Faculty Total. 8, 8 full-time; 85% of full-time faculty have terminal degrees. Graduate students do not teach undergraduate courses. Undergraduate student–faculty ratio: 11:1.

Expenses for 1994–95 Application fee: $20. Canadian resident tuition: $2890 full-time, $580 per course part-time. Nonresident tuition: $6035 full-time, $1210 per course part-time. (All figures are in Canadian dollars.). Full-time mandatory fees: $378. College room and board: $5055. Special program-related fees: $600–$1,500 for supplies.

Financial Aid Program-specific awards for Fall of 1994 available.

Application Procedures Deadline—freshmen: April 1; transfers: July 1. Required: high school transcript, minimum 3.0 high school GPA, 2 letters of recommendation, portfolio. Portfolio reviews held 1 time on campus; the submission of slides may be substituted for portfolios.

Undergraduate Contact Jeffrey Hollett, Director of Admissions, Mount Allison University, Gairdner Building, Sackville, New Brunswick E0A 3C0, Canada; 506-364-2270, fax: 506-364-2262, E-mail address: jhollett@mta.ca.

Murray State University

Murray, Kentucky

State-supported, coed. Small-town campus. Total enrollment: 7,960.

Degrees Bachelor of Fine Arts in the areas of studio art, art education. Majors: art education, ceramic art and design, design, graphic design, jewelry and metalsmithing, painting/drawing, photography, printmaking, sculpture, weaving/surface design, wood.

Art Student Profile Fall 1994: 193 total; all matriculated undergraduate; 3% minorities, 46% females, 1% international.

Art Faculty Total: 16; 14 full-time, 2 part-time; 100% of full-time faculty have terminal degrees. Graduate students do not teach undergraduate courses. Undergraduate student–faculty ratio: 14:1.

Expenses for 1995–96 Application fee: $15. State resident tuition: $1680 full-time, $72 per credit hour part-time. Nonresident tuition: $5040 full-time, $210 per credit hour part-time. Full-time mandatory fees: $260. College room and board: $3000. College room only: $1275.

Financial Aid Program-specific awards for Fall of 1994: 15–20 Department of Art Scholarships for program majors ($500–$1000).

Application Procedures Deadline—freshmen and transfers: continuous. Required: high school transcript, ACT test score only, minimum composite ACT score of 18.

Undergraduate Contact Dick Dougherty, Chair, Department of Art, Murray State University, P.O. Box 9, Murray, Kentucky 42071; 502-762-3784, fax: 502-762-3920.

New England School of Art and Design

Boston, Massachusetts

Independent. Total enrollment: 118.

Degrees Bachelor of Fine Arts in the areas of graphic design, interior design, fine arts. Majors: graphic design, illustration, interior design. Mandatory cross-registration with Suffolk University.

Art Student Profile Fall 1994: 100 total; all matriculated undergraduate.

Art Faculty Total: 46; 6 full-time, 40 part-time. Graduate students do not teach undergraduate courses.

Student Life Student groups include American Society of Interior Designers.

Expenses for 1995–96 Application fee: $25. Tuition: $10,240 full-time, $490 per credit part-time. Part-time mandatory fees: $25 per term. Full-time mandatory fees: $810.

Financial Aid Program-specific awards for Fall of 1994: 8–15 J. W. S. Cox Scholarships for program majors ($1000–$1500).

Application Procedures Deadline—freshmen and transfers: continuous. Required: essay, high school transcript, 2 letters of recommendation, portfolio. Recommended: interview. Portfolio reviews held when interviews are also scheduled on campus; the submission of slides may be substituted for portfolios when distance is prohibitive.

Undergraduate Contact Anne Blevins, Director of Admissions, New England School of Art and Design, 28 Newbury Street, Boston, Massachusetts 02116; 617-536-0383 ext. 11.

New Mexico Highlands University

Las Vegas, New Mexico

State-supported, coed. Small-town campus. Total enrollment: 2,797.

Degrees Bachelor of Fine Arts in the areas of sculpture, printmaking, painting, foundry, ceramics, jewelry. Majors: applied art, art/fine arts, ceramic art and design, computer graphics, graphic arts, illustration, jewelry and metalsmithing, painting/drawing, photography, printmaking, sculpture, studio art.

Art Student Profile Fall 1994: 135 total; 70 matriculated undergraduate, 65 nondegree; 80% minorities, 55% females, 5% international.

Art Faculty Total: 8; 3 full-time, 5 part-time; 67% of full-time faculty have terminal degrees. Graduate students do not teach undergraduate courses. Undergraduate student–faculty ratio: 12:1.

Expenses for 1995–96 Application fee: $15. State resident tuition: $1506 full-time, $62.75 per semester hour part-time. Nonresident tuition: $6204 full-time. Nonresident part-time tuition per semester hour ranges from $62.75 to $258.50. College room and board: $2796. College room only: $1200. Special program-related fees: $45 for studio fees.

Financial Aid Program-specific awards for Fall of 1994: 2 Shula Awards for program majors ($1500).

Application Procedures Deadline—freshmen and transfers: May 15. Notification date—freshmen and transfers: continuous. Required: high school transcript, minimum 2.0 high school GPA.

Undergraduate Contact Secretary, Fine Arts Department, New Mexico Highlands University, Burris Hall, Las Vegas, New Mexico 87701; 505-454-3238.

New Mexico State University

Las Cruces, New Mexico

State-supported, coed. Suburban campus. Total enrollment: 15,645.

Degrees Bachelor of Fine Arts in the area of studio art. Majors: ceramic art and design, graphic design, jewelry and metalsmithing, painting/drawing, photography, printmaking, sculpture. Graduate degrees offered: Master of Fine Arts in the area of studio art.

Art Student Profile Fall 1994: 1,118 total; 160 matriculated undergraduate, 20 matriculated graduate, 938 nondegree.

Art Faculty Total: 12; 10 full-time, 2 part-time; 100% of full-time faculty have terminal degrees. Graduate students teach about a quarter undergraduate courses.

Expenses for 1994–95 Application fee: $10. State resident tuition: $1980 full-time, $76 per credit part-time. Nonresident tuition: $6432 full-time, $251 per credit part-time. Full-time mandatory fees: $48. College room and board: $2592 (minimum). College room only: $1486 (minimum).

New Mexico State University *(continued)*

Application Procedures Deadline—freshmen and transfers: August 14. Required: high school transcript.

Contact Joshua Rose, Head, Art Department, New Mexico State University, Box 30001, Department 3572, Las Cruces, New Mexico 88003-0001; 505-646-1705, fax: 505-646-8036.

Parsons School of Design

New School for Social Research

New York, New York

Independent, coed. Urban campus. Total enrollment: 1,912.

Degrees Bachelor of Fine Arts in the areas of fine art, illustration, communication design, fashion design, product design, environmental design, interior design, photography. Majors: applied art, art/fine arts, ceramic art and design, commercial art, drafting and design, fashion design, furniture design, glass, graphic arts, illustration, interior design, jewelry and metalsmithing, painting/drawing, photography, sculpture, studio art, textile arts. Graduate degrees offered: Master of Fine Arts in the areas of painting, sculpture, lighting design. Cross-registration with Eugene Lang College, New School for Social Research.

Art Student Profile Fall 1994: 4,311 total; 2,017 matriculated undergraduate, 151 matriculated graduate, 2,143 nondegree; 42% minorities, 67% females, 33% international.

Art Faculty Total: 399; 34 full-time, 365 part-time. Graduate students teach a few undergraduate courses. Undergraduate student–faculty ratio: 15:1.

Student Life Student groups include Student Gallery. Special housing available for art students.

Expenses for 1994–95 Application fee: $30. Comprehensive fee of $22,600 includes full-time tuition ($15,030), mandatory fees ($150), and college room and board ($7420). College room only: $5170. Part-time tuition: $510 per credit. Part-time mandatory fees: $150 per year. Special program-related fees: $100 for studio materials or equipment fees.

Financial Aid Program-specific awards for Fall of 1994: 750 Parsons Scholarships for those demonstrating need ($4000–$12,000), 45 University Scholars Scholarships for African-American and Latino students demonstrating need ($3000), 70 Parsons Restricted Scholarships for those demonstrating need and academic achievement ($1500–$7000).

Application Procedures Deadline—freshmen and transfers: July 1. Notification date—freshmen and transfers: August 1. Required: high school transcript, college transcript(s) for transfer students, minimum 2.0 high school GPA, interview, portfolio, SAT I or ACT test scores, home examination. Recommended: minimum 3.0 high school GPA. Portfolio reviews held continuously by appointment on campus; the submission of slides may be substituted for portfolios when distance is prohibitive.

Contact Nadine Bourgeois, Director of Admissions, Parsons School of Design, New School for Social Research, 66 Fifth Avenue, New York, New York 10011; 212-229-8910, fax: 212-229-8975.

More about the School

Program Facilities Black-and-white and color darkrooms; image enhancement technology; computer illustration; animation; painting, sculpture, printmaking studios; welding; fashion design studios; computer-aided fashion design; jewelry/metals, clay, mass-production, furniture/wood shops; ALIAS 3-D computer design; AutoCAD; exhibition systems; drafting studios; desktop publishing; computer graphics; Design Library; resource/materials libraries.

Faculty, Critics, and Alumni Donna Karan '68, visiting critic: CDFA lifetime recipient, Coty Hall of Fame; Fred Woodward, faculty: art director, *Rolling Stone,* two gold medals—1994 Society of Publication; Isaac Mizrahi '82, visiting critic: *New York Times* 1989 leading fashion designer; Kevin Walz, faculty: cover, *Interiors* magazine, April 1994; Joan Snyder, faculty: painter, Hirschl & Adler gallery; Barbara Nessim, department chair: cover illustrator, *Time,* Levi's campaign; Jill Ciment, faculty: author, *The Law of Falling Bodies;* Adrian '22: MGM costume designer, *Wizard of Oz;* Albert Hadley '49: Parish-Hadley interior design; Michael Donovan '69 and Nancye Green '73: interior/graphic design, Ronald Reagan Presidential Library; Peter de Seve '81: cover illustrator, *New Yorker, New York Times Magazine;* David Spada '83: jewelry designer to performers such as Madonna.

Student Performance/Exhibition Opportunities Student gallery, senior exhibitions, Fashion Critics Awards Show.

Special Programs Internships/career placement; competitions/collaborations with Dupont, Reebok, Perry Ellis, Kodak, and Samsung; summer and freshman ESL; Summer College and High School: Paris, New York; Exchange/Mobility: Parsons Paris, U.S., Amsterdam, London, Stockholm, the Netherlands; Affiliates: Japan, Dominican Republic, Korea; HEOP: financial and tutoring support for eligible students; lecture series on contemporary art/design issues.

In 1996 Parsons School of Design will turn 100 years old. Throughout its history, the School has added academic programs, students, and campuses. Parsons has responded to and anticipated shifts in art and design by changing curriculum and adding new technologies and vital faculty members.

Specialization remains a feature of the business landscape, but interdisciplinary design is gaining value. To achieve both aims from the start, freshmen are immersed in historical and contemporary ideas, visual analysis, and personal exploration, and they complete projects in various design disciplines before selecting a major.

The main campus at Greenwich Village in New York City is surrounded by brownstones, tree-lined streets, unique shops, restaurants, and galleries. Within walking distance of the campus are three residence halls that house primarily undergraduates. The Housing Office assists students in finding apartments. The Student Center Gallery and Health Clinic are recent improvements. New clubs emerge each year—such as the Student

Gallery Committee, Polar Surf Club, Parsons Film Society, Parson Volunteers, and ethnic and religious clubs. The Student Advisory Council meets regularly with the Dean.

Parsons has computer facilities for nearly every area of art and design. The Fashion Design Department unveiled Phase I of its new computing center. The School added freshman and continuing education labs to its computer graphics and design facility.

Parsons also has a midtown campus in the fashion district. At both locations, New York City is a main resource. The museums, galleries, exhibitions, and stores that students frequent also show the work of faculty members, who are working professionals in their field.

In turn, industry approaches Parsons. In 1993–1994, Parsons began working with Perry Ellis International on new products and on designing with computers. Internships and competitions with Reebok, Dupont, Kodak, and The Gap are typical. David Dworkin, president and CEO of Carter Hawley Hale Stores, Inc. has said, "No one unlocks that creativity—and gives it the tools that touch us—better than Parsons. It's an international treasure."

Parsons' perspective is global. The School has a Paris B.F.A. program and study-abroad option; affiliates in Japan, the Dominican Republic, and Korea; students from seventy countries; and exchange programs in London, Amsterdam, Stockholm, and Sweden. English as a second language courses are integrated with studio curricula, but Parsons' teaching method is primarily American. Students complete and pitch real-world design assignments. Summer programs in New York and Paris give college and high school students an intensive sample of this approach. In all programs, the work of artists and designers from all over the world, past and present, inspires students to find their own voices.

Many Parsons graduates become leaders in their field—some achieving brand-name status like Donna Karan, Isaac Mizrahi, and Albert Hadley. Graduates have completed prestigious design projects such as the Ronald Reagan Presidential Library and Hillary Clinton's inaugural gown. They have produced cable TV's *Nickelodeon* and designed for *Time* magazine and CBS records.

Midge Karr Fine Art Department

New York Institute of Technology

Old Westbury, New York

Independent, coed. Suburban campus. Total enrollment: 10,221.

Degrees Bachelor of Fine Arts in the areas of fine art, design graphics, computer graphics, interior design, photographics, teacher education. Majors: art education, art/fine arts, computer graphics, graphic arts, interior design, painting/drawing, photography, printmaking, sculpture, studio art.

Art Student Profile Fall 1994: 242 total; all matriculated undergraduate.

Art Faculty Total: 27; 7 full-time, 20 part-time; 90% of full-time faculty have terminal degrees. Graduate students teach about a quarter undergraduate courses. Undergraduate student–faculty ratio: 8:1.

Student Life Student groups include American Society of Interior Designers, United Artists.

Estimated Expenses for 1995–96 Application fee: $30. Comprehensive fee of $15,960 includes full-time tuition ($9190 minimum), mandatory fees ($850), and college room and board ($5920). College room only: $2980. Part-time tuition: $306 per credit. Part-time mandatory fees per semester range from $140 to $210. Special program-related fees: .

Financial Aid Program-specific awards for Fall of 1994: Presidential Awards for academically qualified applicants ($2200–$2600), Academic Achievement Awards for academically qualified applicants ($1200–$1800), Academic Incentive Awards for academically qualified applicants ($600).

Application Procedures Deadline—freshmen and transfers: continuous. Required: high school transcript, college transcript(s) for transfer students, minimum 2.0 high school GPA, interview, portfolio. Recommended: 2 letters of recommendation. Portfolio reviews held continuously on campus; the submission of slides may be substituted for portfolios for out-of-state applicants.

Undergraduate Contact Antonella Natale, Administrative Assistant, Midge Karr Fine Art Department, New York Institute of Technology, P.O. Box 8000, Old Westbury, New York 11568-8000; 516-686-7542.

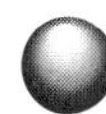

New York School of Interior Design

New York, New York

Independent, coed. Urban campus. Total enrollment: 399.

Degrees Bachelor of Fine Arts in the area of interior design. Majors: interior design.

Art Student Profile Fall 1994: 700 total; 400 matriculated undergraduate, 300 nondegree; 20% minorities, 90% females, 10% international.

Art Faculty Total: 100; 5 full-time, 95 part-time. Graduate students do not teach undergraduate courses.

Student Life Student groups include American Society of Interior Designers Student Chapter.

Expenses for 1995–96 Tuition: $11,520 full-time, $360 per credit part-time. Part-time mandatory fees: $25 per semester. Full-time mandatory fees: $50. Special program-related fees: $800 for supplies.

Financial Aid Program-specific awards for Fall of 1994: Institutional and Endowed Scholarships for program majors ($1000–$5000).

Application Procedures Deadline—freshmen and transfers: continuous. Required: essay, high school transcript, minimum 2.0 high school GPA, letter of recommendation, portfolio, SAT I or ACT test scores. Recommended: minimum 3.0 high school GPA, interview. Portfolio reviews held continuously on campus; the submission of slides may be substituted for portfolios when distance is prohibitive.

Undergraduate Contact Elaine M. Anton, Director of Admissions, New York School of Interior Design, 170

New York School of Interior Design *(continued)*

East 70th Street, New York, New York 10021; 212-472-1500 ext. 19, fax: 212-472-1867.

More about the School

Throughout its history, the New York School of Interior Design (NYSID) has devoted all of its resources to a single field of study—interior design. NYSID is specifically designed for those who wish to pursue a career in one or more of the various fields of interior design and wish to do so under the guidance of a faculty composed of practicing designers, architects, and art and architectural historians. The various academic programs compose an integrated curriculum covering interior design concepts, history of art, architecture, interiors and furniture, technical and communication skills, materials and methods, philosophy and theory, professional design procedures, and design problem solving.

Because of its select faculty and established reputation, the School continues to maintain a close relationship with the interior design industry. This provides an excellent means for students to develop associations that offer opportunities to move into the profession after completing their degree program at NYSID.

In 1994 the School moved to a new facility twice as large as its previous home. The school is located on Manhattan's upper East Side. Many of the world's most important museums, galleries, and showrooms are close by within walking distance. The city is world-renowned for its cultural activities, architecture, historic districts, and cosmopolitan urban experience.

NYSID is located on a quiet, tree-lined street in Manhattan's Upper East Side Landmark District. The School has two auditorium spaces, 10 classrooms, and is in the process of expanding its already substantial CADD lab by purchasing more state-of-the-art computer equipment and software. NYSID also has a two-story library containing a comprehensive collection of books, journals, periodicals, and trade and auction catalogs specifically devoted to the interior design field and related fine arts; a materials library; a 3,000-square-foot atelier studio; a gallery; a rooftop terrace; and on the lower-level, a full-service Cafe and dining area, an exhibition space, a faculty lounge, and an ASID student chapter office.

NYSID has an active student chapter of the American Society of Interior Designers (ASID). ASID organizes lectures, tours, workshops, and other events throughout the school year, providing an inside view of the interior design industry. Guest lecturers included Mario Buatta, Niels Diffrient, Anne Eisenhower, Charles Gwathmey, Osamo Hashimoto, Dakota Jackson, Sarah Tomerlin Lee, Renny B. Saltzman, Jay Spectre, Alexandra Stoddard, Adam Tibany, Massimo Vignelli, and James Wines.

One of the strengths of NYSID is its gallery. The Gallery under the direction of David Garrard Lowe, Director, and Sally Forbes, Assistant Director, is the setting for exciting exhibitions relating to architecture and design. Open to both students and the public, the Gallery has mounted such highly praised shows as *Perspective on Perspective, Paris in the Belle Epoque, The Grand Canal/Il Canal Grande, The Great Age of Fairs, Beaux-Arts New York,* and *Dublin: A Grand Tour.* In conjunction with its exhibitions, the Gallery sponsors lectures, symposia, and walking tours. Recent lecture subjects have included "Elsie de Wolfe and the Stanford White Connection," "Designs for a Beaux-Arts Building," "Gustave Eiffel & His Wonderful Tower," and "Palladio from Venice to Dublin." In conjunction with the exhibition, the gallery organizes an evening lecture series that students are encouraged to attend.

The New York School of Interior Design offers a two-week summer study abroad program that focuses on different European cities each year. Each area's distinctive artistic, architectural, and cultural characteristics are studied through visits to museums and historic sites as well as lectures.

The school maintains an active placement service for graduates and all current students. Students are placed in a wide variety of positions that reflect the full spectrum of job opportunities in the interior design profession. Because of its reputation in the design field, many NYSID graduates find work in the best design, architectural, and industry-related firms in New York City, across the United States, and around the world.

Tisch School of the Arts

New York University

New York, New York

Independent, coed. Urban campus. Total enrollment: 33,428.

Degrees Bachelor of Fine Arts in the area of photography. Majors: photography.

Art Student Profile Fall 1994: 120 total; all matriculated undergraduate; 19% minorities, 64% females, 10% international.

Art Faculty Total: 17; 5 full-time, 12 part-time; 80% of full-time faculty have terminal degrees. Graduate students do not teach undergraduate courses. Undergraduate student–faculty ratio: 8:1.

Student Life Student groups include Artists in the Community, Out Artists, United Artists of Color.

Expenses for 1994–95 Application fee: $45. Comprehensive fee of $26,001 includes full-time tuition ($18,739) and college room and board ($7262). Part-time tuition: $513 per credit. Part-time mandatory fees per semester range from $96 to $426. Special program-related fees: $174 for photo lab fee.

Financial Aid Program-specific awards for Fall of 1994: 3 Goddard Awards for those demonstrating financial need ($1500), 1 Wasserman Award ($3500).

Application Procedures Deadline—freshmen: January 15; transfers: April 1. Notification date—freshmen: April 1; transfers: May 15. Required: essay, high school transcript, college transcript(s) for transfer students, letter of recommendation, portfolio, SAT I or ACT test scores, resume. Recommended: minimum 3.0 high school GPA, interview. Portfolio reviews held 2 times and by appointment on campus; the submission of slides may be substituted for portfolios.

Undergraduate Contact Office of Undergraduate Admissions, New York University, 22 Washington Square North, New York, New York 10011; 212-998-4500.

Northeast Missouri State University

Kirksville, Missouri

State-supported, coed. Small-town campus. Total enrollment: 6,317.

Degrees Bachelor of Fine Arts in the areas of studio art, visual communications. Majors: art history, art/fine arts, ceramic art and design, commercial art, painting, photography, printmaking, sculpture, textile arts.

Art Student Profile Fall 1994: 149 total; all matriculated undergraduate; 2% minorities, 53% females, 2% international.

Art Faculty Total: 18; 12 full-time, 6 part-time; 84% of full-time faculty have terminal degrees. Graduate students do not teach undergraduate courses. Undergraduate student–faculty ratio: 9:1.

Student Life Student groups include Student Art History Society, Missouri Art Education Association, Art Club.

Expenses for 1995–96 State resident tuition: $2872 full-time, $120 per credit part-time. Nonresident tuition: $5152 full-time, $215 per credit part-time. Full-time mandatory fees: $18. College room and board: $3624. Special program-related fees: $10–$30 for art supplies.

Financial Aid Program-specific awards for Fall of 1994: 5 Endowed Scholarships for outstanding program majors ($200–$950), 30 Service Scholarships for program majors ($400–$700).

Application Procedures Deadline—freshmen: November 15; transfers: May 1. Notification date—freshmen: December 15. Required: essay, high school transcript, college transcript(s) for transfer students, minimum 3.0 high school GPA, SAT I or ACT test scores.

Undergraduate Contact John M. Lee, Head, Division of Fine Arts, Northeast Missouri State University, Baldwin Hall #118, Kirksville, Missouri 63501; 816-785-4417, fax: 816-785-7463, E-mail address: fa01%nemomus@academic.nemostate.edu.

Northern Illinois University

De Kalb, Illinois

State-supported, coed. Small-town campus. Total enrollment: 22,881.

Degrees Bachelor of Fine Arts in the areas of crafts, design, fine arts. Majors: applied art, art/fine arts, ceramic art and design, commercial art, computer graphics, craft design, design, graphic arts, illustration, interior design, intermedia, jewelry and metalsmithing, painting/drawing, photography, printmaking, sculpture, studio art, textile arts. Graduate degrees offered: Master of Fine Arts in the area of studio and design.

Art Student Profile Fall 1994: 1,045 total; 896 matriculated undergraduate, 149 matriculated graduate; 13% minorities, 54% females, 1% international.

Art Faculty Total: 62; 53 full-time, 9 part-time; 92% of full-time faculty have terminal degrees. Graduate students teach a few undergraduate courses. Undergraduate student–faculty ratio: 18:1.

Student Life Student groups include National Art Education Association Student Chapter, American Center for Design Student Chapter. Special housing available for art students.

Expenses for 1995–96 State resident tuition: $2930 full-time, $89.70 per credit hour part-time. Nonresident tuition: $8611 full-time, $269.10 per credit hour part-time. Part-time mandatory fees: $32 per credit hour. Full-time mandatory fees: $777. College room and board: $3416. Special program-related fees: $5–$105 for lab/materials fees.

Financial Aid Program-specific awards for Fall of 1994: 6–12 Tuition Waivers for high school seniors ($2136–$3204).

Application Procedures Deadline—freshmen and transfers: continuous. Notification date—freshmen and transfers: continuous. Required: high school transcript, college transcript(s) for transfer students, ACT test score only, minimum composite ACT score of 19, standing in top half of graduating class, completion of college preparatory courses.

Undergraduate Contact Office of Admissions, NIU, Northern Illinois University, Williston Hall Room 101, De Kalb, Illinois 60115; 815-753-0446.

Graduate Contact Robert Bornhuetter, Coordinator of Graduate Admissions in Art, School of Art, Northern Illinois University, De Kalb, Illinois 60115-2883; 815-753-0292, fax: 815-753-7701.

Northern Kentucky University

Highland Heights, Kentucky

State-supported, coed. Suburban campus. Total enrollment: 11,978.

Degrees Bachelor of Fine Arts in the areas of studio art, graphic design. Majors: ceramic art and design, graphic design, intermedia, painting/drawing, photography, printmaking, sculpture, studio art. Cross-registration with Northern Kentucky/Cincinnati Consortium of Colleges and Universities.

Art Student Profile Fall 1994: 256 total; all matriculated undergraduate.

Art Faculty Total: 27; 12 full-time, 15 part-time; 100% of full-time faculty have terminal degrees. Graduate students do not teach undergraduate courses. Undergraduate student–faculty ratio: 17:1.

Student Life Student groups include Students in Design, Mudd Club, Print Club.

Expenses for 1995–96 Application fee: $25. State resident tuition: $1960 full-time, $83 per semester hour part-time. Nonresident tuition: $5320 full-time, $223 per semester hour part-time. College room and board: $3480 (minimum). Special program-related fees: $20 for in-studio expenses, $20 for lab fees.

Financial Aid Program-specific awards for Fall of 1994: 1–2 Friends of Fine Arts Awards for continuing students ($2000), 4 University Art Awards for continuing students ($2000), 1 Schiff Scholarship for continuing students ($2000).

Northern Kentucky University *(continued)*

Application Procedures Deadline—freshmen: continuous; transfers: August 1. Required: high school transcript, portfolio, ACT test score only, minimum 3.0 college GPA. Portfolio reviews held 2 times upon completion of 60 hours of coursework or 18 hours of art on campus.

Undergraduate Contact Barbara Houghton, Chairwoman, Art Department, Northern Kentucky University, Fine Arts Center 312, Highland Heights, Kentucky 41099; 606-572-6952, fax: 606-572-6185, E-mail address: houghton@nku.edu.

Nova Scotia College of Art and Design

Halifax, Nova Scotia

Province-supported, coed. Urban campus. Total enrollment: 601.

Degrees Bachelor of Fine Arts in the areas of fine arts, studio art, crafts. Majors: art/fine arts, ceramic art and design, computer graphics, jewelry and metalsmithing, painting/drawing, photography, printmaking, sculpture, studio art, textile arts, visual communication. Graduate degrees offered: Master of Fine Arts in the areas of fine arts, design. Cross-registration with Dalhousie University, St. Mary's University, Mount St. Vincent University.

Art Student Profile Fall 1994: 566 total; 509 matriculated undergraduate, 20 matriculated graduate, 37 nondegree; 60% females, 7% international.

Art Faculty Total: 87; 42 full-time, 45 part-time; 95% of full-time faculty have terminal degrees. Graduate students teach a few undergraduate courses. Undergraduate student–faculty ratio: 13:1.

Student Life Student groups include "Rewire" (college publication), Women's Collective, Mosaic (minority ethnic group).

Expenses for 1994–95 Canadian resident tuition: $2904 full-time, $145.20 per credit part-time. Nonresident tuition: $4604 full-time, $230.20 per credit part-time. (All figures are in Canadian dollars.). Full-time mandatory fees: $148.

Financial Aid Program-specific awards for Fall of 1994: 50 Merit Scholarships for those demonstrating talent and academic achievement ($700), 10 Joseph Beuys Memorial Scholarships for those demonstrating talent and academic achievement ($1500).

Application Procedures Deadline—freshmen: May 15; transfers: May 1. Notification date—freshmen and transfers: June 20. Required: essay, high school transcript, college transcript(s) for transfer students, portfolio. Recommended: interview. Portfolio reviews held 2 times on campus; the submission of slides may be substituted for portfolios.

Undergraduate Contact Jane Harmon, Director, Student Affairs, Nova Scotia College of Art and Design, 5163 Duke Street, Halifax, Nova Scotia B3J 3J6, Canada; 902-422-7381 ext. 188, fax: 902-425-2420, E-mail address: jane@nscad6000.nscad.ns.ca.

Graduate Contact MFA Admissions, Nova Scotia College of Art and Design, 5163 Duke Street, Halifax, Nova Scotia B3J3J6, Canada; 902-422-7381 ext. 129, fax: 902-425-2420.

Ohio Northern University

Ada, Ohio

Independent-religious, coed. Small-town campus. Total enrollment: 2,872.

Degrees Bachelor of Fine Arts in the area of art. Majors: ceramic art and design, drawing, graphic design, painting, sculpture.

Art Faculty Total: 6; 4 full-time, 2 part-time; 100% of full-time faculty have terminal degrees.

Student Life Student groups include Kappa Pi, Polaris (art magazine), Art Club.

Expenses for 1995–96 Application fee: $30. Comprehensive fee of $21,240 includes full-time tuition ($16,950 minimum) and college room and board ($4290). College room only: $1875. Full-time tuition ranges up to $17,985 according to program. Part-time tuition per quarter hour ranges from $395 to $500 according to program.

Financial Aid Program-specific awards for Fall of 1994: 2 Petrillo Scholarships ($700), 5 Performance Scholarships for performance majors ($1000–$3000).

Application Procedures Deadline—freshmen and transfers: continuous. Notification date—freshmen and transfers: continuous. Required: high school transcript, SAT I or ACT test scores, minimum 2.5 high school GPA. Recommended: minimum 3.0 high school GPA. Portfolio reviews held by request on campus.

Undergraduate Contact Bruce Chesser, Chairman, Department of Art, Ohio Northern University, South Main Street, Ada, Ohio 45810; 419-772-2160, fax: 419-772-1932, E-mail address: bchesser@onu.edu.

Ohio State University

Columbus, Ohio

State-supported, coed. Urban campus. Total enrollment: 49,542.

Degrees Bachelor of Fine Arts in the areas of ceramics, glass, sculpture, painting, drawing, printmaking, photography. Majors: art/fine arts, ceramics, glass, painting/drawing, photography, printmaking, sculpture. Graduate degrees offered: Master of Fine Arts in the areas of ceramics, glass, sculpture, painting, drawing, printmaking, photography, computer art, media art.

Art Student Profile Fall 1994: 225 total; 150 matriculated undergraduate, 50 matriculated graduate, 25 nondegree.

Art Faculty Total: 25; 19 full-time, 6 part-time; 100% of full-time faculty have terminal degrees. Graduate stu-

dents teach more than half undergraduate courses. Undergraduate student–faculty ratio: 10:1.

Student Life Student groups include Student League of Independent Potters, Student Printmakers Association, Undergraduate Student Art League.

Expenses for 1995–96 Application fee: $30. State resident tuition: $3273 full-time. Nonresident tuition: $9813 full-time. Part-time tuition per quarter ranges from $179 to $1001 for state residents, $361 to $2999 for nonresidents. College room and board: $4668.

Application Procedures Deadline—freshmen and transfers: continuous. Portfolio reviews held upon completion of foundation year on campus.

Undergraduate Contact University Admissions, Ohio State University, 1800 Cannon Drive, 3rd Floor Lincoln Tower, Columbus, Ohio 43210; 614-292-5995, fax: 614-292-4818.

Graduate Contact Cathy Ellis, Administrative Secretary, Art Department, Ohio State University, 146 Hopkins Hall, 128 North Oval Mall, Columbus, Ohio 43210; 614-292-5072, fax: 614-292-1674, E-mail address: ellis.11@osu.edu.

Ohio University

Athens, Ohio

State-supported, coed. Small-town campus. Total enrollment: 18,855.

Degrees Bachelor of Fine Arts in the areas of printmaking, photography, art education, art history, ceramics, painting, graphic design, sculpture. Majors: art education, art history, ceramic art and design, graphic arts, painting/drawing, photography, printmaking, sculpture. Graduate degrees offered: Master of Fine Arts in the areas of printmaking, photography, art history, ceramics, sculpture, painting.

Art Student Profile Fall 1994: 480 total; 400 matriculated undergraduate, 80 matriculated graduate; 3% minorities, 64% females, 4% international.

Art Faculty Total: 30; 27 full-time, 3 part-time; 98% of full-time faculty have terminal degrees. Graduate students teach a few undergraduate courses. Undergraduate student–faculty ratio: 17:1.

Student Life Student groups include Students in Design, Undergraduate Art League, National Art Educators Association.

Expenses for 1995–96 Application fee: $25. State resident tuition: $3666 full-time, $118 per quarter hour part-time. Nonresident tuition: $7905 full-time, $259 per quarter hour part-time. College room and board: $4260. College room only: $2094. Special program-related fees: $5–$100 for materials fees.

Financial Aid Program-specific awards for Fall of 1994: 3–4 L. C. Mitchell Memorial Scholarships for art majors ($1000), 1 Mary Nelson Stephenson Art Memorial Award for program majors ($1500), 1 Kenneth B. Clifford Memorial Scholarship for junior/senior painting or printmaking majors ($500), 1–4 Mannaseh Cutler Memorial Scholarship for incoming students ($1000).

Application Procedures Deadline—freshmen: March 1; transfers: June 1. Required: high school transcript, SAT I test score only. Recommended: ACT test score only.

Undergraduate Contact Dianne Bouvier, Student Services Coordinator, School of Art, Ohio University, Seigfred 527, Athens, Ohio 45701; 614-593-0274, fax: 614-593-0457, E-mail address: bouvier@ouvaxa.cats.ohiou.edu.

Graduate Contact Mary Manusos, Assistant Director for Graduate Affairs, School of Art, Ohio University, Seigfred Hall, Athens, Ohio 45701; 800-766-8278, fax: 614-593-0457, E-mail address: manusos@art.ohiou.edu.

Ohio Wesleyan University

Delaware, Ohio

Independent-religious, coed. Small-town campus. Total enrollment: 1,732.

Degrees Bachelor of Fine Arts. Majors: art history, ceramic art and design, computer art, graphic design, jewelry and metalsmithing, painting/drawing, photography, printmaking, sculpture.

Art Student Profile Fall 1994: 120 total; all matriculated undergraduate.

Art Faculty Total: 10; 7 full-time, 3 part-time.

Expenses for 1995–96 Application fee: $35. Comprehensive fee of $23,445 includes full-time tuition ($17,569) and college room and board ($5876). College room only: $2974. Part-time tuition: $1950 per course.

Application Procedures Deadline—freshmen and transfers: May 1. Notification date—freshmen and transfers: continuous. Required: essay, high school transcript, 2 letters of recommendation, SAT I or ACT test scores. Recommended: interview, portfolio. Portfolio reviews held by request on campus; the submission of slides may be substituted for portfolios for large works of art.

Undergraduate Contact Justin Kronewetter, Chairperson, Fine Arts Department, Ohio Wesleyan University, 60 South Sandusky Street, Delaware, Ohio 43015; 614-368-3602, fax: 614-368-3299.

Oklahoma Baptist University

Shawnee, Oklahoma

Independent-religious, coed. Small-town campus. Total enrollment: 2,440.

Degrees Bachelor of Fine Arts in the area of studio art. Majors: studio art. Cross-registration with St. Gregory's College.

Art Student Profile Fall 1994: 17 total; all matriculated undergraduate; 10% minorities, 50% females, 10% international.

Oklahoma Baptist University *(continued)*

Art Faculty Total: 4; 2 full-time, 2 part-time; 50% of full-time faculty have terminal degrees. Graduate students do not teach undergraduate courses. Undergraduate student–faculty ratio: 9:1.

Expenses for 1995–96 Application fee: $25. Comprehensive fee of $9734 includes full-time tuition ($5960), mandatory fees ($564), and college room and board ($3210). College room only: $1380. Part-time tuition: $200 per credit hour. Part-time mandatory fee per semester (6 to 11 credits) range from $140 to $177.50. Special program-related fees: $10–$15 for material fees.

Financial Aid Program-specific awards for Fall of 1994: 10 Talentships for program majors ($500–$1500).

Application Procedures Deadline—freshmen and transfers: continuous. Required: high school transcript, college transcript(s) for transfer students, minimum 2.0 high school GPA, SAT I or ACT test scores. Recommended: portfolio. Portfolio reviews held continuously on campus; the submission of slides may be substituted for portfolios when distance is prohibitive.

Undergraduate Contact Jody Johnson, Dean of Admissions, Oklahoma Baptist University, 500 West University, Shawnee, Oklahoma 74801; 405-878-2030, fax: 405-878-2069.

Oklahoma State University

Stillwater, Oklahoma

State-supported, coed. Small-town campus. Total enrollment: 18,561.

Degrees Bachelor of Fine Arts in the areas of graphic design, studio art. Majors: graphic arts, illustration, jewelry and metalsmithing, painting/drawing, printmaking, sculpture.

Art Student Profile Fall 1994: 159 total; all matriculated undergraduate; 8% minorities, 58% females, 5% international.

Art Faculty Total: 13; 12 full-time, 1 part-time; 100% of full-time faculty have terminal degrees. Graduate students do not teach undergraduate courses. Undergraduate student–faculty ratio: 20:1.

Expenses for 1995–96 Application fee: $15. Part-time mandatory fees: $9.66 per credit hour. Full-time tuition ranges from $1458 to $1555 for state residents, $4698 to $5208 for nonresidents, according to class level. Part-time tuition per credit hour ranges from $48.60 to $51.84 for state residents, $156.60 to $173.61 for nonresidents, according to class level. Full-time mandatory fees: $290. College room and board: $3136 (minimum). College room only: $1488 (minimum). Special program-related fees: $5–$85 for consumable materials, $25–$185 for computer lab use, $25 for model fees.

Financial Aid Program-specific awards for Fall of 1994: 5 Freshmen/Transfer Scholarships for freshmen and transfer students ($1000), 5 Medical Heritage Gallery Scholarships for continuing students ($1500).

Application Procedures Deadline—freshmen and transfers: continuous. Required: high school transcript, college transcript(s) for transfer students, minimum 2.0 high school GPA, SAT I or ACT test scores, minimum combined SAT I score of 1,020, minimum composite ACT score of 21.

Undergraduate Contact Nancy B. Wilkinson, Head, Art Department, Oklahoma State University, 108 Bartlett Center, Stillwater, Oklahoma 74078; 405-744-6016.

Old Dominion University

Norfolk, Virginia

State-supported, coed. Urban campus. Total enrollment: 16,500.

Degrees Bachelor of Fine Arts in the area of studio art. Majors: art education, art/fine arts, clay and metal, fibers, graphic arts, graphic design, jewelry and metalsmithing, painting/drawing, photography, printmaking, sculpture, studio art. Graduate degrees offered: Master of Fine Arts in the area of visual studies. Cross-registration with Tidewater Community College, Norfolk State University.

Art Student Profile Fall 1994: 1,082 total; 1,025 matriculated undergraduate, 32 matriculated graduate, 25 nondegree; 29% minorities, 57% females, 17% international.

Art Faculty Total: 17; 13 full-time, 4 part-time; 100% of full-time faculty have terminal degrees. Graduate students teach a few undergraduate courses. Undergraduate student–faculty ratio: 20:1.

Student Life Student groups include Student Art League, Technoart.

Expenses for 1995–96 Application fee: $30. State resident tuition: $3990 full-time, $133 per semester hour part-time. Nonresident tuition: $10,350 full-time, $345 per semester hour part-time. Full-time mandatory fees: $96. College room and board: $4676.

Financial Aid Program-specific awards for Fall of 1994: 3 Sibley Scholarships for enrolled program students by portfolio competition ($1000), 2 Margolious Scholarships for enrolled program students by portfolio competition ($700), 1–2 Gorlinsky Scholarships for enrolled program students by portfolio competition ($300–$500).

Application Procedures Deadline—freshmen: May 1; transfers: July 1. Required: high school transcript, college transcript(s) for transfer students, minimum 2.0 high school GPA, portfolio. Portfolio reviews held 1 time for transfer applicants on campus; the submission of slides may be substituted for portfolios.

Undergraduate Contact Michael Fanizza, Chair, Art Department, Old Dominion University, Visual Arts Building, 49th Street, Norfolk, Virginia 23529; 804-683-4047, fax: 804-683-5923, E-mail address: maf100f@elvis.va.odu.edu.

Graduate Contact Ron Snapp, Graduate Program Director, Art Department, Old Dominion University,

Visual Arts Building, 49th Street, Norfolk, Virginia 23529; 804-683-4047, fax: 804-683-5923, E-mail address: rws100f@ elvis.fpa.odu.edu.

Oregon School of Arts and Crafts

Portland, Oregon

Independent, coed. Urban campus. Total enrollment: 27.

Degrees Bachelor of Fine Arts in the area of crafts. Majors: book arts, ceramic art and design, fibers, furniture design, jewelry and metalsmithing, painting/ drawing, woodworking design. Cross-registration with Pacific Northwest College of Art, Portland State University, Portland Community College.

Art Student Profile Fall 1994: 55 total; 26 matriculated undergraduate, 29 nondegree.

Art Faculty Total: 19; 14 full-time, 5 part-time; 86% of full-time faculty have terminal degrees. Graduate students do not teach undergraduate courses. Undergraduate student–faculty ratio: 10:1.

Expenses for 1995–96 Tuition: $9000 full-time, $250 per credit part-time. Part-time mandatory fees: $90 per year. Full-time mandatory fees: $490. Special program-related fees: $350–$450 for studio fees.

Financial Aid Program-specific awards for Fall of 1994: 15 Tuition Scholarships for those demonstrating need ($1465), 19 Tuition Work Study Awards for those demonstrating need ($960).

Application Procedures Deadline—freshmen and transfers: August 1. Notification date—freshmen and transfers: August 15. Required: essay, high school transcript, college transcript(s) for transfer students, 2 letters of recommendation, interview, minimum 2.5 high school GPA, slides of portfolio. Recommended: minimum 3.0 high school GPA. Portfolio reviews held as needed on campus; the submission of slides may be substituted for portfolios.

Undergraduate Contact Penelope Hunter, Director of Admissions, Oregon School of Arts and Crafts, 8245 Southwest Barnes Road, Portland, Oregon 97225; 503-297-5544, fax: 503-297-9651.

More about the Schools

Program Facilities The campus is on the site of an 8-acre orchard 3 miles west of downtown Portland; separate and specially equipped studios for each medium; papermaking, equipment includes Hollander beater, facilities for salt, raku, and pit fringe; tapestry (including 12-foot Shamrock) and floor looms; fully equipped surface design studio; individual workbenches in metal; the central building houses library (region's most extensive collection of books, slides, and periodicals on crafts), exhibition gallery, sales shop, and cafe.

Faculty, Resident Artists, and Alumni All studio faculty are exhibiting artists. Artist-in-Residence programs bring 7 to 10 emerging and midcareer artists to campus each year for extended stays. Our year-round workshop program has recently included these visiting faculty members: Peter Beasecker, Jim Bassler, Bob Ebendorf, Timothy Ely, Warren MacKenzie, Tim McCreight, Stephen Proctor, Buzz Spector, and Barbara Lee Smith. In recent years faculty members have helped organize national conferences of their professional associations in Portland, including the Society of North American Goldsmiths, Surface Design Association, and Handweavers Guild of America.

Student Exhibit Opportunities Annual juried student exhibition in the Hoffman Gallery each May; group exhibition of thesis work each June; annual sale of student work each December.

Special Programs B.F.A. students take general education classes and some art history courses off campus. The School helps facilitate registration at other local colleges, including Portland State University. Departments may offer the option of an internship with a local artist as part of the final year of the program.

Oregon State University

Corvallis, Oregon

State-supported, coed. Small-town campus. Total enrollment: 14,336.

Degrees Bachelor of Fine Arts in the areas of art history, studio art. Majors: applied art, art/fine arts, ceramic art and design, graphic design, photography, printmaking, sculpture, studio art.

Art Student Profile Fall 1994: 545 total; 195 matriculated undergraduate, 350 nondegree.

Art Faculty Total: 20; 16 full-time, 4 part-time; 100% of full-time faculty have terminal degrees. Graduate students do not teach undergraduate courses. Undergraduate student–faculty ratio: 20:1.

Estimated Expenses for 1995–96 Application fee: $50. State resident tuition: $3048 full-time. Nonresident tuition: $9096 full-time. Part-time tuition per quarter ranges from $199 to $939 for state residents, $367 to $2787 for nonresidents. College room and board: $3830. Special program-related fees: $5–$75 for material fees.

Financial Aid Program-specific awards for Fall of 1994: 1 Fine Arts Award in Painting for freshmen and Oregon Community College transfers ($1000), 1 Matsen-Davidson Art Scholarship for freshmen or sophomore program majors ($1500), 1 Norma Siebert Print Scholarship in Art for undergraduate program majors in printmaking ($1000), 1 Yaquina Art Association Scholarship for junior or senior program majors ($1500), 1 Art Department Faculty Award for program majors ($1000), 1 Wayne Takami Memorial Scholarship for returning students ($1000).

Application Procedures Deadline—freshmen and transfers: continuous.

Contact Director of Admissions, Oregon State University, Administration Building, 14th and Jefferson, Corvallis, Oregon 97331; 503-737-4411.

Otis College of Art and Design

Los Angeles, California

Independent, coed. Urban campus. Total enrollment: 714.

Degrees Bachelor of Fine Arts in the areas of fine arts, ceramics, environmental arts, fashion design, communication arts, illustration, photography, surface design. Majors: art/fine arts, ceramic art and design, fashion design and technology, graphic design, illustration, photography, surface design. Graduate degrees offered: Master of Fine Arts in the areas of painting, sculpture, ceramics, photography.

Art Student Profile Fall 1994: 720 total; 698 matriculated undergraduate, 22 matriculated graduate; 60% minorities, 62% females, 18% international.

Art Faculty Total: 234; 28 full-time, 206 part-time; 60% of full-time faculty have terminal degrees. Graduate students teach a few undergraduate courses. Undergraduate student–faculty ratio: 14:1.

Expenses for 1995–96 Application fee: $40. Tuition: $13,950 full-time, $465 per credit part-time. Part-time mandatory fees: $360 per semester. Full-time mandatory fees: $720. College room only: $2700. Special program-related fees: $100 for departmental supply fee, $50 for lab or shop fees.

Financial Aid Program-specific awards for Fall of 1994: 535 Otis Institutional Grants for undergraduates ($4000).

Application Procedures Deadline—freshmen and transfers: continuous. Notification date—freshmen and transfers: September 1. Required: essay, high school transcript, minimum 2.0 high school GPA, portfolio. Recommended: letter of recommendation, interview. Portfolio reviews held continuously on campus and off campus on National Portfolio Days and high school visits; the submission of slides may be substituted for portfolios.

Undergraduate Contact Michael Fuller, Director of Admissions, Otis College of Art and Design, 2401 WIlshire Boulevard, Los Angeles, California 90057; 213-251-0505, fax: 213-480-0059.

Graduate Contact Roy Dowell, Chair, Graduate Studies, Otis College of Art and Design, 2401 Wilshire Boulevard, Los Angeles, California 90057; 213-251-0577, fax: 213-480-0059.

More about the College

Program Facilities The oldest and most renowned college fine arts letterpress in the city; computer labs with advanced communication tools and graphics systems; specialized interior, set, architectural, and furniture design workshops; woodworking and metalworking shops; bronze and aluminum foundry; editorial and product photography studio; video studio and video editing lab; thirty black-and-white and ten photo enlargers with mural-size developing facilities; studio- and commercial-size gas and electric kilns; lithography and etching presses; individual senior studios and on-campus graduate studios; extensive library holdings in fine art, design, art history, architecture, and critical studies and periodical subscriptions to 120 international and multidisciplinary publications.

Faculty and Guests Designers, architects, ceramicists, photographers, critical writers, and fine artists, including Michelle Clinton, Georganne Deen, Michael Davis, Amy Gerstler, Lyle Ashton Harris, Larry Johnson, Tom Knechtel, Linda Nishio, Renee Petropolis, Benjamin Weissman, Roy Dowell, Nancy Barton, and Carole Caroompas. Guest lecturers and visiting artists include Kim Abeles, Nayland Blake, Benjamin Buchloh, Jack Flam, Lynn Foulkes, David Hickey, Lauren Lesko, Donald Lipski, Robert Longo, Robert Pincus-Witten, Lari Pittman, Abigail Solomon-Godeau, Alexis Smith, Kiki Smith, Annie Sprinkle, and Millie Wilson.

Student Exhibit Opportunities Abe and Helen Bolsky Student Gallery, Otis Gallery, annual Senior Open Studio and M.F.A. Exhibition, Student Lounge.

Special Programs Spring Paris trip, Writing Lab, Tutoring Center, the only menswear program on the West Coast, study abroad and a visiting/exchange student program, summer of art program, and an extensive graphic design and illustration internship program.

Otis College of Art and Design has a 75-year reputation for its energetic assault against the status quo, whether it be in fine arts, fashion, graphic arts, photography, or the environmental arts. Founded in 1918, Otis was the first college of art in the then young city of Los Angeles and today is the only urban college of art design in southern California.

By positioning themselves in one of the world's pace-setting cities, students can draw upon the resources of the vital artistic community that fuels the Los Angeles fashion, film, fine arts, and design worlds—and enjoy the support of a welcoming professional network of Otis faculty and alumni.

The network includes individuals who have created such cultural icons as the first Walt Disney animated cartoons; videos, posters, and product design for Columbia, A&M, and Virgin Records; editorial cartoons and covers for the *Los Angeles Times, Time, Omni, the New Yorker, Buzz and American Film;* costumes for *Hoffa, Hook* and *Legends of the Fall,* and a host of Academy Award-winning films costumed by almuna Edith Head; production design for Spike Lee; and the fashion-forward imagery of such industry leaders as NIKE, Guess? Esprit, Richard Tyler, and Carole Little.

Otis alumni are featured in major museums—Whitney Museum of American Art, Museum of Modern Art, Guggenheim Museum, Museum of the Art Institute of Chicago, Corcoran Gallery of Art, L.A.'s Museum of Contemporary Art—and in galleries and artist-run exhibition spaces throughout the world.

Today's Otis students join a community dedicated to expanding artistic skills and developing personal and

Dean Mitchell

Columbus College of Art and Design—Artist

Mitchell creates works in many media. He has won numerous awards since his training at the Columbus College. He states that the visual arts must communicate to the human spirit, forcing man/woman to reflect on themselves, and their existence beyond their own self-interest to explore beauty, love, fear, hate, and greed, elements that have enriched and entrapped us since the beginning of time.

critical insight. This process is fostered by a liberal arts program that emphasizes cultural and intellectual history and provides a meaningful integration of writing and studio skills. Studio visits, lectures, hands-on instruction, and critiques from the more than 125 professional artists, designers, and architects who teach at the College maintain a student's dynamic relationship with contemporary culture. The campus is filled with student work, and student shows are hosted at the campus' Bolsky Gallery, its main gallery, and at galleries and businesses around Los Angeles.

Located within minutes of all the major Los Angeles museums, Otis is also close to established and alternative galleries and performance spaces. The campus is convenient to a host of cultural resources, from the Philharmonic to cutting-edge contemporary music, outstanding theater, dance, video, and an intense inter-media and literary scene.

The rich mix of creativity is central to life at Otis. Visiting artists, writers, and lecturers bring a wealth of added expertise and insight to the educational experience. And, committed to providing students with every opportunity to succeed, Otis offers a Tutoring Center and Writing Lab to support writing, reading, and speaking skills; build confidence; and strengthen individual vision.

Through small group discussion and individualized instruction, Otis forges multidimensional creative leaders as well as successful artists and designers.

Otis takes its students' futures seriously.

Pacific Lutheran University

Tacoma, Washington

Independent-religious, coed. Suburban campus. Total enrollment: 3,257.

Degrees Bachelor of Fine Arts in the areas of 2–dimensional media, 3–dimensional media, graphic design. Majors: art/fine arts, ceramic art and design, graphic arts, painting/drawing, photography, printmaking, sculpture.

Art Student Profile Fall 1994: 354 total; all matriculated undergraduate; 3% minorities, 7% international.

Art Faculty Total: 8; 6 full-time, 2 part-time; 100% of full-time faculty have terminal degrees. Graduate students do not teach undergraduate courses. Undergraduate student–faculty ratio: 15:1.

Student Life Student groups include Art Guild.

Expenses for 1994–95 Application fee: $35. Comprehensive fee of $17,800 includes full-time tuition ($13,312) and college room and board ($4488). Part-time tuition: $416 per semester hour. Special program-related fees: $20–$45 for supplies.

Financial Aid Program-specific awards for Fall of 1994: 5–15 Talent Awards for freshmen and sophomores ($500–$1000), 1 Lila Moe Scholarship for female seniors ($1500), 1 Cheney Scholarship for juniors and seniors ($3000), 1–5 Knudsen Scholarship for juniors and seniors ($300–$1500), 1 Undergraduate Fellow Award for juniors and seniors ($2000).

Application Procedures Deadline—freshmen and transfers: February 15. Notification date—freshmen and transfers: March 1. Required: essay, high school transcript, college transcript(s) for transfer students, 2 letters of recommendation, SAT I or ACT test scores. Recommended: minimum 3.0 high school GPA, portfolio. Portfolio reviews held continuously on campus; the submission of slides may be substituted for portfolios.

Undergraduate Contact John Hallam, Chair, Art Department, Pacific Lutheran University, Tacoma, Washington 98447; 206-535-7575, E-mail address: hallamjs@plu.edu.

Pacific Northwest College of Art

Portland, Oregon

Independent, coed. Urban campus. Total enrollment: 269.

Degrees Bachelor of Fine Arts in the areas of ceramics, drawing, painting, graphic design, illustration, photography, printmaking, sculpture, general fine arts, individualized major. Majors: art/fine arts, ceramic art and design, graphic arts, illustration, painting/drawing, photography, printmaking, sculpture. Cross-registration with Oregon Independent Colleges Association.

Art Student Profile Fall 1994: 269 total; 259 matriculated undergraduate, 10 nondegree; 10% minorities, 58% females, 7% international.

Art Faculty Total: 41; 18 full-time, 23 part-time; 63% of full-time faculty have terminal degrees. Graduate students do not teach undergraduate courses. Undergraduate student–faculty ratio: 10:1.

Expenses for 1995–96 Application fee: $30. Tuition: $8836 full-time, $380 per semester hour part-time. Full-time mandatory fees: $267.

Financial Aid Program-specific awards for Fall of 1994: 1 Robert Wiener Travel Award for seniors ($750), 1 Gamblin Painting Award for sophomores and juniors ($500), 3 Nancy Tonkin Memorial Scholarship for freshmen, sophomores, juniors ($6000), 3 Leta Kennedy Scholarships for freshmen ($6000), 2 Robert C. Lee Printmaking Scholarships for sophomores and juniors ($4000), 2 Jacob and Ruth Kainen Printmaking Scholarships for sophomores and juniors ($2000), 1 Ed and Sandy Martin Award for freshmen, sophomores, juniors ($500), 1 Jane Chase Memorial Scholarship for freshmen, sophomores, juniors ($1000), 1 William Jamison Scholarship for freshmen, sophomores, juniors ($500), 1 Fashion Group Scholarship for freshmen, sophomores, juniors ($500), 1 Alumni and Friends Scholarship for freshmen, sophomores, juniors ($3000), 1 Agnes Prentis Memorial Scholarship for freshmen, sophomores, juniors ($1000), 3 Rachael Griffin Memorial Scholarships for freshmen, sophomores, juniors ($3000), 1 Helen Director Scholarship for freshmen, sophomores, juniors ($1000), 1 Louis Bunce Memorial Scholarship for freshmen, sophomores, juniors ($1000), 1 Stephen Eberly Thompson Scholarship for freshmen, sophomores, juniors ($500), 1 Hearst Foundation Scholarship for freshmen, sophomores, juniors ($500–$1000).

Application Procedures Deadline—freshmen and transfers: continuous. Notification date—freshmen and trans-

Pacific Northwest College of Art *(continued)*

fers: August 15. Required: essay, 3 letters of recommendation, portfolio, documentation of high school graduation. Portfolio reviews held continuously (student need not be present) on campus; the submission of slides may be substituted for portfolios.

Undergraduate Contact Colin Page, Director of Admission, Pacific Northwest College of Art, 1219 Southwest Park Avenue, Portland, Oregon 97205; 503-226-0462, fax: 503-226-3587.

More about the College

Program Facilities Macintosh computer lab accessible to all students, student art gallery, comprehensive art library with 22,500 volumes on art and 54 periodical subscriptions, a 14,000-square-foot sculpture/ceramic studio, individual spaces for fourth-year thesis students.

Visiting Artist/Speaker Program The 1994 program included John Ahearn, Jim Buonocoursi, Dale Chihuly, Robbie Conal, Baba Wague Diakite, Diane Fenster, Coco Fusco, Paul Green, James Lavadour, Helen Lessick, James McGarrell, James Rosenquist, Keiji Shinohara, Devorah Sperber, Rigoberto Torres, Judith Wyss, Da Hang Zhou, and Shan Zuo Zhou.

Special Programs New York Studio School, a summer semester in New York under the aegis of the association of Independent Colleges of art and Design; Cooperative Training Program for Graphic Design Students, a semester program of real-world experience in design agency during the senior year; Annual American Institute of Graphic Arts (AIGA) Portfolio Evaluation Program for graphic design and illustration students.

The Pacific Northwest College of Art has been providing art students a rich education in studio art since 1909. The College was started by supporters of the Portland Art Museum and continues to remain affiliated with the Museum. Through this relationship the PNCA student has firsthand acquaintance with artwork from African and Pre-Columbian art to contemporary conceptual art. The Art Museum also houses the Gilkey Print Center, which is a preservation and study facility for the Museum's noteworthy print collection and a support facility for the College's Printmaking Department. The Museum's Northwest Film Center is an added feature of the Museum that enriches the experience of PNCA students through its film programs. For the art student, the close relationship between the College and Museum provides an exceptional environment rarely found in art schools.

Community and environment are essential ingredients in the art student's experience. Portland's cultural life centers around the downtown South Park Blocks, in which are located the Pacific Northwest College of Art and Portland Art Museum; Portland's Performing Art Center, home of the Oregon Symphony and Oregon Shakespeare Theatre; the Schnitzer Concert Hall; Oregon Historical Society and its Historical Museum; the county's Main Library; and Portland State University. Within walking distance of the College are major art galleries, live theaters, movie theaters, jazz clubs, and excellent public transportation that brings the entire city within easy reach of the PNCA student.

PNCA's curriculum comes from a strong historical foundation based on structured and sequential courses and centered on the development of skills and visual intelligence. However, PNCA also offers its students the opportunity to explore options beyond the structured curriculum, to use the resources of all departments in their studies, and, in some instances, to develop individualized curricula using the strengths of the students' motivation and special interests. To further expand opportunities for its students, PNCA has an arrangement with Oregon independent colleges such as Reed College, Lewis and Clark College, and the University of Portland that allows students to cross-register. In addition, because of PNCA's membership in the Association of Independent Colleges of Art and Design, students in their junior year may also spend a semester or year at another art college elsewhere in the country. This reciprocal program also contributes to the diversity and depth of the College's student body.

PNCA has more transfer students than students directly from high school. This singular circumstance, coupled with the small size of the student body, facilitates generous exchange between students of varying experiences and backgrounds, raises the level of intellectual exchange among students and between students and faculty, and raises the faculty's level of expectations for student achievement in the classroom and studio. The Pacific Northwest College of Art expects its students to be intellectually and visually challenged and to consider their work relative to the contemporary world and to the community.

Paier College of Art, Inc.

Hamden, Connecticut

Proprietary, coed. Suburban campus. Total enrollment: 292.

Degrees Bachelor of Fine Arts in the areas of graphic design, illustration, interior design. Majors: art/fine arts, graphic design, illustration, interior design.

Art Student Profile Fall 1994: 248 total; 200 matriculated undergraduate, 48 nondegree; 8% minorities, 55% females, 6% international.

Art Faculty Total: 37; 9 full-time, 28 part-time; 55% of full-time faculty have terminal degrees. Graduate students do not teach undergraduate courses. Undergraduate student–faculty ratio: 7:1.

Expenses for 1995–96 Application fee: $25. Tuition: $9760 full-time, $305 per semester hour part-time. Full-time mandatory fees: $340. Special program-related fees: $100–$250 for lab fees and model fees.

Financial Aid Program-specific awards for Fall of 1994: 1 Paier Minority Scholarship for minority undergraduates ($5000), 4 PCA Tuition Reduction for undergraduates demonstrating need ($1500).

Application Procedures Deadline—freshmen and transfers: continuous. Required: high school transcript, college transcript(s) for transfer students, letter of recommendation, interview, portfolio, SAT I or ACT test scores.

Portfolio reviews held 2 times and by appointment on campus; the submission of slides may be substituted for portfolios.

Undergraduate Contact Lynn Pascale, Admissions Department, Paier College of Art, Inc., 20 Gorham Avenue, Hamden, Connecticut 06514-3902; 203-287-3031, fax: 203-287-3021.

Parsons School of Design

See New School for Social Research, Parsons School of Design

Pennsylvania Academy of the Fine Arts

Philadelphia, Pennsylvania

Degrees Bachelor of Fine Arts in the areas of painting, sculpture, printmaking. Majors: painting/drawing, printmaking, sculpture. Graduate degrees offered: Master of Fine Arts in the areas of painting, sculpture, printmaking. Mandatory cross-registration with University of Pennsylvania, University of the Arts.

Art Student Profile Fall 1994: 325 total; 300 matriculated undergraduate, 25 matriculated graduate.

Art Faculty Total: 44; 25 full-time, 19 part-time; 85% of full-time faculty have terminal degrees. Graduate students teach a few undergraduate courses.

Financial Aid Program-specific awards for Fall of 1994: 9 Travel Scholarships for juniors and seniors ($5000), 155–200 Institutional Scholarships for those demonstrating need and merit ($3550).

Application Procedures Deadline—freshmen and transfers: August 15. Notification date—freshmen and transfers: August 30. Required: high school transcript, college transcript(s) for transfer students, 2 letters of recommendation, interview, portfolio. Auditions held on campus and off campus. Portfolio reviews held 11 times on campus and off campus; the submission of slides may be substituted for portfolios.

Contact Michael Smith, Acting Director of Admissions, Pennsylvania Academy of the Fine Arts, 118 North Broad Street, Philadelphia, Pennsylvania 19102; 215-972-7625, fax: 215-569-0153.

More about the Academy

Almost everyone in the visual arts world knows the Academy's reputation for educating artists to achieve at the highest possible level. The Academy's objective is to assist individuals who aspire to be artists in reaching their goals. To this end, the Academy offers a two-year M.F.A. degree program, a one-year postbaccalaureate program, a four-year certificate program, and a coordinated B.F.A. program with several institutions. Each program has majors in painting and drawing, printmaking, and sculpture.

The Academy programs are all studio-based and require each participant to make an unequivocal commitment to the creative process. The instructional program fosters and protects the special empathy that must be struck between an instructor and student for the educational process to be meaningful.

The faculty members' professional lives as artists are considered central at the Academy and teaching schedules are created so as not to interrupt the continuity of the instructors' personal studio time. There are also twelve private studios within the Academy buildings that are reserved for faculty use, which enhances the life of the school community.

Students at the Academy come from all walks of life, all ages, and widely varying backgrounds. This creates a high-energy enriching community bound together by a passion for art and the creative act.

Most who seek the advantages of higher education have limited means to access the opportunity. Every student who is accepted at the Academy automatically receives a scholarship covering over one-third of the tuition cost. The Academy is privileged to provide this support from its endowment and development efforts. For this reason, the Academy can still offer one of the lowest tuitions in the country. In addition, it has an extensive financial aid program, including fifty-two named funds that provide tuition assistance, and $30,000 in merit prizes are awarded each spring.

The certificate program has a unique structure. In the last two years of the program, students are assigned their own private studios. Those years are devoted to the independent development of a personal approach to their work, under the guidance of faculty critics selected by the student. The first two years are characterized by rigor and discipline in the techniques and concepts on which the tradition of western art has been built. Drawing, painting, clay modeling, and using the life model are dominant activities. Courses in portrait, still life, landscape, abstract sculpture principles, and traditional printmaking media are all required as is the classical training embodied in anatomy, perspective, and cast drawing from the Academy's famous cast collection.

In recent years, it has become imperative to prepare graduates to manage the realities of the art world. The Academy accomplishes this in many ways. There are continuous juried student exhibitions, and other opportunities for students to expose themselves to formal competition. The Visiting Artists Program contributes dimensions to the curriculum not inherent in the program. A series of lectures specifically focusing on the business of art is presented each year. But, perhaps most importantly, there is a strong tradition of mentoring at the Academy; and through that system, students learn how to construct a strong, supportive environment for themselves. **Faculty and Alumni** The critics and instructors are often the reason students choose to study at the Academy. Students are presented with some of the most distinguished mentors available–public works artist Jody Pinto; sculptor Joel Fisher; painters Sidney Goodman, Yvonne Jacquette, and Irving Petlin, to name a few.

Because the Academy was the first art school in the country, its alumni list reads like a "Who's Who," from painters Thomas Eakins and Mary Cassatt in the late 1800s to architect Louis Kahn and filmmaker David Lynch in the latter half of this century.

Pennsylvania State University University Park Campus

University Park, Pennsylvania

State-related, coed. Small-town campus. Total enrollment: 38,294.

Degrees Bachelor of Fine Arts in the area of studio art. Majors: ceramic art and design, graphic arts, metals, painting/drawing, photography, printmaking, sculpture. Graduate degrees offered: Master of Fine Arts in the area of studio art.

Expenses for 1994–95 Application fee: $35. State resident tuition: $4966 full-time, $208 per credit part-time. Nonresident tuition: $10,654 full-time, $445 per credit part time. Part time mandatory fees per semester range from $12 to $25. Full-time mandatory fees: $70. College room and board: $3920.

Application Procedures Deadline—freshmen: November 30; transfers: March 1. Notification date—freshmen and transfers: continuous. Required: high school transcript, college transcript(s) for transfer students, SAT I or ACT test scores. Auditions held on campus and off campus. Portfolio reviews held on campus and off campus.

Contact Kitty Haupt, Secretary, College of Arts and Architecture, School of Visual Arts, Pennsylvania State University University Park Campus, 210 Paterson Building, University Park, Pennsylvania 16802; 814-865-0444, fax: 814-863-8664.

Pittsburg State University

Pittsburg, Kansas

State-supported, coed. Small-town campus. Total enrollment: 6,377.

Degrees Bachelor of Fine Arts in the area of art. Majors: art/fine arts, ceramic art and design, jewelry and metalsmithing, painting/drawing, photography, printmaking, sculpture.

Art Student Profile Fall 1994: 100 total; all matriculated undergraduate; 1% minorities, 60% females, 4% international.

Art Faculty Total: 8; 7 full-time, 1 part-time; 100% of full-time faculty have terminal degrees. Graduate students teach a few undergraduate courses. Undergraduate student–faculty ratio: 20:1.

Student Life Student groups include senior and graduate exhibits, judging of art exhibits.

Expenses for 1995–96 Application fee: $15. State resident tuition: $1806 full-time, $66 per semester hour part-time. Nonresident tuition: $5788 full-time, $199 per semester hour part-time. College room and board: $3126.

Financial Aid Program-specific awards for Fall of 1994: 4 Bertha Spencer Scholarships for program majors ($100), 1 Laurence A. Wooster Scholarship for program majors ($100), 1 University Arts Association Scholarship for program majors ($100), 1 E. V. and F. B. Baxter Scholarship for program majors ($200).

Application Procedures Deadline—freshmen and transfers: August 15. Required: high school transcript, minimum 2.0 high school GPA, GED if applicable.

Undergraduate Contact Dr. Larrie Moody, Acting Chairperson, Art Department, Pittsburg State University, 1701 South Broadway, Pittsburgh, Kansas 66762; 316-235-4302, fax: 316-232-7515.

Pratt Institute

Brooklyn, New York

Independent, coed. Urban campus. Total enrollment: 2,979.

Degrees Bachelor of Fine Arts in the areas of communications design, fine arts, fashion design, interior design, art and design education, photography, computer graphics, criticism and history of art, design and architecture, illustration; Bachelor of Industrial Design in the area of industrial design. Majors: art direction, art education, commercial art, computer graphics, fashion design and technology, graphic design, illustration, industrial design, interior design, painting/drawing, photography, printmaking, sculpture. Graduate degrees offered: Master of Fine Arts in the areas of fine arts, computer graphics; Master of Industrial Design in the area of industrial design.

Art Student Profile Fall 1994: 1,952 total; 1,082 matriculated undergraduate, 851 matriculated graduate, 19 nondegree; 22% minorities, 52% females, 31% international.

Art Faculty Total: 590; 112 full-time, 478 part-time; 51% of full-time faculty have terminal degrees. Graduate students do not teach undergraduate courses. Undergraduate student–faculty ratio: 9:1.

Student Life Student groups include Industrial Design Society of America, American Society of Interior Designers, American Institute of Graphic Artists.

Expenses for 1995–96 Application fee: $30. Comprehensive fee of $22,480 includes full-time tuition ($14,814), mandatory fees ($400), and college room and board ($7266). College room only: $4666. Part-time tuition: $471 per credit. Part-time mandatory fees: $117.50 per semester.

Financial Aid Program-specific awards for Fall of 1994: 12 National Talent Search Awards for freshmen and transfer students ($14,000), President's Scholarship for freshmen and transfer students ($1000–$3000), Merit Award for freshmen and transfer students ($1000–$3000).

Application Procedures Deadline—freshmen and transfers: continuous. Required: essay, high school transcript, college transcript(s) for transfer students, minimum 2.0 high school GPA, letter of recommendation, portfolio, SAT I or ACT test scores. Recommended: minimum 3.0 high school GPA, interview. Portfolio reviews held continuously on campus and off campus on National Portfolio Days.

Contact Judith Aaron, Dean, Admissions, Pratt Institute, 200 Willoughby Avenue, Brooklyn, New York 11205; 718-636-3669, fax: 718-636-3670.

More about the Institute

Pratt Institute is located on a 25-acre tree-lined campus, with twenty-seven buildings of differing architectural styles in Brooklyn's historic Clinton Hill section. Approximately 75 percent of freshmen live in one of Pratt's six residence halls. Parking is available for residents and commuters. Pratt's proximity to New York City is a distinct advantage to students. Through Pratt's optional internship program, qualified students are offered challenging on-the-job experience in Manhattan's top art galleries and design firms, giving them firsthand work experience as well as credit toward their professional degree. This extension of the classroom into the professional world adds a practical dimension to their education.

Pratt has one of the largest undergraduate and graduate art and design schools in the United States, which is a distinct advantage in that students can combine B.F.A. and M.F.A. degrees in several programs, saving money and time and obtaining the necessary edge to advance professionally. Pratt offers B.F.A.'s in the following programs: art history, art and design education, fine arts (ceramics, drawing, jewelry, painting, photography, printmaking, and sculpture), fashion design, graphic design, illustration, and interior design.

Student services include career planning and placement, counseling, and student development. There are more than thirty-five student organizations, including fraternities, sororities, honorary societies, professional societies, and clubs. Pratt also has intramural sport teams as well as NCAA and ECAC men's and women's varsity athletic teams. The art history, art and design education, fine arts, graphic design, computer graphics, industrial design, and interior design programs are also offered on the graduate level. Additional graduate art design programs include packaging design and creative art therapy.

Pratt Institute has educated professionals for productive careers in artistic and technical fields since its founding in 1887. Pratt's School of Art and Design offers one of the best professional art and design educations in the world, with an excellent faculty of practicing professionals and state-of-the art facilities.

Pratt's faculty, most of whom are practicing professionals, bring to the classroom a "real-world" expertise, a strong theoretical base, and the high standard of their professional work. The faculty members have received more than eighteen Tiffany, Fulbright, and Guggenheim awards as well as other prestigious professional awards.

For over 100 years, the Institute has produced some of the world's greatest artists and designers. The following are just a few of Pratt's alumni and their outstanding accomplishments: Bob Giraldi, director of award-wining TV commercials, including Michael Jackson Pepsi commercials; Betsey Johnson, fashion designer; Ellsworth Kelly, painter; Max Weber, Modernist painter; David Sarnoff, CEO and president of RCA Corporation; Peter Max, pop artist; and Paul Rand, designer of IBM, Westinghouse, and NEXT Computer logos.

Pratt has numerous studio, shop, and technical facilities for work in all media as well as state-of-the-art computer facilities. Graphics labs include color Macintosh IIs and SEs, Cubicoms, Targa TIPS PCs with digitizer tablets, ALIAS labs, and a Quantel graphics system. Pratt also has extensive gallery space, which features throughout the academic year the work of students, alumni, faculty, and other well-known artists and designers.

The educational goal of the School of Art and Design is to educate whole artists and designers. A Pratt education focuses primarily on two objectives: professional training—emphasizing the learning of skills, techniques, and the methodology necessary for students to perform in the professional community as productive artists or designers—and building students' critical awareness through the exposure to a strong liberal arts curriculum and a number of concepts and learning experiences that are not within the formal realm of art and design. Students from all of Pratt's programs are encouraged to take courses in other art and design major areas of study as well as in architecture so that they have the opportunity to examine the interrelationships of art, design, technology, and human need. Students also have the opportunity to study abroad through one of Pratt's many travel programs in places such as Venice, Copenhagen, and Tuscany.

At Pratt, future art teachers also discover themselves by teaching classes in the Department of Art and Design Education's Saturday Art School. For almost a century, this laboratory school has provided New York City children, adolescents, and, more recently, adults and senior citizens with a quality art program.

In educating more than four generations of students to be creative, technically skilled, and adaptable professionals, Pratt has gained an international reputation that attracts more than 3,100 undergraduate and graduate students annually from more than forty-seven states and seventy countries.

Purchase College, State University of New York

Purchase, New York

State-supported, coed. Small-town campus. Total enrollment: 2,498.

Degrees Bachelor of Fine Arts in the areas of painting/drawing, printmaking, photography, design, sculpture, art of the book. Majors: art/fine arts, graphic design, painting/drawing, photography, printmaking, sculpture, studio art. Graduate degrees offered: Master of Fine Arts in the areas of painting/drawing, printmaking, sculpture, art of the book. Cross-registration with Manhattanville College.

Art Student Profile Fall 1994: 412 total; 400 matriculated undergraduate, 12 matriculated graduate; 12% minorities, 52% females, 3% international.

Art Faculty Total: 50; 19 full-time, 31 part-time; 100% of full-time faculty have terminal degrees. Graduate students teach a few undergraduate courses. Undergraduate student–faculty ratio: 16:1.

Purchase College, State University of New York
(continued)

Student Life Student groups include Visual Artists for Visual Arts, Sonodanza (interdisciplinary performing arts/visual arts group), senior show.

Expenses for 1995–96 Application fee: $25. State resident tuition: $3400 full-time, $137 per credit part-time. Nonresident tuition: $8300 full-time, $346 per credit part-time. Part-time mandatory fees: $13.30 per credit. Full-time mandatory fees: $399. College room and board: $4872. College room only: $3130. Special program-related fees: $25–$250 for lab fees for consumable materials.

Financial Aid Program-specific awards for Fall of 1994: 2 Dean's Merit Scholarships for those demonstrating high academic and artistic achievement ($1000), 1–4 A. I. Friedman Scholarships for those demonstrating need ($500–$1000), 2–4 Empire Minority Scholarships for minority students from New York State ($2500), 5–10 Reed Scholarships for those demonstrating high academic and artistic achievement ($500–$1000).

Application Procedures Deadline—freshmen and transfers: continuous. Notification date—freshmen and transfers: continuous. Required: essay, high school transcript, minimum 2.0 high school GPA, 2 letters of recommendation, slide portfolio. Recommended: minimum 3.0 high school GPA, SAT I or ACT test scores. Auditions held on campus.

Contact Merrill Grinnell, Admissions Counselor, Admissions Department, Purchase College, State University of New York, 735 Anderson Hill Road, Purchase, New York 10577-1400; 914-251-6300, fax: 914-251-6314.

Purchase College considers itself an experiment in the history of postsecondary education. Many major conservatory programs in Fine and Performing Arts coexist with a "Public Ivy" Liberal Arts College. Philosophically as well as pragmatically, the purpose of the Visual Arts program is to provide an educational atmosphere in which students and artists work together, engage in critical dialogue, experiment, test their ideas, and learn. The curriculum is based on the belief that the artist and designer who will be practicing into the twenty-first century must have both the traditional tools and emerging skills of the painter, photographer, sculptor, designer, and printmaker; an understanding of contemporary society and technology; and the educational opportunity to explore their own talents through the development of skills, the training of the eye, and the cultivation of the mind. The visual arts curriculum attempts, therefore, to remain responsive to the established traditions and categories of art and to the expanding new concepts, materials, and technologies of the contemporary world of art and design.

In the Visual Arts program all students complete a Foundation year that includes two semesters of drawing and one semester each of design, sculpture, and visual language. Visual language is an introduction to art history and helps students understand the various approaches to art-making as well as the shared terminology within the arts. Students also investigate introductory courses within different visual arts disciplines: graphic design, painting/drawing, photography, printmaking, and sculpture. In the course of four years, students specialize in one area of study. Four-year programs have been developed in each area. Some students may wish to pursue a synthesis of several areas. Each student works closely with an assigned faculty adviser to establish a program of study that allows the student to develop particular areas of interest.

Purchase also requires that students complete a senior project. In many ways similar to a graduate thesis, the senior project is undertaken as the culminating experience of students graduating from Purchase. In the visual arts, students create a body of work of their choosing, sponsored by a faculty mentor. The work is documented and accompanied by a written thesis statement. The senior project allows for in-depth exploration of a particular content area and provides a critical focus for a student to leave their mark at Purchase. Senior projects are kept on file in the library as a reference resource for the entire campus community.

Just over twenty years old, Purchase already counts major filmmakers, musicians, actors, artists, and writers among its alumni. The interaction of artists in conservatory programs and scholars in the College of Liberal Arts makes for a cross-fertilization that is mutually beneficial. This then is the premise and promise of Purchase College, and the culture of the campus reflects it. On any given day one can attend a lecture on medieval literature, a dance rehearsal, a gallery opening, and more. This environment is stimulating and a springboard for the individual imagination.

Queen's University at Kingston

Kingston, Ontario

Province-supported, coed. Urban campus. Total enrollment: 18,656.

Degrees Bachelor of Fine Arts in the area of studio art with an art history component. Majors: painting/drawing, printmaking, sculpture.

Art Student Profile Fall 1994: 125 total; all matriculated undergraduate.

Art Faculty Total: 6; 4 full-time, 2 part-time.

Expenses for 1994–95 Application fee: $50. Canadian resident tuition: $2730 (minimum) full-time, $445.60 per course part-time. Nonresident tuition: $8024 (minimum) full-time. Full-time tuition ranges up to $3363 for Canadian residents, $13,080 for nonresidents, according to program. (All figures are in Canadian dollars.). College room and board: $5463. Special program-related fees: $400 for gallery tour to New York City.

Financial Aid Program-specific awards for Fall of 1994 available.

Application Procedures Deadline—freshmen: May 13; transfers: June 1. Required: high school transcript, interview, portfolio. Portfolio reviews held 6 times on campus; the submission of slides may be substituted for portfolios when distance is prohibitive.

Undergraduate Contact Art Department, Queen's University at Kingston, Ontario Hall, Kingston, Ontario K7L 3N6, Canada; 613-545-6166.

Quincy University

Quincy, Illinois

Independent-religious, coed. Small-town campus. Total enrollment: 1,164.

Degrees Bachelor of Fine Arts in the area of art. Majors: art/fine arts, ceramic art and design, commercial art, computer graphics, painting/drawing, photography, printmaking, sculpture, studio art.

Art Student Profile Fall 1994: 14 total; all matriculated undergraduate; 1% minorities, 65% females, 1% international.

Art Faculty Total: 6; 2 full-time, 4 part-time; 100% of full-time faculty have terminal degrees. Graduate students do not teach undergraduate courses. Undergraduate student–faculty ratio: 10:1.

Student Life Student groups include Student Show, senior show.

Expenses for 1995–96 Application fee: $20. Comprehensive fee of $15,290 includes full-time tuition ($10,700), mandatory fees ($210), and college room and board ($4380). College room only: $1750. Part-time tuition: $315 per credit hour. Tuition guaranteed not to increase for student's term of enrollment. Special program-related fees: $10–$25 for lab fees.

Financial Aid Program-specific awards for Fall of 1994: 1 de Mero Scholarship for program majors ($1025), 1 Helmer Fine Arts Scholarship for program majors ($300), 1 Mejer Visual Arts Scholarship for program majors ($100).

Application Procedures Deadline—freshmen and transfers: continuous. Required: high school transcript, college transcript(s) for transfer students, minimum 2.0 high school GPA, portfolio, SAT I or ACT test scores. Recommended: minimum 3.0 high school GPA, 2 letters of recommendation, interview. Portfolio reviews held continuously on campus; the submission of slides may be substituted for portfolios if a campus visit is impossible, with permission of the chair.

Undergraduate Contact Frank P. Bevec, Director of Admissions, Quincy University, 1800 College Avenue, Quincy, Illinois 62301-2699; 217-228-5210, fax: 217-228-5479, E-mail address: frank@quincy.edu.

Radford University

Radford, Virginia

State-supported, coed. Small-town campus. Total enrollment: 9,105.

Degrees Bachelor of Fine Arts in the area of art. Majors: 2-dimensional studies, 3-dimensional studies, art/fine arts, ceramic art and design, fibers, graphic design, jewelry and metalsmithing, painting/drawing, photography, printmaking, sculpture, studio art, video art, watercolors. Graduate degrees offered: Master of Fine Arts in the area of art.

Art Student Profile Fall 1994: 197 total; 179 matriculated undergraduate, 18 matriculated graduate; 5% minorities, 60% females, 10% international.

Art Faculty Total: 16; 15 full-time, 1 part-time; 93% of full-time faculty have terminal degrees. Graduate students teach a few undergraduate courses. Undergraduate student–faculty ratio: 18:1.

Student Life Student groups include Student Art Guild.

Expenses for 1995–96 Application fee: $15. State resident tuition: $3114 full-time, $130 per semester hour part-time. Nonresident tuition: $7688 full-time, $321 per semester hour part-time. College room and board: $4250.

Financial Aid Program-specific awards for Fall of 1994: 7 Arts Society Scholarships for undergraduates ($500).

Application Procedures Deadline—freshmen: April 1; transfers: June 1. Notification date—freshmen and transfers: continuous. Required: high school transcript, SAT I or ACT test scores.

Undergraduate Contact Dr. Arthur F. Jones, Chairperson, Art Department, Radford University, Box 6965, Radford, Virginia 24142; 703-831-5475, fax: 703-831-6313.

Ray College of Design

Chicago, Illinois

Proprietary, coed. Urban campus. Total enrollment: 610.

Degrees Bachelor of Fine Arts in the areas of fashion design, interior design, advertising design, illustration, fashion merchandising. Majors: advertising design, fashion design and technology, fashion merchandising, illustration, interior design, textiles and clothing.

Art Student Profile Fall 1994: 543 total; 435 matriculated undergraduate, 108 nondegree; 40% minorities, 60% females, 10% international.

Art Faculty Total: 62; 10 full-time, 52 part-time; 70% of full-time faculty have terminal degrees. Undergraduate student–faculty ratio: 16:1.

Student Life Student groups include American Society of Interior Designers, Fashion Group Student Chapter, Center for Design Student Chapter.

Expenses for 1995–96 Application fee: $50. Tuition: $8880 full-time, $296 per credit part-time. Part-time mandatory fees: $15 per semester. Full-time mandatory fees: $50. Special program-related fees: $50–$100 for computer lab fee, $50–$100 for photography lab fee.

Financial Aid Program-specific awards for Fall of 1994: 12 High School Scholarships for incoming freshmen ($2000), 12 Transfer Student Scholarships for transfer students ($2000), 40 Ray College Grants for those demonstrating need ($1776).

Application Procedures Deadline—freshmen and transfers: continuous. Notification date—freshmen and transfers: continuous. Required: essay, high school transcript, college transcript(s) for transfer students, minimum 2.0 high school GPA, portfolio. Recommended: letter of recommendation, interview, SAT I or ACT test scores. Portfolio reviews held continuously on campus and off campus in various high schools in the region; the

Ray College of Design *(continued)*

submission of slides may be substituted for portfolios when distance is prohibitive.

Undergraduate Contact Mindy Spritz, Director of Admissions, Ray College of Design, 350 North Orleans Street, #136, Chicago, Illinois 60654; 312-280-3500, fax: 312-280-3528.

Rhode Island College

Providence, Rhode Island

State-supported, coed. Urban campus. Total enrollment: 9,900.

Degrees Bachelor of Fine Arts in the area of studio art. Majors: ceramic art and design, graphic design, jewelry and metalsmithing, painting, photography, printmaking, sculpture.

Art Faculty Total: 24; 10 full-time, 14 part-time.

Estimated Expenses for 1995–96 Application fee: $25. State resident tuition: $2477 full-time, $112 per semester hour part-time. Nonresident tuition: $6995 full-time, $290 per semester hour part-time. Part-time mandatory fees per semester range from $55 to $200. Full-time mandatory fees: $493. College room and board: $5380.

Application Procedures Deadline—freshmen and transfers: April 1. Required: essay, high school transcript, portfolio, SAT I or ACT test scores. Recommended: interview. Portfolio reviews held 1 time on campus; the submission of slides may be substituted for portfolios for large works of art or when distance is prohibitive.

Undergraduate Contact Harriet Brisson, Studio Coordinator, Art Department, Rhode Island College, 600 Mount Pleasant Avenue, Providence, Rhode Island 02908; 401-456-9687.

Rhode Island School of Design

Providence, Rhode Island

Independent, coed. Urban campus. Total enrollment: 2,011.

Degrees Bachelor of Fine Arts in the areas of painting, sculpture, glass, jewelry and metals, textiles, apparel design, graphic design, industrial design, architecture, interior architecture, landscape architecture, printmaking, ceramics, illustration, photography, furniture design. Majors: apparel design, architecture, ceramics, furniture design, glass, graphic design, illustration, industrial design, interior architecture, jewelry and metalsmithing, landscape architecture, landscape architecture/design, painting/drawing, photography, printmaking, sculpture, textiles. Graduate degrees offered: Master of Fine Arts in the areas of ceramics, furniture design, graphic design, glass, jewelry and metals, painting/printmaking, photography, sculpture, textiles, landscape architecture; Master of Industrial Design in the area of industrial design. Cross-registration with Brown University.

Art Student Profile Fall 1994: 2,170 total; 1,860 matriculated undergraduate, 151 matriculated graduate, 159 nondegree; 12% minorities, 55% females, 19% international.

Art Faculty Total: 293; 121 full-time, 172 part-time; 71% of full-time faculty have terminal degrees. Graduate students do not teach undergraduate courses. Undergraduate student–faculty ratio: 12:1.

Student Life Special housing available for art students.

Expenses for 1995–96 Application fee: $35. Comprehensive fee of $24,218 includes full-time tuition ($17,600) and college room and board ($6618). Special program-related fees: $10–$100 for lab fees.

Financial Aid Program-specific awards for Fall of 1994: 5–7 Trustees Scholarships for above-average students with exceptional artistic ability ($2500–$8800).

Application Procedures Deadline—freshmen: February 15; transfers: March 31. Notification date—freshmen: April 1; transfers: May 7. Required: essay, high school transcript, college transcript(s) for transfer students, portfolio, SAT I or ACT test scores, 3 original drawings. Recommended: minimum 3.0 high school GPA, letter of recommendation. the submission of slides may be substituted for portfolios.

Contact Admissions Office, Rhode Island School of Design, 2 College Street, Providence, Rhode Island 02903; 401-454-6300, fax: 401-454-6309, E-mail address: admissions@risd.edu.

More about the School

Facilities Forty buildings with more than 500,000 square feet of space, including specialized studio spaces and equipment; access to studio spaces, with upperclass students often having a private studio space; thirteen residence halls offering a variety of living environments; Museum of Art with more than 100,000 objects frequently used for study purposes by faculty and students; library with more than 80,000 volumes, including artist's and rare books, and an image research collection of 410,000 clippings and photographs and 125,000 slides; Nature Lab with 70,000 objects available for study and research; more than 200 computer systems available in departmental and specialized labs.

Faculty and Resident Artists RISD has 280 faculty members, 120 of them full-time and readily available to students on campus. More than 200 artists and guest critics visit the campus on average each year. Among recent visitors were Laurie Anderson, artist/performer; Bread and Puppet Theater; Jane Alexander, Chairperson of the NEA; Pat Olezko, performance artist; and Frank Gehry, architect.

Student Exhibit Opportunities Two college-wide galleries and eight departmental exhibition spaces on campus with an average of 125 shows staged each year.

Special Programs The European Honors Program allows students to study in Rome for their junior or senior year. Study-abroad exchange agreements are in place with 18 other art and design colleges around the world. Wintersession term provides unique study opportunities each year, including travel abroad courses (recently to Italy, Switzerland, Paris, and Fiji). Mobility program available with 32 other arts colleges. Professional internships are available with 170 students participating yearly. Recently, students have interned at WGBH, Cannondale, Chermayeff & Geismar, and Pentagram.

Students who come to RISD (riz-dee) join an intense creative artists' community that has been internationally respected for its excellent education for more than 118 years. This dynamic atmosphere—created among people with similar interests, talents, and focus—is frequently noted by many sources as a distinguishing feature of RISD, which was cited again in 1994 as the best visual arts college in the country by *U.S. News & World Report*.

RISD'S 2,000 students, coming from more than 50 nations around the world find an extensive range of majors in areas of architecture, design, and the fine arts. This diverse choice of disciplines creates an enriched environment of ideas and personal directions. Students find balance in the curriculum between focus on their major interest, experimentation in related studios, and innovative cross-disciplinary study. For example, the annual Cabaret combines students from a variety of majors in the study of the social and artistic happenings of a time in history, resulting in a multimedia performance work at the end of the class. It is a frequent happening at RISD for a student in one studio major to work jointly with a classmate from another department on a single project, broadening understanding of the creative opportunities between disciplines. There are a growing number of real-world applications at RISD of design to industry, involving research studios sponsored by Frigidare, Rubbermaid, Virtual I/O, and Nissan and innovative courses taught jointly with other colleges, such as the product development collaboration between Industrial Design and MBA students from MIT.

Liberal arts form an important component of each student's study as well, and RISD invests notably in the quality of its academic course offerings. There are 18 full-time faculty members in liberal arts departments, all holding the highest degree in their discipline, and 24 part-time faculty members who specialize in certain areas; this number and quality of academic faculty is unusual for a visual arts college and results in a varied selection of more than 180 courses yearly.

RISD's 240 studio faculty members are among the leaders in the visual arts, passionate about the fulfillment that the arts bring to the individual and the role of the arts and design in society. They include designers of products found in most homes, award-winning authors and illustrators, painters and sculptors whose work can be seen in major museums and galleries, and acclaimed architects, filmmakers, and textile artists.

RISD alumni consistently win major competitions, prestigious awards, and recognition for their works in the arts, industry, and education. Chris Van Allsburg is a two-time winner of the nationally acclaimed Caldecott Medal for his books. Architects Anthony Belluschi and Deborah Berke have been recognized for outstanding design work. Designer Nicole Miller is noted for her lines of women's apparel and men's accessories. Glass artists Dale Chihuly and Howard Ben Tre, musician David Byrne, actor and painter Martin Mull, gallery director Mary Boone, and filmmakers Gus van Sant and Martha Coolidge are but a few of the successes among RISD's 12,000 alumni. The RISD community is a continuing tradition, having an impact well beyond the years and the walls of each student's education on the campus in Providence.

Ringling School of Art and Design

Sarasota, Florida

Independent, coed. Urban campus. Total enrollment: 805.

Degrees Bachelor of Fine Arts in the areas of computer animation, fine arts, graphic design, illustration, interior design, photography. Majors: art/fine arts, computer animation, graphic design, illustration, interior design, photography.

Art Student Profile Fall 1994: 805 total; 799 matriculated undergraduate, 6 nondegree; 13% minorities, 38% females, 5% international.

Art Faculty Total: 97; 39 full-time, 58 part-time; 70% of full-time faculty have terminal degrees. Graduate students do not teach undergraduate courses. Undergraduate student–faculty ratio: 13:1.

Student Life Student groups include Campus Activities Board, Phi Delta Theta, preprofessional organizations.

Expenses for 1995–96 Application fee: $30. Comprehensive fee of $17,650 includes full-time tuition ($11,500), mandatory fees ($200), and college room and board ($5950). Part-time tuition: $1590 per course. Part-time mandatory fees: $65 per year.

Financial Aid Program-specific awards for Fall of 1994: Portfolio Scholarships for incoming students.

Application Procedures Deadline—freshmen and transfers: continuous. Notification date—freshmen and transfers: continuous. Required: essay, high school transcript, college transcript(s) for transfer students, minimum 2.0 high school GPA, 2 letters of recommendation, slides or photographs of portfolio. Recommended: interview, SAT I or ACT test scores. Portfolio reviews held continuously on campus and off campus on National Portfolio Days.

Undergraduate Contact James H. Dean, Dean of Admissions, Ringling School of Art and Design, 2700 North Tamiami Trail, Sarasota, Florida 34234; 941-351-5100, fax: 941-359-7517.

More about the School

Program Facilities Academic facilities: Verman Kimbrough Memorial Library, with 17,000 volumes, 50,000 slides, 3,000 periodicals, videotapes; Selby Gallery, with annual juried student and faculty exhibitions, national and regional shows; specialized studios for painting, printmaking, sculpture, wood, graphic design, computer animation, illustration, figure drawing, interior design, and CADD; Deborah M. Cooley Photography Center, with studios and black-and-white and color darkrooms.

Computer classroom facilities include sixteen Silicon Graphics XS24 workstations, three IBM RISC 6000 workstations, one SUN IPX workstation, eight SGI INDY R 4400 SC workstations, one SGI Webforce Challenge S Internet Server, one Novell Server, twenty-five Power PC

Ringling School of Art and Design *(continued)*

7100 computers, sixteen Macintosh LC II computers, twenty-two Macintosh II ci/cx computers, 13 Pentium P-90 computers, and a variety of scanning, display, presentation, and printing technologies. Software includes: Wavefront Advanced Visualizer, Side Effects Software, Prisms, SOFTIMAGE Creative Environment, Adobe Freehand, QuarkXpress, Adobe PageMaker, Macromedia Director, Adobe Photoshop, Adobe Persuasion, Fractal Design Painter, Debabelizer, Autocad XIII, Deluxe Paint, Soundedit 16.

The following corporations support the curriculum through a variety of resources: Silicon Graphics, Inc., IBM Corporation, Pacific Data Images, Side Effects Software, Adobe, SOFTIMAGE, Sun Microsystems, Inc., Wavefront Technologies.

Located on a residential campus on Florida's Gulf Coast, Ringling School of Art and Design is a fully accredited four-year college of visual art. Approximately 800 students from around the world pursue the Bachelor of Fine Arts degree (B.F.A.) in six majors: computer animation, fine arts, graphic design, illustration, interior design, or photography. A minor program in photography is also available.

The B.F.A. curriculum is a four-year sequence of studio art, art history, and liberal arts courses with the concentration in studio work. Studio faculty members are professional artists and designers who are actively committed to their own work as well as to teaching. Students begin their studies in the foundation program, concentrating on the development of basic drawing and design skills. They begin to specialize in their major fields in the sophomore year. Ringling School of Art and Design emphasizes professional portfolio development and career preparation and provides extensive career-related services for students and alumni.

Ringling's Center for Career Services provides a variety of services to help students learn about full-time, part-time, and freelance job opportunities. The Center provides students with opportunities to develop professional skills to prepare for specific careers or to research additional training and graduate education. A variety of internships are available to qualified students, both locally and nationally. Companies that have offered internships to Ringling students include Walt Disney Animation; *The St. Petersburg Times*; Gametek, Inc.; the Peters Creative Group ("Mother Goose & Grimm" creators); Carole Korn Interiors, Inc.; Interprise; Corporate Office Systems; The Florida State University Conservatory of Motion Picture, Television, and Recording Arts; Advent Design Group; Walt Disney Imagineering; Rhythm & Hues; The BronzArt Foundry of Sarasota; and Lamb & Company.

Recent graduates are currently employed by such firms as Walt Disney Animation; Hallmark Greeting Cards; SOFTIMAGE; Gannett Corporation; CGI Systems; Dan Miller Design; Electronic Data Systems; Bausch & Lomb Pharmaceutical; Wagner Office Furniture, Inc.; Warner Brothers Feature Animation; The Franklin Mint; Industrial Light & Magic; Leo Burnett; Sega Genesis; and Magnet Design, Inc.

Ringling School of Art and Design recognizes that education also takes place outside of the classroom or studio. A number of student organizations provide a well-balanced calendar of cocurricular events, leadership opportunities, and activities to suit all types of interests. Campus organizations include those focusing on student governance, recreational and intramural sports, special interests, social and community service, and departmental/preprofessional concerns. There are opportunities for students to form organizations at any time based on current concerns and interests. Some of the permanent ongoing student activities are Phi Delta Theta International Fraternity, Campus Activities Board, American Society of Interior Designers, Residence Hall Council, Theatre Production Guild, Outdoor Recreation, and an International Student Association.

Additionally, Ringling has a number of traditions involving the entire campus community. Annual programs include Parents' Weekend, the Goombay Festival (a Bahamian-style Mardi Gras), and Founder's Day festivities. These are supplemented by beach parties, Halloween and holiday parties, and the senior graduation party.

On-campus housing is available for approximately 160 students. The air-conditioned residence hall rooms are mostly doubles, although some private rooms are available for women students. In addition to the convenience of campus living, residents benefit from a variety of programs, residence hall support staff, and campus food service.

A weeklong orientation program is conducted prior to the start of the fall semester. The week includes opportunities to meet other students, meetings with department heads and other faculty, presentations on academic expectations, an introduction to student organizations, a parents' orientation, and a variety of social activities.

Ringling School of Art and Design welcomes applications from students with a serious commitment to the visual arts. Admission is based on a review of the student's portfolio, academic record, essay, and teacher recommendations. All applicants are reviewed individually, with special consideration given to creative ability and potential for success in college-level studies.

Rivier College

Nashua, New Hampshire

Independent-religious, coed. Suburban campus. Total enrollment: 2,759.

Degrees Bachelor of Fine Arts in the areas of studio art, visual communication design. Majors: digital imaging, graphic design, illustration, painting/drawing, photography. Cross-registration with New Hampshire Consortium of Universities and Colleges.

Art Student Profile Fall 1994: 50 total; all matriculated undergraduate; 8% minorities, 75% females, 2% international.

Art Faculty Total: 14; 4 full-time, 10 part-time; 100% of full-time faculty have terminal degrees. Graduate students do not teach undergraduate courses. Undergraduate student–faculty ratio: 10:1.

Student Life Student groups include Rivier Fine Arts Society, "Adopt a School" Program, Rivier Theatre Company.

Expenses for 1995–96 Application fee: $25. Comprehensive fee of $16,400 includes full-time tuition ($11,010), mandatory fees ($140), and college room and board ($5250). College room only: $2835. Part-time tuition per credit: $367 for day division, $179 for evening division. Special program-related fees: $15 for art history field trips, $50 for sculpture studio materials, $60 for color and design course materials, $70 for 3-dimensional design and course materials.

Application Procedures Deadline—freshmen and transfers: continuous. Required: essay, high school transcript, college transcript(s) for transfer students, letter of recommendation, portfolio, SAT I test score only. Recommended: interview. Portfolio reviews held by appointment on campus; the submission of slides may be substituted for portfolios when distance is prohibitive.

Undergraduate Contact Darlene Nadeau, Assistant to the Chair for Promotion and Advancement, Art and Music Department, Rivier College, 420 Main Street, Nashua, New Hampshire 03060-5086; 603-888-1311 ext. 8269, fax: 603-888-6447.

Rochester Institute of Technology

Rochester, New York

Independent, coed. Suburban campus. Total enrollment: 12,250.

Degrees Bachelor of Fine Arts in the areas of medical illustration, printmaking, graphic design, illustration, industrial design, painting, interior design, furniture design, glass, textiles, ceramics. Majors: ceramics, computer graphics, furniture design, glass, graphic arts, illustration, industrial design, interior design, medical illustration, painting/drawing, printmaking, textile arts. Graduate degrees offered: Master of Fine Arts in the areas of graphic design, industrial design, interior design, medical illustration, painting, printmaking, illustration, furniture design, glass, textiles, ceramics.

Expenses for 1995–96 Application fee: $35. Comprehensive fee of $20,835 includes full-time tuition ($14,670), mandatory fees ($267), and college room and board ($5898). College room only: $3189. Part-time tuition: $350 per credit hour.

Application Procedures Deadline—freshmen and transfers: continuous. Notification date—freshmen and transfers: continuous. Required: high school transcript, college transcript(s) for transfer students, portfolio, SAT I or ACT test scores. Auditions held on campus and off campus. Portfolio reviews held on campus and off campus.

Contact Lorna Mullins, Secretary, School of Art and Design, School for American Crafts, Rochester Institute of Technology, Booth Building #7, P.O. Box 9887, Rochester, New York 14623-5604; 716-475-6114, fax: 716-475-6447.

Rocky Mountain College of Art & Design

Denver, Colorado

Proprietary, coed. Urban campus. Total enrollment: 366.

Degrees Bachelor of Fine Arts in the areas of advertising and graphic design, illustration, environmental graphic design, interior design, painting and drawing, sculpture and drawing. Majors: commercial art, illustration, interior design, painting/drawing, sculpture.

Art Student Profile Fall 1994: 350 total; 315 matriculated undergraduate, 35 nondegree; 5% minorities, 50% females, 2% international.

Art Faculty Total: 49; 4 full-time, 45 part-time; 75% of full-time faculty have terminal degrees. Graduate students do not teach undergraduate courses. Undergraduate student–faculty ratio: 20:1.

Student Life Student groups include American Society of Interior Designers, Society for Environmental Graphic Designers, Art Directors Club of Denver.

Expenses for 1994–95 Tuition: $6180 full-time, $206 per credit part-time. Part-time mandatory fees: $15 per trimester. Full-time mandatory fees: $30. Special program-related fees: $1,000 for supplies.

Financial Aid Program-specific awards for Fall of 1994: 15 RMCAD Scholarships for continuing students ($750).

Application Procedures Deadline—freshmen and transfers: continuous. Notification date—freshmen and transfers: continuous. Required: essay, high school transcript, college transcript(s) for transfer students, minimum 2.0 high school GPA, letter of recommendation, portfolio, SAT I or ACT test scores. Recommended: interview. Portfolio reviews held continuously on campus; the submission of slides may be substituted for portfolios.

Undergraduate Contact Rex Whisman, Director of Admissions, Rocky Mountain College of Art & Design, 6875 East Evans Avenue, Denver, Colorado 80224; 800-888-2787, fax: 303-759-4970.

Roland Dille Center for the Arts

See Moorhead State University, Roland Dille Center for the Arts

Mason Gross School of Arts

Rutgers, The State University of New Jersey

New Brunswick, New Jersey

State-supported, coed. Small-town campus. Total enrollment: 647.

Degrees Bachelor of Fine Arts in the area of visual art. Majors: ceramics, graphic design, painting/drawing, photography, printmaking, sculpture. Graduate degrees offered: Master of Fine Arts in the area of visual art.

Rutgers, The State University of New Jersey
(continued)

Art Student Profile Fall 1994: 225 total; 175 matriculated undergraduate, 50 matriculated graduate.

Art Faculty Total: 29; 23 full-time, 6 part-time; 100% of full-time faculty have terminal degrees. Graduate students teach a few undergraduate courses.

Expenses for 1995–96 Application fee: $50. State resident tuition: $3786 full-time, $122.50 per credit hour part-time. Nonresident tuition: $7707 full-time, $249.75 per credit hour part-time. Mandatory fees range from $105 to $1045 full-time, $155 to $187 per year part-time, according to college of affiliation. College room and board: $4253.

Financial Aid Program-specific awards for Fall of 1994: 2–3 Betts Scholarships for upperclassmen ($500).

Application Procedures Deadline—freshmen: January 15; transfers: March 15. Notification date—freshmen: June 1; transfers: July 1. Required: essay, high school transcript, portfolio. Portfolio reviews held 1 time on campus; the submission of slides may be substituted for portfolios when distance is prohibitive.

Undergraduate Contact Emma Amos, Undergraduate Director, Rutgers, The State University of New Jersey, 33 Livingston Avenue, New Brunswick, New Jersey 08901; 908-445-9078.

Graduate Contact Toby MacLennan, Graduate Director, Rutgers, The State University of New Jersey, 33 Livingston Avenue, New Brunswick, New Jersey 08901; 908-445-9078.

Saint Mary's College

Notre Dame, Indiana

Independent-religious, women only. Suburban campus. Total enrollment: 1,545.

Degrees Bachelor of Arts/Bachelor of Fine Arts in the areas of fine arts (painting, drawing, photography, printmaking, sculpture, fiber, ceramics). Majors: art education, art/fine arts, ceramic art and design, painting/drawing, photography, printmaking, sculpture, textile arts. Cross-registration with University of Notre Dame, Indiana Technical College, Indiana University South Bend, Goshen College, Bethel College.

Art Student Profile Fall 1994: 45 total; all matriculated undergraduate; 10% minorities, 100% females, 10% international.

Art Faculty Total: 8; 5 full-time, 3 part-time; 100% of full-time faculty have terminal degrees. Graduate students do not teach undergraduate courses. Undergraduate student–faculty ratio: 10:1.

Expenses for 1995–96 Application fee: $30. Comprehensive fee of $18,968 includes full-time tuition ($13,494), mandatory fees ($740), and college room and board ($4734 minimum). Part-time tuition: $562 per semester hour. Special program-related fees: $40 for studio supplies.

Financial Aid Program-specific awards for Fall of 1994: Art Talent Awards for art majors demonstrating need ($500), 1 Theresa McLaughlin Award for freshmen art major demonstrating need ($1000).

Application Procedures Deadline—freshmen: March 1; transfers: April 15. Notification date—freshmen and transfers: continuous. Required: essay, high school transcript, college transcript(s) for transfer students, minimum 3.0 high school GPA, letter of recommendation, SAT I or ACT test scores. Recommended: interview, portfolio. Auditions held on campus and off campus. Portfolio reviews held 2 times on campus and off campus.

Undergraduate Contact Admissions Office, Saint Mary's College, Notre Dame, Indiana 46556; 219-284-4587, fax: 219-284-4716.

Saint Vincent College

Latrobe, Pennsylvania

Independent-religious, coed. Rural campus.

Degrees Bachelor of Fine Arts in the areas of painting, sculpture, graphic design, printmaking, ceramics. Majors: art/fine arts, ceramic art and design, fashion design and technology, graphic arts, interior design, painting/drawing, photography, printmaking, sculpture, studio art. Mandatory cross-registration with Seton Hill College.

Art Student Profile Fall 1994: 21 total; all matriculated undergraduate; 4% minorities, 50% females, 1% international.

Art Faculty Total: 7; 4 full-time, 3 part-time; 90% of full-time faculty have terminal degrees. Graduate students do not teach undergraduate courses. Undergraduate student–faculty ratio: 13:1.

Expenses for 1995–96 Application fee: $25. Comprehensive fee of $16,200 includes full-time tuition ($12,000) and college room and board ($4200). Part-time tuition: $375 per credit. Special program-related fees: $50 for supplies.

Application Procedures Deadline—freshmen and transfers: continuous. Notification date—freshmen and transfers: continuous. Required: high school transcript, college transcript(s) for transfer students, minimum 2.0 high school GPA, interview, portfolio, SAT I or ACT test scores. Recommended: essay, minimum 3.0 high school GPA, letter of recommendation. Portfolio reviews held continuously off campus in Greensburg, PA; the submission of slides may be substituted for portfolios.

Undergraduate Contact Maureen Vissat, Chair, Art Department, Saint Vincent College, 300 Fraser Purchase Road, Greensburg, Pennsylvania 15601; 412-834-2200, fax: 412-830-4611.

Sam Houston State University

Huntsville, Texas

State-supported, coed. Small-town campus. Total enrollment: 12,906.

Degrees Bachelor of Fine Arts in the areas of studio arts, advertising/graphic design. Majors: studio art. Graduate degrees offered: Master of Fine Arts in the areas of drawing, painting, printmaking, sculpture, ceramics.

Art Student Profile Fall 1994: 287 total; 275 matriculated undergraduate, 10 matriculated graduate, 2 nondegree; 7% minorities, 60% females, 2% international.

Art Faculty Total: 12; 10 full-time, 2 part-time; 90% of full-time faculty have terminal degrees. Graduate students teach a few undergraduate courses. Undergraduate student–faculty ratio: 20:1.

Expenses for 1994–95 State resident tuition: $896 full-time. Nonresident tuition: $5472 full-time, $171 per semester hour part-time. State resident part-time tuition per semester ranges from $100 to $308. Part-time mandatory fees per semester range from $76 to $303. Full-time mandatory fees: $706. College room and board: $3070. College room only: $1530.

Financial Aid Program-specific awards for Fall of 1994: 1 Clem Otis Memorial Scholarship for enrolled students ($350), 1 Elkins Lake/Kuntz Nelson Scholarship for enrolled students ($200), 1 Harry Ahysen Scholarship/Art Endowment for enrolled students ($300), 1 Marion St. John Baker Scholarship for enrolled students ($250).

Application Procedures Deadline—freshmen and transfers: August 1. Required: high school transcript, college transcript(s) for transfer students, SAT I or ACT test scores, minimum combined SAT I score of 900, minimum composite ACT score of 21, minimum 2.0 college GPA for transfer students.

Undergraduate Contact Joey Chandler, Director, Undergraduate Admissions, Sam Houston State University, Box 2418, Huntsville, Texas 77341; 409-294-1315, fax: 409-294-3668.

Graduate Contact Kathy Ellisor, Secretary, College of Arts and Sciences, Sam Houston State University, Box 2209, Huntsville, Texas 77341; 409-294-3727, fax: 409-294-1598.

San Francisco Art Institute

San Francisco, California

Independent, coed. Urban campus. Total enrollment: 664.

Degrees Bachelor of Fine Arts in the areas of painting, photography, printmaking, sculpture, new genres. Majors: art/fine arts, ceramic art and design, new genre, painting/drawing, photography, printmaking, sculpture, studio art. Graduate degrees offered: Master of Fine Arts in the areas of painting, photography, printmaking, sculpture, new genres.

Art Student Profile Fall 1994: 662 total; 513 matriculated undergraduate, 129 matriculated graduate, 20 nondegree; 15% minorities, 50% females, 11% international.

Art Faculty Total: 63; 29 full-time, 34 part-time; 100% of full-time faculty have terminal degrees. Graduate students do not teach undergraduate courses. Undergraduate student–faculty ratio: 9:1.

Student Life Student groups include Multicultural Art Students, Gay and Lesbian Students, Artists for Social Responsibility.

Expenses for 1995–96 Application fee: $50. Tuition: $15,486 full-time, $646 per semester hour part-time.

Financial Aid Program-specific awards for Fall of 1994: 40 Sobel Scholarships for undergraduates ($4500), 24 Community College Scholarships for undergraduates ($4000).

Application Procedures Deadline—freshmen and transfers: continuous. Notification date—freshmen and transfers: September 1. Required: essay, high school transcript, college transcript(s) for transfer students, portfolio, SAT I or ACT test scores. Recommended: minimum 2.0 high school GPA, letter of recommendation, interview. Portfolio reviews held continuously on campus and off campus on National Portfolio Days; the submission of slides may be substituted for portfolios.

Contact Tim Robison, Vice President for Enrollment Services, San Francisco Art Institute, 800 Chestnut Street, San Francisco, California 94133; 415-749-4500, fax: 415-749-4590.

More about the Institute

Program Facilities Painting facilities include four large painting studios, an area for spray painting, and two spacious drawing studios. Photography facilities include eighteen private darkrooms, a group laboratory, and a Cibachrome room. Printmaking maintains complete facilities for silkscreen, etching, lithography, relief, book arts, and related photo-process printmaking. Sculpture occupies 6,840 square feet of classroom and shop space, including facilities for working in steel, wood, plaster, and ceramics. Film has facilities for shooting Super-8 and 16mm film, silent or with sync sound; two studios; and complete editing facilities. New Genres maintains three video-editing suites and a studio with special effects generation and mixing ability between live camera and tape. Facilities also include a state-of-the-art Digital Imaging Lab.

Faculty and Alumni Art Institute faculty and alumni include many important artists, including Stan Brackhage, Karen Finley, Dawn Fryling, David Ireland, George Kuchar, Annie Leibovitz, Bruce Nauman, and Sabina Ott.

Student Exhibition Opportunities The Diego Rivera Gallery, a showcase for work by students, provides opportunities for presenting work in a gallery setting, installations, or experimenting in a public venue.

Special Programs The Core Program: First-year study at the Art Institute provides the basic skills and information necessary to begin work in a primary field of studio interest, the basic language skills and historical and cultural information necessary to begin college-level work in liberal arts and art history, and a nurturing community that shares a common vocabulary for description, analysis and criticism, and the nature of art and the artist's role in society.

San Jose State University

San Jose, California

State-supported, coed. Urban campus. Total enrollment: 26,299.

Degrees Bachelor of Fine Arts in the area of art. Majors: art/fine arts, computer graphics, graphic design, illustration, industrial design, interior design, painting/drawing, photography, printmaking, studio art, textile arts. Graduate degrees offered: Master of Fine Arts in the area of art. Cross-registration with California State University System.

Art Student Profile Fall 1994: 1,320 total; 1,200 matriculated undergraduate, 120 matriculated graduate; 55% minorities, 55% females, 5% international.

Art Faculty Total: 84; 34 full-time, 50 part-time; 92% of full-time faculty have terminal degrees. Graduate students teach a few undergraduate courses. Undergraduate student–faculty ratio: 16:1.

Student Life Student groups include American Society of Interior Designers, Industrial Design Society of America, American Institute of Graphic Artists.

Expenses for 1995–96 Application fee: $55. State resident tuition: $0 full-time. Nonresident tuition: $7626 full-time, $246 per unit part-time. Part-time mandatory fees: $655 per semester. Full-time mandatory fees: $1976. College room and board: $4875 (minimum).

Financial Aid Program-specific awards for Fall of 1994: 10–15 Speddy Urban Awards for program students ($500–$1000), 5–10 Dooley Awards for program students ($500–$1000), 15–25 Art Scholarships for artistically talented program majors ($300).

Application Procedures Deadline—freshmen and transfers: August 1. Required: high school transcript, college transcript(s) for transfer students, minimum 2.0 high school GPA, portfolio, SAT I or ACT test scores, standing in upper 30% of graduating class. Portfolio reviews held 2 times on campus; the submission of slides may be substituted for portfolios.

Undergraduate Contact Office of Admissions and Records, San Jose State University, One Washington Square, San Jose, California 95192-0089; 408-924-2080.

Graduate Contact Paul Staiger, Graduate Advisor, School of Art and Design, San Jose State University, One Washington Square, San Jose, California 95192-0089; 408-924-4346, fax: 408-924-4326.

Savannah College of Art and Design

Savannah, Georgia

Independent, coed. Urban campus. Total enrollment: 2,488.

Degrees Bachelor of Fine Arts in the areas of architectural history, architecture, art history, computer art, fashion, fibers, furniture design, graphic design, historic preservation, illustration, industrial design, interior design, metals and jewelry, painting, photography, sequential art. Majors: art history, cartooning, computer graphics, fashion design and technology, furniture design, graphic arts, illustration, interior design, jewelry and metalsmithing, painting/drawing, photography, textile arts. Graduate degrees offered: Master of Fine Arts in the areas of architectural history, architecture, art history, computer art, fashion, fibers, furniture design, graphic design, historic preservation, illustration, industrial design, interior design, metals and jewelry, painting, photography, sequential art.

Art Student Profile Fall 1994: 2,488 total; 2,206 matriculated undergraduate, 271 matriculated graduate, 11 nondegree; 13% minorities, 46% females, 10% international.

Art Faculty Total: 143; 113 full-time, 30 part-time; 97% of full-time faculty have terminal degrees. Graduate students do not teach undergraduate courses. Undergraduate student–faculty ratio: 17:1.

Student Life Student groups include Graphic Union, Society of Computer Artists. Special housing available for art students.

Expenses for 1995–96 Application fee: $50. Comprehensive fee of $16,550 includes full-time tuition ($10,800) and college room and board ($5750). Part-time tuition: $1200 per course. College room only ranges from $3100 to $3600. Special program-related fees: $30 for photography lab fee.

Financial Aid Program-specific awards for Fall of 1994: Henderson Scholarships for undergraduates ($6000), Whelan Scholarships for undergraduates ($10,000), Friedman Scholarships for undergraduates ($20,000), Portfolio Scholarships for undergraduates ($10,000), Dorsey Scholarships for Selected Governors' Program ($10,000), Effing Scholarships for transfer students ($10,000), Fleming Scholarships for international students ($10,000), McCommon/White Scholarships for International Competition for Student Artists contest winners ($10,000), Trustees Scholarships for undergraduates ($10,000).

Application Procedures Deadline—freshmen and transfers: continuous. Notification date—freshmen and transfers: continuous. Required: high school transcript, college transcript(s) for transfer students, minimum 2.0 high school GPA, 3 letters of recommendation, SAT I or ACT test scores. Recommended: interview, portfolio. Portfolio reviews held by request on campus and off campus in various cities; the submission of slides may be substituted for portfolios.

Undergraduate Contact Admissions Office, Savannah College of Art and Design, P.O. Box 3146, Savannah, Georgia 31402-3146; 912-238-2483, fax: 912-238-2456, E-mail address: admissions@scad.edu.

Graduate Contact Vice President for Graduate Admissions, Admissions Office, Savannah College of Art and Design, P.O. Box 3146, Savannah, Georgia 31402-3146; 912-238-2424, fax: 912-238-2456, E-mail address: admissions@scad.edu.

More about the College

Program Facilities Fully equipped studios and classrooms with state-of-the-art equipment are available in each major. Among facilities are group and private black-and-white darkrooms, color darkrooms, and electronic imaging equipment; a complete resource lab for interior designers; CIAD computer lab for the building arts; skylit painting studios with oversized easels; a fully equipped graphic design production lab with Xerox 5775 digital color copier with a Fiery interface to a Macintosh computer; video production studios and a chromokey studio with a Super Panther production dolly system as well as editing and sound studios; computer labs equipped with Amiga, Macintosh, and IBM-compatible computers as well as Silicon Graphics workstations, color monitors, and color printers; a fabrication shop equipped with facilities for wood, metal, and plastics fabrication; a metals and jewelry lab; professional floor looms, including computerized AVL production dobby looms; the new Lectra computer systems for fashion design, complete with the "Graphic Instinct" program; and a comprehensive slide library of over 140,000 slides.

Student Performance/Exhibit Opportunities The College maintains many gallery spaces that feature constantly changing exhibits of works by internationally recognized professional artists in every discipline and medium. The work of students and faculty is displayed in the Bergen Galleries and at annual student-faculty shows. In addition, student work is continually displayed in gallery space dedicated to each major.

Special Programs In 1995 SCAD faculty will direct off-campus studies in the United States and Europe. Locations include Italy, France, England, and New York. Courses in art and architectural history, fashion photography, video, computer art, graphic design, drawing and painting, interior design, the fine arts, and theater add an exciting dimension to this college program. Also throughout the year, SCAD spotlights different majors through a week of seminars, guest lecturers, workshops, and/or exhibits. Students meet and learn from professionals successful in their fields.

The goal of the College is to nurture and cultivate the unique qualities of each student through the influence of an interesting curriculum, an inspiring environment, and the leadership of involved professors. The College exists for the purpose of preparing talented students for careers in the arts. Classes are student-centered, with the number one priority being the student's success in school and beyond.

Since its inception, the College has enjoyed a phenomenal rate of growth. Approximately 2500 students attend SCAD from virtually every state and fifty-four countries. At SCAD learning is a partnership between teacher and student. The focus is on the individual; classes average about 14 students each, and professors encourage active student involvement in learning. This "partnership learning" approach to education, combined with a dedicated corps of talented professors stressing career preparation, demonstrates the College's commitment to helping students succeed.

The College is located in the heart of Savannah's picturesque historic landmark district, providing a stimulating environment for the visually oriented student of art and design. Savannah is a living laboratory of architecturally and historically significant buildings. Only minutes from the ocean, Savannah's mild climate allows for many outdoor activities. Normal mean temperatures range from 81 degrees in July to 51 degrees in December. Because of its history as a thriving coastal port, Savannah has a cultural diversity unique among Southern cities. The city calendar is full of cultural and commemorative events and festivals offering a variety of local cuisine, musical performances, and artistic exhibitions, from Oktoberfest and St. Patrick's Day to the Coastal Jazz Festival and the College's own spring Sidewalk Arts Festival. Charleston, Jacksonville, Atlanta, and coastal islands such as Hilton Head Island are within driving distance and are pleasant to visit.

SCAD developed its curriculum around the belief that the serious art student wishes to maximize time spent on art-related subjects and minimize time spent on other subjects. The total course of study for a Bachelor of Fine Arts degree consists of 180 quarter hours (thirty-six courses). Of these, a student takes approximately 50 hours in the foundation program, 60 hours in liberal arts courses, 60 hours in the major area of study, and 10 hours of electives. The Bachelor of Architecture degree requires 225 hours, which include 35 foundation hours, 60 hours of liberal arts study, 95 hours in the major program, and 35 hours of electives. Independent study programs are also available to students wishing to pursue a highly specialized area of study.

Residence hall accommodations, with meal plans, are available for students who wish to reside in the College area. While students are not required to live in College housing, some consider the camaraderie and intellectual stimulation of residence hall life a highlight of their college experience. The housing fee includes furnishings (including drafting tables) and utilities and is payable in advance for the entire academic year. Early reservations are strongly recommended.

The College competes at the NCAA Division III level in baseball, basketball, golf, soccer, softball, tennis, and volleyball. The College sponsors rowing and rugby teams and a variety of intramural games.

Schmidt College of Arts and Humanities

See Florida Atlantic University, Schmidt College of Arts and Humanities

School of the Art Institute of Chicago

Chicago, Illinois

Independent, coed. Urban campus. Total enrollment: 2,891.

Degrees Bachelor of Fine Arts in the area of studio art. Majors: art education, art/fine arts, ceramic art and design, computer graphics, fashion design and technology, graphic arts, interior design, painting/drawing, performance art, photography, printmaking, sculpture, sound design, studio art, textile arts. Graduate degrees offered: Master of Fine Arts in the area of studio art. Cross-registration with Roosevelt University.

Art Student Profile Fall 1994: 2,832 total; 1,422 matriculated undergraduate, 210 matriculated graduate, 1,200 nondegree; 17% minorities, 5% international.

Art Faculty Total: 329; 95 full-time, 234 part-time; 84% of full-time faculty have terminal degrees. Graduate students teach a few undergraduate courses. Undergraduate student–faculty ratio: 14:1.

School of the Art Institute of Chicago *(continued)*

Student Life Student groups include Student Union, student newspaper, Artists of Color United. Special housing available for art students.

Expenses for 1995–96 Tuition: $15,300 full-time, $510 per semester hour part-time. Full-time mandatory fees: $600. College room only: $5100.

Financial Aid Program-specific awards for Fall of 1994: 29 Presidential Scholarships for academically qualified applicants ($5352), 86 Recognition Scholarships for academically qualified applicants ($2675), 20 Incentive Scholarships for academically qualified applicants ($1338), 11 Minority Scholarships for minority students ($2675), 765 School of the Art Institute of Chicago Grants for those demonstrating need ($3370).

Application Procedures Deadline—freshmen and transfers: continuous. Required: essay, high school transcript, minimum 2.0 high school GPA, letter of recommendation, portfolio. Recommended: minimum 3.0 high school GPA, interview. Portfolio reviews held continuously on campus and off campus on National Portfolio Days and several school-sponsored events; the submission of slides may be substituted for portfolios and required for transfer credit evaluation.

Undergraduate Contact Anne Morley, Director of Admissions, School of the Art Institute of Chicago, 37 South Wabash Avenue, Chicago, Illinois 60603; 312-899-5219, fax: 312-899-1840.

Graduate Contact Jennifer Stein, Graduate Coordinator, Admissions Department, School of the Art Institute of Chicago, 37 South Wabash Avenue, Chicago, Illinois 60603; 312-899-5219, fax: 312-263-0141.

More about the School

Program Facilities Computer studios: Macintosh II computers, Amiga 2000 computers, IBM computers with Lumena software, Silicon Graphics personal Iris computers, Silicon Graphics Indigo computers and Soft Image software, full color computers with CD-Rom drives. Fiber: Macomber computer loom and AVL computer loom. Filmmaking, video, and sound: Oxberry animation stand, mixing and transfer facilities, Steenbeck flatbeds, Bell & Howell contact printer, HI-8 cameras, 8mm video cameras, 3-chip HI-8 and ¾-inch cameras, hybrid 8mm to ¾-inch editing units, ¾-inch to ¾-inch editing units, 8mm to 8mm editing unit, HI-8 to HI-8 system, large scale video synthesis system, Yamaha SPX, Fairlight computer video instrument, 8-track recording/dubbing system, E Max digital sampling instrument, Yamaha DX7 digital synthesizer.

Faculty, Resident Artists, and Alumni During the past two decades, 9 SAIC faculty members have received John Simon Guggenheim Memorial Foundation Fellowships; many others have been recognized by the National Endowment for the Arts. Studio faculty are working artists/designers. Notable alumni: Grant Wood, Claes Oldenburg, Ivan Albright, Vincente Minnelli, Georgia O'Keeffe, Elizabeth Murray.

Student Performance/Exhibit Opportunities SAIC has two professional galleries; the Betty Rymer Gallery on campus, and Gallery 2 is located in the River West Gallery district. Many other student-run spaces are available throughout the School. The Fashion Department hosts a fashion show, in late spring, for students in their second, third, and fourth year.

Special Programs Foreign exchanges include: Ecole Nationale Superieure Des Beaux-Arts, Paris; Royal College of Art, London; Universitat De Barcelona; Staatliche Hochschule fur Bildende Kunste, Frankfurt. National schools: Minneapolis College of Art, San Francisco Art Institute, and more.

The School of the Art Institute of Chicago is an accredited college of the visual-related arts whose primary purpose is to foster the conceptual and technical education of the artist in a highly professional and studio-oriented environment. Believing that the artist's success is dependent on both creative vision and technical expertise, the School encourages excellence, critical inquiry, and experimentation.

Graduate and undergraduate students and the faculty of artists and scholars work closely, sharing resources and establishing a forum for critiquing and refining technical abilities and conceptual concerns.

The first-year program is the beginning of an art education that encourages exploration of various concepts and media. Along with 2-D and 3-D design, there are the challenges of 4-D design, which include filmmaking, performance, and video. With no declared majors, the student is allowed and encouraged to continue this exploration throughout the four years of study. The teaching of studio art, the complementary program in art history theory and criticism and liberal arts, the visiting artists, and the collections and exhibitions of one of the world's finest museums all contribute to the variety, the challenge, and the resonance of the educational experience.

The School, founded in 1866, offers students wishing to attain a degree at either the undergraduate or graduate level an opportunity to study in one of the most exciting cities in the world. The School's campus is situated within a five-block radius and is composed of three state-of-the art facilities in the heart of downtown Chicago.

About one half of the new students who enroll at the School will live in the Wolberg Residences. Located on Chicago's magnificent Michigan Avenue, the Wolberg residence hall is conveniently located, directly across the street from the museum of the Art Institute of Chicago and only a three-minute walk from the School's other studios, classrooms, and libraries. Each room has a refrigerator, private bath, custom-designed loft bed and work tables, and an individually controlled heating and cooling unit. Each floor has a common studio space as well as a common kitchen area with an oven and microwave.

The museum, galleries, and libraries (including the second-largest art research library in the country), undergraduate studios, school galleries, and classrooms create a lively and stimulating environment that facilitates the exchange of ideas among students at all levels. An education of this sort is rare and, for the artist, irreplaceable.

School of the Museum of Fine Arts

Boston, Massachusetts

Independent, coed. Urban campus. Total enrollment: 705.

Degrees Bachelor of Arts/Bachelor of Fine Arts in the area of fine arts. Majors: animation, art education, art/fine arts, ceramic art and design, computer graphics, electronic arts, illustration, jewelry and metalsmithing, painting/drawing, performance, photography, printmaking, sculpture, stained glass, studio art, video art. Graduate degrees offered: Master of Fine Arts in the area of fine arts. Cross-registration with ProArts Consortium, Association of Independent Colleges of Art and Design.

Art Student Profile Fall 1994: 705 total; 181 matriculated undergraduate, 89 matriculated graduate, 435 nondegree; 11% minorities, 58% females, 11% international.

Art Faculty Total: 182; 56 full-time, 126 part-time. Graduate students teach a few undergraduate courses. Undergraduate student–faculty ratio: 10:1.

Student Life Student groups include School Senate. Special housing available for art students.

Expenses for 1995–96 Application fee: $35. Tuition: $13,995 full-time. Part-time tuition for all students: $840 per 3-hour period. Full-time mandatory fees: $320.

Financial Aid Program-specific awards for Fall of 1994: 5 Art Merit Scholarships for freshmen ($3000), 230 School of the Museum of Fine Arts Grants for those demonstrating need ($3749).

Application Procedures Deadline—freshmen and transfers: continuous. Required: essay, college transcript(s) for transfer students, portfolio, interview for applicants within 150 miles of Boston, MA. Recommended: high school transcript, letter of recommendation, interview. Portfolio reviews held weekly on campus and off campus on National Portfolio Days; the submission of slides may be substituted for portfolios for large works of art.

Contact Admissions Office, School of the Museum of Fine Arts, 230 The Fenway, Boston, Massachusetts 02115; 617-267-6100 ext. 3626, fax: 617-424-6271, E-mail address: smfa_info@flo.org.

More about the School

Program Facilities A formal gallery, auditorium, lobby, and corridors are used as exhibition spaces for students of all levels and from every area of study during the academic year. Under special circumstances, students have twenty-four hour access to the studio facilities.

Faculty, Visiting Artists, and Alumni All studio faculty members are practicing professional artists with regional, national, and, in some cases, international reputations. The Visiting Artists Program encourages students to interact with prominent artists who have included John Baldessari, Karen Finley, Guillermo Gomez Pena, The Guerrilla Girls, Dennis Oppenheim, Lorna Simpson, Janine Antoni, and Bruce Nauman.

Exhibit Opportunities There are annual student exhibitions, including the Fall Boit Scholarship Competition, the Dana Pond Scholarship Competition, the December Exhibition and Sale, the January Exhibition, Annual Exhibition, Graduating Student Exhibition, Fifth Year Competition, and Traveling Scholars Exhibition held at the Museum of Fine Arts.

Special Programs The Fifth Year Certificate Program is a year of intensive independent study in studio art available to students who have earned the School's diploma. The School is a member of the ProArts Consortium of visual and performing arts institutions in Boston and participates in Mobility Programs through the Association of Independent Colleges of Art and Design (AICAD). The Career Services Office produces an Artists' Resources Letter every other week that lists various opportunities for artists.

Students at the School of the Museum of Fine Arts enjoy the unique opportunity to design their own programs of study and explore every area of the School, from animation to sculpture, ceramics to video, painting to photography, computers to printmaking, metals to stained glass, and more. There is no traditional departmental structure in the all-studio elective, diploma, and postbaccalaureate programs, so students are not limited to the course requirements of a major.

The portfolio for admission can consist of one or a number of techniques or media, depending on the interests and background of the applicant. The diversity of the faculty and the range of facilities allow the student to develop a very personal and individual means of expression. Many studio courses operate as open workshops in which students with a high degree of self-motivation excel. Course teaching methods range from structured classes, with regular attendance, to individual instruction for work done independently outside the School. Class sizes are generally small, and every area of study is supported by an accomplished, professional faculty; extensive visiting artists programs; and an energetic exhibitions schedule. At the end of each semester the student presents a body of art work from all classes to a review board consisting of faculty and students. There is a discussion of the total semester experience, and suggestions are made for future study. A block of credits is awarded, appropriate to the term's accomplishments, and a written evaluation is made.

Students and alumni can access information on local, national, and international job opportunities, exhibitions, competitions, grants, and more through the School's Career Services Office. Boston and its neighbor Cambridge are cities devoted to education and the arts. Many schools, museums, galleries, theaters, and music and dance spaces provide constant inspiration and entertainment to students. The Museum School is a part of Boston's Museum of Fine Arts, which allows the School to access the educational facilities, collections, and special programs of one of the most comprehensive and outstanding collections of art in the world. All undergraduate and graduate degrees are offered in affiliation with Tufts University. This long-standing affiliation provides a broad range of academic resources at a university of top national rank. The possibilities are limitless at the Museum School.

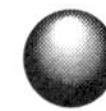

School of Visual Arts

New York, New York

Proprietary, coed. Urban campus. Total enrollment: 3,049.

Degrees Bachelor of Fine Arts in the areas of advertising and graphic design, art education, illustration and cartooning, interior design, photography, computer art, animation. Majors: advertising design, animation, applied art, art education, art/fine arts, cartooning, commercial art, computer art, computer graphics, graphic arts, illustration, interior design, painting/drawing, photography, printmaking, sculpture, studio art. Graduate degrees offered: Master of Fine Arts in the areas of computer art, illustration, photography.

Art Student Profile Fall 1994: 5,212 total; 2,745 matriculated undergraduate, 304 matriculated graduate, 2,163 nondegree; 26% minorities, 40% females, 20% international.

Art Faculty Total: 621; 87 full-time, 534 part-time; 36% of full-time faculty have terminal degrees. Graduate students do not teach undergraduate courses. Undergraduate student–faculty ratio: 13:1.

Student Life Student groups include Visual Arts Student Association, Photography Club. Special housing available for art students.

Expenses for 1995–96 Application fee: $30. Tuition: $12,400 full-time, $525 per credit part-time. Full-time mandatory fees: $200. College room only: $4800. Special program-related fees: $75–$350 for departmental fee.

Financial Aid Program-specific awards for Fall of 1994: 1042 Institutional Scholarships for undergraduates ($1920), 155 wages for undergraduates ($2700).

Application Procedures Deadline—freshmen and transfers: continuous. Required: essay, high school transcript, college transcript(s) for transfer students, portfolio, SAT I or ACT test scores. Recommended: minimum 2.0 high school GPA, interview. Portfolio reviews held 6 times and by appointment on campus; the submission of slides may be substituted for portfolios for large works of art (sculpture, painting, etc..

Contact Lawrence E. Wilson III, Director of Admissions, School of Visual Arts, 209 East 23rd Street, New York, New York 10010; 212-592-2100, fax: 212-725-3584.

More about the School

Program Facilities The School operates six student galleries and a professional gallery in SoHo at 137 Wooster Street for the exhibition and sale of advanced student work. Studio space and equipment are offered in different departments, varying in availability upon such factors as class seniority and the major of study. The SVA Library holds approximately 60,000 books, 110,000 35mm slides, and a picture file of 350,000 pieces. Other significant resources include a videotape collection and more than 50 original film scripts. The library subscribes to 255 periodicals.

Faculty, Resident Artists, and Alumni The School's roster of 700 faculty members, all of whom are working professionals, includes award-winning designers, critics, scholars, and artists. SVA's Alumni Society provides information, support services, and programs of general interest to artists.

Exhibit Opportunities SVA students are given numerous opportunities to exhibit their work twelve months a year in the main gallery space and in six student galleries. There are also many opportunities for students to have their work included in Visual Arts Press publications. Students are encouraged to show their work outside of SVA's framework by participating in exhibits and competitions held in New York City and throughout the United States.

Special Programs In addition to its campus in New York City, SVA has a branch campus in Savannah, Georgia, which opened in the Fall of 1994. SVA/Savannah offers programs in computer art, design, fine arts, and illustration to approximately 100 students who desire the SVA education in a historic, coastal, and less urban environment. Its resident faculty combines with visiting working professionals from the School's New York campus to provide SVA/Savannah students with opportunities that until now were available only to art students in New York.

Founded in 1947, the School of Visual Arts has grown steadily and is, today, one of the largest and best-equipped undergraduate colleges of art in the country. This growth is due principally to SVA's pioneering role in bringing outstanding working professionals to the classroom to teach what they know best. In addition, SVA's student advisement system not only adds close personal contact and strengthens its flexible programs but also seeks to ensure that the School will always have the best attributes of a small college. Taken together, these structures and the commitment to professionalism enable the School to bring to students some of the very best artists and designers in the world, directly from their studios, offices, and agencies in Manhattan. SVA's faculty, which numbers over 700, offers the benefits of size. Students have a broad choice of faculty within a curriculum that allows for many electives. At the same time the programs require that all students master the core of each of the disciplines taught. SVA also offers a broad range of course offerings not only in the arts, as might be expected, but also in art history, the humanities, and even computer science. SVA's faculty and courses foster that spirit of independence that is so necessary for creative work. But freedom requires self-discipline. Consequently, SVA expects the same commitment from its entering freshmen as from the most advanced graduate students.

SVA strives to prepare its students for professional careers in their field of study. In doing so, the School operates six student galleries and a professional gallery in SoHo at 137 Wooster Street for the exhibition and sale of advanced student work. A minimum of 20 group exhibitions are presented annually at the SoHo Gallery. The Visual Arts Museum at 209 East 23rd Street, also used at times to display student work, actively undertakes to improve visual awareness and increase aesthetic understanding by presenting the work of noted professionals working in the applied arts. As a result, over 13,000 SVA alumni are working in their field of study, and in the past four years alone, over 87 percent of the School's graduates have been employed in their major fields. As noted in *Advertising Age* magazine, SVA's foresight in staffing the School with professionals helps to prepare students for the real-life professional world. Many prominent artists have graduated with degrees from SVA, including graphic designer Paul Davis, fine artist Keith Haring, and the well-known painter of 60's psychedelia, Peter Max.

SVA offers workshops, one-week seminars, concentrated studio residencies, public lectures, panel discussion series, professional symposiums, international study programs, and a one-year Asian student program which serves as a vehicle for Chinese, Japanese, and Korean art students to make an effective transition into our education culture.

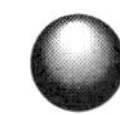

School of Visual Arts/Savannah

Savannah, Georgia

Proprietary, coed. Small-town campus. Total enrollment: 30.

Degrees Bachelor of Fine Arts in the areas of design, illustration. Majors: applied art, commercial art, design, graphic arts, illustration, painting/drawing, printmaking, sculpture, studio art.

Art Student Profile Fall 1994: 30 total; all matriculated undergraduate; 9% minorities, 30% females, 3% international.

Art Faculty Total: 5; 2 full-time, 3 part-time; 100% of full-time faculty have terminal degrees. Graduate students do not teach undergraduate courses. Undergraduate student–faculty ratio: 6:1.

Student Life Student groups include Visual Arts Student Association.

Expenses for 1995–96 Application fee: $30. Tuition: $9400 full-time. Full-time mandatory fees: $220. College room only: $3200. Special program-related fees: $30 for class fee.

Financial Aid Program-specific awards for Fall of 1994: 25 Institutional Scholarships for undergraduates ($1900), 6 wages for undergraduates ($1000).

Application Procedures Deadline—freshmen and transfers: continuous. Required: essay, high school transcript, college transcript(s) for transfer students, portfolio, SAT I or ACT test scores. Recommended: minimum 2.0 high school GPA, interview. Auditions held on campus and off campus. Portfolio reviews held 6 times and by appointment on campus and off campus; the submission of slides may be substituted for portfolios for large works of art (sculpture, painting, etc.).

Undergraduate Contact Lawrence E. Wilson III, Director of Admissions, School of Visual Arts/Savannah, 209 East 23rd Street, New York, New York 10010; 212-592-2100, fax: 212-725-3584.

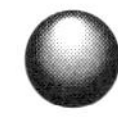

Seton Hill College

Greensburg, Pennsylvania

Independent-religious, primarily women. Small-town campus. Total enrollment: 923.

Degrees Bachelor of Fine Arts in the areas of painting, sculpture, graphic design, printmaking, ceramics, metalsmithing. Majors: art education, art history, art/fine arts, arts management, ceramic art and design, fabric styling, fashion design and technology, graphic arts, interior design, metals, painting/drawing, photography, printmaking, sculpture, studio art. Cross-registration with Saint Vincent College.

Art Student Profile Fall 1994: 100 total; all matriculated undergraduate; 80% females, 10% international.

Art Faculty Total: 7; 4 full-time, 3 part-time; 90% of full-time faculty have terminal degrees. Graduate students do not teach undergraduate courses. Undergraduate student–faculty ratio: 13:1.

Student Life Student groups include Student Art Society.

Expenses for 1994–95 Application fee: $30. Comprehensive fee of $15,520 includes full-time tuition ($11,090), mandatory fees ($250), and college room and board ($4180). Part-time tuition: $318 per credit. Part-time mandatory fees: $6 per credit. Special program-related fees: $50 for supplies.

Financial Aid Program-specific awards for Fall of 1994: 1–2 Hensler-Irwin Scholarships for freshmen program majors ($1000).

Application Procedures Deadline—freshmen and transfers: July 30. Notification date—freshmen and transfers: continuous. Required: high school transcript, minimum 2.0 high school GPA, letter of recommendation, portfolio. Recommended: essay, interview. Portfolio reviews held continuously on campus; the submission of slides may be substituted for portfolios when distance is prohibitive.

Undergraduate Contact Peter Egan, Director of Admissions, Seton Hill College, Greensburg, Pennsylvania 15601; 412-834-2200 ext. 4255.

Shannon Rodgers/Jerry Silverman School of Fashion Design and Merchandising

See Kent State University, Shannon Rodgers/Jerry Silverman School of Fashion Design and Merchandising

Shepherd College

Shepherdstown, West Virginia

State-supported, coed. Small-town campus. Total enrollment: 3,648.

Degrees Bachelor of Fine Arts. Majors: art/fine arts, graphic design, painting/drawing, photography, printmaking.

Art Student Profile Fall 1994: 210 total; all matriculated undergraduate.

Art Faculty Total: 10; 5 full-time, 5 part-time; 100% of full-time faculty have terminal degrees. Graduate students do not teach undergraduate courses. Undergraduate student–faculty ratio: 15:1.

Shepherd College *(continued)*

Expenses for 1995–96 Application fee: $20. State resident tuition: $2064 full-time. Nonresident tuition: $4694 full-time. Part-time tuition per semester ranges from $86 to $946 for state residents, $196 to $2153 for nonresidents. College room and board: $3960. College room only: $1910. Special program-related fees: $25 for studio fee.

Financial Aid Program-specific awards for Fall of 1994: 7 Art Scholarships for West Virginia resident program majors ($1800).

Application Procedures Deadline—freshmen and transfers: April 1. Required: minimum 2.0 high school GPA.

Undergraduate Contact Rhonda Smith, Chair, Art Department, Shepherd College, Frank Arts Center, Shepherdstown, West Virginia 25443; 304-876-2511 ext. 265, fax: 304-876-3101.

Siena Heights College

Adrian, Michigan

Independent-religious, coed. Small-town campus. Total enrollment: 1,141.

Degrees Bachelor of Fine Arts in the area of art. Majors: ceramics, graphic arts, metals, painting, photography, printmaking, sculpture.

Expenses for 1995–96 Application fee: $15. Comprehensive fee of $13,920 includes full-time tuition ($9810) and college room and board ($4110). Part-time tuition per semester hour ranges from $250 to $290.

Application Procedures Auditions held on campus and off campus. Portfolio reviews held on campus and off campus.

Undergraduate Contact Department of Art, Siena Heights College, 1247 East Siena Heights Drive, Adrian, Michigan 49221; 517-263-0731, fax: 517-265-3380.

Simon Fraser University

Burnaby, British Columbia

Province-supported, coed. Suburban campus. Total enrollment: 18,252.

Degrees Bachelor of Fine Arts in the area of visual arts. Majors: art/fine arts. Graduate degrees offered: Master of Fine Arts in the area of interdisciplinary studies.

Art Student Profile Fall 1994: 227 total; 225 matriculated undergraduate, 2 matriculated graduate.

Art Faculty Total: 4; 4 full-time; 100% of full-time faculty have terminal degrees. Graduate students teach a few undergraduate courses. Undergraduate student–faculty ratio: 50:1.

Expenses for 1994–95 Application fee: $20. Canadian resident tuition: $2190 full-time, $73 per credit hour part-time. Nonresident tuition: $6570 full-time, $219 per credit hour part-time. Part-time mandatory fees: $50 per trimester. (All figures are in Canadian dollars.). Full-time mandatory fees: $178. College room only: $2120. Special program-related fees: $50–$100 for studio lab fee.

Financial Aid Program-specific awards for Fall of 1994: 1 Marcia Scholarship for music students, 1 Murray Farr Scholarship for program majors ($500), 1 Adaline Clark Scholarships for program majors ($500), 1 SCA Scholarship for program majors, 1 Helen Pitt Scholarship for program majors.

Application Procedures Deadline—freshmen and transfers: May 1. Required: high school transcript, college transcript(s) for transfer students, minimum 3.0 high school GPA, interview, video, portfolio. Auditions held on campus; videotaped performances are permissible as a substitute for live auditions for international applicants. Portfolio reviews held 2 times (or portfolio may be sent by mail) on campus; the submission of slides may be substituted for portfolios.

Undergraduate Contact Admissions Office, Simon Fraser University, Burnaby, British Columbia V5A 156, Canada; 604-291-3224, fax: 604-291-4969.

Graduate Contact Donna Zapf, Chair, MFA Program, School for the Contemporary Arts, Simon Fraser University, Burnaby, British Columbia V5A 156, Canada; 604-291-3603, fax: 604-291-5907, E-mail address: mfa_grad_office@sfu.ca.

Sonoma State University

Rohnert Park, California

State-supported, coed. Small-town campus. Total enrollment: 6,610.

Degrees Bachelor of Fine Arts in the areas of painting, printmaking, sculpture, photography. Majors: art/fine arts, painting/drawing, photography, printmaking, sculpture. Cross-registration with San Francisco State University.

Art Student Profile Fall 1994: 17 total; all matriculated undergraduate; 19% minorities, 65% females, 5% international.

Art Faculty Total: 8; 6 full-time, 2 part-time; 100% of full-time faculty have terminal degrees. Graduate students do not teach undergraduate courses. Undergraduate student–faculty ratio: 24:1.

Student Life Student groups include BFA Student Exhibition, Student Art Exhibition.

Expenses for 1994–95 Application fee: $55. State resident tuition: $0 full-time. Nonresident tuition: $7380 full-time, $246 per unit part-time. Part-time mandatory fees: $702 per semester. Full-time mandatory fees: $2070. College room and board: $5450. College room only: $4030. Special program-related fees: $25–$50 for supplies.

Financial Aid Program-specific awards for Fall of 1994: 1 William Smith Award for ceramics majors ($500), 1 William Smith Award for studio art majors ($500), 1 Les and Alexis Brooks Award for art history majors ($400), 1 John Bolles Scholarship for program majors ($750).

Application Procedures Deadline—freshmen and transfers: November 30. Required: essay, college transcript(s) for transfer students, minimum 3.0 high school GPA, 2 letters of recommendation, portfolio. Portfolio reviews held 2 times (students apply in junior year) on campus.

Undergraduate Contact William Guynn, Chair, Art Department, Sonoma State University, 1801 East Cotati Avenue, Rohnert Park, California 94928; 707-664-2151, fax: 707-664-2505, E-mail address: william.guynn@sonoma.edu.

Southern Illinois University at Carbondale

Carbondale, Illinois

State-supported, coed. Small-town campus. Total enrollment: 23,162.

Degrees Bachelor of Fine Arts in the area of art. Majors: ceramic art and design, jewelry and metalsmithing, painting/drawing, printmaking, sculpture, weaving and fibers. Graduate degrees offered: Master of Fine Arts in the area of art.

Art Student Profile Fall 1994: 118 total; 63 matriculated undergraduate, 55 matriculated graduate; 7% minorities, 40% females, 5% international.

Art Faculty Total: 30; 26 full-time, 4 part-time; 100% of full-time faculty have terminal degrees. Graduate students teach about a quarter undergraduate courses. Undergraduate student–faculty ratio: 5:1.

Expenses for 1995–96 State resident tuition: $2400 full-time, $80 per semester hour part-time. Nonresident tuition: $7200 full-time, $240 per semester hour part-time. Part-time mandatory fees: $241.64 per semester. Full-time mandatory fees: $936. College room and board: $3352. Special program-related fees: $50 for model fees, $3–$75 for studio materials.

Financial Aid Program-specific awards for Fall of 1994: 5–7 Talent Scholarships for incoming students ($1000), 2 Mitchell Scholarships for incoming students from Southern Illinois ($1000).

Application Procedures Deadline—freshmen and transfers: continuous. Notification date—freshmen and transfers: continuous. Required: high school transcript, SAT I or ACT test scores.

Undergraduate Contact Joyce Jolliff, Academic Adviser, School of Art and Design, Southern Illinois University at Carbondale, Carbondale, Illinois 62901-4301; 618-453-4315, fax: 618-453-7710, E-mail address: ge1085@siucvmb.edu.

Graduate Contact Michael Onken, Head of Graduate Programs, School of Art and Design, Southern Illinois University at Carbondale, Carbondale, Illinois 62901-4301; 618-453-4315, fax: 618-453-7710.

Southern Illinois University at Edwardsville

Edwardsville, Illinois

State-supported, coed. Small-town campus. Total enrollment: 10,938.

Degrees Bachelor of Fine Arts in the area of art studio. Majors: applied art, art/fine arts, ceramic art and design, commercial art, computer graphics, drafting and design, glassworking, graphic arts, jewelry and metalsmithing, painting/drawing, photography, printmaking, sculpture, studio art, textile arts. Graduate degrees offered: Master of Fine Arts in the area of art studio.

Art Student Profile Fall 1994: 332 total; 255 matriculated undergraduate, 67 matriculated graduate, 10 nondegree; 20% minorities, 55% females, 10% international.

Art Faculty Total: 27; 17 full-time, 10 part-time; 100% of full-time faculty have terminal degrees. Graduate students teach a few undergraduate courses. Undergraduate student–faculty ratio: 17:1.

Expenses for 1995–96 State resident tuition: $1842 full-time, $76.75 per credit part-time. Nonresident tuition: $5526 full-time, $230.25 per credit part-time. Part-time mandatory fees per semester range from $97.65 to $243.65. Full-time mandatory fees: $488. College room and board: $3498. College room only: $2028. Special program-related fees: $12–$22 for studio fee.

Application Procedures Deadline—freshmen and transfers: continuous. Notification date—freshmen and transfers: continuous. Required: essay, high school transcript, college transcript(s) for transfer students, minimum 2.0 high school GPA.

Undergraduate Contact Director of Admission, Southern Illinois University at Edwardsville, Campus Box 1047, Edwardsville, Illinois 62026; 618-692-3705.

Graduate Contact Daniel Anderson, Graduate Advisor, Art and Design Department, Southern Illinois University at Edwardsville, Campus Box 1774, Edwardsville, Illinois 62026; 618-692-3071, fax: 618-692-3096.

Meadows School of the Arts

Southern Methodist University

Dallas, Texas

Independent-religious, coed. Suburban campus. Total enrollment: 9,014.

Degrees Bachelor of Fine Arts in the area of art. Majors: studio art. Graduate degrees offered: Master of Fine Arts in the area of art.

Art Student Profile Fall 1994: 98 total; 68 matriculated undergraduate, 7 matriculated graduate, 23 nondegree; 22% minorities, 50% females, 5% international.

Art Faculty Total: 14; 13 full-time, 1 part-time; 90% of full-time faculty have terminal degrees. Graduate stu-

Southern Methodist University *(continued)*

dents do not teach undergraduate courses. Undergraduate student–faculty ratio: 7:1.

Student Life Student groups include Student Art Association. Special housing available for art students.

Expenses for 1994–95 Application fee: $40. Comprehensive fee of $19,474 includes full-time tuition ($12,772), mandatory fees ($1624), and college room and board ($5078). College room only: $2426. Part-time tuition: $532 per credit hour. Part-time mandatory fees: $68 per semester. Special program-related fees: $10 for model and supply fees.

Financial Aid Program-specific awards for Fall of 1994: 10 Meadows Artistic Scholarships for talented program majors ($1000–$6000).

Application Procedures Deadline—freshmen and transfers: continuous. Required: essay, high school transcript, college transcript(s) for transfer students, letter of recommendation, SAT I or ACT test scores. Recommended: interview, portfolio. Portfolio reviews held 1 time on campus.

Undergraduate Contact Charles J. Helfert, Associate Dean, Meadows School of the Arts, Southern Methodist University, P.O. Box 750356, Dallas, Texas 75275-0356; 214-768-3217, fax: 214-768-3272.

Graduate Contact Jeannette Garnsey, Director, Graduate Admissions and Records, Meadows School of the Arts, Southern Methodist University, P.O. Box 750356, Dallas, Texas 75275-0356; 214-768-3765, fax: 214-768-3272.

Southern Oregon State College

Ashland, Oregon

State-supported, coed. Small-town campus. Total enrollment: 4,554.

Degrees Bachelor of Fine Arts in the areas of painting, printmaking, photography, ceramics, sculpture, fibers. Majors: ceramic art and design, painting/drawing, photography, printmaking, sculpture, studio art, textile arts. Cross-registration with National Student Exchange.

Art Student Profile Fall 1994: 140 total; all matriculated undergraduate.

Art Faculty Total: 18; 11 full-time, 7 part-time; 100% of full-time faculty have terminal degrees. Graduate students do not teach undergraduate courses. Undergraduate student–faculty ratio: 20:1.

Student Life Student groups include Society of Fine Arts Students.

Expenses for 1994–95 Application fee: $50. State resident tuition: $2835 full-time. Nonresident tuition: $7824 full-time. Part-time tuition per quarter ranges from $114 to $875 for state residents, $114 to $2399 for nonresidents. College room and board: $3562. Special program-related fees: $5–$50 for materials.

Application Procedures Deadline—freshmen and transfers: continuous. Notification date—freshmen and transfers: continuous. Required: high school transcript, portfolio, minimum 2.75 high school GPA. Recommended: minimum 3.0 high school GPA, 3 letters of recommendation, interview. Portfolio reviews held 2 times during junior year on campus; the submission of slides may be substituted for portfolios for transfer applicants.

Undergraduate Contact Director, Admissions and Records Department, Southern Oregon State College, 1250 Siskiyou Boulevard, Ashland, Oregon 97520; 503-552-6411, fax: 503-552-6329.

Southwest Missouri State University

Springfield, Missouri

State-supported, coed. Suburban campus. Total enrollment: 17,310.

Degrees Bachelor of Fine Arts in the areas of design, fine arts. Majors: ceramic art and design, computer graphics, digital imaging, fibers, graphic arts, illustration, jewelry and metalsmithing, painting/drawing, photography, printmaking, sculpture, studio art.

Art Student Profile Fall 1994: 388 total; all matriculated undergraduate; 10% minorities, 50% females, 5% international.

Art Faculty Total: 33; 25 full-time, 8 part-time; 95% of full-time faculty have terminal degrees. Graduate students do not teach undergraduate courses. Undergraduate student–faculty ratio: 16:1.

Expenses for 1995–96 Application fee: $15. State resident tuition: $2370 full-time, $79 per credit hour part-time. Nonresident tuition: $4898 full-time. Part-time mandatory fees per semester range from $41 to $88. Part-time tuition per credit hour for nonresidents: $79 for the first 3 credits, $158 for the next 8 credits. Full-time mandatory fees: $176. College room and board: $2722 (minimum). College room only: $1755 (minimum).

Financial Aid Program-specific awards for Fall of 1994: 10 Department Awards for program majors ($500–$800).

Application Procedures Deadline—freshmen and transfers: August 1. Notification date—freshmen and transfers: continuous. Required: high school transcript, minimum 2.0 high school GPA. Portfolio reviews held at end of sophomore year on campus; the submission of slides may be substituted for portfolios.

Undergraduate Contact James K. Hill, Head, Art and Design Department, Southwest Missouri State University, 901 South National, Springfield, Missouri 65804; 417-836-5110.

More about the University

The Departments of Arts and Design, Music and Theatre, and Dance are in the College of Arts and Letters and are among the largest and most active arts departments at state-supported institutions in Missouri.

The Department of Art and Design has a gallery for exhibitions by faculty and guests and another for students. Microcomputers, a mainframe terminal, and video systems support the programs in applied design technology and art education. Other facilities include a completely equipped applied design studio, black-and-

white and color photography processing labs, a metals casting foundry, precious metals studios, and a slide collection consisting of approximately 75,000 transparencies.

The Department of Music is accredited by the National Association of Schools of Music. Faculty members and student present concerts in the new Juanita K. Hammons Hall for Performing Arts and the smaller Ellis Recital Hall. There are an electronic music laboratory, a computer-assisted instruction laboratory, a listening laboratory with Apple computers to assist students in the development of skills in music, and a piano laboratory to help develop keyboard skills. The marching band, with over 350 members, is one of the largest in the nation.

The Department of Theatre and Dance presents eight major productions a year, including contemporary and period plays, musicals, operas, dance concerts, and plays for young people. Summer Tent Theatre presents two musicals and a comedy playing in repertory for six weeks. Productions are presented in a 500-seat proscenium theater, a 400-seat proscenium theater, and a 100-seat thrust studio and in the summer in the 350-seat open stage of the Tent. The Department sponsors a number of student touring groups: In-School Players consists of 6 to 8 performers who create their own material and then tour the area elementary schools during the late fall and spring. Inertia Dance Company consists of students who develop materials to present as programs in communities and schools in southwest Missouri and northern Arkansas. Bear Stages is a peer education troupe that develops materials concerning social and health issues to present before campus organizations. Footnotes Entertainment Troupe develops musical and dance programs to present for university public relations and scholarship fundraising purposes.

Southwest Texas State University

San Marcos, Texas

State-supported, coed. Small-town campus. Total enrollment: 20,899.

Degrees Bachelor of Fine Arts in the areas of studio art, commercial art, art education. Majors: art education, art/fine arts, ceramic art and design, commercial art, computer graphics, graphic arts, illustration, jewelry and metalsmithing, painting/drawing, photography, printmaking, sculpture, studio art, textile arts.

Art Student Profile Fall 1994: 456 total; all matriculated undergraduate; 22% minorities, 53% females, 1% international.

Art Faculty Total: 33; 19 full-time, 14 part-time; 100% of full-time faculty have terminal degrees. Graduate students do not teach undergraduate courses. Undergraduate student–faculty ratio: 18:1.

Estimated Expenses for 1995–96 Application fee: $25. State resident tuition: $900 full-time. Nonresident tuition: $5280 full-time, $176 per semester hour part-time. State resident part-time tuition per semester ranges from $100 to $330. Part-time mandatory fees per semester range from $207 to $407. Full-time mandatory fees: $906. College room and board: $3676. College room only: $2198. Special program-related fees: $10–$35 for material fees.

Financial Aid Program-specific awards for Fall of 1994: 1 Dr. Francis Henry Scholarship for art education majors ($500), 1 Louise Eckerd McGehee Scholarship for program majors ($500), 8–12 Student Services Fee Scholarships for program majors ($200–$400), 10 Research/Materials Grants for program majors ($200), 1 Presidential Upper Level Scholarship for program majors ($1200), 1 Turner Endowed Scholarship for painting majors ($500).

Application Procedures Deadline—freshmen and transfers: July 1. Required: high school transcript, college transcript(s) for transfer students, minimum 2.0 high school GPA, SAT I or ACT test scores.

Undergraduate Contact Brian Row, Chair, Art Department, Southwest Texas State University, 601 University Drive, San Marcos, Texas 78666; 512-245-2611, fax: 512-245-3040, E-mail address: br01@swt.edu.

St. Cloud State University

St. Cloud, Minnesota

State-supported, coed. Suburban campus. Total enrollment: 14,673.

Degrees Bachelor of Fine Arts in the areas of studio art, graphic design. Majors: applied art, art education, art/fine arts, ceramic art and design, computer graphics, graphic arts, jewelry and metalsmithing, painting/drawing, photography, printmaking, sculpture, studio art, textile arts.

Art Student Profile Fall 1994: 340 total; all matriculated undergraduate; 2% minorities, 60% females, 3% international.

Art Faculty Total: 16; 13 full-time, 3 part-time; 80% of full-time faculty have terminal degrees. Graduate students teach a few undergraduate courses. Undergraduate student–faculty ratio: 20:1.

Expenses for 1995–96 Application fee: $15. State resident tuition: $2376 full-time, $49.50 per quarter hour part-time. Nonresident tuition: $5160 full-time, $107.50 per quarter hour part-time. Part-time mandatory fees: $9.68 per quarter hour. Full-time mandatory fees: $465. College room and board: $2937. Special program-related fees: $15–$25 for lab fees.

Financial Aid Program-specific awards for Fall of 1994: 2–3 Bill Ellingson Awards for program majors ($500), 4 May Bowle Awards for program majors ($500).

Application Procedures Deadline—freshmen and transfers: August 15. Required: high school transcript, minimum 2.0 high school GPA.

Undergraduate Contact Art Department, St. Cloud State University, Kiehle Visual Arts Building, St. Cloud, Minnesota 56301; 612-255-4283.

St. John's University

Jamaica, New York

Independent-religious, coed. Urban campus. Total enrollment: 17,820.

Degrees Bachelor of Fine Arts in the areas of fine arts, graphic design, photography. Majors: art/fine arts, graphic design, photography. Mandatory cross-registration with International Center of Photography.

Art Student Profile Fall 1994: 100 total; all matriculated undergraduate.

Art Faculty Total: 16; 8 full-time, 8 part-time; 100% of full-time faculty have terminal degrees. Graduate students do not teach undergraduate courses. Undergraduate student–faculty ratio: 15:1.

Student Life Student groups include New Vision Art Society, Art Exhibits in University Gallery, Senior Citizens Art Program.

Expenses for 1995–96 Application fee: $20. Tuition: $10,050 full-time, $335 per credit part-time. Part-time mandatory fees per semester range from $70 to $155. Full-time mandatory fees: $400. Special program-related fees: $30 for studio lab fee.

Financial Aid Program-specific awards for Fall of 1994: 2 Fine Arts Scholarships for incoming freshmen, 3 Visual Arts Awards for incoming freshmen ($1000).

Application Procedures Deadline—freshmen and transfers: continuous. Required: high school transcript, college transcript(s) for transfer students, letter of recommendation, portfolio, SAT I or ACT test scores, minimum 3.0 high school GPA or minimum 1000 SAT combined score. Portfolio reviews held continuously by appointment on campus; the submission of slides may be substituted for portfolios for foreign students and U.S. students from great distance.

Undergraduate Contact Jeanne Umland, Associate Vice President and Executive Director, Admissions, St. John's University, 8000 Utopia Parkway, Jamaica, New York 11439; 718-990-6250, fax: 718-990-1677.

State University of New York College at Purchase

See Purchase College, State University of New York

State University of New York at Buffalo

Buffalo, New York

State-supported, coed. Suburban campus. Total enrollment: 24,943.

Degrees Bachelor of Fine Arts in the area of fine art. Majors: communication design, computer art, illustration, painting/drawing, photography, printmaking, sculpture. Graduate degrees offered: Master of Fine Arts in the area of fine art.

Art Student Profile Fall 1994: 266 total; 199 matriculated undergraduate, 24 matriculated graduate, 43 nondegree; 10% minorities.

Art Faculty Total: 20; 14 full-time, 6 part-time; 90% of full-time faculty have terminal degrees. Graduate students teach about a quarter undergraduate courses. Undergraduate student–faculty ratio: 18:1.

Student Life Student groups include Art Department Gallery exhibits, University Gallery exhibits.

Estimated Expenses for 1995–96 Application fee: $25. State resident tuition: $2650 full-time, $105 per credit hour part-time. Nonresident tuition: $6550 full-time, $274 per credit hour part-time. Part-time mandatory fees: $23.50 per credit hour. Full-time mandatory fees: $594. College room and board: $5024. College room only: $2874. Special program-related fees: $15–$75 for lab fees, supplies, models.

Application Procedures Deadline—freshmen and transfers: January 1. Notification date—freshmen and transfers: April 15. Required: college transcript(s) for transfer students, portfolio. Recommended: essay, letter of recommendation. Portfolio reviews held 1 time on campus; the submission of slides may be substituted for portfolios whenever needed.

Undergraduate Contact Coordinator of Student Affairs, Art Department, State University of New York at Buffalo, 202 Center for the Arts, Buffalo, New York 14260-6010; 716-645-6882, fax: 716-645-6970.

Graduate Contact Director of Graduate Studies, Art Department, State University of New York at Buffalo, 202 Center for the Arts, Buffalo, New York 14260-6010; 716-645-6878, fax: 716-645-6970.

State University of New York at New Paltz

New Paltz, New York

State-supported, coed. Rural campus. Total enrollment: 7,897.

Degrees Bachelor of Fine Arts in the areas of ceramics, metals, painting, photography, printmaking, sculpture, graphic design. Majors: art education, ceramic art and design, graphic design, jewelry and metalsmithing, painting/drawing, photography, printmaking, sculpture. Graduate degrees offered: Master of Fine Arts in the areas of ceramics, metals, painting, photography, printmaking, sculpture, graphic design, interdisciplinary studies. Cross-registration with State University of New York system.

Art Student Profile Fall 1994: 530 total; 450 matriculated undergraduate, 80 matriculated graduate.

Art Faculty Total: 31; 22 full-time, 9 part-time. Graduate students teach a few undergraduate courses.

Student Life Student groups include Student Art Alliance, National Art Educators Association.

Expenses for 1995–96 Application fee: $25. State resident tuition: $3400 full-time, $142 per credit part-time. Nonresident tuition: $8300 full-time, $346 per credit part-time. Part-time mandatory fees per semester range from $40.60 to $148.60. Full-time mandatory fees: $351. College room and board: $4918. College room only: $2920. Special program-related fees: $45–$80 for lab fees.

Financial Aid Program-specific awards for Fall of 1994: Resnick Scholarship for incoming freshmen.

Application Procedures Deadline—freshmen: May 1; transfers: June 1. Required: high school transcript, portfolio, SAT I or ACT test scores. Portfolio reviews held 10 times on campus and off campus in Albany, NY; the submission of slides may be substituted for portfolios.

Contact Art Department, State University of New York at New Paltz, SAB 106, South Manheim Boulevard, New Paltz, New York 12561; 914-257-3830.

Stephen F. Austin State University

Nacogdoches, Texas

State-supported, coed. Small-town campus. Total enrollment: 12,206.

Degrees Bachelor of Fine Arts in the area of art. Majors: art education, art/fine arts, ceramic art and design, computer graphics, graphic arts, jewelry and metalsmithing, painting/drawing, photography, printmaking, sculpture, studio art. Graduate degrees offered: Master of Fine Arts in the area of art.

Art Student Profile Fall 1994: 181 total; 157 matriculated undergraduate, 24 matriculated graduate; 45% females.

Art Faculty Total: 15; 15 full-time; 93% of full-time faculty have terminal degrees. Graduate students teach a few undergraduate courses. Undergraduate student–faculty ratio: 18:1.

Expenses for 1994–95 State resident tuition: $896 full-time. Nonresident tuition: $5472 full-time, $171 per semester hour part-time. State resident part-time tuition per semester ranges from $100 to $308. Part-time mandatory fees per semester range from $32.25 to $166.50. Full-time mandatory fees: $832. College room and board: $3542. Special program-related fees: $5–$40 for supplies.

Financial Aid Program-specific awards for Fall of 1994: 6–10 Art Scholarships for program majors ($200–$600).

Application Procedures Deadline—freshmen and transfers: August 15. Required: high school transcript, college transcript(s) for transfer students, SAT I or ACT test scores, minimum combined SAT I score of 800, minimum composite ACT score of 19.

Contact John D. Wink, Chairman, Art Department, Stephen F. Austin State University, Box 13001 SFA Station, Nacogdoches, Texas 75962-3001; 409-568-4804, fax: 409-568-4041, E-mail address: f_priceep@titan.sfasu.edu.

Stephens College

Columbia, Missouri

Independent, women only. Urban campus. Total enrollment: 600.

Degrees Bachelor of Fine Arts in the area of visual arts. Majors: art/fine arts, ceramic art and design, computer graphics, fashion design and technology, graphic arts, painting/drawing, printmaking, studio art. Cross-registration with University of Missouri&–Columbia, Columbia College, William Woods College, Westminster College, Lincoln University.

Art Student Profile Fall 1994: 30 total; all matriculated undergraduate; 6% minorities, 100% females.

Art Faculty Total: 5; 5 full-time; 100% of full-time faculty have terminal degrees. Graduate students do not teach undergraduate courses. Undergraduate student–faculty ratio: 10:1.

Student Life Student groups include Fine Arts Club.

Expenses for 1995–96 Application fee: $25. Comprehensive fee of $19,770 includes full-time tuition ($14,400) and college room and board ($5370). College room only: $2900. Part-time tuition: $1140 per course.

Financial Aid Program-specific awards for Fall of 1994: 1 Gardiner Nettleton Materials Scholarship for those demonstrating need ($750).

Application Procedures Deadline—freshmen and transfers: continuous. Required: high school transcript, minimum 2.0 high school GPA, letter of recommendation, SAT I or ACT test scores. Recommended: minimum 3.0 high school GPA, portfolio. Portfolio reviews held 1 time on campus; the submission of slides may be substituted for portfolios.

Undergraduate Contact Rosalind Kimball Moulton, Chair, Visual Arts and Humanities Department, Stephens College, Box 2012, Columbia, Missouri 65215; 314-876-7251, fax: 314-876-7237.

Sul Ross State University

Alpine, Texas

State-supported, coed. Small-town campus. Total enrollment: 3,145.

Degrees Bachelor of Fine Arts in the area of art. Majors: applied art, art education, art/fine arts, ceramic art and design, computer graphics, drafting and design, graphic arts, illustration, jewelry and metalsmithing, painting/drawing, printmaking, sculpture, studio art, textile arts.

Art Student Profile Fall 1994: 37 total; 30 matriculated undergraduate, 7 nondegree; 40% minorities, 50% females.

Art Faculty Total: 7; 3 full-time, 4 part-time; 100% of full-time faculty have terminal degrees. Graduate students do not teach undergraduate courses. Undergraduate student–faculty ratio: 15:1.

Student Life Student groups include Art Club, Student Art Show.

Sul Ross State University *(continued)*

Expenses for 1995–96 State resident tuition: $960 full-time. Nonresident tuition: $5632 full-time, $176 per semester part-time. State resident part-time tuition per semester ranges from $100 to $330. Part-time mandatory fees per semester range from $29 to $292. Full-time mandatory fees: $612. College room and board: $3160. College room only: $1500.

Financial Aid Program-specific awards for Fall of 1994: 6 Boatright Scholarships for undergraduates ($100–$300).

Application Procedures Deadline—freshmen and transfers: continuous. Required: high school transcript, minimum 2.0 high school GPA, portfolio. Recommended: interview. Portfolio reviews held 1 time on campus.

Undergraduate Contact Director of Admissions, Sul Ross State University, Box C-2, Alpine, Texas 79832; 915-837-8050.

Syracuse University

Syracuse, New York

Independent, coed. Urban campus. Total enrollment: 14,550.

Degrees Bachelor of Fine Arts in the areas of advertising design, art education, ceramics, computer graphics, communications design, fibers, history of art, interior design, metalsmithing, painting, photography, printmaking, sculpture, surface pattern design, illustration; Bachelor of Industrial Design in the area of industrial design. Majors: advertising design, art education, art history, ceramic art and design, communication design, computer graphics, fibers, illustration, industrial design, interior design, jewelry and metalsmithing, painting/drawing, photography, printmaking, sculpture, surface design. Graduate degrees offered: Master of Fine Arts in the areas of advertising design, ceramics, computer graphics, fibers, film, illustration, interior design, metalsmithing, museum studies, painting, photography, printmaking, sculpture, surface pattern design, video; Master of Industrial Design in the area of industrial design.

Art Student Profile Fall 1994: 1,227 total; 1,124 matriculated undergraduate, 103 matriculated graduate; 14% minorities, 48% females, 2% international.

Art Faculty Total: 103; 60 full-time, 43 part-time; 88% of full-time faculty have terminal degrees. Graduate students teach a few undergraduate courses. Undergraduate student–faculty ratio: 18:1.

Student Life Student groups include American Society of Interior Designers, Art Education Association, Industrial Design Society of America.

Expenses for 1995–96 Application fee: $40. Comprehensive fee of $23,190 includes full-time tuition ($15,910), mandatory fees ($370), and college room and board ($6910). College room only: $3760. Special program-related fees: $10–$300 for lab fees.

Financial Aid Program-specific awards for Fall of 1994: 15 Art Merit Scholarships for incoming freshmen ($1000), 50 Chancellor's Awards for incoming freshmen ($6000), 160 Deans Awards for incoming freshmen ($4000), 1 National Scholastic Award for Art National Scholarship winner ($2000).

Application Procedures Deadline—freshmen: February 1; transfers: July 1. Notification date—freshmen: March 15; transfers: August 15. Required: essay, high school transcript, college transcript(s) for transfer students, minimum 2.0 high school GPA, portfolio, SAT I or ACT test scores, high school counselor evaluation. Recommended: minimum 3.0 high school GPA, interview. Portfolio reviews held continuously on campus and off campus in New York, NY; Boston, MA; Chicago, IL; Philadelphia, PA; Baltimore, MD; Hartford, CT; the submission of slides may be substituted for portfolios.

Undergraduate Contact Judy McCumber, Coordinator of Recruiting, College of Visual and Performing Arts, Syracuse University, 202P Crouse College, Syracuse, New York 13244-1010; 315-443-2769, fax: 315-443-1935, E-mail address: admissu@vpa.syr.edu.

Graduate Contact Graduate School, Syracuse University, Suite 303 Bowne Hall, Syracuse, New York 13244; 315-443-4492.

More about the University

Program Facilities Comstock Art Facility: studios for ceramics, fibers, metalsmithing, printmaking, and sculpture and three-dimensional design studios; Crouse College: drawing and design studios and classrooms; Dorothea Ilgen Shaffer Art Building: Joe and Emily Lowe Art Gallery; Shemin auditorium (300 seats); Green and Seifter Lecture Hall (60 seats); facilities for advertising design, communications design, illustration, photography, video, computer graphics, film, drawing and painting; and studios for undergraduates; Smith Hall (Center for Design): studios for industrial, interior, and surface pattern design; M-17 Skytop Building: art education program facilities.

Faculty, Resident Artists, and Alumni Faculty members are well-established professional artists and designers who are active locally, nationally, and internationally; several are Guggenheim, Pulitzer, and Fulbright fellows and recipients of grants from the National Endowment for the Arts, Ford Foundation, and the Rockefeller Foundation. Alumni are prestigious figures in the museum and gallery world who exhibit locally, nationally, and internationally, as well as professionals and executives in prominent agencies, firms, and corporations in the area of industrial design, interior design, surface pattern design, advertising, computer graphics, and filmmaking.

Student Exhibit Opportunities Exhibit space is in Joe and Emily Lowe Art Gallery, Comstock Art Facility, Schine Student Center, Community Darkrooms, Smith Hall, Shaffer Art Building, and Crouse College.

Special Programs Weekly visiting artist programs in studio arts and visual communications feature lectures and critiques of student work and are open to all; study abroad in Florence or London through Division of International Programs Abroad (DIPA); internships through the school, Community Internship program, and the Placement Center at galleries, museums, newspapers and magazines, design agencies, and local television stations; honors program available for students who desire a rigorous academic challenge.

The School of Art and Design encourages students to reach their creative and intellectual potential and prepares them as professional artists, designers, and educators. All students in the School of Art and Design start with a one-year foundation program that offers studio work in drawing, 2-D and 3-D problem solving, academic courses in art history and issues in art, and a writing studio. In the sophomore year, students begin specialization toward their major; typically each semester, they take studio courses in their major, studio electives, and academic electives. The studio electives allow them to experiment in disciplines and media outside the major. The academic electives may be selected from the broad range of courses offered by the University. All degree paths are accredited by the National Association of Schools of Art and Design.

Students benefit from a faculty of practicing professionals whose work is included in the permanent collections of the Art Institute of Chicago; the International Polaroid Collection in Cambridge, Massachusetts; the Museum of Fine Art in Houston; the Museum of Modern Art in New York City; the National Gallery of Canada in Ottawa; the Gallerie Degli Uffici in Florence, Italy; and the Museo Nacional Centro de Arte Reina Sofia in Madrid, Spain. Faculty have also contributed to such publications as *Time, Scientific American, Audubon Magazine, Reader's Digest,* and *National Lampoon*. Their work is commissioned by clients in the United States and abroad, and many publish and exhibit in Europe and Asia.

Several features set SU's School of Art and Design apart from other schools and increase students' contact with the professional art and design world. An extensive network of active and successful alumni, comprehensive visiting artist programs, well-known faculty, and University programs and organizations all contribute to the internship and professional opportunities for students. Students also have the opportunity to study abroad in Florence or London through SU's Division of International Programs Abroad (DIPA).

The creative activities of the School of Art and Design are an integral part of the College of Visual and Performing Arts, which also governs programs in drama, music, and speech communication. The College serves as the center of SU's cultural life, on a campus whose lively and diverse schedule of events could only be found at a large university.

The city of Syracuse offers a rich culture of its own. The Everson Museum of Art, designed by architect I. M. Pei, houses one of the foremost ceramic collections in the United States and offers a diverse exhibition schedule. The Syracuse Symphony Orchestra, Syracuse Opera, and the Society for New Music as well as nationally known comedians, rock groups, and dance companies perform frequently. And, nestled between the Finger Lakes, the Adirondacks, and the many historical and natural landmarks in central New York State, Syracuse is within a day's drive of New York City, Philadelphia, Boston, and of Toronto and Montreal in Canada.

Tyler School of Art

Temple University

Philadelphia, Pennsylvania

State-related, coed. Urban campus. Total enrollment: 26,952.

Degrees Bachelor of Fine Arts in the areas of ceramics/glass, fibers/fabric design, graphic design/illustration, jewelry/metals, painting/drawing, photography, printmaking, sculpture. Majors: art education, ceramic art and design, glass, graphic arts, illustration, jewelry and metalsmithing, painting/drawing, photography, printmaking, sculpture, textile arts. Graduate degrees offered: Master of Fine Arts in the areas of ceramics/glass, fibers/fabric design, graphic design/illustration, jewelry/metals, painting/drawing, photography, printmaking, sculpture. Cross-registration with East Coast Consortium of Art Schools.

Art Student Profile Fall 1994: 698 total; 604 matriculated undergraduate, 79 matriculated graduate, 15 nondegree; 14% minorities, 52% females, 4% international.

Art Faculty Total: 82; 52 full-time, 30 part-time; 95% of full-time faculty have terminal degrees. Graduate students teach a few undergraduate courses. Undergraduate student–faculty ratio: 11:1.

Student Life Special housing available for art students.

Expenses for 1995–96 Application fee: $30. State resident tuition: $5314 full-time, $185 per semester hour part-time. Nonresident tuition: $10,096 full-time, $286 per semester hour part-time. Part-time mandatory fees per semester range from $15 to $45. Full-time mandatory fees: $200. College room and board: $5282. College room only: $3492. Special program-related fees: $25–$50 for lab fees.

Financial Aid Program-specific awards for Fall of 1994: 10–25 Merit Scholarships for undergraduates ($1000–$3500).

Application Procedures Deadline—freshmen and transfers: continuous. Notification date—freshmen and transfers: continuous. Required: essay, high school transcript, college transcript(s) for transfer students, minimum 2.0 high school GPA, portfolio, SAT I or ACT test scores, slides for transfer applicants. Recommended: minimum 3.0 high school GPA, interview. Portfolio reviews held 25 times on campus and off campus on National Portfolio Days; the submission of slides may be substituted for portfolios for freshman applicants for large works of art or if distance is prohibitive.

Contact Carmina Cianciulli, Assistant Dean for Admissions, Tyler School of Art, Temple University, Beech and Penrose Avenues, Elkins Park, Pennsylvania 19027; 215-782-2875, fax: 215-782-2711.

More about the School

Faculty, Resident Artists, and Alumni Tyler has a faculty of practicing artists, many of whom have been granted prestigious awards and fellowships through such foundations as the national Endowment for the Humanities, the Guggenheim Foundation, the Fulbright Foundation, and others. The careers of Tyler faculty are recognized throughout the professional art and design

Temple University *(continued)*

world. An extensive lecture series by visiting and exhibiting artists is an important part of a Tyler education. Invitations to lectures and exhibitions are extended to Tyler's alumni, a diverse group of arts professionals living throughout the country and abroad.

Program Facilities All studio facilities at Tyler are designed for extensive research and the creation of works in each major. Facilities include the computer labs for both graphic design/illustration and jewelry/metals, a fully equipped offset printing facility, and modern studios for each major. Tyler has three on-campus galleries, one on the main campus of Temple University, and one in central Philadelphia. These galleries not only show student work but also exhibit work from important national and international artists. Additional spaces include an auditorium that functions as a lecture hall, exhibition space, and theatre, and a dormitory.

Special Programs Temple University's Rome, Italy program, with its outstanding faculty, staff, and facilities, attracts students from colleges and universities throughout the country and abroad. In conjunction with the Glasgow School of Art, Tyler offers a summer program abroad in Great Britain. Temple University also has a campus in Japan.

For more than sixty years, Tyler School of Art has offered the combination of a world-renowned faculty and the resources of a major university within a small-school atmosphere. Because Tyler is situated on an independent campus in suburban Elkins Park, students experience the intimacy of Tyler's art community while benefiting from the facilities, curriculum, and activities of Temple University. A Tyler education is one that will distinguish each student as an artist who is both visually and intellectually prepared for diverse opportunities in the visual arts.

Tyler alumni are recipients of many prestigious awards and fellowships; are writers and critics; own galleries and businesses; teach in schools, colleges, and universities; and are involved in much more. Tyler's graduates have produced a collective record of achievement that is one of the prime reasons for the School's excellent reputation among institutions of higher learning.

The Bachelor of Fine Arts program is divided into a four-year sequence of planned study that provides a solid base in the fundamentals, the opportunity to explore a variety of curricular options, and an intensive and professional major concentration. Intensive studio work is complemented by an academic education with strong art history and liberal arts components in the belief that artists should be grounded in a broad base of knowledge. A highly motivated and talented student body, an extensive visiting and exhibitions program, and access to museums and galleries contribute to this challenging educational experience. The School's graduate program is highly competitive and extremely well respected. More information about all Tyler programs can be found in the Tyler catalog.

In addition to the B.F.A., M.F.A., and M.Ed. programs on the Elkins Park campus, students may also wish to investigate the programs available on the main campus of Temple University. These include the B.A. in studio art, the B.S. in art education, and the B.A., M.A., and Ph.D. in art history.

Tyler is a member of the Consortium of East Coast Art Schools. This program allows selected students in good standing to spend a semester during their junior year at any of the cooperating art schools. Tyler also nominates students for participation in the Yale Norfolk Summer School of Art and Music, the Black Hills Print Symposium, the Pilchuck Glass School, and the Skowhegan School of Painting and Sculpture, and, in the area of glass, the West Surrey College of Art and Design.

An important resource for Tyler students is Philadelphia's great wealth of museums and galleries. Students have an easy commute to the Philadelphia Museum of Art, the Pennsylvania Academy of the Fine Arts, the Rodin Museum, the Barnes Foundation, and the Institute of Contemporary Art. Philadelphia has many prestigious galleries, art spaces, and artists' cooperatives, as well as the largest number of public works in the country. Students also have easy access to the art collections, galleries, and cultural events in New York and Washington, D.C.

It is this combination of exceptional faculty, dedicated students, and a richly diverse setting that make Tyler School of Art an excellent choice for a professional education in art.

Texas Christian University

Fort Worth, Texas

Independent-religious, coed. Suburban campus. Total enrollment: 6,706.

Degrees Bachelor of Fine Arts in the areas of studio art, communication graphics, art education. Majors: art education, art history, graphic communication, painting/drawing, photography, printmaking, sculpture. Graduate degrees offered: Master of Fine Arts in the areas of painting, printmaking, sculpture. Cross-registration with Universidad de las Americas in Mexico.

Art Student Profile Fall 1994: 200 total; 180 matriculated undergraduate, 10 matriculated graduate, 10 nondegree.

Art Faculty Total: 18; 12 full-time, 6 part-time; 100% of full-time faculty have terminal degrees. Graduate students do not teach undergraduate courses. Undergraduate student–faculty ratio: 18:1.

Student Life Student groups include Visual Arts Committee of the Student Programming Council.

Expenses for 1995–96 Application fee: $30. Comprehensive fee of $13,840 includes full-time tuition ($9000), mandatory fees ($1000), and college room and board ($3840). Part-time tuition: $300 per semester hour. Part-time mandatory fees: $25 per semester hour. Special program-related fees: $50 for computer use.

Financial Aid Program-specific awards for Fall of 1994: 2 Nordan Scholarships for freshmen ($3000).

Application Procedures Deadline—freshmen and transfers: April 15. Required: essay, high school transcript, minimum 3.0 high school GPA, 3 letters of recommendation, interview.

Contact Ronald Watson, Chairman, Department of Art and Art History, Texas Christian University, 2800 South University Drive, Fort Worth, Texas 76129; 817-921-7643, fax: 817-921-7703.

Texas Southern University

Houston, Texas

State-supported, coed. Urban campus. Total enrollment: 10,872.

Degrees Bachelor of Fine Arts. Majors: art history, ceramic art and design, computer art, design, painting/drawing, printmaking, sculpture, weaving.

Art Student Profile Fall 1994: 45 total; all matriculated undergraduate.

Art Faculty Total: 6; 5 full-time, 1 part-time.

Expenses for 1995–96 State resident tuition: $900 full-time. Nonresident tuition: $6660 full-time, $222 per semester hour part-time. State resident part-time tuition per semester ranges from $100 to $330. Part-time mandatory fees per semester range from $64.50 to $249.50. Full-time mandatory fees: $570. College room and board: $3320.

Application Procedures Deadline—freshmen and transfers: August 10. Required: high school transcript, interview, portfolio. Portfolio reviews held 2 times on campus.

Undergraduate Contact Dr. Sarah Trotty, Chair, Fine Arts Department, Texas Southern University, 3100 Cleburne, Houston, Texas 77004; 713-527-7337, fax: 713-527-7539.

Texas Tech University

Lubbock, Texas

State-supported, coed. Urban campus. Total enrollment: 24,083.

Degrees Bachelor of Fine Arts in the areas of studio art, design communication, art education. Majors: art education, ceramics, communication design, jewelry and metalsmithing, painting/drawing, photography, printmaking, sculpture, studio art, textile arts. Graduate degrees offered: Master of Fine Arts in the area of art. Doctor of Arts in the area of fine arts.

Art Student Profile Fall 1994: 368 total; 320 matriculated undergraduate, 48 matriculated graduate; 14% minorities, 52% females, 1% international.

Art Faculty Total: 33; 28 full-time, 5 part-time; 82% of full-time faculty have terminal degrees. Graduate students teach about a quarter undergraduate courses. Undergraduate student–faculty ratio: 13:1.

Student Life Student groups include National Art Educators Association Student Chapter, Masterpiece (student art organization), Design Communication Association.

Estimated Expenses for 1995–96 Application fee: $25. State resident tuition: $900 full-time. Nonresident tuition: $5280 full-time, $176 per semester hour part-time. State resident part-time tuition per semester ranges from $100 to $330. Part-time mandatory fees: $25 per semester hour. Full-time mandatory fees: $870. College room and board: $3851. Special program-related fees: $26–$95 for art supplies.

Financial Aid Program-specific awards for Fall of 1994: 20–25 Art Scholarships for undergraduates ($200–$500), 3–5 H.Y. Price Scholarships for undergraduates ($2000).

Application Procedures Deadline—freshmen and transfers: continuous. Notification date—freshmen and transfers: continuous. Required: high school transcript, college transcript(s) for transfer students, minimum 2.0 high school GPA, SAT I or ACT test scores, TOEFL score for international applicants. Portfolio reviews held 2 times on campus and off campus in Junction, TX; the submission of slides may be substituted for portfolios for large works of art and 3-dimensional pieces.

Undergraduate Contact Office of New Student Relations, Texas Tech University, Mailstop 45005, Lubbock, Texas 79409-5005; 806-742-1482.

Graduate Contact Graduate Admissions, Texas Tech University, Box 41030, Lubbock, Texas 79409-1030; 806-742-2787, fax: 806-742-1746.

Texas Woman's University

Denton, Texas

State-supported, primarily women. Suburban campus. Total enrollment: 10,090.

Degrees Bachelor of Fine Arts in the areas of painting, photography, ceramics, sculpture, jewelry/metalsmithing, fibers, advertising design. Majors: applied art, art/fine arts, ceramic art and design, commercial art, graphic arts, illustration, jewelry and metalsmithing, painting/drawing, photography, sculpture, studio art, textile arts. Graduate degrees offered: Master of Fine Arts in the areas of painting, photography, ceramics, sculpture, jewelry/metalsmithing, fibers. Cross-registration with University of North Texas.

Art Student Profile Fall 1994: 245 total; 140 matriculated undergraduate, 70 matriculated graduate, 35 nondegree; 11% minorities, 100% females, 3% international.

Art Faculty Total: 28; 18 full-time, 10 part-time; 100% of full-time faculty have terminal degrees. Graduate students teach about a quarter undergraduate courses. Undergraduate student–faculty ratio: 13:1.

Student Life Student groups include Delta Phi Delta, Fine Arts Guild, American Advertising Federation Student Chapter. Special housing available for art students.

Expenses for 1994–95 Application fee: $25. State resident tuition: $868 full-time. Nonresident tuition: $5301 full-time, $171 per semester hour part-time. State resident part-time tuition per semester ranges from $100 to $308. Part-time mandatory fees per semester range

Texas Woman's University *(continued)*

from $74.55 to $322.85. Full-time mandatory fees: $670. College room and board: $3102. College room only: $1440. Special program-related fees: $20–$30 for studio courses.

Financial Aid Program-specific awards for Fall of 1994: 2 Marie Delleney Awards for art majors ($200–$500), 2 Helen Thomas Perry Awards for junior or senior art majors ($1000), 1 Hazel Snodgrass Award for art majors ($200–$300), 1 Lucie Clark Thompson Award for art majors ($200), 2 Noreen Kitsinger Awards for art education students ($200), 2 Sue Comer Awards for art majors ($200), 2 Weller-Washmon Awards for art majors ($200), 1 Dorothy Laselle Award for art majors ($300), 6 Coreen Spellman Awards for Delta Phi Delta members ($100–$200).

Application Procedures Deadline—freshmen and transfers: July 15. Notification date—freshmen and transfers: August 1. Required: high school transcript, minimum 2.0 high school GPA, portfolio, SAT I or ACT test scores, artist's statement or letter of intent. Recommended: letter of recommendation, interview. Portfolio reviews held 8 times on campus and off campus in various high schools in Texas; the submission of slides may be substituted for portfolios.

Contact Dr. Betty D. Copeland, Chair, Department of Visual Arts, Texas Woman's University, P.O. Box 425469, TWU Station, Denton, Texas 76204; 817-898-2530, fax: 817-898-2496, E-mail address: d_copeland@twu.edu.

Tisch School of the Arts

See New York University, Tisch School of the Arts

Trenton State College

Trenton, New Jersey

State-supported, coed. Suburban campus. Total enrollment: 6,981.

Degrees Bachelor of Fine Arts in the areas of fine arts, graphic design, interior design. Majors: art/fine arts, graphic design, interior design.

Art Student Profile Fall 1994: 350 total; all matriculated undergraduate.

Art Faculty Total: 30; 18 full-time, 12 part-time; 100% of full-time faculty have terminal degrees. Graduate students do not teach undergraduate courses. Undergraduate student–faculty ratio: 15:1.

Student Life Student groups include Art Directors Club of New Jersey, National Art Educators Association, American Society of Interior Designers Student Chapter.

Expenses for 1995–96 Application fee: $50. State resident tuition: $4240 full-time, $143 per semester hour part-time. Nonresident tuition: $6657 full-time, $227 per semester hour part-time. College room and board: $5600. Special program-related fees: $10–$25 for supplemental materials.

Application Procedures Deadline—freshmen and transfers: March 1. Notification date—freshmen and transfers: April 1. Required: essay, high school transcript, college transcript(s) for transfer students, portfolio, SAT I test score only. Recommended: minimum 3.0 high school GPA, letter of recommendation. Portfolio reviews held 5 times on campus; the submission of slides may be substituted for portfolios for international applicants.

Undergraduate Contact Office of Admissions, Trenton State College, Green Hall, Trenton, New Jersey 08650-4700; 609-771-2131.

Tyler School of Art

See Temple University, Tyler School of Art

University of Akron

Akron, Ohio

State-supported, coed. Urban campus. Total enrollment: 26,009.

Degrees Bachelor of Fine Arts in the areas of drawing, painting, photography, printmaking, crafts, metalsmithing, graphics, sculpture, ceramics. Majors: art/fine arts, ceramic art and design, graphic design, jewelry and metalsmithing, painting/drawing, photography, printmaking, sculpture.

Art Student Profile Fall 1994: 700 total; 444 matriculated undergraduate, 256 nondegree; 10% minorities, 50% females, 1% international.

Art Faculty Total: 50; 24 full-time, 26 part-time; 99% of full-time faculty have terminal degrees. Graduate students do not teach undergraduate courses. Undergraduate student–faculty ratio: 14:1.

Student Life Student groups include Student Art League.

Expenses for 1995–96 Application fee: $35. State resident tuition: $3192 full-time, $123.65 per credit part-time. Nonresident tuition: $7954 full-time, $282.40 per credit part-time. Full-time mandatory fees: $380. College room and board: $3844. Special program-related fees: $25 for ceramics supplies, $35 for photography supplies, $35 for printmaking materials, $30 for metalsmithing materials, $20 for weaving supplies.

Financial Aid Program-specific awards for Fall of 1994: 1–2 Scholastics Art and Writing Award for incoming freshmen program majors ($3000–$12,000), 1–2 Governor's Art Youth Award for Ohio resident program majors ($500–$750), 3–5 Incoming Freshmen Awards for incoming freshmen program majors ($500–$2000), 13–15 School of Art Scholarships for continuing program majors based on portfolio and GPA ($1000–$3000).

Application Procedures Deadline—freshmen: June 30; transfers: July 30. Required: high school transcript, college transcript(s) for transfer students, minimum 2.0 high school GPA, SAT I or ACT test scores, portfolio for transfer students, 3.0 college GPA in art courses for transfer students. Auditions held on campus. Portfolio reviews held as needed on campus; the submission of slides may be substituted for portfolios.

Undergraduate Contact Admissions Office, University of Akron, 381 Buchtel Common, Akron, Ohio 44325-2001; 216-972-7100.

University of Alabama

Tuscaloosa, Alabama

State-supported, coed. Small-town campus. Total enrollment: 19,366.

Degrees Bachelor of Fine Arts in the areas of painting, printmaking, graphic design, ceramics, sculpture, photography. Majors: art history, art/fine arts, ceramic art and design, graphic design, painting/drawing, photography, printmaking, sculpture. Graduate degrees offered: Master of Fine Arts in the areas of painting, printmaking, ceramics, sculpture, photography.

Art Student Profile Fall 1994: 864 total; 156 matriculated undergraduate, 28 matriculated graduate, 680 nondegree; 16% minorities, 56% females, 3% international.

Art Faculty Total: 19; 14 full-time, 5 part-time; 100% of full-time faculty have terminal degrees. Graduate students teach a few undergraduate courses. Undergraduate student–faculty ratio: 20:1.

Expenses for 1995–96 Application fee: $25. State resident tuition: $2374 full-time. Nonresident tuition: $5924 full-time. Part-time tuition per semester ranges from $322 to $1187 for state residents, $474 to $2962 for nonresidents. College room and board: $3658. College room only: $2000. Special program-related fees: $20–$40 for studio fees.

Financial Aid Program-specific awards for Fall of 1994: 3 Mary M. Morgan Scholarships for program students ($1141), 2 Bradley Endowed Scholarships for program students ($1141), 2 Society for the Fine Arts Scholarships for program students ($1141), 1 Ann Lary Scholarship for program students ($1000).

Application Procedures Deadline—freshmen and transfers: continuous. Required: high school transcript, minimum 2.0 high school GPA.

Contact W. Lowell Baker, Chairman, Art and Art History Department, University of Alabama, Box 870270, Tuscaloosa, Alabama 35487-0270; 205-348-5967, fax: 205-348-9642, E-mail address: wbaker@woodsquad.ualvm.ya.edu.

University of Alabama at Birmingham

Birmingham, Alabama

State-supported, coed. Urban campus. Total enrollment: 16,252.

Degrees Bachelor of Fine Arts in the area of visual arts. Majors: art/fine arts, studio art. Cross-registration with Birmingham&–Southern College, Samford University.

Art Student Profile Fall 1994: 501 total; 431 matriculated undergraduate, 70 nondegree; 13% minorities, 75% females, 2% international.

Art Faculty Total: 16; 11 full-time, 5 part-time; 100% of full-time faculty have terminal degrees. Graduate students do not teach undergraduate courses. Undergraduate student–faculty ratio: 15:1.

Student Life Student groups include The Art Guild.

Expenses for 1995–96 Application fee: $20. State resident tuition: $2604 full-time, $86.80 per hour part-time. Nonresident tuition: $5208 full-time, $173.60 per hour part-time. College room and board: $5490. Special program-related fees: $40 for lab fees.

Financial Aid Program-specific awards for Fall of 1994: 1 Senior Scholarship for seniors ($1700), 1 Frohock Scholarship for juniors ($300), 1 Hulsey Prize for seniors ($100).

Application Procedures Deadline—freshmen and transfers: continuous. Notification date—freshmen and transfers: continuous. Required: high school transcript, college transcript(s) for transfer students, minimum 2.0 high school GPA, portfolio, SAT I or ACT test scores, minimum combined SAT I score of 832, minimum composite ACT score of 20. Portfolio reviews held 2 times at end of college sophomore year on campus; the submission of slides may be substituted for portfolios.

Undergraduate Contact Sonja Rieger, Chair, Department of Art, University of Alabama at Birmingham, 900 13th Street South, Birmingham, Alabama 35294-1260; 205-934-4941, fax: 205-975-6639.

University of Alaska Anchorage

Anchorage, Alaska

State-supported, coed. Urban campus. Total enrollment: 15,113.

Degrees Bachelor of Fine Arts in the area of art. Majors: art/fine arts, ceramic art and design, graphic arts, illustration, jewelry and metalsmithing, painting/drawing, photography, printmaking, sculpture, textile arts.

Art Student Profile Fall 1994: 1,028 total; 325 matriculated undergraduate, 703 nondegree; 6% minorities, 70% females, 2% international.

Art Faculty Total: 25; 10 full-time, 15 part-time; 90% of full-time faculty have terminal degrees. Graduate students do not teach undergraduate courses. Undergraduate student–faculty ratio: 12:1.

Student Life Student groups include Art Student Association, Student National Art Educators Association, Camera Club.

Expenses for 1995–96 Application fee: $35. Full-time tuition ranges from $2070 to $2250 for state residents, $6210 to $6750 for nonresidents, according to class level. Part-time tuition per credit hour ranges from $69 to $75

University of Alaska Anchorage *(continued)*

for state residents, $207 to $225 for nonresidents, according to class level. Part-time mandatory fees per semester range from $54 for 3 to 5 credits, $74 for 5 to 9 credits, $79 for 10 credits or above. Full-time mandatory fees: $158. College room only: $2500. Special program-related fees: $20–$50 for lab fees for materials, equipment maintenance, and models.

Financial Aid Program-specific awards for Fall of 1994: 2 Saradell Ard Scholarships for upper-division program majors ($850), 2 Muriel Hannah Scholarships for program majors with preference to Native-American Alaskans ($750), 2 Tuition Waivers for upper-division program majors ($1250), 1 Sam Kimura Scholarship for photography majors, 1 Ken Gray Scholarship for incoming freshmen, 1 Joan Kimura Scholarship for illustration majors.

Application Procedures Deadline—freshmen and transfers: continuous. Notification date—freshmen and transfers: continuous. Required: high school transcript, minimum 2.0 high school GPA, portfolio. Portfolio reviews held at the end of sophomore year for admission to BFA program on campus.

Undergraduate Contact Office of Enrollment Services, University of Alaska Anchorage, 3211 Providence Drive, Anchorage, Alaska 99508; 907-786-1480, fax: 907-786-4888.

University of Arizona

Tucson, Arizona

State-supported, coed. Urban campus. Total enrollment: 35,306.

Degrees Bachelor of Fine Arts in the area of art. Majors: art education, art history, art/fine arts, ceramic art and design, computer graphics, graphic arts, illustration, jewelry and metalsmithing, new genre, painting/drawing, photography, printmaking, sculpture, studio art, textile arts. Graduate degrees offered: Master of Fine Arts in the area of art.

Art Student Profile Fall 1994: 770 total; 650 matriculated undergraduate, 120 matriculated graduate; 10% minorities, 60% females, 10% international.

Art Faculty Total: 98; 43 full-time, 55 part-time; 95% of full-time faculty have terminal degrees. Graduate students teach about a quarter undergraduate courses. Undergraduate student–faculty ratio: 17:1.

Expenses for 1995–96 State resident tuition: $1950 full-time. Nonresident tuition: $7978 full-time. Part-time tuition per semester ranges from $103 to $975 for state residents, $334 to $3989 for nonresidents. College room and board: $4400. College room only: $2400. Special program-related fees: $5–$25 for supplies for some studio courses.

Financial Aid Program-specific awards for Fall of 1994: 1 Arizona Porcelain Artists Scholarship for program majors ($500), 1 Robert C. Brown Memorial Scholarship for program majors ($750), Edward Francis Dunn Scholarships for program majors ($4600), Albert and Kathryn Haldeman Scholarships for program majors ($3600), 1 Hudson Foundation Scholarship for program majors ($1200), Samuel Latta Kingan Scholarships for program majors ($2300), 1 Stephen Langmade Scholarship for program majors ($950), 8 Regents In-State Registration Scholarships for state resident program majors ($922), 5 Regents In-State Registration Scholarships for state resident program majors demonstrating need ($922), 10 Regents Non-Resident Tuition Scholarships for non-resident program majors ($3675), 1 Santa Rita Art League Scholarship for program majors ($500), 1 Mary C. Sloan Fine Arts Scholarship for program majors ($922), 1 Sandy Truett Memorial Scholarship for program majors ($1050).

Application Procedures Deadline—freshmen: March 15; transfers: April 15. Required: high school transcript, minimum 2.0 high school GPA, 3 letters of recommendation.

Undergraduate Contact Sheila Pitt, Undergraduate Advisor, Art Department, University of Arizona, Art Building, Room 108, Tucson, Arizona 85721; 602-621-7570, fax: 602-621-2955, E-mail address: artadvr@gas.uug.arizona.edu.

Graduate Contact Dennis Jones, Graduate Advisor, Art Department, University of Arizona, Art Building, Room 108, Tucson, Arizona 85721; 602-621-7570, fax: 602-621-2955, E-mail address: aggie@ccit.arizona.edu.

J. William Fulbright College of Arts and Sciences

University of Arkansas

Fayetteville, Arkansas

State-supported, coed. Small-town campus. Total enrollment: 14,655.

Degrees Bachelor of Fine Arts in the area of art. Majors: art/fine arts, ceramic art and design, graphic arts, jewelry and metalsmithing, painting/drawing, photography, printmaking, sculpture. Graduate degrees offered: Master of Fine Arts in the area of art.

Art Student Profile Fall 1994: 162 total; 125 matriculated undergraduate, 10 matriculated graduate, 27 nondegree; 5% minorities, 62% females, 5% international.

Art Faculty Total: 12; 12 full-time; 98% of full-time faculty have terminal degrees. Graduate students teach a few undergraduate courses. Undergraduate student–faculty ratio: 15:1.

Expenses for 1995–96 Application fee: $15. State resident tuition: $2200 full-time, $95.33 per credit hour part-time. Nonresident tuition: $5392 full-time, $228.33 per credit hour part-time. Mandatory fees for engineering program: $277. Full-time mandatory fees: $130 (minimum). College room and board: $3468 (minimum). Special program-related fees: $4 for teaching equipment.

Application Procedures Deadline—freshmen and transfers: August 15. Required: high school transcript, minimum 2.0 high school GPA, portfolio. Recommended: minimum 3.0 high school GPA. Portfolio reviews held 1 time on campus.

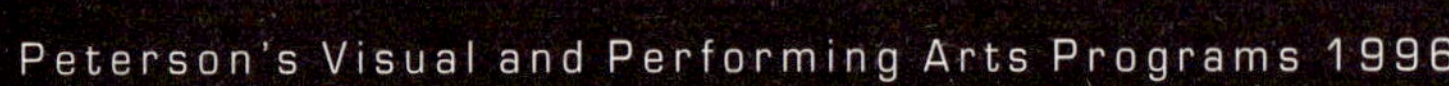

Contact Michael Peven, Chairman, Art Department, University of Arkansas, 116 Fine Arts Center, Fayetteville, Arkansas 72701; 501-575-5202, fax: 501-575-2062, E-mail address: mpeven@comp.uark.edu.

University of Bridgeport

Bridgeport, Connecticut

Independent, coed. Urban campus. Total enrollment: 1,939.

Degrees Bachelor of Fine Arts in the areas of fine art, graphic design, illustration. Majors: art/fine arts, graphic design, illustration, studio art.

Art Student Profile Fall 1994: 26 total; all matriculated undergraduate.

Art Faculty Total: 12; 5 full-time, 7 part-time.

Student Life Student groups include Art Shows.

Expenses for 1994–95 Application fee: $35. Comprehensive fee of $19,934 includes full-time tuition ($12,500), mandatory fees ($624), and college room and board ($6810). College room only: $3700. Part-time tuition: $260 per credit. Part-time mandatory fees: $75 per year.

Application Procedures Deadline—freshmen and transfers: continuous. Required: essay, high school transcript, portfolio, SAT I or ACT test scores. Recommended: interview. Portfolio reviews held as needed; the submission of slides may be substituted for portfolios for international applicants.

Undergraduate Contact Dr. Clayton Lee, Director, School of Fine and Applied Arts, University of Bridgeport, 180 University Avenue, Bridgeport, Connecticut 06601; 203-576-4412.

University of British Columbia

Vancouver, British Columbia

Province-supported, coed. Urban campus. Total enrollment: 31,118.

Degrees Bachelor of Fine Arts in the area of visual arts. Majors: art/fine arts, painting/drawing, photography, printmaking, sculpture, studio art. Graduate degrees offered: Master of Fine Arts in the area of visual arts.

Art Student Profile Fall 1994: 364 total; 300 matriculated undergraduate, 54 matriculated graduate, 10 nondegree.

Art Faculty Total: 23; 19 full-time, 4 part-time; 90% of full-time faculty have terminal degrees. Graduate students teach a few undergraduate courses. Undergraduate student–faculty ratio: 15:1.

Student Life Student groups include Graduate Student Art History Symposium, Alma Mater Drawing Club.

Expenses for 1995–96 Canadian resident tuition: $2295 full-time, $76.50 per credit part-time. Nonresident tuition: $5738 full-time, $191.25 per credit part-time. Part-time mandatory fees: $11.45 per credit. (All figures are in Canadian dollars.). Full-time mandatory fees: $205. College room and board: $4300 (minimum). College room only: $2000 (minimum).

Financial Aid Program-specific awards for Fall of 1994: 1 Faculty Women's Club Ida Green Award for academically qualified applicants ($2500), 1 Florence Muriel Meltzer Scholarship for academically qualified applicants ($2000), 1 Helen Pitt Graduating Award for academically qualified applicants ($1000), 1 IODE Fine Arts Foundation Scholarship for academically qualified applicants ($1000), 1 Sharon Yacawer Frohlinger Memorial Scholarship for academically qualified applicants ($325), 1 CATA Coerner Memorial Scholarship for academically qualified applicants ($1650).

Application Procedures Deadline—freshmen and transfers: March 31. Required: minimum 3.0 high school GPA, portfolio. Portfolio reviews held 1 time on campus.

Undergraduate Contact Patsi Longmire, Undergraduate Secretary, Department of Fine Arts, University of British Columbia, 6333 Memorial Road, Vancouver, British Columbia V6T 1Z2, Canada; 604-822-2757.

Graduate Contact Jennifer Cullen, Graduate Administrator, Department of Fine Arts, University of British Columbia, 6333 Memorial Road, Vancouver, British Columbia V6T 1Z2, Canada; 604-822-2757.

University of Calgary

Calgary, Alberta

Province-supported, coed. Urban campus. Total enrollment: 21,885.

Degrees Bachelor of Fine Arts in the areas of art, art education. Majors: art education, painting/drawing, photography, printmaking, sculpture. Graduate degrees offered: Master of Fine Arts in the area of art.

Art Student Profile Fall 1994: 200 total; 189 matriculated undergraduate, 11 matriculated graduate; 63% females, 2% international.

Art Faculty Total: 32; 22 full-time, 10 part-time; 82% of full-time faculty have terminal degrees. Graduate students do not teach undergraduate courses. Undergraduate student–faculty ratio: 52:1.

Student Life Student groups include on campus exhibitions in two venues.

Estimated Expenses for 1995–96 Application fee: $60. Canadian resident tuition: $2660 full-time, $532 per course part-time. Nonresident tuition: $5320 full-time, $1064 per course part-time. Part-time mandatory fees: $48.35 per semester. (All figures are in Canadian dollars.). Full-time mandatory fees: $348. College room and board: $2900 (minimum).

Financial Aid Program-specific awards for Fall of 1994: 1 Alberta Printmakers Society Award for printmakers ($100), 1 Continuing Arts Association Travel Scholarship for those demonstrating academic achievement ($700), 1 Bow Fort Chapter I.O.D.E. Bursary for those demonstrating academic achievement ($250), 1 Heinz Jordan

University of Calgary *(continued)*

Memorial Scholarship for those demonstrating academic achievement ($500), 2 Santo Mignosa Awards for printmakers ($500), 1 George Milne Award for printmakers ($1000), 1 Sadie M. Nelson Bursary in Art for those demonstrating need and academic merit ($500), 1 Western Silk Screen Prize for silk screen majors ($300).

Application Procedures Deadline—freshmen and transfers: June 1. Required: high school transcript, college transcript(s) for transfer students. Recommended: SAT I test score only. Portfolio reviews held on campus; the submission of slides may be substituted for portfolios.

Undergraduate Contact Bernice Peterson, Academic Advisor, Department of Art, University of Calgary, 2500 University Drive, NW, Calgary, Alberta T2N 1N4, Canada; 403-220-6260, fax: 403-282-6925, E-mail address: 19052@ucdasvm1.admin.ucalgary.ca.

Graduate Contact Helen Miller, Graduate Secretary, Department of Art, University of Calgary, 2500 University Drive, NW, Calgary, Alberta T2N 1N4, Canada; 403-220-3299.

University of Central Florida

Orlando, Florida

State-supported, coed. Suburban campus. Total enrollment: 25,363.

Degrees Bachelor of Fine Arts in the area of art. Majors: ceramic art and design, fibers, graphic design, painting/drawing, photography, printmaking, sculpture.

Art Student Profile Fall 1994: 270 total; all matriculated undergraduate.

Art Faculty Total: 21; 11 full-time, 10 part-time; 100% of full-time faculty have terminal degrees. Graduate students do not teach undergraduate courses. Undergraduate student–faculty ratio: 15:1.

Student Life Student groups include Arts Alliance.

Expenses for 1995–96 Application fee: $20. State resident tuition: $1842 full-time, $58.19 per credit hour part-time. Nonresident tuition: $6743 full-time, $221.60 per credit hour part-time. Part-time mandatory fees: $47.30 per semester. Full-time mandatory fees: $95. College room and board: $4310. College room only: $2500. Special program-related fees: $75 for ceramic supplies.

Financial Aid Program-specific awards for Fall of 1994: 2 San Miguel Awards for Hispanic art students ($600), 2 Altrusa Club Awards for art students ($500).

Application Procedures Deadline—freshmen and transfers: July 15. Notification date—freshmen and transfers: continuous. Required: college transcript(s) for transfer students. Auditions held on campus and off campus. Portfolio reviews held 1 time at end of college junior year for entrance into BFA program on campus.

Undergraduate Contact University Admissions, University of Central Florida, 4000 Central Florida Boulevard, Orlando, Florida 32816; 407-823-3000.

University of Cincinnati

Cincinnati, Ohio

State-supported, coed. Urban campus. Total enrollment: 18,473.

Degrees Bachelor of Fine Arts in the area of fine arts. Majors: ceramic art and design, electronic arts, fibers, painting/drawing, photography, printmaking, sculpture. Graduate degrees offered: Master of Fine Arts in the area of fine arts.

Art Student Profile Fall 1994: 280 total; 170 matriculated undergraduate, 50 matriculated graduate, 60 nondegree; 3% minorities, 55% females, 2% international.

Art Faculty Total: 19; 17 full-time, 2 part-time; 100% of full-time faculty have terminal degrees. Graduate students teach about a quarter undergraduate courses. Undergraduate student–faculty ratio: 11:1.

Expenses for 1994–95 Application fee: $30. State resident tuition: $3732 full-time, $104 per credit hour part-time. Nonresident tuition: $9405 full-time, $261 per credit hour part-time. Full-time mandatory fees: $166. College room and board: $4698.

Application Procedures Deadline—freshmen: December 31; transfers: continuous. Required: high school transcript, college transcript(s) for transfer students, minimum 2.5 high school GPA, standing in top third of graduating class. Recommended: interview.

Undergraduate Contact Derrick Woodham, Director, School of Art, University of Cincinnati, Mail Location 0016, Cincinnati, Ohio 45221; 513-556-2962, fax: 513-556-2887.

Graduate Contact Kim Burleigh, Director, Graduate Studies, School of Art, University of Cincinnati, Mail Location 0016, Cincinnati, Ohio 45221; 513-556-2075.

University of Colorado at Boulder

Boulder, Colorado

State-supported, coed. Urban campus. Total enrollment: 24,548.

Degrees Bachelor of Fine Arts in the area of studio arts. Majors: art/fine arts, ceramic art and design, painting/drawing, photography, printmaking, sculpture, studio art. Graduate degrees offered: Master of Fine Arts in the area of studio arts.

Art Student Profile Fall 1994: 566 total; 466 matriculated undergraduate, 100 matriculated graduate.

Art Faculty Total: 64; 30 full-time, 34 part-time; 100% of full-time faculty have terminal degrees. Graduate students teach about a quarter undergraduate courses. Undergraduate student–faculty ratio: 20:1.

Expenses for 1995–96 Application fee: $40. Part-time tuition per credit hour ranges from $138 to $165 for state residents, $741 to $776 for nonresidents. Part-time mandatory fees per semester range from $55.99 to $243.70. Full-time tuition ranges from $2216 to $2672 for state residents, $12,780 to $13,374 for nonresidents according to program. Full-time mandatory fees: $487. College room and board: $4162. Special program-related fees: $10–$200 for equipment repair and maintenance, supplies, model fees.

Financial Aid Program-specific awards for Fall of 1994: 20 Scholarships for program majors ($500).

Application Procedures Deadline—freshmen and transfers: continuous. Required: high school transcript, minimum 2.0 high school GPA.

Undergraduate Contact Office of Admissions, University of Colorado at Boulder, Campus Box 30, Boulder, Colorado 80309; 303-492-6301, fax: 303-492-7115.

Graduate Contact Dona Uyeno, Graduate Secretary and Assistant to Chair, Fine Arts Department, University of Colorado at Boulder, Campus Box 318, Boulder, Colorado 80309-0318; 303-492-6504, fax: 303-492-4886.

University of Colorado at Denver

Denver, Colorado

State-supported, coed. Urban campus. Total enrollment: 9,537.

Degrees Bachelor of Fine Arts in the area of creative arts. Majors: art/fine arts, painting/drawing, photography, sculpture. Cross-registration with Metropolitan State College of Denver.

Art Faculty Total: 16; 9 full-time, 7 part-time; 100% of full-time faculty have terminal degrees. Graduate students do not teach undergraduate courses.

Expenses for 1995–96 Part-time mandatory fees: $128.76 per semester. Full-time tuition ranges from $1828 to $2126 for state residents, $9244 to $9620 for nonresidents according to program. Part-time tuition per semester hour ranges from $110 to $128 for state residents, $555 to $577 for nonresidents according to program. Full-time mandatory fees: $257.52. Special program-related fees: $45–$75 for photography lab fee, $40 for general sculpture fee, $5 for studio class fee.

Application Procedures Deadline—freshmen and transfers: July 22. Notification date—freshmen and transfers: August 18. Required: high school transcript, minimum 2.0 high school GPA, 3 letters of recommendation.

Undergraduate Contact Judith Thorpe, Chairperson, Department of Fine Arts, University of Colorado at Denver, Campus Box 177, P.O. Box 173364, Denver, Colorado 80217; 303-556-2809, fax: 303-556-2335.

University of Connecticut

Storrs, Connecticut

State-supported, coed. Rural campus. Total enrollment: 15,626.

Degrees Bachelor of Fine Arts in the areas of art, graphic design, illustration, painting, photography, printmaking, sculpture. Majors: art/fine arts, graphic design, illustration, painting/drawing, photography, printmaking, sculpture. Graduate degrees offered: Master of Fine Arts in the areas of art, printmaking, sculpture, graphic design, drawing, painting, photography.

Art Student Profile Fall 1994: 239 total; 229 matriculated undergraduate, 10 matriculated graduate.

Art Faculty Total: 30; 23 full-time, 7 part-time; 100% of full-time faculty have terminal degrees. Graduate students teach a few undergraduate courses. Undergraduate student–faculty ratio: 16:1.

Expenses for 1995–96 Application fee: $40. State resident tuition: $3900 full-time. Nonresident tuition: $11,890 full-time. Part-time tuition per semester ranges from $163 to $1950 for state residents, $495 to $5945 for nonresidents. Part-time mandatory fees per semester range from $104 to $414. Full-time mandatory fees: $949. College room and board: $5124.

Financial Aid Program-specific awards for Fall of 1994: 2 University Scholarships for incoming freshmen ($2200), 1 Victor Borge Scholarship for incoming freshmen ($1000), 8 University Scholarships for undergraduates ($2200), 1 Anniversary Scholarship for undergraduates ($1500), 1 Alaimo Scholarship for undergraduates ($1000).

Application Procedures Deadline—freshmen: April 1; transfers: May 1. Required: essay, high school transcript. Recommended: letter of recommendation.

Undergraduate Contact David C. Kelly, Head, Art Department, University of Connecticut, Box U-99, 875 Coventry Road, Storrs, Connecticut 06269-1099; 203-486-3930, fax: 203-486-3869, E-mail address: dkelly@finearts.sfa.uconn.edu.

Graduate Contact Laurie Sloan, Graduate Program Coordinator, Art Department, University of Connecticut, Box U-99, 875 Coventry Road, Storrs, Connecticut 06269-1099; 203-486-3930, fax: 203-486-3869.

University of Dayton

Dayton, Ohio

Independent-religious, coed. Suburban campus. Total enrollment: 10,204.

Degrees Bachelor of Fine Arts in the areas of art education, studio art, visual communication design, photography. Majors: art education, art history, art/fine arts, computer graphics, graphic arts, illustration, photography, studio art. Cross-registration with Miami Valley Consortium.

Art Student Profile Fall 1994: 158 total; all matriculated undergraduate; 4% minorities, 66% females, 1% international.

Art Faculty Total: 29; 11 full-time, 18 part-time; 100% of full-time faculty have terminal degrees. Graduate students do not teach undergraduate courses. Undergraduate student–faculty ratio: 5:1.

Student Life Student groups include Horvath Student Art Show, Stander Symposium, American Center for Design Student Chapter.

University of Dayton *(continued)*

Expenses for 1994–95 Comprehensive fee of $16,050 includes full-time tuition ($11,380), mandatory fees ($450), and college room and board ($4220). College room only: $2160. Part-time tuition per semester ranges from $380 to $4270. Part-time mandatory fees per semester range from $25 to $225. Special program-related fees: $20–$60 for studio/lab fees.

Financial Aid Program-specific awards for Fall of 1994: 5–10 Visual Arts Scholarships for freshmen ($2500), 1 Gordon Richardson Scholarship for juniors ($1500), 1 Horvath Scholarship for sophomores ($1250), 1 Anne Perman Scholarship for upperclassmen ($1000).

Application Procedures Deadline—freshmen: continuous; transfers: August 1. Required: essay, high school transcript, college transcript(s) for transfer students, minimum 2.0 high school GPA, SAT I or ACT test scores. Recommended: interview, portfolio. Portfolio reviews held as needed on campus and off campus in various cities in Indiana, Ohio, Kentucky.

Undergraduate Contact Office of Admission, University of Dayton, 300 College Park, Dayton, Ohio 45469-1611; 513-229-4411.

University of Delaware

Newark, Delaware

State-related, coed. Small-town campus. Total enrollment: 18,080.

Degrees Bachelor of Fine Arts in the areas of ceramics, painting, photography, printmaking, sculpture, advertising design, applied photography, fibers, graphic design, illustration, metals. Majors: advertising design, applied photography, art/fine arts, ceramics, fibers, graphic design, illustration, jewelry and metalsmithing, painting/drawing, photography, printmaking, sculpture. Graduate degrees offered: Master of Fine Arts in the areas of ceramics, painting, photography, printmaking, sculpture.

Art Student Profile Fall 1994: 399 total; 364 matriculated undergraduate, 27 matriculated graduate, 8 nondegree; 9% minorities, 5% international.

Art Faculty Total: 20; 18 full-time, 2 part-time; 88% of full-time faculty have terminal degrees. Graduate students teach about a quarter undergraduate courses. Undergraduate student–faculty ratio: 15:1.

Student Life Student groups include Art Community Interest Housing, Refinery Art Group. Special housing available for art students.

Expenses for 1995–96 Application fee: $40. State resident tuition: $3860 full-time, $161 per credit hour part-time. Nonresident tuition: $10,730 full-time, $447 per credit hour part-time. Full-time mandatory fees: $426. College room and board: $4420. Special program-related fees: $20–$60 for studio materials and supplies.

Financial Aid Program-specific awards for Fall of 1994: 3–5 Calloway Awards for those demonstrating talent, academic achievement, and need ($3000–$5000).

Application Procedures Deadline—freshmen and transfers: March 1. Required: high school transcript, college transcript(s) for transfer students, SAT I test score only. Recommended: essay. Portfolio reviews held on campus.

Contact Martha Carothers, Chair, Department of Art, University of Delaware, 203 54 West Delaware Avenue, Newark, Delaware 19716; 302-831-2244, fax: 302-831-8000, E-mail address: martha.carothers@mvs.udel.edu.

University of Denver

Denver, Colorado

Independent, coed. Suburban campus. Total enrollment: 8,522.

Degrees Bachelor of Fine Arts in the areas of printmaking, ceramics, sculpture, photography, painting, graphic design. Majors: art education, ceramic art and design, commercial art, painting/drawing, photography, printmaking, sculpture. Graduate degrees offered: Master of Fine Arts in the areas of printmaking, ceramics, sculpture, photography, painting, graphic design.

Art Student Profile Fall 1994: 120 total; 90 matriculated undergraduate, 15 matriculated graduate, 15 nondegree; 12% minorities, 50% females, 20% international.

Art Faculty Total: 14; 10 full-time, 4 part-time; 100% of full-time faculty have terminal degrees. Graduate students teach a few undergraduate courses. Undergraduate student–faculty ratio: 10:1.

Student Life Special housing available for art students.

Expenses for 1994–95 Application fee: $35. Comprehensive fee of $19,995 includes full-time tuition ($15,192), mandatory fees ($108), and college room and board ($4695). Part-time tuition: $422 per quarter hour.

Financial Aid Program-specific awards for Fall of 1994: 2–4 Harrison Scholarships for those demonstrating need ($5000–$12,000), 2–4 Art Scholarships for those demonstrating talent and academic achievement ($5000–$12,000).

Application Procedures Deadline—freshmen and transfers: March 1. Notification date—freshmen and transfers: continuous. Required: essay, high school transcript, college transcript(s) for transfer students, minimum 2.0 high school GPA, letter of recommendation, SAT I or ACT test scores. Recommended: interview, portfolio.

Contact Michael L. Griffin, Director of Student Recruitment, School of Art and Art History, University of Denver, 2121 East Asbury, Denver, Colorado 80208; 303-871-2846, fax: 303-871-4112, E-mail address: m.griffin@du.edu.

University of Evansville

Evansville, Indiana

Independent-religious, coed. Suburban campus. Total enrollment: 3,162.

Degrees Bachelor of Fine Arts in the areas of ceramics, graphic design, painting, sculpture. Majors: art/fine arts, ceramic art and design, graphic design, painting/drawing, sculpture.

Art Student Profile Fall 1994: 61 total; 55 matriculated undergraduate, 6 nondegree; 1% minorities, 70% females, 10% international.

Art Faculty Total: 8; 4 full-time, 4 part-time; 100% of full-time faculty have terminal degrees. Graduate students do not teach undergraduate courses. Undergraduate student–faculty ratio: 13:1.

Student Life Student groups include Student Art Association.

Expenses for 1995–96 Application fee: $30. Comprehensive fee of $16,570 includes full-time tuition ($12,400) and college room and board ($4170 minimum). Part-time tuition: $365 per semester hour. Special program-related fees: $15–$25 for ceramics, photography and printmaking fees.

Financial Aid Program-specific awards for Fall of 1994: 15 Art Scholarships for program majors ($4316).

Application Procedures Deadline—freshmen: March 1; transfers: June 1. Notification date—freshmen and transfers: continuous. Required: essay, high school transcript, college transcript(s) for transfer students, minimum 2.0 high school GPA, SAT I or ACT test scores. Recommended: minimum 3.0 high school GPA, letter of recommendation, interview, portfolio. Portfolio reviews held 5 times on campus; the submission of slides may be substituted for portfolios.

Undergraduate Contact William Richmond, Student Recruitment Coordinator, Art Department, University of Evansville, 1800 Lincoln Avenue, Evansville, Indiana 47722; 812-479-2043, fax: 812-479-2320.

University of Florida

Gainesville, Florida

State-supported, coed. Suburban campus. Total enrollment: 38,277.

Degrees Bachelor of Fine Arts in the areas of ceramics, drawing, graphic design, painting, creative photography, printmaking, sculpture, electronic intermedia. Majors: art education, ceramic art and design, graphic arts, painting/drawing, photography, printmaking, sculpture. Graduate degrees offered: Master of Fine Arts in the areas of ceramics, drawing, graphic design, painting, creative photography, printmaking, sculpture, electronic intermedia. Cross-registration with Penland School of Crafts, New World School of the Arts.

Art Student Profile Fall 1994: 313 total; 249 matriculated undergraduate, 47 matriculated graduate, 17 nondegree; 7% minorities, 55% females.

Art Faculty Total: 39; 36 full-time, 3 part-time; 100% of full-time faculty have terminal degrees. Graduate students teach a few undergraduate courses. Undergraduate student–faculty ratio: 8:1.

Expenses for 1995–96 Application fee: $20. State resident tuition: $1820 full-time, $56.83 per semester hour part-time. Nonresident tuition: $7090 full-time, $220.24 per semester hour part-time. College room and board: $4310. College room only: $2050. Special program-related fees: $15 for lab fee for studio courses.

Financial Aid Program-specific awards for Fall of 1994: 2 Amy DeGrove Scholarships for freshmen and juniors ($2500), 1 Ann Marston Scholarship for female art students ($500).

Application Procedures Deadline—freshmen: February 1; transfers: June 7. Notification date—freshmen and transfers: continuous. Required: high school transcript, college transcript(s) for transfer students, minimum 3.0 high school GPA, portfolio, SAT I or ACT test scores. Auditions held on campus and off campus. Portfolio reviews held 1 time on campus and off campus.

Undergraduate Contact Dr. Louise S. Rothman, Undergraduate Coordinator/Academic Advisor, Department of Art, University of Florida, FAC 302, P.O. Box 115801, Gainesville, Florida 32611-5801; 904-392-0211, fax: 904-392-8453.

Graduate Contact Joseph J. Sabatella, Professor, Department of Art, University of Florida, FAC 302, P.O. Box 115801, Gainesville, Florida 32611-5801; 904-392-0211, fax: 904-392-8453.

University of Georgia

Athens, Georgia

State-supported, coed. Suburban campus. Total enrollment: 29,469.

Degrees Bachelor of Fine Arts in the area of art. Majors: art education, ceramics, graphic design, interior design, jewelry and metalsmithing, painting/drawing, photography, printmaking, sculpture. Graduate degrees offered: Master of Fine Arts in the area of art.

Art Student Profile Fall 1994: 435 total; 376 matriculated undergraduate, 53 matriculated graduate, 6 nondegree; 4% minorities, 63% females, 2% international.

Art Faculty Total: 59; 53 full-time, 6 part-time; 98% of full-time faculty have terminal degrees. Graduate students teach a few undergraduate courses. Undergraduate student–faculty ratio: 18:1.

Student Life Student groups include American Society of Interior Designers Student Chapter, National Art Education Association Student Chapter.

Expenses for 1995–96 Application fee: $25. State resident tuition: $2508 full-time, $56 per quarter hour part-time. Nonresident tuition: $6795 full-time, $176 per quarter hour part-time. College room and board: $3876. College room only: $1776. Special program-related fees: $10–$75 for supplies.

Financial Aid Program-specific awards for Fall of 1994: 16 Art Awards for undergraduates ($500–$1000).

Application Procedures Deadline—freshmen: March 1; transfers: July 1. Notification date—freshmen: March 31. Required: high school transcript, college transcript(s) for transfer students, minimum 2.0 high school GPA, SAT I or ACT test scores. Portfolio reviews held 1 time during sophomore year for entrance into BFA program on campus.

University of Georgia *(continued)*

Undergraduate Contact Dr. Claire Swann, Director of Admissions, University of Georgia, 114 Academic Building, Athens, Georgia 30602; 706-542-2112, fax: 706-542-1466.

Graduate Contact Betty Andrews, Degree Program Specialist, School of Art, University of Georgia, Visual Arts Building, Athens, Georgia 30602; 706-542-1636, fax: 706-542-0226.

The Hartford Art School

University of Hartford

West Hartford, Connecticut

Independent, coed. Suburban campus. Total enrollment: 7,253.

Degrees Bachelor of Fine Arts in the areas of ceramic art and design, graphic arts, illustration, painting/drawing, photography, sculpture, printmaking, video production. Majors: experimental studies, graphic arts, illustration, painting/drawing, photography, printmaking, sculpture, studio art, video production. Graduate degrees offered: Master of Fine Arts in the areas of ceramic art and design, painting/drawing, printmaking, sculpture, photography. Cross-registration with Greater Hartford Consortium for Higher Education.

Art Student Profile Fall 1994: 379 total; 325 matriculated undergraduate, 14 matriculated graduate, 40 nondegree; 5% minorities, 45% females, 5% international.

Art Faculty Total: 29; 22 full-time, 7 part-time; 86% of full-time faculty have terminal degrees. Graduate students do not teach undergraduate courses. Undergraduate student–faculty ratio: 12:1.

Student Life Student groups include Student Association, student newspaper and yearbook staff, fraternities and sororities. Special housing available for art students.

Expenses for 1995–96 Comprehensive fee of $21,875 includes full-time tuition ($14,860), mandatory fees ($750), and college room and board ($6265). College room only: $3865. Part-time tuition: $310 per credit. Part-time mandatory fees: $50 per semester.

Financial Aid Program-specific awards for Fall of 1994: 25 Endowed Scholarships for those demonstrating need ($2000).

Application Procedures Deadline—freshmen and transfers: continuous. Notification date—freshmen and transfers: continuous. Required: high school transcript, college transcript(s) for transfer students, minimum 2.0 high school GPA, 2 letters of recommendation, portfolio, SAT I or ACT test scores. Recommended: essay, interview. Portfolio reviews held by appointment on campus and off campus on National Portfolio Days; the submission of slides may be substituted for portfolios when distance is prohibitive.

Undergraduate Contact Wendy Jackson, Admissions Officer, Hartford Art School, University of Hartford, 200 Bloomfield Avenue, West Hartford, Connecticut 06117; 203-768-4827.

Graduate Contact Stephen Keller, Associate Dean, Hartford Art School, University of Hartford, 200 Bloomfield Avenue, West Hartford, Connecticut 06117; 203-768-4396, fax: 203-768-5296.

University of Hawaii at Manoa

Honolulu, Hawaii

State-supported, coed. Urban campus. Total enrollment: 19,983.

Degrees Bachelor of Fine Arts in the area of art. Majors: ceramics, fibers, glass, graphic design, painting/drawing, photography, printmaking, sculpture. Graduate degrees offered: Master of Fine Arts in the area of art.

Art Student Profile Fall 1994: 1,888 total; 434 matriculated undergraduate, 36 matriculated graduate, 1,418 nondegree; 78% minorities, 55% females, 8% international.

Art Faculty Total: 47; 27 full-time, 20 part-time; 93% of full-time faculty have terminal degrees. Graduate students teach a few undergraduate courses. Undergraduate student–faculty ratio: 15:1.

Student Life Student groups include art shows, juried exhibitions.

Expenses for 1995–96 Application fee: $10. State resident tuition: $1631 full-time, $68 per credit part-time. Nonresident tuition: $4825 full-time, $201 per credit part-time. College room and board: $4210. College room only: $2400. Special program-related fees: $20–$100 for material fees.

Financial Aid Program-specific awards for Fall of 1994: 14 Tuition Waivers for above-average students with exceptional artistic ability ($1500).

Application Procedures Deadline—freshmen and transfers: May 1. Required: high school transcript, portfolio, SAT I or ACT test scores, minimum combined SAT I score of 860. Portfolio reviews held 2 times on campus; the submission of slides may be substituted for portfolios.

Undergraduate Contact Frank Beaver II, Associate Chair, Department of Art, University of Hawaii at Manoa, 2535 The Mall, Honolulu, Hawaii 96822; 808-956-8251, fax: 808-956-9043.

Graduate Contact Fred Roster, Graduate Chair, Department of Art, University of Hawaii at Manoa, 2535 The Mall, Honolulu, Hawaii 96822; 808-956-8251, fax: 808-956-9043.

University of Houston

Houston, Texas

State-supported, coed. Urban campus. Total enrollment: 31,298.

Degrees Bachelor of Fine Arts in the areas of graphic communication, interior design, photography, art history, sculpture, painting. Majors: art education, art history, graphic design, interior design, painting/drawing, photography, sculpture. Graduate degrees offered: Master of Fine Arts in the areas of graphic communication, interior design, photography, painting, sculpture. Cross-registration with North Houston Institute.

Art Student Profile Fall 1994: 720 total; 676 matriculated undergraduate, 44 matriculated graduate.

Art Faculty Total: 49; 24 full-time, 25 part-time. Graduate students teach about a quarter undergraduate courses. Undergraduate student–faculty ratio: 20:1.

Expenses for 1994–95 Application fee: $25. State resident tuition: $840 full-time. Nonresident tuition: $5130 full-time, $171 per semester hour part-time. State resident part-time tuition per semester ranges from $100 to $308. Part-time mandatory fees per semester range from $93 to $333. Full-time mandatory fees: $754. College room and board: $4608. College room only: $2340. Special program-related fees: $30–$40 for equipment maintenance and supplies.

Financial Aid Program-specific awards for Fall of 1994: 7 Flaxman Scholarships for seniors ($500), 3 Flaxman Competitive Scholarships for sophomores and juniors ($500), 2 Peter Guenther Scholarships for art history majors ($1000–$1500), 1 George Bunker Scholarship for program majors ($600).

Application Procedures Deadline—freshmen and transfers: July 15. Notification date—freshmen and transfers: continuous. Required: high school transcript, SAT I or ACT test scores. Recommended: letter of recommendation.

Undergraduate Contact Admission Office, University of Houston, 4800 Calhoun, Houston, Texas 77204; 713-743-1010.

Graduate Contact Cathy Hunt, Graduate Advisor, Art Department, University of Houston, Room 348 Fine Arts Building, Houston, Texas 77204-4893; 713-743-3001, fax: 713-743-2823.

University of Illinois at Chicago

Chicago, Illinois

State-supported, coed. Urban campus. Total enrollment: 24,865.

Degrees Bachelor of Fine Arts in the areas of art education, studio arts, industrial design, graphic design, photo/film/electronic media. Majors: art education, electronic arts, graphic arts, industrial design, painting/drawing, photography, printmaking, sculpture, studio art. Graduate degrees offered: Master of Fine Arts in the areas of studio arts, graphic design, industrial design, photography, film/animation/video, electronic visualization.

Art Student Profile Fall 1994: 685 total; 550 matriculated undergraduate, 135 matriculated graduate.

Art Faculty Total: 45; 37 full-time, 8 part-time; 100% of full-time faculty have terminal degrees. Graduate students teach a few undergraduate courses.

Expenses for 1994–95 Application fee: $30. Part-time mandatory fees: $554 per year. Full-time tuition ranges from $2520 to $3060 for state residents, $7230 to $8050 for nonresidents, according to class level. Part-time tuition per year ranges from $880 to $2060 for state residents, $2490 to $5406 for nonresidents, according to class level and course load. Full-time mandatory fees: $1108. College room and board: $5033.

Application Procedures Deadline—freshmen and transfers: June 9. Required: high school transcript, college transcript(s) for transfer students, SAT I or ACT test scores, English competency, minimum 3.25 college GPA for transfer students. Recommended: interview. Auditions held on campus and off campus. Portfolio reviews held on campus and off campus.

Contact Office of Admissions and Records, University of Illinois at Chicago, Box 5220, Chicago, Illinois 60680; 312-996-4350.

University of Illinois at Urbana-Champaign

Champaign, Illinois

State-supported, coed. Small-town campus. Total enrollment: 36,191.

Degrees Bachelor of Fine Arts in the areas of art education, art history, ceramics, glass, graphic design, industrial design, metals, painting, photography, sculpture. Majors: art education, ceramic art and design, glass, graphic arts, industrial design, jewelry and metalsmithing, painting/drawing, photography, sculpture. Graduate degrees offered: Master of Fine Arts in the areas of ceramics, glass, graphic design, industrial design, metals, painting, photography, printmaking, sculpture. Doctor of Arts in the areas of art education, art history.

Art Student Profile Fall 1994: 4,190 total; 600 matriculated undergraduate, 190 matriculated graduate, 3,400 nondegree; 23% minorities, 52% females, 1% international.

Art Faculty Total: 65; 65 full-time; 100% of full-time faculty have terminal degrees. Graduate students teach a few undergraduate courses. Undergraduate student–faculty ratio: 15:1.

Student Life Student groups include organizations for crafts, photography, industrial design, graphic design.

Expenses for 1994–95 Application fee: $30. Part-time mandatory fees per semester range from $201 to $474. Full-time tuition ranges from $2760 to $2900 for state residents, $7560 to $7980 for nonresidents, according to class level. Part-time tuition per semester ranges from $480 to $977 for state residents, $1300 to $2607 for nonresidents, according to class level and course load. Full-time mandatory fees: $920. College room and board: $4260. Special program-related fees: $100–$200 for equipment and materials fees.

Financial Aid Program-specific awards for Fall of 1994: 60–70 Tuition Waivers for program majors ($2000).

Application Procedures Deadline—freshmen: January 1; transfers: March 15. Required: essay, high school transcript, SAT I or ACT test scores.

University of Illinois at Urbana-Champaign
(continued)

Undergraduate Contact Robin Douglas, Associate Director, School of Art and Design, University of Illinois at Urbana-Champaign, 408 East Peabody Drive, Champaign, Illinois 61820; 217-333-7261, fax: 217-244-7688.

Graduate Contact Don Pilcher, Coordinator of Graduate Programs, School of Art and Design, University of Illinois at Urbana-Champaign, 408 East Peabody Drive, Champaign, Illinois 61820; 217-333-3083, fax: 217-244-7688.

University of Iowa

Iowa City, Iowa

State-supported, coed. Small-town campus. Total enrollment: 26,932.

Degrees Bachelor of Fine Arts in the area of studio arts. Majors: art education, art history, art/fine arts, ceramics, design, intermedia, jewelry and metalsmithing, painting/drawing, photography, printmaking, sculpture, studio art, video art. Graduate degrees offered: Master of Fine Arts in the area of studio arts.

Art Student Profile Fall 1994: 566 total; 421 matriculated undergraduate, 145 matriculated graduate; 8% minorities, 61% females, 7% international.

Art Faculty Total: 41; 34 full-time, 7 part-time; 97% of full-time faculty have terminal degrees. Graduate students teach a few undergraduate courses. Undergraduate student–faculty ratio: 13:1.

Student Life Student groups include Art History Society, College Art Association, art exhibitions.

Expenses for 1995–96 Application fee: $20. State resident tuition: $2386 full-time. Nonresident tuition: $8636 full-time. Part-time tuition per semester ranges from $192 to $1193 for state residents, $192 to $4318 for nonresidents. Part-time mandatory fees per semester range from $22 to $44. Full-time mandatory fees: $172. College room and board: $3550. Special program-related fees: $3–$55 for model fees, $10 for props, $3–$60 for material fees.

Financial Aid Program-specific awards for Fall of 1994: 1 Iowa Center for Art Scholarship for freshmen program majors ($2500), 1 Mary Sue Miller Memorial Award for freshmen program majors ($600–$800), 1 Emma McAllister Novel Award for minority program majors ($1000), 1–3 Schumacher Awards for program majors ($1800).

Application Procedures Deadline—freshmen and transfers: continuous. Required: high school transcript, SAT I or ACT test scores, minimum 2.25 high school GPA. Recommended: interview.

Contact Laura Jorgensen, Academic Secretary, School of Art and Art History, University of Iowa, E100 Art Building, Iowa City, Iowa 52242; 319-335-1758, fax: 319-335-1774.

University of Kansas

Lawrence, Kansas

State-supported, coed. Suburban campus. Total enrollment: 28,046.

Degrees Bachelor of Fine Arts in the areas of painting, sculpture, printmaking. Majors: painting/drawing, printmaking, sculpture. Graduate degrees offered: Master of Fine Arts in the area of art.

Art Student Profile Fall 1994: 175 total; 150 matriculated undergraduate, 15 matriculated graduate, 10 nondegree.

Art Faculty Total: 17; 17 full-time; 100% of full-time faculty have terminal degrees. Graduate students teach a few undergraduate courses. Undergraduate student–faculty ratio: 9:1.

Expenses for 1995–96 Application fee: $15. State resident tuition: $1766 full-time, $59 per credit hour part-time. Nonresident tuition: $7484 full-time, $249 per credit hour part-time. Part-time mandatory fees: $22 per credit hour. Full-time mandatory fees: $416. College room and board: $3544. Special program-related fees.

Application Procedures Deadline—freshmen and transfers: February 15. Required: high school transcript, SAT I or ACT test scores.

Undergraduate Contact Judith McCrea, Chairperson, Art Department, University of Kansas, 300 Art and Design Building, Lawrence, Kansas 66045; 913-864-4401.

Graduate Contact Cima Katz, Graduate Studies Director, Art Department, University of Kansas, 300 Art and Design Building, Lawrence, Kansas 66045; 913-864-4401.

Allen R. Hite Art Institute

University of Louisville

Louisville, Kentucky

State-supported, coed. Urban campus. Total enrollment: 21,377.

Degrees Bachelor of Fine Arts in the areas of painting, drawing, printmaking, sculpture, ceramics, fibers, photography, graphic design. Majors: art education, art/fine arts, ceramic art and design, graphic arts, painting/drawing, photography, printmaking, sculpture, textile arts. Cross-registration with Metroversity.

Art Student Profile Fall 1994: 363 total; all matriculated undergraduate; 6% minorities, 71% females, 5% international.

Art Faculty Total: 28; 21 full-time, 7 part-time; 100% of full-time faculty have terminal degrees. Graduate students teach a few undergraduate courses. Undergraduate student–faculty ratio: 13:1.

Student Life Student groups include Student Art League, American Society of Interior Designers, Louisville Graphic Design Association.

Estimated Expenses for 1995–96 Application fee: $25. State resident tuition: $2670 full-time, $106.50 per credit hour part-time. Nonresident tuition: $7550 full-time, $288 per credit hour part-time. College room and board: $3800. College room only: $2000. Special program-related fees: $13–$18 for supplies.

Financial Aid Program-specific awards for Fall of 1994: 26 Hite Scholarships for enrolled students ($500–$1500).

Application Procedures Deadline—freshmen and transfers: continuous. Required: high school transcript, college transcript(s) for transfer students, minimum 2.0 high school GPA, portfolio, SAT I or ACT test scores. Portfolio reviews held as needed for graphic design and interior design applicants on campus; the submission of slides may be substituted for portfolios.

Undergraduate Contact Matt Landrus, Program Assistant, Fine Arts Department, University of Louisville, 104 Schneider Hall, Louisville, Kentucky 40292; 502-852-6794, fax: 502-852-6791, E-mail address: mhland01@ulkyvm.louisville.edu.

University of Manitoba

Winnipeg, Manitoba

Province-supported, coed. Suburban campus. Total enrollment: 25,462.

Degrees Bachelor of Fine Arts in the areas of studio art, art history. Majors: ceramic art and design, graphic design, painting/drawing, photography, printmaking, sculpture.

Art Student Profile Fall 1994: 385 total; all matriculated undergraduate.

Art Faculty Total: 27; 18 full-time, 9 part-time; 78% of full-time faculty have terminal degrees. Graduate students do not teach undergraduate courses. Undergraduate student–faculty ratio: 20:1.

Expenses for 1994–95 Application fee: $25. Canadian resident tuition: $1956 full-time. Nonresident tuition: $3423 full-time. Part-time tuition and fees vary according to program. (All figures are in Canadian dollars.). Full-time mandatory fees: $390 (minimum). College room and board: $3840 (minimum).

Application Procedures Deadline—freshmen and transfers: May 1. Notification date—freshmen and transfers: continuous. Required: high school transcript, portfolio, letter of intent. Portfolio reviews held 1 time on campus; the submission of slides may be substituted for portfolios for large works of art.

Undergraduate Contact Shawn Anderson, Administrative Assistant, School of Art, University of Manitoba, 203 Fitz-Gerald Building, Fort Garry Campus, Winnipeg, Manitoba R3T2N2, Canada; 204-474-9367.

University of Mary Hardin-Baylor

Belton, Texas

Independent-religious, coed. Small-town campus. Total enrollment: 2,244.

Degrees Bachelor of Fine Arts in the area of art. Majors: art education, art/fine arts.

Art Student Profile Fall 1994: 301 total; 41 matriculated undergraduate, 260 nondegree.

Art Faculty Total: 5; 2 full-time, 3 part-time; 100% of full-time faculty have terminal degrees. Graduate students do not teach undergraduate courses. Undergraduate student–faculty ratio: 50:1.

Student Life Student groups include Kappa Pi (art fraternity).

Expenses for 1995–96 Comprehensive fee of $9274 includes full-time tuition ($5850), mandatory fees ($12), and college room and board ($3412). Part-time tuition: $195 per semester hour. Special program-related fees: $25 for lab fees/studio courses.

Application Procedures Deadline—freshmen and transfers: continuous. Required: high school transcript, SAT I or ACT test scores.

Undergraduate Contact Hershall Seals, Chair, Art Department, University of Mary Hardin-Baylor, UMHB-Station Box 8413, Belton, Texas 76513; 817-939-4675, fax: 817-939-4943.

University of Massachusetts Dartmouth

North Dartmouth, Massachusetts

State-supported, coed. Suburban campus. Total enrollment: 5,245.

Degrees Bachelor of Fine Arts in the areas of visual design, painting, printmaking, sculpture, textile design/fibers, art education. Majors: art education, ceramics, electronic imaging, fibers, graphic design, illustration, jewelry and metalsmithing, painting/drawing, photography, printmaking, sculpture, textile arts, textiles and clothing. Graduate degrees offered: Master of Fine Arts in the areas of design, artisanry, art education, fine arts. Cross-registration with University of Massachusetts System, Southeastern Association for Cooperation in Higher Education in Massachusetts.

Art Student Profile Fall 1994: 550 total; all matriculated undergraduate.

Art Faculty Total: 51; 34 full-time, 17 part-time; 92% of full-time faculty have terminal degrees. Graduate students teach a few undergraduate courses. Undergraduate student–faculty ratio: 18:1.

Student Life Student groups include Illustration Club, Campus Design: Omni Ad, Ceramics Club.

Expenses for 1995–96 Application fee: $20. State resident tuition: $1836 full-time, $76.50 per credit hour part-time. Nonresident tuition: $6919 full-time, $288.29 per credit hour part-time. Part-time mandatory fees: $230.90 per credit hour. Full-time mandatory fees per year: $1989 for state residents, $2693 for nonresidents. College room and board: $4890. College room only: $2628 (minimum). Special program-related fees: $20 for studio lab fees.

University of Massachusetts Dartmouth
(continued)

Financial Aid Program-specific awards for Fall of 1994: 25 Art Auction Awards for studio majors ($150–$400), 3–4 Neugebauer Awards for studio majors ($200).

Application Procedures Deadline—freshmen and transfers: continuous. Required: essay, high school transcript, college transcript(s) for transfer students. Recommended: letter of recommendation, portfolio, slides, minimum 2.7 high school GPA. Portfolio reviews held continuously on campus and off campus in Boston, MA.

Undergraduate Contact Jeffrey Feroce, Admissions Advisor, Office of Admissions, University of Massachusetts Dartmouth, Old Westport Road, North Dartmouth, Massachusetts 02747-2300; 508-999-8605, fax: 508-999-8901.

Graduate Contact Carol Novo, Secretary, Graduate Admissions Department, University of Massachusetts Dartmouth, Old Westport Road, North Dartmouth, Massachusetts 02747-2300; 508-999-8026, fax: 508-999-8901, E-mail address: cnovo@umassd.edu.

University of Massachusetts Lowell

Lowell, Massachusetts

State-supported, coed. Urban campus. Total enrollment: 12,731.

Degrees Bachelor of Fine Arts in the areas of fine arts, graphic design. Majors: applied art, art/fine arts, computer graphics, graphic arts, painting/drawing, photography, printmaking, sculpture, studio art.

Art Student Profile Fall 1994: 110 total; all matriculated undergraduate; 2% minorities, 45% females, 1% international.

Art Faculty Total: 8; 7 full-time, 1 part-time; 100% of full-time faculty have terminal degrees. Graduate students do not teach undergraduate courses. Undergraduate student–faculty ratio: 10:1.

Student Life Student groups include Art History Club.

Expenses for 1994–95 State resident tuition: $1884 full-time, $78.50 per credit part-time. Nonresident tuition: $7028 full-time, $293 per credit part-time. Part-time mandatory fees: $110.25 per credit. Full-time mandatory fees: $2718. College room and board: $4300 (minimum). College room only: $2520.

Financial Aid Program-specific awards for Fall of 1994: 8 Talent Scholarships for undergraduates ($500).

Application Procedures Deadline—freshmen and transfers: continuous. Required: high school transcript, minimum 2.0 high school GPA, portfolio. Portfolio reviews held 2 times on campus; the submission of slides may be substituted for portfolios when distance is prohibitive.

Undergraduate Contact Dr. Gerald J. Lloyd, Dean, College of Fine Arts, University of Massachusetts Lowell, Durgin Hall, South Campus, 1 University Avenue, Lowell, Massachusetts 01854; 508-934-3850, fax: 508-934-3034, E-mail address: lloydg@woods.vmi.edu.

University of Memphis

Memphis, Tennessee

State-supported, coed. Urban campus. Total enrollment: 19,848.

Degrees Bachelor of Fine Arts in the areas of art education, graphic design, interior design, ceramics, painting, printmaking, photography, sculpture. Majors: art education, art/fine arts, ceramic art and design, graphic design, interior design, painting/drawing, photography, printmaking, sculpture. Graduate degrees offered: Master of Fine Arts in the areas of ceramics, graphic design, interior design, painting, printmaking/photography.

Art Student Profile Fall 1994: 393 total; 331 matriculated undergraduate, 62 matriculated graduate; 11% minorities, 62% females, 3% international.

Art Faculty Total: 50; 28 full-time, 22 part-time; 100% of full-time faculty have terminal degrees. Graduate students teach a few undergraduate courses.

Student Life Student groups include Art History Student Organization, Photography Club, Clay Club.

Expenses for 1995–96 Application fee: $5. State resident tuition: $2094 full-time. Nonresident tuition: $6224 full-time. Part-time tuition per semester ranges from $92 to $989 for state residents, $273 to $2980 for nonresidents. College room and board: $2200 (minimum). Special program-related fees: $5–$125 for material fees.

Financial Aid Program-specific awards for Fall of 1994: 3 Visual Arts Performance Awards for incoming freshmen ($2000–$5975), 1 Dana D. Johnson Scholarship for program majors ($500), 1 M. M. Ross Art Alumni Award for program majors ($1000), 1 Industrial Design Alumni Scholarship for program majors ($500), 1 Art Directors Club of Memphis Award for graphic design majors ($500).

Application Procedures Deadline—freshmen and transfers: August 1. Required: high school transcript, minimum 3.0 high school GPA, portfolio, ACT test score only. Portfolio reviews held 1 time on campus; the submission of slides may be substituted for portfolios for 3-dimensional work.

Undergraduate Contact Brenda Landman, Assistant to the Chairman, Art Department, University of Memphis, Jones Hall 201, Memphis, Tennessee 38152; 901-678-2216, fax: 901-678-3299, E-mail address: blandman@adminl.memst.edu.

Graduate Contact Rodger S. Langdon, Coordinator, Graduate Programs, Art Department, University of Memphis, Jones Hall 201, Memphis, Tennessee 38152; 901-678-2216, fax: 901-678-3299, E-mail address: rlangdon@adminl.memst.edu.

University of Miami

Coral Gables, Florida

Independent, coed. Suburban campus. Total enrollment: 13,410.

Degrees Bachelor of Fine Arts in the areas of ceramics, graphic design/illustration, painting, photography, sculpture, printmaking. Majors: ceramic art and design, graphic arts, illustration, painting/drawing, photography, printmaking, sculpture. Graduate degrees offered: Master of Fine Arts in the areas of ceramics, graphic design/illustration, painting, photography, sculpture, printmaking.

Art Student Profile Fall 1994: 258 total; 225 matriculated undergraduate, 30 matriculated graduate, 3 nondegree; 35% minorities, 47% females, 12% international.

Art Faculty Total: 33; 17 full-time, 16 part-time; 100% of full-time faculty have terminal degrees. Graduate students teach a few undergraduate courses. Undergraduate student–faculty ratio: 15:1.

Student Life Student groups include Annual Student Show.

Estimated Expenses for 1995–96 Application fee: $35. Comprehensive fee of $24,552 includes full-time tuition ($17,340), mandatory fees ($360), and college room and board ($6852). College room only: $3830. Part-time tuition: $672 per credit.

Financial Aid Program-specific awards for Fall of 1994: 6 Art Scholarships for those demonstrating talent ($6000).

Application Procedures Deadline—freshmen: March 1; transfers: continuous. Notification date—freshmen: April 15; transfers: continuous. Required: essay, high school transcript, college transcript(s) for transfer students, letter of recommendation, SAT I or ACT test scores. Recommended: minimum 3.0 high school GPA. Portfolio reviews held on campus; the submission of slides may be substituted for portfolios.

Contact Telma Estrada, Senior Secretary, Art and Art History Department, University of Miami, P.O. Box 248106, Coral Gables, Florida 33124-4410; 305-284-2542, fax: 305-284-2115.

More about the University

A wonderful place to study art, Miami is warm year round. The Department of Art and Art History is part of the University of Miami, which is recognized among the nation's best private universities. It is located in the lush tropical paradise of Coral Gables, the "City Beautiful," minutes away from dynamic Miami and exotic Miami Beach.

Miami has one of the best foundation programs in the country. When students finish the 100-level courses, they know how to draw realistically and design in two and three dimensions. They learn the principles of abstract painting and have a good grasp of world art history. On the 200-levels, each area offers systematic, thorough instruction on the basics of the craft. Students begin to evolve under the guidance of talented and devoted instructors, many of them internationally recognized artists and scholars. Several young, dynamic new faculty members have come on board recently. Every art major studies with full-time, tenured faculty. There is continuous creative interchange with a large group of excellent graduate students, especially in the intense Friday critiques, open to everyone.

Facilities are first-rate and getting better. Recently the University added glassblowing and entered computer imaging into the curriculum. A new art library has been built, and a twenty-station computer lab in graphic design has been installed. There is a large new advanced painting studio in one of the most beautiful buildings on campus. The Lowe Art Museum, one of the top University museums in the country, is host to the student and M.F.A. exhibitions. The University also has its own gallery, which shows nationally prominent artists as well as students and faculty. The visiting artist/lecturer program is very active.

University of Michigan

Ann Arbor, Michigan

State-supported, coed. Suburban campus. Total enrollment: 36,543.

Degrees Bachelor of Fine Arts. Majors: art/fine arts, ceramic art and design, fibers, graphic design, industrial design, jewelry and metalsmithing, painting/drawing, photography, printmaking, sculpture. Graduate degrees offered: Master of Fine Arts in the areas of fine arts, medical and biological illustration.

Art Student Profile Fall 1994: 611 total; 562 matriculated undergraduate, 44 matriculated graduate, 5 nondegree; 60% females, 4% international.

Art Faculty Total: 53; 27 full-time, 26 part-time; 90% of full-time faculty have terminal degrees. Graduate students teach a few undergraduate courses. Undergraduate student–faculty ratio: 18:1.

Student Life Student groups include Art Students League, Industrial Design Society of America Student Chapter.

Expenses for 1994–95 Application fee: $40. Full-time tuition ranges from $5040 to $6698 for state residents, $15,732 to $17,850 for nonresidents according to class level and program. Part-time tuition and fees per term (1 to 11 credits) range from $525 to $3204 for state residents, $970 to $8530 for nonresidents according to course load, class level, and program. Full-time mandatory fees: $175. College room and board: $4659.

Financial Aid Program-specific awards for Fall of 1994: 2 Scholastic Art Awards for those participating in the National Art Honor Society competition ($2000), 2 National Art Honor Society Awards for Michigan high school seniors belonging to Michigan Art Honor Society ($1000).

Application Procedures Deadline—freshmen and transfers: February 1. Notification date—freshmen and transfers: May 1. Required: essay, high school transcript, college transcript(s) for transfer students, minimum 3.0 high school GPA, letter of recommendation, portfolio, SAT I or ACT test scores, minimum combined SAT I score of 1000, minimum composite ACT score of 24. Recommended: interview. Portfolio reviews held continuously on campus and off campus on National Portfolio Days; the submission of slides may be substituted for portfolios.

Undergraduate Contact Gene Pijanowski, Associate Dean for Student Affairs, School of Art, University of Michigan, 2000 Bonisteel, Ann Arbor, Michigan 48109-

University of Michigan *(continued)*

2069; 313-763-5249, fax: 313-936-0469, E-mail address: eugene_pijanowski@um.cc.umich.edu.

Graduate Contact Ed West, Associate Dean for Graduate Studies, School of Art, University of Michigan, 2000 Bonisteel, Ann Arbor, Michigan 48109-2069; 313-936-0667, fax: 313-936-0469, E-mail address: ed_west@um.cc.umich.edu.

More about the University

Program Facilities The University of Michigan School of Art is located in the Art & Architecture Building on North Campus. Opened in 1974, the spacious building houses programs in art, design, architecture, and urban planning. Studios enjoy natural light and air conditioning, and an interior courtyard provides a place to relax outdoors. The Jean Paul Slusser Gallery is a handsome showcase for exhibitions. Resources include individual and group darkrooms and facilities for lithography and intaglio, ceramics, wood, metal, plastic, bronze casting, and electronic imaging. The Art & Architecture Library includes a collection of 55,000 books, 600 journals and periodicals, 82,000 slides, and audiovideo tapes. In addition, the six-million-volume University Library network includes the History of Fine Arts Library and Undergraduate and Graduate Libraries. Computers are widely available, with easy access to extensive software and research databases.

Faculty, Visiting Artists, and Alumni Distinguished faculty members include international printmakers Paul Stewart and Takeshi Takahara, metalsmiths Hiroko and Eugene Pijanowski, photographer Joanne Leonard, fiber artist Sherri Smith, ceramist Georgette Zirbes, painter Al Hinton, and multimedia artist Carol Ann Carter. Gerome Kamrowski, professor emeritus, is considered one of this century's more important artists of the Surrealist school. Visiting artists in 1994-1995 included Francoise Gilot and Art Spiegelman. Significant alumni are Michele Oka Doner and Pat Oleszko of New York City and Ruth Weisberg and Mike Kelley of Los Angeles.

Student Exhibit Opportunities The Jean Paul Slusser Gallery and numerous exhibition areas throughout the building provide interesting display spaces for student work, and in May 1995 the gallery was host to an extraordinary Mondrian show.

Special Programs International programs are available in Kyoto, Japan, and Florence, Italy. Kyoto Seika University offers ceramics, papermaking, and wood block printing, and students experience cultural opportunities—festivals, gardens, shrines, and temples. In Florence, students sketch and paint in the picturesque gardens of Villa Corsi-Salviati and explore the surrounding Tuscany landscape. Summer workshops on the Ann Arbor campus include calligraphy, photography, quilt making, handmade books, metals, CAD, and furniture design.

University of Michigan–Flint

Flint, Michigan

State-supported, coed. Urban campus. Total enrollment: 6,236.

Degrees Bachelor of Fine Arts in the area of studio art. Majors: art education, studio art. Mandatory cross-registration with Charles Stewart Mott Community College.

Art Student Profile Fall 1994: 205 total; 55 matriculated undergraduate, 150 nondegree; 10% minorities, 60% females.

Art Faculty Total: 7; 3 full-time, 4 part-time; 100% of full-time faculty have terminal degrees. Graduate students do not teach undergraduate courses. Undergraduate student–faculty ratio: 18:1.

Student Life Student groups include Annual Student Exhibition, BFA Exhibits.

Expenses for 1995–96 State resident tuition: $3184 full-time. Nonresident tuition: $9454 full-time. Part-time mandatory fees: $50 per semester. Part-time tuition per credit hour: $166 for the first credit hour, $126 for the next 10 credit hours for state residents; $434 for the first credit hour, $394 for the next 10 credit hours for nonresidents. Full-time mandatory fees: $120.

Application Procedures Deadline—freshmen and transfers: August 21. Notification date—freshmen: September 18; transfers: September 1. Required: high school transcript, minimum 2.0 high school GPA, portfolio. Portfolio reviews held as needed for transfer applicants on campus; the submission of slides may be substituted for portfolios.

Undergraduate Contact David James, Director, Admissions, University of Michigan–Flint, University Pavillion, Flint, Michigan 48502; 810-762-3300, fax: 810-762-3687, E-mail address: james-d@pavillion.flint.umich.edu.

University of Minnesota, Duluth

Duluth, Minnesota

State-supported, coed. Suburban campus. Total enrollment: 7,497.

Degrees Bachelor of Fine Arts. Majors: art education, art history, graphic design, studio art. Cross-registration with University of Wisconsin&–Superior, College of St. Scholastica.

Art Student Profile Fall 1994: 266 total; 258 matriculated undergraduate, 6 matriculated graduate, 2 nondegree; 1% minorities, 50% females.

Art Faculty Total: 14; 12 full-time, 2 part-time; 92% of full-time faculty have terminal degrees. Graduate students teach a few undergraduate courses. Undergraduate student–faculty ratio: 19:1.

Student Life Student groups include American Institute of Graphic Arts.

Expenses for 1994–95 Application fee: $25. State resident tuition: $2995 full-time, $71.30 per credit part-time. Nonresident tuition: $8828 full-time, $210.20 per credit part-time. Part-time mandatory fees (6 to 11 credits): $103.45 per quarter. Full-time mandatory fees: $310. College room and board: $3474. Special program-related fees: $3–$35 for expendable supplies, computer lab fees.

Financial Aid Program-specific awards for Fall of 1994: 10–15 Raymond W. Darland Art Awards for program majors ($250–$1000), 2 Gershgol Awards for program majors ($750), 1–2 Mitchell and Schissell Awards for program majors ($250), 1 Edith M. Nelson Award for program majors ($500).

Application Procedures Deadline—freshmen: February 1; transfers: June 15. Required: high school transcript, college transcript(s) for transfer students, ACT test score only.

Undergraduate Contact Gerald Allen, Director, Admissions, University of Minnesota, Duluth, 184 Darland Administration Building, Duluth, Minnesota 55812; 218-726-7171, E-mail address: admis@ua.d.umn.edu.

University of Minnesota, Twin Cities Campus

Minneapolis, Minnesota

State-supported, coed. Urban campus. Total enrollment: 36,699.

Degrees Bachelor of Fine Arts in the area of art. Majors: ceramic art and design, painting/drawing, photography, printmaking, sculpture. Graduate degrees offered: Master of Fine Arts in the area of art.

Art Student Profile Fall 1994: 1,390 total; 350 matriculated undergraduate, 40 matriculated graduate, 1,000 nondegree.

Art Faculty Total: 29; 19 full-time, 10 part-time; 85% of full-time faculty have terminal degrees. Graduate students teach a few undergraduate courses. Undergraduate student–faculty ratio: 20:1.

Student Life Student groups include Studio Arts Student Society.

Expenses for 1994–95 Application fee: $25. Full-time tuition ranges from $3395 to $3482 for state residents, $9190 to $10,794 for nonresidents, according to class level and program. Part-time tuition per credit ranges from $70.80 to $82.90 for state residents, $208.80 to $244.40 for nonresidents, according to class level and program. Full-time tuition for pharmacy program ranges from $2478 to $6077 for state residents, $4687 to $12,150 for nonresidents according to class level. Part-time tuition per credit for pharmacy program ranges from $59 to $144.70 for state residents, $111.60 to $289.30 for nonresidents according to class level. Full-time mandatory fees: $431. College room and board: $3774.

Financial Aid Program-specific awards for Fall of 1994: 10–20 Department of Art Scholarships for program majors ($200–$1000).

Application Procedures Deadline—freshmen: December 15; transfers: June 1. Notification date—freshmen: January 15; transfers: July 15. Required: high school transcript, college transcript(s) for transfer students, SAT I or ACT test scores, minimum 2.8 high school GPA. Portfolio reviews held 2 times in junior year of college for BFA on campus; the submission of slides may be substituted for portfolios.

Undergraduate Contact Office of Admissions, University of Minnesota, Twin Cities Campus, 240 Williamson, 231 Pillsbury Avenue SE, Minneapolis, Minnesota 55455; 612-625-2008.

Graduate Contact Department of Art Graduate Program, University of Minnesota, Twin Cities Campus, 216 21st Avenue South, Minneapolis, Minnesota 55455; 612-625-8096.

University of Mississippi

University, Mississippi

State-supported, coed. Small-town campus. Total enrollment: 10,075.

Degrees Bachelor of Fine Arts in the area of art. Majors: art education, art history, ceramic art and design, painting/drawing, printmaking, sculpture, visual communication. Graduate degrees offered: Master of Fine Arts in the area of art.

Art Student Profile Fall 1994: 230 total; 42 matriculated undergraduate, 18 matriculated graduate, 170 nondegree; 9% minorities, 46% females, 2% international.

Art Faculty Total: 17; 12 full-time, 5 part-time; 100% of full-time faculty have terminal degrees. Graduate students teach about a quarter undergraduate courses. Undergraduate student–faculty ratio: 12:1.

Student Life Student groups include Student Art Association, Mud Daubbers.

Expenses for 1994–95 Application fee: $25. State resident tuition: $2546 full-time, $83 per semester hour part-time. Nonresident tuition: $5006 full-time, $186 per semester hour part-time. Part-time mandatory fees per semester (7 to 11 semester hours): $275. Full-time mandatory fees: $550. College room only: $1560.

Financial Aid Program-specific awards for Fall of 1994: 10 Art Merit Scholarships for portfolio students ($4750).

Application Procedures Deadline—freshmen and transfers: July 31. Notification date—freshmen and transfers: continuous. Required: essay, high school transcript, college transcript(s) for transfer students, minimum 2.0 high school GPA, ACT test score only. Portfolio reviews held 2 times (upon completion of 30 semester hours in studio art) on campus; the submission of slides may be substituted for portfolios.

Contact Margaret J. Gorove, Chair, Art Department, University of Mississippi, University, Mississippi 38677; 601-232-7193, fax: 601-232-5013.

University of Montana–Missoula

Missoula, Montana

State-supported, coed. Urban campus. Total enrollment: 11,067.

University of Montana–Missoula *(continued)*

Degrees Bachelor of Fine Arts in the area of art. Majors: art/fine arts, ceramics, painting/drawing, printmaking, sculpture. Graduate degrees offered: Master of Fine Arts in the area of art.

Art Student Profile Fall 1994: 254 total; 235 matriculated undergraduate, 19 matriculated graduate; 3% minorities, 40% females, 5% international.

Art Faculty Total: 16; 12 full-time, 4 part-time; 83% of full-time faculty have terminal degrees. Graduate students teach a few undergraduate courses. Undergraduate student–faculty ratio: 19:1.

Student Life Student groups include Artists Collective.

Expenses for 1994–95 Application fee: $30. State resident tuition: $2251 full-time. Nonresident tuition: $6311 full-time. Part-time tuition per semester ranges from $99.10 to $943.10 for state residents, $244.10 to $2538 for nonresidents. College room and board: $3667. Special program-related fees: $30 for materials, student aides, minor tools and repairs for ceramics and sculpture courses, $45 for chemicals, lab monitors, minor tools and repairs for printmaking and photography courses, $30 for basic supplies, models, photo development, studio upkeep for art fundamentals courses, $30 for models, equipment, studio upkeep for painting courses, $10 for slide replacement, library monitoring, copying for art history courses.

Financial Aid Program-specific awards for Fall of 1994: 2 Wallace Awards for sophomore or junior program majors ($500), 1 Pat Williams Scholarship for sophomore or junior program majors ($400), 1 Christopher Parker Scholarship for sophomore or junior program majors ($500), 1 Walter Hook Scholarship for sophomore or junior program majors ($600), 1 Briggs Scholarship for sophomore or junior program majors ($500).

Application Procedures Deadline—freshmen and transfers: continuous. Required: high school transcript, college transcript(s) for transfer students, SAT I or ACT test scores, minimum combined SAT I score of 920, minimum 2.5 high school GPA. Auditions held on campus and off campus. Portfolio reviews held on campus and off campus.

Undergraduate Contact New Student Services, University of Montana–Missoula, The Lodge, Missoula, Montana 59812; 406-243-6266.

Graduate Contact Rhea Blanchard, Administrative Assistant, Department of Art, University of Montana–Missoula, Missoula, Montana 59812-1057; 406-243-4181, fax: 406-243-4968.

University of Montevallo

Montevallo, Alabama

State-supported, coed. Small-town campus. Total enrollment: 3,282.

Degrees Bachelor of Fine Arts in the area of studio art. Majors: ceramic art and design, graphic design, painting/drawing, printmaking, sculpture.

Art Student Profile Fall 1994: 154 total; all matriculated undergraduate.

Art Faculty Total: 9; 8 full-time, 1 part-time; 100% of full-time faculty have terminal degrees. Graduate students do not teach undergraduate courses. Undergraduate student–faculty ratio: 17:1.

Expenses for 1994–95 Application fee: $15. State resident tuition: $2340 full-time, $78 per semester hour part-time. Nonresident tuition: $4680 full-time, $156 per semester hour part-time. Full-time mandatory fees: $67. College room and board: $2964.

Financial Aid Program-specific awards for Fall of 1994: Dean's Fine Arts Awards for visual arts students.

Application Procedures Deadline—freshmen and transfers: continuous. Required: high school transcript, minimum 2.0 high school GPA, SAT I or ACT test scores, minimum 2.0 college GPA for transfer students. Recommended: interview.

Undergraduate Contact Dr. Sandra Jordan, Chairperson, Art Department, University of Montevallo, Station 6400, Montevallo, Alabama 35115; 205-665-6400, fax: 205-665-6383, E-mail address: jordan@um.montevallo.edu.

University of Nebraska–Lincoln

Lincoln, Nebraska

State-supported, coed. Urban campus. Total enrollment: 23,854.

Degrees Bachelor of Fine Arts in the area of studio art. Majors: art/fine arts, ceramic art and design, commercial art, computer graphics, graphic arts, illustration, painting/drawing, photography, printmaking, sculpture, studio art. Graduate degrees offered: Master of Fine Arts in the area of studio art. Cross-registration with University of Nebraska at Omaha, University of Nebraska at Kearney.

Art Student Profile Fall 1994: 1,672 total; 292 matriculated undergraduate, 21 matriculated graduate, 1,359 nondegree; 52% females.

Art Faculty Total: 26; 18 full-time, 8 part-time; 100% of full-time faculty have terminal degrees. Graduate students teach a few undergraduate courses. Undergraduate student–faculty ratio: 20:1.

Expenses for 1994–95 Application fee: $25. State resident tuition: $2415 full-time, $68.50 per credit hour part-time. Nonresident tuition: $5955 full-time, $186.50 per credit hour part-time. Part-time mandatory fees per semester range from $85 to $180. Full-time mandatory fees: $360. College room and board: $3145. College room only: $1375. Special program-related fees: $5–$50 for lab fees.

Application Procedures Deadline—freshmen and transfers: July 15. Notification date—freshmen and transfers: August 7. Required: high school transcript.

Undergraduate Contact Department of Art and Art History, University of Nebraska–Lincoln, 207 Nelle Cochrane Woods Hall, Lincoln, Nebraska 68588-0114; 402-472-2631, fax: 402-472-9746.

Graduate Contact David Routon, Graduate Committee Chairperson, Department of Art and Art History, University of Nebraska–Lincoln, 207 Nelle Cochrane Woods Hall, Lincoln, Nebraska 68588-0114; 402-472-5543, fax: 402-472-9746.

University of Nevada, Las Vegas

Las Vegas, Nevada

State-supported, coed. Urban campus. Total enrollment: 20,239.

Degrees Bachelor of Fine Arts in the area of art. Majors: ceramic art and design, painting/drawing, photography, printmaking, sculpture, studio art. Graduate degrees offered: Master of Fine Arts in the area of art.

Art Student Profile Fall 1994: 260 total; 240 matriculated undergraduate, 20 matriculated graduate.

Art Faculty Total: 21; 11 full-time, 10 part-time. Graduate students teach a few undergraduate courses.

Student Life Student groups include Art Club.

Estimated Expenses for 1995–96 Application fee: $40. State resident tuition: $1800 full-time, $60 per credit hour part-time. Nonresident tuition: $6800 full-time. Nonresident part-time tuition per semester ranges from $62 to $3400. Part-time mandatory fees: $25 per semester. Tuition for nonresidents who are eligible for the Western Undergraduate Exchange: $2700 full-time, $90 per credit hour part-time. Full-time mandatory fees: $50. College room and board: $5000. Special program-related fees: .

Financial Aid Program-specific awards for Fall of 1994: Scholarships for those demonstrating need/talent.

Application Procedures Deadline—freshmen and transfers: continuous. Required: high school transcript, portfolio. Portfolio reviews held 1 time on campus; the submission of slides may be substituted for portfolios.

Undergraduate Contact Lee Sido, Chair, Department of Art, University of Nevada, Las Vegas, 4505 Maryland Parkway, Las Vegas, Nevada 89154-5002; 702-895-3237.

Graduate Contact Jim Pink, Graduate Advisor, Department of Art, University of Nevada, Las Vegas, 4505 Maryland Parkway, Las Vegas, Nevada 89154-5002; 702-895-3237.

University of New Hampshire

Durham, New Hampshire

State-supported, coed. Small-town campus. Total enrollment: 12,518.

Degrees Bachelor of Fine Arts. Majors: ceramic art and design, furniture design, painting/drawing, photography, printmaking, sculpture.

Art Student Profile Fall 1994: 6 total; all matriculated undergraduate.

Art Faculty Total: 23; 17 full-time, 6 part-time.

Expenses for 1994–95 State resident tuition: $3670 full-time, $157 per credit part-time. Nonresident tuition: $11,990 full-time, $500 per credit part-time. Part-time mandatory fees per semester (6 to 11 credits): $235.25. Full-time mandatory fees: $889. College room and board: $4038. College room only: $2326.

Application Procedures Deadline—freshmen: February 1; transfers: March 1. Notification date—freshmen: April 15; transfers: May 15. Required: portfolio. Portfolio reviews held 2 times on campus.

Undergraduate Contact Daniel Valenza, Chair, Department of Art and Art History, University of New Hampshire, Paul Arts Center, Durham, New Hampshire 03824; 603-862-2190.

University of New Mexico

Albuquerque, New Mexico

State-supported, coed. Urban campus. Total enrollment: 24,344.

Degrees Bachelor of Fine Arts in the area of art studio. Graduate degrees offered: Master of Fine Arts in the area of art studio.

Art Student Profile Fall 1994: 190 total; all matriculated undergraduate; 20% minorities, 64% females, 2% international.

Art Faculty Total: 27; 27 full-time; 89% of full-time faculty have terminal degrees. Graduate students teach about a quarter undergraduate courses.

Student Life Student groups include Associated Students of Arts.

Expenses for 1995–96 Application fee: $15. State resident tuition: $2080 full-time, $83.20 per semester hour part-time. Nonresident tuition: $7856 full-time, $314.25 per semester hour part-time. College room and board: $4176.

Application Procedures Deadline—freshmen and transfers: July 21. Required: essay, high school transcript, college transcript(s) for transfer students, minimum 2.25 high school GPA. Auditions held on campus and off campus. Portfolio reviews held on campus and off campus.

Undergraduate Contact Office of Admissions and Outreach Services, University of New Mexico, Albuquerque, New Mexico 87131; 505-277-2446.

University of North Alabama

Florence, Alabama

State-supported, coed. Urban campus. Total enrollment: 5,221.

University of North Alabama *(continued)*

Degrees Bachelor of Fine Arts in the area of art. Majors: art education, art/fine arts, graphic arts, painting/drawing, photography, printmaking, sculpture.

Art Student Profile Fall 1994: 485 total; 85 matriculated undergraduate, 400 nondegree; 5% minorities, 60% females, 1% international.

Art Faculty Total: 9; 8 full-time, 1 part-time; 90% of full-time faculty have terminal degrees. Graduate students do not teach undergraduate courses. Undergraduate student–faculty ratio: 12:1.

Student Life Student groups include Student Art Association, W.C. Handy Music Festival Poster Competition, Floala (student newspaper) and Diorama (yearbook).

Expenses for 1995–96 State resident tuition: $1800 full-time, $75 per semester hour part-time. Nonresident tuition: $3600 full-time, $150 per semester hour part-time. Part-time mandatory fees per year range from $23 to $86. Full-time mandatory fees: $92. College room and board: $3150. College room only: $1400. Special program-related fees: $30 for studio lab fee.

Financial Aid Program-specific awards for Fall of 1994: 4 Endowed Scholarships for program majors ($300–$500).

Application Procedures Deadline—freshmen and transfers: August 30. Notification date—freshmen and transfers: continuous. Required: high school transcript, college transcript(s) for transfer students, SAT I or ACT test scores, minimum combined SAT I score of 700, minimum composite ACT score of 18. Recommended: minimum 2.0 high school GPA. Portfolio reviews held 2 times for admission to BFA program after 45 hours prescribed courses on campus.

Undergraduate Contact Dr. G. Daniel Howard, Dean of Enrollment Management, Admissions Office, University of North Alabama, Box 5058, Florence, Alabama 35632-0001; 205-760-4680, fax: 205-760-4329, E-mail address: kbenson@unaalpha.una.edu.

University of North Carolina at Charlotte

Charlotte, North Carolina

State-supported, coed. Urban campus. Total enrollment: 15,513.

Degrees Bachelor of Fine Arts in the areas of ceramics, painting, drawing, photography, graphic design/illustration, fiber, printmaking, sculpture, art education, art history, museum studies. Majors: art education, art history, art/fine arts, ceramic art and design, commercial art, computer graphics, graphic arts, illustration, jewelry and metalsmithing, museum studies, painting/drawing, photography, printmaking, sculpture, studio art, textile arts. Cross-registration with area universities.

Art Student Profile Fall 1994: 300 total; all matriculated undergraduate; 11% minorities, 54% females, 2% international.

Art Faculty Total: 25; 14 full-time, 11 part-time; 100% of full-time faculty have terminal degrees. Undergraduate student–faculty ratio: 14:1.

Student Life Student groups include National Art Education Association Student Chapter, Sculpture Guild.

Expenses for 1994–95 Application fee: $25. State resident tuition: $764 full-time. Nonresident tuition: $7248 full-time. Part-time tuition per semester ranges from $96 to $287 for state residents, $906 to $2718 for nonresidents. Part-time mandatory fees per semester range from $87 to $178.50. Full-time mandatory fees: $695. College room and board: $3260. College room only: $1670.

Application Procedures Deadline—freshmen and transfers: continuous. Required: high school transcript, minimum 3.0 high school GPA, portfolio, SAT I or ACT test scores. Portfolio reviews held on campus; the submission of slides may be substituted for portfolios.

Undergraduate Contact Director, Admissions Office, University of North Carolina at Charlotte, Reese Administration Building, 1st Floor, Charlotte, North Carolina 28223; 704-547-2213, fax: 704-547-3340.

University of North Carolina at Greensboro

Greensboro, North Carolina

State-supported, coed. Urban campus. Total enrollment: 12,094.

Degrees Bachelor of Fine Arts in the area of studio art. Majors: art education, ceramic art and design, design, graphic design, painting/drawing, photography, printmaking, sculpture. Graduate degrees offered: Master of Fine Arts in the area of studio art.

Art Student Profile Fall 1994: 408 total; 379 matriculated undergraduate, 29 matriculated graduate; 10% minorities, 60% females, 2% international.

Art Faculty Total: 23; 19 full-time, 4 part-time; 99% of full-time faculty have terminal degrees. Graduate students teach a few undergraduate courses. Undergraduate student–faculty ratio: 22:1.

Student Life Student groups include Student Art Alliance, Student Government.

Expenses for 1994–95 Application fee: $35. State resident tuition: $874 full-time. Nonresident tuition: $8400 full-time. Part-time tuition per semester ranges from $109 to $328 for state residents, $1050 to $3150 for nonresidents. Full-time mandatory fees: $891. College room and board: $3505. College room only: $1791.

Financial Aid Program-specific awards for Fall of 1994: 3 Reeves/Howard/Falk Awards for junior program majors ($500–$1500).

Application Procedures Deadline—freshmen and transfers: August 1. Required: high school transcript, college transcript(s) for transfer students, SAT I or ACT test scores, minimum combined SAT I score of 800, minimum composite ACT score of 20. Portfolio reviews held on campus.

Contact K. Porter Aichele, Head, Art Department, University of North Carolina at Greensboro, 162 McIver Building, Greensboro, North Carolina 27412; 910-334-5248.

University of North Dakota

Grand Forks, North Dakota

State-supported, coed. Small-town campus. Total enrollment: 11,521.

Degrees Bachelor of Fine Arts in the area of visual arts. Majors: art education, ceramic art and design, jewelry and metalsmithing, painting/drawing, photography, printmaking, sculpture. Graduate degrees offered: Master of Fine Arts in the area of visual arts.

Art Student Profile Fall 1994: 95 total; 75 matriculated undergraduate, 20 matriculated graduate.

Art Faculty Total: 13; 10 full-time, 3 part-time.

Expenses for 1995–96 Application fee: $25. State resident tuition: $2878 full-time, $119.92 per credit hour part-time. Nonresident tuition: $6402 full-time, $266.75 per credit hour part-time. Full-time mandatory fees: $318. College room and board: $2816.

Application Procedures Deadline—freshmen and transfers: continuous.

Undergraduate Contact Mackelroy Edwards, Chair, Visual Art Department, University of North Dakota, Box 7099, Grand Forks, North Dakota 58202; 701-777-2257, fax: 701-777-3395.

Graduate Contact Dr. Ronald Shaefer, Director of Graduate Program, Visual Arts Department, University of North Dakota, Box 7099, Grand Forks, North Dakota 58202; 701-777-2903, fax: 701-777-3395.

University of North Florida

Jacksonville, Florida

State-supported, coed. Urban campus. Total enrollment: 10,064.

Degrees Bachelor of Fine Arts in the areas of painting, drawing, ceramics, photography, sculpture, graphic design. Majors: art/fine arts, ceramic art and design, commercial art, computer graphics, digital imaging, graphic arts, painting/drawing, photography, sculpture, studio art.

Estimated Expenses for 1995–96 Application fee: $20. State resident tuition: $1820 full-time, $55.01 per semester hour part-time. Nonresident tuition: $6390 full-time, $213.66 per semester hour part-time. College room and board: $3800.

Application Procedures

Undergraduate Contact Registrar, University of North Florida, 4567 St. Johns Bluff Road South, Jacksonville, Florida 32224; 904-646-2624.

University of North Texas

Denton, Texas

State-supported, coed. Urban campus. Total enrollment: 25,605.

Degrees Bachelor of Fine Arts in the areas of advertising art, art history, ceramics, drawing and painting, fashion design, fibers, interior design, metalsmithing and jewelry, photography, printmaking, sculpture, visual arts studies. Majors: art education, ceramic art and design, communication design, fashion design and technology, fibers, interior design, jewelry and metalsmithing, painting/drawing, photography, printmaking, sculpture. Graduate degrees offered: Master of Fine Arts in the areas of art education, art history, ceramics, communication design, drawing and painting, fashion design, fibers, interior design, metalsmithing and jewelry, photography, printmaking, sculpture.

Art Student Profile Fall 1994: 1,558 total; 1,439 matriculated undergraduate, 119 matriculated graduate; 5% minorities, 62% females, 5% international.

Art Faculty Total: 101; 36 full-time, 65 part-time; 98% of full-time faculty have terminal degrees. Graduate students teach about a quarter undergraduate courses. Undergraduate student–faculty ratio: 16:1.

Expenses for 1995–96 Application fee: $25. State resident tuition: $900 full-time. Nonresident tuition: $6660 full-time, $222 per semester hour part-time. State resident part-time tuition per semester ranges from $120 to $330. Part-time mandatory fees per semester range from $92.30 to $332.30. Full-time mandatory fees: $813. College room and board: $3659. College room only: $1877. Special program-related fees: $25–$75 for materials fee.

Financial Aid Program-specific awards for Fall of 1994: 3–6 John D. Murchison Scholarships for upperclassmen program majors ($500), 3–6 Helen Voertman Scholarships for upperclassmen program majors ($500), 2–4 Nelda Lee Scholarships for upperclassmen program majors ($250), 2–4 Cora Stafford Scholarships for upperclassmen program majors ($250), 1 Roger Thomason Scholarship for upperclassmen weaving majors ($250), 3–6 Jean Andrews Awards for program majors ($500), 1 Edward and Betty Mattil Scholarship for undergraduates ($500), 1 Mozelle Rawson Brown Scholarship for undergraduates ($250), 1 J. Robert Egan Scholarship for photography majors ($250), 1 Paramount Pictures Scholarship for undergraduates ($250), 1 President's Council Scholarship for undergraduates ($250).

Application Procedures Deadline—freshmen and transfers: June 15. Required: high school transcript, college transcript(s) for transfer students, SAT I or ACT test scores, minimum 2.5 high school GPA.

Undergraduate Contact Mickey McCarter, Coordinator of Undergraduate Studies, School of Visual Arts,

University of North Texas *(continued)*

University of North Texas, P.O. Box 5098, Denton, Texas 76203; 817-565-4007, fax: 817-565-4717.

Graduate Contact Jerry Austin, Coordinator of Graduate Studies, School of Visual Arts, University of North Texas, P.O. Box 5098, Denton, Texas 76203; 817-565-4004, fax: 817-565-4717.

University of Northern Iowa

Cedar Falls, Iowa

State-supported, coed. Small-town campus. Total enrollment: 12,572.

Degrees Bachelor of Fine Arts in the area of studio arts. Majors: ceramic art and design, graphic design, jewelry and metalsmithing, painting/drawing, papermaking, photography, printmaking, sculpture.

Expenses for 1995–96 Application fee: $20. State resident tuition: $2390 full-time, $100 per semester hour part-time. Nonresident tuition: $6462 full-time, $270 per semester hour part-time. Part-time mandatory fees per semester range from $11 to $32. Full-time mandatory fees: $172. College room and board: $3112. Special program-related fees.

Application Procedures Portfolio reviews held on campus.

Undergraduate Contact Dr. William Lew, Head, Department of Art, University of Northern Iowa, 1227 West 27th Street, Cedar Falls, Iowa 50614-0362; 319-273-2077, fax: 319-273-2731.

University of Notre Dame

Notre Dame, Indiana

Independent-religious, coed. Suburban campus. Total enrollment: 10,000.

Degrees Bachelor of Fine Arts in the areas of studio art, design. Majors: art/fine arts, ceramic art and design, computer graphics, graphic arts, painting/drawing, photography, printmaking, sculpture, studio art. Graduate degrees offered: Master of Fine Arts in the areas of studio art, design.

Art Student Profile Fall 1994: 145 total; 120 matriculated undergraduate, 25 matriculated graduate; 5% minorities, 50% females.

Art Faculty Total: 18; 16 full-time, 2 part-time; 100% of full-time faculty have terminal degrees. Graduate students teach about a quarter undergraduate courses. Undergraduate student–faculty ratio: 15:1.

Student Life Student groups include student exhibitions.

Expenses for 1995–96 Application fee: $40. Comprehensive fee of $22,467 includes full-time tuition ($17,830), mandatory fees ($137), and college room and board ($4500). Part-time tuition: $743 per credit hour. Special program-related fees: $15–$50 for studio materials.

Application Procedures Deadline—freshmen and transfers: January 4. Notification date—freshmen and transfers: April 10. Required: essay, high school transcript, minimum 3.0 high school GPA, 2 letters of recommendation. Recommended: slide portfolio. the submission of slides may be substituted for portfolios.

Undergraduate Contact Admissions Office, University of Notre Dame, 113 Main Building, Notre Dame, Indiana 46556; 219-631-7505.

Graduate Contact Richard Gray, Director of Graduate Studies, Art, Art History and Design Department, University of Notre Dame, Notre Dame, Indiana 46556; 219-631-7602, fax: 219-631-6312.

University of Oklahoma

Norman, Oklahoma

State-supported, coed. Suburban campus. Total enrollment: 19,683.

Degrees Bachelor of Fine Arts in the areas of art, art history. Majors: art/fine arts, ceramic art and design, commercial art, painting/drawing, photography, printmaking, sculpture. Graduate degrees offered: Master of Fine Arts in the areas of art, design.

Art Student Profile Fall 1994: 283 total; 265 matriculated undergraduate, 18 matriculated graduate; 22% minorities, 49% females, 8% international.

Art Faculty Total: 20; 19 full-time, 1 part-time; 100% of full-time faculty have terminal degrees. Graduate students teach a few undergraduate courses. Undergraduate student–faculty ratio: 20:1.

Expenses for 1994–95 Application fee: $15. Part-time mandatory fees: $91 per semester. Full-time tuition ranges from $1688 to $1785 for state residents, $4928 to $5438 for nonresidents according to class level. Part-time tuition per credit hour ranges from $56.25 to $59.49 for state residents, $164.25 to $181.26 for nonresidents according to class level. Full-time mandatory fees: $182. College room and board: $3526. Special program-related fees: $10–$80 for material fees.

Financial Aid Program-specific awards for Fall of 1994: 8–12 Ben Barnett Scholarships for undergraduates ($500), 1–2 DeLoe Memorial Awards for undergraduates ($250–$500).

Application Procedures Deadline—freshmen and transfers: continuous. Recommended: high school transcript, college transcript(s) for transfer students, SAT I or ACT test scores, minimum 2.5 high school GPA. Portfolio reviews held 2 times on campus and off campus in various cities.

Undergraduate Contact Andrew Phelam, Director, School of Art, University of Oklahoma, 520 Parrington Oval, Room 202, Norman, Oklahoma 73019-0550; 405-325-2691, fax: 405-325-1668.

Graduate Contact Graduate Liaison, School of Art, University of Oklahoma, 520 Parrington Oval, Room 202, Norman, Oklahoma 73019-0550; 405-325-2691, fax: 405-325-1668.

University of Oregon

Eugene, Oregon

State-supported, coed. Urban campus. Total enrollment: 16,681.

Degrees Bachelor of Fine Arts in the areas of painting, sculpture, ceramics, fibers, metals and jewelry, printmaking, visual design. Majors: animation, art/fine arts, ceramic art and design, computer graphics, fibers, graphic design, jewelry and metalsmithing, painting/drawing, photography, printmaking, sculpture. Graduate degrees offered: Master of Fine Arts in the areas of painting, sculpture, ceramics, fibers, metals and jewelry, printmaking, visual design.

Art Student Profile Fall 1994: 570 total; 500 matriculated undergraduate, 50 matriculated graduate, 20 nondegree; 10% minorities, 50% females, 3% international.

Art Faculty Total: 24; 20 full-time, 4 part-time; 90% of full-time faculty have terminal degrees. Graduate students teach a few undergraduate courses. Undergraduate student–faculty ratio: 20:1.

Estimated Expenses for 1995–96 Application fee: $50. State resident tuition: $2590 full-time. Nonresident tuition: $10,300 full-time. Part-time tuition per quarter ranges from $250 to $1112 for state residents, $481 to $3652 for nonresidents. Full-time mandatory fees: $790. College room and board: $3900. Special program-related fees: $50 for material fees.

Financial Aid Program-specific awards for Fall of 1994: 4 Phillip Johnson Scholarships for continuing painting and printmaking students ($200–$400), 4 LaVerne Krause Scholarships for continuing printmaking students ($200–$400), 1 Merz Memorial Scholarship for continuing students ($200–$400), 4 David McCosh Painting Scholarships for continuing painting students ($200–$400), 1 Jack Wilkinson Paint Award for continuing students ($200–$400), 2 Molly Muntzel Awards for continuing students ($200–$400).

Application Procedures Deadline—freshmen and transfers: March 1. Required: minimum 3.0 high school GPA, letter of recommendation. Recommended: portfolio. Portfolio reviews held 3 times on campus; the submission of slides may be substituted for portfolios.

Undergraduate Contact Fine Arts Admissions, Fine and Applied Arts Department, University of Oregon, 5232 University of Oregon, Eugene, Oregon 97403-5232; 503-346-3610, fax: 503-346-3626.

Graduate Contact Graduate Fine Arts Admissions, Fine and Applied Arts Department, University of Oregon, 5232 University of Oregon, Eugene, Oregon 97403-5232; 503-346-3610, fax: 503-346-3626.

University of Regina

Regina, Saskatchewan

Province-supported, coed. Urban campus. Total enrollment: 11,537.

Degrees Bachelor of Fine Arts in the areas of drawing, painting, sculpture, ceramics, printmaking, intermedia. Majors: ceramics, painting/drawing, printmaking, sculpture. Graduate degrees offered: Master of Fine Arts in the areas of drawing, painting, sculpture, ceramics, printmaking, intermedia.

Art Student Profile Fall 1994: 91 total; 85 matriculated undergraduate, 6 matriculated graduate; 2% minorities, 65% females, 5% international.

Art Faculty Total: 9; 8 full-time, 1 part-time; 80% of full-time faculty have terminal degrees. Graduate students teach a few undergraduate courses. Undergraduate student–faculty ratio: 15:1.

Expenses for 1994–95 Application fee: $25. Canadian resident tuition: $2490 full-time, $83 per credit hour part-time. Nonresident tuition: $4110 full-time, $137 per credit hour part-time. Full-time mandatory fees: $50. College room and board: $3759. College room only: $1542. Special program-related fees: $15–$75 for materials.

Financial Aid Program-specific awards for Fall of 1994: 3 Endowed Scholarships for program majors ($50–$250), 4 Funded Scholarships for program majors ($250–$1000).

Application Procedures Deadline—freshmen and transfers: April 1. Notification date—freshmen and transfers: April 15. Required: high school transcript, minimum 2.0 high school GPA, portfolio. Recommended: letter of recommendation, interview. Portfolio reviews held 2 times on campus; the submission of slides may be substituted for portfolios.

Undergraduate Contact Leesa Streifler, Head, Department of Visual Arts, University of Regina, Room 108 Fine Arts Building, Regina, Saskatchewan S4S0A2, Canada; 306-585-5752, fax: 306-585-5744.

Graduate Contact Department of Graduate Studies and Research, Admissions Office, University of Regina, Regina, Saskatchewan S4S0A2, Canada; 306-585-4161, fax: 306-585-4893.

University of South Alabama

Mobile, Alabama

State-supported, coed. Suburban campus. Total enrollment: 12,386.

Degrees Bachelor of Fine Arts in the area of studio art. Majors: ceramics, graphic design, painting/drawing, printmaking, sculpture.

Art Student Profile Fall 1994: 142 total; all matriculated undergraduate; 46% females.

Art Faculty Total: 15; 11 full-time, 4 part-time; 91% of full-time faculty have terminal degrees. Graduate stu-

University of South Alabama *(continued)*

dents do not teach undergraduate courses. Undergraduate student–faculty ratio: 12:1.

Student Life Student groups include Student Art Association.

Expenses for 1995–96 Application fee: $20. State resident tuition: $2352 full-time, $49 per quarter hour part-time. Nonresident tuition: $3402 full-time. Nonresident part-time tuition per quarter ranges from $424 to $1214. Part-time mandatory fees per quarter range from $123 to $147. Full-time mandatory fees: $189. College room and board: $2940. College room only: $1440. Special program-related fees: $10–$50 for lab fees.

Application Procedures Deadline—freshmen and transfers: continuous. Required: high school transcript, college transcript(s) for transfer students, portfolio, SAT I or ACT test scores. Portfolio reviews held continuously for transfer students on campus; the submission of slides may be substituted for portfolios.

Undergraduate Contact John H. Cleverdon, Acting Chair, Art and Art History Department, University of South Alabama, 172 Visual Arts Building, Mobile, Alabama 36688; 334-460-6336, fax: 334-460-7928.

University of South Carolina

Columbia, South Carolina

State-supported, coed. Urban campus. Total enrollment: 26,754.

Degrees Bachelor of Fine Arts. Majors: 3-dimensional studies, ceramic art and design, design, fibers, painting/drawing, photography, printmaking. Graduate degrees offered: Master of Fine Arts.

Art Faculty Total: 40; 26 full-time, 14 part-time.

Expenses for 1995–96 Application fee: $35. State resident tuition: $3280 full-time, $148 per credit hour part-time. Nonresident tuition: $8324 full-time, $366 per credit hour part-time. College room and board: $3428 (minimum). College room only: $1646 (minimum).

Application Procedures Deadline—freshmen and transfers: continuous. Required: portfolio. Portfolio reviews held 2 times upon completion of 45 hours of course work on campus.

Undergraduate Contact Dr. John O'Neil, Chair, Art Department, University of South Carolina, Sloan College, Columbia, South Carolina 29208; 803-777-4236.

Graduate Contact Director of Graduate Studies, Art Department, University of South Carolina, Columbia, South Carolina 29208; 803-777-4236.

University of South Dakota

Vermillion, South Dakota

State-supported, coed. Small-town campus. Total enrollment: 7,739.

Degrees Bachelor of Fine Arts in the areas of graphics, photography, ceramics, painting, sculpture, printmaking, art education. Majors: art/fine arts, photography, printmaking, sculpture. Graduate degrees offered: Master of Fine Arts in the areas of painting, printmaking, sculpture.

Art Student Profile Fall 1994: 652 total; 98 matriculated undergraduate, 10 matriculated graduate, 544 nondegree; 8% minorities, 51% females.

Art Faculty Total: 13; 11 full-time, 2 part-time; 91% of full-time faculty have terminal degrees. Graduate students teach a few undergraduate courses. Undergraduate student–faculty ratio: 10:1.

Student Life Student groups include Art Students Organization, Art Student Co-op.

Expenses for 1995–96 Application fee: $15. State resident tuition: $1648 full-time, $51.50 per credit hour part-time. Nonresident tuition: $4480 full-time, $140 per credit hour part-time. Part-time mandatory fees per semester range from $74.56 to $440.96. Minnesota residents pay state resident tuition. Tuition for nonresidents who are eligible for the Western Undergraduate Exchange: $2182 full-time, $68.18 per credit hour part-time. Full-time mandatory fees: $1105. College room and board: $2572. College room only: $1247. Special program-related fees: $15–$100 for consumable materials, $100 for computer graphics course fees, $5–$10 for art appreciation/art history hand-outs.

Financial Aid Program-specific awards for Fall of 1994: 5–6 Oscar Howe Scholarships for upperclass Native Americans ($300), 1 A.B. Gunderson Fine Arts Scholarship for upperclassmen ($750), 3 Louise Hansen Art Scholarships for upperclassmen ($300), 1 Lance Hyde Memorial Art Scholarship for upperclassmen ($200).

Application Procedures Deadline—freshmen and transfers: continuous. Required: high school transcript, SAT I or ACT test scores, minimum composite ACT score of 22.

Undergraduate Contact David Lorenz, Director, Admissions Office, University of South Dakota, Slagle 12, 414 East Clark Street, Vermillion, South Dakota 57069-2390; 605-677-5434, fax: 605-677-5073.

Graduate Contact Charles N. Kaufman, Dean, Graduate School, University of South Dakota, Slagel 105, 414 East Clark Street, Vermillion, South Dakota 57069-2390; 605-677-6498, fax: 605-677-5073.

University of Southern California

Los Angeles, California

Independent, coed. Urban campus. Total enrollment: 27,864.

Degrees Bachelor of Fine Arts in the area of studio arts. Majors: art/fine arts, ceramic art and design, computer imaging, painting/drawing, photography, printmaking, sculpture, studio art. Graduate degrees offered: Master of Fine Arts in the area of studio arts.

Art Student Profile Fall 1994: 148 total; 123 matriculated undergraduate, 11 matriculated graduate, 14 nondegree; 17% minorities, 65% females, 20% international.

Art Faculty Total: 30; 10 full-time, 20 part-time; 80% of full-time faculty have terminal degrees. Graduate students do not teach undergraduate courses. Undergraduate student–faculty ratio: 3:1.

Student Life Student groups include Students of Fine Arts Organization, Annual Student Art Exhibition.

Expenses for 1995–96 Application fee: $50. Comprehensive fee of $25,988 includes full-time tuition ($19,198), mandatory fees ($352), and college room and board ($6438 minimum). College room only: $3502. Part-time tuition: $614 per unit. Part-time mandatory fees per year (6 to 11 units): $330. Special program-related fees: $30 for lab/studio materials fee.

Financial Aid Program-specific awards for Fall of 1994: 30 Fine Art Scholarships for program majors ($2000).

Application Procedures Deadline—freshmen and transfers: continuous. Notification date—freshmen: July 15; transfers: August 1. Required: essay, high school transcript, college transcript(s) for transfer students, 3 letters of recommendation, portfolio, SAT I or ACT test scores, slides for transfer aplicants, minimum 2.8 college GPA for transfer applicants. Recommended: minimum 3.0 high school GPA, interview. Portfolio reviews held continuously on campus; the submission of slides may be substituted for portfolios.

Contact Penelope Jones, Director of Admissions, School of Fine Arts, University of Southern California, Watt Hall 104, Los Angeles, California 90089-0292; 213-740-9153, fax: 213-749-9703, E-mail address: penelope@mizar.usc.edu.

University of Southern Maine

Gorham, Maine

State-supported, coed. Urban campus. Total enrollment: 9,628.

Degrees Bachelor of Fine Arts in the areas of studio art, art education. Majors: art education, ceramic art and design, painting/drawing, photography, printmaking, sculpture. Cross-registration with Maine College of Art, University of New England, St. Joseph's College, Westbrook College, Southern Maine Technical College.

Art Student Profile Fall 1994: 290 total; all matriculated undergraduate; 5% minorities, 55% females, 1% international.

Art Faculty Total: 22; 12 full-time, 10 part-time; 80% of full-time faculty have terminal degrees. Graduate students do not teach undergraduate courses. Undergraduate student–faculty ratio: 24:1.

Expenses for 1995–96 Application fee: $25. State resident tuition: $3180 full-time, $106 per credit hour part-time. Nonresident tuition: $9000 full-time, $300 per credit hour part-time. Part-time mandatory fees per semester range from $7 to $123. Tuition for nonresidents who are eligible for the New England Regional Student Program: $4545 full-time, $151 per credit hour part-time. Full-time mandatory fees: $290. College room and board: $4494. College room only: $2298.

Application Procedures Deadline—freshmen and transfers: continuous. Notification date—freshmen and transfers: July 15. Required: essay, high school transcript, letter of recommendation, portfolio. Recommended: minimum 2.0 high school GPA, interview. Portfolio reviews held 2 times on campus.

Undergraduate Contact Susan Roberts, Acting Director of Admissions, University of Southern Maine, 37 College Ave, Gorham, Maine 04038; 207-780-5670, fax: 207-780-5640.

University of Southern Mississippi

Hattiesburg, Mississippi

State-supported, coed. Suburban campus. Total enrollment: 11,587.

Degrees Bachelor of Fine Arts in the area of art. Majors: 3-dimensional studies, art education, graphic communication, painting/drawing. Graduate degrees offered: Master of Fine Arts in the areas of drawing, painting.

Art Student Profile Fall 1994: 120 total; 115 matriculated undergraduate, 5 nondegree; 27% minorities, 30% females, 4% international.

Art Faculty Total: 11; 10 full-time, 1 part-time; 100% of full-time faculty have terminal degrees. Graduate students teach a few undergraduate courses. Undergraduate student–faculty ratio: 15:1.

Student Life Student groups include Student Art Club.

Expenses for 1994–95 State resident tuition: $2428 full-time. Nonresident tuition: $4892 full-time. Part-time tuition per semester ranges from $100 to $970 for state residents, $202 to $2092 for nonresidents. College room and board: $2430. College room only: $1250 (minimum).

Financial Aid Program-specific awards for Fall of 1994: 5 Endowed Scholarships for program majors ($370), 1 Mississippi Gulf Coast Scholarship for program majors ($600–$900).

Application Procedures Deadline—freshmen and transfers: July 31. Notification date—freshmen and transfers: continuous. Required: high school transcript, portfolio, ACT test score only. Portfolio reviews held as needed for transfers on campus and off campus in Jackson, MS; the submission of slides may be substituted for portfolios.

Undergraduate Contact Admissions Office, University of Southern Mississippi, Box 5011, Hattiesburg, Mississippi 39406-5033; 601-266-5555.

Graduate Contact Graduate Admissions, University of Southern Mississippi, Box 10066, Hattiesburg, Mississippi 39406-1006; 601-266-5137.

University of Tennessee at Chattanooga

Chattanooga, Tennessee

State-supported, coed. Urban campus. Total enrollment: 8,281.

University of Tennessee at Chattanooga *(continued)*

Degrees Bachelor of Fine Arts in the areas of graphic design, painting and drawing, sculpture. Majors: art education, graphic design, painting/drawing, sculpture.

Art Student Profile Fall 1994: 721 total; 140 matriculated undergraduate, 581 nondegree; 2% minorities, 57% females.

Art Faculty Total: 15; 9 full-time, 6 part-time; 100% of full-time faculty have terminal degrees. Graduate students do not teach undergraduate courses. Undergraduate student–faculty ratio: 45:1.

Student Life Student groups include Student Art Cooperative.

Expenses for 1994–95 Application fee: $15. State resident tuition: $1850 full-time, $76 per semester hour part-time. Nonresident tuition: $5782 full-time, $208 per semester hour part-time. College room only: $1360 (minimum). Special program-related fees: $10–$35 for supplies.

Financial Aid Program-specific awards for Fall of 1994: 1 Wayne Hannah Award for freshmen graphic design majors ($1800), 1 Doug Griffith Award for continuing student graphic design majors ($1800), 2 Lillian B. Fernstein Awards for program majors ($1800).

Application Procedures Deadline—freshmen and transfers: continuous. Notification date—freshmen and transfers: continuous. Required: high school transcript, minimum 2.0 high school GPA.

Undergraduate Contact Patsy Reynolds, Admissions Director, University of Tennessee at Chattanooga, 615 Mc Callie Avenue, Chattanooga, Tennessee 37403; 615-755-4662, fax: 615-755-4157, E-mail address: patsyrenolds/admin/ug@hpdeskutc.edu.

University of Tennessee at Martin

Martin, Tennessee

State-supported, coed. Small-town campus. Total enrollment: 5,627.

Degrees Bachelor of Fine Arts in the area of fine and performing arts. Majors: art/fine arts.

Art Student Profile Fall 1994: 24 total; all matriculated undergraduate; 5% minorities, 60% females, 5% international.

Art Faculty Total: 2; 2 full-time; 100% of full-time faculty have terminal degrees. Graduate students do not teach undergraduate courses. Undergraduate student–faculty ratio: 12:1.

Student Life Student groups include Visual Arts Society.

Expenses for 1994–95 Application fee: $15. State resident tuition: $1900 full-time, $76 per semester hour part-time. Nonresident tuition: $5832 full-time, $240 per semester hour part-time. College room and board: $2890 (minimum). College room only: $1490 (minimum).

Application Procedures Deadline—freshmen and transfers: continuous. Required: high school transcript, minimum 2.0 high school GPA, SAT I or ACT test scores. Auditions held on campus. Portfolio reviews held on campus; the submission of slides may be substituted for portfolios.

Undergraduate Contact Dr. Earl Norwood, Director, Division of Fine and Performing Arts, University of Tennessee at Martin, 102 Fine Arts Building, Martin, Tennessee 38238; 901-587-7400, fax: 901-587-7415, E-mail address: norwood@utm.edu.

University of Tennessee, Knoxville

Knoxville, Tennessee

State-supported, coed. Urban campus. Total enrollment: 25,890.

Degrees Bachelor of Fine Arts in the areas of studio art, graphic design. Majors: art/fine arts, ceramics, graphic arts, interrelated media, painting/drawing, photography, printmaking, sculpture, watercolors. Graduate degrees offered: Master of Fine Arts in the area of studio art. Cross-registration with Arrowmont School of Art and Crafts.

Art Faculty Total: 31; 27 full-time, 4 part-time; 100% of full-time faculty have terminal degrees. Graduate students teach a few undergraduate courses.

Expenses for 1994–95 Application fee: $15. State resident tuition: $2052 full-time, $87 per semester hour part-time. Nonresident tuition: $5986 full-time, $241 per semester hour part-time. College room and board: $3398. College room only: $1600. Special program-related fees: $10–$100 for lab fees.

Financial Aid Program-specific awards for Fall of 1994: 1 Buck Ewing Undergraduate Scholarship for juniors, seniors ($2000), Dille Scholarships for undergraduates.

Application Procedures Deadline—freshmen and transfers: continuous. Required: high school transcript, college transcript(s) for transfer students, minimum 3.0 high school GPA, ACT test score only. Portfolio reviews held one per semester for studio arts students and once each Spring for graphic design students on campus.

Contact Norman Magden, Head, Art Department, University of Tennessee, Knoxville, 1715 Volunteer Boulevard, Knoxville, Tennessee 37996-2410; 615-974-3408, fax: 615-974-3198.

University of Texas at Arlington

Arlington, Texas

State-supported, coed. Suburban campus. Total enrollment: 23,280.

Degrees Bachelor of Fine Arts in the areas of art, media arts. Majors: art history, art/fine arts, ceramic art and design, commercial art, glass, graphic arts, jewelry and metalsmithing, painting/drawing, photography, printmaking, sculpture, studio art.

Art Student Profile Fall 1994: 385 total; all matriculated undergraduate.

Art Faculty Total: 27; 21 full-time, 6 part-time; 100% of full-time faculty have terminal degrees. Graduate students do not teach undergraduate courses. Undergraduate student–faculty ratio: 18:1.

Student Life Student groups include Student Art Association, Student Film and Video Association.

Expenses for 1995–96 State resident tuition: $930 full-time. Nonresident tuition: $5456 full-time, $176 per semester hour part-time. State resident part-time tuition per semester ranges from $100 to $330. Part-time mandatory fees per semester range from $89 to $289. Full-time mandatory fees: $706. College room and board: $2560. College room only: $1180 (minimum). Special program-related fees: $25–$75 for materials fee.

Application Procedures Deadline—freshmen and transfers: August 5.

Undergraduate Contact Director of Admissions, University of Texas at Arlington, P.O. Box 19088-A, Arlington, Texas 76019; 817-273-3565.

University of Texas at Austin

Austin, Texas

State-supported, coed. Urban campus. Total enrollment: 47,957.

Degrees Bachelor of Fine Arts in the areas of design, studio art. Majors: ceramic art and design, design, intaglio, jewelry and metalsmithing, lithography, painting/drawing, performance art, photography, printmaking, sculpture, seriography, studio art, video art. Graduate degrees offered: Master of Fine Arts in the area of studio art.

Art Student Profile Fall 1994: 459 total; 424 matriculated undergraduate, 35 matriculated graduate.

Art Faculty Total: 40; 40 full-time; 99% of full-time faculty have terminal degrees. Graduate students do not teach undergraduate courses.

Expenses for 1995–96 Application fee: $35. State resident tuition: $900 full-time. Nonresident tuition: $6660 full-time, $222 per semester hour part-time. State resident part-time tuition per semester ranges from $120 to $330. Part-time mandatory fees per semester range from $169.85 to $570.14. Full-time mandatory fees: $1308. College room and board: $3632. Special program-related fees: $16–$144 for lab fees.

Application Procedures Deadline—freshmen and transfers: March 1. Required: high school transcript, college transcript(s) for transfer students, SAT I or ACT test scores.

Undergraduate Contact Rachel Hindshaw, Student Development Specialist, Department of Art and Art History, University of Texas at Austin, Austin, Texas 78712-1285; 512-475-7718, fax: 514-471-7801.

Graduate Contact Graduate Advisor, Department of Art and Art History, University of Texas at Austin, Austin, Texas 78712-1285; 512-471-3377, fax: 512-471-7801.

More about the University

Founded in 1938, the Department of Art and Art History enjoys a strong reputation across the country. Today with over 90 undergraduate art majors and 165 graduate students, it is one of the largest and most comprehensive in the country.

Program Facilities The studio art program has eight areas of concentration: ceramics, metals, painting, drawing, photography, printmaking, sculpture, and transmedia. All studio areas are well-equipped and a centralized shop is maintained. In the design area, students have access to numerous labs, each tailored to a specific technology including photography, graphic arts photography, and a new and constantly expanding digital technology laboratory.

Faculty, Visiting Artists Programs Over 40 full-time faculty members, all practicing artists. Approximately 20 visiting artists per year. *Viewpoint Series* is a distinguished critics program occurring during the spring semester and presents lectures and seminars. *Guest Artist in Printmaking* program brings a nationally recognized artist for a two-week residency, and numerous other symposiums, such as *Beyond Identity: Latin American Art in the 21st Century* in 1995.

Student Exhibition Opportunities Several student exhibition spaces are open to all students to show their work on a regular basis. The Performing Arts Center's mezzanine levels are set aside for student exhibitions. An annual student exhibition is sponsored by the University's art museum.

Special Programs The *Study in Italy* program allows students to take departmental courses during the summer and receive university credit in the Tuscany region of Italy.

University of Texas at San Antonio

San Antonio, Texas

State-supported, coed. Suburban campus. Total enrollment: 17,579.

Degrees Bachelor of Fine Arts in the area of art. Majors: ceramic art and design, painting/drawing, photography, printmaking, sculpture. Graduate degrees offered: Master of Fine Arts in the area of art.

Art Student Profile Fall 1994: 232 total; 200 matriculated undergraduate, 32 matriculated graduate; 39% minorities, 60% females, 2% international.

Art Faculty Total: 16; 13 full-time, 3 part-time; 100% of full-time faculty have terminal degrees. Graduate students teach a few undergraduate courses. Undergraduate student–faculty ratio: 18:1.

Student Life Student groups include Art Guild, Printmaking Club.

Expenses for 1995–96 Application fee: $20. State resident tuition: $900 full-time. Nonresident tuition:

University of Texas at San Antonio *(continued)*

$6660 full-time, $222 per semester part-time. State resident part-time tuition per semester ranges from $120 to $330. Part-time mandatory fees per semester range from $121 to $496. Full-time mandatory fees: $1168. College room only: $2724. Special program-related fees: $20 for studio supplies.

Application Procedures Deadline—freshmen and transfers: July 1. Required: high school transcript, SAT I or ACT test scores.

Undergraduate Contact Kent Rush, Associate Professor of Art, Division of Art and Architecture, University of Texas at San Antonio, 6900 North Loop 1604 West, San Antonio, Texas 78249-1130; 210-691-4352.

Graduate Contact Ken Little, Chair, Graduate Studies, Division of Art and Architecture, University of Texas at San Antonio, 6900 North Loop 1604 West, San Antonio, Texas 78249-1130; 210-691-4352.

University of Texas–Pan American

Edinburg, Texas

State-supported, coed. Rural campus. Total enrollment: 13,298.

Degrees Bachelor of Fine Arts in the areas of studio art, advertising design, biological illustration, secondary art education. Majors: advertising design, art education, ceramic art and design, jewelry and metalsmithing, lithography, painting/drawing, printmaking, sculpture.

Art Student Profile Fall 1994: 220 total; all matriculated undergraduate.

Art Faculty Total: 12; 8 full-time, 4 part-time.

Estimated Expenses for 1995–96 State resident tuition: $900 full-time. Nonresident tuition: $5280 full-time, $176 per semester hour part-time. State resident part-time tuition per semester ranges from $100 to $330. Part-time mandatory fees per semester range from $35.48 to $285.28. Full-time mandatory fees: $693. College room and board: $2050.

Application Procedures Deadline—freshmen: July 1; transfers: continuous. Required: high school transcript, SAT I or ACT test scores.

Undergraduate Contact Nancy Moyer, Chair, Art Department, University of Texas–Pan American, 1201 West University Drive, Edinburg, Texas 78539; 210-381-3480.

University of the Arts

Philadelphia, Pennsylvania

Independent, coed. Urban campus. Total enrollment: 1,298.

Degrees Bachelor of Fine Arts in the areas of graphic design, painting, printmaking, sculpture, illustration, photography, animation. Majors: animation, applied art, art education, art/fine arts, ceramic art and design, graphic arts, illustration, industrial design, jewelry and metalsmithing, painting/drawing, photography, printmaking, sculpture, studio art, textile arts, wood. Graduate degrees offered: Master of Fine Arts in the areas of museum exhibition planning and design, book arts/printmaking, painting, sculpture, ceramics; Master of Industrial Design in the area of industrial design.

Art Student Profile Fall 1994: 828 total; 728 matriculated undergraduate, 100 matriculated graduate; 18% minorities, 45% females, 10% international.

Art Faculty 60% of full-time faculty have terminal degrees. Graduate students teach a few undergraduate courses. Undergraduate student–faculty ratio: 9:1.

Student Life Special housing available for art students.

Expenses for 1995–96 Application fee: $30. Tuition: $13,170 full-time, $570 per credit part-time. Full-time mandatory fees: $500. College room only: $3860.

Financial Aid Program-specific awards for Fall of 1994: 50 Merit Scholarships for undergraduates ($500–$5000).

Application Procedures Deadline—freshmen and transfers: continuous. Required: essay, high school transcript, college transcript(s) for transfer students, minimum 2.0 high school GPA, letter of recommendation, portfolio, SAT I or ACT test scores. Recommended: minimum 3.0 high school GPA, interview, resume. Portfolio reviews held continuously by appointment on campus and off campus on National Portfolio Days; the submission of slides may be substituted for portfolios.

Contact Barbara Elliott, Director of Admissions, University of the Arts, 320 South Broad Street, Philadelphia, Pennsylvania 19102; 800-616-ARTS, fax: 215-875-5458.

More about the University

Program Facilities Music: new recording studio, three MIDI studios, editing suites, chamber music studios, Challis harpsichords, Moog synthesizer, computer music calligraphy facility, four grand piano studios, music library; Theatre/Dance: several theatres, including the 1,668-seat merriam: light-filled studios with barres, mirrors, resilient 4-inch suspended floors; Art: public galleries maintained by UArts include the Rosenwald-Wolf, Haviland Hall, the Great Hall galleries, and the Mednick.

Faculty, Resident Artists, and Alumni Faculty members (334) are professionals, most with advanced degrees, who perform and exhibit regularly. Visiting artists have included dance: Edward Villela, Donna McKechnie, Oleg Briansky, Gabriella Darvash, James Truitt, Meredith Monk, Ronnie Favors; music: Andre Watts, Victor Borge, Wynton Marsalis, Pierre Boulez, Billy Joel, George Crumb, Beverly Sills, Placido Domingo, Klaus Tennstedt, Ricardi Muti, Thad Joones, Mel Lewis, Peter Erskine, Stanley Clarke; theatre: Elizabeth Ashley, Laurie Anderson, Tommy Hicks,David Henry Hwang. Alumni include Philadelphia orchestra violinist Michael Ludwig, Alvin Ailey Dance member Antonio Carlos Scott, artist Sidney Goodman, Tony-Award-nominated dancer/actress Rhonda LaChanze Sapp, illustrator Arnold Roth, jazz artist/composer Stanley Clarke, illustrator

Charles Santore, dancer/choreographer Judith Jamison, actress Sophia Maletsky, and concert pianist Lydia Artymiw.

Student Performance/Exhibit Opportunities Ensemble productions, student composition concerts featuring original choreography, repertory concerts, exhibitions in University galleries, recitals, appearances with visiting artists. **Special Programs** Student exchange with eleven other U.S. schools and colleges, foreign and summer studies, career planning and placement, personal counseling, academic support, professional and peer tutoring, services for the disabled, international student services.

The University The University of the Arts sits in the heart of Philadelphia's professional arts community and is surrounded by everything a major city should offer: theaters, museums, galleries, night life, and restaurants. The city, long a supporter of the arts, is urban and sophisticated, yet also features a diversity of small neighborhoods and ethnic enclaves.

UArts is among a few universities in the nation devoted exclusively to education and training in design and in the visual and performing arts. Composing the Philadelphia College of Art and Design and the Philadelphia College of Performing Arts. UArts offers intensive concentration within its major and other creative possibilities for exploration and growth. More than 1,400 undergraduate and graduate students from thirty-seven states and thirty countries are enrolled, and what they come to Philadelphia for is an educational atmosphere dedicated to the aesthetic experience.

The University docs, however, sponsor many activities–dances and other social events, talent shows, and regular gallery and museum trips in Philadelphia itself and in New York and Washington.

Philadelphia College of Art and Design faculty members are practicing professionals and are deeply committed to the development of their students. As active participants in the arts, they have achieved recognition in their specific fields of study. Members of the art and design faculty regularly exhibit their work in galleries and museums across the country. It is this real-world experience, in a most demanding environment, that gives them the knowledge and understanding so vital in the training of young, emerging artists–not just professionally but also in terms of personal growth. The faculty has 178 full- and part-time members. The majority hold advanced degrees. The faculty-student ration is approximately 1:9.

Members of the music faculty of the Philadelphia College of Performing Arts hold first-chair positions in major orchestras such as the Philadelphia orchestra and the New York Philharmonic and have international reputations as concert soloists and jazz artists. Members of the dance faculty have distinguished careers in ballet and modern, jazz, and tap dance. Members of the theatre faculty have acting and directing experience that ranges from Broadway shows to European companies. There are 156 full- and part-time members. Again, the faculty-student ratio is about 1:9.

UArts is a different kind of university, defined by students with a passion for what they want to do and where they want to go. The University is looking for student talent and potential; it provides formal exposure to the great ideas that shape the arts, focused practice and coaching in a student's chosen discipline, and an environment that frees imagination, stimulates creativity, and encourages change.

Student housing, with coed apartment-style accommodations, complete kitchen and bath facilities, and laundry rooms on the premises, is available. Resident advisers are on each floor.

Please see the University of the Art's other programs listed under Dance, Music, and Theater.

University of the Pacific

Stockton, California

Independent, coed. Suburban campus. Total enrollment: 4,140.

Degrees Bachelor of Fine Arts in the areas of studio art, graphic design. Majors: art/fine arts, graphic design, studio art.

Art Student Profile Fall 1994: 80 total; all matriculated undergraduate; 20% minorities, 60% females, 5% international.

Art Faculty Total: 10; 9 full-time, 1 part-time; 85% of full-time faculty have terminal degrees. Undergraduate student–faculty ratio: 18:1.

Expenses for 1995–96 Application fee: $50. Comprehensive fee of $22,876 includes full-time tuition ($17,220), mandatory fees ($330), and college room and board ($5326). Part-time tuition per unit ranges from $530 to $673 according to course load. Full-time tuition for pharmacy program: $25,830.

Application Procedures Deadline—freshmen: March 1; transfers: June 1. Notification date—freshmen: April 15. Required: essay, high school transcript, college transcript(s) for transfer students, minimum 2.0 high school GPA, SAT I or ACT test scores. Recommended: minimum 3.0 high school GPA, letter of recommendation, SAT II writing test. Auditions held on campus and off campus. Portfolio reviews held on campus and off campus.

Undergraduate Contact Alex McDavid, Assistant Director, Admissions, University of the Pacific, 3601 Pacific Avenue, Stockton, California 95211-0197; 209-946-2211.

University of Utah

Salt Lake City, Utah

State-supported, coed. Urban campus. Total enrollment: 25,226.

Degrees Bachelor of Fine Arts in the area of art. Majors: art education, ceramic art and design, graphic arts, illustration, painting/drawing, photography, printmaking, sculpture. Graduate degrees offered: Master of Fine Arts in the area of art.

University of Utah *(continued)*

Art Student Profile Fall 1994: 808 total; 447 matriculated undergraduate, 11 matriculated graduate, 350 nondegree; 5% minorities, 53% females, 2% international.

Art Faculty Total: 37; 19 full-time, 18 part-time; 70% of full-time faculty have terminal degrees. Graduate students teach a few undergraduate courses. Undergraduate student–faculty ratio: 20:1.

Student Life Student groups include student exhibitions, intercollegiate exhibitions, interdepartmental collaborative classes.

Expenses for 1994–95 Application fee: $30. State resident tuition: $2298 full-time. Nonresident tuition: $6795 full-time. Part-time tuition per quarter ranges from $206 to $766 for state residents, $597 to $2265 for nonresidents. College room and board: $4570. College room only: $1570. Special program-related fees: $20 for models, $30–$45 for materials, tools and equipment maintenance.

Financial Aid Program-specific awards for Fall of 1994: 4 Special Departmental Scholarships for incoming freshmen ($7515), 5 Continuing Student Scholarships for continuing students ($9393), 2 Ann Cannon Scholarships for continuing students ($1000), 1 Ethel A. Rolapp Award for graduating students ($2000), 1 Speess Memorial Award for continuing students ($1000).

Application Procedures Deadline—freshmen and transfers: continuous. Notification date—freshmen and transfers: continuous. Required: minimum 2.0 high school GPA, portfolio for transfer students. Portfolio reviews held 1 time for graphic design and illustration majors and throughout the year for placement of transfer on campus and off campus in Springville, UT; the submission of slides may be substituted for portfolios for large works of art and 3-D pieces and for out-of-state applicants.

Undergraduate Contact Carol Warner, Undergraduate Counselor, Art Department, University of Utah, AAC161, Salt Lake City, Utah 84112; 801-581-8677, fax: 801-585-6171, E-mail address: carol.warner@art.utah.edu.

Graduate Contact Michelle Marthia, Secretary, Art Department, University of Utah, AAC161, Salt Lake City, Utah 84112; 801-581-8677, fax: 801-585-6171.

University of Washington

Seattle, Washington

State-supported, coed. Urban campus. Total enrollment: 33,719.

Degrees Bachelor of Fine Arts in the areas of ceramics, fibers, graphic design, industrial design, metals, painting, photography, printmaking, sculpture. Majors: ceramic art and design, graphic arts, industrial design, jewelry and metalsmithing, painting/drawing, photography, printmaking, sculpture, textile arts. Graduate degrees offered: Master of Fine Arts in the areas of ceramics, fibers, graphic design, industrial design, metals, painting, photography, printmaking, sculpture.

Art Student Profile Fall 1994: 900 total; 850 matriculated undergraduate, 50 matriculated graduate; 10% minorities, 65% females.

Art Faculty Total: 41; 41 full-time; 95% of full-time faculty have terminal degrees. Graduate students teach a few undergraduate courses. Undergraduate student–faculty ratio: 22:1.

Expenses for 1995–96 Application fee: $35. State resident tuition: $3021 full-time. Nonresident tuition: $8523 full-time. Part-time tuition per 2 credit. College room and board: $4329. Special program-related fees: $35–$95 for materials fee.

Financial Aid Program-specific awards for Fall of 1994: 51 School of Art Scholarships for program majors ($800).

Application Procedures Deadline—freshmen: February 1; transfers: July 1. Notification date—freshmen: March 15; transfers: continuous. Required: high school transcript, portfolio, SAT I or ACT test scores. Portfolio reviews held continuously on campus; the submission of slides may be substituted for portfolios.

Undergraduate Contact Admissions Office, University of Washington, Box 355840, Seattle, Washington 98195-5840; 206-543-9686.

Graduate Contact Graduate Program Coordinator, School of Art, University of Washington, Box 353440, Seattle, Washington 98195-3440; 206-685-1714, fax: 206-685-1657, E-mail address: patd@u.washington.edu.

University of West Florida

Pensacola, Florida

State-supported, coed. Suburban campus. Total enrollment: 7,816.

Degrees Bachelor of Fine Arts in the area of studio arts. Majors: art/fine arts, studio art.

Art Student Profile Fall 1994: 221 total; 207 matriculated undergraduate, 14 nondegree; 4% minorities, 67% females, 3% international.

Art Faculty Total: 12; 8 full-time, 4 part-time. Graduate students teach a few undergraduate courses. Undergraduate student–faculty ratio: 15:1.

Expenses for 1995–96 Application fee: $20. State resident tuition: $1711 full-time, $57.04 per semester hour part-time. Nonresident tuition: $6614 full-time, $220.45 per semester hour part-time. College room and board: $4134. College room only: $1760.

Financial Aid Program-specific awards for Fall of 1994: 8 Talent Scholarships for incoming students ($1000).

Application Procedures Deadline—freshmen and transfers: continuous. Required: high school transcript, college transcript(s) for transfer students, minimum 2.0 high school GPA, SAT I or ACT test scores.

Undergraduate Contact Jim Jipson, Chair, Art Department, University of West Florida, 11000 University Parkway, Pensacola, Florida 32514; 904-474-2045, E-mail address: jjipson@uwf.cc.uwf.edu.

University of Wisconsin–Eau Claire

Eau Claire, Wisconsin

State-supported, coed. Urban campus. Total enrollment: 10,331.

Degrees Bachelor of Fine Arts in the areas of graphic design, illustration, painting, drawing and printmaking, photography, sculpture, ceramics. Majors: ceramic art and design, graphic design, painting, painting/drawing, photography, printmaking, sculpture.

Art Student Profile Fall 1994: 225 total; all matriculated undergraduate; 5% minorities.

Art Faculty Total: 17; 17 full-time; 95% of full-time faculty have terminal degrees. Graduate students do not teach undergraduate courses. Undergraduate student–faculty ratio: 14:1.

Student Life Student groups include Art Student Association, None of the Above (arts magazine).

Expenses for 1994–95 Application fee: $25. State resident tuition: $2312 full-time, $96.25 per credit part-time. Nonresident tuition: $7100 full-time, $295.75 per credit part-time. Minnesota residents pay tuition at the rate they would pay if attending a comparable state-supported institution in Minnesota. College room and board: $2705 (minimum). College room only: $1565. Special program-related fees: $20 for studio materials, lab fees.

Financial Aid Program-specific awards for Fall of 1994: 1 Patrick Danen Memorial Scholarship for upper division photography majors ($100), 1 Edward Fish Art Scholarship for academically qualified juniors or seniors ($450), 1 Ruth Foster Scholarship for academically qualified upperclassmen ($100), 5–6 Gerald Newton Scholarships for academically qualified seniors ($50), 1 Sigrid Rasmussen Memorial Art Scholarship for academically qualified program majors ($100).

Application Procedures Deadline—freshmen: February 1; transfers: April 1. Required: ACT score for state residents, SAT or ACT score for out-of-state residents. Recommended: portfolio. Portfolio reviews held 2 times on campus; the submission of slides may be substituted for portfolios.

Undergraduate Contact Admissions Office, University of Wisconsin–Eau Claire, P.O. Box 4004, Eau Claire, Wisconsin 54702-4004; 715-836-5415, fax: 715-836-2380.

University of Wisconsin–Madison

Madison, Wisconsin

State-supported, coed. Urban campus. Total enrollment: 38,139.

Degrees Bachelor of Fine Arts in the area of art. Majors: art/fine arts. Graduate degrees offered: Master of Fine Arts in the area of art.

Art Student Profile Fall 1994: 1,084 total; 454 matriculated undergraduate, 130 matriculated graduate, 500 nondegree.

Art Faculty Total: 41; 28 full-time, 13 part-time; 100% of full-time faculty have terminal degrees. Graduate students teach about a quarter undergraduate courses. Undergraduate student–faculty ratio: 23:1.

Student Life Student groups include Friends of Art Metal, Friends of Typography, Clay Club.

Expenses for 1994–95 Application fee: $25. State resident tuition: $2737 full-time, $115 per semester hour part-time. Nonresident tuition: $9096 full-time, $379.75 per semester hour part-time. Minnesota residents pay tuition at the rate they would pay if attending University of Minnesota, Twin Cities Campus. College room and board: $2925. Special program-related fees: $10–$90 for special course materials and field trips.

Financial Aid Program-specific awards for Fall of 1994: 2 Edith Gilbertson Scholarships for continuing undergraduates ($1000), 2 Ethel Odegaard Schoalrships for continuing undergraduates ($1250), 1 Carrie Jones Cady Scholarship for continuing undergraduates ($350).

Application Procedures Deadline—freshmen and transfers: February 1. Required: high school transcript, college transcript(s) for transfer students, minimum 3.0 high school GPA.

Undergraduate Contact Keith White, Assistant Director, Undergraduate Admissions, University of Wisconsin–Madison, 750 University Avenue, Madison, Wisconsin 53706; 608-262-3961, E-mail address: keith.white@mail.admin.wisc.edu.

Graduate Contact Carla Leskinen, Graduate Secretary, Art Department, University of Wisconsin–Madison, 6241 Humanities Building, 455 North Park Street, Madison, Wisconsin 53706; 608-262-1958, E-mail address: leskinen@mail.soemadison.wisc.edu.

University of Wisconsin–Milwaukee

Milwaukee, Wisconsin

State-supported, coed. Urban campus. Total enrollment: 22,984.

Degrees Bachelor of Fine Arts in the area of art. Majors: art education, ceramic art and design, fibers, graphic design, jewelry and metalsmithing, painting/drawing, photography, printmaking, sculpture. Graduate degrees offered: Master of Fine Arts in the area of art.

Art Student Profile Fall 1994: 685 total; 600 matriculated undergraduate, 85 matriculated graduate; 2% minorities, 50% females, 3% international.

Art Faculty Total: 60; 30 full-time, 30 part-time; 99% of full-time faculty have terminal degrees. Graduate students teach a few undergraduate courses.

Expenses for 1994–95 State resident tuition: $2772 full-time. Nonresident tuition: $8787 full-time. Part-time tuition per semester ranges from $212 to $1287 for state residents, $465.75 to $4046 for nonresidents. Minnesota residents pay tuition at the rate they would pay if attending a comparable state-supported institution in Minnesota. College room and board: $3000.

Application Procedures Deadline—freshmen: June 30; transfers: August 1. Required: high school transcript,

University of Wisconsin–Milwaukee *(continued)*

college transcript(s) for transfer students, SAT I or ACT test scores, ACT score for state residents.

Undergraduate Contact Patricia Busalacchi, Administrative Assistant, Art Department, University of Wisconsin–Milwaukee, P.O. Box 413, 2400 East Kenwood Boulevard, Milwaukee, Wisconsin 53201; 414-229-6054, fax: 414-229-6154, E-mail address: pats@csd.uwm.edu.

Graduate Contact Denis Sargent, Head of Graduate Studies, Art Department, University of Wisconsin–Milwaukee, P.O. Box 413, 2400 East Kenwood Boulevard, Milwaukee, Wisconsin 53201; 414-229-6053, fax: 414-229-6154.

University of Wisconsin–Oshkosh

Oshkosh, Wisconsin

State-supported, coed. Suburban campus. Total enrollment: 10,567.

Degrees Bachelor of Fine Arts in the areas of art education, studio/fine arts. Majors: art education, ceramic art and design, fibers, furniture design, graphic communication, jewelry and metalsmithing, painting/drawing, photography, printmaking, sculpture.

Expenses for 1994–95 Application fee: $25. State resident tuition: $2162 full-time, $89.91 per credit part-time. Nonresident tuition: $6950 full-time, $289.41 per credit part-time. Minnesota residents pay tuition at the rate they would pay if attending a comparable state-supported institution in Minnesota. College room and board: $2256. College room only: $1396.

Application Procedures

Undergraduate Contact David Hodge, Academic Advisor, Art Department, University of Wisconsin–Oshkosh, Art and Communication Building, Oshkosh, Wisconsin 54901, 414; 414-424-2236.

University of Wisconsin–Stevens Point

Stevens Point, Wisconsin

State-supported, coed. Small-town campus. Total enrollment: 8,424.

Degrees Bachelor of Fine Arts in the area of art. Majors: ceramic art and design, computer graphics, graphic design, painting/drawing, photography, printmaking, sculpture.

Art Student Profile Fall 1994: 250 total; all matriculated undergraduate; 60% females, 5% international.

Art Faculty Total: 15; 13 full-time, 2 part-time. Undergraduate student–faculty ratio: 18:1.

Estimated Expenses for 1995–96 Application fee: $25. State resident tuition: $2395 full-time. Nonresident tuition: $7422 full-time. Minnesota residents pay tuition at the rate they would pay if attending a comparable state-supported institution in Minnesota. College room and board: $3150. College room only: $1800.

Application Procedures Deadline—freshmen and transfers: continuous. Required: high school transcript, ACT test score only. Recommended: interview, portfolio. Portfolio reviews held 3 times on campus; the submission of slides may be substituted for portfolios if original work not available.

Undergraduate Contact Gary Hagen, Chair, Department of Art and Design, University of Wisconsin–Stevens Point, College of Fine Arts and Communication, Stevens Point, Wisconsin 54481; 715-346-2669.

University of Wisconsin–Stout

Menomonie, Wisconsin

State-supported, coed. Small-town campus. Total enrollment: 7,413.

Degrees Bachelor of Fine Arts in the area of art. Majors: graphic design, industrial design, interior design, studio art.

Art Student Profile Fall 1994: 642 total; all matriculated undergraduate; 4% minorities, 56% females, 1% international.

Art Faculty Total: 32; 24 full-time, 8 part-time; 88% of full-time faculty have terminal degrees. Graduate students do not teach undergraduate courses. Undergraduate student–faculty ratio: 13:1.

Student Life Student groups include Industrial Design Society of America Student Chapter, American Society of Interior Designers Student Chapter, Graphic Design Association Student Chapter.

Expenses for 1994–95 Application fee: $25. State resident tuition: $1916 full-time, $79.75 per credit part-time. Nonresident tuition: $6704 full-time, $279.25 per credit part-time. Minnesota residents pay tuition at the rate they would pay if attending a comparable state-supported institution in Minnesota. Full-time mandatory fees: $400. College room and board: $2592 (minimum). College room only: $1404.

Financial Aid Program-specific awards for Fall of 1994: 2 John and Frances Furlong Art Scholarships for art/art education majors ($250), 2 Bud and Betty Micheels Student Artist-in-Residence Grants for undergraduates ($1300).

Application Procedures Deadline—freshmen and transfers: continuous. Notification date—freshmen and transfers: continuous. Required: high school transcript, college transcript(s) for transfer students. Recommended: letter of recommendation, ACT test score only.

Undergraduate Contact Charles Kell, Director of Admissions, University of Wisconsin–Stout, 124 Bowman Hall, Menomonie, Wisconsin 54751; 715-232-1293, fax: 715-232-1667, E-mail address: kellc@uwstout.edu.

University of Wisconsin-Whitewater

Whitewater, Wisconsin

State-supported, coed. Small-town campus. Total enrollment: 10,438.

Degrees Bachelor of Fine Arts in the area of art. Majors: art education, art/fine arts, ceramic art and design, computer graphics, graphic arts, illustration, jewelry and metalsmithing, painting/drawing, printmaking, sculpture, studio art. Cross-registration with University of Wisconsin Center System.

Art Student Profile Fall 1994: 270 total; all matriculated undergraduate; 7% minorities, 54% females, 1% international.

Art Faculty Total: 17; 16 full-time, 1 part-time; 100% of full-time faculty have terminal degrees. Graduate students do not teach undergraduate courses. Undergraduate student–faculty ratio: 13:1.

Student Life Student groups include Juried Student Art Exhibition, Student Design Association, Student Art Association.

Expenses for 1994–95 State resident tuition: $2327 full-time, $96.90 per credit part-time. Nonresident tuition: $7115 full-time, $296.40 per credit part-time. Minnesota residents pay tuition at the rate they would pay if attending a comparable state-supported institution in Minnesota. College room and board: $2496. College room only: $1460. Special program-related fees: $5–$300 for studio materials.

Financial Aid Program-specific awards for Fall of 1994: 1 Roberta Fiskum Award for returning program majors, graphic design ($600), 10 Art Department Scholarships for artistically talented returning program majors ($100), 1 Mary Wiser Award for returning program majors, excellence in ceramics ($100).

Application Procedures Deadline—freshmen and transfers: continuous. Required: high school transcript, minimum 2.0 high school GPA. Recommended: interview.

Undergraduate Contact Amy Arntson, Chair, Art Department, University of Wisconsin–Whitewater, College of Arts and Communications, Whitewater, Wisconsin 53190; 414-472-1324, fax: 414-472-2808.

Utah State University

Logan, Utah

State-supported, coed. Urban campus. Total enrollment: 20,371.

Degrees Bachelor of Fine Arts in the area of art. Majors: advertising design, art education, art history, ceramic art and design, graphic design, illustration, painting/drawing, photography, printmaking, sculpture. Graduate degrees offered: Master of Fine Arts in the area of art.

Art Student Profile Fall 1994: 362 total; 326 matriculated undergraduate, 36 matriculated graduate.

Art Faculty Total: 15; 15 full-time. Graduate students teach a few undergraduate courses.

Expenses for 1995–96 Application fee: $35. State resident tuition: $1992 full-time. Nonresident tuition: $6042 full-time. Part-time tuition per quarter ranges from $146 to $625 for state residents, $418 to $1877 for nonresidents. Part-time mandatory fees per quarter range from $38 to $121. Full-time mandatory fees: $381. College room and board: $3069.

Application Procedures Deadline—freshmen and transfers: continuous.

Contact Head, Art Department, Utah State University, Logan, Utah 84322-4000; 801-797-3460.

Valdosta State University

Valdosta, Georgia

State-supported, coed. Small-town campus. Total enrollment: 9,160.

Degrees Bachelor of Fine Arts in the areas of art, art education. Majors: art education, art/fine arts.

Art Student Profile Fall 1994: 130 total; 112 matriculated undergraduate, 18 nondegree; 8% minorities, 52% females, 4% international.

Art Faculty Total: 13; 10 full-time, 3 part-time; 100% of full-time faculty have terminal degrees. Graduate students do not teach undergraduate courses. Undergraduate student–faculty ratio: 13:1.

Student Life Student groups include Art Students League, National Art Educators Association Student Chapter.

Expenses for 1995–96 Application fee: $10. State resident tuition: $1887 full-time. Nonresident tuition: $5097 full-time. Part-time tuition per quarter ranges from $42 to $593 for state residents, $132 to $1583 for nonresidents. College room and board: $3165. College room only: $1440.

Financial Aid Program-specific awards for Fall of 1994: 5 Freshman Art Scholarships for incoming students ($300–$500), 3 Fortner Scholarships for continuing students ($1275), 1 Art Department Assistantship for program majors ($1000).

Application Procedures Deadline—freshmen and transfers: continuous. Required: high school transcript, college transcript(s) for transfer students, SAT I or ACT test scores, minimum combined SAT I score of 800. Recommended: minimum 2.0 high school GPA, portfolio. Portfolio reviews held 1 time on campus; the submission of slides may be substituted for portfolios.

Undergraduate Contact Walter Peacock, Director, Admissions Office, Valdosta State University, 1500 North Patterson Street, Valdosta, Georgia 31698; 912-333-5791.

Virginia Commonwealth University

Richmond, Virginia

State-supported, coed. Urban campus. Total enrollment: 21,523.

Virginia Commonwealth University *(continued)*

Degrees Bachelor of Fine Arts in the areas of art education, art history, communications, crafts, fashion, interior design, painting/printmaking, sculpture. Majors: art education, art/fine arts, ceramic art and design, commercial art, computer graphics, drafting and design, fashion design and technology, graphic arts, illustration, interior design, jewelry and metalsmithing, painting/drawing, printmaking, sculpture, studio art, textile arts, textiles and clothing. Graduate degrees offered: Master of Fine Arts in the areas of art education, art history, communications, crafts, fashion, interior design, painting/printmaking, photography, sculpture. Doctor of Arts in the area of art history.

Art Student Profile Fall 1994: 2,407 total; 2,197 matriculated undergraduate, 210 matriculated graduate; 18% minorities, 61% females, 11% international.

Art Faculty Total: 231; 136 full-time, 95 part-time; 97% of full-time faculty have terminal degrees. Graduate students teach a few undergraduate courses. Undergraduate student–faculty ratio: 22:1.

Estimated Expenses for 1995–96 Application fee: $20. State resident tuition: $3034 full-time, $126 per credit part-time. Nonresident tuition: $10,217 full-time, $426 per credit part-time. Part-time mandatory fees: $30.50 per credit. Full-time mandatory fees: $880. College room and board: $4182. College room only: $2416 (minimum). Special program-related fees: $150 for comprehensive arts fee.

Application Procedures Deadline—freshmen: February 1; transfers: May 1. Notification date—freshmen and transfers: continuous. Required: essay, high school transcript, letter of recommendation, portfolio. Recommended: interview. Portfolio reviews held continuously on campus and off campus on National Portfolio Days.

Undergraduate Contact Lydia Thompson, Assistant Dean of Student Affairs, School of the Arts, Virginia Commonwealth University, 325 North Harrison Street, Richmond, Virginia 23284-2519; 804-828-2787, fax: 804-828-6469.

Graduate Contact Dr. Daniel Reeves, Director of Graduate Studies and Assistant Dean, School of the Arts, Virginia Commonwealth University, 325 North Harrison Street, Richmond, Virginia 23284-2519; 804-828-2787, fax: 804-828-6469.

More about the University

Virginia Commonwealth University, with 2,300 full-time students, is one of the largest art schools in the nation. The urban Richmond School hosts more than 300 on-campus public performances and exhibitions each year, and its faculty and students are involved in hundreds more throughout the greater Richmond community.

The School of the Arts has a three-part mission: teaching, research, and services. Students invest many hours in serious creative pursuit of the arts disciplines. Artistic freedom is stressed, and students are exposed to a wide variety of artistic sensibilities and techniques. All students are exposed to the artistic applications of computers, and departments have fully equipped multistation laboratories. The Department of Communication Arts and Design now has a Virtual Reality Lab.

VCU's School of the Arts offers degree programs in virtually every visual and performing arts discipline. The School is organized into twelve departments: Art Education, Art History, Communication Arts and Design, Crafts, Dance and Choreography, Fashion, Interior Design, Music, Painting and Printmaking, Photography and Film, Sculpture, and Theatre. Within the departments are various tracks of study. For example, crafts students can major in any of five areas: fiber, clay, metal, wood, and glass. Painting and printmaking students can major in lithography, screenprinting, etching, and various paint and mixed mediums.

The School has 139 full-time faculty members and 85 part-time faculty members. Many are recognized for significant accomplishments both nationally and internationally. Phillip B. Meggs is the author of *A History of Graphic Design,* and Martha Curtis' video performance, "Three Dances with Martha Curtis," has been seen by PBS audiences in every major national market. Robert Hobbs is the author of eleven books on art history, including landmarks on Robert Smithson and Milton Avery. Richard Carlyon received the College Art Association of America's highest award for teaching and the 1993 Award for Distinguished Teaching of Art, and Richard Newdick received the Southern Theatre Conference highest honor, the Davis Award for Distinguished Service to Theater in the Southeast.

Among the School's strengths is its Sculpture Department, which is among the nation's largest. Over the past four years its students have received four of the valuable and prestigious Jacob Javitts Awards in the Arts. Another is the Jazz Studies program. The student Jazz Orchestra I has recorded three acclaimed albums and was named Outstanding Big Band three times at the Notre Dame Intercollegiate Jazz Festival.

The School's alumni include Kenneth Smith, Oscar winner for visual effects for *E.T.;* Signe Girgus, interior designer for the White House; Phil Jordan, art director for *Smithsonian Air and Space Magazine;* Stephen Furst, star of *Animal House;* Thomas Moser, soloist for New York's Metropolitan Opera Company; and Tony Cokes, three-time exhibitor at the Whitney Museum of American Art.

The School of the Arts is part of Virginia Commonwealth University—a 20,000 student urban university located on the edge of downtown Richmond. The University's schools include such areas of study as medicine, dentistry, mass communication, social work, community and public affairs, nursing, humanities and sciences, business, and a newly announced School of Engineering which will open in 1996.

The University has on-campus housing facilities, and there are additional housing opportunities throughout the historic Fan residential district, which borders the campus. Most students come from Virginia, but students have come from all states and dozens of countries. The School of the Arts has initiated educational exchange agreements and/or on-site opportunities in Russia, Germany, Italy, England, and Latin America.

The School's Anderson Gallery is recognized internationally as a major exhibitor of contemporary art. It has a track record of grants from the National Endowment for the Arts and the Institute of Museum Services. Its 1994 premier exhibition of the works of the late Tomas Gonda is accompanied by a full-color 96-page catalog and will travel to Germany, Argentina, and Italy and throughout the United States.

The city of Richmond has a great number of art galleries and clubs, music and theatre performance groups, ballet, symphony, opera, and museums. Richmond is a 2-hour drive from Washington, D.C. and 1 hour from historic Williamsburg.

Virginia Intermont College

Bristol, Virginia

Independent-religious, coed. Small-town campus. Total enrollment: 682.

Degrees Bachelor of Fine Arts in the areas of fine arts, photography, graphic design. Majors: art education, art/fine arts, computer graphics, computer imaging, graphic arts, photography. Cross-registration with King College.

Art Student Profile Fall 1994: 73 total; all matriculated undergraduate.

Art Faculty Total: 14; 6 full-time, 8 part-time. Graduate students do not teach undergraduate courses.

Expenses for 1995–96 Application fee: $15. Comprehensive fee of $13,850 includes full-time tuition ($9500), mandatory fees ($100), and college room and board ($4250). Part-time mandatory fees: $25 per semester. Part-time tuition and fees per credit: $125 for the first 6 hours, $300 for the next 5 hours. Special program-related fees: $40 for lab fees, $40 for computer lab use.

Financial Aid Program-specific awards for Fall of 1994: 15 Room Grants for program majors ($1800).

Application Procedures Deadline—freshmen and transfers: continuous. Notification date—freshmen and transfers: continuous. Required: high school transcript, minimum 2.0 high school GPA. Recommended: portfolio. Auditions held on campus and off campus. Portfolio reviews held by request on campus and off campus; the submission of slides may be substituted for portfolios.

Undergraduate Contact Robin Cozart, Acting Admissions Director, Virginia Intermont College, Box D-460, Bristol, Virginia 24201; 703-669-6101 ext. 207, fax: 703-669-5763.

Virginia State University

Petersburg, Virginia

State-supported, coed. Suburban campus. Total enrollment: 4,007.

Degrees Bachelor of Fine Arts in the areas of art education, visual communications arts and design. Majors: art education, commercial art.

Expenses for 1995–96 State resident tuition: $1951 full-time, $82 per credit hour part-time. Nonresident tuition: $5960 full-time, $252 per credit hour part-time. Part-time mandatory fees: $20 per credit hour. Full-time mandatory fees: $1305. College room and board: $4845. College room only: $2750.

Application Procedures

Undergraduate Contact Gary Knight, Director of Admissions, Virginia State University, P.O. Box 9018, Petersburg, Virginia 23806; 804-524-5902.

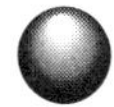

Washburn University of Topeka

Topeka, Kansas

City-supported, coed. Urban campus. Total enrollment: 6,439.

Degrees Bachelor of Fine Arts. Majors: 3-dimensional studies, art history, computer graphics, design, painting/drawing, photography, printmaking.

Art Student Profile Fall 1994: 50 total; all matriculated undergraduate.

Art Faculty Total: 12; 5 full-time, 7 part-time.

Expenses for 1995–96 State resident tuition: $2790 full-time, $93 per credit hour part-time. Nonresident tuition: $5730 full-time, $191 per credit hour part-time. Part-time mandatory fees: $8 per semester. Full-time mandatory fees: $32. College room and board: $3410.

Application Procedures Deadline—freshmen and transfers: continuous. Required: high school transcript, portfolio. Portfolio reviews held 2 times during sophomore year on campus; the submission of slides may be substituted for portfolios for transfer applicants.

Undergraduate Contact John Hunter, Chair, Department of Art and Theater Arts, Washburn University of Topeka, 1700 College Street, Topeka, Kansas 66621; 913-231-1010 ext. 1639.

Washington State University

Pullman, Washington

State-supported, coed. Rural campus. Total enrollment: 19,314.

Degrees Bachelor of Fine Arts in the areas of painting, sculpture, printmaking, ceramics, photography, computer art, drawing. Majors: art/fine arts, ceramic art and design, computer graphics, painting/drawing, photography, printmaking, sculpture, studio art. Graduate degrees offered: Master of Fine Arts in the areas of painting, sculpture, printmaking, ceramics, photography, computer art, drawing. Cross-registration with institutions in the state of Washington, University of Idaho.

Art Student Profile Fall 1994: 191 total; 178 matriculated undergraduate, 13 matriculated graduate; 30% minorities, 10% international.

Art Faculty Total: 18; 13 full-time, 5 part-time; 100% of full-time faculty have terminal degrees. Graduate students teach a few undergraduate courses. Undergraduate student–faculty ratio: 20:1.

Washington State University *(continued)*

Expenses for 1994–95 Application fee: $35. State resident tuition: $2908 full-time, $145 per credit part-time. Nonresident tuition: $8200 full-time, $410 per credit part-time. Full-time mandatory fees: $245. College room and board: $4050. Special program-related fees: $25–$60 for materials.

Financial Aid Program-specific awards for Fall of 1994: 1 John Ludwig Memorial Scholarship for program majors ($300–$500), 2–3 James Balyeat Awards for program majors ($200–$300), 3 Fine Arts Development Fund Scholarships for program majors ($200–$500), 2 Fine Arts Faculty Fund Scholarships for program majors ($200–$300).

Application Procedures Deadline—freshmen and transfers: continuous. Required: high school transcript, minimum 2.0 high school GPA.

Undergraduate Contact Chris Watts, Chair, Fine Arts Department, Washington State University, 5072 Fine Arts Center, Pullman, Washington 99164-7450; 509-335-8686.

Graduate Contact Ross Coates, Graduate Advisor, Fine Arts Department, Washington State University, 5072 Fine Arts Center, Pullman, Washington 99164-7450; 509-335-8686.

Washington University

St. Louis, Missouri

Independent, coed. Suburban campus. Total enrollment: 11,655.

Degrees Bachelor of Fine Arts in the areas of ceramics/glass, fashion design, graphic communications, painting, printmaking, photography, sculpture. Majors: advertising design, ceramics, fashion design and technology, glass, graphic design, illustration, painting/drawing, photography, printmaking, sculpture. Graduate degrees offered: Master of Fine Arts in the areas of ceramics/glass, painting, printmaking, photography, sculpture.

Art Student Profile Fall 1994: 343 total; 300 matriculated undergraduate, 39 matriculated graduate, 4 nondegree; 14% minorities, 1% international.

Art Faculty Total: 40; 25 full-time, 15 part-time; 92% of full-time faculty have terminal degrees. Graduate students teach a few undergraduate courses. Undergraduate student–faculty ratio: 11:1.

Student Life Student groups include American Institute for Graphic Arts Student Chapter, Mid-America College Art Association.

Expenses for 1994–95 Application fee: $50. Comprehensive fee of $24,643 includes full-time tuition ($18,350), mandatory fees ($450), and college room and board ($5843). Special program-related fees: $3–$150 for material fees.

Financial Aid Program-specific awards for Fall of 1994: 1 Conway/Proetz Award for high academic and artistic achievement.

Application Procedures Deadline—freshmen: January 15; transfers: June 1. Notification date—freshmen: April 1; transfers: August 1. Required: essay, high school transcript, college transcript(s) for transfer students, minimum 2.0 high school GPA, 2 letters of recommendation, SAT I or ACT test scores, portfolio for transfer students. Recommended: minimum 3.0 high school GPA, portfolio. Portfolio reviews held 1 time on campus and off campus on National Portfolio Days; the submission of slides may be substituted for portfolios.

Undergraduate Contact Georgia Binnington, Assistant Director, Undergraduate Admissions, Washington University, Campus Box 1089, One Brookings Drive, St. Louis, Missouri 63130; 314-935-6000.

Graduate Contact Cris Baldwin, Assistant to Director, Graduate Studies, Washington University, Campus Box 1031, St. Louis, Missouri 63130; 314-935-4761.

More about the University

Program Facilities The School of Art is housed in two buildings, Bixby Hall and Lewis Center. Combined, these facilities offer approximately 49,000 square feet of studio space, including Bixby Gallery. Each of the School's major areas has a studio space equipped with professional tools and equipment. Majors work in their own studio space. The Carolyne Roehm Electronic Media Center serves all areas and contains sophisticated hardware and software, video cameras, and editing equipment. Next door to Bixby Hall is Steinberg Hall, which contains the Gallery of Art and the Art and Architecture Library. The Art and Architecture library, part of the University's library system, contains over 60,000 volumes, 457 periodicals, and a rare book room.

Faculty and Alumni Faculty artists have received fellowship and grant support from the NEA and the Guggenheim Foundation, among others. Two emeritus professors are elected members of the prestigious American Academy of Arts and letters. Selected School of Art alumni include Erika Beckman, Mike Peters, Bernie Fuchs, Carolyne Roehm, Judy Pfaff, Jack Unruh, Adam Niklewicz, and Jay Krueger. Quondam visiting artists: Susan Crile, Frida Baranek, Tom Nakashima, Robert Andrew Parker, and Catherine Wagner.

Student Exhibit Opportunities Student Arts Council Juried Show; Junior Major, Core, B.F.A., Annual Fashion, and Painting Major shows; the University City Sculpture Project Show.

Special Programs Study abroad, internship, and volunteer opportunities are offered. Special programs in learning, health, counseling, and career development are all available.

Wayne State University

Detroit, Michigan

State-supported, coed. Urban campus. Total enrollment: 32,906.

Degrees Bachelor of Fine Arts in the areas of ceramics, drawing, fibers, graphic design, industrial design, metal arts, painting, photography, printmaking, sculpture, interior design, design. Majors: ceramic art and design, computer art, design, fibers, graphic design, industrial design, interior design, jewelry and metalsmithing, painting/drawing, photography, printmaking, sculpture, textile arts. Graduate degrees offered: Master of Fine Arts in the areas of ceramics, drawing, design, metal arts, painting, photography, printmaking, sculpture, fibers. Cross-registration with University of Windsor.

Art Student Profile Fall 1994: 25% minorities, 50% females, 5% international.

Art Faculty Total: 68; 28 full-time, 40 part-time; 100% of full-time faculty have terminal degrees. Graduate students teach a few undergraduate courses. Undergraduate student–faculty ratio: 20:1.

Student Life Student groups include American Society of Interior Designers, American Ceramic Design, Fashion Merchandising Group.

Expenses for 1994–95 Application fee: $20. State resident tuition: $3060 (minimum) full-time. Nonresident tuition: $6810 (minimum) full-time. Part-time mandatory fees: $70 per semester. Full-time tuition ranges up to $3705 for state residents, $8169 for nonresidents, according to class level. Part-time tuition per credit hour ranges from $98 to $115 for state residents, $218 to $259 for nonresidents, according to class level. Full-time mandatory fees: $70.

Financial Aid Program-specific awards for Fall of 1994: 5 Talent Awards for program majors ($1000), 1 Becker Award for program majors ($1500), 12–15 Endowed Scholarships for program majors ($1000).

Application Procedures Deadline—freshmen and transfers: continuous. Required: high school transcript, minimum 2.0 high school GPA. Portfolio reviews held continuously on campus.

Undergraduate Contact Carolyn J. Hooper, Associate Chair, Art and Art History Department, Wayne State University, 150 Art Building, Detroit, Michigan 48202; 313-577-2980, fax: 313-577-3491.

Graduate Contact Stanley I. Rosenthal, Graduate Officer, Art and Art History Department, Wayne State University, 150 Art Building, Detroit, Michigan 48202; 313-577-2980, fax: 313-577-3491.

Webster University

St. Louis, Missouri

Independent, coed. Suburban campus. Total enrollment: 10,834.

Degrees Bachelor of Fine Arts in the area of studio art. Majors: applied art, ceramic art and design, painting/drawing, photography, printmaking, sculpture, studio art. Cross-registration with various colleges in St. Louis.

Art Student Profile Fall 1994: 176 total; 173 matriculated undergraduate, 3 matriculated graduate; 11% minorities, 60% females, 2% international.

Art Faculty Total: 19; 9 full-time, 10 part-time; 100% of full-time faculty have terminal degrees. Graduate students do not teach undergraduate courses. Undergraduate student–faculty ratio: 20:1.

Expenses for 1994–95 Application fee: $25. Comprehensive fee of $13,500 includes full-time tuition ($9160) and college room and board ($4340). Part-time tuition: $280 per credit hour. Special program-related fees: $50–$75 for studio lab fee.

Application Procedures Deadline—freshmen and transfers: continuous. Required: essay, high school transcript, college transcript(s) for transfer students, 2 letters of recommendation, interview, portfolio, SAT I or ACT test scores. Auditions held on campus. Portfolio reviews held 8 times on campus; the submission of slides may be substituted for portfolios when distance is prohibitive.

Undergraduate Contact Mary Walz, Auditions Coordinator, Office of Admissions, Webster University, 470 East Lockwood Avenue, St. Louis, Missouri 63119-3194; 314-968-7001, fax: 314-968-7115.

West Georgia College

Carrollton, Georgia

State-supported, coed. Small-town campus. Total enrollment: 8,310.

Degrees Bachelor of Fine Arts in the area of art. Majors: art education, ceramic art and design, commercial art, interior design, painting/drawing, photography, printmaking, sculpture, studio art.

Art Student Profile Fall 1994: 142 total; 130 matriculated undergraduate, 12 nondegree; 15% minorities, 60% females, 1% international.

Art Faculty Total: 11; 8 full-time, 3 part-time; 100% of full-time faculty have terminal degrees. Graduate students do not teach undergraduate courses. Undergraduate student–faculty ratio: 35:1.

Student Life Student groups include Georgia Art Education Association Student Chapter, professional artists organizations, Art Students League.

Expenses for 1995–96 Application fee: $10. State resident tuition: $1884 full-time, $42 per quarter hour part-time. Nonresident tuition: $5094 full-time, $132 per quarter hour part-time. College room and board: $3093. College room only: $1545. Special program-related fees: $10 for ceramics fee, $15 for photography fee.

Financial Aid Program-specific awards for Fall of 1994: 1 Artist-Scholar Award for academically qualified program majors ($1500), 20–30 Departmental Awards for those demonstrating talent and need ($200–$300).

Application Procedures Deadline—freshmen and transfers: continuous. Notification date—freshmen and transfers: continuous. Required: high school transcript, college transcript(s) for transfer students, SAT I or ACT test scores, minimum combined SAT I score of 700, minimum composite ACT score of 17.

Undergraduate Contact Bruce Bobick, Chairman, Department of Art, West Georgia College, 1600 Maple Street, Carrollton, Georgia 30118; 404-836-6521, fax: 404-836-6791.

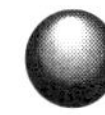

Western Carolina University

Cullowhee, North Carolina

State-supported, coed. Rural campus. Total enrollment: 6,619.

Degrees Bachelor of Fine Arts in the area of fine arts. Majors: art/fine arts, arts administration, ceramic art and design, graphic arts, illustration, painting/drawing, photography, printmaking, sculpture, studio art. Cross-registration with Penland School of Crafts.

Art Student Profile Fall 1994: 120 total; all matriculated undergraduate; 8% minorities, 50% females, 1% international.

Art Faculty Total: 16; 10 full-time, 6 part-time; 100% of full-time faculty have terminal degrees. Graduate students do not teach undergraduate courses. Undergraduate student–faculty ratio: 16:1.

Student Life Student groups include Annual Student Exhibition, Nomad (student art and literature publication), Cullowhee Arts Festival.

Expenses for 1994–95 Application fee: $20. State resident tuition: $764 full-time. Nonresident tuition: $7248 full-time. Part-time tuition per semester ranges from $96 to $287 for state residents, $906 to $2718 for nonresidents. Full-time mandatory fees: $787. College room and board: $2454.

Financial Aid Program-specific awards for Fall of 1994: 4 University Art Scholarships for those demonstrating talent ($500).

Application Procedures Deadline—freshmen and transfers: continuous. Notification date—freshmen and transfers: August 20. Required: high school transcript, minimum 2.0 high school GPA, letter of recommendation. Recommended: interview, portfolio. Portfolio reviews held continuously on campus.

Undergraduate Contact Robert Godfrey, Head, Department of Art, Western Carolina University, Cullowhee, North Carolina 28723; 704-227-7210, fax: 704-227-7705.

Western Illinois University

Macomb, Illinois

State-supported, coed. Small-town campus. Total enrollment: 12,599.

Degrees Bachelor of Fine Arts in the area of art. Majors: art/fine arts, ceramic art and design, commercial art, jewelry and metalsmithing, painting/drawing, printmaking, sculpture, studio art.

Art Student Profile Fall 1994: 174 total; all matriculated undergraduate; 12% minorities, 43% females, 10% international.

Art Faculty Total: 18; 16 full-time, 2 part-time; 100% of full-time faculty have terminal degrees. Graduate students do not teach undergraduate courses. Undergraduate student–faculty ratio: 11:1.

Student Life Student groups include Student Art League, National Art Educators Association Student Chapter. Special housing available for art students.

Expenses for 1995–96 State resident tuition: $1968 full-time, $82 per credit hour part-time. Nonresident tuition: $5904 full-time, $246.75 per credit hour part-time. Part-time mandatory fees: $24.25 per credit hour. Full-time mandatory fees: $734. College room and board: $3413. Special program-related fees: $10–$35 for material fees.

Financial Aid Program-specific awards for Fall of 1994: 3 Bulkeley Scholarships for program majors ($800), 7 Talent Grants for program majors ($500), 8 Tuition Waivers for program majors ($550).

Application Procedures Deadline—freshmen and transfers: August 10. Notification date—freshmen and transfers: continuous. Required: high school transcript, college transcript(s) for transfer students, minimum 2.0 high school GPA, SAT I or ACT test scores, minimum combined SAT I score of 720, minimum composite ACT score of 18. Recommended: portfolio. Portfolio reviews held continuously on campus; the submission of slides may be substituted for portfolios when distance is prohibitive.

Undergraduate Contact Ed Gettinger, Chair, Department of Art, Western Illinois University, 32 Garwood Hall, Macomb, Illinois 61455; 309-298-1549, fax: 309-298-2695.

Western Michigan University

Kalamazoo, Michigan

State-supported, coed. Urban campus. Total enrollment: 25,673.

Degrees Bachelor of Fine Arts in the areas of painting, watercolor, ceramics, sculpture, photography, graphic design, printmaking. Majors: art education, art/fine arts, ceramic art and design, graphic design, jewelry and metalsmithing, painting/drawing, photography, printmaking, sculpture, studio art, watercolors. Graduate degrees offered: Master of Fine Arts in the areas of painting, printmaking, graphic design, sculpture. Cross-registration with Michigan colleges and universities.

Art Student Profile Fall 1994: 536 total; 517 matriculated undergraduate, 19 matriculated graduate.

Art Faculty Total: 39; 21 full-time, 18 part-time; 90% of full-time faculty have terminal degrees. Graduate students teach a few undergraduate courses. Undergraduate student–faculty ratio: 20:1.

Student Life Student groups include VASAC (local student art group), Students in Design.

Expenses for 1994–95 Application fee: $25. Part-time mandatory fees: $85 per semester. Full-time tuition ranges from $2705 to $3046 for state residents, $6936 to $7804 for nonresidents, according to class level. Part-time tuition per credit hour ranges from $87.25 to $98.25 for state residents, $223.75 to $251.75 for nonresidents, according to class level. Full-time mandatory fees: $455. College room and board: $4097.

Financial Aid Program-specific awards for Fall of 1994 available.

Application Procedures Deadline—freshmen and transfers: continuous. Required: high school transcript, college transcript(s) for transfer students, minimum 2.0 high school GPA, ACT test score only. Recommended: minimum 3.0 high school GPA.

Undergraduate Contact Academic Advisor, Art Department, Western Michigan University, 1201 Oliver Street, Kalamazoo, Michigan 49008; 616-387-2440, fax: 616-387-2477.

Graduate Contact Patricia Opel, Art Department, Western Michigan University, 1201 Oliver Street, Kalamazoo, Michigan 49008; 616-387-2440, fax: 616-387-2477.

More about the University

A computer lab specializing in computer graphics/visual art is housed right in the department. It is equipped with color Macintosh, PC, and NEXT UNIX computers, laser and color printers, scanner, video cameras, digitizing drawing tablet and computer graphics–oriented software. The Design Center, housed within the department, provides B.F.A./Graphic Design Intern students the opportunity to work with real clients. The photography facilities are equipped to do black and white, color, and alternative process work. The printmaking facilities include studios for lithography and etching. The department contains a significant permanent print collection with specific emphasis on major twentieth-century works of international import. The sculpture facilities include appropriate equipment for a large-scale foundry, metal fabrication, wood working, and clay modeling. The Art History area maintains a collection of over 70,000 slides of works from all periods of art. The department annually awards in excess of $45,000 in grants, scholarships, and awards to all levels of students.

The Visiting Artist/Exhibitions Program brings to campus a variety of nationally prominent professionals. Some highlights in the last few years include visits by: Hollis Sigler, Mel Edwards, Al Hinton, Audrey Skuodas, Ryoji Koie, Doug Moran, Jean Van Harlingen, Dennis Adrian, Jerald Jacquard, Katherine Carter, Ron Porter, Eric Maakestad, Howard Watler, Mindy Faber, and Daniel Leary. East Hall gallery is a student-operated facility designed specifically for the display of student work. Gallery II is located in the heart of Sangren Hall, where faculty, visiting artist, student, and occasional international shows are scheduled.

West Virginia University

Morgantown, West Virginia

State-supported, coed. Small-town campus. Total enrollment: 22,500.

Degrees Bachelor of Fine Arts in the areas of painting, printmaking, sculpture, ceramics, graphic design. Majors: art education, art/fine arts, ceramic art and design, graphic arts, painting/drawing, printmaking, sculpture. Graduate degrees offered: Master of Fine Arts in the areas of painting, printmaking, sculpture, ceramics, new forms (experimental).

Art Student Profile Fall 1994: 257 total; 239 matriculated undergraduate, 18 matriculated graduate; 6% minorities, 49% females, 4% international.

Art Faculty Total: 17; 14 full-time, 3 part-time; 95% of full-time faculty have terminal degrees. Graduate students teach a few undergraduate courses. Undergraduate student–faculty ratio: 17:1.

Student Life Student groups include Women's Caucus for the Arts, Student Art Association.

Expenses for 1995–96 Application fee: $10. State resident tuition: $2192 full-time, $93 per credit hour part-time. Nonresident tuition: $6784 full-time, $284 per credit hour part-time. College room and board: $4434. Special program-related fees: $45 for expendable supplies for studio courses.

Financial Aid Program-specific awards for Fall of 1994: 14 Performance Grants for undergraduates ($2000–$6000), 3 Loyalty Permanent Endowment Awards for state residents ($1000), 1 Gabriel Fellowship for state residents ($1000).

Application Procedures Deadline—freshmen and transfers: continuous. Notification date—freshmen and transfers: continuous. Required: high school transcript, college transcript(s) for transfer students, minimum 2.0 high school GPA.

Undergraduate Contact Victoria Fergus, Undergraduate Advisor, Art Department, West Virginia University, College of Creative Arts, P.O. Box 6111, Morgantown, West Virginia 26506-6111; 304-293-2140 ext. 138, fax: 304-293-3550.

Graduate Contact Paul Krainak, Graduate Advisor, Art Department, West Virginia University, College of Creative Arts, P.O. Box 6111, Morgantown, West Virginia 26506-6111; 304-293-2140 ext. 138, fax: 304-293-3550.

Wichita State University

Wichita, Kansas

State-supported, coed. Urban campus. Total enrollment: 14,558.

Degrees Bachelor of Fine Arts in the areas of ceramics, painting/drawing, printmaking, sculpture. Majors: art history, ceramic art and design, painting/drawing, printmaking, sculpture, studio art. Graduate degrees offered: Master of Fine Arts in the areas of ceramics, painting/drawing, printmaking, sculpture.

Art Faculty Total: 16; 15 full-time, 1 part-time; 100% of full-time faculty have terminal degrees. Graduate students teach a few undergraduate courses. Undergraduate student–faculty ratio: 32:1.

Expenses for 1994–95 Application fee: $15. State resident tuition: $2090 full-time, $69.65 per credit hour part-time. Nonresident tuition: $7434 full-time, $247.80 per credit hour part-time. Part-time mandatory fees: $13 per semester. Full-time mandatory fees: $26. College room and board: $3121 (minimum). Special program-related fees: $15–$50 for lab fees.

Financial Aid Program-specific awards for Fall of 1994: 20 Miller Trust Awards for undergraduates ($500), 1

Wichita State University *(continued)*

Budge Trust Award for program majors ($300), 1 Lair Trust Award for junior watercolorists ($1200), 2 Paulson Endowment Awards for sculpture majors ($450).

Application Procedures Deadline—freshmen and transfers: continuous. Required: high school transcript, minimum 2.0 high school GPA.

Undergraduate Contact Donald R. Byrum, Chair, School of Art and Design, Wichita State University, 1845 Fairmount, Wichita, Kansas 67260-0067; 316-689-3551, fax: 316-689-3951.

Graduate Contact Kathleen Shanahan, Graduate Coordinator, School of Art and Design, Wichita State University, 1845 Fairmount, Wichita, Kansas 67260-0067; 316-689-3555, fax: 316-689-3951.

Williams Baptist College

Walnut Ridge, Arkansas

Independent-religious, coed. Rural campus. Total enrollment: 607.

Degrees Bachelor of Fine Arts in the areas of painting, printmaking, ceramics. Majors: ceramics, painting, printmaking.

Art Student Profile Fall 1994: 10 total; all matriculated undergraduate; 60% females.

Art Faculty Total: 2; 1 full-time, 1 part-time; 100% of full-time faculty have terminal degrees. Graduate students do not teach undergraduate courses. Undergraduate student–faculty ratio: 5:1.

Student Life Student groups include Art Club.

Expenses for 1995–96 Application fee: $20. Comprehensive fee of $7072 includes full-time tuition ($4400), mandatory fees ($150), and college room and board ($2522). Part-time tuition: $150 per hour. Part-time mandatory fees: $150 per year. Special program-related fees: $25 for lab fees.

Financial Aid Program-specific awards for Fall of 1994: 1 Art Scholarship for program majors ($3952).

Application Procedures Deadline—freshmen and transfers: May 1. Required: high school transcript, 2 letters of recommendation, portfolio, SAT I or ACT test scores, minimum combined SAT I score of 750, minimum composite ACT score of 19, 2.5 college GPA. Recommended: minimum 2.0 high school GPA, interview. Portfolio reviews held once per semester after completion of foundation courses for entrance into BFA program on campus; the submission of slides may be substituted for portfolios when distance is prohibitive.

Undergraduate Contact Dr. David Midkiff, Chairman, Department of Art, Williams Baptist College, P.O. Box 3536 WBC, Walnut Ridge, Arkansas 72476; 501-886-6741 ext. 157.

Winthrop University

Rock Hill, South Carolina

State-supported, coed. Small-town campus. Total enrollment: 5,164.

Degrees Bachelor of Fine Arts in the areas of ceramics, sculpture, printmaking, painting, photography, interior design, graphic design, general studio. Majors: ceramic art and design, graphic arts, interior design, jewelry and metalsmithing, painting/drawing, photography, printmaking, sculpture, studio art. Graduate degrees offered: Master of Fine Arts in the areas of ceramics, sculpture, printmaking, painting, photography, interior design, graphic design, crafts. Cross-registration with York Technical College.

Art Student Profile Fall 1994: 360 total; 330 matriculated undergraduate, 20 matriculated graduate, 10 nondegree; 5% minorities, 65% females, 2% international.

Art Faculty Total: 32; 20 full-time, 12 part-time; 100% of full-time faculty have terminal degrees. Graduate students do not teach undergraduate courses. Undergraduate student–faculty ratio: 15:1.

Student Life Student groups include American Society of Interior Designers Student Chapter, National Art Educators Association.

Estimated Expenses for 1995–96 Application fee: $35. State resident tuition: $3801 full-time, $158 per credit hour part-time. Nonresident tuition: $6601 full-time, $274 per credit hour part-time. Part-time mandatory fees: $10 per semester. Full-time mandatory fees: $20. College room and board: $3780. College room only: $2058. Special program-related fees: $10–$35 for lab fees.

Financial Aid Program-specific awards for Fall of 1994: 1 Clara Barres Strait Award for incoming freshmen ($500), 1 Hovermale Award for interior design majors ($500), 1 Bell Theodore Award for juniors ($500).

Application Procedures Deadline—freshmen and transfers: continuous. Notification date—freshmen and transfers: continuous. Required: high school transcript, portfolio, minimum 2..2 college GPA for transfer students. Recommended: interview. Portfolio reviews held 4 times for transfer applicants on campus.

Undergraduate Contact Jerome Walden, Chair, Art and Design Department, Winthrop University, 140 McLaurin, Rock Hill, South Carolina 29733; 803-323-2126.

Xavier University

Cincinnati, Ohio

Independent-religious, coed. Suburban campus. Total enrollment: 6,180.

Degrees Bachelor of Fine Arts in the area of art. Majors: art education, art history, art therapy, art/fine arts, ceramic art and design, graphic arts, painting/drawing, printmaking, sculpture, studio art, textile arts. Cross-registration with Greater Cincinnati Consortium of Colleges and Universities.

Art Student Profile Fall 1994: 55 total; all matriculated undergraduate; 3% minorities, 55% females, 3% international.

Art Faculty Total: 9; 5 full-time, 4 part-time; 80% of full-time faculty have terminal degrees. Graduate students do not teach undergraduate courses. Undergraduate student–faculty ratio: 13:1.

Expenses for 1995–96 Application fee: $25. Comprehensive fee of $17,460 includes full-time tuition ($12,270) and college room and board ($5190). College room only: $2760. Part-time tuition per semester ranges from $300 to $4400. Special program-related fees: $20–$30 for studio fees.

Financial Aid Program-specific awards for Fall of 1994: 3 McAuley Scholarships for incoming freshmen ($6135–$12,270).

Application Procedures Deadline—freshmen and transfers: continuous. Required: high school transcript, college transcript(s) for transfer students, minimum 3.0 high school GPA, letter of recommendation, SAT I or ACT test scores, minimum combined SAT I score of 1000, minimum composite ACT score of 23. Recommended: interview. Portfolio reviews held 4 times on campus; the submission of slides may be substituted for portfolios.

Undergraduate Contact Bernard L. Schmidt, Chair, Department of Art, Xavier University, 3800 Victory Parkway, Cincinnati, Ohio 45207-5311; 513-745-3811, fax: 513-745-4301.

York University

North York, Ontario

Province-supported, coed. Urban campus. Total enrollment: 38,313.

Degrees Bachelor of Fine Arts in the area of visual arts. Majors: design, painting/drawing, photography, printmaking, sculpture. Graduate degrees offered: Master of Fine Arts in the area of visual arts.

Art Student Profile Fall 1994: 616 total; 600 matriculated undergraduate, 16 matriculated graduate.

Art Faculty Total: 42; 22 full-time, 20 part-time. Graduate students teach about a quarter undergraduate courses. Undergraduate student–faculty ratio: 15:1.

Expenses for 1994–95 Application fee: $75. Canadian resident tuition: $2720 full-time, $90.67 per credit part-time. Nonresident tuition: $8894 full-time, $296.47 per credit part-time. (All figures are in Canadian dollars.). Full-time mandatory fees: $140. College room and board: $3796. College room only: $3201. Special program-related fees: $20–$100 for lab fees for photography, sculpture and printmaking.

Financial Aid Program-specific awards for Fall of 1994: 3 Talent Awards for students with outstanding portfolios ($1000).

Application Procedures Deadline—freshmen and transfers: March 1. Notification date—freshmen: June 30; transfers: July 15. Required: essay, high school transcript, minimum 3.0 high school GPA, portfolio, SAT, ACT or Canadian equivalent. Portfolio reviews held 1 time on campus and off campus; the submission of slides may be substituted for portfolios.

Undergraduate Contact Don Murdoch, Liaison Officer, Liaison and Advising, Faculty of Fine Arts, York University, 213 CFA, 4700 Keele Street, North York, Ontario M3J 1P3, Canada; 416-736-5135, fax: 416-736-5447, E-mail address: donm@vm2.yorku.ca.

Graduate Contact Judith Schwarz, MFA Director, Visual Arts Department, York University, 213 CFA, 4700 Keele Street, North York, Ontario M3J 1P3; 416-736-5187, fax: 416-736-5447.

Youngstown State University

Youngstown, Ohio

State-supported, coed. Urban campus. Total enrollment: 13,979.

Degrees Bachelor of Fine Arts in the area of studio art. Majors: art education, ceramic art and design, graphic arts, painting/drawing, photography, printmaking, sculpture, studio art.

Art Student Profile Fall 1994: 307 total; all matriculated undergraduate; 10% minorities, 50% females, 1% international.

Art Faculty Total: 45; 15 full-time, 30 part-time; 90% of full-time faculty have terminal degrees. Graduate students do not teach undergraduate courses. Undergraduate student–faculty ratio: 12:1.

Student Life Student groups include Student Art Association.

Expenses for 1994–95 Application fee: $25. State resident tuition: $2910 full-time, $81 per credit part-time. Tuition for nonresidents residing within a 100-mile radius: $4926 full-time, $137 per credit part-time. Tuition for nonresidents residing outside a 100-mile radius: $5430 full-time, $151 per credit part-time. College room and board: $3750. Special program-related fees: $20 for studio lab fees, $35 for computer class lab fees.

Financial Aid Program-specific awards for Fall of 1994: 4 Beecher Talent Scholarships for freshmen ($1000).

Application Procedures Deadline—freshmen and transfers: continuous. Required: high school transcript, college transcript(s) for transfer students. Recommended: SAT I or ACT test scores. Auditions held on campus and off campus. Portfolio reviews held on campus and off campus; the submission of slides may be substituted for portfolios.

Undergraduate Contact Susan Russo, Chairperson, Department of Art, Youngstown State University, 410 Wick Avenue, Youngstown, Ohio 44555; 216-742-3627, fax: 216-742-7183, E-mail address: scrusso@cc.ysu.edu.

DANCE PROGRAMS

DANCE PROGRAMS

Different Undergraduate Programs in Dance

Every program is different. It's important for students looking at dance programs to research *every* school they're considering to see what's offered and required. Many colleges/universities offer one or two kinds of programs in dance: a Bachelor of Arts (B.A.), a Bachelor of Science, (B.S.), and a Bachelor of Fine Arts (B.F.A.). These degrees are offered as part of the larger four-year university program. For a B.A., you usually take 30–45 credits (out of a total of 120) in your major. Some programs offer a B.S. degree, which is much like a B.A. in terms of program balance. There are also distribution requirements and a series of electives. It's a broad curriculum that emphasizes learning as much as you can about all aspects of dance while pursuing a general liberal arts education.

B.F.A. Programs

A university Bachelor of Fine Arts program is more specialized and often emphasizes professional training. It usually requires somewhere between 45 and 60 credits in the major as well as a general education component—some science, social science, humanities, and so on. With a B.F.A., you have more studio work than for a B.A. or B.S., and there's probably a more stringent process of leveling—putting you in a class based on your level of ability. The advanced class will be much more rigorous, and the school's performing group is usually chosen from the B.F.A. students (although some schools also audition B.A. students). B.F.A. programs usually require students to complete some sort of senior project in their area of specialization.

Many B.F.A. programs have a very defined focus. It may be performance, the physiology of movement, dance notation, or the body sciences (such as the Alexander technique). Some schools emphasize learning a little bit about all kinds of dance—jazz, tap, ethnic, modern, ballet, and more—and others concentrate on just one or two types.

The B.F.A. programs in some schools, like those at Purchase, Juilliard, and the North Carolina School for the Arts, are set up as conservatory programs offering professional training in different performing arts (such as dance, music, theater, and film) as well as visual arts. These schools for the arts are accredited degree-granting institutions that may or may not be part of a larger university. They require that about 90 of the 120 credits that must be taken are in the professional field. These conservatory dance programs primarily focus on ballet and modern dance.

Evaluating Programs and Your Goals

There are programs full of advantages on paper that could be all wrong for somebody else, so there has to be a match between the program and your goals. Students must also determine if they have has what it takes to pursue a performing career.

If you think you want to be a performer, audition for B.F.A. programs. Seeing if you get in is one of the very first steps to finding out whether your professional goals are realistic. You might also get guidance from your own dance teachers, who know about how you work and something about the range of differences that exist in the various B.F.A. programs. If someone has the passion to become a professional performer, and evaluations by their current teachers and success at their auditions for major performing institutions speak positively to them, they should go for it. And, if a dance program is doing its job, it will evaluate students and their potential honestly and help them make this decision.

Dance requires commitment at a very young age. If you're at all interested in becoming a performing artist, you must do it now. Choose a school where you have opportunities to go in the direction you wish to pursue. Once you get there, it's your daily and annual progress, initiative, and ability to absorb the technique and the corrections and the connections between all of these courses that are going to move you forward.

Going Directly into a Performance Company

At the end of their junior year of high school such students should get themselves into a very top-flight summer program and have their potential to become a professional assessed. In the ballet world, fewer dancers have degrees. In the modern world, more dancers have degrees. They've all attended at least a couple of years of school because it allows them to work in a professional training program where everything is in one place, progressively and sequentially organized—access to studios, musicians who accompany class, a curriculum that surrounds the studio work, ongoing evaluation by the faculty—rather than having to go from studio to studio putting together a schedule of classes on their own.

The Application Process: B.A. and B.F.A. Programs

For most B.A. programs, students apply through the office of admissions to be accepted by the university or the college. The procedure would be the same as that for any other discipline—there aren't any special criteria. When you get there, you go to the dance department and enroll in classes. Every department has its own standards in accepting majors. Some let you declare yourself a major right away, in some you must wait two years, and sometimes you must go through a pre-dance curriculum for a year.

Admission procedures for university B.F.A. programs vary. Some schools use the process just described—you're admitted to the university, and then you enter the dance department. (In some schools you eventually have to audition to become a major.) Others have a dual admission process—you have to audition to be accepted into the program, and you must be accepted by the university as well.

Student Self-Evaluation

Questions To Ask Yourself Before Applying to a Dance Program

What area of dance do I want to study? Do I want to be a performer, a choreographer, a writer, a teacher, a theorist? You begin by looking into the future to figure out where you want to be. Then find the program that will help you get there. Finding the right program should be your first priority.

Do I know enough about my particular area of interest to determine if this is the career I really want? It might be helpful to talk with several people working in the field for an honest assessment of both its positive and negative aspects so you clearly understand what it will entail.

If I choose a B.F.A. program, do I want the very focused professional training a conservatory would give me, or do I want to study dance within a broader liberal arts context at a university? A conservatory offers the company of like minded and equally dedicated people, while a university program will offer more of a diverse "college experience."

What are my strengths and weaknesses? What areas of my craft do I want and need to develop? It's very important to be honest with yourself and seek advice from a fairly broad spectrum of people.

What size school do I want? Will I be most comfortable in a smaller, more intimate setting, or do I want the diversity of a large school?

What geographic area do I want to be in? A major urban cultural center? Near a specific company with which I'd like to work?

Auditions

The audition process itself usually includes taking one technique class (sometimes two) in ballet and/or modern dance. Some schools may also require a performance, a showing of your choreographic work, improvisations, an essay, and/or an interview. Every school has a different combination. You have to be able to demonstrate how much training you've had, where you are as a dancer, your ability to take correction, and your ability to phrase musically.

There's usually a panel of dance faculty members who judge the students. How much weight the audition carries depends on the program. For the performance-oriented programs, the admissions officers go out and talk to students and distribute or collect material, but it's usually the dance faculty that makes the admission determination. Most schools will try, if possible, to have U.S. students come to campus for an audition; many schools travel around and either hold regional auditions or attend various high school dance festivals to look at students. Most (but not all) schools accept videotapes from international students or from those who can't afford to travel; each school has its own requirements for videotapes. It's very important for students to find out what each school requires. If you can possibly audition in person, it's by far the best way to do it. Students should also inquire about the dress code for auditions.

The Admissions Process

There are a few factors that schools—conservatory and B.F.A. programs in particular—consider when they look at dancers: What are your physical proportions? How fit are you? Are you injury-free?

Contacts and Networking

If you're in the performance field, it's a distinct handicap to attend a college or university where you don't have an opportunity to go see professional companies and to take classes and interact with professional dancers. You need to be near a major metropolitan area. If you're not, try to get there during the summer.

There are schools that do a very good job of developing a network, especially through faculty members. And there are pockets outside of New York—in Utah, California, Arizona, and Texas, for example—where there's a lot of networking going on.

Guest Artists

Some schools have guest artists who come in for three or six weeks during a semester, and this is really valuable. They teach, they set a piece, they evaluate the students, they really work with them. Others have outside professionals drop in and teach one master class; that's nice, but that's not teaching—it's

Program Evaluation

Questions to Ask About a Dance Program to Determine if It's the Right One for You

What is the focus of the program? Is this program going to help get you where you want to go? For example, some programs focus exclusively on modern dance, others primarily on ballet, and still others on both. It's important to understand that there are differences and to inquire about them.

What kinds of classes will I take? What requirements, outside of dance, will I have? How many technique classes will I have each week? How does the program determine in which technique class students will be?

What repertory will I perform? Works by students? Faculty? Guest artists? Major American and international choreographers?

How much performing will I be able to do? How are performers selected?

Is a final project required? It is very important for students to do a senior project that synthesizes and pulls together their four years of education.

How many professional companies come to the school or nearby that I will be able to see?

Does the program feature guest artists, artists-in-residence, or industry visitors so I can meet practicing professionals and learn the latest theories and techniques? How long do they stay on campus? Do they give lectures, teach classes, or offer workshops? Do they work with all students or just those at a certain level?

Does the program allow time off for professional leave or internships?

What kind of facilities are available to me to practice my craft? Is there adequate rehearsal space? Is the equipment state-of-the-art?

How large is the school or university? How many people are in the program in which you're interested? What's the student-faculty ratio in your area of study?

Does the school's location suit my needs and preferences?

Who is on the faculty? Are faculty members practicing in their field?

Are alumni of the program working in their chosen field? If most of the alumni of a performance program are teaching instead of performing, this tells you something. You have to ask, How many students did you graduate in the last five years, where are they, and what are they doing? Every program will have a couple of people who managed to make it. You really have to look at the larger number, the percentages. This is particularly true of the B.F.A. programs. Speak to some alumni of the program, if possible, to find out how they feel about their experiences.

What kind of placement help does the program or school offer?

Does the program or school offer opportunities to study abroad?

exposure. If a program says it has lots of guest artists, you need to find out how they define "guest artist."

Performance Majors and Internships

Some companies have apprentices chosen solely by company audition. Usually it's not something the school arranges—the student has to take the initiative. In many cases students will take a leave of absence from school to work with a professional company. In a few instances, apprenticeships may be incorporated into the program of study. In administration, an internship may be required as part of the degree program.

Career Paths After Performance Programs

You start by auditioning for companies. Very lucky students will already have something by the time they graduate. In the dance world, as in theater and music, you have very intense competition for jobs.

Many students have fears about choosing a performing career. Some worry about having their careers cut short by injuries. This really doesn't happen much these days because there are so many medical procedures for care and prevention. Others think that you can only dance for ten years and then your career is over. This is not true either. Some ballerinas have been performing with the same company for twenty or twenty-five years. Longevity is not the issue it used to be.

Geography and Job Prospects

When there are an abundance of companies and a diversity of techniques and styles in one area, there are many more options. In areas with only a few companies, it depends so much on whether a company has vacancies. It's a pretty dynamic profession, so dancers have to stay very tuned in and be flexible in terms of going where the jobs are—and that means around the world, not just in this country.

Options for Performance Graduates

In addition to performing or while you are preparing for a performing career, some graduates produce their own concerts—they find space, make a budget, choreograph a work, and select their dancers. Dancers can work for arts councils, in the box office in performing spaces, or as assistant managers in dance companies in exchange for taking classes. Some have opened their own schools or founded their own companies.

Beyond that, performance majors who have a degree can do practically anything. Studying the arts is one of the best preparations for the rest of life because students learn how to evaluate themselves, meet deadlines, develop a sense of responsibility, work with groups, develop skills in creative thinking and "thinking on their feet," and locate information that they need. Performance students also have degrees—they've learned how to write papers, they speak well, they have all kinds of skills. They are prepared! Depending on your area of specialization in dance, many other career options are available. Arts administration and dance production (lighting and costuming) are the two fairly hot areas right now. In a lot of areas—history, notation, sports medicine, dance ethnology (documenting dances indigenous to different cultures), dance or movement therapy, and body therapies—you probably need a master's degree or the equivalent. In the field of dance history, there are a lot of part-time jobs available at universities, but there are very few full-time jobs. Some of these positions will require a Ph.D. Dance notation is usually something you teach along with something else. If you get a teacher's certification as part of your undergraduate work, that entitles you to teach in the public school system. If you want to proceed in the educational world, you really need a professional performing career. Some university positions require this as well as an M.F.A. degree to qualify as a faculty member. Conservatory programs primarily hire professionals of the highest caliber in dance, choreography, music, history, and other fields. To open your own studio, you need initiative, knowledge of dance training, and administrative skills.

Arizona State University

Tempe, Arizona

State-supported, coed. Suburban campus. Total enrollment: 42,189.

Degrees Bachelor of Fine Arts in the areas of dance, dance education. Majors: choreography and performance, modern dance. Graduate degrees offered: Master of Fine Arts in the area of dance.

Dance Student Profile Fall 1994: 109 total; 92 matriculated undergraduate, 17 matriculated graduate; 9% minorities, 96% females, 3% international.

Dance Faculty Total: 13; 10 full-time, 3 part-time; 60% of full-time faculty have terminal degrees. Graduate students teach about a quarter undergraduate courses. Undergraduate student–faculty ratio: 16:1.

Student Life Student groups include Dance Arizona Repertory Theatre.

Expenses for 1994–95 State resident tuition: $1894 full-time. Nonresident tuition: $7500 full-time, $310 per credit part-time. State resident part-time tuition per semester ranges from $96 to $576. Part-time mandatory fees: $32 per year. College room and board: $4690. College room only: $3090.

Financial Aid Program-specific awards for Fall of 1994: 4 In-State Tuition Scholarships for those demonstrating need/talent ($914), 7 Friends of Dance Scholarships for those demonstrating need/talent ($800), 1 Sun Angel Scholarship for those demonstrating need/talent ($700), 5 Out-of-State Tuition Scholarships for those demonstrating need/talent ($2800).

Application Procedures Deadline—freshmen and transfers: continuous. Required: college transcript(s) for transfer students, minimum 2.0 high school GPA, SAT I or ACT test scores. Recommended: minimum 3.0 high school GPA.

Undergraduate Contact Sally Flanigan, Student Academic Specialist, Dance Department, Arizona State University, P.O. Box 870304, Tempe, Arizona 85287-0304; 602-965-5029, fax: 602-965-2247.

Graduate Contact Ann Ludwig, Graduate Coordinator, Dance Department, Arizona State University, P.O. Box 870304, Tempe, Arizona 85287-0304; 602-965-3914, fax: 602-965-2247.

Barat College

Lake Forest, Illinois

Independent-religious, coed. Suburban campus. Total enrollment: 729.

Degrees Bachelor of Fine Arts in the area of performance and choreography. Majors: ballet, modern dance.

Dance Student Profile Fall 1994: 240 total; 40 matriculated undergraduate, 200 nondegree; 20% minorities, 90% females, 2% international.

Dance Faculty Total: 9; 2 full-time, 7 part-time; 100% of full-time faculty have terminal degrees. Graduate students do not teach undergraduate courses. Undergraduate student–faculty ratio: 10:1.

Student Life Student groups include Barat Repertory Dance Company, Choreographers' Showcase. Special housing available for dance students.

Expenses for 1995–96 Application fee: $20. Comprehensive fee of $15,980 includes full-time tuition ($11,190), mandatory fees ($110), and college room and board ($4680). Part-time tuition: $373 per credit hour.

Financial Aid Program-specific awards for Fall of 1994: 8–10 Dance Talent Awards ($2500–$3000).

Application Procedures Deadline—freshmen and transfers: continuous. Required: essay, high school transcript, minimum 2.0 high school GPA, 2 letters of recommendation, audition, SAT I or ACT test scores, minimum 2.0 college GPA for transfer students. Recommended: minimum 3.0 high school GPA. Auditions held 4 times and by appointment on campus; videotaped performances are permissible as a substitute for live auditions if a campus visit is impossible.

Undergraduate Contact Jennifer McDermott, Admissions Office, Barat College, 700 East Westleigh Road, Lake Forest, Illinois 60045; 708-234-3000, fax: 708-615-5000.

Boston Conservatory

Boston, Massachusetts

Independent, coed. Urban campus. Total enrollment: 414.

Degrees Bachelor of Fine Arts in the area of dance. Majors: ballet, modern dance. Graduate degrees offered: Master of Fine Arts in the areas of performance, choreography. Cross-registration with Emerson College, Massachusetts College of Art, Berklee College of Music, Boston Architectural Center, School of the Museum of Fine Arts.

Dance Student Profile Fall 1994: 80 total; 73 matriculated undergraduate, 7 matriculated graduate; 10% minorities, 85% females, 5% international.

Dance Faculty Total: 30; 3 full-time, 27 part-time. Graduate students teach a few undergraduate courses.

Student Life Student groups include Boston Dance Theater.

Expenses for 1995–96 Comprehensive fee of $20,130 includes full-time tuition ($13,400), mandatory fees ($450), and college room and board ($6280). Part-time tuition: $555 per credit. Part-time mandatory fees per semester range from $56.25 to $168.75.

Financial Aid Program-specific awards for Fall of 1994: 44 Conservatory Scholarships for those passing audition evaluations ($5000), 5 Jan Veen Memorial Scholarships for continuing students ($2000), 1 Ruth S. Ambrose Award for juniors ($2000).

Application Procedures Deadline—freshmen and transfers: continuous. Notification date—freshmen and transfers: September 1. Required: essay, high school transcript, 3 letters of recommendation, interview, audition, minimum 2.7 high school GPA. Recommended: video.

Auditions held 10 times on campus and off campus in St. Petersburg, FL; Washington, DC; San Diego, CA; Los Angeles, CA; Dallas, TX; Houston, TX; videotaped performances are permissible as a substitute for live auditions when distance is prohibitive.

Contact Richard Wallace, Director of Admissions, Boston Conservatory, 8 The Fenway, Boston, Massachusetts 02215; 617-536-6340, fax: 617-536-3176.

More about the Conservatory

Program Facilities Five dance studios plus annex studios, Mainstage Proscenium arch theater (400 seats), Seully Hall (200 seats), costume shop, computer lab (Apple), library of 60,000 volumes and scores, and interlibrary loan availability with college network of Boston.

Faculty and Alumni Professional artist faculty represents all styles of dance and teaching methods. Alumni can be seen in professional dance companies in the United States and Europe, Broadway companies, industrials, and television.

Student Performance Opportunities Three mainstage concerts yearly, studio recitals (various), student choreographed recitals, road company performances in greater Boston area, guest appearances with Boston Pops and Boston Symphony Open House.

Special Programs Gig office providing performance opportunities throughout the greater Boston area, career seminar series, counseling and health services, international student ESL classes/orientation program, academic year ESL course work, and tutorial assistance.

The Boston Conservatory, founded in 1867, is one of the oldest colleges offering training to serious students of the performing arts. The three divisions of the college—Music, Dance, and Theater—take full advantage of the wealth of cultural and academic offerings Boston has to offer. Guest artists, master classes, performance opportunities, and professional contacts and networking are provided to all students of the college. These experiences seek to ensure that each student receives a varied and professional level of education to augment the intensive study of the prescribed curriculum.

The Boston Conservatory Dance Division is the oldest degree-granting dance program in the United States. Founded in 1943 by the dance innovator and teacher, Jan Veen, the Dance Division was the first to offer ballet and modern training as a core curriculum of study. This tradition continues today with additional study in all styles of dance performance.

Daily technique classes provide professional training in ballet and modern dance. In addition, dancers study choreography, pedagogy, music, laban, jazz, tap, and ethnic dance styles.

Versatility for a dancer translates into work and performance opportunities; therefore, the Boston Conservatory curriculum requires students to extend themselves and be knowledgeable about music, literature, dance repertory, danced history, and anatomy. To support the inner dancer, seminars in health and nutrition are scheduled throughout the academic year.

Faculty members are current or former members of some of the most prestigious dance organizations in the United States. Their artistry and professional qualifications offer students a full range of dance technique and teaching methods. Faculty members serve as mentors to a core of dancers, forming a nurturing and supportive relationship. Students are thus able to grow and achieve their dreams within a caring, artistic environment.

Performance experience is provided in both studio and mainstage concerts. The range of work performed runs the gamut of dance repertory, in addition to frequent premieres of new works choreographed by artist faculty members or commissioned by the school. Mainstage concerts are held in collaboration with the Music Division, offering a unique opportunity to interact with musicians as part of the performance preparation.

Boston is a major center of higher education in America, with over fifty major colleges and universities. This provides a diverse student population and an endless array of courses, lectures, concerts, and social opportunities. The Conservatory is in the Pro-Arts Consortium with five area colleges (Emerson College, Berklee College of Music, Museum School, Massachusetts College of Art, and Boston Architectural Center), which offers extensive cross-registration course possibilities to all students.

On-campus housing is provided to all interested students, offering brownstone-style living accommodations just a few steps from the main training and rehearsal buildings. For those students interested in off-campus housing, Boston offers a wide range of architectural styles and rent prices in neighborhoods throughout the city, which are all within easy access to the school by public transportation.

The Boston Conservatory strives to meet each student's needs, musically and personally, and provides a nurturing, safe environment in which to study, learn, and grow. The supportive atmosphere of the college extends to student life areas as well. Over a dozen special interest groups and organizations exist on campus, with new ones developing constantly as the student population grows and needs change. As part of the student services, a number of career seminars are given each year ranging from résumé writing and audition anxiety to grant writing and tax laws for the performing artist. In addition, there is an active student government and a student-run newspaper.

Brenau University

Gainesville, Georgia

Independent, primarily women. Small-town campus. Total enrollment: 2,241.

Degrees Bachelor of Fine Arts in the areas of arts management, dance pedagogy, dance performance. Majors: performance.

Dance Student Profile Fall 1994: 15 total; all matriculated undergraduate; 20% minorities, 100% females, 20% international.

Dance Faculty Total: 3; 2 full-time, 1 part-time; 100% of full-time faculty have terminal degrees. Graduate students do not teach undergraduate courses. Undergraduate student–faculty ratio: 10:1.

Student Life Student groups include Tau Sigma, Brenau Opera Company, Gainesville Theatre Alliance.

Brenau University *(continued)*

Estimated Expenses for 1995–96 Application fee: $30. Comprehensive fee of $16,040 includes full-time tuition ($9855) and college room and board ($6185). Part-time tuition: $205 per semester hour.

Financial Aid Program-specific awards for Fall of 1994: Dance Scholarships for program majors ($3000).

Application Procedures Deadline—freshmen and transfers: continuous. Required: high school transcript, college transcript(s) for transfer students, letter of recommendation, audition. Recommended: interview. Auditions held 5 times on campus; videotaped performances are permissible as a substitute for live auditions when distance is prohibitive.

Undergraduate Contact John D. Upchurch, Dean of Admissions, Brenau University, One Centennial Circle, Gainesville, Georgia 30501; 800-252-5119, fax: 404-534-6114.

Jordan College of Fine Arts

Butler University

Indianapolis, Indiana

Independent, coed. Urban campus. Total enrollment: 3,758.

Degrees Bachelor of Fine Arts in the area of dance performance. Majors: ballet, dance, jazz dance, modern dance. Cross-registration with Consortium for Urban Education.

Dance Student Profile Fall 1994: 205 total; 80 matriculated undergraduate, 125 nondegree; 9% minorities, 90% females, 2% international.

Dance Faculty Total: 22; 12 full-time, 10 part-time; 50% of full-time faculty have terminal degrees. Graduate students do not teach undergraduate courses. Undergraduate student–faculty ratio: 8:1.

Student Life Student groups include Butler Ballet, senior production concerts, Summer dance concert.

Expenses for 1995–96 Comprehensive fee of $18,720 includes full-time tuition ($13,990) and college room and board ($4730). College room only: $2120. Part-time tuition: $585 per semester hour.

Financial Aid Program-specific awards for Fall of 1994: 8–12 Talent Awards for freshmen ($2000–$10,000).

Application Procedures Deadline—freshmen and transfers: April 15. Notification date—freshmen and transfers: August 20. Required: essay, high school transcript, minimum 2.0 high school GPA, audition. Auditions held 23 times on campus and off campus in Hartford, CT; Princeton, NJ; Miami, FL; San Francisco, CA; St. Petersburg, FL; Los Angeles, CA; videotaped performances are permissible as a substitute for live auditions for international applicants.

Undergraduate Contact Chair, Department of Dance, Jordan College of Fine Arts, Butler University, 4600 Sunset Avenue, Indianapolis, Indiana 46208; 317-283-9346, fax: 317-283-9658.

More about the College

Program Facilities Because computers play an increasingly important role for Butler fine arts majors, a computer lab especially for fine arts students is located in Lilly Hall. Department of Music: Clowes Memorial Hall, a 2,200-seat multifaceted performing arts center, the hub of the performing arts at Butler, offers its own season of varied performing arts events. Department of Dance: Dance studios and rehearsal space are state-of-the-art, with resilient flooring designed to meet the specific needs of dancers. The Butler Ballet, the department's preprofessional company, performs a full season in Clowes Memorial Hall with a number of symphonies, including the Indianapolis Chamber Orchestra and the Butler Symphony Orchestra. The dance department has one of the highest production budgets of any dance school in the nation. Department of Theatre: Most of the works produced by the theater department take place in Butler's Studio Theatre, a large black box theater located in Lilly Hall, the University's performing arts complex, or in a small proscenium theater in Robertson Hall. Additional facilities include a rehearsal room, which serves as a studio classroom for courses in acting and directing; a costume shop; a scenery studio; and a makeup room. Department of Telecommunications Arts: Butler operates WTBU-TV Channel 69, a full-power educational television station affiliated with the Corporation for Public Broadcasting. The department also operates two radio stations: WRBU-1, a student operation available on the sideband of WTBU-TV; and WRBU-2, a campus-limited station serving the Butler community.

Faculty and Resident Artists Faculty-in-Residence: Panayis Lyras, artist-in-residence (piano); Laurence Shapiro, artist-in-residence (violin); Michael Schelle, composer-in-residence, Pulitzer Price nominee (composition).

Butler University's Jordan College of Fine Arts (JCFA) continues a 100-year tradition of educating students as emerging professionals in the arts. JCFA has established its educational tradition in the arts through a dynamic faculty, creative and talented students from around the nation, and outstanding facilities, including Clowes Memorial Hall, a 2,200-seat multifaceted performing arts center. The Butler Ballet, Butler Symphony Orchestra, Symphonic Wind Ensemble, Chorale, Jazz Ensemble, and Jordan Jazz Singers perform annually in Clowes Hall and enjoy the benefits of professional stagehands and box office staff members.

As freshmen, students are admitted to JCFA and make the transition into the academic area of their choice with a wide range of programs within the Departments of Dance, Music, Theatre, and Telecommunication Arts. Programs in these areas include arts administration, dance/pedagogy concentration, dance performance, music, music business, music education, music performance, music theory and composition, performing arts, piano pedagogy, telecommunication arts, theater performance, and theater/pedagogy concentration.

The Department of Dance is counted among the nation's leading dance schools. Butler dance alumni are currently with the Boston Ballet, Paris Opera Ballet, and Joffrey Ballet; in Broadway shows; and on the faculty of leading dance departments and studios around the country. Among the first in the nation to offer a university dance program centered on classical ballet technique, Butler continues to offer professional-level training combined with a liberal arts education. In addition, faculty members of the Department of Dance are highly qualified artists whose range of experience contributes to the diversity of the dance program. With rigorous classes in dance studios, theoretical studies, and a strong choreography program, the serious dance student is prepared for a professional career in dance. Butler Ballet, the department's dance company, performs a full season with a number of local professional music organizations. Past performances have included *The Sleeping Beauty, Cinderella, Swan Lake,* and an annual performance of *The Nutcracker* that draws more than 15,000 patrons each year.

Within the Department of Music, Butler offers extensive programs in both instrumental and vocal music with artists-in-residence such as Van Cliburn silver medalist Panayis Lyras in piano, Laurence Shapiro in violin, and Pulitzer Prize–nominee composer Michael Schelle. All students have the opportunity to study one-on-one with recognized artist-teachers who teach throughout the music curriculum, including the freshman year. The highly diversified music faculty, mixed with a wide range of curricular offerings, attracts students in the performance areas of voice, piano, orchestral instruments, organ, guitar, piano pedagogy, conducting, music education, music theory, and composition. In addition, students may request a specific instructor for their private study, and freshmen often have more contact with their primary teacher than any other faculty member. Butler's instrumental and vocal groups—eighteen in all—perform professional-level works for campus concerts in Clowes Hall, and freshmen through seniors join together to perform popular annual events such as the "Rejoice!" concert, the Butler Symphony Orchestra's Halloween concert, and a student concerto competition.

The Department of Theatre offers programs in performing arts, professional theater, technical theater, arts administration, and theater pedagogy. Faculty members within the theater department have extensive experience, and all have professional theater backgrounds. In addition to classroom study, theater majors are required to have firsthand experience creating theater, since all students are required to audition and accept crew assignments for all major productions. The department produces at least four faculty-directed shows each year. Some of the past productions have included *Hedda Gabler, Oklahoma, Over a Glass of Wine, Equus, 1959 Pink Thunderbird,* and *a Midsummer Night's Dream.* Additional productions during the year give juniors and seniors valuable directing experience and give faculty the opportunity to present works in progress. Theater majors also have the opportunity to provide technical assistance for productions and concerts within the music and dance departments. Most of the work produced by the theater department is done in a large black box theater located in Lilly Hall, Butler's performing arts complex. Also located in Lilly Hall are rehearsal rooms, a costume shop, and a makeup room.

The Department of Telecommunication Arts offers students hands-on experience in electronic media production, management, and news. With a television station and two radio stations owned and operated by Butler, students may begin work in video and audio as early as their freshman year. Telecommunication Arts operates WTBU-TV Channel 69, a full-power educational television station, which airs many student-produced programs. WTBU-TV is also affiliated with the Corporation for Public Broadcasting and is carried by most cable systems in central Indiana. In addition, students have access to professional studios and remote production equipment, including a live remote truck. The telecommunication arts department also operates two radio stations: WRBU-1, a student operation available on the sideband of WTBU-TV reaching all of Indianapolis, and WRBU-2, a campus-limited station serving the Butler community. Students learn audio production using new digital workstations that harness computer technology and spend 360 hours on the job, as part of the department's internship program, at a broadcast, cable, or other telecommunications facility in a major-market city. Indianapolis has network affiliate, independent, and public television stations and is the twenty-sixth-largest television market in the nation. In addition, Indianapolis is home to twenty-two radio stations and various production facilities.

The performing arts are a vital part of the Indianapolis community, and the city is developing its niche as a growing arts center. JCFA enjoys a cooperative relationship with the Indianapolis arts community, including the American Pianists Association, the Indianapolis Chamber Orchestra, the Indianapolis Ballet Theatre, and the Indianapolis Opera.

Butler University is an independent, coeducational, nonsectarian university with a total enrollment of about 4,000 students. Students at Butler are exposed to both breadth and depth in academic programs, and a core curriculum encourages students to gain a broad knowledge in government, the arts, social sciences, natural sciences, humanities, and mathematics. Butler students can take advantage of more than 100 different activities, which include but are not limited to social groups, service clubs, honorary societies, performance groups, fraternities and sororities, intramural sports, and varsity teams.

California Institute of the Arts

Valencia, California

Independent, coed. Suburban campus. Total enrollment: 1,051.

Degrees Bachelor of Fine Arts in the area of dance. Majors: dance. Graduate degrees offered: Master of Fine Arts in the area of dance.

Dance Student Profile Fall 1994: 60 total; 53 matriculated undergraduate, 7 matriculated graduate; 35% minorities, 75% females, 6% international.

Dance Faculty Total: 13; 7 full-time, 6 part-time; 100% of full-time faculty have terminal degrees. Graduate students do not teach undergraduate courses. Undergraduate student–faculty ratio: 6:1.

Student Life Student groups include American College Dance Festival Association. Special housing available for dance students.

California Institute of the Arts *(continued)*

Expenses for 1995–96 Comprehensive fee of $21,225 includes full-time tuition ($15,450), mandatory fees ($75), and college room and board ($5700). College room only: $2550 (minimum).

Financial Aid Program-specific awards for Fall of 1994: Sharon Lund Scholarship for program majors ($10,000).

Application Procedures Deadline—freshmen and transfers: September 2. Required: essay, high school transcript, college transcript(s) for transfer students, audition. Auditions held 15 times on campus and off campus in New York, NY; Baltimore, MD; Dallas, TX; Houston, TX; Atlanta, GA; San Francisco, CA; Chicago, IL; Minneapolis, MN; videotaped performances are permissible as a substitute for live auditions with approval from the department.

Undergraduate Contact Stuart Horn, Admissions Officer, California Institute of the Arts, 24700 McBean Parkway, Valencia, California 91355; 805-255-1050.

Graduate Contact Larry Attaway, Associate Dean, School of Dance, California Institute of the Arts, 24700 McBean Parkway, Valencia, California 91355; 805-222-2774, fax: 805-253-1562, E-mail address: lattaway@muse.calarts.edu.

California State University, Long Beach

Long Beach, California

State-supported, coed. Suburban campus. Total enrollment: 26,227.

Degrees Bachelor of Fine Arts in the area of dance. Majors: dance. Graduate degrees offered: Master of Fine Arts in the area of dance: performance and/or choreography.

Dance Student Profile Fall 1994: 594 total; 90 matriculated undergraduate, 4 matriculated graduate, 500 nondegree; 40% minorities, 70% females, 10% international.

Dance Faculty Total: 24; 6 full-time, 18 part-time; 50% of full-time faculty have terminal degrees. Graduate students do not teach undergraduate courses. Undergraduate student–faculty ratio: 15:1.

Student Life Student groups include Off 7th Dancers.

Expenses for 1995–96 State resident tuition: $0 full-time. Nonresident tuition: $7626 full-time, $246 per unit part-time. Part-time mandatory fees: $542.50 per semester. Full-time mandatory fees: $1751. College room and board: $5300.

Financial Aid Program-specific awards for Fall of 1994: 1 Fine Arts Affiliates Awards for program majors ($1000), 1 Dramatic Allied Arts Guild Award for program majors ($1000), 10–15 Adopt A Dancer Scholarships for all dancers demonstrating need ($200–$500), 2 Rotating Awards for program majors ($1000–$1200).

Application Procedures Deadline—freshmen and transfers: continuous. Required: high school transcript, college transcript(s) for transfer students, minimum 2.0 high school GPA, audition, SAT I or ACT test scores. Auditions held 4 times on campus; videotaped performances are permissible as a substitute for live auditions for out-of-state and international applicants.

Undergraduate Contact Tryntje Shapli, Professor/ BFA Advisor, California State University, Long Beach, 1250 Bellflower Boulevard, Long Beach, California 90840; 310-985-4747, fax: 310-985-7896.

Graduate Contact Jeff Slayton, Professor/ MFA Advisor, California State University, Long Beach, 1250 Bellflower Boulevard, Long Beach, California 90840; 310-985-4747, fax: 310-985-7896.

Chapman University

Orange, California

Independent-religious, coed. Suburban campus. Total enrollment: 3,285.

Degrees Bachelor of Fine Arts in the areas of dance performance, dance theater. Majors: dance, performance.

Dance Student Profile Fall 1994: 40 total; all matriculated undergraduate; 36% minorities, 65% females, 4% international.

Dance Faculty Total: 6; 1 full-time, 5 part-time. Graduate students do not teach undergraduate courses. Undergraduate student–faculty ratio: 15:1.

Student Life Student groups include Orange County Choreographers Showcase, American Celebration, Performing Arts Society of Chapman.

Estimated Expenses for 1995–96 Application fee: $30. Comprehensive fee of $24,136 includes full-time tuition ($17,372), mandatory fees ($544), and college room and board ($6220). Part-time tuition: $538 per credit.

Financial Aid Program-specific awards for Fall of 1994: 20 Talent Awards for incoming students ($10,000).

Application Procedures Deadline—freshmen and transfers: continuous. Required: high school transcript, minimum 2.0 high school GPA, letter of recommendation. Recommended: essay, interview.

Undergraduate Contact Cyrus Parker-Geannette, Dance Director, Theatre and Dance Department, Chapman University, 333 North Glassell Street, Orange, California 92666; 714-744-7087.

Columbia College

Columbia, South Carolina

Independent-religious, women only. Suburban campus. Total enrollment: 1,229.

Degrees Bachelor of Fine Arts in the area of dance performance and choreography. Majors: choreography and performance.

Dance Student Profile Fall 1994: 43 total; 42 matriculated undergraduate, 1 nondegree; 10% minorities, 100% females.

Dance Faculty Total: 8; 4 full-time, 4 part-time; 100% of full-time faculty have terminal degrees. Graduate students do not teach undergraduate courses. Undergraduate student–faculty ratio: 11:1.

Student Life Student groups include American College Dance Festival Association, Dance Major's Club.

Expenses for 1995–96 Application fee: $20. Comprehensive fee of $15,755 includes full-time tuition ($10,995) and college room and board ($4760). Part-time tuition: $310 per credit.

Financial Aid Program-specific awards for Fall of 1994: 30 Dance Scholarships for program majors ($1000–$2500).

Application Procedures Deadline—freshmen and transfers: continuous. Required: high school transcript, 3 letters of recommendation, audition, SAT I or ACT test scores. Recommended: essay, interview. Auditions held 1 time on campus; videotaped performances are permissible as a substitute for live auditions for out-of-state applicants.

Undergraduate Contact Patty Graham, Assistant Professor of Dance, Dance Department, Columbia College, 1301 Columbia College Drive, Columbia, South Carolina 29203; 803-786-3668, fax: 803-786-3868.

More about the College

Program Facilities Cottingham Theater is a 375-seat hall in which all major productions are held. In addition, Godbold Studio Theater provides the feel of a smaller, New York "loft" space where less formal, more experimental works are shown. The well-equipped dance studio areas have state-of-the-art flooring and full wall mirrors.

Faculty, Resident Artists, and Alumni Faculty members are all artist-educators who continue to perform and choreograph. An aggressive professional residency program brings three to four dance companies or solo artists to the campus for residencies lasting from one-half to two full weeks. Residencies provide students the opportunity to train with these current professional artists in master technique classes, composition workshops, informal discussions, and other meaningful activities. Past artists in residence include Dan Wagoner and Dancers, BeBe Miller, Urban Bush Women, and Joe Goode Performance Company. Alumnae have gone on to perform professionally with such nationally recognized choreographers as Dan Wagoner, Mark Dendy, and Randy James, as well as several regional companies such as the South Carolina Ballet Theater and Marcus Alford's Jazz Theatre South.

Student Performance Opportunities Dance majors have the opportunity to perform in three formal and two informal concert productions annually. In addition, selected works are presented through participation in the American College Dance Festival conferences and Piccolo Spoleto productions. Special choreographic residencies provide students the opportunity to perform in works by such leading choreographers as Laura Dean and David Dorfman. Choreographic residencies range from one to four weeks in length.

Special Programs Generous dance scholarships are available for students who have outstanding technical and creative talents in dance. Academically strong dancers have the benefit of additional scholarship opportunities.

Cornish College of the Arts

Seattle, Washington

Independent, coed. Urban campus. Total enrollment: 623.

Degrees Bachelor of Fine Arts in the area of dance. Majors: ballet, choreography and performance, dance, modern dance.

Dance Student Profile Fall 1994: 57 total; all matriculated undergraduate; 14% minorities, 80% females.

Dance Faculty Total: 16; 4 full-time, 12 part-time; 70% of full-time faculty have terminal degrees. Graduate students do not teach undergraduate courses. Undergraduate student–faculty ratio: 7:1.

Student Life Student groups include Northwest Regional American College Dance Festival Association, Cornish Dance Theatre.

Expenses for 1995–96 Application fee: $30. Tuition: $10,540 full-time, $405 per credit part-time.

Financial Aid Program-specific awards for Fall of 1994: Merit Awards for continuing students ($1000), Endowed/Restricted Awards for continuing students ($1000), Trustee Grants for all students ($800–$1500), Cornish Scholarships for new students ($1000), 1–4 Minority Dance Scholarships for new minority students ($1000), 1–5 Kreielsheimer Scholarships for new students from Washington, Oregon, or Alaska ($15,000), Male Dance Scholarships for new and continuing male students ($2000).

Application Procedures Deadline—freshmen and transfers: continuous. Required: essay, high school transcript, minimum 2.0 high school GPA, audition. Auditions held 10 times on campus and off campus in Riverside, CA; videotaped performances are permissible as a substitute for live auditions when distance is prohibitive.

Undergraduate Contact Jane Buckman, Director, Admissions Office, Cornish College of the Arts, 710 East Roy Street, Seattle, Washington 98102; 206-323-1400, fax: 206-720-1011.

More about the College

The Dance Department at Cornish College of the Arts provides demanding but nurturing training for professional artists to create graduates with proficient technique, creative voice, self-assurance, and a willingness to take risks. The training is designed to give students a thorough knowledge of the craft of the past while preparing them to become artistic innovators of the twenty-first century.

Student pursuing a B.F.A. in dance will participate in daily ballet and modern dance classes, which form the core of the technique curriculum. Other courses offered include pointe, partnering, character, and African dance. Strength and flexibility exercises are incorporated into all technique classes to prevent injuries. A three-year sequence of courses in composition and improvisation

Cornish College of the Arts *(continued)*

develops choreographic craft. A senior project, typically involving and advanced level of choreography and a public performance, is the final requirement of the B.F.A. program.

Faculty members and guest artists choreograph for Cornish Dance Theatre, the department's performing ensemble, which presents two concert seasons each year. Additional performance and choreographic opportunities arise from an annual concert of student choreography, senior projects, and collaborations with the Theatre and Music departments.

There is a two-way dialogue between the professional dance community and the department. Students have the chance to intern with several local companies. Seattle offers many opportunities to present choreography, while visiting artists such as Mark Morris, and members of the Martha Graham, Merce Cunningham, and Paul Taylor Dance companies provide a vital connection to the national dance world.

East Carolina University

Greenville, North Carolina

State-supported, coed. Urban campus. Total enrollment: 16,373.

Degrees Bachelor of Fine Arts in the area of dance. Majors: ballet, dance, jazz dance, modern dance.

Expenses for 1994–95 Application fee: $35. State resident tuition: $764 full-time. Nonresident tuition: $7248 full-time. Part-time tuition per semester ranges from $96 to $287 for state residents, $906 to $2718 for nonresidents. Part-time mandatory fees per semester range from $99 to $298. Full-time mandatory fees: $793. College room and board: $3030. College room only: $1590 (minimum).

Application Procedures Deadline—freshmen: March 15; transfers: April 15. Required: high school transcript, SAT I test score only. Recommended: minimum 2.0 high school GPA, letter of recommendation, audition.

Undergraduate Contact Undergraduate Admissions, East Carolina University, Wichard Building, Greenville, North Carolina 27858-4353; 919-328-6640.

Florida State University

Tallahassee, Florida

State-supported, coed. Suburban campus. Total enrollment: 29,630.

Degrees Bachelor of Fine Arts in the area of dance. Majors: choreography and performance, dance. Graduate degrees offered: Master of Fine Arts in the area of dance. Cross-registration with Florida Agricultural and Mechanical University.

Dance Student Profile Fall 1994: 562 total; 54 matriculated undergraduate, 18 matriculated graduate, 490 nondegree; 1% minorities, 75% females, 1% international.

Dance Faculty Total: 12; 11 full-time, 1 part-time; 55% of full-time faculty have terminal degrees. Graduate students teach about a quarter undergraduate courses. Undergraduate student–faculty ratio: 5:1.

Student Life Student groups include American College Dance Festival Association, Florida Dance Association.

Expenses for 1995–96 Application fee: $20. State resident tuition: $1798 full-time, $59.93 per semester hour part-time. Nonresident tuition: $6700 full-time, $223.34 per semester hour part-time. College room and board: $4500. College room only: $2360.

Financial Aid Program-specific awards for Fall of 1994: 34 Out-of-State Tuition Waivers for program majors.

Application Procedures Deadline—freshmen: March 1; transfers: June 20. Required: high school transcript, college transcript(s) for transfer students, minimum 2.0 high school GPA, audition, SAT I or ACT test scores. Recommended: minimum 3.0 high school GPA, letter of recommendation. Auditions held 3 times on campus; videotaped performances are permissible as a substitute for live auditions for international applicants or in special circumstances.

Contact Dr. Nancy Smith Fichter, Chairperson, Dance Department, Florida State University, Room 404 Montgomery Gym, Tallahassee, Florida 32306-2012; 904-644-1023, fax: 904-644-1277.

Friends University

Wichita, Kansas

Independent, coed. Urban campus. Total enrollment: 2,326.

Degrees Bachelor of Fine Arts in the area of ballet. Majors: ballet, dance. Cross-registration with Kansas Newman College.

Dance Student Profile Fall 1994: 30 total; all matriculated undergraduate; 5% minorities, 55% females, 10% international.

Dance Faculty Total: 2; 1 full-time, 1 part-time; 50% of full-time faculty have terminal degrees. Graduate students do not teach undergraduate courses.

Expenses for 1995–96 Application fee: $15. Comprehensive fee of $11,876 includes full-time tuition ($8631), mandatory fees ($115), and college room and board ($3130). Part-time tuition: $289 per semester hour.

Financial Aid Program-specific awards for Fall of 1994: 5 Miller Scholarships for program majors ($1000), 15 Departmental Scholarships for program majors ($1000).

Application Procedures Deadline—freshmen: August 1; transfers: August 26. Required: high school transcript, minimum 2.0 high school GPA, interview, audition. Auditions held 4 times on campus; videotaped performances are permissible as a substitute for live auditions if a campus visit is impossible.

Undergraduate Contact Stan Rogers, Director, Department of Dance, Friends University, 2100 University Drive, Wichita, Kansas 67213; 316-261-5848.

The Hartt School

See University of Hartford, The Hartt School

Jacksonville University

Jacksonville, Florida

Independent, coed. Suburban campus. Total enrollment: 2,480.

Degrees Bachelor of Fine Arts in the area of dance. Majors: dance.

Dance Student Profile Fall 1994: 44 total; all matriculated undergraduate; 99% females, 1% international.

Dance Faculty Total: 9; 2 full-time, 7 part-time; 100% of full-time faculty have terminal degrees. Undergraduate student–faculty ratio: 12:1.

Student Life Student groups include Jacksonville University Dance Theatre, Jacksonville University Dance Ensemble.

Expenses for 1995–96 Application fee: $25. Comprehensive fee of $15,178 includes full-time tuition ($10,080), mandatory fees ($500), and college room and board ($4598). Part-time tuition: $336 per semester hour. Part-time mandatory fees: $80 per semester.

Financial Aid Program-specific awards for Fall of 1994: 20 Dance Scholarships for those demonstrating need/talent ($1000).

Application Procedures Deadline—freshmen and transfers: continuous. Notification date—freshmen and transfers: August 31. Required: essay, high school transcript, minimum 2.0 high school GPA, 3 letters of recommendation, audition. Recommended: minimum 3.0 high school GPA. Auditions held by appointment on campus; videotaped performances are permissible as a substitute for live auditions if a campus visit is impossible.

Undergraduate Contact Angelus Hollis, Director, Dance Department, Jacksonville University, 2800 University Boulevard North, Jacksonville, Florida 32211; 904-744-7374, fax: 904-745-7375.

More about the University

Program Facilities All classes are held in the two studios in the Alexander Brest Dance Pavilion on the Jacksonville University campus. The University's dance studio complex was built in 1987 and contains two large, airy studios with professionally designed dance flooring, floor-to-ceiling windows and extensive mirrors, plus dressing rooms with showers and lockers. All ballet technique and modern classes have live musical accompaniment.

Faculty, Resident Artists, and Alumni The faculty represents some of the best in academic and performing traditions in classical ballet, modern dance, and jazz. It consists of 2 full-time, 2 half-time, and several adjunct faculty members plus 3 accompanists. Guest faculty members have included Donlin Forman, Ernestine Stodelle, Bojan Spassoff, Phyllis Lamhut, Rachel Lampert, Edward Villela, Russel Sultzback, Carl Ratcliff, Twyla Tharp, Alvin Ailey, among others.

Student Performance Opportunities Performance opportunities are offered each semester, including the Student Choreography Concert, Spring Dance Concert, special choreography set by guest artists, and opportunities to perform in Jacksonville's First Coast *Nutcracker*. There are also opportunities for performance before audiences by participation in the Jacksonville University Dance Theatre, the dance performing ensemble of the University.

Special Programs The curriculum at Jacksonville University is based on the guidelines of the National Association of Dance of which the University is an accredited member. Students may choose to pursue a B.A., B.S., or B.F.A. in dance or receive dance certification with a B.A. or B.S. in dance education.

Jordan College of Fine Arts

See Butler University, Jordan College of Fine Arts

Juilliard School

New York, New York

Independent, coed. Urban campus. Total enrollment: 825.

Degrees Bachelor of Fine Arts in the area of dance. Majors: ballet, modern dance.

Dance Student Profile Fall 1994: 80 total; 77 matriculated undergraduate, 3 nondegree; 35% minorities, 65% females, 20% international.

Dance Faculty Total: 30; 8 full-time, 22 part-time. Graduate students do not teach undergraduate courses.

Student Life Special housing available for dance students.

Expenses for 1995–96 Application fee: $75. Comprehensive fee of $19,900 includes full-time tuition ($13,000), mandatory fees ($600), and college room and board ($6300).

Financial Aid Program-specific awards for Fall of 1994: 70 The Juilliard Scholarship Fund Awards for program majors ($7200–$12,200).

Application Procedures Deadline—freshmen and transfers: December 15. Notification date—freshmen and transfers: April 1. Required: essay, high school transcript, letter of recommendation, audition, health form. Recommended: minimum 2.0 high school GPA, interview, video. Auditions held 2 times on campus and off campus in Chicago, IL; San Francisco, CA; Dallas, TX; St. Petersburg, FL.

Undergraduate Contact Mary K. Gray, Director of Admissions, Juilliard School, 60 Lincoln Center Plaza, New York, New York 10023-6590; 212-799-5000 ext. 223.

Juilliard School *(continued)*

More about the College

The Juilliard Dance Division was established in 1951 by William Schuman during his tenure as President of the School. Under the guidance of Martha Hill, founding director of the division, Juilliard became the first major teaching institution ever to combine equal dance instruction in both modern and ballet techniques, an idea that was considered heretical in its day. Combining the best from the past and the present opens the dancer's eye and mind to exploring the new choreographic possibilities that lie ahead. Her program was a forecast of the future of dance in America, where ballet and modern dance companies routinely cross into one another's territory. Ms. Hill became Artistic Director Emeritus with the appointment of Muriel Topaz as Director in 1985. Since 1992, noted choreographer and artistic director Benjamin Harkarvy has been Director of the Juilliard Dance Division.

Graduates of the division have gone on to dance with virtually every established modern dance company in the United States and many others abroad. Juilliard graduates are also among the directors and administrators of respected companies. Among its alumni are noted dancers and choreographers such as Pina Bausch, Gregory Burge, Martha Clarke, Christine Dakin, Mercedes Ellington, Saeko Ichinohe, Lar Lubovitch, Francis Patrelle, Sebastian Prantl, and Paul Taylor.

The Dance Division offers a four-year course of study, its goal is to give dancers the essential tools enabling them to cross the bridge from dance studio to stage. Students may choose between pursuing a Bachelor of Fine Arts degree or a diploma. The core curriculum requires intensive technical study and performance in classical ballet and modern dance, and includes courses in repertory, pas de deux, point or mend's class, dance composition, Labanotation, anatomy, dance history, stagecraft, production, music theory, and keyboard studies. The dancers work in an enormous variety of repertory styles and techniques. Electives such as acting, voice, and tap are also offered. Juilliard dancers are expected to develop versatility, a keen stylistic sense, and an ease when working with choreographers, which makes them inspiring and desirable collaborators. Of particular note is the School's choreography training from beginning studies through advanced seminars with the renowned Bessie Schoöberg. The dance facilities at Juilliard include four specialized performance halls, two-story studios, classrooms, and teaching studios.

Throughout their four-year program, students participate in approximately 75 performances a year, including eight full-staged concerts and workshop presentations in the Juilliard Theater, informal workshops and tours with the Lincoln Center and Juilliard Student Programs. Masterworks are performed frequently and students are encouraged to present their own choreographed works in informal concerts and workshop showings, as well as in Juilliard's Alice Tully Hall *Wednesdays at One* series.

Next season, the Juilliard Dance Division will present a concert performance series in the Juilliard Theatre performed by the students enrolled in the Division. These concert series often feature major repertory works in addition to world premieres created for the Dance Division by noted choreographers, many of whom are Juilliard alumni. Last season's series featured the world premier of Lila York's *Rapture,* and revivals of Agnes De Mille's *Rodeo,* staged by Terrence Orr, and Benjamin Harkarvy's *Recital for Cello and Eight Dancers.* The annual workshop series to be conducted this season in conjunction with the Joseé Limon Dance Company, culminates a semester of study of the Limon technique, highlighted in performance by Juilliard Dance Ensemble members and the Limon Company. The workshops also will offer dance performance previews of the Spring series repertoire as well as ballet excerpts from the dance repertory workshops and works that tour as part of the Juilliard Dance Ensemble's program in metropolitan-area schools. In addition, student choreography from both the choreographers/composers collaborations as well as the advance composition projects (whose participants work with faculty member Bessie Schoöberg) will be included. The final dance workshops in the Juilliard Theatre, in May, spotlight both the performing skills and choreographic crafts of the Dance Division's soon-to-graduate class of 1996.

Student Performance Opportunities On the basis of capacity and achievement, students audition or are assigned to participate in several performances throughout the year. Each year there are fully staged public dance concerts, monthly workshop performances, and special projects. Students also tour local schools and perform in area hospitals and community centers. Fully staged performances feature standard repertory and commissioned works by both recognized and emerging choreographers, in a wide range of styles. Workshop performances are presented either on stage or in the studio, with programming selected from advanced classes, student choreography, and studies prepared in composition, notation, and other classes. In addition, Juilliard may host dance companies from across the United States and other countries who participate in discussions and informal workshops with students during their visits.

Alumni Juilliard's alumni are among the world's best-known dancers, choreographers, and company directors. Among its alumni are illustrious artists such as: Pina Bausch, Greg Burge, Martha Clarke, Mercedes Ellington, Richard Englund, Saeko Ichinohe, Lar Lubovitch, Carla Maxwell, Gregory Mitchell, Francis Patrelle, Joel Schnee, Paul Taylor, and Michael Utoff.

Lake Erie College

Painesville, Ohio

Independent, coed. Small-town campus. Total enrollment: 732.

Degrees Bachelor of Fine Arts in the area of dance. Majors: choreography and performance, dance.

Dance Student Profile Fall 1994: 6 total; all matriculated undergraduate.

Dance Faculty Total: 2; 2 part-time.

Expenses for 1995–96 Application fee: $20. Comprehensive fee of $17,226 includes full-time tuition ($11,840), mandatory fees ($480), and college room and board ($4906). Part-time tuition: $356 per semester hour. Part-time mandatory fees: $15 per semester.

Application Procedures Deadline—freshmen: July 1; transfers: August 20. Required: essay, high school transcript, minimum 2.0 high school GPA, 2 letters of recommendation, SAT I or ACT test scores. Recommended: interview.

Undergraduate Contact Paul Gothard, Director, Fine Arts Department, Lake Erie College, 391 West Washington Street, Painesville, Ohio 44077; 216-639-7856.

Marymount Manhattan College

New York, New York

Independent, coed. Urban campus. Total enrollment: 1,973.

Degrees Bachelor of Fine Arts in the area of dance. Majors: ballet, modern dance.

Dance Student Profile Fall 1994: 75 total; all matriculated undergraduate.

Dance Faculty Total: 15; 3 full-time, 12 part-time.

Expenses for 1995–96 Application fee: $30. Tuition: $11,200 full-time, $325 per credit part-time. Part-time mandatory fees: $85 per term. Full-time mandatory fees: $250. College room only: $5200.

Application Procedures Deadline—freshmen and transfers: March 15. Required: high school transcript, 2 letters of recommendation, audition, SAT I or ACT test scores. Auditions held 4 times on campus; videotaped performances are permissible as a substitute for live auditions when distance is prohibitive.

Undergraduate Contact Haila Strauss, Director, Department of Dance, Marymount Manhattan College, 221 East 71st Street, New York, New York 10021; 212-517-0651.

Mason Gross School of the Arts

See Rutgers, The State University of New Jersey, Mason Gross School of the Arts

Meadows School of the Arts

See Southern Methodist University, Meadows School of the Arts

Montclair State University

Upper Montclair, New Jersey

State-supported, coed. Suburban campus. Total enrollment: 12,675.

Degrees Bachelor of Fine Arts in the area of dance.

Dance Student Profile Fall 1994: 30 total; all matriculated undergraduate; 2% minorities, 97% females, 2% international.

Dance Faculty Total: 8; 2 full-time, 6 part-time; 50% of full-time faculty have terminal degrees. Graduate students do not teach undergraduate courses. Undergraduate student–faculty ratio: 7:1.

Student Life Student groups include Danceworks, Musicals, American College Dance Festival.

Expenses for 1994–95 Application fee: $35. State resident tuition: $3000 full-time, $94.50 per semester hour part-time. Nonresident tuition: $4248 full-time, $133.50 per semester hour part-time. College room and board: $4834. College room only: $3160.

Application Procedures Deadline—freshmen: March 1; transfers: May 1. Required: high school transcript, minimum 2.0 high school GPA, interview, audition. Auditions held continuously on campus; videotaped performances are permissible as a substitute for live auditions for international students and U.S. students when distance is prohibitive.

Undergraduate Contact Lori Katterhenry, Program Coordinator, Division of Dance, Montclair State University, Normal Avenue, Upper Montclair, New Jersey 07043; 201-655-7080, fax: 201-256-4260.

Tisch School of the Arts

New York University

New York, New York

Independent, coed. Urban campus. Total enrollment: 33,428.

Degrees Bachelor of Fine Arts in the area of dance. Majors: dance. Graduate degrees offered: Master of Fine Arts in the area of dance.

Dance Student Profile Fall 1994: 107 total; 75 matriculated undergraduate, 32 matriculated graduate.

Dance Faculty Total: 21; 7 full-time, 14 part-time. Graduate students do not teach undergraduate courses. Undergraduate student–faculty ratio: 5:1.

Student Life Student groups include Artists in the Community, Out Artists, United Artists of Color.

Expenses for 1994–95 Application fee: $45. Comprehensive fee of $26,001 includes full-time tuition ($18,739) and college room and board ($7262). Part-time tuition: $513 per credit. Part-time mandatory fees per semester range from $96 to $426.

Financial Aid Program-specific awards for Fall of 1994 available.

Application Procedures Deadline—freshmen: January 15; transfers: April 1. Notification date—freshmen: April 1; transfers: May 15. Required: essay, high school transcript, college transcript(s) for transfer students, letter of recommendation, audition, SAT I or ACT test scores. Recommended: minimum 3.0 high school GPA, interview. Auditions held continuously November through April on campus and off campus in Chicago, IL; San Francisco, CA; videotaped performances are permissible

New York University *(continued)*

as a substitute for live auditions for international applicants or with approval from the department.

Undergraduate Contact Dan Sandford, Office of Graduate Admissions, New York University, 721 Broadway, 7th Floor, New York, New York 10003-6807; 212-998-1918.

More about the Department

Program Facilities Tisch students study ballet and contemporary techniques and explore choreographic skills in six spacious sprung-floor studios equipped with pianos. Tisch dancers give approximately fifteen concerts a year in their own recently renovated 200-seat proscenium theater. Although students are enrolled in a conservatory program, they have access to all the educational opportunities offered at New York University.

Permanent Faculty Kay Cummings, Chair, Susan Aberth, Andre Bernard, Sergio Cervetti, Elizabeth Frankel, Kathy Grant, Mark Haim, Deborah Jowitt, Phyllis Lamhut, Cherylyn Lavagnino, James Martin, Chad McArver, William Moulton, Tere O'Connor, Cassandra Phifer, JoAnna Mendl Shaw, Gus Solomons Jr., James Sutton, Linda Tarnay, Jennifer Way, Gwen Welliver.

Recent Guest Choreographers Bill T. Jones, Ralph Lemon, Bebe Miller, Mark Morris, David Parsons, Paul Taylor, Twyla Tharp, Doug Varone.

Student Performance Opportunities Performance opportunities are plentiful. In the final year, students can gain professional experience with the Second Avenue Dance Company, which presents a series of performances featuring works by students and noted guest choreographers. Concerts have won favorable reviews in *The New York Times, the Village Voice,* and other newspapers.

Special Programs Tisch students may earn a B.F.A degree in dance in an intensive three-year, two-summer program as well as the traditional four-year curriculum. The department offers 2 three-week intensive summer workshops to serve the intermediate-to-advanced dance student who is preparing to enter the profession. The department selects six different companies to be in residence. The 1995 Summer Residency Festival companies are Creach/Koester, David Dorfman Dance, Doug Elkins Dance Company, Bebe Miller company, Shapiro & Smith Dance, and Doug Varone and Dancers.

North Carolina School of the Arts

Winston-Salem, North Carolina

State-supported, coed. Urban campus. Total enrollment: 613.

Degrees Bachelor of Fine Arts in the area of dance. Majors: ballet.

Dance Student Profile Fall 1994: 183 total; 75 matriculated undergraduate, 108 nondegree.

Dance Faculty Total: 15; 13 full-time, 2 part-time. Graduate students do not teach undergraduate courses. Undergraduate student–faculty ratio: 8:1.

Expenses for 1994–95 State resident tuition: $1233 full-time. Nonresident tuition: $8640 full-time. Full-time mandatory fees: $766. College room and board: $3600. College room only: $2376. Special program-related fees: $135 for instructional fees.

Financial Aid Program-specific awards for Fall of 1994: Talent Scholarships for artistically talented.

Application Procedures Deadline—freshmen and transfers: March 1. Required: high school transcript, 2 letters of recommendation, interview, audition. Auditions held by request on campus and off campus in various cities in the U.S.; videotaped performances are permissible as a substitute for live auditions for provisional acceptance.

Undergraduate Contact Carol J. Palm, Director of Admissions, North Carolina School of the Arts, 200 Waughtown Street, Winston-Salem, North Carolina 27117; 910-770-3291, fax: 910-770-3370, E-mail address: palmc@ ncsavx.ncarts.edu.

More about the School

Program Facilities Dance concerts featuring ballet and contemporary dance are presented at the Stevens Center, a magnificently restored 1920s movie palace seating 1,380 in downtown Winston-Salem. On campus, Agnes de Mille Theatre is a 188-seat performance space used mainly for dance concerts. Dance classes and rehearsals are conducted in modern, clerestory-lit, air-conditioned dance studios, which feature "sprung" floors specially designed for dancers. The School of the Arts also has a dance costume shop and provides complete dance production support through its own School of Design and Production.

Faculty, Guest Artists and Alumni The resident faculty of artist-teachers features distinguished professionals who have danced and/or choreographed for some of the world's finest companies, including American Ballet Theatre, New York City Ballet, Netherlands Dance Theatre, Martha Graham, and Murray Louis. In addition, internationally renowned guest artists frequently visit to teach, coach, choreograph, or restage works for performance by students. The Lucia Chase Endowed Fellowship supports week-long residencies by some of the world's most respected dancers; these have included Margot Fonteyn, Agnes de Mille, Jacques d'Amboise, and Arthur Mitchell. School of Dance graduates are currently performing in major companies throughout the world and can be found at the creative vanguard of contemporary dance. Noted alumni include Janie Parker, principal, Houston Ballet; Victor Barbee, principal, American Ballet Theatre; Mark Dendy, Dendy Dance; and Peter Pucci, artistic director, Peter Pucci Plus Dancers.

Student Performance Opportunities The School of Dance has a growing repertory of classical and contemporary dance unsurpassed in its diversity and challenge. Each year, students perform more than forty workshops and public performances, including an annual tour of *The Nutcracker*. These performance opportunities develop the dance student's versatility, a trademark of the School's alumni.

Ohio State University

Columbus, Ohio

State-supported, coed. Urban campus. Total enrollment: 49,542.

Degrees Bachelor of Fine Arts in the areas of performance, dance education. Majors: modern dance. Graduate degrees offered: Master of Fine Arts in the areas of choreography, performance, lighting, directing in Labanotation.

Dance Student Profile Fall 1994: 110 total; 80 matriculated undergraduate, 30 matriculated graduate; 20% minorities, 90% females, 4% international.

Dance Faculty Total: 22; 15 full-time, 7 part-time; 75% of full-time faculty have terminal degrees. Graduate students teach a few undergraduate courses. Undergraduate student–faculty ratio: 4:1.

Expenses for 1995–96 Application fee: $30. State resident tuition: $3273 full-time. Nonresident tuition: $9813 full-time. Part-time tuition per quarter ranges from $179 to $1001 for state residents, $361 to $2999 for nonresidents. College room and board: $4668.

Application Procedures Deadline—freshmen: February 15; transfers: June 25. Required: high school transcript, college transcript(s) for transfer students, audition, SAT I or ACT test scores. Recommended: letter of recommendation, interview. Auditions held 2 times on campus; videotaped performances are permissible as a substitute for live auditions for international applicants.

Contact Ellie Breckman, Graduate Secretary, Dance Department, Ohio State University, Sullivant Hall, 1813 North High Street, Columbus, Ohio 43210-1307; 614-292-7977.

Ohio University

Athens, Ohio

State-supported, coed. Small-town campus. Total enrollment: 18,855.

Degrees Bachelor of Fine Arts in the area of dance. Majors: dance.

Dance Student Profile Fall 1994: 48 total; all matriculated undergraduate; 8% minorities, 96% females, 3% international.

Dance Faculty Total: 7; 6 full-time, 1 part-time; 66% of full-time faculty have terminal degrees. Undergraduate student–faculty ratio: 10:1.

Student Life Student groups include The Movement (student performance organization), Dance Factory (local dance studio).

Expenses for 1995–96 Application fee: $25. State resident tuition: $3666 full-time, $118 per quarter hour part-time. Nonresident tuition: $7905 full-time, $259 per quarter hour part-time. College room and board: $4260. College room only: $2094.

Financial Aid Program-specific awards for Fall of 1994: 4–5 Provost Scholarships for talented students ($1000), 1 Ruiz-Lewis Scholarship for minorities and males ($500), 1 Bailin-Stern Scholarship for talented students ($400–$500), 1 Hazeland Carr Liggett Award for talented students ($800), 1–2 Shirley Wimmer Award for talented students ($1000–$1200), 1 Betsy Milhandler Award for talented students ($500).

Application Procedures Deadline—freshmen: February 1; transfers: May 30. Notification date—freshmen: March 15; transfers: June 15. Required: college transcript(s) for transfer students, 3 letters of recommendation, audition, SAT I or ACT test scores. Recommended: high school transcript, minimum 3.0 high school GPA, interview. Auditions held 2 times on campus; videotaped performances are permissible as a substitute for live auditions when distance is prohibitive.

Undergraduate Contact Teresa Holland, School Secretary, School of Dance, Ohio University, Putnam Hall 222, Athens, Ohio 45701; 614-593-1826, fax: 614-593-0749.

Point Park College

Pittsburgh, Pennsylvania

Independent, coed. Urban campus. Total enrollment: 2,397.

Degrees Bachelor of Fine Arts in the areas of ballet, modern dance, jazz, arts management. Majors: arts management, ballet, jazz dance, modern dance. Cross-registration with Carnegie Mellon University, University of Pittsburgh, Chatham College, Robert Morris College, Duquesne University, Carlow College.

Dance Student Profile Fall 1994: 143 total; all matriculated undergraduate; 20% minorities, 90% females, 10% international.

Dance Faculty Total: 16; 9 full-time, 7 part-time; 80% of full-time faculty have terminal degrees. Graduate students do not teach undergraduate courses. Undergraduate student–faculty ratio: 24:1.

Student Life Student groups include Student Choreography Showcase, American College Dance Festival.

Expenses for 1995–96 Application fee: $20. Comprehensive fee of $15,624 includes full-time tuition ($10,552) and college room and board ($5072). Part-time tuition: $275 per credit. Special program-related fees: $265 for voice/piano private lessons, $20–$60 for music course fees, $335 for lab fees.

Financial Aid Program-specific awards for Fall of 1994: 8–42 Golden Key and Academic Scholarships for those demonstrating talent and academic achievement ($2500–$9000), 24–35 Dance Scholarships for those demonstrating talent and academic achievement ($500–$2000), 39–50 Talent Scholarships for those demonstrating academic achievement and talent ($500–$3500).

Application Procedures Deadline—freshmen and transfers: June 1. Required: college transcript(s) for transfer students, minimum 2.0 high school GPA, letter of recommendation, audition, SAT I or ACT test scores. Auditions held 5 times on campus and off campus in Louisville, KY; San Juan, PR; Miami, FL; Arizona;

Point Park College *(continued)*

videotaped performances are permissible as a substitute for live auditions if distance is prohibitive or in special circumstances.

Undergraduate Contact Joseph McGoldrick, Assistant to the Chair, Department of Fine, Applied and Performing Arts, Point Park College, 201 Wood Street, Pittsburgh, Pennsylvania 15222; 800-321-0129.

More about the College

The program of Fine, Applied, and Performing Arts (FAPA) is conservatory-oriented within a liberal arts context. Students receive intense grounding in their specialty and a well-rounded education. Because the faculty of PAPA believes that performing arts majors develop best in front of a live audience, the program offers many performing opportunities for students at The Playhouse of Point Park College.

Nationally renowned, The Playhouse (formerly called "The Pittsburgh Playhouse") is the performance facility for the Department of Fine, Applied, and Performing Arts. Here, students participate in live theater experiences before a subscription audience. Containing three working theaters, this sixty-year-old facility is fully staffed by a production team of designers and artisans who train and supervise student apprentices in building, designing, lighting, and managing shows. The front-of-house staff, box office, and public relations personnel engage all students in the full range of theater operations. The season, which features student actors, dancers, designers and stage managers, consists of five Playhouse Junior Shows for children; four College Theater Company dramas and musicals; and two Playhouse Theater Company presentations for professional faculty, alumni, visiting artists, and selected undergraduates, who perform in them.

The dance students are featured in three Playhouse Dance Theater productions, plus a Playhouse Junior Children's Ballet, as well as public school outreach program in cooperation with the Gateway to Music organization.

Arts management majors receive practical on-stage experience as well as training in business, public relations, and budgeting, which culminate in two major internships with arts groups outside the College.

The newly formed stage management concentration similarly requires outside internships.

The innovative children's theater degree provides opportunities for majors to plan, teach, and direct creative drama activities. Venues for these opportunities exist within the Children's School of the Education Department, Playhouse Junior, and classes offered by the Community Conservatories of Dance, Music, and Theater.

Pittsburgh is a vibrant arts and education center. FAPA students can reach the Pittsburgh Symphony, Opera, Ballet, Dance Council, and public theaters, as well as eight other institutions of higher learning, within a 15-minute drive. The whole city is, in a sense, a performance laboratory.

Faculty FAPA teachers are working professionals in their specialties of acting, singing, dancing, choreographing, writing, composing, painting, designing, and more. Additional guest and master teachers in musical theater, voice and speech, and dance are a regular feature. Guest artists have included Cicely Berry, Paul Gavert, Albert Poland, Barbara Pontecorvo, Edward Villella, Maxine Sherman, and Claire Bataille.

Alumni FAPA has over 150 graduates performing in touring companies, on Broadway, in dance groups, in movies, on television, and in other theaters, as well as many more teaching in schools, on faculties, choreographing, writing, directing, and stage managing across the world. Within the last eighteen months, our graduates have had roles in New York and national touring productions of *Carousel, Cats, Gentleman Prefer Blondes, Joseph and the Technicolor Dreamcoat, Tommy, Damn Yankees, The rink, and Kiss of the Spider Women.* Others have also appeared on screen in *Pulp Fiction* and *NYPD Blue.*

Special Programs Eight dance studios; three theater complexes at The Playhouse of Point Park College; performance opportunities for students in front of subscription audiences; on-site costume/set construction apprenticeships; nine private signing and piano instructors; college choir; art and design classes; 100 dance classes per week, 12:1 student faculty ratio.

During the summer, there is an International Summer Dance program (open by audition and special registration only) featuring renowned performers in the world of dance. The six-week session offers jazz, ballet, and modern dance from a distinguished faculty including Laura Alonso, Roberto Muniz, Miguel Canpaneira, Alexander Filipov, Michael Uthoff, and Whilheim Burman.

Prospective students must apply and be accepted by the College. An audition or an interview by faculty members are required of all majors. Training scholarships and apprenticeships ranging from $750 to $2500 are available. Additional scholarship support may be available to students with distinguished academic credentials.

Fees and Tuition Full-time tuition: $10,000; room and board: $5,072; private voice and/or piano: $265 per term, performing arts fee: $356 per term.

Potter College of Arts, Humanities, and Social Sciences

See Western Kentucky University, Potter College of Arts, Humanities, and Social Sciences

Purchase College, State University of New York

Purchase, New York

State-supported, coed. Small-town campus. Total enrollment: 2,498.

Degrees Bachelor of Fine Arts in the area of dance. Majors: ballet, composition, modern dance, production.

Dance Student Profile Fall 1994: 120 total; all matriculated undergraduate; 20% minorities, 4% international.

Dance Faculty Total: 17; 9 full-time, 8 part-time; 100% of full-time faculty have terminal degrees. Graduate students do not teach undergraduate courses. Undergraduate student–faculty ratio: 16:1.

Student Life Student groups include lecture/demonstrations to local schools, national and international performance tours, Purchase Dance Corps.

Expenses for 1995–96 Application fee: $25. State resident tuition: $3400 full-time, $137 per credit part-time. Nonresident tuition: $8300 full-time, $346 per credit part-time. Part-time mandatory fees: $13.30 per credit. Full-time mandatory fees: $399. College room and board: $4872. College room only: $3130.

Financial Aid Program-specific awards for Fall of 1994: 1–5 In Praise of Merit Scholarships for those demonstrating need/talent ($500–$1000), 2 Bales/Fernandez Scholarships for talented students ($1000), 2 Jane Falk Scholarships for talented students ($500).

Application Procedures Deadline—freshmen and transfers: June 1. Notification date—freshmen and transfers: August 1. Required: high school transcript, college transcript(s) for transfer students, audition. Recommended: SAT I or ACT test scores. Auditions held 7 times on campus and off campus in Miami, FL; Chicago, IL; San Francisco, CA: Los Angeles, CA; Interlochen, MI; videotaped performances are permissible as a substitute for live auditions for international applicants and applicants from Hawaii.

Undergraduate Contact Meryl Wiener, Dance Admissions Counselor, Office of Admissions, Purchase College, State University of New York, 735 Anderson Hill Road, Purchase, New York 10577-1400; 914-251-6307, fax: 914-251-6314.

More about the College

Facilities Award-winning dance building; largest specially built facility designed in the United States exclusively for the training and performance of dance; nine fully equipped, light-filled studios; 270-seat Dance Theatre Lab; two Pilates studios, Performing Arts Center, with four theaters for student concerts.

Faculty Faculty have performed with Martha Graham, Merce Cunningham, Alvin Ailey, Jose Limon, Viola Farber, New York City Ballet, The American Ballet Theatre, and the Joffrey Ballet. They choreography, teach, or set masterworks in Asia, Europe, or South America. They produce their own work in Manhattan. They teach the students daily. Musicians accompany every technique class. Alumni perform with major American and international companies, are founders of their own company, or are freelance choreographers. Classes are held with guest teachers from the Professional Performing Arts Center Dance Series.

Performance Opportunities Students are required to perform. The Purchase Dance Corps is the performing company of the Dance Division. Students, selected by audition, present two concerts annually of major professional repertory, including modern works by Paul Taylor and Mark Morris, ballets by George Balanchine and Lew Christianson, reconstructions by Doris Humphrey and Charles Weidman, international choreographers Lin Hwai Min and Robert Cohan, and emerging choreographers and faculty works created especially for the Purchase Dance Corps in the Performing Arts Center. Additional performing opportunities: seven weekends of senior project concerts in the Dance Theatre Lab, special fund-raising events and galas.

Special Programs Student exchange programs in dance in London, Amsterdam, Rotterdam, or Taipei; Arts Management certificate; physical therapist available two days per week.

Purchase is an excellent conservatory program from which to launch a career in dance. Why? Because it offers professional, comprehensive, in-depth, personalized training in modern dance and classical ballet.

Performance credits are required for graduation. Students may perform in the Purchase Dance Corps concerts, tours, senior projects, lecture demonstrations, galas and fund-raising events, student concerts, studio showings, and workshops. Performance of a major professional repertory piece is required for the senior project. Purchase Dance Corps Tours have included Hong Kong (1987 and 1990); Amsterdam (1991); Taipei (1992); Beijing, China (1994); and Taiwan (1995).

The four-year composition program involves each student in performance of a sophomore, junior, and senior project which is mentored by a faculty member and monitored by the faculty project committee. The senior project concerts, coproduced by 3 to 4 seniors in the Dance Theatre Lab, are the culminating events that serve as a bridge to the profession.

The Dance Division faculty is active in the profession as choreographers, teachers, coaches, musicians, and performers. Alumni are performing or have performed in the Martha Graham Dance Co., the Merce Cunningham Dance Co., the Trisha Brown Dance Co., the Frankfurt Ballet, the Houston Ballet, the Parsons Co., the Mark Morris Dance Co., American Ballet Theatre, the Feld Ballets N.Y., the Paul Taylor Dance Co., and the Bill T. Jones/Arnie Zane Co. An extensive listing of alumni accomplishments is available upon request.

The Performing Arts Center provides professional theaters in which students perform and concerts are sponsored by major contemporary and classical companies. Each company provides a master class for students. These have included the Miami City Ballet, Alvin Ailey, Dance Theatre of Harlem, Paul Taylor, Brenda Daniels, and Bill T. Jones.

The B.F.A. degree conservatory professional training program requires 120 credits to graduate: 90 credits in the professional dance curriculum, 30 credits in liberal arts. The program emphasizes modern dance technique, classical ballet technique, performance, and choreography. Students take classical ballet and modern dance technique daily, anatomy for dance, music for dance, dance history, dance production, improvisation, ballet and modern partnering, and pointe.

Purchase College is 45 minutes north of New York City in a suburban setting where students have the best of both worlds. They reside on campus in residence halls or apartment complexes with students from the Music, Theatre Arts and Film, Visual Arts, and Letters and Science Divisions. The ease of living in a campus setting combined with the cultural advantages of Manhattan allows the student's artistic stimulation and knowledge of the real challenges they will face upon graduation. They travel to the city to attend concerts, take classes, go to auditions, visit museums, and absorb the rich culture.

Purchase College, State University of New York
(continued)

New York City serves an important purpose in the education of these future artists. It is the reality check and the constant reminder of what the College works for in its program.

"For a number of years, the Dance Division of the State University College at Purchase has been turning out more than its fair share of the most interesting and skillful professional dancers working in New York City."—Jennifer Dunning, *The New York Times.*

Radford University

Radford, Virginia

State-supported, coed. Small-town campus. Total enrollment: 9,105.

Degrees Bachelor of Fine Arts in the areas of classical dance, contemporary dance. Majors: ballet, dance, modern dance.

Dance Student Profile Fall 1994: 9% minorities, 91% females.

Dance Faculty Total: 5; 4 full-time, 1 part-time; 75% of full-time faculty have terminal degrees. Graduate students do not teach undergraduate courses. Undergraduate student–faculty ratio: 18:1.

Expenses for 1995–96 Application fee: $15. State resident tuition: $3114 full-time, $130 per semester hour part-time. Nonresident tuition: $7688 full-time, $321 per semester hour part-time. College room and board: $4250.

Financial Aid Program-specific awards for Fall of 1994: 7 Arts Society Scholarships for talented program students ($700).

Application Procedures Deadline—freshmen and transfers: continuous. Required: essay, high school transcript, minimum 2.0 high school GPA, audition. Auditions held continuously by appointment on campus; videotaped performances are permissible as a substitute for live auditions when distance is prohibitive.

Undergraduate Contact Chris Knauer, Director of Admissions, Radford University, P.O. Box 6904, Radford, Virginia 24142; 540-831-5271, fax: 540-831-5138.

Mason Gross School of the Arts

Rutgers, The State University of New Jersey

New Brunswick, New Jersey

State-supported, coed. Small-town campus. Total enrollment: 647.

Degrees Bachelor of Fine Arts in the area of dance. Majors: modern dance.

Dance Student Profile Fall 1994: 364 total; 39 matriculated undergraduate, 325 nondegree; 10% minorities, 95% females, 1% international.

Dance Faculty Total: 9; 6 full-time, 3 part-time; 100% of full-time faculty have terminal degrees. Graduate students do not teach undergraduate courses. Undergraduate student–faculty ratio: 15:1.

Student Life Student groups include University Dance Works.

Expenses for 1995–96 Application fee: $50. State resident tuition: $3786 full-time, $122.50 per credit hour part-time. Nonresident tuition: $7707 full-time, $249.75 per credit hour part-time. Mandatory fees range from $105 to $1045 full-time, $155 to $187 per year part-time, according to college of affiliation. College room and board: $4253.

Application Procedures Deadline—freshmen: February 15; transfers: March 15. Notification date—freshmen and transfers: continuous. Required: high school transcript, college transcript(s) for transfer students, interview, video, audition, SAT I or ACT test scores. Recommended: letter of recommendation. Auditions held 5 times on campus and off campus in Baltimore, MD: Minneapolis, MN; videotaped performances are permissible as a substitute for live auditions when distance is prohibitive. Portfolio reviews held on campus and off campus.

Undergraduate Contact Office of Undergraduate Admissions, Rutgers, The State University of New Jersey, P.O. Box 2101, New Brunswick, New Jersey 08903-2101; 908-932-3777.

Sam Houston State University

Huntsville, Texas

State-supported, coed. Small-town campus. Total enrollment: 12,906.

Degrees Bachelor of Fine Arts in the area of dance. Majors: dance. Graduate degrees offered: Master of Fine Arts in the area of dance.

Dance Student Profile Fall 1994: 464 total; 44 matriculated undergraduate, 5 matriculated graduate, 415 nondegree.

Dance Faculty Total: 4; 3 full-time, 1 part-time; 100% of full-time faculty have terminal degrees. Graduate students teach about a quarter undergraduate courses. Undergraduate student–faculty ratio: 14:1.

Student Life Student groups include Chi Tau Epsilon (dance honor society).

Expenses for 1994–95 State resident tuition: $896 full-time. Nonresident tuition: $5472 full-time, $171 per semester hour part-time. State resident part-time tuition per semester ranges from $100 to $308. Part-time mandatory fees per semester range from $76 to $303. Full-time mandatory fees: $706. College room and board: $3070. College room only: $1530.

Application Procedures Deadline—freshmen and transfers: continuous. Required: high school transcript, college

transcript(s) for transfer students, minimum 2.0 high school GPA, SAT I or ACT test scores, minimum combined SAT I score of 900, minimum composite ACT score of 21. Recommended: 2 letters of recommendation, audition. Auditions held 2 times on campus; videotaped performances are permissible as a substitute for live auditions with permission of the Program Coordinator.

Contact Dana Eugene Nicolay, Program Coordinator, Dance Program, Division of Theatre and Dance, Sam Houston State University, P.O. Box 2269, Huntsville, Texas 77341-2269; 409-294-1875, fax: 409-294-1598, E-mail address: dnc_dxn@shsu.edu.

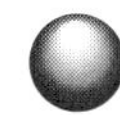

San Diego State University

San Diego, California

State-supported, coed. Urban campus. Total enrollment: 27,787.

Degrees Bachelor of Arts/Bachelor of Fine Arts in the area of dance. Majors: dance.

Dance Student Profile Fall 1994: 225 total; 25 matriculated undergraduate, 200 nondegree; 20% minorities, 90% females, 5% international.

Dance Faculty Total: 7; 4 full-time, 3 part-time; 2% of full-time faculty have terminal degrees. Undergraduate student–faculty ratio: 21:1.

Student Life Student groups include TRIBE (student organization composed of visual and performing arts students).

Expenses for 1994–95 State resident tuition: $0 full-time. Nonresident tuition: $7646 full-time, $246 per unit part-time. Part-time mandatory fees: $618 per semester. Full-time mandatory fees: $1902. College room and board: $4397.

Financial Aid Program-specific awards for Fall of 1994: 2 Scholarships for dance majors ($300).

Application Procedures Deadline—freshmen and transfers: continuous. Notification date—freshmen and transfers: continuous. Required: high school transcript, college transcript(s) for transfer students, minimum 2.0 high school GPA, SAT I or ACT test scores. Recommended: interview, audition. Auditions held on campus and off campus. Portfolio reviews held on campus and off campus.

Undergraduate Contact Melissa Nunn, Undergraduate Advisor - Dance, School of Music and Dance, San Diego State University, San Diego, California 92182-7902; 619-594-6031, fax: 619-594-1692.

Shenandoah University

Winchester, Virginia

Independent-religious, coed. Small-town campus. Total enrollment: 1,652.

Degrees Bachelor of Fine Arts in the areas of dance, dance education. Majors: dance, dance education.

Dance Student Profile Fall 1994: 19 total; all matriculated undergraduate; 11% minorities, 95% females.

Dance Faculty Total: 9; 3 full-time, 6 part-time; 67% of full-time faculty have terminal degrees. Graduate students do not teach undergraduate courses. Undergraduate student–faculty ratio: 2:1.

Student Life Student groups include Dance Sensations, Outreach Programs (Show Makers), American College Dance Festival Association.

Expenses for 1995–96 Application fee: $30. Comprehensive fee of $16,270 includes full-time tuition ($11,470)

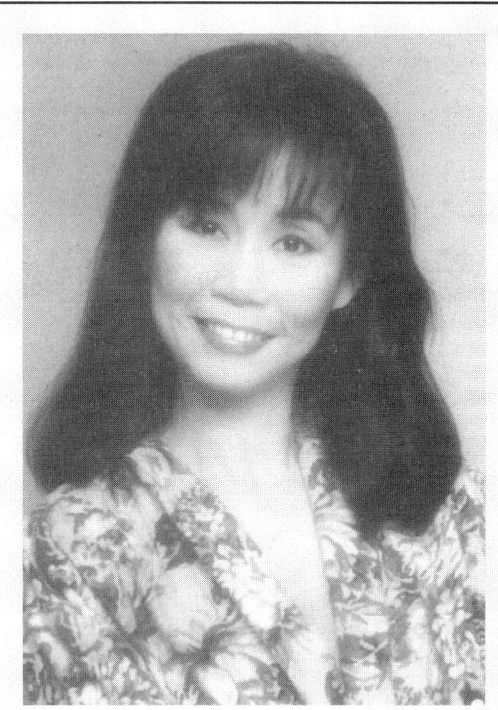

Lai Keun, Leong

University of Hawaii, Manoa—Lecturer, School of Physical Education, National Institute of Education/Nanyang Technological University

The University of Hawaii, Manoa, Department of Dance and Theatre offers not only classes in modern dance and ballet but also ethnic dances and Hula. In addition, drama courses, such as creative drama and puppetry are offered. Most of the ethnic dance courses are run by staff who are established artists with years of performance and teaching experience. Students in the dance department are given much freedom in the planning of course work to suit their interests and ability. The student population is a truly international mix.

Shenandoah University *(continued)*

and college room and board ($4800). Part-time tuition: $360 per semester hour.

Financial Aid Program-specific awards for Fall of 1994: 12 Talent Scholarships for program majors ($1000).

Application Procedures Deadline—freshmen and transfers: continuous. Required: high school transcript, college transcript(s) for transfer students, minimum 2.0 high school GPA, interview, video, audition, SAT I or ACT test scores. Recommended: letter of recommendation. Auditions held 5 times on campus and off campus in various cities; videotaped performances are permissible as a substitute for live auditions if a campus visit is impossible.

Undergraduate Contact Michael Carpenter, Director, Admissions Office, Shenandoah University, 1460 University Drive, Winchester, Virginia 22601-5195; 540-665-4581, fax: 540-665-4627, E-mail address: admit@su.edu.

Simon Fraser University

Burnaby, British Columbia

Province-supported, coed. Suburban campus. Total enrollment: 18,252.

Degrees Bachelor of Fine Arts in the area of contemporary dance. Majors: dance. Graduate degrees offered: Master of Fine Arts in the area of interdisciplinary studies.

Dance Student Profile Fall 1994: 168 total; all matriculated undergraduate.

Dance Faculty Total: 7; 7 full-time; 42% of full-time faculty have terminal degrees. Graduate students teach a few undergraduate courses. Undergraduate student–faculty ratio: 24:1.

Student Life Student groups include Off Centre Dance Company.

Expenses for 1994–95 Application fee: $20. Canadian resident tuition: $2190 full-time, $73 per credit hour part-time. Nonresident tuition: $6570 full-time, $219 per credit hour part-time. Part-time mandatory fees: $50 per trimester. (All figures are in Canadian dollars.). Full-time mandatory fees: $178. College room only: $2120.

Financial Aid Program-specific awards for Fall of 1994: 5 Adaline May Clark Scholarships for program majors ($100–$500), 1 Murray Farr Award for program majors ($500).

Application Procedures Deadline—freshmen and transfers: May 1. Required: high school transcript, college transcript(s) for transfer students, minimum 3.0 high school GPA, interview, audition. Auditions held 2 times on campus and off campus; videotaped performances are permissible as a substitute for live auditions for international applicants. Portfolio reviews held on campus and off campus.

Undergraduate Contact Admissions Office, Simon Fraser University, Burnaby, British Columbia V5A 1S6, Canada; 604-291-3224, fax: 604-291-4969.

Meadows School of the Arts

Southern Methodist University

Dallas, Texas

Independent-religious, coed. Suburban campus. Total enrollment: 9,014.

Degrees Bachelor of Fine Arts in the area of dance performance. Majors: ballet, jazz dance, modern dance. Graduate degrees offered: Master of Fine Arts in the area of choreographic theory and practice.

Dance Student Profile Fall 1994: 100 total; 82 matriculated undergraduate, 3 matriculated graduate, 15 nondegree; 16% minorities, 85% females, 1% international.

Dance Faculty Total: 11; 8 full-time, 3 part-time; 80% of full-time faculty have terminal degrees. Graduate students do not teach undergraduate courses. Undergraduate student–faculty ratio: 10:1.

Student Life Student groups include American Dance Festival. Special housing available for dance students.

Expenses for 1994–95 Application fee: $40. Comprehensive fee of $19,474 includes full-time tuition ($12,772), mandatory fees ($1624), and college room and board ($5078). College room only: $2426. Part-time tuition: $532 per credit hour. Part-time mandatory fees: $68 per semester.

Financial Aid Program-specific awards for Fall of 1994: 20 Meadows Artistic Scholarships for talented program majors ($1000–$5000).

Application Procedures Deadline—freshmen and transfers: continuous. Required: essay, high school transcript, college transcript(s) for transfer students, letter of recommendation, audition, SAT I or ACT test scores. Recommended: interview. Auditions held 20 times on campus and off campus in various locations; videotaped performances are permissible as a substitute for live auditions when distance is prohibitive.

Undergraduate Contact Charles J. Helfert, Associate Dean, Meadows School of the Arts, Southern Methodist University, P.O. Box 750356, Dallas, Texas 75275-0356; 214-768-3217, fax: 214-768-3272.

Graduate Contact Jeannette Garnsey, Director, Graduate Admissions and Records, Meadows School of the Arts, Southern Methodist University, P.O. Box 750356, Dallas, Texas 75275-0356; 214-768-3765, fax: 214-768-3272.

Southwest Missouri State University

Springfield, Missouri

State-supported, coed. Suburban campus. Total enrollment: 17,310.

Degrees Bachelor of Fine Arts in the area of dance. Majors: dance.

Dance Student Profile Fall 1994: 26 total; all matriculated undergraduate; 5% minorities, 90% females.

Dance Faculty Total: 5; 4 full-time, 1 part-time; 67% of full-time faculty have terminal degrees. Graduate students do not teach undergraduate courses. Undergraduate student–faculty ratio: 12:1.

Student Life Student groups include Inertia Dance Company, Footnotes Entertainment Troupe.

Expenses for 1995–96 Application fee: $15. State resident tuition: $2370 full-time, $79 per credit hour part-time. Nonresident tuition: $4898 full-time. Part-time mandatory fees per semester range from $41 to $88. Part-time tuition per credit hour for nonresidents: $79 for the first 3 credits, $158 for the next 8 credits. Full-time mandatory fees: $176. College room and board: $2722 (minimum). College room only: $1755 (minimum).

Financial Aid Program-specific awards for Fall of 1994: 4 Dance Activity Awards for program majors ($1700), 2 Out-of-State Waivers for program majors ($2550), 8 Footnotes Entertainment Troupe Awards for program majors ($1700).

Application Procedures Deadline—freshmen and transfers: August 1. Notification date—freshmen and transfers: continuous. Required: high school transcript, minimum 2.0 high school GPA, ACT test score only, minimum composite ACT score of 18, standing in top 67% of graduating class.

Undergraduate Contact Robert H. Bradley, Head, Department of Theatre and Dance, Southwest Missouri State University, 901 South National, Springfield, Missouri 65804; 417-836-5268, fax: 417-836-6940.

State University of New York College at Brockport

Brockport, New York

State-supported, coed. Small-town campus. Total enrollment: 7,910.

Degrees Bachelor of Fine Arts in the areas of dance, dance education. Majors: dance. Graduate degrees offered: Master of Fine Arts in the areas of dance, dance education.

Dance Student Profile Fall 1994: 91 total; 70 matriculated undergraduate, 15 matriculated graduate, 6 nondegree; 15% minorities, 90% females, 10% international.

Dance Faculty Total: 15; 11 full-time, 4 part-time; 75% of full-time faculty have terminal degrees. Graduate students teach a few undergraduate courses. Undergraduate student–faculty ratio: 10:1.

Student Life Student groups include Dance Club.

Expenses for 1995–96 Application fee: $25. State resident tuition: $3400 full-time, $137 per credit hour part-time. Nonresident tuition: $8304 full-time, $346 per credit hour part-time. Part-time mandatory fees: $16.45 per credit hour. Full-time mandatory fees: $395. College room and board: $4660. College room only: $2840.

Financial Aid Program-specific awards for Fall of 1994: 2 Friars Scholarship for talented students ($1100).

Application Procedures Deadline—freshmen and transfers: continuous. Required: high school transcript, college transcript(s) for transfer students, minimum 2.0 high school GPA, audition, SAT I or ACT test scores. Recommended: minimum 3.0 high school GPA, letter of recommendation, interview. Auditions held 3 times on campus and off campus in Miami, FL; videotaped performances are permissible as a substitute for live auditions when distance is prohibitive.

Undergraduate Contact Jacqueline Davis, Undergraduate Program Director, Dance Department, State University of New York College at Brockport, Hartwell Hall, Brockport, New York 14420; 716-395-2153.

Graduate Contact Sondra Fraleigh, Graduate Program Director, Dance Department, State University of New York College at Brockport, Hartwell Hall, Brockport, New York 14420; 716-395-2219.

State University of New York College at Purchase

See Purchase College, State University of New York

Stephens College

Columbia, Missouri

Independent, women only. Urban campus. Total enrollment: 600.

Degrees Bachelor of Fine Arts in the area of dance. Majors: dance. Cross-registration with University of Missouri&–Columbia.

Dance Student Profile Fall 1994: 35 total; all matriculated undergraduate; 100% females.

Dance Faculty Total: 5; 3 full-time, 2 part-time; 40% of full-time faculty have terminal degrees. Graduate students do not teach undergraduate courses.

Student Life Student groups include Chi Tau Epsilon. Special housing available for dance students.

Expenses for 1995–96 Application fee: $25. Comprehensive fee of $19,770 includes full-time tuition ($14,400) and college room and board ($5370). College room only: $2900. Part-time tuition: $1140 per course.

Financial Aid Program-specific awards for Fall of 1994 available.

Application Procedures Deadline—freshmen and transfers: April 1. Notification date—freshmen and transfers: August 1. Required: essay, high school transcript, minimum 2.0 high school GPA, 2 letters of recommendation, interview. Auditions held as needed on campus.

Undergraduate Contact Office of Admission, Stephens College, Box 2121, Columbia, Missouri 65215-0002; 800-876-7207, fax: 314-876-7237, E-mail address: apply@sc.stephens.edu.

Stephens College *(continued)*

More about the College

Professionals in dance, both men and women, each with a background rich from experience, offer the dance student the chance to work with and learn from some of the best. The B.F.A. is earned in three years and two summers.

Program Facilities Stephens Summer Dance: Held on campus, the SSD program is composed of two sessions, The Workshop and The Technique, which culminate in two public performances. This conservatory setting ensures technical growth and provides performing opportunities. In The Workshop, the studio becomes a laboratory representing a professional environment where choreographer and student explore the dynamics of the creative process. The Technique is open to students high school–age and above. Students study with professional faculty in an intensive and comprehensive program of three to four classes daily.

Facilities The Anchor of the Stephens Performing Arts Program is the Macklanburg Playhouse, a state-of-the-art facility with a fully trapped stage, a computerized lighting system, and a hydraulic lift. In addition, there's the Stephens Warehouse Theatre, a theater company managed and run by students. Dance productions are held both in the Macklanburg Playhouse and in the Warehouse. The Harriette Ann Gray Dance Studio is housed in the newly renovated Historic Senior Hall. Light and airy with walls of windows and mirrors, the studio has floors specially designed for dance, ample dressing rooms, and an observation deck on the second floor. A smaller studio is also housed in the elegant hall as well as a recital hall for voice and piano performances.

Sybil B. Harrington College of Fine Arts and Humanities

See West Texas A&M University, Sybil B. Harrington College of Fine Arts and Humanities

Temple University

Philadelphia, Pennsylvania

State-related, coed. Urban campus. Total enrollment: 26,952.

Degrees Bachelor of Fine Arts in the area of dance. Majors: dance. Graduate degrees offered: Master of Fine Arts in the area of dance.

Dance Student Profile Fall 1994: 115 total; 41 matriculated undergraduate, 74 matriculated graduate; 24% minorities, 88% females, 6% international.

Dance Faculty Total: 13; 8 full-time, 5 part-time; 65% of full-time faculty have terminal degrees. Graduate students teach a few undergraduate courses. Undergraduate student–faculty ratio: 10:1.

Expenses for 1995–96 Application fee: $30. State resident tuition: $5314 full-time, $185 per semester hour part-time. Nonresident tuition: $10,096 full-time, $286 per semester hour part-time. Part-time mandatory fees per semester range from $15 to $45. Full-time mandatory fees: $200. College room and board: $5282. College room only: $3492.

Financial Aid Program-specific awards for Fall of 1994: 3 Department Scholarships for freshmen ($1000).

Application Procedures Deadline—freshmen and transfers: June 15. Notification date—freshmen and transfers: August 1. Required: essay, high school transcript, college transcript(s) for transfer students, minimum 2.0 high school GPA, letter of recommendation, interview, video, audition, SAT I or ACT test scores. Recommended: minimum 3.0 high school GPA. Auditions held 5 times on campus; videotaped performances are permissible as a substitute for live auditions for international applicants.

Undergraduate Contact Ed Groff, Coordinator, BFA Program, Dance Department, Temple University, 309 Seltzer Hall, Philadelphia, Pennsylvania 19122; 215-204-6284.

Graduate Contact Admissions Coordinator, Dance Department, Temple University, 309 Seltzer Hall, Philadelphia, Pennsylvania 19122; 215-204-5169.

Texas Christian University

Fort Worth, Texas

Independent-religious, coed. Suburban campus. Total enrollment: 6,706.

Degrees Bachelor of Fine Arts in the areas of modern dance, ballet. Majors: ballet, modern dance. Graduate degrees offered: Master of Fine Arts in the areas of modern dance, ballet.

Dance Student Profile Fall 1994: 48 total; 45 matriculated undergraduate, 3 matriculated graduate; 6% minorities, 90% females, 2% international.

Dance Faculty Total: 8; 5 full-time, 3 part-time; 80% of full-time faculty have terminal degrees. Graduate students do not teach undergraduate courses. Undergraduate student–faculty ratio: 15:1.

Expenses for 1995–96 Application fee: $30. Comprehensive fee of $13,840 includes full-time tuition ($9000), mandatory fees ($1000), and college room and board ($3840). Part-time tuition: $300 per semester hour. Part-time mandatory fees: $25 per semester hour.

Financial Aid Program-specific awards for Fall of 1994: 2 Nordan Awards for dance majors ($3000).

Application Procedures Deadline—freshmen: February 5; transfers: August 1. Notification date—freshmen: April 1; transfers: continuous. Required: essay, high school transcript, college transcript(s) for transfer students, 2 letters of recommendation, audition, SAT I or ACT test scores. Auditions held 3 times and by appointment on campus and off campus; videotaped performances are permissible as a substitute for live auditions for international applicants.

Undergraduate Contact Ellen Page Garrison, Chair, Ballet and Modern Dance Department, Texas Christian

University, P.O. Box 32889, Fort Worth, Texas 76129; 817-921-7615, fax: 817-921-7333.

Graduate Contact John Burton, Director of Graduate Studies, College of Fine Arts and Communication, Texas Christian University, P.O. Box 30793, Fort Worth, Texas 76129; 817-921-7603, fax: 817-921-7703.

Tisch School of the Arts

See New York University, Tisch School of the Arts

Towson State University

Towson, Maryland

State-supported, coed. Suburban campus. Total enrollment: 14,551.

Degrees Bachelor of Fine Arts in the areas of dance performance, dance performance and education. Majors: dance.

Expenses for 1995–96 Application fee: $25. State resident tuition: $3530 full-time, $132 per credit hour part-time. Nonresident tuition: $6932 full-time, $218 per credit hour part-time. College room and board: $4480. College room only: $2620.

Application Procedures Deadline—freshmen and transfers: April 1. Notification date—freshmen and transfers: continuous. Required: high school transcript, college transcript(s) for transfer students, audition, SAT I test score only, minimum 2.5 high school GPA. Auditions held 2 times on campus and off campus. Portfolio reviews held on campus and off campus.

Undergraduate Contact C. Trent Owings, Admissions Officer, Department of Dance, Towson State University, Burdick Hall, Room 125, Towson, Maryland 21204-7097; 410-830-3333, fax: 410-830-3030.

University of Akron

Akron, Ohio

State-supported, coed. Urban campus. Total enrollment: 26,009.

Degrees Bachelor of Fine Arts in the areas of dance, musical theater–dance. Majors: dance.

Dance Student Profile Fall 1994: 138 total; 58 matriculated undergraduate, 80 nondegree; 5% minorities, 90% females, 3% international.

Dance Faculty Total: 14; 5 full-time, 9 part-time; 80% of full-time faculty have terminal degrees. Graduate students do not teach undergraduate courses. Undergraduate student–faculty ratio: 10:1.

Student Life Student groups include Ohio Association of Health, Physical Education, Recreation and Dance, American College Dance Festival.

Expenses for 1995–96 Application fee: $35. State resident tuition: $3192 full-time, $123.65 per credit part-time. Nonresident tuition: $7954 full-time, $282.40 per credit part-time. Full-time mandatory fees: $380. College room and board: $3844. Special program-related fees: $5 for trainer and supplies.

Financial Aid Program-specific awards for Fall of 1994: 1 Muehlstein Award for applicants living within 100 miles of New York City ($7000).

Application Procedures Deadline—freshmen and transfers: continuous. Required: high school transcript, college transcript(s) for transfer students. Recommended: audition. Auditions held 2 times on campus; videotaped performances are permissible as a substitute for live auditions if a campus visit is impossible.

Undergraduate Contact Lucinda Lavelli, Director, School of Dance, University of Akron, 354 East Market Street, Akron, Ohio 44325-2502; 216-972-7948.

University of Arizona

Tucson, Arizona

State-supported, coed. Urban campus. Total enrollment: 35,306.

Degrees Bachelor of Fine Arts in the area of dance. Majors: ballet, modern dance. Graduate degrees offered: Master of Fine Arts in the area of theater arts.

Expenses for 1995–96 State resident tuition: $1950 full-time. Nonresident tuition: $7978 full-time. Part-time tuition per semester ranges from $103 to $975 for state residents, $334 to $3989 for nonresidents. College room and board: $4400. College room only: $2400.

Application Procedures Required: high school transcript, college transcript(s) for transfer students, minimum 3.0 high school GPA, audition, SAT I or ACT test scores. Auditions held on campus and off campus. Portfolio reviews held on campus and off campus.

Undergraduate Contact Office of Admissions and New Student Enrollment, University of Arizona, Robert L. Nugent Building, Tucson, Arizona 85721; 602-621-7783.

University of California, Santa Barbara

Santa Barbara, California

State-supported, coed. Suburban campus. Total enrollment: 17,834.

Degrees Bachelor of Fine Arts in the areas of performance, choreography. Majors: choreography and performance, modern dance.

Dance Student Profile Fall 1994: 12 total; all matriculated undergraduate.

University of California, Santa Barbara *(continued)*

Dance Faculty Total: 9; 7 full-time, 2 part-time; 28% of full-time faculty have terminal degrees. Graduate students do not teach undergraduate courses. Undergraduate student–faculty ratio: 5:1.

Student Life Student groups include American College Dance Festival, Intercampus Arts Festival.

Expenses for 1995–96 Application fee: $40. State resident tuition: $0 full-time. Nonresident tuition: $7699 full-time. Full-time mandatory fees: $4098. College room and board: $5990.

Financial Aid Program-specific awards for Fall of 1994: 1–3 M. Plaskett Scholarships for incoming males ($1000), 1 Drama and Dance Affiliate Scholarship for seniors ($200–$400).

Application Procedures Deadline—freshmen and transfers: November 30. Notification date—freshmen: March 15; transfers: April 1. Required: essay, high school transcript, minimum 3.0 high school GPA, audition. Auditions held 3 times on campus; videotaped performances are permissible as a substitute for live auditions if a campus visit is impossible.

Undergraduate Contact Marilyn Romine, Undergraduate Advisor, Department of Dramatic Art and Dance, University of California, Santa Barbara, Snidecor 2645, Santa Barbara, California 93106; 805-893-3241, fax: 805-893-3242, E-mail address: romine@humanitas.ucsb.edu.

University of Cincinnati

Cincinnati, Ohio

State-supported, coed. Urban campus. Total enrollment: 18,473.

Degrees Bachelor of Fine Arts in the area of dance. Majors: ballet, dance. Cross-registration with Greater Cincinnati Consortium of Colleges and Universities.

Dance Student Profile Fall 1994: 37 total; all matriculated undergraduate; 8% minorities, 1% international.

Dance Faculty Total: 8; 3 full-time, 5 part-time; 33% of full-time faculty have terminal degrees. Graduate students do not teach undergraduate courses. Undergraduate student–faculty ratio: 9:1.

Student Life Student groups include Choreographer's Showcase.

Expenses for 1994–95 Application fee: $30. State resident tuition: $3732 full-time, $104 per credit hour part-time. Nonresident tuition: $9405 full-time, $261 per credit hour part-time. Full-time mandatory fees: $166. College room and board: $4698.

Financial Aid Program-specific awards for Fall of 1994: Honor Awards for program majors ($890–$8000).

Application Procedures Deadline—freshmen and transfers: continuous. Notification date—freshmen and transfers: continuous. Required: high school transcript, college transcript(s) for transfer students, minimum 2.0 high school GPA, letter of recommendation, audition, SAT I or ACT test scores. Recommended: minimum 3.0 high school GPA. Auditions held 7 times on campus and off campus in Interlochen, MI; Washington, DC; Montgomery, AL; Orlando, FL; videotaped performances are permissible as a substitute for live auditions with approval of division head when distance is prohibitive.

Undergraduate Contact Paul R. Hillner, Assistant Dean, College Conservatory of Music, University of Cincinnati, P.O. Box 210003, Cincinnati, Ohio 45221-0003; 513-556-5463, fax: 513-556-1028, E-mail address: paul.hillner@uc.edu.

University of Colorado at Boulder

Boulder, Colorado

State-supported, coed. Urban campus. Total enrollment: 24,548.

Degrees Bachelor of Fine Arts in the area of dance. Majors: modern dance. Graduate degrees offered: Master of Fine Arts in the area of dance.

Dance Student Profile Fall 1994: 49 total; 38 matriculated undergraduate, 11 matriculated graduate; 7% minorities, 91% females.

Dance Faculty Total: 8; 6 full-time, 2 part-time; 80% of full-time faculty have terminal degrees. Graduate students teach about a quarter undergraduate courses. Undergraduate student–faculty ratio: 6:1.

Student Life Student groups include American College Dance Festival.

Expenses for 1995–96 Application fee: $40. Part-time tuition per credit hour ranges from $138 to $165 for state residents, $741 to $776 for nonresidents. Part-time mandatory fees per semester range from $55.99 to $243.70. Full-time tuition ranges from $2216 to $2672 for state residents, $12,780 to $13,374 for nonresidents according to program. Full-time mandatory fees: $487. College room and board: $4162. Special program-related fees: $25 for accompanist fee, $15 for tapes and compact discs.

Financial Aid Program-specific awards for Fall of 1994: 10–12 University Dance Awards for program majors ($250–$500), 1 Redmond Scholarship for upperclass program majors demonstrating talent and academic achievement ($1300), 1 Katherine J. Lamont Scholarship for program majors ($450).

Application Procedures Deadline—freshmen: February 15; transfers: April 1. Required: high school transcript, college transcript(s) for transfer students, minimum 2.0 high school GPA, SAT I or ACT test scores.

Undergraduate Contact Admissions Office, University of Colorado at Boulder, Box 30, Boulder, Colorado 80309; 303-492-6301, fax: 303-492-7115.

Graduate Contact Graduate Secretary, Theatre and Dance Department, University of Colorado at Boulder, Box 261, Boulder, Colorado 80309; 303-492-7356, fax: 303-492-7722.

The Hartt School

University of Hartford

West Hartford, Connecticut

Independent, coed. Suburban campus. Total enrollment: 7,253.

Degrees Bachelor of Fine Arts in the areas of dance performance, dance pedagogy, children's dance. Majors: ballet pedagogy, children's dance, performance. Cross-registration with Trinity College, Saint Joseph College, The Hartford Graduate Center, Hartford Seminary.

Dance Faculty Total: 12; 4 full-time, 8 part-time. Graduate students do not teach undergraduate courses. Undergraduate student–faculty ratio: 1:1.

Expenses for 1995–96 Comprehensive fee of $21,875 includes full-time tuition ($14,860), mandatory fees ($750), and college room and board ($6265). College room only: $3865. Part-time tuition: $310 per credit. Part-time mandatory fees: $50 per semester.

Financial Aid Program-specific awards for Fall of 1994: 8 Merit Scholarships for students passing audition evaluations ($1000–$3000).

Application Procedures Deadline—freshmen and transfers: continuous. Required: high school transcript, minimum 2.0 high school GPA, 3 letters of recommendation, interview, audition. Recommended: essay, minimum 3.0 high school GPA. Auditions held 6 times on campus and off campus in Hartford, CT; Boston, MA; New York, NY; videotaped performances are permissible as a substitute for live auditions when distance is prohibitive.

Undergraduate Contact James Jacobs, Director of Admissions, The Hartt School, University of Hartford, 200 Bloomfield Avenue, West Hartford, Connecticut 06117; 203-768-4465, fax: 203-768-4441.

University of Hawaii at Manoa

Honolulu, Hawaii

State-supported, coed. Urban campus. Total enrollment: 19,983.

Degrees Bachelor of Fine Arts in the areas of dance, theater. Majors: dance. Graduate degrees offered: Master of Fine Arts in the area of dance.

Dance Student Profile Fall 1994: 39 total; 27 matriculated undergraduate, 12 matriculated graduate.

Dance Faculty Total: 15; 5 full-time, 10 part-time; 50% of full-time faculty have terminal degrees. Graduate students teach a few undergraduate courses.

Expenses for 1995–96 Application fee: $10. State resident tuition: $1631 full-time, $68 per credit part-time. Nonresident tuition: $4825 full-time, $201 per credit part-time. College room and board: $4210. College room only: $2400.

Application Procedures Deadline—freshmen and transfers: May 1. Required: minimum 2.0 high school GPA, audition. Auditions held 1 time on campus; videotaped performances are permissible as a substitute for live auditions.

Contact Gregg Lizenbery, Director of Dance, Department of Theatre and Dance, University of Hawaii at Manoa, 1770 East West Road, Honolulu, Hawaii 96822; 808-956-2464, fax: 808-956-4234, E-mail address: lgreg@uhunix.uhcc.hawaii.edu.

University of Illinois at Urbana-Champaign

Champaign, Illinois

State-supported, coed. Small-town campus. Total enrollment: 36,191.

Degrees Bachelor of Fine Arts in the area of dance. Majors: choreography and performance. Graduate degrees offered: Master of Fine Arts in the area of dance.

Dance Student Profile Fall 1994: 57 total; 40 matriculated undergraduate, 16 matriculated graduate, 1 nondegree; 7% minorities, 87% females, 9% international.

Dance Faculty Total: 8; 7 full-time, 1 part-time; 100% of full-time faculty have terminal degrees. Graduate students do not teach undergraduate courses. Undergraduate student–faculty ratio: 7:1.

Student Life Student groups include Illinois Dance Theatre.

Expenses for 1994–95 Application fee: $30. Part-time mandatory fees per semester range from $201 to $474. Full-time tuition ranges from $2760 to $2900 for state residents, $7560 to $7980 for nonresidents, according to class level. Part-time tuition per semester ranges from $480 to $977 for state residents, $1300 to $2607 for nonresidents, according to class level and course load. Full-time mandatory fees: $920. College room and board: $4260.

Financial Aid Program-specific awards for Fall of 1994: Talented Student Awards for talented students ($1000).

Application Procedures Deadline—freshmen and transfers: continuous. Notification date—freshmen and transfers: continuous. Required: high school transcript, college transcript(s) for transfer students, audition, portfolio, SAT I or ACT test scores, minimum combined SAT I score of 790, minimum composite ACT score of 20. Recommended: letter of recommendation. Auditions held 5 times on campus and off campus in Louisville, KY; Chicago, IL; videotaped performances are permissible as a substitute for live auditions when distance is prohibitive.

Undergraduate Contact Rebecca Nettl-Fiol, Assistant Professor, Department of Dance, University of Illinois at

University of Illinois at Urbana-Champaign
(continued)

Urbana-Champaign, 4-501 Krannert Center for the Performing Arts, 500 South Goodwin Avenue, Urbana, Illinois 61801; 217-333-1010, fax: 217-244-0810, E-mail address: rnettl@ux].cso.uiuc.edu.

Graduate Contact Patricia Knowles, Head, Department of Dance, University of Illinois at Urbana-Champaign, 4-501 Krannert Center for the Performing Arts, 500 South Goodwin Avenue, Urbana, Illinois 61801; 217-333-1010, fax: 217-244-0810, E-mail address: kmatting@uiuc.edu.

University of Iowa

Iowa City, Iowa

State-supported, coed. Small-town campus. Total enrollment: 26,932.

Degrees Bachelor of Fine Arts in the area of dance. Majors: ballet, modern dance. Graduate degrees offered: Master of Fine Arts in the area of dance.

Dance Student Profile Fall 1994: 753 total; 45 matriculated undergraduate, 8 matriculated graduate, 700 nondegree; 3% minorities, 80% females, 2% international.

Dance Faculty Total: 7; 7 full-time; 95% of full-time faculty have terminal degrees. Graduate students teach more than half undergraduate courses. Undergraduate student–faculty ratio: 10:1.

Student Life Student groups include American College Dance Festival Association.

Expenses for 1995–96 Application fee: $20. State resident tuition: $2386 full-time. Nonresident tuition: $8636 full-time. Part-time tuition per semester ranges from $192 to $1193 for state residents, $192 to $4318 for nonresidents. Part-time mandatory fees per semester range from $22 to $44. Full-time mandatory fees: $172. College room and board: $3550.

Financial Aid Program-specific awards for Fall of 1994: 1 Iowa Center for the Arts Scholarship for incoming freshmen ($3000), 1 T. J. Myers Memorial Scholarship for male incoming freshmen ($1000).

Application Procedures Deadline—freshmen and transfers: May 13. Required: high school transcript, college transcript(s) for transfer students, minimum 2.0 high school GPA, letter of recommendation, interview, video, portfolio, SAT I or ACT test scores. Recommended: essay, minimum 3.0 high school GPA, audition. Auditions held 6 times on campus; videotaped performances are permissible as a substitute for live auditions when distance is prohibitive or for financial reasons.

Undergraduate Contact Alicia Brown, Chair, Dance Department, University of Iowa, E114 Halsey Hall, Iowa City, Iowa 52242; 319-335-2228, fax: 319-335-3246.

Graduate Contact David Berkey, Dance Department, University of Iowa, E114 Halsey Hall, Iowa City, Iowa 52242; 319-335-2190.

University of Massachusetts Amherst

Amherst, Massachusetts

State-supported, coed. Small-town campus. Total enrollment: 22,332.

Degrees Bachelor of Fine Arts in the area of dance. Majors: dance. Cross-registration with Amherst College, Hampshire College, Mount Holyoke College, Smith College.

Dance Student Profile Fall 1994: 65 total; all matriculated undergraduate; 1% minorities, 99% females.

Dance Faculty Total: 5; 2 full-time, 3 part-time; 100% of full-time faculty have terminal degrees. Graduate students do not teach undergraduate courses. Undergraduate student–faculty ratio: 13:1.

Expenses for 1995–96 Application fee: $20. State resident tuition: $2220 full-time, $92.50 per credit part-time. Nonresident tuition: $8566 full-time, $357 per credit part-time. Part-time mandatory fees per semester range from $489.25 to $1198. Tuition for nonresidents who are eligible for the New England Regional Student Program: $3330 full-time, $138.75 per credit part-time. Full-time mandatory fees: $3355. College room and board: $4184. College room only: $2376. Special program-related fees: $20 for lab fee for technique and some academic courses.

Financial Aid Program-specific awards for Fall of 1994: 4–6 Chancellor's Talent Awards for undergraduates ($2200), 2 cash awards for undergraduates ($1100).

Application Procedures Deadline—freshmen: February 15; transfers: April 1. Notification date—freshmen: April 15; transfers: July 1. Required: audition. Auditions held 4 times on campus; videotaped performances are permissible as a substitute for live auditions when distance is prohibitive or in special circumstances.

Undergraduate Contact Mariah Lilly, Acting Director of Dance Admissions, Dance Program, University of Massachusetts Amherst, 11 Totman, Amherst, Massachusetts 01003; 413-545-2413, fax: 413-545-2092.

University of Memphis

Memphis, Tennessee

State-supported, coed. Urban campus. Total enrollment: 19,848.

Degrees Bachelor of Fine Arts in the area of dance. Majors: dance.

Dance Student Profile Fall 1994: 13 total; all matriculated undergraduate.

Dance Faculty Total: 5; 3 full-time, 2 part-time.

Expenses for 1995–96 Application fee: $5. State resident tuition: $2094 full-time. Nonresident tuition: $6224 full-time. Part-time tuition per semester ranges from $92 to $989 for state residents, $273 to $2980 for nonresidents. College room and board: $2200 (minimum).

Application Procedures Deadline—freshmen and transfers: August 1. Required: high school transcript, audition, ACT test score only. Auditions held continuously on campus; videotaped performances are permissible as a substitute for live auditions when distance is prohibitive.

Undergraduate Contact John McFadden, Chair, Dance/Theater Department, University of Memphis, 3745 Central Avenue, Memphis, Tennessee 38152; 901-678-2565.

University of Michigan

Ann Arbor, Michigan

State-supported, coed. Suburban campus. Total enrollment: 36,543.

Degrees Bachelor of Fine Arts in the area of dance. Majors: modern dance, performance. Graduate degrees offered: Master of Fine Arts in the area of dance.

Dance Student Profile Fall 1994: 366 total; 57 matriculated undergraduate, 9 matriculated graduate, 300 nondegree.

Dance Faculty Total: 9; 6 full-time, 3 part-time; 83% of full-time faculty have terminal degrees. Graduate students teach a few undergraduate courses. Undergraduate student–faculty ratio: 8:1.

Expenses for 1994–95 Application fee: $40. Full-time tuition ranges from $5040 to $6698 for state residents, $15,732 to $17,850 for nonresidents according to class level and program. Part-time tuition and fees per term (1 to 11 credits) range from $525 to $3204 for state residents, $970 to $8530 for nonresidents according to course load, class level, and program. Full-time mandatory fees: $175. College room and board: $4659.

Financial Aid Program-specific awards for Fall of 1994: 3 Dance Merit Scholarships for incoming students ($1500).

Application Procedures Deadline—freshmen and transfers: continuous. Required: essay, high school transcript, college transcript(s) for transfer students, minimum 3.0 high school GPA, audition, SAT I or ACT test scores. Auditions held 5 times on campus and off campus in New York, NY; videotaped performances are permissible as a substitute for live auditions with permission of the chair.

Undergraduate Contact Laura Strozeski, Senior Admissions Counselor, School of Music, University of Michigan, Moore Building, Ann Arbor, Michigan 48109-2085; 313-764-0593, fax: 313-763-5097, E-mail address: laura.strozeski@um.cc.umich.edu.

Graduate Contact Suzanne Jones, Administrative Associate, Dance Department, University of Michigan, 1310 North University Court, Ann Arbor, Michigan 48109; 313-763-5460, fax: 313-763-5962, E-mail address: smjones@umich.edu.

University of Minnesota, Twin Cities Campus

Minneapolis, Minnesota

State-supported, coed. Urban campus. Total enrollment: 36,699.

Degrees Bachelor of Fine Arts in the area of dance. Majors: dance.

Dance Student Profile Fall 1994: 1,019 total; 44 matriculated undergraduate, 975 nondegree; 9% minorities, 68% females, 10% international.

Dance Faculty Total: 24; 5 full-time, 19 part-time; 65% of full-time faculty have terminal degrees. Graduate students do not teach undergraduate courses. Undergraduate student–faculty ratio: 5:1.

Student Life Student groups include Student Dance Coalition.

Expenses for 1994–95 Application fee: $25. Full-time tuition ranges from $3395 to $3482 for state residents, $9190 to $10,794 for nonresidents, according to class level and program. Part-time tuition per credit ranges from $70.80 to $82.90 for state residents, $208.80 to $244.40 for nonresidents, according to class level and program. Full-time tuition for pharmacy program ranges from $2478 to $6077 for state residents, $4687 to $12,150 for nonresidents according to class level. Part-time tuition per credit for pharmacy program ranges from $59 to $144.70 for state residents, $111.60 to $289.30 for nonresidents according to class level. Full-time mandatory fees: $431. College room and board: $3774.

Financial Aid Program-specific awards for Fall of 1994: 1 Nadine Jette-Sween Scholarship for dance majors ($800), 1 Marion Haynes Andrus Scholarship for dance majors ($800), 1 Advisory Council Scholarship for dance majors ($800), 1 Tom and Ellie Crosby Scholarship for incoming freshmen or newly declared dance majors ($800), 1 Robert Moulton Memorial Scholarship for dance majors ($800).

Application Procedures Deadline—freshmen and transfers: continuous. Required: audition. Auditions held 2 times on campus; videotaped performances are permissible as a substitute for live auditions if a campus visit is impossible.

Undergraduate Contact Paul Meierant, Coordinator, Office of Admissions, University of Minnesota, Twin Cities Campus, 240 Williamson Hall, 231 Pillsbury Drive, SE, Minneapolis, Minnesota 55455; 612-625-2008, E-mail address: meier010@gold.tc.umn.edu.

Cornelius Carter

**University of Hawaii, Manoa, M.F.A.—
Assistant Professor of Dance,
University of Alabama**

The University of Hawaii, Manoa, gave me, as an African American, opportunities other schools didn't seem to offer, even as a graduate student I took independent study classes. At this school I learned as many life lessons as dance lessons.

University of Minnesota, Twin Cities Campus
(continued)

More about the University

Faculty, Resident Artists, and Alumni The University Dance Program is particularly proud of its distinguished faculty. All technique teachers are professional artists, many of whom have been or are directors of dance companies. In addition, the Dance Program annually hosts an average of five internationally renowned dance artists in residencies as an integral component of technical and creative training. Past guest artists include Sally Banes, Merce Cunningham, Douglas Dunn, Barbara Mahler, Bebe Miller, Shapiro & Smith, Billy Siegenfeld, Joan Skinner, Peter Sparling, Dan Wagoner, David White, and Mel Wong. Dance graduates have entered the professional companies of Ralph Lemon, Creach and Koester, Paul Taylor, and Jose Limon. Still others have advanced to graduate school, become teachers, and established their own studios.

Student Performance Students give close to two dozen performances per year, from workshop showings to fully produced concerts by the student repertory company, University Dance Theatre (UDT). In addition, UDT annually collaborates with a major presenter and/or guest artists on a work of national significance. Examples include Bill T. Jones's "The Promised Land," Susan Marshall's "Spectators at an Event," and Kei Takei's "24 Hours of Light."

Program Facilities/Environment The program has four studios, two classrooms, video equipment, and full production facilities shared with the Theatre Program. The campus is situated in a major metropolitan area minutes away from the downtowns of Minneapolis and St. Paul. Both cities are noted for their extraordinary arts community. Professional dance companies include Zenon, 45 CHARTREUSE, Paula Mann & Dancers, JAZZDANCE, Corning Dancers & Company, Ethnic Dance Theatre, and the Flying Foot Forum. Current dance majors and past graduates are performing with all of these companies.

University of Missouri-Kansas City

Kansas City, Missouri

State-supported, coed. Urban campus. Total enrollment: 9,962.

Degrees Bachelor of Fine Arts in the area of dance. Majors: dance.

Dance Student Profile Fall 1994: 80 total; 40 matriculated undergraduate, 40 nondegree.

Dance Faculty Total: 5; 5 full-time.

Expenses for 1995–96 Application fee: $25. State resident tuition: $3330 full-time, $111 per credit hour part-time. Nonresident tuition: $9954 full-time, $331.80 per credit hour part-time. Part-time mandatory fees per semester range from $45.70 to $202.55. Full-time mandatory fees: $469.20. College room and board: $3750.

Application Procedures Deadline—freshmen and transfers: continuous. Notification date—freshmen and transfers: continuous. Required: high school transcript, college transcript(s) for transfer students, 3 letters of recommendation, audition, SAT I or ACT test scores. Auditions held 4 times on campus and off campus. Portfolio reviews held on campus and off campus.

Undergraduate Contact James T. Elswick, Admissions Coordinator, University of Missouri–Kansas City, 4949 Cherry, Kansas City, Missouri 64110-2229; 816-235-2900, fax: 816-235-5264, E-mail address: cadmissions@cctr.umkc.edu.

University of Montana-Missoula

Missoula, Montana

State-supported, coed. Urban campus. Total enrollment: 11,067.

Degrees Bachelor of Fine Arts in the area of dance. Majors: choreography and performance, dance education.

Dance Student Profile Fall 1994: 228 total; 28 matriculated undergraduate, 200 nondegree; 1% minorities, 90% females, 2% international.

Dance Faculty Total: 7; 3 full-time, 4 part-time; 100% of full-time faculty have terminal degrees. Graduate students do not teach undergraduate courses. Undergraduate student–faculty ratio: 20:1.

Student Life Student groups include Associated Students of the University of Montana.

Expenses for 1994–95 Application fee: $30. State resident tuition: $2251 full-time. Nonresident tuition: $6311 full-time. Part-time tuition per semester ranges from $99.10 to $943.10 for state residents, $244.10 to $2538 for nonresidents. College room and board: $3667. Special program-related fees: $20–$60 for class fees.

Financial Aid Program-specific awards for Fall of 1994: 2 Department Scholarships for program majors ($500), 2 Alexander Dean Awards for program majors ($600).

Application Procedures Deadline—freshmen and transfers: March 1. Required: essay, high school transcript, audition, SAT I test score only. Auditions held 1 time at the end of freshman year on campus.

Undergraduate Contact Terri Denney, Administrative Assistant, Department of Drama/Dance, University of Montana–Missoula, Missoula, Montana 59812; 406-243-4481.

University of Nebraska-Lincoln

Lincoln, Nebraska

State-supported, coed. Urban campus. Total enrollment: 23,854.

Degrees Bachelor of Fine Arts in the area of dance. Majors: ballet, modern dance.

Dance Faculty Total: 5; 3 full-time, 2 part-time.

Expenses for 1994–95 Application fee: $25. State resident tuition: $2415 full-time, $68.50 per credit hour part-time. Nonresident tuition: $5955 full-time, $186.50 per credit hour part-time. Part-time mandatory fees per semester range from $85 to $180. Full-time mandatory fees: $360. College room and board: $3145. College room only: $1375.

Application Procedures Deadline—freshmen and transfers: July 15. Required: high school transcript, SAT I or ACT test scores.

Undergraduate Contact Dr. Lisa Fusillo, Director, Dance Department, University of Nebraska–Lincoln, 215 Temple Building, P.O. Box 880201, Lincoln, Nebraska 68588-0201; 402-472-5803.

University of North Carolina at Greensboro

Greensboro, North Carolina

State-supported, coed. Urban campus. Total enrollment: 12,094.

Degrees Bachelor of Fine Arts in the area of dance. Majors: dance. Graduate degrees offered: Master of Fine Arts in the area of dance. Cross-registration with North Carolina Agricultural and Technical State University, Guilford College, Greensboro College, Bennett College.

Dance Student Profile Fall 1994: 384 total; 70 matriculated undergraduate, 14 matriculated graduate, 300 nondegree; 13% minorities, 68% females, 3% international.

Dance Faculty Total: 12; 9 full-time, 3 part-time; 78% of full-time faculty have terminal degrees. Graduate students teach about a quarter undergraduate courses. Undergraduate student–faculty ratio: 5:1.

Student Life Student groups include Prime Movers (student dance association).

Expenses for 1994–95 Application fee: $35. State resident tuition: $874 full-time. Nonresident tuition: $8400 full-time. Part-time tuition per semester ranges from $109 to $328 for state residents, $1050 to $3150 for nonresidents. Full-time mandatory fees: $891. College room and board: $3505. College room only: $1791.

Financial Aid Program-specific awards for Fall of 1994: 1–2 Virginia Moomaw Scholarships for continuing program students ($150–$300), 1 Joseph Levinoff Scholarship for continuing program students ($150), 1 Feinstein Scholarship for minority program students ($150), 1–3 Burns Scholarship for students with career interest in musical theater ($750–$2500).

Application Procedures Deadline—freshmen and transfers: continuous. Required: high school transcript, college transcript(s) for transfer students, SAT I or ACT test scores, minimum 2.5 college GPA and minimum 3.0 college GPA in dance. Recommended: minimum 3.0 high school GPA, letter of recommendation.

Undergraduate Contact Dr. Sue Stinson, Head, Department of Dance, University of North Carolina at Greensboro, 323 HHP Building, Greensboro, North Carolina 27412-5001; 910-334-3046, fax: 910-334-3238, E-mail address: stinsons@uncg.edu.

Graduate Contact Dr. Jan Van Dyke, Director of Graduate Studies, Department of Dance, University of North Carolina at Greensboro, 323 HHP Building, Greensboro, North Carolina 27412-5001; 910-334-3266, fax: 910-334-3238.

University of Oklahoma

Norman, Oklahoma

State-supported, coed. Suburban campus. Total enrollment: 19,683.

Degrees Bachelor of Fine Arts in the area of dance. Majors: ballet, modern dance. Graduate degrees offered: Master of Fine Arts in the area of dance.

Dance Student Profile Fall 1994: 528 total; 70 matriculated undergraduate, 8 matriculated graduate, 450 nondegree; 26% minorities, 80% females, 15% international.

Dance Faculty Total: 11; 6 full-time, 5 part-time; 83% of full-time faculty have terminal degrees. Graduate students teach a few undergraduate courses. Undergraduate student–faculty ratio: 12:1.

Student Life Student groups include Drama and Dance Student Association, Student Advisory Council.

Expenses for 1994–95 Application fee: $15. Part-time mandatory fees: $91 per semester. Full-time tuition ranges from $1688 to $1785 for state residents, $4928 to $5438 for nonresidents according to class level. Part-time tuition per credit hour ranges from $56.25 to $59.49 for state residents, $164.25 to $181.26 for nonresidents according to class level. Full-time mandatory fees: $182. College room and board: $3526. Special program-related fees: $50 for accompanying fee.

Financial Aid Program-specific awards for Fall of 1994: 4–6 Fee Waivers for state residents ($500–$800), 15–20 Tuition Waivers for non-residents ($1500–$3000), 10–20 Barnett Foundation Scholarships for excellent dancers ($300–$800), 2–6 Everett Foundation Scholarships for male ballet majors ($1000).

Application Procedures Deadline—freshmen and transfers: continuous. Notification date—freshmen and transfers: continuous. Required: high school transcript, minimum 3.0 high school GPA, audition, SAT I or ACT test scores. Recommended: interview. Auditions held 2 times and by appointment on campus and off campus in Houston, TX; Louisville, KY; videotaped performances are permissible as a substitute for live auditions when distance is prohibitive.

Undergraduate Contact Kathleen Burnett, Assistant Professor, Dance Department, University of Oklahoma, 563 Elm Avenue, Room 209, Norman, Oklahoma 73019; 405-325-4021.

Graduate Contact Ko Yukihiro, Assistant Chair, Dance Department, University of Oklahoma, 563 Elm Avenue, Room 209, Norman, Oklahoma 73019; 405-325-4021.

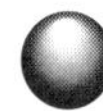

University of Southern Mississippi

Hattiesburg, Mississippi

State-supported, coed. Suburban campus. Total enrollment: 11,587.

Degrees Bachelor of Fine Arts in the area of dance. Majors: choreography and performance.

Dance Student Profile Fall 1994: 150 total; 25 matriculated undergraduate, 125 nondegree; 3% minorities, 99% females.

Dance Faculty Total: 4; 3 full-time, 1 part-time; 100% of full-time faculty have terminal degrees. Graduate students do not teach undergraduate courses. Undergraduate student–faculty ratio: 9:1.

Student Life Student groups include Southern Arts Pro Musica, Opera Theatre, Theatre Productions.

Expenses for 1994–95 State resident tuition: $2428 full-time. Nonresident tuition: $4892 full-time. Part-time tuition per semester ranges from $100 to $970 for state residents, $202 to $2092 for nonresidents. College room and board: $2430. College room only: $1250 (minimum).

Financial Aid Program-specific awards for Fall of 1994: 1–2 J. Clinton Endowment Award for those demonstrating talent ($380–$500), 1–2 Dean's Endowment Award for those demonstrating talent ($250–$500), 20–25 Service Awards for program majors ($100–$600), 10–15 Out-of-State Awards for program majors ($2460), 1–2 Myer's Endowment Awards for program majors ($500–$1000).

Application Procedures Deadline—freshmen and transfers: continuous. Required: high school transcript, college transcript(s) for transfer students, minimum 2.0 high school GPA, 2 letters of recommendation, interview, SAT I or ACT test scores. Recommended: video. Auditions held 2 times on campus; videotaped performances are permissible as a substitute for live auditions if a campus visit is impossible.

Undergraduate Contact Janet Prieur, Coordinator of Dance, Dance Program, University of Southern Mississippi, Box 5052, Hattiesburg, Mississippi 39406-5052; 601-266-4161.

University of Tennessee at Martin

Martin, Tennessee

State-supported, coed. Small-town campus. Total enrollment: 5,627.

Degrees Bachelor of Fine Arts in the area of fine and performing arts. Majors: dance.

Dance Student Profile Fall 1994: 6 total; all matriculated undergraduate; 100% females.

Dance Faculty Total: 1; 1 full-time; 100% of full-time faculty have terminal degrees. Graduate students do not teach undergraduate courses. Undergraduate student–faculty ratio: 6:1.

Student Life Student groups include UTM Dance Ensemble.

Expenses for 1994–95 Application fee: $15. State resident tuition: $1900 full-time, $76 per semester hour part-time. Nonresident tuition: $5832 full-time, $240 per semester hour part-time. College room and board: $2890 (minimum). College room only: $1490 (minimum).

Application Procedures Deadline—freshmen and transfers: continuous. Required: high school transcript, minimum 2.0 high school GPA, audition, SAT I or ACT test scores. Auditions held 1 time on campus; videotaped performances are permissible as a substitute for live auditions.

Undergraduate Contact Dr. Earl Norwood, Director, Division of Fine and Performing Arts, University of Tennessee at Martin, 102 Fine Arts Building, Martin, Tennessee 38238; 901-587-7400, fax: 901-587-7415, E-mail address: norwood@utm.edu.

University of Texas at Austin

Austin, Texas

State-supported, coed. Urban campus. Total enrollment: 47,957.

Degrees Bachelor of Fine Arts in the areas of modern dance, ballet. Majors: ballet, modern dance.

Dance Student Profile Fall 1994: 79 total; all matriculated undergraduate; 36% minorities, 90% females, 1% international.

Dance Faculty Total: 11; 7 full-time, 4 part-time; 71% of full-time faculty have terminal degrees. Graduate students do not teach undergraduate courses. Undergraduate student–faculty ratio: 7:1.

Student Life Student groups include Dance Repertory Theatre.

Expenses for 1995–96 Application fee: $35. State resident tuition: $900 full-time. Nonresident tuition: $6660 full-time, $222 per semester hour part-time. State resident part-time tuition per semester ranges from $120 to $330. Part-time mandatory fees per semester range from $169.85 to $570.14. Full-time mandatory fees: $1308. College room and board: $3632. Special program-related fees: $40 for performance and production fee.

Financial Aid Program-specific awards for Fall of 1994 available.

Application Procedures Deadline—freshmen: March 1; transfers: February 1. Notification date—freshmen and transfers: continuous. Required: high school transcript, SAT I or ACT test scores.

Undergraduate Contact Sharon Vasquez, Chair, Department of Theatre and Dance, University of Texas at Austin, WIN 1.142, Austin, Texas 78712; 512-471-5793, fax: 512-471-0824.

University of the Arts

Philadelphia, Pennsylvania

Independent, coed. Urban campus. Total enrollment: 1,298.

Degrees Bachelor of Fine Arts in the area of dance. Majors: ballet, dance education, jazz dance, modern dance.

Dance Student Profile Fall 1994: 230 total; 150 matriculated undergraduate, 80 nondegree; 27% minorities, 92% females, 2% international.

Dance Faculty Total: 28; 3 full-time, 25 part-time; 33% of full-time faculty have terminal degrees. Graduate students do not teach undergraduate courses. Undergraduate student–faculty ratio: 5:1.

Expenses for 1995–96 Application fee: $30. Tuition: $13,170 full-time, $570 per credit part-time. Full-time mandatory fees: $500. College room only: $3860.

Financial Aid Program-specific awards for Fall of 1994: 25 Talent Scholarships for program majors ($500–$5000).

Application Procedures Deadline—freshmen and transfers: continuous. Required: essay, high school transcript, college transcript(s) for transfer students, letter of recommendation, audition, SAT I or ACT test scores. Recommended: minimum 2.0 high school GPA, interview. Auditions held 8 times on campus; videotaped performances are permissible as a substitute for live auditions if a campus visit is impossible.

Undergraduate Contact Barbara Elliott, Director of Admissions, University of the Arts, 320 South Broad Street, Philadelphia, Pennsylvania 19102; 800-626-ARTS, fax: 215-875-4836.

University of Utah

Salt Lake City, Utah

State-supported, coed. Urban campus. Total enrollment: 25,226.

Degrees Bachelor of Fine Arts in the area of ballet. Majors: ballet, ballet pedagogy, dance education, performance. Graduate degrees offered: Master of Fine Arts in the area of ballet.

Dance Student Profile Fall 1994: 212 total; 112 matriculated undergraduate, 10 matriculated graduate, 90 nondegree; 10% minorities, 90% females, 5% international.

Dance Faculty Total: 13; 6 full-time, 7 part-time; 50% of full-time faculty have terminal degrees. Graduate students teach a few undergraduate courses. Undergraduate student–faculty ratio: 10:1.

Expenses for 1994–95 Application fee: $30. State resident tuition: $2298 full-time. Nonresident tuition: $6795 full-time. Part-time tuition per quarter ranges from $206 to $766 for state residents, $597 to $2265 for nonresidents. College room and board: $4570. College room only: $1570. Special program-related fees: $8 for hydrostatic weighing of students.

Financial Aid Program-specific awards for Fall of 1994: 3 William F. Christensen Scholarships for resident incoming freshmen ($2000), 25–40 Departmental Scholarships for undergraduates ($600–$5000).

Application Procedures Deadline—freshmen and transfers: May 30. Required: high school transcript, college transcript(s) for transfer students, minimum 2.0 high school GPA, 2 letters of recommendation, video, audition, SAT I or ACT test scores, 2 photographs in ballet poses - women on pointe. Recommended: essay, minimum 3.0 high school GPA. Auditions held 1 time and as needed on campus; videotaped performances are permissible as a substitute for live auditions when distance is prohibitive or time constraints exist.

Undergraduate Contact Anne Bagley, Executive Secretary, Ballet Department, University of Utah, 110 Marriott Center for Dance, Salt Lake City, Utah 84112; 801-587-8231, fax: 801-581-5442.

Graduate Contact Bene Arnold, Graduate Advisor, Ballet Department, University of Utah, 110 Marriott Center for Dance, Salt Lake City, Utah 84112; 801-581-8231, fax: 801-581-5442.

University of Wisconsin-Milwaukee

Milwaukee, Wisconsin

State-supported, coed. Urban campus. Total enrollment: 22,984.

Degrees Bachelor of Fine Arts in the area of dance. Majors: modern dance.

Dance Student Profile Fall 1994: 50 total; all matriculated undergraduate.

Dance Faculty Total: 7; 5 full-time, 2 part-time. Graduate students do not teach undergraduate courses.

Expenses for 1994–95 State resident tuition: $2772 full-time. Nonresident tuition: $8787 full-time. Part-time tuition per semester ranges from $212 to $1287 for state residents, $465.75 to $4046 for nonresidents. Minnesota residents pay tuition at the rate they would pay if attending a comparable state-supported institution in Minnesota. College room and board: $3000.

Application Procedures Deadline—freshmen and transfers: continuous. Required: high school transcript, ACT score for state residents.

Undergraduate Contact Undergraduate Admissions, University of Wisconsin–Milwaukee, P.O. Box 413, Milwaukee, Wisconsin -0413; 414-229-1122.

University of Wisconsin-Stevens Point

Stevens Point, Wisconsin

State-supported, coed. Small-town campus. Total enrollment: 8,424.

University of Wisconsin–Stevens Point *(continued)*

Degrees Bachelor of Fine Arts in the area of dance. Majors: dance.

Dance Student Profile Fall 1994: 40 total; all matriculated undergraduate.

Dance Faculty Total: 4; 4 full-time; 75% of full-time faculty have terminal degrees. Graduate students do not teach undergraduate courses. Undergraduate student–faculty ratio: 10:1.

Estimated Expenses for 1995–96 Application fee: $25. State resident tuition: $2395 full-time. Nonresident tuition: $7422 full-time. Minnesota residents pay tuition at the rate they would pay if attending a comparable state-supported institution in Minnesota. College room and board: $3150. College room only: $1800.

Financial Aid Program-specific awards for Fall of 1994: 2 Dance Scholarships for incoming students ($500–$800).

Application Procedures Deadline—freshmen and transfers: January 20. Required: high school transcript, audition, ACT test score only, minimum composite ACT score of 24, standing in top 35% of graduating class. Auditions held 1 time on campus.

Undergraduate Contact Arthur B. Hopper, Chair, Department of Theater and Dance, University of Wisconsin–Stevens Point, COFAC– Fine Arts Building, Stevens Point, Wisconsin 54481; 715-346-4429, fax: 715-346-2718.

Virginia Commonwealth University

Richmond, Virginia

State-supported, coed. Urban campus. Total enrollment: 21,523.

Degrees Bachelor of Fine Arts in the area of dance and choreography. Majors: modern dance.

Dance Student Profile Fall 1994: 60 total; all matriculated undergraduate; 20% minorities, 80% females, 2% international.

Dance Faculty Total: 16; 6 full-time, 10 part-time. Graduate students do not teach undergraduate courses. Undergraduate student–faculty ratio: 10:1.

Estimated Expenses for 1995–96 Application fee: $20. State resident tuition: $3034 full-time, $126 per credit part-time. Nonresident tuition: $10,217 full-time, $426 per credit part-time. Part-time mandatory fees: $30.50 per credit. Full-time mandatory fees: $880. College room and board: $4182. College room only: $2416 (minimum). Special program-related fees: $5 for musician/ accompanists fees.

Financial Aid Program-specific awards for Fall of 1994: Departmental Awards for continuing students, 4 Carpenter Fellow Awards for incoming students ($2500).

Application Procedures Deadline—freshmen and transfers: June 1. Required: high school transcript, minimum 2.0 high school GPA, 2 letters of recommendation, audition, SAT I or ACT test scores. Recommended: interview. Auditions held 8 times on campus and off campus in various high schools in the Mid-Atlantic region; videotaped performances are permissible as a substitute for live auditions when distance is prohibitive.

Undergraduate Contact Chris Burnside, Chair, Department of Dance, Virginia Commonwealth University, 1315 Floyd Avenue, Richmond, Virginia 23284-3007; 804-828-1711, fax: 804-828-7356.

Virginia Intermont College

Bristol, Virginia

Independent-religious, coed. Small-town campus. Total enrollment: 682.

Degrees Bachelor of Fine Arts in the area of performing arts (dance). Majors: dance. Cross-registration with King College.

Dance Student Profile Fall 1994: 6 total; all matriculated undergraduate.

Dance Faculty Total: 6; 2 full-time, 4 part-time; 100% of full-time faculty have terminal degrees. Graduate students do not teach undergraduate courses.

Expenses for 1995–96 Application fee: $15. Comprehensive fee of $13,850 includes full-time tuition ($9500), mandatory fees ($100), and college room and board ($4250). Part-time mandatory fees: $25 per semester. Part-time tuition and fees per credit: $125 for the first 6 hours, $300 for the next 5 hours. Special program-related fees: $300 for instruction fee.

Financial Aid Program-specific awards for Fall of 1994: 15 Room Grants for program majors ($1800).

Application Procedures Deadline—freshmen and transfers: continuous. Notification date—freshmen and transfers: continuous. Required: high school transcript, minimum 2.0 high school GPA, audition. Auditions held on campus.

Undergraduate Contact Robin Cozart, Acting Director of Admissions, Virginia Intermont College, Box D-460, Bristol, Virginia 24201; 703-669-6101 ext. 207, fax: 703-669-5763.

Webster University

St. Louis, Missouri

Independent, coed. Suburban campus. Total enrollment: 10,834.

Degrees Bachelor of Fine Arts in the area of dance. Majors: dance. Cross-registration with various colleges in St. Louis.

Dance Student Profile Fall 1994: 15 total; all matriculated undergraduate; 15% minorities, 90% females, 15% international.

Dance Faculty Total: 8; 2 full-time, 6 part-time; 50% of full-time faculty have terminal degrees. Graduate students do not teach undergraduate courses. Undergraduate student–faculty ratio: 10:1.

Student Life Student groups include Dance Club.

Expenses for 1994–95 Application fee: $25. Comprehensive fee of $13,500 includes full-time tuition ($9160) and college room and board ($4340). Part-time tuition: $280 per credit hour.

Application Procedures Deadline—freshmen and transfers: continuous. Required: essay, high school transcript, college transcript(s) for transfer students, 2 letters of recommendation, audition, SAT I or ACT test scores. Recommended: minimum 2.0 high school GPA. Auditions held 8 times on campus; videotaped performances are permissible as a substitute for live auditions when distance is prohibitive.

Undergraduate Contact Mary Walz, Auditions Coordinator, Office of Admissions, Webster University, 470 East Lockwood Avenue, St. Louis, Missouri 63119-3194; 314-968-7001, fax: 314-968-7115.

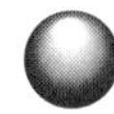

Potter College of Arts, Humanities, and Social Sciences

Western Kentucky University

Bowling Green, Kentucky

State-supported, coed. Suburban campus. Total enrollment: 14,765.

Degrees Bachelor of Fine Arts in the area of performing arts (dance). Majors: ballet, jazz dance, music theater, tap dance.

Dance Student Profile Fall 1994: 18 total; all matriculated undergraduate; 5% minorities, 75% females, 5% international.

Dance Faculty Total: 8; 8 full-time; 80% of full-time faculty have terminal degrees. Graduate students do not teach undergraduate courses. Undergraduate student–faculty ratio: 12:1.

Student Life Student groups include Dance Company, Musical Theatre Ensemble.

Expenses for 1995–96 Application fee: $15. State resident tuition: $1910 full-time, $78 per semester hour part-time. Nonresident tuition: $5270 full-time, $218 per semester hour part-time. Full-time mandatory fees: $125. College room and board: $2456 (minimum). College room only: $1316 (minimum).

Application Procedures Deadline—freshmen and transfers: June 1. Required: high school transcript, minimum 2.0 high school GPA. Auditions held 1 time on campus; recorded music is permissible as a substitute for live auditions and videotaped performances are permissible as a substitute for live auditions. 20 Lone Star Ballet Scholarships for dancers ($1200).

Undergraduate Contact Office of Admissions, Western Kentucky University, 101 Cravens Center, One Big Red Way, Bowling Green, Kentucky 42101-3576; 502-745-5422.

Western Michigan University

Kalamazoo, Michigan

State-supported, coed. Urban campus. Total enrollment: 25,673.

Degrees Bachelor of Fine Arts in the area of dance. Majors: dance.

Dance Student Profile Fall 1994: 406 total; 83 matriculated undergraduate, 323 nondegree; 6% minorities, 87% females.

Dance Faculty Total: 15; 6 full-time, 9 part-time; 66% of full-time faculty have terminal degrees. Graduate students do not teach undergraduate courses. Undergraduate student–faculty ratio: 13:1.

Expenses for 1994–95 Application fee: $25. Part-time mandatory fees: $85 per semester. Full-time tuition ranges from $2705 to $3046 for state residents, $6936 to $7804 for nonresidents, according to class level. Part-time tuition per credit hour ranges from $87.25 to $98.25 for state residents, $223.75 to $251.75 for nonresidents, according to class level. Full-time mandatory fees: $455. College room and board: $4097. Special program-related fees: $10–$25 for accompanying fee, $6–$18 for enrichment fee.

Financial Aid Program-specific awards for Fall of 1994: 1–2 Dalton New Dance Major Scholarships for incoming students ($500), 1–2 Male Dance Major Scholarships for male undergraduates ($300–$500), 1 Ethnic Dance Major Scholarship for under-represented groups ($200–$400), 1–2 Exceptional Dance Major Scholarships for talented students ($750), 4–6 Outstanding Dance Major Scholarships for outstanding program majors ($1000).

Application Procedures Deadline—freshmen and transfers: March 15. Notification date—freshmen: continuous. Required: high school transcript, college transcript(s) for transfer students, minimum 2.0 high school GPA, audition, ACT test score only. Auditions held 3 times on campus; videotaped performances are permissible as a substitute for live auditions if student resides on the west coast.

Undergraduate Contact Jane Baas, Associate Professor of Dance and Academic Advisor, Dance Department, Western Michigan University, Kalamazoo, Michigan 49008-3833; 616-387-5840, fax: 616-387-5809.

Sybil B. Harrington College of Fine Arts and Humanities

West Texas A&M University

Canyon, Texas

State-supported, coed. Small-town campus. Total enrollment: 6,738.

Degrees Bachelor of Fine Arts in the area of dance. Majors: ballet, dance, jazz dance, modern dance, tap dance. Graduate degrees offered: Master of Fine Arts in the area of interdisciplinary studies: dance emphasis.

Dance Student Profile Fall 1994: 94 total; 32 matriculated undergraduate, 2 matriculated graduate, 60 nondegree; 16% minorities, 55% females.

West Texas A&M University *(continued)*

Dance Faculty Total: 2; 1 full-time, 1 part-time; 100% of full-time faculty have terminal degrees. Graduate students teach a few undergraduate courses. Undergraduate student–faculty ratio: 10:1.

Student Life Student groups include American College Dance Festival, University Ballet Expo.

Expenses for 1995–96 State resident tuition: $900 full-time. Nonresident tuition: $5280 full-time, $176 per semester hour part-time. State resident part-time tuition per semester ranges from $100 to $330. Full-time mandatory fees: $634. College room and board: $2900. College room only: $1400.

Financial Aid Program-specific awards for Fall of 1994:

Application Procedures Deadline—freshmen and transfers: August 1. Notification date—freshmen and transfers: August 1. Required: high school transcript, college transcript(s) for transfer students, minimum 2.0 high school GPA, SAT I or ACT test scores. Recommended: letter of recommendation, interview, audition. Auditions held at various times on campus; videotaped performances are permissible as a substitute for live auditions when distance is prohibitive.

Contact Neil Hess, Director, Dance Department, West Texas A&M University, Box 879, Canyon, Texas 79015; 806-656-2820, fax: 806-656-2779.

Wichita State University

Wichita, Kansas

State-supported, coed. Urban campus. Total enrollment: 14,558.

Degrees Bachelor of Fine Arts in the area of performing arts/dance. Majors: modern dance.

Dance Student Profile Fall 1994: 264 total; 22 matriculated undergraduate, 242 nondegree; 35% minorities, 85% females, 15% international.

Dance Faculty Total: 7; 3 full-time, 4 part-time; 100% of full-time faculty have terminal degrees. Graduate students do not teach undergraduate courses. Undergraduate student–faculty ratio: 10:1.

Student Life Student groups include Kansas Dance Festival, Mid-America Dance Network, American College Dance Festival.

Expenses for 1994–95 Application fee: $15. State resident tuition: $2090 full-time, $69.65 per credit hour part-time. Nonresident tuition: $7434 full-time, $247.80 per credit hour part-time. Part-time mandatory fees: $13 per semester. Full-time mandatory fees: $26. College room and board: $3121 (minimum). Special program-related fees: $12 for live accompanying fees.

Financial Aid Program-specific awards for Fall of 1994: 16–18 Miller Dance Scholarships for incoming students ($600–$1200).

Application Procedures Deadline—freshmen and transfers: continuous. Required: high school transcript, college transcript(s) for transfer students, minimum 2.0 high school GPA, audition, SAT I or ACT test scores. Auditions held 2 times on campus.

Undergraduate Contact Christine Schneikart-Luebbe, Director of Admissions, Office of Undergraduate Admissions, Wichita State University, 1845 Fairmount, Wichita, Kansas 67260-0124; 316-689-3085.

Wright State University

Fairborn, Ohio

State-supported, coed. Suburban campus. Total enrollment: 16,823.

Degrees Bachelor of Fine Arts in the area of dance. Majors: dance.

Dance Student Profile Fall 1994: 40 total; all matriculated undergraduate.

Dance Faculty Total: 4; 3 full-time, 1 part-time; 33% of full-time faculty have terminal degrees. Graduate students do not teach undergraduate courses.

Student Life Student groups include Dayton Ballet II Company, Dayton Contemporary Dance Company II.

Expenses for 1995–96 Application fee: $30. State resident tuition: $3429 full-time, $107 per credit hour part-time. Nonresident tuition: $6858 full-time, $214 per credit hour part-time. College room and board: $4806. Special program-related fees: $125 for private voice lessons.

Financial Aid Program-specific awards for Fall of 1994: Wright State/Dayton Ballet, Dayton Contemporary Dance Company II Awards for program majors ($1000–$2000).

Application Procedures Deadline—freshmen and transfers: continuous. Required: high school transcript, video, audition, SAT I or ACT test scores, dance photograph. Auditions held by appointment on campus; videotaped performances are permissible as a substitute for live auditions.

Undergraduate Contact Victoria Oleen, Administrative Coordinator, Department of Theatre Arts, Wright State University, 3640 Colonel Glenn Highway, T148 CAC, Dayton, Ohio 45435; 513-873-3072, fax: 513-873-3787.

York University

North York, Ontario

Province-supported, coed. Urban campus. Total enrollment: 38,313.

Degrees Bachelor of Fine Arts in the area of dance. Majors: ballet, composition, modern dance.

Dance Student Profile Fall 1994: 120 total; all matriculated undergraduate.

Dance Faculty Total: 15; 9 full-time, 6 part-time. Graduate students teach a few undergraduate courses. Undergraduate student–faculty ratio: 8:1.

Expenses for 1994–95 Application fee: $75. Canadian resident tuition: $2720 full-time, $90.67 per credit part-time. Nonresident tuition: $8894 full-time, $296.47 per credit part-time. (All figures are in Canadian dollars.). Full-time mandatory fees: $140. College room and board: $3796. College room only: $3201.

Financial Aid Program-specific awards for Fall of 1994: 1 Talent Award for students with outstanding audition ($1000).

Application Procedures Deadline—freshmen and transfers: March 1. Notification date—freshmen: June 30; transfers: July 15. Required: high school transcript, college transcript(s) for transfer students, minimum 3.0 high school GPA, interview, audition, SAT, ACT or Canadian equivalent. Recommended: letter of recommendation. Auditions held 1 time on campus and off campus; videotaped performances are permissible as a substitute for live auditions when distance is prohibitive. Portfolio reviews held on campus and off campus.

Undergraduate Contact Don Murdoch, Liaison Officer, Liaison and Advising, Faculty of Fine Arts, York University, 213 CFA, 4700 Keele Street, North York, Ontario M3J 1P3; 416-736-5135, fax: 416-736-5447, E-mail address: donm@vm2.yorku.ca.

MUSIC PROGRAMS

MUSIC PROGRAMS

Interested in pursuing a music degree? Your first step will be to decide which type of program and setting is right for you. Professional degree programs, which are the main subject of this book, most often lead to the Bachelor of Music (B.M.) or the Bachelor of Music Education (B.M.E.). Offered at conservatories, liberal arts colleges, and universities, these programs emphasize acquiring professional skills in either performance or education. Enroll in one of them and you can expect to devote about 75 percent of your work to music and 25 percent to studying other areas.

Where to Study for a Professional Degree

If you go the liberal arts route, on the other hand, you'll earn a Bachelor of Arts (B.A.) in music. About half your course work will be in music and half will be spent on other subjects.

A few schools offer a Bachelor of Fine Arts (B.F.A.) degree program, where two thirds of the course work is in your area and one third is outside of it. Some schools also have a double-degree program, which usually offers both a B.A. and a B.M.

Once you know the type of degree you'd like to earn, you'll need to consider the setting in which you'll live, study, grow, and have fun 24 hours each day, week after week, for the next several years. Curriculum alone won't tell you whether you'll be happiest at a conservatory, small liberal arts college, or a large urban campus of a major university—the required coursework may not be that different among institutions. What you really need to think about is the overall environment and mindset schools offer. Do you want to go where students eat, breathe, and sleep music? Are you charged up by the thought of living in a large city and studying with professional musicians who make their living performing? If you are, a conservatory may be your first choice.

Or would you prefer a university or college, which may offer more diverse course offerings, and social and sports activities, as well as students with different majors. To make the best choice, don't just ask, "What's the best school for me musically?" but rather consider, "What's the best school for me musically *and* academically and socially and emotionally?"

Looking for a Mentor?

Still undecided between conservatory and college settings? Consider with whom you'd like to study. Most professors at conservatories are working professionals who teach part-time, while most university faculties tend to be made up of full-time teachers. Faculty members are probably more available to students in a university setting, since they're committing their life's work to teaching. In the conservatory, on the other hand, you're going to work with people who live what they teach every day. As practicing professionals, they may be able to provide a different kind of guidance than university professors. They also may have different employment contacts.

Career Implications

A good majority of people who are playing in orchestras in America probably graduated from conservatories, simply because the training is so focused and oriented toward preparing students for that career. However, a significant number of professionals attended non-conservatory institutions. Most people who choose liberal arts colleges and universities tend to have more diverse interests.

Whatever program you choose, keep in mind that 99 percent of the people doing anything in music have extensive formal training. Music is much more structured than a lot of the other arts. Theoretical studies provide the structure that puts music together. If you don't know theory, you're going to have big holes in your knowledge. Pursuing a degree will not only make you a better, more well-rounded musician, it also provides an automatic connection to the arts world that's much more difficult to get on your own.

Student Self-Evaluation

Questions to Ask Yourself before Applying to a Music Program

How strongly am I committed to devoting my life to music? If you believe you want to be an artist, you cannot do it halfway. You must devote every ounce of your energy to it or it will never happen. You must believe that you can do it and feel that you must do it.

What are my strengths and weaknesses? What areas of my craft do I want and need to develop? Seek evaluation from other people. Ask the music teachers you have in school, because they know you well and have watched you grow. Also try to consult other people, such as a conductor or principal player in your instrument in the local symphony or an opera singer or jazz musician in your area. Take a lesson with them for evaluation and ask, "What do you think of me? What do you think I can do? What are my problems?" You'll start hearing some common themes about your strengths and weaknesses.

Do I want the very focused professional training a conservatory would give me, or do I want to study music within a broader liberal arts context at a college or university? A university program will offer more of a diverse "college experience," while a conservatory offers the company of like-minded and equally dedicated people. This is an important choice. You have to look at the social and emotional dimensions and see what would be right for you at this stage in your life, because getting the right musical training in the wrong environment may not serve you well.

What size school do I want? Will I be most comfortable in a smaller, more intimate setting, or do I want the diversity of a large school?

What geographic area do I want to be in? A particular section of the country? In a major cultural center? Near an organization with which I'd like to work? In a quiet rural area where I won't be distracted?

Program Evaluation

Questions to Ask About a Program to Determine if It's the Right One for You

What is the focus of the program? Every program has a different emphasis. One school may be more rooted in a nineteenth-century tradition, while another may be avant-garde in its approach. Each institution has a very different bent, and you'll want to find out what that is.

What kind of atmosphere does the school have? Consider the feeling of the place, the environment in which you'll be studying. The best school for you is the one that will enable you to grow as thoroughly and quickly as possible.

What opportunities are there for me to perform? How many student performance groups—orchestras, bands, jazz ensembles, chamber music groups, opera productions—are there? How many concerts or recitals do students take part in each semester? How many recitals are required for graduation?

How large is the school or university? How many people are in the program in which I'm interested? In my instrument? What's the student-faculty ratio in my area of study? Does the school's location suit my needs and preferences?

Does the program feature guest artists, artists-in-residence, or industry visitors so I can meet practicing professionals and learn the latest theories and techniques? How long do they stay on campus? Do they give lectures, teach classes, or offer workshops? Do they work with all students or just those at a certain level?

How many faculty members teach my instrument? Who is on the faculty? Are they practicing in their field? Are they the best choice for my particular needs at this time?

What are alumni of the program doing? Any school of any name or size can always have one or two stars. It is important to look at the total number of people actually working in their chosen field or a related field.

What kind of facilities are available to me to practice my craft? Is there adequate practice space? Is the equipment state-of-the-art?

What kind of placement help does the program or school offer?

The Application Process

In addition to transcripts, test scores, and the usual forms, music students have to audition. Of course, every school is different and the importance of the audition in the admissions process varies. But in general, the more selective the institution, the more important the audition. Apply to a conservatory, then the audition will be the critical factor, followed by grades and test scores or interviews. When looking at a university or liberal arts college, by contrast, you'll usually find the admission criteria are more equally weighted—you'll need to pass both academic and performance requirements to get in.

Auditions

Some schools hold regional auditions in different cities, while others, like Juilliard in New York and Curtis Institute of Music in Philadelphia, require students to go to them. When schools hold auditions in different cities, a representative—either an admissions officer or faculty member—makes a videotape or audiotape to bring back for review.

Auditions are usually judged by teachers of your instrument. Whether it's one person or 10 depends on the institution's philosophy and the size of the faculty. Let's say you're auditioning in flute. Here are three examples of what might happen: At a conservatory, the flute faculty will all listen to the audition. At a college or university with a much smaller faculty—say with only one flute teacher—the whole woodwind faculty will listen. At yet another college, only one teacher will listen to tapes and/or auditions.

What are Judges Listening for?

First and foremost, judges are looking for raw talent and second, technique. And third, they are listening for something special—a musicality and artistry that sets you apart.

As a rule, the more applicants a school has, the shorter the audition. An audition at most high-powered schools can be as short as 5 to 15 minutes. A liberal arts college with a smaller applicant pool is often able to take a more personal approach. They may take a ½ hour with you, listening to you play and then interviewing you. Generally you go in and they'll ask for your first piece. They'll probably stop you somewhere along the way and ask you for a second piece. They'll stop you along the way and, if time permits, they'll ask you for part of a third piece. And that's about it. The school will usually let applicants know if the audition will include sight reading (playing a piece you haven't prepared).

As far as the audition repertoire goes, usually it's stated in general terms, such as: "Play a piece from the eighteenth, nineteenth, and twentieth centuries in contrasting styles." But some schools ask for very specific things, like a Mozart concerto, for example.

Never play pieces that you can't handle yet. Teachers are much more impressed with seeing what you can do rather than what you can't. It's better to pick an easier piece that you play extremely well. And definitely don't play something you don't like even though you may be able to play it technically well and you think the teacher is going to like it. When auditioning, if you can't sell it, don't play it.

Never play pieces that you can't handle yet. . . . It's better to pick an easier piece that you play extremely well.

Will I Get a Job?

With 300 or 500 people auditioning for one spot in an orchestra, competition is often incredibly intense. Some instruments, such as the flute, the trumpet, and the clarinet, are more popular and more competitive than others. The bassoon, viola, and double bass are not as competitive. But it's still competitive—it's just that a bassoon position might only have 100 applicants. And that holds true, by the way, with getting into college, too. If you're a flutist, you're going to have a harder time getting into a selective school than if you're a bassoonist. When a school says it accepts x percent of the number of people who apply, that's an overall figure. It may accept 100 percent of the double bassists and 5 percent of the flutists.

In the area of jazz and commercial music the way to jobs is not quite so structured. Most often there are no formal auditions; you get recommended from other professionals or a contractor may call you for a particular gig. You may audition for a contractor and he/she may call you to do a Broadway show. Then through contacts you have made on other gigs you may do a European tour with a group for six months. Then you're back in the United States substituting for someone in the Radio City Music Hall Orchestra.

Other Career Tracks

Besides performance, music students can prepare for careers in teaching, sound engineering, music therapy, and arts administration. With an undergraduate degree in music education, you can teach elementary and secondary school. To teach at the college level, however, you'll probably need performance and/or music education training up through a doctoral degree.

When considering the future, don't rule out nonmusic career opportunities. The analytical skills music students acquire are often quite useful in other fields, including computer science, medicine, or law.

Studying Abroad

Most of the conservatories have large international populations, but very few have significant study programs in any other countries. A college or university may have a general study abroad program, but usually not one specifically in music.

Guest Artists/ Artists-in-Residence

It's important for a school to offer students exposure to the professional world. Whether schools bring in guest conductors or have visiting artists hold master classes, such contacts allow students to look at the world a bit differently and get a fresh perspective from the outside.

Internships

At the undergraduate level, internships are almost nonexistent. Metropolitan areas, however, will have secondary orchestras, churches and synagogues, and regional jazz bands that hire students. Some smaller cities may have a regional symphony that welcomes student enrollment.

Advice for Studying Music

Students should be involved as much as they can not only in their own high school music activities but also in local, district, and state youth orchestras and performance ensembles. The more you perform and study, the deeper and richer your musical experience becomes and the more confident you will be on stage. These experiences will clearly show in your auditions and you'll be a better candidate for admission at your schools of choice.

Aaron Copland School of Music

See Queens College of the City University of New York, Aaron Copland School of Music

Abilene Christian University

Abilene, Texas

Independent-religious, coed. Urban campus. Total enrollment: 4,207.

Degrees Bachelor of Music in the areas of music education, performance. Majors: piano, stringed instruments, voice, wind and percussion instruments. Cross-registration with Hardin–Simmons University.

Music Student Profile Fall 1994: 80 total; all matriculated undergraduate; 60% females, 3% international.

Music Faculty Total: 24; 12 full-time, 12 part-time; 60% of full-time faculty have terminal degrees. Graduate students do not teach undergraduate courses.

Student Life Student groups include Children's Theater, Sing Song, Homecoming Musical.

Expenses for 1995–96 Application fee: $10. Comprehensive fee of $12,150 includes full-time tuition ($8320), mandatory fees ($200), and college room and board ($3630). College room only: $1600. Part-time tuition: $260 per semester hour.

Financial Aid Program-specific awards for Fall of 1994: 10–15 Budgeted Awards for musically qualified ($750), 5 Endowed Awards for program majors ($800).

Application Procedures Deadline—freshmen and transfers: continuous. Required: high school transcript, letter of recommendation, audition, ACT test score only, minimum composite ACT score of 19. Recommended: interview. Auditions held 2 times on campus; recorded music is permissible as a substitute for live auditions when distance is prohibitive and videotaped performances are permissible as a substitute for live auditions when scheduling is difficult.

Undergraduate Contact Dr. Ed George, Chair, Music Department, Abilene Christian University, ACU Station, Box 8274, Abilene, Texas 79699; 915-674-2199.

Acadia University

Wolfville, Nova Scotia

Province-supported, coed. Rural campus. Total enrollment: 4,115.

Degrees Bachelor of Music in the areas of performance, composition, music theory/history, 18th century studies, music education. Majors: composition, harpsichord, music, music education, music history, music theory, piano/organ, stringed instruments, voice, wind and percussion instruments.

Music Student Profile Fall 1994: 106 total; 94 matriculated undergraduate, 12 nondegree; 7% minorities, 60% females, 8% international.

Music Faculty Total: 25; 12 full-time, 13 part-time; 100% of full-time faculty have terminal degrees. Graduate students do not teach undergraduate courses. Undergraduate student–faculty ratio: 7:1.

Financial Aid Program-specific awards for Fall of 1994: Alumni Awards for program majors, Endowed Awards for program majors.

Application Procedures Deadline—freshmen and transfers: August 1. Notification date—freshmen and transfers: September 1. Required: high school transcript, college transcript(s) for transfer students, 2 letters of recommendation, interview, audition, music theory test. Recommended: minimum 3.0 high school GPA. Auditions held 6 times on campus; recorded music is permissible as a substitute for live auditions when distance is prohibitive and videotaped performances are permissible as a substitute for live auditions when distance is prohibitive.

Undergraduate Contact Director, School of Music, Acadia University, Wolfville, Nova Scotia B0P 1X0, Canada; 902-542-2201 ext. 1512, E-mail address: bjordan@ace.acadia.ca.

Alcorn State University

Lorman, Mississippi

State-supported, coed. Rural campus. Total enrollment: 2,742.

Degrees Bachelor of Music in the area of performance; Bachelor of Music Education in the area of music education. Majors: guitar, music education, piano/organ, voice, wind and percussion instruments.

Music Student Profile Fall 1994: 60 total; all matriculated undergraduate.

Music Faculty Total: 12; 12 full-time.

Expenses for 1995–96 State resident tuition: $2589 full-time, $108 per semester hour part-time. Nonresident tuition: $5091 full-time, $213 per semester hour part-time. College room and board: $2029.

Application Procedures Deadline—freshmen and transfers: July 31. Required: high school transcript, audition, SAT I or ACT test scores. Auditions held as needed on campus and off campus in various sites in southern United States; recorded music is permissible as a substitute for live auditions when distance is prohibitive.

Undergraduate Contact Dr. Joyce Bolden, Chair, Department of Fine Arts, Alcorn State University, 1000 ASU Drive #29, Lorman, Mississippi 39096-9402; 601-877-6261, fax: 601-877-6256.

Alverno College

Milwaukee, Wisconsin

Independent-religious, women only. Suburban campus. Total enrollment: 1,876.

Degrees Bachelor of Music in the areas of music education, music therapy, music pedagogy, music performance and pedagogy. Majors: music education, music pedagogy, music therapy, performance.

Music Student Profile Fall 1994: 45 total; all matriculated undergraduate; 5% minorities, 100% females.

Music Faculty Total: 16; 5 full-time, 11 part-time; 50% of full-time faculty have terminal degrees. Undergraduate student–faculty ratio: 3:1.

Student Life Student groups include Music Therapy Club, Music Educators National Conference Student Chapter, Delta Omicron.

Expenses for 1995–96 Application fee: $10. Comprehensive fee of $12,698 includes full-time tuition ($8928 minimum) and college room and board ($3770). Part-time tuition: $372 per unit (minimum). Tuition for nursing and engineering programs: $8964 full-time, $373.50 per unit part-time. Special program-related fees: $100–$200 for private lessons.

Application Procedures Deadline—freshmen and transfers: continuous. Required: audition. Auditions held 5 times on campus; recorded music is permissible as a substitute for live auditions for out-of-state applicants and videotaped performances are permissible as a substitute for live auditions for out-of-state applicants. Portfolio reviews held 2 times on campus.

Undergraduate Contact Colleen Hayes, Director, Admissions Department, Alverno College, 3401 South 39th Street, Milwaukee, Wisconsin 53234-3922; 414-382-6100, fax: 414-382-6354.

American Conservatory of Music

Chicago, Illinois

Independent, coed. Urban campus. Total enrollment: 117.

Degrees Bachelor of Music in the areas of jazz, classical music. Majors: classical music, composition, jazz, music theory, piano/organ, stringed instruments, voice, wind and percussion instruments. Graduate degrees offered: Master of Music in the areas of jazz, classical music. Doctor of Musical Arts in the areas of jazz, classical music.

Music Student Profile Fall 1994: 160 total; 47 matriculated undergraduate, 60 matriculated graduate, 53 nondegree; 50% minorities, 60% females, 70% international.

Music Faculty Total: 35; 10 full-time, 25 part-time; 90% of full-time faculty have terminal degrees. Graduate students teach a few undergraduate courses. Undergraduate student–faculty ratio: 5:1.

Expenses for 1995–96 Application fee: $50. Tuition: $7000 (minimum) full-time, $195 per credit part-time. Full-time mandatory fees: $75.

Application Procedures Deadline—freshmen and transfers: continuous. Required: essay, audition. Recommended: high school transcript, minimum 2.0 high school GPA, 2 letters of recommendation, interview, video, portfolio. Auditions held 10–12 times on campus; recorded music is permissible as a substitute for live auditions when distance is prohibitive and videotaped performances are permissible as a substitute for live auditions when distance is prohibitive.

Undergraduate Contact Joseph Miller, Director of Admissions, American Conservatory of Music, 16 North Wabash, Chicago, Illinois 60602; 312-263-4161.

Graduate Contact Patrick Riley, Director, Graduate Programs, American Conservatory of Music, 16 North Wabash, Chicago, Illinois 60602; 312-263-4161.

American University

Washington, District of Columbia

Independent-religious, coed. Suburban campus. Total enrollment: 11,708.

Degrees Bachelor of Music. Majors: classical music. Graduate degrees offered: Master of Music.

Music Student Profile Fall 1994: 35 total; 20 matriculated undergraduate, 15 matriculated graduate; 20% minorities, 50% females, 40% international.

Music Faculty Total: 36; 6 full-time, 30 part-time; 60% of full-time faculty have terminal degrees. Undergraduate student–faculty ratio: 5:1.

Student Life Student groups include Music Club.

Expenses for 1995–96 Application fee: $45. Comprehensive fee of $23,808 includes full-time tuition ($16,890), mandatory fees ($220), and college room and board ($6698). College room only: $4160. Part-time tuition: $563 per semester hour. Part-time mandatory fees: $220 per year. Special program-related fees: $75–$150 for applied music fee.

Financial Aid Program-specific awards for Fall of 1994: 5 Endowed Scholarships for program majors ($1000), 4 Music Awards for string instrumentalists ($1250–$15,000).

Application Procedures Deadline—freshmen: February 1; transfers: July 1. Notification date—freshmen: April 1; transfers: continuous. Required: essay, high school transcript, minimum 2.0 high school GPA, 3 letters of recommendation, SAT I or ACT test scores. Recommended: minimum 3.0 high school GPA, interview, audition. Auditions held by appointment on campus; recorded music is permissible as a substitute for live auditions when distance is prohibitive and videotaped performances are permissible as a substitute for live auditions when distance is prohibitive.

Undergraduate Contact Elizabeth Vrenios, Director, Music Division, Department of Performing Arts, American University, 4400 Massachusetts Avenue, NW, Washington, District of Columbia 20016; 202-885-3431.

Anderson College

Anderson, South Carolina

Independent-religious, coed. Small-town campus. Total enrollment: 932.

Degrees Bachelor of Music Education in the areas of choral music education, instrumental music education. Majors: instrumental music, music education, piano/organ, stringed instruments, voice, wind and percussion instruments.

Music Student Profile Fall 1994: 23 total; all matriculated undergraduate; 15% minorities, 59% females, 4% international.

Music Faculty Total: 11; 5 full-time, 6 part-time; 80% of full-time faculty have terminal degrees. Graduate students do not teach undergraduate courses. Undergraduate student–faculty ratio: 11:1.

Student Life Student groups include Music Educators National Conference, Anderson College Playhouse.

Estimated Expenses for 1995–96 Application fee: $20. Comprehensive fee of $13,060 includes full-time tuition ($8026), mandatory fees ($862), and college room and board ($4172). College room only: $2086. Part-time tuition: $208 per semester hour. Special program-related fees: $400–$600 for private music lessons.

Financial Aid Program-specific awards for Fall of 1994: 46 Music Scholarships for program majors ($1500), 13 Choir Scholarships for non-music majors ($500), 12 Anderson College Music Scholarships for freshmen ($1600).

Application Procedures Deadline—freshmen and transfers: August 15. Required: high school transcript, college transcript(s) for transfer students, minimum 2.0 high school GPA, interview, audition, SAT I or ACT test scores. Recommended: minimum 3.0 high school GPA. Auditions held 5 times on campus; recorded music is permissible as a substitute for live auditions when distance is prohibitive.

Undergraduate Contact Dr. Janet L. Roberts, Coordinator, BME Program, Anderson College, 316 Boulevard, Anderson, South Carolina 29621; 803-231-2127, fax: 803-231-2004, E-mail address: sopsinger@aol.com.

Andrews University

Berrien Springs, Michigan

Independent-religious, coed. Small-town campus. Total enrollment: 2,952.

Degrees Bachelor of Music in the areas of music education, performance. Majors: music, music education, piano/organ, stringed instruments, voice, wind and percussion instruments. Graduate degrees offered: Master of Music in the areas of music education, performance.

Music Student Profile Fall 1994: 33 total.

Music Faculty Total: 25; 7 full-time, 18 part-time. Graduate students do not teach undergraduate courses.

Student Life Student groups include Collegiate Music Educators National Conference, Composers Club.

Expenses for 1995–96 Application fee: $30. Comprehensive fee of $13,833 includes full-time tuition ($10,476), mandatory fees ($147), and college room and board ($3210). College room only: $1890. Part-time tuition: $262 per quarter hour.

Financial Aid Program-specific awards for Fall of 1994: Named Scholarships for program majors ($500–$1000), Performance Scholarship for Ensembles for ensemble performers ($500–$1000).

Application Procedures Deadline—freshmen and transfers: continuous. Required: high school transcript, college transcript(s) for transfer students, 3 letters of recommendation, audition. Auditions held by request on campus and off campus. Portfolio reviews held on campus and off campus.

Undergraduate Contact Department of Music, Andrews University, Berrien Springs, Michigan 49104-0230; 616-471-3600.

Graduate Contact Graduate Admissions, Department of Music, Andrews University, Berrien Springs, Michigan 49104-0230; 616-471-3600.

Angelo State University

San Angelo, Texas

State-supported, coed. Urban campus. Total enrollment: 6,276.

Degrees Bachelor of Music in the area of music education. Majors: music, music education, piano/organ, voice, wind and percussion instruments.

Music Student Profile Fall 1994: 90 total; all matriculated undergraduate; 10% minorities, 50% females.

Music Faculty Total: 13; 10 full-time, 3 part-time; 40% of full-time faculty have terminal degrees. Graduate students do not teach undergraduate courses. Undergraduate student–faculty ratio: 7:1.

Student Life Student groups include Kappa Kappa Psi, Phi Mu Alpha, Sigma Alpha Iota.

Expenses for 1995–96 State resident tuition: $900 full-time. Nonresident tuition: $6660 full-time, $222 per semester hour part-time. State resident part-time tuition per semester ranges from $120 to $330. Part-time mandatory fees per semester range from $92 to $374. Full-time mandatory fees: $884. College room and board: $3500 (minimum). Special program-related fees: $25 for private lessons.

Financial Aid Program-specific awards for Fall of 1994: Carr Academic Scholarships for academically qualified applicants ($3000), Band Awards for instrumentalists ($300), Choral Awards for vocalists ($300).

Application Procedures Deadline—freshmen and transfers: August 5. Notification date—freshmen and transfers: August 15. Required: high school transcript, college transcript(s) for transfer students, audition, SAT I or ACT test scores. Recommended: minimum 2.0 high school GPA, letter of recommendation. Auditions held continuously on campus; recorded music is permissible as a substitute for live auditions for out-of-state applicants and videotaped performances are permissible as a substitute for live auditions for out-of-state applicants.

Undergraduate Contact Dean of Admissions and Registrar, Angelo State University, Administration and Journalism Building, San Angelo, Texas 76909; 915-942-2042.

Anna Maria College

Paxton, Massachusetts

Independent-religious, coed. Small-town campus. Total enrollment: 1,797.

Degrees Bachelor of Music in the areas of music education, music therapy, music education and music therapy, piano performance, vocal performance. Majors: music, music education, music therapy, piano/organ, voice. Cross-registration with Worcester Consortium.

Music Student Profile Fall 1994: 33 total; all matriculated undergraduate; 1% minorities, 42% females, 1% international.

Music Faculty Total: 13; 5 full-time, 8 part-time; 50% of full-time faculty have terminal degrees. Graduate students do not teach undergraduate courses. Undergraduate student–faculty ratio: 8:1.

Student Life Student groups include Music Club, Music Educators National Conference, Music Therapy Club. Special housing available for music students.

Expenses for 1995–96 Application fee: $30. Comprehensive fee of $16,808 includes full-time tuition ($11,280), mandatory fees ($500), and college room and board ($5028). Part-time tuition: $151 per credit hour. Special program-related fees: $30 for private lessons.

Financial Aid Program-specific awards for Fall of 1994: 4 Music Scholarships for program majors ($1000).

Application Procedures Deadline—freshmen and transfers: continuous. Required: essay, high school transcript, college transcript(s) for transfer students, minimum 2.0 high school GPA, 3 letters of recommendation, audition, SAT I or ACT test scores. Recommended: interview. Auditions held as needed on campus.

Undergraduate Contact David Pirani, Director of Admissions, Anna Maria College, Box 78, Paxton, Massachusetts 01612-1198; 508-849-3360, fax: 508-849-3362.

More about the College

The chief goal of music study at Anna Maria College is continuing growth of technique, sensitivity, and intellectual background, whereby each student's potential for musical self expression and communication is realized to the greatest possible extent. AMC's music programs and campus-wide commitment to developing the total person cultivate not only fine musicians, but well-rounded professionals.

The College is accredited by The New England Association of Schools and Colleges (NEASC) and is a full member of the National Association of Schools of Music (NASM). The music therapy program is approved by the National Association for Music Therapy (NAMT); the music education program is approved by the Massachusetts Department of Education. AMC is one of only a few colleges in the Northeast with a music therapy major.

AMC's small-college environment fosters close, personal contact with faculty and with other students. The comradery among music students is reflected in the fact that many choose to reside in the same dormitory wing. Most music classes have under 12 students, allowing maximum individual attention. In terms of music facilities, the College compares favorably with larger institutions. The 350-seat Zecco Performing Arts Center and the 75-seat Payer Concert Room are ideal for student and faculty concerts; they are also popular venues for guest performers.

Students sing in the chorus and participate as soloists, ensemble performers, or accompanists in recitals and department concerts. Instrumentalists have additional ensemble and orchestral performance opportunities through nearby colleges of Worcester Consortium of which AMC is a member. Active clubs on campus include the Music Club, the student chapter of Music Educators National Conference (MENC), and the Music Therapy Club. Concerts sponsored by these clubs are widely appreciated by the AMC community and the general public. High achievers are candidates for the Delta Epsilon Sigma honor society.

The advantage of studying music at AMC, which offers over thirty academic programs, is exposure to a wider spectrum of perspective and thought than found at more specialized institutions. Some music majors participate in NCAA Division III athletics together with art, business, criminal justice, English, psychology, science, social work, and other majors. Some act in AMC Theater Club plays. Still others serve with the Student Government Association or the AMC Cultural Committee.

Opportunities abound on the College's very safe, rural 180-acre campus, and other exciting activities are just 15 minutes away in Worcester, New England's second-largest city. Musical events in the city include the Worcester County Music Association's Music Festival, the Community Concerts series, concerts at the Worcester Art Museum, and performances at various other locations, including Mechanics Hall and the Worcester Centrum.

At the heart of the AMC music program are the dedicated, distinguished music professionals of the department's faculty. Many have performed nationally and internationally, yet all remain true to their chosen vocation of educating students. At AMC, the focus is always on the students.

The College offers counseling services, English as a Second Language (ESL) for international students, a Learning Center, and a Career Development Center.

Program Facilities Zecco Performing Arts Center (350 seats), Payer Concert Room (75 seats), a separate building exclusively for music, fifteen practice rooms, all with windows; several grand pianos available for practice, a computer lab with high-speed laser printers, World Wide Web access, and a variety of CD-ROM selections, a library media room with scores, recordings, and audio/video equipment, and interlibrary loan of materials from other Worcester Consortium colleges.

Faculty and Alumni Members of the faculty have made significant contributions to music through their perfor-

MUSIC

248

Anna Maria College *(continued)*

mances, recordings, books, and papers, as well as through their active participation in professional organizations. Many alumni are conspicuously placed in the musical world as faculty members at major universities and colleges, administrators in elementary and secondary schools, solo and ensemble performers, and members/directors of opera companies.

Student Performance/Ensemble Opportunities Students sing in the chorus and participate as soloists, ensemble performers, or accompanists in recitals and department concerts. Instrumentalists have additional ensemble and orchestral performance opportunities through nearby colleges of Worcester Consortium for Higher Education.

Special Programs Counseling and health services, music education prepracticum and student teaching, music therapy clinical experiences and six-month internship, ESL program for international students, including academic-year ESL classes and tutorial assistance.

Appalachian State University

Boone, North Carolina

State-supported, coed. Small-town campus. Total enrollment: 11,866.

Degrees Bachelor of Music in the areas of music education, performance, composition, sacred music. Majors: classical music, music, musical instrument technology, piano/organ, stringed instruments, voice, wind and percussion instruments. Graduate degrees offered: Master of Music in the areas of music education, performance.

Music Student Profile Fall 1994: 355 total; 325 matriculated undergraduate, 30 matriculated graduate; 5% minorities, 47% females, 2% international.

Music Faculty Total: 42; 30 full-time, 12 part-time; 90% of full-time faculty have terminal degrees. Graduate students teach a few undergraduate courses. Undergraduate student–faculty ratio: 10:1.

Student Life Student groups include Music Educators National Conference, Music and Entertainment Industry Student Association, music fraternities and sororities.

Estimated Expenses for 1995–96 Application fee: $25. State resident tuition: $800 full-time. Nonresident tuition: $7600 full-time. Full-time mandatory fees: $870. College room and board: $2630. College room only: $1470.

Financial Aid Program-specific awards for Fall of 1994: 20 School of Music Awards for program majors ($750–$1000), 6 Fletcher Scholarships for program majors ($1000–$5000), 1 Presser Award for program majors ($2250).

Application Procedures Deadline—freshmen and transfers: April 1. Notification date—freshmen and transfers: May 1. Required: high school transcript, college transcript(s) for transfer students, minimum 3.0 high school GPA, audition, SAT I or ACT test scores, minimum combined SAT I score of 800. Auditions held 4 times on campus; recorded music is permissible as a substitute for live auditions when distance is prohibitive and videotaped performances are permissible as a substitute for live auditions when distance is prohibitive.

Undergraduate Contact Olive Reece, Director, Undergraduate Admissions, School of Music, Appalachian State University, Rivers Street, Boone, North Carolina 28608; 704-262-3020, fax: 704-262-6446.

Graduate Contact William Harbinson, Director, Graduate Studies, School of Music, Appalachian State University, Rivers Street, Boone, North Carolina 28608; 704-262-3020, fax: 704-262-6446.

Aquinas College

Grand Rapids, Michigan

Independent-religious, coed. Suburban campus. Total enrollment: 2,443.

Degrees Bachelor of Music in the areas of choral supervision, instrumental supervision, organ performance, piano performance, voice performance, instrumental performance, liturgical music, jazz. Majors: jazz, liturgical music, music, music education, piano/organ.

Music Faculty Total: 12; 2 full-time, 10 part-time. Graduate students do not teach undergraduate courses.

Student Life Student groups include Music Educators National Conference.

Expenses for 1995–96 Application fee: $25. Comprehensive fee of $15,976 includes full-time tuition ($11,852 minimum) and college room and board ($4124). College room only: $1864. Part-time tuition per credit: $240 for the first 6 credits, $350 for the next 5 credits. Special program-related fees: $100 for voice student lab fees.

Financial Aid Program-specific awards for Fall of 1994: Departmental Awards for program majors.

Application Procedures Deadline—freshmen and transfers: continuous. Notification date—freshmen and transfers: continuous. Required: high school transcript, letter of recommendation.

Undergraduate Contact John Baird, Admissions Office, Aquinas College, 1607 Robinson Road, SE, Grand Rapids, Michigan 49506; 616-459-5193.

Arizona State University

Tempe, Arizona

State-supported, coed. Suburban campus. Total enrollment: 42,189.

Degrees Bachelor of Music in the areas of choral music, general music, instrumental music, music theater, performance, music theory and composition, music therapy, jazz performance, piano accompanying. Majors: jazz,

music education, music theater, piano/organ, stringed instruments, voice, wind and percussion instruments. Graduate degrees offered: Master of Music in the areas of choral music, general music, instrumental music, music theater, performance, music theater direction, performance pedagogy, music theory, composition, piano accompanying; Master of Music Education in the area of music education. Doctor of Musical Arts in the areas of choral music, instrumental music, performance.

Music Student Profile Fall 1994: 712 total; 436 matriculated undergraduate, 276 matriculated graduate; 5% minorities, 50% females, 5% international.

Music Faculty Total: 71; 62 full-time, 9 part-time; 75% of full-time faculty have terminal degrees. Graduate students teach a few undergraduate courses. Undergraduate student–faculty ratio: 16:1.

Expenses for 1994–95 State resident tuition: $1894 full-time. Nonresident tuition: $7500 full-time, $310 per credit part-time. State resident part-time tuition per semester ranges from $96 to $576. Part-time mandatory fees: $32 per year. College room and board: $4690. College room only: $3090.

Financial Aid Program-specific awards for Fall of 1994: 165 Tuition Waivers for non-residents ($8000), 167 Tuition Waivers for residents ($2000), 100 Cash Awards for program students ($500).

Application Procedures Deadline—freshmen and transfers: June 15. Required: high school transcript, audition. Auditions held 3 times on campus; recorded music is permissible as a substitute for live auditions if distance is prohibitive or in special circumstances and videotaped performances are permissible as a substitute for live auditions if distance is prohibitive or in special circumstances.

Contact Delores Thompson, Admissions Officer, School of Music, Arizona State University, Box 870405, Tempe, Arizona 85287-0405; 602-965-2816, fax: 602-965-2659.

Arkansas State University

State University, Arkansas

State-supported, coed. Urban campus. Total enrollment: 9,631.

Degrees Bachelor of Music in the areas of vocal music, instrumental music, keyboard performance, composition; Bachelor of Music Education in the areas of vocal music, instrumental music. Majors: music, music education, piano/organ, stringed instruments, voice, wind and percussion instruments. Graduate degrees offered: Master of Music in the areas of performance, composition; Master of Music Education in the area of music education.

Music Faculty Total: 38; 36 full-time, 2 part-time; 55% of full-time faculty have terminal degrees. Graduate students teach a few undergraduate courses. Undergraduate student–faculty ratio: 20:1.

Expenses for 1995–96 Application fee: $25. State resident tuition: $1950 full-time, $82 per credit hour part-time. Nonresident tuition: $3600 full-time, $150 per credit hour part-time. College room and board: $2590. Special program-related fees: $35–$55 for private lessons.

Application Procedures Deadline—freshmen and transfers: August 15. Required: high school transcript, audition. Recommended: minimum 2.0 high school GPA. Auditions held 2 times and by appointment on campus; recorded music is permissible as a substitute for live auditions by request and videotaped performances are permissible as a substitute for live auditions by request.

Undergraduate Contact Dr. William Holmes, Chair, Music Department, Arkansas State University, P.O. Box 779, State University, Arkansas 72467; 501-972-2094, fax: 501-972-3932.

Graduate Contact Dr. Neale Bartee, Graduate Music Coordinator, Music Department, Arkansas State University, P.O. Box 779, State University, Arkansas 72467; 501-972-2094, fax: 501-972-3932.

Armstrong State College

Savannah, Georgia

State-supported, coed. Suburban campus. Total enrollment: 5,040.

Degrees Bachelor of Music Education in the areas of instrumental music education, choral music education, general music education. Majors: music education.

Music Student Profile Fall 1994: 55 total; all matriculated undergraduate.

Music Faculty Total: 22; 9 full-time, 13 part-time; 78% of full-time faculty have terminal degrees. Graduate students do not teach undergraduate courses.

Expenses for 1995–96 Application fee: $10. State resident tuition: $1719 full-time. Nonresident tuition: $4929 full-time. Part-time tuition per quarter hour ranges from $285 to $495 for state residents, $735 to $1395 for nonresidents. College room and board: $3726.

Application Procedures Deadline—freshmen and transfers: continuous. Required: high school transcript, audition, SAT I or ACT test scores, music theory placement test. Auditions held continuously on campus; recorded music is permissible as a substitute for live auditions for out-of-state applicants and videotaped performances are permissible as a substitute for live auditions for out-of-state applicants.

Undergraduate Contact Dr. Jim Anderson, Head, Department of Art and Music, Armstrong State College, 11935 Abercorn Street, Savannah, Georgia 31419; 912-927-5325, fax: 912-912-5492, E-mail address: jim_anderson@mailgate.armstrong.edu.

Ashland University

Ashland, Ohio

Independent-religious, coed. Small-town campus. Total enrollment: 5,826.

Ashland University *(continued)*

Degrees Bachelor of Music in the area of music education. Majors: music education, piano/organ, stringed instruments, voice, wind and percussion instruments.

Music Faculty Graduate students do not teach undergraduate courses.

Student Life Student groups include Music Educators National Conference.

Expenses for 1995–96 Application fee: $15. Comprehensive fee of $17,258 includes full-time tuition ($12,174), mandatory fees ($248), and college room and board ($4836). College room only: $2547. Part-time tuition: $375 per credit hour. Part-time mandatory fees: $8 per credit hour. Special program-related fees: $150 for private music lessons, $20 for instrumental lab fees.

Financial Aid Program-specific awards for Fall of 1994: Scholarships for program majors.

Application Procedures Deadline—freshmen and transfers: continuous. Required: high school transcript, college transcript(s) for transfer students, letter of recommendation, SAT I or ACT test scores. Recommended: interview. Auditions held on campus and off campus. Portfolio reviews held on campus and off campus.

Undergraduate Contact Department of Music, Ashland University, 401 College Avenue, Ashland, Ohio 44805; 419-289-4142.

Atlantic Union College

South Lancaster, Massachusetts

Independent-religious, coed. Small-town campus. Total enrollment: 704.

Degrees Bachelor of Music in the areas of performance, music education. Majors: music education, piano/organ, stringed instruments, voice, wind and percussion instruments.

Music Student Profile Fall 1994: 13 total; all matriculated undergraduate.

Music Faculty Total: 25; 2 full-time, 23 part-time; 100% of full-time faculty have terminal degrees. Graduate students do not teach undergraduate courses. Undergraduate student–faculty ratio: 8:1.

Expenses for 1995–96 Application fee: $15. Comprehensive fee of $15,350 includes full-time tuition ($11,750) and college room and board ($3600). College room only: $2000. Part-time tuition: $442 per hour.

Application Procedures Deadline—freshmen and transfers: August 15. Required: high school transcript, minimum 2.0 high school GPA, 2 letters of recommendation, audition, SAT I or ACT test scores, 3 musical references. Auditions held as needed on campus and off campus; recorded music is permissible as a substitute for live auditions if a campus visit is impossible.

Undergraduate Contact Enrollment Management Office, Atlantic Union College, P.O. Box 1000, South Lancaster, Massachusetts 01561-1000; 508-368-2255, fax: 508-368-2015.

Auburn University

Auburn University, Alabama

State-supported, coed. Small-town campus. Total enrollment: 21,226.

Degrees Bachelor of Music in the areas of music performance, piano pedagogy, jazz studies, composition; Bachelor of Music Education in the areas of choral music, band. Majors: composition, jazz, performance, piano pedagogy.

Music Student Profile Fall 1994: 70 total; all matriculated undergraduate; 5% minorities, 50% females, 1% international.

Music Faculty Total: 28; 24 full-time, 4 part-time; 85% of full-time faculty have terminal degrees.

Student Life Student groups include Phi Mu Alpha.

Expenses for 1994–95 Application fee: $25. State resident tuition: $2100 full-time. Nonresident tuition: $6300 full-time. Part-time tuition per quarter ranges from $178 to $758 for state residents, $534 to $2274 for nonresidents. College room only: $1410 (minimum). Special program-related fees: $72 for applied music fees.

Financial Aid Program-specific awards for Fall of 1994: 5–10 Music Scholarships for music majors ($1000).

Application Procedures Deadline—freshmen and transfers: September 1. Required: audition. Auditions held on campus and off campus. Portfolio reviews held on campus and off campus.

Undergraduate Contact Joseph Stephenson, Head, Department of Music, Auburn University, 101 Goodwin Music Building, Auburn University, Alabama 36849-5420; 334-844-4164, fax: 334-844-3168.

Augsburg College

Minneapolis, Minnesota

Independent-religious, coed. Urban campus. Total enrollment: 2,958.

Degrees Bachelor of Music in the area of performance; Bachelor of Music Education in the area of music education. Majors: music, music education. Cross-registration with Associated Colleges of the Twin Cities.

Music Student Profile Fall 1994: 55 total; all matriculated undergraduate; 1% minorities, 70% females.

Music Faculty Total: 31; 7 full-time, 24 part-time; 70% of full-time faculty have terminal degrees. Graduate students do not teach undergraduate courses. Undergraduate student–faculty ratio: 8:1.

Student Life Student groups include Mu Phi Epsilon.

Expenses for 1995–96 Application fee: $20. Comprehensive fee of $17,193 includes full-time tuition ($12,490), mandatory fees ($112), and college room and board ($4591). Part-time tuition: $1350 per course.

Financial Aid Program-specific awards for Fall of 1994: 35 Scholarships for program majors ($200–$1500).

Application Procedures Deadline—freshmen and transfers: continuous. Required: essay, high school transcript, minimum 2.0 high school GPA, audition. Recommended: letter of recommendation. Auditions held 1 time on campus.

Undergraduate Contact Admissions, Augsburg College, 2211 Riverside Avenue, Minneapolis, Minnesota 55454; 612-330-1001, fax: 612-330-1649.

Augusta College

Augusta, Georgia

State-supported, coed. Urban campus. Total enrollment: 5,673.

Degrees Bachelor of Music in the area of performance; Bachelor of Music Education in the area of music education. Majors: music, music education, piano/organ, stringed instruments, voice, wind and percussion instruments.

Music Student Profile Fall 1994: 70 total; all matriculated undergraduate.

Music Faculty Total: 8; 8 full-time; 100% of full-time faculty have terminal degrees. Graduate students do not teach undergraduate courses. Undergraduate student–faculty ratio: 10:1.

Expenses for 1994–95 Application fee: $10. State resident tuition: $1632 full-time. Nonresident tuition: $4476 full-time. Part-time tuition per quarter ranges from $270 to $470 for state residents, $670 to $1270 for nonresidents. Special program-related fees: $25–$45 for applied music fee.

Financial Aid Program-specific awards for Fall of 1994: 12–15 Maxwell Fund Awards for program majors ($300–$600), 2 Storyland Theater Awards for music theater participants ($2000), 4 William Boyd Scholarships for program majors ($1650), 4–6 Church Scholarships for choir singers ($1200–$1650), 2 Mary Bird Scholarships for students from Columbia County, Georgia.

Application Procedures Deadline—freshmen and transfers: August 15. Required: high school transcript, minimum 2.0 high school GPA, 2 letters of recommendation. Recommended: audition. Auditions held 6 times on campus; recorded music is permissible as a substitute for live auditions when distance is prohibitive and videotaped performances are permissible as a substitute for live auditions when distance is prohibitive. Portfolio reviews held on campus.

Undergraduate Contact Dr. Clayton Shotwell, Chairman, Fine Arts Department, Augusta College, 2500 Walton Way, Augusta, Georgia 30904-2200; 706-737-1453.

Baker University

Baldwin City, Kansas

Independent-religious, coed. Small-town campus. Total enrollment: 1,997.

Degrees Bachelor of Music in the area of performance; Bachelor of Music Education in the area of music education. Majors: music, music education, piano/organ, voice, wind and percussion instruments.

Music Student Profile Fall 1994: 30 total; all matriculated undergraduate.

Music Faculty Total: 9; 6 full-time, 3 part-time; 83% of full-time faculty have terminal degrees. Graduate students do not teach undergraduate courses. Undergraduate student–faculty ratio: 15:1.

Student Life Student groups include Collegiate Music Educators National Conference.

Expenses for 1995–96 Application fee: $20. Comprehensive fee of $14,970 includes full-time tuition ($9600), mandatory fees ($270), and college room and board ($5100). Part-time tuition: $400 per credit hour.

Financial Aid Program-specific awards for Fall of 1994: 3 Music Department Scholarships for program majors ($3700).

Application Procedures Deadline—freshmen and transfers: continuous. Required: high school transcript, minimum 2.0 high school GPA, letter of recommendation, interview, audition. Recommended: minimum 3.0 high school GPA. Auditions held on campus; recorded music is permissible as a substitute for live auditions when distance is prohibitive and videotaped performances are permissible as a substitute for live auditions when distance is prohibitive.

Undergraduate Contact Dr. Roger Kugler, Chairman, Department of Music, Baker University, P.O. Box 65, Baldwin City, Kansas 66006-0065; 913-594-6451, fax: 913-594-6721.

Baldwin-Wallace College

Berea, Ohio

Independent-religious, coed. Suburban campus. Total enrollment: 4,716.

Degrees Bachelor of Music in the areas of performance, musical theater, music therapy, music theory, composition, music history and literature; Bachelor of Music Education in the areas of instrumental music education, vocal music education. Majors: classical music, composition, music, music education, music history and literature, music theater, music theory, music therapy, piano/organ, stringed instruments, voice, wind and percussion instruments.

Music Student Profile Fall 1994: 190 total; all matriculated undergraduate; 6% minorities, 60% females, 1% international.

Music Faculty Total: 52; 21 full-time, 31 part-time; 75% of full-time faculty have terminal degrees. Graduate students do not teach undergraduate courses. Undergraduate student–faculty ratio: 14:1.

Expenses for 1994–95 Application fee: $15. Comprehensive fee of $15,990 includes full-time tuition ($10,995), mandatory fees ($585), and college room and board ($4410). College room only: $2175. Part-time mandatory

Baldwin-Wallace College *(continued)*

fees per quarter range from $62 to $124. Part-time tuition per quarter hour: $238 for daytime classes, $163 for evening and weekend classes. Special program-related fees: $1,020 for private lessons.

Financial Aid Program-specific awards for Fall of 1994: 40–70 Talent Scholarships for program majors ($2000).

Application Procedures Deadline—freshmen and transfers: continuous. Notification date—freshmen and transfers: August 30. Required: essay, high school transcript, college transcript(s) for transfer students, 2 letters of recommendation, audition, SAT I or ACT test scores, minimum 2.5 high school GPA. Recommended: interview. Auditions held 5 times on campus and off campus in Interlochen, MI; Chicago, IL; recorded music is permissible as a substitute for live auditions if all application materials are complete and videotaped performances are permissible as a substitute for live auditions if all application materials are complete.

Undergraduate Contact Grace Hong, Admission Counselor, Conservatory of Music, Baldwin-Wallace College, 275 Eastland Road, Berea, Ohio 44017; 216-826-2367, fax: 216-826-3239, E-mail address: ghong@rs6000.baldwinw.edu.

More about the College

The reputation of The Conservatory at Baldwin-Wallace College is due in large part to an exceptional faculty of performing artists, scholars, and composers who are committed to developing the highest performance standards in students. The faculty of over 40 members includes members of both The Cleveland Orchestra and Ohio Chamber Orchestra.

The Conservatory offers the Bachelor of Music degree with concentration in performance, musical theater, music therapy, history and literature, composition, and theory. The Bachelor of Music Education degree offers concentrations in either vocal or instrumental music. Students desiring a stronger liberal arts emphasis may elect the Bachelor of Arts degree with concentrations in either general music or arts management.

Of special note are the programs in music therapy and musical theater. B-W is the home site of the Cleveland Music Therapy Consortium and maintains one of the most highly respected undergraduate music therapy programs in the United States. Therapy majors benefit from the fact that Cleveland leads the nation in its development and implementation of this discipline, and students have opportunities to work with many Registered Music Therapists in a variety of clinical settings. The musical theater program is Conservatory based with additional requirements in the dance and theater areas. Performance opportunities are abundant and include musical, drama, opera, and dance productions.

Performance is an integral part of all Conservatory degree programs. Numerous ensembles include orchestra, wind ensemble, three choirs and a stage choir, jazz ensemble, brass choir, percussion ensemble, collegium musicum, and many more.

With over ninety years of professional music training, the Baldwin-Wallace College Conservatory of Music assumes an established position among the nation's finest conservatories and schools of music. A sincere commitment to provide undergraduate students with the very best training within a supportive and highly personalized environment is the foundation upon which all degree programs are based.

The Baldwin-Wallace Conservatory truly is "more than a music school." A Conservatory student body of approximately 200 is enriched through interaction with professional musicians, scholars, and peers within the Conservatory as well as faculty and students from the Liberal Arts College. It is this greater College community that fosters individual growth—not just as a musician, but as a complete person.

At the B-W Conservatory, students do not compete with graduate students for performance opportunities, nor do they receive instruction from graduate teaching assistants. The faculty has a passion for teaching and working with undergraduate students, and the College is committed to providing the finest resources for its undergraduate students.

The Conservatory facilities have recently been extensively renovated in keeping with this institutional commitment. Kulas Musical Arts Building houses two concert halls, a 650-seat air-conditioned hall of superb acoustical design, and a 100-seat chamber hall. Kulas also houses a choral rehearsal room, faculty studios, classrooms, and an electronic music studio. Fifty practice rooms are well-maintained, many with brand new grand pianos. The adjoining Merner-Pfeiffer Hall houses administrative offices, faculty studios, the Jones Music Library, classrooms, the Music Therapy Center, and The Riemenschneider Bach Institute, one of the finest Bach research centers in the western hemisphere.

Two music festivals offer Conservatory students the opportunity to collaborate with prominent guest artists. The annual Bach Festival is the oldest collegiate Bach festival in the United States, with a high standard of performance that has resulted in worldwide recognition. Each spring world-renowned soloists come to B-W, joining with students to present two days of concerts. The biennial FOCUS Festival of Contemporary Music features the music of a contemporary composer who has a weeklong residency on the B-W campus. Past featured composers have included Witold Lutoslawski, Karel Husa, and Gunther Schuller.

Students find that B-W's location is a tremendous asset. Although situated in the small college town of Berea, Ohio, the picturesque campus is just 20 minutes away from the cultural wealth of Cleveland. Proximity to The Cleveland Orchestra, Ohio Chamber Orchestra, Cleveland Opera, Lyric Opera Cleveland, Cleveland Ballet, Ohio Ballet, The Cleveland Museum of Art, Great Lakes Theater Festival, The Cleveland Play House, and many other arts organizations has clear advantages for music students. Whether studying privately with members of The Cleveland Orchestra or Ohio Chamber Orchestra, attending cultural events with tickets made available through the Conservatory, or enjoying the beauty, serenity, and security of the campus and surrounding metroparks system, students truly benefit from the best of both worlds.

Ball State University

Muncie, Indiana

State-supported, coed. Urban campus. Total enrollment: 19,515.

Degrees Bachelor of Music in the areas of guitar, composition, organ, piano, music engineering technology, symphonic instruments, voice. Majors: composition, music, music education, music technology, piano/organ, stringed instruments, voice, wind and percussion instruments. Graduate degrees offered: Master of Music in the areas of performance, conducting, woodwinds, piano chamber music/accompanying, music history and musicology, music education, music theory, music composition. Doctor of Arts in the areas of performance, conducting, woodwinds, piano chamber music/accompanying, music history and musicology, music education, music theory, music composition.

Music Student Profile Fall 1994: 487 total; 403 matriculated undergraduate, 84 matriculated graduate; 8% minorities, 34% females, 3% international.

Music Faculty Total: 60; 60 full-time. Graduate students teach a few undergraduate courses. Undergraduate student–faculty ratio: 20:1.

Student Life Student groups include Music Educators National Conference.

Expenses for 1995–96 Application fee: $25. State resident tuition: $3048 full-time. Nonresident tuition: $7824 full-time. Part-time tuition per semester ranges from $458 to $1224 for state residents, $1260 to $2955 for nonresidents. College room and board: $3768. Special program-related fees: $8 for instrument rental, $40 for applied music lesson fee.

Financial Aid Program-specific awards for Fall of 1994: 60 Young Artist Scholarships for undergraduates ($1000), 60 General Music Scholarships for undergraduates ($500).

Application Procedures Deadline—freshmen and transfers: March 1. Required: high school transcript, college transcript(s) for transfer students, audition, SAT I or ACT test scores. Recommended: 2 letters of recommendation, interview. Auditions held 7 times on campus; recorded music is permissible as a substitute for live auditions when distance is prohibitive and videotaped performances are permissible as a substitute for live auditions when distance is prohibitive.

Undergraduate Contact Ruth Vedvik, Director of Admissions, Ball State University, Muncie, Indiana 47306; 317-285-8279.

Graduate Contact Kirby Koriath, Graduate Programs Coordinator, Music Department, Ball State University, School of Music, Muncie, Indiana 47306; 317-285-5502.

Baylor University

Waco, Texas

Independent-religious, coed. Urban campus. Total enrollment: 12,240.

Degrees Bachelor of Music in the area of classical music; Bachelor of Music Education in the area of classical music. Majors: classical music, music, music education, opera, piano/organ, sacred music, stringed instruments, voice, wind and percussion instruments. Graduate degrees offered: Master of Music in the area of classical music.

Music Student Profile Fall 1994: 331 total; 269 matriculated undergraduate, 62 matriculated graduate; 13% minorities, 54% females, 4% international.

Music Faculty Total: 55; 46 full-time, 9 part-time; 65% of full-time faculty have terminal degrees. Graduate students teach a few undergraduate courses. Undergraduate student–faculty ratio: 5:1.

Student Life Student groups include fraternities and sororities, Music Educators National Conference Student Chapter, Baylor Association of Church Musicians.

Expenses for 1995–96 Application fee: $25. Comprehensive fee of $12,533 includes full-time tuition ($7740), mandatory fees ($654), and college room and board ($4139). College room only: $1790. Part-time tuition: $258 per semester hour. Part-time mandatory fees: $21 per semester hour. Special program-related fees: $25 for lab fees, $70 for applied music fee.

Financial Aid Program-specific awards for Fall of 1994: 1 Competitive Scholarship for organ majors, 27 General Scholarships for program majors, 100 Incentive Scholarships for program majors.

Application Procedures Deadline—freshmen and transfers: continuous. Required: high school transcript, college transcript(s) for transfer students, minimum 2.0 high school GPA, audition, SAT I or ACT test scores. Recommended: minimum 3.0 high school GPA. Auditions held 7 times on campus and off campus in Atlanta, GA; Chicago, IL; Los Angeles, CA; recorded music is permissible as a substitute for live auditions if a campus visit is impossible.

Undergraduate Contact Celia Austin, Secretary, School of Music, Baylor University, P.O. Box 97408, Waco, Texas 76798-7408; 817-755-1161, fax: 817-755-3843, E-mail address: couaustin@baylor.edu.

Graduate Contact Harry Elzinga, Director of Graduate Studies, School of Music, Baylor University, P.O. Box 97408, Waco, Texas 76798-7408; 817-755-1161, fax: 817-755-3843.

Belhaven College

Jackson, Mississippi

Independent-religious, coed. Suburban campus. Total enrollment: 1,109.

Degrees Bachelor of Music in the area of performance. Majors: piano/organ, voice.

Music Student Profile Fall 1994: 12 total; all matriculated undergraduate; 15% minorities, 55% females, 5% international.

Music Faculty Total: 5; 2 full-time, 3 part-time; 50% of full-time faculty have terminal degrees. Graduate stu-

Belhaven College *(continued)*

dents do not teach undergraduate courses. Undergraduate student–faculty ratio: 6:1.

Student Life Student groups include Mu Phi Epsilon.

Estimated Expenses for 1995–96 Application fee: $15. Comprehensive fee of $10,520 includes full-time tuition ($7490), mandatory fees ($130), and college room and board ($2900). Part-time tuition: $195 per semester hour.

Financial Aid Program-specific awards for Fall of 1994: 20 Music Scholarships for program majors ($4500), 8 Music Awards for program majors ($500), 30 Choir Scholarships for choir singers ($3500).

Application Procedures Deadline—freshmen and transfers: continuous. Required: high school transcript, minimum 2.0 high school GPA, interview, audition, SAT I or ACT test scores, minimum composite ACT score of 20. Recommended: minimum 3.0 high school GPA. Auditions held throughout the year on campus; recorded music is permissible as a substitute for live auditions when distance is prohibitive and videotaped performances are permissible as a substitute for live auditions when distance is prohibitive.

Undergraduate Contact Roy E. Stillwell, Chairman, Department of Music/Fine Arts, Belhaven College, 1500 Peachtree Street, Jackson, Mississippi 39202-1789; 601-968-8707.

Belmont University

Nashville, Tennessee

Independent-religious, coed. Urban campus. Total enrollment: 2,961.

Degrees Bachelor of Music in the areas of church music, commercial music, composition, performance, piano pedagogy, music theory, music education; Bachelor of Music Education in the area of music education. Majors: classical performance, commercial music, composition, music, music education, music theory, piano pedagogy. Graduate degrees offered: Master of Music Education in the area of music education.

Music Student Profile Fall 1994: 289 total; 265 matriculated undergraduate, 12 matriculated graduate, 12 nondegree; 45% females, 1% international.

Music Faculty Total: 60; 24 full-time, 36 part-time; 70% of full-time faculty have terminal degrees. Graduate students do not teach undergraduate courses. Undergraduate student–faculty ratio: 10:1.

Student Life Student groups include International Association of Jazz Educators, Phi Mu Alpha, Sigma Alpha Iota.

Expenses for 1995–96 Application fee: $25. Comprehensive fee of $12,482 includes full-time tuition ($8500), mandatory fees ($250), and college room and board ($3732 minimum). Part-time tuition: $354 per semester hour. Part-time mandatory fees: $90 per semester. Special program-related fees: $60–$200 for applied lessons, $30–$100 for material fees.

Financial Aid Program-specific awards for Fall of 1994: 2 Dean's Scholarships for academically qualified/talented applicants ($3000), 6 Endowed Scholarships for talented applicants ($1000–$1500), 20 Music Scholarships for talented applicants ($1000–$1500).

Application Procedures Deadline—freshmen and transfers: June 30. Required: high school transcript, college transcript(s) for transfer students, minimum 2.0 high school GPA, letter of recommendation, audition, SAT I or ACT test scores, minimum combined SAT I score of 800, minimum composite ACT score of 20. Auditions held 6 times on campus; recorded music is permissible as a substitute for live auditions if a campus visit is impossible and videotaped performances are permissible as a substitute for live auditions if a campus visit is impossible.

Undergraduate Contact Rebecca Ownby, Admissions Counselor, School of Music, Belmont University, 1900 Belmont Boulevard, Nashville, Tennessee 37212, 3757; 615-385-6408, fax: 615-386-0239, E-mail address: belmontmusic@belmont.edu.

Graduate Contact Shawna Butler, Secretary, School of Music, Belmont University, 1900 Belmont Boulevard, Nashville, Tennessee 37212-3757; 615-385-6408, fax: 615-386-0239, E-mail address: belmontmusic@belmont.edu.

More about the University

Program Facilities The new School of Music Sam A. Wilson Building is the first success of a three-phase master plan of providing ample rehearsal and practice rooms; spacious teaching studios; fully equipped classrooms; computer, piano, and music technology labs; and multiple performance areas, including a recital hall and a large theater.

Faculty Under the leadership of 60 faculty members, more than 250 music students from thirty--five states and five countries prepare at Belmont for careers as performers, church musicians, composers, music teachers, and studio musicians. Faculty are graduates of some of the most prestigious institutions and hold such honors as Composer of the Year awards, listings in *Who's Who in Music,* Outstanding Educator of America, Nashville Composer of the Year, Grammy Award nominations, professionally released recordings, and Metropolitan Opera Regional Finalist.

Student Performance More than twenty ensemble opportunities include Oratorio Chorus, Chorale, Chamber Singers, Women's Choir and Men's Chorus, Company, Jazzmin, Image, Opera and Musical Theater workshops, University Band and Orchestra, Jazz Ensemble and small groups, Brass and Woodwind Quintets, String Quartet, Rock Combo, New Music Ensembles, Pops, and Bluegrass Ensemble. Belmont's proximity to downtown Nashville and Music Row allows for involvement in professional recording projects and productions of leading arts organizations.

Special Programs International music opportunities are growing with The Russian Academy of Music in Moscow and with Germany's Hochschule für Musik Dresden, Karl Maria von Weber. The Commercial Music Program, a unique approach to the study of popular styles, includes course work in music technology to stay

current with developing technological advances as they impact music composition, copying, and performance.

Benedictine College

Atchison, Kansas

Independent-religious, coed. Small-town campus. Total enrollment: 843.

Degrees Bachelor of Music Education in the area of music education. Majors: music, music education, music management.

Music Student Profile Fall 1994: 50 total; all matriculated undergraduate.

Music Faculty Total: 6; 3 full-time, 3 part-time. Graduate students do not teach undergraduate courses.

Expenses for 1995–96 Application fee: $25. Comprehensive fee of $12,350 includes full-time tuition ($10,020) and college room and board ($2330). College room only: $1870. Part-time tuition: $200 per credit hour. Special program-related fees: $25–$50 for private music lessons.

Financial Aid Program-specific awards for Fall of 1994: Music Scholarships for program majors ($500–$4000), Academic Music Scholarships for academically qualified applicants ($500–$4000).

Application Procedures Deadline—freshmen and transfers: continuous. Required: high school transcript, college transcript(s) for transfer students, audition, SAT I or ACT test scores. Auditions held by appointment on campus and off campus; recorded music is permissible as a substitute for live auditions if a campus visit is impossible. Portfolio reviews held on campus and off campus.

Undergraduate Contact Music Department, Benedictine College, Atchison, Kansas 66002-1499; 800-467-5340.

Benjamin T. Rome School of Music

See Catholic University of America, Benjamin T. Rome School of Music

Berklee College of Music

Boston, Massachusetts

Independent, coed. Urban campus. Total enrollment: 2,686.

Degrees Bachelor of Music in the areas of performance, music writing, music technology, music business, music education. Majors: composition/songwriting, film scoring, music engineering, music management. Graduate degrees offered: Master of Music in the areas of jazz studies, composition, pedagogy, performance. Cross-registration with ProArts Consortium.

Music Student Profile Fall 1994: 2,696 total; 2,686 matriculated undergraduate, 10 matriculated graduate; 18% females, 33% international.

Music Faculty Total: 280; 138 full-time, 142 part-time. Graduate students do not teach undergraduate courses. Undergraduate student–faculty ratio: 9:1.

Student Life Student groups include Arts/Berklee Coalition.

Expenses for 1995–96 Application fee: $50. Comprehensive fee of $19,580 includes full-time tuition ($12,390) and college room and board ($7190). Tuition for summer program: $5095. Special program-related fees: $50–$395 for lab fees.

Application Procedures Deadline—freshmen and transfers: continuous. Required: high school transcript, college transcript(s) for transfer students, 2 letters of recommendation, SAT I or ACT test scores. Recommended: minimum 2.0 high school GPA.

Undergraduate Contact Emily Woolf Economou, Director of Admissions, Berklee College of Music, 1140 Boylston Street, Boston, Massachusetts 02215-3693; 617-266-1400, fax: 617-536-2632.

More about the College

Performance Facilities Berklee Performance Center, a 1,200-seat concert hall servicing over 200 student, faculty, and other concerts each year, three recital halls equipped with a variety of second reinforcement systems; over 40 ensemble rooms; 75 private instruction studios; 250 private practice rooms; and an outdoor concert pavilion.

Technological Facilities Recording Studio Complex consisting of ten studio facilities that include 8-, 16-, and 24-track digital and analog recording capability, automated mixdown, digital editing, video postproduction, and comprehensive signal processing facilities; Synthesis Labs featuring over 250 MIDI and digitally equipped synthesizers, expanders, drum machines, sequencers, and computers, including hard-disk recording; Learning Center equipped with forty computer-based MIDI workstations; Professional Writing Division MIDI Lab, offering the ability to produce high-quality demos of compositions, arrangements, and songs at individual workstations; and Film Scoring Labs providing professional training in the areas of film music composition, editing, sequencing, and computer applications.

Faculty, Visiting Artists, Alumni, and More Faculty members are all experienced musicians and educators who bring to the classroom a thorough knowledge of music and the wisdom that comes from professional music experience. Through the Visiting Artist Series, students are exposed to valuable firsthand career insights from every sector of the industry. Berklee alumni can be found in every music profession: in education, business, technology, film, and television—to name just a few. *The Berklee Prospectus* lists some of the renowned faculty, visiting artists, and alumni who have contributed to the college over the years, as well as information on housing, financial aid, student activities, counseling services, and more.

Students come to a music school to master instrumental skills and to develop creative abilities. They need a place that offers numerous opportunities to pursue their own paths across a vast musical landscape, a

Berklee College of Music *(continued)*

place that will help them excel in whatever musical field they choose to explore—a place like Berklee College of Music.

Whether it be performance, production and synthesis, composition and arranging, business and management, or music education, there is a wealth of possibilities for the contemporary musician, all of which can be studied at Berklee.

The broad-based curriculum includes majors in performance, music production and engineering, songwriting, music business/management, film scoring, music education, jazz composition, commercial arranging, music synthesis, composition, and professional music. The dual major allows students to combine two majors and graduate with a more marketable degree that expands their career options in the music industry. A new major in music therapy will be launched in the fall of 1996.

Over 350 ensembles rehearse and perform throughout the year, offering students countless opportunities to play or sing lead or provide instrumental or vocal support for their classmates and friends. Berklee students at all levels of ability have the chance to participate in instrumental labs, ensembles, public performances, special college musical events, recording sessions, informal jam sessions, and student-led groups.

During students' time at Berklee, they have the chance to work in the College's state-of-the-art music technology facilities, using some of the most sophisticated recording and synthesis equipment currently available, in addition to facilities specially designed for the areas of composition, arranging, and film scoring. The facilities at Berklee are equipped with the instruments and equipment that are being used in the world beyond the classroom.

Berklee students learn from the professionals. Like the technology, the faculty at Berklee is highly regarded. Professionals from every field of music make up the faculty, most of whom teach on a full-time basis.

Berklee is located in Boston, Massachusetts, in the heart of historic Back Bay. An international hub of intellectual and creative activity, Boston hosts many of the world's finest colleges and universities (and an estimated 240,000 students), a lively club and concert scene, treasure-filled museums and avant-garde galleries, and world-class performing arts centers.

For fifty years, Berklee has prepared students for the many challenges presented in the contemporary music industry. The Berklee mission is to provide the best possible academic and professional career preparation for its students. That preparation includes teaching students to be ethical, global citizens. Berklee celebrates human diversity, nurtures the artistic spirit, and encourages intellectual curiosity as the rest of that preparation, for each student brings to Berklee something new—a new sound, a new idea, a new song.

Berry College

Mount Berry, Georgia

Independent, coed. Small-town campus. Total enrollment: 1,876.

Degrees Bachelor of Music in the areas of music education, music business. Majors: brass, music and business, music education, piano/organ, voice, wind and percussion instruments.

Music Student Profile Fall 1994: 47 total; all matriculated undergraduate; 2% minorities, 50% females.

Music Faculty Total: 10; 5 full-time, 5 part-time; 40% of full-time faculty have terminal degrees. Graduate students do not teach undergraduate courses. Undergraduate student–faculty ratio: 10:1.

Student Life Student groups include Music to the People Projects, Church Concerts.

Expenses for 1995–96 Application fee: $20. Comprehensive fee of $13,320 includes full-time tuition ($9216) and college room and board ($4104). College room only: $2224. Part-time tuition: $307 per semester hour. Special program-related fees: $90–$175 for lessons.

Financial Aid Program-specific awards for Fall of 1994: 40 Music Scholarships for performers/program majors ($2000), 10 Performance Grants for performers/program minors ($500).

Application Procedures Deadline—freshmen and transfers: continuous. Required: high school transcript, college transcript(s) for transfer students, minimum 2.0 high school GPA, audition, SAT I or ACT test scores. Auditions held on a case-by-case basis on campus; recorded music is permissible as a substitute for live auditions when distance is prohibitive and videotaped performances are permissible as a substitute for live auditions when distance is prohibitive.

Undergraduate Contact George Gaddie, Dean of Admissions, Berry College, 159 Mount Berry Station, Mount Berry, Georgia 30149-0159; 706-236-2215, fax: 706-236-2248.

Bethel College

St. Paul, Minnesota

Independent-religious, coed. Suburban campus. Total enrollment: 2,208.

Degrees Bachelor of Music in the areas of applied performance, composition; Bachelor of Music Education in the areas of vocal music education, instrumental music education. Majors: composition, music education, piano/organ, stringed instruments, voice, wind and percussion instruments.

Music Student Profile Fall 1994: 80 total; 50 matriculated undergraduate, 30 nondegree; 65% females.

Music Faculty Total: 28; 4 full-time, 24 part-time; 75% of full-time faculty have terminal degrees. Graduate students do not teach undergraduate courses. Undergraduate student–faculty ratio: 15:1.

Student Life Student groups include Music Educators National Conference.

Expenses for 1995–96 Application fee: $20. Comprehensive fee of $16,720 includes full-time tuition ($12,260) and college room and board ($4460). College room only: $2490. Part-time tuition: $466 per credit hour. Special program-related fees: $30 for music purchase, $15 for robe rental.

Financial Aid Program-specific awards for Fall of 1994: 6 Music Scholarships for performers ($1000), 65–75 free music lessons for freshmen and sophomore members of performance organizations ($250).

Application Procedures Deadline—freshmen and transfers: continuous. Required: essay, high school transcript, 2 letters of recommendation, SAT I or ACT test scores, minimum combined SAT I score of 920, minimum composite ACT score of 21. Recommended: audition. Auditions held 1 time on campus; recorded music is permissible as a substitute for live auditions when distance is prohibitive.

Undergraduate Contact Dr. Dennis Port, Chair, Department of Music, Bethel College, 3900 Bethel Drive, St. Paul, Minnesota 55112; 612-638-6486, fax: 612-638-6001.

Biola University

La Mirada, California

Independent-religious, coed. Suburban campus. Total enrollment: 2,961.

Degrees Bachelor of Music in the areas of performance, composition, music education. Majors: classical music, music, music education, piano/organ, stringed instruments, voice, wind and percussion instruments.

Music Student Profile Fall 1994: 107 total; all matriculated undergraduate; 30% minorities, 65% females, 10% international.

Music Faculty Total: 15; 11 full-time, 4 part-time; 50% of full-time faculty have terminal degrees. Graduate students do not teach undergraduate courses. Undergraduate student–faculty ratio: 9:1.

Student Life Student groups include American Choral Directors Association, Music Educators National Conference.

Expenses for 1995–96 Application fee: $35. Comprehensive fee of $17,120 includes full-time tuition ($12,652) and college room and board ($4468 minimum). Part-time tuition: $528 per unit. Special program-related fees: $220 for private applied lessons.

Financial Aid Program-specific awards for Fall of 1994: 100 Biola Music Awards for program majors, music ensemble members ($2500–$6000).

Application Procedures Deadline—freshmen and transfers: June 1. Notification date—freshmen and transfers: August 15. Required: high school transcript, college transcript(s) for transfer students, 2 letters of recommendation, interview, audition. Auditions held continuously on campus; recorded music is permissible as a substitute for live auditions when distance is prohibitive and videotaped performances are permissible as a substitute for live auditions if distance is prohibitive.

Undergraduate Contact Gail Neal, Admissions Counselor, Music Department, Biola University, 13800 Biola Avenue, LaMirada, California 90639; 310-903-4892, fax: 310-903-4746.

Birmingham-Southern College

Birmingham, Alabama

Independent-religious, coed. Urban campus. Total enrollment: 1,583.

Degrees Bachelor of Music in the areas of classical performance, composition, music history, church music; Bachelor of Music Education in the area of music education. Majors: classical music, opera, piano/organ, stringed instruments, voice, wind and percussion instruments. Cross-registration with University of Alabama at Birmingham.

Music Student Profile Fall 1994: 250 total; 50 matriculated undergraduate, 200 nondegree; 20% minorities, 60% females, 10% international.

Music Faculty Total: 24; 9 full-time, 15 part-time; 100% of full-time faculty have terminal degrees. Graduate students do not teach undergraduate courses. Undergraduate student–faculty ratio: 8:1.

Student Life Student groups include GALA, Opera Productions, Music Theater Productions.

Expenses for 1995–96 Application fee: $25. Comprehensive fee of $17,109 includes full-time tuition ($12,360), mandatory fees ($164), and college room and board ($4585). Special program-related fees: $160–$300 for private lessons.

Financial Aid Program-specific awards for Fall of 1994: 2–3 Music Theater Scholarships for program majors and minors ($3000–$4000), 7–8 Music Performance Scholarships for program majors and minors ($4000–$6000), 1–2 Music Composition Awards for program majors ($4000–$6000).

Application Procedures Deadline—freshmen and transfers: May 1. Required: essay, high school transcript, college transcript(s) for transfer students, minimum 2.0 high school GPA, SAT I or ACT test scores, minimum combined SAT I score of 1,110, minimum composite ACT score of 21. Recommended: letter of recommendation, interview, audition. Auditions held 2 times on campus; recorded music is permissible as a substitute for live auditions when distance is prohibitive and videotaped performances are permissible as a substitute for live auditions when distance is prohibitive.

Undergraduate Contact Bob Dortch, Vice President for Admissions Services, Birmingham-Southern College, 900 Arkadelphia Road, Birmingham, Alabama 35254; 205-226-4686, fax: 205-226-4931.

Blair School of Music

See Vanderbilt University, Blair School of Music

Boise State University

Boise, Idaho

State-supported, coed. Urban campus. Total enrollment: 14,647.

Degrees Bachelor of Music in the area of performance; Bachelor of Music Education in the areas of elementary music education, secondary music education. Majors: classical music, jazz, music, music and business, music education, opera, piano/organ, sacred music, stringed instruments, voice, wind and percussion instruments. Graduate degrees offered: Master of Music in the areas of pedagogy, performance; Master of Music Education in the areas of elementary music education, secondary music education.

Music Student Profile Fall 1994: 167 total; 151 matriculated undergraduate, 16 matriculated graduate; 76% females, 1% international.

Music Faculty Total: 35; 20 full-time, 15 part-time; 100% of full-time faculty have terminal degrees. Graduate students teach a few undergraduate courses. Undergraduate student–faculty ratio: 25:1.

Student Life Student groups include Music Educators National Conference, Kappa Kappa Psi.

Expenses for 1994–95 Application fee: $15. State resident tuition: $0 full-time, $82 per semester hour part-time. Nonresident tuition: $6062 full-time, $82 per semester hour part-time. Full-time mandatory fees: $1876. College room and board: $3106 (minimum).

Financial Aid Program-specific awards for Fall of 1994: 112 Music Scholarships for those demonstrating talent and academic achievement ($200–$1500).

Application Procedures Deadline—freshmen and transfers: July 27. Required: high school transcript, minimum 2.0 high school GPA, 2 letters of recommendation, audition, portfolio. Recommended: minimum 3.0 high school GPA, interview, video. Auditions held 2 times on campus and off campus in Boise, ID; recorded music is permissible as a substitute for live auditions when distance is prohibitive and videotaped performances are permissible as a substitute for live auditions when distance is prohibitive. Portfolio reviews held 2 times for BM applicants on campus.

Undergraduate Contact Office of Admissions, Boise State University, 1910 University Drive, Boise, Idaho 83725; 208-385-1156.

Graduate Contact Graduate Admissions Office, Boise State University, 1910 University Drive, Boise, Idaho 83725; 208-385-3903.

Boston Conservatory

Boston, Massachusetts

Independent, coed. Urban campus. Total enrollment: 414.

Degrees Bachelor of Music in the areas of composition, performance, music education, opera; Bachelor of Music Education in the area of music education. Majors: music, music education, opera, piano/organ, stringed instruments, voice, wind and percussion instruments. Graduate degrees offered: Master of Music in the areas of composition, choral conducting, performance, music education, jazz studies, opera, musical theater. Cross-registration with ProArts Consortium.

Music Student Profile Fall 1994: 433 total; 323 matriculated undergraduate, 110 matriculated graduate; 9% minorities, 70% females, 20% international.

Music Faculty Total: 88; 23 full-time, 65 part-time; 10% of full-time faculty have terminal degrees. Graduate students teach a few undergraduate courses.

Student Life Student groups include Music Educators National Conference, Phi Mu Alpha Sinfonia, Sigma Alpha Iota. Special housing available for music students.

Expenses for 1995–96 Comprehensive fee of $20,130 includes full-time tuition ($13,400), mandatory fees ($450), and college room and board ($6280). Part-time tuition: $555 per credit. Part-time mandatory fees per semester range from $56.25 to $168.75. Special program-related fees: $60 for lab fees, $500 for opera studio surcharge for part-time students.

Financial Aid Program-specific awards for Fall of 1994: 45–70 Merit Scholarships for artistically talented students ($2000–$10,500).

Application Procedures Deadline—freshmen and transfers: continuous. Notification date—freshmen and transfers: April 1. Required: essay, high school transcript, college transcript(s) for transfer students, 4 letters of recommendation, audition, SAT I or ACT test scores, minimum 2.7 high school GPA. Auditions held on campus and off campus in Chicago, IL; St. Louis, MO; Minneapolis, MN; Seattle, WA; Los Angeles, CA; Houston, TX; Tampa, FL; Washington, DC; Pittsburgh, PA; Boston, MA; Tokyo, Japan; Kyoto, Japan; Osaka, Japan; Hong Kong; Sydney, Australia; Adelaide, Australia; Melbourne, Australia; Brisbane, Australia; Perth, Australia; Wellington, New Zealand; Auckland, New Zealand; recorded music is permissible as a substitute for live auditions when distance is prohibitive and videotaped performances are permissible as a substitute for live auditions when distance is prohibitive. Portfolio reviews held continuously on campus.

Contact Richard Wallace, Director of Admissions, Boston Conservatory, 8 The Fenway, Boston, Massachusetts 02215; 617-536-6340 ext. 16, fax: 617-536-3176.

More about the Conservatory

Program Facilities Two recital halls (400 and 75 seats); computer lab (Apple and print stations); library of 60,000 volumes and scores, and interlibrary loan availability with college network of Boston; twenty-five practice rooms.

Faculty and Alumni Faculty are members of the Boston Symphony Orchestra, Boston Pops, and Boston Ballet orchestras as well as concern, chamber, and recording artists. The Atlantic Brass Quintet is in residence. Alumni are represented in major orchestras, opera companies, and faculty of college and university music programs in the United States and Europe.

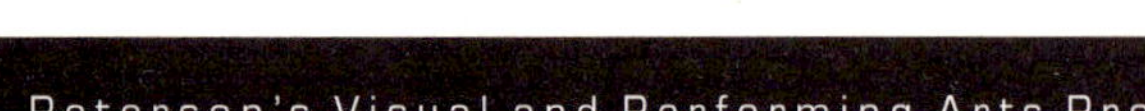

Robert Rinehart

San Francisco Conservatory of Music—Member of the New York Philharmonic Orchestra

Besides being located in one of the world's most inspiring cities, the San Francisco Conservatory has a first-rate faculty that includes distinguished artists who belong to the mainstream of American musical life. Judging from my experiences at the Conservatory, I would say that it certainly compares very favorably with the better known music schools on the East Coast. Bigger schools often can't offer students the kind of performance opportunities that I had in San Francisco. I got the foundation of my chamber music experience there—the language, the basic skills—and I was active in the music ensemble. Also, the general atmosphere was warm, attentive, and encouraging. There was a nice sense of camaraderie. At the Conservatory, no one was lost in the woodwork.

Student Performance Opportunities Orchestra, wind ensemble, opera orchestra, musical theater orchestra, dance orchestra, chorale, chamber choir, opera theater, percussion ensemble, chamber music groups (numerous), jazz ensembles (with Berklee College of Music).

Special Programs Gig office providing performance opportunities throughout the greater Boston area, career seminar series, counseling and health services, international student ESL classes/orientation program, academic year ESL course work, and tutorial assistance.

The Boston Conservatory, founded in 1867, is one of the oldest colleges offering training to serious students of the performing arts. The three divisions of the college—Music, Dance, and Theater—take full advantage of the wealth of cultural and academic offerings Boston has to offer. Guest artists, master classes, performance opportunities, and professional contacts and networking are provided to all students of the college. These experiences seek to ensure that each student receives a varied and professional level of education to augment the intensive study of the prescribed curriculum.

Music students work with artist faculty members and teachers who are truly interested in working to develop students' musical abilities to their utmost potential. With over 300 concerts being offered each year, performance experience is a core part of the curriculum. Students participate in orchestra, wind ensemble, chamber ensembles, choral ensembles, and pit work for the dance, opera, and musical theater mainstage productions produced several times throughout the academic year. Pianists are involved with accompanying and can choose to expand their skills and work with dance and/or musical theater studio classes.

In addition to the school's performance opportunities, the greater Boston area provides numerous playing possibilities for solo, small chamber, and orchestral musicians that students may choose to further expand both their performance experience and knowledge of the repertory.

Boston is a major center of higher education in America, with over fifty major colleges and universities. The city provides a diverse student population and an endless array of courses, lectures, concerts, and social opportunities. The Conservatory is in the Pro-Arts Consortium with five area colleges (Emerson College, Berklee College of Music, Museum School, Massachusetts College of Art, and Boston Architectural Center), which offers extensive cross-registration course possibilities to all students.

On-campus housing is provided to all interested students, offering brownstone-style living accommodations just a few steps from the main training and rehearsal buildings. For those students interested in off-campus housing, Boston offers a wide range of architectural styles and rent prices in neighborhoods throughout the city, which are all within easy access to the school by public transportation.

The Boston Conservatory strives to meet each student's needs, musically and personally, and provides a nurturing, safe environment in which to study, learn, and grow. The supportive atmosphere of the college extends to student life areas as well. Over a dozen special interest groups and organizations exist on campus, with new ones developing constantly as the student population grows and needs change. As part of the student services, a number of career seminars are given each year ranging from résumé writing and audition anxiety to grant writing and tax laws for the performing artist. In addition, there is an active student government and a student-run newspaper.

Boston University

Boston, Massachusetts

Independent, coed. Urban campus. Total enrollment: 28,664.

Degrees Bachelor of Music in the areas of performance, music education, music theory and composition, music history and literature. Majors: music education, music history and literature, music theory and composition, piano/organ, stringed instruments, voice, wind and percussion instruments. Graduate degrees offered: Master of Music in the areas of performance, music education, music theory and composition, music history and literature, orchestral and choral conducting, historical performance, collaborative piano. Doctor of Musical Arts in the areas of performance, music education, music theory and composition, music history and literature, orchestral and choral conducting, historical performance, collaborative piano.

Music Student Profile Fall 1994: 600 total; 250 matriculated undergraduate, 300 matriculated graduate, 50 nondegree; 15% minorities, 50% females, 20% international.

Music Faculty Total: 90; 40 full-time, 50 part-time; 100% of full-time faculty have terminal degrees. Graduate students teach a few undergraduate courses. Undergraduate student–faculty ratio: 6:1.

Student Life Student groups include Jazz Ensemble, Concert Band, Choral Union. Special housing available for music students.

Expenses for 1995–96 Application fee: $50. Comprehensive fee of $26,800 includes full-time tuition ($19,420), mandatory fees ($280), and college room and board ($7100). College room only: $4110. Part-time tuition: $607 per credit. Part-time mandatory fees: $40 per semester. Special program-related fees: $990 for applied music fee.

Financial Aid Program-specific awards for Fall of 1994: 126 Grants–Need/Performance Awards for undergraduates ($10,321), 81 Grants–Performance Awards for undergraduates ($8499).

Application Procedures Deadline—freshmen: January 15; transfers: May 1. Notification date—freshmen: March 15; transfers: June 1. Required: essay, high school transcript, college transcript(s) for transfer students, 2 letters of recommendation, audition, SAT I or ACT test scores. Recommended: interview. Auditions held 24 times on campus and off campus in various cities; recorded music is permissible as a substitute for live auditions when distance is prohibitive.

Undergraduate Contact Halley Shefler, Director of Admissions, Music Division, Boston University, 855 Commonwealth Avenue, Boston, Massachusetts 02215; 617-353-3341, fax: 617-353-7455, E-mail address: hshefler@uism.bu.edu.

Graduate Contact Jay deFrank, Graduate Coordinator, School for the Arts, Boston University, 855 Commonwealth Avenue, Boston, Massachusetts 02215; 617-353-3500, fax: 617-353-7455.

More about the University

Program Facilities Performance spaces include a 485-seat concert hall in the School for the Arts and the 650-seat Tsai Performance Center on the Boston University campus. There are 3 rehearsal halls for orchestra, wind ensemble, band, and choral groups; over 100 soundproof practice rooms; a recording studio; and 3 electronic music studios. Opera rehearsal and coaching studios are adjacent to the School for the Arts.

Faculty, Resident Artists, and Alumni Bruce MacCombie, a noted composer and former Dean of the Juilliard School, has served as Dean of the Boston University School for the Arts since 1992. The faculty includes many members of the Boston Symphony Orchestra. Phyllis Curtin, one of the world's leading sopranos, is Dean Emerita of the School for the Arts and founder of the Opera Institute at Boston University. Artists-in-residence include the Muir String Quartet, the Atlantic Brass Quintet, and Alea III, a contemporary music ensemble. Boston University is a member of The Robert Shaw Institute, a consortium which includes The Ohio State University and the University of California at Los Angeles.

Student Performance Opportunities Ensembles include the Symphony Orchestra, Chamber Orchestra, Wind Ensemble, Symphonic Chorus, Women's Chorus, New Music Ensemble, Collegium in Early Music, Baroque Ensemble, Early Music Series, and Opera Theatre. All-University organizations include the Jazz Ensemble, Concert Band, and Choral Union.

Special Programs Students at the Boston University School for the Arts may take advantage of a wide range of academic and extracurricular activities. Through the Collaborative Degree Program (BUCOP), students may obtain a dual degree in two of the University's schools and colleges. Boston University also offers intensive English programs for international students.

Bowling Green State University

Bowling Green, Ohio

State-supported, coed. Small-town campus. Total enrollment: 17,564.

Degrees Bachelor of Music in the areas of music education, performance, music history and literature, composition. Majors: classical music, jazz, music, music education, piano/organ, sound recording technology, stringed instruments, voice, wind and percussion instruments. Graduate degrees offered: Master of Music in the areas of music education, performance, composition, music theory, music history. Cross-registration with University of Toledo.

Music Student Profile Fall 1994: 4% minorities, 60% females, 4% international.

Music Faculty Total: 60; 52 full-time, 8 part-time; 100% of full-time faculty have terminal degrees. Graduate students teach a few undergraduate courses. Undergraduate student–faculty ratio: 7:1.

Student Life Student groups include Phi Mu Alpha, Sigma Alpha Iota, Music Educators National Conference.

Expenses for 1995–96 Application fee: $30. State resident tuition: $3954 full-time, $197 per credit hour part-time. Nonresident tuition: $8512 full-time, $414 per credit hour part-time. College room and board: $3522. College room only: $2068. Special program-related fees: $70 for music equipment fee, $180 for applied music lesson fee.

Financial Aid Program-specific awards for Fall of 1994: 30 Music Talent Awards for top musicians ($1200).

Application Procedures Deadline—freshmen and transfers: continuous. Notification date—transfers: August 1. Required: high school transcript, audition. Recommended: minimum 3.0 high school GPA, interview. Auditions held 5 times on campus; recorded music is permissible as a substitute for live auditions when distance is prohibitive and videotaped performances are permissible as a substitute for live auditions when distance is prohibitive.

Contact Dr. Richard Kennell, Associate Dean, College of Musical Arts, Bowling Green State University, 1031 Moore Musical Arts Center, Bowling Green, Ohio 43403; 419-372-2182, fax: 419-372-2938, E-mail address: kennel@opie.bgsu.edu.

Bradley University

Peoria, Illinois

Independent, coed. Urban campus. Total enrollment: 5,882.

Degrees Bachelor of Music in the areas of performance, music education, composition. Majors: music, music education.

Music Student Profile Fall 1994: 55 total; all matriculated undergraduate.

Music Faculty Total: 28; 10 full-time, 18 part-time; 70% of full-time faculty have terminal degrees. Graduate students do not teach undergraduate courses.

Student Life Student groups include Music Educators National Conference, Phi Mu Alpha Sinfonia, Sigma Alpha Iota.

Expenses for 1995–96 Application fee: $35. Comprehensive fee of $16,110 includes full-time tuition ($11,410), mandatory fees ($80), and college room and board ($4620). Part-time tuition per credit: $295 for the first 7 credits, $368 for the next 4 credits. Special program-related fees: $115 for private lessons.

Financial Aid Program-specific awards for Fall of 1994: 50 Music Scholarships for program majors.

Application Procedures Deadline—freshmen and transfers: continuous. Required: high school transcript, letter of recommendation, audition. Auditions held continuously on campus; recorded music is permissible as a substitute for live auditions when distance is prohibitive and videotaped performances are permissible as a substitute for live auditions when distance is prohibitive.

Undergraduate Contact Office of Undergraduate Admissions, Bradley University, Swords Hall, Peoria, Illinois 61625; 800-447-6460, fax: 309-677-2797.

Brenau University

Gainesville, Georgia

Independent, primarily women. Small-town campus. Total enrollment: 2,241.

Degrees Bachelor of Music in the area of music. Majors: music education, performance.

Music Student Profile Fall 1994: 29 total; 25 matriculated undergraduate, 4 nondegree; 10% minorities, 100% females, 6% international.

Music Faculty Total: 4; 2 full-time, 2 part-time; 100% of full-time faculty have terminal degrees. Graduate students do not teach undergraduate courses. Undergraduate student–faculty ratio: 10:1.

Student Life Student groups include Opera Company.

Estimated Expenses for 1995–96 Application fee: $30. Comprehensive fee of $16,040 includes full-time tuition ($9855) and college room and board ($6185). Part-time tuition: $205 per semester hour.

Financial Aid Program-specific awards for Fall of 1994: 20 Music Scholarships for program majors ($2000).

Application Procedures Deadline—freshmen and transfers: continuous. Required: high school transcript, interview, audition. Auditions held at various times on campus; recorded music is permissible as a substitute for live auditions when distance is prohibitive and videotaped performances are permissible as a substitute for live auditions when distance is prohibitive.

Undergraduate Contact John D. Upchurch, Dean of Admissions, Brenau University, One Centennial Circle, Gainesville, Georgia 30501; 800-252-5119, fax: 404-534-6114.

Brewton-Parker College

Mt. Vernon, Georgia

Independent-religious, coed. Rural campus. Total enrollment: 2,250.

Degrees Bachelor of Music in the area of music education. Majors: brass, music education, piano/organ, voice, wind and percussion instruments.

Music Student Profile Fall 1994: 62 total; all matriculated undergraduate; 6% minorities, 50% females.

Music Faculty Total: 8; 6 full-time, 2 part-time; 60% of full-time faculty have terminal degrees. Graduate students do not teach undergraduate courses. Undergraduate student–faculty ratio: 10:1.

Student Life Student groups include Students' Professional Association of Georgia Educators.

Expenses for 1995–96 Application fee: $15. Comprehensive fee of $7251 includes full-time tuition ($4731), mandatory fees ($150), and college room and board ($2370). Part-time tuition: $100 per quarter hour. Part-time mandatory fees: $50 per quarter.

Financial Aid Program-specific awards for Fall of 1994: 50–60 Music Scholarships for ensemble participants ($300–$600).

Brewton-Parker College *(continued)*

Application Procedures Deadline—freshmen and transfers: continuous. Required: high school transcript, college transcript(s) for transfer students, letter of recommendation, audition. Auditions held 3 times on campus.

Undergraduate Contact Don Buckner, Director of Admissions, Brewton-Parker College, Highway 280, Mt. Vernon, Georgia 30445; 912-583-2241, fax: 912-583-4498.

Brigham Young University

Provo, Utah

Independent-religious, coed. Suburban campus. Total enrollment: 30,413.

Degrees Bachelor of Music in the areas of composition, music education (K–12), elementary music specialist, performance. Majors: brass, composition, jazz, music, music education, opera, piano/organ, sound recording technology, stringed instruments, voice, wind and percussion instruments. Graduate degrees offered: Master of Music in the areas of composition, conducting, music education, performance, pedagogy.

Music Student Profile Fall 1994: 729 total; 667 matriculated undergraduate, 62 matriculated graduate.

Music Faculty Total: 87; 48 full-time, 39 part-time; 74% of full-time faculty have terminal degrees. Graduate students teach a few undergraduate courses. Undergraduate student–faculty ratio: 12:1.

Expenses for 1995–96 Application fee: $25. Comprehensive fee of $6190 includes full-time tuition ($2450 minimum) and college room and board ($3740 minimum). Part-time tuition: $125 per credit (minimum). Tuition for non-church members: $3510 full-time, $180 per credit part-time. Special program-related fees: $200 for private lessons.

Financial Aid Program-specific awards for Fall of 1994: 225 Talent Awards for program majors ($800), 225 Talent Awards for marching band students ($400).

Application Procedures Deadline—freshmen: February 15; transfers: March 15. Required: essay, high school transcript, minimum 3.0 high school GPA, letter of recommendation, audition, ACT test score only, music theory examination. Auditions held 2 times on campus; recorded music is permissible as a substitute for live auditions if a campus visit is impossible and videotaped performances are permissible as a substitute for live auditions if a campus visit is impossible.

Undergraduate Contact Academic Advisement Center, Brigham Young University, D-444 HFAC, Provo, Utah 84602; 801-378-3777.

Graduate Contact Glenn Williams, Music Department, Brigham Young University, E-466 HFAC, Provo, Utah 84602; 801-378-3317.

More about the University

Brigham Young University—founded, supported, and guided by The Church of Jesus Christ of Latter-day Saints—is dedicated to the education of the whole person. The arts play an important role in the university's unique synthesis of religious, humanistic, scientific, and professional education. BYU students enjoy a distinctive environment derived from the university's commitment to Christian virtues and academic excellence, cultivation of the arts, and a beautiful campus. The University itself, both through its facilities and through its students and faculty, symbolizes a fundamental article of faith of the Mormon church: "We believe in being honest, true, chaste, benevolent, virtuous, and in doing good to all men.... If there is anything virtuous, lovely, or of good report or praiseworthy, we seek after these things."

The Department of Music serves both the university community and those diligent and highly gifted students accepted as music majors. In the broadest sense, the department's purpose is to preserve and develop an art that is essential to human progress and well-being. Professional degrees offered at BYU prepare future leaders to serve others in the artistic aspect of their humanity. These leadership roles may take the form of careers in performance, studio teaching, music education, composition, or higher education, among others.

The department fulfills the University's goal of "preparing our students to compete with the best in their field." Nearly all full-time faculty hold doctoral degrees from distinguished universities. The department is a fully accredited member of the National Association of Schools of Music. Weekly studio master classes and practicum courses allow students to benefit both from the insight and emotional support of their peers as well as expert advice and gentle guidance from the faculty. Students receive many opportunities to apply their intensive study to live performance.

BYU music graduates who seek advanced studies meet or exceed entrance requirements at internationally recognized graduate schools. Music alumni are professional musicians, opera and musical theater soloists, composers, arrangers, music industry professionals, recording engineers, educators, college professors, and arts managers. They can be found on the stage of the Metropolitan Opera (currently two contract soloists), the Vienna Volksoper (one soloist), on the Broadway stage (one soloist), in major symphony orchestras, and as recording artists. Many alumni are nationally recognized educators, education administrators, and successful businessmen (both in the music industry and in other industries). Two BYU composition graduates have won Emmys, another has written scores for Emmy award–winning productions. BYU graduates can be found in the credits of major motion picture scores, acclaimed recordings, and in musical theater productions. Other alumni—while making their primary living outside of music in such fields as law, business, software development, or as homemakers—employ their musical artistry and knowledge toward the cultural enrichment of their communities.

Program Facilities The Department of Music is housed in two comprehensive fine arts complexes with five theaters, four large rehearsal halls, practice rooms, two piano labs, a 24-channel digital recording studio, electronic music studios, and television and radio broadcast facilities. Nineteen of the 42 practice rooms contain grand pianos. Nine-foot concert grands are located in teaching studios, large rehearsal rooms, and in the concert hall and recital hall. Two harpsichords, ten pipe organs (three tracker), and a four-manual digital organ are available for majors. The music library contains over 20,000 sound recordings and over 36,000 monographs and periodical titles. Special collections include the Primrose International Viola Archive, the Pratt International Harp Archive, and the Bartok-Serly, Max Steiner, Capitol Records, Percy Faith, and Bruning Sheet Music collections.

Faculty The Department employs resident faculty for every keyboard, orchestral instrument, and vocal specialty, all of whom meet high standards of teaching and performing experience and skill. Academic faculty are respected scholars in composition, musicology, music education, and music media.

Student Performance Opportunities The department supports four audition choirs, three orchestras, three bands, three jazz ensembles, fully staged opera and musical productions, as well as percussion ensemble, group for new music, folk ensemble, vocal jazz, and chamber music. The University sponsors extensive performing tours (half of which are overseas) for a musical theater troupe (annually), and for a wind ensemble, chamber orchestra, jazz ensemble, and choir (biannually).

The University's study-abroad program includes half-year residencies in Vienna, London, and Jerusalem.

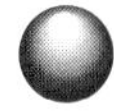

Brock University

St. Catharines, Ontario

Province-supported, coed. Urban campus. Total enrollment: 11,324.

Degrees Bachelor of Music in the area of performance. Majors: applied music, composition, directing, music theory, musicology.

Music Student Profile Fall 1994: 30 total; all matriculated undergraduate.

Music Faculty Total: 15; 4 full-time, 11 part-time. Graduate students do not teach undergraduate courses. Undergraduate student–faculty ratio: 20:1.

Expenses for 1995–96 Canadian resident tuition: $2666 full-time, $527 per course part-time. Nonresident tuition: $9456 full-time, $1916 per course part-time. (All figures are in Canadian dollars.). Full-time mandatory fees: $30. College room and board: $4770 (minimum). College room only: $2800. Special program-related fees: $20 for practice room rental, $500 for music lesson fee.

Application Procedures Deadline—freshmen and transfers: June 1. Required: high school transcript, minimum 3.0 high school GPA, audition, 4 years of keyboard study, 2 years of theory study. Auditions held by appointment on campus; recorded music is permissible as a substitute for live auditions for international applicants and videotaped performances are permissible as a substitute for live auditions for international applicants.

Undergraduate Contact Dr. Peter Landey, Chairman, Department of Music, Brock University, 500 Glenridge Avenue, St. Catharines, Ontario L2S 3A1, Canada; 905-688-5550 ext. 3824, fax: 905-688-2789, E-mail address: plandey@spartan.ac.brocku.ca.

Brooklyn College of the City University of New York

Brooklyn, New York

State and locally supported, coed. Urban campus. Total enrollment: 13,045.

Degrees Bachelor of Music in the areas of performance, composition. Majors: classical music, composition, music, music education, opera, stringed instruments, voice, wind and percussion instruments. Graduate degrees offered: Master of Music in the areas of performance, composition. Cross-registration with City University of New York System.

Music Faculty Total: 36; 16 full-time, 20 part-time; 100% of full-time faculty have terminal degrees. Graduate students teach a few undergraduate courses. Undergraduate student–faculty ratio: 5:1.

Expenses for 1995–96 State resident tuition: $2450 full-time, $100 per credit part-time. Nonresident tuition: $5050 full-time, $210 per credit part-time. Part-time mandatory fees: $53.35 per semester. Full-time mandatory fees: $181.

Application Procedures Deadline—freshmen and transfers: continuous. Required: high school transcript, audition. Recommended: minimum 3.0 high school GPA. Auditions held 3 times on campus; recorded music is permissible as a substitute for live auditions when distance is prohibitive and videotaped performances are permissible as a substitute for live auditions when distance is prohibitive.

Contact Nancy Hager, Director, Conservatory of Music, Brooklyn College of the City University of New York, 2900 Bedford Avenue, Brooklyn, New York 11210; 718-951-5286, fax: 718-951-4858.

More about the College

Young musicians from all over the world come to Brooklyn College's Conservatory of Music to study with a professional faculty, to learn in a liberal arts environment, and to experience the dynamic and diverse cultural life of New York Cityat a fraction of the tuition at private institutions.

Conservatory students complete a full curriculum in history and theory, attend master classes with violin virtuoso Itzhak Perlman, take composition tutorials with Tania Leon, explore the rich traditions of American music with historian Carol Oja, study performance with concert pianist Agustin Anievas and New York Philharmonic percussionist Morris Lang, and perform on the opera stage under director Richard Barrett. Music majors are also encouraged to venture into collaborative projects with young artists in the College's fine programs in film and video, theater, dance, and television/radio.

A calendar of more than 150 performances by students and faculty is integral to the life of the Conservatory and has featured critically acclaimed

Brooklyn College of the City University of New York *(continued)*

premieres of operas by Darius Milhaud and Francis Thorne. Invitations for off-campus performances have led to a Taiwan tour and a Kennedy Center appearance by the Conservatory orchestra, two European tours by the Percussion Ensemble, and a Columbus quincentenary production by the Opera Theatre at the Empire Center in Albany. The Conservatory's Schooltime program for area children and Sounds of Brooklyn series celebrating Brooklyn's diverse musical traditions contribute to the musical vitality on campus.

Special features include a performing arts center (auditorium, theatre, and recital hall), a state-of-the-art Center for Computer Music, the Institute for Studies in American Music with a comprehensive research library, and a professional recording studio.

Bucknell University

Lewisburg, Pennsylvania

Independent, coed. Small-town campus. Total enrollment: 3,528.

Degrees Bachelor of Music in the areas of performance, music education, music history, music composition. Majors: composition, music education, piano/organ, stringed instruments, voice, wind instruments.

Music Student Profile Fall 1994: 40 total; all matriculated undergraduate; 7% minorities, 52% females.

Music Faculty Total: 18; 9 full-time, 9 part-time; 88% of full-time faculty have terminal degrees. Graduate students do not teach undergraduate courses.

Expenses for 1995–96 Application fee: $45. Comprehensive fee of $24,395 includes full-time tuition ($19,360), mandatory fees ($110), and college room and board ($4925). College room only: $2640. Part-time tuition: $2420 per course. Part-time mandatory fees: $110 per year. Special program-related fees: .

Financial Aid Program-specific awards for Fall of 1994: Preferential Awards for program majors ($2000).

Application Procedures Deadline—freshmen: January 1; transfers: April 1. Notification date—freshmen: April 1; transfers: July 1. Required: essay, high school transcript, minimum 3.0 high school GPA, audition. Recommended: 3 letters of recommendation, interview. Auditions held 4 times on campus; recorded music is permissible as a substitute for live auditions if a campus visit is impossible and videotaped performances are permissible as a substitute for live auditions if a campus visit is impossible.

Undergraduate Contact Christopher Para, Associate Professor of Music, Music Department, Bucknell University, Lewisburg, Pennsylvania 17837; 717-524-3191, fax: 717-524-3760, E-mail address: para@bucknell.edu.

Jordan College of Fine Arts

Butler University

Indianapolis, Indiana

Independent, coed. Urban campus. Total enrollment: 3,758.

Degrees Bachelor of Music in the areas of performance, piano pedagogy, music theory/composition; Bachelor of Music Education in the areas of music education, choral music education, instrumental music education. Majors: music, music education, music theory and composition, piano pedagogy, piano/organ, stringed instruments, voice, wind and percussion instruments. Graduate degrees offered: Master of Music in the areas of performance, composition, conducting, music theory, music history, piano pedagogy; Master of Music Education in the area of music education. Cross-registration with Indianapolis Consortium for Urban Education.

Music Student Profile Fall 1994: 10% minorities, 58% females, 2% international.

Music Faculty Total: 66; 32 full-time, 34 part-time; 90% of full-time faculty have terminal degrees. Graduate students do not teach undergraduate courses. Undergraduate student–faculty ratio: 12:1.

Student Life Student groups include Music Educators National Conference Student Chapter, American String Teachers Association Student Chapter, music fraternities and sororities.

Expenses for 1995–96 Comprehensive fee of $18,720 includes full-time tuition ($13,990) and college room and board ($4730). College room only: $2120. Part-time tuition: $585 per semester hour.

Financial Aid Program-specific awards for Fall of 1994: 40 Performance Audition Awards for program majors ($3500).

Application Procedures Deadline—freshmen and transfers: continuous. Required: high school transcript, audition. Recommended: essay, letter of recommendation. Auditions held 4–6 times on campus; recorded music is permissible as a substitute for live auditions when distance is prohibitive and videotaped performances are permissible as a substitute for live auditions when distance is prohibitive.

Undergraduate Contact Margaret Hayworth, Admissions Secretary, Jordan College of Fine Arts, Butler University, 4600 Sunset Avenue, Indianapolis, Indiana 46208; 317-940-9656, fax: 317-940-9246.

Graduate Contact Annie Paulmer, Graduate Admissions Secretary, Jordan College of Fine Arts, Music Department, Butler University, 4600 Sunset Avenue, Indianapolis, Indiana 46208; 317-940-9657.

California Institute of the Arts

Valencia, California

Independent, coed. Suburban campus. Total enrollment: 1,051.

Degrees Bachelor of Fine Arts in the areas of music composition, musical arts, performance, world music. Majors: classical music, composition, jazz, music, piano, stringed instruments, voice, wind and percussion instruments. Graduate degrees offered: Master of Fine Arts in the areas of music composition, musical arts, performance, world music.

Music Student Profile Fall 1994: 175 total; 102 matriculated undergraduate, 70 matriculated graduate, 3 nondegree; 20% minorities, 23% females, 15% international.

Music Faculty Total: 43; 25 full-time, 18 part-time; 80% of full-time faculty have terminal degrees. Graduate students do not teach undergraduate courses. Undergraduate student–faculty ratio: 5:1.

Student Life Student groups include Community Arts Partnership, off-campus performance groups.

Expenses for 1995–96 Comprehensive fee of $21,225 includes full-time tuition ($15,450), mandatory fees ($75), and college room and board ($5700). College room only: $2550 (minimum).

Application Procedures Deadline—freshmen and transfers: February 1. Required: essay, high school transcript, audition. Recommended: interview. Auditions held by appointment on campus; recorded music is permissible as a substitute for live auditions and videotaped performances are permissible as a substitute for live auditions.

Contact Kenneth Young, Director of Admissions, California Institute of the Arts, 24700 McBean Parkway, Valencia, California 91355; 805-253-7863, fax: 805-254-8352, E-mail address: kyoung@indy1.calarts.edu.

California State University, Fullerton

Fullerton, California

State-supported, coed. Suburban campus. Total enrollment: 22,097.

Degrees Bachelor of Music in the areas of voice, piano/organ, stringed instruments, wind/percussion instruments, composition. Majors: composition, music, music education, music history, music theory, piano/organ, stringed instruments, voice, wind and percussion instruments. Graduate degrees offered: Master of Music in the areas of performance, composition. Cross-registration with California State University System.

Music Student Profile Fall 1994: 270 total; 225 matriculated undergraduate, 35 matriculated graduate, 10 nondegree; 40% minorities, 50% females, 5% international.

Music Faculty Total: 100; 80 full-time, 20 part-time; 85% of full-time faculty have terminal degrees. Graduate students do not teach undergraduate courses. Undergraduate student–faculty ratio: 10:1.

Student Life Student groups include American Choral Directors Association Student Chapter, Phi Mu Alpha Sinfonia, Mu Phi Epsilon.

Expenses for 1994–95 Application fee: $55. State resident tuition: $0 full-time. Nonresident tuition: $7380 full-time, $246 per unit part-time. Part-time mandatory fees: $567 per semester. Full-time mandatory fees: $1800. College room only: $3476. Special program-related fees: $25 for piano maintenance fee, $25 for instrument use fee.

Financial Aid Program-specific awards for Fall of 1994: 15–20 Department Scholarships for performers ($1000).

Application Procedures Deadline—freshmen and transfers: continuous. Required: essay, high school transcript, college transcript(s) for transfer students, minimum 2.0 high school GPA, SAT I or ACT test scores. Auditions held 3 times on campus. Portfolio reviews held 3 times on campus.

Contact Gordon Paine, Chair, Music Department, California State University, Fullerton, Box 34080, Fullerton, California 92654-9480; 714-773-3511, fax: 714-449-5956, E-mail address: gpaine@fullerton.edu.

California State University, Long Beach

Long Beach, California

State-supported, coed. Suburban campus. Total enrollment: 26,227.

Degrees Bachelor of Music in the areas of performance, music history and literature, composition; Bachelor of Music Education in the area of music education. Majors: classical music, composition, jazz, music, music education, opera, piano/organ, stringed instruments, voice, wind and percussion instruments. Graduate degrees offered: Master of Music in the areas of composition, conducting, performance, music history, music theory, opera; Master of Music Education in the area of music education. Cross-registration with California State University System.

Music Student Profile Fall 1994: 250 total; 175 matriculated undergraduate, 65 matriculated graduate, 10 nondegree; 15% minorities, 55% females, 5% international.

Music Faculty Total: 59; 14 full-time, 45 part-time; 95% of full-time faculty have terminal degrees. Graduate students teach a few undergraduate courses. Undergraduate student–faculty ratio: 16:1.

Student Life Student groups include American Choral Directors Association, Music Educators National Conference.

Expenses for 1995–96 State resident tuition: $0 full-time. Nonresident tuition: $7626 full-time, $246 per unit part-time. Part-time mandatory fees: $542.50 per semester. Full-time mandatory fees: $1751. College room and board: $5300. Special program-related fees: $20 for practice room and instrument fee.

Financial Aid Program-specific awards for Fall of 1994: 60 Music Scholarships for program majors ($750).

California State University, Long Beach *(continued)*

Application Procedures Deadline—freshmen and transfers: March 15. Required: high school transcript, minimum 3.0 high school GPA, audition. Auditions held 4 times on campus; recorded music is permissible as a substitute for live auditions when distance is prohibitive and videotaped performances are permissible as a substitute for live auditions when distance is prohibitive.

Undergraduate Contact Coordinator of Undergraduate Studies, Music Department, California State University, Long Beach, 1250 Bellflower Boulevard, Long Beach, California 90840-7101; 310-985-4781.

Graduate Contact Graduate Advisor, Music Department, California State University, Long Beach, 1250 Bellflower Boulevard, Long Beach, California 90840-7101; 310-984-4781.

California State University, Los Angeles

Los Angeles, California

State-supported, coed. Urban campus. Total enrollment: 18,224.

Degrees Bachelor of Music in the areas of performance, composition, jazz studies. Majors: classical music, commercial music, jazz, music, music education, piano/organ, stringed instruments, voice, wind and percussion instruments. Graduate degrees offered: Master of Music in the areas of commercial music, composition, performance, conducting. Cross-registration with California State University System.

Music Student Profile Fall 1994: 200 total; 150 matriculated undergraduate, 50 matriculated graduate; 80% minorities, 50% females.

Music Faculty Total: 39; 19 full-time, 20 part-time; 100% of full-time faculty have terminal degrees. Graduate students do not teach undergraduate courses. Undergraduate student–faculty ratio: 14:1.

Student Life Student groups include Music Educators National Conference, American Choral Directors Association, International Association of Jazz Educators.

Expenses for 1995–96 State resident tuition: $0 full-time. Nonresident tuition: $7626 full-time, $164 per unit part-time. Part-time mandatory fees: $351 per quarter. Full-time mandatory fees: $1749. Special program-related fees: $25 for instrument use fee.

Application Procedures Deadline—freshmen and transfers: June 30. Required: essay, high school transcript, college transcript(s) for transfer students, minimum 2.0 high school GPA, audition, portfolio. Recommended: SAT I or ACT test scores. Auditions held 3 times on campus and off campus; recorded music is permissible as a substitute for live auditions when distance is prohibitive and videotaped performances are permissible as a substitute for live auditions. Portfolio reviews held 1 time on campus and off campus.

Contact H. David Caffey, Chair, Department of Music, California State University, Los Angeles, Los Angeles, California 90052; 213-343-4060, fax: 213-343-6440, E-mail address: dcaffey@calstatela.edu.

California State University, Northridge

Northridge, California

State-supported, coed. Urban campus. Total enrollment: 24,310.

Degrees Bachelor of Music in the areas of performance, jazz, choral performance, composition/music theory; Bachelor of Music Education in the area of music education. Majors: classical music, jazz, music, music business, music education, music theory and composition, music therapy, performance, piano/organ, stringed instruments, voice, wind and percussion instruments. Graduate degrees offered: Master of Music in the areas of performance, conducting, composition. Cross-registration with California State University System.

Music Student Profile Fall 1994: 471 total; 381 matriculated undergraduate, 49 matriculated graduate, 41 nondegree.

Music Faculty Total: 71; 24 full-time, 47 part-time; 42% of full-time faculty have terminal degrees. Graduate students do not teach undergraduate courses. Undergraduate student–faculty ratio: 15:1.

Student Life Student groups include Sigma Alpha Iota, California Music Educators Association Student Chapter, American Association of Music Therapy Student Chapter.

Expenses for 1994–95 Application fee: $55. State resident tuition: $0 full-time. Nonresident tuition: $7592 full-time, $246 per unit part-time. Part-time mandatory fees: $625 per semester. Full-time mandatory fees: $1916. College room and board: $5760. College room only: $3250.

Financial Aid Program-specific awards for Fall of 1994: 25 University Scholarships for undergraduates ($1000), 70 Department Scholarships for undergraduates ($750).

Application Procedures Deadline—freshmen and transfers: continuous. Required: essay, high school transcript, minimum 2.0 high school GPA, letter of recommendation, audition. Auditions held 2 times on campus; recorded music is permissible as a substitute for live auditions when distance is prohibitive and videotaped performances are permissible as a substitute for live auditions when distance is prohibitive.

Contact Mary Shamrock, Assistant Chair, Music Department, California State University, Northridge, 18111 Nordhoff Street, Northridge, California 91330-8314; 818-885-3181, fax: 818-885-3164, E-mail address: mshamrock@huey.csun.edu.

California State University, Sacramento

Sacramento, California

State-supported, coed. Urban campus. Total enrollment: 22,726.

Degrees Bachelor of Music in the areas of voice, piano, organ, orchestral instruments, guitar, music theory/ composition. Majors: guitar, music, music theory and composition, piano/organ, stringed instruments, voice, wind and percussion instruments. Graduate degrees offered: Master of Music in the areas of conducting, composition, music education, music history and literature, performance. Cross-registration with Sacramento City College, American River College, Cosumnes River College, Sierra College.

Music Student Profile Fall 1994: 180 total; 125 matriculated undergraduate, 30 matriculated graduate, 25 nondegree; 36% minorities, 59% females, 5% international.

Music Faculty Total: 64; 41 full-time, 23 part-time; 100% of full-time faculty have terminal degrees. Graduate students do not teach undergraduate courses. Undergraduate student–faculty ratio: 12:1.

Student Life Student groups include Music Educators National Conference, Mu Phi Epsilon, Pi Kappa Lambda.

Expenses for 1994–95 Application fee: $55. State resident tuition: $0 full-time. Nonresident tuition: $7380 full-time, $246 per semester part-time. Part-time mandatory fees: $597 per semester. Full-time mandatory fees: $1860. College room and board: $4899. Special program-related fees: $20 for practice room fee.

Financial Aid Program-specific awards for Fall of 1994: 30–50 various awards for program majors ($500–$1500).

Application Procedures Deadline—freshmen and transfers: continuous. Required: high school transcript, college transcript(s) for transfer students, minimum 2.0 high school GPA, audition, SAT I or ACT test scores. Recommended: essay, minimum 3.0 high school GPA, video. Auditions held 4 times on campus; recorded music is permissible as a substitute for live auditions if a campus visit is impossible and videotaped performances are permissible as a substitute for live auditions if a campus visit is impossible.

Undergraduate Contact Margaret Buggy, Admissions Coordinator, Music Department, California State University, Sacramento, 6000 J Street, Sacramento, California 95819-6015; 916-278-6543, fax: 916-278-7217, E-mail address: mbuggy@saclink1.csus.edu.

Graduate Contact Dr. Carole Delaney, California State University, Sacramento, 6000 J Street, Sacramento, California 95819-6015; 916-278-6558, fax: 916-278-7217, E-mail address: cdelaney@csus.edu.

Calvary Bible College and Theological Seminary

Kansas City, Missouri

Independent-religious, coed. Suburban campus. Total enrollment: 272.

Degrees Bachelor of Music Education in the areas of keyboard, voice. Majors: conducting, music education, piano/organ, voice.

Music Student Profile Fall 1994: 16 total; all matriculated undergraduate; 68% females.

Music Faculty Total: 5; 1 full-time, 4 part-time; 100% of full-time faculty have terminal degrees. Graduate students do not teach undergraduate courses. Undergraduate student–faculty ratio: 5:1.

Expenses for 1995–96 Comprehensive fee of $6570 includes full-time tuition ($3460), mandatory fees ($380), and college room and board ($2730). College room only: $1130. Part-time tuition: $137 per semester hour. Special program-related fees: $100 for private lessons.

Application Procedures Deadline—freshmen and transfers: continuous. Required: high school transcript, 2 letters of recommendation. Recommended: audition. Auditions held whenever needed on campus; recorded music is permissible as a substitute for live auditions if a campus visit is impossible and videotaped performances are permissible as a substitute for live auditions if a campus visit is impossible.

Undergraduate Contact Brian Krause, Director of Admissions, Calvary Bible College and Theological Seminary, 15800 Calvary Road, Kansas City, Missouri 64147; fax: 816-331-4474.

Cameron University

Lawton, Oklahoma

State-supported, coed. Suburban campus. Total enrollment: 5,927.

Degrees Bachelor of Music in the areas of vocal music education, instrumental music education, composition, performance. Majors: composition, music education, performance, piano/organ, stringed instruments, voice, wind and percussion instruments. Cross-registration with Oklahoma University, State Board of Regents University System.

Music Student Profile Fall 1994: 72 total; all matriculated undergraduate.

Music Faculty Total: 16; 11 full-time, 5 part-time. Graduate students do not teach undergraduate courses.

Student Life Student groups include Kappa Kappa Psi, Tau Beta Sigma.

Expenses for 1994–95 Application fee: $15. State resident tuition ranges from $1665 to $1691 full-time, $54.04 to $54.85 per semester hour part-time, according to class level. Nonresident tuition ranges from $3865 to $4122 full-time, $122.79 to $130.82 per semester hour part-time, according to class level. College room and board: $2276 (minimum). Special program-related fees: $18 for private music lessons.

Financial Aid Program-specific awards for Fall of 1994: Leslie Powell Scholarship for above-average students with exceptional artistic ability, 1 Presser Scholarship for above-average students with exceptional artistic ability ($1500), McMann Scholarships for academically qualified applicants.

Application Procedures Deadline—freshmen and transfers: continuous. Required: essay, college transcript(s) for transfer students, SAT I or ACT test scores. Auditions held on campus and off campus. Portfolio reviews held on campus and off campus.

Cameron University *(continued)*

Undergraduate Contact Tammy Johnson, Secretary, Department of Music, Cameron University, Lawton, Oklahoma 73505; 405-581-2440.

Campbellsville College

Campbellsville, Kentucky

Independent-religious, coed. Small-town campus. Total enrollment: 1,260.

Degrees Bachelor of Music in the areas of church music, music education. Majors: music education, piano/organ, sacred music, stringed instruments, voice, wind and percussion instruments.

Music Student Profile Fall 1994: 85 total; all matriculated undergraduate; 1% minorities, 55% females, 1% international.

Music Faculty Total: 9; 7 full-time, 2 part-time; 90% of full-time faculty have terminal degrees. Graduate students do not teach undergraduate courses. Undergraduate student–faculty ratio: 9:1.

Student Life Student groups include Fall Drama, Spring Musical Drama, Children's Theater.

Expenses for 1995–96 Application fee: $10. Comprehensive fee of $9630 includes full-time tuition ($6420) and college room and board ($3210). Part-time tuition: $268 per credit.

Financial Aid Program-specific awards for Fall of 1994: 3 Competitive Music Scholarships for program majors ($1600).

Application Procedures Deadline—freshmen and transfers: continuous. Required: high school transcript, college transcript(s) for transfer students, audition, SAT I or ACT test scores. Recommended: essay, letter of recommendation. Auditions held by request on campus; recorded music is permissible as a substitute for live auditions when distance is prohibitive and videotaped performances are permissible as a substitute for live auditions when distance is prohibitive.

Undergraduate Contact Dr. Robert Gaddis, Chair, Division of Fine Arts, Campbellsville College, 200 West College Street, C.P.O. 1314, Campbellsville, Kentucky 42718; 502-789-5269, fax: 502-789-5020.

Capital University

Columbus, Ohio

Independent-religious, coed. Suburban campus. Total enrollment: 3,924.

Degrees Bachelor of Music in the areas of music education, composition, jazz studies, music industry, performance, keyboard pedagogy, music theater. Majors: classical music, piano/organ, stringed instruments, voice, wind and percussion instruments.

Music Student Profile Fall 1994: 160 total; all matriculated undergraduate; 2% minorities, 49% females, 1% international.

Music Faculty Total: 38; 19 full-time, 19 part-time. Graduate students do not teach undergraduate courses. Undergraduate student–faculty ratio: 5:1.

Student Life Student groups include Ohio Student Music Educators Association, Phi Mu Alpha, Phi Beta.

Expenses for 1995–96 Application fee: $15. Comprehensive fee of $17,700 includes full-time tuition ($13,700) and college room and board ($4000). Part-time tuition: $457 per semester hour. Special program-related fees: $225–$300 for private lessons.

Financial Aid Program-specific awards for Fall of 1994: Performance Awards for program majors ($500–$3500), Participation Awards for non-music majors ($500–$3500), Music Grants for program majors needing instruments ($500–$1000).

Application Procedures Deadline—freshmen and transfers: continuous. Required: high school transcript, college transcript(s) for transfer students, audition, SAT I or ACT test scores, minimum 2.5 high school GPA. Recommended: minimum 3.0 high school GPA, letter of recommendation, interview. Auditions held 5 times on campus; recorded music is permissible as a substitute for live auditions when distance is prohibitive and videotaped performances are permissible as a substitute for live auditions when distance is prohibitive.

Undergraduate Contact Steve Crawford, Assistant Director, Admissions, Capital University, 2199 East Main Street, Columbus, Ohio 43209; 614-236-6101, fax: 614-236-6820, E-mail address: admissions@capital.edu.

Carleton University

Ottawa, Ontario

Province-supported, coed. Urban campus. Total enrollment: 22,412.

Degrees Bachelor of Music in the areas of performance, composition, musical research. Majors: classical music, ethnomusicology, jazz, music, piano/organ, sociology of music, stringed instruments, voice, wind and percussion instruments. Cross-registration with University of Ottawa.

Music Student Profile Fall 1994: 37 total; all matriculated undergraduate; 46% females.

Music Faculty Total: 11; 7 full-time, 4 part-time; 85% of full-time faculty have terminal degrees. Graduate students teach a few undergraduate courses. Undergraduate student–faculty ratio: 18:1.

Student Life Student groups include Art Gallery Concert Series performers.

Expenses for 1994–95 Application fee: $50. Canadian resident tuition: $2577 (minimum) full-time. Nonresident tuition: $8752 (minimum) full-time. Full-time tuition and fees range up to $2833 for Canadian residents, $14,113 for

nonresidents, according to program. Part-time tuition and fees per course range from $493.96 to $505.46 for Canadian residents, $1738.46 to $2810.96 for nonresidents, according to program. (All figures are in Canadian dollars.). College room and board: $4903.

Financial Aid Program-specific awards for Fall of 1994: 3 Jack Barwick Awards for program majors ($350), 2 MacDonald Club Awards for upperclassmen ($500), 2 Bettina Oppenheimer Awards for seniors ($600), 1 Music Award for sophomores ($185).

Application Procedures Deadline—freshmen and transfers: April 1. Notification date—freshmen: June 15. Required: high school transcript, college transcript(s) for transfer students, audition, Canadian OAC of 6. Recommended: essay, interview. Auditions held 1 time on campus; recorded music is permissible as a substitute for live auditions when distance is prohibitive and videotaped performances are permissible as a substitute for live auditions when distance is prohibitive.

Undergraduate Contact Victor Chapman, Director of Admissions, Office of Admissions and Academic Records, Carleton University, 1125 Colonel By Drive, Ottawa, Ontario K1S 5B6, Canada; 613-788-3663, fax: 613-788-3517, E-mail address: vic_chapman@carleton.ca.

Carnegie Mellon University

Pittsburgh, Pennsylvania

Independent, coed. Urban campus. Total enrollment: 7,141.

Degrees Bachelor of Fine Arts in the areas of music, music performance. Majors: composition, instrumental music, piano/organ, voice. Graduate degrees offered: Master of Music in the areas of composition, conducting, performance. Cross-registration with Pittsburgh Council on Higher Education.

Music Student Profile Fall 1994: 165 total; 107 matriculated undergraduate, 47 matriculated graduate, 11 nondegree; 2% minorities, 56% females, 21% international.

Music Faculty Total: 86; 66 full-time, 20 part-time; 33% of full-time faculty have terminal degrees. Graduate students do not teach undergraduate courses. Undergraduate student–faculty ratio: 4:1.

Student Life Student groups include Greek Sing, Carnival.

Expenses for 1995–96 Application fee: $45. Comprehensive fee of $24,610 includes full-time tuition ($18,600), mandatory fees ($160), and college room and board ($5850). College room only: $3610.

Financial Aid Program-specific awards for Fall of 1994: Music Scholarships for program majors.

Application Procedures Deadline—freshmen and transfers: January 1. Notification date—freshmen and transfers: March 15. Required: essay, high school transcript, 3 letters of recommendation, audition, SAT I or ACT test scores. Recommended: minimum 3.0 high school GPA, interview, video. Auditions held 22 times on campus and off campus in Atlanta, GA; Boston, MA; Charlotte, NC; Chicago, IL; Dallas, TX; Detroit, MI; Houston, TX; Interlochen, MI; Miami, FL; New York, NY; Philadelphia, PA; Washington, DC; Los Angeles, CA; San Francisco, CA; recorded music is permissible as a substitute for live auditions if a campus visit is impossible and videotaped performances are permissible as a substitute for live auditions if a campus visit is impossible.

Contact Sharon Johnston, Director of Student Services, Music Department, Carnegie Mellon University, College of Fine Arts, 5000 Forbes Avenue, Pittsburgh, Pennsylvania 15213-3890; 412-268-2385, fax: 412-268-1431, E-mail address: sj1j+@andrew.cmu.edu.

Carson-Newman College

Jefferson City, Tennessee

Independent-religious, coed. Small-town campus. Total enrollment: 2,163.

Degrees Bachelor of Music in the areas of applied music, church music, music education, performance. Majors: music, music education, piano/organ, sacred music, voice.

Music Student Profile Fall 1994: 94 total; all matriculated undergraduate; 60% females.

Music Faculty Total: 16; 11 full-time, 5 part-time; 50% of full-time faculty have terminal degrees. Graduate students do not teach undergraduate courses. Undergraduate student–faculty ratio: 8:1.

Student Life Student groups include Delta Omicron Benefit recitals, American Guild of Organists projects, Center for Church Music workshops. Special housing available for music students.

Expenses for 1995–96 Application fee: $25. Comprehensive fee of $12,220 includes full-time tuition ($8550), mandatory fees ($450), and college room and board ($3220). College room only: $1330. Part-time tuition: $360 per semester hour. Part-time mandatory fees: $126 per semester. Special program-related fees: $90–$170 for applied music lesson fees.

Financial Aid Program-specific awards for Fall of 1994: 1 Ersa Davis Organ Scholarship for organists ($800), 25 Performance Scholarships for program majors ($1300).

Application Procedures Deadline—freshmen and transfers: continuous. Required: high school transcript, college transcript(s) for transfer students, minimum 2.0 high school GPA, 2 letters of recommendation, audition, SAT I or ACT test scores, minimum combined SAT I score of 800, minimum composite ACT score of 19, 24 hours of credit and minimum college GPA of 2.0 for transfer students. Auditions held 3 times and by appointment on campus; recorded music is permissible as a substitute for live auditions when distance is prohibitive and videotaped performances are permissible as a substitute for live auditions when distance is prohibitive.

Undergraduate Contact Sheryl Gray, Director, Undergraduate Admissions, Carson-Newman College, Box 72025, Jefferson City, Tennessee 37760; 800-678-9061, fax: 615-471-3502.

Casebolt School of Fine Arts

See Southwest Baptist University, Casebolt School of Fine Arts

Benjamin T. Rome School of Music

Catholic University of America

Washington, District of Columbia

Independent-religious, coed. Urban campus. Total enrollment: 6,128.

Degrees Bachelor of Music in the areas of vocal performance, instrumental performance, composition, musical theater, general–choral music education, instrumental music education, combined general choral and instrumental music education, music history and literature. Majors: composition, music education, music theater, piano/organ, stringed instruments, voice, wind and percussion instruments. Graduate degrees offered: Master of Music in the areas of vocal performance, instrumental performance, accompanying, chamber music, pedagogy, composition, instrumental conducting, music education; Master of Liturgical Music in the area of liturgical music. Doctor of Musical Arts in the areas of vocal performance, instrumental performance, accompanying, chamber music, composition, instrumental conducting, liturgical music, music education, pedagogy. Cross-registration with Consortium of Universities of the Washington Metropolitan Area.

Music Student Profile Fall 1994: 322 total; 159 matriculated undergraduate, 163 matriculated graduate; 11% minorities, 55% females, 7% international.

Music Faculty Total: 127; 17 full-time, 110 part-time; 71% of full-time faculty have terminal degrees. Graduate students teach a few undergraduate courses.

Student Life Student groups include drama department productions and student-run productions, Music Educators National Conference Student Chapter, Sigma Alpha Iota.

Expenses for 1995–96 Application fee: $30. Comprehensive fee of $21,577 includes full-time tuition ($14,612 minimum), mandatory fees ($440), and college room and board ($6525). College room only: $3730 (minimum). Part-time tuition: $563 per credit. Part-time mandatory fees: $220 per semester. Full-time tuition for architecture and engineering programs: $13,830. Special program-related fees: $340 for applied music fee, $50 for recital fee, $35–$50 for practice room fee.

Financial Aid Program-specific awards for Fall of 1994: 45 University Scholarships for academically qualified applicants ($6500), 80 Music Performance Scholarships for musically qualified applicants ($4500).

Application Procedures Deadline—freshmen: February 15; transfers: April 1. Required: essay, high school transcript, college transcript(s) for transfer students, minimum 3.0 high school GPA, letter of recommendation, audition, SAT I or ACT test scores. Recommended: interview, SAT II. Auditions held approximately once per month on campus; recorded music is permissible as a substitute for live auditions if a campus visit is impossible and videotaped performances are permissible as a substitute for live auditions if a campus visit is impossible.

Undergraduate Contact Dr. Amy Antonelli, Assistant Dean, Benjamin T. Rome School of Music, Catholic University of America, Washington, District of Columbia 20064; 202-319-5414.

Graduate Contact Dr. Paul Taylor, Assistant Dean, Benjamin T. Rome School of Music, Catholic University of America, Washington, District of Columbia 20064; 202-319-5414.

More about the University

Special Programs Qualified CUA students may enroll in dual-degree (double major) programs within the School of Music or between the School of Music and other schools of the University. The University is part of a consortium of universities in the Washington, D.C., area, and students may elect to take courses at any of these universities as well. The Summer Opera Theatre Company, a professional company national in scope, resides at the University and hires many qualified students annually.

Faculty, Resident Artists, and Alumni The 100-member full-time/part-time faculty of artists and scholars includes members of The National Symphony Orchestra, Kennedy Center Orchestra, Philadelphia Orchestra, Baltimore Symphony Orchestra, and The Metropolitan Opera. Piano faculty members perform internationally in solo, chamber, and orchestral programs. Many of the world's greatest concert performers and conductors visit Washington, D.C., and The Catholic University of America on their concert tours. Alberto Ginastera, Horacio Gutierrez, Mstislav Rostropovich, Gian Carlo Menotti, Lorin Hollander, Birgit Nielson, and Renata Scotto are among the artists who have performed or given master classes at the school. Alumni hold positions in many of the major orchestras and opera houses in the world.

Student Performance Opportunities The CUA Symphony Orchestra and Chorus, Concert Choir, Chamber Winds, and other ensembles perform throughout the academic year. These concerts are highlighted annually by a nationally televised Christmas Concert, a Kennedy Center Concert, a concerto/vocal competition (which entitles the winner to solo with the CUA Symphony Orchestra), and opera and musical theater performances. More than 200 student solo and chamber recitals are presented each year in addition to performances by faculty, resident and visiting artists, and alumni.

Program Facilities Performance spaces include Ward Recital Hall (120 seats), Hartke Theatre (590 seats), and St. Vincent's Chapel (400 seats), as well as annual access to the Kennedy Center, Basilica of The National Shrine, and other churches; recording studio; electronic piano lab; thirty practice rooms; classrooms; and studios. An on-line catalog combines the music library's collection of approximately 25,000 books, scores, CDs, and videotapes with the collection of the consortium of university libraries in the Washington, D.C., metropolitan area. Students may borrow materials from any of the libraries in the consortium system.

Cedarville College

Cedarville, Ohio

Independent-religious, coed. Rural campus. Total enrollment: 2,378.

Degrees Bachelor of Music Education in the areas of choral music education, instrumental music education. Majors: music education, piano/organ, stringed instruments, voice, wind and percussion instruments.

Music Student Profile Fall 1994: 55 total; all matriculated undergraduate.

Music Faculty Total: 21; 7 full-time, 14 part-time. Graduate students do not teach undergraduate courses.

Student Life Student groups include Music Educators National Conference.

Expenses for 1995–96 Application fee: $30. Comprehensive fee of $12,576 includes full-time tuition ($7872), mandatory fees ($132), and college room and board ($4572). College room only: $2460. Part-time tuition: $164 per quarter hour. Special program-related fees: $25 for pratice room.

Financial Aid Program-specific awards for Fall of 1994: Music Scholarships for those demonstrating musical achievement.

Application Procedures Deadline—freshmen and transfers: continuous. Required: essay, high school transcript, minimum 2.0 high school GPA, 2 letters of recommendation, audition. Auditions held 7 times and by appointment on campus; videotaped performances are permissible as a substitute for live auditions if a campus visit is impossible.

Undergraduate Contact Cheryl Sims, Secretary, Music Department, Cedarville College, P.O. Box 601, Cedarville, Ohio 45314; 513-766-7728.

Hurley School of Music

Centenary College of Louisiana

Shreveport, Louisiana

Independent-religious, coed. Suburban campus. Total enrollment: 1,014.

Degrees Bachelor of Music in the areas of performance, sacred music, music theory/composition; Bachelor of Music Education in the areas of vocal music education, instrumental music education. Majors: classical music, music, music education, piano/organ, sacred music, stringed instruments, voice, wind and percussion instruments.

Music Student Profile Fall 1994: 62 total; all matriculated undergraduate; 8% minorities, 65% females, 5% international.

Music Faculty Total: 19; 8 full-time, 11 part-time; 70% of full-time faculty have terminal degrees. Graduate students do not teach undergraduate courses. Undergraduate student–faculty ratio: 11:1.

Student Life Student groups include Sigma Alpha Iota, Music Educators National Conference.

Expenses for 1995–96 Comprehensive fee of $13,812 includes full-time tuition ($9800), mandatory fees ($322), and college room and board ($3690). Part-time tuition: $325 per semester hour. Part-time mandatory fees: $30 per term. Special program-related fees: $125 for applied music fee.

Financial Aid Program-specific awards for Fall of 1994: 50–70 Hurley Foundation Scholarships for incoming freshmen and program majors ($3500–$6000), 1–4 Mary C. White Awards for program majors ($9000–$13,600).

Application Procedures Deadline—freshmen and transfers: continuous. Required: essay, high school transcript, minimum 2.0 high school GPA, letter of recommendation, interview, audition, SAT I or ACT test scores. Auditions held 4 times on campus; recorded music is permissible as a substitute for live auditions when distance is prohibitive and videotaped performances are permissible as a substitute for live auditions when distance is prohibitive.

Undergraduate Contact Director of Admissions, Centenary College of Louisiana, P.O. Box 41188, Shreveport, Louisiana 71134; 318-869-5131.

Central Methodist College

Fayette, Missouri

Independent-religious, coed. Small-town campus. Total enrollment: 1,134.

Degrees Bachelor of Music in the areas of piano, organ, voice; Bachelor of Music Education in the area of instrumental and vocal music (K–12). Majors: classical music, music education, piano/organ, voice.

Music Student Profile Fall 1994: 51 total; all matriculated undergraduate; 2% minorities, 55% females.

Music Faculty Total: 12; 5 full-time, 7 part-time; 67% of full-time faculty have terminal degrees. Graduate students teach a few undergraduate courses.

Student Life Student groups include Phi Mu Alpha, Phi Beta, Music Educators National Conference.

Expenses for 1995–96 Application fee: $10. Comprehensive fee of $13,030 includes full-time tuition ($9160), mandatory fees ($270), and college room and board ($3600). College room only: $1650. Part-time tuition: $385 per credit hour. Part-time mandatory fees: $10 per credit hour.

Financial Aid Program-specific awards for Fall of 1994: Scholarships for those demonstrating need.

Application Procedures Deadline—freshmen and transfers: continuous. Required: high school transcript, college transcript(s) for transfer students, minimum 2.0 high school GPA, interview, audition. Recommended: letter of recommendation, SAT I or ACT test scores. Auditions held on campus and off campus; recorded music is permissible as a substitute for live auditions and videotaped performances are permissible as a substitute for live auditions. Portfolio reviews held on campus and off campus.

Central Methodist College *(continued)*

Undergraduate Contact Tony Boes, Director of Admissions, Central Methodist College, Fayette, Missouri 65248; 816-248-3391.

Central Michigan University

Mount Pleasant, Michigan

State-supported, coed. Small-town campus. Total enrollment: 16,126.

Degrees Bachelor of Music in the areas of performance, music theory/composition; Bachelor of Music Education in the area of music education. Majors: classical music, music, music education, piano/organ, stringed instruments, voice, wind and percussion instruments. Graduate degrees offered: Master of Music in the areas of music education, performance.

Music Student Profile Fall 1994: 329 total; 291 matriculated undergraduate, 38 matriculated graduate.

Music Faculty Total: 36; 30 full-time, 6 part-time; 80% of full-time faculty have terminal degrees. Graduate students do not teach undergraduate courses. Undergraduate student–faculty ratio: 9:1.

Student Life Student groups include Music Educators National Conference Student Chapter, Phi Mu Alpha Sinfonia, music fraternity and sorority.

Expenses for 1994–95 State resident tuition: $2767 full-time, $89.25 per credit part-time. Nonresident tuition: $6882 full-time, $231.75 per credit part-time. Full-time mandatory fees: $270. College room and board: $3900. Special program-related fees: $40–$70 for private lessons.

Financial Aid Program-specific awards for Fall of 1994: 85–125 Music Scholarships for program majors ($800–$1600).

Application Procedures Deadline—freshmen and transfers: May 1. Required: high school transcript, college transcript(s) for transfer students, minimum 2.0 high school GPA, audition, SAT I or ACT test scores. Recommended: minimum 3.0 high school GPA. Auditions held 4 times on campus; recorded music is permissible as a substitute for live auditions for out-of-state applicants and videotaped performances are permissible as a substitute for live auditions for out-of-state applicants.

Undergraduate Contact Roger Rehm, Assistant Director, School of Music, Central Michigan University, 102 Powers Music Building, Mount Pleasant, Michigan 48859; 517-774-3281, fax: 517-774-3766.

Graduate Contact Daniel Steele, Graduate Coordinator, School of Music, Central Michigan University, 102 Powers Music Building, Mount Pleasant, Michigan 48859; 517-774-3281, fax: 517-774-3766.

Central Missouri State University

Warrensburg, Missouri

State-supported, coed. Small-town campus. Total enrollment: 10,805.

Degrees Bachelor of Music in the areas of instrumental music, jazz/commercial music, piano,piano pedagogy, voice; Bachelor of Music Education in the areas of instrumental music education, vocal music education. Majors: commercial music, jazz, music education, piano pedagogy, piano/organ, stringed instruments, voice, wind and percussion instruments.

Music Student Profile Fall 1994: 149 total; 129 matriculated undergraduate, 20 matriculated graduate; 1% minorities, 54% females, 1% international.

Music Faculty Total: 23; 22 full-time, 1 part-time; 95% of full-time faculty have terminal degrees. Graduate students do not teach undergraduate courses. Undergraduate student–faculty ratio: 7:1.

Student Life Student groups include Phi Mu Alpha Sinfonia, Sigma Alpha Iota, Music Educators National Conference.

Expenses for 1995–96 State resident tuition: $2460 full-time, $82 per credit hour part-time. Nonresident tuition: $4920 full-time, $164 per credit hour part-time. College room and board: $3578 (minimum). College room only: $2328 (minimum).

Financial Aid Program-specific awards for Fall of 1994: 10–12 Achievement Awards for program majors ($300), 30–35 Foundation Awards for program majors and minors ($200–$500), 150 Service Awards for ensemble performers ($150–$350).

Application Procedures Deadline—freshmen and transfers: continuous. Required: high school transcript, college transcript(s) for transfer students, minimum 2.0 high school GPA, ACT test score only. Recommended: letter of recommendation, audition. Auditions held at student's convenience on campus and off campus in Kansas City, MO; St. Louis, MO; recorded music is permissible as a substitute for live auditions if a campus visit is impossible and videotaped performances are permissible as a substitute for live auditions if a campus visit is impossible.

Undergraduate Contact Delores Hudson, Director of Admissions, Central Missouri State University, Administration Building 104, Warrensburg, Missouri 64093; 816-543-4290, fax: 816-543-8517.

Graduate Contact Dr. J. Franklin Fenley, Department of Music, Central Missouri State University, Warrensburg, Missouri 64093.

Central State University

Wilberforce, Ohio

State-supported, coed. Rural campus. Total enrollment: 3,068.

Degrees Bachelor of Music in the areas of music education, performance, jazz studies. Majors: jazz, music education, performance, piano/organ, stringed instruments, voice, wind and percussion instruments. Cross-registration with Consortium of Ohio State Universities.

Music Student Profile Fall 1994: 125 total; all matriculated undergraduate.

Music Faculty Total: 14; 10 full-time, 4 part-time. Graduate students do not teach undergraduate courses.

Student Life Student groups include Phi Mu Alpha, Kappa Kappa Psi.

Expenses for 1995–96 Application fee: $15.

Financial Aid Program-specific awards for Fall of 1994: scholarships for above-average students with exceptional artistic ability.

Application Procedures Deadline—freshmen: June 15. Required: high school transcript, college transcript(s) for transfer students, ACT test score only, placement test in theory, audition for transfer students. Auditions held on campus and off campus. Portfolio reviews held on campus and off campus.

Undergraduate Contact Admissions Department, Central State University, Zenia, Ohio 45384; 513-376-6011.

Central Washington University

Ellensburg, Washington

State-supported, coed. Small-town campus. Total enrollment: 8,468.

Degrees Bachelor of Music in the areas of music education, performance, composition, conducting, music theory, pedagogy. Majors: classical music, jazz, music, music education, piano/organ, stringed instruments, voice, wind and percussion instruments. Graduate degrees offered: Master of Music in the areas of music education, performance, composition, conducting, music theory, pedagogy.

Music Student Profile Fall 1994: 5% minorities, 50% females, 1% international.

Music Faculty Total: 26; 20 full-time, 6 part-time; 75% of full-time faculty have terminal degrees. Graduate students teach a few undergraduate courses. Undergraduate student–faculty ratio: 20:1.

Student Life Student groups include Music Educators National Conference Student Chapter, Pi Kappa Lambda (music honorary fraternity), International Association of Jazz Educators.

Expenses for 1995–96 Application fee: $35. State resident tuition: $2346 full-time, $78 per credit part-time. Nonresident tuition: $8292 full-time, $276 per credit part-time. Part-time mandatory fees: $25 per quarter. Full-time mandatory fees: $75. College room and board: $4200.

Financial Aid Program-specific awards for Fall of 1994: 12 Music Department Scholarships for program majors ($600).

Application Procedures Deadline—freshmen and transfers: May 1. Required: high school transcript, minimum 2.0 high school GPA, 2 letters of recommendation, audition. Auditions held throughout the school year on campus; recorded music is permissible as a substitute for live auditions when distance is prohibitive and videotaped performances are permissible as a substitute for live auditions when distance is prohibitive.

Contact Myrna Antonich, Secretary, Music Department, Central Washington University, Hertz Hall, Ellensburg, Washington 98926; 509-963-1216, fax: 509-963-1239, E-mail address: antonicm@cwu.edu.

Chapman University

Orange, California

Independent-religious, coed. Suburban campus. Total enrollment: 3,285.

Degrees Bachelor of Music in the areas of performance, conducting, composition, music therapy; Bachelor of Music Education in the area of music education. Majors: composition, conducting, music, music education, music therapy, piano/organ, stringed instruments, voice, wind and percussion instruments.

Music Student Profile Fall 1994: 160 total; 110 matriculated undergraduate, 50 nondegree; 15% minorities, 60% females, 10% international.

Music Faculty Total: 40; 10 full-time, 30 part-time; 70% of full-time faculty have terminal degrees. Graduate students do not teach undergraduate courses. Undergraduate student–faculty ratio: 4:1.

Student Life Student groups include American Choral Director Association Student Chapter, American Association of Music Therapy Student Chapter.

Estimated Expenses for 1995–96 Application fee: $30. Comprehensive fee of $24,136 includes full-time tuition ($17,372), mandatory fees ($544), and college room and board ($6220). Part-time tuition: $538 per credit. Special program-related fees: $190 for private lessons.

Financial Aid Program-specific awards for Fall of 1994: 24 Master Talent Grants for talented students ($12,000), 12 Talent Awards for talented students ($8000).

Application Procedures Deadline—freshmen and transfers: March 1. Required: essay, high school transcript, college transcript(s) for transfer students, letter of recommendation, audition, SAT I or ACT test scores. Auditions held by appointment on campus; recorded music is permissible as a substitute for live auditions when distance is prohibitive and videotaped performances are permissible as a substitute for live auditions when distance is prohibitive.

Undergraduate Contact Michael Drummy, Director of Admissions, Undergraduate Admissions, Chapman University, Orange, California 92666; 714-997-6711.

Chicago Musical College

See Roosevelt University, Chicago Musical College

Christopher Newport University

Newport News, Virginia

State-supported, coed. Urban campus. Total enrollment: 4,705.

Degrees Bachelor of Music in the areas of performance, music history and literature, music theory and composition, music education. Majors: choral music education, instrumental music education, music history and literature, music theory and composition, piano/organ, stringed instruments, voice, wind and percussion instruments.

Music Student Profile Fall 1994: 50 total; all matriculated undergraduate; 14% minorities, 63% females.

Music Faculty Total: 22; 5 full-time, 17 part-time; 100% of full-time faculty have terminal degrees. Graduate students do not teach undergraduate courses. Undergraduate student–faculty ratio: 10:1.

Expenses for 1995–96 Application fee: $25. State resident tuition: $3350 full-time, $140 per semester hour part-time. Nonresident tuition: $7946 full-time, $331 per semester hour part-time. College room and board: $4750. Special program-related fees: $105 for applied music fees.

Financial Aid Program-specific awards for Fall of 1994: 1 Ed D'Alfonso Scholarship for instrumental majors ($500), 5 Friends of Music Scholarships for program majors ($500).

Application Procedures Deadline—freshmen and transfers: August 1. Required: essay, high school transcript, college transcript(s) for transfer students, minimum 2.0 high school GPA, interview, audition, SAT I test score only, minimum combined SAT I score of 1000. Auditions held 4 times on campus; recorded music is permissible as a substitute for live auditions when distance is prohibitive.

Undergraduate Contact Dr. Mark Reimer, Director of Music, Christopher Newport University, Newport News, Virginia 23606; 804-594-7074.

Cincinnati Bible College and Seminary

Cincinnati, Ohio

Independent-religious, coed. Urban campus. Total enrollment: 922.

Degrees Bachelor of Music in the area of church music. Majors: brass, piano/organ, sacred music, voice. Cross-registration with College of Mount St. Joseph, Miami University, Northern Kentucky University, University of Cincinnati, Xavier University.

Music Student Profile Fall 1994: 40 total; all matriculated undergraduate.

Music Faculty Total: 8; 3 full-time, 5 part-time. Graduate students do not teach undergraduate courses.

Expenses for 1995–96 Application fee: $35. Comprehensive fee of $8845 includes full-time tuition ($5445) and college room and board ($3400). Part-time tuition: $165 per semester hour. Special program-related fees: $127 for applied fees.

Application Procedures Deadline—freshmen and transfers: August 10. Required: essay, high school transcript, college transcript(s) for transfer students, 3 letters of recommendation, audition. Recommended: minimum 2.0 high school GPA, interview. Auditions held by appointment on campus; recorded music is permissible as a substitute for live auditions if a campus visit is impossible.

Undergraduate Contact Gary Gregory, Chair, Music Department, Cincinnati Bible College and Seminary, 2700 Glenway Avenue, Cincinnati, Ohio 45204; 513-244-8174, fax: 513-244-8140.

Division of the Arts: The Leonard Davis Center

City College of the City University of New York

New York, New York

State and locally supported, coed. Urban campus. Total enrollment: 14,885.

Degrees Bachelor of Fine Arts in the areas of jazz performance, classical performance. Majors: classical music, jazz, music, performance.

Music Student Profile Fall 1994: 105 total; 80 matriculated undergraduate, 25 matriculated graduate; 60% minorities, 40% females, 30% international.

Music Faculty Total: 28; 15 full-time, 13 part-time; 90% of full-time faculty have terminal degrees. Graduate students teach a few undergraduate courses. Undergraduate student–faculty ratio: 8:1.

Student Life Student groups include Friends of Music.

Expenses for 1995–96 Application fee: $35. State resident tuition: $3200 full-time, $135 per credit part-time. Nonresident tuition: $6800 full-time, $285 per credit part-time. Part-time mandatory fees: $31.35 per semester. Full-time mandatory fees: $104.70. Special program-related fees: $200–$400 for off-campus private instruction.

Financial Aid Program-specific awards for Fall of 1994: 2 Friar Foundation Awards for BFA applicants passing audition evaluation ($750).

Application Procedures Deadline—freshmen and transfers: continuous. Required: high school transcript, college transcript(s) for transfer students, minimum 3.0 high school GPA, audition. Auditions held 2 times on campus; recorded music is permissible as a substitute for live auditions when distance is prohibitive and videotaped performances are permissible as a substitute for live auditions when distance is prohibitive.

Undergraduate Contact Music Department, City College of the City University of New York, Shepard Hall 72,

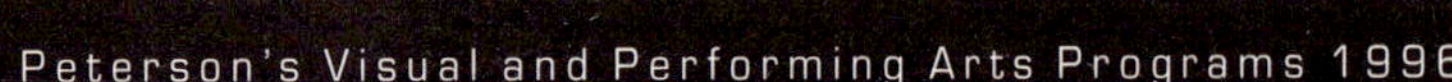

Convent Avenue at West 138th Street, New York, New York 10031; 212-650-5411, fax: 212-650-5428.

Clarion University of Pennsylvania

Clarion, Pennsylvania

State-supported, coed. Rural campus. Total enrollment: 5,367.

Degrees Bachelor of Music in the areas of music performance, music marketing. Majors: music marketing, performance.

Music Student Profile Fall 1994: 69 total; all matriculated undergraduate; 42% females.

Music Faculty Total: 13; 13 full-time; 77% of full-time faculty have terminal degrees. Graduate students do not teach undergraduate courses. Undergraduate student–faculty ratio: 5:1.

Student Life Student groups include Pennsylvania Collegiate Music Educators Association, Kappa Kappa Psi, Tau Beta Sigma.

Expenses for 1994–95 State resident tuition: $3086 full-time, $129 per credit part-time. Nonresident tuition: $7844 full-time, $327 per credit part-time. Part-time mandatory fees: $46.45 per credit. Full-time mandatory fees: $792. College room and board: $2924. College room only: $1710.

Financial Aid Program-specific awards for Fall of 1994: 1 Dr. John A. Mooney Scholarship for upperclassmen ($700), 1 Department Foundation Scholarship for program majors ($500), 4 Trunzo Memorial Scholarships for freshmen ($700), 1 Presser Foundation Award for program seniors ($2770).

Application Procedures Deadline—freshmen and transfers: continuous. Required: high school transcript, audition. Auditions held 7 times and by appointment on campus; recorded music is permissible as a substitute for live auditions when distance is prohibitive and videotaped performances are permissible as a substitute for live auditions when distance is prohibitive.

Undergraduate Contact Dr. Lawrence J. Wells, Chair, Music Department, Clarion University of Pennsylvania, 215 Fine Arts, Clarion, Pennsylvania 16214; 814-226-2287, fax: 814-226-2723, E-mail address: wells@vaxb.clarion.edu.

Clayton State College

Morrow, Georgia

State-supported, coed. Suburban campus. Total enrollment: 4,760.

Degrees Bachelor of Music in the areas of performance, composition, instrument building. Majors: classical music, early instruments, instrument building, music education, stringed instruments, voice, wind and percussion instruments.

Music Student Profile Fall 1994: 104 total; all matriculated undergraduate; 10% minorities, 55% females, 5% international.

Music Faculty Total: 20; 6 full-time, 14 part-time; 100% of full-time faculty have terminal degrees. Graduate students do not teach undergraduate courses. Undergraduate student–faculty ratio: 12:1.

Student Life Student groups include American Choral Directors Association, Music Club.

Estimated Expenses for 1995–96 State resident tuition: $1440 full-time, $40 per quarter hour part-time. Nonresident tuition: $4320 full-time, $120 per quarter hour part-time. Part-time mandatory fees: $42 per quarter. Full-time mandatory fees: $126.

Financial Aid Program-specific awards for Fall of 1994: 45 Spivey Scholarships for program majors ($2000).

Application Procedures Deadline—freshmen and transfers: August 25. Notification date—freshmen and transfers: September 16. Required: high school transcript, minimum 2.0 high school GPA. Recommended: audition. Auditions held continuously on campus; recorded music is permissible as a substitute for live auditions for out-of-state applicants and videotaped performances are permissible as a substitute for live auditions for out-of-state applicants.

Undergraduate Contact Dr. Lyle Nordstrom, Chair, Music Department, Clayton State College, 5900 North Lee Street, Morrow, Georgia 30260; 404-961-3609, fax: 404-961-3700, E-mail address: nordstrom@gg.csc.peachnet.edu.

Cleveland Institute of Music

Cleveland, Ohio

Independent, coed. Urban campus. Total enrollment: 335.

Degrees Bachelor of Music in the areas of piano, harpsichord, organ, voice, violin, viola, cello, double bass, harp, classical guitar, flute, oboe, clarinet, bassoon, trumpet, horn, trombone, bass trombone, tuba, percussion, audio recording, composition, music theory, eurythmics. Majors: audio recording technology, classical music, composition, eurythmics, music education, music theory, piano/organ, stringed instruments, wind and percussion instruments. Graduate degrees offered: Master of Music in the areas of piano, harpsichord, organ, accompanying, voice, violin, viola, cello, double bass, harp, classical guitar, flute, oboe, clarinet, bassoon, trumpet, horn, trombone, bass trombone, tuba, Suzuki violin pedagogy, percussion, composition, orchestral conducting, choral conducting. Doctor of Musical Arts in the areas of piano, organ, accompanying, voice, violin, viola, cello, double bass, harp, classical guitar, flute, oboe, clarinet, bassoon, trombone, bass trombone, tuba, timpani, percussion, composition, horn. Mandatory cross-registration with Case Western Reserve University.

Music Student Profile Fall 1994: 335 total; 201 matriculated undergraduate, 134 matriculated graduate; 21% minorities, 53% females, 19% international.

Music Faculty Total: 107; 29 full-time, 78 part-time. Graduate students do not teach undergraduate courses. Undergraduate student–faculty ratio: 10:1.

Cleveland Institute of Music *(continued)*

Expenses for 1995–96 Application fee: $50. Comprehensive fee of $20,766 includes full-time tuition ($14,756), mandatory fees ($1155), and college room and board ($4855). College room only: $3025.

Financial Aid Program-specific awards for Fall of 1994: 140 Cleveland Institute of Music Scholarships for undergraduates ($1000–$12,000), 110 Cleveland Institute of Music Loans for undergraduates ($1000–$6000).

Application Procedures Deadline—freshmen and transfers: December 15. Required: essay, high school transcript, college transcript(s) for transfer students, 2 letters of recommendation, audition, SAT I or ACT test scores. Recommended: minimum 3.0 high school GPA, interview. Auditions held several times on campus; recorded music is permissible as a substitute for live auditions with approval from the department and videotaped performances are permissible as a substitute for live auditions with approval from the department.

Contact William Fay, Director of Admission, Cleveland Institute of Music, 11021 East Boulevard, Cleveland, Ohio 44106; 216-795-3107, fax: 216-791-1530, E-mail address: ewf3@po.cwru.edu.

More about the Institute

Program Facilities CIM's main building includes two concert and recital halls, classrooms, teaching studios, practice rooms, library, eurhythmics studio, orchestra library, opera theater workshop and studio, electronic music studios, conference room, performers' lounge, and music store. Through connection of the entire facility to Case Western Reserve University's fiber-optic computer network, CWRUnet, CIM also provides a Technology Learning Center that enables students to become aware of and accustomed to the ways in which music and technology go hand in hand. The library contains 47,000 books and scores, 110 periodical subscriptions, and an audiovisual collection of 16,000 items. Through the Institute's relationship with CWRU, CIM students have access to additional library resources, especially those at the CWRU Music Department. CWRU holdings include 1.2 million volumes, 1.8 million microforms, and 8,000 current serial subscriptions. A share on-line system permits access to public catalogs in the CIM library and to OhioLink, a planned statewide information network. The dormitory, Cutter House, is adjacent to CIM's main building. In addition to the usual amenities, each room is connected to CWRUnet. Adjacent to CIM's main building is the Hazel Road Annex, an additional facility for individual practice, chamber music, rehearsal and coaching, master classes, and class recitals.

Faculty The distinguished faculty includes the principals and many section players of The Cleveland Orchestra, with which CIM has a close relationship. All collegiate-level music instruction is conducted by CIM faculty and not by teaching assistants; however, there are occasional opportunities for graduate students to teach within CIM's Preparatory and Continuing Education Department. Liberal arts, music education, and music history courses are taught by the faculty of Case Western Reserve University.

The mission of the Cleveland Institute of Music is to provide its students with a thoroughly professional, world-class education in instrumental and vocal performance, composition, music theory, and audio technology. The Institute challenges its students to achieve the ultimate within their potential and provides an outstanding setting in which they may prepare for success. Ranked as one of the foremost schools of music in the United States, CIM bases its curriculum on solid, traditional musical values while incorporating substantial liberal arts instruction and new technologies designed to equip students to meet the challenges of the twenty-first century. Graduates routinely attend leading graduate schools, are winners of major competitions, and occupy important performance and teaching positions throughout the world.

Founded in 1920, the Cleveland Institute of Music maintains its current size of approximately 340 undergraduate and graduate students and 90 full- and part-time faculty members by controlling enrollment through carefully balanced admission policies. In admitting the optimum rather than an unlimited number of students to each performance area, CIM seeks to provide personal, individual attention for each student and to maximize performance opportunities.

The unusually intense performance environment encourages students to develop multifaceted skills that include solo, chamber, orchestral, and operatic literature. This approach leads students to focus on solo expertise as well as to develop the collaborative abilities necessary for small and large ensemble work. The key is access to faculty and visiting artists in a challenging but supportive atmosphere of private lessons, master classes, repertoire classes, concerts, and recitals.

Orchestral studies are designed to develop and maintain the discipline and skill necessary to make the smoothest possible transition from school to professional life. Regularly scheduled sectional rehearsals and orchestral repertoire classes are conducted by principals of The Cleveland Orchestra. The Institute's symphony and chamber orchestras present approximately twenty concerts during the academic year, including multiple performances of two fully staged operas. These ensembles also provide a vehicle through which student composers may hear and record readings of their works.

CIM is located in University Circle, a cultural, educational, and scientific research center situated approximately 3 miles east of downtown Cleveland. University Circle comprises over thirty institutions that together constitute one of the largest diversified cultural complexes in the world. Located within easy walking distance of CIM are Case Western Reserve University, where CIM students have access to all facilities and liberal arts course offerings, and Severance Hall, home of The Cleveland Orchestra, the rehearsals of which are open to CIM students by special arrangement. Also easily accessible are numerous other University Circle institutions, such as the Cleveland Museum of Art, Cleveland Institute of Art, Cleveland Playhouse, Cleveland Museum of Natural History, Western Reserve Historical Society, and Cleveland Botanical Garden.

Cleveland State University

Cleveland, Ohio

State-supported, coed. Urban campus. Total enrollment: 16,504.

Degrees Bachelor of Music in the areas of performance, education, composition, history. Majors: classical music, music, music education, stringed instruments, voice, wind and percussion instruments. Graduate degrees offered: Master of Music in the areas of performance, education, composition, history.

Music Student Profile Fall 1994: 197 total; 142 matriculated undergraduate, 55 matriculated graduate; 16% minorities, 52% females, 3% international.

Music Faculty Total: 57; 12 full-time, 45 part-time; 100% of full-time faculty have terminal degrees. Graduate students do not teach undergraduate courses. Undergraduate student–faculty ratio: 15:1.

Student Life Student groups include Ohio Collegiate Music Educators Association, Mu Phi Epsilon, American Choral Directors Association.

Expenses for 1994–95 Application fee: $25. State resident tuition: $3231 full-time, $90 per quarter hour part-time. Nonresident tuition: $6462 full-time, $180 per quarter hour part-time. College room and board: $4161. Special program-related fees: $165 for music lessons.

Financial Aid Program-specific awards for Fall of 1994: 60 Music Scholarships for program majors ($1500).

Application Procedures Deadline—freshmen and transfers: continuous. Notification date—freshmen and transfers: continuous. Required: high school transcript, interview, audition. Recommended: minimum 2.0 high school GPA. Auditions held by appointment on campus; recorded music is permissible as a substitute for live auditions when distance is prohibitive and videotaped performances are permissible as a substitute for live auditions when distance is prohibitive.

Undergraduate Contact Howard Meeker, Chair, Department of Music, Cleveland State University, Euclid Avenue at East 24th Street, Cleveland, Ohio 44115; 216-687-2301, fax: 216-687-9279.

Graduate Contact Dr. Judith Eckelmeyer, Coordinator of Graduate Studies in Music, Department of Music, Cleveland State University, Euclid Avenue at East 24th Street, Cleveland, Ohio 44115; 216-687-2033, fax: 216-687-9279.

Coe College

Cedar Rapids, Iowa

Independent-religious, coed. Urban campus. Total enrollment: 1,343.

Degrees Bachelor of Music in the areas of performance, music education, music theory/composition. Majors: classical music, guitar, harpsichord, music, music education, music theory and composition, piano/organ, stringed instruments, voice, wind and percussion instruments.

Music Student Profile Fall 1994: 33 total; all matriculated undergraduate; 2% minorities, 64% females.

Music Faculty Total: 22; 6 full-time, 16 part-time; 80% of full-time faculty have terminal degrees. Graduate students do not teach undergraduate courses. Undergraduate student–faculty ratio: 12:1.

Student Life Student groups include Music Educators National Conference, Mu Phi Epsilon, Phi Mu Alpha.

Expenses for 1995–96 Application fee: $25. Comprehensive fee of $19,330 includes full-time tuition ($14,750), mandatory fees ($125), and college room and board ($4455). College room only: $1990. Part-time tuition: $765 per course.

Financial Aid Program-specific awards for Fall of 1994: 5–8 Bachelor of Music Full Tuition Scholarships for program majors ($13,000), 20–30 Music Scholarships for program majors ($4500).

Application Procedures Deadline—freshmen and transfers: continuous. Required: essay, high school transcript, college transcript(s) for transfer students, SAT I or ACT test scores, minimum combined SAT I score of 840, minimum composite ACT score of 20, minimum 2.75 high school GPA. Recommended: 2 letters of recommendation, interview, audition. Auditions held 2 times on campus; recorded music is permissible as a substitute for live auditions when distance is prohibitive and videotaped performances are permissible as a substitute for live auditions when distance is prohibitive.

Undergraduate Contact Sharon K. Stang, Recruiting Coordinator, Music Department, Coe College, 1220 1st Avenue, NE, Cedar Rapids, Iowa 52402; 319-399-8640, fax: 319-399-8830.

College of Notre Dame

Belmont, California

Independent-religious, coed. Suburban campus. Total enrollment: 1,707.

Degrees Bachelor of Music in the area of performance. Majors: classical music, music education, piano/organ, stringed instruments, voice, wind and percussion instruments. Graduate degrees offered: Master of Music in the areas of performance, pedagogy. Cross-registration with Trinity College, Emmanuel College.

Music Student Profile Fall 1994: 31 total; 18 matriculated undergraduate, 13 matriculated graduate; 85% females, 34% international.

Music Faculty Total: 17; 4 full-time, 13 part-time; 100% of full-time faculty have terminal degrees. Graduate students teach a few undergraduate courses. Undergraduate student–faculty ratio: 8:1.

Student Life Student groups include Music Club.

Expenses for 1995–96 Application fee: $35. Comprehensive fee of $19,582 includes full-time tuition ($13,482) and college room and board ($6100). Part-time tuition: $500 per unit. Special program-related fees: $385–$425 for private applied lessons.

Financial Aid Program-specific awards for Fall of 1994: 5 Brooks Memorial Scholarships for those demonstrating

College of Notre Dame *(continued)*

need/talent ($1100), 13 Music Assistance Grants for those demonstrating need/talent ($745), 1 LaRatta Scholarship for freshmen pianist ($790), 1 Rudin Scholarship for string students ($850).

Application Procedures Deadline—freshmen: July 1; transfers: August 1. Notification date—freshmen: August 1; transfers: September 1. Required: essay, high school transcript, college transcript(s) for transfer students, letter of recommendation, audition, SAT I or ACT test scores. Recommended: minimum 3.0 high school GPA. Auditions held 2 times on campus; recorded music is permissible as a substitute for live auditions when distance is prohibitive and videotaped performances are permissible as a substitute for live auditions when distance is prohibitive.

Undergraduate Contact Undergraduate Admissions, College of Notre Dame, 1500 Ralston Avenue, Belmont, California 94002-1997; 415-508-3589, fax: 415-637-0493.

Graduate Contact Graduate Admissions, College of Notre Dame, 1500 Ralston Avenue, Belmont, California 94002-1997; 415-508-3523, fax: 415-508-3736.

College of Santa Fe

Santa Fe, New Mexico

Independent, coed. Small-town campus. Total enrollment: 1,365.

Degrees Bachelor of Fine Arts in the area of contemporary music. Majors: performance, production.

Music Student Profile Fall 1994: 57 total; all matriculated undergraduate; 27% minorities, 62% females, 2% international.

Music Faculty Total: 4; 1 full-time, 3 part-time; 100% of full-time faculty have terminal degrees. Graduate students do not teach undergraduate courses. Undergraduate student–faculty ratio: 12:1.

Student Life Student groups include Music Club.

Expenses for 1995–96 Application fee: $25. Comprehensive fee of $16,006 includes full-time tuition ($11,796) and college room and board ($4210). College room only: $2036. Part-time tuition: $371 per semester hour. Part-time mandatory fees: $50 per year.

Application Procedures Deadline—freshmen and transfers: continuous. Required: high school transcript, minimum 2.0 high school GPA, letter of recommendation, interview, audition. Recommended: minimum 3.0 high school GPA. Auditions held as needed on campus; recorded music is permissible as a substitute for live auditions and videotaped performances are permissible as a substitute for live auditions.

Undergraduate Contact Kevin Zoernig, Director, Contemporary Music Program, College of Santa Fe, 1600 Saint Michael's Drive, Santa Fe, New Mexico 87505; 505-473-6196, fax: 505-473-6127.

More about the College

The Contemporary Music Program at the College of Santa Fe explores music tradition and innovation and exposes today's students to the global language of music. The program embraces the merit of all musical traditions. Students choose the scope of musical lineages they wish to explore under intensive and highly personalized instruction. The program also requires the study of Western theory. However, the scope of contemporary music includes much that is not classical; the program creates a blend of traditional principles that are confirmed, enhanced, and updated, and the gap between traditional theory and contemporary practice is bridged.

The College of Santa Fe Contemporary Music Program, begun in 1991, combines the best elements of music education with a focus on individual expression in a highly personalized and supportive environment. A Bachelor of Fine Arts degree is offered in contemporary music, with concentrations in either performance or production. Course work includes a variety of theory, practicum, individual lessons, and hands-on projects.

The program's core is the Contemporary Music Forum, a weekly lecture and demonstration event. The Forum also serves as a performance venue that models situations musicians will face in professional life. In the weekly Forum, students hear presentations by faculty members and guest speakers and schedule performances of their own throughout each semester. The Contemporary Music Program also sponsors the Collaborations Concert Series each semester. Nationally and internationally recognized musicians from all genres perform in these concerts, often offering workshops to students. Contemporary music students are directly involved in the production of the concerts, assisting in the technical, production, and management facets of the performances. In addition to working on the Collaborations concerts, contemporary music students work closely with other departments of the College, including the Moving Image Arts Department, the Art Department, and the theater and dance divisions of Performing Arts. In this way, contemporary music students learn first hand music's roles in the "big picture."

Many students are members of on- and off-campus bands and participate in an all-day music festival produced by students each spring.

College of Wooster

Wooster, Ohio

Independent-religious, coed. Small-town campus. Total enrollment: 1,644.

Degrees Bachelor of Music in the areas of performance, music theory/composition, music history; Bachelor of Music Education in the areas of public school teaching, music therapy. Majors: music, music education, piano/organ, stringed instruments, voice, wind and percussion instruments.

Music Student Profile Fall 1994: 56 total; all matriculated undergraduate; 5% minorities, 50% females, 10% international.

Music Faculty Total: 21; 9 full-time, 12 part-time; 55% of full-time faculty have terminal degrees. Graduate students do not teach undergraduate courses. Undergraduate student–faculty ratio: 11:1.

Student Life Student groups include Student Music Association.

Expenses for 1995–96 Comprehensive fee of $22,240 includes full-time tuition ($17,600) and college room and board ($4640). College room only: $2110. Special program-related fees: $385 for music lessons.

Financial Aid Program-specific awards for Fall of 1994: 4 Music Performance Scholarships for program majors ($5000).

Application Procedures Deadline—freshmen: February 15; transfers: June 1. Notification date—freshmen: March 25. Required: essay, high school transcript, college transcript(s) for transfer students, 2 letters of recommendation, SAT I or ACT test scores. Recommended: minimum 2.0 high school GPA, interview.

Undergraduate Contact Dean of Admissions, College of Wooster, 1101 North Bever Street, Wooster, Ohio 44691; 800-877-9905.

Colorado Christian University

Lakewood, Colorado

Independent-religious, coed. Suburban campus. Total enrollment: 2,568.

Degrees Bachelor of Music in the area of performance; Bachelor of Music Education in the areas of choral music education, instrumental music education, general music education; Bachelor of Church Music in the area of music ministry. Majors: classical music, jazz, music, piano/organ, production, stringed instruments, voice, wind and percussion instruments.

Music Student Profile Fall 1994: 75 total; 45 matriculated undergraduate, 30 nondegree; 7% minorities, 67% females, 2% international.

Music Faculty Total: 18; 6 full-time, 12 part-time; 66% of full-time faculty have terminal degrees. Graduate students do not teach undergraduate courses. Undergraduate student–faculty ratio: 12:1.

Student Life Student groups include Mainstage Productions, Music Ministry in local churches, Music Educators National Conference.

Expenses for 1995–96 Application fee: $35. Comprehensive fee of $11,310 includes full-time tuition ($7080), mandatory fees ($520), and college room and board ($3710). College room only: $2390. Part-time tuition: $295 per semester hour. Special program-related fees: $65 for vocal accompanying fee.

Financial Aid Program-specific awards for Fall of 1994: 41 Music Scholarships for undergraduates ($750), 22 Ensemble Scholarships for undergraduates ($300).

Application Procedures Deadline—freshmen and transfers: continuous. Notification date—freshmen and transfers: continuous. Required: high school transcript, college transcript(s) for transfer students, minimum 2.0 high school GPA, 3 letters of recommendation, audition, SAT I or ACT test scores. Recommended: minimum 3.0 high school GPA, interview, video. Auditions held 3 times on campus; videotaped performances are permissible as a substitute for live auditions if a campus visit is impossible.

Undergraduate Contact Anna Di Torrice, Admissions Department, Colorado Christian University, 180 South Garrison Street, Lakewood, Colorado 80226; 303-238-5386 ext. 125, fax: 303-274-7560.

More about the University

A unique, progressive, creative, and distinctively Christian philosophy guides the music program. Integrated offerings combine all aspects of classical, jazz, folk, multi-cultural, popular, and contemporary Christian music with the blend of musical growth, Biblical ethics, and Christian living.

The music program provides world-class preparation for life, the opportunity to tour internationally, on- and off-campus production studios, computer-assisted instruction, an emphasis on Christian ministry, and personal attention by an exceptional, creative, and caring faculty.

State-of-the-Art Offerings: Courses such as Computers in Music and Studio Production balance first-rate traditions in Music Theory, Music History, and Music Performance. The Music Center offers a music information technologies laboratory with Power Macintosh color computers and multi-timbral synthesizers using the latest software for music composition and transcription. It also provides a *Tap Master* rhythm laboratory and a keyboard laboratory with *Roland* full 88-key keyboards.

Tours to New York City, Europe, and the Far East are taken by the larger ensembles in alternate years. Membership in ensembles is by audition only. A partial listing of available ensembles follows: University Choir, University Band, Orchestra and Chamber Ensembles, Mainstream (an elite instrumental jazz ensemble), Profile (an elite vocal jazz ensemble), Flute Choir (a small, select ensemble), and Chronical (a Contemporary Christian Band).

Majors offered in the School of Music, Theater, and Arts provide an integrated, life-enriching, well-rounded education. Graduates excel in a wide variety of careers throughout the world.

Colorado State University

Fort Collins, Colorado

State-supported, coed. Urban campus. Total enrollment: 21,461.

Degrees Bachelor of Music in the areas of music therapy, music education, performance. Majors: music, music education, music therapy, piano/organ, stringed instruments, voice, wind and percussion instruments. Graduate degrees offered: Master of Music in the areas of conducting, music theory, music history and literature, music therapy, music education, performance.

Music Student Profile Fall 1994: 184 total; 158 matriculated undergraduate, 26 matriculated graduate; 7% minorities, 59% females, 1% international.

Music Faculty Total: 35; 20 full-time, 15 part-time; 90% of full-time faculty have terminal degrees. Graduate students teach a few undergraduate courses. Undergraduate student–faculty ratio: 20:1.

Colorado State University *(continued)*

Student Life Student groups include Music Therapy Student Association, Music Educators National Conference Student Chapter, Phi Mu Alpha Sinfonia. Special housing available for music students.

Expenses for 1994–95 Application fee: $30. State resident tuition: $2124 full-time, $89 per credit part-time. Nonresident tuition: $8412 full-time, $351 per credit part-time. Part-time mandatory fees: $25.80 per credit. Full-time mandatory fees: $585. College room and board: $4180. Special program-related fees: $17 for practice room fee, $25 for instrument fee, $5 for locker fee.

Financial Aid Program-specific awards for Fall of 1994: 1 Walter Charles Scholarship for cello majors ($1000), 1 Wendel Diebel Scholarship for pianists ($1000), 2 Sallee Performance Awards for program majors ($1500).

Application Procedures Deadline—freshmen and transfers: April 1. Required: essay, high school transcript, college transcript(s) for transfer students, audition, SAT I or ACT test scores. Recommended: minimum 3.0 high school GPA, 2 letters of recommendation. Auditions held 4 times on campus; recorded music is permissible as a substitute for live auditions and videotaped performances are permissible as a substitute for live auditions.

Undergraduate Contact William E. Runyan, Chairman, Department of Music, Theatre, and Dance, Colorado State University, Fort Collins, Colorado 80523; 970-491-5529, fax: 970-491-7541.

Columbia College

Columbia, South Carolina

Independent-religious, women only. Suburban campus. Total enrollment: 1,229.

Degrees Bachelor of Music in the areas of music education, sacred music, piano/voice pedagogy, performance. Majors: music education, piano/organ, sacred music, stringed instruments, voice, wind and percussion instruments.

Music Student Profile Fall 1994: 65 total; all matriculated undergraduate; 100% females.

Music Faculty Total: 27; 7 full-time, 20 part-time.

Expenses for 1995–96 Application fee: $20. Comprehensive fee of $15,755 includes full-time tuition ($10,995) and college room and board ($4760). Part-time tuition: $310 per credit.

Application Procedures Deadline—freshmen and transfers: continuous. Required: high school transcript, 3 letters of recommendation, audition, SAT I or ACT test scores. Auditions held 3 times and by appointment on campus; recorded music is permissible as a substitute for live auditions when distance is prohibitive.

Undergraduate Contact James Caldwell, Chair, Music Department, Columbia College, 1301 Columbia College Drive, Columbia, South Carolina 29203; 803-786-3810.

Columbus College

Columbus, Georgia

State-supported, coed. Suburban campus. Total enrollment: 5,534.

Degrees Bachelor of Music in the areas of performance, piano pedagogy, music education. Majors: music education, piano pedagogy, piano/organ, stringed instruments, voice, wind and percussion instruments. Graduate degrees offered: Master of Music in the areas of music education, piano pedagogy.

Music Student Profile Fall 1994: 116 total; 97 matriculated undergraduate, 13 matriculated graduate, 6 nondegree; 6% minorities, 7% international.

Music Faculty Total: 32; 16 full-time, 16 part-time; 41% of full-time faculty have terminal degrees. Graduate students do not teach undergraduate courses. Undergraduate student–faculty ratio: 4:1.

Student Life Student groups include Music Educators National Conference Student Chapter, Mu Phi Epsilon, Pi Kappa Lambda.

Expenses for 1995–96 Application fee: $20. State resident tuition: $1740 full-time, $78 per quarter hour part-time. Nonresident tuition: $4950 full-time, $168 per quarter hour part-time. Full-time mandatory fees: $291. College room and board: $3486. Special program-related fees: $30–$55 for lessons.

Financial Aid Program-specific awards for Fall of 1994: 70–85 Music Fund Awards for program majors ($2750–$5400).

Application Procedures Deadline—freshmen and transfers: continuous. Required: high school transcript, college transcript(s) for transfer students, interview, audition, SAT I or ACT test scores, minimum combined SAT I score of 800. Recommended: minimum 3.0 high school GPA, 2 letters of recommendation. Auditions held 3 times and by appointment on campus; recorded music is permissible as a substitute for live auditions for out-of-state applicants and videotaped performances are permissible as a substitute for live auditions for out-of-state applicants.

Undergraduate Contact Paul N. Weise, Assistant to the Chair, Schwob Department of Music, Columbus College, 4225 University Avenue, Columbus, Georgia 31907-5645; 706-568-2049, fax: 706-568-2409, E-mail address: weise.paul@mercury.csg.peachnet.edu.

Graduate Contact William Bullock, Coordinator of Graduate Studies, Schwob Department of Music, Columbus College, 4225 University Avenue, Columbus, Georgia 31907-5645; 706-568-2049, fax: 706-568-2409.

Concordia College

Bronxville, New York

Independent-religious, coed. Small-town campus. Total enrollment: 614.

Degrees Bachelor of Music in the area of church music. Majors: sacred music.

Expenses for 1995–96 Application fee: $15.

Application Procedures Deadline—freshmen and transfers: continuous. Auditions held by appointment on campus; recorded music is permissible as a substitute for live auditions when distance is prohibitive.

Undergraduate Contact Admissions Office, Concordia College, South Building, Bronxville, New York 10708; 914-337-9300 ext. 2150.

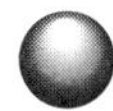

Concordia College

Moorhead, Minnesota

Independent-religious, coed. Suburban campus. Total enrollment: 2,970.

Degrees Bachelor of Music in the areas of music education, performance, music theory. Majors: music education, music theory, piano/organ, stringed instruments, voice, wind and percussion instruments. Cross-registration with Moorhead State University, North Dakota State University.

Music Student Profile Fall 1994: 143 total; all matriculated undergraduate; 3% minorities, 56% females, 2% international.

Music Faculty Total: 36; 19 full-time, 17 part-time; 53% of full-time faculty have terminal degrees. Graduate students do not teach undergraduate courses. Undergraduate student–faculty ratio: 5:1.

Student Life Student groups include Music Educators National Conference Student Chapter, Mu Phi Epsilon, American Choral Directors Student Chapter.

Expenses for 1995–96 Application fee: $20. Comprehensive fee of $14,000 includes full-time tuition ($10,620), mandatory fees ($100), and college room and board ($3280). College room only: $1450. Part-time tuition: $1660 per course. Part-time mandatory fees: $50 per year. Special program-related fees: $225 for private lessons.

Financial Aid Program-specific awards for Fall of 1994: 30 Music Performance Scholarships for freshmen ($7000).

Application Procedures Deadline—freshmen and transfers: continuous. Notification date—freshmen and transfers: September 1. Required: high school transcript, minimum 2.0 high school GPA, SAT I or ACT test scores, proficiency exams for transfer students.

Undergraduate Contact Lee E. Johnson, Director of Admissions, Concordia College, 901 8th Street South, Moorhead, Minnesota 56562; 218-299-3004.

Converse College

Spartanburg, South Carolina

Independent, women only. Urban campus. Total enrollment: 1,160.

Degrees Bachelor of Music in the areas of performance (vocal, instrumental), music theory, composition, music history, music education, piano pedagogy. Majors: classical music, music, music education, piano/organ, stringed instruments, voice, wind and percussion instruments. Graduate degrees offered: Master of Music in the areas of performance (vocal, instrumental), music theory, composition, musicology, piano pedagogy, music education. Cross-registration with Wofford College.

Music Student Profile Fall 1994: 98 total; 80 matriculated undergraduate, 15 matriculated graduate, 3 nondegree; 10% minorities, 100% females, 2% international.

Music Faculty Total: 22; 16 full-time, 6 part-time; 55% of full-time faculty have terminal degrees. Graduate students do not teach undergraduate courses. Undergraduate student–faculty ratio: 4:1.

Student Life Student groups include Delta Omicron, Pi Kappa Lambda.

Expenses for 1995–96 Application fee: $35. Comprehensive fee of $16,975 includes full-time tuition ($13,150) and college room and board ($3825).

Financial Aid Program-specific awards for Fall of 1994: 1 Daniel Music Scholarship for program majors ($10,000), Music Honor Awards for program majors ($1000–$9000).

Application Procedures Deadline—freshmen and transfers: continuous. Notification date—freshmen and transfers: September 1. Required: essay, high school transcript, minimum 2.0 high school GPA, letter of recommendation, audition. Recommended: minimum 3.0 high school GPA. Auditions held 1 time or by appointment on campus and off campus in various cities in the Southeast; recorded music is permissible as a substitute for live auditions when distance is prohibitive.

Undergraduate Contact Gindi V. Prutzman, Director of Music Admissions, Converse College, 580 East Main, Spartanburg, South Carolina 29302; 803-596-9708, fax: 803-596-9226.

Graduate Contact Lynn Stalnaker, Assistant Dean, School of Music, Converse College, 580 East Main, Spartanburg, South Carolina 29302; 803-596-9021, fax: 803-596-9158.

Cornell College

Mount Vernon, Iowa

Independent-religious, coed. Small-town campus. Total enrollment: 1,133.

Degrees Bachelor of Music in the area of performance; Bachelor of Music Education in the area of music education. Majors: music education, performance, piano/organ, stringed instruments, voice, wind and percussion instruments.

Music Student Profile Fall 1994: 25 total; all matriculated undergraduate.

Music Faculty Total: 18; 5 full-time, 13 part-time.

Expenses for 1995–96 Comprehensive fee of $20,892 includes full-time tuition ($16,300), mandatory fees ($140), and college room and board ($4452). College room only: $2037.

Cornell College *(continued)*

Application Procedures Deadline—freshmen and transfers: March 1. Notification date—freshmen and transfers: April 1. Required: essay, high school transcript, letter of recommendation, audition, SAT I or ACT test scores. Recommended: interview. Auditions held as needed on campus.

Undergraduate Contact Dean of Admissions, Cornell College, 600 First Street West, Mount Vernon, Iowa 52314-1098; 319-895-4477.

Cornerstone College

Grand Rapids, Michigan

Independent-religious, coed. Suburban campus. Total enrollment: 791.

Degrees Bachelor of Music in the areas of performance, church music, music theory/composition; Bachelor of Music Education in the areas of vocal music education, instrumental music education. Majors: music education, music theory and composition, piano/organ, sacred music, stringed instruments, voice, wind and percussion instruments.

Music Student Profile Fall 1994: 85 total; all matriculated undergraduate; 2% minorities, 60% females, 1% international.

Music Faculty Total: 15; 7 full-time, 8 part-time; 100% of full-time faculty have terminal degrees. Graduate students do not teach undergraduate courses. Undergraduate student–faculty ratio: 15:1.

Expenses for 1995–96 Application fee: $25. Comprehensive fee of $11,598 includes full-time tuition ($7050), mandatory fees ($466), and college room and board ($4082). College room only: $1890. Part-time tuition: $270 per credit hour. Part-time mandatory fees per year (7 to 11 credit hours): $466. Special program-related fees: $15 for practice room fee.

Financial Aid Program-specific awards for Fall of 1994: 1 Bateman Award for top freshmen music majors ($1500), 1 Scripps Award for top freshmen brass players ($1500).

Application Procedures Deadline—freshmen and transfers: continuous. Required: essay, high school transcript, letter of recommendation, audition, ACT test score only. Recommended: minimum 3.0 high school GPA, interview. Auditions held continuously on campus; recorded music is permissible as a substitute for live auditions when distance is prohibitive and videotaped performances are permissible as a substitute for live auditions when distance is prohibitive.

Undergraduate Contact Dr. W. Bruce Curlette, Chair, Division of Fine Arts, Cornerstone College, 1001 East Beltline Avenue, NE, Grand Rapids, Michigan 49505; 616-285-1522, fax: 616-949-0875, E-mail address: bcurlette@cornerstone.edu.

Cornish College of the Arts

Seattle, Washington

Independent, coed. Urban campus. Total enrollment: 623.

Degrees Bachelor of Music in the areas of jazz vocal performance, jazz instrumental performance, classical/new music vocal performance, instrumental performance, composition. Majors: classical music, composition, instrumental music, jazz, piano/organ, stringed instruments, voice, wind and percussion instruments.

Music Student Profile Fall 1994: 106 total; all matriculated undergraduate; 12% minorities, 36% females, 3% international.

Music Faculty Total: 27; 13 full-time, 14 part-time; 11% of full-time faculty have terminal degrees. Graduate students do not teach undergraduate courses. Undergraduate student–faculty ratio: 7:1.

Expenses for 1995–96 Application fee: $30. Tuition: $10,540 full-time, $405 per credit part-time. Special program-related fees: $120–$220 for private lessons.

Financial Aid Program-specific awards for Fall of 1994: Merit Awards for continuing students ($1000), Endowed/Restricted Awards for continuing students ($1000), Trustee Grants for all students ($800–$1500), Cornish Scholarships for new students ($1000), 2–5 Kreielsheimer Scholarships for new students from Washington, Oregon, or Alaska ($15,000).

Application Procedures Deadline—freshmen and transfers: continuous. Required: essay, high school transcript, minimum 2.0 high school GPA, audition. Auditions held 7 times on campus; recorded music is permissible as a substitute for live auditions when distance is prohibitive.

Undergraduate Contact Jane Buckman, Director, Admissions Office, Cornish College of the Arts, 710 East Roy Street, Seattle, Washington 98102; 206-323-1400, fax: 206-720-1011.

More about the College

Cornish College of the Arts is an exciting place for musicians who want to play a role in shaping the music of the twenty-first century. Students can pursue a Bachelor of Music degree with a major emphasis in jazz vocal or instrumental performance, or classical/new music vocal performance, instrumental performance, or composition. Both the jazz and classical/new music programs are alive with fresh musical influences from around the world, which build on a solid understanding of tradition and past masters.

The Music Department provides individualized instruction and a flexible curriculum that encourages students to become fluent in a variety of musical dialects. Students work with a renowned faculty of professional musicians who are leaders in their fields on a regional, national, and international level. The Music Department also maintains an active visiting artist program, which in recent years has brought John Cage, Larry Coryell, Malcolm Goldstein, Bud Shank, and Chinary Ung.

Each year students are featured in over 100 music performances. These include twice-weekly noon concerts, junior and senior recitals, an annual opera, and evening performances for ensemble classes and student composers.

Cornish College music facilities include twelve teaching studios, five classrooms with grand pianos, and an electronic music studio. Most Music Department performances take place in the 230-seat PONCHO Concert hall. Eight additional practice rooms with pianos, and a state-of-the-art electronic piano lab are also available. A percussion building houses the gamelan, percussion instruments, Chinese instrument collection, and a grand piano.

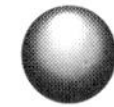

Covenant College

Lookout Mountain, Georgia

Independent-religious, coed. Small-town campus. Total enrollment: 707.

Degrees Bachelor of Music in the area of performance. Majors: piano/organ, stringed instruments, voice, wind and percussion instruments. Cross-registration with University of Tennessee at Chattanooga.

Music Student Profile Fall 1994: 122 total; 22 matriculated undergraduate, 100 nondegree.

Music Faculty Total: 9; 3 full-time, 6 part-time; 66% of full-time faculty have terminal degrees. Graduate students do not teach undergraduate courses. Undergraduate student–faculty ratio: 7:1.

Expenses for 1995–96 Application fee: $20. Comprehensive fee of $14,916 includes full-time tuition ($10,600), mandatory fees ($320), and college room and board ($3996). College room only: $1976. Part-time tuition: $440 per unit. Special program-related fees: $60–$120 for lessons.

Financial Aid Program-specific awards for Fall of 1994: 4 Keyboard Scholarships for musically qualified ($825), 34 Instrument Scholarships for musically qualified ($875), 35 Vocal Scholarships for musically qualified ($791).

Application Procedures Deadline—freshmen and transfers: continuous. Required: essay, high school transcript, 2 letters of recommendation, interview, audition, SAT I or ACT test scores, minimum combined SAT I score of 900, minimum composite ACT score of 24, minimum 2.5 high school GPA. Auditions held 2 times and by appointment on campus; videotaped performances are permissible as a substitute for live auditions when distance is prohibitive.

Undergraduate Contact Admissions Office, Covenant College, Lookout Mountain, Georgia 30750; 706-820-1560, fax: 706-820-2165.

Crane School of Music

See State University of New York College at Potsdam, Crane School of Music

Crown College

St. Bonifacius, Minnesota

Independent-religious, coed. Suburban campus. Total enrollment: 620.

Degrees Bachelor of Music Education in the areas of vocal music education, instrumental music education; Bachelor of Church Music in the area of church music. Majors: music, music education, piano/organ, voice.

Music Student Profile Fall 1994: 36 total; 32 matriculated undergraduate, 4 nondegree; 9% minorities, 67% females.

Music Faculty Total: 15; 4 full-time, 11 part-time; 66% of full-time faculty have terminal degrees. Graduate students do not teach undergraduate courses. Undergraduate student–faculty ratio: 14:1.

Student Life Student groups include American Choral Directors Association Student Chapter, Music Educators National Conference Student Chapter. Special housing available for music students.

Expenses for 1995–96 Application fee: $35. Comprehensive fee of $12,006 includes full-time tuition ($7650), mandatory fees ($436), and college room and board ($3920). College room only: $1996. Part-time tuition: $265 per credit hour. Special program-related fees: $25 for practice room rental, $50 for music computer center fee, $15 for concert tickets for classes.

Financial Aid Program-specific awards for Fall of 1994: 130 Music Participation Grants for music performers ($200–$600), 3 Scholarships for program majors ($600–$2000).

Application Procedures Deadline—freshmen and transfers: continuous. Notification date—freshmen and transfers: continuous. Required: high school transcript, minimum 2.0 high school GPA, 4 letters of recommendation, interview. Recommended: minimum 3.0 high school GPA, audition. Auditions held as needed on campus; recorded music is permissible as a substitute for live auditions and videotaped performances are permissible as a substitute for live auditions.

Undergraduate Contact Lynn Hauger, Vice President of Enrollment Division, Admissions Office, Crown College, 6425 County Road 30, St. Bonifacius, Minnesota 55375; 612-446-4142, fax: 612-446-4149.

Culver-Stockton College

Canton, Missouri

Independent-religious, coed. Small-town campus. Total enrollment: 1,057.

Degrees Bachelor of Music Education in the areas of vocal music education, instrumental and vocal music education, instrumental music education. Majors: music, music education, piano/organ, voice, wind and percussion instruments.

Music Student Profile Fall 1994: 46 total; 41 matriculated undergraduate, 5 nondegree; 5% minorities, 60% females, 2% international.

Music Faculty Total: 9; 5 full-time, 4 part-time; 70% of full-time faculty have terminal degrees. Graduate students do not teach undergraduate courses. Undergraduate student–faculty ratio: 8:1.

Student Life Student groups include Music Educators National Conference, Sigma Phi Zeta (honorary music fraternity).

Culver-Stockton College *(continued)*

Expenses for 1995–96 Comprehensive fee of $12,200 includes full-time tuition ($8400) and college room and board ($3800). College room only: $1700. Part-time tuition: $350 per hour.

Financial Aid Program-specific awards for Fall of 1994: 130 Music Grants for program majors and non-majors ($1200–$2000).

Application Procedures Deadline—freshmen: May 1; transfers: June 1. Notification date—freshmen: June 1; transfers: July 1. Required: high school transcript, college transcript(s) for transfer students, minimum 2.0 high school GPA, interview, audition, ACT test score only. Auditions held as needed on campus; recorded music is permissible as a substitute for live auditions if a campus visit is impossible and videotaped performances are permissible as a substitute for live auditions if a campus visit is impossible.

Undergraduate Contact Betty Smith, Dean of Admissions, Culver-Stockton College, Henderson Hall, South College Hill, Canton, Missouri 63435; 314-288-5221.

Cumberland College

Williamsburg, Kentucky

Independent-religious, coed. Rural campus. Total enrollment: 1,550.

Degrees Bachelor of Music in the areas of music education, church music, music business. Majors: music business, music education, sacred music.

Music Student Profile Fall 1994: 61 total; all matriculated undergraduate; 2% minorities, 2% international.

Music Faculty Total: 9; 8 full-time, 1 part-time; 50% of full-time faculty have terminal degrees. Graduate students do not teach undergraduate courses. Undergraduate student–faculty ratio: 13:1.

Student Life Student groups include Collegiate Music Educators National Conference, American Choral Directors Association.

Estimated Expenses for 1995–96 Application fee: $25. Comprehensive fee of $10,656 includes full-time tuition ($7098), mandatory fees ($32), and college room and board ($3526). Part-time tuition: $240 per credit hour. Part-time mandatory fees: $16 per semester. Special program-related fees: $75–$150 for applied lesson fee, $500 for locker rental, $50 for instrument maintenance.

Financial Aid Program-specific awards for Fall of 1994: Music Scholarships for program majors ($400–$800).

Application Procedures Deadline—freshmen and transfers: continuous. Required: essay, high school transcript, college transcript(s) for transfer students, minimum 2.0 high school GPA, 3 letters of recommendation, SAT I or ACT test scores. Recommended: interview, audition. Auditions held continuously on campus and off campus in Louisville, KY; recorded music is permissible as a substitute for live auditions when distance is prohibitive and videotaped performances are permissible as a substitute for live auditions when distance is prohibitive.

Undergraduate Contact Dr. Joseph Tarry, Chair, Music Department, Cumberland College, 7525 College Station Drive, Williamsburg, Kentucky 40769; 606-539-4332, fax: 606-539-4317.

Curtis Institute of Music

Philadelphia, Pennsylvania

Independent, coed. Urban campus. Total enrollment: 156.

Degrees Bachelor of Music in the area of performance. Majors: composition, conducting, piano/organ, stringed instruments, voice, wind and percussion instruments. Graduate degrees offered: Master of Music in the area of opera.

Music Student Profile Fall 1994: 158 total; 147 matriculated undergraduate, 11 matriculated graduate.

Music Faculty Total: 82; 2 full-time, 80 part-time. Graduate students do not teach undergraduate courses.

Expenses for 1994–95 Tuition: $0 full-time. Full-time mandatory fees: $600.

Application Procedures Deadline—freshmen and transfers: January 15. Required: high school transcript, letter of recommendation, audition, SAT I test score only. Auditions held 1 time on campus.

Contact Director of Admissions, Curtis Institute of Music, 1726 Locust Street, Philadelphia, Pennsylvania 19103; 215-893-5262.

Dalhousie University

Halifax, Nova Scotia

Province-supported, coed. Urban campus. Total enrollment: 10,910.

Degrees Bachelor of Music in the areas of composition, history, church music, performance; Bachelor of Music Education in the areas of vocal music education, instrumental music education. Majors: classical guitar, classical music, harpsichord, jazz, music education, opera, piano/organ, sacred music, stringed instruments, voice, wind and percussion instruments.

Music Student Profile Fall 1994: 108 total; all matriculated undergraduate; 1% minorities, 70% females, 30% international.

Music Faculty Total: 31; 11 full-time, 20 part-time; 90% of full-time faculty have terminal degrees. Undergraduate student–faculty ratio: 5:1.

Expenses for 1994–95 Application fee: $30. Full-time tuition ranges from $3124 to $4144 for Canadian residents, $5824 to $6844 for nonresidents, according to program. Part-time tuition and fees per course range from $630 to $830 for Canadian residents. (All figures are in Canadian dollars.). College room and board: $4500. College room only: $2200. Special program-related fees: $750 for applied skills class.

Financial Aid Program-specific awards for Fall of 1994: 2 Don Wright Scholarships for music education majors ($1000), 1 Halifax Ladies Club Scholarship for first year students ($200).

Application Procedures Deadline—freshmen and transfers: June 1. Required: high school transcript, interview, audition, SAT I test score only, . Recommended: letter of recommendation, video, portfolio. Auditions held 8 times from March through June on campus; recorded music is permissible as a substitute for live auditions when distance is prohibitive and videotaped performances are permissible as a substitute for live auditions when distance is prohibitive. Portfolio reviews held on campus.

Undergraduate Contact Dr. Walter H. Kemp, Chair, Music Department, Dalhousie University, Room 514 Arts Center, Halifax, Nova Scotia B3H 3J5, Canada; 902-494-2418, E-mail address: kstanfor@is.dal.ca.

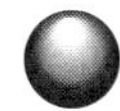

Dallas Baptist University

Dallas, Texas

Independent-religious, coed. Urban campus. Total enrollment: 2,989.

Degrees Bachelor of Music in the areas of performance, church music, music education. Majors: music education, piano/organ, sacred music, voice.

Music Student Profile Fall 1994: 70 total; all matriculated undergraduate; 2% minorities, 50% females, 4% international.

Music Faculty Total: 16; 5 full-time, 11 part-time; 85% of full-time faculty have terminal degrees. Graduate students do not teach undergraduate courses. Undergraduate student–faculty ratio: 12:1.

Student Life Student groups include American Choral Directors Association Student Chapter, Church Music Conference, Hymn Society of America.

Expenses for 1995–96 Application fee: $25. Comprehensive fee of $10,390 includes full-time tuition ($7140) and college room and board ($3250 minimum). College room only: $1390. Part-time tuition: $238 per credit hour. Special program-related fees: $113 for practice room fee.

Financial Aid Program-specific awards for Fall of 1994: 14–16 Boettcher Awards for vocalists ($2000), 6 Leonore Kirk Awards for minority program majors ($4000), 53 Music Department Scholarships for those demonstrating need/talent ($1500).

Application Procedures Deadline—freshmen and transfers: continuous. Required: essay, high school transcript, audition, standing in top half of graduating class. Recommended: letter of recommendation, interview, portfolio. Auditions held 2 times on campus; recorded music is permissible as a substitute for live auditions if a campus visit is impossible and videotaped performances are permissible as a substitute for live auditions if a campus visit is impossible. Portfolio reviews held on campus; the submission of slides may be substituted for portfolios.

Undergraduate Contact Dr. John Plotts, Director, Admissions Department, Dallas Baptist University, 3000 Mountain Creek Parkway, Dallas, Texas 75211; 214-333-5360.

Dana School of Music

See Youngstown State University, Dana School of Music

DePaul University

Chicago, Illinois

Independent-religious, coed. Urban campus. Total enrollment: 16,747.

Degrees Bachelor of Music in the areas of composition, jazz studies, music/business, music education, performance. Majors: piano, stringed instruments, voice, wind and percussion instruments. Graduate degrees offered: Master of Music in the areas of composition, music education, performance, jazz studies.

Music Student Profile Fall 1994: 387 total; 305 matriculated undergraduate, 73 matriculated graduate, 9 nondegree; 15% minorities, 44% females, 4% international.

Music Faculty Total: 102; 18 full-time, 84 part-time; 88% of full-time faculty have terminal degrees. Graduate students do not teach undergraduate courses. Undergraduate student–faculty ratio: 8:1.

Student Life Student groups include Music Educators National Conference.

Expenses for 1995–96 Application fee: $25. Comprehensive fee of $16,575 includes full-time tuition ($11,856 minimum), mandatory fees ($30), and college room and board ($4689 minimum). College room only: $3489 (minimum). Part-time tuition: $247 per quarter hour (minimum). Part-time mandatory fees: $10 per quarter. Tuition for music program: $12,048 full-time, $302 per quarter hour part-time. Tuition for theater program: $13,077 full-time, $326 per quarter hour part-time. Special program-related fees: $20 for music education instrument rental.

Financial Aid Program-specific awards for Fall of 1994: 250 Music Performance Awards for program majors ($3000).

Application Procedures Deadline—freshmen: continuous; transfers: August 15. Required: essay, high school transcript, college transcript(s) for transfer students, minimum 2.0 high school GPA, letter of recommendation, interview, audition. Recommended: minimum 3.0 high school GPA. Auditions held continuously on campus and off campus; recorded music is permissible as a substitute for live auditions when distance is prohibitive and with approval from the Admissions Department and videotaped performances are permissible as a substitute for live auditions when distance is prohibitive and with approval from Admissions.

DePaul University *(continued)*

Contact Robert Shamo, Coordinator of Admissions, School of Music, DePaul University, 804 West Belden Avenue, Chicago, Illinois 60614-3296; fax: 312-325-7444.

More about the University

Program Facilities The School of Music offers impressive modern facilities. There are ample classrooms, spacious rehearsal areas, a 140-seat lecture-recital hall, and a 500-seat Concert Hall. A fully integrated MIDI electronic studio and 16-track recording facility permits remote recording of rehearsals and performances from a professional control room. The studio contains state-of-the-art equipment, such as a DAT machine, effects and processing units, and multitrack sound modules. The DePaul Symphony Orchestra annually performs in Chicago's famed Orchestra Hall. The DePaul Opera Theatre offers a major production each spring at the Merle Reskin Theatre. Sound recording technology students learn their craft in one of the most advanced professional recording studios. Prospective teachers undertake clinical experiences in the area's top schools. In effect, DePaul turns the city into a vast classroom and a wonderful laboratory.

Faculty DePaul's music faculty includes many of the world's finest professionals. More than 20 members of the Chicago Symphony, Chicago Lyric Opera, Grant Park Symphony orchestras, and a dozen of the city's foremost studio performers and recording artists teach at DePaul.

Student Performances In addition to the standard student performing organizations, many DePaul students play in the Chicago Civic Orchestra (training orchestra of the CSO) and local professional orchestras; sing in the Chicago Symphony, Grant Park, and Lyric Opera choruses; and gig in local jazz clubs and recording studios.

Special Programs Office of Career Planning and Placement, music business and sound recording technology internships.

DePauw University

Greencastle, Indiana

Independent-religious, coed. Small-town campus. Total enrollment: 2,042.

Degrees Bachelor of Music in the areas of performance, composition, music education, music/business; Bachelor of Arts/Bachelor of Fine Arts in the area of music. Majors: classical music, jazz, music, music education, piano/organ, stringed instruments, voice, wind and percussion instruments.

Music Student Profile Fall 1994: 140 total; all matriculated undergraduate; 10% minorities, 60% females, 3% international.

Music Faculty Total: 40; 20 full-time, 20 part-time; 50% of full-time faculty have terminal degrees. Graduate students do not teach undergraduate courses. Undergraduate student–faculty ratio: 5:1.

Student Life Student groups include Music Educators National Conference, Pi Kappa Lambda, Mu Phi Epsilon.

Expenses for 1995–96 Application fee: $25. Comprehensive fee of $20,720 includes full-time tuition ($15,175), mandatory fees ($300), and college room and board ($5245).

Financial Aid Program-specific awards for Fall of 1994: Music Honor Performance Awards for enrolled students ($5700).

Application Procedures Deadline—freshmen: February 15; transfers: April 1. Notification date—freshmen: April 1; transfers: May 1. Required: essay, high school transcript, college transcript(s) for transfer students, 2 letters of recommendation, audition, SAT I or ACT test scores. Recommended: minimum 3.0 high school GPA, interview. Auditions held 5 times on campus and off campus in Interlochen, MI; recorded music is permissible as a substitute for live auditions and videotaped performances are permissible as a substitute for live auditions. Portfolio reviews held on campus and off campus.

Undergraduate Contact Kent Cleland, Coordinator of Music Admission, DePauw University, Performing Arts Center, 600 South Locust, Greencastle, Indiana 46135; 800-447-2495, fax: 317-658-4007, E-mail address: kcleland%admin@depauw.edu.

Delta State University

Cleveland, Mississippi

State-supported, coed. Small-town campus. Total enrollment: 3,775.

Degrees Bachelor of Music Education in the areas of vocal music education, instrumental music education. Majors: music education, piano/organ, voice, wind and percussion instruments. Graduate degrees offered: Master of Music Education in the areas of vocal music education, instrumental music education.

Music Student Profile Fall 1994: 71 total; 69 matriculated undergraduate, 2 matriculated graduate.

Music Faculty Total: 18; 15 full-time, 3 part-time; 80% of full-time faculty have terminal degrees. Graduate students do not teach undergraduate courses.

Expenses for 1995–96 State resident tuition: $2294 full-time, $83 per semester hour part-time. Nonresident tuition: $4888 full-time, $176 per semester hour part-time. College room and board: $2180.

Application Procedures Deadline—freshmen and transfers: continuous. Required: high school transcript, audition, SAT I or ACT test scores. Auditions held by appointment on campus; recorded music is permissible as a substitute for live auditions when distance is prohibitive.

Contact Douglas Wheeler, Chair, Department of Music, Delta State University, P.O. Box 3256, Cleveland, Mississippi 38733; 601-846-4606, fax: 601-846-4605, E-mail address: dwheeler@dsu.deltast.edu.

Division of the Arts: The Leonard Davis Center

See City College of the City University of New York, Division of the Arts: The Leonard Davis Center

Drake University

Des Moines, Iowa

Independent, coed. Suburban campus. Total enrollment: 5,954.

Degrees Bachelor of Music in the area of performance; Bachelor of Music Education in the areas of choral music education, instrumental music education. Majors: classical music, piano/organ, sacred music, stringed instruments, voice, wind and percussion instruments. Graduate degrees offered: Master of Music in the areas of performance, conducting; Master of Music Education in the area of music education.

Music Student Profile Fall 1994: 125 total; 80 matriculated undergraduate, 20 matriculated graduate, 25 nondegree; 5% minorities, 65% females.

Music Faculty Total: 21; 17 full-time, 4 part-time; 100% of full-time faculty have terminal degrees. Graduate students do not teach undergraduate courses. Undergraduate student–faculty ratio: 10:1.

Student Life Student groups include Music Educators National Conference Student Chapter, Phi Mu Alpha, Sigma Alpha Iota.

Expenses for 1995–96 Application fee: $25. Comprehensive fee of $18,830 includes full-time tuition ($14,100) and college room and board ($4730 minimum). College room only: $2500. Part-time tuition per semester hour: $325 for daytime classes, $210 for evening classes. Special program-related fees: $90 for applied music lesson fee.

Financial Aid Program-specific awards for Fall of 1994: 60 Fine Arts Scholarships for program majors ($2000–$3000).

Application Procedures Deadline—freshmen and transfers: continuous. Required: high school transcript, minimum 2.0 high school GPA, 2 letters of recommendation, audition. Auditions held continuously on campus; recorded music is permissible as a substitute for live auditions when distance is prohibitive and videotaped performances are permissible as a substitute for live auditions when distance is prohibitive.

Contact Dr. James Cox, Chair, Music Department, Drake University, FAC 260, 25th and Carpenter, Des Moines, Iowa 50311; 515-271-3975.

Duquesne University

Pittsburgh, Pennsylvania

Independent-religious, coed. Urban campus. Total enrollment: 9,001.

Degrees Bachelor of Music in the areas of performance, recording arts and sciences, music technology. Majors: guitar, music, music education, musical instrument technology, piano/organ, stringed instruments, voice, wind and percussion instruments. Graduate degrees offered: Master of Music in the areas of performance, sacred music, music theory/composition, vocal coaching/accompanying; Master of Music Education in the area of music education. Cross-registration with Pittsburgh Council of Higher Education.

Music Student Profile Fall 1994: 550 total; 200 matriculated undergraduate, 100 matriculated graduate, 250 nondegree; 20% minorities, 50% females, 10% international.

Music Faculty Total: 93; 25 full-time, 68 part-time; 90% of full-time faculty have terminal degrees. Graduate students do not teach undergraduate courses. Undergraduate student–faculty ratio: 8:1.

Student Life Student groups include Mu Phi Epsilon, Music Educators National Conference, American Guild of Organists.

Expenses for 1995–96 Application fee: $45. Comprehensive fee of $18,158 includes full-time tuition ($11,662), mandatory fees ($916), and college room and board ($5580). Part-time tuition: $393 per credit. Part-time mandatory fees: $33 per credit.

Financial Aid Program-specific awards for Fall of 1994: 70 School of Music Talent Awards for undergraduates ($6000).

Application Procedures Deadline—freshmen and transfers: May 1. Notification date—freshmen and transfers: August 15. Required: essay, high school transcript, college transcript(s) for transfer students, minimum 2.0 high school GPA, 2 letters of recommendation, audition, SAT I or ACT test scores, theory examination, musicianship examination. Recommended: interview. Auditions held 12 times on campus and off campus in Washington, DC, area; recorded music is permissible as a substitute for live auditions if a campus visit is impossible and videotaped performances are permissible as a substitute for live auditions if a campus visit is impossible.

Undergraduate Contact Thomas G. Schaefer, Director of Admissions, Duquesne University, 600 Forbes Avenue, Pittsburgh, Pennsylvania 15282; 412-396-6222, fax: 412-396-5644, E-mail address: schaefer@duq2.cc.duq.edu.

Graduate Contact Nicholas Jordanoff, Administrator for Music Enrollment, School of Music, Duquesne University, Pittsburgh, Pennsylvania 15282; 412-396-5983, E-mail address: jordanof@duq2.cc.duq.edu.

More about the University

Program Facilities More than eighty pianos; eight organs; extensive array of band and orchestra instruments; numerous practice rooms, a recital hall, and large ensemble rehearsal/performance room; computerized Music Learning Resource Center; interactive electronic piano/computer laboratory; state-of-the-art synthesizer and MIDI studio; 24-track digital recording studio.

Visiting and Resident Artists 1994–95 Keiko Abe, Colorado Quartet, Jeanne Galway, Sherrill Milnes, Don Muro, Aaron Shearer, Janos Starker, Charles Treger, Jim Walker. **Student Performance Opportunities** Brass ensemble, chamber music, choirs, contemporary ensemble, electronic ensemble, guitar ensembles, jazz band, opera workshop, orchestra, percussion ensemble, trombone ensemble, tuba/euphorium ensemble, wind symphony.

Duquesne University *(continued)*

Special Programs Student teaching abroad, national and international tours, internships and practice for music therapy and technology majors, opera training in association with the Pittsburgh Opera, an energetic summer program featuring dozens of workshops with nationally renowned faculty, comprehensive career preparation for performers and composers, including courses, seminars, and computer referrals.

Pittsburgh is known as one of America's great "melting pots," where immigrants from many nations and backgrounds joined to create an industrial powerhouse. More recently, the city has adapted to changing times, broadening its business interests and becoming recognized as a center for technology and innovation.

Like the community surrounding it, the Duquesne University School of Music offers a lively, eclectic atmosphere. Classical, jazz, and sacred musicians; music educators; and music therapists all advance their crafts, celebrating the history and tradition of music while they shape its future.

At Duquesne, students' talents are nurtured by a faculty that includes 16 members of the world-renowned Pittsburgh Symphony Orchestra and more than 50 other exceptional performers, teachers, and scholars. The depth and breadth of their experience are shared in a caring, personal atmosphere.

The knowledge imparted in classes and private lessons is enhanced by modern technology, including a state-of-the-art interactive piano laboratory and a computerized music learning resource center. Students' performing skills are honed through individual recitals and participation in the school's fourteen ensembles, which appear regularly on campus, in venues throughout the Pittsburgh area, and on national and international tours.

A close association with Pittsburgh's cultural community is a hallmark of Duquesne's music school. Pittsburgh is home to a world-class symphony orchestra and opera company as well as hundreds of other professional and community ensembles and organizations, many of which perform in the nearby downtown cultural district. Students have the opportunity not only to attend concerts but also to perform on local stages and to learn from the many international artists who appear in the area each year. Chamber and orchestral performers, opera singers, and jazz artists visiting Pittsburgh frequently present lectures and master classes on Duquesne's campus.

In its traditional strengths, music at Duquesne is better than ever. Its Music Education Department is a recognized leader in curriculum development, striving to prepare the teachers of today and tomorrow to pass on the appreciation and performance of music. Its Music Therapy program reaches out in new directions to employ the healing power of music. And its Sacred Music program has established itself as a national resource for the preservation, study, and performance of the church's musical tradition.

At the same time, Duquesne has adapted to music's future, introducing an Artist Diploma program and the Pittsburgh Opera Center at Duquesne to serve the most talented rising performers. Duquesne supports the composers of today and tomorrow through its contemporary ensemble and through a close association with the Pittsburgh New Music Ensemble. The school has invested heavily in music technology and in the recording arts and sciences, offering new degree programs taught in the region's most advanced facilities.

All of this is offered in the context of Duquesne University's 116-year tradition of a broad, liberal education and a commitment to an ethic of moral growth and service to others. Duquesne's education for the heart, mind, and soul seeks to enrich and enlighten music students' understanding of their art.

East Carolina University

Greenville, North Carolina

State-supported, coed. Urban campus. Total enrollment: 16,373.

Degrees Bachelor of Music in the areas of performance, music education, piano pedagogy, church music, theory/composition, music therapy, music theater. Majors: music education, music theater, music theory and composition, music therapy, piano pedagogy, piano/organ, sacred music, stringed instruments, voice, wind and percussion instruments. Graduate degrees offered: Master of Music in the areas of accompanying, church music, music education, composition, performance, piano pedagogy, Suzuki pedagogy, music therapy, choral conducting, jazz performance.

Music Student Profile Fall 1994: 315 total; 239 matriculated undergraduate, 42 matriculated graduate, 34 nondegree; 6% minorities, 51% females, 1% international.

Music Faculty Total: 53; 50 full-time, 3 part-time; 90% of full-time faculty have terminal degrees. Graduate students teach a few undergraduate courses. Undergraduate student–faculty ratio: 5:1.

Student Life Student groups include music sororities and fraternities, Music Educators National Conference, American Choral Directors Association.

Expenses for 1994–95 Application fee: $35. State resident tuition: $764 full-time. Nonresident tuition: $7248 full-time. Part-time tuition per semester ranges from $96 to $287 for state residents, $906 to $2718 for nonresidents. Part-time mandatory fees per semester range from $99 to $298. Full-time mandatory fees: $793. College room and board: $3030. College room only: $1590 (minimum).

Application Procedures Deadline—freshmen: March 15; transfers: April 15. Required: high school transcript, college transcript(s) for transfer students, minimum 2.0 high school GPA, audition, SAT I or ACT test scores, minimum combined SAT I score of 900. Recommended: 2 letters of recommendation. Auditions held at various times on campus; recorded music is permissible as a substitute for live auditions if a campus visit is impossible and videotaped performances are permissible as a substitute for live auditions if a campus visit is impossible.

Undergraduate Contact Brad Foley, Dean, School of Music, East Carolina University, A.J. Fletcher Music

Center, Greenville, North Carolina 27858-4353; 919-328-6851, fax: 919-328-6258, E-mail address: mufoley@ecuvm.cis.ecu.edu.

Graduate Contact Rodney Schmidt, Assistant Dean, Graduate Studies, School of Music, East Carolina University, A.J. Fletcher Music Center, Greenville, North Carolina 27858; 919-328-6851, fax: 919-328-6258, E-mail address: muschmidt@ecuvm.cis.ecu.edu.

East Central University

Ada, Oklahoma

State-supported, coed. Small-town campus. Total enrollment: 4,538.

Degrees Bachelor of Music. Majors: music education, piano/organ, voice, wind and percussion instruments.

Music Student Profile Fall 1994: 59 total; all matriculated undergraduate.

Music Faculty Total: 15; 9 full-time, 6 part-time.

Expenses for 1994–95 State resident tuition: $1212 (minimum) full-time. Nonresident tuition: $3274 (minimum) full-time. Part-time mandatory fees: $10.55 per semester hour. Part-time tuition per semester hour ranges from $40.39 to $41.20 for state residents, $109.14 to $117.17 for nonresidents, according to class level. Full-time mandatory fees: $317. College room and board: $2068 (minimum). College room only: $660.

Application Procedures Deadline—freshmen and transfers: August 17. Required: high school transcript, audition, SAT I or ACT test scores. Auditions held continuously on campus; recorded music is permissible as a substitute for live auditions if a campus visit is impossible.

Undergraduate Contact Dr. Doug Nelson, Chair, Music Department, East Central University, Box M5, Ada, Oklahoma 74820; 405-332-8000 ext. 471, fax: 405-332-1623.

East Tennessee State University

Johnson City, Tennessee

State-supported, coed. Small-town campus. Total enrollment: 11,512.

Degrees Bachelor of Music in the areas of music education, performance. Majors: music education, piano/organ, stringed instruments, voice, wind and percussion instruments.

Music Student Profile Fall 1994: 105 total; all matriculated undergraduate.

Music Faculty Total: 22; 17 full-time, 5 part-time. Graduate students do not teach undergraduate courses.

Student Life Student groups include Pi Kappa Lambda.

Expenses for 1995–96 Application fee: $5. State resident tuition: $1870 full-time, $87 per semester hour part-time. Nonresident tuition: $6000 full-time, $268 per semester hour part-time. College room and board: $2550 (minimum). College room only: $1450 (minimum). Special program-related fees: $55 for private music lessons.

Financial Aid Program-specific awards for Fall of 1994: 5–10 Floyd Cramer Scholrships for those passing audition evaluations ($200–$1500), 5–10 Lamar Alexander Scholarships for those passing audition evaluations ($200–$1500), 2 Theresa Bowers Endowment Awards for those passing audition evaluations ($500), 17 APS Awards for above-average students with exceptional artistic ability ($750–$1500).

Application Procedures Deadline—freshmen and transfers: continuous. Required: high school transcript, audition, SAT I or ACT test scores. Auditions held 4 times on campus and off campus in high schools in northeast Tennessee; recorded music is permissible as a substitute for live auditions.

Undergraduate Contact Dr. James O'Donnell, Chair, Music Department, East Tennessee State University, Box 70661, Johnson City, Tennessee 37614; 615-929-6948.

East Texas Baptist University

Marshall, Texas

Independent-religious, coed. Small-town campus. Total enrollment: 1,333.

Degrees Bachelor of Music in the areas of music education, sacred music, applied voice; Bachelor of Sacred Music in the area of sacred music. Majors: music education, piano/organ, sacred music, voice.

Music Student Profile Fall 1994: 165 total; 65 matriculated undergraduate, 100 nondegree; 5% minorities, 60% females, 5% international.

Music Faculty Total: 17; 8 full-time, 9 part-time; 40% of full-time faculty have terminal degrees. Graduate students do not teach undergraduate courses. Undergraduate student–faculty ratio: 10:1.

Student Life Student groups include Sigma Alpha Iota. Special housing available for music students.

Expenses for 1995–96 Application fee: $25. Comprehensive fee of $8750 includes full-time tuition ($5460), mandatory fees ($500), and college room and board ($2790). College room only: $1260. Part-time tuition: $182 per semester hour. Part-time mandatory fees: $20 per semester hour. Special program-related fees: $50 for applied music fee.

Financial Aid Program-specific awards for Fall of 1994: 35 Music Scholarships for program majors ($300–$1000), 50 Ensemble Scholarships for band and choral majors ($100–$400).

Application Procedures Deadline—freshmen and transfers: August 31. Required: high school transcript, college transcript(s) for transfer students, minimum 2.0 high school GPA, letter of recommendation, audition. Recommended: SAT I or ACT test scores. Auditions held 5 times on campus; recorded music is permissible as a substitute for live auditions when distance is prohibitive and

David Tanenbaum

San Francisco Conservatory of Music—Chair, Guitar Department, San Francisco Conservatory of Music, and his most recent recording is *El Porteno,* guitar music of Astor Piazzolla.

The San Francisco Conservatory's undergraduate school is like a graduate school because students have so much contact with their teachers. My teachers took me under their wing when I was a student and they allowed me the flexibility to find a way of my own. In my last year my major teacher was not even a guitar teacher. I specialized in baroque music and transcribed Scarlatti with my harpsichord teacher—transcriptions we both still use today. Guitarists tend to isolate themselves in trying to be soloists, but the world is changing. In order to make a real life in music now, guitarists need to be versatile. Besides providing a technical foundation, conservatories need to train guitarists to be chamber players, to sightread well, and to be fluent in contemporary and earlier styles. San Francisco is arguably the most active guitar city in the country. There are always a lot of gigs for our students, so much so that we sometimes have trouble keeping them in class.

East Texas Baptist University *(continued)*

videotaped performances are permissible as a substitute for live auditions when distance is prohibitive.

Undergraduate Contact Mike Davis, Director of Admissions, East Texas Baptist University, 1209 North Grove, Marshall, Texas 75670; 903-935-7963.

East Texas State University

Commerce, Texas

State-supported, coed. Small-town campus. Total enrollment: 7,952.

Degrees Bachelor of Music in the areas of performance, composition, piano pedagogy; Bachelor of Music Education in the areas of instrumental music education, choral music education. Majors: classical music, music, piano/organ, voice, wind and percussion instruments. Graduate degrees offered: Master of Music in the areas of performance, composition; Master of Music Education in the areas of choral music education, instrumental music education, piano pedagogy.

Music Student Profile Fall 1994: 160 total; 120 matriculated undergraduate, 40 matriculated graduate; 10% minorities, 50% females, 2% international.

Music Faculty Total: 21; 11 full-time, 10 part-time; 50% of full-time faculty have terminal degrees. Graduate students do not teach undergraduate courses. Undergraduate student–faculty ratio: 11:1.

Student Life Student groups include Phi Mu Alpha, fraternities and sororities.

Expenses for 1994–95 State resident tuition: $840 full-time. Nonresident tuition: $5130 full-time, $171 per semester hour part-time. State resident part-time tuition per semester ranges from $100 to $308. Part-time mandatory fees per semester range from $57 to $376. Full-time mandatory fees: $914. College room and board: $3600 (minimum). Special program-related fees: $25 for applied music fees.

Financial Aid Program-specific awards for Fall of 1994: 120 Music Scholarships for undergraduates ($200–$1000).

Application Procedures Deadline—freshmen and transfers: August 1. Required: high school transcript, audition. Recommended: minimum 2.0 high school GPA, letter of recommendation, interview. Auditions held by appointment on campus; recorded music is permissible as a substitute for live auditions if a campus visit is impossible.

Undergraduate Contact Director of Admissions, East Texas State University, 2600 Neal Street, Commerce, Texas 75429; 903-886-5102.

Graduate Contact Graduate School Admissions, East Texas State University, Commerce, Texas 75429; 903-886-5163.

Eastern Illinois University

Charleston, Illinois

State-supported, coed. Small-town campus. Total enrollment: 11,301.

Degrees Bachelor of Music in the areas of music education, performance, jazz studies. Majors: classical music, jazz, music, music education, piano/organ, stringed instruments, voice, wind and percussion instruments. Graduate degrees offered: Master of Music in the areas of composition, performance.

Music Student Profile Fall 1994: 130 total; all matriculated undergraduate; 6% minorities.

Music Faculty Total: 31; 31 full-time; 40% of full-time faculty have terminal degrees. Graduate students teach a few undergraduate courses. Undergraduate student–faculty ratio: 4:1.

Student Life Student groups include Sigma Alpha Iota, Phi Mu Alpha, Tau Beta Sigma.

Expenses for 1995–96 Application fee: $25. State resident tuition: $2776 full-time, $110 per semester hour part-time. Nonresident tuition: $6712 full-time, $274 per semester hour part-time. College room and board: $3244.

Financial Aid Program-specific awards for Fall of 1994: 25 Endowed Scholarships for program majors ($250–$1900).

Application Procedures Deadline—freshmen and transfers: continuous. Required: high school transcript, college transcript(s) for transfer students, minimum 2.0 high school GPA, audition, SAT I or ACT test scores. Recommended: interview. Auditions held 6 times on campus; recorded music is permissible as a substitute for live auditions if a campus visit is impossible and videotaped performances are permissible as a substitute for live auditions if a campus visit is impossible.

Undergraduate Contact Herman D. Taylor, Chair, Music Department, Eastern Illinois University, Charleston, Illinois 61920; 217-581-3010, fax: 217-581-2722, E-mail address: cfhdt@ux1.cts.eiu.edu.

Graduate Contact Peter D. Hesterman, Graduate Chair, Music Department, Eastern Illinois University, Charleston, Illinois 61920; 217-581-3010, fax: 217-581-2722.

Eastern Kentucky University

Richmond, Kentucky

State-supported, coed. Small-town campus. Total enrollment: 16,060.

Degrees Bachelor of Music in the area of performance; Bachelor of Music Education. Majors: instrumental music, voice. Graduate degrees offered: Master of Music in the areas of choral conducting, performance, theory/composition; Master of Music Education.

Expenses for 1995–96 State resident tuition: $1900 full-time, $80 per semester hour part-time. Nonresident tuition: $5260 full-time, $220 per semester hour part-time. College room and board: $2636 (minimum). College room only: $1276 (minimum).

Application Procedures Required: high school transcript, college transcript(s) for transfer students, audition, ACT test score only. Auditions held on campus and off campus. Portfolio reviews held on campus and off campus.

Undergraduate Contact Admissions Office, Eastern Kentucky University, 203 Jones Building, Richmond, Kentucky 40475-3101; 606-622-1000.

Eastern Michigan University

Ypsilanti, Michigan

State-supported, coed. Suburban campus. Total enrollment: 23,321.

Degrees Bachelor of Music in the area of performance; Bachelor of Music Education in the areas of vocal music education, instrumental music education; Bachelor of Music Therapy in the area of music therapy. Majors: guitar, music education, music therapy, piano/organ, stringed instruments, voice, wind and percussion instruments.

Music Student Profile Fall 1994: 200 total; all matriculated undergraduate.

Music Faculty Total: 40; 32 full-time, 8 part-time; 60% of full-time faculty have terminal degrees. Graduate students do not teach undergraduate courses.

Expenses for 1995–96 Application fee: $20. Part-time mandatory fees per semester range from $53.33 to $226.62. State resident tuition ranges from $2610 to $2820 full-time, $87 to $94 per semester hour part-time, according to class level. Nonresident tuition ranges from $6750 to $7200 full-time, $225 to $240 per semester hour part-time, according to class level. Ohio residents pay state resident tuition. Full-time mandatory fees: $400. College room and board: $4148. College room only: $1924.

Financial Aid Program-specific awards for Fall of 1994 available.

Application Procedures Deadline—freshmen and transfers: continuous. Required: high school transcript, minimum 2.0 high school GPA, audition, SAT I or ACT test scores. Auditions held 8 times on campus; recorded music is permissible as a substitute for live auditions when distance is prohibitive.

Undergraduate Contact David Pierce, Coordinator of Undergraduate Advising, Department of Music, Eastern Michigan University, Alexander Music Building, Ypsilanti, Michigan 48197; 313-487-1044, fax: 313-487-6939.

Eastern New Mexico University

Portales, New Mexico

State-supported, coed. Small-town campus. Total enrollment: 3,853.

Degrees Bachelor of Music in the areas of piano performance and pedagogy, string performance, vocal performance and pedagogy, winds or percussion performance, music therapy, music business; Bachelor of Music Education in the areas of choral music education, elementary music education, string music education, winds music education, percussion music education. Majors: music, music business, music education, music therapy, piano/organ, stringed instruments, voice, wind and percussion instruments. Graduate degrees offered: Master of Music in the area of music education.

Music Student Profile Fall 1994: 150 total; 90 matriculated undergraduate, 10 matriculated graduate, 50 nondegree.

Music Faculty Total: 16; 14 full-time, 2 part-time; 88% of full-time faculty have terminal degrees. Graduate students teach a few undergraduate courses. Undergraduate student–faculty ratio: 10:1.

Student Life Student groups include Music Educators National Conference, American Choral Directors Association, music sorority and fraternity.

Expenses for 1995–96 Application fee: $15. State resident tuition: $2258 full-time, $94 per credit hour part-time. Nonresident tuition: $6500 full-time, $270.80 per credit hour part-time. College room and board: $2728. College room only: $1268. Special program-related fees: $50 for applied music lesson fee.

Financial Aid Program-specific awards for Fall of 1994: Symphony League Awards for strings/winds majors ($100–$1000), 8 Talent Day Scholarships for program majors ($400), 45 Participation Grants for program majors ($200).

Application Procedures Deadline—freshmen and transfers: July 23. Required: high school transcript, minimum 2.0 high school GPA, audition. Auditions held continuously on campus; recorded music is permissible as a substitute for live auditions when distance is prohibitive and videotaped performances are permissible as a substitute for live auditions when distance is prohibitive.

Undergraduate Contact David Gerig, Director, School of Music, Eastern New Mexico University, Station #16, Portales, New Mexico 88130; 505-562-2376, fax: 505-562-2500.

Graduate Contact Dr. William Wood, Graduate Coordinator, School of Music, Eastern New Mexico University, Station #16, Portales, New Mexico 88130; 505-562-2376, fax: 505-562-2500.

Eastern Washington University

Cheney, Washington

State-supported, coed. Small-town campus. Total enrollment: 8,360.

Degrees Bachelor of Music in the areas of instrumental music, vocal performance. Majors: music, music theory and composition, musical instrument technology, piano/organ, stringed instruments, voice, wind and percussion instruments.

Music Student Profile Fall 1994: 100 total; 80 matriculated undergraduate, 20 nondegree; 3% minorities, 2% international.

Music Faculty Total: 21; 13 full-time, 8 part-time; 92% of full-time faculty have terminal degrees. Graduate students teach a few undergraduate courses. Undergraduate student–faculty ratio: 15:1.

Student Life Student groups include Music Educators National Conference Student Chapter, National Association of String Teachers, Music Teachers National Association.

Expenses for 1995–96 Application fee: $35. State resident tuition: $2343 full-time, $78 per quarter hour part-time. Nonresident tuition: $8289 full-time, $276 per quarter hour part-time. Full-time mandatory fees: $120. College room and board: $3903.

Financial Aid Program-specific awards for Fall of 1994: Instrumental Scholars Program awards for instrumentalists, 1 George W. Lotzenhiser Scholarship for artistically talented brass instrumentalists, 1 Lloyd and Thekla Rowles Scholarship for artistically talented vocalists, 1 Ann Harder Wyatt Scholarship for artistically talented juniors or seniors, 1 Marvin Mutchnik Scholarship for artistically talented strings students, 1 Eastern Washington University Scholarship for artistically talented woodwind students, Meritorious Music Awards for artistically talented program majors, 1 Gwendoline Harper Scholarship for artistically talented pianists, Pep Band Awards for band students ($100).

Application Procedures Deadline—freshmen and transfers: continuous. Required: high school transcript, college transcript(s) for transfer students, audition, SAT I or ACT test scores, minimum 2.5 high school GPA. Recommended: interview. Auditions held continuously off campus in Seattle, WA; recorded music is permissible as a substitute for live auditions when distance is prohibitive and videotaped performances are permissible as a substitute for live auditions when distance is prohibitive.

Undergraduate Contact Lynn Brinckmeyer, Director of Music Education, Music Department, Eastern Washington University, MS-100, Cheney, Washington 99004; 509-359-2330, fax: 509-359-7028.

Eastman School of Music

See University of Rochester, Eastman School of Music

Elmhurst College

Elmhurst, Illinois

Independent-religious, coed. Suburban campus. Total enrollment: 2,775.

Degrees Bachelor of Music in the areas of music education, music business. Majors: music, music business, music education.

Music Student Profile Fall 1994: 95 total; all matriculated undergraduate; 8% minorities, 53% females, 5% international.

Music Faculty Total: 45; 5 full-time, 40 part-time; 100% of full-time faculty have terminal degrees. Graduate students do not teach undergraduate courses. Undergraduate student–faculty ratio: 15:1.

Student Life Student groups include Music Educators National Conference, Music and Entertainment Industry Student Association, Student Recording Services.

Estimated Expenses for 1995–96 Application fee: $15. Comprehensive fee of $14,654 includes full-time tuition ($10,184), mandatory fees ($80), and college room and board ($4390). College room only: $2310. Part-time tuition: $299 per credit hour.

Financial Aid Program-specific awards for Fall of 1994: 20–30 Music Scholarship/Talent Awards for performers ($500–$3000), 1 National Association of Music Merchants Scholarship for academically qualified/talented applicants ($1000), 1 National Academy of Recording Arts and Sciences Scholarship for academically qualified/talented applicants ($1000).

Application Procedures Deadline—freshmen and transfers: August 15. Notification date—freshmen and transfers: August 20. Required: high school transcript, college transcript(s) for transfer students, minimum 2.0 high school GPA, audition, SAT I or ACT test scores. Auditions held continuously on campus; recorded music is permissible as a substitute for live auditions for international students and U.S. students from great distance and videotaped performances are permissible as a substitute for live auditions for international students and U.S. students from great distance.

Undergraduate Contact Doug Beach, Director of Music Admissions, Music Department, Elmhurst College, 190 Prospect Avenue, Elmhurst, Illinois 60126; 708-617-3515, fax: 708-617-3738.

Emporia State University

Emporia, Kansas

State-supported, coed. Small-town campus. Total enrollment: 6,075.

Degrees Bachelor of Music in the area of performance; Bachelor of Music Education in the areas of instrumental music education, vocal music education. Majors: music education, piano/organ, stringed instruments, voice, wind and percussion instruments. Graduate degrees offered: Master of Music in the area of performance; Master of Music Education in the area of music education.

Music Student Profile Fall 1994: 95 total; 80 matriculated undergraduate, 15 matriculated graduate; 5% minorities.

Music Faculty Total: 20; 13 full-time, 7 part-time; 70% of full-time faculty have terminal degrees. Graduate students teach a few undergraduate courses. Undergraduate student–faculty ratio: 6:1.

Student Life Student groups include Collegiate Music Educators National Conference, Kappa Kappa Psi, Tau Beta Sigma.

Expenses for 1995–96 Application fee: $15. State resident tuition: $1782 full-time, $65 per credit hour part-time. Nonresident tuition: $5764 full-time, $198 per credit hour part-time. College room and board: $3220.

Financial Aid Program-specific awards for Fall of 1994: 60 Endowed Scholarships for talented students ($800–$1500).

Application Procedures Deadline—freshmen and transfers: continuous. Required: high school transcript, college transcript(s) for transfer students, SAT I or ACT test scores, theory skills evaluation. Recommended: audition. Auditions held by appointment on campus and off campus in various cities in Kansas; recorded music is permissible as a substitute for live auditions and videotaped performances are permissible as a substitute for live auditions.

Undergraduate Contact Dr. Marie Miller, Chair, Division of Music, Emporia State University, Box 4029, Emporia, Kansas 66801; 316-341-5431, fax: 316-341-5073.

Graduate Contact Dr. Penelope Speedie, Division of Music, Emporia State University, Box 4029, Emporia, Kansas 66801; 316-341-5438.

Esther Boyer College of Music

See Temple University, Esther Boyer College of Music

Evangel College

Springfield, Missouri

Independent-religious, coed. Urban campus. Total enrollment: 1,541.

Degrees Bachelor of Music in the areas of music education, sacred music, performance. Majors: classical music, music, music education, piano/organ, sacred music, stringed instruments, voice, wind and percussion instruments.

Music Student Profile Fall 1994: 106 total; all matriculated undergraduate; 5% minorities, 55% females, 5% international.

Music Faculty Total: 27; 11 full-time, 16 part-time; 60% of full-time faculty have terminal degrees. Graduate students do not teach undergraduate courses. Undergraduate student–faculty ratio: 10:1.

Student Life Student groups include Music Educators National Conference Student Chapter, Pi Kappa Lambda, Mu Phi Epsilon.

Expenses for 1995–96 Application fee: $25. Comprehensive fee of $10,470 includes full-time tuition ($7120), mandatory fees ($180), and college room and board ($3170). College room only: $1550. Part-time tuition: $277 per credit hour. Part-time mandatory fees per semester

Evangel College *(continued)*

range from $40 to $50. Special program-related fees: $10 for techniques classes, instrument rental.

Financial Aid Program-specific awards for Fall of 1994: 50 Music Performance Awards for undergraduates ($1500–$2000), 12 Endowed Awards for upperclassmen ($300–$1000).

Application Procedures Deadline—freshmen and transfers: August 15. Required: high school transcript, college transcript(s) for transfer students, minimum 2.0 high school GPA, letter of recommendation, audition, ACT test score only. Auditions held 4–6 times on campus; recorded music is permissible as a substitute for live auditions when distance is prohibitive and videotaped performances are permissible as a substitute for live auditions.

Undergraduate Contact John Shows, Chairman, Department of Music, Evangel College, 1111 North Glenstone, Springfield, Missouri 65802; 417-865-2811 ext. 7211, fax: 417-865-9599.

Fisk University

Nashville, Tennessee

Independent-religious, coed. Urban campus. Total enrollment: 872.

Degrees Bachelor of Music in the area of classical music. Cross-registration with Vanderbilt University.

Music Student Profile Fall 1994: 25 total; all matriculated undergraduate; 100% minorities.

Music Faculty Total: 5; 4 full-time, 1 part-time; 50% of full-time faculty have terminal degrees. Graduate students do not teach undergraduate courses. Undergraduate student–faculty ratio: 6:1.

Student Life Student groups include Jazz Ensemble, Opera Workshop, Jubilee Singers.

Expenses for 1995–96 Application fee: $25. Comprehensive fee of $11,003 includes full-time tuition ($6740), mandatory fees ($315), and college room and board ($3948). College room only: $2266. Full-time mandatory fees for freshmen: $100. Special program-related fees: $20 for piano practice fee, $40 for class lessons, $60–$100 for applied music lesson fee, $40 for organ practice fee.

Application Procedures Deadline—freshmen and transfers: June 15. Required: essay, high school transcript, college transcript(s) for transfer students, minimum 2.0 high school GPA, 2 letters of recommendation, SAT I or ACT test scores. Recommended: audition. Auditions held by appointment on campus.

Undergraduate Contact Valija Mellins-Bumbulis, Chairman, Department of Music, Fisk University, 1000 17th Avenue North, Nashville, Tennessee 37208-3051; 615-329-8700.

Five Towns College

Dix Hills, New York

Independent, coed. Suburban campus. Total enrollment: 732.

Degrees Bachelor of Music in the area of jazz/commercial music; Bachelor of Music Education in the area of music education. Majors: audio recording technology, composition/songwriting, jazz, music, music business, music education, music theater, musical instrument technology, performance, video music. Cross-registration with Long Island Regional Advisory Council on Higher Education.

Music Student Profile Fall 1994: 300 total; all matriculated undergraduate; 27% minorities, 35% females, 1% international.

Music Faculty Total: 37; 18 full-time, 19 part-time; 38% of full-time faculty have terminal degrees. Graduate students do not teach undergraduate courses. Undergraduate student–faculty ratio: 11:1.

Student Life Student groups include Music Theatre Production Society, Audio Recording Club, Music Educators National Conference Student Chapter.

Expenses for 1995–96 Application fee: $25. Comprehensive fee of $12,790 includes full-time tuition ($8100), mandatory fees ($300), and college room and board ($4390). College room only: $3790. Part-time tuition: $335 per credit. Special program-related fees: $450 for private music instruction, $10 for piano lab fee, $25–$150 for audio/video lab fees.

Financial Aid Program-specific awards for Fall of 1994: 7 Mickey Sheen Awards for percussion majors ($1000), 40 Music Program Awards for musical performers ($1200), 8 Brass and Woodwind Awards for brass/woodwind majors ($1200), 9 Long Island Superintendent Awards for music education majors ($4300).

Application Procedures Deadline—freshmen and transfers: continuous. Required: high school transcript, college transcript(s) for transfer students, minimum 2.0 high school GPA, interview, audition. Recommended: essay, minimum 3.0 high school GPA, 2 letters of recommendation, SAT I or ACT test scores. Auditions held 7 times on campus; recorded music is permissible as a substitute for live auditions for international applicants.

Undergraduate Contact Jennifer Roemer, Director of Admissions, Five Towns College, Dix Hills, New York 11746-6055; 516-424-7000 ext. 110, fax: 516-424-7006.

More about the College

Program Facilities Performance spaces include the Dix Hills Center for the Performing Arts (600 seats), College athletic center (1,000-seat arena), The Upbeat Café (132 seats), and the College television center (70-seat hall/television studio). In addition, the College is equipped with 8-, 16-, 24-, and 48-track state-of-the-art recording studios as well as a MIDI technology laboratory.

Faculty, Resident Artists, and Alumni The many gifted and talented musicians and educators who comprise the Five Towns College faculty bring a vast array of backgrounds and experiences to campus. The faculty is exemplary in both their academic and performance credentials. Artists-in-residence include the

Sound Symphony Orchestra, the International Art of Jazz, and the Allegro Chamber Ensemble. Representative visiting artists include the Sea Cliff Chamber Players, Atlantic Wind Symphony, Township Theatre Group, and Gilbert & Sullivan Light Opera Theatre Company of Long Island. Alumni work throughout the music industry in numerous capacities, such as musicians, business managers, audio recording engineers, and music educators.

Student Performance Students have the opportunity to perform in ensembles of every size and instrumentation. The most popular ensembles include the Concert Choir, Stage Band, Guitar Ensemble, and Percussion Ensemble. Students are invited to participate in any of the six major theatrical productions produced on campus each year. These include three musicals, one operetta, one comedy, and one drama. The Upbeat Café provides an informal atmosphere for students to gather, perform, and collaborate each afternoon.

Special Programs The College is a member of the Phi Sigma National Honor Society and hosts a student chapter of the Music Educators National Conference (MENC). Each spring, the College hosts the Classic American Guitar Show, which brings thousands of guitarists from around the world together for a conference and exposition. Numerous other festivals and performances are held each year, including a Stage Band Festival and Music Industry Conference.

Nestled on nearly 40 rolling acres at Dix Hills, Long Island, New York, Five Towns College is a comprehensive institution of higher education with a well-rounded music and performing arts environment. Through its three major divisions—Music, Business, and Liberal Arts—the College offers twenty-seven different programs of study leading to associate and bachelor degrees.

The College awards a Bachelor of Music degree in jazz/commercial music, with major areas of concentration in performance, composition/songwriting, musical theater, audio recording technology, music business, and video music. These programs are designed for students pursuing careers as professional performers, composers, recording engineers, music business executives, or producers of video music.

The College also offers a Bachelor of Music degree program in music education. The Music Education program is designed for students interested in a career as a teacher of music in a public or private school (K–12), leads to New York State Certification, and prepares students for the National Teacher Education (NTE) Core Battery Tests.

For students interested in nonperforming careers in the music industry, Five Towns College offers the Bachelor of Professional Studies (B.P.S.) degree program in business management, with major areas of concentration in audio recording technology, music business, and video arts. These programs are designed for students planning to pursue careers in management and marketing with firms in the areas of record and music production, broadcasting, concert promotion, radio, television, theater, and communications. The program is intended for students who are interested in developing their business and technical expertise.

Students who attend Five Towns College benefit from the institution's excellent reputation for preparing students for entry into the music industry. In addition to its highly qualified faculty, the College has facilities that are state-of-the-art. The College is equipped with 8-, 16-, 24-, and 48-track modern recording studios designed by the well-known Walters-Storyk design team. The College is also equipped with a television production facility and sound stages of various sizes. The Dix Hills Center for the Performing Arts has been described as "acoustically perfect." The Five Towns College library consists of nearly 30,000 print and nonprint materials and has a significant collection of recorded music.

Five Towns College is fully accredited by the Middle States Association and the New York State Board of Regents.

Schmidt College of Arts and Humanities

Florida Atlantic University

Boca Raton, Florida

State-supported, coed. Suburban campus. Total enrollment: 17,484.

Degrees Bachelor of Music in the areas of music performance, music education, jazz studies. Majors: accompanying, classical music, piano/organ, stringed instruments, voice, wind and percussion instruments.

Music Student Profile Fall 1994: 115 total; 90 matriculated undergraduate, 25 matriculated graduate; 10% minorities, 50% females, 2% international.

Music Faculty Total: 28; 8 full-time, 20 part-time; 75% of full-time faculty have terminal degrees. Graduate students teach a few undergraduate courses. Undergraduate student–faculty ratio: 10:1.

Student Life Student groups include Collegiate Music Educators National Conference, International Jazz Educators Association.

Expenses for 1994–95 Application fee: $20. State resident tuition: $1791 full-time, $59.69 per semester hour part-time. Nonresident tuition: $6693 full-time, $223.10 per semester hour part-time. College room and board: $3930.

Financial Aid Program-specific awards for Fall of 1994: 30 Music Scholarships for program majors ($300–$1500).

Application Procedures Deadline—freshmen and transfers: August 1. Required: high school transcript, college transcript(s) for transfer students, minimum 3.0 high school GPA, audition, SAT I or ACT test scores. Auditions held 8 times on campus; recorded music is permissible as a substitute for live auditions when distance is prohibitive and videotaped performances are permissible as a substitute for live auditions when distance is prohibitive.

Undergraduate Contact Stuart Glazer, Chair, Music Department, Florida Atlantic University, 777 Glades Road, Boca Raton, Florida 33431; 407-367-3820, fax: 407-367-2752.

Florida Baptist Theological College

Graceville, Florida

Independent-religious, coed. Small-town campus. Total enrollment: 491.

Degrees Bachelor of Music in the area of church music. Majors: sacred music.

Music Student Profile Fall 1994: 70 total; all matriculated undergraduate; 5% minorities, 37% females, 3% international.

Music Faculty Total: 5; 5 full-time; 60% of full-time faculty have terminal degrees. Graduate students do not teach undergraduate courses. Undergraduate student–faculty ratio: 14:1.

Student Life Student groups include Spring Concert, Christmas Concert, Florida Baptist Convention.

Expenses for 1995–96 Application fee: $20. Tuition: $2700 full-time, $90 per semester hour part-time. Part-time mandatory fees: $42 per term. Full-time mandatory fees: $84. College room only: $1500. Special program-related fees: $2–$3 for practice room fee, $25 for class instruction, $45–$80 for private lessons, $20–$30 for recital fee, $90–$200 for applied music fees.

Application Procedures Deadline—freshmen and transfers: August 1. Notification date—freshmen and transfers: August 15. Required: high school transcript, minimum 2.0 high school GPA, 3 letters of recommendation, interview, audition. Auditions held 2 times on campus.

Undergraduate Contact Lavan Wilson, Director of Admissions, Florida Baptist Theological College, P.O. Box 1306, Graceville, Florida 32440; 904-263-3261 ext. 62, fax: 904-263-7506.

Florida Southern College

Lakeland, Florida

Independent-religious, coed. Suburban campus. Total enrollment: 1,820.

Degrees Bachelor of Music in the areas of winds, percussion, voice; Bachelor of Music Education in the area of music education; Bachelor of Sacred Music in the area of sacred music. Majors: classical music, music, music education, piano/organ, sacred music, stringed instruments, voice, wind and percussion instruments.

Music Student Profile Fall 1994: 246 total; 96 matriculated undergraduate, 150 nondegree; 4% minorities, 60% females, 1% international.

Music Faculty Total: 31; 10 full-time, 21 part-time; 40% of full-time faculty have terminal degrees. Graduate students do not teach undergraduate courses. Undergraduate student–faculty ratio: 8:1.

Student Life Student groups include Music Educators National Conference Student Chapter, Phi Mu Alpha Sinfonia, Delta Omicron.

Expenses for 1995–96 Application fee: $30. Comprehensive fee of $14,500 includes full-time tuition ($8760), mandatory fees ($640), and college room and board ($5100). Part-time tuition: $240 per semester hour. Special program-related fees: $275 for applied lesson fee, $150–$300 for applied music fee for non-music majors.

Financial Aid Program-specific awards for Fall of 1994: 28 Davidson Scholarships for program majors ($2000), 1 Presser Scholarship for program majors ($2000), 1 Gannaway Award for program majors ($4000), 2 Pickard Scholarships for program majors ($2000), 4 Wolff/MacDonald Scholarships for program majors ($4000), 1 Bösendorfer Award for program majors ($1000), 1 Schimmel Award for program majors ($1000), 1 Woodard Scholarship for program majors ($650), 1 Houts Scholarship for program majors ($600).

Application Procedures Deadline—freshmen and transfers: continuous. Required: essay, high school transcript, college transcript(s) for transfer students, minimum 2.0 high school GPA, 3 letters of recommendation, audition, SAT I or ACT test scores. Recommended: minimum 3.0 high school GPA, interview. Auditions held by appointment on campus; recorded music is permissible as a substitute for live auditions when distance is prohibitive and videotaped performances are permissible as a substitute for live auditions when distance is prohibitive.

Undergraduate Contact William Stephens, Director of Admissions, Florida Southern College, 111 Lake Hollingsworth Drive, Lakeland, Florida 33801-5698; 813-680-4131, fax: 813-680-4120.

Florida State University

Tallahassee, Florida

State-supported, coed. Suburban campus. Total enrollment: 29,630.

Degrees Bachelor of Music in the areas of performance, piano pedagogy, composition, music history/literature, music theory, music theater, music therapy; Bachelor of Music Education in the areas of instrumental music education, choral music education. Majors: classical music, jazz, music, music education, music theater, music therapy, piano/organ, stringed instruments, voice, wind and percussion instruments. Graduate degrees offered: Master of Music in the areas of performance, accompanying, piano pedagogy, choral conducting, opera, instrumental conducting, jazz, theory, composition, musicology, music therapy; Master of Music Education in the areas of instrumental music education, choral music education, arts administration. Doctor of Musical Arts in the areas of composition, performance; Doctor of Music Education in the area of music education. Cross-registration with Tallahassee Community College.

Music Student Profile Fall 1994: 850 total; 550 matriculated undergraduate, 300 matriculated graduate; 12% minorities, 53% females, 2% international.

Music Faculty Total: 92; 85 full-time, 7 part-time; 94% of full-time faculty have terminal degrees. Graduate students teach about a quarter undergraduate courses. Undergraduate student–faculty ratio: 8:1.

Student Life Student groups include Collegiate Music Educators National Conference, American Choral Directors Association.

Expenses for 1995–96 Application fee: $20. State resident tuition: $1798 full-time, $59.93 per semester hour part-time. Nonresident tuition: $6700 full-time, $223.34 per semester hour part-time. College room and board: $4500. College room only: $2360.

Financial Aid Program-specific awards for Fall of 1994: 59 Out-of-state Awards for program majors ($3735), 180 General Scholarships for program majors ($250–$2500).

Application Procedures Deadline—freshmen: March 1; transfers: May 20. Required: high school transcript, college transcript(s) for transfer students, minimum 3.0 high school GPA, audition, SAT I or ACT test scores, minimum combined SAT I score of 1000, minimum composite ACT score of 24. Auditions held 7 times on campus; recorded music is permissible as a substitute for live auditions when distance is prohibitive and videotaped performances are permissible as a substitute for live auditions when distance is prohibitive.

Undergraduate Contact Roger K. Duncan, Director for Undergraduate Studies, School of Music, Florida State University, Tallahassee, Florida 32306-2098; 904-644-4833, fax: 904-644-2033.

Graduate Contact Dr. John Deal, Assistant Dean of Graduate Programs, School of Music, Florida State University, Tallahassee, Florida 32306-2098; 904-644-5848, fax: 904-644-2033.

Fort Hays State University

Hays, Kansas

State-supported, coed. Small-town campus. Total enrollment: 5,496.

Degrees Bachelor of Music in the areas of performance, music education. Majors: classical music, music, music education, piano/organ, stringed instruments, voice, wind and percussion instruments.

Music Student Profile Fall 1994: 72 total; all matriculated undergraduate; 10% minorities, 50% females, 10% international.

Music Faculty Total: 16; 13 full-time, 3 part-time; 38% of full-time faculty have terminal degrees. Graduate students do not teach undergraduate courses. Undergraduate student–faculty ratio: 5:1.

Student Life Student groups include Collegiate Music Educators National Conference, Phi Mu Alpha Sinfonia, Sigma Alpha Iota.

Estimated Expenses for 1995–96 Application fee: $15. State resident tuition: $1902 full-time, $61.15 per credit hour part-time. Nonresident tuition: $6169 full-time, $193.85 per credit hour part-time. College room and board: $3172. College room only: $1600. Special program-related fees: $32 for applied lessons.

Financial Aid Program-specific awards for Fall of 1994: 20–30 Awards of Excellence in Music for freshmen ($400), 40–60 Music Scholarships for undergraduates ($500–$700).

Application Procedures Deadline—freshmen and transfers: continuous. Required: high school transcript, 2 letters of recommendation, audition. Auditions held 3 times and by appointment on campus and off campus in various locations in Kansas; recorded music is permissible as a substitute for live auditions when distance is prohibitive and videotaped performances are permissible as a substitute for live auditions when distance is prohibitive.

Undergraduate Contact Pat Mahon, Director, Admissions Department, Fort Hays State University, 600 Park Street, Hays, Kansas 67601; 913-628-5666, E-mail address: adpm@fhsuvm.fhsu.edu.

Friends University

Wichita, Kansas

Independent, coed. Urban campus. Total enrollment: 2,326.

Degrees Bachelor of Music in the areas of voice, piano; Bachelor of Music Education in the areas of vocal music education, instrumental music education. Majors: music, music education, piano/organ, voice. Graduate degrees offered: Master of Music in the area of church music. Cross-registration with Kansas Newman College.

Music Student Profile Fall 1994: 75 total; 70 matriculated undergraduate, 5 matriculated graduate; 10% minorities, 55% females, 5% international.

Music Faculty Total: 14; 10 full-time, 4 part-time; 33% of full-time faculty have terminal degrees. Graduate students do not teach undergraduate courses.

Student Life Student groups include Mu Phi Epsilon, American Choral Directors Association, Music Educators National Conference.

Expenses for 1995–96 Application fee: $15. Comprehensive fee of $11,876 includes full-time tuition ($8631), mandatory fees ($115), and college room and board ($3130). Part-time tuition: $289 per semester hour.

Financial Aid Program-specific awards for Fall of 1994: 10 Miller Scholarships for program majors ($1000), 35 Departmental Scholarships for program majors ($1000).

Application Procedures Deadline—freshmen: August 1; transfers: August 26. Required: high school transcript, minimum 2.0 high school GPA, interview, audition. Auditions held 4 times on campus; recorded music is permissible as a substitute for live auditions if a campus visit is impossible.

Contact Dr. Cecil Riney, Dean, Fine Arts Department, Friends University, 2100 University, Wichita, Kansas 67213; 316-261-5849, fax: 316-262-5027.

Furman University

Greenville, South Carolina

Independent, coed. Suburban campus. Total enrollment: 2,663.

Furman University *(continued)*

Degrees Bachelor of Music in the areas of performance, church music, music education, music theory. Majors: music, music education, music theory, performance, piano/organ, stringed instruments, voice, wind and percussion instruments.

Music Faculty Total: 28; 18 full-time, 10 part-time. Graduate students do not teach undergraduate courses.

Student Life Student groups include Mu Phi Epsilon, Phi Mu Alpha.

Expenses for 1995–96 Application fee: $25. Comprehensive fee of $18,744 includes full-time tuition ($14,432), mandatory fees ($144), and college room and board ($4168). College room only: $2160. Part-time tuition: $451 per credit hour.

Financial Aid Program-specific awards for Fall of 1994: 1 Daniel Scholarship for program majors ($1000–$2000), 1 Timmons Scholarship for program majors ($1000–$2000), 10 Music Scholarships for instrumentalists ($1000–$2000).

Application Procedures Deadline—freshmen and transfers: February 1. Notification date—freshmen: March 15. Required: essay, high school transcript, college transcript(s) for transfer students, SAT I or ACT test scores. Auditions held on campus and off campus. Portfolio reviews held on campus and off campus.

Undergraduate Contact Department of Music, Furman University, Greenville, South Carolina 29613; 803-294-2086.

George Mason University

Fairfax, Virginia

State-supported, coed. Suburban campus. Total enrollment: 21,774.

Degrees Bachelor of Music in the area of music. Majors: music education, performance.

Music Student Profile Fall 1994: 192 total; 146 matriculated undergraduate, 46 matriculated graduate; 12% minorities.

Music Faculty Total: 31; 11 full-time, 20 part-time; 95% of full-time faculty have terminal degrees. Graduate students do not teach undergraduate courses. Undergraduate student–faculty ratio: 20:1.

Expenses for 1995–96 Application fee: $30. State resident tuition: $4212 full-time, $175.50 per credit hour part-time. Nonresident tuition: $11,604 full-time, $483.50 per credit hour part-time. College room and board: $5050. College room only: $3150.

Application Procedures Deadline—freshmen: February 1; transfers: March 15. Required: essay, high school transcript, minimum 2.0 high school GPA, audition, SAT I or ACT test scores. Recommended: minimum 3.0 high school GPA, letter of recommendation. Auditions held 8 times on campus; recorded music is permissible as a substitute for live auditions and videotaped performances are permissible as a substitute for live auditions.

Undergraduate Contact Dr. Joseph D. Shirk, Chair, Music Department, George Mason University, Mail Stop 3E3, Fairfax, Virginia 22030-4444; 703-993-1380.

George Washington University

Washington, District of Columbia

Independent, coed. Urban campus. Total enrollment: 19,298.

Degrees Bachelor of Music in the area of performance. Majors: brass, classical guitar, music, piano/organ, stringed instruments, voice, wind and percussion instruments. Cross-registration with universities of the Washington metropolitan area.

Music Student Profile Fall 1994: 686 total; 40 matriculated undergraduate, 646 nondegree.

Music Faculty Total: 50; 5 full-time, 45 part-time; 60% of full-time faculty have terminal degrees. Graduate students do not teach undergraduate courses.

Student Life Student groups include Creative and Performing Arts Residential Learning Program, Chamber Players, Kappa Kappa Psi.

Expenses for 1994–95 Application fee: $50. Comprehensive fee of $23,768 includes full-time tuition ($17,450), mandatory fees ($720), and college room and board ($5598). College room only: $3998. Part-time tuition: $575 per semester hour. Part-time mandatory fees: $30 per semester hour. Full-time mandatory fees for freshmen: $845.

Financial Aid Program-specific awards for Fall of 1994: 5 Presidential Arts Scholarships for program majors and non-majors ($7500).

Application Procedures Deadline—freshmen: February 1; transfers: June 1. Notification date—freshmen: March 15; transfers: September 1. Required: essay, high school transcript, minimum 2.0 high school GPA, 2 letters of recommendation, audition, SAT I or ACT test scores, minimum 2.7 college GPA for transfer students. Recommended: minimum 3.0 high school GPA. Auditions held 2 times and by appointment on campus; recorded music is permissible as a substitute for live auditions when distance is prohibitive or scheduling is difficult and videotaped performances are permissible as a substitute for live auditions when distance is prohibitive or if scheduling is difficult.

Undergraduate Contact Dr. Roy J. Guenther, Chairman, Department of Music, George Washington University, Academic Center B-144, 801 22nd Street, NW, Washington, District of Columbia 20052; 202-994-6245, fax: 202-994-9038.

Georgetown College

Georgetown, Kentucky

Independent-religious, coed. Small-town campus. Total enrollment: 1,405.

Degrees Bachelor of Music in the area of church music; Bachelor of Music Education in the areas of vocal music education, instrumental music education. Majors: music education, piano/organ, sacred music, voice, wind and percussion instruments.

Music Student Profile Fall 1994: 50 total; all matriculated undergraduate; 3% minorities, 60% females.

Music Faculty Total: 11; 6 full-time, 5 part-time; 50% of full-time faculty have terminal degrees. Graduate students do not teach undergraduate courses. Undergraduate student–faculty ratio: 13:1.

Student Life Student groups include Music Educators National Conference Student Chapter.

Expenses for 1995–96 Application fee: $20. Comprehensive fee of $12,840 includes full-time tuition ($8840), mandatory fees ($50 minimum), and college room and board ($3950). College room only: $1975. Full-time mandatory fees range from $50 to $150. Part-time tuition per semester hour ranges from $250 to $330. Special program-related fees: $125–$200 for applied fees, $100 for piano class.

Financial Aid Program-specific awards for Fall of 1994: 12–15 Music Department Scholarships ($500–$2000), 15–25 College Grants in Music ($500–$2000).

Application Procedures Deadline—freshmen and transfers: April 15. Required: essay, high school transcript, college transcript(s) for transfer students, interview, audition, SAT I or ACT test scores. Recommended: ACT test score only. Auditions held 3 times and by appointment on campus; recorded music is permissible as a substitute for live auditions when distance is prohibitive and videotaped performances are permissible as a substitute for live auditions when distance is prohibitive.

Undergraduate Contact Dr. Sonny Burnette, Chair, Music Department, Georgetown College, 400 East College Street, Georgetown, Kentucky 40324-1696; 502-863-8117, E-mail address: sburnett@gtc.georgetown.ky.us.

Georgia College

Milledgeville, Georgia

State-supported, coed. Small-town campus. Total enrollment: 5,655.

Degrees Bachelor of Music in the areas of wind and percussion, voice, keyboard, guitar, brass; Bachelor of Music Education in the areas of choral music, instrumental music; Bachelor of Music Therapy in the area of music therapy. Majors: brass, choral music education, guitar, instrumental music education, music therapy, piano/organ, voice, wind and percussion instruments.

Music Student Profile Fall 1994: 80 total; 65 matriculated undergraduate, 15 nondegree.

Music Faculty Total: 21; 7 full-time, 14 part-time; 43% of full-time faculty have terminal degrees. Graduate students teach a few undergraduate courses. Undergraduate student–faculty ratio: 4:1.

Expenses for 1995–96 Application fee: $10. State resident tuition: $1494 full-time, $47 per quarter hour part-time. Nonresident tuition: $4704 full-time, $137 per quarter hour part-time. Full-time mandatory fees: $326. College room and board: $3150. Special program-related fees: $20–$40 for applied music fees.

Application Procedures Deadline—freshmen and transfers: continuous. Required: high school transcript, audition, completion of College Preparatory Curriculum (CPC) with no deficiencies. Auditions held 2 times and by appointment on campus; recorded music is permissible as a substitute for live auditions on a case-by-case basis and videotaped performances are permissible as a substitute for live auditions on a case-by-case basis.

Undergraduate Contact Jim Willoughby, Chairman, Department of Music and Theatre, Georgia College, Box 066, Milledgeville, Georgia 31061; 912-453-4346.

Gordon College

Wenham, Massachusetts

Independent-religious, coed. Small-town campus. Total enrollment: 1,178.

Degrees Bachelor of Music in the areas of music performance, music education. Majors: classical music, music, music education, piano/organ, stringed instruments, voice, wind and percussion instruments. Cross-registration with Christian College Coalition, Northeast Consortium of Colleges and Universities in Massachusetts.

Music Student Profile Fall 1994: 63 total; all matriculated undergraduate; 10% minorities, 65% females, 15% international.

Music Faculty Total: 31; 7 full-time, 24 part-time; 70% of full-time faculty have terminal degrees. Graduate students do not teach undergraduate courses. Undergraduate student–faculty ratio: 10:1.

Student Life Student groups include Music Educators National Conference Student Chapter.

Expenses for 1995–96 Application fee: $40. Comprehensive fee of $18,390 includes full-time tuition ($13,380), mandatory fees ($570), and college room and board ($4440). College room only: $2850. Special program-related fees: $360 for applied music fee.

Financial Aid Program-specific awards for Fall of 1994: 40 Music Leadership Grants for program majors and non-majors ($750–$1000).

Application Procedures Deadline—freshmen and transfers: continuous. Required: essay, high school transcript, college transcript(s) for transfer students, interview, audition, SAT I or ACT test scores. Recommended: minimum 2.0 high school GPA, 2 letters of recommendation. Auditions held continuously by appointment on campus; recorded music is permissible as a substitute for live auditions when distance is prohibitive and videotaped performances are permissible as a substitute for live auditions when distance is prohibitive.

Gordon College *(continued)*

Undergraduate Contact David W. Rox, Chair, Music Department, Gordon College, 255 Grapevine Road, Wenham, Massachusetts 01984; 508-927-2300 ext. 4369, fax: 508-524-3706.

Grace College

Winona Lake, Indiana

Independent-religious, coed. Small-town campus. Total enrollment: 680.

Degrees Bachelor of Music. Majors: classical music, music, piano/organ, stringed instruments, voice, wind and percussion instruments.

Music Student Profile Fall 1994: 25 total; all matriculated undergraduate.

Music Faculty Total: 19; 4 full-time, 15 part-time; 25% of full-time faculty have terminal degrees. Undergraduate student–faculty ratio: 5:1.

Student Life Student groups include Music Educators National Conference.

Expenses for 1995–96 Application fee: $20. Comprehensive fee of $13,300 includes full-time tuition ($9230) and college room and board ($4070). College room only: $1920. Part-time tuition per semester ranges from $172 to $3303. Special program-related fees: $50 for studio fee.

Financial Aid Program-specific awards for Fall of 1994: 5 Grace Honors Brass Quintet Scholarships for freshmen program majors ($2240), 5 Grace Honors Woodwind Quintet Scholarships for freshmen program majors ($2240), 4 Grace Honors String Quartet Scholarships for freshmen program majors ($2240), 13 Music Talent Scholarships for freshmen program majors ($500).

Application Procedures Deadline—freshmen and transfers: August 1. Required: audition. Auditions held 4 times on campus; recorded music is permissible as a substitute for live auditions when distance is prohibitive and videotaped performances are permissible as a substitute for live auditions when distance is prohibitive.

Undergraduate Contact Ron Henry, Dean of Enrollment, Admissions Office, Grace College, 200 Seminary Drive, Winona Lake, Indiana 46590; 219-372-5131, fax: 219-372-5265.

Grand Valley State University

Allendale, Michigan

State-supported, coed. Small-town campus. Total enrollment: 13,553.

Degrees Bachelor of Music in the area of performance; Bachelor of Music Education in the areas of vocal music education, instrumental music education. Majors: music, music education, piano/organ, stringed instruments, voice, wind and percussion instruments.

Music Student Profile Fall 1994: 65 total; all matriculated undergraduate; 1% minorities, 51% females.

Music Faculty Total: 30; 7 full-time, 23 part-time; 25% of full-time faculty have terminal degrees. Graduate students do not teach undergraduate courses. Undergraduate student–faculty ratio: 9:1.

Student Life Student groups include Music Educators National Conference, Mu Phi Epsilon.

Expenses for 1995–96 State resident tuition: $2780 full-time, $124 per semester hour part-time. Nonresident tuition: $6462 full-time, $279 per semester hour part-time. Part-time mandatory fees per semester range from $48 to $128. Full-time mandatory fees: $360. College room and board: $4181. Special program-related fees: $25 for practice room rental, $50 for recital recording programs, $25 for instrument rental.

Financial Aid Program-specific awards for Fall of 1994: 1 Blodgett Piano Award for pianists ($1000), 1 Eitzen Voice Award for vocalists ($1000).

Application Procedures Deadline—freshmen and transfers: July 30. Required: high school transcript, college transcript(s) for transfer students, minimum 3.0 high school GPA, 2 letters of recommendation, interview, audition, theory placement examination. Recommended: essay. Auditions held 6 times on campus; recorded music is permissible as a substitute for live auditions when distance is prohibitive and videotaped performances are permissible as a substitute for live auditions when distance is prohibitive.

Undergraduate Contact Director of Admissions, Grand Valley State University, 1 Campus Drive, Allendale, Michigan 49401; 616-895-2025.

Grove City College

Grove City, Pennsylvania

Independent-religious, coed. Small-town campus. Total enrollment: 2,280.

Degrees Bachelor of Music in the areas of music education, music and religion, music and business, music and performing arts. Majors: music, music and religion, music education, performance art.

Music Student Profile Fall 1994: 80 total; all matriculated undergraduate; 60% females.

Music Faculty Total: 20; 4 full-time, 16 part-time; 100% of full-time faculty have terminal degrees. Graduate students do not teach undergraduate courses. Undergraduate student–faculty ratio: 4:1.

Student Life Student groups include Music Educators National Conference Student Chapter. Special housing available for music students.

Expenses for 1995–96 Application fee: $25. Comprehensive fee of $9648 includes full-time tuition ($6174 minimum) and college room and board ($3474). Full-time tuition ranges up to $6012 according to program.

Financial Aid Program-specific awards for Fall of 1994: 6 Music Awards for upperclassmen.

Application Procedures Deadline—freshmen: February 15. Notification date—freshmen: March 15. Required: essay, high school transcript, college transcript(s) for transfer students, minimum 3.0 high school GPA, 2 letters of recommendation, interview, audition, SAT I or ACT test scores. Auditions held 5 times and by appointment on campus; recorded music is permissible as a substitute for live auditions when distance is prohibitive and videotaped performances are permissible as a substitute for live auditions when distance is prohibitive.

Undergraduate Contact Dr. Edwin Arnold, Chair, Department of Music and Fine Arts, Grove City College, 100 Campus Drive, Grove City, Pennsylvania 16127; 412-458-2263, fax: 412-458-2190.

Hardin-Simmons University

Abilene, Texas

Independent-religious, coed. Urban campus. Total enrollment: 2,133.

Degrees Bachelor of Music in the areas of performance, music education, church music, music theory/composition. Majors: music education, music theory and composition, piano/organ, sacred music, stringed instruments, voice, wind and percussion instruments. Graduate degrees offered: Master of Music in the areas of performance, music education, music theory/composition. Cross-registration with Abilene Christian University.

Music Student Profile Fall 1994: 165 total; 110 matriculated undergraduate, 10 matriculated graduate, 45 nondegree; 10% minorities, 55% females.

Music Faculty Total: 20; 16 full-time, 4 part-time; 56% of full-time faculty have terminal degrees. Graduate students teach a few undergraduate courses. Undergraduate student–faculty ratio: 10:1.

Student Life Student groups include Music Educators National Conference Student Chapter, Phi Mu Alpha, Sigma Alpha Iota.

Expenses for 1995–96 Application fee: $25. Comprehensive fee of $10,148 includes full-time tuition ($6600), mandatory fees ($480), and college room and board ($3068). Part-time tuition: $220 per semester hour. Part-time mandatory fees per semester (9 to 11 semester hours): $240. Tuition guaranteed not to increase for student's term of enrollment. Special program-related fees: $15 for performance–music facilities fee, $100 for private instruction.

Financial Aid Program-specific awards for Fall of 1994: 1 Irl Allison Award for pianists ($400), 6 Foreman Awards for cowboy band students ($1890), 1 Hamilton Award for vocalists ($1600), 1 Lacewell Award for church music majors ($2500), 4 Reeves Awards for program majors ($2475), 1 Shaw Award for church music majors ($1400).

Application Procedures Deadline—freshmen and transfers: continuous. Required: high school transcript, college transcript(s) for transfer students, minimum 2.0 high school GPA, 2 letters of recommendation, audition, SAT I or ACT test scores. Auditions held 4 times on campus; recorded music is permissible as a substitute for live auditions if a campus visit is impossible and videotaped performances are permissible as a substitute for live auditions if a campus visit is impossible.

Undergraduate Contact Laura Moore, Director of Admissions, Hardin-Simmons University, Box 16050, Abilene, Texas 79698-6050; 915-670-1207, fax: 915-670-1527.

Graduate Contact Dr. Paul Sorrels, Dean, Graduate School, Hardin-Simmons University, Box 16210, Abilene, Texas 79698-6210; 915-670-1298.

Harding University

Searcy, Arkansas

Independent-religious, coed. Small-town campus. Total enrollment: 3,817.

Degrees Bachelor of Music Education in the areas of instrumental music, vocal/choral music. Majors: instrumental music.

Estimated Expenses for 1995–96 Application fee: $25. Comprehensive fee of $10,200 includes full-time tuition ($5450), mandatory fees ($1000), and college room and board ($3750). College room only: $1800. Part-time tuition: $180 per semester hour. Part-time mandatory fees: $33 per semester hour.

Application Procedures Auditions held on campus and off campus. Portfolio reviews held on campus and off campus.

Undergraduate Contact Director of Admissions, Harding University, Box 2255, Searcy, Arkansas 72149-0001; 800-477-4407.

The Hartt School

See University of Hartford, The Hartt School

Hastings College

Hastings, Nebraska

Independent-religious, coed. Small-town campus. Total enrollment: 1,064.

Degrees Bachelor of Music in the areas of performance, music education, piano pedagogy. Majors: music, music education, piano pedagogy, piano/organ, stringed instruments, voice, wind and percussion instruments. Cross-registration with National Association of Schools of Music.

Music Student Profile Fall 1994: 336 total; 68 matriculated undergraduate, 268 nondegree; 2% minorities, 54% females.

Hastings College *(continued)*

Music Faculty Total: 16; 9 full-time, 7 part-time; 40% of full-time faculty have terminal degrees. Graduate students do not teach undergraduate courses. Undergraduate student–faculty ratio: 13:1.

Student Life Student groups include Sigma Alpha Iota, Music Educators National Conference, Phi Mu Alpha Sinfonia.

Expenses for 1995–96 Application fee: $20. Comprehensive fee of $13,636 includes full-time tuition ($9754), mandatory fees ($410), and college room and board ($3472 minimum). College room only: $1472. Part-time tuition: $404 per semester hour. Part-time mandatory fees per semester (4 to 11 semester hours): $104. Special program-related fees: $150 for private lessons.

Financial Aid Program-specific awards for Fall of 1994: 150 Music Scholarships for vocalists and instrumentalists ($860).

Application Procedures Deadline—freshmen and transfers: August 15. Required: essay, high school transcript, college transcript(s) for transfer students, minimum 2.0 high school GPA, letter of recommendation, interview, audition, SAT I or ACT test scores, minimum composite ACT score of 15. Auditions held by request on campus; recorded music is permissible as a substitute for live auditions when distance is prohibitive and videotaped performances are permissible as a substitute for live auditions.

Undergraduate Contact Mike Karloff, Admissions Department, Hastings College, 7th and Turner, Hastings, Nebraska 68901; 402-461-7315, fax: 402-463-3002.

Heidelberg College

Tiffin, Ohio

Independent-religious, coed. Small-town campus. Total enrollment: 1,372.

Degrees Bachelor of Music in the areas of composition, performance, pedagogy, music business; Bachelor of Music Education in the area of music education. Majors: classical music, music, music business, music education, piano/organ, stringed instruments, voice, wind and percussion instruments.

Music Student Profile Fall 1994: 85 total; all matriculated undergraduate; 2% minorities, 60% females, 10% international.

Music Faculty Total: 22; 9 full-time, 13 part-time; 80% of full-time faculty have terminal degrees. Graduate students do not teach undergraduate courses. Undergraduate student–faculty ratio: 6:1.

Student Life Student groups include Ohio Collegiate Music Educators National Conference, National Association of Teachers of Singing, Tau Mu Sigma.

Expenses for 1995–96 Application fee: $20. Comprehensive fee of $19,280 includes full-time tuition ($14,606) and college room and board ($4674). College room only: $2124. Part-time tuition: $340 per semester hour.

Financial Aid Program-specific awards for Fall of 1994: 25–30 Music Scholarships for program majors ($1500), 20 Ensemble Scholarships for ensemble performers ($250–$400), 10 Endowed Music Awards for program majors ($500–$1000).

Application Procedures Deadline—freshmen and transfers: continuous. Required: high school transcript, college transcript(s) for transfer students, minimum 2.0 high school GPA, letter of recommendation, interview, audition, SAT I or ACT test scores. Recommended: essay. Auditions held 5 times on campus; recorded music is permissible as a substitute for live auditions when distance is prohibitive and videotaped performances are permissible as a substitute for live auditions when distance is prohibitive.

Undergraduate Contact Dr. John E. Owen, Chair, Department of Music, Heidelberg College, 310 East Market Street, Tiffin, Ohio 44883; 419-448-2073, fax: 419-448-2124, E-mail address: jowen@nike.heidelberg.edu.

Henderson State University

Arkadelphia, Arkansas

State-supported, coed. Small-town campus. Total enrollment: 3,796.

Degrees Bachelor of Music in the area of performance; Bachelor of Music Education in the area of music education. Majors: music education, piano/organ, voice, wind and percussion instruments. Cross-registration with Ouachita Baptist University.

Music Student Profile Fall 1994: 75 total; all matriculated undergraduate; 1% minorities, 47% females.

Music Faculty Total: 16; 14 full-time, 2 part-time; 100% of full-time faculty have terminal degrees. Graduate students do not teach undergraduate courses.

Expenses for 1995–96 State resident tuition: $1832 full-time, $76 per semester hour part-time. Nonresident tuition: $3456 full-time, $152 per semester hour part-time. Part-time mandatory fees: $110 per year. Full-time mandatory fees: $110. College room and board: $2600. Special program-related fees: $40–$60 for applied music fees.

Financial Aid Program-specific awards for Fall of 1994: 55–100 Band Scholarships for band members ($1000), 30 Music Scholarships for program majors/non-majors ($1000).

Application Procedures Deadline—freshmen and transfers: continuous. Required: high school transcript, minimum 2.0 high school GPA. Recommended: interview.

Undergraduate Contact Tom Gattin, Registrar, Admissions Office, Henderson State University, Box 7534, Arkadelphia, Arkansas 71999-0001; 501-230-5135, fax: 501-230-5144.

Holy Names College

Oakland, California

Independent-religious, coed. Urban campus. Total enrollment: 975.

Degrees Bachelor of Music in the areas of piano performance, vocal performance, instrumental performance, piano pedagogy. Majors: classical music, harp, music, music education, piano/organ, stringed instruments, voice, wind and percussion instruments. Graduate degrees offered: Master of Music in the areas of performance, piano pedagogy, vocal performance, music education with Kodaly emphasis. Cross-registration with Mills College, University of California at Berkeley, California State University &– Hayward.

Music Student Profile Fall 1994: 45 total; 20 matriculated undergraduate, 20 matriculated graduate, 5 nondegree; 40% minorities, 90% females, 25% international.

Music Faculty Total: 10; 4 full-time, 6 part-time; 100% of full-time faculty have terminal degrees. Graduate students do not teach undergraduate courses. Undergraduate student–faculty ratio: 7:1.

Student Life Student groups include Mu Phi Epsilon.

Expenses for 1995–96 Application fee: $35. Comprehensive fee of $18,030 includes full-time tuition ($12,400), mandatory fees ($300), and college room and board ($5330). Part-time tuition: $450 per unit. Part-time mandatory fees: $170 per year. Special program-related fees: $10 for practice room fee, $45 for recital fee, $490–$990 for private music lessons.

Financial Aid Program-specific awards for Fall of 1994: 12 Shaklee Awards for vocalists ($250–$600), 4 Cotton Awards for those demonstrating need ($570–$1500), 1–2 Trutner Awards for instrumentalists ($430), 1 Abramowitsch Award for program majors ($150), 1–3 Cadenasso Awards for pianists ($190–$500).

Application Procedures Deadline—freshmen and transfers: continuous. Required: essay, high school transcript, college transcript(s) for transfer students, minimum 2.0 high school GPA, 2 letters of recommendation, audition. Recommended: interview. Auditions held as needed on campus; recorded music is permissible as a substitute for live auditions when distance is prohibitive.

Undergraduate Contact Joe McDevitt, Admissions Director, Holy Names College, 3500 Mountain Boulevard, Oakland, California 94619; 510-436-1324, fax: 510-436-1199.

Graduate Contact Caryl Mutti, Senior Graduate Admissions Officer, Holy Names College, 3500 Mountain Boulevard, Oakland, California 94619; 510-436-1361, fax: 510-436-1199.

Hope College

Holland, Michigan

Independent-religious, coed. Small-town campus. Total enrollment: 2,825.

Degrees Bachelor of Music in the area of performance; Bachelor of Music Education in the areas of vocal music education, instrumental music education. Majors: music, music education, piano/organ, stringed instruments, voice, wind and percussion instruments.

Music Student Profile Fall 1994: 75 total; all matriculated undergraduate; 5% minorities, 65% females.

Music Faculty Total: 34; 11 full-time, 23 part-time; 75% of full-time faculty have terminal degrees. Graduate students do not teach undergraduate courses. Undergraduate student–faculty ratio: 15:1.

Student Life Student groups include Music Educators National Conference.

Expenses for 1995–96 Application fee: $25. Comprehensive fee of $17,834 includes full-time tuition ($13,234), mandatory fees ($84), and college room and board ($4516). College room only: $2060. Part-time tuition per credit hour: $190 for the first 4 credit hours, $275 for the next 3 credit hours, $420 for the next 4 credit hours. Special program-related fees: $65–$80 for lessons.

Financial Aid Program-specific awards for Fall of 1994: 12–15 Distinguished Artist Awards for program majors ($2500), 3 Swaby Awards for program majors ($2000), 1 Hughes Award for organists ($5000).

Application Procedures Deadline—freshmen and transfers: continuous. Required: essay, high school transcript, audition, SAT I or ACT test scores. Recommended: minimum 2.0 high school GPA. Auditions held 2 times on campus; recorded music is permissible as a substitute for live auditions if a campus visit is impossible and videotaped performances are permissible as a substitute for live auditions if a campus visit is impossible.

Undergraduate Contact Linda Strouf, Music Recruitment Coordinator, Music Department, Hope College, 127 East 12th Street, Holland, Michigan 49422-9000; 616-395-7106, fax: 616-395-7922, E-mail address: strouf@hope.cit.hope.edu.

Hope School of Fine Arts

See Indiana University Bloomington, Hope School of Fine Arts

Houghton College

Houghton, New York

Independent-religious, coed. Rural campus. Total enrollment: 1,332.

Degrees Bachelor of Music in the areas of applied music, music education, music theory/composition. Majors: brass, classical music, music, music education, music theory and composition, piano/organ, stringed instruments, voice, wind and percussion instruments.

Music Student Profile Fall 1994: 100 total; all matriculated undergraduate.

Music Faculty Total: 25; 10 full-time, 15 part-time; 60% of full-time faculty have terminal degrees. Graduate

Houghton College *(continued)*

students do not teach undergraduate courses. Undergraduate student–faculty ratio: 6:1.

Student Life Student groups include Student Music Education Association. Special housing available for music students.

Expenses for 1994–95 Comprehensive fee of $13,850 includes full-time tuition ($9990), mandatory fees ($310), and college room and board ($3550). College room only: $1700. Part-time tuition per credit hour: $225 for the first 6 credit hours, $274 for the next 3 credit hours, $322 for the next 2 credit hours.

Financial Aid Program-specific awards for Fall of 1994: 20–30 Performance Grants for program majors ($1000–$1500), 1 Presidential Scholarship for program majors ($2500).

Application Procedures Deadline—freshmen and transfers: continuous. Required: essay, high school transcript, college transcript(s) for transfer students, minimum 2.0 high school GPA, 2 letters of recommendation, audition. Recommended: minimum 3.0 high school GPA, interview, SAT I or ACT test scores. Auditions held 10 times on campus; recorded music is permissible as a substitute for live auditions when distance is prohibitive and videotaped performances are permissible as a substitute for live auditions when distance is prohibitive.

Undergraduate Contact Robert Galloway, Director, School of Music, Houghton College, 1 Willard Avenue, Houghton, New York 14744; 716-567-9400, fax: 716-567-9570.

Howard Payne University

Brownwood, Texas

Independent-religious, coed. Small-town campus. Total enrollment: 1,488.

Degrees Bachelor of Music in the areas of piano, organ, voice, instrumental music, piano pedagogy and accompanying, church music, choral music education, instrumental music education. Majors: music, music education, piano/organ, sacred music, voice, wind and percussion instruments.

Music Student Profile Fall 1994: 81 total; 74 matriculated undergraduate, 7 nondegree; 2% minorities, 45% females, 1% international.

Music Faculty Total: 16; 12 full-time, 4 part-time; 50% of full-time faculty have terminal degrees. Graduate students do not teach undergraduate courses. Undergraduate student–faculty ratio: 5:1.

Student Life Student groups include Music Educators National Conference, American Choral Directors Association.

Expenses for 1995–96 Application fee: $25. Comprehensive fee of $9590 includes full-time tuition ($5790), mandatory fees ($450), and college room and board ($3350). Part-time tuition: $193 per semester hour. Part-time mandatory fees: $15 per semester hour. Special program-related fees: $10 for computer lab use, $100 for piano accompanying fees.

Financial Aid Program-specific awards for Fall of 1994: 1 Turner Music Award ($500), 1 Presser Award ($2250), 1 Schubert Music Award ($100), 93 Music Scholarships for program majors/minors ($400–$1500).

Application Procedures Deadline—freshmen and transfers: continuous. Required: high school transcript, college transcript(s) for transfer students, audition. Recommended: minimum 3.0 high school GPA. Auditions held 2 times and at student's convenience on campus; recorded music is permissible as a substitute for live auditions if a campus visit is impossible and videotaped performances are permissible as a substitute for live auditions if a campus visit is impossible.

Undergraduate Contact Veta Young, Director, Recruiting and Admissions, Howard Payne University, 1000 Fisk Street, HPU Station 828, Brownwood, Texas 76801-2494; 915 649 8020, fax: 915-649-8901.

Howard University

Washington, District of Columbia

Independent, coed. Urban campus. Total enrollment: 10,961.

Degrees Bachelor of Music in the areas of vocal performance, instrumental performance, music history, jazz studies, music business, music therapy; Bachelor of Music Education in the area of music education. Majors: classical music, jazz, music business, music education, music history, music theory and composition, music therapy, piano/organ, stringed instruments, voice, wind and percussion instruments. Graduate degrees offered: Master of Music in the areas of performance, jazz studies; Master of Music Education in the area of music education.

Music Student Profile Fall 1994: 157 total; 153 matriculated undergraduate, 4 matriculated graduate.

Music Faculty Total: 41; 21 full-time, 20 part-time; 43% of full-time faculty have terminal degrees. Graduate students teach a few undergraduate courses. Undergraduate student–faculty ratio: 7:1.

Expenses for 1994–95 Comprehensive fee of $11,676 includes full-time tuition ($7130), mandatory fees ($401), and college room and board ($4145). Part-time tuition: $275 per credit hour. Part-time mandatory fees: $401 per year.

Application Procedures Deadline—freshmen and transfers: continuous. Required: high school transcript, college transcript(s) for transfer students, audition, SAT I or ACT test scores, GED if applicable. Auditions held 6 times and by appointment on campus; recorded music is permissible as a substitute for live auditions when distance is prohibitive and videotaped performances are permissible as a substitute for live auditions when distance is prohibitive.

Contact Dr. J. Weldon Norris, Chairman, Department of Music, Howard University, College of Fine Arts, Washington, District of Columbia 20059; 202-806-7082, fax: 202-806-6503.

Hugh A. Glauser School of Music

See Kent State University, Hugh A. Glauser School of Music

Hunter College of the City University of New York

New York, New York

State and locally supported, coed. Urban campus. Total enrollment: 18,390.

Degrees Bachelor of Music in the area of performance. Majors: classical music, piano/organ, stringed instruments, voice, wind and percussion instruments. Cross-registration with senior colleges of the City University of New York System.

Music Student Profile Fall 1994: 143 total; 15 matriculated undergraduate, 128 nondegree; 50% minorities, 70% females, 40% international.

Music Faculty Total: 38; 13 full-time, 25 part-time; 100% of full-time faculty have terminal degrees. Graduate students teach a few undergraduate courses. Undergraduate student–faculty ratio: 15:1.

Student Life Student groups include Performance Club, Music Theater Workshop, Beethoven Club.

Expenses for 1994–95 Application fee: $35. State resident tuition: $2450 full-time, $100 per credit part-time. Nonresident tuition: $5050 full-time, $210 per credit part-time. Part-time mandatory fees: $53.60 per semester. Full-time mandatory fees: $107.

Financial Aid Program-specific awards for Fall of 1994: 10 Alumni Awards for students taking private lessons ($500).

Application Procedures Deadline—freshmen: November 1; transfers: March 15. Notification date—freshmen and transfers: June 1. Required: high school transcript, college transcript(s) for transfer students, audition, minimum 2.2 high school GPA, minimum 2.0 college GPA for transfer students with 24 credits. Recommended: minimum 3.0 high school GPA. Auditions held 2 times on campus; recorded music is permissible as a substitute for live auditions for provisional admission and videotaped performances are permissible as a substitute for live auditions for provisional admission.

Undergraduate Contact Jewel Thompson, Director of Undergraduate Studies, Music Department, Hunter College of the City University of New York, 695 Park Avenue, New York, New York 10021; 212-772-5020, fax: 212-772-5022.

Huntington College

Huntington, Indiana

Independent-religious, coed. Small-town campus. Total enrollment: 638.

Degrees Bachelor of Music in the areas of music performance, music education. Majors: music, music education.

Music Student Profile Fall 1994: 17 total; all matriculated undergraduate; 6% minorities, 76% females, 6% international.

Music Faculty Total: 20; 3 full-time, 17 part-time; 100% of full-time faculty have terminal degrees. Graduate students do not teach undergraduate courses. Undergraduate student–faculty ratio: 13:1.

Expenses for 1994–95 Application fee: $15. Comprehensive fee of $14,120 includes full-time tuition ($9950), mandatory fees ($250), and college room and board ($3920). Part-time tuition: $300 per semester hour. Tuition guaranteed not to increase for student's term of enrollment. Special program-related fees: $15 for instrument use fee, $135 for private instruction and practice room fee.

Financial Aid Program-specific awards for Fall of 1994: 25 Performance Grants for program majors/minors ($600).

Application Procedures Deadline—freshmen and transfers: continuous. Required: high school transcript, college transcript(s) for transfer students, minimum 2.0 high school GPA, audition. Auditions held as needed on campus.

Undergraduate Contact Jeffrey Berggren, Executive Director of Enrollment Management, Admissions Department, Huntington College, 2303 College Avenue, Huntington, Indiana 46750; 219-356-6000, fax: 219-356-9448.

Hurley School of Music

See Centenary College of Louisiana, Hurley School of Music

Idaho State University

Pocatello, Idaho

State-supported, coed. Small-town campus. Total enrollment: 11,877.

Degrees Bachelor of Music in the area of performance; Bachelor of Music Education in the area of music education. Majors: music, music education, piano/organ, stringed instruments, voice, wind and percussion instruments.

Music Student Profile Fall 1994: 56 total; all matriculated undergraduate; 1% minorities, 65% females, 1% international.

Music Faculty Total: 16; 8 full-time, 8 part-time; 100% of full-time faculty have terminal degrees. Graduate students do not teach undergraduate courses. Undergraduate student–faculty ratio: 12:1.

Student Life Student groups include Music Educators National Conference Student Chapter, American Guild of Organists.

Expenses for 1995–96 Application fee: $20. State resident tuition: $0 full-time, $78.50 per credit part-time. Nonresident tuition: $4710 full-time, $157 per credit

Idaho State University *(continued)*

part-time. Full-time mandatory fees: $1820. College room and board: $3100. Special program-related fees: $125–$250 for applied music fee.

Financial Aid Program-specific awards for Fall of 1994: 80 Ensemble Scholarships for program majors ($350), 1 Missal Band Scholarship for band majors ($810), 4 Berryman Endowment Awards for program majors ($500), 2 Phoenix Endowment Awards for program majors ($500), 4 Department Music Endowment Awards for program majors ($500).

Application Procedures Deadline—freshmen: August 1; transfers: continuous. Required: high school transcript, college transcript(s) for transfer students, minimum 2.0 high school GPA, letter of recommendation, interview, audition. Recommended: essay, minimum 3.0 high school GPA. Auditions held 3–4 times on campus and off campus in various Idaho locations; recorded music is permissible as a substitute for live auditions when distance is prohibitive and videotaped performances are permissible as a substitute for live auditions when distance is prohibitive.

Undergraduate Contact Alan E. Stanek, Chairman, Department of Music, Idaho State University, Box 8099, Pocatello, Idaho 83209-8099; 208-236-3636, fax: 208-236-4529, E-mail address: stanalan@isu.edu.

Illinois State University

Normal, Illinois

State-supported, coed. Urban campus. Total enrollment: 19,166.

Degrees Bachelor of Music in the areas of performance, music therapy, music theory/composition; Bachelor of Music Education in the area of music education. Majors: classical music, music, music education, music therapy, piano/organ, stringed instruments, voice, wind and percussion instruments. Graduate degrees offered: Master of Music in the areas of performance, music theory/composition, music therapy; Master of Music Education in the area of music education.

Music Student Profile Fall 1994: 270 total; 225 matriculated undergraduate, 45 matriculated graduate.

Music Faculty Total: 40; 40 full-time; 65% of full-time faculty have terminal degrees. Graduate students teach a few undergraduate courses. Undergraduate student–faculty ratio: 6:1.

Student Life Student groups include National Association of Music Therapy, Music Educators National Conference, Tau Beta Sigma.

Expenses for 1995–96 State resident tuition: $3572 full-time, $119.05 per credit part-time. Nonresident tuition: $8954 full-time, $298.45 per credit part-time. College room and board: $3782. College room only: $1984.

Financial Aid Program-specific awards for Fall of 1994: 16 Tuition Waivers for program majors and minors ($300–$1200), 20 Talent Grants-in-Aid for program majors and minors ($100–$500), 20 Endowed Scholarships for enrolled music majors.

Application Procedures Deadline—freshmen and transfers: continuous. Required: high school transcript, college transcript(s) for transfer students, audition. Auditions held 6 times on campus; recorded music is permissible as a substitute for live auditions for out-of-state applicants.

Undergraduate Contact Judy Thomas, Recruiting Secretary, Music Department, Illinois State University, Campus Box 5660, Normal, Illinois 61790-5660; 309-438-7633.

Graduate Contact Don Armstrong, Graduate Coordinator, Music Department, Illinois State University, Campus Box 5660, Normal, Illinois 61790-5660; 309-438-7633.

Illinois Wesleyan University

Bloomington, Illinois

Independent, coed. Suburban campus. Total enrollment: 1,855.

Degrees Bachelor of Music in the areas of performance, composition; Bachelor of Music Education in the areas of vocal music education, instrumental music education; Bachelor of Fine Arts in the area of music theater. Majors: classical music, music, music education, music theater, piano/organ, sacred music, stringed instruments, voice, wind and percussion instruments.

Music Student Profile Fall 1994: 147 total; all matriculated undergraduate; 5% minorities, 55% females, 5% international.

Music Faculty Total: 33; 18 full-time, 15 part-time; 100% of full-time faculty have terminal degrees. Graduate students do not teach undergraduate courses. Undergraduate student–faculty ratio: 8:1.

Student Life Student groups include Music Educators National Conference Student Chapter, music fraternities and sororities, Delta Omicron.

Expenses for 1995–96 Comprehensive fee of $19,800 includes full-time tuition ($15,410), mandatory fees ($100), and college room and board ($4290). College room only: $2450. Part-time tuition: $1925 per course.

Financial Aid Program-specific awards for Fall of 1994: 40 Music Talent Awards for incoming students ($4500), 4 Music Talent Awards for program majors ($15,000).

Application Procedures Deadline—freshmen and transfers: April 1. Notification date—freshmen and transfers: May 1. Required: essay, high school transcript, college transcript(s) for transfer students, minimum 3.0 high school GPA, interview, audition, SAT I or ACT test scores, minimum combined SAT I score of 900, minimum composite ACT score of 23, portfolio for composition majors. Recommended: 2 letters of recommendation. Auditions held by appointment on campus and off campus in Chicago, IL; recorded music is permissible as a substitute for live auditions when distance is prohibitive and videotaped performances are permissible as a substitute for live auditions when distance is prohibitive. Portfolio reviews held by appointment on campus.

Undergraduate Contact Laura Dolan, Recruiting Coordinator, School of Music, Illinois Wesleyan University, P.O. Box 2900, Bloomington, Illinois 61702; 309-556-3063, fax: 309-556-3411.

Immaculata College

Immaculata, Pennsylvania

Independent-religious, primarily women. Suburban campus. Total enrollment: 2,088.

Degrees Bachelor of Music in the area of music therapy; Bachelor of Music Education in the area of music education. Majors: music, music education, music therapy. Graduate degrees offered: Master of Music in the area of music therapy.

Music Student Profile Fall 1994: 97 total; 47 matriculated undergraduate, 39 matriculated graduate, 11 nondegree; 8% minorities, 95% females, 8% international.

Music Faculty Total: 25; 7 full-time, 18 part-time; 100% of full-time faculty have terminal degrees. Graduate students do not teach undergraduate courses. Undergraduate student–faculty ratio: 7:1.

Expenses for 1995–96 Application fee: $25. Comprehensive fee of $16,558 includes full-time tuition ($10,700), mandatory fees ($180), and college room and board ($5678). College room only: $3024. Part-time mandatory fees: $40 per year. Part-time tuition and fees per credit: $279 for daytime classes, $217 for evening classes. Special program-related fees: $250–$300 for private music lessons.

Financial Aid Program-specific awards for Fall of 1994: 19 Music Talent Scholarships for program majors ($2700), 1 Presser Award for outstanding seniors ($2250), 1 Borelli Award for juniors or seniors ($1000).

Application Procedures Deadline—freshmen and transfers: continuous. Required: high school transcript, college transcript(s) for transfer students, minimum 2.0 high school GPA, 2 letters of recommendation, audition. Recommended: essay, interview, video. Auditions held 6 times on campus; recorded music is permissible as a substitute for live auditions if a campus visit is impossible and videotaped performances are permissible as a substitute for live auditions if a campus visit is impossible.

Undergraduate Contact James P. Sullivan, Director of Undergraduate Admission, Immaculata College, King Road, Immaculata, Pennsylvania 19345; 610-647-4400 ext. 3015, fax: 610-251-1668.

Graduate Contact Director of Graduate Admission, Graduate School, Immaculata College, King Road, Immaculata, Pennsylvania 19345; 610-647-4400 ext. 3216, fax: 610-251-1668.

Incarnate Word College

San Antonio, Texas

Independent-religious, coed. Urban campus. Total enrollment: 2,801.

Degrees Bachelor of Music in the areas of classical music, composition, music, performance; Bachelor of Music Education in the area of music education; Bachelor of Music Therapy in the area of music therapy. Majors: classical music, composition, music, music business, music education, music therapy, piano/organ, stringed instruments, voice, wind and percussion instruments. Cross-registration with Our Lady of the Lake University of San Antonio, St. Mary's University of San Antonio.

Music Student Profile Fall 1994: 44 total; 39 matriculated undergraduate, 5 nondegree.

Music Faculty Total: 14; 5 full-time, 9 part-time; 100% of full-time faculty have terminal degrees. Graduate students do not teach undergraduate courses. Undergraduate student–faculty ratio: 4:1.

Student Life Student groups include American Association of Music Therapy.

Expenses for 1995–96 Application fee: $20. Comprehensive fee of $14,117 includes full-time tuition ($9500), mandatory fees ($135), and college room and board ($4482). College room only: $2290. Part-time tuition: $290 per semester hour. Part-time mandatory fees per term range from $40.50 to $108. Special program-related fees: $150 for private lessons.

Financial Aid Program-specific awards for Fall of 1994: 1 Sarah Eliz Bell Endowed Scholarship for program majors ($1200), 1 Hortense Buchanan Award for program majors ($100), 1 Lamar Moreau Award for program majors ($100).

Application Procedures Deadline—freshmen and transfers: continuous. Required: high school transcript, college transcript(s) for transfer students, minimum 2.0 high school GPA, letter of recommendation, audition, SAT I or ACT test scores. Auditions held 5 times on campus and off campus in McAllen, TX; Laredo, TX; recorded music is permissible as a substitute for live auditions with 3 letters of recommendation and videotaped performances are permissible as a substitute for live auditions with 3 letters of recommendation.

Undergraduate Contact D. E. Bussineau, Coordinator, Music Department, Incarnate Word College, Box 67, 4301 Broadway, San Antonio, Texas 78209; 210-829-3858, fax: 210-829-3880.

Indiana State University

Terre Haute, Indiana

State-supported, coed. Urban campus. Total enrollment: 11,641.

Degrees Bachelor of Music in the area of performance; Bachelor of Music Education in the area of music education. Majors: music education, piano, stringed

Indiana State University *(continued)*

instruments, voice, wind and percussion instruments. Graduate degrees offered: Master of Music in the area of performance; Master of Music Education in the area of music education. Cross-registration with Saint Mary–of–the–Woods College.

Music Student Profile Fall 1994: 200 total; 180 matriculated undergraduate, 20 matriculated graduate; 5% minorities, 50% females, 4% international.

Music Faculty Total: 34; 28 full-time, 6 part-time; 83% of full-time faculty have terminal degrees. Graduate students teach a few undergraduate courses. Undergraduate student–faculty ratio: 8:1.

Expenses for 1995–96 Application fee: $20. State resident tuition: $2928 full-time, $104.50 per credit hour part-time. Nonresident tuition: $7224 full-time, $252.50 per credit hour part-time. College room and board: $3859. Special program-related fees: $30 for applied music fee.

Application Procedures Deadline—freshmen and transfers: June 1. Required: high school transcript, audition, SAT I or ACT test scores, minimum 2.0 college GPA for transfer students. Recommended: essay, minimum 2.0 high school GPA. Auditions held 8 times and by appointment on campus and off campus in Indianapolis, IN; Evansville, IN; South Bend, IN; Fort Wayne, IN, and other Indiana cities; recorded music is permissible as a substitute for live auditions when distance is prohibitive or for international applicants and videotaped performances are permissible as a substitute for live auditions when distance is prohibitive or for international applicants.

Contact Robert L. Cowden, Chair, Department of Music, Indiana State University, Terre Haute, Indiana 47809; 812-237-2771, fax: 812-237-3009.

Hope School of Fine Arts

Indiana University Bloomington

Bloomington, Indiana

State-supported, coed. Small-town campus. Total enrollment: 35,594.

Degrees Bachelor of Music in the areas of composition, early music, jazz studies, performance; Bachelor of Music Education in the areas of choral–general teaching, instrumental teaching, teaching area. Majors: classical music, early music, jazz, music, music education, musical instrument technology, opera, piano/organ, sacred music, stringed instruments, voice, wind and percussion instruments. Graduate degrees offered: Master of Music in the areas of brass, choral conducting, composition, early music, guitar, harp, jazz, music theory, musicology, organ, organ and church music, percussion, piano, strings, voice, wind conducting, woodwinds; Master of Music Education in the areas of band conducting and literature, choral methods, general music, instrumental methods, Kodaly, Orff. Doctor of Musical Arts in the areas of brass, choral conducting, composition, early music, guitar, harp, instrumental conducting, music theory, musicology, opera coaching, conducting, performance and literature, organ, organ and church music, percussion, piano, strings, voice, wind conducting.

Music Student Profile Fall 1994: 1,362 total; 743 matriculated undergraduate, 619 matriculated graduate.

Music Faculty Total: 152; 137 full-time, 15 part-time; 100% of full-time faculty have terminal degrees. Graduate students teach a few undergraduate courses. Undergraduate student–faculty ratio: 18:1.

Expenses for 1995–96 Application fee: $35. State resident tuition: $3582 full-time, $98.65 per credit hour part-time. Nonresident tuition: $10,770 full-time, $323.50 per credit hour part-time. College room and board: $4148. Special program-related fees: $132 for applied music fee, $32 for instrument rental, $27–$38 for recital program printing, $30 for recital recording.

Financial Aid Program-specific awards for Fall of 1994: 50 Music Performance Awards for talented students ($3000).

Application Procedures Deadline—freshmen and transfers: May 1. Required: essay, high school transcript, college transcript(s) for transfer students, minimum 2.0 high school GPA, 3 letters of recommendation, audition, SAT I or ACT test scores, minimum combined SAT I score of 860, minimum composite ACT score of 21. Auditions held 5 times on campus; recorded music is permissible as a substitute for live auditions with later audition on campus.

Contact Gwyn Richards, Director of Recruitment, School of Music, Indiana University Bloomington, Bloomington, Indiana 47405; 812-855-7998, fax: 812-855-4936.

More about the University

Program Facilities The School of Music facilities consists of the Musical Arts Center, a 1,460-seat performing auditorium and technical complex; four buildings housing more than 100 offices and studio, 180 practice rooms, choral and instrumental rehearsal rooms, a recital hall, a library with more than 380,000 books, scores, microfilms, and periodicals and nearly 160,000 recordings; and a performance practice building with 80 soundproof rooms. The School of Music has just completed construction of a music library and recital center. The Music Library integrates the music collection into a technological environment, including a computer classroom and a media center. The building also houses a grand concert hall featuring a tracker organ and a chamber recital hall.

Faculty and Alumni There are over 142 internationally known teachers and scholars on the School's faculty, including David Baker, jazz; Atar Arad, viola; Martina Arroyo, voice; Janos Starker, cello; James Campbell, clarinet; Menahem Pressler, piano; Eugene Rousseau, saxophone; Gyorgy Sebok, piano; Leonard Hokanson, piano; Susann McDonald, harp; Franco Gulli, violin; Giorgio Tozzi, voice; Virginia Zeani, voice; Miriam Fried, violin; Ray Cramer, conducting; Patricia McBride, ballet; Daniel Perantoni, tuba; Claude Baker, composition; Kim Walker, bassoon; Jacques Zoon, flute; Tsuyoshi Tsutsumi, cello.

Student Performance Opportunities Nearly 1,000 different programs are presented annually, including recitals by students, faculty, and guest artists and performances by the School's four symphony orchestras,

chamber orchestra, Baroque orchestra, three bands, jazz ensembles, fifteen choral ensembles, New Music Ensemble, Early Music Institute Ensembles, Opera Theater, and Ballet Theater. Eight full-scale operas are presented in the Musical Arts Center each year.

Special Programs Placement services for graduates of the School of Music are available. Special classes and programs are offered for international students needing additional help in English. Options for students wishing to have advanced study without pursuing a degree or diploma are available.

The Indiana University School of Music is widely respected as one of the most comprehensive institutions for musical studies and has been ranked three times as the best in the nation by the deans and faculty members of the country's music schools. By providing the academic programs of a major university with the atmosphere of a conservatory, the School offers students a well-balanced program consisting of both study and performance.

The facilities of the School of Music include four buildings housing more than 100 offices and studios, 180 practice rooms, rehearsal rooms, a recital hall, a library with more than 380,000 print resources and nearly 160,000 recordings, and a practice building with 80 soundproof rooms.

Facilities of the School of Music are highlighted by the Musical Arts Center, which features an acoustically refined auditorium and a stage with technical capabilities extraordinary for a university facility. The School of Music had just completed construction of a new music library and recital center at the cost of $19 million. The Music Library integrates its existing music collection into a technological environment that includes a computer classroom and a media center. This new technology allows users to unite all aspects of a musical work—score, sound, and textual information. A new grand concert hall and a chamber recital hall accommodates musical performances of all types—from solo student recitals to large ensemble events with orchestra and chorus. The concert hall features a tracker organ for solo concerts as well as choral and orchestral events.

Perhaps the greatest asset of the School of Music is its over 142 teachers and scholars on the School's faculty, including some of the world's most renowned performers: David Baker, jazz; Atar Arad, viola; Martina Arroyo, voice; Janos Starker, cello; James Campell, clarinet; Miriam Fried, violin; Ray Cramer, conducting; Daniel Perantoni, tuba; Patricia McBride, ballet; Claude Baker, composition; Kim Walker, bassoon; Jacques Zoon, flute; Tsuyoshi Tsutsumi, cello; Menahem Pressler, piano; Eugene Rousseau, saxophone; Gyorgy Sebok, piano; Leonard Hokanson, piano; Susann McDonald, harp; Franco Gulli, violin; Giorgio Tozzi, voice; and Virginia Zeani, voice. Internationally recognized alumni include Sylvia McNair, soprano; Joshua Bell, violin; Timothy Noble, baritone; Andres Cardenes, concertmaster of Pittsburgh Symphony Orchestra; Elizabeth Hainen, principal harp of Philadelphia Orchestra; Daniel Gaede, concertmaster of Vienna Philharmonic; Hank Dutt; Joan Jeanrehaud of the Kronos Quartet; and seventeen alumni on the 1994–95 Metropolitan Opera roster.

The School of Music presents nearly 1,000 different programs annually. These include recitals by students, faculty, and guest artists and performances by the School's four symphony orchestras, chamber orchestra, Baroque orchestra, three bands, jazz ensembles, fifteen choral ensembles, New Music Ensemble, Early Music Institute Ensembles, Opera Theater, and Ballet Theater. The Opera Theater of the School of Music has given more than 1,000 performances of 250 different operas, including many premieres. Eight full-scale operas are presented in the Musical Arts Center each year.

The School of Music hosts numerous international music workshops, master classes, and conferences. During the summer months, special workshops and clinics are offered for young musicians in many different performing areas. More than 1,500 students from throughout the United States and from thirty-five other countries attend the School of Music during the school year.

Indiana University South Bend

South Bend, Indiana

State-supported, coed. Suburban campus. Total enrollment: 7,936.

Degrees Bachelor of Music in the areas of piano, orchestral instruments, guitar, composition, voice; Bachelor of Music Education in the areas of piano, orchestral instruments, guitar, composition, voice. Majors: classical music, guitar, jazz, music, music education, opera, piano/organ, sacred music, stringed instruments, voice, wind and percussion instruments. Graduate degrees offered: Master of Music in the areas of piano, orchestral instruments, guitar, composition, voice; Master of Music Education in the areas of piano, orchestral instruments, guitar, composition, voice. Cross-registration with Indiana University System, Bethel College.

Music Student Profile Fall 1994: 67 total; 50 matriculated undergraduate, 12 matriculated graduate, 5 nondegree; 5% minorities, 60% females, 20% international.

Music Faculty Total: 22; 7 full-time, 15 part-time; 100% of full-time faculty have terminal degrees. Graduate students teach a few undergraduate courses. Undergraduate student–faculty ratio: 8:1.

Expenses for 1995–96 State resident tuition: $2544 full-time, $84.80 per credit hour part-time. Nonresident tuition: $6957 full-time, $231.90 per credit hour part-time. Part-time mandatory fees: $2.00 per credit hour. Full-time mandatory fees range. Full-time mandatory fees range from $120 to $150. Special program-related fees: $135 for applied music.

Financial Aid Program-specific awards for Fall of 1994: 15–20 Music Scholarships for pianists and string instrumentalists ($500).

Application Procedures Deadline—freshmen and transfers: August 15. Notification date—freshmen and transfers: September 1. Required: high school transcript, minimum 2.0 high school GPA, audition. Auditions held 2 times on campus; recorded music is permissible as a substitute for live auditions for international applicants and videotaped performances are permissible as a substitute for live auditions for international applicants.

Indiana University South Bend *(continued)*

Undergraduate Contact Christine Seitz, Academic Coordinator, Division of the Arts, Indiana University South Bend, 1700 Mishawaka Avenue, P.O. Box 7111, South Bend, Indiana 46634; 219-237-4306.

Graduate Contact Dr. Michael J. Esselstrom, Director of Instruction, Division of the Arts, Indiana University South Bend, 1700 Mishawaka Avenue, P.O. Box 7111, South Bend, Indiana 46634; 219-237-4562.

Indiana University of Pennsylvania

Indiana, Pennsylvania

State-supported, coed. Small-town campus. Total enrollment: 13,814.

Degrees Bachelor of Fine Arts in the area of music performance.

Expenses for 1995–96 State resident tuition: $3224 full-time, $134 per semester hour part-time. Nonresident tuition: $8198 full-time, $342 per semester hour part-time. Part-time mandatory fees: $125 per semester. Full-time mandatory fees: $639. College room and board: $3258. College room only: $1858.

Application Procedures Deadline—freshmen and transfers: continuous. Required: high school transcript, college transcript(s) for transfer students, letter of recommendation, SAT I or ACT test scores. Auditions held on campus and off campus. Portfolio reviews held on campus and off campus.

Undergraduate Contact Calvin E. Weber, Chair, Department of Music, Indiana University of Pennsylvania, 101 Cogswell Hall, Indiana, Pennsylvania 15705; 412-357-2390, fax: 412-357-7899.

Indiana University–Purdue University Fort Wayne

Fort Wayne, Indiana

State-supported, coed. Urban campus. Total enrollment: 11,513.

Degrees Bachelor of Music in the areas of piano, voice, orchestral instruments; Bachelor of Music Education in the area of choral and/or instrumental teaching; Bachelor of Music Therapy in the area of music therapy. Majors: music, music education, music therapy, piano/organ, stringed instruments, voice, wind and percussion instruments.

Music Student Profile Fall 1994: 78 total; 70 matriculated undergraduate, 8 nondegree; 5% minorities, 55% females.

Music Faculty Total: 20; 10 full-time, 10 part-time; 100% of full-time faculty have terminal degrees. Graduate students do not teach undergraduate courses. Undergraduate student–faculty ratio: 8:1.

Student Life Student groups include Sigma Alpha Iota, Music Educators National Conference, Music Therapy Club.

Expenses for 1994–95 Application fee: $30. State resident tuition: $2408 full-time, $80.25 per semester hour part-time. Nonresident tuition: $5966 full-time, $198.85 per semester hour part-time. Part-time mandatory fees: $2.90 per semester hour. Full-time mandatory fees: $87. Special program-related fees: $72 for applied lesson fee.

Financial Aid Program-specific awards for Fall of 1994: 1–2 Ator Scholarships for instrumental majors ($800), 1–2 Loessi Scholarships for vocal/choral majors ($800), 6–8 Whitney Scholarships for program majors ($400), 10–15 Departmental Merit Awards for program majors ($500).

Application Procedures Deadline—freshmen and transfers: August 1. Notification date—freshmen and transfers: August 21. Required: high school transcript, college transcript(s) for transfer students, minimum 2.0 high school GPA, interview, audition, SAT I or ACT test scores. Auditions held continuously on campus and off campus; recorded music is permissible as a substitute for live auditions if a campus visit is impossible and videotaped performances are permissible as a substitute for live auditions if a campus visit is impossible. Portfolio reviews held on campus and off campus.

Undergraduate Contact Steven T. Sarratore, Interim Chair, Music Department, Indiana University–Purdue University Fort Wayne, 2101 Coliseum Boulevard East, Fort Wayne, Indiana 46805-1499; 219-481-6712, fax: 219-481-6985, E-mail address: sarrator@cvax.ipfw.indiana.edu.

Iowa State University of Science and Technology

Ames, Iowa

State-supported, coed. Suburban campus. Total enrollment: 24,728.

Degrees Bachelor of Music in the areas of music education, performance, composition; Bachelor of Music Education in the areas of vocal music education, instrumental music education. Majors: music, music education, piano/organ, stringed instruments, voice, wind and percussion instruments.

Music Student Profile Fall 1994: 122 total; all matriculated undergraduate; 5% minorities, 57% females, 3% international.

Music Faculty Total: 26; 23 full-time, 3 part-time; 30% of full-time faculty have terminal degrees. Graduate students do not teach undergraduate courses. Undergraduate student–faculty ratio: 19:1.

Student Life Student groups include Phi Mu Alpha Sinfonia, Sigma Alpha Iota.

Estimated Expenses for 1995–96 Application fee: $20. State resident tuition: $2386 full-time, $100 per semester hour part-time. Nonresident tuition: $8004

full-time, $334 per semester hour part-time. Full-time mandatory fees: $188. College room and board: $3386.

Financial Aid Program-specific awards for Fall of 1994: Department Scholarships for program majors.

Application Procedures Deadline—freshmen and transfers: continuous. Required: high school transcript, college transcript(s) for transfer students, minimum 2.0 high school GPA, 2 letters of recommendation, interview, audition, SAT I or ACT test scores. Auditions held continuously on campus and off campus; recorded music is permissible as a substitute for live auditions if a campus visit is impossible and videotaped performances are permissible as a substitute for live auditions if a campus visit is impossible. Portfolio reviews held on campus and off campus.

Undergraduate Contact Mahlon Darlington, Chair, Admissions and Scholarship Committee, Department of Music, Iowa State University of Science and Technology, 229 Music Hall, Ames, Iowa 50011; 515-294-8016, fax: 315-294-6409.

Iowa Wesleyan College

Mount Pleasant, Iowa

Independent-religious, coed. Small-town campus. Total enrollment: 887.

Degrees Bachelor of Music Education in the area of music education. Majors: music, music education.

Music Student Profile Fall 1994: 19 total; all matriculated undergraduate; 10% minorities, 59% females, 5% international.

Music Faculty Total: 10; 4 full-time, 6 part-time; 75% of full-time faculty have terminal degrees. Graduate students do not teach undergraduate courses. Undergraduate student–faculty ratio: 3:1.

Student Life Student groups include Music Educators National Conference Student Chapter, American Choral Directors Association Student Chapter.

Expenses for 1995–96 Application fee: $15. Comprehensive fee of $14,760 includes full-time tuition ($10,920) and college room and board ($3840). College room only: $1660. Part-time tuition per credit hour: $225 for day students, $150 for evening students.

Financial Aid Program-specific awards for Fall of 1994: 6 Goodell Music Scholarships for incoming students ($6000).

Application Procedures Deadline—freshmen and transfers: continuous. Required: essay, high school transcript, college transcript(s) for transfer students, minimum 2.0 high school GPA, letter of recommendation, interview, audition, ACT test score only, minimum composite ACT score of 17. Auditions held continuously on campus; recorded music is permissible as a substitute for live auditions when distance is prohibitive and videotaped performances are permissible as a substitute for live auditions when distance is prohibitive.

Undergraduate Contact Tony Damewood, Director, Admissions Department, Iowa Wesleyan College, 601 North Main Street, Mount Pleasant, Iowa 52641.

Ithaca College

Ithaca, New York

Independent, coed. Small-town campus. Total enrollment: 5,556.

Degrees Bachelor of Music in the areas of composition, jazz studies, music education, performance, performance music education, music theory. Majors: composition, conducting, jazz, music, music education, music theory, performance, piano/organ, stringed instruments, voice, wind and percussion instruments. Graduate degrees offered: Master of Music in the areas of brasses, composition, conducting, music education, performance, strings, Suzuki pedagogy, music theory, woodwinds. Cross-registration with Cornell University.

Music Student Profile Fall 1994: 473 total; 435 matriculated undergraduate, 38 matriculated graduate; 5% minorities, 54% females, 7% international.

Music Faculty Total: 74; 56 full-time, 18 part-time; 84% of full-time faculty have terminal degrees. Graduate students do not teach undergraduate courses. Undergraduate student–faculty ratio: 6:1.

Student Life Student groups include American Choral Directors Association, Phi Mu Alpha Sinfonia, Music Educators National Conference. Special housing available for music students.

Expenses for 1995–96 Application fee: $40. Comprehensive fee of $21,844 includes full-time tuition ($15,250) and college room and board ($6594). Part-time tuition: $477 per credit hour.

Financial Aid Program-specific awards for Fall of 1994: Jephson Educational Trust Scholarship for outstanding program majors ($500–$1500), Leo A. and Frances MacArthur Keilocker Scholarship for talented stringed instrumentalists ($500–$1500), Herbert C. Mueller Memorial Scholarship for trumpeters ($500–$1000), Brigid A. Porter Scholarship for music education or performance/music education majors ($500), Presser Foundation Scholarship for program majors ($1000), Celia Slocum Blair Scholarship for vocal or instrumental music education majors ($500–$1500), Elenita M. Benjamin Fitch Scholarship for members of Mu Phi Epsilon ($500–$1500), Charlotte C. and James M. Fitzgerald Scholarship for program majors ($500–$2000), Clinton B. Ford Scholarship for talented stringed instrumentalists ($500–$1500), Kathleen Kimple Houghton Memorial Scholarship for upperclass violinists ($500–$1500), Iola Angood Taylor Scholarship for students from public school music programs ($500–$1500), Josephine Southwick Award for program majors ($1000–$2000), Kathryn A.C. Martin Music Scholarship for program majors ($500–$1500).

Application Procedures Deadline—freshmen: March 1; transfers: July 15. Notification date—freshmen: April 15. Required: essay, high school transcript, college transcript(s) for transfer students, minimum 2.0 high

Ithaca College *(continued)*

school GPA, letter of recommendation, audition, SAT I or ACT test scores. Recommended: interview. Auditions held 13 times on campus and off campus in New York, NY; Interlochen, MI; Chicago, IL; Tampa, FL; Washington, DC; Philadelphia, PA; Boston, MA; Pittsburgh, PA; recorded music is permissible as a substitute for live auditions if distance is prohibitive or scheduling is difficult and videotaped performances are permissible as a substitute for live auditions if distance is prohibitive or scheduling is difficult.

Undergraduate Contact Paula J. Mitchell, Director, Admissions, Ithaca College, 100 Job Hall, Ithaca, New York 14850-7020; 800-429-4274, fax: 607-274-1900.

Graduate Contact Mary Lee Seibert, Associate Provost and Dean, Graduate Studies and Continuing Education, Ithaca College, 111 Towers Concourse, Ithaca, New York 14850-7142; 607-274-3527.

More about the College

Program facilities Performance spaces include Ford Hall auditorium (735 seats) and Nabenhauer Recital Hall (150 seats). Three electroacoustic music studios, computer-assisted instruction facilities, and a full complement of practice instruments are available. More than 90 practice room spaces are open to students, and there are 4 concert grands for performances as well as 17 practice grands included in the 141 pianos at the school. The library has extensive holdings of music and recordings.

Faculty, Resident Artists, and Alumni Faculty perform nationally and regionally; many are scholars in the fields of music education, theory, composition, and history. Resident faculty ensembles include the Ithaca Brass, Ithaca Wind Quintet, and Ithaca College String Quartet. Alumni hold positions in major orchestras and opera companies, perform in many prestigious chamber ensembles, sing on Broadway, and are recognized jazz recording artists. They also hold teaching positions in secondary schools and universities and are successful in arts administration, music publishing, audio technology, and music business.

Student Performance Opportunities Every student is required to perform in a major ensemble; many participate in more than one. There are twenty-four student ensembles, including wind ensemble, concert band, symphony orchestra, chamber orchestra, brass choir, percussion ensemble, guitar ensemble, choir, chorus, women's chorale, madrigal singers, vocal jazz ensemble, opera workshop, and jazz ensemble, as well as numerous chamber ensembles.

Special Programs Students may study abroad at the Ithaca College London Center or elsewhere. Programs in Suzuki string and piano pedagogy are available, and teacher certification is offered in 15 areas, including music. The Office of Career Planning and Placement offers special assistance geared to music students, and alumni also actively serve as career opportunity resources.

Since its founding in 1892 as a conservatory of music, Ithaca College has been nurturing and developing its musical character. The College remains dedicated to the goals of its founder, W. Grant Egbert, who said, "It is my plan to build a school of music second to none in the excellence of its faculty, the soundness of its educational ideals, and the superior quality of instruction."

As the conservatory evolved into a college with expanded academic offerings, the programs in music retained their position of prominence. Today, Ithaca's School of Music is counted among the nation's leading schools.

Devoted primarily to undergraduate study, the School of Music is steadfastly committed to providing a high level of music education. Students benefit from a blend of first-class faculty, innovative programs, and outstanding facilities.

Students in the School of Music take one quarter of their academic work in the liberal arts, primarily through the School of Humanities and Sciences. Additional electives from Ithaca's other professional schools—Business, Communications, and Health Sciences and Human Performance—are also available. The interaction among the schools is another advantage to an Ithaca education: physics majors can be found working in the electroacoustic music studios, television-radio majors take courses such as Music and Media, and music students play in the pit orchestra for theater productions and perform on soundtracks for student filmmakers. The Planned Studies option allows students to create their own degree programs that take advantage of the broad array of courses and majors—some 2,000 courses and more than 100 majors are offered.

Students who come to the Ithaca College School of Music are already dedicated to the idea of mastering voice or any of the standard orchestral musical instruments. At Ithaca they continue their training under a faculty of performing professionals. Students prepare for their musical performances through weekly private lessons and 1-hour repertory classes with their major teachers and fellow students. Repertory classes provide opportunities for students to perform for each other, review performance techniques, and meet guest artists such as Phyllis Curtin, Ruth Laredo, Garrick Ohlsson, Barry Tuckwell, Lukas Foss, and the Guarneri String Quartet. As soloists and with ensembles, students become part of the rich musical life of the School, where more than 300 recitals, concerts, musicals, and operas are given each year.

All degree programs emphasize performance. Each year, some 450 undergraduate and 40 graduate students are involved in live performances—on campus, in the Ithaca community, and throughout the northeastern United States. In addition, several ensembles tour annually and have won critical acclaim for their work in New York at Lincoln Center's Alice Tully Hall, St. Patrick's Cathedral, and Carnegie Hall, as well as throughout the rest of the state; in Boston and throughout New England; in Washington, D.C.; and in other cities.

The city of Ithaca is one of the country's premier college towns, with nearly 25,000 students at Ithaca College and Cornell University. Surrounded by magnificent gorges, lakes, and countryside in the Finger Lakes region of New York State, Ithaca is a thriving cultural center. The community supports an impressive array of concerts, art galleries, movies, and theater productions. Among the artists who have performed in town recently are Itzhak Perlman, James Galway, Mstislav Rostropovich, and Kathleen Battle.

Ithaca College's combination of a resident faculty, an emphasis on undergraduate performance, and access to a wide spectrum of liberal arts courses makes it an excellent choice among the major music schools in the nation.

J. William Fulbright College of Arts and Sciences

See University of Arkansas, J. William Fulbright College of Arts and Sciences

Jackson State University

Jackson, Mississippi

State-supported, coed. Urban campus. Total enrollment: 6,224.

Degrees Bachelor of Music in the area of piano performance; Bachelor of Music Education in the areas of instrumental music education, vocal music education, piano music education, jazz music education. Majors: jazz, music education, piano/organ, stringed instruments, voice, wind and percussion instruments. Graduate degrees offered: Master of Music Education in the area of music education.

Music Student Profile Fall 1994: 107 total; 89 matriculated undergraduate, 8 matriculated graduate, 10 nondegree; 4% minorities, 40% females, 3% international.

Music Faculty Total: 22; 18 full-time, 4 part-time; 62% of full-time faculty have terminal degrees. Graduate students do not teach undergraduate courses. Undergraduate student–faculty ratio: 5:1.

Student Life Student groups include Music Educators National Conference, Music Teachers National Association, Kappa Kappa Psi.

Expenses for 1995–96 State resident tuition: $2380 full-time, $99 per credit hour part-time. Nonresident tuition: $4974 full-time. College room and board: $2988. College room only: $1706.

Financial Aid Program-specific awards for Fall of 1994: 134 Music Scholarships for talented program majors ($2000).

Application Procedures Deadline—freshmen and transfers: August 1. Notification date—freshmen and transfers: August 15. Required: high school transcript, minimum 2.0 high school GPA, audition. Recommended: letter of recommendation, interview, video. Auditions held 3 times on campus and off campus in St. Louis, MO; East St. Louis, IL; Chicago, IL; Detroit, MI; Atlanta, GA; Hattiesburg, MS; Natchez, MS; Clarksdale, MS; Meridian, MS; recorded music is permissible as a substitute for live auditions when distance is prohibitive and videotaped performances are permissible as a substitute for live auditions when distance is prohibitive.

Contact Dr. Jimmie J. James Jr., Chair, Music Department, Jackson State University, P.O. Box 17055, Jackson, Mississippi 39217; 601-968-2141, fax: 601-968-2568.

Jacksonville State University

Jacksonville, Alabama

State-supported, coed. Small-town campus. Total enrollment: 7,553.

Degrees Bachelor of Music in the area of performance; Bachelor of Music Education in the area of music education. Majors: classical music, music, music education, piano/organ, voice, wind and percussion instruments. Graduate degrees offered: Master of Music in the area of performance; Master of Music Education in the area of music education.

Music Student Profile Fall 1994: 190 total; 162 matriculated undergraduate, 18 matriculated graduate, 10 nondegree; 10% minorities, 45% females, 5% international.

Music Faculty Total: 16; 16 full-time; 75% of full-time faculty have terminal degrees. Graduate students do not teach undergraduate courses. Undergraduate student–faculty ratio: 12:1.

Student Life Student groups include Music Educators National Conference Student Chapter, Phi Mu Alpha Sinfonia, Sigma Alpha Iota.

Expenses for 1995–96 Application fee: $20. State resident tuition: $1840 full-time, $77 per semester hour part-time. Nonresident tuition: $2760 full-time, $116 per semester hour part-time. Residents of Georgia counties contiguous to Alabama pay state resident tuition. College room and board: $2320. Special program-related fees: $25 for individual applied music fee, $5 for class applied music fee.

Financial Aid Program-specific awards for Fall of 1994: 75–100 Band Scholarships for wind/percussion majors ($800–$1000), 25–50 Choral Scholarships for vocal/choral majors ($800–$1000), 10–15 Vocal Scholarships for voice majors ($800–$1000), 10–15 Piano Scholarships for piano majors ($800–$1000).

Application Procedures Deadline—freshmen and transfers: continuous. Required: high school transcript, college transcript(s) for transfer students, minimum 2.0 high school GPA, SAT I or ACT test scores. Recommended: interview, audition. Auditions held 3 times on campus; recorded music is permissible as a substitute for live auditions if a campus visit is impossible and videotaped performances are permissible as a substitute for live auditions if a campus visit is impossible.

Undergraduate Contact Dr. Jerry D. Smith, Dean of Admissions and Records, Jacksonville State University, 700 Pelham Road North, Jacksonville, Alabama 36265; 205-782-5400.

Graduate Contact Dr. William D. Carr, Dean, College of Graduate Studies, Jacksonville State University, 700 Pelham Road North, Jacksonville, Alabama 36265; 205-782-5329.

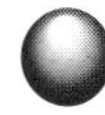

MUSIC

314

Jacksonville University

Jacksonville, Florida

Independent, coed. Suburban campus. Total enrollment: 2,480.

Degrees Bachelor of Music in the areas of performance, composition and theory; Bachelor of Music Education in the area of music education; Bachelor of Fine Arts in the areas of music, music theater. Majors: classical music, music, music education, music theater, music theory and composition, piano/organ, sacred music, stringed instruments, voice, wind and percussion instruments.

Music Student Profile Fall 1994: 89 total; all matriculated undergraduate; 14% minorities, 54% females.

Music Faculty Total: 40; 9 full-time, 31 part-time; 33% of full-time faculty have terminal degrees. Graduate students do not teach undergraduate courses. Undergraduate student–faculty ratio: 9:1.

Student Life Student groups include Mu Phi Epsilon, Florida National Music Educators Conference Student Chapter.

Expenses for 1995–96 Application fee: $25. Comprehensive fee of $15,178 includes full-time tuition ($10,080), mandatory fees ($500), and college room and board ($4598). Part-time tuition: $336 per semester hour. Part-time mandatory fees: $80 per semester. Special program-related fees: $30 for instrumental methods instructional material assessment, $80–$110 for private music lessons.

Financial Aid Program-specific awards for Fall of 1994: 30 Music Grants for undergraduates ($4800), 56 Service Awards for chorus, band orchestra students ($1150), 6 Accompanying Grants for pianists ($1835), 20 Awards for the musically talented ($1000).

Application Procedures Deadline—freshmen and transfers: continuous. Required: high school transcript, minimum 2.0 high school GPA, audition. Recommended: essay, minimum 3.0 high school GPA, 2 letters of recommendation. Auditions held 5 times on campus; recorded music is permissible as a substitute for live auditions if a campus visit is impossible and videotaped performances are permissible as a substitute for live auditions if a campus visit is impossible.

Undergraduate Contact Artie Clifton, Associate Chair, Division of Music, Jacksonville University, 2800 University Boulevard North, Jacksonville, Florida 32211; 904-745-7370 ext. 7386, fax: 904-745-7375.

More about the University

Program Facilities Terry Concert Hall, opened in 1991, is a state-of-the-art 400-seat concert hall with excellent acoustics. Swisher Auditorium seats 550 and is used for staging the dramatic and musical productions presented by the College of Fine Arts students. The Phillips Fine Arts Building houses three classrooms, eighteen teaching studios, fifteen practice rooms, two large rehearsal rooms, an electronic music studio, a recital hall/art museum, and an ear training lab.

Faculty, Resident Artists, and Alumni JU faculty are members of the Jacksonville Symphony Orchestra and St. Johns River City Band as well as active concert artists, recitalists, and church musicians. Aaron Krosnick, violin, and Mary Lou Krosnick, piano, present over forty recitals and master classes each year throughout the state of Florida. Master classes and/or lectures in 1994–95 were presented by Maurice Hinson, piano; Nneena Freelon, voice; Texas Boys Choir; and David Shaffer-Gottschalk, piano. JU alumni include George Massey, Carole Clifford, Byron Adams, Mary Ann Farrell, and Tim Kidder.

Student Performance Opportunities JU has eight formal student ensembles and other smaller ensembles. Students participate in University-Community Orchestra, University Wind Ensemble, Jazz Ensemble, Percussion Ensemble, Pep Band, Concert Choir, Chamber Singers, and Dolphinaires, a vocal jazz ensemble.

Special Programs Many scholarships are available for ensemble participation and accompanying. It is possible for music majors to receive one-half to full tuition scholarships.

James Madison University

Harrisonburg, Virginia

State-supported, coed. Small-town campus. Total enrollment: 11,539.

Degrees Bachelor of Music in the areas of music industry, music education, performance, composition, musical theater. Majors: composition, jazz, music, music business, music education, music theater, piano/organ, stringed instruments, voice, wind and percussion instruments. Graduate degrees offered: Master of Music in the areas of performance, music education, conducting, music theory/composition.

Music Student Profile Fall 1994: 349 total; 324 matriculated undergraduate, 25 matriculated graduate; 6% minorities, 49% females, 7% international.

Music Faculty Total: 42; 33 full-time, 9 part-time; 94% of full-time faculty have terminal degrees. Graduate students teach a few undergraduate courses. Undergraduate student–faculty ratio: 8:1.

Student Life Student groups include Music Educators National Conference, Phi Mu Alpha Sinfonia, Sigma Alpha Iota.

Expenses for 1995–96 Application fee: $25. State resident tuition: $4014 full-time. Nonresident tuition: $8294 full-time. Part-time tuition per semester ranges from $264 to $1660 for state residents, $689 to $3238 for nonresidents. College room and board: $4576. College room only: $2474.

Financial Aid Program-specific awards for Fall of 1994: 55 Music Performance Awards for program majors ($1000).

Application Procedures Deadline—freshmen and transfers: January 15. Notification date—freshmen and transfers: April 1. Required: essay, high school transcript, college transcript(s) for transfer students, 3 letters of recommendation, audition, SAT I or ACT test scores. Recommended: minimum 3.0 high school GPA. Auditions held 3 times on campus and off campus; recorded music is permissible as a substitute for live auditions when distance is prohibitive. Portfolio reviews held on campus and off campus.

Undergraduate Contact Music Admissions, School of Music, James Madison University, Harrisonburg, Virginia 22807; 703-568-6197, fax: 703-568-7819, E-mail address: fac_mmorris@vax1.acs.jmu.edu.

Graduate Contact Carol K. Noe, Graduate Coordinator, School of Music, James Madison University, Harrisonburg, Virginia 22807; 703-568-6972, fax: 703-568-7819.

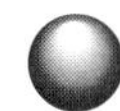

Peabody Conservatory of Music

Johns Hopkins University

Baltimore, Maryland

Independent, coed. Urban campus. Total enrollment: 4,812.

Degrees Bachelor of Music in the areas of composition, performance, recording arts sciences, music education. Majors: composition, early music, guitar, music education, piano/organ, recording arts and sciences, stringed instruments, voice, wind and percussion instruments. Graduate degrees offered: Master of Music in the areas of composition, performance, conducting, pedagogy, music education, music history, computer music, performance, ensemble arts. Doctor of Musical Arts in the areas of composition, performance, conducting, ensemble arts, pedagogy.

Music Student Profile Fall 1994: 575 total; 10% minorities, 55% females, 35% international.

Music Faculty Total: 153; 76 full-time, 77 part-time; 32% of full-time faculty have terminal degrees. Graduate students do not teach undergraduate courses. Undergraduate student–faculty ratio: 20:1.

Student Life Special housing available for music students.

Estimated Expenses for 1995–96 Application fee: $50. Comprehensive fee of $26,750 includes full-time tuition ($19,700) and college room and board ($7050). One-time mandatory fee: $500.

Application Procedures Deadline—freshmen and transfers: April 1. Required: essay, high school transcript, minimum 3.0 high school GPA, 3 letters of recommendation, audition. Recommended: interview. Auditions held 2 times on campus and off campus in New York, NY; Boston, MA; Atlanta, GA; Chicago, IL; San Francisco, CA; Los Angeles, CA; recorded music is permissible as a substitute for live auditions when distance is prohibitive. Portfolio reviews held on campus and off campus.

Undergraduate Contact David Lane, Director of Admissions, Peabody Conservatory of Music, Johns Hopkins University, 1 East Mount Vernon Place, Baltimore, Maryland 21202; 410-659-8110.

More about the Conservatory

This is the place in which schools are supposed to tell you about their wonderful facilities, famous faculty members, and excellent performing ensembles. The trouble is, all prominent music schools have these attributes. Instead, Peabody would like to help you understand two of the key philosophies on which a Peabody education is based.

First, Peabody believes in liberal arts for musicians. Some music schools feel the best way to develop musicians is to direct all their energy into practice. Practice alone is not enough. The world already has a surplus of musicians with fast fingers. It takes a broader knowledge of culture, art, and philosophy to really understand what you are doing. That is one of the reasons Peabody includes liberal arts courses in its programs. Even better, all required courses are taught at Peabody so they can be tailored to the needs of serious musicians.

Second, Peabody does not promote cut-throat competition. Occasionally one hears about music conservatories being nasty places—students fighting over practice rooms and trying to "psych" each other out at auditions. You may be the kind of person who thrives in a competitive atmosphere like that. Peabody has a different philosophy. Certainly it has auditions and competitions, but Peabody believes that each student has his or her own unique musical gift to develop. And it will develop better in an atmosphere that promotes cooperation and growth. Sometimes, you might even see one participant accompanying another at a competition. Peabody is exceptionally proud of that.

The Admissions Office at the Peabody Conservatory understands how daunting the college search process can be to an aspiring artist. Readers of this guide are likely to be collecting literature from many colleges, conservatories, and universities. The college viewbooks they receive generally paint a wholly appealing picture of life at the school—no scheduling problems, an exquisite campus, incredibly talented students and understanding faculty members—one could imagine that a Carnegie Hall debut is only a step away. How does a student make a wise choice and separate the fantasies from the realities?

As the Director of Admissions at Peabody has said, "We can't be everything to everybody. If a student and I do our jobs well, it is likely he or she will be happy with the final school selected. We need to see if what Peabody has to offer fits a student's needs."

Of course, Peabody has much to offer. The school was founded in 1857 but did not actually open its doors until 1866. The advantage of this age is that Peabody has been turning out top-quality musicians for a century or so, and the music world has come to assume that anyone who graduates from Peabody is a good performer. When students are asked how they heard about the school, they often reply, "I don't know. I think I've always known about Peabody."

In 1977 the Conservatory entered into an affiliation with The Johns Hopkins University, giving Peabody students access to all facilities and activities at the School of Arts and Sciences. In 1986 the Peabody Conservatory officially became a division of the University system. Thus, Peabody graduates are simultaneously graduates of JHU. If the Carnegie Hall fantasy doesn't work out, a Peabody/Hopkins diploma is a powerful credential to have on a resumé.

The focus of Peabody's 600 or so students is entirely "classical," so a student interested in jazz, musical theater, or music therapy should look at some of the other schools in this guide. On the other hand, within the field of classical music, Peabody is quite diverse.

Johns Hopkins University *(continued)*

Students can write or call Peabody for application materials or to learn details about the school's philosophy, audition requirements, who is on the faculty, and the financial side of things. In any case, the Peabody Conservatory wishes every student planning to pursue a music career the best of luck in finding the right school.

Jordan College of Fine Arts

See Butler University, Jordan College of Fine Arts

Juilliard School

New York, New York

Independent, coed. Urban campus. Total enrollment: 825.

Degrees Bachelor of Music in the area of classical music. Majors: accompanying, composition, conducting, guitar, harp, harpsichord, piano, voice. Graduate degrees offered: Master of Music in the area of classical music. Doctor of Musical Arts in the area of classical music. Cross-registration with Columbia University, Barnard College.

Music Student Profile Fall 1994: 619 total; 306 matriculated undergraduate, 213 matriculated graduate, 100 nondegree; 30% minorities, 53% females, 35% international.

Music Faculty Total: 232; 100 full-time, 132 part-time. Graduate students teach a few undergraduate courses. Undergraduate student–faculty ratio: 3:1.

Student Life Special housing available for music students.

Expenses for 1995–96 Application fee: $75. Comprehensive fee of $19,900 includes full-time tuition ($13,000), mandatory fees ($600), and college room and board ($6300).

Financial Aid Program-specific awards for Fall of 1994: 300–400 The Juilliard Scholarship Fund Awards for program majors ($6362–$12,200).

Application Procedures Deadline—freshmen and transfers: December 15. Notification date—freshmen and transfers: April 1. Required: high school transcript, interview, video, audition. Recommended: essay, letter of recommendation. Auditions held 2 times on campus.

Contact Mary K. Gray, Director of Admissions, Juilliard School, 60 Lincoln Center Plaza, New York, New York 10023-6590; 212-799-5000 ext. 223, fax: 212-873-4085.

Kansas State University

Manhattan, Kansas

State-supported, coed. Suburban campus. Total enrollment: 20,664.

Degrees Bachelor of Music in the areas of performance, composition, music theater; Bachelor of Music Education in the area of music education. Majors: composition, music, music education, music theater, piano/organ, stringed instruments, voice, wind and percussion instruments. Graduate degrees offered: Master of Music in the areas of music education, performance, music history and literature, composition.

Music Student Profile Fall 1994: 175 total; 150 matriculated undergraduate, 25 matriculated graduate; 5% minorities, 55% females, 5% international.

Music Faculty Total: 26; 24 full-time, 2 part-time; 90% of full-time faculty have terminal degrees. Graduate students teach a few undergraduate courses. Undergraduate student–faculty ratio: 15:1.

Student Life Student groups include Music Educators National Conference Student Chapter, American Choral Directors Association, music fraternity and sorority.

Expenses for 1995–96 Application fee: $15. State resident tuition: $1766 full-time, $59 per semester hour part-time. Nonresident tuition: $7484 full-time, $249 per semester hour part-time. Full-time mandatory fees: $433. College room and board: $3370.

Financial Aid Program-specific awards for Fall of 1994: 50 Music Service Guild Awards for freshmen program majors ($400).

Application Procedures Deadline—freshmen and transfers: continuous. Required: high school transcript. Recommended: video, audition. Auditions held 3 times on campus; recorded music is permissible as a substitute for live auditions if a campus visit is impossible.

Undergraduate Contact Jack Flouer, Head, Music Department, Kansas State University, McCain 109, Manhattan, Kansas 66506; 913-532-5740, fax: 913-532-5709, E-mail address: flouer@ksuvm.ksu.edu.

Graduate Contact Craig Parker, Professor, Music Department, Kansas State University, McCain 109, Manhattan, Kansas 66506; 913-537-0168, fax: 913-532-5709.

Keene State College

Keene, New Hampshire

State-supported, coed. Small-town campus. Total enrollment: 3,931.

Degrees Bachelor of Music in the areas of music education, performance. Majors: classical guitar, music education, piano/organ, voice, wind and percussion instruments.

Music Student Profile Fall 1994: 111 total; 86 matriculated undergraduate, 25 nondegree; 3% minorities, 55% females, 1% international.

Music Faculty Total: 24; 7 full-time, 17 part-time; 71% of full-time faculty have terminal degrees. Graduate students do not teach undergraduate courses. Undergraduate student–faculty ratio: 10:1.

Student Life Student groups include Music Educators National Conference Student Chapter, Society of Composers Student Chapter, Music Teachers National Association Student Chapter.

Expenses for 1995–96 State resident tuition: $2740 full-time, $140 per credit part-time. Nonresident tuition: $8230 full-time, $412 per credit part-time. Part-time mandatory fees: $33 per credit. Full-time mandatory fees: $864. College room and board: $4350. College room only: $2853. Special program-related fees: $80–$160 for applied music fees.

Financial Aid Program-specific awards for Fall of 1994: 3 Talent Scholarships for incoming freshmen ($2700), 1 Jesse Davis Scholarship for upperclassmen ($500).

Application Procedures Deadline—freshmen and transfers: April 15. Notification date—freshmen and transfers: May 1. Required: high school transcript, college transcript(s) for transfer students, 2 letters of recommendation, audition, SAT I or ACT test scores. Recommended: interview. Auditions held continuously on campus; recorded music is permissible as a substitute for live auditions if a campus visit is impossible and videotaped performances are permissible as a substitute for live auditions if a campus visit is impossible.

Undergraduate Contact Douglas A. Nelson, Coordinator, Music Department, Keene State College, Box 2402, Keene, New Hampshire 03435; 603-358-2177, fax: 603-358-2257.

Kennesaw State College

Marietta, Georgia

State-supported, coed. Suburban campus. Total enrollment: 11,915.

Degrees Bachelor of Music in the area of performance; Bachelor of Music Education in the area of music education. Majors: classical guitar, music education, piano/organ, stringed instruments, voice, wind and percussion instruments. Cross-registration with University System of Georgia.

Music Student Profile Fall 1994: 90 total; all matriculated undergraduate; 5% minorities, 50% females, 5% international.

Music Faculty Total: 24; 9 full-time, 15 part-time; 100% of full-time faculty have terminal degrees. Graduate students do not teach undergraduate courses. Undergraduate student–faculty ratio: 15:1.

Student Life Student groups include Music Educators National Conference, Drama Club.

Expenses for 1995–96 Application fee: $20. State resident tuition: $1776 full-time, $42 per quarter hour part-time. Nonresident tuition: $4986 full-time, $132 per quarter hour part-time. Special program-related fees: $50–$100 for applied music fee, $100 for applied music techniques fee.

Financial Aid Program-specific awards for Fall of 1994: 1 Gibson Scholarship for voice/piano majors ($500), 1 Sullivan Scholarship for voice majors ($800), 1 Miller and Wilhiot Scholarship for program majors ($1000), 20 Kennesaw State College Foundation Scholarships for program majors ($300).

Application Procedures Deadline—freshmen and transfers: continuous. Required: high school transcript, minimum 2.0 high school GPA. Recommended: audition. Auditions held 3 times on campus; videotaped performances are permissible as a substitute for live auditions with approval from the department.

Undergraduate Contact Music and Performing Arts, Kennesaw State College, P.O. Box 444, Marietta, Georgia 30061; 404-423-6151, fax: 404-423-6368.

Hugh A. Glauser School of Music

Kent State University

Kent, Ohio

State-supported, coed. Small-town campus. Total enrollment: 21,413.

Degrees Bachelor of Music in the areas of performance, music theory, composition, music education. Majors: classical music, composition, music, music education, music theory, piano/organ, stringed instruments, voice, wind and percussion instruments. Graduate degrees offered: Master of Music in the areas of performance, conducting, piano pedagogy, music education.

Music Student Profile Fall 1994: 282 total; 189 matriculated undergraduate, 93 matriculated graduate; 2% minorities, 50% females, 3% international.

Music Faculty Total: 42; 32 full-time, 10 part-time; 50% of full-time faculty have terminal degrees. Graduate students teach a few undergraduate courses. Undergraduate student–faculty ratio: 14:1.

Student Life Student groups include Music Educators National Conference, music fraternities and sororities.

Expenses for 1995–96 State resident tuition: $4084 full-time, $185.75 per semester hour part-time. Nonresident tuition: $8168 full-time, $371.50 per semester hour part-time. College room and board: $3834. College room only: $2242. Special program-related fees: $23 for applied music lesson fee.

Financial Aid Program-specific awards for Fall of 1994: 20 Departmental Awards for program majors ($1500), 10 Orchestra Society Awards for orchestra participants ($500), 1 L. Wallach Award for program majors ($1000), 1 A. Wallach Award for program majors ($1000), 1 D. Morgan Award for program majors ($1000).

Application Procedures Deadline—freshmen and transfers: continuous. Notification date—freshmen and transfers: continuous. Required: high school transcript, audition, minimum 2.5 high school GPA. Auditions held 6 times on campus; recorded music is permissible as a substitute for live auditions when distance is prohibitive.

Undergraduate Contact Kent Larmee, Coordinator of Undergraduate Studies, Hugh A. Glauser School of Music, Kent State University, P.O. Box 5190, Kent, Ohio 44242; 216-672-2172, fax: 216-672-7837.

Graduate Contact Dr. James Waters, Coordinator of Graduate Studies, Hugh A. Glauser School of Music, Kent State University, P.O. Box 5190, Kent, Ohio 44242; 216-672-2172, fax: 216-672-7837.

Kentucky State University

Frankfort, Kentucky

State-related, coed. Small-town campus. Total enrollment: 2,564.

Degrees Bachelor of Music in the areas of vocal performance, instrumental performance; Bachelor of Music Education in the areas of vocal music education, instrumental music education. Majors: music, music education, voice, wind and percussion instruments.

Music Student Profile Fall 1994: 227 total; 67 matriculated undergraduate, 160 nondegree; 98% minorities, 67% females.

Music Faculty Total: 11; 11 full-time; 85% of full-time faculty have terminal degrees. Graduate students do not teach undergraduate courses. Undergraduate student–faculty ratio: 26:1.

Student Life Student groups include Music Educators National Conference Student Chapter, Tau Beta Sigma, Kappa Kappa Psi.

Expenses for 1995–96 Application fee: $5. State resident tuition: $1680 full-time, $77 per credit hour part-time. Nonresident tuition: $5040 full-time, $217 per credit hour part-time. Part-time mandatory fees: $7 per credit hour. Full-time mandatory fees: $180. College room and board: $2984. College room only: $1364.

Financial Aid Program-specific awards for Fall of 1994: 50 Performance Scholarships for program majors ($2000), 100 Ensemble Scholarships for ensemble performers ($500).

Application Procedures Deadline—freshmen and transfers: July 10. Notification date—freshmen and transfers: July 15. Required: high school transcript, college transcript(s) for transfer students, minimum 2.0 high school GPA, 3 letters of recommendation, audition, SAT I or ACT test scores, minimum composite ACT score of 18. Recommended: essay, minimum 3.0 high school GPA, interview. Auditions held 4 times on campus; recorded music is permissible as a substitute for live auditions for provisional admission and videotaped performances are permissible as a substitute for live auditions.

Undergraduate Contact Dr. Roosevelt O. Shelton, Chairperson, Division of Fine Arts, Kentucky State University, G5-Bradford Hall, Frankfort, Kentucky 40601; 502-227-6496, fax: 502-227-5999.

Kentucky Wesleyan College

Owensboro, Kentucky

Independent-religious, coed. Suburban campus. Total enrollment: 740.

Degrees Bachelor of Music in the areas of performance, church music; Bachelor of Music Education in the area of music education. Majors: guitar, music, music education, piano/organ, sacred music, voice. Cross-registration with Brescia College.

Music Student Profile Fall 1994: 30 total; all matriculated undergraduate; 4% minorities, 58% females, 2% international.

Music Faculty Total: 11; 3 full-time, 8 part-time; 100% of full-time faculty have terminal degrees. Graduate students do not teach undergraduate courses. Undergraduate student–faculty ratio: 8:1.

Student Life Student groups include Music Educators National Conference, Kentucky Wesleyan Singers, Kentucky Wesleyan Players.

Expenses for 1995–96 Application fee: $20. Comprehensive fee of $13,400 includes full-time tuition ($8950), mandatory fees ($150), and college room and board ($4300). College room only: $1950. Part-time tuition: $280 per semester hour.

Financial Aid Program-specific awards for Fall of 1994: 30–35 Music Scholarships for program majors ($2500).

Application Procedures Deadline—freshmen and transfers: continuous. Required: high school transcript, minimum 2.0 high school GPA, audition, SAT I or ACT test scores. Recommended: essay, minimum 3.0 high school GPA, 3 letters of recommendation, interview. Auditions held 4 times and by appointment on campus and off campus in various cities by special arrangement; recorded music is permissible as a substitute for live auditions and videotaped performances are permissible as a substitute for live auditions.

Undergraduate Contact Dr. Diane K. Earle, Associate Professor of Music, Music Department, Kentucky Wesleyan College, 3000 Frederica Street, Owensboro, Kentucky 42302-1039; 502-926-3111 ext. 245.

Lake Erie College

Painesville, Ohio

Independent, coed. Small-town campus. Total enrollment: 732.

Degrees Bachelor of Fine Arts in the area of music. Majors: composition, music history, music theory, piano/organ, voice.

Expenses for 1995–96 Application fee: $20. Comprehensive fee of $17,226 includes full-time tuition ($11,840), mandatory fees ($480), and college room and board ($4906). Part-time tuition: $356 per semester hour. Part-time mandatory fees: $15 per semester.

Application Procedures

Undergraduate Contact Paul Gothard, Director, Fine Arts Department, Lake Erie College, Box 354, 391 West Washington Street, Painesville, Ohio 44077; 216-639-7856.

Lakehead University

Thunder Bay, Ontario

Province-supported, coed. Suburban campus. Total enrollment: 7,918.

Degrees Bachelor of Music. Majors: classical music. Cross-registration with Confederation College.

Music Student Profile Fall 1994: 90 total; all matriculated undergraduate; 5% minorities, 50% females.

Music Faculty Total: 20; 2 full-time, 18 part-time; 100% of full-time faculty have terminal degrees. Graduate students do not teach undergraduate courses. Undergraduate student–faculty ratio: 30:1.

Expenses for 1994–95 Application fee: $50. Canadian resident tuition: $2228 (minimum) full-time, $460 per course part-time. Nonresident tuition: $8402 (minimum) full-time, $1736 per course part-time. Part-time mandatory fees: $40.40 per course. (All figures are in Canadian dollars.). Full-time mandatory fees: $333. College room and board: $4325. College room only: $3338.

Financial Aid Program-specific awards for Fall of 1994: 1 Munro Family Memorial Prize for program majors ($725), 5 A.L. Musselman Awards for program majors ($297–$800), 1 Westlake Music Scholarship for continuing students ($450), 1 Ranta Entrance Award for incoming students ($300).

Application Procedures Deadline—freshmen and transfers: continuous. Required: high school transcript, minimum 2.0 high school GPA, interview, audition. Auditions held by appointment on campus; recorded music is permissible as a substitute for live auditions for out-of-town applicants and videotaped performances are permissible as a substitute for live auditions for out-of-town applicants.

Undergraduate Contact Registrar's Office, Lakehead University, 955 Oliver Road, Thunder Bay, Ontario P7B 5E1, Canada; 807-343-8500, fax: 807-343-8156.

Lamar University–Beaumont

Beaumont, Texas

State-supported, coed. Urban campus.

Degrees Bachelor of Music in the areas of performance, composition, music education. Majors: composition, music education, piano/organ, stringed instruments, voice, wind and percussion instruments. Graduate degrees offered: Master of Music in the area of performance; Master of Music Education in the area of music education.

Music Student Profile Fall 1994: 326 total; 123 matriculated undergraduate, 9 matriculated graduate, 194 nondegree; 20% minorities, 50% females, 5% international.

Music Faculty Total: 22; 12 full-time, 10 part-time; 84% of full-time faculty have terminal degrees. Graduate students teach a few undergraduate courses. Undergraduate student–faculty ratio: 13:1.

Student Life Student groups include Delta Omicron, Phi Mu Alpha Sinfonia, International Association of Jazz Educators.

Expenses for 1995–96 State resident tuition: $900 full-time. Nonresident tuition: $6660 full-time, $222 per semester hour part-time. State resident part-time tuition per semester ranges from $100 to $330. Part-time mandatory fees per semester range from $73 to $370. Full-time mandatory fees: $836. College room and board: $3060. College room only: $1576. Special program-related fees: $50–$150 for applied music fee.

Financial Aid Program-specific awards for Fall of 1994: 45–50 Band Scholarships for band students ($300–$1900), 20–25 Choir Scholarships for choir students ($300–$1000), 5–10 Orchestra Scholarships for orchestra students ($700–$2000), 20–30 scholarships for program majors ($300–$1900).

Application Procedures Deadline—freshmen and transfers: continuous. Required: high school transcript, audition. Recommended: interview. Auditions held continuously on campus; recorded music is permissible as a substitute for live auditions when distance is prohibitive and videotaped performances are permissible as a substitute for live auditions when distance is prohibitive.

Undergraduate Contact Dr. Robert Culbertson, Chair, Department of Music and Theatre, Lamar University–Beaumont, P.O. Box 10044, Beaumont, Texas 77710; 409-880-8144, fax: 409-880-2286.

Graduate Contact Dr. Kurt Gilman, Director of Graduate Music, Department of Music and Theatre, Lamar University–Beaumont, P.O. Box 10044, Beaumont, Texas 77710; 409-880-8077, fax: 409-880-2286.

Lambuth University

Jackson, Tennessee

Independent-religious, coed. Urban campus. Total enrollment: 1,209.

Degrees Bachelor of Music in the areas of church music, instrumental music education, vocal music education, performance, piano pedagogy. Majors: classical music, music, music education, piano pedagogy, piano/organ, sacred music, voice, wind and percussion instruments. Cross-registration with Union University, Freed–Hardeman University.

Music Student Profile Fall 1994: 175 total; 25 matriculated undergraduate, 150 nondegree; 14% minorities, 52% females, 5% international.

Music Faculty Total: 6; 3 full-time, 3 part-time; 80% of full-time faculty have terminal degrees. Graduate students do not teach undergraduate courses.

Expenses for 1995–96 Application fee: $10. Comprehensive fee of $9170 includes full-time tuition ($5380), mandatory fees ($220), and college room and board ($3570). Part-time tuition: $185 per credit hour. Part-time tuition per credit hour for students over 25: $130. Special program-related fees: $90–$180 for applied music lesson fee.

Financial Aid Program-specific awards for Fall of 1994: 75–100 Leadership Grants in Music for band/choir majors ($200–$2000), 20–25 Endowed Music Majors Awards for program majors ($250).

Application Procedures Deadline—freshmen and transfers: continuous. Required: high school transcript, minimum 2.0 high school GPA, 2 letters of recommendation.

Lambuth University *(continued)*

Recommended: audition. Auditions held 3 times and by appointment on campus; recorded music is permissible as a substitute for live auditions when distance is prohibitive and videotaped performances are permissible as a substitute for live auditions when distance is prohibitive.

Undergraduate Contact Nancy Callis, Director of Admissions, Admissions Office, Lambuth University, 705 Lambuth Boulevard, Jackson, Tennessee 38301; 901-425-3223, fax: 901-423-1990.

Lamont School of Music

See University of Denver, Lamont School of Music

Lander University

Greenwood, South Carolina

State-supported, coed. Small-town campus. Total enrollment: 2,779.

Degrees Bachelor of Music Education in the areas of instrumental music education, vocal music education. Majors: classical music, guitar, music education, piano/organ, wind and percussion instruments. Cross-registration with University of Plymouth, Trent Polytechnic University.

Music Student Profile Fall 1994: 45 total; all matriculated undergraduate; 16% minorities, 68% females.

Music Faculty Total: 9; 6 full-time, 3 part-time; 80% of full-time faculty have terminal degrees. Graduate students do not teach undergraduate courses. Undergraduate student–faculty ratio: 7:1.

Student Life Student groups include University Pep Band, Music Educators National Conference.

Expenses for 1995–96 Application fee: $25. State resident tuition: $3400 full-time, $136 per semester hour part-time. Nonresident tuition: $5026 full-time, $181 per semester hour part-time. Full-time mandatory fees: $50. College room and board: $3350. College room only: $2200. Special program-related fees: $40 for applied music fee.

Financial Aid Program-specific awards for Fall of 1994: 1 Kerhoulas Award for incoming students ($500), 1 White Award for instrumentalists ($300), 1 Hutto Award for voice majors ($225), 2 Lenti Awards for piano majors ($225).

Application Procedures Deadline—freshmen and transfers: continuous. Required: audition. Auditions held 2–3 times on campus; recorded music is permissible as a substitute for live auditions when distance is prohibitive and videotaped performances are permissible as a substitute for live auditions when distance is prohibitive.

Undergraduate Contact Jackie Roark, Director of Admissions, Lander University, Stanley Avenue, Greenwood, South Carolina 29649; 803-229-8307, fax: 803-229-8890.

The Lawrence Conservatory of Music

Lawrence University

Appleton, Wisconsin

Independent, coed. Small-town campus. Total enrollment: 1,161.

Degrees Bachelor of Music in the areas of music education, music theory–composition, performance. Majors: classical guitar, classical music, harp, harpsichord, jazz, music education, music theory and composition, performance, piano/organ, stringed instruments, voice, wind and percussion instruments.

Music Student Profile Fall 1994: 250 total; all matriculated undergraduate; 5% minorities, 50% females, 5% international.

Music Faculty Total: 31; 25 full-time, 6 part-time; 93% of full-time faculty have terminal degrees. Graduate students do not teach undergraduate courses. Undergraduate student–faculty ratio: 8:1.

Student Life Student groups include Lawrence International, Lawrence Theatre and Film Festival.

Expenses for 1995–96 Application fee: $25. Comprehensive fee of $22,095 includes full-time tuition ($17,937), mandatory fees ($120), and college room and board ($4038).

Financial Aid Program-specific awards for Fall of 1994: 15–25 Performance Awards for top auditions ($2000–$5000), 5–8 Trustee Awards for top auditions ($10,000).

Application Procedures Deadline—freshmen: February 1; transfers: May 15. Notification date—freshmen: April 1; transfers: June 1. Required: essay, high school transcript, college transcript(s) for transfer students, 2 letters of recommendation, audition, SAT I or ACT test scores, interview for music theory applicants. Recommended: minimum 3.0 high school GPA, interview. Auditions held 16 times on campus and off campus in Boston, MA; Denver, CO; Interlochen, MI; Los Angeles, CA; Minneapolis, MN; New York, NY; Portland, OR; San Francisco, CA; St. Louis, MO; Seattle, WA; Washington, DC; recorded music is permissible as a substitute for live auditions when distance is prohibitive and videotaped performances are permissible as a substitute for live auditions when distance is prohibitive.

Undergraduate Contact David Stull, Director of Conservatory Admissions, Lawrence University, P.O. Box 599, Appleton, Wisconsin 54912-0599; fax: 414-832-6782, E-mail address: excel@lawrence.edu.

More about the University

Program facilities Memorial Chapel (concert hall of 1,250 seats); Harper Recital Hall (250 seats); Miller Hall (150 seats/choral rehearsal hall); orchestral rehearsal hall (315 seats); jazz rehearsal studio; percussion studios; recording studio, including 16-track digital system, with compact disk recording, editing, and production capabilities; Macintosh-based computer lab, including MIDI technology in conjunction with Finale, Symphony, and Vivace programs; Cloak Theatre (experimental black box); Stansbury Theatre (proscenium theater of 500 seats); outdoor amphitheater; WLFM campus radio station affiliated with Wisconsin Public Radio; historical instruments such as 41-stop mechanical action organ by John Brombaugh, 1815 Broadway piano, Guarneri violin.

Faculty and Resident Artists 25 full-time faculty members, 6 part-time faculty members; artists-in-residence include faculty chamber ensembles and Dale Duesing ('67), Grammy award-winning lyric baritone; recent visiting artists include Richard Goode, Emanuel Ax, Joshua Bell, The Chamber Music Society of Lincoln Center, Marilyn Horne, Joe Henderson, Wynton Marsalis, and Nadja Salerno-Sonnenberg.

Student Performance Opportunities Major ensembles include Symphony Orchestra, Contemporary Music Ensemble, Wind Ensemble, Percussion Ensemble, Jazz Ensemble, Concert Choir, Opera Theatre, Musical Theatre, Jazz Singers, and numerous chamber ensembles.

Special Programs Twenty-three off-campus programs, both domestic and international; academic advising; residence hall life; counseling center; career center; writing skills lab; seventy campus clubs and organizations; twenty-three varsity sports; fifteen club and intramural sports; and a strong commitment to volunteerism.

The Lawrence Conservatory of Music is a nationally recognized conservatory devoted exclusively to the education of undergraduate musicians within a college of the liberal arts and sciences.

A faculty of performers, composers, scholars, and teachers prides itself on the individual attention given to the 250 music majors and the many college students who participate in the Conservatory's activities.

Music facilities are housed within three contiguous buildings: the Music-Drama Center, the Memorial Chapel, and the Ruth Harwood Shattuck Hall of Music, completed in 1991. The music library, located in the Media Center of the main university library, holds more than 31,000 recordings and scores as well as music reference works.

At Lawrence, music is not isolated from the other disciplines. All music majors complete a core curriculum in the college in addition to their conservatory course work. Conservatory students live in the same residence halls and dine with college students, taking full advantage of the residential nature of the liberal arts institution. While the degree curriculum within the Conservatory is intense and focused in music, it allows students to explore the liberal arts and sciences through an array of courses taught by an accomplished faculty. The study of music at Lawrence occurs within the context of the liberal arts, thereby providing a well-rounded, broad-based understanding of music and its place within society.

Music students choose from five degree programs: the Bachelor of Music degree in performance, the Bachelor of Music degree in music education (instrumental or choral/general), the Bachelor of Music degree in theory-composition, the Bachelor of Arts degree in music, and the double degree. One of the oldest double-degree programs in the country, the Lawrence five-year program permits students to earn a Bachelor of Music degree and a Bachelor of Arts degree in a discipline other than music. The combined degree program provides both professional-level study of music and engagement and a rigorous academic program of study. As a very challenging program, it is one that many students find rewarding. In addition, Lawrence students may design their own majors with the approval of and supervision by faculty and may also pursue a double major within the Bachelor of Music degree. The curriculum in the Conservatory of Music seeks to ensure that all students graduate with a thorough and firm grounding in music theory and analysis, music history and literature, and both solo and ensemble performance.

Such preparation and training has allowed Lawrence's students and ensembles to receive awards such as *Down Beat* magazine's "Outstanding Performance" and "Best Original Jazz Composition" and the National Bandmasters Association top honors. All major ensembles have performed at regional and national music conferences, the result of adjudicated competitions, and have recorded CDs for national distribution. Individual students consistently place as finalists and winners in the Metropolitan Opera auditions; the National Association of Teachers of Singing auditions; and a variety of other district, regional, and national instrumental competitions. Each summer a high percentage of conservatory students continue their studies at festivals such as Eastern, Brevard, Tanglewood, and Aspen.

Lawrence University is committed to the development of intellect and talent, the acquisition of knowledge and understanding, and the cultivation of judgment and values. The University prepares students for lives of service, achievement, leadership, and personal fulfillment. Established in 1847, Lawrence will celebrate its 150th anniversary in 1997 and is now in its second century of awarding the Bachelor of Music degree. Lawrence Conservatory graduates are counted not only among the ranks of professional orchestras and opera companies, Grammy Award winners, university faculty, elementary and high school teachers, college administrators, and composers, but also among authors, medical and law professionals, and public servants.

Lebanon Valley College

Annville, Pennsylvania

Independent-religious, coed. Small-town campus. Total enrollment: 1,754.

Degrees Bachelor of Music in the area of sound recording technology. Majors: sound recording technology.

Music Student Profile Fall 1994: 45 total; all matriculated undergraduate; 12% females, 10% international.

Music Faculty Total: 3; 1 full-time, 2 part-time. Graduate students do not teach undergraduate courses. Undergraduate student–faculty ratio: 15:1.

Student Life Student groups include Audio Engineering Society.

Lebanon Valley College *(continued)*

Expenses for 1995–96 Comprehensive fee of $19,540 includes full-time tuition ($14,785) and college room and board ($4755). Part-time tuition per semester ranges from $195 to $300. Part-time tuition and fees per credit: $295 for daytime classes, $190 for evening classes.

Application Procedures Deadline—freshmen and transfers: June 1. Required: high school transcript, college transcript(s) for transfer students, audition. Recommended: essay, 2 letters of recommendation, interview. Auditions held by appointment on campus; recorded music is permissible as a substitute for live auditions for international applicants and videotaped performances are permissible as a substitute for live auditions for international applicants.

Undergraduate Contact Barry Hill, Director, Sound Recording Technology, Music Department, Lebanon Valley College, Blair Music Center, Annville, Pennsylvania 17003; 717-867-6285.

Lee College

Cleveland, Tennessee

Independent-religious, coed. Small-town campus. Total enrollment: 2,197.

Degrees Bachelor of Music Education in the areas of vocal/general music education, instrumental music education. Majors: guitar, piano/organ, sacred music, stringed instruments, voice, wind and percussion instruments.

Music Student Profile Fall 1994: 172 total; all matriculated undergraduate; 12% minorities, 55% females, 12% international.

Music Faculty Total: 35; 10 full-time, 25 part-time; 40% of full-time faculty have terminal degrees. Graduate students do not teach undergraduate courses. Undergraduate student–faculty ratio: 17:1.

Student Life Student groups include Music Drama Workshop.

Expenses for 1995–96 Application fee: $25. Comprehensive fee of $8782 includes full-time tuition ($5172), mandatory fees ($190), and college room and board ($3420). College room only: $1710. Part-time tuition: $208 per semester hour. Part-time mandatory fees: $20 per semester. Special program-related fees: $150 for practice room rental, lesson fee.

Financial Aid Program-specific awards for Fall of 1994: 20 Endowed Scholarships for program majors ($500).

Application Procedures Deadline—freshmen and transfers: continuous. Required: high school transcript, audition, SAT I or ACT test scores. Auditions held 3 times on campus; recorded music is permissible as a substitute for live auditions when distance is prohibitive and videotaped performances are permissible as a substitute for live auditions when distance is prohibitive.

Undergraduate Contact Mary Beth Wickes, Administrative Assistant, Music Department, Lee College, P.O. Box 3450, Cleveland, Tennessee 37320-3450; 615-478-7384, fax: 615-478-7075.

Lenoir-Rhyne College

Hickory, North Carolina

Independent-religious, coed. Small-town campus. Total enrollment: 1,418.

Degrees Bachelor of Music Education in the areas of vocal music education, choral music education, keyboard music education, instrumental music education. Majors: piano/organ, voice, wind and percussion instruments.

Music Faculty Total: 8; 5 full-time, 3 part-time.

Expenses for 1995–96 Application fee: $25. Comprehensive fee of $14,886 includes full-time tuition ($10,450), mandatory fees ($436), and college room and board ($4000). Part-time tuition: $165 per credit.

Application Procedures Deadline—freshmen and transfers: continuous. Required: high school transcript, SAT I or ACT test scores, minimum 2.5 high school GPA. Recommended: essay, 2 letters of recommendation, interview. Auditions held 4 times and by appointment on campus and off campus in various locations in North Carolina and Florida; recorded music is permissible as a substitute for live auditions if distance is prohibitive or scheduling is difficult.

Undergraduate Contact Ray McNeely, Chairman, Music Department, Lenoir-Rhyne College, Box 7355, Hickory, North Carolina 28603; 704-328-1741 ext. 7151.

Liberty University

Lynchburg, Virginia

Independent-religious, coed. Suburban campus. Total enrollment: 4,879.

Degrees Bachelor of Music in the areas of choral music, instrumental music, instrumental music education, choral music education. Majors: music, music education, piano/organ, voice, wind and percussion instruments.

Music Student Profile Fall 1994: 120 total; all matriculated undergraduate.

Music Faculty Total: 18; 12 full-time, 6 part-time; 55% of full-time faculty have terminal degrees. Graduate students do not teach undergraduate courses. Undergraduate student–faculty ratio: 20:1.

Student Life Student groups include Music Educators National Conference, American Choral Directors Association.

Expenses for 1995–96 Application fee: $35. Comprehensive fee of $12,150 includes full-time tuition ($6450), mandatory fees ($900), and college room and board

($4800). Part-time tuition: $215 per semester hour. Part-time mandatory fees: $30 per semester hour. Special program-related fees: $15 for practice room rental.

Financial Aid Program-specific awards for Fall of 1994: Fine Arts Scholarships for program majors ($500–$1000).

Application Procedures Deadline—freshmen and transfers: August 1. Required: high school transcript, 3 letters of recommendation, audition. Recommended: interview. Auditions held 4 times on campus; recorded music is permissible as a substitute for live auditions and videotaped performances are permissible as a substitute for live auditions.

Undergraduate Contact Raymond S. Locy, Chairman, Fine Arts Department, Liberty University, Box 20000, Lynchburg, Virginia 24506; 804-582-2318.

Lincoln University

Jefferson City, Missouri

State-supported, coed. Small-town campus. Total enrollment: 3,512.

Degrees Bachelor of Music Education in the areas of instrumental music, vocal music, piano. Majors: instrumental music, music education, voice.

Music Student Profile Fall 1994: 42 total.

Music Faculty Total: 10; 6 full-time, 4 part-time; 50% of full-time faculty have terminal degrees.

Student Life Student groups include Music Educators National Conference, Kappa Kappa Psi.

Expenses for 1995–96 Application fee: $17. State resident tuition: $2016 full-time, $84 per credit hour part-time. Nonresident tuition: $4032 full-time, $168 per credit hour part-time. College room and board per year: $2728 for women, $2676 for men. College room only: $1030.

Application Procedures Deadline—freshmen and transfers: July 15. Required: high school transcript, college transcript(s) for transfer students, audition, ACT test score only, theory test, performance on piano. Auditions held on campus and off campus. Portfolio reviews held on campus and off campus.

Undergraduate Contact Office of Admissions, Lincoln University, 820 Chestnut Street, Jefferson City, Missouri 65102-0029; 314-681-5599, fax: 314-681-5566.

Lionel Hampton School of Music

See University of Idaho, Lionel Hampton School of Music

Lock Haven University of Pennsylvania

Lock Haven, Pennsylvania

State-supported, coed. Small-town campus. Total enrollment: 3,687.

Degrees Bachelor of Fine Arts in the area of music. Majors: music, stringed instruments, wind and percussion instruments.

Expenses for 1994–95 Application fee: $25. State resident tuition: $3086 full-time, $129 per semester hour part-time. Nonresident tuition: $7844 full-time, $327 per semester hour part-time. Full-time mandatory fees: $576. College room and board: $3716.

Application Procedures Deadline—freshmen and transfers: continuous. Required: high school transcript, college transcript(s) for transfer students, audition, SAT I or ACT test scores. Recommended: minimum 3.0 high school GPA, standing in top 40% of graduating class. Auditions held at student's convenience on campus.

Undergraduate Contact Dr. Glenn Hosterman, Chairman, Music Department, Lock Haven University of Pennsylvania, 233 Sloan Fine Arts Center, Lock Haven, Pennsylvania 17745; 717-893-2127.

Longwood College

Farmville, Virginia

State-supported, coed. Small-town campus. Total enrollment: 3,277.

Degrees Bachelor of Music in the areas of choral music, instrumental music, music education. Majors: composition, harpsichord, jazz, music education, piano/organ, stringed instruments, voice, wind and percussion instruments.

Music Student Profile Fall 1994: 35 total; all matriculated undergraduate.

Music Faculty Total: 13; 8 full-time, 5 part-time.

Expenses for 1995–96 Application fee: $25. State resident tuition: $2684 full-time, $112 per credit hour part-time. Nonresident tuition: $8156 full-time, $340 per credit hour part-time. Part-time mandatory fees: $25 per credit hour. Full-time mandatory fees: $1686. College room and board: $3934. College room only: $2352.

Application Procedures Deadline—freshmen and transfers: May 1. Required: essay, high school transcript, audition, SAT I or ACT test scores. Recommended: letter of recommendation. Auditions held 6 times on campus; recorded music is permissible as a substitute for live auditions for out-of-state applicants.

Undergraduate Contact Dr. Donald Trott, Chair, Music Department, Longwood College, 201 High Street, Wygal Building, Farmville, Virginia 23909; 804-395-2504.

Louisiana College

Pineville, Louisiana

Independent-religious, coed. Small-town campus. Total enrollment: 1,013.

Louisiana College *(continued)*

Degrees Bachelor of Music in the areas of voice, piano, organ, church music, piano pedagogy, music education, performance. Majors: classical music, music, music education, opera, piano/organ, sacred music, voice, wind and percussion instruments.

Music Student Profile Fall 1994: 40 total; all matriculated undergraduate.

Music Faculty Total: 12; 6 full-time, 6 part-time; 90% of full-time faculty have terminal degrees. Graduate students do not teach undergraduate courses. Undergraduate student–faculty ratio: 7:1.

Student Life Student groups include Music Educators National Conference, Phi Mu Alpha Sinfonia.

Expenses for 1995–96 Comprehensive fee of $9142 includes full-time tuition ($5664), mandatory fees ($454), and college room and board ($3024). Part-time tuition: $177 per semester hour. Part-time mandatory fees per semester range from $18.50 to $161. Special program-related fees: $85 for applied music fee, $40 for accompanying fee, $15 for materials fee.

Financial Aid Program-specific awards for Fall of 1994: 10 Music Scholarships for freshmen ($1000), 2 Piano Majors Scholarships for freshmen ($2000).

Application Procedures Deadline—freshmen: March 1; transfers: continuous. Notification date—freshmen and transfers: continuous. Required: essay, high school transcript, minimum 2.0 high school GPA, 2 letters of recommendation, interview, audition. Auditions held 2 times on campus; recorded music is permissible as a substitute for live auditions when distance is prohibitive and videotaped performances are permissible as a substitute for live auditions when distance is prohibitive.

Undergraduate Contact Admissions, Louisiana College, Pineville, Louisiana 71359; 318-487-7259, fax: 318-487-7191.

Louisiana State University and Agricultural and Mechanical College

Baton Rouge, Louisiana

State-supported, coed. Urban campus. Total enrollment: 25,317.

Degrees Bachelor of Music in the areas of performance, composition; Bachelor of Music Education in the areas of instrumental music education, vocal music education. Majors: composition, harp, piano/organ, stringed instruments, voice, wind and percussion instruments. Graduate degrees offered: Master of Music in the areas of performance, theory, musicology, music education, piano pedagogy, conducting. Doctor of Musical Arts in the areas of performance, composition. Cross-registration with Southern University and Agricultural and Mechanical College.

Music Student Profile Fall 1994: 430 total; 280 matriculated undergraduate, 145 matriculated graduate, 5 nondegree.

Music Faculty Total: 51; 48 full-time, 3 part-time. Graduate students teach a few undergraduate courses. Undergraduate student–faculty ratio: 10:1.

Student Life Student groups include music fraternities and sororities.

Expenses for 1995–96 Application fee: $25. State resident tuition: $2648 full-time. Nonresident tuition: $5948 full-time. Part-time tuition per semester ranges from $285 to $860 for state residents, $435 to $2215 for nonresidents. College room and board: $3310. College room only: $1500 (minimum). Special program-related fees: $75 for senior recital fee.

Financial Aid Program-specific awards for Fall of 1994: School of Music Scholarships for talented students ($600–$6000).

Application Procedures Deadline—freshmen and transfers: June 1. Required: high school transcript, college transcript(s) for transfer students, audition, SAT I or ACT test scores, minimum 2.3 high school GPA. Recommended: 2 letters of recommendation. Auditions held 3 times and by appointment on campus; recorded music is permissible as a substitute for live auditions and videotaped performances are permissible as a substitute for live auditions.

Undergraduate Contact Dr. William Grimes, Assistant Dean, School of Music, Louisiana State University and Agricultural and Mechanical College, 102 School of Music, Baton Rouge, Louisiana 70803; 504-388-3261, fax: 504-388-2562, E-mail address: mugrim@lsuvm.sncc.lsu.edu.

Graduate Contact Kathleen Rountree, Associate Dean, School of Music, Louisiana State University and Agricultural and Mechanical College, 102 School of Music, Baton Rouge, Louisiana 70803; 504-388-3261, fax: 504-388-2562, E-mail address: muroun@lsuvm.sncc.lsu.edu.

Louisiana Tech University

Ruston, Louisiana

State-supported, coed. Small-town campus. Total enrollment: 10,023.

Degrees Bachelor of Fine Arts in the areas of voice, keyboard, instruments of symphony orchestra or band. Majors: instrumental music, keyboard, voice.

Expenses for 1994–95 Application fee: $20. State resident tuition: $2262 full-time. Nonresident tuition: $3957 full-time. Part-time tuition per quarter ranges from $218 to $634 for state residents, $218 to $1124 for nonresidents. College room and board: $2325. College room only: $1245.

Application Procedures Auditions held on campus and off campus. Portfolio reviews held on campus and off campus.

Undergraduate Contact Admissions Office, Louisiana Tech University, P.O. Box 3178 Tech Station, Ruston, Louisiana 71272; 318-257-0211.

Loyola University, New Orleans

New Orleans, Louisiana

Independent-religious, coed. Urban campus. Total enrollment: 5,634.

Degrees Bachelor of Music in the areas of performance, piano pedagogy, jazz studies; Bachelor of Music Education in the area of music education; Bachelor of Music Therapy in the area of music therapy. Majors: classical music, jazz, music education, music therapy, piano/organ, stringed instruments, voice, wind and percussion instruments. Graduate degrees offered: Master of Music in the areas of performance, piano pedagogy; Master of Music Education in the area of music education; Master of Music Therapy in the area of music therapy. Cross-registration with Xavier University of Louisiana.

Music Student Profile Fall 1994: 262 total; 237 matriculated undergraduate, 20 matriculated graduate, 5 nondegree; 15% minorities, 55% females, 2% international.

Music Faculty Total: 39; 21 full-time, 18 part-time; 55% of full-time faculty have terminal degrees. Graduate students do not teach undergraduate courses. Undergraduate student–faculty ratio: 6:1.

Student Life Student groups include Loyola Association of Music Therapy Students, Music Educators National Conference Student Chapter, Loyola University Community Action Program.

Expenses for 1995–96 Comprehensive fee of $17,316 includes full-time tuition ($11,766), mandatory fees ($250), and college room and board ($5300). Part-time mandatory fees: $126.50 per year. Part-time tuition per credit hour: $390 for daytime classes, $180 for evening classes.

Financial Aid Program-specific awards for Fall of 1994: 30 Music Scholarships for music majors ($4500).

Application Procedures Deadline—freshmen and transfers: continuous. Required: essay, high school transcript, college transcript(s) for transfer students, letter of recommendation, audition, SAT I or ACT test scores, minimum combined SAT I score of 810, minimum composite ACT score of 21, minimum 2.25 high school GPA. Auditions held 3 times and by appointment on campus and off campus in Las Vegas, NV; Fairfield, CT; Chicago, IL; recorded music is permissible as a substitute for live auditions when distance is prohibitive and videotaped performances are permissible as a substitute for live auditions when distance is prohibitive. Portfolio reviews held 3 times on campus.

Contact Dr. Anthony Decuir, Associate Dean, College of Music, Loyola University, New Orleans, 6363 Saint Charles Avenue, New Orleans, Louisiana 70118; 504-865-3037.

Manhattan School of Music

New York, New York

Independent, coed. Urban campus. Total enrollment: 921.

Degrees Bachelor of Music in the areas of classical performance, classical composition, jazz/commercial music. Majors: classical music, jazz, piano/organ, stringed instruments, voice, wind and percussion instruments. Graduate degrees offered: Master of Music in the areas of classical performance, classical composition, jazz/commercial music. Doctor of Musical Arts in the areas of classical performance, classical composition. Cross-registration with Barnard College.

Music Student Profile Fall 1994: 881 total; 408 matriculated undergraduate, 467 matriculated graduate, 6 nondegree; 19% minorities, 55% females, 41% international.

Music Faculty Total: 250; 20 full-time, 230 part-time; 30% of full-time faculty have terminal degrees. Graduate students teach a few undergraduate courses. Undergraduate student–faculty ratio: 11:1.

Student Life Special housing available for music students.

Expenses for 1995–96 Application fee: $85. Tuition: $14,200 full-time. Full-time mandatory fees: $680. College room only: $4160 (minimum).

Financial Aid Program-specific awards for Fall of 1994: 300 Scholarships ($6000).

Application Procedures Deadline—freshmen and transfers: April 1. Notification date—freshmen and transfers: July 1. Required: essay, high school transcript, college transcript(s) for transfer students, minimum 2.0 high school GPA, audition. Recommended: minimum 3.0 high school GPA, letter of recommendation, interview, SAT I or ACT test scores. Auditions held 2 times on campus; recorded music is permissible as a substitute for live auditions for international applicants and videotaped performances are permissible as a substitute for live auditions for international applicants.

Contact Carolyn Disnew, Director of Admission, Office of Admission and Financial Aid, Manhattan School of Music, 120 Claremont Avenue, New York, New York 10027-4698; 212-749-2802, fax: 212-749-5471.

More about the School

Program Facilities Borden Auditorium (1,000 seats), Hubbard Hall (300 seats), Pforzheimer Hall (75 seats), Myers Hall and recording Studio (35 seats); library with 21,000 recordings, 61,000 volumes, 125 periodical subscriptions; two electronic music studios.

Faculty, Resident artists, and Alumni Faculty are members of the New York Philharmonic, Metropolitan Opera and Orchestra, New York City Opera, chamber Music Society of Lincoln Center, and Orpheus Chamber Orchestra, as well as concert, chamber, jazz, and recording artists. Artists-in-residence: American String Quartet, New York Wind Soloists, New Music Consort. 1994–95 master classes: Manuel Barrueco, classical guitar; Yefim Bronfman, piano; Michel Debost, flute; Eduardo Fernandez, classical guitar; Leon Fleisher, piano; Milton Hinton, jazz bassist; Eugene Istomin, piano; Byron Janis, piano; Martin Katz, voice and accompanying; Christopher Lamb, percussion; Stanley Leonard, percussion; Michael Lorimer, classical guitar; "Marimolin", percussion; Wynton Marsalis, visiting guest artist; John O'Connor, piano; Duncan Patton, timpani; Herman Prey, baritone; Paul Robison, flute; Sylvia Rosenberg, violin; David Russell, classical guitar; Karl Ulrich Schnabel, piano;

Manhattan School of Music *(continued)*

Arnold Steinhardt, violin; David Tanenbaum, classical guitar; David Taylor, trombone; André Watts, piano.

Student Performance Opportunities Classical ensembles: Symphony; Philharmonica; Chamber Sinfonia; Chamber Winds; Opera Theater; Handel Project (opera); American Musical Theater Ensemble; Contemporary Ensemble; Baroque Aria Ensemble; Percussion Ensemble: Brass Ensemble; Guitar Ensemble; Early Music Ensemble; numerous chamber ensembles. Jazz/commercial music ensembles: Jazz Orchestra; Big Bands II & III; Jazz Choir; numerous jazz combos.

Special Programs The Office of Career Planning offers students gig information throughout the metro area, information about summer festivals, competitions and graduate schools, and one-on-one counseling regarding career preparation and marketing.

Since 1917 Manhattan School of Music has prepared gifted young musicians to assume their place on the world's stages.

In selecting MSM, students choose to work with faculty who are themselves performers with international reputations. They choose to be with students from around the world who come together to create an environment remarkable not just for its intensity but for genuine friendliness and cooperation. And, of course, they choose New York itself, a major center of music and art in America.

While many fine music conservatories are acknowledged for their ability to develop talents and skills, MSM has a particular combination of strengths that make it an excellent place from which to launch a career.

With extensive performance opportunities on campus as well as the chance to freelance and begin to develop a network of professional contacts, students undergo remarkable changes here: they start to function as professional musicians while they are still in school. It is this powerful convergence of opportunity and training that gives students the chance to go as far as their talent, intelligence, and courage can take them.

Alumni are the School's best examples of this training. Here are just a few of MSM alumni from 1970 to the present: Laura Albeck, Metropolitan Opera Orchestra; Robert Anderson, Minnesota Orchestra; Gerald Appleman, New York Philharmonic; Karen Beardsley, soprano, New York City Opera; Elizabeth Burkhardt, Atlanta Symphony; John Carabella, New York Philharmonic; Todd Coolman, jazz bassist; Harry Connick Jr., singer; Alison Dalton, Chicago Symphony; Jacqui Danilow, Metropolitan Opera Orchestra; Garry Dial, jazz pianist; James Dooley, San José Symphony; Desiree Elsevier, Metropolitan Opera Orchestra; Mary Ewing, New York Philharmonic; Lauren Flannigan, soprano, Metropolitan Opera; Susan Graham, mezzo-soprano, Metropolitan Opera; Andrea Gruber, soprano, Metropolitan Opera; Laura Hamilton, Metropolitan Opera Orchestra; Herbie Hancock, jazz pianist; Louella Hasbun, San José Symphony; Douglas Hedwig, Metropolitan Opera Orchestra; Donald Hilsberg, Denver Chamber Orchestra; Frank Hosticka, Metropolitan Opera Orchestra; Simon James, Seattle Symphony; Richard Jensen, Cincinnati Symphony; Henry Kao, New Jersey Symphony; Gilad Karni, New York Philharmonic; Motti Kaston, baritone; Kemal Khan, Assistant Conductor, Metropolitan Opera; Christopher Komer, New Jersey Symphony; Dawn Kotoski, soprano, Metropolitan Opera; Morris Lang, New York Philharmonic; Michael Leonhart, Grammy Award winner; Roy Lewis, Manhattan String Quartet; Douglas Lindsay, Cincinnati Symphony; George Manahan, Music Director, Minnesota Opera; Marvis Martin, soprano, Metropolitan Opera; Kerri McDermott, New York Philharmonic; Peter McGinnis, jazz trombonist; Sharon Meekins, Metropolitan Opera Orchestra; Warren Mok, tenor, Berlin Opera; Frank Morelli, Orpheus Chamber Orchestra; June Morganstern, Chicago Lyric Opera Orchestra; Elmar Oliveira, concert violinist; Susan Quittmeyer, mezzo-soprano, Metropolitan Opera; Mary Kay Robinson, New Jersey Symphony; Bruce Smith, Detroit Symphony; Dawn Stahler, Dallas Symphony; James Stubbs, Metropolitan Opera Orchestra; Stewart Taylor, Israel Philharmonic; Dawn Upshaw, soprano, Metropolitan Opera; Roland Vasquez, jazz drummer; Rosa Vento, soprano, Vienna State Opera; Bing Wang, Los Angeles Philharmonic; Mark Wells, Canadian Opera Orchestra; Virginia Chen Wells, Toronto Symphony; Thomas Wetzel, Milwaukee Symphony; Timothy Wilson, San Francisco Opera Orchestra; Carol Wincenc, concert flutist; Hai Xim Wu, Detroit Symphony; Naomi Youngstein, New Jersey Symphony; and Dolara Zajick, mezzo-soprano, Metropolitan Opera.

Manhattanville College

Purchase, New York

Independent, coed. Suburban campus. Total enrollment: 909.

Degrees Bachelor of Music in the area of music education. Majors: music, music education, music management. Cross-registration with Purchase College, State University of New York.

Music Student Profile Fall 1994: 50 total; all matriculated undergraduate.

Music Faculty Total: 20; 3 full-time, 17 part-time; 100% of full-time faculty have terminal degrees. Graduate students do not teach undergraduate courses. Undergraduate student–faculty ratio: 10:1.

Student Life Student groups include Music Educators National Conference, Music Teachers National Association.

Expenses for 1995–96 Application fee: $35. Comprehensive fee of $23,370 includes full-time tuition ($15,500), mandatory fees ($500), and college room and board ($7370). Part-time tuition: $345 per credit. Special program-related fees: $150–$295 for applied music lesson fee, $35 for practice room rental.

Financial Aid Program-specific awards for Fall of 1994: Departmental Awards ($2000–$5000).

Application Procedures Deadline—freshmen and transfers: continuous. Required: essay, high school transcript, college transcript(s) for transfer students, minimum 2.0 high school GPA, letter of recommendation, audition, SAT I or ACT test scores, high school transcript for transfer applicants with fewer than 45 credits. Recommended: minimum 3.0 high school GPA, interview. Auditions held 6 times on campus; recorded music is permissible as a substitute for live auditions for international applicants and in special circumstances and videotaped performances are permissible as a substitute for live auditions for international applicants and in special circumstances.

Undergraduate Contact Robin Beth Askins, Admissions Counselor, Manhattanville College, 2900 Purchase Street, Purchase, New York 10577; 800-328-4553.

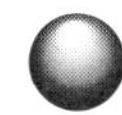

Mankato State University

Mankato, Minnesota

State-supported, coed. Small-town campus. Total enrollment: 12,624.

Degrees Bachelor of Music in the areas of voice, piano, winds, strings, percussion, organ. Majors: classical music, music, music education, piano/organ, stringed instruments, voice, wind and percussion instruments. Graduate degrees offered: Master of Music in the areas of performance, music education.

Music Student Profile Fall 1994: 110 total; 90 matriculated undergraduate, 10 matriculated graduate, 10 nondegree; 8% minorities, 30% females, 4% international.

Music Faculty Total: 20; 12 full-time, 8 part-time; 65% of full-time faculty have terminal degrees. Graduate students teach a few undergraduate courses. Undergraduate student–faculty ratio: 15:1.

Student Life Student groups include Music Educators National Conference, American Choral Directors Association, Pi Kappa Lambda.

Estimated Expenses for 1995–96 Application fee: $15. State resident tuition: $2355 full-time, $58.45 per quarter hour part-time. Nonresident tuition: $4893 full-time, $115.90 per quarter hour part-time. Full-time mandatory fees: $340. College room and board: $2905. Special program-related fees: $10–$30 for instrument rental.

Financial Aid Program-specific awards for Fall of 1994: 1 Stewart Ross Band Scholarship ($600), 1 Nancy Cora Williams Scholarship ($500), 1 Hickory Tech Award for music majors ($1000), 1 President's Scholarship for program majors ($1000), 1 Van Sickle Endowment for string majors ($600), 1 Een Endowment for program majors ($470), 16 Talent Grants ($9600), 7 Stein Scholarships ($2400), 7 Music Foundation Awards ($3190), 4 Mankato Symphony Awards ($5000).

Application Procedures Deadline—freshmen and transfers: August 1. Required: high school transcript, minimum 2.0 high school GPA, 3 letters of recommendation, interview, audition. Recommended: minimum 3.0 high school GPA. Auditions held as needed on campus; recorded music is permissible as a substitute for live auditions when distance is prohibitive and videotaped performances are permissible as a substitute for live auditions when distance is prohibitive.

Undergraduate Contact Dr. John Lindberg, Undergraduate Coordinator, Music Department, Mankato State University, Box 5, Mankato, Minnesota 56002-8400; 507-389-1523, fax: 507-389-2922, E-mail address: bassoon@vax1.mankato.msus.edu.

Graduate Contact Dr. Stewart Ross, Director of Band, Music Department, Mankato State University, Box 5, Mankato, Minnesota 56002-8400; 507-389-5800, fax: 507-389-2922, E-mail address: stewart_ross@ms1.mankato.msu.edu.

Mannes College of Music

See New School for Social Research, Mannes College of Music

Mansfield University of Pennsylvania

Mansfield, Pennsylvania

State-supported, coed. Small-town campus. Total enrollment: 2,992.

Degrees Bachelor of Music in the areas of music education, music therapy, performance, elective studies in business. Majors: music, music education, piano/organ, stringed instruments, voice, wind and percussion instruments. Graduate degrees offered: Master of Music in the area of music education.

Music Student Profile Fall 1994: 180 total; 160 matriculated undergraduate, 20 matriculated graduate; 1% minorities, 60% females, 1% international.

Music Faculty Total: 22; 17 full-time, 5 part-time; 60% of full-time faculty have terminal degrees. Graduate students do not teach undergraduate courses. Undergraduate student–faculty ratio: 8:1.

Student Life Student groups include Music Educators National Conference Student Chapter, Mid-Atlantic Regional Association of Music Therapy Students, Music Entertainment and Industry Education Association.

Expenses for 1994–95 Application fee: $25. State resident tuition: $3086 full-time, $129 per credit part-time. Nonresident tuition: $7844 full-time, $327 per credit part-time. Full-time mandatory fees: $538. College room and board: $3324. College room only: $1872.

Financial Aid Program-specific awards for Fall of 1994: 5 Kreuscher Awards for freshmen program majors ($1000), 1 Darrin-Dye Award for freshmen program majors ($1000), 1 GSA Award for program majors ($1000), 1 Doud Award for freshmen program majors ($5000).

Application Procedures Deadline—freshmen and transfers: continuous. Required: high school transcript, college transcript(s) for transfer students, minimum 2.0 high school GPA, interview, audition, SAT I or ACT test scores. Auditions held 8 times on campus; recorded music is permissible as a substitute for live auditions when distance is prohibitive.

Contact Chairperson, Music Department, Mansfield University of Pennsylvania, Butler Center 110, Mansfield, Pennsylvania 16933; 717-662-4710, fax: 717-662-4114.

Margaret E. Petree School of Music and Performing Arts

See Oklahoma City University, Margaret E. Petree School of Music and Performing Arts

Mars Hill College

Mars Hill, North Carolina

Independent-religious, coed. Small-town campus. Total enrollment: 1,056.

Degrees Bachelor of Music in the areas of music education, performance; Bachelor of Fine Arts in the area of music. Majors: music education, piano/organ, voice, wind and percussion instruments.

Music Student Profile Fall 1994: 62 total; all matriculated undergraduate; 5% minorities, 55% females.

Music Faculty Total: 19; 10 full-time, 9 part-time; 25% of full-time faculty have terminal degrees. Graduate students do not teach undergraduate courses. Undergraduate student–faculty ratio: 8:1.

Student Life Student groups include Music Educators National Conference Student Chapter, American Choral Directors Association Student Chapter, music societies.

Expenses for 1995–96 Application fee: $15. Comprehensive fee of $12,050 includes full-time tuition ($7850), mandatory fees ($550), and college room and board ($3650). College room only: $1650. Part-time tuition: $250 per credit. Special program-related fees: $100 for private instruction.

Financial Aid Program-specific awards for Fall of 1994: 1 Theodore Presser Award for upperclassmen ($2250), 2 Corbett Awards for undergraduates/upper classmen ($1000), 1 Alexander Award for undergraduates ($1000), 1 Cornwell Award for undergraduates ($1000), 2 Gentile Awards for percussion majors ($500).

Application Procedures Deadline—freshmen and transfers: continuous. Notification date—freshmen and transfers: continuous. Required: essay, high school transcript, college transcript(s) for transfer students, minimum 2.0 high school GPA, 3 letters of recommendation, audition, SAT I or ACT test scores. Recommended: interview. Auditions held 4 times on campus and off campus; recorded music is permissible as a substitute for live auditions when distance is prohibitive and videotaped performances are permissible as a substitute for live auditions when distance is prohibitive. Portfolio reviews held 1 time off campus.

Undergraduate Contact Rick Hinshaw, Dean of Admissions, Mars Hill College, Mars Hill, North Carolina 28754; 704-689-1201, fax: 704-689-1474.

Marshall University

Huntington, West Virginia

State-supported, coed. Urban campus. Total enrollment: 12,659.

Degrees Bachelor of Fine Arts in the area of music. Majors: music history and literature, music theory and composition, piano/organ, stringed instruments, voice, wind and percussion instruments.

Music Student Profile Fall 1994: 148 total; 130 matriculated undergraduate, 18 nondegree; 3% minorities, 48% females, 1% international.

Music Faculty Total: 24; 21 full-time, 3 part-time; 75% of full-time faculty have terminal degrees. Graduate students teach a few undergraduate courses. Undergraduate student–faculty ratio: 11:1.

Student Life Student groups include Kappa Kappa Psi, Music Educators National Conference Student Chapter.

Expenses for 1995–96 Application fee: $10. State resident tuition: $2050 full-time, $85.75 per semester hour part-time. Nonresident tuition: $5696 full-time, $237.50 per semester hour part-time. Tuition for Kentucky residents. College room and board: $4050.

Financial Aid Program-specific awards for Fall of 1994: 32 Tuition Waivers for program majors ($520–$5146), 6 Endowed Scholarships for program majors ($400–$600), 5 Marching Band Tuition Awards for marching band members ($520–$5146), 25 Marching Band Awards for marching band members ($200).

Application Procedures Deadline—freshmen and transfers: continuous. Notification date—freshmen and transfers: continuous. Required: high school transcript, minimum 2.0 high school GPA, audition. Recommended: letter of recommendation, interview. Auditions held 7 times on campus; recorded music is permissible as a substitute for live auditions with approval from the department and videotaped performances are permissible as a substitute for live auditions if a campus visit is impossible.

Undergraduate Contact Donald A. Williams, Chairman, Music Department, Marshall University, 400 Hal Greer Boulevard, Huntington, West Virginia 25755; 304-696-3117, fax: 304-696-3333, E-mail address: dfa004@marshall.wvnet.edu.

Marygrove College

Detroit, Michigan

Independent-religious, coed. Urban campus. Total enrollment: 1,218.

Degrees Bachelor of Music. Majors: music education, music theory, performance, piano pedagogy, sacred music.

Expenses for 1995–96 Comprehensive fee of $12,876 includes full-time tuition ($8496), mandatory fees ($220), and college room and board ($4160). Part-time tuition: $307 per credit hour. Part-time mandatory fees per semester range from $59 to $99.

Undergraduate Contact Elaine Grover, Head, Music Department, Marygrove College, 8425 West McNichols Road, Detroit, Michigan 48221; 313-862-8000 ext. 354.

Marylhurst College

Marylhurst, Oregon

Independent-religious, coed. Suburban campus. Total enrollment: 1,183.

Degrees Bachelor of Music. Majors: composition, performance art, sacred music.

Expenses for 1994–95 Application fee: $73. Tuition: $8505 full-time, $189 per quarter hour part-time. Part-time mandatory fees: $14 per quarter. Full-time mandatory fees: $42.

Application Procedures Auditions held on campus and off campus. Portfolio reviews held on campus and off campus.

Undergraduate Contact Department of Music, Marylhurst College, Marylhurst, Oregon 97036; 503-636-8141 ext. 362.

Maryville College

Maryville, Tennessee

Independent-religious, coed. Small-town campus. Total enrollment: 843.

Degrees Bachelor of Music in the areas of vocal music education, instrumental music education, piano performance, vocal performance. Majors: music education, piano/organ, voice.

Music Student Profile Fall 1994: 26 total; all matriculated undergraduate; 19% minorities, 65% females, 12% international.

Music Faculty Total: 11; 3 full-time, 8 part-time; 100% of full-time faculty have terminal degrees. Graduate students do not teach undergraduate courses.

Student Life Student groups include Delta Omicron.

Expenses for 1995–96 Application fee: $25. Comprehensive fee of $16,626 includes full-time tuition ($12,098), mandatory fees ($150), and college room and board ($4378). College room only: $2058. Part-time tuition: $504 per semester hour. Special program-related fees: $160–$340 for applied music lesson fees.

Financial Aid Program-specific awards for Fall of 1994: 20–35 Music Performance Scholarships for program majors ($4000).

Application Procedures Deadline—freshmen and transfers: continuous. Required: essay, high school transcript, college transcript(s) for transfer students, minimum 2.0 high school GPA, letter of recommendation, audition, SAT I or ACT test scores. Auditions held on a case-by-case basis on campus; recorded music is permissible as a substitute for live auditions if a campus visit is impossible and videotaped performances are permissible as a substitute for live auditions if a campus visit is impossible.

Undergraduate Contact Donna Davis, Vice President of Admissions and Enrollment, Maryville College, Anderson 210, 502 East Lamar Alexander Parkway, Maryville, Tennessee 37804-5907; 615-981-8111, fax: 615-983-0581.

Marywood College

Scranton, Pennsylvania

Independent-religious, coed. Suburban campus. Total enrollment: 3,068.

Degrees Bachelor of Music in the areas of performance, music therapy, church music, music education. Majors: music education, music therapy, performance, sacred music.

Music Student Profile Fall 1994: 110 total; 60 matriculated undergraduate, 50 nondegree; 1% international.

Music Faculty Total: 16; 8 full-time, 8 part-time; 100% of full-time faculty have terminal degrees. Graduate students do not teach undergraduate courses. Undergraduate student–faculty ratio: 9:1.

Student Life Student groups include Music Educators National Conference Student Chapter, National Association of Music Therapy Student Chapter, American Choral Association.

Expenses for 1995–96 Application fee: $20. Comprehensive fee of $17,040 includes full-time tuition ($11,840), mandatory fees ($400), and college room and board ($4800). Part-time tuition: $370 per credit. Special program-related fees: $100–$350 for applied music lesson fees and practice room rental.

Financial Aid Program-specific awards for Fall of 1994 available.

Application Procedures Deadline—freshmen and transfers: continuous. Required: high school transcript, letter of recommendation, interview, audition. Recommended: minimum 2.5 high school GPA. Auditions held continuously on campus; recorded music is permissible as a substitute for live auditions when distance is prohibitive and videotaped performances are permissible as a substitute for live auditions when distance is prohibitive.

Undergraduate Contact Joan Paskert, IHM, Chairperson, Music Department, Marywood College, Adams Avenue, Scranton, Pennsylvania 18509; 717-348-6268, fax: 717-348-1817.

Mason Gross School of the Arts

See Rutgers, The State University of New Jersey, Mason Gross School of the Arts

McNeese State University

Lake Charles, Louisiana

State-supported, coed. Small-town campus. Total enrollment: 8,729.

McNeese State University *(continued)*

Degrees Bachelor of Music in the area of performance; Bachelor of Music Education in the areas of vocal school music, instrumental school music. Majors: jazz, music education, piano/organ, stringed instruments, voice, wind and percussion instruments. Graduate degrees offered: Master of Music Education in the areas of vocal school music, instrumental school music.

Music Student Profile Fall 1994: 100 total; 97 matriculated undergraduate, 2 matriculated graduate, 1 nondegree.

Music Faculty Total: 23; 19 full-time, 4 part-time; 37% of full-time faculty have terminal degrees. Graduate students teach a few undergraduate courses. Undergraduate student–faculty ratio: 7:1.

Student Life Student groups include music sorority and fraternity, Phi Mu Alpha Sinfonia, Music Educators National Conference.

Expenses for 1995–96 Application fee: $10. State resident tuition: $1966 full-time. Nonresident tuition: $5166 full-time. Part-time tuition per semester ranges from $302.50 to $778.50 for state residents, $302.50 to $2380 for nonresidents. College room and board: $2864.

Financial Aid Program-specific awards for Fall of 1994 available.

Application Procedures Deadline—freshmen and transfers: continuous. Required: high school transcript, college transcript(s) for transfer students, audition, SAT I or ACT test scores. Auditions held continuously on campus and off campus in selected locations; recorded music is permissible as a substitute for live auditions and videotaped performances are permissible as a substitute for live auditions. Portfolio reviews held on campus and off campus.

Undergraduate Contact Michele Martin, Head, Department of Music, McNeese State University, P.O. Box 92175, Lake Charles, Louisiana 70609-2175; 318-475-5028, fax: 318-475-5922.

Meadows School of the Arts

See Southern Methodist University, Meadows School of the Arts

Mercer University

Macon, Georgia

Independent-religious, coed. Suburban campus. Total enrollment: 6,823.

Degrees Bachelor of Music in the areas of performance, sacred music; Bachelor of Music Education in the area of music education. Majors: music education, piano/organ, sacred music, voice, wind and percussion instruments. Cross-registration with Wesleyan College.

Music Faculty Total: 20; 8 full-time, 12 part-time.

Student Life Student groups include Phi Mu Alpha Sinfonia.

Expenses for 1995–96 Application fee: $25. Comprehensive fee of $17,352 includes full-time tuition ($12,987) and college room and board ($4365). College room only: $2085. Part-time tuition: $288.60 per quarter hour.

Application Procedures Deadline—freshmen and transfers: continuous. Notification date—freshmen and transfers: continuous. Required: high school transcript, college transcript(s) for transfer students, letter of recommendation, portfolio, SAT I or ACT test scores, list of extracurricular activities. Auditions held on campus and off campus. Portfolio reviews held on campus and off campus.

Undergraduate Contact Office of Undergraduate Admission, Mercer University, 1400 Coleman Avenue, Macon, Georgia 31207-0003; 912-752-2650, fax: 912-752-4120.

Meredith College

Raleigh, North Carolina

Independent-religious, women only. Urban campus. Total enrollment: 2,336.

Degrees Bachelor of Music in the areas of applied music, music education. Majors: classical music, music, music education, piano/organ, stringed instruments, voice, wind and percussion instruments. Graduate degrees offered: Master of Music in the areas of performance, pedagogy, music education. Cross-registration with North Carolina State University and Cooperating Raleigh Colleges Consortium.

Music Student Profile Fall 1994: 604 total; 70 matriculated undergraduate, 15 matriculated graduate, 519 nondegree; 10% minorities, 100% females, 5% international.

Music Faculty Total: 37; 7 full-time, 30 part-time; 90% of full-time faculty have terminal degrees. Graduate students do not teach undergraduate courses. Undergraduate student–faculty ratio: 5:1.

Student Life Student groups include Sigma Alpha Iota, Collegiate Music Educators National Conference, Pi Kappa Lambda.

Expenses for 1995–96 Application fee: $25. Comprehensive fee of $10,500 includes full-time tuition ($7100) and college room and board ($3400). Part-time tuition: $200 per semester hour.

Application Procedures Deadline—freshmen and transfers: continuous. Required: high school transcript, college transcript(s) for transfer students, minimum 2.0 high school GPA, 2 letters of recommendation, SAT I test score only. Recommended: interview, audition. Auditions held at various times on campus and off campus; recorded music is permissible as a substitute for live auditions when distance is prohibitive or scheduling is difficult and videotaped performances are permissible as a substitute for live auditions when distance is prohibitive or scheduling is difficult. Portfolio reviews held on campus and off campus.

Undergraduate Contact Sue Kearney, Director, Office of Admissions, Meredith College, 3700 Hillsborough Street, Raleigh, North Carolina 27607-5298; 800-637-3348, fax: 919-829-2348, E-mail address: admissions@meredith.edu.

Graduate Contact Dr. James Fogle, Director of Graduate Studies, Department of Music, Meredith College, 3700 Hillsborough Street, Raleigh, North Carolina 27607-5298; 919-829-8576, fax: 919-829-2828, E-mail address: foglej@mercury.interpath.net.

Methodist College

Fayetteville, North Carolina

Independent-religious, coed. Suburban campus. Total enrollment: 1,612.

Degrees Bachelor of Music in the areas of music education, performance. Majors: classical music, music education, piano/organ, stringed instruments, voice, wind and percussion instruments.

Music Student Profile Fall 1994: 18 total; all matriculated undergraduate; 17% minorities, 68% females, 1% international.

Music Faculty Total: 9; 5 full-time, 4 part-time; 20% of full-time faculty have terminal degrees. Graduate students do not teach undergraduate courses. Undergraduate student–faculty ratio: 5:1.

Student Life Student groups include American Choral Directors Association, Intercollegiate Choral Festival, Music Educators National Conference.

Expenses for 1995–96 Application fee: $25. Comprehensive fee of $13,925 includes full-time tuition ($9950) and college room and board ($3975). College room only: $1750. Part-time tuition: $325 per semester hour.

Financial Aid Program-specific awards for Fall of 1994: 7 Rainbow's End Awards for recent high school graduates ($3000), 5 Monarch Quarted Awards for recent high school graduates ($3000).

Application Procedures Deadline—freshmen and transfers: continuous. Notification date—freshmen and transfers: August 15. Required: high school transcript, audition, SAT I or ACT test scores. Recommended: essay, letter of recommendation, interview. Auditions held 3 times and by appointment on campus; recorded music is permissible as a substitute for live auditions when distance is prohibitive and videotaped performances are permissible as a substitute for live auditions when distance is prohibitive.

Undergraduate Contact Alan Porter, Head, Department of Music, Methodist College, 5400 Ramsey Street, Fayetteville, North Carolina 28311; 910-630-7101.

Miami University

Oxford, Ohio

State-related, coed. Small-town campus. Total enrollment: 15,882.

Degrees Bachelor of Music in the areas of performance, music education. Majors: music, music education, piano/organ, stringed instruments, voice, wind and percussion instruments. Graduate degrees offered: Master of Music in the areas of performance, music education.

Music Student Profile Fall 1994: 220 total; 200 matriculated undergraduate, 20 matriculated graduate; 5% minorities, 50% females, 1% international.

Music Faculty Total: 39; 30 full-time, 9 part-time; 50% of full-time faculty have terminal degrees. Graduate students teach a few undergraduate courses. Undergraduate student–faculty ratio: 6:1.

Student Life Student groups include Music Educators National Conference, American Choral Directors Association, Pi Kappa Lambda.

Expenses for 1995–96 Application fee: $30. State resident tuition: $3964 full-time, $166 per credit hour part-time. Nonresident tuition: $9394 full-time, $393 per credit hour part-time. Part-time mandatory fees: $45.50 per credit hour. Full-time mandatory fees: $920. College room and board: $4210. College room only: $1950.

Financial Aid Program-specific awards for Fall of 1994 available.

Application Procedures Deadline—freshmen: January 31; transfers: May 1. Notification date—freshmen: March 15; transfers: June 1. Required: essay, high school transcript, college transcript(s) for transfer students, minimum 2.0 high school GPA, audition, SAT I or ACT test scores. Recommended: minimum 3.0 high school GPA, letter of recommendation, interview. Auditions held 15 times on campus; recorded music is permissible as a substitute for live auditions when distance is prohibitive and videotaped performances are permissible as a substitute for live auditions when distance is prohibitive.

Contact John Heard, Chair, Department of Music, Miami University, 119 Center for the Performing Arts, Oxford, Ohio 45056; 513-529-3014.

Michigan State University

East Lansing, Michigan

State-supported, coed. Small-town campus. Total enrollment: 40,254.

Degrees Bachelor of Music in the areas of performance, theory/composition, music therapy, music education. Majors: classical music, music, music education, music history, music theory, music therapy, piano/organ, stringed instruments, voice, wind and percussion instruments. Graduate degrees offered: Master of Music. Doctor of Musical Arts in the areas of performance, composition.

Michigan State University *(continued)*

Music Student Profile Fall 1994: 500 total; 350 matriculated undergraduate, 150 matriculated graduate; 10% minorities, 55% females, 10% international.

Music Faculty Total: 56; 50 full-time, 6 part-time; 70% of full-time faculty have terminal degrees. Graduate students teach a few undergraduate courses. Undergraduate student–faculty ratio: 7:1.

Expenses for 1994–95 Application fee: $30. State resident tuition: $4102 full-time. Nonresident tuition: $10,658 full-time. Part-time tuition per semester hour ranges from $129.50 to $144 for state residents, $349 to $361.50 for nonresidents, according to class level. Full-time mandatory fees: $524. College room and board: $3764.

Financial Aid Program-specific awards for Fall of 1994: 200 Scholarships for those passing audition evaluations ($500–$10,000).

Application Procedures Deadline—freshmen and transfers: continuous. Required: high school transcript, college transcript(s) for transfer students, audition, SAT I or ACT test scores. Auditions held 4 times on campus and off campus; recorded music is permissible as a substitute for live auditions and videotaped performances are permissible as a substitute for live auditions. Portfolio reviews held on campus and off campus.

Contact Dorothy Bartholic, Secretary, Music Department, Michigan State University, 102 Music Building, East Lansing, Michigan 48824; 517-355-2140, fax: 517-432-2880.

Middle Tennessee State University

Murfreesboro, Tennessee

State-supported, coed. Suburban campus. Total enrollment: 17,120.

Degrees Bachelor of Music in the areas of music education, performance, music industry, music theory/composition. Majors: music business, music education, music theory and composition, piano/organ, stringed instruments, voice, wind and percussion instruments.

Music Student Profile Fall 1994: 225 total; all matriculated undergraduate.

Music Faculty Total: 46; 26 full-time, 20 part-time.

Expenses for 1995–96 Application fee: $5. State resident tuition: $1972 full-time, $74 per semester hour part-time. Nonresident tuition: $6102 full-time, $255 per semester hour part-time. College room and board: $2438. College room only: $1376.

Financial Aid Program-specific awards for Fall of 1994 available.

Application Procedures Deadline—freshmen and transfers: continuous. Required: high school transcript, minimum 2.0 high school GPA, audition, SAT I or ACT test scores. Auditions held 5 times and by appointment for performance applicants on campus.

Undergraduate Contact Dr. John Bingham, Chair, Department of Music, Middle Tennessee State University, Box 47, Murfreesboro, Tennessee 37132; 615-898-2469.

Midwestern State University

Wichita Falls, Texas

State-supported, coed. Small-town campus. Total enrollment: 5,819.

Degrees Bachelor of Music in the areas of performance, music education. Majors: music, music education, piano/organ, voice, wind and percussion instruments.

Music Student Profile Fall 1994: 100 total; all matriculated undergraduate; 5% minorities, 40% females, 5% international.

Music Faculty Total: 14; 9 full-time, 5 part-time; 80% of full-time faculty have terminal degrees. Undergraduate student–faculty ratio: 10:1.

Student Life Student groups include Mu Phi Epsilon, Kappa Kappa Psi, Tau Beta Sigma.

Expenses for 1995–96 State resident tuition: $1646 full-time. Nonresident tuition: $7406 full-time. Part-time tuition per semester ranges from $184.05 to $822.75 for state residents, $286.05 to $3703 for nonresidents. College room and board: $3430 (minimum). College room only: $1830.

Financial Aid Program-specific awards for Fall of 1994: 50 Music Scholarships for program majors ($1600).

Application Procedures Deadline—freshmen and transfers: April 1. Notification date—freshmen and transfers: August 15. Required: high school transcript, college transcript(s) for transfer students, minimum 2.0 high school GPA, audition, SAT I or ACT test scores. Recommended: 3 letters of recommendation, interview, portfolio. Auditions held 5 times on campus and off campus; recorded music is permissible as a substitute for live auditions when distance is prohibitive. Portfolio reviews held on campus and off campus.

Undergraduate Contact Dr. Larry Archambo, Coordinator, Department of Music, Midwestern State University, 3410 Taft, Wichita Falls, Texas 76308; 817-689-4210, fax: 817-689-4511, E-mail address: farchmbl@nexus.mwsu.edu.

Millikin University

Decatur, Illinois

Independent-religious, coed. Suburban campus. Total enrollment: 1,863.

Degrees Bachelor of Music in the areas of performance, church music, music education, commercial music; Bachelor of Music Education in the areas of instrumental music education, instrumental music education with jazz emphasis, vocal music education. Majors: commercial music, jazz, music, music education, opera, piano/organ, sacred music, stringed instruments, voice, wind and percussion instruments.

Music Student Profile Fall 1994: 197 total; all matriculated undergraduate.

Music Faculty Total: 56; 22 full-time, 34 part-time; 100% of full-time faculty have terminal degrees. Graduate students do not teach undergraduate courses. Undergraduate student–faculty ratio: 8:1.

Student Life Student groups include Music Educators National Conference Student Chapter, music fraternity and sorority, Music and Entertainment Industry Educators Association.

Expenses for 1995–96 Application fee: $25. Comprehensive fee of $17,283 includes full-time tuition ($12,596), mandatory fees ($91), and college room and board ($4596). College room only: $2392. Part-time tuition: $364 per credit.

Financial Aid Program-specific awards for Fall of 1994: Talent Awards for those passing audition evaluations ($5400).

Application Procedures Deadline—freshmen and transfers: continuous. Required: high school transcript, college transcript(s) for transfer students, minimum 2.0 high school GPA, 2 letters of recommendation, interview, audition, SAT I or ACT test scores, minimum combined SAT I score of 950, minimum composite ACT score of 20. Auditions held 9 times on campus and off campus in St. Louis, MO; Indianapolis, IN; Interlochen, MI; Chicago, IL; recorded music is permissible as a substitute for live auditions when distance is prohibitive and videotaped performances are permissible as a substitute for live auditions when distance is prohibitive.

Undergraduate Contact School of Music Admissions, School of Music, Millikin University, 1184 West Main Street, Decatur, Illinois 62522; 217-424-6300, fax: 217-424-3993.

Mississippi College

Clinton, Mississippi

Independent-religious, coed. Small-town campus. Total enrollment: 3,781.

Degrees Bachelor of Music in the areas of vocal performance, piano, organ, instrumental music, church music, composition; Bachelor of Music Education in the areas of vocal music education, instrumental music education. Majors: music, music education, piano/organ, sacred music, stringed instruments, voice, wind and percussion instruments. Graduate degrees offered: Master of Music in the areas of performance, composition, vocal pedagogy; Master of Music Education in the area of music education.

Music Student Profile Fall 1994: 77 total; 65 matriculated undergraduate, 12 matriculated graduate; 1% minorities, 50% females, 1% international.

Music Faculty Total: 19; 11 full-time, 8 part-time; 70% of full-time faculty have terminal degrees. Graduate students teach a few undergraduate courses. Undergraduate student–faculty ratio: 12:1.

Student Life Student groups include Music Educators National Conference.

Expenses for 1995–96 Comprehensive fee of $9390 includes full-time tuition ($6000), mandatory fees ($350), and college room and board ($3040). Part-time tuition: $200 per credit hour. Special program-related fees: $160 for private studio fee.

Financial Aid Program-specific awards for Fall of 1994: 30 Endowed Scholarships for program majors ($2000), 110 Ensemble Scholarships for ensemble performers ($1000).

Application Procedures Deadline—freshmen and transfers: continuous. Notification date—freshmen and transfers: continuous. Required: essay, high school transcript, minimum 2.0 high school GPA, interview, audition. Auditions held at various times on campus.

Undergraduate Contact Admissions Director, Mississippi College, Box 4203, Clinton, Mississippi 39058; 601-925-3240, fax: 601-925-3804.

Graduate Contact Edwin MacMillan, Graduate School Admissions, Mississippi College, Box 4185, Clinton, Mississippi 39058; 601-925-3225, fax: 601-925-3804.

Mississippi University for Women

Columbus, Mississippi

State-supported, primarily women. Small-town campus. Total enrollment: 3,020.

Degrees Bachelor of Music in the area of music education. Majors: music education. Cross-registration with Mississippi State University.

Music Student Profile Fall 1994: 31 total; all matriculated undergraduate; 30% minorities, 60% females.

Music Faculty Total: 7; 5 full-time, 2 part-time; 20% of full-time faculty have terminal degrees. Graduate students do not teach undergraduate courses. Undergraduate student–faculty ratio: 6:1.

Student Life Student groups include Music Educators National Conference.

Expenses for 1995–96 State resident tuition: $2244 full-time, $93.50 per semester hour part-time. Nonresident tuition: $4746 full-time, $197.66 per semester hour part-time. Full-time mandatory fees: $505. College room and board: $2450. College room only: $1160.

Financial Aid Program-specific awards for Fall of 1994: 30 Service Awards for ensemble performers ($400), 12 Scholarships for program majors ($500).

Application Procedures Deadline—freshmen and transfers: continuous. Required: high school transcript, college transcript(s) for transfer students, ACT test score only, minimum composite ACT score of 18. Recommended: minimum 2.0 high school GPA, interview, audition. Auditions held 4 times and by appointment on campus.

Mississippi University for Women *(continued)*

Undergraduate Contact Office of Admissions, Mississippi University for Women, W-1613, Columbus, Mississippi 39701; 601-329-7106.

Mississippi Valley State University

Itta Bena, Mississippi

State-supported, coed. Small-town campus. Total enrollment: 2,182.

Degrees Bachelor of Music Education in the areas of vocal music education, instrumental music education, keyboard music education. Majors: music education.

Music Student Profile Fall 1994: 48 total; all matriculated undergraduate; 100% minorities, 21% females.

Music Faculty Total: 11; 9 full-time, 2 part-time; 27% of full-time faculty have terminal degrees. Graduate students do not teach undergraduate courses. Undergraduate student–faculty ratio: 3:1.

Student Life Student groups include Music Educators National Conference, senior recitals, local/state/national competitions and programs.

Expenses for 1994–95 State resident tuition: $2278 full-time. Nonresident tuition: $4420 full-time. College room and board: $2300.

Financial Aid Program-specific awards for Fall of 1994: 120 Band/Choir Scholarships for those demonstrating need/talent ($3500).

Application Procedures Deadline—freshmen and transfers: continuous. Required: high school transcript, minimum 2.0 high school GPA, interview, audition. Recommended: 2 letters of recommendation. Auditions held as needed on campus and off campus in Jackson, MS; Greenville, MS; Greenwood, MS; Indianola, MS; recorded music is permissible as a substitute for live auditions when distance is prohibitive and videotaped performances are permissible as a substitute for live auditions when distance is prohibitive.

Undergraduate Contact Dr. Sandra C. Scott, Head, Fine Arts Department, Mississippi Valley State University, Box 1301, 14000 Highway 82 West, Itta Bena, Mississippi 38941-1400; 601-254-3485 ext. 6259, fax: 601-254-6704.

Montana State University–Bozeman

Bozeman, Montana

State-supported, coed. Small-town campus. Total enrollment: 10,962.

Degrees Bachelor of Music Education in the area of music education. Majors: music education, piano/organ, stringed instruments, voice, wind and percussion instruments.

Music Student Profile Fall 1994: 80 total; all matriculated undergraduate; 53% females.

Music Faculty Total: 17; 15 full-time, 2 part-time; 100% of full-time faculty have terminal degrees. Graduate students do not teach undergraduate courses. Undergraduate student–faculty ratio: 17:1.

Student Life Student groups include Kappa Kappa Psi.

Expenses for 1995–96 Application fee: $30. State resident tuition: $2378 full-time. Nonresident tuition: $6796 full-time. Part-time tuition per semester ranges from $100.35 to $1119 for state residents, $238.15 to $3170 for nonresidents. College room and board: $3598. Special program-related fees: $60 for applied music fee, $10 for lab fee/instrument maintenance.

Financial Aid Program-specific awards for Fall of 1994: 60 Fee Waivers for program majors ($700), 8 Intermountain Opera Awards for state resident program majors ($700), 20 Music Performance Awards for program majors ($100–$500).

Application Procedures Deadline—freshmen and transfers: continuous. Required: high school transcript, audition for scholarship consideration. Auditions held continuously on campus; recorded music is permissible as a substitute for live auditions when distance is prohibitive and videotaped performances are permissible as a substitute for live auditions when distance is prohibitive.

Undergraduate Contact Carol Oeschger, Administrative Assistant, Department of Music, Montana State University–Bozeman, Howard Hall, Bozeman, Montana 59717-0342; 406-994-3561.

Montclair State University

Upper Montclair, New Jersey

State-supported, coed. Suburban campus. Total enrollment: 12,675.

Degrees Bachelor of Music in the areas of performance, music theory/composition. Majors: classical music, music, music education, music theory and composition, music therapy, piano/organ, stringed instruments, voice, wind and percussion instruments.

Music Student Profile Fall 1994: 123 total; all matriculated undergraduate; 30% minorities, 60% females, 10% international.

Music Faculty Total: 60; 16 full-time, 44 part-time; 100% of full-time faculty have terminal degrees. Graduate students teach a few undergraduate courses. Undergraduate student–faculty ratio: 2:1.

Student Life Student groups include Sigma Alpha Iota, Phi Mu Alpha Sinfonia, Music Educators National Conference.

Expenses for 1994–95 Application fee: $35. State resident tuition: $3000 full-time, $94.50 per semester hour part-time. Nonresident tuition: $4248 full-time, $133.50 per semester hour part-time. College room and board: $4834. College room only: $3160. Special program-related fees: $300 for applied music fees, $20 for instrument rental, $50 for recital recording fee.

Financial Aid Program-specific awards for Fall of 1994: 1–10 Griffiths Piano Scholarships for piano majors ($100–$500), 1–10 Ravina Strings Awards for strings majors ($100–$500), 1–10 Howe Scholarships for music majors ($100–$500).

Application Procedures Deadline—freshmen: March 1; transfers: May 1. Required: high school transcript, college transcript(s) for transfer students, interview, audition, SAT I or ACT test scores, minimum combined SAT I score of 1000, portfolio for theory/composition applicants. Recommended: essay, letter of recommendation. Auditions held 4 times on campus; recorded music is permissible as a substitute for live auditions when distance is prohibitive or scheduling is difficult and videotaped performances are permissible as a substitute for live auditions when distance is prohibitive or scheduling is difficult.

Undergraduate Contact Admissions Chairperson, Department of Music, Montclair State University, 1 Normal Avenue, Upper Montclair, New Jersey 07043; 201-655-7610.

Moody Bible Institute

Chicago, Illinois

Independent-religious, coed. Urban campus. Total enrollment: 1,532.

Degrees Bachelor of Music in the area of sacred music. Majors: sacred music.

Music Student Profile Fall 1994: 7% minorities, 45% females, 10% international.

Music Faculty Total: 18; 15 full-time, 3 part-time; 50% of full-time faculty have terminal degrees. Graduate students do not teach undergraduate courses. Undergraduate student–faculty ratio: 6:1.

Student Life Student groups include Campus Radio Station, National Association of Teachers of Singing. Special housing available for music students.

Expenses for 1995–96 Application fee: $35. Comprehensive fee of $5409 includes full-time tuition ($0), mandatory fees ($1209), and college room and board ($4200). Special program-related fees: $160–$195 for lessons, $45 for organ practice, $20 for piano practice.

Financial Aid Program-specific awards for Fall of 1994: 1 Wilfred Burton Award for upperclassmen ($500), 1 Howard Hermansen Award for upperclassmen ($300).

Application Procedures Deadline—freshmen and transfers: March 1. Notification date—freshmen and transfers: May 1. Required: high school transcript, college transcript(s) for transfer students, minimum 2.0 high school GPA, letter of recommendation, audition, ACT test score only. Recommended: minimum 3.0 high school GPA. Auditions held 2 times on campus.

Undergraduate Contact Annette Moy, Recruiter, Enrollment Management, Moody Bible Institute, 820 North LaSalle Boulevard, Chicago, Illinois 60610; 312-329-4400, fax: 312-329-2035.

Roland Dille Center for the Arts

Moorhead State University

Moorhead, Minnesota

State-supported, coed. Urban campus. Total enrollment: 7,037.

Degrees Bachelor of Music in the areas of voice, keyboard, instrumental music, composition, music industry; Bachelor of Music Education in the area of music education. Majors: music, music business, music education, performance. Graduate degrees offered: Master of Music in the areas of performance, vocal music, instrumental music; Master of Music Education in the area of music education. Cross-registration with Concordia College, North Dakota State University.

Music Student Profile Fall 1994: 188 total; all matriculated undergraduate; 4% minorities, 60% females, 2% international.

Music Faculty Total: 19; 17 full-time, 2 part-time; 71% of full-time faculty have terminal degrees. Graduate students do not teach undergraduate courses. Undergraduate student–faculty ratio: 10:1.

Student Life Student groups include Snowfire/Choir Group, Music and Entertainment Industry Club, Opera Workshop.

Estimated Expenses for 1995–96 Application fee: $15. State resident tuition: $2332 full-time, $72.85 per credit part-time. Nonresident tuition: $5060 full-time, $101.40 per credit part-time. Part-time mandatory fees: $15.75 per credit. Wisconsin and South Dakota residents pay tuition at the rate they would pay if attending a comparable state-supported institution in their home state. North Dakota residents pay approximately 25% above Minnesota state tuition. Full-time mandatory fees: $378. College room and board: $2912. College room only: $1695.

Financial Aid Program-specific awards for Fall of 1994: 40–50 Talent Awards for program majors ($300–$500).

Application Procedures Deadline—freshmen and transfers: August 7. Required: high school transcript, college transcript(s) for transfer students, minimum 2.0 high school GPA, SAT I or ACT test scores, minimum composite ACT score of 21. Recommended: audition. Auditions held continuously on campus; recorded music is permissible as a substitute for live auditions with permission of the chair and videotaped performances are permissible as a substitute for live auditions with permission of the chair.

Undergraduate Contact Jean Lange, Director of Admissions, Moorhead State University, 1104 7th Avenue South, Moorhead, Minnesota 56563; 218-236-2161, fax: 218-236-2168.

Moorhead State University *(continued)*

Graduate Contact John Tandberg, Registrar, Moorhead State University, 1104 7th Avenue South, Moorhead, Minnesota 56563; 218-236-2566, fax: 218-236-2168.

Moravian College

Bethlehem, Pennsylvania

Independent-religious, coed. Suburban campus. Total enrollment: 1,353.

Degrees Bachelor of Music in the areas of performance, composition, music education. Majors: classical music, composition, jazz, music, music education, piano/organ, stringed instruments, voice, wind and percussion instruments. Cross-registration with Lehigh University, Lafayette College, Muhlenberg College, Allentown College.

Music Student Profile Fall 1994: 66 total; all matriculated undergraduate; 10% minorities, 55% females.

Music Faculty Total: 37; 5 full-time, 32 part-time; 60% of full-time faculty have terminal degrees. Graduate students do not teach undergraduate courses. Undergraduate student–faculty ratio: 13:1.

Student Life Student groups include Music Educators National Conference.

Expenses for 1995–96 Application fee: $30. Comprehensive fee of $21,010 includes full-time tuition ($15,880), mandatory fees ($180), and college room and board ($4950). Part-time tuition and fees per course: $1665 for day division, $648 for evening division.

Financial Aid Program-specific awards for Fall of 1994: 15 Ina Love Thursby Scholarships for those demonstrating need ($1000).

Application Procedures Deadline—freshmen: September 1; transfers: continuous. Required: essay, high school transcript, college transcript(s) for transfer students, minimum 2.0 high school GPA, 3 letters of recommendation, audition. Recommended: interview. Auditions held continuously at student's convenience on campus.

Undergraduate Contact James Earl Barnes, Director of Instrumental Music, Music Department, Moravian College, 1200 Main Street, Bethlehem, Pennsylvania 18018; 610-861-1672, fax: 610-861-1657.

Morehead State University

Morehead, Kentucky

State-supported, coed. Small-town campus. Total enrollment: 8,697.

Degrees Bachelor of Music in the areas of voice, piano, organ, strings, winds, music theory/composition, jazz; Bachelor of Music Education in the area of music education. Majors: jazz, music education, music theory and composition, piano/organ, stringed instruments, voice, wind and percussion instruments. Graduate degrees offered: Master of Music in the areas of performance, music education.

Music Student Profile Fall 1994: 169 total; 154 matriculated undergraduate, 7 matriculated graduate, 8 nondegree; 6% minorities, 54% females, 2% international.

Music Faculty Total: 24; 23 full-time, 1 part-time; 57% of full-time faculty have terminal degrees. Graduate students do not teach undergraduate courses. Undergraduate student–faculty ratio: 14:1.

Student Life Special housing available for music students.

Estimated Expenses for 1995–96 State resident tuition: $1900 full-time, $80 per credit hour part-time. Nonresident tuition: $5060 full-time, $211 per credit hour part-time. College room and board: $2950. College room only: $1380 (minimum). Special program-related fees: $45–$75 for private lessons, $11–$16 for instrumental rental.

Financial Aid Program-specific awards for Fall of 1994: 60 Music Scholarships for program majors ($700).

Application Procedures Deadline—freshmen and transfers: June 15. Notification date—freshmen: August 1. Required: high school transcript, college transcript(s) for transfer students, SAT I or ACT test scores. Recommended: 2 letters of recommendation, interview, audition. Auditions held 4 times on campus; recorded music is permissible as a substitute for live auditions when distance is prohibitive.

Contact Christopher Gallaher, Chair, Music Department, Morehead State University, Morehead, Kentucky 40351; 606-783-2473, fax: 606-783-2678, E-mail address: c.gallah@msuacad.morehead-st.edu.

Morningside College

Sioux City, Iowa

Independent-religious, coed. Suburban campus. Total enrollment: 1,214.

Degrees Bachelor of Music in the areas of piano, voice, instrumental music; Bachelor of Music Education in the area of music education. Majors: classical music, jazz, music education, musical instrument technology, opera, piano/organ, stringed instruments, voice, wind and percussion instruments. Cross-registration with Western Iowa Tech Community College.

Music Student Profile Fall 1994: 175 total; 45 matriculated undergraduate, 130 nondegree; 10% minorities, 55% females, 2% international.

Music Faculty Total: 13; 6 full-time, 7 part-time; 90% of full-time faculty have terminal degrees. Undergraduate student–faculty ratio: 15:1.

Expenses for 1995–96 Application fee: $15. Comprehensive fee of $15,096 includes full-time tuition ($11,050), mandatory fees ($176), and college room and board ($3870). College room only: $2000. Part-time tuition per semester hour: $230 for the first 6 semester hours, $370

for the next 4 semester hours for day classes, $230 for evening classes. Special program-related fees: $160 for lessons.

Financial Aid Program-specific awards for Fall of 1994: 10–12 Talent Grants for freshmen ($4500–$5500), 7–8 Endowed Scholarships for program majors ($50–$2000).

Application Procedures Deadline—freshmen and transfers: continuous. Notification date—freshmen and transfers: September 1. Required: high school transcript, college transcript(s) for transfer students, interview, audition, SAT I or ACT test scores. Recommended: essay, minimum 2.0 high school GPA. Auditions held 3 times on campus; videotaped performances are permissible as a substitute for live auditions with approval from the department.

Undergraduate Contact Lance Lehmberg, Chair, Music Department, Morningside College, 1501 Morningside Avenue, Sioux City, Iowa 51106; 712-274-5218, fax: 712-274-5101, E-mail address: hllool@chief.morningside.edu.

Mount Allison University

Sackville, New Brunswick

Province-supported, coed. Small-town campus. Total enrollment: 2,376.

Degrees Bachelor of Music. Majors: composition, music education, music history, music theory, performance.

Music Student Profile Fall 1994: 125 total; all matriculated undergraduate.

Music Faculty Total: 17; 14 full-time, 3 part-time.

Expenses for 1994–95 Application fee: $20. Canadian resident tuition: $2890 full-time, $580 per course part-time. Nonresident tuition: $6035 full-time, $1210 per course part-time. (All figures are in Canadian dollars.). Full-time mandatory fees: $378. College room and board: $5055.

Application Procedures Deadline—freshmen: March 15; transfers: May 1. Required: high school transcript, minimum 3.0 high school GPA, audition, music theory examination. Recommended: 2 letters of recommendation. Auditions held 2 times and by appointment on campus; recorded music is permissible as a substitute for live auditions if a campus visit is impossible.

Undergraduate Contact Head, Department of Music, Mount Allison University, Sackville, New Brunswick E0A 3C0, Canada; 506-364-2374, fax: 506-364-2376.

Mount Senario College

Ladysmith, Wisconsin

Independent, coed. Small-town campus. Total enrollment: 475.

Degrees Bachelor of Music in the areas of vocal performance, piano performance; Bachelor of Music Education in the area of vocal music education. Majors: music education, piano/organ, voice.

Music Faculty Total: 2; 2 full-time; 100% of full-time faculty have terminal degrees. Graduate students do not teach undergraduate courses.

Student Life Student groups include Music Educators National Conference.

Expenses for 1995–96 Comprehensive fee of $11,527 includes full-time tuition ($8167), mandatory fees ($110), and college room and board ($3250). Part-time tuition per credit hour ranges from $260 to $340 according to course load. Tuition guaranteed not to increase for student's term of enrollment.

Application Procedures Deadline—freshmen and transfers: continuous. Required: high school transcript, 2 letters of recommendation. Recommended: interview.

Undergraduate Contact Jeanne Gentry Waits, Chair, Music Department, Mount Senario College, 1500 College Avenue West, Ladysmith, Wisconsin 54848; 715-532-5511 ext. 218.

Mount St. Mary's College

Los Angeles, California

Independent-religious, primarily women. Suburban campus. Total enrollment: 1,621.

Degrees Bachelor of Music in the areas of vocal performance, instrumental performance, liturgical music, music education. Majors: music education, music theory and composition, sacred music, stringed instruments, voice, wind and percussion instruments. Cross-registration with University of California, Los Angeles.

Music Student Profile Fall 1994: 30 total; all matriculated undergraduate; 33% minorities, 96% females.

Music Faculty Total: 9; 2 full-time, 7 part-time; 50% of full-time faculty have terminal degrees. Graduate students do not teach undergraduate courses. Undergraduate student–faculty ratio: 11:1.

Student Life Student groups include Campus Liturgies in Mary Chapel, Spring Sing, trips to off campus concerts.

Expenses for 1994–95 Application fee: $30. Comprehensive fee of $18,214 includes full-time tuition ($12,474), mandatory fees ($440), and college room and board ($5300 minimum). Part-time tuition: $475 per unit. Part-time mandatory fees: $20 per semester.

Financial Aid Program-specific awards for Fall of 1994 available.

Application Procedures Required: essay, high school transcript, college transcript(s) for transfer students, minimum 3.0 high school GPA, SAT I or ACT test scores. Auditions held 2 times on campus and off campus. Portfolio reviews held on campus and off campus.

Mount St. Mary's College *(continued)*

Undergraduate Contact Admissions Office, Mount St. Mary's College, 12001 Chalon Road, Los Angeles, California 90049; 310-471-9546.

Mount Union College

Alliance, Ohio

Independent-religious, coed. Suburban campus. Total enrollment: 1,481.

Degrees Bachelor of Music in the area of performance; Bachelor of Music Education in the area of music education. Majors: classical music, music education, piano/organ, stringed instruments, voice, wind and percussion instruments.

Music Student Profile Fall 1994: 40 total; all matriculated undergraduate; 55% females.

Music Faculty Total: 25; 6 full-time, 19 part-time; 100% of full-time faculty have terminal degrees. Graduate students do not teach undergraduate courses. Undergraduate student–faculty ratio: 9:1.

Student Life Student groups include Kappa Kappa Psi, Mu Phi Epsilon.

Expenses for 1995–96 Application fee: $20. Comprehensive fee of $17,130 includes full-time tuition ($12,750), mandatory fees ($730), and college room and board ($3650). Part-time tuition: $500 per semester hour. Special program-related fees: $150 for private music lessons.

Financial Aid Program-specific awards for Fall of 1994: 40 Music Proficiency Awards for those demonstrating musical achievement ($1000–$3000).

Application Procedures Deadline—freshmen and transfers: continuous. Required: essay, high school transcript, college transcript(s) for transfer students, minimum 2.0 high school GPA, letter of recommendation, interview, audition, SAT I or ACT test scores. Auditions held 5 times on campus; recorded music is permissible as a substitute for live auditions when distance is prohibitive and videotaped performances are permissible as a substitute for live auditions when distance is prohibitive.

Undergraduate Contact Dr. Victoria Harris, Chairperson, Music Department, Mount Union College, 1972 Clark Avenue, Alliance, Ohio 44601; 216-823-2180.

Murray State University

Murray, Kentucky

State-supported, coed. Small-town campus. Total enrollment: 7,960.

Degrees Bachelor of Music in the area of performance; Bachelor of Music Education in the area of music education. Majors: classical music, jazz, music, music education, opera, piano/organ, stringed instruments, voice, wind and percussion instruments. Graduate degrees offered: Master of Music Education in the area of music education.

Music Student Profile Fall 1994: 198 total; 150 matriculated undergraduate, 31 matriculated graduate, 17 nondegree; 2% minorities, 55% females.

Music Faculty Total: 26; 20 full-time, 6 part-time; 50% of full-time faculty have terminal degrees. Graduate students teach a few undergraduate courses. Undergraduate student–faculty ratio: 8:1.

Student Life Student groups include Music Educators National Conference, Kentucky Music Educators Association, Music Teachers National Association.

Expenses for 1995–96 Application fee: $15. State resident tuition: $1680 full-time, $72 per credit hour part-time. Nonresident tuition: $5040 full-time, $210 per credit hour part-time. Full-time mandatory fees: $260. College room and board: $3000. College room only: $1275. Special program-related fees: $40–$75 for lesson fees.

Financial Aid Program-specific awards for Fall of 1994: 30–58 Music/University Scholarships for program majors.

Application Procedures Deadline—freshmen and transfers: continuous. Required: high school transcript, college transcript(s) for transfer students, letter of recommendation, interview, audition, ACT test score only. Auditions held 4 times on campus; recorded music is permissible as a substitute for live auditions when distance is prohibitive and videotaped performances are permissible as a substitute for live auditions when distance is prohibitive.

Undergraduate Contact Raymond L. Conklin, Chair, Department of Music, Murray State University, Box 9, Murray, Kentucky 42071-0009; 502-762-6339, fax: 502-762-6335.

Graduate Contact Roger Reichmuth, Coordinator/Director, Graduate Program in Music, Department of Music, Murray State University, College of Fine Arts and Communication, Box 9, Murray, Kentucky 42071-0009; 502-762-4669, fax: 502-762-6335.

Nazareth College of Rochester

Rochester, New York

Independent, coed. Suburban campus. Total enrollment: 2,723.

Degrees Bachelor of Music in the areas of music education, music therapy, performance, music theory, music history. Majors: music education, music history, music theory, music therapy, performance. Cross-registration with State University of New York College at Brockport, University of Rochester, St. John Fisher College.

Music Student Profile Fall 1994: 70 total; all matriculated undergraduate; 1% minorities, 60% females.

Music Faculty Total: 26; 8 full-time, 18 part-time; 100% of full-time faculty have terminal degrees. Graduate

students do not teach undergraduate courses. Undergraduate student–faculty ratio: 10:1.

Expenses for 1995–96 Application fee: $25. Comprehensive fee of $17,002 includes full-time tuition ($11,380), mandatory fees ($202), and college room and board ($5420). College room only: $3060. Part-time tuition: $329 per credit hour. Special program-related fees: $190 for voice or instrument lessons for majors, $105 for voice or instrument lessons for minors, $105 for group lessons, $33 for music therapy clinic fee.

Financial Aid Program-specific awards for Fall of 1994: 15 Honors Music Scholarships for incoming freshmen passing audition evaluations ($17,067), 5 Gerald Wilmot Music Scholarships for honors juniors or seniors ($17,010), 2 Lewis Dollinger Scholarships for honors juniors or seniors ($1000).

Application Procedures Deadline—freshmen and transfers: continuous. Required: high school transcript, minimum 2.0 high school GPA, 2 letters of recommendation, interview, audition. Auditions held 5 times on campus.

Undergraduate Contact Tom DaRin, Admissions Office, Nazareth College of Rochester, 4245 East Avenue, Rochester, New York 14618; 716-586-2525 ext. 265, fax: 716-586-2452.

Nebraska Wesleyan University

Lincoln, Nebraska

Independent-religious, coed. Suburban campus. Total enrollment: 1,610.

Degrees Bachelor of Music in the areas of applied music, music education. Majors: music, music education.

Music Student Profile Fall 1994: 60 total; all matriculated undergraduate; 2% minorities, 50% females.

Music Faculty Total: 17; 8 full-time, 9 part-time; 90% of full-time faculty have terminal degrees. Graduate students do not teach undergraduate courses. Undergraduate student–faculty ratio: 7:1.

Student Life Student groups include Mu Phi Epsilon, Music Educators National Conference, National Music Educators Association.

Expenses for 1995–96 Application fee: $20. Comprehensive fee of $13,736 includes full-time tuition ($9890), mandatory fees ($426), and college room and board ($3420 minimum). Part-time tuition: $400 per hour. Part-time mandatory fees: $48 per semester. Part-time tuition per hour for Wesleyan PM program: $125.

Financial Aid Program-specific awards for Fall of 1994: 10 Bennett Music Scholarships for program majors ($1000–$1500).

Application Procedures Deadline—freshmen and transfers: continuous. Required: high school transcript, audition. Auditions held 1 time on campus; recorded music is permissible as a substitute for live auditions if a campus visit is impossible.

Undergraduate Contact Ken Sieg, Director of Admissions, Nebraska Wesleyan University, 5000 St. Paul Avenue, Lincoln, Nebraska 68504; 402-465-2141.

New England Conservatory of Music

Boston, Massachusetts

Independent, coed. Urban campus. Total enrollment: 774.

Degrees Bachelor of Music in the areas of composition, historical performance, music history, music theory. Majors: classical music, composition, conducting, directing, jazz, music, music education, music theory, musical instrument technology, opera, performance, piano/organ, sacred music, stringed instruments, voice, wind and percussion instruments. Graduate degrees offered: Master of Music in the areas of composition, historical performance, music history, music theory, accompaniment, conducting, musicology, vocal pedagogy; Master of Music Education in the area of music education. Doctor of Musical Arts in the areas of performance, composition, music education. Cross-registration with Northeastern University, Tufts University, Simmons College.

Music Student Profile Fall 1994: 765 total; 379 matriculated undergraduate, 386 matriculated graduate; 10% minorities, 55% females, 37% international.

Music Faculty Total: 180; 50 full-time, 130 part-time; 100% of full-time faculty have terminal degrees. Graduate students do not teach undergraduate courses. Undergraduate student–faculty ratio: 4:1.

Expenses for 1994–95 Application fee: $60. Comprehensive fee of $22,700 includes full-time tuition ($15,300), mandatory fees ($100), and college room and board ($7300). Part-time tuition: $496 per credit hour. Part-time mandatory fees: $100 per year. Tuition for studio instruction: $3800 per semester.

Application Procedures Deadline—freshmen and transfers: January 15. Notification date—freshmen and transfers: April 1. Required: essay, high school transcript, college transcript(s) for transfer students, letter of recommendation, audition, SAT I or ACT test scores. Auditions held 10 times on campus; recorded music is permissible as a substitute for live auditions when distance is prohibitive and videotaped performances are permissible as a substitute for live auditions when distance is prohibitive. Portfolio reviews held on campus.

Contact Office of Admissions, New England Conservatory of Music, 290 Huntington Avenue, Boston, Massachusetts 02115; 617-262-1120 ext. 430, fax: 617-262-0500.

New Mexico State University

Las Cruces, New Mexico

State-supported, coed. Suburban campus. Total enrollment: 15,645.

Degrees Bachelor of Music in the areas of performance, music theory/composition; Bachelor of Music Education in the areas of vocal music education, instrumental music education, piano pedagogy. Majors: classical music, music, music education, music theory and composition, piano/organ, stringed instruments, voice, wind and percussion instruments. Graduate degrees offered: Mas-

New Mexico State University *(continued)*

ter of Music in the areas of accompanying, music theory/composition, music history, performance, music education, conducting.

Music Student Profile Fall 1994: 178 total; 158 matriculated undergraduate, 20 matriculated graduate; 2% minorities, 40% females, 1% international.

Music Faculty Total: 21; 15 full-time, 6 part-time; 85% of full-time faculty have terminal degrees. Graduate students teach a few undergraduate courses. Undergraduate student–faculty ratio: 15:1.

Student Life Student groups include Phi Mu Alpha, Sigma Alpha Iota.

Expenses for 1994–95 Application fee: $10. State resident tuition: $1980 full-time, $76 per credit part-time. Nonresident tuition: $6432 full-time, $251 per credit part-time. Full-time mandatory fees: $48. College room and board: $2592 (minimum). College room only: $1486 (minimum).

Financial Aid Program-specific awards for Fall of 1994: 1 Theodore Presser Scholarship for program majors ($1500), 3 Jack Ward Scholarships for wind or percussion students ($600), 2 Vivien B. Head Scholarships for program majors ($1500), 1 Ray Tross Scholarship for woodwind majors ($300), 300 Ray Tross Band, Choir, and Orchestra Service Grants for musically talented performers ($500).

Application Procedures Deadline—freshmen and transfers: April 15. Notification date—freshmen and transfers: July 1. Required: high school transcript, minimum 3.0 high school GPA, interview, audition. Recommended: 3 letters of recommendation. Auditions held continuously on campus and off campus in various New Mexico cities.

Contact William Clark, Head, Music Department, New Mexico State University, Box 3F, Las Cruces, New Mexico 88003; 505-646-1290, fax: 505-646-8199, E-mail address: music@nmsu.edu.

New School/Mannes Jazz and Contemporary Music Program

New School for Social Research

New York, New York

Degrees Bachelor of Fine Arts in the area of jazz. Majors: composition/songwriting, jazz.

Music Student Profile Fall 1994: 216 total; 136 matriculated undergraduate, 80 nondegree; 18% minorities, 18% females, 36% international.

Music Faculty Total: 62; 4 full-time, 58 part-time; 33% of full-time faculty have terminal degrees. Graduate students do not teach undergraduate courses. Undergraduate student–faculty ratio: 3:1.

Expenses for 1994–95 Application fee: $30. Comprehensive fee of $22,600 includes full-time tuition ($15,030), mandatory fees ($150), and college room and board ($7420). College room only: $5170. Part-time tuition: $510 per credit. Part-time mandatory fees: $150 per year. Special program-related fees: $5–$15 for cassette tapes.

Financial Aid Program-specific awards for Fall of 1994: 97 Jazz Scholarships for those demonstrating need ($3600), 15 University Scholar Awards for minority students ($3000).

Application Procedures Deadline—freshmen and transfers: continuous. Required: essay, high school transcript, college transcript(s) for transfer students, minimum 2.0 high school GPA, audition. Recommended: 2 letters of recommendation, interview, SAT I or ACT test scores. Auditions held 15 times on campus; recorded music is permissible as a substitute for live auditions when distance is prohibitive and videotaped performances are permissible as a substitute for live auditions when distance is prohibitive.

Undergraduate Contact L. E. Howell, Coordinator of Admissions, New School for Social Research, 55 West 13th Street, New York, New York 10011; 212-229-5896, fax: 212-229-8936.

More about the School

The metropolitan New York region is home for most of the great jazz artists in the world. It is also one of America's two centers for the recording and television industry, and as a consequence, is the most active environment, internationally, for jazz and related contemporary music. The New School's Bachelor of Fine Arts curriculum in jazz draws both its faculty members and its inspiration from this extraordinary resource. It provides a comprehensive musical education, coupled with specialized work in the performance, writing, and recording of jazz and its related musical forms. Students work in the classroom and private studio with world-class professionals, and they are able to follow the great tradition of jazz at first hand, learning through intense exposure to the finest musicians, as they perform throughout the New York metropolitan area, live in concert, in jazz clubs, and in recording studios.

Students of jazz and contemporary music at the New School find themselves in an energetic and diversified college community, offering many opportunities to learn from instructors and students in a variety of disciplines and areas of inquiry. The Jazz Program is a component of the Mannes College of Music, one of the academic divisions of the New School for Social Research. Mannes, as one of New York's three major classical conservatories, provides curricular depth, enhanced credibility for instruction in musicianship, and dialogue between musicians with distinctly different professional experiences. All of this takes place within the context of New York City itself, whose vast cultural and intellectual resources offer endless opportunities for intellectual and creative development.

The program proudly announces the September 1995 opening of new facilities, offering greatly expanded space and services, including the addition of an intimate performance/recording space and MIDI/computer facilities. This new state of the art facility, located within the jazz environs of Greenwich Village, constitutes a direct investment in the future of jazz and contemporary music, and promises a new level of artistic opportunity and excellence.

Performance, and the artist as educator and mentor, are the heart of the program's philosophy. The curriculum begins with a comprehensive musical foundation which becomes more flexible as the student advances to graduation. Advanced students have the opportunity to apprentice with one or more jazz masters, gaining a realistic view of the art form, not only through its daily practice, but also through close observation of the artist's working environment and lifestyle.

The key to this program's success, however, lies in its use of the finest professionals available anywhere to supervise an intense involvement in small group playing. Students work closely with the creators, not the interpreters, of jazz–an art form that is continually reaching toward, and achieving, new technical and conceptual horizons. *Faculty: Classroom and Ensemble* Richie Beirach, Bob Belden, Joanne Brackeen, Cecil Bridgewater, Joe Chambers, Andrew Cyrille, Harold Danko, Garry Dial, Armen Donelian, Mario Escalera, Gil Goldstein, Jamey Haddad, Chico Hamilton, Billy Harper, Richard Harper, Sheila Jordan, Vic Juris, Bill Kirchner, Arnie Lawrence, David Lopato, Junior Mance, Phil Markowitz, Henry Martin, Cecil McBee, Makanda McIntyre, Mike Mossman, Steve Neil, Jimmy Owens, Charli Persip, Lewis Porter, Benny Powell, Loren Schoenberg, Steve Slagle, Rory Stuart, Francesca Tanksley, Charles Tolliver, Buster Williams, Reggie Workman. *Instrumental Faculty* (partial list): **Trombone** Slide Hampton, Benny Powell, Steve Turre, Craig Harris, **Trumpet** Jimmy Owens, Cecil Bridgewater, Brian Lynch, **Saxophone and Woodwinds** Charles Davis, George Garzone, Joe Lovano, Dewey Redman, Frank Wess, **Bass** Eddie Gomez, Andy McKee, Reggie Workman, Buster Williams, **Guitar** John Abercrombie, Ted Dunbar, Jim Hall, Vic Juris, **Percussion** Horacee Arnold, Joe Chambers, Kenwood Dennard, Billy Hart, Bernard Purdie, Kenny Washington, **Piano** Jaki Byard, George Cables, Richie Beirach, Fred Hersch, Joanne Brackeen, **Composition and Arranging** Bob Belden, Gil Goldstein, Maria Schneider, Henry Martin, **Vocals** Sheila Jordan, Anne Marie Moss, Andy Bey, Janet Lawson, **Master Class and Special Guests** (partial list): Toshiko Akiyoshi, Victor Bailey, Lester Bowie, Randy Brecker, Benny Carter, Art Farmer, Tommy Flanagan, Frank Foster, Benny Golson, Sir Roland Hanna, Billy Hart, Jon Hendricks, Milt Hinton, Milt Jackson, Etta James, Steve Lacey, John Lewis, Branford Marsalis, Hugh Masakela, Charlie Palmieri, Wallace Rooney, Badal Roy, Clark Terry, Cedar Walton, Joe Williams.

Mannes College of Music

New School for Social Research

New York, New York

Independent, coed. Urban campus. Total enrollment: 267. **Degrees** Bachelor of Music in the areas of orchestral instruments, piano, organ, voice, composition, music theory, orchestral and choral conducting, historical performance, guitar. Majors: classical music, composition, conducting, guitar, music, music theory, opera, performance, piano/organ, stringed instruments, voice, wind and percussion instruments. Graduate degrees offered: Master of Music in the areas of orchestral instruments, piano, organ, voice, composition, music theory, orchestral and choral conducting, historical performance, guitar. Cross-registration with New School for Social Research.

Music Student Profile Fall 1994: 269 total; 131 matriculated undergraduate, 84 matriculated graduate, 54 nondegree; 13% minorities, 55% females, 42% international.

Music Faculty Total: 150; 25 full-time, 125 part-time; 100% of full-time faculty have terminal degrees. Graduate students do not teach undergraduate courses. Undergraduate student–faculty ratio: 8:1.

Expenses for 1994–95 Application fee: $60. Tuition: $12,750 full-time, $300 per credit part-time. Part-time mandatory fees: $225 per year. Part-time students pay a minimum of $3400 for lessons. Full-time mandatory fees: $225. College room only: $5500.

Application Procedures Deadline—freshmen and transfers: continuous. Required: high school transcript, letter of recommendation, audition. Recommended: essay, minimum 3.0 high school GPA, interview. Auditions held 5 times on campus and off campus in Chicago, IL; Los Angeles, CA; San Francisco, CA.

Contact Marilyn Groves, Director of Admissions, New School for Social Research, 150 West 85th Street, New York, New York 10024; 212-580-0210, fax: 212-580-1738.

Founded in 1916 by David and Clara Mannes, world renowned as a violin-piano duo, the Mannes College of Music is recognized internationally as being among the finest professional music conservatories.

Throughout its existence, Mannes has taken a leading role with programs known for broad musical training and the encouragement of artistic growth. Its distinguished faculty includes some of the world's most prominent musicians and ensembles. Current faculty members include Peter Serkin, Richard Goode, Vladimir Feltsman, Grant Johannesen, Felix Galimir, Walter Trampler, Timothy Eddy, Ruth Falcon, Theodor Uppman, and principal players from the New York Philharmonic, Metropolitan Opera Orchestra, and New York City Opera and Ballet orchestras. Mannes graduates include Frederica von Stade, Julius Rudel, Murray Perahia, Eugene Istomin, Richard Goode, Semyon Bychkov, and Myung Whun Chung.

Mannes offers the Bachelor of Music, Bachelor of Science, and Master of Music degrees and a Professional Studies Diploma. Major instructional fields include all keyboard and orchestral instruments, guitar, voice, theory, composition, orchestral and choral conducting, and historical performance.

Performance is the main activity of Mannes students, and the training of aspirant professional musicians is the College's mission. Mannes has developed a distinctive approach and environment in which to implement it. Through an intensive curriculum in ear-training, dictation, theory, harmony, composition, and analysis, Mannes students are provided with a thorough understanding of the theory, structure, and history of music. The enrollment limit of about 250 students seeks to ensure highly personalized instruction and close interaction among students, faculty, and administrators. Students receive individual lessons from their major teachers and participate in small performance groups. Class size is kept small to maximize individual attention. Mannes prides itself on being a community of musicians dedicated to advancing art through a personal and humanistic approach to education.

The Mannes Orchestra gives four to five concerts yearly in Symphony Space, a major New York City

New School for Social Research *(continued)*

facility; performs at Lincoln Center; and takes part in choral concerts and opera presentations. Each concert features a student performance of a solo work with orchestra.

Participation in chamber music ensembles is an essential part of the performance training of any musician, and Mannes activities include performances for all standard instrumental groups as well as Percussion Ensemble, Piano Ensemble, Guitar Ensemble, Baroque Chamber Players, and the Contemporary Ensemble. Student chamber music groups regularly perform works by student composers.

The Opera Department presents programs of opera scenes and excerpts, and, in the spring, a full chamber opera production is mounted. A concert presentation of vocal repertory is included in one orchestral concert.

Mannes's location is particularly well suited for students and musicians. Manhattan's West Side is one of the most vibrant areas of New York and is the site of most of the city's major musical and cultural activities. Within blocks of the College are Lincoln Center, Merkin Hall, Symphony Space, the Museum of Natural History, and the New York Historical Society as well as recreational centers such as Central Park and Riverside Park.

In an age of mass education, Mannes maintains an intimate atmosphere that permits a close and sustained contact among all members of the College. In the larger context, students have the benefit of full access to the richness of New York City's musical and cultural life.

New School/Mannes Jazz and Contemporary Music Program

See New School for Social Research, New School/ Mannes Jazz and Contemporary Music Program

Tisch School of the Arts

New York University

New York, New York

Independent, coed. Urban campus. Total enrollment: 33,428.

Degrees Bachelor of Music in the areas of performance, composition, music business, jazz studies, music technology. Majors: classical music, jazz, music, music business, music education, music theater, music theory and composition, musical instrument technology, opera, orchestral instruments, piano/organ, sacred music, stringed instruments, voice, wind and percussion instruments. Graduate degrees offered: Master of Music in the area of music technology; Master of Music Therapy in the area of music therapy. Doctor of Arts in the areas of music therapy, performance, composition.

Music Student Profile Fall 1994: 500 total; 250 matriculated undergraduate, 250 matriculated graduate.

Music Faculty Total: 160; 20 full-time, 140 part-time; 90% of full-time faculty have terminal degrees. Graduate students teach a few undergraduate courses. Undergraduate student–faculty ratio: 20:1.

Student Life Student groups include American Association of Music Therapists, New York State Music Association.

Expenses for 1994–95 Application fee: $45. Comprehensive fee of $26,001 includes full-time tuition ($18,739) and college room and board ($7262). Part-time tuition: $513 per credit. Part-time mandatory fees per semester range from $96 to $426.

Application Procedures Deadline—freshmen: February 1; transfers: April 1. Notification date—freshmen and transfers: continuous. Required: essay, high school transcript, college transcript(s) for transfer students, minimum 3.0 high school GPA, 3 letters of recommendation, audition, portfolio, SAT I test score only. Recommended: interview. Auditions held 8 times on campus and off campus in Dallas, TX; Houston, TX; recorded music is permissible as a substitute for live auditions when distance is prohibitive and videotaped performances are permissible as a substitute for live auditions when distance is prohibitive. Portfolio reviews held continuously on campus and off campus in Houston, TX; Dallas, TX; Boston, MA.

Undergraduate Contact Peter Farell, Director of Undergraduate Admissions, School of Education, New York University, 22 Washington Square North, New York, New York 10012; 212-998-4500, fax: 212-995-4902.

Graduate Contact Stan Greidus, Director of Graduate Admissions, School of Education, New York University, 32 Washington Place, 2nd Floor, New York, New York 10012; 212-998-5030.

More about the University

Facilities and resources include the education building (private practice rooms, ensemble rehearsal rooms, teaching studios, University Theatre); computer music studios (MacIntosh-based computer music, audio for video, film music studios; multimedia laboratories using IBM, NeXT, and Apple computers; digital recording and editing rooms featuring Digidesign Pro-tools and Sonic Solutions multitrack systems. Rollnick Recording Studios (multitrack facility featuring analog and digital recording, DAT facilities and sound processing units, outboard effects, and MIDI processing for live and studio performance): MBT Records (a full-service NYU-based record company providing experience in all aspects of record production); Nordoff-Robbins Music Therapy Clinic (an international outreach and training center for music therapists); Center for Women in Music (a research and resource center for the advancement of women composers, performers, scholars and administrators); NYU Arts and Media Studio (advanced hardware platforms for computer music, graphics, and animation); Elmer Holmes Bobst Library (open-stack; over 2.5 million volumes; includes the Avery Fisher Center for Music and Media)

Faculty, Resident Artists, and Alumni Faculty members are internationally acclaimed artists, composers, scholars, and members of such renowned music organizations as the New York Philharmonic and the Metropolitan Opera Company. Currently in residence: The Brentano String Quartet, Reimann Opera Theatre; Leonard Roseman, composer-in-residence. Guest artists

have included Arlene Saunders, Michel Singher, Emil Sein, Judy Collins, Claudette Sorel, and JoAnn Fulletta.

Student Performance Opportunities Student composers and performers are involved in national and international tours and are regularly featured in concerts and recitals at NYU, Carnegie Recital Hall, Merkin Hall, Lincoln Center and landmark jazz clubs and new music venues in Greenwich Village and SoHo. Performance ensembles include: Chamber Music Ensemble; Symphony Orchestra; Concert Band; Washington Square Woodwind Ensemble; Jazz Ensembles; New Music Ensemble; Percussion Ensembles; Choral Arts Society; Opera Workshop; All-University Gospel Choir, University Singers. The Center for Music Performance sponsors music events and serves as a referral service for the entire NYU musical community. An active NYU composers' forum features visiting composers and provides ongoing opportunities for students' work to be performed.

Special Programs Interactive Performance Series; Stephen F. Temmer Tonmeister Studies (advanced recording technology); Annual Summer Composers Seminar; Summer Musical Theatre and Opera, Music in Italy, a summer study abroad program, includes participation in an international music festival and study with distinguished NYU faculty and Italian performers and composers.

The Department of Music and Performing Arts Professions at New York University's School of Education offers the finest professional training for your career combined with academic studies at a preeminent university. Alongside the music programs described above, our department also offers: Dance Education (B.S., M.A., Ed.D, Ph.D), education theater (B.S., M.A., Ed.D, Ph.D), Drama Therapy (M.S.), and performing arts administration (M.A.). Baccalaureate programs combine intense professional training in music, technology, music business, dance, or theater with a solid liberal arts core in the humanities and the social and natural sciences. In our classrooms, undergraduate students join advanced master's and doctoral degree students and faculty members in a collaborative environment that fosters creativity.

Studies in music performance and composition prepare students for the demands of a professional career in music by providing them with the breadth of skills to perform in a wide range of styles and contexts. Whatever their musical interests, you benefit from being part of a department that thrives on a variety of styles–from the Western musical tradition to contemporary multicultural music.

Added to this, is the excitement and opportunities of New York City. Well-known musicians from New York City's professional world of music routinely join our students in performances on- and off-campus. Music business and technology students gain hands-on experience through internships at leading recording companies, publishing houses, and concert management, and public relations firms. Students in music education gain the finest student experiences in the country's largest public school system. Being in New York City helps you build a network of contacts for your professional career.

NYU attracts talented high achievers from across the country and around the world. The diverse course offerings of NYU's 13 schools and colleges provide unparalleled opportunities to pursue many academic interests during our studies. For those interested in careers in the visual arts, the Department of Arts and Arts

Mike Stern

Berklee College of Music—*Standards* was named "Best Jazz Album" in the 1993 *Guitar Player* reader poll. He has made seven records as lead player.

Berklee was terrific—just what I needed. It is what you make of it. Some people say you sound too much like everybody else if you go to a music school. But I never felt that. There is this atmosphere there where everyone is trying to develop their musical potential. For me it was a way to enhance my vocabulary and musical options. Today, I often play with musicians I met at Berklee.

New York University *(continued)*

Professions at NYU's School of Education offers: studio art (B.S., M.F.A., M.A., D.A.) including painting, drawing, sculpture, printmaking, photography, and art and media; art education (B.S., M.A., Ed.D, Ph.D), visual arts administration and (M.A.), decorative arts (M.A.) including folk art studies and costume studies.

Newberry College

Newberry, South Carolina

Independent-religious, coed. Small-town campus. Total enrollment: 624.

Degrees Bachelor of Music in the area of music performance; Bachelor of Music Education in the areas of choral music, instrumental music. Majors: music education, piano/organ, voice, wind and percussion instruments.

Music Student Profile Fall 1994: 32 total; all matriculated undergraduate; 7% minorities, 55% females, 1% international.

Music Faculty Total: 8; 5 full-time, 3 part-time; 20% of full-time faculty have terminal degrees. Undergraduate student–faculty ratio: 6:1.

Student Life Student groups include Phi Mu Alpha, Delta Omicron.

Expenses for 1995–96 Application fee: $25. Comprehensive fee of $13,350 includes full-time tuition ($10,950) and college room and board ($2400 minimum). College room only: $1000. Part-time tuition: $350 per semester hour. Special program-related fees: $50 for instrument maintenance, $75 for private lessons.

Financial Aid Program-specific awards for Fall of 1994: 40 Music Scholarships for program majors ($1500).

Application Procedures Deadline—freshmen and transfers: continuous. Required: audition. Auditions held 4 times on campus; recorded music is permissible as a substitute for live auditions if a campus visit is impossible and videotaped performances are permissible as a substitute for live auditions if a campus visit is impossible.

Undergraduate Contact Dr. John W. Wagner, Chairman, Music Department, Newberry College, 2100 College Street, Newberry, South Carolina 29108; 803-321-5174, fax: 803-321-5232.

Nicholls State University

Thibodaux, Louisiana

State-supported, coed. Small-town campus. Total enrollment: 7,205.

Degrees Bachelor of Music Education in the areas of instrumental music, vocal music. Majors: music education.

Music Student Profile Fall 1994: 37 total; all matriculated undergraduate; 16% minorities, 50% females.

Music Faculty Total: 10; 8 full-time, 2 part-time; 50% of full-time faculty have terminal degrees. Graduate students do not teach undergraduate courses. Undergraduate student–faculty ratio: 5:1.

Student Life Student groups include Phi Mu Alpha Sinfonia.

Expenses for 1994–95 State resident tuition: $1990 full-time. Nonresident tuition: $4579 full-time. Part-time tuition per semester ranges from $253.25 to $924.50 for state residents, $253.25 to $2113 for nonresidents. College room and board: $2550.

Financial Aid Program-specific awards for Fall of 1994: 12 Band Service Awards for instrumental ensemble members ($300), 20 Choir Service Awards for choir members ($100), 25 Music Department Scholarships for program majors ($600).

Application Procedures Deadline—freshmen and transfers: continuous. Required: high school transcript, audition. Recommended: 3 letters of recommendation. Auditions held 3 times on campus; recorded music is permissible as a substitute for live auditions if a campus visit is impossible and videotaped performances are permissible as a substitute for live auditions if a campus visit is impossible.

Undergraduate Contact Dr. James Fields, Head, Department of Music, Nicholls State University, P.O. Box 2017, Thibodaux, Louisiana 70310; 504-448-4600.

Norfolk State University

Norfolk, Virginia

State-supported, coed. Urban campus. Total enrollment: 8,667.

Degrees Bachelor of Music in the area of media. Majors: jazz, piano/organ, stringed instruments, voice, wind and percussion instruments. Graduate degrees offered: Master of Music in the areas of performance, theory and composition, music education. Cross-registration with Old Dominion University.

Music Student Profile Fall 1994: 75 total; 50 matriculated undergraduate, 25 matriculated graduate; 90% minorities, 40% females.

Music Faculty Total: 24; 20 full-time, 4 part-time; 60% of full-time faculty have terminal degrees. Graduate students do not teach undergraduate courses.

Expenses for 1995–96 Application fee: $20. State resident tuition: $2865 full-time, $126 per semester hour part-time. Nonresident tuition: $6392 full-time, $279 per semester hour part-time. College room and board: $3720. Special program-related fees.

Application Procedures Deadline—freshmen and transfers: continuous. Required: high school transcript, college transcript(s) for transfer students, minimum 2.0 high school GPA, 3 letters of recommendation, audition, SAT I or ACT test scores. Auditions held 4 times on campus.

Undergraduate Contact Dr. Carl Harris, Head, Department of Music, Norfolk State University, 2401 Corprew Avenue, Norfolk, Virginia 23504; 804-683-8544, fax: 804-683-8213.

Graduate Contact Dr. William Schaffer, Coordinator of Graduate Studies, Department of Music, Norfolk State University, 2401 Corprew Avenue, Norfolk, Virginia 23504-8213; 804-683-9521, fax: 804-683-9521.

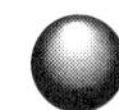

North Carolina Central University

Durham, North Carolina

State-supported, coed. Urban campus. Total enrollment: 5,634.

Degrees Bachelor of Music in the areas of jazz studies, sacred music. Majors: jazz, piano/organ, sacred music, stringed instruments, voice, wind and percussion instruments.

Expenses for 1994–95 Application fee: $15. State resident tuition: $1518 full-time. Nonresident tuition: $8002 full-time. Part-time tuition per semester ranges from $212 to $479 for state residents, $1022 to $2910 for nonresidents. College room and board: $3010.

Undergraduate Contact Dr. Charles H. Gilchrist, Chair, Department of Music, North Carolina Central University, 1801 Fayetteville Street, Durham, North Carolina 27707; 919-560-6319.

North Carolina School of the Arts

Winston-Salem, North Carolina

State-supported, coed. Urban campus. Total enrollment: 613.

Degrees Bachelor of Music in the area of music performance. Majors: classical music, composition, harp, performance, piano/organ, saxophone, stringed instruments, voice, wind and percussion instruments. Graduate degrees offered: Master of Music in the areas of music performance, opera, film music composition.

Music Student Profile Fall 1994: 250 total; 133 matriculated undergraduate, 30 matriculated graduate, 87 nondegree.

Music Faculty Total: 47; 26 full-time, 21 part-time. Graduate students do not teach undergraduate courses. Undergraduate student–faculty ratio: 8:1.

Expenses for 1994–95 State resident tuition: $1233 full-time. Nonresident tuition: $8640 full-time. Full-time mandatory fees: $766. College room and board: $3600. College room only: $2376. Special program-related fees: $135 for instructional fees.

Financial Aid Program-specific awards for Fall of 1994: Talent Scholarships for artistically talented.

Application Procedures Deadline—freshmen and transfers: March 1. Required: high school transcript, 2 letters of recommendation, interview, audition. Auditions held by request on campus and off campus in Washington, DC; Philadelphia, PA; New York, NY; Atlanta, GA; Fort Lauderdale, FL; Jacksonville, FL; recorded music is permissible as a substitute for live auditions for provisional acceptance.

Contact Carol J. Palm, Director of Admissions, North Carolina School of the Arts, 200 Waughtown Street, Winston-Salem, North Carolina 27117; 910-770-3291, fax: 910-770-3370, E-mail address: palmc@ncsavx.ncart.edu.

More about the School

Program Facilities A major performance center for the School of Music is the Stevens Center, a magnificently restored 1920s movie palace seating 1,380 in downtown Winston-Salem. Crawford Hall, a 590-seat auditorium, houses the Sarah Graham Kenan organ (designed specifically for the hall by Charles Fisk), a Dowd harpsichord, a Hamburg Steinway, and a Baldwin concert grand. Chamber and solo recitals are presented in the more intimate Recital Hall, which accommodates 60 people. Reference materials are found in the Semans Library, which contains a growing selection of 2,000 CDs, 24,000 LPs, and 700 videocassettes, as well as more than 100,000 volumes on music and the other arts. The music school also maintains two electronic studios, including a composite analog/MIDI digital studio.

Faculty, Guest Artists and Alumni The resident faculty is composed of outstanding artist-teachers who actively pursue professional careers while offering individual attention and personal guidance to students. Their careers have spanned the New York City Opera Orchestra to the Crackow Philharmonic of Poland to the Saugatuck Chamber Music Festival to the recording studios of 20th Century Fox. Throughout the year, distinguished guest artists visit the campus for performances and master classes. They have included Leonard Bernstein, John Cage, Itzhak Perlman, Menahem Pressler, and William Schuman. The standard of training at the School is reflected in the accomplishments of the alumni, who are currently employed by such institutions as the Berlin Philharmonic, Metropolitan Opera, San Francisco Symphony, and Solisti New York. Noted alumni include soloist John Cheek, flutist/conductor Ransom Wilson, and composer Kenneth Frazelle.

Student Performance Opportunities The music program is designed to provide the broadest possible performance opportunities for each student. The Symphony Orchestra, Cantata Singers, Jazz Ensemble, Percussion Ensemble, Contemporary Ensemble, opera productions, and chamber groups in every medium provide ensemble performance opportunities through rehearsals and frequent public performances.

Special Programs Music ensembles and soloists are often involved in performance tours throughout the Southeastern United States and beyond. The School of the Arts is the only American school that offers students a chance to perform in a multi-week European tour (International Music Program) each summer.

Since it opened in 1965 as the first state-assisted residential conservatory in the nation, the North Carolina School of the Arts has provided students with solid professional training for careers as performing artists.

North Carolina School of the Arts *(continued)*

Today, the school's mission has grown to encompass not only the performing arts, but the moving image and visual arts as well.

At the School of the Arts, students of all arts disciplines live, learn, practice, and perform together on one campus. A musician's roommate may be a dancer or filmmaker. Scene designers and actors and cellists debate philosophical points or work calculus problems in the same classes. Interdisciplinary collaborations, both structured and spontaneous, are part of daily life at the School of the Arts. The inclusion of all the arts makes for a unique vitality and richness of creative expression.

The relationship between students and their teachers, that of apprentice to master, is the heart of the School of the Arts. Students and teachers are engaged in classes, rehearsals, and shoots from morning to late evening six days a week, and weekends are filled with performances and screenings. The resident faculty of 100 artists have had successful careers on Broadway, in Hollywood, as members of the great orchestras and dance companies and theaters of the world. Most continued to perform, direct, choreograph, coach, write, and produce professionally. In the tradition of artists throughout human history, they pass on their knowledge and experience to their students, one-on-one, face-to-face. Their close, sustained work with students is supplemented with residencies by more than 150 guest artists each year.

For aspiring performers, there is no substitute for performing. The 300 performances presented each year by students provide an unparalleled learning experience. Music students participate in jazz ensemble and orchestral performances, operas, solo recitals and chamber groups in every medium. Dance students perform a repertory of ballet and contemporary works that is unsurpassed in its diversity. Actors are cast in challenging works from the world's repertory of classical and contemporary plays. Theatrical design and production students light the shows, design and build costumes and sets, and manage the productions.

As the School's alumni know, there is no better preparation for careers in the arts than performing in professionally mounted productions, in performance places designed to professional standards. Graduates emerge ready to go on stage, because they have been on stage, all through their training.

Students are intimately connected to the professional world that awaits them through many channels, including their faculty, guest artists, and touring performances around the country and abroad. Also vital to the emerging artist is the professional network of thousands of successful North Carolina School of the Arts alumni who are putting their training to work on the stages and screens of the world.

School of the Arts alumni have distinguished themselves from the Metropolitan Opera to the Houston Ballet, from the Great Lakes Theater Festival to Merce Cunningham Dance Company, from Broadway to Hollywood. Virtually every orchestra in this country has had a School of the Arts alumnus in its ranks. Some of the finest ballet, theater, and opera companies the world over feature School alumni in the corps, the chorus, in starring roles, and behind the scenes. Alumni continually enrich the lives of the people in the communities where they perform, live, or work as artists in residence.

The School of the Arts is located in Winston-Salem, a medium-sized city in the central Piedmont of scenic North Carolina. The city has a tradition of appreciation for the arts dating back to the 18th century, when the area was settled by European members of the Moravian church, many of whom were highly skilled classical musicians, artisans, and craftsmen. The first arts council in America was established in Winston-Salem, and the city relied on its strong support of the arts in its quest to become the home of the School of the Arts.

Today, the North Carolina School of the Arts enrolls more than 900 students—from middle school through graduate school—in the Schools of Dance, Design and Production, Drama, Filmmaking, and Music. A high school Visual Arts Program is part of the School of Design and Production. Long considered part of the School's mission, filmmaking was added in 1993; this unique program focuses on creative rather than technical aspects of the industry.

At the School of the Arts, arts courses are balanced with academic courses to give students a solid grounding in the humanities and sciences, and to deepen their understanding of the role of the artist in society. The School is part of the highly regarded, 16-campus University of North Carolina. Both the high school and the college programs are accredited.

North Park College

Chicago, Illinois

Independent-religious, coed. Urban campus. Total enrollment: 1,647.

Degrees Bachelor of Music in the areas of voice, piano, strings; Bachelor of Music Education in the area of music education. Majors: music, music education.

Music Student Profile Fall 1994: 35 total; all matriculated undergraduate; 3% minorities, 54% females, 34% international.

Music Faculty Total: 26; 6 full-time, 20 part-time; 40% of full-time faculty have terminal degrees. Graduate students do not teach undergraduate courses. Undergraduate student–faculty ratio: 15:1.

Expenses for 1995–96 Application fee: $20. Comprehensive fee of $17,680 includes full-time tuition ($13,280) and college room and board ($4400). College room only: $2450. Part-time tuition: $465 per semester hour.

Financial Aid Program-specific awards for Fall of 1994: 15 Music Scholarships for freshmen and transfer students ($1000–$4000), 14 Named Music Scholarships for continuing students ($300–$1500).

Application Procedures Deadline—freshmen and transfers: continuous. Required: high school transcript, interview, audition. Auditions held at least 2 times and by appointment on campus; recorded music is permissible as a substitute for live auditions if a campus visit is impossible and videotaped performances are permissible as a substitute for live auditions if a campus visit is impossible.

Undergraduate Contact Joseph Lill, Admissions Coordinator, Music Department, North Park College, 3225 West Foster Avenue, Chicago, Illinois 60625; 312-244-5634, fax: 312-583-0858.

Northeast Louisiana University

Monroe, Louisiana

State-supported, coed. Urban campus. Total enrollment: 11,379.

Degrees Bachelor of Music in the areas of performance, pedagogy, music theory, composition, music history/literature, music theater; Bachelor of Music Education in the area of music education. Majors: classical music, music, music education, music history and literature, music theater, music theory and composition, piano pedagogy, piano/organ, stringed instruments, voice, wind and percussion instruments. Graduate degrees offered: Master of Music in the areas of performance, music education, music theory/composition, conducting.

Music Student Profile Fall 1994: 92 total; 66 matriculated undergraduate, 26 matriculated graduate; 5% minorities, 55% females, 10% international.

Music Faculty Total: 26; 23 full-time, 3 part-time; 55% of full-time faculty have terminal degrees. Graduate students teach a few undergraduate courses. Undergraduate student–faculty ratio: 3:1.

Student Life Student groups include Music Educators National Conference Student Chapter, music sorority, band fraternity and sorority.

Expenses for 1994–95 Application fee: $25. State resident tuition: $1644 full-time. Nonresident tuition: $3804 full-time. Part-time tuition per semester ranges from $207 to $759 for state residents, $207 to $1749 for nonresidents. Part-time mandatory fees per semester range from $48 to $140.75. Full-time mandatory fees: $282. College room and board: $2060.

Financial Aid Program-specific awards for Fall of 1994: 250 Music Talent Grants for members of major ensembles ($900).

Application Procedures Deadline—freshmen and transfers: continuous. Notification date—freshmen and transfers: continuous. Required: high school transcript, college transcript(s) for transfer students, audition, ACT test score only. Recommended: interview. Auditions held throughout the year on campus; recorded music is permissible as a substitute for live auditions when distance is prohibitive or scheduling is difficult and videotaped performances are permissible as a substitute for live auditions when distance is prohibitive or scheduling is difficult.

Contact Dr. Larry W. Edwards, Director, School of Music, Northeast Louisiana University, Monroe, Louisiana 71209-0250; 318-342-1570, fax: 318-342-1369, E-mail address: muedwards@alpha.nlu.edu.

Northeast Missouri State University

Kirksville, Missouri

State-supported, coed. Small-town campus. Total enrollment: 6,317.

Degrees Bachelor of Music in the area of performance. Majors: composition, piano, stringed instruments, voice, wind and percussion instruments.

Music Student Profile Fall 1994: 120 total; all matriculated undergraduate; 1% minorities, 50% females, 1% international.

Music Faculty Total: 25; 20 full-time, 5 part-time; 80% of full-time faculty have terminal degrees. Graduate students teach a few undergraduate courses. Undergraduate student–faculty ratio: 5:1.

Student Life Student groups include Phi Mu Alpha, Sigma Alpha Iota, Pi Kappa Lambda.

Expenses for 1995–96 State resident tuition: $2872 full-time, $120 per credit part-time. Nonresident tuition: $5152 full-time, $215 per credit part-time. Full-time mandatory fees: $18. College room and board: $3624. Special program-related fees: $40–$80 for private lessons.

Financial Aid Program-specific awards for Fall of 1994: 10 Endowed Scholarships for program majors ($200–$950), 100 Service Scholarships for program majors and non-majors ($300–$1500).

Application Procedures Deadline—freshmen: November 15; transfers: May 1. Notification date—freshmen: December 5. Required: essay, high school transcript, college transcript(s) for transfer students, audition, SAT I or ACT test scores. Auditions held continuously on campus and off campus in Kansas City, MO; St. Louis, MO; Chicago, IL; Des Moines, IA; recorded music is permissible as a substitute for live auditions with approval from the department and videotaped performances are permissible as a substitute for live auditions with approval from the department. Portfolio reviews held 2 times on campus.

Undergraduate Contact John M. Lee, Head, Division of Fine Arts, Northeast Missouri State University, Baldwin Hall #118, Kirksville, Missouri 63501; 816-785-4417, fax: 816-785-7463, E-mail address: fa01%nemomus@academic.nemostate.edu.

Northern Arizona University

Flagstaff, Arizona

State-supported, coed. Small-town campus. Total enrollment: 19,242.

Degrees Bachelor of Music in the area of performance; Bachelor of Music Education in the area of music education. Majors: music, music education, opera, piano/organ, stringed instruments, voice, wind and percussion instruments. Graduate degrees offered: Master of Music in the areas of performance, music education, music history/musicology, music theory/composition.

Northern Arizona University *(continued)*

Music Student Profile Fall 1994: 316 total; 276 matriculated undergraduate, 40 matriculated graduate; 5% minorities, 50% females, 8% international.

Music Faculty Total: 47; 32 full-time, 15 part-time; 90% of full-time faculty have terminal degrees. Graduate students teach a few undergraduate courses. Undergraduate student–faculty ratio: 15:1.

Student Life Student groups include music fraternities and sororities, Music Educators National Conference Student Chapter, American Choral Directors Association.

Expenses for 1995–96 Application fee: $35. State resident tuition: $1914 full-time, $99 per semester hour part-time. Nonresident tuition: $7086 full-time, $304 per semester hour part-time. College room and board: $3286. College room only: $1576.

Financial Aid Program-specific awards for Fall of 1994: Tuition Waiver Scholarships for program majors and minors ($1770–$1826), Lesson Only Scholarships for program majors and minors.

Application Procedures Deadline—freshmen and transfers: continuous. Required: high school transcript, minimum 2.0 high school GPA, audition, SAT I or ACT test scores. Recommended: 3 letters of recommendation, video. Auditions held 3 times and in special circumstances with approval from the department; recorded music is permissible as a substitute for live auditions when distance is prohibitive and videotaped performances are permissible as a substitute for live auditions when distance is prohibitive.

Undergraduate Contact Band and Choral Department, Northern Arizona University, P.O. Box 6040, Flagstaff, Arizona 86011-6040; 520-523-8413.

Graduate Contact Dr. C. T. Aufdemberge, Director of Graduate Studies, Department of Music, Northern Arizona University, P.O. Box 6040, Flagstaff, Arizona 86011-6040; 520-523-3538.

Northern Illinois University

De Kalb, Illinois

State-supported, coed. Small-town campus. Total enrollment: 22,881.

Degrees Bachelor of Music in the areas of performance, music education. Majors: jazz, music education, piano/organ, stringed instruments, voice, wind and percussion instruments. Graduate degrees offered: Master of Music in the areas of performance, music education, individualized studies.

Music Faculty 100% of full-time faculty have terminal degrees. Graduate students do not teach undergraduate courses. Undergraduate student–faculty ratio: 10:1.

Student Life Student groups include professional fraternities and sororities, Music Educators National Conference, National Association of Jazz Educators.

Expenses for 1995–96 State resident tuition: $2930 full-time, $89.70 per credit hour part-time. Nonresident tuition: $8611 full-time, $269.10 per credit hour part-time. Part-time mandatory fees: $32 per credit hour. Full-time mandatory fees: $777. College room and board: $3416. Special program-related fees: $20–$50 for applied fees.

Financial Aid Program-specific awards for Fall of 1994: Scholarships for program majors ($250–$1000).

Application Procedures Deadline—freshmen: August 1; transfers: July 15. Required: high school transcript, college transcript(s) for transfer students, audition, ACT test score only. Auditions held 3 times on campus and off campus; recorded music is permissible as a substitute for live auditions and videotaped performances are permissible as a substitute for live auditions. Portfolio reviews held on campus and off campus.

Undergraduate Contact Coordinator of Undergraduate Admissions, School of Music, Northern Illinois University, De Kalb, Illinois 60115; 815-753-7976.

Graduate Contact Coordinator of Graduate Admissions, School of Music, Northern Illinois University, De Kalb, Illinois 60115; 815-753-7976.

Northern Kentucky University

Highland Heights, Kentucky

State-supported, coed. Suburban campus. Total enrollment: 11,978.

Degrees Bachelor of Music in the area of performance; Bachelor of Music Education in the area of music education. Majors: guitar, harp, music education, piano, stringed instruments, voice, wind and percussion instruments.

Music Student Profile Fall 1994: 90 total; all matriculated undergraduate; 1% minorities, 1% international.

Music Faculty Total: 22; 10 full-time, 12 part-time; 100% of full-time faculty have terminal degrees. Undergraduate student–faculty ratio: 10:1.

Student Life Student groups include Sigma Alpha Iota, Phi Mu Alpha, Music Educators National Conference Student Chapter.

Expenses for 1995–96 Application fee: $25. State resident tuition: $1960 full-time, $83 per semester hour part-time. Nonresident tuition: $5320 full-time, $223 per semester hour part-time. College room and board: $3480 (minimum). Special program-related fees: $160 for private music lessons.

Financial Aid Program-specific awards for Fall of 1994: 18 University Scholarships ($1500), 3 Private Scholarships ($1200).

Application Procedures Deadline—freshmen and transfers: continuous. Required: high school transcript, college transcript(s) for transfer students, SAT I or ACT test scores, minimum composite ACT score of 18. Recommended: 2 letters of recommendation, audition. Auditions held 4 times on campus; recorded music is permissible as a substitute for live auditions and videotaped performances are permissible as a substitute for live auditions.

Undergraduate Contact John Westlund, Chairman, Music Department, Northern Kentucky University, Fine

Arts Center, Room 253, Highland Heights, Kentucky 41099-1005; 606-572-5649, fax: 606-572-5566, E-mail address: westlund@nku.edu.

Northern Michigan University

Marquette, Michigan

State-supported, coed. Small-town campus. Total enrollment: 7,898.

Degrees Bachelor of Music Education in the areas of choral music education, instrumental music education. Majors: music, music education.

Music Student Profile Fall 1994: 33 total; all matriculated undergraduate; 55% females, 3% international.

Music Faculty Total: 10; 10 part-time; 90% of full-time faculty have terminal degrees. Graduate students do not teach undergraduate courses. Undergraduate student–faculty ratio: 3:1.

Estimated Expenses for 1995–96 Application fee: $25. State resident tuition: $2900 full-time, $89 per credit hour part-time. Nonresident tuition: $5200 full-time, $164 per credit hour part-time. Part-time mandatory fees per semester range from $2 to $39.10. Full-time mandatory fees: $98. College room and board: $4100.

Financial Aid Program-specific awards for Fall of 1994: 12 Scholarships for talented program majors ($800).

Application Procedures Deadline—freshmen and transfers: continuous. Required: high school transcript, minimum 2.25 high school GPA. Recommended: audition. Auditions held as needed for voice and instrumental applicants on campus; recorded music is permissible as a substitute for live auditions and videotaped performances are permissible as a substitute for live auditions.

Undergraduate Contact Dr. Elda Tate, Head, Music Department, Northern Michigan University, 1401 Presque Isle Avenue, Marquette, Michigan 49855; 906-227-2563, fax: 906-227-2204.

Northern State University

Aberdeen, South Dakota

State-supported, coed. Small-town campus. Total enrollment: 3,078.

Degrees Bachelor of Music Education in the areas of instrumental music, vocal music. Majors: instrumental music, stringed instruments, voice.

Music Student Profile Fall 1994: 100 total; 75 matriculated undergraduate, 25 nondegree.

Music Faculty Total: 13; 12 full-time, 1 part-time; 58% of full-time faculty have terminal degrees.

Student Life Student groups include Music Educators National Conference.

Expenses for 1995–96 Application fee: $15. State resident tuition: $1508 full-time, $47.10 per semester hour part-time. Nonresident tuition: $3797 full-time, $118.65 per semester hour part-time. Part-time mandatory fees: $26 per semester hour. Minnesota residents pay state resident tuition rates. Tuition for nonresidents who are eligible for the Western Undergraduate Exchange Program: $2198 full-time, $68.67 per semester hour part-time. Full-time mandatory fees: $832. College room and board: $2202. College room only: $1128.

Financial Aid Program-specific awards for Fall of 1994: 30 Music Scholarships for incoming freshmen/transfers ($400).

Application Procedures Deadline—freshmen and transfers: September 1. Notification date—freshmen and transfers: continuous. Required: high school transcript, college transcript(s) for transfer students, ACT test score only. Auditions held on campus and off campus. Portfolio reviews held on campus and off campus.

Undergraduate Contact Admissions Office, Northern State University, 1200 South Jay Street, Aberdeen, South Dakota 57401-7198; 605-626-2544, fax: 605-626-2431.

Northwestern Oklahoma State University

Alva, Oklahoma

State-supported, coed. Small-town campus. Total enrollment: 1,861.

Degrees Bachelor of Music in the area of performance; Bachelor of Music Education in the areas of vocal music education, instrumental music education. Majors: music education, piano/organ, voice, wind and percussion instruments.

Music Student Profile Fall 1994: 25 total; all matriculated undergraduate.

Music Faculty Total: 7; 4 full-time, 3 part-time; 75% of full-time faculty have terminal degrees. Graduate students do not teach undergraduate courses.

Expenses for 1994–95 State resident tuition: $1556 full-time. Nonresident tuition: $3756 full-time. Part-time tuition per semester hour ranges from $48.64 to $49.45 for state residents, $117.39 to $125.42 for nonresidents, according to class level. Full-time mandatory fees: $30. College room and board: $1876 (minimum). Special program-related fees.

Financial Aid Program-specific awards for Fall of 1994 available.

Application Procedures Deadline—freshmen and transfers: continuous. Required: high school transcript, college transcript(s) for transfer students, ACT test score only, minimum composite ACT score of 19. Recommended: audition. Auditions held by appointment on campus; recorded music is permissible as a substitute for live auditions when distance is prohibitive and videotaped performances are permissible as a substitute for live auditions when distance is prohibitive.

Undergraduate Contact Dr. Ed Huckeby, Chair, Music Department, Northwestern Oklahoma State Univer-

Northwestern Oklahoma State University
(continued)

sity, 709 Oklahoma Boulevard, Alva, Oklahoma 73717; 405-327-8411 ext. 302, fax: 405-327-1881.

Northwestern State University of Louisiana

Natchitoches, Louisiana

State-supported, coed. Small-town campus. Total enrollment: 8,762.

Degrees Bachelor of Music in the area of performance; Bachelor of Music Education in the areas of instrumental music education, vocal music education, piano music education. Majors: music, music education, piano/organ, voice, wind and percussion instruments. Graduate degrees offered: Master of Music in the areas of instrumental music, vocal music, piano. Cross-registration with Louisiana State University in Shreveport, Louisiana State University and Agricultural and Mechanical College.

Music Student Profile Fall 1994: 141 total; 125 matriculated undergraduate, 16 matriculated graduate; 10% minorities, 40% females, 1% international.

Music Faculty Total: 25; 14 full-time, 11 part-time; 80% of full-time faculty have terminal degrees. Graduate students teach a few undergraduate courses. Undergraduate student–faculty ratio: 18:1.

Student Life Student groups include professional fraternities and sororities, Music Educators National Conference.

Expenses for 1995–96 Application fee: $5. State resident tuition: $2067 full-time. Nonresident tuition: $4497 full-time. Part-time tuition per semester ranges from $321.25 to $906.50 for state residents, $405 to $1114 for nonresidents. Full-time mandatory fees: $187. College room and board: $2216 (minimum). College room only: $980.

Financial Aid Program-specific awards for Fall of 1994: 200–250 Band Awards for incoming freshmen ($800–$1200), 75–100 Music Awards for incoming freshmen ($800–$1200).

Application Procedures Deadline—freshmen and transfers: August 15. Notification date—freshmen: August 15. Required: college transcript(s) for transfer students, minimum 2.0 high school GPA, 3 letters of recommendation, audition, SAT I or ACT test scores. Auditions held 5 times on campus; recorded music is permissible as a substitute for live auditions with approval from the department and videotaped performances are permissible as a substitute for live auditions with approval from the department.

Undergraduate Contact Chris Maggio, Director, Office of Admissions, Northwestern State University of Louisiana, College Avenue, Natchitoches, Louisiana 71497; 318-357-4503, fax: 318-357-5906.

Graduate Contact Dr. Randy Webb, Dean, Graduate School, Northwestern State University of Louisiana, College Avenue, Natchitoches, Louisiana 71497; 318-357-4522, fax: 318-357-5906.

Northwestern University

Evanston, Illinois

Independent, coed. Suburban campus. Total enrollment: 12,179.

Degrees Bachelor of Music in the areas of church music, composition, music history, music education, music technology, percussion, piano, strings, music theory, voice, winds. Majors: classical music, composition, jazz, music, music education, music history and literature, music technology, music theory, opera, piano/organ, sacred music, stringed instruments, voice, wind and percussion instruments. Graduate degrees offered: Master of Music in the areas of church music, composition, conducting, music history, jazz pedagogy, music education, music technology, percussion, piano, strings, music theory, voice, winds; Master of Music Education. Doctor of Musical Arts in the areas of composition, conducting, percussion, piano, strings, voice, winds.

Music Student Profile Fall 1994: 589 total; 358 matriculated undergraduate, 231 matriculated graduate; 14% minorities, 53% females, 9% international.

Music Faculty Total: 110; 50 full-time, 60 part-time; 98% of full-time faculty have terminal degrees. Graduate students teach a few undergraduate courses. Undergraduate student–faculty ratio: 3:1.

Student Life Student groups include Phi Mu Alpha, Sigma Alpha Iota, Pi Kappa Lambda. Special housing available for music students.

Expenses for 1994–95 Application fee: $50. Comprehensive fee of $21,924 includes full-time tuition ($16,404) and college room and board ($5520).

Financial Aid Program-specific awards for Fall of 1994 available.

Application Procedures Deadline—freshmen: January 1; transfers: June 1. Notification date—freshmen: April 15; transfers: July 1. Required: essay, high school transcript, minimum 3.0 high school GPA, letter of recommendation, audition, SAT I or ACT test scores. Recommended: interview, SAT II. Auditions held 34 times on campus and off campus in Detroit, MI; Kansas City, MO; New Orleans, LA; Denver, CO; Boston, MA; Seattle, WA; St. Louis, MO; Minneapolis, MN; Miami, FL; Orlando, FL; Atlanta, GA; Nashville, TN; Cincinnati, OH; Philadelphia, PA; New York, NY; Washington, DC; Houston, TX; Albuquerque, NM; Phoenix, AZ; Interlochen, MI; Cleveland, OH; Portland, OR; San Francisco, CA; Palo Alto, CA; Los Angeles, CA; recorded music is permissible as a substitute for live auditions if a live audition is impossible and videotaped performances are permissible as a substitute for live auditions if a live audition is impossible.

Undergraduate Contact Heather Landes, Coordinator of Undergraduate Music Admissions, School of

Music, Northwestern University, 711 Elgin Road, Evanston, Illinois 60208-1200; 708-491-3141, fax: 708-491-5260, E-mail address: hlandes@nwu.edu.

Graduate Contact Wayne Gordon, Coordinator of Graduate Music Admissions, School of Music, Northwestern University, 711 Elgin Road, Evanston, Illinois 60208-1200; 708-491-3141, fax: 708-491-5260, E-mail address: wgordon@nwu.edu.

More about the University

The School of Music consists of six buildings. The Music Administration Building houses administrative offices, classrooms, studios, and practice rooms. The faculty of the Department of Academic Studies and Composition as well as the faculty of the Voice and Opera Program and the Piano Program have offices in this building. Regenstein Hall houses rehearsal facilities, practice rooms, a 200-seat lecture/recital room, and the library and offices for the University bands. The Department of Music Performance Studies office and studios for faculty of the Conducting and Ensembles, String Instruments, and Wind and Percussion Instruments programs are also located in Regenstein Hall. The Practice Hall contains thirty-five practice rooms. Lutkin Hall, seating 400, is used for student and faculty recitals and lecture classes. Pick-Staiger Concert Hall provides a 1,000-seat concert hall, rehearsal facilities, and offices and library for the University Symphony Orchestra. The School of Music maintains two computer labs, an electronic music studio, and a computer music studio. The Music Library, internationally recognized for its collection of contemporary music, is one of the country's finest academic music libraries. It has spacious, aesthetically pleasing facilities, including a multidimensional listening center. Holdings include 142,000 books, music, journals, and microforms, and the Recorded Sound Collection, consisting of 53,000 disks and tapes. The library's special collections, consisting of over 2,000 items, include a manuscript collection documenting contemporary notation compiled by John Cage for use in his book, *Notations;* additional holographic scores, sketches, and letters of musicians; the Fritz Reiner Library; and rare printed resources.

Since its establishment in 1895, the School of Music has been highly ranked among the nations's prestigious music schools, providing an environment in which young musicians can dedicate themselves to their art. The School educates its students to become highly proficient in performance and to acquire the broad cultural knowledge that will make them well-rounded musicians. The School of Music is a professional school within the University; students accepted into the School are also accepted into the University and consequently have the advantage of pursuing academic study through a variety of courses and with distinguished faculty. As part of a private institution, the School of Music has developed distinctive programs to meet the artistic and professional needs of its students, preparing them for careers as instrumentalists, singers, teachers, composers, conductors, theorists, historians, critics, managers, and others needing a specialized knowledge of music. These programs are responsive to new directions, recognizing that a thriving institution of musical learning preserves the riches of past practices while it encourages its students to explore the practices that will produce the music of the future.

Faculty members strive to be inspiring teachers as well as musical and intellectual leaders. They are actively engaged in expanding knowledge about music through their research and scholarship; in preparing students to be performers, composers, teachers, scholars, and informed audiences; and in enriching their community's culture through their own artistry. The faculty believe that each undergraduate should be given a comprehensive musical background, that the education should be centered on performance founded on scholarly studies in music theory and history, and that all musical training should be accompanied by a broad cultural background in the humanities. In addition to providing instruction in voice and all principal instruments, composition, and music technology, the School supports orchestras, bands, choral ensembles, opera, musical theatre, and a wide variety of small ensembles that give students experience in all avenues of musical expression.

The graduate division of the School is open to students who are deemed capable of advanced study. Graduate courses emphasize scholarly performance and include concentrated work and research in students' major fields of interest. The ultimate aim is to develop informed musicians, independent scholars, and inspired teachers.

Although the excellence of any school depends mainly upon the quality of its faculty and students and the soundness of its curriculum, distinguished personages in the field of music are brought to the campus from time to time to enrich the regular programs and to give a special impetus to study. In past years, guess have included Dmitri Shostakovich, Witold Lutoslowsky, John Cage, Sherrill Milnes, James Galway, Pierre Boulez, Erich Leinsdorf, and Sir Georg Solti, among others. An annual performing arts series presents concert artists in performance and master classes for students.

In addition to outstanding instruction and significant platform experience at the University, the School offers excellent opportunities for professional associations in the Chicago metropolitan area. Students can gain valuable experience in performance while studying toward a degree, and the richness of Chicago's musical life can enhance their education as developing musicians.

Nyack College

Nyack, New York

Independent-religious, coed. Small-town campus. Total enrollment: 790.

Degrees Bachelor of Music in the areas of performance, music education; Bachelor of Sacred Music in the area of sacred music. Majors: classical music, music, music education, piano/organ, sacred music, stringed instruments, voice, wind and percussion instruments. Cross-registration with Sarah Lawrence College.

Music Student Profile Fall 1994: 50 total; all matriculated undergraduate; 40% minorities, 60% females, 16% international.

Music Faculty Total: 20; 4 full-time, 16 part-time; 75% of full-time faculty have terminal degrees. Graduate students do not teach undergraduate courses.

Nyack College *(continued)*

Student Life Student groups include Music Educators National Conference, American Guild of Organists, American Choral Directors Association.

Expenses for 1995–96 Application fee: $15. Comprehensive fee of $13,580 includes full-time tuition ($8950), mandatory fees ($500), and college room and board ($4130). Part-time tuition: $375 per credit hour. Part-time mandatory fees per semester range from $50 to $100. Special program-related fees: $135 for private lessons.

Financial Aid Program-specific awards for Fall of 1994: 6 Music Achievement Grants for talented performers ($3000).

Application Procedures Deadline—freshmen and transfers: continuous. Notification date—freshmen: continuous. Required: essay, high school transcript, college transcript(s) for transfer students, 3 letters of recommendation, interview, audition, SAT I or ACT test scores, minimum combined SAT I score of 850. Recommended: minimum 2.0 high school GPA, portfolio. Auditions held 4 times and by appointment on campus and off campus in New York, NY; recorded music is permissible as a substitute for live auditions when distance is prohibitive and videotaped performances are permissible as a substitute for live auditions when distance is prohibitive.

Undergraduate Contact Miguel Sanchez, Head, Admissions Office, Nyack College, 1 South Boulevard, Nyack, New York 10960; 800-366-9225.

Oakland City University

Oakland City, Indiana

Independent-religious, coed. Rural campus. Total enrollment: 983.

Degrees Bachelor of Music Education in the areas of choral music education, general music education. Majors: music, music education, piano/organ, sacred music, voice.

Music Student Profile Fall 1994: 18 total; all matriculated undergraduate; 5% minorities, 50% females, 3% international.

Music Faculty Total: 3; 2 full-time, 1 part-time; 50% of full-time faculty have terminal degrees. Undergraduate student–faculty ratio: 6:1.

Student Life Student groups include Music Educators National Conference, Music Club.

Expenses for 1995–96 Application fee: $25. Comprehensive fee of $10,662 includes full-time tuition ($7500), mandatory fees ($166), and college room and board ($2996). College room only: $998. Part-time tuition: $250 per semester hour.

Financial Aid Program-specific awards for Fall of 1994: 1 Voice Scholarship for vocalists ($300), 1 Instrumental Scholarship for piano, organ, or flute players ($300), 6 Tuition Scholarships for program majors and minors ($1700–$5100), 1 Piano Accompanying Scholarship for pianists ($6800).

Application Procedures Deadline—freshmen and transfers: continuous. Notification date—freshmen and transfers: continuous. Required: high school transcript, interview, audition. Recommended: portfolio. Auditions held by appointment on campus; recorded music is permissible as a substitute for live auditions when distance is prohibitive and videotaped performances are permissible as a substitute for live auditions when distance is prohibitive.

Undergraduate Contact Dr. Jean Cox, Associate Professor, Music Department, Oakland City University, Lucretia Street, Oakland City, Indiana 47660; 812-749-4781.

Oakland University

Rochester, Michigan

State-supported, coed. Suburban campus. Total enrollment: 13,165.

Degrees Bachelor of Music in the areas of music education, sacred music, voice performance, piano performance. Majors: composition, music education, piano, sacred music, voice. Graduate degrees offered: Master of Music in the areas of music education, conducting, performance, composition, pedagogy.

Music Student Profile Fall 1994: 174 total; 140 matriculated undergraduate, 30 matriculated graduate, 4 nondegree; 6% minorities, 52% females, 1% international.

Music Faculty Total: 40; 15 full-time, 25 part-time; 87% of full-time faculty have terminal degrees. Graduate students teach a few undergraduate courses. Undergraduate student–faculty ratio: 16:1.

Student Life Student groups include Music Educators National Conference.

Expenses for 1995–96 Application fee: $25. State resident tuition: $3154 (minimum) full-time. Nonresident tuition: $9292 (minimum) full-time. Part-time mandatory fees: $121 per semester. Full-time tuition ranges up to $3271 for state residents, $9455 for nonresidents according to class level. Part-time tuition per credit ranges from $96 to $105.50 for state residents, $283 to $305 for nonresidents according to class level. Full-time mandatory fees: $242. College room and board: $4165.

Application Procedures Deadline—freshmen and transfers: July 15. Required: high school transcript, college transcript(s) for transfer students, SAT I or ACT test scores, minimun 2.5 high school GPA. Auditions held on campus; recorded music is permissible as a substitute for live auditions if a campus visit is impossible.

Contact David Daniels, Chief Advisor, Music, Theater and Dance Department, Oakland University, 315 Varner, Rochester, Michigan 48309; 810-370-2034, fax: 810-370-2041.

Oberlin College

Oberlin, Ohio

Independent, coed. Small-town campus. Total enrollment: 2,744.

Degrees Bachelor of Music in the areas of performance, music education, composition, music history, electronic and computer music, jazz studies, music theory, accompanying. Majors: accompanying, classical music, composition, historical performance, jazz, music education, music theory, musical instrument technology, musicology, piano/organ, stringed instruments, voice, wind and percussion instruments. Graduate degrees offered: Master of Music in the area of historical performance; Master of Music Education in the area of music education.

Music Student Profile Fall 1994: 567 total; 550 matriculated undergraduate, 5 matriculated graduate, 12 nondegree; 16% minorities, 52% females, 13% international.

Music Faculty Total: 120; 60 full-time, 60 part-time. Graduate students do not teach undergraduate courses. Undergraduate student–faculty ratio: 8:1.

Expenses for 1995–96 Application fee: $45. Comprehensive fee of $26,862 includes full-time tuition ($20,600), mandatory fees ($146), and college room and board ($6116). College room only: $2970. Part-time tuition: $830 per credit hour.

Financial Aid Program-specific awards for Fall of 1994: 220 Oberlin College Scholarships for those demonstrating need ($2000–$24,000), 120 Oberlin Conservatory Dean's Scholarships for those demonstrating talent and academic achievement ($4000–$24,000), 10 Oberlin College Prize Funds for those with academic merit ($50–$4000), 15 Oberlin Conservatory/Aspen-John H. Stern Scholarships for enrolled students ($1500), 220 Work Study Awards for program majors ($500–$1500).

Application Procedures Deadline—freshmen and transfers: February 15. Notification date—freshmen and transfers: April 1. Required: essay, high school transcript, college transcript(s) for transfer students, minimum 2.0 high school GPA, 2 letters of recommendation, audition, SAT I or ACT test scores. Recommended: minimum 3.0 high school GPA, interview, video. Auditions held 28 times on campus and off campus in Atlanta, GA; Boston, MA; Chicago, IL; Denver, CO; Houston, TX; Interlochen, MI; Los Angeles, CA; Miami, FL; Minneapolis, MN; New York, NY; Portland, OR; San Diego, CA; San Francisco, CA; Seattle, WA; Washington, DC; Hong Kong; Seoul, Korea; Singapore; Taipei, Taiwan; Tokyo, Japan; recorded music is permissible as a substitute for live auditions if of good quality and videotaped performances are permissible as a substitute for live auditions if of good quality.

Contact Michael Manderen, Director of Conservatory Admissions, Conservatory of Music, Oberlin College, 77 West College Street, Oberlin, Ohio 44074; 216-775-8413, fax: 216-775-6972, E-mail address: ad_mail@ocvaxc.cc.oberlin.edu.

More about the College

Facilities Within the Conservatory, which is housed in a modern complex designed by Minoru Yamasaki, are ensemble rehearsal rooms, two excellent concert halls, and 153 individual practice rooms. The Conservatory houses the largest collection of Steinway pianos in the world, and the campus is also home to 25 organs. Other features include numerous instrument collections, seven acoustically isolated and optimized electronic music studios, and a library that rivals those in the nation's largest university music schools.

Special Programs The Conservatory of Music and the College of Arts and Sciences share the same campus. As a result, Conservatory students can take courses in both the College and the Conservatory in the same semester and can simultaneously pursue majors in both divisions, completing majors leading to both the B.Mus. and the B.A. degrees after five years. Twenty-five to thirty percent of the Conservatory's students are in the Double Degree Program. Additionally, the Conservatory offers four dual-degree programs, open only to Oberlin's own undergraduates which combine bachelor's degree study in performance or music education with graduate study leading to the master's degree in conducting, opera theater, music education, or music teaching.

The Oberlin Conservatory is one of the few major music schools in the country devoted primarily to the education of undergraduate musicians. As a division of Oberlin College, the Conservatory is also recognized for being paired with a preeminent college of the liberal arts and sciences. These factors allow the conservatory to offer its students the essential components of excellent musical training: an accomplished faculty, outstanding facilities, an extensive curriculum drawing on both divisions of Oberlin College, and an active cultural life centered on campus and drawing on Cleveland as well.

"You're at Oberlin? What do you play?" Every Oberlinian has heard this question even though the Conservatory of Music is but one fourth the size of its partner, the College of Arts and Sciences. Yet it is natural that the name Oberlin should evoke thoughts of music. Built up by an amateur cellist (Charles Grandison Finney) and funded mainly by a former piano student (Charles Martin Hall), Oberlin College created America's first professorship in music in 1835. Oberlin's Conservatory of Music, established in 1865, is the country's first continuously operating conservatory. Even before the Civil War, a visitor, Thomas Hastings, pronounced the Oberlin choir "the finest in the land." A century later Igor Stravinsky was similarly effusive over the Conservatory's young instrumentalists.

Oberlin has been the source of much innovation in American musical education. It established the country's first full-time chair in music history (1892); offered the country's first four-year degree program in public school music (1921); introduced to the United States the renowned Suzuki method of string pedagogy (1958); pioneered a program in electronic music (1969); and created the American-Soviet Youth Orchestra, composed of 100 young musicians from the United States and the former U.S.S.R., the first arts exchange produced jointly by the two countries (1988).

Conservatory alumni include well-known composers, conductors, performers, and teachers. Some, like David Zinman, conductor of the Baltimore Orchestra, have gained public renown. Others, like jazz pioneer Will Marion Cook–whom Duke Ellington called "my conservatory"–are revered mainly by specialists. Today's Oberlin graduates are to be found in virtually every major American orchestra as well as in foreign orchestras from

Oberlin College *(continued)*

Berlin to Hong Kong. Its singers and pianists are no less ubiquitous, as are Oberlinians in the many new allied fields of music.

The Oberlin Conservatory of Music has taken great pains to both educate and train its students. More than ever, technical proficiency is essential to success in music; however, the day when a pianist could simply perfect a limited repertoire of classics in order to launch a career is past. Increasingly, musicians will have to master worlds of sound that were scarcely imaginable when they were students. Only the most well-educated minds will attain such flexibility. Oberlin is committed to providing its students a balanced combination of professional training and deep education.

Ohio Northern University

Ada, Ohio

Independent-religious, coed. Small-town campus. Total enrollment: 2,872.

Degrees Bachelor of Music in the areas of performance, composition, music education. Majors: composition, music education, performance.

Music Student Profile Fall 1994: 58 total; all matriculated undergraduate; 70% females.

Music Faculty Total: 21; 6 full-time, 15 part-time; 67% of full-time faculty have terminal degrees. Undergraduate student–faculty ratio: 3:1.

Student Life Student groups include Ohio Music Educators Association, National Association of Teachers of Singing.

Expenses for 1995–96 Application fee: $30. Comprehensive fee of $21,240 includes full-time tuition ($16,950 minimum) and college room and board ($4290). College room only: $1875. Full-time tuition ranges up to $17,985 according to program. Part-time tuition per quarter hour ranges from $395 to $500 according to program. Special program-related fees: $50 for private lessons.

Financial Aid Program-specific awards for Fall of 1994: 8 Snyder Scholarships for top musicians ($7000–$10,000), 20 Dean's Talent Awards for top musicians ($3000–$3500).

Application Procedures Deadline—freshmen and transfers: continuous. Required: high school transcript, college transcript(s) for transfer students, minimum 2.0 high school GPA, audition, SAT I or ACT test scores, minimum combined SAT I score of 950, minimum composite ACT score of 20. Auditions held continuously at the convenience of the auditionee on campus; recorded music is permissible as a substitute for live auditions for out-of-state applicants and videotaped performances are permissible as a substitute for live auditions for out-of-state applicants.

Undergraduate Contact Dr. Edwin L. Williams, Chairman, Music Department, Ohio Northern University, 525 South Main Street, Ada, Ohio 45810; 419-772-2151, fax: 419-772-1932.

Ohio State University

Columbus, Ohio

State-supported, coed. Urban campus. Total enrollment: 49,542.

Degrees Bachelor of Music in the areas of performance, music theory–composition, jazz studies, music history; Bachelor of Music Education in the area of music education. Majors: jazz, music, music education, music history, music theory and composition, piano/organ, stringed instruments, voice, wind and percussion instruments. Graduate degrees offered: Master of Music in the areas of voice, piano, orchestral instruments, instrument family, composition, instrumental conducting, choral conducting. Doctor of Musical Arts in the areas of performance, composition, conducting. Cross-registration with Capital University, Columbus State Community College, Ohio Dominican College, Otterbein College.

Music Student Profile Fall 1994: 550 total; 350 matriculated undergraduate, 200 matriculated graduate; 10% minorities, 54% females.

Music Faculty Total: 67; 60 full-time, 7 part-time. Graduate students teach about a quarter undergraduate courses. Undergraduate student–faculty ratio: 6:1.

Student Life Student groups include Ohio Collegiate Music Education Association, Sigma Alpha Iota, Phi Mu Alpha Sinfonia.

Expenses for 1995–96 Application fee: $30. State resident tuition: $3273 full-time. Nonresident tuition: $9813 full-time. Part-time tuition per quarter ranges from $179 to $1001 for state residents, $361 to $2999 for nonresidents. College room and board: $4668.

Financial Aid Program-specific awards for Fall of 1994: 30 Music Achievement Scholarships for program majors ($1500), 20 Academic Achievement Scholarships for academically qualified applicants ($300–$2940).

Application Procedures Deadline—freshmen: February 15; transfers: June 25. Required: high school transcript, college transcript(s) for transfer students, audition. Recommended: essay, SAT I or ACT test scores. Auditions held 4 days for group auditions and by appointment on campus; recorded music is permissible as a substitute for live auditions for out-of-state and international applicants and videotaped performances are permissible as a substitute for live auditions for out-of-state and international applicants.

Undergraduate Contact Dr. Judith K. Delzell, Assistant Director, School of Music, Ohio State University, 1866 College Road, Columbus, Ohio 43210-1170; 614-292-2870, fax: 614-292-1102, E-mail address: jdelzell@magnus.acs.ohio-state.edu.

Graduate Contact Dr. Patricia Flowers, Chair of Graduate Studies, School of Music, Ohio State University, 1866 College Road, Columbus, Ohio 43210-1770; 614-292-6389, fax: 614-292-1102.

Ohio University

Athens, Ohio

State-supported, coed. Small-town campus. Total enrollment: 18,855.

Degrees Bachelor of Music in the areas of performance, composition, theory, history, education, therapy. Majors: classical music, music, music education, music theory and composition, music therapy, piano/organ, stringed instruments, voice, wind and percussion instruments. Graduate degrees offered: Master of Music in the areas of performance, composition, theory, history, education, therapy.

Music Student Profile Fall 1994: 230 total; 175 matriculated undergraduate, 55 matriculated graduate; 4% minorities, 46% females, 3% international.

Music Faculty Total: 32; 29 full-time, 3 part-time; 100% of full-time faculty have terminal degrees. Graduate students do not teach undergraduate courses.

Student Life Student groups include Music Educators National Conference Student Chapter, American Association of Music Therapy Student Chapter, National Association of Music Therapy Student Chapter.

Expenses for 1995–96 Application fee: $25. State resident tuition: $3666 full-time, $118 per quarter hour part-time. Nonresident tuition: $7905 full-time, $259 per quarter hour part-time. College room and board: $4260. College room only: $2094. Special program-related fees: $12 for applied music lesson fee.

Financial Aid Program-specific awards for Fall of 1994: 15–20 Talent Scholarships for the artistically talented ($1000–$3600).

Application Procedures Deadline—freshmen and transfers: February 1. Notification date—freshmen and transfers: March 15. Required: high school transcript, college transcript(s) for transfer students, minimum 2.0 high school GPA, letter of recommendation, audition. Recommended: minimum 3.0 high school GPA, interview. Auditions held 4–6 times on campus; recorded music is permissible as a substitute for live auditions when distance is prohibitive and videotaped performances are permissible as a substitute for live auditions when distance is prohibitive.

Undergraduate Contact Harold Robison, Associate Director, School of Music, Ohio University, Music Building, Athens, Ohio 45701-2979; 614-593-4244, fax: 614-593-1429, E-mail address: robisonh@ohiou.edu.

Graduate Contact Richard Wetzel, Chair, Graduate Studies, School of Music, Ohio University, Music Building, Athens, Ohio 45701-2979; 614-593-4244, fax: 614-593-1429.

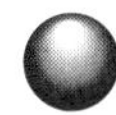

Ohio Wesleyan University

Delaware, Ohio

Independent-religious, coed. Small-town campus. Total enrollment: 1,732.

Degrees Bachelor of Music in the areas of performance, music education. Majors: music, music education, piano/organ, stringed instruments, voice, wind and percussion instruments.

Music Student Profile Fall 1994: 39 total; all matriculated undergraduate; 1% minorities, 53% females, 1% international.

Music Faculty Total: 16; 7 full-time, 9 part-time; 100% of full-time faculty have terminal degrees. Graduate students do not teach undergraduate courses. Undergraduate student–faculty ratio: 4:1.

Student Life Student groups include Mu Phi Epsilon Student Chapter, Music Educators National Conference Student Chapter.

Expenses for 1995–96 Application fee: $35. Comprehensive fee of $23,445 includes full-time tuition ($17,569) and college room and board ($5876). College room only: $2974. Part-time tuition: $1950 per course.

Financial Aid Program-specific awards for Fall of 1994: 1 Ruth Wilson Music Scholarship for program majors ($2000), 1 Edward D. and Laura Rich Cleary Music Education Memorial Scholarship for music education majors ($1000), 1 Edith Mahon Davis Music Education Scholarship for music education majors ($500), 10–15 Ohio Wesleyan University Merit Scholarships for program majors ($3000–$15,000), 1–2 Edith M. Keller Scholarship in Music Education for music education majors ($2500).

Application Procedures Deadline—freshmen and transfers: March 1. Required: essay, high school transcript, college transcript(s) for transfer students, letter of recommendation, audition, SAT I or ACT test scores. Recommended: interview, video. Auditions held 4 scheduled times and by appointment on campus; recorded music is permissible as a substitute for live auditions and videotaped performances are permissible as a substitute for live auditions.

Undergraduate Contact Doug Thompson, Dean of Admission, Ohio Wesleyan University, Slocum Hall, Delaware, Ohio 43015; 614-368-3020, fax: 614-368-3314.

Oklahoma Baptist University

Shawnee, Oklahoma

Independent-religious, coed. Small-town campus. Total enrollment: 2,440.

Degrees Bachelor of Music in the areas of voice/keyboard, music performance, church music, theory/composition; Bachelor of Music Education in the areas of vocal music education, instrumental music education. Majors: music education, piano/organ, sacred music, stringed instruments, voice, wind and percussion instruments. Cross-registration with St. Gregory's College.

Music Student Profile Fall 1994: 122 total; all matriculated undergraduate; 5% minorities, 50% females, 3% international.

Music Faculty Total: 30; 22 full-time, 8 part-time; 41% of full-time faculty have terminal degrees. Graduate

Oklahoma Baptist University *(continued)*

students do not teach undergraduate courses. Undergraduate student–faculty ratio: 9:1.

Student Life Student groups include Music Educators National Conference, Sigma Alpha Iota, Phi Mu Alpha Sinfonia.

Expenses for 1995–96 Application fee: $25. Comprehensive fee of $9734 includes full-time tuition ($5960), mandatory fees ($564), and college room and board ($3210). College room only: $1380. Part-time tuition: $200 per credit hour. Part-time mandatory fee per semester (6 to 11 credits) range from $140 to $177.50. Special program-related fees: $900 for applied music fee.

Financial Aid Program-specific awards for Fall of 1994: 100 Talentships for program majors ($500–$1500).

Application Procedures Deadline—freshmen and transfers: continuous. Required: high school transcript, minimum 2.0 high school GPA, SAT I or ACT test scores. Recommended: audition. Auditions held 4 times on campus; recorded music is permissible as a substitute for live auditions when distance is prohibitive and videotaped performances are permissible as a substitute for live auditions when distance is prohibitive.

Undergraduate Contact Jody Johnson, Dean of Admissions, Oklahoma Baptist University, Box 61174, 500 West University, Shawnee, Oklahoma 74801; 800-654-3285, fax: 405-878-2069.

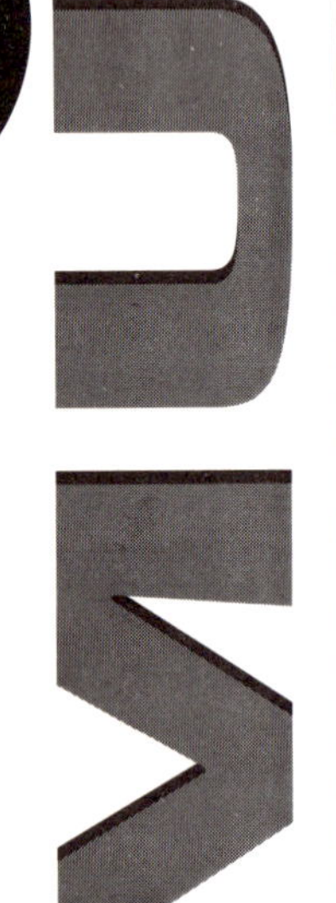

Oklahoma Christian University of Science and Arts

Oklahoma City, Oklahoma

Independent-religious, coed. Suburban campus. Total enrollment: 1,508.

Degrees Bachelor of Music Education in the areas of vocal music education, instrumental music education. Majors: music education. Cross-registration with University of Central Oklahoma.

Music Student Profile Fall 1994: 35 total; all matriculated undergraduate; 8% minorities, 55% females.

Music Faculty Total: 14; 4 full-time, 10 part-time; 50% of full-time faculty have terminal degrees. Graduate students do not teach undergraduate courses. Undergraduate student–faculty ratio: 10:1.

Student Life Student groups include Collegiate Music Educators National Conference.

Expenses for 1995–96 Application fee: $25. Comprehensive fee of $10,500 includes full-time tuition ($6700), mandatory fees ($460), and college room and board ($3340 minimum). College room only: $1590 (minimum). Part-time tuition: $282 per hour. Special program-related fees: $180 for private instruction, $35 for ensemble tour expenses, $35 for instrument maintenance.

Financial Aid Program-specific awards for Fall of 1994: 5 Distinguished Performer Awards for program majors ($6000), 10 Music Performance Scholarships for vocalists/instrumentalists ($500).

Application Procedures Deadline—freshmen and transfers: continuous. Required: high school transcript. Recommended: interview, audition. Auditions held 2 times on campus; recorded music is permissible as a substitute for live auditions if a campus visit is impossible and videotaped performances are permissible as a substitute for live auditions if a campus visit is impossible.

Undergraduate Contact Tom Clark, Vice President of Admissions, Oklahoma Christian University of Science and Arts, Box 11000, Oklahoma City, Oklahoma 73136; 800-877-5010, fax: 405-425-5316.

Margaret E. Petree School of Music and Performing Arts

Oklahoma City University

Oklahoma City, Oklahoma

Independent-religious, coed. Suburban campus. Total enrollment: 4,571.

Degrees Bachelor of Music in the areas of performance, musical theater, composition; Bachelor of Music Education in the areas of vocal music education, instrumental music education. Majors: composition, music, music education, music theater, piano/organ, stringed instruments, voice, wind and percussion instruments. Graduate degrees offered: Master of Music in the areas of performance, composition, music theater, opera performance.

Music Student Profile Fall 1994: 273 total; 225 matriculated undergraduate, 48 matriculated graduate.

Music Faculty Total: 48; 16 full-time, 32 part-time; 40% of full-time faculty have terminal degrees. Graduate students do not teach undergraduate courses. Undergraduate student–faculty ratio: 25:1.

Student Life Student groups include American String Teachers Association, Sigma Alpha Iota, Music Educators National Conference.

Expenses for 1995–96 Application fee: $20. Comprehensive fee of $11,265 includes full-time tuition ($7350), mandatory fees ($85), and college room and board ($3830). College room only: $1750. Part-time tuition: $245 per semester hour. Part-time mandatory fees per semester range from $35.85 to $44.35. Special program-related fees: $45 for practice room fee, $165 for accompanist fee.

Financial Aid Program-specific awards for Fall of 1994: 30 Endowed Scholarships for program majors and performers ($500–$7000), 100–150 General Music Scholarships for program majors and performers ($500–$7000).

Application Procedures Deadline—freshmen and transfers: continuous. Notification date—freshmen and transfers: August 15. Required: high school transcript, minimum 2.0 high school GPA, 3 letters of recommendation, video, audition. Recommended: essay, minimum 3.0 high school GPA, interview. Auditions held 2 times on campus; recorded music is permissible as a substitute for live auditions if a campus visit is impossible and videotaped performances are permissible as a substitute for live auditions if a campus visit is impossible.

Undergraduate Contact Keith Hackett, Dean, Admissions Department, Oklahoma City University, 2501 North Blackwelder, Oklahoma City, Oklahoma 73106; 405-521-5050.

Graduate Contact Laura Mitchell, Director, Graduate Admissions, Oklahoma City University, 2501 North Blackwelder, Oklahoma City, Oklahoma 73106; 405-521-5351.

Chartered in 1904, Oklahoma City University is a highly respected educational institution and was selected as one of the top liberal arts universities in the United States by the *National Review College Guide.* OCU maintains the reputation by combining a unique blend of tradition, quality, community, and innovation.

The Margaret E. Petree School of Music and Performing Arts is known as an excellent learning and training center for aspiring young artists. The number of graduates achieving international recognition for their performances in professional endeavors attests to a reputation enjoyed for many years. Students from OCU are also recognized for their leadership in music education and creativity in music composition and arranging. The Dance Department, whose focus is American Musical Theater dance, is emerging as one of the most active and vital components of the School.

The School hosts two companies that give regular performances. The Oklahoma Opera and Music Theater Company presents a season of four all-student productions, and the American Spirit Dance Company presents an annual production; both companies have toured internationally. The American Spirit Dance Company continues to join the Oklahoma City Philharmonic and the Canterbury Choral Society to present a Yuletide Festival. OCU singers provide back-up for Philharmonic "Pops" concerts.

A vital choral music program is fostered through the Chamber Singers, the University Singers, and the Women's Choral Union. Instrumental music ensembles include the University Orchestra, Symphonic Band, Jazz Arts Ensemble, chamber ensembles, and Pep Band. Each performs with regularity throughout the academic year and tours regionally. Instrumentalists are the pit orchestra for the opera and musical theater productions.

The University's Composition Program provides students with a broad educational experience. Computerized equipment and software have been added to the composition studio. Two classes in sound engineering introduce students to professional recording and film scoring.

OCU offers a Bachelor of Science in music business, a Bachelor of Music with elective studies in business administration and dance management, and a Master of Business Administration with arts management track degrees. An International Advisory Board of top professionals from the business world serve as guest speakers and oversee the program. The University has established internships with professional entities in business and performance. Oklahoma City University is a community cultural center as well as a highly respected institution of education.

OCU's programs in speech and theater are offered through the College of Arts and Sciences. As part of the liberal arts tradition, the broad education of speech and theater students uses great dramatic literature to expand students' understanding of life. OCU presents four plays and two children's plays to the general public each academic season.

The visual art degrees at OCU provide a strong foundation of knowledge in a wide variety of art forms and media. The program prepares the career-minded student to work professionally within many fields of art. Various aspects of commercial and fine art are closely related, and, therefore, many skills and media can be applied to both. It is important for OCU graduates to have a wide range of knowledge and skills that can be useful in many artistic endeavors. Former OCU students are working professionally throughout the United States, Europe, South America, and Asia.

Oklahoma Panhandle State University

Goodwell, Oklahoma

State-supported, coed. Rural campus. Total enrollment: 1,259.

Degrees Bachelor of Music Education in the areas of vocal music education, instrumental music education. Majors: music education, piano/organ, voice, wind and percussion instruments.

Expenses for 1995–96 Part-time mandatory fees per semester range from $21 to $101. Full-time tuition ranges from $1212 to $1238 for state residents, $3274 to $3517 for nonresidents according to class level. Part-time tuition per credit hour ranges from $40.39 to $41.25 for state residents, $109.14 to $117.22 for nonresidents, according to class level. Full-time mandatory fees: $323. College room and board: $1870 (minimum). College room only: $600.

Undergraduate Contact Jesse Henkla, Chair, Fine Arts Department, Oklahoma Panhandle State University, P.O. Box 430, Goodwell, Oklahoma 73939; 405-349-2611 ext. 260.

Oklahoma State University

Stillwater, Oklahoma

State-supported, coed. Small-town campus. Total enrollment: 18,561.

Degrees Bachelor of Music in the areas of performance, music education, music business. Majors: piano/organ, stringed instruments, voice, wind and percussion instruments.

Music Student Profile Fall 1994: 110 total; all matriculated undergraduate.

Music Faculty Total: 24; 20 full-time, 4 part-time.

Expenses for 1995–96 Application fee: $15. Part-time mandatory fees: $9.66 per credit hour. Full-time tuition ranges from $1458 to $1555 for state residents, $4698 to $5208 for nonresidents, according to class level. Part-time

Oklahoma State University *(continued)*

tuition per credit hour ranges from $48.60 to $51.84 for state residents, $156.60 to $173.61 for nonresidents, according to class level. Full-time mandatory fees: $290. College room and board: $3136 (minimum). College room only: $1488 (minimum).

Application Procedures Deadline—freshmen and transfers: continuous. Required: high school transcript, minimum 3.0 high school GPA, audition, SAT I or ACT test scores. Auditions held continuously on campus and off campus in various locations in Oklahoma; recorded music is permissible as a substitute for live auditions if a campus visit is impossible.

Undergraduate Contact Dr. William Ballenger, Head, Music Department, Oklahoma State University, 132 Seratean Center, Stillwater, Oklahoma 74078; 405-744-6133.

Old Dominion University

Norfolk, Virginia

State-supported, coed. Urban campus. Total enrollment: 16,500.

Degrees Bachelor of Music in the areas of performance, composition; Bachelor of Music Education in the area of music education. Majors: classical music, music education, piano/organ, stringed instruments, voice, wind and percussion instruments. Cross-registration with Norfolk State University, Hampton University, Tidewater Community College, College of William and Mary, Virginia Wesleyan College.

Music Student Profile Fall 1994: 110 total; 100 matriculated undergraduate, 10 matriculated graduate; 10% minorities, 50% females, 5% international.

Music Faculty Total: 38; 16 full-time, 22 part-time; 100% of full-time faculty have terminal degrees. Graduate students do not teach undergraduate courses.

Student Life Student groups include Phi Mu Alpha, Sigma Alpha Iota.

Expenses for 1995–96 Application fee: $30. State resident tuition: $3990 full-time, $133 per semester hour part-time. Nonresident tuition: $10,350 full-time, $345 per semester hour part-time. Full-time mandatory fees: $96. College room and board: $4676. Special program-related fees: $85 for applied music fee.

Financial Aid Program-specific awards for Fall of 1994: 16–50 Ensemble Scholarships for performers ($500–$750), 5–7 Stamos Scholarships for vocalists ($300–$600), 1 Vogan Scholarship for keyboard players ($1800).

Application Procedures Deadline—freshmen: May 1; transfers: July 5. Required: high school transcript, college transcript(s) for transfer students, minimum 2.0 high school GPA, letter of recommendation, audition, SAT I or ACT test scores, minimum combined SAT I score of 950. Auditions held 4 times on campus; recorded music is permissible as a substitute for live auditions when distance is prohibitive and videotaped performances are permissible as a substitute for live auditions when distance is prohibitive.

Undergraduate Contact Dennis Zeisler, Chair, Music Department, Old Dominion University, Room 244 Fine Arts Building, Norfolk, Virginia 23529-0187; 804-683-4061, fax: 804-683-5457, E-mail address: djz300f@barbados.cc.odu.edu.

Graduate Contact Dr. Nancy Klein, Graduate Program Director, Music Department, Old Dominion University, Room 244 Fine Arts Building, Norfolk, Virginia 23529-0187; 804-683-4061, fax: 804-683-5457.

Oral Roberts University

Tulsa, Oklahoma

Independent-religious, coed. Urban campus. Total enrollment: 3,318.

Degrees Bachelor of Music in the areas of sacred music, composition, performance, composition/technology; Bachelor of Music Education in the areas of vocal music education, instrumental music education. Majors: composition, music education, music technology, piano/organ, sacred music, stringed instruments, voice, wind and percussion instruments.

Music Student Profile Fall 1994: 153 total; 145 matriculated undergraduate, 8 matriculated graduate; 30% minorities, 60% females, 10% international.

Music Faculty Total: 39; 15 full-time, 24 part-time; 70% of full-time faculty have terminal degrees. Undergraduate student–faculty ratio: 10:1.

Student Life Student groups include Franco Autori Concert, Family Christmas Concert.

Expenses for 1995–96 Application fee: $35. Comprehensive fee of $13,204 includes full-time tuition ($8538), mandatory fees ($192), and college room and board ($4474 minimum). College room only: $2124. Part-time tuition: $365 per credit. Tuition guaranteed not to increase for student's term of enrollment. Special program-related fees: $30 for music equipment.

Financial Aid Program-specific awards for Fall of 1994: Talent Awards for music majors or participants ($500).

Application Procedures Deadline—freshmen and transfers: continuous. Required: essay, minimum 2.0 high school GPA, 2 letters of recommendation, audition, SAT I or ACT test scores. Recommended: college transcript(s) for transfer students. Auditions held by appointment on campus; recorded music is permissible as a substitute for live auditions when distance is prohibitive and videotaped performances are permissible as a substitute for live auditions when distance is prohibitive.

Undergraduate Contact Music Department, Oral Roberts University, 7777 South Lewis Avenue, Tulsa, Oklahoma 74171; 918-495-7500.

Graduate Contact Graduate Theology Department, Oral Roberts University, 7777 South Lewis Avenue, Tulsa, Oklahoma 74171; 918-495-6096.

Otterbein College

Westerville, Ohio

Independent-religious, coed. Suburban campus. Total enrollment: 2,599.

Degrees Bachelor of Music Education in the area of vocal and instrumental music education; Bachelor of Fine Arts in the area of musical theater. Majors: classical music, music, music and business, music education, music history, music theater, music theory and composition, piano/organ, stringed instruments, voice, wind and percussion instruments. Cross-registration with Ohio State University, Capital University, Columbus State Community College.

Music Student Profile Fall 1994: 110 total; all matriculated undergraduate; 2% minorities, 55% females, 1% international.

Music Faculty Total: 33; 8 full-time, 25 part-time; 88% of full-time faculty have terminal degrees. Graduate students do not teach undergraduate courses. Undergraduate student–faculty ratio: 4:1.

Student Life Student groups include Ohio Student Music Educators Association, Delta Omicron.

Expenses for 1995–96 Application fee: $15. Comprehensive fee of $18,180 includes full-time tuition ($13,611) and college room and board ($4569). College room only: $2019. Part-time tuition: $182 per credit hour. Special program-related fees: $504–$1,260 for private applied music lessons.

Financial Aid Program-specific awards for Fall of 1994: 20–30 Music Talent Grants for program majors ($1250–$3000).

Application Procedures Deadline—freshmen and transfers: continuous. Required: high school transcript, college transcript(s) for transfer students, minimum 2.0 high school GPA, audition, SAT I or ACT test scores. Recommended: interview. Auditions held continuously on campus; recorded music is permissible as a substitute for live auditions when distance is prohibitive and videotaped performances are permissible as a substitute for live auditions when distance is prohibitive.

Undergraduate Contact Morton Achter, Chairperson, Department of Music, Otterbein College, Battelle Fine Arts Center, Westerville, Ohio 43081; 614-823-1508, fax: 614-823-1118.

Ouachita Baptist University

Arkadelphia, Arkansas

Independent-religious, coed. Small-town campus. Total enrollment: 1,440.

Degrees Bachelor of Music in the areas of performance, musical theater, church music, music theory/composition; Bachelor of Music Education in the areas of choral music education, instrumental music education. Majors: classical music, music, music education, music theater, piano/organ, sacred music, voice, wind and percussion instruments. Cross-registration with Henderson State University.

Music Student Profile Fall 1994: 119 total; all matriculated undergraduate; 2% minorities, 51% females, 3% international.

Music Faculty Total: 26; 15 full-time, 11 part-time; 70% of full-time faculty have terminal degrees. Graduate students do not teach undergraduate courses. Undergraduate student–faculty ratio: 6:1.

Student Life Student groups include Phi Mu Alpha Sinfonia, Sigma Alpha Iota, Pi Kappa Lambda. Special housing available for music students.

Expenses for 1995–96 Application fee: $25. Comprehensive fee of $9970 includes full-time tuition ($6970), mandatory fees ($100), and college room and board ($2900). College room only: $1250. Part-time tuition: $192 per semester hour. Special program-related fees: $70–$140 for private instruction.

Financial Aid Program-specific awards for Fall of 1994: 125 Music Scholarships for program majors ($2000–$3000), 1 Presidential Scholarship for freshmen program majors ($6000).

Application Procedures Deadline—freshmen and transfers: continuous. Notification date—freshmen and transfers: continuous. Required: high school transcript, college transcript(s) for transfer students, letter of recommendation, audition, SAT I or ACT test scores, minimum composite ACT score of 19, minimum 2.5 high school GPA. Auditions held 2 times and by appointment on campus; recorded music is permissible as a substitute for live auditions and videotaped performances are permissible as a substitute for live auditions if a campus visit is impossible.

Undergraduate Contact Charles W. Wright, Dean, School of Music, Ouachita Baptist University, Box 3771, Arkadelphia, Arkansas 71998-0001; 501-245-5129.

Pacific Lutheran University

Tacoma, Washington

Independent-religious, coed. Suburban campus. Total enrollment: 3,257.

Degrees Bachelor of Music in the area of performance; Bachelor of Music Education in the areas of choral music, band, orchestra; Bachelor of Musical Arts in the area of music combined with an outside field. Majors: composition, music education, performance.

Music Student Profile Fall 1994: 110 total; all matriculated undergraduate.

Music Faculty Total: 45; 15 full-time, 30 part-time; 33% of full-time faculty have terminal degrees. Graduate students do not teach undergraduate courses. Undergraduate student–faculty ratio: 15:1.

Expenses for 1994–95 Application fee: $35. Comprehensive fee of $17,800 includes full-time tuition ($13,312) and college room and board ($4488). Part-time tuition: $416 per semester hour. Special program-related fees: $125–$175 for private lessons, $75–$250 for ensemble tours.

Pacific Lutheran University *(continued)*

Financial Aid Program-specific awards for Fall of 1994: Music Scholarships for music students ($2000).

Application Procedures Deadline—freshmen and transfers: continuous. Required: essay, high school transcript, college transcript(s) for transfer students, 2 letters of recommendation, audition, SAT I or ACT test scores, minimum 2.5 high school GPA. Auditions held by request on campus; recorded music is permissible as a substitute for live auditions if a campus visit is impossible and videotaped performances are permissible as a substitute for live auditions if a campus visit is impossible.

Undergraduate Contact Pam Deacon, Administrative Assistant, Department of Music, Pacific Lutheran University, Tacoma, Washington 98447; 206-535-7603, fax: 206-535-8669.

Pacific Union College

Angwin, California

Independent-religious, coed. Rural campus. Total enrollment: 1,597.

Degrees Bachelor of Music in the areas of music education, performance. Majors: classical music, music, music education, piano/organ, stringed instruments, voice, wind and percussion instruments.

Music Student Profile Fall 1994: 40 total; all matriculated undergraduate; 45% minorities, 65% females, 15% international.

Music Faculty Total: 13; 6 full-time, 7 part-time; 85% of full-time faculty have terminal degrees. Graduate students do not teach undergraduate courses. Undergraduate student–faculty ratio: 5:1.

Student Life Student groups include California Music Educators Association.

Expenses for 1995–96 Comprehensive fee of $16,315 includes full-time tuition ($12,360) and college room and board ($3955). College room only: $2310. Special program-related fees: $125 for lesson fees for non-music majors/minors.

Financial Aid Program-specific awards for Fall of 1994: 5 Proficiency in Performance Scholarships for ensemble participants ($1000), 6 Loye Scholarships for organists ($1000), 1–2 Mayes Music Ministry Scholarships for organ/voice majors ($500–$1000), 1–2 Coltrin Lewis Scholarships for musicians ($500–$1000).

Application Procedures Deadline—freshmen and transfers: continuous. Notification date—freshmen and transfers: September 28. Required: high school transcript, 3 letters of recommendation, audition, minimum 2.3 high school GPA. Auditions held 3 times on campus.

Undergraduate Contact Al Trace, Admissions Director, Pacific Union College, 100 Howell Mountain Road, Angwin, California 94508; 707-965-6336, fax: 707-965-6432.

Pacific University

Forest Grove, Oregon

Independent, coed. Small-town campus. Total enrollment: 1,837.

Degrees Bachelor of Music in the area of music education. Majors: music education. Cross-registration with Oregon Graduate Institute.

Music Student Profile Fall 1994: 5 total; all matriculated undergraduate; 28% minorities, 60% females, 6% international.

Music Faculty Total: 17; 5 full-time, 12 part-time. Graduate students do not teach undergraduate courses. Undergraduate student–faculty ratio: 13:1.

Expenses for 1995–96 Application fee: $30. Comprehensive fee of $19,240 includes full-time tuition ($14,920), mandatory fees ($220), and college room and board ($4100). College room only: $1850. Part-time tuition: $500 per semester hour. Part-time mandatory fees: $110 per term.

Financial Aid Program-specific awards for Fall of 1994: 15 Endowed Scholarships for program majors ($700), 32 Music Talent Awards for program majors ($4000).

Application Procedures Deadline—freshmen and transfers: continuous. Required: essay, high school transcript, minimum 3.0 high school GPA, 2 letters of recommendation. Recommended: interview.

Undergraduate Contact George Harschbarger, Chair, Music Department, Pacific University, 2043 College Way, Forest Grove, Oregon 97116-1797; 503-357-6151 ext. 2508, fax: 503-359-2910.

Palm Beach Atlantic College

West Palm Beach, Florida

Independent-religious, coed. Urban campus. Total enrollment: 1,894.

Degrees Bachelor of Music in the areas of performance, church music. Majors: piano/organ, sacred music, stringed instruments, voice, wind and percussion instruments.

Music Student Profile Fall 1994: 100 total; all matriculated undergraduate; 16% minorities, 55% females, 7% international.

Music Faculty Total: 20; 8 full-time, 12 part-time; 63% of full-time faculty have terminal degrees. Graduate students do not teach undergraduate courses. Undergraduate student–faculty ratio: 17:1.

Expenses for 1995–96 Application fee: $25. Comprehensive fee of $12,350 includes full-time tuition ($8600) and college room and board ($3750). Part-time tuition per credit hour: $220 for the first 6 credit hours, $230 for the next 5 credit hours. Special program-related fees: $75–$150 for applied fees.

Financial Aid Program-specific awards for Fall of 1994: 50–80 Music Scholarships for program majors ($1000–$2000), 1 Brown Vargas Scholarship for music theater students ($400), 1 Sylvia Brainen Piano Quartet Scholarship for piano students ($300).

Application Procedures Deadline—freshmen and transfers: continuous. Required: essay, high school transcript, minimum 2.0 high school GPA, 2 letters of recommendation, audition, SAT I or ACT test scores. Recommended: minimum 3.0 high school GPA, interview, video. Auditions held continuously on campus; recorded music is permissible as a substitute for live auditions when distance is prohibitive and videotaped performances are permissible as a substitute for live auditions when distance is prohibitive.

Undergraduate Contact Dean, Admissions Department, Palm Beach Atlantic College, P.O. Box 24708, West Palm Beach, Florida 33416; 800-238-3998, fax: 407-835-4342.

More about the College

Program Facilities The historic PBA Auditorium building houses the School of Music & Fine Arts. PBA has two performance facilities for drama: a 200-seat off-Broadway-style auditorium and a small black box for student-directed one-act plays and scene work. The Art House features a state-of-the-art computerized gas kiln.

Faculty, Resident Artists, and Alumni PBA's tradition of music education has attracted one of the finest faculty groups in the nation, including alumni of Juilliard, Indiana University, Westminster Choir College, Manhattan School of Music, University of Chicago, and Florida State University. Several alumni are professional recording artists, church musicians, and teachers.

Student Performance Opportunities Students study in metropolitan Palm Beach County, home to over 200 arts organizations. On campus, music students may participate in numerous groups, including two choirs, the PBA Symphony, and several vocal and instrumental ensembles. Off campus, students may participate in productions at a new $55-million performing arts center, and many have the opportunity to perform with professional groups such as the Palm Beach Opera. Theater arts students take part in three major productions annually. Students also may audition for Living Proof, a traveling Christian drama troupe. The Burt Reynolds Institute for Theater Training is accessible from campus. Art students may take part in the annual student art exhibit.

Special Programs Students may study overseas with PBA's Semester in London program. They also may participate in a variety of cooperative programs with the Christian College Coalition, including a Film Studies Program in Los Angeles.

Kurt Bestor

Brigham Young University—Winner, Emmy Award, for music used on televised network coverage of 1988 Olympics

My music experience at BYU was a study in contrasts. One moment would find me studying the history of symphonic form with one of the country's top musicologists, while in the next, playing progressive jazz in the award-winning ensemble, Synthesis. Much of my time was spent composing music for the University's many performing groups—from a renaissance recorder consort to large philharmonic orchestra. Many times these compositions would eventually be recorded in Studio Y—the music department's state-of-the-art recording studio. These "hands-on" experiences have proved to be invaluable in my career as a composer of film and television music.

Peabody Conservatory of Music

See Johns Hopkins University, Peabody Conservatory of Music

Pembroke State University

Pembroke, North Carolina

State-supported, coed. Rural campus. Total enrollment: 3,017.

Degrees Bachelor of Music in the area of music education. Majors: music education.

Music Student Profile Fall 1994: 40 total; all matriculated undergraduate.

Music Faculty Total: 13; 6 full-time, 7 part-time; 100% of full-time faculty have terminal degrees. Undergraduate student–faculty ratio: 16:1.

Student Life Student groups include Phi Mu Alpha, Sigma Alpha Iota, Music Educators National Conference.

Expenses for 1994–95 Application fee: $25. State resident tuition: $628 full-time. Nonresident tuition: $6360 full-time. Part-time tuition per semester ranges from $79 to $236 for state residents, $795 to $2385 for nonresidents. Part-time mandatory fees per semester range from $52 to $208. Full-time mandatory fees: $518. College room and board: $2760. College room only: $1410.

Financial Aid Program-specific awards for Fall of 1994: 5–15 Non-majors Scholarships for freshmen ensemble performers ($300), 10–20 Majors Scholarships for program majors ($600).

Application Procedures Deadline—freshmen and transfers: July 15. Required: high school transcript, 3 letters of recommendation, SAT I test score only, minimum combined SAT I score of 750. Recommended: interview, audition. Auditions held continuously on campus and off campus in various locations; recorded music is permissible as a substitute for live auditions for out-of-state applicants and videotaped performances are permissible as a substitute for live auditions for out-of-state applicants.

Undergraduate Contact George Walter, Chair, Music Department, Pembroke State University, 1 University Drive, Pembroke, North Carolina 28372-1510; 910-521-6230.

Pennsylvania State University University Park Campus

University Park, Pennsylvania

State-related, coed. Small-town campus. Total enrollment: 38,294.

Degrees Bachelor of Music in the areas of performance, composition; Bachelor of Musical Arts in the area of performance. Majors: classical music, music education, piano/organ, stringed instruments, voice, wind and percussion instruments. Graduate degrees offered: Master of Music in the areas of performance, composition, conducting, piano pedagogy and performance; Master of Music Education in the area of music education.

Music Student Profile Fall 1994: 303 total; 250 matriculated undergraduate, 53 matriculated graduate; 5% minorities, 47% females, 2% international.

Music Faculty Total: 37; 37 full-time; 100% of full-time faculty have terminal degrees. Graduate students teach a few undergraduate courses. Undergraduate student–faculty ratio: 6:1.

Expenses for 1994–95 Application fee: $35. State resident tuition: $4966 full-time, $208 per credit part-time. Nonresident tuition: $10,654 full-time, $445 per credit part-time. Part-time mandatory fees per semester range from $12 to $25. Full-time mandatory fees: $70. College room and board: $3920. Special program-related fees: $100 for applied music lesson fee.

Financial Aid Program-specific awards for Fall of 1994: 110 Music Scholarships for program majors ($1800).

Application Procedures Deadline—freshmen: April 1; transfers: June 1. Notification date—freshmen and transfers: continuous. Required: high school transcript, minimum 2.0 high school GPA, audition. Auditions held 4 times on campus; recorded music is permissible as a substitute for live auditions when distance is prohibitive and videotaped performances are permissible as a substitute for live auditions when distance is prohibitive.

Undergraduate Contact Irene Lucas, Staff Assistant V, School of Music, Pennsylvania State University University Park Campus, 233 Music Building, University Park, Pennsylvania 16802-1503; 814-865-0431, fax: 814-865-7140.

Graduate Contact Nancy Erdley, Staff Assistant, School of Music, Pennsylvania State University University Park Campus, 233 Music Building, University Park, Pennsylvania 16802-1503; 814-865-0431, fax: 814-865-7140.

Philadelphia College of Bible

Langhorne, Pennsylvania

Independent-religious, coed. Suburban campus. Total enrollment: 1,050.

Degrees Bachelor of Music in the areas of performance, music education, church music, composition. Majors: composition, guitar, music education, piano/organ, sacred music, stringed instruments, voice, wind and percussion instruments.

Music Student Profile Fall 1994: 70 total; all matriculated undergraduate; 20% minorities, 54% females, 11% international.

Music Faculty Total: 22; 7 full-time, 15 part-time; 50% of full-time faculty have terminal degrees. Graduate students do not teach undergraduate courses. Undergraduate student–faculty ratio: 10:1.

Student Life Student groups include Music Educators National Conference.

Expenses for 1995–96 Application fee: $15. Comprehensive fee of $12,304 includes full-time tuition ($7800), mandatory fees ($260), and college room and board ($4244 minimum). College room only: $2060. Part-time tuition per credit ranges from $248 to $331. Part-time mandatory fees: $6 per credit hour.

Financial Aid Program-specific awards for Fall of 1994: 80 Music Scholarships for freshmen ($5000).

Application Procedures Deadline—freshmen and transfers: continuous. Required: high school transcript, college transcript(s) for transfer students, interview, audition, SAT I or ACT test scores, minimum combined SAT I score of 800, minimum composite ACT score of 19. Auditions held continuously on campus; recorded music is permissible as a substitute for live auditions when distance is prohibitive and videotaped performances are permissible as a substitute for live auditions when distance is prohibitive.

Undergraduate Contact Dr. Al Lunde, Chair, Music Department, Philadelphia College of Bible, 200 Manor Avenue, Langhorne, Pennsylvania 19047; 215-752-5800 ext. 330, fax: 215-752-5812.

Phillips University

Enid, Oklahoma

Independent-religious, coed. Small-town campus. Total enrollment: 905.

Degrees Bachelor of Music Education in the areas of instrumental music education, vocal music education; Bachelor of Music Therapy in the area of music therapy. Majors: brass, guitar, harpsichord, music business, music education, music therapy, piano/organ, stringed instruments, voice, wind and percussion instruments. Cross-registration with Phillips University in Japan, Regent's College, United Kingdom.

Music Student Profile Fall 1994: 85 total; 35 matriculated undergraduate, 50 nondegree; 10% minorities, 60% females, 40% international.

Music Faculty Total: 18; 3 full-time, 15 part-time; 20% of full-time faculty have terminal degrees. Graduate students do not teach undergraduate courses. Undergraduate student–faculty ratio: 6:1.

Student Life Student groups include Mu Phi Epsilon, Music Therapy Club, Music Educators National Conference Student Chapter.

Expenses for 1995–96 Comprehensive fee of $10,454 includes full-time tuition ($6000), mandatory fees ($550), and college room and board ($3904). Part-time tuition: $200 per credit hour. Special program-related fees: $150 for private music lessons.

Financial Aid Program-specific awards for Fall of 1994: 15 Music Major Scholarships for music majors ($1500), 20 Music Participant Scholarships for ensemble participants ($1000).

Application Procedures Deadline—freshmen and transfers: continuous. Notification date—freshmen and transfers: continuous. Required: essay, high school transcript, college transcript(s) for transfer students, letter of recommendation, audition, SAT I or ACT test scores. Recommended: interview, minimum 2.75 high school GPA. Auditions held continuously on campus; recorded music is permissible as a substitute for live auditions if a campus visit is impossible and videotaped performances are permissible as a substitute for live auditions if a campus visit is impossible.

Undergraduate Contact Lois Bender, Vice President for Enrollment Management, Undergraduate Admissions, Phillips University, 100 South University Avenue, Enid, Oklahoma 73701; 800-238-1185, fax: 405-237-1607.

Pittsburg State University

Pittsburg, Kansas

State-supported, coed. Small-town campus. Total enrollment: 6,377.

Degrees Bachelor of Music in the areas of jazz, classical, music performance; Bachelor of Music Education in the area of instrumental and vocal music education (grades K–12). Majors: classical music, jazz, music education, piano/organ, stringed instruments, voice, wind and percussion instruments. Graduate degrees offered: Master of Music in the areas of music theory/composition, performance, music history/literature; Master of Music Education in the areas of vocal music education, instrumental music education.

Music Student Profile Fall 1994: 135 total; 85 matriculated undergraduate, 20 matriculated graduate, 30 nondegree; 4% minorities, 55% females, 10% international.

Music Faculty Total: 18; 14 full-time, 4 part-time; 100% of full-time faculty have terminal degrees. Graduate students do not teach undergraduate courses. Undergraduate student–faculty ratio: 8:1.

Student Life Student groups include Music Educators National Conference Student Chapter, International Association of Jazz Educators.

Expenses for 1995–96 Application fee: $15. State resident tuition: $1806 full-time, $66 per semester hour part-time. Nonresident tuition: $5788 full-time, $199 per semester hour part-time. College room and board: $3126.

Financial Aid Program-specific awards for Fall of 1994: 50–60 Music Scholarships for program majors and minors ($400–$2000).

Application Procedures Deadline—freshmen and transfers: July 1. Required: high school transcript, minimum 2.0 high school GPA, audition. Auditions held continuously on campus; recorded music is permissible as a substitute for live auditions when distance is prohibitive and videotaped performances are permissible as a substitute for live auditions when distance is prohibitive.

Undergraduate Contact Gene E. Vollen, Chair, Music Department, Pittsburg State University, 1701 South Broadway, Pittsburg, Kansas 66762; 316-235-4466, fax: 316-232-7515.

Graduate Contact James Poulos, Director, Graduate Studies in Music, Music Department, Pittsburg State University, 1701 South Broadway, Pittsburg, Kansas 66762; 316-235-4479.

Portland State University

Portland, Oregon

State-supported, coed. Urban campus. Total enrollment: 14,426.

Degrees Bachelor of Music in the area of classical performance. Majors: classical music, music, music education, performance, piano/organ, stringed instruments, voice, wind and percussion instruments.

Music Student Profile Fall 1994: 100 total; all matriculated undergraduate; 5% minorities, 55% females, 5% international.

Music Faculty Total: 24; 12 full-time, 12 part-time; 67% of full-time faculty have terminal degrees. Graduate students do not teach undergraduate courses. Undergraduate student–faculty ratio: 10:1.

Student Life Student groups include Music Educators National Conference, Mu Phi Epsilon.

Expenses for 1994–95 Application fee: $50. State resident tuition: $3060 full-time. Nonresident tuition: $9108 full-time. Part-time tuition per quarter ranges from $128 to $938 for state residents, $128 to $2786 for nonresidents. College room only: $2700. Special program-related fees: $40 for applied music fee.

Financial Aid Program-specific awards for Fall of 1994: 14 Laurel Awards for program majors ($3000).

Application Procedures Deadline—freshmen and transfers: June 1. Notification date—freshmen and transfers: continuous. Required: high school transcript, minimum 2.5 high school GPA. Recommended: letter of recommendation, interview, audition. Auditions held 2–3 times on campus; recorded music is permissible as a substitute for live auditions when distance is prohibitive.

Undergraduate Contact Music Department, Portland State University, P.O. Box 751, Portland, Oregon 97207-0751; 503-725-3011, fax: 503-725-3351.

More about the University

Program Facilities New Kawai piano lab, MIDI lab, Hamburg Steinway grand piano.

Faculty, Resident Artists, and Alumni Floristan Trio; Ensemble Viento; Jerome Hines, Metropolitan Opera; James DePriest, Oregon Symphony, Michael Foxman, Oregon Symphony; Beaux Arts Trio; Takacs Quartet; Tokyo Quartet; Rudolph Firkusny; Bella Davodovich; Emanuel Ax; Steve Lacy; David Shifrin; New York

Portland State University *(continued)*

Chamber Soloists. PSU faculty performs with Oregon Symphony and Portland Opera.

Student Performance Opportunities Portland Opera, Portland Youth Philharmonic, Portland Symphonic Choir, numerous community and university opportunities to perform in bands, choirs, orchestras, and ensembles.

Special Programs Chamber Choir and Orchestra European tours, student competitions in international instrumental and vocal competitions.

Potter College of Arts, Humanities, and Social Sciences

See Western Kentucky University, Potter College of Arts, Humanities, and Social Sciences

Prairie View A&M University

Prairie View, Texas

State-supported, coed. Small-town campus. Total enrollment: 5,849.

Degrees Bachelor of Music in the areas of applied music, music education. Majors: music, music education, piano/organ, voice, wind and percussion instruments.

Music Student Profile Fall 1994: 65 total; 60 matriculated undergraduate, 5 matriculated graduate; 90% minorities, 50% females, 3% international.

Music Faculty Total: 8; 8 full-time; 50% of full-time faculty have terminal degrees. Graduate students do not teach undergraduate courses. Undergraduate student–faculty ratio: 10:1.

Student Life Student groups include Music Educators National Conference Student Chapter, Kappa Kappa Psi, Tau Beta Sigma.

Expenses for 1995–96 State resident tuition: $900 full-time. Nonresident tuition: $6660 full-time, $222 per credit hour part-time. State resident part-time tuition per semester ranges from $120 to $330. Part-time mandatory fees per semester range from $66.89 to $385.79. Full-time mandatory fees: $1000. College room and board: $3620. Special program-related fees: $12 for applied music fees, $10 for lab fees.

Financial Aid Program-specific awards for Fall of 1994: 5–15 Jesse Jones Scholarships for talented students ($600–$2000), 3 University Talent Scholarships for program majors ($1000–$2500).

Application Procedures Deadline—freshmen and transfers: May 1. Notification date—freshmen and transfers: August 1. Required: high school transcript, minimum 2.0 high school GPA, letter of recommendation, interview, audition. Auditions held 4 times on campus and off campus in Dallas, TX; Houston, TX; Fort Worth, TX; San Antonio, TX; recorded music is permissible as a substitute for live auditions when distance is prohibitive and videotaped performances are permissible as a substitute for live auditions when distance is prohibitive.

Undergraduate Contact Director of Admissions, Prairie View A&M University, P.O. Box 3089, Prairie View, Texas 77446; 409-857-2618.

Purchase College, State University of New York

Purchase, New York

State-supported, coed. Small-town campus. Total enrollment: 2,498.

Degrees Bachelor of Fine Arts in the areas of performance, composition. Majors: classical music, composition, guitar, harp, jazz, music, opera, piano/organ, sacred music, stringed instruments, voice, wind and percussion instruments. Graduate degrees offered: Master of Fine Arts in the areas of performance, composition.

Music Student Profile Fall 1994: 250 total; 200 matriculated undergraduate, 50 matriculated graduate; 10% minorities, 55% females, 5% international.

Music Faculty Total: 110; 10 full-time, 100 part-time; 100% of full-time faculty have terminal degrees. Graduate students teach a few undergraduate courses. Undergraduate student–faculty ratio: 9:1.

Student Life Student groups include Ballet and Arts in Education performances, performances in the community.

Expenses for 1995–96 Application fee: $25. State resident tuition: $3400 full-time, $137 per credit part-time. Nonresident tuition: $8300 full-time, $346 per credit part-time. Part-time mandatory fees: $13.30 per credit. Full-time mandatory fees: $399. College room and board: $4872. College room only: $3130. Special program-related fees: $35 for audition.

Financial Aid Program-specific awards for Fall of 1994: 80 Scholarships for undergraduates ($500–$8000).

Application Procedures Deadline—freshmen and transfers: June 1. Notification date—freshmen and transfers: July 1. Required: high school transcript, college transcript(s) for transfer students, audition, SAT I or ACT test scores, TOEFL score for international applicants. Recommended: minimum 3.0 high school GPA, letter of recommendation, interview. Auditions held 4 times on campus; recorded music is permissible as a substitute for live auditions when distance is prohibitive or in special circumstances and videotaped performances are permissible as a substitute for live auditions when distance is prohibitive or in special circumstances.

Contact Sandra Corday, Divisional Secretary, Division of Music, Purchase College, State University of New York, 735 Anderson Hill Road, Purchase, New York 10577-1400; 914-251-6700, fax: 914-251-6739.

The Division of Music at Purchase College offers a comprehensive musical education at both the undergraduate and graduate level for a limited number of gifted students who wish to pursue the art of music at a professional level. It is a small community of about 250 students and faculty members dedicated to professional training in performance and composition in a conservatory setting. Music students have the opportunity to work very closely on an individual basis with many wonderful musicians who care deeply about them and who are passionately committed to teaching. Faculty members have active professional careers as performers and composers, and the College's performance affiliates include some of the most prestigious artist-teachers in the metropolitan area. Programs—instrumental (including jazz), voice/opera, piano, organ, composition, and studio composition—are designed to prepare students for a professional career.

The young artist aspiring to master the craft of musical performance or composition soon discovers the need for knowledge, insight, and imagination in addition to technical skill. The core undergraduate curriculum is similar throughout the four years for all areas of study: all students are required to take private or small-group study; ensemble; a set of courses in music theory, history, and musicianship; and courses specific to their area—all this, with sufficient time to practice. Further effort is made, in cooperation with the College of Letters and Science, to acquaint students with landmarks of cultural and social history as well as of scientific and philosophical thought. It is assumed that musical and cultural studies can be realistically undertaken together, given both desire and discipline. The Master of Fine Arts degree is an intensive program of approximately 60 credits designed to provide advanced training for students clearly destined for professional careers.

Each curriculum has a strong and vital component of specialized professional training; for example, the voice/opera program has courses in song repertoire, diction, languages (Italian, French, and German), acting, body movement, modern dance, dance improvisation and composition, opera history, opera workshop, and coaching. The jazz and studio composition curricula have courses in jazz harmony and arranging; jazz repertoire, ensemble, and chorus; the history of recorded music; world music survey and ensemble; AfroCuban and Indian music; composers' forum; songwriting; orchestration; commercial arranging; advanced studio production; film scoring; and hard drive digital recording.

Private lessons are taken with an affiliate artist-teacher selected by agreement of the student, the private teacher, and the Dean. Guidance in the choice of teacher is available from the resident faculty, in particular the head of the student's discipline area. The student may choose, subject to approval by the Dean, any established teacher in the New York City metropolitan area. Many students take their lessons with teachers in the city and use the opportunity to attend concerts and rehearsals and to taste the extraordinary richness that this cultural center has to offer.

Queens College

Charlotte, North Carolina

Independent-religious, coed. Suburban campus. Total enrollment: 1,572.

Degrees Bachelor of Music in the areas of music therapy, applied music performance. Majors: classical music, music therapy, piano/organ, stringed instruments, voice, wind and percussion instruments. Cross-registration with 13 member colleges of the Charlotte Area Educational Consortium.

Music Student Profile Fall 1994: 135 total; 35 matriculated undergraduate, 100 nondegree; 8% minorities, 96% females, 4% international.

Music Faculty Total: 19; 5 full-time, 14 part-time; 80% of full-time faculty have terminal degrees. Graduate students do not teach undergraduate courses. Undergraduate student–faculty ratio: 5:1.

Student Life Student groups include Music Therapy Club, Delta Omicron, Drama Club.

Expenses for 1995–96 Application fee: $25. Comprehensive fee of $16,690 includes full-time tuition ($11,520) and college room and board ($5170). Part-time tuition: $195 per credit hour. Part-time mandatory fees: $15 per semester. Special program-related fees: $75 for private music instruction.

Financial Aid Program-specific awards for Fall of 1994: 15 Music Major Awards for freshmen program majors ($1000), 8 Music Minor Awards for freshmen program minors ($500), 1 Stegner Music Scholarship for undergraduates ($5000), 1 Presser Award for seniors who demonstrate musical talent and academic achievement ($2250), 1 Lammers Music Scholarship for program majors ($5000).

Application Procedures Deadline—freshmen and transfers: continuous. Required: essay, high school transcript, minimum 2.0 high school GPA, 2 letters of recommendation. Recommended: interview, audition. Auditions held 4 times and by appointment on campus; recorded music is permissible as a substitute for live auditions if student has already visited the campus or when distance is prohibitive and videotaped performances are permissible as a substitute for live auditions if student has already visited the campus or when distance is prohibitive.

Undergraduate Contact Elizabeth B. Yancey, Associate Director of Admissions, Queens College, 1900 Selwyn Avenue, Charlotte, North Carolina 28274; 704-337-2355, fax: 704-337-2503, E-mail address: yancey@queens.edu.

Aaron Copland School of Music

Queens College of the City University of New York

Flushing, New York

State and locally supported, coed. Urban campus. Total enrollment: 17,958.

Queens College of the City University of New York *(continued)*

Degrees Bachelor of Music in the area of performance. Majors: piano/organ, stringed instruments, voice, wind and percussion instruments.

Music Student Profile Fall 1994: 100 total; all matriculated undergraduate.

Music Faculty Total: 73; 29 full-time, 44 part-time; 85% of full-time faculty have terminal degrees. Graduate students teach a few undergraduate courses. Undergraduate student–faculty ratio: 12:1.

Student Life Student groups include Music Educators National Conference.

Expenses for 1994–95 Application fee: $35. State resident tuition: $2450 full-time, $100 per credit part-time. Nonresident tuition: $5050 full-time, $210 per credit part-time. Part-time mandatory fees: $93.25 per semester. Full-time mandatory fees: $187.

Financial Aid Program-specific awards for Fall of 1994: 1–3 Boris Schwarz Scholarships for string majors ($500–$2200), 2 Zatkin Scholarships–Opera for voice majors ($250–$500), 1 Edward Downes Scholarship for voice majors ($700).

Application Procedures Deadline—freshmen and transfers: March 15. Required: high school transcript, minimum 3.0 high school GPA, audition. Auditions held 2 times on campus; recorded music is permissible as a substitute for live auditions when distance is prohibitive and videotaped performances are permissible as a substitute for live auditions when distance is prohibitive.

Undergraduate Contact Dr. Jonathan Irving, Special Assistant to the Director, Aaron Copland School of Music, Queens College of the City University of New York, 65-30 Kissena Boulevard, Flushing, New York 11367; 718-997-3800, fax: 718-997-3849.

Radford University

Radford, Virginia

State-supported, coed. Small-town campus. Total enrollment: 9,105.

Degrees Bachelor of Music in the areas of music education, music business, performance, composition; Bachelor of Music Therapy in the area of music therapy. Majors: composition, music business, music education, music therapy, piano/organ.

Music Student Profile Fall 1994: 153 total; 141 matriculated undergraduate, 12 matriculated graduate; 2% minorities, 56% females, 2% international.

Music Faculty Total: 29; 17 full-time, 12 part-time; 50% of full-time faculty have terminal degrees. Graduate students teach a few undergraduate courses. Undergraduate student–faculty ratio: 5:1.

Student Life Student groups include Music Therapy Club, Music Educators National Conference Student Chapter.

Expenses for 1995–96 Application fee: $15. State resident tuition: $3114 full-time, $130 per semester hour part-time. Nonresident tuition: $7688 full-time, $321 per semester hour part-time. College room and board: $4250.

Financial Aid Program-specific awards for Fall of 1994: 2–4 Arts Society Awards for freshmen ($4000), 1 Ingram-Lee Award for program majors ($2500), 5 Liebgrace Awards for program majors ($1000), 1 Presser Award for seniors ($2250).

Application Procedures Deadline—freshmen: April 1; transfers: June 1. Notification date—freshmen and transfers: continuous. Required: essay, high school transcript, minimum 2.0 high school GPA, audition. Recommended: minimum 3.0 high school GPA. Auditions held continuously by appointment on campus; recorded music is permissible as a substitute for live auditions if unedited and videotaped performances are permissible as a substitute for live auditions if unedited.

Undergraduate Contact Chris Knauer, Director, Office of Admissions, Radford University, East Norwood Street, Radford, Virginia 24142; 703-831-5371, fax: 703-831-5138, E-mail address: cknauer@ruscad.ac.runet.edu.

More about the University

The College of Visual and Performing Arts at Radford University contains six academic departments, two support centers, and the University Galleries to form a comprehensive arts complex that includes all of the principal art disciplines. The departments are Visual Art, Dance, Fashion, Interior Design, Music, and Theater. The support centers are the Center for Media Arts Technology and the Center for Music Technology. The University galleries include the Flossie Martin Gallery and the Corinna de la Burde Sculpture Court and routinely exhibit faculty, undergraduate, and graduate student shows in addition to entertaining exhibits from outside the University. The College has a faculty of 70, all of whom are active artists, musicians, researchers, and performers. The facilities include a 1,500-seat concert hall, a 500-seat theater, and a black box theater. The Department of Music features a 12-station MIDI theory lab and a state-of-the-art music technology lab. The Department of Art contains 2-D and 3-D facilities, including a computer graphics lab, photo and darkroom facilities and jewelry studio. In addition to traditional drawing, painting, ceramics, fibers, and sculpture studios. Both Fashion and Interior Design departments feature state-of-the-art equipment supporting the digital based technology used in their respective fields. The College offers two study-abroad programs exclusive to the fine arts, a semester-long program at Middlesex Polytech in London and a summer program with the University of Antwerp, Belgium, in addition to many special program opportunities offered in theater and music.

The Department of Art offers three undergraduate degrees: B.A., B.S., and B.F.A. Bachelor of Science students may earn certification in art education. The programs in art are characterized by flexibility of studio opportunities in both 2-D and 3-D areas, including drawing, painting, graphic design, computer graphics, ceramics, sculpture, crafts, jewelry, watercolor, photography, and fibers.

The Department of Dance offers a well-rounded curriculum emphasizing technique, performance, and theory. Students take one technique class per day in both

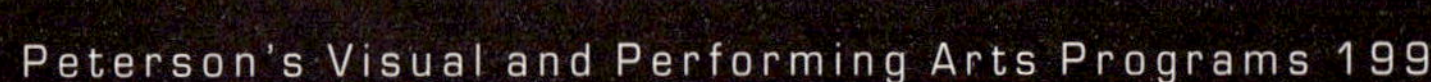

ballet and contemporary dance. Creative aspects of dance are explored through courses in composition and choreographic studies. In addition to continuing study in dance technique, upper division majors take courses in dance history, production, accompaniment for movement, and teaching methodology and selected theater courses. The R.U. Dance Theater, the performing company, presents three mainstage productions per year. One is a ballet program, which may be a full-length work such as the biennial production of *The Nutcracker* or one-act ballets from the classical repertoire. Ballets are accompanied by an orchestra, and students have the opportunity to perform with renowned guest artists. The other productions feature original contemporary choreography by faculty and guest choreographers. The department is presently exploring the new area of dance and technology, both in the classroom and in live performance.

The Department of Music offers four undergraduate degrees in music: the B.M., with concentrations in music education, music business, performance, or composition; the Bachelor of Music Therapy; the B.A.; and the B.S. Performance experiences include traditional instrumental and choral (solo and ensembles), jazz, and electronic music. The music education concentration is designed to provide students with stimulating professional music education course work along with extensive field experience in a variety of settings. The concentration in music business incorporates business core courses into a professional music degree program. The music therapy program is uniquely structured to provide not only an intensive study of music but also an in-depth understanding of the biological and behavioral sciences. The Center for Music Technology serves as a nucleus for activities involving music and technology within the department. Radford University is an accredited institutional member of the National Association of Schools of Music.

The Theater Department covers all aspects of drama and is combined with a challenging variety of performance opportunities, including major studio and children's theatrical productions for the campus community and the general public. The program provides a variety of areas of study, including vocal and physical training, technical theater, dance, makeup, acting, costume design and construction, playwriting, film, directing, stage lighting, and history literature. The department also hosts a guest artist each spring as a lead for the spring production. Past guest artists include William Christopher, Lee Meriwether, Marion Ross, Karen Grassle, John Amos, William Windom, and Tammy Grimes, to name a few. Internships with professional theaters available.

The Departments of Interior Design and Fashion offer B.A. and B.S. degrees in either design or merchandising. Both contain many field trips to major market locations, including New York, Atlanta, and Washington.

Please see Radford University's other programs listed under Art, Theater, and Dance.

Rhode Island College

Providence, Rhode Island

State-supported, coed. Urban campus. Total enrollment: 9,900.

Degrees Bachelor of Music in the area of performance. Majors: performance. Graduate degrees offered: Master of Music Education in the area of music education.

Music Student Profile Fall 1994: 962 total; 86 matriculated undergraduate, 7 matriculated graduate, 869 nondegree; 6% minorities, 58% females.

Music Faculty Total: 29; 11 full-time, 18 part-time; 100% of full-time faculty have terminal degrees. Graduate students do not teach undergraduate courses. Undergraduate student–faculty ratio: 75:1.

Estimated Expenses for 1995–96 Application fee: $25. State resident tuition: $2477 full-time, $112 per semester hour part-time. Nonresident tuition: $6995 full-time, $290 per semester hour part-time. Part-time mandatory fees per semester range from $55 to $200. Full-time mandatory fees: $493. College room and board: $5380. Special program-related fees: $300 for applied music fees.

Financial Aid Program-specific awards for Fall of 1994: 25 Special Talent Awards for program majors ($600–$1500).

Application Procedures Deadline—freshmen and transfers: continuous. Required: essay, high school transcript, minimum 3.0 high school GPA, video, audition. Auditions held 4 times on campus; recorded music is permissible as a substitute for live auditions if a campus visit is impossible and videotaped performances are permissible as a substitute for live auditions.

Undergraduate Contact Dr. Francis Marciniak, Professor, Music Department, Rhode Island College, 600 Mt. Pleasant Avenue, Providence, Rhode Island 02908; 401-456-8244.

Graduate Contact Dr. Philip McClintock, Professor, Music Department, Rhode Island College, 600 Mt. Pleasant Avenue, Providence, Rhode Island 02908; 401-456-8244.

Shepherd School of Music

Rice University

Houston, Texas

Independent, coed. Urban campus. Total enrollment: 4,073.

Degrees Bachelor of Music in the areas of performance, music theory, composition, musicology. Majors: classical music, composition, music, music history, music theory, opera, piano/organ, stringed instruments, voice, wind and percussion instruments. Graduate degrees offered: Master of Music in the areas of performance, music theory, composition, musicology. Doctor of Musical Arts in the areas of performance, composition.

Rice University *(continued)*

Music Student Profile Fall 1994: 278 total; 130 matriculated undergraduate, 148 matriculated graduate; 6% minorities, 49% females, 10% international.

Music Faculty Total: 54; 34 full-time, 20 part-time; 99% of full-time faculty have terminal degrees. Graduate students teach a few undergraduate courses. Undergraduate student–faculty ratio: 5:1.

Expenses for 1994–95 Application fee: $25. Comprehensive fee of $16,500 includes full-time tuition ($10,400), mandatory fees ($375), and college room and board ($5725).

Financial Aid Program-specific awards for Fall of 1994: Merit Awards for program majors ($1000–$10,400).

Application Procedures Deadline—freshmen: January 2; transfers: April 1. Notification date—freshmen: April 1; transfers: May 1. Required: essay, high school transcript, college transcript(s) for transfer students, 2 letters of recommendation, interview, audition, portfolio, SAT I or ACT test scores. Recommended: minimum 3.0 high school GPA. Auditions held as needed on campus; recorded music is permissible as a substitute for live auditions and videotaped performances are permissible as a substitute for live auditions. Portfolio reviews held as needed for composition students on campus.

Contact Gary Smith, Assistant Dean, Shepherd School of Music, Rice University, P.O. Box 1892, Houston, Texas 77251; 713-527-4047, fax: 713-285-5317.

Westminster Choir College of Rider University

Rider University

Lawrenceville, New Jersey

Independent, coed. Suburban campus. Total enrollment: 5,026.

Degrees Bachelor of Music in the areas of sacred music, music education, piano pedagogy, piano accompanying, piano performance, theory and composition, organ performance, voice performance. Majors: accompanying, music education, music theory and composition, piano, piano pedagogy, sacred music, voice. Graduate degrees offered: Master of Music in the areas of sacred music, music education, choral conducting, piano performance, piano pedagogy and performance, piano accompanying and coaching, composition, organ performance, voice pedagogy and performance. Cross-registration with Princeton University, Princeton Ballet School, Rider University.

Music Student Profile Fall 1994: 344 total; 227 matriculated undergraduate, 86 matriculated graduate, 31 nondegree; 12% minorities, 49% females, 11% international.

Music Faculty Total: 69; 38 full-time, 31 part-time; 80% of full-time faculty have terminal degrees. Graduate students do not teach undergraduate courses. Undergraduate student–faculty ratio: 7:1.

Student Life Special housing available for music students.

Expenses for 1995–96 Application fee: $35. Comprehensive fee of $19,570 includes full-time tuition ($13,800), mandatory fees ($140), and college room and board ($5630). Part-time tuition: $456 per semester hour. Special program-related fees: $245 for senior student teaching.

Financial Aid Program-specific awards for Fall of 1994: 12 Presidential Awards for undergraduates ($10,000), 20 J.F. Williamson Awards for undergraduates ($3000), 35 Dean's Awards for undergraduates ($3500), 141 Endowed Scholarships for undergraduates ($1300).

Application Procedures Deadline—freshmen and transfers: continuous. Required: high school transcript, college transcript(s) for transfer students, 3 letters of recommendation, audition, SAT I or ACT test scores. Recommended: essay, minimum 3.0 high school GPA, interview. Auditions held 20 times on campus and off campus in Atlanta, GA; Houston, TX; Richmond, VA; Lakeland, FL; Chicago, IL; Los Angeles, CA; Denver, CO; recorded music is permissible as a substitute for live auditions when distance is prohibitive or in special circumstances and videotaped performances are permissible as a substitute for live auditions when distance is prohibitive or in special circumstances. Portfolio reviews held on campus and off campus.

Contact Anne Farmer Meservey, Director of Admissions, Rider University, 101 Walnut Lane, Princeton, New Jersey 08540-3899; 609-921-7144, fax: 609-921-7144.

More about the School

Program Facilities Performance halls include the fine Arts Theatre (550 seats), Bristol Hall (350 seats), Williamson Hall (100 seats), Scheide Hall (100 seats), and the Playhouse/Opera Theatre (300 seats). Students play 120 pianos and 21 pipe organs. Talbott Library houses 55,000 scores and books, a state-of-the-art electronic music computer laboratory with fifteen Kurzweil synthesizers, sixteen Macintosh Power PCs running Finale and Performer, a multimedia center with CD-ROM and laser disc, computers customized for music theory and sight-singing programs, and 100 music fundamental programs.

Faculty and Alumni Faculty are all distinguished performers and scholars. Leonard Bernstein described Joseph Flummerfelt, principal Conductor and Artistic Director, as "the greatest choral conductor in the world." Joan Lippincott, organ chair and internationally known recitalist was recently appointed University Organist at Princeton University. Recent Composers-in-Residence include Daniel Pinkham, Peter Schikele, and John Corigliano. Westminster's distinguished alumni include a senior winning the 1994 Metropolitan Opera National Competition; professors at Rice, Notre Dame, Manhattan School of Music, and the Cincinnati Conservatory; performers with the Metropolitan Opera, New York City Opera, and Chicago Lyric opera; and leading music ministers and teachers worldwide.

Student Performance opportunities. All Westminster students perform in professional concerts each year. The 200-student Westminster Symphonic Choir (all upperclass and graduate students) regularly performs and records with the New York Philharmonic and Philadelphia and New Jersey symphony orchestras. Moreover, students perform in Chapel Choir, Westminster Signers, Westminster Concert Bell Choir, and The Westminster Choir (Choir-in-Residence at the Spoleto Festival USA), which all tour nationally.

Special Programs Westminster students can take classes at Westminster, Rider University, Princeton University, Princeton Theological Seminary, and the Princeton Ballet School. Rider offers intensive English language instruction on the Lawrenceville campus at the American Language Academy. Rider and Westminster Career Development Offices provide specialized career services for musicians. **Westminster Choir College,** home of the famed Westminster Symphonic Choir, integrates music study with professional choral performances conducted in concert with major symphony orchestras. The Westminster Symphonic Choir performs regularly at Lincoln Center, Carnegie Hall, and the Philadelphia Academy of Music with the New York Philharmonic Orchestra, the Philadelphia Orchestra, and the New Jersey Symphony Orchestra. The Westminster Symphonic Choir has performed and recorded with such notable conductors as Toscanini, Bernstein, Leinsdorf, Mehta, Ozawa, and Muti.

Additional performance and touring opportunities include the Westminster Choir, freshman Chapel Choir, Westminster Singers, and Westminster Concert Bell Choir. Students who play orchestral instruments can participate in the Westminster Conservatory Community Orchestra and chamber ensembles. Westminster students can also perform with orchestral musicians in Princeton, New Jersey.

Westminster's scenic 23-acre campus, ideally situated in picturesque Princeton within walking distance of charming Palmer Square, is an outstanding example for living, performing, and learning.

Westminster's campus centers around elegant Williamson Hall in the original Georgian Quadrangle, providing an intimate seating for recitals and chamber ensembles. Stately Bristol Hall, housing a 50-rank Aeolian-Skinner organ, a 16-rank Fisk organ, a 14-rank Noack organ, and a 9-foot Steinway grand piano, is a large recital facility for student, faculty, and guest performers. Nestled among the trees, the Playhouse/Opera Theatre offers a stage and two Steinway grand pianos. Beyond Bristol Chapel, Scheide Recital hall showcases a 44-rank Casavant organ.

Westminster offers practice rooms in each residence hall and has over 120 pieces and 21 pipe organs, including practice organs by Flentrop, Holtkamp, Schantz, Moller, and Noack.

Talbott Library/Learning Center houses 55,000 books, scores, periodicals, and microforms, plus 23,000 music scores and 160 periodical titles. The Performance Collection contains 6,000 titles in multiple copies for student study, class assignments, student teaching, and church choirs. A single-copy reference file of 45,000 individual octavos is the largest collection of its type in the United States. Voice students use a state-of-the-art voice laboratory, an invaluable resource for vocal pedagogy, for the scientific study of the vocal mechanism and singing. The Media Center contains over 9,000 recordings and videos, with facilities for student playback. The Music Education Resource Collection contains 1,000 textbooks, recordings, filmstrips, charts, and resource materials, plus listening equipment and an electronic piano.

Princeton, 40 miles from New York and Philadelphia, is within easy reach by train or bus, offering students a wealth of educational, cultural, and recreational activities. Princeton University, a short walk from Westminster, offers lectures, art exhibits, recitals, and concerts. Through a cooperative agreement, Westminster students may enroll in courses at Princeton University and the university's athletic and recreational facilities. Near Westminster, the Tony Award-Winning McCarter Theatre stages several major productions each year and hosts guest artists and performers.

Performances scheduled for the 1995–96 school year include the Hindemith *Requiem,* Grieg's *Peer Gynt,* Stravinsky's *Symphony of Psalms,* the Bach *St. John Passion,* and a recording of the Dvorak *Te Deum.*

Roland Dille Center for the Arts

See Moorhead State University, Roland Dille Center for the Arts

Chicago Musical College

Roosevelt University

Chicago, Illinois

Independent, coed. Urban campus. Total enrollment: 6,709.

Degrees Bachelor of Music in the areas of jazz performance, classical performance, music education, composition, theory, music history, piano pedagogy, music business. Majors: classical music, jazz, music, music business, music education, piano/organ, stringed instruments, voice, wind and percussion instruments. Graduate degrees offered: Master of Music in the areas of classical performance, music education, theory, composition, musicology, vocal pedagogy, piano pedagogy. Cross-registration with School of the Art Institute of Chicago.

Music Student Profile Fall 1994: 320 total; 231 matriculated undergraduate, 81 matriculated graduate, 8 nondegree; 45% minorities, 42% females, 18% international.

Music Faculty Total: 97; 22 full-time, 75 part-time; 55% of full-time faculty have terminal degrees. Graduate students do not teach undergraduate courses. Undergraduate student–faculty ratio: 11:1.

Student Life Student groups include Music Educators National Conference, Mu Phi Epsilon (music honorary fraternity). Special housing available for music students.

Expenses for 1995–96 Application fee: $25. Comprehensive fee of $14,485 includes full-time tuition ($9450), mandatory fees ($85), and college room and board ($4950). College room only: $3850. Part-time tuition: $315 per semester hour. Part-time mandatory fees: $85 per year. Special program-related fees: $40 for practice room rental.

Financial Aid Program-specific awards for Fall of 1994: 100 Music Scholarships for music majors ($3000), 40 Roosevelt Tuition Grants for those demonstrating need ($1200).

Application Procedures Deadline—freshmen and transfers: continuous. Required: high school transcript, college transcript(s) for transfer students, minimum 2.0 high

Roosevelt University *(continued)*

school GPA, interview, audition, SAT I or ACT test scores, minimum composite ACT score of 20. Auditions held 10 times on campus and off campus. Portfolio reviews held on campus and off campus.

Contact Bryan Shilander, Assistant Dean, Chicago Musical College, Roosevelt University, 430 South Michigan Avenue, Chicago, Illinois 60605; 312-341-3789, fax: 312-341-6358.

More about the College

Program Facilities Chicago Musical College was founded in 1867 and joined Roosevelt University in 1954. Students make the most of the city's vast musical and cultural activities. Within walking distance are the Chicago Symphony Orchestra, the Lyric Opera of Chicago, the Grant Park Symphony, the Auditorium Theatre, Jazz Showcase, theaters, museums, and parks. Located in Roosevelt University's landmark Auditorium Building, the college features air conditioned practice studios, MIDI instruments and computers, the historic Ganz Recital Hall, well-equipped studios and classrooms, and a large music library. Secure modern dormitory, dining, meeting, and recreational facilities. Special unlimited practice privileges for resident students.

Faculty, Resident Artists, and Alumni Many faculty perform on national and international concert stages. Notables include Ludmila Lazar and Pawel Checinski, piano, Bruce Berr, piano pedagogy, David Schrader, organ and harpsichord, Cyrus Forough, violin, Kim Scholes, cello, Paul Henry, classical guitar, Gregory Smith, clarinet, Judith Haddon, Maria Lagios and Jeffrey Gall, voice, Rob Parton, jazz, Edward Poremba, percussion, Robert Lombardo, composition, Anne Heider, choral conducting. Recent master classes with Jerry Hadley, Samuel Remey, Thomas Hampson, Josef Gingold, Ramsey Lewis, Leonard Hokanson, Jeffrey Gall, Dalton Baldwin, Radoslav Kvapil.

Student Performance/Exhibit Opportunities Over 140 concerts, recitals, operas, and musicals presented each year. Ensembles include Chorus, Chamber Singers, Symphony, Wind Ensemble, Opera, Jazz Ensembles, Chamber Music, Early Music, New Music, Two-Piano, Guitar Ensemble, Collegium Musicum. Off-campus performance opportunities for advanced students.

Special Programs A diverse student body from 19 states and 23 foreign countries. Particularly accommodating to international students. Admission with or without TOEFL and TWE scores. Roosevelt University offers extensive ESL preparation for students without TOEFL. Music scholarship program open to both U.S. and international applicants. Music business internship, MENC, and Mu Phi Epsilon chapters.

Rowan College of New Jersey

Glassboro, New Jersey

State-supported, coed. Small-town campus. Total enrollment: 8,936.

Degrees Bachelor of Music. Majors: composition, jazz, music education, performance.

Music Faculty Total: 26; 16 full-time, 10 part-time.

Expenses for 1994–95 Application fee: $35. State resident tuition: $3095 full-time, $103.60 per credit part-time. Nonresident tuition: $4356 full-time, $171.10 per credit part-time. College room and board: $4830. College room only: $2880.

Application Procedures Deadline—freshmen: March 15; transfers: April 15. Required: essay, high school transcript, audition, portfolio, SAT I or ACT test scores. Auditions held 4 times on campus; recorded music is permissible as a substitute for live auditions when distance is prohibitive. Portfolio reviews held throughout the year for composition applicants on campus.

Undergraduate Contact Thomas Wade, Chair, Music Department, Rowan College of New Jersey, 201 Mullica Hill Road, Glassboro, New Jersey 08028; 609-863-6478.

Mason Gross School of the Arts

Rutgers, The State University of New Jersey

New Brunswick, New Jersey

State-supported, coed. Small-town campus. Total enrollment: 647.

Degrees Bachelor of Music in the areas of music education, jazz, performance. Majors: classical music, jazz, music education. Graduate degrees offered: Master of Music in the areas of performance, jazz. Doctor of Musical Arts in the area of performance.

Music Student Profile Fall 1994: 260 total; 126 matriculated undergraduate, 94 matriculated graduate, 40 nondegree; 10% minorities, 40% females, 15% international.

Music Faculty Total: 55; 37 full-time, 18 part-time; 100% of full-time faculty have terminal degrees. Graduate students teach a few undergraduate courses. Undergraduate student–faculty ratio: 3:1.

Student Life Student groups include National Association of Teachers.

Expenses for 1995–96 Application fee: $50. State resident tuition: $3786 full-time, $122.50 per credit hour part-time. Nonresident tuition: $7707 full-time, $249.75 per credit hour part-time. Mandatory fees range from $105 to $1045 full-time, $155 to $187 per year part-time, according to college of affiliation. College room and board: $4253.

Financial Aid Program-specific awards for Fall of 1994: 4 Benefit Series Awards for those with artistic merit ($1500), 8 Nicholas Awards for those with artistic merit ($1300), 3 Naumberg Awards for those with artistic merit ($800), 3 Pee Wee Russell Awards for those with artistic merit ($400), Music Excellence Awards for those with artistic merit ($1500), 3 Rutgers Trio Awards for those with artistic merit ($1000), 5 Douglass Noe Awards for those with artistic merit ($1500), 3 Douglass Shaw

Awards for those with artistic merit ($500), 4 Douglass Waxman Awards for those with artistic merit ($600).

Application Procedures Deadline—freshmen: February 15; transfers: March 15. Notification date—freshmen and transfers: May 1. Required: high school transcript, minimum 2.0 high school GPA, interview, audition. Auditions held 5 times on campus and off campus; recorded music is permissible as a substitute for live auditions for out-of-state applicants and videotaped performances are permissible as a substitute for live auditions for out-of-state applicants. Portfolio reviews held on campus and off campus.

Contact Chairman, Music Department, Rutgers, The State University of New Jersey, Marryott Music Building, P.O. Box 270, New Brunswick, New Jersey 08903; 908-932-9302, fax: 908-932-1517.

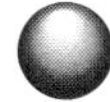

Saint Mary's College

Notre Dame, Indiana

Independent-religious, women only. Suburban campus. Total enrollment: 1,545.

Degrees Bachelor of Music in the areas of performance, music theory and literature, music education. Majors: music education, music literature, music theory, performance. Cross-registration with University of Notre Dame.

Music Student Profile Fall 1994: 20 total; all matriculated undergraduate; 100% females, 15% international.

Music Faculty Total: 15; 5 full-time, 10 part-time; 100% of full-time faculty have terminal degrees. Undergraduate student–faculty ratio: 4:1.

Student Life Student groups include Music Educators National Conference Student Chapter.

Expenses for 1995–96 Application fee: $30. Comprehensive fee of $18,968 includes full-time tuition ($13,494), mandatory fees ($740), and college room and board ($4734 minimum). Part-time tuition: $562 per semester hour. Special program-related fees: $150–$200 for private lessons.

Financial Aid Program-specific awards for Fall of 1994: 1–3 Presidential Merit Scholarships for exceptionally talented students ($2500).

Application Procedures Deadline—freshmen and transfers: continuous. Required: essay, high school transcript, college transcript(s) for transfer students, minimum 3.0 high school GPA, letter of recommendation, audition, SAT I or ACT test scores, minimum 3.0 college GPA for transfer students. Recommended: interview. Auditions held continuously on campus; recorded music is permissible as a substitute for live auditions when distance is prohibitive and videotaped performances are permissible as a substitute for live auditions when distance is prohibitive.

Undergraduate Contact Dr. Nancy Menk, Chair, Department of Music, Saint Mary's College, 313 Moreau Hall, Notre Dame, Indiana 46556-5001; 219-284-4632, fax: 219-284-4716.

Saint Vincent College

Latrobe, Pennsylvania

Independent-religious, coed. Rural campus.

Degrees Bachelor of Music in the areas of performance, music education, sacred music. Majors: music education, sacred music. Mandatory cross-registration with Seton Hill College.

Music Student Profile Fall 1994: 12 total; all matriculated undergraduate; 4% minorities, 50% females, 1% international.

Music Faculty Total: 22; 4 full-time, 18 part-time; 75% of full-time faculty have terminal degrees. Graduate students do not teach undergraduate courses.

Student Life Student groups include Saint Vincent College Singers, Saint Vincent Troubadours, Westmoreland Symphony, Youth Orchestra.

Expenses for 1995–96 Application fee: $25. Comprehensive fee of $16,200 includes full-time tuition ($12,000) and college room and board ($4200). Part-time tuition: $375 per credit. Special program-related fees: $100 for private instruction.

Financial Aid Program-specific awards for Fall of 1994: 1 Gabriel Burda Award for program majors ($1000).

Application Procedures Deadline—freshmen and transfers: continuous. Required: high school transcript, college transcript(s) for transfer students, minimum 2.0 high school GPA, audition, SAT I or ACT test scores. Recommended: essay, minimum 3.0 high school GPA, letter of recommendation, interview. Auditions held on a case-by-case basis off campus in Greensburg, PA; recorded music is permissible as a substitute for live auditions if a campus visit is impossible and videotaped performances are permissible as a substitute for live auditions if a campus visit is impossible.

Undergraduate Contact Joseph Bronder, Chair, Music Department, Saint Vincent College, 300 Fraser Purchase Road, Latrobe, Pennsylvania 15650; 412-539-9761.

Saint Xavier University

Chicago, Illinois

Independent-religious, coed. Urban campus. Total enrollment: 4,060.

Degrees Bachelor of Music in the areas of performance, music education. Majors: music education, piano/organ, stringed instruments, voice, wind and percussion instruments.

Music Student Profile Fall 1994: 235 total; 35 matriculated undergraduate, 200 nondegree.

Music Faculty Total: 22; 6 full-time, 16 part-time; 100% of full-time faculty have terminal degrees. Graduate students do not teach undergraduate courses. Undergraduate student–faculty ratio: 5:1.

Student Life Student groups include Collegiate Music Educators National Conference.

Saint Xavier University *(continued)*

Expenses for 1995–96 Application fee: $20. Comprehensive fee of $16,400 includes full-time tuition ($11,490), mandatory fees ($110), and college room and board ($4800). Part-time tuition: $383 per semester hour. Special program-related fees: $100 for accompanist fee, $45 for computer lab for theory courses, $45 for piano lab fee for keyboard musicianship courses, $45 for instrument rental fee for methods courses.

Financial Aid Program-specific awards for Fall of 1994: 3 Sinon Catherine O'Donohue Keyboard Scholarships for keyboard students ($2000), 7 Sister Gabrielle McShane Awards for vocalists/instrumentalists ($2000), Band Scholarships for ensemble performers ($750–$4000).

Application Procedures Deadline—freshmen and transfers: continuous. Required: essay, high school transcript, letter of recommendation, audition, SAT I or ACT test scores, minimum 2.5 high school GPA. Recommended: interview. Auditions held 4–5 times and by appointment on campus; videotaped performances are permissible as a substitute for live auditions for out-of-state and international applicants.

Undergraduate Contact Martha Morris, Chair, Music Department, Saint Xavier University, 3700 West 103rd Street, Chicago, Illinois 60655; 312-298-3420, fax: 312-779-9061.

Salem College

Winston-Salem, North Carolina

Independent-religious, primarily women. Small-town campus. Total enrollment: 901.

Degrees Bachelor of Music in the areas of piano, organ, voice, flute. Majors: piano/organ, voice. Cross-registration with Wake Forest University.

Music Student Profile Fall 1994: 37 total; 29 matriculated undergraduate, 8 nondegree; 8% minorities, 100% females.

Music Faculty Total: 8; 4 full-time, 4 part-time; 100% of full-time faculty have terminal degrees. Graduate students do not teach undergraduate courses. Undergraduate student–faculty ratio: 7:1.

Student Life Student groups include Pierrette's Players (drama club), Archways Choral Group, Salem College Arts Society.

Expenses for 1995–96 Application fee: $25. Comprehensive fee of $17,885 includes full-time tuition ($11,060), mandatory fees ($185), and college room and board ($6640). Part-time tuition: $560 per course.

Financial Aid Program-specific awards for Fall of 1994: 3 Dunford Scholarships for program majors ($2500–$3000), 3 Christian Gregor Awards for program majors ($5000–$6000), 3 Fletcher Foundation Awards for program majors ($7000), 5 Vardell Music Scholarships for program majors ($1000–$1500).

Application Procedures Deadline—freshmen and transfers: continuous. Required: essay, high school transcript, college transcript(s) for transfer students, minimum 2.0 high school GPA, 2 letters of recommendation, audition, SAT I or ACT test scores. Recommended: interview. Auditions held 3–4 times and by appointment on campus; recorded music is permissible as a substitute for live auditions if a campus visit is impossible and videotaped performances are permissible as a substitute for live auditions if a campus visit is impossible.

Undergraduate Contact Dr. David Schildkret, Director, School of Music, Salem College, P.O. Box 10548, Winston-Salem, North Carolina 27108; 910-721-2637, fax: 910-721-2683.

Sam Houston State University

Huntsville, Texas

State-supported, coed. Small-town campus. Total enrollment: 12,906.

Degrees Bachelor of Music in the areas of performance, music theory/composition, music literature, music therapy; Bachelor of Music Education in the area of music education. Majors: classical music, jazz, music, music education, music therapy, opera, piano/organ, stringed instruments, voice, wind and percussion instruments. Graduate degrees offered: Master of Music in the areas of performance, music theory/composition, conducting, musicology, Kodaly pedagogy; Master of Music Education in the area of music education.

Music Student Profile Fall 1994: 365 total; 285 matriculated undergraduate, 15 matriculated graduate, 65 nondegree; 30% minorities, 45% females, 10% international.

Music Faculty Total: 52; 28 full-time, 24 part-time; 70% of full-time faculty have terminal degrees. Graduate students teach a few undergraduate courses. Undergraduate student–faculty ratio: 10:1.

Student Life Student groups include American Association of Music Therapy Student Chapter, Sigma Alpha Iota, Kappa Kappa Psi.

Expenses for 1994–95 State resident tuition: $896 full-time. Nonresident tuition: $5472 full-time, $171 per semester hour part-time. State resident part-time tuition per semester ranges from $100 to $308. Part-time mandatory fees per semester range from $76 to $303. Full-time mandatory fees: $706. College room and board: $3070. College room only: $1530. Special program-related fees: $20 for recital recording fee, $30 for recital hall rental fee.

Financial Aid Program-specific awards for Fall of 1994: 120 scholarships for undergraduates ($200–$1700).

Application Procedures Deadline—freshmen and transfers: continuous. Required: high school transcript, 2 letters of recommendation, interview, audition. Recommended: minimum 2.0 high school GPA. Auditions held a minimum of 6 times on campus and off campus in various locations; recorded music is permissible as a substitute for live auditions with permission of the chair and videotaped performances are permissible as a substitute for live auditions when distance is prohibitive.

Contact Rodney M. Cannon, Chair, Music Department, Sam Houston State University, P.O. Box 2208, Huntsville,

Texas 77341-2208; 409-294-1360, fax: 409-294-3765, E-mail address: mus_rmc@shsu.edu.

Samford University

Birmingham, Alabama

Independent-religious, coed. Suburban campus. Total enrollment: 4,571.

Degrees Bachelor of Music in the areas of performance, church music, music theory/composition; Bachelor of Music Education in the areas of vocal music education, instrumental music education. Majors: music education, music theory and composition, piano/organ, sacred music, stringed instruments, voice, wind and percussion instruments. Graduate degrees offered: Master of Music in the areas of church music, music education.

Music Student Profile Fall 1994: 127 total; 118 matriculated undergraduate, 9 matriculated graduate; 55% females.

Music Faculty Total: 24; 16 full-time, 8 part-time; 62% of full-time faculty have terminal degrees. Graduate students do not teach undergraduate courses. Undergraduate student–faculty ratio: 8:1.

Student Life Student groups include Phi Mu Alpha Sinfonia, Delta Omicron, Music Educators National Conference Student Chapter.

Expenses for 1995–96 Application fee: $25. Comprehensive fee of $12,492 includes full-time tuition ($8648) and college room and board ($3844). Part-time tuition: $284 per semester hour. Special program-related fees: $25 for applied music fee.

Financial Aid Program-specific awards for Fall of 1994: 30 Music Scholarships for program majors ($300–$1500), 20 Band Scholarships for band members ($400–$1500).

Application Procedures Deadline—freshmen and transfers: continuous. Notification date—freshmen and transfers: May 1. Required: high school transcript, college transcript(s) for transfer students, 2 letters of recommendation, audition, SAT I or ACT test scores. Recommended: minimum 3.0 high school GPA. Auditions held 3 times on campus; recorded music is permissible as a substitute for live auditions in special circumstances and videotaped performances are permissible as a substitute for live auditions in special circumstances.

Undergraduate Contact Dr. Billy Strickland, Assistant Dean for Undergraduate Studies, School of Music, Samford University, 800 Lakeshore Drive, P.O. Box 2242, Birmingham, Alabama 35229; 205-870-2826, fax: 205-870-2165.

Graduate Contact Paul Richardson, Assistant Dean for Graduate Studies, School of Music, Samford University, 800 Lakeshore Drive, P.O. Box 2242, Birmingham, Alabama 35229; 205-870-2496, fax: 205-870-2165.

San Diego State University

San Diego, California

State-supported, coed. Urban campus. Total enrollment: 27,787.

Degrees Bachelor of Music in the areas of performance, jazz studies, composition; Bachelor of Arts/Bachelor of Fine Arts in the areas of general music, music education. Majors: classical music, composition, jazz, music, music education, piano/organ, stringed instruments, voice, wind and percussion instruments. Graduate degrees offered: Master of Music in the areas of performance, jazz studies, composition, conducting; Master of Musical Arts in the areas of ethnomusicology, musicology, theory, vocal pedagogy, piano pedagogy, history and literature. Cross-registration with University of California–San Diego.

Music Student Profile Fall 1994: 250 total; 190 matriculated undergraduate, 60 matriculated graduate; 40% minorities, 50% females, 5% international.

Music Faculty Total: 58; 21 full-time, 37 part-time; 12% of full-time faculty have terminal degrees. Graduate students teach a few undergraduate courses. Undergraduate student–faculty ratio: 21:1.

Student Life Student groups include Phi Mu Alpha, Kappa Kappa Psi, Sigma Alpha Iota.

Expenses for 1994–95 State resident tuition: $0 full-time. Nonresident tuition: $7646 full-time, $246 per unit part-time. Part-time mandatory fees: $618 per semester. Full-time mandatory fees: $1902. College room and board: $4397. Special program-related fees: $20 for piano practice room, $20 for instrument use fee.

Financial Aid Program-specific awards for Fall of 1994: Scholarships for music majors ($400–$2000).

Application Procedures Deadline—freshmen and transfers: continuous. Notification date—freshmen and transfers: continuous. Required: high school transcript, college transcript(s) for transfer students, minimum 2.0 high school GPA, audition, SAT I or ACT test scores. Auditions held 2 times on campus and off campus; videotaped performances are permissible as a substitute for live auditions. Portfolio reviews held on campus and off campus.

Undergraduate Contact Dr. Marian Liebowitz, Undergraduate Advisor - Music, School of Music and Dance, San Diego State University, San Diego, California 92182-7902; 619-594-6031, fax: 619-594-1692.

Graduate Contact Thomas Stauffer, Graduate Advisor - Music, School of Music and Dance, San Diego State University, San Diego, California 92182-7902; 619-594-6031, fax: 619-594-1692.

San Francisco Conservatory of Music

San Francisco, California

Independent, coed. Urban campus. Total enrollment: 273.

San Francisco Conservatory of Music *(continued)*

Degrees Bachelor of Music in the areas of classical guitar, composition, keyboard instruments, orchestral instruments, voice. Majors: classical guitar, classical music, composition, piano/organ, stringed instruments, voice, wind and percussion instruments. Graduate degrees offered: Master of Music in the areas of chamber music, classical guitar, composition, instrumental conducting, keyboard instruments, orchestral instruments, piano accompanying, voice.

Music Student Profile Fall 1994: 273 total; 143 matriculated undergraduate, 122 matriculated graduate, 8 nondegree; 20% minorities, 62% females, 23% international.

Music Faculty Total: 79; 27 full-time, 52 part-time; 30% of full-time faculty have terminal degrees. Graduate students do not teach undergraduate courses. Undergraduate student–faculty ratio: 6:1.

Student Life Student groups include Student Government Organization.

Expenses for 1995–96 Application fee: $60. Tuition: $14,500 full-time, $650 per semester hour part-time. Part-time mandatory fees: $250 per year. Full-time mandatory fees: $250.

Financial Aid Program-specific awards for Fall of 1994: 85 Conservatory Scholarships for undergraduates ($6100).

Application Procedures Deadline—freshmen and transfers: March 1. Notification date—freshmen and transfers: July 15. Required: high school transcript, college transcript(s) for transfer students, minimum 2.0 high school GPA, 2 letters of recommendation, audition, SAT I or ACT test scores. Auditions held 6 times on campus and off campus in Boston, MA; New York, NY; Chicago, IL; Oberlin, OH; Interlochen, MI; Miami, FL; Los Angeles, CA; Phoenix, AZ; Houston, TX; Portland, OR; Seattle, WA; recorded music is permissible as a substitute for live auditions for non-voice applicants if distance is prohibitive and videotaped performances are permissible as a substitute for live auditions if distance is prohibitive.

Contact Joan Gordon, Admission Officer, Office of Student Services, San Francisco Conservatory of Music, 1201 Ortega Street, San Francisco, California 94122-4498; 415-759-3431, fax: 415-759-3499.

More about the Conservatory

Program Facilities Hellman Hall (333 seats), considered one of the finest concert halls of its size in northern California, and Agnes Albert Hall (60 seats), a multiuse performance/teaching space: Bothin Library, offering over 35,000 volumes, scores, and periodicals and nearly 9,000 recordings; E. L. Wieland Computer Laboratory and the Electronic Composition Studio: additional feature, including a professional recording studio, bookstore, and 63 practice rooms.

Faculty, Resident Artists, and Alumni SFCM faculty are members of the San Francisco Symphony, San Francisco Opera, San Francisco Ballet, and Philharmonia Baroque Orchestras and perform internationally as soloists and chamber musicians. Recent visiting artists include Isaac Stern, Elliott Carter, John Adams, Leon Fleischer, Thompson Hampson, and the Juilliard String Quartet. Nationally known alumni include pianist Jeffrey Kahane, guitarist David Tanenbaum, mezzo-soprano Wendy Hillhouse, and Naumburg Award-winning cellist Hai-Yi Ni. Isaac Stern and Yehudi Menuhin studied at the Conservatory as children.

Student Performance Opportunities Approximately 400 events are presented at SFCM each year, featuring solo recitals by students and faculty, small ensembles, a fully staged opera, and symphonic programs. Ensembles: the Conservatory Orchestra, Conservatory Opera Theatre, Cantata Singers, Conservatory Baroque, and special ensembles focusing on brass and woodwinds, new music, guitar, and percussion. Concentrated studies: chamber music and baroque performance.

The San Francisco Conservatory of Music was founded in 1917 as a small piano school and has become a nationally prominent conservatory with an international reputation. The Conservatory enrolls approximately 250 students from all over the United States and the world in the undergraduate and graduate programs each year. Students work both one-on-one with their major instrument teacher and in small classes with other faculty members. In addition to their teaching, faculty members coach students for their recitals and often perform with alumni and students in concerts throughout the year. The Conservatory offers a great deal of personal attention for each student, in part because of a low student-teacher ratio of 6:1. In the school's friendly and intimate atmosphere, students receive an intense and intellectually rigorous preparation for a career in music.

Most students live near the Conservatory, which is in a quiet, affordable residential neighborhood near Golden Gate Park about 2 miles from the Pacific Ocean. Convenient public transportation provides access to downtown San Francisco and the Civic Center, the city's performing arts center.

San Francisco's performing arts offerings range from world-class symphony, opera and ballet, avant-garde music, theater, dance and performance. Free tickets to many performances are available to students. Museums, galleries, and the great physical beauty of San Francisco–its parks, beaches, views, and neighborhoods–provide much to explore.

Performing is a major aspect of student life at the Conservatory. Students perform recitals required for their degrees and perform with the orchestra, opera theater, and numerous ensembles based at the Conservatory.

Every year, the Conservatory's Community Service Program sends students out into the community to perform concerts at convalescent homes, hospitals and other institutions, while the Job Placement Program offers approximately 1,000 paid performance opportunities. Outside the Conservatory, students can augment their studies by performing with a wide range of professional groups including many regional symphony orchestras, chamber music ensembles, opera companies, and choruses in the San Francisco Bay Area. With this opportunity to build a professional network while still in school, students from the Conservatory have a head start in the highly competitive field of music. Students at the Conservatory fulfill their early promise by going on to work directly in the music profession. Conservatory alumni have distinguished themselves in many facets of music. Alumni perform with a wide range of music organizations, including the following: Arditti String Quartet, Boston Symphony, Chicago Symphony, Cleveland Orchestra, Glyndebourne Festival Opera, Israel

Philharmonic, Metropolitan Opera, Minnesota Orchestra, National Symphony Orchestra, New York City Opera, New Zealand String quartet, New York Philharmonic, Peabody Trio, Philharmonia Baroque, Philip Glass Ensemble, San Francisco Ballet Orchestra, San Francisco Opera and Opera Orchestra, San Francisco Symphony, and Santa Fe Opera.

The San Francisco Conservatory was the first conservatory in the United States to offer a degree program in chamber music and also offers a significant undergraduate experience in chamber music.

The Conservatory travels to many U.S. cities to hear auditions. The 1995-96 regional audition tours include stops in Boston, New York City, Chicago, Oberlin, Interlochen, Miami, Los Angeles, Phoenix, San Antonio, Houston, Portland, and Seattle.

San Francisco State University

San Francisco, California

State-supported, coed. Urban campus. Total enrollment: 26,552.

Degrees Bachelor of Music in the areas of music education, piano, organ, orchestral instrument performance, classical guitar performance, composition, music history and literature. Majors: classical music, commercial music, composition, electronic music, jazz, music education, music history and literature, piano/organ, stringed instruments, voice, wind and percussion instruments. Graduate degrees offered: Master of Music in the areas of solo performance. chamber music, conducting, composition.

Music Student Profile Fall 1994: 875 total; 275 matriculated undergraduate, 50 matriculated graduate, 550 nondegree; 25% minorities, 54% females, 5% international.

Music Faculty Total: 43; 19 full-time, 24 part-time; 100% of full-time faculty have terminal degrees. Graduate students do not teach undergraduate courses. Undergraduate student–faculty ratio: 18:1.

Student Life Student groups include California Music Educators Association, National Association of Schools of Music.

Expenses for 1995–96 Application fee: $55. State resident tuition: $0 full-time. Nonresident tuition: $7380 full-time, $246 per unit part-time. Part-time mandatory fees per semester range from $658 to $991. Full-time mandatory fees: $1982. College room and board: $5435.

Financial Aid Program-specific awards for Fall of 1994: Music Scholarships for academically and artistically talented program majors.

Application Procedures Deadline—freshmen and transfers: continuous. Required: high school transcript, minimum 3.0 high school GPA, audition, SAT I or ACT test scores, TOEFL score for international applicants. Auditions held 4 times on campus and off campus; recorded music is permissible as a substitute for live auditions when distance is prohibitive and videotaped performances are permissible as a substitute for live auditions when distance is prohibitive. Portfolio reviews held on campus and off campus.

Undergraduate Contact Enrollment Services, San Francisco State University, 1600 Holloway Avenue, San Francisco, California 94132-1722; 415-338-1431, fax: 415-338-6159.

Graduate Contact Patricia Taylor Lee, Chair, Music Department, San Francisco State University, 1600 Holloway Avenue, San Francisco, California 94132-1722; 415-338-1431, fax: 415-338-6159.

San Jose State University

San Jose, California

State-supported, coed. Urban campus. Total enrollment: 26,299.

Degrees Bachelor of Music in the areas of instrumental performance, vocal performance, composition. Majors: classical music, electronic music, jazz, music, music education, opera, piano/organ, stringed instruments, voice, wind and percussion instruments, world music.

Music Student Profile Fall 1994: 240 total; all matriculated undergraduate; 30% minorities, 50% females, 10% international.

Music Faculty Total: 55; 20 full-time, 35 part-time; 90% of full-time faculty have terminal degrees. Graduate students do not teach undergraduate courses. Undergraduate student–faculty ratio: 4:1.

Student Life Student groups include Music Educators National Conference Student Chapter.

Expenses for 1995–96 Application fee: $55. State resident tuition: $0 full-time. Nonresident tuition: $7626 full-time, $246 per unit part-time. Part-time mandatory fees: $655 per semester. Full-time mandatory fees: $1976. College room and board: $4875 (minimum). Special program-related fees: $25 for equipment use fee.

Financial Aid Program-specific awards for Fall of 1994: 25 Music Scholarships for freshmen ($750).

Application Procedures Deadline—freshmen and transfers: continuous. Notification date—freshmen and transfers: continuous. Required: essay, audition. Recommended: minimum 2.0 high school GPA. Auditions held 2 times on campus.

Contact Susan Schadek, Clerical Assistant, School of Music, San Jose State University, One Washington Square, San Jose, California 95192-0095; 408-924-4673, fax: 408-924-4773.

Schmidt College of Arts and Humanities

See Florida Atlantic University, Schmidt College of Arts and Humanities

Seton Hall University

South Orange, New Jersey

Independent-religious, coed. Suburban campus. Total enrollment: 8,400.

Seton Hall University *(continued)*

Degrees Bachelor of Music in the areas of voice, piano, classical instruments, historical musicology; Bachelor of Music Education in the areas of vocal music education, instrumental music education. Majors: applied music, music.

Music Student Profile Fall 1994: 50 total; all matriculated undergraduate.

Music Faculty Total: 31; 6 full-time, 25 part-time. Graduate students do not teach undergraduate courses.

Expenses for 1995–96 Application fee: $25. Comprehensive fee of $19,740 includes full-time tuition ($12,480), mandatory fees ($550), and college room and board ($6710). Part-time tuition: $390 per credit. Part-time mandatory fees: $85 per semester.

Financial Aid Program-specific awards for Fall of 1994: 1 O'Connor Award for those demonstrating talent and academic achievement ($1000).

Application Procedures Deadline—freshmen and transfers: continuous. Required: essay, high school transcript, minimum 2.0 high school GPA, 3 letters of recommendation, audition. Recommended: interview. Auditions held by appointment on campus; recorded music is permissible as a substitute for live auditions for out-of-state applicants.

Undergraduate Contact Dr. Jeanette Hile, Professor of Applied Music, Music Department, Seton Hall University, 400 South Orange Avenue, South Orange, New Jersey 07079; 201-761-9417, fax: 201-275-2368.

Seton Hill College

Greensburg, Pennsylvania

Independent-religious, primarily women. Small-town campus. Total enrollment: 923.

Degrees Bachelor of Music in the areas of performance, music education, sacred music. Majors: music, music education, sacred music. Cross-registration with Saint Vincent College.

Music Student Profile Fall 1994: 64 total; 53 matriculated undergraduate, 11 nondegree; 3% minorities, 50% females, 3% international.

Music Faculty Total: 22; 3 full-time, 19 part-time; 100% of full-time faculty have terminal degrees. Graduate students do not teach undergraduate courses. Undergraduate student–faculty ratio: 10:1.

Student Life Student groups include Music Educators National Conference, Pennsylvania Music Educators Association Student Chapter, American Guild of Organists.

Expenses for 1994–95 Application fee: $30. Comprehensive fee of $15,520 includes full-time tuition ($11,090), mandatory fees ($250), and college room and board ($4180). Part-time tuition: $318 per credit. Part-time mandatory fees: $6 per credit. Special program-related fees: $12–$50 for music education methods course fee, $12 for large ensembles, $150 for private instruction on a major instrument, $75 for private instruction on a secondary instrument.

Financial Aid Program-specific awards for Fall of 1994: 2 Gabriel Burda Scholarships for incoming students ($4000), 4 String Quartet Scholarships for string players ($1500), 1 Highberger Scholarship for incoming students ($1000), 1 Choral Society Scholarship for incoming students ($500), 1 Symphonic Winds Scholarship for incoming students ($1000), 1–4 Mildred Gardner Music Scholarships for incoming students from Westmoreland County, PA ($1000–$4000).

Application Procedures Deadline—freshmen and transfers: continuous. Notification date—freshmen and transfers: continuous. Required: high school transcript, college transcript(s) for transfer students, minimum 2.0 high school GPA, audition, SAT I or ACT test scores, minimum combined SAT I score of 800, minimum composite ACT score of 19. Recommended: essay, minimum 3.0 high school GPA, letter of recommendation, interview. Auditions held by appointment on campus; recorded music is permissible as a substitute for live auditions if a campus visit is impossible and videotaped performances are permissible as a substitute for live auditions if a campus visit is impossible.

Undergraduate Contact Peter Egan, Director, Admissions Office, Seton Hill College, College Avenue, Greensburg, Pennsylvania 15601; 412-834-2200, fax: 412-830-4611.

Shenandoah University

Winchester, Virginia

Independent-religious, coed. Small-town campus. Total enrollment: 1,652.

Degrees Bachelor of Music in the areas of church music, composition, jazz studies, music education, pedagogy performance, piano accompanying; Bachelor of Music Therapy in the area of music therapy. Majors: composition, jazz, music education, music therapy, piano/organ, sacred music, stringed instruments, voice, wind and percussion instruments. Graduate degrees offered: Master of Music in the areas of composition, conducting, performance, church music, dance accompanying, piano accompanying; Master of Music Education in the area of music education.

Music Student Profile Fall 1994: 301 total; 253 matriculated undergraduate, 31 matriculated graduate, 17 nondegree; 8% minorities, 54% females, 10% international.

Music Faculty Total: 57; 31 full-time, 26 part-time; 55% of full-time faculty have terminal degrees. Graduate students teach a few undergraduate courses. Undergraduate student–faculty ratio: 4:1.

Student Life Student groups include music fraternities and sororities, Music Educators National Conference Student Chapter, Student Association of Music Therapy.

Expenses for 1995–96 Application fee: $30. Comprehensive fee of $16,270 includes full-time tuition ($11,470) and college room and board ($4800). Part-time tuition: $360 per semester hour. Special program-related fees: $350 for private music lessons for majors, $175 for private voice and piano lessons.

Financial Aid Program-specific awards for Fall of 1994: 75 Talent Scholarships for program students ($500–$1000).

Application Procedures Deadline—freshmen and transfers: continuous. Required: high school transcript, college transcript(s) for transfer students, minimum 2.0 high school GPA, interview, video, audition, SAT I or ACT test scores. Recommended: letter of recommendation, portfolio. Auditions held 12 times on campus and off campus in various cities; recorded music is permissible as a substitute for live auditions if a campus visit is impossible and videotaped performances are permissible as a substitute for live auditions if a campus visit is impossible. Portfolio reviews held throughout the year for composition students on campus and off campus in various cities.

Contact Michael Carpenter, Director, Admissions Office, Shenandoah University, 1460 University Drive, Winchester, Virginia 22601-5195; 540-665-4581, fax: 540-665-4627, E-mail address: admit@su.edu.

Shepherd School of Music

See Rice University, Shepherd School of Music

Shorter College

Rome, Georgia

Independent-religious, coed. Small-town campus. Total enrollment: 1,455.

Degrees Bachelor of Music in the areas of voice, piano, organ, music and business, piano pedagogy; Bachelor of Music Education in the area of music education; Bachelor of Fine Arts in the area of musical theater; Bachelor of Church Music in the area of church music. Majors: music and business, music education, music theater, piano pedagogy, piano/organ, voice.

Music Student Profile Fall 1994: 92 total; all matriculated undergraduate; 75% females.

Music Faculty Total: 14; 12 full-time, 2 part-time; 50% of full-time faculty have terminal degrees. Graduate students do not teach undergraduate courses. Undergraduate student–faculty ratio: 13:1.

Expenses for 1995–96 Application fee: $20. Comprehensive fee of $11,535 includes full-time tuition ($7500), mandatory fees ($110), and college room and board ($3925). Part-time tuition: $180 per semester hour. Special program-related fees: $220 for private applied lessons.

Application Procedures Deadline—freshmen and transfers: continuous. Required: essay, high school transcript, college transcript(s) for transfer students, minimum 2.0 high school GPA, interview, audition, SAT I or ACT test scores, music theory examination. Recommended: letter of recommendation. Auditions held 4 times and by appointment on campus; recorded music is permissible as a substitute for live auditions for international students and U.S. students from great distance and videotaped performances are permissible as a substitute for live auditions for international students and U.S. students from great distance.

Undergraduate Contact School of the Arts, Shorter College, 315 Shorter Avenue, Rome, Georgia 30165; 706-291-2121, fax: 706-236-1515.

Silver Lake College

Manitowoc, Wisconsin

Independent-religious, coed. Rural campus. Total enrollment: 990.

Degrees Bachelor of Music in the area of music education.

Expenses for 1995–96 Comprehensive fee of $12,850 includes full-time tuition ($8950) and college room and board ($3900). College room only: $2100. Part-time tuition per semester ranges from $165 to $3025.

Application Procedures Auditions held on campus and off campus. Portfolio reviews held on campus and off campus.

Undergraduate Contact Admissions Office, Silver Lake College, 2406 South Alverno Road, Manitowoc, Michigan 54220-9319; 414-684-6691.

Simon Fraser University

Burnaby, British Columbia

Province-supported, coed. Suburban campus. Total enrollment: 18,252.

Degrees Bachelor of Fine Arts in the area of music. Majors: music. Graduate degrees offered: Master of Fine Arts in the area of interdisciplinary studies.

Music Student Profile Fall 1994: 271 total; all matriculated undergraduate.

Music Faculty Total: 6; 6 full-time; 100% of full-time faculty have terminal degrees. Graduate students teach a few undergraduate courses. Undergraduate student–faculty ratio: 45:1.

Expenses for 1994–95 Application fee: $20. Canadian resident tuition: $2190 full-time, $73 per credit hour part-time. Nonresident tuition: $6570 full-time, $219 per credit hour part-time. Part-time mandatory fees: $50 per trimester. (All figures are in Canadian dollars.). Full-time mandatory fees: $178. College room only: $2120.

Financial Aid Program-specific awards for Fall of 1994: 5 Adaline May Clark Scholarships for program majors ($100–$500), 1 Murray Farr Award for program majors ($500).

Application Procedures Deadline—freshmen and transfers: May 1. Required: high school transcript, college transcript(s) for transfer students, minimum 3.0 high school GPA, interview. Auditions held 2 times on campus and off campus. Portfolio reviews held on campus and off campus.

Simon Fraser University *(continued)*

Undergraduate Contact Admissions Office, Simon Fraser University, Burnaby, British Columbia V5A 1S6, Canada; 604-291-3224, fax: 604-291-4969.

Simpson College

Indianola, Iowa

Independent-religious, coed. Small-town campus. Total enrollment: 1,613.

Degrees Bachelor of Music in the areas of classical music, piano/organ, voice, winds and percussion music, vocal music education, instrumental music education. Majors: classical music, music education, piano/organ, voice, wind and percussion instruments.

Music Student Profile Fall 1994: 175 total; 90 matriculated undergraduate, 85 nondegree; 4% minorities.

Music Faculty Total: 23; 8 full-time, 15 part-time; 75% of full-time faculty have terminal degrees. Graduate students do not teach undergraduate courses. Undergraduate student–faculty ratio: 7:1.

Student Life Student groups include Phi Mu Alpha Sinfonia, Mu Phi Epsilon, Music Educators National Conference.

Expenses for 1995–96 Comprehensive fee of $16,255 includes full-time tuition ($12,170), mandatory fees ($105), and college room and board ($3980). Part-time tuition: $170 per credit hour. Special program-related fees: $40 for accompanist fee, $160 for lesson fee.

Financial Aid Program-specific awards for Fall of 1994: 70–80 Music Scholarships for program majors ($2000–$4000).

Application Procedures Deadline—freshmen and transfers: August 1. Notification date—freshmen and transfers: August 15. Required: high school transcript, college transcript(s) for transfer students, minimum 2.0 high school GPA, letter of recommendation, audition, SAT I or ACT test scores, minimum combined SAT I score of 910, minimum composite ACT score of 19. Recommended: essay, minimum 3.0 high school GPA, interview, video. Auditions held 2 times plus special auditions on campus; recorded music is permissible as a substitute for live auditions if a campus visit is impossible and videotaped performances are permissible as a substitute for live auditions if a campus visit is impossible.

Undergraduate Contact Dr. Robert L. Larsen, Chairman, Music Department, Simpson College, 701 North Street, Indianola, Iowa 50125-1297; 515-961-1637, fax: 515-961-1498.

The Simpson College Conservatory of Music was founded in 1891. In 1940 it became the Music Department at Simpson and has developed and maintained a position of preeminence among schools offering serious musical training in the Midwest.

Simpson combines the atmosphere of a fine small liberal arts college with a distinguished program in music education and musical performance. Students at Simpson are given the opportunity of working with superior teachers in private study and small classes and are given extraordinary opportunities for both ensemble and solo performance. Here, every student is an individual and treated as such, often having the opportunity for upper division directed studies in such areas as conducting, vocal repertory, ethnomusicology, Kodaly and Orff techniques, and opera coaching.

Instrumentalists sing and singers play instruments, if they choose. The Middle Ages, the Renaissance, the great operatic repertory of the nineteenth century, and the vitality of twentieth-century musical thought and American jazz are living, breathing, exciting, and viable entities in the music department. Visiting artists such as Russian pianist Oleg Volkov and soprano Evelyn Lear give recitals and master classes. Alumni artists like Brad Cresswell, tenor with the New York City Opera and the Sante Fe Festival, and Kimm Julian, well-known baritone with regional opera companies and in Europe, also return for recitals and master classes each season. Distinguished music educators on the national scene appear regularly in seminars for students and area teachers.

Indianola and the Blank Performing Arts Center are the home of the Des Moines Metro Opera, one of America's leading regional opera companies, and a number of students become a part of its staff each summer.

Simpson is a remarkable place for a young musician to watch, listen, and grow. It is a place where each student is challenged to develop his or her musical and artistic gifts to the fullest and counseled carefully on realistic career goals and the steps to be taken beyond the Simpson years.

Slippery Rock University of Pennsylvania

Slippery Rock, Pennsylvania

State-supported, coed. Rural campus. Total enrollment: 7,563.

Degrees Bachelor of Music in the area of music theory. Majors: music theory.

Student Life Student groups include Pennsylvania Collegiate Music Educators Association, National Association of Music Therapy Regional Association Student Chapter, National Association of Music Therapy Student Chapter.

Expenses for 1994–95 State resident tuition: $3086 full-time, $129 per credit part-time. Nonresident tuition: $7844 full-time, $327 per credit part-time. Part-time mandatory fees per semester range from $30.50 to $318. Full-time mandatory fees: $751. College room and board: $3374. College room only: $1854.

Financial Aid Program-specific awards for Fall of 1994: 1 Swope Scholarship for sophomores and juniors ($500), 6 Madrigal Scholarships for freshmen ($500), 1 Winder Scholarship for freshmen ($500), 1 Chapin Scholarship for freshmen ($500), 2 Governor's School of Performing Arts Scholarships for alumni of Governor's Schools of Excellence ($500), 1 Williamson Scholarship for undergraduates ($500).

Application Procedures Deadline—freshmen and transfers: May 15. Required: minimum 2.0 high school GPA, interview, audition. Recorded music is permissible as a substitute for live auditions for international applicants.

Undergraduate Contact Audition Committee Chairperson, Department of Music, Slippery Rock University of Pennsylvania, Swope Music Hall, Slippery Rock, Pennsylvania 16057; 412-738-2063.

South Dakota State University

Brookings, South Dakota

State-supported, coed. Rural campus. Total enrollment: 9,140.

Degrees Bachelor of Music Education in the areas of vocal music education, instrumental music education, general music education. Majors: music education, music marketing.

Music Student Profile Fall 1994: 809 total; 104 matriculated undergraduate, 705 nondegree; 2% minorities, 56% females.

Music Faculty Total: 14; 11 full-time, 3 part-time; 45% of full-time faculty have terminal degrees. Graduate students do not teach undergraduate courses. Undergraduate student–faculty ratio: 15:1.

Student Life Student groups include Music Educators National Conference, Music Industry Club. Special housing available for music students.

Expenses for 1995–96 Application fee: $15. State resident tuition: $1648 full-time, $51.50 per credit part-time. Nonresident tuition: $4480 full-time, $140 per credit part-time. Part-time mandatory fees: $36.12 per credit. Tuition for nonresidents who are eligible for the Western Undergraduate Exchange: $2264 full-time, $70.77 per credit part-time. Minnesota residents pay in-state tuition rates. Full-time mandatory fees: $1047. College room and board: $2210 (minimum).

Financial Aid Program-specific awards for Fall of 1994: 20–30 Music Scholarships for music majors and minors ($600).

Application Procedures Deadline—freshmen and transfers: June 23. Notification date—freshmen and transfers: continuous. Required: ACT test score only, minimum composite ACT score of 18, minimum GPA of 2.6 or standing in top 60% of graduating class. Auditions held 2 times on campus and off campus; recorded music is permissible as a substitute for live auditions. Portfolio reviews held on campus and off campus.

Undergraduate Contact Dr. Corliss Johnson, Head, Department of Music, South Dakota State University, LMH Box 2212, Brookings, South Dakota 57007; 605-688-5188.

Southeast Missouri State University

Cape Girardeau, Missouri

State-supported, coed. Small-town campus. Total enrollment: 7,921.

Degrees Bachelor of Music in the areas of performance, composition; Bachelor of Music Education in the areas of instrumental music education, vocal music education. Majors: composition, electronic music, music, music education, piano/organ, stringed instruments, voice, wind and percussion instruments. Graduate degrees offered: Master of Music Education in the area of music education.

Music Student Profile Fall 1994: 575 total; 105 matriculated undergraduate, 20 matriculated graduate, 450 nondegree; 5% minorities, 50% females, 5% international.

Music Faculty Total: 23; 17 full-time, 6 part-time; 95% of full-time faculty have terminal degrees. Graduate students do not teach undergraduate courses. Undergraduate student–faculty ratio: 9:1.

Student Life Student groups include Collegiate Music Educators National Conference, Phi Mu Alpha Sinfonia Fraternity of America, Sigma Alpha Iota International Music Fraternity.

Expenses for 1995–96 State resident tuition: $2760 full-time, $92 per credit hour part-time. Nonresident tuition: $4980 full-time, $166 per credit hour part-time. College room and board: $3860. Special program-related fees: $50 for applied music lesson fee, $5 for locker rental, $10 for instrument rental.

Financial Aid Program-specific awards for Fall of 1994: 2 Bea Limbaugh Scholarships for music students ($1200–$1500), 4 Margaret Woods Allen Piano Scholarships for piano students ($7500), Music Scholarships for music and non-music students ($800).

Application Procedures Deadline—freshmen and transfers: May 1. Required: high school transcript, minimum 2.0 high school GPA, 2 letters of recommendation, audition, SAT I or ACT test scores, minimum composite ACT score of 20, completion of music education courses by junior year for BME, minimum 2.0 college GPA for transfer students. Auditions held continuously on campus and off campus; recorded music is permissible as a substitute for live auditions when distance is prohibitive and videotaped performances are permissible as a substitute for live auditions when distance is prohibitive.

Undergraduate Contact Barry W. Bernhardt, Undergraduate Admissions, Department of Music, Southeast Missouri State University, 1 University Plaza, Cape Girardeau, Missouri 63701; 314-651-2141, fax: 314-651-2321.

Graduate Contact Gary L. Miller, Graduate Admissions, Department of Music, Southeast Missouri State University, 1 University Plaza, Cape Girardeau, Missouri 63701; 314-651-2141, fax: 314-651-2321.

Southeastern Louisiana University

Hammond, Louisiana

State-supported, coed. Small-town campus. Total enrollment: 13,912.

Degrees Bachelor of Music in the areas of instrumental music, vocal music, keyboard; Bachelor of Music Education in the areas of instrumental music education, vocal music education. Majors: music education, piano/organ, stringed instruments, voice, wind and percussion instruments. Graduate degrees offered: Master of Music in the areas of theory, performance.

Music Student Profile Fall 1994: 116 total; 104 matriculated undergraduate, 12 matriculated graduate; 10% minorities, 25% females, 2% international.

Music Faculty Total: 27; 12 full-time, 15 part-time; 50% of full-time faculty have terminal degrees. Graduate students teach a few undergraduate courses. Undergraduate student–faculty ratio: 4:1.

Expenses for 1995–96 Application fee: $10. State resident tuition: $1910 full-time. Nonresident tuition: $3998 full-time. Part-time tuition per semester ranges from $267.25 to $884.50 for state residents, $267.25 to $1842 for nonresidents. Part-time mandatory fees per semester range from $12 to $48. Mandatory fee for international students: $60. Full-time mandatory fees: $120. College room and board: $2230 (minimum).

Financial Aid Program-specific awards for Fall of 1994: 72 Performance Grants for music majors ($1000).

Application Procedures Deadline—freshmen and transfers: July 15. Required: high school transcript, college transcript(s) for transfer students, audition, ACT test score only. Auditions held 10 times on campus and off campus in various locations; recorded music is permissible as a substitute for live auditions.

Undergraduate Contact Dr. David Evenson, Head, Music Department, Southeastern Louisiana University, SLU Box 815, Hammond, Louisiana 70402; 504-549-2184, E-mail address: fmus2156@admin.selu.edu.

Graduate Contact Dr. David Evenson, Graduate Coordinator, Music Department, Southeastern Louisiana University, SLU Box 815, Hammond, Louisiana 70402; 504-549-2249, E-mail address: fmus2156@admin.selu.edu.

Southeastern Oklahoma State University

Durant, Oklahoma

State-supported, coed. Small-town campus. Total enrollment: 4,104.

Degrees Bachelor of Music in the areas of performance, sacred music; Bachelor of Music Education in the areas of vocal music education, instrumental music education. Majors: music education, sacred music, voice, wind and percussion instruments.

Music Student Profile Fall 1994: 36 total; all matriculated undergraduate; 25% minorities, 60% females, 6% international.

Music Faculty Total: 11; 8 full-time, 3 part-time; 62% of full-time faculty have terminal degrees. Graduate students do not teach undergraduate courses. Undergraduate student–faculty ratio: 6:1.

Student Life Student groups include Music Educators National Conference Student Chapter, Kappa Kappa Psi.

Expenses for 1995–96 Part-time mandatory fees: $9.50 per credit hour. Full-time tuition ranges from $1252 to $1277 for state residents, $3383 to $3632 for nonresidents, according to class level. Part-time tuition per credit hour ranges from $40.39 to $41.20 for state residents, $109.14 to $117.17 for nonresidents, according to class level. Full-time mandatory fees: $307. College room and board: $2619. College room only: $888. Special program-related fees: $28 for applied music fee.

Financial Aid Program-specific awards for Fall of 1994: 50 partial tuition waivers for ensemble performers ($900–$1200), 8 endowed scholarships for upperclassmen ($200–$300).

Application Procedures Deadline—freshmen and transfers: August 15. Required: high school transcript, college transcript(s) for transfer students, minimum 2.0 high school GPA, interview, audition, ACT test score only, minimum composite ACT score of 19. Auditions held 3 times on campus; recorded music is permissible as a substitute for live auditions when distance is prohibitive and videotaped performances are permissible as a substitute for live auditions when distance is prohibitive. Portfolio reviews held 1 time on campus.

Undergraduate Contact Dr. Walter Britt, Chairman, Department of Music, Southeastern Oklahoma State University, Box 4126, Durant, Oklahoma 74701-0609; 405-924-0121 ext. 2244, fax: 405-920-7475, E-mail address: wintle@marcie.sosu.edu.

Southern Arkansas University–Magnolia

Magnolia, Arkansas

State-supported, coed. Small-town campus. Total enrollment: 2,957.

Degrees Bachelor of Music Education in the area of music education. Majors: music education.

Expenses for 1995–96 State resident tuition: $1680 full-time, $70 per semester hour part-time. Nonresident tuition: $2616 full-time, $109 per semester hour part-time. Full-time mandatory fees: $48. College room and board: $2420. College room only: $620.

Application Procedures Deadline—freshmen and transfers: August 15. Required: high school transcript, interview, audition. Recommended: minimum 2.0 high school GPA.

Undergraduate Contact Dr. David Krouse, Chair, Music Department, Southern Arkansas University– Magnolia, Box 1241, Magnolia, Arkansas 71753-5000; 501-235-4250, fax: 501-235-5005.

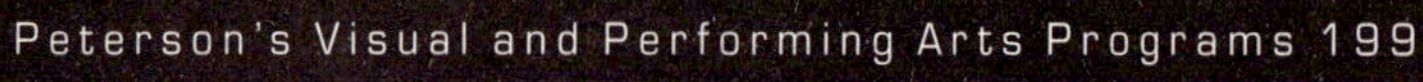

Southern College of Seventh-day Adventists

Collegedale, Tennessee

Independent-religious, coed. Small-town campus. Total enrollment: 1,652.

Degrees Bachelor of Music Education in the areas of vocal music education, instrumental music education. Majors: classical music, music education, piano/organ, stringed instruments, voice, wind and percussion instruments.

Music Student Profile Fall 1994: 428 total; 28 matriculated undergraduate, 400 nondegree; 20% minorities, 57% females, 7% international.

Music Faculty Total: 21; 6 full-time, 15 part-time; 33% of full-time faculty have terminal degrees. Graduate students do not teach undergraduate courses. Undergraduate student–faculty ratio: 4:1.

Expenses for 1995–96 Application fee: $20. Comprehensive fee of $12,522 includes full-time tuition ($8880) and college room and board ($3642). College room only: $1580. Part-time tuition: $377 per semester hour. Special program-related fees: $130 for lesson fee.

Financial Aid Program-specific awards for Fall of 1994: 28 Symphony Scholarships for string, wind, and percussion students ($1700), 15 Band Scholarships for wind, percussion students ($800), 19 Choral/Vocal Scholarships for vocal students ($420), 5 Keyboard Awards for organ/piano students ($500).

Application Procedures Deadline—freshmen and transfers: continuous. Required: high school transcript, college transcript(s) for transfer students, audition, SAT I or ACT test scores. Auditions held 2 times on campus.

Undergraduate Contact Vice President for Admissions and College Relations, Southern College of Seventh-day Adventists, P.O. Box 370, Collegedale, Tennessee 37315; 800-768-8437, fax: 615-238-3005.

Southern Illinois University at Carbondale

Carbondale, Illinois

State-supported, coed. Small-town campus. Total enrollment: 23,162.

Degrees Bachelor of Music in the areas of performance, piano pedagogy, music theory/composition, music education. Majors: classical music, guitar, jazz, music education, opera, piano/organ, stringed instruments, voice, wind and percussion instruments. Graduate degrees offered: Master of Music in the areas of performance, piano pedagogy, music theory/composition, music history/literature, opera/music theater, music education.

Music Student Profile Fall 1994: 155 total; 130 matriculated undergraduate, 25 matriculated graduate; 5% minorities, 48% females, 20% international.

Music Faculty Total: 25; 24 full-time, 1 part-time; 100% of full-time faculty have terminal degrees. Graduate students teach a few undergraduate courses. Undergraduate student–faculty ratio: 7:1.

Student Life Student groups include Collegiate Music Educators National Conference, Phi Mu Alpha Sinfonia, Mu Phi Epsilon.

Expenses for 1995–96 State resident tuition: $2400 full-time, $80 per semester hour part-time. Nonresident tuition: $7200 full-time, $240 per semester hour part-time. Part-time mandatory fees: $241.64 per semester. Full-time mandatory fees: $936. College room and board: $3352. Special program-related fees: $25 for instrument rental.

Financial Aid Program-specific awards for Fall of 1994: 20–30 Music Scholarships for musically talented students ($300–$2000).

Application Procedures Deadline—freshmen and transfers: continuous. Notification date—freshmen: August 15. Required: high school transcript, audition. Recommended: letter of recommendation, video. Auditions held 4 times and by appointment on campus; recorded music is permissible as a substitute for live auditions for international applicants and out-of-state applicants and videotaped performances are permissible as a substitute for live auditions for international applicants and out-of-state applicants.

Undergraduate Contact Dr. Daniel Mellado, Undergraduate Advisor, School of Music, Southern Illinois University at Carbondale, Mailcode 4302, Carbondale, Illinois 62901; 618-536-8742, fax: 618-453-5808.

Graduate Contact Dr. Helen Poulos, Graduate Coordinator, School of Music, Southern Illinois University at Carbondale, Mailcode 4302, Carbondale, Illinois 62901; 618-536-8742.

Southern Illinois University at Edwardsville

Edwardsville, Illinois

State-supported, coed. Small-town campus. Total enrollment: 10,938.

Degrees Bachelor of Music in the areas of performance, music education, jazz performance, musical theater, theory/composition. Majors: classical music, jazz, music, music education, music history and literature, music marketing, music theater, music theory and composition, performance. Graduate degrees offered: Master of Music in the areas of music education, performance.

Music Student Profile Fall 1994: 180 total; 120 matriculated undergraduate, 40 matriculated graduate, 20 nondegree; 16% minorities, 55% females, 5% international.

Music Faculty Total: 48; 21 full-time, 27 part-time; 90% of full-time faculty have terminal degrees. Graduate students teach a few undergraduate courses. Undergraduate student–faculty ratio: 6:1.

Student Life Student groups include Sigma Alpha Iota, Student Experimental Theater. Special housing available for music students.

Southern Illinois University at Edwardsville
(continued)

Expenses for 1995–96 State resident tuition: $1842 full-time, $76.75 per credit part-time. Nonresident tuition: $5526 full-time, $230.25 per credit part-time. Part-time mandatory fees per semester range from $97.65 to $243.65. Full-time mandatory fees: $488. College room and board: $3498. College room only: $2028.

Financial Aid Program-specific awards for Fall of 1994: 20–40 Music Talent Awards for those demonstrating talent and academic achievement ($100–$1000), 6–12 Provost Scholarships for those demonstrating talent and academic achievement ($400–$900).

Application Procedures Deadline—freshmen and transfers: August 1. Notification date—freshmen and transfers: August 19. Required: high school transcript, college transcript(s) for transfer students, minimum 3.0 high school GPA, audition, SAT I or ACT test scores, minimum composite ACT score of 18. Recommended: letter of recommendation. Auditions held 5 times and by appointment on campus; recorded music is permissible as a substitute for live auditions when distance is prohibitive and videotaped performances are permissible as a substitute for live auditions when distance is prohibitive.

Undergraduate Contact Ronald D. Abraham, Chair, Music Department, Southern Illinois University at Edwardsville, Box 1771, Edwardsville, Illinois 62026-1771; 618-692-3900, fax: 618-692-2233.

Graduate Contact R. Kent Perry, Graduate Advisor, Music Department, Southern Illinois University at Edwardsville, Box 1771, Edwardsville, Illinois 62026-1771; 618-692-3900.

Meadows School of the Arts

Southern Methodist University

Dallas, Texas

Independent-religious, coed. Suburban campus. Total enrollment: 9,014.

Degrees Bachelor of Music in the areas of performance, music education, music theory, composition, piano pedagogy, music therapy. Majors: composition, guitar, harp, harpsichord, music education, music theory, music therapy, piano, piano pedagogy, saxophone. Graduate degrees offered: Master of Music in the areas of performance, music education, music theory, composition, music history, sacred music, piano accompanying, piano performance and pedagogy; Master of Music Therapy in the area of music therapy.

Music Student Profile Fall 1994: 284 total; 162 matriculated undergraduate, 97 matriculated graduate, 25 nondegree.

Music Faculty Total: 59; 34 full-time, 25 part-time.

Student Life Student groups include Music Educators National Conference, National Association for Music Therapy. Special housing available for music students.

Expenses for 1994–95 Application fee: $40. Comprehensive fee of $19,474 includes full-time tuition ($12,772), mandatory fees ($1624), and college room and board ($5078). College room only: $2426. Part-time tuition: $532 per credit hour. Part-time mandatory fees: $68 per semester. Special program-related fees: $15 for practice room fee, $30 for recital recording fee, $17 for concert fee.

Financial Aid Program-specific awards for Fall of 1994: 40 Meadows Artistic Scholarships for talented program majors and minors ($2000–$12,000).

Application Procedures Deadline—freshmen and transfers: April 1. Required: essay, high school transcript, college transcript(s) for transfer students, letter of recommendation, audition, SAT I or ACT test scores. Recommended: interview. Auditions held 24 times on campus and off campus in various locations; recorded music is permissible as a substitute for live auditions if a campus visit is impossible and videotaped performances are permissible as a substitute for live auditions if a campus visit is impossible.

Undergraduate Contact Charles J. Helfert, Associate Dean, Meadows School of the Arts, Southern Methodist University, P.O. Box 750356, Dallas, Texas 75275-0356; 214-768-3217, fax: 214-768-3272.

Graduate Contact Jeannette Garnsey, Director, Graduate Admissions and Records, Meadows School of the Arts, Southern Methodist University, P.O. Box 750356, Dallas, Texas 75275-0356; 214-768-3765, fax: 214-768-3272.

Southern University and Agricultural and Mechanical College

Baton Rouge, Louisiana

State-supported, coed. Suburban campus. Total enrollment: 9,800.

Degrees Bachelor of Music in the area of performance; Bachelor of Music Education in the area of music education. Majors: jazz, music, music education, piano/organ, voice, wind and percussion instruments. Cross-registration with Louisiana State University.

Music Student Profile Fall 1994: 90 total; all matriculated undergraduate; 99% minorities, 35% females.

Music Faculty Total: 15; 12 full-time, 3 part-time; 25% of full-time faculty have terminal degrees. Graduate students do not teach undergraduate courses. Undergraduate student–faculty ratio: 12:1.

Student Life Student groups include Music Educators National Conference, Phi Mu Alpha Sinfonia, Mu Phi Epsilon.

Estimated Expenses for 1995–96 State resident tuition: $2028 full-time. Nonresident tuition: $4150 full-time. Part-time tuition per semester ranges from $440 to $866 for state residents, $1501 to $1927 for nonresidents. College room and board: $2375.

Financial Aid Program-specific awards for Fall of 1994: 12 Choir/Vocal Awards for choir singers ($2500), 5 Music (Jazz) Awards for jazz majors ($2500), 10–15 Music Awards for program majors ($100–$500).

Application Procedures Deadline—freshmen and transfers: continuous. Notification date—freshmen: July 1.

Required: high school transcript, college transcript(s) for transfer students, minimum 2.0 high school GPA, audition, SAT I or ACT test scores. Auditions held 1 time on campus; recorded music is permissible as a substitute for live auditions for out-of-state applicants.

Undergraduate Contact Henry Bellaire, Director of Admissions, Southern University and Agricultural and Mechanical College, P.O. Box 9901, Southern University Branch Post Office, Baton Rouge, Louisiana 70813; 504-771-2430.

Casebolt School of Fine Arts

Southwest Baptist University

Bolivar, Missouri

Independent-religious, coed. Small-town campus. Total enrollment: 3,202.

Degrees Bachelor of Music in the area of church music; Bachelor of Music Education in the areas of vocal music education, instrumental music education, vocal/instrumental music education. Majors: music, music education, sacred music.

Music Student Profile Fall 1994: 95 total; all matriculated undergraduate; 4% minorities, 60% females, 3% international.

Music Faculty Total: 17; 11 full-time, 6 part-time; 73% of full-time faculty have terminal degrees. Graduate students do not teach undergraduate courses. Undergraduate student–faculty ratio: 5:1.

Student Life Student groups include Music Educators National Conference, Church Music Conference, Tau Beta Sigma.

Expenses for 1995–96 Application fee: $25. Comprehensive fee of $9981 includes full-time tuition ($7344), mandatory fees ($137), and college room and board ($2500). Part-time tuition: $306 per credit hour. Part-time mandatory fees: $5 per credit hour. Special program-related fees: $130 for applied music fees, $25 for practice room fee.

Financial Aid Program-specific awards for Fall of 1994: 110 Music Performance Scholarships for program majors ($500).

Application Procedures Deadline—freshmen and transfers: continuous. Required: high school transcript, audition. Auditions held 3–4 times on campus and off campus in St. Louis, MO; Kansas City, MO; recorded music is permissible as a substitute for live auditions when distance is prohibitive or by request and videotaped performances are permissible as a substitute for live auditions when distance is prohibitive or by request.

Undergraduate Contact Office of Admissions, Southwest Baptist University, 1600 University Avenue, Bolivar, Missouri 65613; 417-326-1810.

Southwest Missouri State University

Springfield, Missouri

State-supported, coed. Suburban campus. Total enrollment: 17,310.

Degrees Bachelor of Music in the areas of performance, composition. Majors: music, piano/organ, stringed instruments, voice, wind and percussion instruments. Graduate degrees offered: Master of Music in the areas of performance, theory/composition, conducting, string/piano pedagogy, music education.

Music Student Profile Fall 1994: 244 total; 231 matriculated undergraduate, 13 matriculated graduate; 5% minorities, 41% females, 2% international.

Music Faculty Total: 37; 24 full-time, 13 part-time; 54% of full-time faculty have terminal degrees. Graduate students do not teach undergraduate courses. Undergraduate student–faculty ratio: 10:1.

Student Life Student groups include Phi Mu Alpha, Mu Phi Epsilon, Pi Kappa Lambda.

Expenses for 1995–96 Application fee: $15. State resident tuition: $2370 full-time, $79 per credit hour part-time. Nonresident tuition: $4898 full-time. Part-time mandatory fees per semester range from $41 to $88. Part-time tuition per credit hour for nonresidents: $79 for the first 3 credits, $158 for the next 8 credits. Full-time mandatory fees: $176. College room and board: $2722 (minimum). College room only: $1755 (minimum).

Financial Aid Program-specific awards for Fall of 1994: 16 Performance Awards for talented students ($1700), Talent Awards for talented students ($100–$1000), Band Grants for band members.

Application Procedures Deadline—freshmen and transfers: August 1. Notification date—freshmen and transfers: continuous. Required: high school transcript, college transcript(s) for transfer students, minimum 2.0 high school GPA, audition, ACT test score only. Recommended: video. Auditions held 5 times for performance applicants on campus and off campus; recorded music is permissible as a substitute for live auditions when distance is prohibitive and videotaped performances are permissible as a substitute for live auditions when distance is prohibitive.

Undergraduate Contact Dr. John Prescott, Head, Department of Music, Southwest Missouri State University, 901 South National, Springfield, Missouri 65804; 417-836-5648, fax: 417-836-7665, E-mail address: jsp304f@vma.smsu.edu.

Graduate Contact Dr. Robert Quebbeman, Graduate Coordinator, Music Department, Southwest Missouri State University, 901 South National, Springfield, Missouri 65804; 417-836-5729, fax: 417-836-7665.

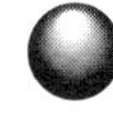

Southwest Texas State University

San Marcos, Texas

State-supported, coed. Small-town campus. Total enrollment: 20,899.

Southwest Texas State University *(continued)*

Degrees Bachelor of Music in the areas of performance, sound recording technology, music education. Majors: classical music, music education, piano/organ, sound recording technology, stringed instruments, voice, wind and percussion instruments. Graduate degrees offered: Master of Music in the areas of music education, performance.

Music Student Profile Fall 1994: 680 total; 315 matriculated undergraduate, 365 nondegree; 40% minorities, 50% females, 1% international.

Music Faculty Total: 45; 31 full-time, 14 part-time; 50% of full-time faculty have terminal degrees. Graduate students teach a few undergraduate courses. Undergraduate student–faculty ratio: 6:1.

Student Life Student groups include Music Educators National Conference Student Chapter, American Choral Directors Association Student Chapter, professional music fraternities.

Estimated Expenses for 1995–96 Application fee: $25. State resident tuition: $900 full-time. Nonresident tuition: $5280 full-time, $176 per semester hour part-time. State resident part-time tuition per semester ranges from $100 to $330. Part-time mandatory fees per semester range from $207 to $407. Full-time mandatory fees: $906. College room and board: $3676. College room only: $2198. Special program-related fees: $35 for private lesson fee.

Financial Aid Program-specific awards for Fall of 1994: 5–10 Schneider Scholarships for Victoria, TX area students ($500–$1000).

Application Procedures Deadline—freshmen and transfers: July 1. Notification date—freshmen and transfers: July 15. Required: high school transcript, college transcript(s) for transfer students, SAT I or ACT test scores. Recommended: audition. Auditions held 5 times on campus; recorded music is permissible as a substitute for live auditions if distance is prohibitive or scheduling is difficult and videotaped performances are permissible as a substitute for live auditions if distance is prohibitive or scheduling is difficult.

Undergraduate Contact Dr. Mary Anne Bruner, Associate Chair, Music Department, Southwest Texas State University, 601 University Drive, San Marcos, Texas 78666-4616; 512-245-2651, fax: 512-245-8181, E-mail address: mb10@academia.swt.edu.

Graduate Contact Dr. Russell C. Riepe, Coordinator of Graduate Studies, Music Department, Southwest Texas State University, 601 University Drive, San Marcos, Texas 78666-4616; 512-245-2651.

Southwestern College

Winfield, Kansas

Independent-religious, coed. Small-town campus. Total enrollment: 752.

Degrees Bachelor of Music in the area of music education. Majors: music education.

Music Student Profile Fall 1994: 26 total; all matriculated undergraduate.

Music Faculty Total: 5; 4 full-time, 1 part-time; 100% of full-time faculty have terminal degrees. Graduate students do not teach undergraduate courses. Undergraduate student–faculty ratio: 12:1.

Student Life Student groups include Music Educators National Conference Student Chapter, Mu Phi Epsilon, Campus Music Teachers Association.

Expenses for 1995–96 Application fee: $15. Comprehensive fee of $11,542 includes full-time tuition ($7850) and college room and board ($3692). Part-time tuition: $330 per semester hour. Special program-related fees: $100 for private lesson fee.

Financial Aid Program-specific awards for Fall of 1994: 1–75 Activity Grants for music majors and minors, participants in music activities ($200–$2800).

Application Procedures Deadline—freshmen and transfers: July 1. Required: high school transcript, minimum 2.0 high school GPA, audition. Recommended: minimum 3.0 high school GPA. Auditions held at student's convenience on campus; recorded music is permissible as a substitute for live auditions for out-of-state applicants and videotaped performances are permissible as a substitute for live auditions for out-of state applicants.

Undergraduate Contact Michael Wilder, Chair, Division of Performing Arts, Southwestern College, Darbeth Fine Arts Center, Winfield, Kansas 67156; 316-221-8272, fax: 316-221-8224.

Southwestern Oklahoma State University

Weatherford, Oklahoma

State-supported, coed. Small-town campus. Total enrollment: 4,737.

Degrees Bachelor of Music in the areas of sacred music, music therapy, music theory/composition; Bachelor of Music Education in the areas of instrumental music education, vocal/keyboard music education. Majors: composition, music, music education, music theory, music therapy, performance, piano/organ, sacred music, stringed instruments, voice, wind and percussion instruments. Graduate degrees offered: Master of Music Education in the area of music education.

Music Student Profile Fall 1994: 200 total; 175 matriculated undergraduate, 25 matriculated graduate.

Music Faculty Total: 24; 16 full-time, 8 part-time. Graduate students teach a few undergraduate courses.

Student Life Student groups include music fraternities and sororities, National Association of Music Therapists, Music Educators National Conference.

Expenses for 1994–95 Application fee: $15. Part-time mandatory fees: $4.50 per semester hour. Full-time tuition ranges from $1422 to $1446 for state residents, $3484 to $3725 for nonresidents, according to class level. Part-time tuition per credit hour ranges from $47.39 to $48.20 for state residents, $116.14 to $124.17 for nonresidents, according to class level. Full-time mandatory fees: $9. College room and board: $1956 (minimum). Special program-related fees: $30 for applied lessons fee.

Financial Aid Program-specific awards for Fall of 1994: Ensemble Music Scholarships for ensemble performers, Music Scholarships for those passing audition evaluations.

Application Procedures Deadline—freshmen and transfers: continuous. Required: high school transcript, college transcript(s) for transfer students, ACT test score only, minimum composite ACT score of 19, auditions for transfer students. Recommended: audition. Auditions held continuously by appointment on campus and off campus; recorded music is permissible as a substitute for live auditions when distance is prohibitive and videotaped performances are permissible as a substitute for live auditions when distance is prohibitive. Portfolio reviews held on campus and off campus.

Undergraduate Contact Barbara Lane, Secretary, Department of Music, Southwestern Oklahoma State University, Weatherford, Oklahoma 73096; 405-774-3708.

Southwestern University

Georgetown, Texas

Independent-religious, coed. Suburban campus. Total enrollment: 1,238.

Degrees Bachelor of Music in the areas of performance, music education, music theory, music literature, sacred music. Majors: music education, music literature, music theory, piano/organ, sacred music, stringed instruments, voice, wind and percussion instruments.

Music Student Profile Fall 1994: 40 total; all matriculated undergraduate; 10% minorities, 60% females, 1% international.

Music Faculty Total: 24; 8 full-time, 16 part-time; 100% of full-time faculty have terminal degrees. Graduate students teach a few undergraduate courses. Undergraduate student–faculty ratio: 12:1.

Student Life Student groups include Pi Kappa Lambda, Delta Omicron, Texas Music Educators Association.

Expenses for 1995–96 Application fee: $25. Comprehensive fee of $17,570 includes full-time tuition ($12,700) and college room and board ($4870). Part-time tuition: $530 per semester hour. Special program-related fees: $150 for half-hour weekly private lessons, $300 for one hour weekly private lessons.

Financial Aid Program-specific awards for Fall of 1994: 18 Music Scholarships for talented program majors ($2000–$3000), 20 Performance Awards for non-music majors ($1000–$1500).

Application Procedures Deadline—freshmen and transfers: March 1. Notification date—freshmen and transfers: May 1. Required: essay, college transcript(s) for transfer students, audition, SAT I or ACT test scores, minimum 3.0 college GPA for transfer students. Recommended: minimum 3.0 high school GPA, letter of recommendation, interview. Auditions held by appointment on campus; recorded music is permissible as a substitute for live auditions when distance is prohibitive and videotaped performances are permissible as a substitute for live auditions when distance is prohibitive.

Undergraduate Contact Dr. Kenneth Sheppard, Chair, Music Department, Southwestern University, Box 6192, Georgetown, Texas 78626; 512-863-1358, fax: 512-863-1422.

St. Cloud State University

St. Cloud, Minnesota

State-supported, coed. Suburban campus. Total enrollment: 14,673.

Degrees Bachelor of Music in the areas of performance, piano pedagogy. Majors: classical music, jazz, music business, music education, opera, piano/organ, stringed instruments, voice, wind and percussion instruments. Graduate degrees offered: Master of Music in the areas of education, conducting, piano pedagogy.

Music Student Profile Fall 1994: 190 total; 110 matriculated undergraduate, 30 matriculated graduate, 50 nondegree; 1% minorities, 50% females, 3% international.

Music Faculty Total: 30; 20 full-time, 10 part-time; 85% of full-time faculty have terminal degrees. Graduate students do not teach undergraduate courses. Undergraduate student–faculty ratio: 10:1.

Student Life Student groups include Sigma Alpha Iota, American Choral Directors Association Student Chapter, Music Educators National Conference Student Chapter.

Expenses for 1995–96 Application fee: $15. State resident tuition: $2376 full-time, $49.50 per quarter hour part-time. Nonresident tuition: $5160 full-time, $107.50 per quarter hour part-time. Part-time mandatory fees: $9.68 per quarter hour. Full-time mandatory fees: $465. College room and board: $2937. Special program-related fees: $10 for computer lab fees for specific music courses.

Financial Aid Program-specific awards for Fall of 1994: 45 Endowed/Foundation Scholarships for talented students ($400), 5 May Bowle Scholarships for talented students ($400), 6 David Swenson Memorial Awards for talented students ($2000), 1 Jane Burkleo Award for talented students ($3500).

Application Procedures Deadline—freshmen and transfers: continuous. Required: high school transcript, college transcript(s) for transfer students, minimum 2.0 high school GPA, ACT test score only.

Contact Sherwood Reid, Director of Admissions, St. Cloud State University, 720 4th Avenue South, St. Cloud, Minnesota 56301-4498; 612-255-2244, fax: 612-654-5367.

St. Francis Xavier University

Antigonish, Nova Scotia

Independent-religious, coed. Small-town campus. Total enrollment: 3,160.

St. Francis Xavier University *(continued)*

Degrees Bachelor of Music in the areas of jazz performance, jazz composition/arranging. Majors: brass, classical guitar, classical music, jazz, jazz guitar, music, piano, voice, wind and percussion instruments.

Music Student Profile Fall 1994: 404 total; 106 matriculated undergraduate, 298 nondegree; 5% minorities, 20% females, 1% international.

Music Faculty Total: 12; 8 full-time, 4 part-time; 50% of full-time faculty have terminal degrees. Graduate students do not teach undergraduate courses. Undergraduate student–faculty ratio: 25:1.

Student Life Student groups include Nova Scotia Music Educators Association.

Expenses for 1994–95 Application fee: $30. Canadian resident tuition: $2925 full-time, $620 per course part-time. Nonresident tuition: $4625 full-time, $960 per course part-time. Part-time mandatory fees: $13 per course. (All figures are in Canadian dollars.). Full-time mandatory fees: $123. College room and board: $4520.

Financial Aid Program-specific awards for Fall of 1994: 3 Music Scholarships for program majors ($1000), 8 Music Bursaries for program majors ($250–$500).

Application Procedures Deadline—freshmen and transfers: June 30. Notification date—freshmen and transfers: August 1. Required: high school transcript, audition. Auditions held continuously on campus; recorded music is permissible as a substitute for live auditions if certified by a teacher and videotaped performances are permissible as a substitute for live auditions if certified by teacher.

Undergraduate Contact Director of Admissions, Admissions Office, St. Francis Xavier University, P.O. Box 5000, Antigonish, Nova Scotia B2G 2W5, Canada; 902-867-2160, fax: 902-867-2329.

St. Norbert College

De Pere, Wisconsin

Independent-religious, coed. Suburban campus. Total enrollment: 2,092.

Degrees Bachelor of Music in the areas of performance, music education. Majors: music, music education, piano/organ, voice, wind and percussion instruments.

Music Student Profile Fall 1994: 51 total; all matriculated undergraduate; 4% minorities, 58% females, 1% international.

Music Faculty Total: 12; 6 full-time, 6 part-time; 50% of full-time faculty have terminal degrees. Graduate students do not teach undergraduate courses. Undergraduate student–faculty ratio: 7:1.

Student Life Student groups include Music Educators National Conference.

Expenses for 1995–96 Application fee: $25. Comprehensive fee of $17,670 includes full-time tuition ($13,015) and college room and board ($4655). College room only: $2455. Part-time tuition: $1626 per course. Tuition guaranteed not to increase for student's term of enrollment.

Financial Aid Program-specific awards for Fall of 1994: 20–25 Music Merit Scholarships for program majors/minors ($2500).

Application Procedures Deadline—freshmen and transfers: continuous. Recommended: audition. Auditions held 4 times and by request on campus; recorded music is permissible as a substitute for live auditions when distance is prohibitive and videotaped performances are permissible as a substitute for live auditions when distance is prohibitive.

Undergraduate Contact Craig S. Wesley, Dean of Admission, St. Norbert College, 316 Third Street, De Pere, Wisconsin 54115; 414-337-3007, fax: 414-337-4072, E-mail address: weslcs@sncad.snc.edu.

St. Olaf College

Northfield, Minnesota

Independent-religious, coed. Small-town campus. Total enrollment: 2,958.

Degrees Bachelor of Music in the areas of performance, music education, church music, theory/composition. Majors: classical guitar, piano/organ, stringed instruments, voice, wind and percussion instruments.

Expenses for 1995–96 Application fee: $25. Comprehensive fee of $18,930 includes full-time tuition ($15,000), mandatory fees ($80), and college room and board ($3850).

Application Procedures Deadline—freshmen: June 1; transfers: July 1. Notification date—freshmen and transfers: continuous. Required: high school transcript, college transcript(s) for transfer students, 2 letters of recommendation, audition, SAT I or ACT test scores. Auditions held on campus and off campus. Portfolio reviews held on campus and off campus.

Undergraduate Contact Catherine Langord Wall, Music Admissions Coordinator, Department of Music, St. Olaf College, 1520 St. Olaf Avenue, Northfield, Minnesota 55057-1098; 507-646-3297, fax: 507-646-3527, E-mail address: music@stolaf.edu.

State University of New York College at Fredonia

Fredonia, New York

State-supported, coed. Small-town campus. Total enrollment: 4,892.

Degrees Bachelor of Music in the areas of music education, performance, composition; Bachelor of Fine Arts in the area of music theater. Majors: music education, music theory, piano/organ, stringed instruments, voice, wind and percussion instruments. Graduate degrees offered: Master of Music in the areas of music education, performance, composition.

Music Student Profile Fall 1994: 351 total; 330 matriculated undergraduate, 21 matriculated graduate; 6% minorities, 50% females, 5% international.

Music Faculty Total: 49; 34 full-time, 15 part-time; 90% of full-time faculty have terminal degrees. Graduate students do not teach undergraduate courses. Undergraduate student–faculty ratio: 10:1.

Student Life Student groups include Music Educators National Conference Student Chapter, Pi Kappa Lambda, Phi Mu Alpha Sinfonia.

Expenses for 1995–96 Application fee: $25. State resident tuition: $3400 full-time, $137 per credit hour part-time. Nonresident tuition: $8300 full-time, $346 per credit hour part-time. Part-time mandatory fees: $17.35 per credit hour. Full-time mandatory fees: $519. College room and board: $4670. College room only: $2750. Special program-related fees: $15 for ensemble fee, $30 for electronic music lab fee, $75 for sound recording fee.

Financial Aid Program-specific awards for Fall of 1994: 30 Hillman Foundation Awards for program majors ($500), 5 Directors Scholarships for program majors ($750), 10 Piano and Voice Scholarships for program majors ($500).

Application Procedures Deadline—freshmen and transfers: continuous. Required: high school transcript, audition, SAT I or ACT test scores. Auditions held 8 times on campus and off campus in various locations in the Albany and Long Island areas; recorded music is permissible as a substitute for live auditions when distance is prohibitive.

Contact Barry Kilpatrick, Assistant Director of Admissions, School of Music, State University of New York College at Fredonia, Mason Hall, Fredonia, New York 14063; 716-673-3153.

More about the University

Facilities Mason Hall, built in 1941 for the School of Music, was the first academic structure on Fredonia's 226-acre campus. Major expansions in 1961 and 1973 produced the present facility, which will soon undergo a $12.5-million renovation. There are plenty of practice rooms (130, most with pianos), four large rehearsal rooms, a 225-seat recital hall, and a magnificent 1,200-seat concert hall.

Faculty Many are active as professional soloists, members of orchestras and chamber ensembles, adjudicators, composers, and writers. An abiding commitment to chamber music is evidenced by faculty ensembles and other ensembles-in-residence, including the Rackham String Quartet, Fredonia Brass Quintet, Fredonia Woodwind Quintet, Buffalo Guitar Quartet, and Fredonia Chamber Players.

Professional Programs The preparation of public school music teachers was Fredonia's original mission and continues to be the School's central focus. The music therapy degree is an intensive and comprehensive program, while the innovative sound recording technology curriculum prepares students for the rapidly developing field of audio engineering.

Performing Opportunities Student ensembles include the College Symphony Orchestra, Wind Symphony, Concert Band, All-College Band, Jazz Workshop, Percussion Ensemble, Chamber Singers, College Choir, Festival Chorus, and a host of smaller groups. Solo recitals are required by the music education, performance, and applied music curricula, and Fredonia is one of the only undergraduate institutions to produce fully staged operas and musicals each year.

Scholarships Significant financial assistance is provided to qualified students by the Hillman Foundation and numerous other endowed funds.

Crane School of Music

State University of New York College at Potsdam

Potsdam, New York

State-supported, coed. Small-town campus. Total enrollment: 4,293.

Degrees Bachelor of Music in the areas of music education, performance, composition, musical studies. Majors: classical music, jazz, keyboard, music, music and business, music education, music theater, opera, piano pedagogy, piano/organ, stringed instruments, voice, wind and percussion instruments. Graduate degrees offered: Master of Music in the areas of music education, performance, composition, music theory, music history. Cross-registration with State University of New York College of Technology at Canton, St. Lawrence University, Clarkson University.

Music Student Profile Fall 1994: 500 total; 475 matriculated undergraduate, 25 matriculated graduate; 8% minorities, 42% females, 1% international.

Music Faculty Total: 52; 38 full-time, 14 part-time; 95% of full-time faculty have terminal degrees. Graduate students do not teach undergraduate courses. Undergraduate student–faculty ratio: 11:1.

Student Life Student groups include Music Educators National Conference, Phi Mu Alpha Sinfonia, Sigma Alpha Iota.

Expenses for 1994–95 Application fee: $25. State resident tuition: $2650 full-time, $105 per credit hour part-time. Nonresident tuition: $6550 full-time, $274 per credit hour part-time. Part-time mandatory fees: $12.35 per credit hour. Full-time mandatory fees: $311. College room and board: $4570. College room only: $2750. Special program-related fees: $183 for instrument maintenance, $60 for community performance series fee.

Financial Aid Program-specific awards for Fall of 1994: 100 Endowed Scholarships for undergraduates ($851).

Application Procedures Deadline—freshmen and transfers: continuous. Required: high school transcript, letter of recommendation, interview, audition. Auditions held 10 times on campus and off campus in Smithtown, NY; Rochester, NY; Buffalo, NY; Albany, NY; recorded music is permissible as a substitute for live auditions for out-of-state and international applicants and videotaped

State University of New York College at Potsdam *(continued)*

performances are permissible as a substitute for live auditions for out-of-state and international applicants.

Undergraduate Contact Karen O'Brien, Interim Director, Admissions Office, State University of New York College at Potsdam, Potsdam, New York 13676; 315-267-2180.

Graduate Contact Jim Madeja, Coordinator of Graduate Program, Graduate and Continuing Education Department, State University of New York College at Potsdam, The Crane School of Music, Potsdam, New York 13676; 315-267-2415, fax: 315-267-2413.

More about the School

Program Facilities The five-building music complex includes a 1,400-seat concert hall, 450-seat music theater, expansive music library, rehearsal halls, classrooms, electronic music studio, and seventy practice rooms. The library, classrooms, and studios are sound equipped, and the school has available over 1,500 instruments, including 150 pianos. All equipment is maintained by a full-time professional staff.

Faculty, Visiting Artists, and Alumni The School of Music's full-time staff of artist-teachers are all active performers as well as leaders in the field of music education. Recent visiting artists include Arturo Sandoval, Richard Stolzman, The Canadian Brass and Empire Brass Quintets, Emanuel Ax, David Burge, Bobbie McFerrin, the Beaux Arts Trio, Gregg Smith Singers, Mark O'Connor and Claude Frank. It is estimated that over 20 percent nationwide and 50 percent of New York State teachers are Crane alumni; graduates perform across the country from regional ensembles to the stage at the Metropolitan Opera.

Student Performance Opportunities Crane School of Music at SUNY College at Potsdam has over fifty performing ensembles that present over 200 concerts each year, including Orchestra, Opera Orchestra, Wind Ensemble, two bands, three jazz ensembles, six choirs, Opera Ensemble, like-ensembles, and woodwind, brass, and string chamber ensembles.

Special Programs Degree minors and concentrations include business of music, piano pedagogy, jazz and commercial music, and special education. Double majors include music education and performance, music education and elementary education, and music education and secondary education. Cross-registration is available with Clarkson University, St. Lawrence University, and SUNY Canton. Study abroad includes sites in England, Germany, and Australia.

State University of New York College at Purchase

See Purchase College, State University of New York

State University of New York at Binghamton

Binghamton, New York

State-supported, coed. Suburban campus. Total enrollment: 12,088.

Degrees Bachelor of Music in the area of performance. Majors: harpsichord, piano/organ, stringed instruments, voice, wind and percussion instruments. Graduate degrees offered: Master of Music in the areas of performance, composition, conducting.

Music Student Profile Fall 1994: 35 total; 5 matriculated undergraduate, 30 matriculated graduate.

Music Faculty Total: 32; 12 full-time, 20 part-time. Graduate students teach more than half undergraduate courses.

Expenses for 1994–95 Application fee: $25. State resident tuition: $2650 full-time, $105 per credit part-time. Nonresident tuition: $6550 full-time, $274 per credit part-time. Part-time mandatory fees per semester range from $29.85 to $141.35. Full-time mandatory fees: $311. College room and board: $5080. Special program-related fees: $10 for practice room fee.

Application Procedures Deadline—freshmen and transfers: January 15. Required: essay, high school transcript, college transcript(s) for transfer students, audition, SAT I or ACT test scores. Auditions held as needed at end of freshman year on campus.

Undergraduate Contact Janet Brady, Director of Undergraduate Studies, Department of Music, State University of New York at Binghamton, P.O. Box 6000, Binghamton, New York 13902-6000; 607-777-2591, fax: 607-777-4425.

Graduate Contact Jonathan Biggers, Director of Graduate Studies, Department of Music, State University of New York at Binghamton, P.O. Box 6000, Binghamton, New York 13908-6000; 607-777-2591, fax: 607-777-4425.

State University of New York at Buffalo

Buffalo, New York

State-supported, coed. Suburban campus. Total enrollment: 24,943.

Degrees Bachelor of Music in the areas of music education, performance. Majors: classical music, harpsichord, music, music education, piano/organ, stringed instruments, voice, wind and percussion instruments. Graduate degrees offered: Master of Music in the areas of music education, music performance. Cross-registration with Buffalo Consortium.

Music Student Profile Fall 1994: 270 total; 150 matriculated undergraduate, 70 matriculated graduate, 50 nondegree; 4% minorities, 60% females, 8% international.

Music Faculty Total: 58; 22 full-time, 36 part-time; 90% of full-time faculty have terminal degrees. Graduate students teach a few undergraduate courses.

Student Life Student groups include Music Educators National Conference.

Estimated Expenses for 1995–96 Application fee: $25. State resident tuition: $2650 full-time, $105 per credit hour part-time. Nonresident tuition: $6550 full-time, $274 per credit hour part-time. Part-time mandatory fees: $23.50 per credit hour. Full-time mandatory fees: $594. College room and board: $5024. College room only: $2874.

Financial Aid Program-specific awards for Fall of 1994: 14 Departmental Scholarships for program majors ($500–$2000), 3 Garahee Awards for program majors ($500).

Application Procedures Deadline—freshmen: February 1; transfers: continuous. Required: high school transcript, minimum 3.0 high school GPA, audition, SAT I or ACT test scores, minimum combined SAT I score of 800, minimum composite ACT score of 23. Recommended: essay, 2 letters of recommendation. Auditions held 3 times on campus; recorded music is permissible as a substitute for live auditions if scheduling is difficult.

Contact Michael Burke, Director of Student Programs, Music Department, State University of New York at Buffalo, 226 Baird Hall, Buffalo, New York 14260; 716-645-2758, fax: 716-645-3824.

Stephen F. Austin State University

Nacogdoches, Texas

State-supported, coed. Small-town campus. Total enrollment: 12,206.

Degrees Bachelor of Music in the areas of performance, composition, music education. Majors: music education, music theory and composition, piano/organ, stringed instruments, voice, wind and percussion instruments. Graduate degrees offered: Master of Music in the areas of performance, conducting.

Music Student Profile Fall 1994: 176 total; 159 matriculated undergraduate, 17 matriculated graduate; 12% minorities, 54% females, 2% international.

Music Faculty Total: 32; 22 full-time, 10 part-time; 64% of full-time faculty have terminal degrees. Graduate students teach a few undergraduate courses. Undergraduate student–faculty ratio: 10:1.

Student Life Student groups include Texas Music Educators Association, National Association of Teachers of Singing, Music Teachers National Association.

Expenses for 1994–95 State resident tuition: $896 full-time. Nonresident tuition: $5472 full-time, $171 per semester hour part-time. State resident part-time tuition per semester ranges from $100 to $308. Part-time mandatory fees per semester range from $32.25 to $166.50. Full-time mandatory fees: $832. College room and board: $3542. Special program-related fees: $20 for applied music lesson fee, $25 for recital fee.

Financial Aid Program-specific awards for Fall of 1994: 12 Young Artist's Competition Awards for incoming freshmen ($4200–$7000), 75 Music Activity Scholarships for undergraduates ($600–$900).

Application Procedures Deadline—freshmen and transfers: continuous. Notification date—freshmen and transfers: continuous. Required: high school transcript, college transcript(s) for transfer students, audition, SAT I or ACT test scores, minimum combined SAT I score of 900, minimum composite ACT score of 21. Auditions held as needed on campus; recorded music is permissible as a substitute for live auditions when distance is prohibitive and videotaped performances are permissible as a substitute for live auditions when distance is prohibitive.

Contact Dr. Ronald E. Anderson, Chair, Music Department, Stephen F. Austin State University, Box 13043, Nacogdoches, Texas 75962; 409-468-4602, fax: 409-468-5810.

Stetson University

DeLand, Florida

Independent, coed. Small-town campus. Total enrollment: 2,883.

Degrees Bachelor of Music in the areas of performance, music theory; Bachelor of Music Education in the areas of vocal music education, instrumental music education. Majors: classical music, music, music education, music theory, piano/organ, stringed instruments, voice, wind and percussion instruments.

Music Student Profile Fall 1994: 159 total; all matriculated undergraduate; 10% minorities, 55% females, 2% international.

Music Faculty Total: 38; 20 full-time, 18 part-time; 95% of full-time faculty have terminal degrees. Graduate students do not teach undergraduate courses. Undergraduate student–faculty ratio: 6:1.

Student Life Student groups include Music Educators National Conference Student Chapter, Phi Mu Alpha, Sigma Alpha Iota.

Expenses for 1995–96 Application fee: $25. Comprehensive fee of $18,502 includes full-time tuition ($13,110), mandatory fees ($590), and college room and board ($4802). College room only: $2500. Part-time tuition: $440 per hour. Special program-related fees: $25 for practice room fee.

Financial Aid Program-specific awards for Fall of 1994: 220 Endowed Music Scholarships for program students ($3500).

Application Procedures Deadline—freshmen: March 1. Notification date—freshmen: April 1. Required: essay, high school transcript, college transcript(s) for transfer students, audition, SAT I or ACT test scores. Recommended: minimum 3.0 high school GPA. Audi-

Stetson University *(continued)*

tions held 4 times and scheduled as needed on campus and off campus; recorded music is permissible as a substitute for live auditions if a campus visit is impossible and videotaped performances are permissible as a substitute for live auditions if a campus visit is impossible.

Undergraduate Contact Jane Wendt, Music Admissions Counselor, School of Music, Stetson University, DeLand, Florida 32720; 904-822-8975, fax: 904-822-8948.

Susquehanna University

Selinsgrove, Pennsylvania

Independent-religious, coed. Small-town campus. Total enrollment: 1,512.

Degrees Bachelor of Music in the areas of performance, music education, church music. Majors: guitar, harpsichord, piano/organ, stringed instruments, voice, wind and percussion instruments.

Music Student Profile Fall 1994: 85 total; all matriculated undergraduate; 1% minorities, 99% females.

Music Faculty Total: 22; 9 full-time, 13 part-time; 45% of full-time faculty have terminal degrees. Graduate students do not teach undergraduate courses.

Student Life Student groups include Music Educators National Conference Student Chapter.

Expenses for 1995–96 Application fee: $25. Comprehensive fee of $21,980 includes full-time tuition ($16,800), mandatory fees ($280), and college room and board ($4900). College room only: $2590. Part-time tuition: $525 per semester hour. Special program-related fees: $115–$185 for private lessons, $25 for organ lessons and practice, $15 for instrument rentals.

Financial Aid Program-specific awards for Fall of 1994: 4 Isaacs Scholarships for program majors ($7500), 10 Music Scholarships for program majors ($3000–$5000), 10 Performance Grants for program majors and nonmajors ($1000–$1500).

Application Procedures Deadline—freshmen and transfers: continuous. Required: high school transcript, audition. Auditions held 4 times on campus.

Undergraduate Contact Rick Ziegler, Director of Admissions, Susquehanna University, 514 University Avenue, Selinsgrove, Pennsylvania 17870; 717-372-4260, E-mail address: ziegler@einstein.susqu.edu.

Sybil B. Harrington College of Fine Arts and Humanities

See West Texas A&M University, Sybil B. Harrington College of Fine Arts and Humanities

Syracuse University

Syracuse, New York

Independent, coed. Urban campus. Total enrollment: 14,550.

Degrees Bachelor of Music in the areas of music composition, music education, music industry, organ, percussion, piano, strings, voice, wind instruments. Majors: composition, music, music business, music education, performance, piano/organ, stringed instruments, voice, wind and percussion instruments. Graduate degrees offered: Master of Music in the areas of music composition, music education, organ, percussion, piano, strings, music theory, voice, wind instruments.

Music Student Profile Fall 1994: 128 total; 109 matriculated undergraduate, 19 matriculated graduate; 12% minorities, 59% females.

Music Faculty Total: 55; 12 full-time, 43 part-time; 92% of full-time faculty have terminal degrees. Graduate students teach a few undergraduate courses. Undergraduate student–faculty ratio: 9:1.

Student Life Student groups include Sigma Alpha Iota, Music Educators National Conference, Pi Kappa Lambda.

Expenses for 1995–96 Application fee: $40. Comprehensive fee of $23,190 includes full-time tuition ($15,910), mandatory fees ($370), and college room and board ($6910). College room only: $3760. Special program-related fees: $172–$345 for private lessons, $15–$20 for practice room fee (piano), $36–$72 for practice room fee (organ).

Financial Aid Program-specific awards for Fall of 1994: 25 Special Music Awards for talented program majors, 9 Chancellor's Awards for those demonstrating academic achievement ($6000), 22 Deans Awards for those demonstrating academic achievement ($4000).

Application Procedures Deadline—freshmen: February 1; transfers: July 1. Notification date—freshmen: March 15; transfers: August 15. Required: essay, high school transcript, college transcript(s) for transfer students, minimum 2.0 high school GPA, audition, SAT I or ACT test scores, high school counselor evaluation. Recommended: minimum 3.0 high school GPA, interview. Auditions held 10 times on campus and off campus in New York, NY; recorded music is permissible as a substitute for live auditions and videotaped performances are permissible as a substitute for live auditions.

Undergraduate Contact Coordinator of Recruiting, College of Visual and Performing Arts, Syracuse University, 202P Crouse College, Syracuse, New York 13244-1010; 315-443-2769, fax: 315-443-1935, E-mail address: admissu@vpa.syr.edu.

Graduate Contact Graduate School, Syracuse University, Suite 303 Bowne Hall, Syracuse, New York 13244; 315-443-4492.

More about the University

Program Facilities Crouse College houses acoustically rich Crouse Auditorium (750 seats), 3,823-pipe Holtkamp organ; classrooms, practice rooms, studios; an electronic music studio with equipment for sampling, FM and analog synthesis, and MIDI-based programming with a MacIntosh Quadra 850; Belfer Audio Archive (newly

refurbished studio that offers study in sound archiving and digital multitrack and live acoustic recording), Music Education Resource Center.

Faculty, Resident Artists, and Alumni Faculty are members of the Syracuse Symphony Orchestra and the Buffalo Philharmonic, active recitalists and performers, published authors, and widely performed composers. Recent visiting artists include Kronos Quartet, Chuck Mangione, Atlantic Brass Quintet, Gunther Schuller, and California EAR Unit. Alumni perform world wide and are active in many areas of the music industry.

Student performances Formal groups include chamber groups and small ensembles. Men's and Women's Glee Clubs, Instrumental Jazz Ensemble, Opera Workshop, orange Opus (new music ensemble that performs works by SU student composers, Oratorio Society, Pride of the Orange marching Band (football, pep band), Sour Sitrus Society (basketball pep band), SU Chimemasters, Symphonic Band, University Orchestra, University Singers, Weekly Convocation, Wind Ensemble, Windjammer (vocal jazz).

Special Programs Guest artists perform and hold lectures and master classes on a regular basis, internships–local or national–in many areas of the music industry, merit scholarships for exceptionally qualified students. Performance honors program for non-performing majors, study abroad in London through SU's Division of International Programs Abroad (DIPA), honors program available for students who desire a rigorous academic challenge.

The School of Music encourages students to reach their musical and intellectual potential through preparation as performers, composers, arrangers, music educators, and music industry professionals. Students are a part of a vibrant creative environment led by faculty members who are absorbed in music making both on and off campus.

Although part of a large university, the School of Music enjoys an intimate atmosphere that allows each student to receive the individual attention and opportunity for regular performance that every serious young musician requires. In this inclusive program with a classic basis, students are also exposed to contemporary music of many genres. Students are immersed in music in many contexts: in private lessons, ensemble rehearsals, recitals, guest artists, master classes, and performance. Qualified composition, music education, music industry, and B.A. music students may participate in a performance honors program that allows them to pursue a high level of proficiency in their instrument.

A wide array of ensembles provides ample variety for performance opportunities. All students in the School of Music are required to be involved in one of the School's ensembles every semester, although many participate in several groups. This experience helps students develop the important skill of functioning in group situations and complements the many hours every dedicated musician spends in solitary practice. A required weekly convocation provides a forum for music students and faculty to convene as a community and features a lively mix of student, faculty, and guest performances. Academic electives, which provide a liberal arts component to the curriculum, can be selected from the broad range of courses offered at the University.

Students benefit from a faculty of active professionals who are members of the Syracuse Symphony Orchestra and the Buffalo Philharmonic,composers whose works have been performed nationally and internationally, and recitalists who have won competitions worldwide and have performed with internationally known orchestras and ensembles. They are dedicated to challenging, inspiring, and encouraging students to explore their realized and untapped abilities.

Music students at SU have the opportunity to study abroad in London, where the University makes special arrangements for private music lessons, internships, which may be obtained through the School of Music, the Placement Center, or the Community Internship Program (CIP), allow students to refine their technical proficiency and develop confidence to bridge the gap between college and the professional music world.

The creative activities of the School of Music are an integral part of the College of Visual and Performing Arts, which also governs programs in art and design, drama, and speech communication. The College serves as the center of SU's cultural life, on a campus whose lively and diverse schedule of events could only be found at a large university.

The city of Syracuse itself offers a rich culture: it is home to the Syracuse Symphony orchestra, the Syracuse opera, and the Society for New Music. Syracuse is also a regular stop for touring companies of Broadway's most popular musical comedies, experimental theatre troupes, nationally known comedians, rock groups, and dance companies.

Tarleton State University

Stephenville, Texas

State-supported, coed. Small-town campus. Total enrollment: 6,460.

Degrees Bachelor of Music in the area of music education. Majors: music education.

Expenses for 1994–95 Application fee: $20. State resident tuition: $896 full-time. Nonresident tuition: $5472 full-time, $171 per semester hour part-time. State resident part-time tuition per semester ranges from $100 to $308. Part-time mandatory fees per semester range from $33.10 to $301.10. Full-time mandatory fees: $738. College room and board: $3180.

Application Procedures Auditions held on campus and off campus. Portfolio reviews held on campus and off campus.

Undergraduate Contact Richard Denning, Head, Department of Fine Arts and Speech, Tarleton State University, Tarleton Station, Stephenville, Texas 76402; 817-968-9245, fax: 817-968-9239, E-mail address: denning@tarleton.edu.

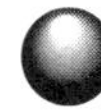

Taylor University

Upland, Indiana

Independent, coed. Rural campus. Total enrollment: 1,831.

Degrees Bachelor of Music in the areas of performance, composition; Bachelor of Music Education in the area of music education. Majors: music education, piano/organ, stringed instruments, voice, wind and percussion instruments.

Music Student Profile Fall 1994: 60 total; all matriculated undergraduate; 5% minorities, 55% females, 5% international.

Music Faculty Total: 28; 8 full-time, 20 part-time; 90% of full-time faculty have terminal degrees. Graduate students do not teach undergraduate courses. Undergraduate student–faculty ratio: 16:1.

Student Life Student groups include Music Educators National Conference, National Association of Schools of Singing, Community Music Development.

Expenses for 1995–96 Application fee: $20. Comprehensive fee of $16,064 includes full-time tuition ($11,700), mandatory fees ($214), and college room and board ($4150). College room only: $1980. Part-time tuition per credit hour ranges from $315 to $395 according to course load. Special program-related fees.

Financial Aid Program-specific awards for Fall of 1994: 3–15 Enrollment Awards for freshmen ($2000–$4000), 6–10 Music Merit Awards for freshmen ($500–$2000), 10–15 Applied Music Awards for freshmen ($250–$500).

Application Procedures Deadline—freshmen and transfers: February 15. Notification date—freshmen and transfers: continuous. Required: essay, high school transcript, college transcript(s) for transfer students, minimum 3.0 high school GPA, 3 letters of recommendation, interview, audition, SAT I or ACT test scores. Auditions held 4 times on campus; recorded music is permissible as a substitute for live auditions when distance is prohibitive and videotaped performances are permissible as a substitute for live auditions when distance is prohibitive.

Undergraduate Contact Steve Mortland, Admissions Department, Taylor University, 500 West Reade Avenue, Upland, Indiana 46989; 317-998-5206.

Teikyo Westmar University

Le Mars, Iowa

Independent, coed. Small-town campus. Total enrollment: 566.

Degrees Bachelor of Music Education in the area of music education. Majors: music education.

Music Student Profile Fall 1994: 2 total; all matriculated undergraduate; 50% females.

Music Faculty Total: 7; 4 full-time, 3 part-time; 50% of full-time faculty have terminal degrees. Graduate students do not teach undergraduate courses.

Expenses for 1995–96 Application fee: $25. Comprehensive fee of $14,026 includes full-time tuition ($9980), mandatory fees ($296), and college room and board ($3750). College room only: $1680. Part-time tuition: $200 per semester hour. Special program-related fees: $125 for lessons.

Financial Aid Program-specific awards for Fall of 1994: 10–15 Music Grants for program majors and non-majors ($2000–$2500), 5 Endowed Scholarships for program majors ($300).

Application Procedures Deadline—freshmen and transfers: continuous. Required: high school transcript, minimum 2.0 high school GPA, audition. Auditions held continuously on campus; recorded music is permissible as a substitute for live auditions if a campus visit is impossible and videotaped performances are permissible as a substitute for live auditions if a campus visit is impossible.

Undergraduate Contact Betty Lou Larson, Chair, Music Program, Teikyo Westmar University, 1002 3rd Avenue, SE, Le Mars, Iowa 51031; 712-546-2564.

Esther Boyer College of Music

Temple University

Philadelphia, Pennsylvania

State-related, coed. Urban campus. Total enrollment: 26,952.

Degrees Bachelor of Music in the areas of classical guitar performance, composition, instrumental performance, jazz arranging/composition, jazz instrumental performance, jazz voice performance, music education, music education/jazz, music history, music theory, music therapy, music therapy/jazz. Majors: classical music, composition, jazz, keyboard, music, music education, music technology, music therapy, opera, stringed instruments, voice. Graduate degrees offered: Master of Music in the areas of choral conducting, composition, music education, music history, music theory, music therapy, opera, organ, piano, piano pedagogy, piano accompanying and chamber music, piano accompanying and opera coaching, stringed instruments, string pedagogy, percussion. Doctor of Musical Arts in the areas of composition, performance.

Music Student Profile Fall 1994: 600 total; 350 matriculated undergraduate, 225 matriculated graduate, 25 nondegree; 12% minorities, 47% females, 25% international.

Music Faculty Total: 149; 50 full-time, 99 part-time; 100% of full-time faculty have terminal degrees. Graduate students do not teach undergraduate courses. Undergraduate student–faculty ratio: 10:1.

Student Life Student groups include Sigma Alpha Iota, Kappa Kappa Psi, Pi Kappa Lambda. Special housing available for music students.

Expenses for 1995–96 Application fee: $30. State resident tuition: $5314 full-time, $185 per semester hour part-time. Nonresident tuition: $10,096 full-time, $286 per semester hour part-time. Part-time mandatory fees per semester range from $15 to $45. Full-time mandatory fees: $200. College room and board: $5282. College room only: $3492. Special program-related fees: $125 for private lesson fee, $50 for instrument rental in music education, $8–$30 for lab fees.

Financial Aid Program-specific awards for Fall of 1994: 40 Boyer Grants for freshmen and transfers ($250–$10,096), 100 Performance Grants for program majors ($250–$10,096).

Application Procedures Deadline—freshmen and transfers: May 1. Notification date—freshmen and transfers: September 1. Required: high school transcript, college transcript(s) for transfer students, minimum 2.0 high school GPA, interview, audition, SAT I or ACT test scores, minimum combined SAT I score of 850. Recommended: essay, 2 letters of recommendation. Auditions held 9 times on campus and off campus; recorded music is permissible as a substitute for live auditions when distance is prohibitive and videotaped performances are permissible as a substitute for live auditions when distance is prohibitive. Portfolio reviews held 9 times on campus and off campus.

Undergraduate Contact Dr. Steven Estrella, Coordinator of Recruitment, Esther Boyer College of Music, Temple University, Box 012-00, Philadelphia, Pennsylvania 19122; 215-204-8301, fax: 215-204-4957, E-mail address: estrella@astro.ocis.temple.edu.

Graduate Contact Dr. Steven Kreinberg, Assistant Dean, Esther Boyer College of Music, Temple University, Box 012-00, Philadelphia, Pennsylvania 19122; 215-204-7609, fax: 215-204-4957.

More about the College

Program Facilities Presser Hall (practice rooms, classrooms, ensemble rehearsal rooms, teaching studios, electronic composition/computer synthesis and recording studios, listening library); Presser Learning Center (multimedia laboratory); Alice Tully Library (scores, ensemble music, records, tapes, books); Rock Hall (practice and performance facilities) and the Presser Creative Music Technology Center; libraries containing over 2 million volumes, 1 million microforms, and 16,000 serials.

Faculty, Resident Artists, and Alumni Fifty full-time and 99 part-time faculty; Philadelphia Orchestra members, world-renowned performers, scholars, educators, and therapists; prominent alumni include Leon Bates, Claudia Catania, Katherine Ciesinski, Robert Fitzpatrick, George Gray, Jeffrey Kirschen, William McGlaughlin, Kirk Muspratt, Lambert Orkis, Marietta Simpson, and Kathleen Viglante. Alumni perform in major symphonies, chamber music ensembles, and opera houses all over the world.

Student Performance Opportunities Bands: Diamond Marching Band, Wind Symphony, Collegiate Band, Big Band; Choirs; Concert Choir, University Singers, University Chorale, Graduate Conductors' Chorus, Recital Chorus; Jazz: Jazz Ensemble, Jazz Lab Band, Jazz Guitar Ensemble, Jazz Keyboard Ensemble, Jazz Brass Ensemble, Jazz Percussion Ensemble, New Music by Temple Jazz Composers; Instrumental: Symphony, Percussion Ensemble, Mixed Chamber Ensembles; Opera: Opera Theater; Other: New Music by Temple Composers, Early Music Ensembles, Contemporary Players and Singers, Piano Ensembles.

Special Programs Undergraduate diploma in performance. Graduate Professional Studies Certificate in performance, certificate in guided imagery and music therapy.

The Esther Boyer College of Music, named in recognition of the generosity of this Temple alumna and benefactress, maintains a tradition of excellent musical training through active and innovative programs designed to focus on the art of music making. Within the framework of a large, multifaceted university, the performance-oriented Boyer College offers a 10:1 student-faculty ratio, which provides each student with a high degree of individual attention. All Boyer College programs draw on the resources of the entire University, while students study privately with members of its outstanding artist-faculty.

The College's fine reputation is founded on the efforts of a distinguished faculty of performers, scholars, and teachers. Temple alumni, in turn, bring renown to the Boyer College in virtually every aspect of the musician's world—as professional members of major metropolitan orchestras, chamber ensembles, and opera companies in this country and abroad and as scholars, researchers, music therapists, and educators in public schools, private schools, colleges, and universities throughout the country.

In addition to a wide array of courses in applied music, composition, computer music synthesis, conducting, music education, music history, music theory, music therapy, and pedagogy, all students are invited to take advantage of the exceptional performance opportunities at the College. The 1986 merger of The New School of Music with the Boyer College—and the resulting creation of The New School Institute—reinforced the College's strong commitment to the education of the ensemble and orchestral musicians of the future. The Temple choral experience includes tours, broadcasts, and numerous concerts and recordings with major American and Western European orchestras. Instrumentalists may perform with several large distinguished ensembles, such as the Temple University Symphony Orchestra, Chamber Orchestra, Symphonic Band, and Diamond Marching Band. Specialized ensemble experience is available to members of the Jazz Ensemble, Big Band, Wind Chamber Symphony, Percussion Ensemble, Guitar Ensemble, and a wide variety of string, wind, brass, keyboard, and mixed chamber groups. Opera Theater provides vocalists with ample opportunity to perform in fully staged opera productions each semester as well as programs of opera scenes and excerpts. Participants in the Early Music Ensembles and the Contemporary Players and Singers enjoy specialized ensemble experiences using reproductions of authentic period instruments, state-of-the-art synthesizers, and coaching in performance practice. Students also benefit from the finest in music technology instruction and equipment available at the Presser Creative Music Technology Center in Rock Hall.

Through its first-rate conservatory-level training, challenging and diverse university curriculums, extraordinary performing opportunities, and the rich cultural resources located in the city of Philadelphia, the Esther Boyer College of Music offers students exceptional opportunities for career growth and enhancement.

Tennessee Wesleyan College

Athens, Tennessee

Independent-religious, coed. Small-town campus. Total enrollment: 633.

Degrees Bachelor of Music Education in the areas of music education, church music. Majors: music education.

Music Faculty Graduate students do not teach undergraduate courses.

Student Life Student groups include Music Educators National Conference.

Expenses for 1995–96 Application fee: $25. Comprehensive fee of $9800 includes full-time tuition ($6100), mandatory fees ($100), and college room and board ($3600). Part-time tuition: $190 per semester hour.

Financial Aid Program-specific awards for Fall of 1994 available.

Application Procedures

Undergraduate Contact Janice Ryberg, Chair, Music Department, Tennessee Wesleyan College, P.O. Box 40, Athens, Tennessee 37371; 615-745-7504, fax: 615-744-9968.

Texas A&M University–Corpus Christi

Corpus Christi, Texas

State-supported, coed. Suburban campus. Total enrollment: 5,152.

Degrees Bachelor of Music in the area of performance. Majors: classical guitar, keyboard, voice, wind and percussion instruments. Mandatory cross-registration with Del Mar College.

Music Student Profile Fall 1994: 50 total.

Music Faculty Total: 31; 21 full-time, 10 part-time; 33% of full-time faculty have terminal degrees.

Estimated Expenses for 1995–96 Application fee: $10. State resident tuition: $900 full-time. Nonresident tuition: $5280 full-time, $176 per semester hour part-time. State resident part-time tuition per semester ranges from $100 to $330. Part-time mandatory fees per semester range from $29 to $269. Full-time mandatory fees: $688. College room only: $2385. Special program-related fees: $40 for applied music fee.

Financial Aid Program-specific awards for Fall of 1994: 30 Fine Arts Studio Scholarships for transfer students ($600).

Application Procedures Deadline—freshmen and transfers: July 1. Notification date—freshmen and transfers: continuous. Required: high school transcript, college transcript(s) for transfer students, audition, SAT I or ACT test scores, theory assessment examination. Auditions held on campus and off campus. Portfolio reviews held on campus and off campus.

Undergraduate Contact Sam Logsdon, Music Program Coordinator, Department of Music, Texas A&M University–Corpus Christi, 6300 Ocean Drive, Corpus Christi, Texas 78412; 512-994-2761, fax: 512-994-5844, E-mail address: logsdons@falcon.tamucc.edu.

Texas A&M University–Kingsville

Kingsville, Texas

State-supported, coed. Small-town campus. Total enrollment: 6,548.

Degrees Bachelor of Music. Majors: applied music, music education. Graduate degrees offered: Master of Music in the area of music education.

Expenses for 1995–96 State resident tuition: $900 full-time. Nonresident tuition: $6660 full-time, $222 per credit hour part-time. State resident part-time tuition per semester ranges from $100 to $330. Part-time mandatory fees per semester range from $71.65 to $346. Full-time mandatory fees: $812. College room and board: $3484. College room only: $1784.

Application Procedures Auditions held on campus and off campus. Portfolio reviews held on campus and off campus.

Undergraduate Contact Department of Music, Texas A&M University–Kingsville, Kingsville, Texas 78363; 512-595-2804.

Texas Christian University

Fort Worth, Texas

Independent-religious, coed. Suburban campus. Total enrollment: 6,706.

Degrees Bachelor of Music in the areas of performance, piano pedagogy, music theory–composition, music history, church music; Bachelor of Music Education in the areas of vocal music education, instrumental music education. Majors: classical music, guitar, music, music education, piano/organ, sacred music, stringed instruments, voice, wind and percussion instruments. Graduate degrees offered: Master of Music in the areas of performance, pedagogy, musicology, music theory/composition/computer music; Master of Music Education in the area of music education.

Music Student Profile Fall 1994: 226 total; 160 matriculated undergraduate, 50 matriculated graduate, 16 nondegree; 10% minorities, 60% females, 20% international.

Music Faculty Total: 50; 26 full-time, 24 part-time; 70% of full-time faculty have terminal degrees. Graduate students do not teach undergraduate courses. Undergraduate student–faculty ratio: 15:1.

Student Life Student groups include Pi Kappa Lambda (music honorary society), American String Teachers Association, Music Educators Organization.

Expenses for 1995–96 Application fee: $30. Comprehensive fee of $13,840 includes full-time tuition ($9000),

mandatory fees ($1000), and college room and board ($3840). Part-time tuition: $300 per semester hour. Part-time mandatory fees: $25 per semester hour.

Financial Aid Program-specific awards for Fall of 1994: Choral Scholarships for vocalists ($800–$8500), Orchestra Scholarships for string players ($800–$8500), Band Scholarships for band instrumentalists ($800–$8500), Music Department Scholarships for program majors ($800–$8500).

Application Procedures Deadline—freshmen: February 15; transfers: August 1. Notification date—freshmen: March 15; transfers: August 15. Required: essay, high school transcript, college transcript(s) for transfer students, audition, SAT I or ACT test scores. Recommended: minimum 3.0 high school GPA, interview. Auditions held continuously by appointment on campus and off campus in various locations; recorded music is permissible as a substitute for live auditions if a campus visit is impossible.

Undergraduate Contact Dr. Kenneth R. Raessler, Chair, Department of Music, Texas Christian University, P.O. Box 32887, Fort Worth, Texas 76129; 817-921-7602, fax: 817-921-7344, E-mail address: mthomas@gamma.is.tcu.edu.

Graduate Contact Dr. John Burton, Director of Graduate Studies, College of Fine Arts and Communication, Texas Christian University, P.O. Box 30793, Fort Worth, Texas 76129; 817-921-7603, fax: 817-921-7703.

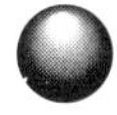

Texas Tech University

Lubbock, Texas

State-supported, coed. Urban campus. Total enrollment: 24,083.

Degrees Bachelor of Music in the areas of performance, composition, music theory, music education. Majors: classical music, music, music education, opera, piano/organ, stringed instruments, voice, wind and percussion instruments. Graduate degrees offered: Master of Music in the areas of performance, music history and literature, music theory; Master of Music Education in the area of music education.

Music Student Profile Fall 1994: 1,283 total; 321 matriculated undergraduate, 62 matriculated graduate, 900 nondegree.

Music Faculty Total: 66; 41 full-time, 25 part-time; 95% of full-time faculty have terminal degrees. Graduate students teach a few undergraduate courses. Undergraduate student–faculty ratio: 7:1.

Student Life Student groups include Texas Music Educators Conference Student Chapter, Music Educators National Conference Student Chapter, Texas Music Educators Association Student Chapter.

Estimated Expenses for 1995–96 Application fee: $25. State resident tuition: $900 full-time. Nonresident tuition: $5280 full-time, $176 per semester hour part-time. State resident part-time tuition per semester ranges from $100 to $330. Part-time mandatory fees: $25 per semester hour. Full-time mandatory fees: $870. College room and board: $3851. Special program-related fees: $15 for private music lessons, $10 for instrument rental, $5 for locker rental, $3–$15 for practice room rental.

Financial Aid Program-specific awards for Fall of 1994: Endowed Scholarships for program majors ($200–$7000).

Application Procedures Deadline—freshmen and transfers: March 1. Required: high school transcript, SAT I or ACT test scores. Recommended: audition. Auditions held 3 times and by request on campus; recorded music is permissible as a substitute for live auditions when distance is prohibitive and videotaped performances are permissible as a substitute for live auditions when distance is prohibitive.

Undergraduate Contact Office of New Student Relations, Texas Tech University, Box 45005, Lubbock, Texas 79409-5005; 806-742-1482.

Graduate Contact Graduate Admissions, Texas Tech University, Box 41030, Lubbock, Texas 79409-1030; 806-742-2787, fax: 806-742-1746.

Tisch School of the Arts

See New York University, Tisch School of the Arts

Trenton State College

Trenton, New Jersey

State-supported, coed. Suburban campus. Total enrollment: 6,981.

Degrees Bachelor of Music in the areas of performance, music education. Majors: classical music, music, music education, piano/organ, stringed instruments, voice, wind and percussion instruments.

Music Student Profile Fall 1994: 180 total; 131 matriculated undergraduate, 49 matriculated graduate; 4% minorities, 3% international.

Music Faculty Total: 33; 13 full-time, 20 part-time; 69% of full-time faculty have terminal degrees. Graduate students do not teach undergraduate courses. Undergraduate student–faculty ratio: 5:1.

Student Life Student groups include Music Educators National Conference, Delta Omicron.

Expenses for 1995–96 Application fee: $50. State resident tuition: $4240 full-time, $143 per semester hour part-time. Nonresident tuition: $6657 full-time, $227 per semester hour part-time. College room and board: $5600.

Financial Aid Program-specific awards for Fall of 1994: 5–10 Talent Scholarships for those demonstrating talent ($750–$1500), 1 Hy Frank Music Scholarship for music education students ($1500).

Application Procedures Deadline—freshmen and transfers: March 1. Notification date—freshmen: April 1; transfers: April 15. Required: essay, high school transcript, minimum 2.0 high school GPA, 2 letters of recommendation, interview, audition. Recommended: minimum 3.0 high school GPA. Auditions held 6 times on campus.

Trenton State College *(continued)*

Contact Robert E. Parrish, Chairperson, Music Department, Trenton State College, Hillwood Lakes, CN4700, Trenton, New Jersey 08650-4700; 609-771-2551, fax: 609-771-3422, E-mail address: bparrish@tscvm.trenton.edu.

Trinity University

San Antonio, Texas

Independent-religious, coed. Urban campus. Total enrollment: 2,479.

Degrees Bachelor of Music in the areas of performance, composition, music education. Majors: guitar, harpsichord, piano/organ, stringed instruments, voice, wind and percussion instruments.

Music Student Profile Fall 1994: 35 total; all matriculated undergraduate; 23% minorities, 45% females, 3% international.

Music Faculty Total: 26; 11 full-time, 15 part-time; 92% of full-time faculty have terminal degrees. Undergraduate student–faculty ratio: 10:1.

Student Life Student groups include Opera Workshop/Musical Theater, Gospel Choir, Pep Band.

Expenses for 1995–96 Application fee: $25. Comprehensive fee of $18,584 includes full-time tuition ($12,900), mandatory fees ($144), and college room and board ($5540). College room only: $3385. Part-time tuition: $537.50 per semester hour. Part-time mandatory fees: $6 per semester hour.

Application Procedures Deadline—freshmen and transfers: February 25. Notification date—freshmen and transfers: April 1. Required: essay, high school transcript, college transcript(s) for transfer students, letter of recommendation, SAT I or ACT test scores. Auditions held 6 times on campus and off campus in Dallas, TX; Houston, TX; recorded music is permissible as a substitute for live auditions if a campus visit is impossible and videotaped performances are permissible as a substitute for live auditions if a campus visit is impossible.

Undergraduate Contact Andrew Mihalso, Chairman, Department of Music, Trinity University, 715 Stadium Drive, San Antonio, Texas 78212-7200; 210-736-8212, fax: 210-736-8512.

Troy State University

Troy, Alabama

State-supported, coed. Small-town campus. Total enrollment: 5,480.

Degrees Bachelor of Music Education in the areas of instrumental music education, vocal/choral music education. Majors: music education.

Music Student Profile Fall 1994: 101 total; all matriculated undergraduate; 4% minorities, 35% females.

Music Faculty Total: 15; 13 full-time, 2 part-time; 46% of full-time faculty have terminal degrees. Graduate students do not teach undergraduate courses. Undergraduate student–faculty ratio: 8:1.

Student Life Student groups include Collegiate Music Educators National Conference, Phi Mu Alpha Sinfonia, Sigma Alpha Iota.

Expenses for 1995–96 Application fee: $15. State resident tuition: $1887 full-time, $50 per quarter hour part-time. Nonresident tuition: $3774 full-time, $100 per quarter hour part-time. Part-time mandatory fees: $40 per quarter. Full-time mandatory fees: $120. College room and board: $3152. College room only: $1290. Special program-related fees: $40 for private lessons.

Financial Aid Program-specific awards for Fall of 1994: 80 Band Scholarships for instrumental majors ($250), 25 Choral Scholarships for singers or pianists ($250).

Application Procedures Deadline—freshmen and transfers: continuous. Required: high school transcript, college transcript(s) for transfer students, minimum 2.0 high school GPA, audition, SAT I or ACT test scores, minimum combined SAT I score of 740, minimum composite ACT score of 18, minimum 2.0 college GPA for transfer students. Recommended: interview. Auditions held by appointment on campus; recorded music is permissible as a substitute for live auditions if a campus visit is impossible and videotaped performances are permissible as a substitute for live auditions if a campus visit is impossible.

Undergraduate Contact Dr. John Long, Dean, School of Fine Arts, Troy State University, Long Hall #1, Troy, Alabama 36082; 334-670-3281.

Union College

Barbourville, Kentucky

Independent-religious, coed. Small-town campus. Total enrollment: 1,003.

Degrees Bachelor of Music in the area of church music; Bachelor of Music Education in the areas of instrumental music education, vocal music education. Majors: music, music education, sacred music, voice, wind and percussion instruments.

Music Student Profile Fall 1994: 23 total; all matriculated undergraduate; 20% minorities, 55% females, 5% international.

Music Faculty Total: 8; 5 full-time, 3 part-time; 80% of full-time faculty have terminal degrees. Graduate students do not teach undergraduate courses. Undergraduate student–faculty ratio: 8:1.

Student Life Student groups include Music Educators National Conference Student Chapter.

Expenses for 1995–96 Application fee: $20. Comprehensive fee of $11,240 includes full-time tuition ($8200) and college room and board ($3040). Part-time tuition: $180 per credit hour.

Financial Aid Program-specific awards for Fall of 1994: 10–20 Department Scholarships for voice/winds/keyboard majors ($2000).

Application Procedures Deadline—freshmen and transfers: August 1. Notification date—freshmen and transfers: August 15. Required: high school transcript, minimum 2.0 high school GPA. Recommended: letter of recommendation, interview, audition. Auditions held 3–4 times on campus; recorded music is permissible as a substitute for live auditions when distance is prohibitive and videotaped performances are permissible as a substitute for live auditions when distance is prohibitive.

Undergraduate Contact Donald Hapward, Dean of Admissions, Union College, 310 College Street, Barbourville, Kentucky 40906; 606-546-1220.

Union University

Jackson, Tennessee

Independent-religious, coed. Small-town campus. Total enrollment: 2,036.

Degrees Bachelor of Music in the areas of voice, piano, organ, music education, sacred music. Majors: choral music education, instrumental music education, performance, piano/organ, sacred music, voice. Cross-registration with Lambuth University, Freed–Hardeman University.

Music Student Profile Fall 1994: 84 total; all matriculated undergraduate; 4% minorities, 60% females.

Music Faculty Total: 17; 10 full-time, 7 part-time; 90% of full-time faculty have terminal degrees. Graduate students do not teach undergraduate courses. Undergraduate student–faculty ratio: 8:1.

Student Life Student groups include Phi Mu Alpha Sinfonia, Sigma Alpha Iota, Music Educators National Conference Student Chapter.

Expenses for 1995–96 Application fee: $10. Comprehensive fee of $9060 includes full-time tuition ($6350), mandatory fees ($80), and college room and board ($2630). Part-time tuition: $265 per semester hour. Part-time mandatory fees: $20 per term. Special program-related fees: $125–$225 for private lessons, $50 for class piano/voice fee.

Financial Aid Program-specific awards for Fall of 1994: 65 Talent Scholarships for program majors ($500), 20 Vocal Ensemble Scholarships for musically qualified ($750), 30 Instrumental Ensemble Scholarships for musically qualified ($300).

Application Procedures Deadline—freshmen and transfers: August 22. Required: high school transcript, college transcript(s) for transfer students, interview, audition. Auditions held 2 times and individually by arrangement on campus; recorded music is permissible as a substitute for live auditions when distance is prohibitive and videotaped performances are permissible as a substitute for live auditions when distance is prohibitive.

Undergraduate Contact Carroll Griffin, Director of Admissions, Union University, 2447 Highway 45 Bypass, Jackson, Tennessee 38305; 901-661-5000, fax: 901-661-5175.

University of Akron

Akron, Ohio

State-supported, coed. Urban campus. Total enrollment: 26,009.

Degrees Bachelor of Music in the areas of theory/composition, jazz studies, music performance, music education, music history and literature. Majors: jazz, music education, music history and literature, music theory and composition, performance.

Music Student Profile Fall 1994: 300 total; all matriculated undergraduate.

Music Faculty Total: 65; 34 full-time, 31 part-time.

Expenses for 1995–96 Application fee: $35. State resident tuition: $3192 full-time, $123.65 per credit part-time. Nonresident tuition: $7954 full-time, $282.40 per credit part-time. Full-time mandatory fees: $380. College room and board: $3844. Special program-related fees: $20 for practice module rental, $75–$150 for applied music lesson fee.

Financial Aid Program-specific awards for Fall of 1994: 2 Music Scholarships for music majors and minors.

Application Procedures Deadline—freshmen: continuous. Required: high school transcript, college transcript(s) for transfer students, audition, SAT I or ACT test scores, tests in rudimentary theory, ear training and keyboard skills. Auditions held 4 times on campus and off campus; recorded music is permissible as a substitute for live auditions for out-of-state applicants. Portfolio reviews held on campus and off campus.

Undergraduate Contact Office of Admissions, University of Akron, Akron, Ohio 44325-2001; 216-972-7100.

University of Alabama

Tuscaloosa, Alabama

State-supported, coed. Small-town campus. Total enrollment: 19,366.

Degrees Bachelor of Music in the areas of performance, music theory, composition, music therapy, arranging. Majors: arranging, composition, music theory, music therapy, piano/organ, stringed instruments, voice, wind and percussion instruments. Graduate degrees offered: Master of Music in the areas of performance, conducting, composition, arranging. Doctor of Musical Arts in the areas of performance, conducting, composition.

Music Student Profile Fall 1994: 265 total; 180 matriculated undergraduate, 70 matriculated graduate, 15 nondegree; 10% minorities, 52% females, 12% international.

University of Alabama *(continued)*

Music Faculty Total: 43; 36 full-time, 7 part-time; 82% of full-time faculty have terminal degrees. Graduate students teach a few undergraduate courses. Undergraduate student–faculty ratio: 6:1.

Expenses for 1995–96 Application fee: $25. State resident tuition: $2374 full-time. Nonresident tuition: $5924 full-time. Part-time tuition per semester ranges from $322 to $1187 for state residents, $474 to $2962 for nonresidents. College room and board: $3658. College room only: $2000. Special program-related fees: $125 for applied music fee.

Financial Aid Program-specific awards for Fall of 1994: 30–40 Music Scholarships for program majors ($500–$5000).

Application Procedures Deadline—freshmen and transfers: continuous. Required: high school transcript, college transcript(s) for transfer students, minimum 2.0 high school GPA, letter of recommendation, audition, SAT I or ACT test scores. Auditions held 5 times on campus; recorded music is permissible as a substitute for live auditions when distance is prohibitive or scheduling is difficult and videotaped performances are permissible as a substitute for live auditions when distance is prohibitive or scheduling is difficult.

Undergraduate Contact Gerald L. Welker, Director, School of Music, University of Alabama, Box 870366, Tuscaloosa, Alabama 35487; 205-348-7110, fax: 205-348-1473.

Graduate Contact Bruce Murray, Director of Graduate Studies, School of Music, University of Alabama, Box 870366, Tuscaloosa, Alabama 35487; 205-348-1463, fax: 205-348-1473.

University of Alaska Anchorage

Anchorage, Alaska

State-supported, coed. Urban campus. Total enrollment: 15,113.

Degrees Bachelor of Music in the area of performance; Bachelor of Music Education in the areas of elementary music education, secondary music education. Majors: classical music, music, piano/organ, stringed instruments, voice, wind and percussion instruments.

Music Student Profile Fall 1994: 453 total; 53 matriculated undergraduate, 400 nondegree; 10% minorities, 3% international.

Music Faculty Total: 17; 6 full-time, 11 part-time; 50% of full-time faculty have terminal degrees. Graduate students do not teach undergraduate courses. Undergraduate student–faculty ratio: 3:1.

Student Life Student groups include Music Educators National Conference Student Chapter.

Expenses for 1995–96 Application fee: $35. Full-time tuition ranges from $2070 to $2250 for state residents, $6210 to $6750 for nonresidents, according to class level. Part-time tuition per credit hour ranges from $69 to $75 for state residents, $207 to $225 for nonresidents, according to class level. Part-time mandatory fees per semester range from $54 for 3 to 5 credits, $74 for 5 to 9 credits, $79 for 10 credits or above. Full-time mandatory fees: $158. College room only: $2500.

Financial Aid Program-specific awards for Fall of 1994: 1 Music Scholarship for incoming students.

Application Procedures Deadline—freshmen and transfers: continuous. Required: high school transcript, college transcript(s) for transfer students. Recommended: minimum 2.0 high school GPA.

Undergraduate Contact Mike Turner, Counseling Coordinator, Advising and Counseling Department, University of Alaska Anchorage, 3211 Providence Drive, Anchorage, Alaska 99508; 907-786-4500, fax: 907-786-4519, E-mail address: anpag@acad2.alaska.edu.

University of Alaska Fairbanks

Fairbanks, Alaska

State-supported, coed. Small-town campus. Total enrollment: 7,807.

Degrees Bachelor of Music in the areas of performance, secondary music education, elementary music education. Majors: classical music, jazz, music education, piano/organ, stringed instruments, voice, wind and percussion instruments.

Music Student Profile Fall 1994: 40 total; 34 matriculated undergraduate, 6 matriculated graduate; 1% minorities, 50% females, 1% international.

Music Faculty Total: 19; 11 full-time, 8 part-time; 90% of full-time faculty have terminal degrees. Graduate students teach a few undergraduate courses.

Expenses for 1995–96 Application fee: $35. State resident tuition: $2070 full-time, $69 per credit hour part-time. Nonresident tuition: $6210 full-time, $207 per credit hour part-time. Part-time mandatory fees: $50 per semester. Full-time mandatory fees: $330. College room and board: $3690. College room only: $1800. Special program-related fees: $145 for private lessons/practice room fee, $75 for class lessons/practice room fee, $30 for class guitar fee, $40 for instrumental rental fee, $5 for locker rental.

Financial Aid Program-specific awards for Fall of 1994: 1–4 Friends of Music Awards for program majors ($500), 1–2 Glenmede Awards for string players ($500), 1–2 Fejes Music Scholarships for program majors ($500).

Application Procedures Deadline—freshmen and transfers: August 1. Required: high school transcript, college transcript(s) for transfer students, 3 letters of recommendation, SAT I or ACT test scores. Recommended: audition. Auditions held 1 time in the fall semester on campus; recorded music is permissible as a substitute for live auditions.

Undergraduate Contact Admissions and Records, University of Alaska Fairbanks, Signers' Hall, Suite 102, Fairbanks, Alaska 99775-0060; 907-474-7521.

University of Alberta

Edmonton, Alberta

Province-supported, coed. Urban campus. Total enrollment: 30,494.

Degrees Bachelor of Music in the areas of school music, performance, music theory and composition, music history and literature. Majors: classical music, composition, music history and literature, music theory and composition, piano/organ, stringed instruments, voice, wind and percussion instruments. Graduate degrees offered: Master of Music in the areas of applied music, composition, choral conducting, theory, musicology, ethnomusicology. Doctor of Music in the area of keyboard. Cross-registration with Grant MacEwan Community College.

Music Student Profile Fall 1994: 204 total; 165 matriculated undergraduate, 39 matriculated graduate; 10% minorities, 4% international.

Music Faculty Total: 38; 20 full-time, 18 part-time; 90% of full-time faculty have terminal degrees. Graduate students teach a few undergraduate courses. Undergraduate student–faculty ratio: 8:1.

Expenses for 1994–95 Application fee: $50. Canadian resident tuition: $2288 full-time, $227.88 per course part-time. Nonresident tuition: $4566 full-time, $455.76 per course part-time. Part-time mandatory fees: $62.78 per term. (All figures are in Canadian dollars.). Full-time mandatory fees: $312. College room and board: $4500. Special program-related fees: $10–$20 for lockers and keys.

Financial Aid Program-specific awards for Fall of 1994: Beryl Barns Memorial Awards for performers ($1000–$1500).

Application Procedures Deadline—freshmen and transfers: May 1. Notification date—freshmen and transfers: June 1. Required: high school transcript, college transcript(s) for transfer students, minimum 2.0 high school GPA, audition. Recommended: minimum 3.0 high school GPA. Auditions held 1 time on campus; recorded music is permissible as a substitute for live auditions when distance is prohibitive and videotaped performances are permissible as a substitute for live auditions when distance is prohibitive.

Undergraduate Contact Donna Maskell, Executive Assistant, Department of Music, University of Alberta, FAB 3-82, Edmonton, Alberta T6G 2C9, Canada; 403-492-3263, fax: 403-492-9246.

Graduate Contact L. Ratzlaff, Graduate Coordinator, Department of Music, University of Alberta, FAB 3-82, Edmonton, Alberta T6G 2C9, Canada; 403-492-3263, fax: 403-492-9246.

University of Arizona

Tucson, Arizona

State-supported, coed. Urban campus. Total enrollment: 35,306.

Degrees Bachelor of Music in the areas of jazz studies, music education, performance, composition. Majors: choral music education, classical guitar, composition, instrumental music education, jazz, keyboard, music theory, stringed instruments, voice, wind and percussion instruments. Graduate degrees offered: Master of Music in the areas of performance, music education, composition, musicology, music theory. Doctor of Musical Arts in the areas of composition, conducting, performance.

Expenses for 1995–96 State resident tuition: $1950 full-time. Nonresident tuition: $7978 full-time. Part-time tuition per semester ranges from $103 to $975 for state residents, $334 to $3989 for nonresidents. College room and board: $4400. College room only: $2400.

Application Procedures Deadline—freshmen: April 1; transfers: June 1. Required: high school transcript, college transcript(s) for transfer students, minimum 3.0 high school GPA, SAT I or ACT test scores. Auditions held on campus and off campus. Portfolio reviews held on campus and off campus.

Undergraduate Contact Jeffrey Showell, Assistant Director, School of Music and Dance, University of Arizona, Tucson, Arizona 85721; 520-621-1454, fax: 520-621-1351.

Graduate Contact Jocelyn Reiter, Director of Graduate Studies, School of Music and Dance, University of Arizona, Tucson, Arizona 85721; 520-621-1454, fax: 520-621-1351.

J. William Fulbright College of Arts and Sciences

University of Arkansas

Fayetteville, Arkansas

State-supported, coed. Small-town campus. Total enrollment: 14,655.

Degrees Bachelor of Music in the areas of performance, music education, composition, music history, music theory. Majors: composition, guitar, harpsichord, music education, music history, music theory, piano/organ, stringed instruments, voice, wind and percussion instruments. Graduate degrees offered: Master of Music in the areas of performance, music education, composition, music history, music theory, accompanying, conducting.

Music Student Profile Fall 1994: 208 total; 175 matriculated undergraduate, 23 matriculated graduate, 10 nondegree.

Music Faculty Total: 29; 25 full-time, 4 part-time; 100% of full-time faculty have terminal degrees. Graduate students teach a few undergraduate courses. Undergraduate student–faculty ratio: 8:1.

Expenses for 1995–96 Application fee: $15. State resident tuition: $2200 full-time, $95.33 per credit hour part-time. Nonresident tuition: $5392 full-time, $228.33 per credit hour part-time. Mandatory fees for engineering program: $277. Full-time mandatory fees: $130 (minimum). College room and board: $3468 (minimum).

Financial Aid Program-specific awards for Fall of 1994 available.

University of Arkansas *(continued)*

Application Procedures Deadline—freshmen and transfers: April 1. Required: high school transcript, audition, SAT I or ACT test scores, minimum composite ACT score of 19, minimum 2.75 high school GPA. Auditions held by appointment on campus; recorded music is permissible as a substitute for live auditions when distance is prohibitive and videotaped performances are permissible as a substitute for live auditions when distance is prohibitive.

Undergraduate Contact Chalon Ragsdale, Chair, Department of Music, University of Arkansas, 201 Music Building, Fayetteville, Arkansas 72701; 501-575-4701, fax: 501-575-5409.

Graduate Contact Dr. Stephen Gates, Associate Chair, Department of Music, University of Arkansas, 201 Music Building, Fayetteville, Arkansas 72701; 501-575-4701, fax: 501-575-5409.

University of Arkansas at Monticello

Monticello, Arkansas

State-supported, coed. Small-town campus. Total enrollment: 2,398.

Degrees Bachelor of Music Education in the areas of vocal music, keyboard, instrumental music. Majors: music education, piano/organ, voice, wind and percussion instruments. Cross-registration with University of Arkansas System.

Music Student Profile Fall 1994: 51 total; all matriculated undergraduate; 8% minorities, 27% females.

Music Faculty Total: 11; 7 full-time, 4 part-time. Graduate students do not teach undergraduate courses. Undergraduate student–faculty ratio: 8:1.

Student Life Student groups include Music Educators National Conference Student Chapter, Kappa Kappa Psi.

Expenses for 1995–96 State resident tuition: $1786 full-time, $74 per hour part-time. Nonresident tuition: $3898 full-time, $162 per hour part-time. Louisiana, Mississippi, and Texas residents pay state resident tuition. College room and board: $2410 (minimum). Special program-related fees: $25–$40 for private lessons.

Financial Aid Program-specific awards for Fall of 1994: 60 Band Grants-in-Aid for band players ($375–$1500), 50 Choir Grants-in-Aid for choir singers ($375–$1500), 5 Keyboard Grants-in-Aid for keyboardists ($375–$1500).

Application Procedures Deadline—freshmen and transfers: August 15. Required: high school transcript, college transcript(s) for transfer students, minimum 2.0 high school GPA, audition, ACT test score only. Auditions held 3 times on campus and off campus in various high schools.

Undergraduate Contact JoBeth Johnson, Director of Admissions, University of Arkansas at Monticello, P.O. Box 3600, Monticello, Arkansas 71656; 501-460-1026, fax: 501-460-1922.

University of Bridgeport

Bridgeport, Connecticut

Independent, coed. Urban campus. Total enrollment: 1,939.

Degrees Bachelor of Music in the areas of jazz studies, performance, music education. Majors: classical music, jazz, music, music education, piano/organ, stringed instruments, voice, wind and percussion instruments.

Music Student Profile Fall 1994: 30% minorities, 20% females, 30% international.

Music Faculty Total: 20; 3 full-time, 17 part-time; 100% of full-time faculty have terminal degrees. Graduate students do not teach undergraduate courses. Undergraduate student–faculty ratio: 9:1.

Student Life Student groups include Music Educators National Conference Student Chapter.

Expenses for 1994–95 Application fee: $35. Comprehensive fee of $19,934 includes full-time tuition ($12,500), mandatory fees ($624), and college room and board ($6810). College room only: $3700. Part-time tuition: $260 per credit. Part-time mandatory fees: $75 per year. Special program-related fees: $300–$700 for private lessons.

Financial Aid Program-specific awards for Fall of 1994: 15 Music Department Scholarships for high academic and musical achievement ($1200).

Application Procedures Deadline—freshmen and transfers: continuous. Required: high school transcript, audition. Recommended: essay, minimum 2.0 high school GPA, 3 letters of recommendation, interview. Auditions held 7 times on campus; recorded music is permissible as a substitute for live auditions and videotaped performances are permissible as a substitute for live auditions.

Undergraduate Contact Director, Admissions Office, University of Bridgeport, 126 Park Avenue, Wahlstrom Library, Bridgeport, Connecticut 06601; 800-898-8278.

University of British Columbia

Vancouver, British Columbia

Province-supported, coed. Urban campus. Total enrollment: 31,118.

Degrees Bachelor of Music in the areas of composition, general studies, elementary education stream, secondary education stream, guitar, music history and literature, music theory, opera, orchestral instruments, organ, piano, voice. Majors: composition, guitar, music history and literature, music theory, opera, orchestral instruments, piano/organ, voice. Graduate degrees offered: Master of Music in the areas of composition, piano, organ, voice, orchestral instruments, opera, guitar. Doctor of Musical Arts in the areas of composition, piano, voice, orchestral instruments.

Music Student Profile Fall 1994: 335 total; 257 matriculated undergraduate, 78 matriculated graduate.

Music Faculty Total: 79; 25 full-time, 54 part-time; 70% of full-time faculty have terminal degrees. Graduate students teach a few undergraduate courses.

Expenses for 1995–96 Canadian resident tuition: $2295 full-time, $76.50 per credit part-time. Nonresident tuition: $5738 full-time, $191.25 per credit part-time. Part-time mandatory fees: $11.45 per credit. (All figures are in Canadian dollars.). Full-time mandatory fees: $205. College room and board: $4300 (minimum). College room only: $2000 (minimum).

Application Procedures Deadline—freshmen and transfers: April 15. Required: essay, high school transcript, college transcript(s) for transfer students, minimum 2.0 high school GPA, 2 letters of recommendation, interview, audition, music theory examination, original music scores for composition applicants. Auditions held 1 time on campus; recorded music is permissible as a substitute for live auditions when distance is prohibitive and videotaped performances are permissible as a substitute for live auditions when distance is prohibitive. Portfolio reviews held 1 time on campus.

Undergraduate Contact Undergraduate Admissions, School of Music, University of British Columbia, 6361 Memorial Road, Vancouver, British Columbia V6T 1Z2, Canada; 604-822-2079, fax: 604-822-4884, E-mail address: isabelm@unixg.ubc.ca.

Graduate Contact Graduate Admissions, School of Music, University of British Columbia, 6361 Memorial Road, Vancouver, British Columbia V6T 1Z2, Canada; 604-822-2079, fax: 604-822-4884, E-mail address: isabelm@unixg.ubc.ca.

University of Calgary

Calgary, Alberta

Province-supported, coed. Urban campus. Total enrollment: 21,885.

Degrees Bachelor of Music in the areas of music education, performance, music theory, composition, music history, jazz studies, studio teaching. Majors: brass, classical music, jazz, music education, piano/organ, stringed instruments, voice, wind and percussion instruments. Graduate degrees offered: Master of Music in the areas of applied performance, composition, pedagogy, conducting, school music. Cross-registration with Mount Royal College.

Music Student Profile Fall 1994: 189 total; 163 matriculated undergraduate, 26 matriculated graduate; 1% minorities, 60% females, 10% international.

Music Faculty Total: 57; 23 full-time, 34 part-time; 80% of full-time faculty have terminal degrees. Graduate students teach a few undergraduate courses. Undergraduate student–faculty ratio: 8:1.

Student Life Student groups include Convocation, President's luncheon.

Estimated Expenses for 1995–96 Application fee: $60. Canadian resident tuition: $2660 full-time, $532 per course part-time. Nonresident tuition: $5320 full-time, $1064 per course part-time. Part-time mandatory fees: $48.35 per semester. (All figures are in Canadian dollars.). Full-time mandatory fees: $348. College room and board: $2900 (minimum). Special program-related fees: $100 for lab fee for recital hour course.

Financial Aid Program-specific awards for Fall of 1994: 30 Music Awards for high academic and musical achievement ($150–$3000).

Application Procedures Deadline—freshmen and transfers: May 1. Notification date—freshmen and transfers: June 15. Required: high school transcript, college transcript(s) for transfer students, minimum 3.0 high school GPA, audition. Auditions held on campus; recorded music is permissible as a substitute for live auditions when distance is prohibitive and videotaped performances are permissible as a substitute for live auditions when distance is prohibitive. Portfolio reviews held 1 for composition applicants on campus.

Undergraduate Contact C. Te Kamp, Undergraduate Academic Advisor, Music Department, University of Calgary, 2500 University Drive, NW, Calgary, Alberta T2N 1N4; 403-220-5379, fax: 403-284-0973.

Graduate Contact T. Ross, Undergraduate Academic Advisor, Music Department, University of Calgary, 2500 University Drive, NW, Calgary, Alberta T2N 1N4, Canada; 403-220-5379, fax: 403-284-0973.

University of California, Santa Barbara

Santa Barbara, California

State-supported, coed. Suburban campus. Total enrollment: 17,834.

Degrees Bachelor of Music in the areas of voice performance, composition, guitar, orchestral and instrumental performance, violin. Majors: composition, guitar, orchestral instruments, stringed instruments, voice, wind and percussion instruments. Graduate degrees offered: Master of Music in the areas of conducting, orchestral winds, percussion, piano, stringed instruments, voice. Doctor of Musical Arts in the areas of conducting, orchestral winds, percussion, piano, stringed instruments.

Music Student Profile Fall 1994: 170 total; 95 matriculated undergraduate, 75 matriculated graduate; 5% international.

Music Faculty Total: 44; 26 full-time, 18 part-time. Graduate students teach a few undergraduate courses.

Student Life Special housing available for music students.

Expenses for 1995–96 Application fee: $40. State resident tuition: $0 full-time. Nonresident tuition: $7699 full-time. Full-time mandatory fees: $4098. College room and board: $5990.

Financial Aid Program-specific awards for Fall of 1994: 10 Excellence in Entrance Awards for incoming freshmen ($300–$1500), 7 Grants-in-Aid for continuing program majors demonstrating need, musical and academic excellence ($300–$1500), 4 Quarterly Performance Awards for outstanding audition performers ($500), 1 Outstanding Early Music Award for early music program majors ($100), 1 Stanley Krebs Memorial Prize in Musicology for program majors ($100), 1 Outstanding Service Award for program majors ($200).

University of California, Santa Barbara *(continued)*

Application Procedures Deadline—freshmen and transfers: November 30. Notification date—freshmen: March 15; transfers: April 1. Required: essay, high school transcript, minimum 3.0 high school GPA, audition. Auditions held 1 time and by appointment on campus and off campus. Portfolio reviews held on campus and off campus.

Undergraduate Contact Robin Zierau-Cooper, Undergraduate Admissions, Department of Music, University of California, Santa Barbara, Santa Barbara, California 93106; 805-893-4603.

University of Central Arkansas

Conway, Arkansas

State-supported, coed. Small-town campus. Total enrollment: 9,192.

Degrees Bachelor of Music in the area of performance; Bachelor of Music Education in the area of music education. Majors: music, music education, piano/organ, stringed instruments, voice, wind and percussion instruments. Graduate degrees offered: Master of Music in the areas of performance, theory, conducting; Master of Music Education in the area of music education.

Music Student Profile Fall 1994: 1,430 total; 121 matriculated undergraduate, 15 matriculated graduate, 1,294 nondegree.

Music Faculty Total: 33; 19 full-time, 14 part-time. Undergraduate student–faculty ratio: 4:1.

Student Life Student groups include Music Teachers National Association competitions, Arkansas Symphony Orchestra, UCA Drama Department.

Expenses for 1995–96 State resident tuition: $2010 full-time, $88 per credit hour part-time. Nonresident tuition: $3834 full-time, $171 per credit hour part-time. Part-time mandatory fees per semester: $7.50 for the first 7 hours, $15 for the next 4 hours. College room and board: $2730. Special program-related fees: $30 for practice room fees.

Financial Aid Program-specific awards for Fall of 1994: 75 Music Scholarships for instrumental, orchestral, vocal, and keyboard students ($500–$1000).

Application Procedures Deadline—freshmen: continuous. Required: college transcript(s) for transfer students, minimum 2.0 high school GPA, audition, portfolio, ACT test score only, minimum composite ACT score of 19. Recommended: high school transcript, 3 letters of recommendation, interview. Auditions held 4 times and by appointment on campus and off campus; recorded music is permissible as a substitute for live auditions when distance is prohibitive or in special circumstances and videotaped performances are permissible as a substitute for live auditions when distance is prohibitive or in special circumstances. Portfolio reviews held as needed on campus and off campus.

Undergraduate Contact Gilbert Baker, Assistant Professor, Department of Music, University of Central Arkansas, UCA P.O. Box 4966, Conway, Arkansas 72035-0001; 501-450-5754, fax: 501-450-5773, E-mail address: gilbertb@ccl.uca.edu.

Graduate Contact Anne Patterson, Assistant Dean, College of Arts and Letters, Department of Music, University of Central Arkansas, UCA P.O. Box 4966, Conway, Arkansas 72035-0001; 501-450-5766, fax: 501-450-5773, E-mail address: annep@ccl.uca.edu.

University of Central Florida

Orlando, Florida

State-supported, coed. Suburban campus. Total enrollment: 25,363.

Degrees Bachelor of Music in the area of performance; Bachelor of Music Education in the areas of instrumental music education, choral music education, elementary music education. Majors: music, music education. Graduate degrees offered: Master of Music Education in the area of music education. Cross-registration with Seminole Community College, Valencia Community College.

Music Student Profile Fall 1994: 488 total; 171 matriculated undergraduate, 17 matriculated graduate, 300 nondegree; 15% minorities, 44% females, 1% international.

Music Faculty Total: 26; 14 full-time, 12 part-time; 80% of full-time faculty have terminal degrees. Graduate students do not teach undergraduate courses. Undergraduate student–faculty ratio: 11:1.

Expenses for 1995–96 Application fee: $20. State resident tuition: $1842 full-time, $58.19 per credit hour part-time. Nonresident tuition: $6743 full-time, $221.60 per credit hour part-time. Part-time mandatory fees: $47.30 per semester. Full-time mandatory fees: $95. College room and board: $4310. College room only: $2500.

Application Procedures Deadline—freshmen and transfers: July 15. Notification date—freshmen and transfers: continuous. Required: high school transcript, college transcript(s) for transfer students, minimum 2.0 high school GPA, audition, SAT I or ACT test scores. Recommended: letter of recommendation. Auditions held 2 times and by appointment on campus; recorded music is permissible as a substitute for live auditions if distance is prohibitive or scheduling is difficult and videotaped performances are permissible as a substitute for live auditions if distance is prohibitive or scheduling is difficult.

Undergraduate Contact Admissions Office, University of Central Florida, P.O. Box 160111, Orlando, Florida 32816-0111; 407-823-3000, fax: 407-823-5625.

Graduate Contact Dr. John Armstrong, Chair, Instructional Programs, College of Education, University of Central Florida, P.O. Box 25000, Orlando, Florida 32816-1250; 407-823-2439, fax: 407-823-5135.

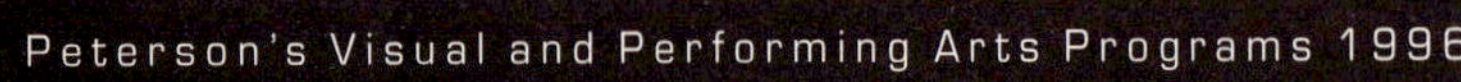

University of Central Oklahoma

Edmond, Oklahoma

State-supported, coed. Suburban campus. Total enrollment: 16,039.

Degrees Bachelor of Music in the areas of instrumental music, piano, voice, music theater; Bachelor of Music Education in the area of music education. Majors: music education, music theater, piano/organ, stringed instruments, voice, wind and percussion instruments. Graduate degrees offered: Master of Music Education in the area of music education.

Music Student Profile Fall 1994: 221 total; 203 matriculated undergraduate, 18 matriculated graduate; 10% minorities, 50% females, 5% international.

Music Faculty Total: 41; 19 full-time, 22 part-time; 58% of full-time faculty have terminal degrees. Graduate students teach a few undergraduate courses. Undergraduate student–faculty ratio: 11:1.

Student Life Student groups include Sigma Alpha Iota, Oklahoma Music Teachers Association, Music Educators National Conference.

Expenses for 1995–96 Application fee: $15. Full-time tuition ranges from $1212 to $1236 for state residents, $3274 to $3515 for nonresidents according to class level. Part-time tuition per credit hour ranges from $40.39 to $41.20 for state residents, $109.14 to $117.17 for nonresidents according to class level. College room and board: $2391. Special program-related fees: $5 for lab fees, $40 for private applied lessons, $18 for lessons.

Application Procedures Deadline—freshmen and transfers: continuous. Required: high school transcript, college transcript(s) for transfer students, minimum 2.0 high school GPA, ACT test score only, minimum composite ACT score of 19. Recommended: minimum 3.0 high school GPA, audition. Auditions held as needed on campus.

Undergraduate Contact Kent Kidwell, Chair, Music Department, University of Central Oklahoma, 100 North University Drive, Edmond, Oklahoma 73034; 405-341-2980 ext. 5004, fax: 405-341-4964.

Graduate Contact Karen Carter, Music Department, University of Central Oklahoma, 100 North University Drive, Edmond, Oklahoma 73034; 405-341-2980 ext. 5743, fax: 405-341-4964.

University of Cincinnati

Cincinnati, Ohio

State-supported, coed. Urban campus. Total enrollment: 18,473.

Degrees Bachelor of Music in the areas of performance, music education, keyboard, jazz, theory/history/composition, instrumental conducting. Majors: classical guitar, classical music, composition, harpsichord, instrumental conducting, jazz, music, music education, music theory, piano/organ, stringed instruments, voice, wind and percussion instruments. Graduate degrees offered: Master of Music in the areas of performance, music education, keyboard, theory/history/composition, conducting, accompanying. Doctor of Musical Arts in the areas of performance, keyboard, composition, conducting; Doctor of Music Education in the area of music education. Cross-registration with Greater Cincinnati Consortium of Colleges and Universities.

Music Student Profile Fall 1994: 876 total; 353 matriculated undergraduate, 523 matriculated graduate; 7% minorities, 43% females, 5% international.

Music Faculty 90% of full-time faculty have terminal degrees. Graduate students teach about a quarter undergraduate courses. Undergraduate student–faculty ratio: 7:1.

Student Life Student groups include Student Artist Program, several music fraternities and sororities.

Expenses for 1994–95 Application fee: $30. State resident tuition: $3732 full-time, $104 per credit hour part-time. Nonresident tuition: $9405 full-time, $261 per credit hour part-time. Full-time mandatory fees: $166. College room and board: $4698.

Financial Aid Program-specific awards for Fall of 1994: 76 Endowed Scholarships for program majors ($1600–$4500).

Application Procedures Deadline—freshmen and transfers: February 15. Notification date—freshmen and transfers: continuous. Required: high school transcript, letter of recommendation, interview, audition. Auditions held 9 times on campus and off campus in Atlanta, GA; Chicago, IL; Interlochen, MI; Los Angeles, CA; New York, NY; San Francisco, CA; recorded music is permissible as a substitute for live auditions with approval from the department and videotaped performances are permissible as a substitute for live auditions with approval from the department.

Contact Paul Hillner, Assistant Dean, Admissions and Student Services, University of Cincinnati, Conservatory of Music, 140 Emery Hall, Cincinnati, Ohio 45221-0003; 513-556-5462, fax: 513-556-1028, E-mail address: paul.hillner@uc.edu.

More about the University

The Corbett Center for the Performing Arts houses the 750-seat Corbett Auditorium, the 400-seat Patricia Corbett Theatre, the 140-seat Watson Recital Hall, three dance studios, four large rehearsal rooms, a large scene shop, three recital organs, 107 practice rooms, teaching studios, and classrooms. The Dieterle Vocal Arts Center, the newest addition to the CCM facility and given by Mr. and Mrs. Louis Nippert, is the home to the Voice, Opera, Choral, and Accompanying departments. It boasts 19 faculty studios, 3 private coaching rooms, the Italo Tajo Archive Room, 2 warm-up rooms, the 100-seat choral rehearsal room, and the choral library. The Center is also the location of the Nipper Rehearsal Studio, a large, grand opera–scale rehearsal space which has dressing rooms and technical support so that the space can double as a performance venue for workshops and concerts. The Gorno Memorial Music Library houses over 110,000 volumes, including books, music scores, periodicals, and numerous special collections of rare books, music, and recordings. The College also has four electronic music studios. The analog studio contains vintage synthesizers

University of Cincinnati *(continued)*

with more than 250 modules of Moog, Oberheim, ARP, and Emu and a Theremin. The Macintosh studio is equipped for automated mixing and synchronization, SMPTE, sampling, digital recording, and a variety of synthesis methods. The digital studio contains a NeXT computer for direct digital synthesis, digital editings, and advanced software development. The multiuser MIDI lab contains six independent synthesis workstations. Under way is an extensive reconstruction project that will result in a new studio theater, a new recital hall, expanded and renovated classroom and rehearsal facilities, studios, and practice rooms.

Faculty, Resident Artists, and Alumni CCM has over 130 faculty members plus numerous adjuncts including Dorothy DeLay and Kurt Sassmannshaus (violin), Masao Kawasaki (viola), Yehuda Hanani (violincello), Al Laszlo (double bass), William Winstead (bassoon), and James Tocco (piano and chamber music). Ensembles-In-Residence include the renowned Tokyo String Quartet and The Percussion Group/Cincinnati. Alumni continue to hold key positions in the performing and media arts. Numbered among them are American and European opera stars Kathleen Battle, Barbara Daniels, Katherine Keen, David Malis, Stanford Olsen, and Mark Oswald; producers Earl Hamner ("The Waltons" and "Falconcrest") and Dan Guntzelman ("Growing Pains"); musical theater stars Faith Prince, Lee Roy Reams, Michele Pawk, Jason Graae, Jim Walton, and Vicki Lewis; prima ballerina Suzanne Farrell; jazz great Al Hirt; composers Albert Hague *(Plain and Fancy, Redhead, How the Grinch Stole Christmas)*, Randy Edelman *(Last of the Mohicans, While You Were Sleeping)*, and Stephen Flaherty *(Once on This Island*, and a host of international competition winners and instrumentalists who hold positions in the major orchestras, both in the United States and in Europe. Over 800 performances a year take place at CCM by two large orchestras, three chamber orchestras, two wind ensembles, five choruses, over forty chamber groups, dance productions and choreographers' workshops, jazz ensembles, early music ensembles, brass choir, and 24 mainstage and workshop productions in opera, musical theater, and drama.

Special Programs The College and the University provide services in placement, counseling, a center for learning disabilities, a concert bureau (gig office), Student Artist performances, and internships as well as special remedial courses in English (not to be misinterpreted as an intensified English as a second language program).

The University of Cincinnati College-Conservatory of Music (CCM) is the result of the merger of two distinguished schools of music–The Cincinnati Conservatory of Music, established in 1867, and The College of Music at Cincinnati, established in 1878. This merger in 1955, and subsequent union with the University of Cincinnati in 1962, brought together the talents of a city long noted for its musical and performing arts.

Cited in the *New York Times* as "one of the nation's leading conservatories," CCM is among the nations most comprehensive conservatories–housing not only the standard disciplines of instrumental performance, voice, musicology, theory, and composition, but also music education, conducting, musical theater, drama, opera, theater design and production (makeup, lighting, scene design, stage management, costuming, and technical), electronic media, jazz and studio music, dance, and a graduate program in arts administration, accompanying, and opera coaching.

Performing groups are continually recognized for their outstanding achievements. The jazz ensemble has regularly won the *Down Beat* magazine award for the best student ensemble; the National Opera Association has honored the CCM opera program with 13 first-place awards in the past six years; and the wind department has been featured at major conventions and conferences in this country and in Japan and currently has eleven CDs on the market. Six additional outstanding CDs have been produced by the CCM Philharmonia orchestra, the Faculty Jazz Ensemble, and the Ensemble for Eighteenth Century Music.

In addition to the strengths of the College-Conservatory of Music, students have the resources of a major university at their disposal. The libraries of the University constitute a nationally recognized research center, with holdings that include 1.8 million bound volumes, 2.6 million microforms, and more than 19,500 serial subscriptions. They also offer access to an expanding number of libraries throughout the state via the OhioLINK on-line catalog.

The CCM Dance Division–the first music school in the United States to offer courses in classical ballet–is the founding institution and affiliate of the Cincinnati Ballet. Both the Cincinnati Ballet Company and the Cincinnati Opera Association offer numerous performance opportunities to dance majors. The Dance Division also offers continual ballet performance experience, featuring works by Division faculty and guest choreographers. Other opportunities exist in productions by the opera and musical theater areas of CCM.

Theater training offers a unique opportunity for CCM students because of the combination of instruction in vocal coaching, dance, opera, musical theater, drama, theater design and production, and arts administration within one division. Students have the opportunity to share in a wide-ranging scope of classes, major productions, workshop productions, master classes, and internships, including the three mainstage and summer productions in the highly successful Hot Summer Nights series. This remarkable sharing of experiences among experts in all areas of theater and arts administration allows students exposure to a wealth of learning opportunities. In addition, the Division manages CCM's three major theater complexes. Technical facilities include a 100′ x 50′ scene shop, costume shop, make-up shop, lighting lab, and state-of-the-art computerized lighting control mechanism for the theaters.

Student support offices serve the entire University population and offer academic counseling and tutoring, resume and interview skills training, psychological and personal counseling, student health clinics, day-care centers; special programming for ethnic groups and women, and a host of activities such as special interest clubs, student government, and intramural sports.

The extensive physical facilities of the University provide residence halls for students; banking services; swimming, tennis, track, volleyball, basketball, racquetball/handball, and bowling; and six restaurants ranging from fast food to table service.

Cincinnati, "North America's most livable city" *Places Rated Almanac*, 1993), is bordered on the south by the Ohio River and truly offers something for everyone.

Nearby Mt. Adams and the adjoining Eden Park, a stylish urban area perched on top of a hill with spectacular views of the city and the Ohio River and the home of the playhouse in the Park, the Cincinnati Art Museum, and the Krohn Conservatory. Within walking distance is University Village, offering inexpensive restaurants and shops. And just beyond is the Ludlow Avenue of Clifton, with its boutiques, restaurants, and gaslit, tree-lined streets. At the heart of downtown, just a 5-minute bus ride, is Fountain Square–the place Cincinnatians go to celebrate, to demonstrate, to welcome hometown heroes, or to bring in the new year. Also downtown are numerous and diverse cultural opportunities–The Cincinnati Symphony Orchestra, the Pops, the Cincinnati Opera, the Cincinnati Ballet, Ensemble Theatre of Cincinnati, the Broadway Series, the Museum Center at Union Terminal, the Contemporary Art Center, and more.

Both of CCM's founding schools, the Cincinnati Conservatory of Music and the College of Music of Cincinnati, were charter members of the National Association of Schools of Music (NASM), in which the present CCM plays a vital leadership role, and all theater programs have received accreditation from the National Association of Schools of Theater (NAST).

University of Colorado at Boulder

Boulder, Colorado

State-supported, coed. Urban campus. Total enrollment: 24,548.

Degrees Bachelor of Music in the areas of performance, music history; Bachelor of Music Education in the areas of instrumental music education, choral music education, general music education. Majors: brass, classical music, composition, jazz, music education, music history, opera, performance, piano/organ, sacred music, stringed instruments, voice, wind and percussion instruments. Graduate degrees offered: Master of Music in the areas of performance, conducting, music history, music theory, composition; Master of Music Education in the areas of choral conducting music education, instrumental conducting music education. Doctor of Musical Arts in the areas of performance, composition, choral conducting, instrumental conducting. Cross-registration with University of Colorado system.

Music Student Profile Fall 1994: 561 total; 320 matriculated undergraduate, 241 matriculated graduate; 14% minorities, 46% females, 8% international.

Music Faculty Total: 53; 53 full-time; 75% of full-time faculty have terminal degrees. Graduate students teach a few undergraduate courses. Undergraduate student–faculty ratio: 6:1.

Student Life Student groups include Sigma Alpha Iota, Phi Mu Alpha, Music Educators National Conference.

Expenses for 1995–96 Application fee: $40. Part-time tuition per credit hour ranges from $138 to $165 for state residents, $741 to $776 for nonresidents. Part-time mandatory fees per semester range from $55.99 to $243.70. Full-time tuition ranges from $2216 to $2672 for state residents, $12,780 to $13,374 for nonresidents according to program. Full-time mandatory fees: $487. College room and board: $4162.

Financial Aid Program-specific awards for Fall of 1994: 120 Music Scholarships for program majors ($500).

Application Procedures Deadline—freshmen and transfers: April 30. Notification date—freshmen and transfers: July 1. Required: high school transcript, minimum 2.0 high school GPA, letter of recommendation, audition. Auditions held weekly in February and by appointment on campus; recorded music is permissible as a substitute for live auditions when distance is prohibitive and videotaped performances are permissible as a substitute for live auditions when distance is prohibitive.

Undergraduate Contact Kevin McCarthy, Associate Dean for Undergraduate Studies, College of Music, University of Colorado at Boulder, Campus Box 301, Boulder, Colorado 80309-0301; 303-492-6354, fax: 303-492-5619.

Graduate Contact Deborah Hayes, Associate Dean for Graduate Studies, College of Music, University of Colorado at Boulder, Campus Box 301, Boulder, Colorado 80309-0301; 303-492-2207, fax: 303-492-5619.

University of Connecticut

Storrs, Connecticut

State-supported, coed. Rural campus. Total enrollment: 15,626.

Degrees Bachelor of Music in the areas of vocal performance, instrumental performance, music theory. Majors: music education, music theory, piano/organ, stringed instruments, voice, wind and percussion instruments. Graduate degrees offered: Master of Music in the areas of performance, performance with chamber music emphasis, performance with conducting (instrumental, choral), performance with Suzuki, composition, music education. Doctor of Musical Arts in the areas of performance, conducting.

Music Student Profile Fall 1994: 270 total; 160 matriculated undergraduate, 90 matriculated graduate, 20 nondegree; 6% minorities, 40% females, 3% international.

Music Faculty Total: 41; 22 full-time, 19 part-time; 100% of full-time faculty have terminal degrees. Graduate students teach a few undergraduate courses. Undergraduate student–faculty ratio: 9:1.

Student Life Student groups include Music Educators National Conference Student Chapter, American Choral Directors Association Student Chapter.

Expenses for 1995–96 Application fee: $40. State resident tuition: $3900 full-time. Nonresident tuition: $11,890 full-time. Part-time tuition per semester ranges from $163 to $1950 for state residents, $495 to $5945 for nonresidents. Part-time mandatory fees per semester range from $104 to $414. Full-time mandatory fees: $949. College room and board: $5124. Special program-related fees: $65–$125 for applied music fee.

Financial Aid Program-specific awards for Fall of 1994: 1–2 Victor Borge Awards for those demonstrating talent

University of Connecticut *(continued)*

and academic achievement ($1000–$3000), 1 Dean's Scholarship for those demonstrating talent and academic achievement ($2000–$5000).

Application Procedures Deadline—freshmen: April 1; transfers: May 1. Notification date—freshmen and transfers: July 1. Required: high school transcript, college transcript(s) for transfer students, 3 letters of recommendation, audition, SAT I test score only. Auditions held 2 times on campus; recorded music is permissible as a substitute for live auditions when distance is prohibitive and videotaped performances are permissible as a substitute for live auditions when distance is prohibitive.

Undergraduate Contact Dr. Thomas Vasil, Director of Undergraduate Studies, Music Department, University of Connecticut, 876 Coventry Road, U-12, Storrs, Connecticut 06269-1012; 203-486-1616, fax: 203-486-5845, E-mail address: tvasil@finearts.sfa.uconn.edu.

Graduate Contact Dr. Richard Bass, Director of Graduate Studies, Music Department, University of Connecticut, 876 Coventry Road, U-12, Storrs, Connecticut 06269-1012; 203-486-4197, fax: 203-486-5845, E-mail address: rbass@finearts.sfa.uconn.edu.

University of Dayton

Dayton, Ohio

Independent-religious, coed. Suburban campus. Total enrollment: 10,204.

Degrees Bachelor of Music in the areas of performance, music therapy, music composition; Bachelor of Music Education in the area of music education. Majors: classical music, composition, music, music education, music therapy, piano/organ, stringed instruments, voice, wind and percussion instruments.

Music Student Profile Fall 1994: 70 total; all matriculated undergraduate; 5% minorities, 60% females.

Music Faculty Total: 38; 15 full-time, 23 part-time; 75% of full-time faculty have terminal degrees. Graduate students do not teach undergraduate courses. Undergraduate student–faculty ratio: 15:1.

Student Life Student groups include music fraternity and sorority, Ohio Student Music Educators Club, Music Therapy Club.

Expenses for 1994–95 Comprehensive fee of $16,050 includes full-time tuition ($11,380), mandatory fees ($450), and college room and board ($4220). College room only: $2160. Part-time tuition per semester ranges from $380 to $4270. Part-time mandatory fees per semester range from $25 to $225. Special program-related fees: $110–$210 for lesson fees, $40 for pedagogy classes.

Financial Aid Program-specific awards for Fall of 1994: 10–13 Music Talent Awards for undergraduates ($3000), Reichard Awards for undergraduates ($500), Band Grants for band members.

Application Procedures Deadline—freshmen and transfers: continuous. Notification date—freshmen and transfers: continuous. Required: essay, high school transcript, 2 letters of recommendation, interview, audition, SAT I or ACT test scores. Recommended: minimum 3.0 high school GPA, portfolio. Auditions held 4 times and by appointment on campus; recorded music is permissible as a substitute for live auditions if a campus visit is impossible and videotaped performances are permissible as a substitute for live auditions if a campus visit is impossible. Portfolio reviews held 1 time for composition and music theory applicants on campus.

Undergraduate Contact Dr. Richard Chenoweth, Coordinator, Music Admissions, Department of Music, University of Dayton, 300 College Park, Dayton, Ohio 45469-0290; 513-229-3936, fax: 513-229-3916.

University of Delaware

Newark, Delaware

State-related, coed. Small-town campus. Total enrollment: 18,080.

Degrees Bachelor of Music in the areas of applied vocal and instrumental music, music theory and composition, music education; Bachelor of Music Education in the areas of instrumental music education, choral music education. Majors: classical music, jazz, music, music education, music theory and composition, opera, piano/organ, stringed instruments, voice, wind and percussion instruments. Graduate degrees offered: Master of Music in the areas of instrumental performance, vocal performance, music education.

Music Student Profile Fall 1994: 113 total; 98 matriculated undergraduate, 15 matriculated graduate; 1% minorities, 55% females, 1% international.

Music Faculty Total: 37; 22 full-time, 15 part-time; 59% of full-time faculty have terminal degrees. Graduate students teach a few undergraduate courses. Undergraduate student–faculty ratio: 2:1.

Student Life Student groups include Sigma Alpha Iota, Phi Mu Alpha, Music Educators National Conference. Special housing available for music students.

Expenses for 1995–96 Application fee: $40. State resident tuition: $3860 full-time, $161 per credit hour part-time. Nonresident tuition: $10,730 full-time, $447 per credit hour part-time. Full-time mandatory fees: $426. College room and board: $4420.

Financial Aid Program-specific awards for Fall of 1994: 7 Jastak-Burgess Awards for those demonstrating musical achievement ($3000), 10–12 Arts and Humanities Awards for state residents demonstrating need/talent ($1500–$2000), 6 Quigley Awards for female state residents ($1000–$2500), 4 Music Department Awards for talented majors in needed instruments ($1000–$2500).

Application Procedures Deadline—freshmen and transfers: March 1. Notification date—freshmen and transfers: April 15. Required: high school transcript, audition. Auditions held 3 times on campus.

Undergraduate Contact Bruce Walker, Associate Provost for Admissions, University of Delaware, 116 Hullihen Hall, Newark, Delaware 19716; 302-831-8125, fax: 302-831-6905.

Graduate Contact Carol Hoffecker, Associate Provost for Graduate Studies, University of Delaware, Willard Hall-Educational Building, Newark, Delaware 19716; 302-831-2129.

More about the University

Program Facilities The modern Amy E. du Pont Music building houses all music classrooms and teaching studios, rehearsal and practice rooms, special laboratories for electric piano and music education, two professional classical recording studios, and the 440-seat Loudis Recital Hall. The on-site music Resource Center contains listening and viewing facilities for sound and video recordings, supplementing the extensive music holdings of the University's main library.

Faculty and Alumni Faculty are members of the Delaware Symphony and other regional orchestras and perform internationally as soloists and chamber artists. Resident Faculty Chamber Ensembles include the Mendelssohn String Quartet, the Del'Arte Wind Quintet, the Delaware Brass, the Taggart-Grycky Flute and Guitar Duo, and the University of Delaware Faculty Jazz.

Student Performance Opportunities Instrumental ensembles: wind ensemble, jazz ensembles, marching band, symphonic band, percussion ensemble, orchestra, small ensembles (brass, winds, guitar, strings). Vocal ensembles: chorale, men's chorus, opera workshop, women's chorus, University Singers. The Collegium Musicum provides vocalists and instrumentalists an opportunity to study and perform music from the Middle Ages, the Renaissance, and the early Baroque period. Non-western musical tradition is represented by a Gamelan Ensemble. solo performance in piano, voice, guitar, and orchestral instruments is highlighted by the university of Delaware Student Concerto Competition, which annually provides several student soloists with the opportunity to perform in concert with a professional symphony orchestra.

Special Programs The University of Delaware provides a full range of services for students with permanent and temporary disabilities and for international students. The University Honors Program provides enriched learning opportunities for those who qualify.

The University of Delaware combines the friendliness, security, personal attention, and emphasis on teaching characteristic of a small-college environment with the stimulating atmosphere of a major state university. Student life is enriched by the attractive campus; the comfortable, college-town setting, the intellectual and social resources of the University; and the ease of access to Philadelphia, New York, Baltimore, and Washington.

For over fifty years, the Department of Music at the University of Delaware, a full member of the National Association of Schools of Music, has provided a broad range of opportunities for students of varied musical backgrounds. The Department offers professional Bachelor of Music degrees in performance, music education, and theory/composition while maintaining a thriving Bachelor of Arts program with a major in music. The Department also has an unusually strong commitment to music minors, who may find that the combination of a minor in applied music, musical studies, or jazz studies while majoring in any of the strong academic programs offered by the University is an attractive option. This flexibility for students at Delaware to incorporate professional training in music with a strong interest in other fields is made possible by the department's position within a college of arts and science.

At the heart of the Department are the music faculty membersall professionally active performers, composers, music educators, and music historians. Their accomplishments are reflected in numerous honors, publications, recordings, and performances that serve to bring much-deserved attention to the quality of instruction available in the University of Delaware Department of Music. A low student-faculty ratio affords all students the opportunity of working closely with this community of artists and scholars, who are personally supportive of each student's goals, providing an ideal atmosphere for study in music.

The University of Delaware Department of Music has an international reputation for achievements in technology-based music instruction. Employed as a supplement to classroom teaching,the systems provide individualized instruction tailored to a student's listening experiences and responses. The Department also utilizes technology allowing for interaction between electronic keyboards, computers, and synthesizers. The award-winning *University of Delaware Videodisc Music Series* is an educational tool that has revolutionized the study of musical masterworks, enhancing instruction at Delaware in the history and appreciation of music. A new computer-based instruction project at the University of Delaware–*Jazz Theory Lessons*– was recently funded by the U.S. Department of Education and will allow the development of an innovative method of teaching the fundamentals of jazz theory at the university level.

Over 12,000 concertgoers attend the nearly 100 recitals, lectures, and master classes presented annually by Music Department faculty, students, and distinguished guest artists who, in recent years, have included John Corigliano, Joan Tower, Gary Burton, John Browning, Igor Kipnis, Martina Arroyo, Robert Mann, Harvey Phillips, Nexus, and Ursula Oppens. Special annual events include the Student Concerto Competition Winners Concert; the University of Delaware Winter Institute for String Quartets; New Music Delaware, a festival of contemporary music; and the Opera Workshop production.

Lamont School of Music

University of Denver

Denver, Colorado

Independent, coed. Suburban campus. Total enrollment: 8,522.

Degrees Bachelor of Music in the areas of performance, jazz, commercial music; Bachelor of Arts/Bachelor of Fine Arts in the area of music. Majors: accordian, classical music, commercial music, jazz, music, music education, piano/organ, stringed instruments, voice, wind and percussion instruments. Graduate degrees offered: Master of Music in the areas of performance, composition; Master of Music Education in the area of music.

University of Denver *(continued)*

Music Student Profile Fall 1994: 160 total; 125 matriculated undergraduate, 35 matriculated graduate; 10% minorities, 50% females, 15% international.

Music Faculty Total: 38; 21 full-time, 17 part-time; 30% of full-time faculty have terminal degrees. Graduate students do not teach undergraduate courses. Undergraduate student–faculty ratio: 6:1.

Student Life Student groups include music specific Greek organizations. Special housing available for music students.

Expenses for 1994–95 Application fee: $35. Comprehensive fee of $19,995 includes full-time tuition ($15,192), mandatory fees ($108), and college room and board ($4695). Part-time tuition: $422 per quarter hour.

Financial Aid Program-specific awards for Fall of 1994: 85 Music Activity Grants for program majors ($5000), 5 Endowed Awards for specific program students ($6000).

Application Procedures Deadline—freshmen and transfers: continuous. Required: essay, high school transcript, college transcript(s) for transfer students, SAT I or ACT test scores. Recommended: interview, audition. Auditions held 4-6 times on campus and off campus in Los Angeles, CA; Chicago, IL; recorded music is permissible as a substitute for live auditions if a campus visit is impossible and videotaped performances are permissible as a substitute for live auditions if a campus visit is impossible. Portfolio reviews held on campus and off campus.

Contact Arthur E. Bouton, Director of Admissions, Lamont School of Music, University of Denver, 7111 Montview Boulevard, Denver, Colorado 80220; 303-871-6400, fax: 303-871-3118, E-mail address: abouton@du.edu.

University of Evansville

Evansville, Indiana

Independent-religious, coed. Suburban campus. Total enrollment: 3,162.

Degrees Bachelor of Music in the areas of performance, performance (Suzuki emphasis), music therapy, music education. Majors: classical guitar, classical music, music, music education, music management, music therapy, piano/organ, stringed instruments, voice, wind and percussion instruments.

Music Student Profile Fall 1994: 120 total; all matriculated undergraduate; 5% minorities, 5% international.

Music Faculty Total: 24; 18 full-time, 6 part-time; 100% of full-time faculty have terminal degrees. Graduate students do not teach undergraduate courses. Undergraduate student–faculty ratio: 8:1.

Student Life Student groups include National Association for Music Therapy Student Chapter, Music Educators National Conference Student Chapter, Phi Mu Alpha/Sigma Alpha Iota.

Expenses for 1995–96 Application fee: $30. Comprehensive fee of $16,570 includes full-time tuition ($12,400) and college room and board ($4170 minimum). Part-time tuition: $365 per semester hour. Special program-related fees: $200 for applied music fee.

Financial Aid Program-specific awards for Fall of 1994: 25–30 Academic Scholarships for those demonstrating talent and academic achievement ($2000–$5000).

Application Procedures Deadline—freshmen: May 1; transfers: June 1. Required: essay, high school transcript, college transcript(s) for transfer students, minimum 2.0 high school GPA, audition, SAT I or ACT test scores. Recommended: minimum 3.0 high school GPA, letter of recommendation. Auditions held 6 times on campus; recorded music is permissible as a substitute for live auditions when distance is prohibitive and videotaped performances are permissible as a substitute for live auditions when distance is prohibitive.

Undergraduate Contact Dr. Alan L. Solomon, Chair, Music Department, University of Evansville, 1800 Lincoln Avenue, Evansville, Indiana 47722; 812-479-2754, fax: 812-479-2101, E-mail address: as7@evansville.edu.

University of Florida

Gainesville, Florida

State-supported, coed. Suburban campus. Total enrollment: 38,277.

Degrees Bachelor of Music in the areas of performance, music history, music theory, composition, church music, music education. Majors: composition, music education, music history and literature, music theory, piano/organ, sacred music, stringed instruments, voice, wind and percussion instruments. Graduate degrees offered: Master of Music in the areas of music education, performance, conducting, composition, music theory, music history and literature, sacred music, pedagogy, accompanying.

Music Student Profile Fall 1994: 184 total; 128 matriculated undergraduate, 46 matriculated graduate, 10 nondegree; 10% minorities, 53% females, 2% international.

Music Faculty Total: 38; 32 full-time, 6 part-time; 75% of full-time faculty have terminal degrees. Graduate students teach a few undergraduate courses. Undergraduate student–faculty ratio: 5:1.

Student Life Student groups include Collegiate Music Educators National Conference, Sigma Alpha Iota, Phi Kappa Phi.

Expenses for 1995–96 Application fee: $20. State resident tuition: $1820 full-time, $56.83 per semester hour part-time. Nonresident tuition: $7090 full-time, $220.24 per semester hour part-time. College room and board: $4310. College room only: $2050.

Financial Aid Program-specific awards for Fall of 1994: 100 Friends of Music Scholarships for program majors ($400–$1500), 40–55 Band Scholarships for band members ($400–$800).

Application Procedures Deadline—freshmen: January 31; transfers: June 1. Notification date—freshmen: May 1; transfers: July 31. Required: high school transcript, college transcript(s) for transfer students, minimum 2.0 high school GPA, letter of recommendation, interview, audition, SAT I or ACT test scores. Auditions held 3–4 times on campus; recorded music is permissible as a substitute for live auditions for out-of-state applicants and videotaped performances are permissible as a substitute for live auditions for out-of-state applicants.

Contact Linda Black, Director of Music Admissions, Music Department, University of Florida, 130 Music Building, P.O. Box 117900, Gainesville, Florida 32611-7900; 904-392-0223, fax: 904-392-0461.

University of Georgia

Athens, Georgia

State-supported, coed. Suburban campus. Total enrollment: 29,469.

Degrees Bachelor of Music in the areas of performance, composition, music therapy, music theory, church music; Bachelor of Music Education in the area of music education. Majors: classical music, composition, conducting, music, music education, music history, music theory, music therapy, piano/organ, sacred music, stringed instruments, voice, wind and percussion instruments. Graduate degrees offered: Master of Music in the areas of musicology, composition, music literature, performance; Master of Music Education in the areas of music education, music therapy. Doctor of Musical Arts in the areas of performance, composition, music education, choral conducting.

Music Student Profile Fall 1994: 386 total; 297 matriculated undergraduate, 80 matriculated graduate, 9 nondegree; 6% minorities, 50% females, 8% international.

Music Faculty Total: 55; 45 full-time, 10 part-time; 97% of full-time faculty have terminal degrees. Graduate students teach a few undergraduate courses. Undergraduate student–faculty ratio: 10:1.

Student Life Student groups include Music Educators National Conference, National Association of Music Therapy, Music Teachers National Association. Special housing available for music students.

Expenses for 1995–96 Application fee: $25. State resident tuition: $2508 full-time, $56 per quarter hour part-time. Nonresident tuition: $6795 full-time, $176 per quarter hour part-time. College room and board: $3876. College room only: $1776. Special program-related fees: $30 for instrument maintenance.

Financial Aid Program-specific awards for Fall of 1994: 40 Band Scholarships for wind and percussion students ($1500), 40 Music Scholarships for voice, piano, and string majors ($1200).

Application Procedures Deadline—freshmen: March 15; transfers: April 15. Notification date—freshmen and transfers: June 15. Required: high school transcript, minimum 3.0 high school GPA, 3 letters of recommendation, interview, audition, SAT I or ACT test scores, minimum combined SAT I score of 900, minimum composite ACT score of 21. Auditions held 6 times on campus; recorded music is permissible as a substitute for live auditions when distance is prohibitive or scheduling is difficult and videotaped performances are permissible as a substitute for live auditions when distance is prohibitive or scheduling is difficult.

Undergraduate Contact David Randolph, Coordinator of Undergraduate Studies, School of Music, University of Georgia, Fine Arts Building, Athens, Georgia 30602; 706-542-2764, fax: 706-542-2773.

Graduate Contact Jolene Davis, Coordinator of Graduate Studies, School of Music, University of Georgia, Fine Arts Building, Athens, Georgia 30602; 706-542-2743, fax: 706-542-2773.

The Hartt School

University of Hartford

West Hartford, Connecticut

Independent, coed. Suburban campus. Total enrollment: 7,253.

Degrees Bachelor of Music in the areas of performance, jazz/African–American music, music theater, music management, composition, music history, music theory, music education, production and technology. Majors: brass, classical music, composition, jazz, music education, music history, music management, music theater, music theory, performance art, performing arts management, piano/organ, production/technology, stringed instruments, voice, wind and percussion instruments. Graduate degrees offered: Master of Music in the areas of performance, opera, liturgical music, conducting, composition, music history, music theory; Master of Music Education in the areas of performance, classroom teaching, conducting, pedagogy. Doctor of Musical Arts in the areas of performance, composition, music education. Cross-registration with Trinity College, Saint Joseph College, The Hartford Graduate Center, Hartford Seminary.

Music Student Profile Fall 1994: 485 total; 365 matriculated undergraduate, 100 matriculated graduate, 20 nondegree; 10% minorities, 60% females, 10% international.

Music Faculty Total: 125; 50 full-time, 75 part-time; 100% of full-time faculty have terminal degrees. Graduate students teach a few undergraduate courses. Undergraduate student–faculty ratio: 5:1.

Student Life Student groups include Music Educators National Conference Student Chapter, music fraternity and sorority, Music Management Association.

Expenses for 1995–96 Comprehensive fee of $21,875 includes full-time tuition ($14,860), mandatory fees ($750), and college room and board ($6265). College room only: $3865. Part-time tuition: $310 per credit. Part-time mandatory fees: $50 per semester.

Financial Aid Program-specific awards for Fall of 1994: 237 Talent Scholarships for undergraduates ($6000).

Application Procedures Deadline—freshmen and transfers: continuous. Required: high school transcript, minimum 2.0 high school GPA, 3 letters of recommendation, audition. Recommended: essay, minimum 3.0 high school

University of Hartford *(continued)*

GPA, interview. Auditions held 5 times on campus; recorded music is permissible as a substitute for live auditions when distance is prohibitive and videotaped performances are permissible as a substitute for live auditions when distance is prohibitive.

Contact James Jacobs, Director of Admissions, The Hartt School, University of Hartford, 200 Bloomfield Avenue, West Hartford, Connecticut 06117; 203-768-4465, fax: 203-768-4441.

University of Hawaii at Manoa

Honolulu, Hawaii

State-supported, coed. Urban campus. Total enrollment: 19,983.

Degrees Bachelor of Music in the areas of composition, performance. Majors: classical music, composition, ethnomusicology, guitar, music, music education, music theory, piano, stringed instruments, voice, wind and percussion instruments. Graduate degrees offered: Master of Music in the areas of composition, performance.

Music Student Profile Fall 1994: 172 total; 118 matriculated undergraduate, 47 matriculated graduate, 7 nondegree; 47% females, 18% international.

Music Faculty Total: 53; 23 full-time, 30 part-time; 100% of full-time faculty have terminal degrees. Graduate students teach a few undergraduate courses. Undergraduate student–faculty ratio: 7:1.

Student Life Student groups include American Choral Directors Association Student Chapter, Circle of Fifths (departmental student organization), Music Educators National Conference Student Chapter.

Expenses for 1995–96 Application fee: $10. State resident tuition: $1631 full-time, $68 per credit part-time. Nonresident tuition: $4825 full-time, $201 per credit part-time. College room and board: $4210. College room only: $2400.

Financial Aid Program-specific awards for Fall of 1994: 197 Tuition Waivers for band and orchestra members ($1400–$4260), 30 Scholarships for program majors ($200–$9000).

Application Procedures Deadline—freshmen and transfers: May 1. Required: high school transcript, college transcript(s) for transfer students, minimum 2.0 high school GPA, SAT I or ACT test scores, standing in top 40% of class for transfer students. Recommended: minimum 3.0 high school GPA, letter of recommendation, interview, audition, portfolio. Auditions held 1 time and by appointment on campus; recorded music is permissible as a substitute for live auditions for out-of-state applicants and videotaped performances are permissible as a substitute for live auditions for out-of-state applicants. Portfolio reviews held 1 time and by appointment for composition applicants on campus.

Undergraduate Contact Dale Hall, Undergraduate Chairman, Music Department, University of Hawaii at Manoa, 2411 Dole Street, Honolulu, Hawaii 96822; 808-956-2129, fax: 808-956-9657.

Graduate Contact Byron K. Yasui, Graduate Chairman, Music Department, University of Hawaii at Manoa, 2411 Dole Street, Honolulu, Hawaii 96822; 808-956-2175, fax: 808-956-9657.

University of Houston

Houston, Texas

State-supported, coed. Urban campus. Total enrollment: 31,298.

Degrees Bachelor of Music in the areas of applied music, music with teaching certificate, music theory, composition. Majors: classical music, composition, music, music education, music theory, opera, piano/organ, stringed instruments, voice, wind and percussion instruments. Graduate degrees offered: Master of Music in the areas of applied music, music theory, composition, musical literature, music education, accompanying and chamber music, performance and pedagogy. Doctor of Musical Arts in the areas of performance, conducting, composition, music education.

Music Student Profile Fall 1994: 503 total; 371 matriculated undergraduate, 132 matriculated graduate; 27% minorities, 53% females, 10% international.

Music Faculty Total: 59; 38 full-time, 21 part-time; 86% of full-time faculty have terminal degrees. Graduate students teach a few undergraduate courses. Undergraduate student–faculty ratio: 11:1.

Student Life Student groups include Phi Mu Alpha Sinfonia, Sigma Alpha Iota.

Expenses for 1994–95 Application fee: $25. State resident tuition: $840 full-time. Nonresident tuition: $5130 full-time, $171 per semester hour part-time. State resident part-time tuition per semester ranges from $100 to $308. Part-time mandatory fees per semester range from $93 to $333. Full-time mandatory fees: $754. College room and board: $4608. College room only: $2340. Special program-related fees: $15 for piano use, $50–$100 for private lessons.

Financial Aid Program-specific awards for Fall of 1994: 150–200 Music Scholarships for undergraduates ($500), 100–125 Band Grants for undergraduates ($200), 20–30 Delores Welder Mitchell Awards for outstanding scholars ($250).

Application Procedures Deadline—freshmen and transfers: July 15. Required: high school transcript, college transcript(s) for transfer students, minimum 2.0 high school GPA, audition, SAT I or ACT test scores. Recommended: minimum 3.0 high school GPA, letter of recommendation, interview. Auditions held 4 times on campus; recorded music is permissible as a substitute for live auditions when distance is prohibitive or scheduling is difficult and videotaped performances are permissible as a substitute for live auditions when distance is prohibitive or scheduling is difficult.

Undergraduate Contact Academic Advisor, School of Music, University of Houston, Houston, Texas 77204-4893; 713-743-3009, fax: 713-743-3166, E-mail address: dkeller@uh.edu.

Graduate Contact Director of Graduate Studies, School of Music, University of Houston, Houston, Texas 77204-4893; 713-743-3151, fax: 713-743-3166.

More about the University

Program Facilities Performance spaces include Cullen Performance Hall (1,200 seats), Dudley Hall (300 seats), Organ Hall (200 seats). Facilities also include an electronic music studio and a computer/synthesizer cluster. The School of Music will move into new $15-million facilities in Summer 1996; these facilities will include an 800-seat auditorium, recording studio, five large and six chamber ensemble rehearsal rooms, and over sixty practice rooms.

Faculty, Resident Artists, and Alumni Faculty are members of the Houston Symphony, the Houston Ballet, and the Houston Grand Opera Orchestra and have held principal positions in the Houston, Pittsburgh, Vancouver, NBC, Indianapolis, Miami Chamber, and Fort Worth symphonies as well as appearing in chamber recitals and as soloists with orchestras and opera companies both in the United States and abroad. Alumni hold positions in major orchestras and opera companies and pursue active solo careers. Music educators from the School of Music are in great demand, receiving numerous honors and awards and directing some of the state's most successful music programs.

Student Performance/Exhibit Opportunities Performance opportunities include the University Orchestra, chamber orchestra, two wind ensembles, concert band, marching band, two jazz ensembles, jazz combos, University Opera Theatre, opera workshop, University Chorus, University Chorale, Chamber Singers, women's chorus, new music ensemble, percussion ensemble, horn ensemble, trombone ensemble, trumpet ensemble, and various chamber ensembles. There are numerous performance and teaching opportunities throughout the city for students.

Special Programs Opera Studio gives select graduate students performing experience with the Houston Grand Opera; Minority Internship in Orchestral Performance is offered in conjunction with the Houston Symphony; an intensive monthlong summer orchestral and chamber music program, the Texas Music Festival, also includes piano, jazz, and junior high band institutes; International Piano Festival brings in 3 artists each year for recitals and master classes; A. I. Lack Music Master Series offers a number of master classes each year with internationally recognized performers.

Lionel Hampton School of Music

University of Idaho

Moscow, Idaho

State-supported, coed. Small-town campus. Total enrollment: 11,730.

Degrees Bachelor of Music in the areas of performance, composition; Bachelor of Music Education in the areas of instrumental music education, choral music education, elementary music education. Majors: composition, music education, piano/organ, stringed instruments, voice, wind and percussion instruments. Graduate degrees offered: Master of Music in the areas of performance, music education, pedagogy, accompanying, composition. Cross-registration with Washington State University.

Music Student Profile Fall 1994: 200 total; 180 matriculated undergraduate, 18 matriculated graduate, 2 nondegree; 3% minorities, 48% females, 4% international.

Music Faculty Total: 23; 20 full-time, 3 part-time; 90% of full-time faculty have terminal degrees. Graduate students teach a few undergraduate courses. Undergraduate student–faculty ratio: 12:1.

Student Life Student groups include Sigma Alpha Iota (music honorary sorority), Pi Kappa Lambda (music honorary fraternity), Music Educators National Conference Student Chapter.

Expenses for 1995–96 Application fee: $25. State resident tuition: $0 full-time, $81 per credit part-time. Nonresident tuition: $5380 full-time, $190 per credit part-time. Full-time mandatory fees: $1620. College room and board: $4280.

Financial Aid Program-specific awards for Fall of 1994: 85 Music Merit Scholarships for those passing audition evaluations ($200–$2500), 12 Out-of-State Tuition Waivers for non-resident program majors ($4614).

Application Procedures Deadline—freshmen and transfers: August 1. Required: high school transcript, college transcript(s) for transfer students, minimum 2.0 high school GPA, audition, SAT I or ACT test scores. Auditions held as needed on campus; recorded music is permissible as a substitute for live auditions by request and videotaped performances are permissible as a substitute for live auditions by request.

Undergraduate Contact Office of New Student Services, University of Idaho, Student Union Building, Moscow, Idaho 83844-4253; 208-885-6163.

Graduate Contact Roger Wallins, Dean, College of Graduate Studies, University of Idaho, 112 Morrill Hall, Moscow, Idaho 83844-4253; 208-885-6243.

University of Illinois at Urbana-Champaign

Champaign, Illinois

State-supported, coed. Small-town campus. Total enrollment: 36,191.

Degrees Bachelor of Music in the areas of performance, composition, music theory, music history; Bachelor of Music Education in the area of music education. Majors: classical music, composition, jazz, music, music history, music theory, piano/organ, stringed instruments, voice, wind and percussion instruments. Graduate degrees offered: Master of Music in the areas of musicology, music theory, composition, performance and literature, choral conducting, instrumental conducting, vocal accompanying and coaching, group piano pedagogy; Master of Music Education in the area of music education. Doctor of Musical Arts in the areas of composition, piano, organ, choral music, voice, violin, cello, wind instruments, percussion instruments.

University of Illinois at Urbana-Champaign
(continued)

Music Student Profile Fall 1994: 683 total; 400 matriculated undergraduate, 283 matriculated graduate; 11% minorities, 52% females, 8% international.

Music Faculty Total: 78; 60 full-time, 18 part-time; 87% of full-time faculty have terminal degrees. Graduate students teach about a quarter undergraduate courses. Undergraduate student–faculty ratio: 9:1.

Student Life Student groups include Music Educators National Conference, Sigma Alpha Iota, Phi Mu Alpha Sinfonia.

Expenses for 1994–95 Application fee: $30. Part-time mandatory fees per semester range from $201 to $474. Full-time tuition ranges from $2760 to $2900 for state residents, $7560 to $7980 for nonresidents, according to class level. Part-time tuition per semester ranges from $480 to $977 for state residents, $1300 to $2607 for nonresidents, according to class level and course load. Full-time mandatory fees: $920. College room and board: $4260. Special program-related fees: $200–$400 for additional music equipment and instructional support.

Financial Aid Program-specific awards for Fall of 1994: 16 Thomas J. Smith Scholarships for female students from Illinois ($3100), Performance Awards for program majors ($2000).

Application Procedures Deadline—freshmen and transfers: continuous. Required: high school transcript, college transcript(s) for transfer students, 3 letters of recommendation, interview, audition, portfolio, SAT I or ACT test scores. Auditions held 6 times on campus; recorded music is permissible as a substitute for live auditions. Portfolio reviews held 6 times for composition applicants on campus.

Undergraduate Contact Mark S. Rabideau, Coordinator of Undergraduate Admissions, School of Music, University of Illinois at Urbana-Champaign, 1114 West Nevada Street, Urbana, Illinois 61801; 217-244-0551, fax: 217-244-4585, E-mail address: axfugad@uicvmc.aiss.uiuc.edu.

Graduate Contact Tom R. Ward, Coordinator of Graduate Studies, School of Music, University of Illinois at Urbana-Champaign, 1114 West Nevada Street, Urbana, Illinois 61801; 217-333-1712, fax: 217-244-4585, E-mail address: tomward@ux1.cso.uiuc.edu.

More about the University

Program Facilities Performance sites (including recording facilities): Foellinger Great Hall (2,100 seats); Tryon Festival Opera Theatre (950 seats); Smith Recital Hall (900 seats, with concert organ); Colwell Playhouse (700 seats); Music Auditorium (250 seats); Studio Theatre (200 seats, for mixed media and contemporary music performances); and Smith Memorial Room (70 seats). Experimental Music Studios (among the largest such facilities in the United States), Computer Music Laboratory, Piano Pedagogy Resource Room, Digital Keyboard Classroom, and computer-assisted instructional labs are available for student use. The Music Library is one of the largest public music libraries in the United States. A. A. Harding Band Building contains John Philip Sousa Collection, Herbert L. Clarke Library and Collection, Busch Instrument Collection, and Harding Archives.

Faculty, Resident Artists, and Alumni Guest artists and scholars, including distinguished alumni, and visiting ensembles provide master classes, lectures, and coaching for students and include the Kronos Quartet; Kalichstein, Laredo, Robinson Trio; members of the San Francisco Symphony; Louis Bellson; Barbara Andress; Samuel Sanders; Toby Twining; Christian Lindberg; and others.

Student Performance Opportunities Eleven choral ensembles, nine bands, two orchestras, two contemporary music ensembles, four jazz bands, year-round opera company, numerous chamber groups, percussion ensemble, and steel drum band. Also features Andean Pipe and African Mbira ensembles, Javanese gamelan, and a Russian Folk Orchestra. Resident faculty present weekly master classes, colloquia, and forums.

Special Programs Student-designed majors in music theater, music business, and others; cooperative curricula in pre-med and pre-law; outstanding ESL and intensive English programs for international students; Public Service Division providing students with additional musical experience and employment; foreign study and performance opportunities available for undergraduate and graduate students.

Founded in 1895 as a department in the College of Literature and Arts, the School of Music is celebrating its first century of distinguished service to higher education and the arts.

The School of Music attracts accomplished students and faculty members in composition/theory, music education, musicology, and performance. It is large enough to provide a wide variety of experience for students seeking professional degrees in music. At the same time, the atmosphere of a smaller school prevails, with emphasis on individualized instruction in performance and comparatively small classes.

The principal strength of the School of Music lies in its faculty. Distinguished and internationally recognized in the areas of teaching, performing, composition, and research, the faculty members contribute substantially to virtually all areas of music. The wealth of experience that they bring to the classroom, concert hall, and studio is complemented by their continuous commitment to excellence. The professional relationship between students and faculty is based upon mutual respect and a common interest in the quest for musical knowledge and artistry.

As a significant cultural resource, the School of Music serves the musical needs of various constituencies, from the local community to an international audience. Two local and many regional professional orchestras and opera companies regularly employ students. Local churches and jazz clubs provide additional performance opportunities for instrumentalists and vocalists. School of Music ensembles recently performed at national meetings of such prestigious organizations as American Bandmasters Association, American Choral Directors Association, International Trombone Association, International Trumpet Guild, Music Educator's National Conference, and the Mid-West International Band and Orchestra Clinic.

One measure of a university's quality is the success of its graduates. Among the nearly 6,000 living alumni of the School of Music are 2 Pulitzer Prize winners in composition; members of major symphony orchestras, opera companies, jazz ensembles, and professional choral groups; and faculty members at many of the nation's most prestigious colleges and universities. Music education graduates direct elementary and secondary music programs in nearly every state in the union as well as in other countries.

The School has a proven record for assisting qualified graduates to assume leadership roles in the music profession through career counseling and professional advising.

The University of Illinois is a residential campus of more than 700 acres, located approximately 130 miles south of Chicago. The University and the surrounding communities of Champaign and Urbana offer a cultural and recreational environment ideally suited to the work of a major research institution. The intellectual life of this international university is further enhanced by its ready access to cultural centers of major cities. The offerings of the University, combined with its geographical location, provide a cosmopolitan atmosphere with nearly unlimited opportunities for professional and personal growth.

University of Iowa

Iowa City, Iowa

State-supported, coed. Small-town campus. Total enrollment: 26,932.

Degrees Bachelor of Music in the areas of performance, composition, music therapy; Bachelor of Fine Arts in the areas of performance, conducting. Majors: music, music education, music therapy, piano/organ, stringed instruments, voice, wind and percussion instruments. Graduate degrees offered: Master of Music in the areas of performance, conducting, composition; Master of Fine Arts in the areas of performance, conducting. Doctor of Musical Arts in the areas of performance, conducting.

Music Student Profile Fall 1994: 456 total; 231 matriculated undergraduate, 225 matriculated graduate.

Music Faculty Total: 54; 50 full-time, 4 part-time. Graduate students teach about a quarter undergraduate courses. Undergraduate student–faculty ratio: 9:1.

Expenses for 1995–96 Application fee: $20. State resident tuition: $2386 full-time. Nonresident tuition: $8636 full-time. Part-time tuition per semester ranges from $192 to $1193 for state residents, $192 to $4318 for nonresidents. Part-time mandatory fees per semester range from $22 to $44. Full-time mandatory fees: $172. College room and board: $3550. Special program-related fees: $224 for applied music fee.

Financial Aid Program-specific awards for Fall of 1994: 50 Music Activities Scholarships for composition and performance majors ($2200).

Application Procedures Deadline—freshmen and transfers: continuous. Required: high school transcript, minimum 2.0 high school GPA, 3 letters of recommendation, audition. Auditions held continuously on campus; recorded music is permissible as a substitute for live auditions if a campus visit is impossible.

Undergraduate Contact Don Coffman, Associate Director for Undergraduate Studies, School of Music, University of Iowa, 1004 MB, Iowa City, Iowa 52242; 319-335-3026.

Graduate Contact Delbert Disselhorst, Associate Director for Graduate Studies, School of Music, University of Iowa, 1004 MB, Iowa City, Iowa 52242; 319-335-1630.

University of Kansas

Lawrence, Kansas

State-supported, coed. Suburban campus. Total enrollment: 28,046.

Degrees Bachelor of Music in the areas of performance, music theory, history, composition, church music; Bachelor of Music Education in the areas of music education, music therapy. Majors: classical music, jazz, music, music education, music therapy, opera, piano/organ, sacred music, stringed instruments, voice, wind and percussion instruments. Graduate degrees offered: Master of Music in the areas of performance, musicology, music theory, composition, conducting; Master of Music Education in the areas of music education, music therapy. Doctor of Musical Arts in the areas of performance, composition, conducting, church music.

Music Student Profile Fall 1994: 463 total; 317 matriculated undergraduate, 146 matriculated graduate; 20% minorities, 50% females, 15% international.

Music Faculty Total: 57; 50 full-time, 7 part-time; 100% of full-time faculty have terminal degrees. Graduate students teach a few undergraduate courses. Undergraduate student–faculty ratio: 6:1.

Student Life Student groups include Kappa Kappa Psi, Tau Beta Sigma, Music Educators National Conference Student Chapter.

Expenses for 1995–96 Application fee: $15. State resident tuition: $1766 full-time, $59 per credit hour part-time. Nonresident tuition: $7484 full-time, $249 per credit hour part-time. Part-time mandatory fees: $22 per credit hour. Full-time mandatory fees: $416. College room and board: $3544.

Financial Aid Program-specific awards for Fall of 1994: 60–100 Piano Performance Awards for program majors ($875–$950), 60–100 Music Scholarships for those passing audition evaluations ($875–$950).

Application Procedures Deadline—freshmen and transfers: April 1. Required: high school transcript, audition. Auditions held at various times on campus; recorded music is permissible as a substitute for live auditions when distance is prohibitive and videotaped performances are permissible as a substitute for live auditions.

Undergraduate Contact Roger Stoner, Associate Chairman, Music and Dance Department, University of Kansas, 452 Murphy Hall, Lawrence, Kansas 66045; 913-864-3436.

Graduate Contact Carole Ross, Associate Dean, School of Fine Arts, University of Kansas, 446 Murphy Hall, Lawrence, Kansas 60045; 913-864-3421, fax: 913-864-5387.

University of Kentucky

Lexington, Kentucky

State-supported, coed. Urban campus. Total enrollment: 23,622.

Degrees Bachelor of Music in the areas of performance, music education. Majors: music, music education, piano/organ, stringed instruments, voice, wind and percussion instruments. Graduate degrees offered: Master of Music in the areas of performance, music composition, music education. Doctor of Musical Arts in the areas of performance, composition.

Music Student Profile Fall 1994: 316 total; 216 matriculated undergraduate, 82 matriculated graduate, 18 nondegree; 7% minorities, 53% females, 2% international.

Music Faculty Total: 44; 39 full-time, 5 part-time; 53% of full-time faculty have terminal degrees. Graduate students teach about a quarter undergraduate courses. Undergraduate student–faculty ratio: 8:1.

Student Life Student groups include Music Educators National Conference Student Chapter, Percussive Arts Society Student Chapter, music fraternities and sororities.

Expenses for 1995–96 Application fee: $15. State resident tuition: $2260 full-time, $95 per semester hour part-time. Nonresident tuition: $6780 full-time, $283 per semester hour part-time. Part-time mandatory fees: $6 per semester hour. Full-time mandatory fees: $330. College room and board: $3226. Special program-related fees: $50 for applied music fee.

Financial Aid Program-specific awards for Fall of 1994: 100 Grants-in-Aid for program majors/minors ($1500–$6000).

Application Procedures Deadline—freshmen and transfers: August 1. Notification date—freshmen and transfers: August 23. Required: high school transcript, college transcript(s) for transfer students, minimum 2.0 high school GPA, audition, SAT I or ACT test scores. Recommended: letter of recommendation, interview. Auditions held 3 times on campus; recorded music is permissible as a substitute for live auditions if a campus visit is impossible and videotaped performances are permissible as a substitute for live auditions if a campus visit is impossible.

Undergraduate Contact Ron Pen, School of Music, University of Kentucky, 105 Fine Arts Building, Lexington, Kentucky 40506-0022; 606-257-8181.

Graduate Contact W. Harry Clarke, School of Music, University of Kentucky, 105 Fine Arts Building, Lexington, Kentucky 40506-0022.

University of Louisville

Louisville, Kentucky

State-supported, coed. Urban campus. Total enrollment: 21,377.

Degrees Bachelor of Music in the areas of performance, music history, music theory, composition; Bachelor of Music Education in the areas of instrumental music education, vocal music education. Majors: classical music, music, music education, piano/organ, stringed instruments, voice, wind and percussion instruments. Graduate degrees offered: Master of Music in the areas of performance, music history, music theory/composition; Master of Music Education in the areas of instrumental music education, vocal music education. Cross-registration with Metroversity.

Music Student Profile Fall 1994: 322 total; 215 matriculated undergraduate, 87 matriculated graduate, 20 nondegree; 5% minorities, 50% females, 2% international.

Music Faculty Total: 50; 30 full-time, 20 part-time; 70% of full-time faculty have terminal degrees. Graduate students teach a few undergraduate courses. Undergraduate student–faculty ratio: 14:1.

Student Life Student groups include Music Educators National Conference Student Chapter, International Trumpet Guild, American Musicological Society.

Estimated Expenses for 1995–96 Application fee: $25. State resident tuition: $2670 full-time, $106.50 per credit hour part-time. Nonresident tuition: $7550 full-time, $288 per credit hour part-time. College room and board: $3800. College room only: $2000.

Financial Aid Program-specific awards for Fall of 1994: 1 Sister Cities Award for program majors ($9000), 1 Presser Award for academically qualified applicants ($2100), 1 Babb Award for composition majors ($2000).

Application Procedures Deadline—freshmen and transfers: continuous. Required: high school transcript, 3 letters of recommendation, audition, SAT I or ACT test scores, minimum combined SAT I score of 650, minimum composite ACT score of 16, minimum 2.25 high school GPA. Recommended: interview. Auditions held 6 times on campus; recorded music is permissible as a substitute for live auditions when distance is prohibitive.

Undergraduate Contact Kate Hickman, Admissions Office, University of Louisville, Louisville, Kentucky 40292; 502-852-6907, fax: 502-852-0520, E-mail address: kmhick01@ulkyvm.louisville.edu.

Graduate Contact Paul R. Blink, Associate Dean, School of Music, University of Louisville, Louisville, Kentucky 40292; 502-852-6907, fax: 502-852-0520, E-mail address: prbrin01@ulkyvm.louisville.edu.

University of Maine

Orono, Maine

State-supported, coed. Small-town campus. Total enrollment: 11,001.

Degrees Bachelor of Music in the areas of classical vocal performance, classical instrumental performance, classical keyboard performance; Bachelor of Music Education in the areas of classical vocal performance, classical instrumental performance, classical keyboard performance. Majors: classical music, music, music education, piano/organ, stringed instruments, voice, wind and percussion instruments. Graduate degrees offered: Master of Music in the areas of performance, music education, instrumental conducting, choral conducting; Master of Music Education in the areas of voice music education, instrumental music education, keyboard music education.

Music Student Profile Fall 1994: 96 total; 85 matriculated undergraduate, 11 matriculated graduate.

Music Faculty Total: 21; 14 full-time, 7 part-time; 43% of full-time faculty have terminal degrees. Graduate students teach a few undergraduate courses.

Expenses for 1995–96 Application fee: $25. State resident tuition: $3420 full-time, $112 per credit hour part-time. Nonresident tuition: $9570 full-time, $317 per credit hour part-time. Tuition for nonresidents who are eligible for the New England Regional Student Program: $5040 full-time, $168 per credit hour part-time. Full-time mandatory fees: $500. College room and board: $4680. Special program-related fees: $30 for applied music lesson fee, $180 for applied music lesson fee (non-music majors).

Application Procedures Deadline—freshmen: February 1; transfers: March 1. Notification date—transfers: continuous. Required: high school transcript, letter of recommendation, audition, SAT I test score only. Recommended: essay. Auditions held continuously on campus; recorded music is permissible as a substitute for live auditions and videotaped performances are permissible as a substitute for live auditions.

Undergraduate Contact Diane Roscetti, Associate Director, Division of Music, University of Maine, 5743 Lord Hall, Room 107, Orono, Maine 04469-5743; 207-581-4700, fax: 207-581-4701.

Graduate Contact Dr. Dennis K. Cox, Professor of Music, Music Department, University of Maine, 5743 Lord Hall, Room 239, Orono, Maine 04469-5743; 207-581-1245, fax: 207-581-4701.

University of Maryland College Park

College Park, Maryland

State-supported, coed. Suburban campus. Total enrollment: 32,493.

Degrees Bachelor of Music in the areas of theory, composition, music performance; Bachelor of Musical Arts in the areas of composition, performance. Majors: opera, piano/organ, stringed instruments, voice, wind and percussion instruments. Graduate degrees offered: Master of Music in the areas of performance, theory/composition, musicology. Cross-registration with University of Maryland System.

Music Student Profile Fall 1994: 375 total; 125 matriculated undergraduate, 250 matriculated graduate.

Music Faculty Total: 60; 37 full-time, 23 part-time; 60% of full-time faculty have terminal degrees. Graduate students teach a few undergraduate courses.

Student Life Student groups include Phi Mu Alpha, Sigma Alpha Iota, Pi Kappa Lambda.

Expenses for 1995–96 Application fee: $30. State resident tuition: $3179 full-time, $160 per semester hour part-time. Nonresident tuition: $9123 full-time, $350 per semester hour part-time. Part-time mandatory fees: $134 per semester. Full-time mandatory fees: $615. College room and board: $5251 (minimum).

Financial Aid Program-specific awards for Fall of 1994: 30 Creative and Performing Arts Scholarships for program majors ($2500–$5000).

Application Procedures Deadline—freshmen: May 1; transfers: July 1. Required: high school transcript, college transcript(s) for transfer students, letter of recommendation, audition, SAT I or ACT test scores, record of co-curricular activities. Auditions held 5 times on campus and off campus. Portfolio reviews held on campus and off campus.

Undergraduate Contact Greg Carpenter, Advising Coordinator, Department of Music, University of Maryland College Park, Tawes Fine Arts Building, College Park, Maryland 20742-9504; 301-314-5563, fax: 301-314-9504.

Graduate Contact Sharon Hunt, Graduate Student Secretary, Department of Music, University of Maryland College Park, Tawes Fine Arts Building, College Park, Maryland 20742-9504; 301-405-5560, fax: 301-314-9504.

University of Massachusetts Amherst

Amherst, Massachusetts

State-supported, coed. Small-town campus. Total enrollment: 22,332.

Degrees Bachelor of Music in the areas of African-American music and jazz, music history, music education, performance, music theory/composition. Majors: classical music, jazz, music, music education, piano/organ, stringed instruments, voice, wind and percussion instruments. Graduate degrees offered: Master of Music in the areas of accompanying, composition, music education, musicology, jazz composition and arranging, music theory, performance. Cross-registration with Amherst College, Hampshire College, Mount Holyoke College, Smith College.

Music Student Profile Fall 1994: 292 total; 200 matriculated undergraduate, 67 matriculated graduate, 25 nondegree; 6% minorities, 43% females, 17% international.

Music Faculty Total: 56; 36 full-time, 20 part-time; 98% of full-time faculty have terminal degrees. Graduate students teach about a quarter undergraduate courses. Undergraduate student–faculty ratio: 5:1.

Student Life Student groups include Music Educators National Conference Student Chapter, Kappa Kappa Psi, Tau Beta Sigma.

Expenses for 1995–96 Application fee: $20. State resident tuition: $2220 full-time, $92.50 per credit part-time. Nonresident tuition: $8566 full-time, $357 per credit part-time. Part-time mandatory fees per semester range from $489.25 to $1198. Tuition for nonresidents who are eligible for the New England Regional Student

University of Massachusetts Amherst *(continued)*

Program: $3330 full-time, $138.75 per credit part-time. Full-time mandatory fees: $3355. College room and board: $4184. College room only: $2376.

Financial Aid Program-specific awards for Fall of 1994: 52 Teaching Assistantships for program majors ($3750), 60 Chancellor's Talent Awards for program majors ($2725), 31 Alumni Scholarships for program majors ($330).

Application Procedures Deadline—freshmen: February 15; transfers: April 1. Notification date—freshmen: May 1; transfers: June 15. Required: essay, high school transcript. Auditions held 5 times and by request on campus; recorded music is permissible as a substitute for live auditions when distance is prohibitive and videotaped performances are permissible as a substitute for live auditions when distance is prohibitive.

Undergraduate Contact Helen Perry, Auditions Coordinator, Department of Music and Dance, University of Massachusetts Amherst, 273 Fine Arts Center, Box 32520, Amherst, Massachusetts 01003-2520, 2520; 413-545-4313, fax: 413-545-2092.

Graduate Contact Miriam Whaples, Graduate Program Director, Department of Music and Dance, University of Massachusetts Amherst, 273 Fine Arts Center, Box 32520, Amherst, Massachusetts 01003-2520, 2520; 413-545-1247, fax: 413-545-2092.

University of Massachusetts Dartmouth

North Dartmouth, Massachusetts

State-supported, coed. Suburban campus. Total enrollment: 5,245.

Degrees Bachelor of Music in the areas of applied music, theory/composition. Majors: composition, electronic music, music theory, piano/organ, stringed instruments, voice, wind and percussion instruments. Cross-registration with University of Massachusetts System, Southeastern Association for Cooperation in Higher Education in Massachusetts.

Music Student Profile Fall 1994: 632 total; 52 matriculated undergraduate, 580 nondegree; 2% minorities, 50% females, 2% international.

Music Faculty Total: 23; 5 full-time, 18 part-time; 100% of full-time faculty have terminal degrees. Graduate students do not teach undergraduate courses. Undergraduate student–faculty ratio: 11:1.

Student Life Student groups include Music Guild, Annual Jazz Festival.

Expenses for 1995–96 Application fee: $20. State resident tuition: $1836 full-time, $76.50 per credit hour part-time. Nonresident tuition: $6919 full-time, $288.29 per credit hour part-time. Part-time mandatory fees: $230.90 per credit hour. Full-time mandatory fees per year: $1989 for state residents, $2693 for nonresidents. College room and board: $4890. College room only: $2628 (minimum). Special program-related fees: $325 for applied music fee, $12–$25 for studio lab fee.

Financial Aid Program-specific awards for Fall of 1994: 2–3 Art Auction Awards for program majors ($200), 1 Neugebauer Award for program majors ($200).

Application Procedures Deadline—freshmen and transfers: continuous. Required: essay, high school transcript, minimum 2.0 high school GPA, audition, SAT I or ACT test scores. Recommended: minimum 3.0 high school GPA, letter of recommendation. Auditions held as needed on campus; recorded music is permissible as a substitute for live auditions when distance is prohibitive or if a campus visit is impossible and videotaped performances are permissible as a substitute for live auditions when distance is prohibitive or if a campus visit is impossible.

Undergraduate Contact Jeffrey Feroce, Admissions Advisor, Office of Admissions, University of Massachusetts Dartmouth, Old Westport Road, North Dartmouth, Massachusetts 02747-2300; 508-999-8605, fax: 508-999-8901.

University of Massachusetts Lowell

Lowell, Massachusetts

State-supported, coed. Urban campus. Total enrollment: 12,731.

Degrees Bachelor of Music in the areas of performance, sound recording technology, music business, music education, music history and literature, music composition. Majors: classical music, guitar, music business, music education, piano/organ, sound recording technology, stringed instruments, voice, wind and percussion instruments. Graduate degrees offered: Master of Music in the areas of performance, conducting, music education.

Music Student Profile Fall 1994: 320 total; 300 matriculated undergraduate, 20 matriculated graduate; 12% minorities, 35% females, 10% international.

Music Faculty Total: 59; 22 full-time, 37 part-time; 80% of full-time faculty have terminal degrees. Graduate students teach a few undergraduate courses. Undergraduate student–faculty ratio: 13:1.

Student Life Student groups include Music Educators National Conference, Audio Engineering Society, Entertainment and Music Industry Association.

Expenses for 1994–95 State resident tuition: $1884 full-time, $78.50 per credit part-time. Nonresident tuition: $7028 full-time, $293 per credit part-time. Part-time mandatory fees: $110.25 per credit. Full-time mandatory fees: $2718. College room and board: $4300 (minimum). College room only: $2520.

Financial Aid Program-specific awards for Fall of 1994: 20 Talent Scholarships for undergraduates ($2000).

Application Procedures Deadline—freshmen and transfers: continuous. Required: high school transcript, 2 letters of recommendation, audition. Recommended: minimum 2.5 high school GPA. Auditions held 4 times on campus; recorded music is permissible as a substitute for live auditions when distance is prohibitive and videotaped performances are permissible as a substitute for live auditions when distance is prohibitive.

Undergraduate Contact Dr. Gerald J. Lloyd, Dean, College of Fine Arts, University of Massachusetts Lowell, Durgin Hall, South Campus, Lowell, Massachusetts 01854; 508-934-3850, fax: 508-934-3034.

Graduate Contact Willis Traphagan, Coordinator, Graduate Studies, College of Fine Arts, University of Massachusetts Lowell, South Campus, Lowell, Massachusetts 01854; 508-934-3858, fax: 508-934-3034.

University of Memphis

Memphis, Tennessee

State-supported, coed. Urban campus. Total enrollment: 19,848.

Degrees Bachelor of Music in the areas of performance, composition, music history, music education, commercial music, sacred music. Majors: composition, jazz, music business, music education, music history, performance, sacred music, sound recording technology. Graduate degrees offered: Master of Music in the areas of performance, sacred music, music history, Orff–Schulberk pedagogy, music education, jazz, studio music. Doctor of Musical Arts in the areas of composition, performance, sacred music, music education.

Music Student Profile Fall 1994: 277 total; 200 matriculated undergraduate, 77 matriculated graduate.

Music Faculty Total: 51; 39 full-time, 12 part-time.

Expenses for 1995–96 Application fee: $5. State resident tuition: $2094 full-time. Nonresident tuition: $6224 full-time. Part-time tuition per semester ranges from $92 to $989 for state residents, $273 to $2980 for nonresidents. College room and board: $2200 (minimum).

Application Procedures Deadline—freshmen and transfers: August 1. Required: high school transcript, audition. Auditions held continuously on campus; recorded music is permissible as a substitute for live auditions when distance is prohibitive.

Undergraduate Contact Dr. Glenn Chandler, Chair, Department of Music, University of Memphis, 3775 Central Avenue, Memphis, Tennessee 38152; 901-678-3764.

Graduate Contact Dr. John Peterson, Coordinator of Graduate Studies, Department of Music, University of Memphis, 3775 Central Avenue, Memphis, Tennessee 38152; 901-678-3532.

University of Miami

Coral Gables, Florida

Independent, coed. Suburban campus. Total enrollment: 13,410.

Degrees Bachelor of Music in the areas of composition, music education, music engineering technology, music business and entertainment industries, music therapy, musical theater, performance, studio music and jazz. Majors: classical music, composition, jazz, music, music business, music education, music engineering, music theater, music therapy, opera, piano/organ, stringed instruments, voice, wind and percussion instruments. Graduate degrees offered: Master of Music in the areas of accompanying and chamber music, conducting, electronic and computer music, jazz pedagogy, jazz performance, keyboard performance and pedagogy, media writing and production, music education, music and business industries, music theory/composition, music theory. Doctor of Musical Arts in the areas of accompanying and chamber music, composition, jazz composition, conducting, keyboard performance and pedagogy, performance, jazz performance.

Music Student Profile Fall 1994: 640 total; 439 matriculated undergraduate, 200 matriculated graduate, 1 nondegree; 23% minorities, 37% females, 4% international.

Music Faculty Total: 90; 63 full-time, 27 part-time; 44% of full-time faculty have terminal degrees. Graduate students teach a few undergraduate courses. Undergraduate student–faculty ratio: 7:1.

Estimated Expenses for 1995–96 Application fee: $35. Comprehensive fee of $24,552 includes full-time tuition ($17,340), mandatory fees ($360), and college room and board ($6852). College room only: $3830. Part-time tuition: $672 per credit.

Financial Aid Program-specific awards for Fall of 1994: 150 Music Scholarships for those demonstrating talent ($8000).

Application Procedures Deadline—freshmen and transfers: March 1. Notification date—freshmen and transfers: April 1. Required: essay, high school transcript, college transcript(s) for transfer students, letter of recommendation, audition, SAT I or ACT test scores. Recommended: minimum 3.0 high school GPA. Auditions held 4 times on campus and off campus in Atlanta, GA; Boston, MA; Charlotte, NC; Chicago, IL; Columbus, OH; Dallas, TX; Denver, CO; Edison, NJ; Houston, TX; Interlochen, MI; Los Angeles, CA; New York, NY; Philadelphia, PA; San Diego, CA; San Francisco, CA; Washington, DC; Hong Kong; Kuala Lumpur, Malaysia; Penang, Malaysia; Seoul, Korea; Singapore, Taipei, Taiwan; Tokyo, Japan; recorded music is permissible as a substitute for live auditions when distance is prohibitive and videotaped performances are permissible as a substitute for live auditions for musical theater students.

Undergraduate Contact Kenneth J. Moses, Director of Admission, School of Music, University of Miami, P.O. Box 248165, Coral Gables, Florida 33124; 305-284-2245, fax: 305-284-6475.

Graduate Contact Dr. J. David Boyle, Associate Dean, School of Music, University of Miami, P.O. Box 248165, Coral Gables, Florida 33124; 305-284-2446, fax: 305-284-6475.

More about the University

Facilities The music complex includes a 600-seat concert hall and 150-seat recital hall, three rehearsal halls, two state-of-the-art recording studios, two computer/MIDI

University of Miami *(continued)*

keyboard labs, music library, instructional studios, and practice rooms and classrooms.

Faculty and Alumni There are over 80 faculty members. Faculty members perform with the Florida Philharmonic, Greater Miami Opera, Miami City Ballet Orchestra, the Naples Philharmonic, and various jazz ensembles. Academic faculty members are widely published and recognized in their various fields. Alumni include Grammy winners Bruce Hornsby and Jon Secada; opera star Marvis Martin; assistant conductor of the St. Louis Symphony, Andre Raphel Smith; television star Dawnn Lewis; Keith Buterbaugh, Raoul in "Phantom of the Opera;" Gary Fry, arranger and producer of over 1,500 commercials; Sam Pilafian, founder of the Empire Brass Quintet and Travelin' Light; and Matt Pierson, Director of A&R/Staff Producer for Warner Brothers Records.

Performance The School of Music serves as a major cultural resource for the Greater Miami area, presenting more than 300 musical events annually. Complementing on-campus recitals and concerts by students and faculty are programs by guest artists, composers, conductors, and lecturers from virtually every corner of the world. Festival Miami, a monthlong international music festival held each fall, typically features performances by an array of faculty and guest artists, student ensembles, composers, and conductors, including many premiere performances of new compositions. Several of the School's more than fifty ensembles have performed in tours around the United States and the world.

Each year, students from across the United States and more than two dozen countries pursue undergraduate and graduate study at the University of Miami School of Music. The School enjoys a reputation as a comprehensive and innovative music school, with more than three dozen degree, certificate, diploma, and international exchange program options available.

Since its founding in 1926 and accreditation in 1939 by the National Association of Schools of Music, the UM School of Music has become one of the largest schools of its kind in a private institution of higher learning in the United States. The School pioneered innovative programs in music industry, music engineering, and studio music and jazz. Since its inception, strong programs in composition/theory, performance, and music education have been a part of the curriculum. Flexible, well-rounded music instruction, designed to give graduates a professional edge, remains a hallmark of the School.

More than 60 full-time faculty members and 25 adjunct faculty members are active in the classroom and as dedicated music professionals. The diverse nature of the programs in the School of Music has attracted a faculty with a broad outlook in its approach to music education who imparts and encourages diversity in the music classroom.

Students choosing the UM School of Music are focused and serious about their studies and are eager for the academic and performance opportunities available to them at UM. The low ratio of students to faculty fosters close academic bonding. Every music student enjoys one-on-one studio instruction.

Many of the more than 3,000 students who have graduated from the UM School of Music have distinguished themselves professionally. Alumni provide a veritable "Who's Who" of both performance and related musical careers. UM graduates perform with major orchestras, operas, and jazz ensembles. Their compositions range from orchestral and operatic music to film and video scores. Some graduates are among the top solo performing artists in the country; others excel as arrangers, recording engineers, editors, therapists, teachers, publishers, distributors, and retailers.

The School of Music is situated on the University's Coral Gables campus, minutes away from the city of Miami, where students enjoy a delightful climate that lends itself to a myriad of activities. All the cultural advantages of a metropolitan center are available to UM music students. In addition to being the home of the Florida Philharmonic Orchestra, the New World Symphony, and the Greater Miami Opera Company, the Miami area is regularly included in concert tours of major symphonies, concert artists, jazz performers, and opera companies. Music students are able to participate in master classes given frequently by visiting artists performing in the greater Miami area.

University of Michigan

Ann Arbor, Michigan

State-supported, coed. Suburban campus. Total enrollment: 36,543.

Degrees Bachelor of Music in the areas of composition, music and technology, music education, music history, music theory, performance; Bachelor of Music Education in the area of music education; Bachelor of Fine Arts in the areas of musical theater, performing arts technology, jazz and improvisational studies; Bachelor of Musical Arts in the areas of composition, jazz studies, music history, music theory, performance. Majors: composition, jazz, music education, music history, music technology, music theater, music theory, piano/organ, stringed instruments, voice, wind and percussion instruments. Graduate degrees offered: Master of Music in the areas of arts administration, church music, composition, conducting, improvisation, music theory, piano pedagogy, performance; Master of Music Education in the area of music education. Doctor of Musical Arts in the areas of composition, conducting, performance.

Music Student Profile Fall 1994: 887 total; 568 matriculated undergraduate, 312 matriculated graduate, 7 nondegree; 14% minorities, 54% females, 7% international.

Music Faculty Total: 134; 99 full-time, 35 part-time; 100% of full-time faculty have terminal degrees. Graduate students teach a few undergraduate courses. Undergraduate student–faculty ratio: 16:1.

Student Life Student groups include Music Educators National Conference, Pi Kappa Lambda, Sigma Alpha Iota/Phi Mu Alpha.

Expenses for 1994–95 Application fee: $40. Full-time tuition ranges from $5040 to $6698 for state residents, $15,732 to $17,850 for nonresidents according to class level and program. Part-time tuition and fees per term (1 to 11 credits) range from $525 to $3204 for state residents,

$970 to $8530 for nonresidents according to course load, class level, and program. Full-time mandatory fees: $175. College room and board: $4659.

Financial Aid Program-specific awards for Fall of 1994: 120 Merit Awards for program students ($4962).

Application Procedures Deadline—freshmen and transfers: continuous. Required: essay, high school transcript, college transcript(s) for transfer students, minimum 3.0 high school GPA, letter of recommendation, audition, SAT I or ACT test scores, minimum combined SAT I score of 1,000, minimum composite ACT score of 24, portfolio for composition and performing arts technology students. Auditions held 12 times on campus and off campus in New York, NY; Washington, DC; Interlochen, MI; recorded music is permissible as a substitute for live auditions when distance is prohibitive and videotaped performances are permissible as a substitute for live auditions when distance is prohibitive.

Contact Laura Strozeski, Senior Admissions Counselor, School of Music, University of Michigan, 1100 Baits Drive, Ann Arbor, Michigan 48109-2085; 313-764-0593, fax: 313-763-5097, E-mail address: lauras@umich.edu.

More about the University

Program Facilities Performance venues: Hill Auditorium (4,200 seats), Power Center for the Performing Arts (1,400 seats), Rackham Auditorium (1,100 seats), Recital Hall, Lydia Mendelssohn Theatre, McIntosh Theatre, Blanche Anderson Moore Hall. Practice/study rooms: 135 practice rooms with pianos; 10 organ practice rooms; special facilities for harp, harpsichord, carillon, and percussion; Rehearsal Hall for ensembles; listening room with ninety stations. The School has a professional-quality Electronic Music Studio, a Microcomputer and Synthesizer Laboratory, and one of the foremost music libraries in the country.

Faculty, Guest Artists, and Alumni Faculty are performers currently active on the international stage; highly experienced musicians who are former members of major orchestras, opera houses, and dance and theatre companies; prize-winning composers; and scholars and theorists who are renowned leaders in their disciplines. Guest artists to visit the school recently include Frederica von Stade, Marilyn Horne, Gene Kelly, Murray Perahia, Arleen Auger, Isaac Stern, and Andre Watts. Well-known alumni include Nessye Norman, Roberta Alexander, George Crumb, Ashley Putnam, Marian Mercer, Bob McGrath, and Michael Maguire.

Student Performance Opportunities Students and faculty present more than 300 concerts, recitals, and staged performances each year. Student ensembles include the University Choir and Chamber Choir, Opera Production, Musical Theatre Production, Digital Music Ensemble, Jazz Orchestra, Men's and Women's Glee Clubs, Percussion Ensemble, Creative Arts Orchestra, Javanese Gamelan, Early Music Ensemble, Contemporary Directions Ensemble, and Composers' Forum. Concerts are frequently presented out of town and occasionally on international tours. Many solo and small-ensemble recitals augment these larger performances.

The University of Michigan School of Music, founded in 1880, is one of the oldest and largest schools of music in the United States. *U.S. News & World Report* (March 14, 1994) ranked it among the top four in its first-ever ranking of conservatories and schools of music in this country. The School of Music has consistently received recognition in a variety of such evaluations. A special strength of the university of Michigan is that in addition to the University as a whole, many of its departments, schools, and colleges rank among the top ten in the nation. The School of Music, as a component of a major university, is advantageously positioned to offer its students a strong combination of breadth and depth of both an artistic and intellectual nature. Students in the School of Music benefit from the personal contact possible in a small unit of 800 students while at the same time taking advantage of the many opportunities and resources available at a major research university.

While conservatories address performance training, some university-based schools emphasize the academic aspects of musicianship, and many state universities provide music teacher training, the University of Michigan School of Music seeks to accomplish all three. Like a conservatory, the School offers studio instruction by some of the finest artist-pedagogues as well as plentiful performance opportunities. The Music Theory, Composition, Music History, and Musicology departments have historically been among the nation's best and continue to draw students who are also recruited by Ivy League schools. The School has long been regarded as an important center for the development of music education. For many decades it has been the overriding goal of the faculty at the School of Music to maintain distinction in all three separate but interrelated categories of music instruction.

An extensive array of degree programs enables each student to choose the curriculum that best meets individual interests and career goals. The Bachelor of Music degree offers intensive professional training in music, while the Bachelor of Fine Arts program provides professional training in dance, theatre, or musical theatre. The Bachelor of Music Arts degree is designed for music students who want a greater emphasis on the liberal arts. Although many members of the Michigan faculty are highly active professionally, they all participate in the life of the School and are in every sense a resident faculty. Notable figures in today's musical world come to the School to present lecture-demonstrations, teach master classes, or meet informally with students to expand their contact with major performing artists. The School enjoys extraordinary facilities and the University and Arbor both provide a rich extracurricular environment with an abundance of performance opportunities. Graduates of the School of Music have distinguished themselves in all areas of performance, composition, directing, choreography, scholarship, teaching, and arts administration.

University of Michigan–Flint

Flint, Michigan

State-supported, coed. Urban campus. Total enrollment: 6,236.

Degrees Bachelor of Music in the areas of music theory and history, classical music; Bachelor of Music Education in the areas of classical music, instrumental music, vocal music, piano, organ. Majors: classical music, music,

University of Michigan–Flint *(continued)*

music education, music history, music theory, piano/organ, stringed instruments, voice, wind and percussion instruments.

Music Student Profile Fall 1994: 40 total; all matriculated undergraduate.

Music Faculty Total: 19; 5 full-time, 14 part-time; 20% of full-time faculty have terminal degrees. Graduate students teach a few undergraduate courses. Undergraduate student–faculty ratio: 12:1.

Student Life Student groups include Music Educators National Conference Student Chapter.

Expenses for 1995–96 State resident tuition: $3184 full-time. Nonresident tuition: $9454 full-time. Part-time mandatory fees: $50 per semester. Part-time tuition per credit hour: $166 for the first credit hour, $126 for the next 10 credit hours for state residents; $434 for the first credit hour, $394 for the next 10 credit hours for nonresidents. Full-time mandatory fees: $120.

Financial Aid Program-specific awards for Fall of 1994: 15–20 Numerous Awards ($400–$600).

Application Procedures Deadline—freshmen and transfers: continuous. Required: high school transcript, college transcript(s) for transfer students, audition, SAT I or ACT test scores. Recommended: essay, minimum 3.0 high school GPA, letter of recommendation. Auditions held 4-5 times on campus and off campus. Portfolio reviews held on campus and off campus.

Undergraduate Contact Christine Waters, Chairperson, Art and Music Department, University of Michigan–Flint, 126 CROB, Flint, Michigan 48502; 810-762-3377, fax: 810-762-3687, E-mail address: maxfield_l@crob.flint.umich.edu.

University of Minnesota, Duluth

Duluth, Minnesota

State-supported, coed. Suburban campus. Total enrollment: 7,497.

Degrees Bachelor of Music in the areas of piano pedagogy, jazz studies, performance, music education, theory–composition. Majors: jazz, music education, music theory and composition, performance, piano pedagogy. Graduate degrees offered: Master of Music in the area of music education. Cross-registration with University of Wisconsin&–Superior, College of St. Scholastica.

Music Student Profile Fall 1994: 325 total; 125 matriculated undergraduate, 200 nondegree; 2% minorities, 50% females.

Music Faculty Total: 30; 15 full-time, 15 part-time; 100% of full-time faculty have terminal degrees. Graduate students teach a few undergraduate courses. Undergraduate student–faculty ratio: 4:1.

Student Life Student groups include Music Educators National Conference, American Choral Directors Association, International Association of Jazz Educators.

Expenses for 1994–95 Application fee: $25. State resident tuition: $2995 full-time, $71.30 per credit part-time. Nonresident tuition: $8828 full-time, $210.20 per credit part-time. Part-time mandatory fees (6 to 11 credits): $103.45 per quarter. Full-time mandatory fees: $310. College room and board: $3474.

Financial Aid Program-specific awards for Fall of 1994: 1 Bernstein Jazz Scholarship for jazz players ($500), 1–3 Comella Scholarships for music education majors ($600), 1–3 Faricy Scholarships for trumpet players ($400), 1–3 Gauger Scholarships for keyboardists ($300), 3 Gendein Scholarships for state residents ($400), 2 Gershgol Scholarships for program majors ($800), 1–2 Oreck Scholarships for program majors ($500), 8 Gregg Johnson Scholarships for program majors ($400).

Application Procedures Deadline—freshmen and transfers: continuous. Required: college transcript(s) for transfer students, interview, audition. Auditions held 2 times and by request on campus; recorded music is permissible as a substitute for live auditions when distance is prohibitive and videotaped performances are permissible as a substitute for live auditions when distance is prohibitive.

Undergraduate Contact Judith Kritzmire, Head, Music Department, University of Minnesota, Duluth, 231 H, 10 University Drive, Duluth, Minnesota 55812; 218-726-8207, fax: 218-726-8503, E-mail address: jkritzmi@ua.d.umn.edu.

University of Minnesota, Twin Cities Campus

Minneapolis, Minnesota

State-supported, coed. Urban campus. Total enrollment: 36,699.

Degrees Bachelor of Music in the areas of performance, music education, music therapy, jazz studies. Majors: jazz, music education, music therapy, piano/organ, stringed instruments, voice, wind and percussion instruments. Graduate degrees offered: Master of Music in the areas of performance, piano pedagogy, choral conducting, orchestral conducting, wind/band conducting, accompanying/coaching. Doctor of Musical Arts in the areas of performance, orchestral conducting, accompanying/coaching.

Music Student Profile Fall 1994: 519 total; 290 matriculated undergraduate, 229 matriculated graduate; 10% minorities, 60% females, 14% international.

Music Faculty Total: 77; 44 full-time, 33 part-time; 80% of full-time faculty have terminal degrees. Graduate students teach a few undergraduate courses.

Student Life Student groups include Music Educators National Conference, Music Therapy Club, music fraternities and sororities.

Expenses for 1994–95 Application fee: $25. Full-time tuition ranges from $3395 to $3482 for state residents, $9190 to $10,794 for nonresidents, according to class level and program. Part-time tuition per credit ranges from $70.80 to $82.90 for state residents, $208.80 to $244.40 for nonresidents, according to class level and program.

Full-time tuition for pharmacy program ranges from $2478 to $6077 for state residents, $4687 to $12,150 for nonresidents according to class level. Part-time tuition per credit for pharmacy program ranges from $59 to $144.70 for state residents, $111.60 to $289.30 for nonresidents according to class level. Full-time mandatory fees: $431. College room and board: $3774. Special program-related fees: $50–$100 for applied music lessons, $22–$44 for practice rooms.

Financial Aid Program-specific awards for Fall of 1994: 50–60 School of Music Scholarships for exceptional talent ($1100–$3000).

Application Procedures Deadline—freshmen and transfers: continuous. Notification date—freshmen and transfers: continuous. Required: high school transcript, college transcript(s) for transfer students, audition, SAT I or ACT test scores, minimum 2.5 college GPA for transfer students. Recommended: 2 letters of recommendation. Auditions held 6 times on campus; recorded music is permissible as a substitute for live auditions when distance is prohibitive.

Undergraduate Contact Rodney Loeffler, Assistant Director, School of Music, University of Minnesota, Twin Cities Campus, 2106 4th Street South, Minneapolis, Minnesota 55455; 612-624-4028, fax: 612-626-2200, E-mail address: loeff001@maroon.tc.umn.edu.

Graduate Contact Janice Porter, Graduate Admissions, School of Music, University of Minnesota, Twin Cities Campus, 2106 4th Street South, Minneapolis, Minnesota 55455; 612-624-0071, fax: 612-626-2200, E-mail address: j-port@maroon.tc.umn.edu.

University of Mississippi

University, Mississippi

State-supported, coed. Small-town campus. Total enrollment: 10,075.

Degrees Bachelor of Music in the areas of performance, music theory, instrumental music education, vocal music education. Majors: classical music, music education, music theory, piano/organ, stringed instruments, voice, wind and percussion instruments. Graduate degrees offered: Master of Music in the areas of performance, music theory, composition, instrumental music education, vocal music education. Doctor of Arts in the areas of music theory, music literature, performance pedagogy, music education.

Music Student Profile Fall 1994: 114 total; 87 matriculated undergraduate, 27 matriculated graduate.

Music Faculty Total: 26; 23 full-time, 3 part-time; 97% of full-time faculty have terminal degrees. Graduate students teach a few undergraduate courses. Undergraduate student–faculty ratio: 12:1.

Expenses for 1994–95 Application fee: $25. State resident tuition: $2546 full-time, $83 per semester hour part-time. Nonresident tuition: $5006 full-time, $186 per semester hour part-time. Part-time mandatory fees per semester (7 to 11 semester hours): $275. Full-time mandatory fees: $550. College room only: $1560.

Financial Aid Program-specific awards for Fall of 1994: 150 Band Scholarships for wind and percussion players ($500), 25 Orchestra Scholarships for stringed instrument players ($750), 75 Chorus Scholarships for vocalists ($300).

Application Procedures Deadline—freshmen and transfers: continuous. Required: high school transcript, minimum 2.0 high school GPA, interview, audition. Recommended: 2 letters of recommendation. Auditions held 4 times and by appointment on campus; recorded music is permissible as a substitute for live auditions with special permission and videotaped performances are permissible as a substitute for live auditions with special permission.

Contact Ronald F. Vernon, Chairman, Music Department, University of Mississippi, 132 Meek Hall, University, Mississippi 38677; 601-232-7268, fax: 601-232-7830.

University of Missouri–Columbia

Columbia, Missouri

State-supported, coed. Small-town campus. Total enrollment: 22,136.

Degrees Bachelor of Music in the areas of piano, strings, winds, percussion, voice, music theory, composition, music education, music history; Bachelor of Music Education in the area of music education. Majors: composition, music education, music history, music theory, piano/organ, stringed instruments, voice, wind and percussion instruments. Graduate degrees offered: Master of Music in the areas of band conducting, choral conducting, orchestra conducting, piano, strings, winds, percussion, voice music theory, composition, music education, music history.

Music Student Profile Fall 1994: 204 total; 137 matriculated undergraduate, 62 matriculated graduate, 5 nondegree; 7% minorities, 6% international.

Music Faculty Total: 36; 32 full-time, 4 part-time; 50% of full-time faculty have terminal degrees. Graduate students teach a few undergraduate courses. Undergraduate student–faculty ratio: 4:1.

Student Life Special housing available for music students.

Estimated Expenses for 1995–96 Application fee: $25. State resident tuition: $3330 full-time, $111 per credit hour part-time. Nonresident tuition: $10,350 full-time, $340 per credit hour part-time. Part-time mandatory fees per semester range from $144 to $196. Full-time mandatory fees: $435. College room and board: $3645. Special program-related fees: $109 for applied music fee.

Financial Aid Program-specific awards for Fall of 1994: 80 Music Scholarships for band, orchestra, chorus participants ($200–$2000).

Application Procedures Deadline—freshmen and transfers: continuous. Notification date—freshmen and transfers: continuous. Required: high school transcript, college transcript(s) for transfer students, minimum 2.0 high school GPA, audition, ACT test score only. Auditions held 9 times on campus and off campus in St. Louis, MO; Kansas City, MO; Springfield, MO; Poplar Bluff, MO; St.

University of Missouri–Columbia *(continued)*

Joseph, MO; recorded music is permissible as a substitute for live auditions when distance is prohibitive and videotaped performances are permissible as a substitute for live auditions when distance is prohibitive.

Contact Charles Kyriakos, Director of Graduate and Undergraduate Studies in Music, Music Department, University of Missouri–Columbia, 150 Fine Arts, Columbia, Missouri 65211; 314-882-2054.

University of Missouri–Kansas City

Kansas City, Missouri

State-supported, coed. Urban campus. Total enrollment: 9,962.

Degrees Bachelor of Music in the areas of composition, instrumental music, music theory, voice; Bachelor of Music Education in the areas of music education, music therapy. Majors: accordian, classical music, composition, guitar, jazz, music education, music theory, opera, piano/organ, stringed instruments, voice, wind and percussion instruments. Graduate degrees offered: Master of Music in the areas of composition, instrumental music, music theory, voice, conducting; Master of Music Education in the area of music education. Doctor of Musical Arts in the areas of performance, composition, conducting.

Music Student Profile Fall 1994: 470 total; 250 matriculated undergraduate, 200 matriculated graduate, 20 nondegree; 50% females.

Music Faculty Total: 65; 47 full-time, 18 part-time; 52% of full-time faculty have terminal degrees. Graduate students teach a few undergraduate courses. Undergraduate student–faculty ratio: 4:1.

Expenses for 1995–96 Application fee: $25. State resident tuition: $3330 full-time, $111 per credit hour part-time. Nonresident tuition: $9954 full-time, $331.80 per credit hour part-time. Part-time mandatory fees per semester range from $45.70 to $202.55. Full-time mandatory fees: $469.20. College room and board: $3750.

Financial Aid Program-specific awards for Fall of 1994: Music Awards for program majors ($200–$3500).

Application Procedures Deadline—freshmen and transfers: March 1. Required: high school transcript, audition, ACT test score only. Auditions held 6–8 times on campus.

Contact Conservatory Admissions, University of Missouri–Kansas City, Conservatory of Music, 4949 Cherry, Kansas City, Missouri 64110; 816-235-2900, fax: 816-235-5264, E-mail address: consadmit@cctr.umkc.edu.

University of Missouri–St. Louis

St. Louis, Missouri

State-supported, coed. Suburban campus. Total enrollment: 12,045.

Degrees Bachelor of Music in the areas of music education, performance. Majors: music, music education, piano/organ, stringed instruments, voice, wind and percussion instruments.

Music Student Profile Fall 1994: 75 total; 60 matriculated undergraduate, 15 nondegree; 8% minorities, 55% females.

Music Faculty Total: 19; 7 full-time, 12 part-time; 85% of full-time faculty have terminal degrees. Graduate students do not teach undergraduate courses. Undergraduate student–faculty ratio: 15:1.

Student Life Student groups include Music Educators National Conference.

Expenses for 1995–96 State resident tuition: $2664 full-time, $111 per credit hour part-time. Nonresident tuition: $7963 full-time, $331.80 per credit hour part-time. Part-time mandatory fees: $16.16 per credit hour. Full-time mandatory fees: $398. College room and board: $3948 (minimum). Special program-related fees: $100 for applied music fee.

Financial Aid Program-specific awards for Fall of 1994: 6 Music Merit Scholarships for talented students ($1000), 4 UM/St. Louis Symphony Scholarships for minorities ($2000).

Application Procedures Deadline—freshmen and transfers: continuous. Required: high school transcript, college transcript(s) for transfer students, minimum 2.0 high school GPA, audition, SAT I or ACT test scores. Recommended: interview. Auditions held 6 times on campus and off campus. Portfolio reviews held on campus and off campus.

Undergraduate Contact John Hylton, Chair, Music Department, University of Missouri–St. Louis, 8001 Natural Bridge, St. Louis, Missouri 63033; 314-516-5980, fax: 314-516-8593.

University of Montana–Missoula

Missoula, Montana

State-supported, coed. Urban campus. Total enrollment: 11,067.

Degrees Bachelor of Music in the areas of performance, theory, composition; Bachelor of Music Education. Majors: instrumental music, piano/organ, voice. Graduate degrees offered: Master of Music in the areas of performance, composition, music history and literature; Master of Music Education. Cross-registration with National Association of Schools of Music.

Music Student Profile Fall 1994: 168 total; 160 matriculated undergraduate, 8 matriculated graduate.

Music Faculty Total: 25; 20 full-time, 5 part-time; 90% of full-time faculty have terminal degrees. Graduate students teach a few undergraduate courses.

Student Life Student groups include Mu Phi Epsilon, College Music Educators National Conference.

Expenses for 1994–95 Application fee: $30. State resident tuition: $2251 full-time. Nonresident tuition: $6311 full-time. Part-time tuition per semester ranges from $99.10 to $943.10 for state residents, $244.10 to $2538 for nonresidents. College room and board: $3667. Special program-related fees: $30 for practice rooms, studio fees.

Financial Aid Program-specific awards for Fall of 1994: 20 various awards for music majors ($300–$500).

Application Procedures Deadline—freshmen and transfers: June 15. Required: high school transcript, college transcript(s) for transfer students, minimum 2.0 high school GPA, SAT I or ACT test scores. Recommended: interview. Auditions held by appointment on campus and off campus; recorded music is permissible as a substitute for live auditions when distance is prohibitive. Portfolio reviews held on campus and off campus.

Contact Thomas H. Cook, Chair, Department of Music, University of Montana–Missoula, Missoula, Montana 59812-1059; 406-243-6880, fax: 406-243-2441.

University of Montevallo

Montevallo, Alabama

State-supported, coed. Small-town campus. Total enrollment: 3,282.

Degrees Bachelor of Music in the areas of performance, composition, piano pedagogy; Bachelor of Music Education in the areas of instrumental music education, choral music education. Majors: classical music, composition, music, music education, piano pedagogy, piano/organ, voice, wind and percussion instruments. Graduate degrees offered: Master of Music in the areas of performance, piano pedagogy, music education.

Music Student Profile Fall 1994: 111 total; 81 matriculated undergraduate, 23 matriculated graduate, 7 nondegree.

Music Faculty Total: 30; 11 full-time, 19 part-time; 63% of full-time faculty have terminal degrees. Graduate students do not teach undergraduate courses. Undergraduate student–faculty ratio: 4:1.

Expenses for 1994–95 Application fee: $15. State resident tuition: $2340 full-time, $78 per semester hour part-time. Nonresident tuition: $4680 full-time, $156 per semester hour part-time. Full-time mandatory fees: $67. College room and board: $2964. Special program-related fees: $50 for applied music fees.

Financial Aid Program-specific awards for Fall of 1994: 35 College of Fine Arts Awards for talented students ($1500), 20 Music Awards for talented students ($750).

Application Procedures Deadline—freshmen and transfers: July 29. Required: high school transcript, interview, audition, portfolio, SAT I or ACT test scores, piano placement examination. Auditions held 2 times in February and March and by appointment on campus. Portfolio reviews held 2 times in February and March for composition students and by appointment on campus.

Undergraduate Contact Dr. J. Ovide DeLage, Chair, Music Department, University of Montevallo, Station 6670, Montevallo, Alabama 35115; 205-665-6670, fax: 205-665-6676.

Graduate Contact Dr. Robert Bean, Director, Graduate Studies in Music, Music Department, University of Montevallo, Station 6670, Montevallo, Alabama 35115; 205-665-6673, fax: 205-665-6676.

University of Nebraska at Kearney

Kearney, Nebraska

State-supported, coed. Small-town campus. Total enrollment: 7,584.

Degrees Bachelor of Fine Arts in the areas of classical music, music performance, music theater. Majors: music, music education, music theater, piano/organ, stringed instruments, voice, wind and percussion instruments.

Music Student Profile Fall 1994: 160 total; 150 matriculated undergraduate, 10 nondegree; 2% minorities, 60% females, 5% international.

Music Faculty Total: 19; 14 full-time, 5 part-time; 93% of full-time faculty have terminal degrees. Graduate students do not teach undergraduate courses. Undergraduate student–faculty ratio: 11:1.

Student Life Student groups include Music Educators National Conference.

Expenses for 1995–96 Application fee: $25. State resident tuition: $1829 full-time, $59 per semester hour part-time. Nonresident tuition: $3426 full-time, $110.50 per semester hour part-time. Part-time mandatory fees per semester range from $17.50 to $102.50. Full-time mandatory fees: $255. College room and board: $2540 (minimum). College room only: $1280 (minimum). Special program-related fees: $20 for practice room fee.

Financial Aid Program-specific awards for Fall of 1994: Music Awards for program majors ($300–$1600).

Application Procedures Deadline—freshmen and transfers: continuous. Required: high school transcript, college transcript(s) for transfer students, minimum 2.0 high school GPA, audition, ACT test score only, minimum composite ACT score of 20. Recommended: minimum 3.0 high school GPA, 2 letters of recommendation, interview. Auditions held 4 times on campus and off campus; recorded music is permissible as a substitute for live auditions when distance is prohibitive and for international applicants and videotaped performances are permissible as a substitute for live auditions when distance is prohibitive and for international applicants. Portfolio reviews held on campus and off campus.

Undergraduate Contact Office of Admissions, University of Nebraska at Kearney, Kearney, Nebraska 68849; 308-865-8526.

University of Nebraska at Omaha

Omaha, Nebraska

State-supported, coed. Urban campus. Total enrollment: 15,570.

University of Nebraska at Omaha *(continued)*

Degrees Bachelor of Music in the areas of music education, music performance. Majors: classical music, music, music education, piano/organ, stringed instruments, voice, wind and percussion instruments. Graduate degrees offered: Master of Music in the areas of music education, music performance. Cross-registration with University of Nebraska System.

Music Student Profile Fall 1994: 170 total; 140 matriculated undergraduate, 30 matriculated graduate; 10% minorities, 52% females, 6% international.

Music Faculty Total: 36; 15 full-time, 21 part-time; 95% of full-time faculty have terminal degrees. Graduate students do not teach undergraduate courses. Undergraduate student–faculty ratio: 9:1.

Student Life Student groups include Music Educators National Conference, Nebraska State Bandmasters Association.

Estimated Expenses for 1995–96 Application fee: $25. State resident tuition: $1995 full-time, $66.50 per semester hour part-time. Nonresident tuition: $5370 full-time, $179 per semester hour part-time. Part-time mandatory fees: $96.50 per semester. Tuition for home economics, en. Full-time mandatory fees: $193. Special program-related fees: $15 for facilities fee.

Financial Aid Program-specific awards for Fall of 1994: 30–40 Music Scholarships for program majors ($200–$1200).

Application Procedures Deadline—freshmen and transfers: continuous. Required: high school transcript, audition. Auditions held 5 times on campus; recorded music is permissible as a substitute for live auditions when distance is prohibitive and videotaped performances are permissible as a substitute for live auditions when distance is prohibitive.

Undergraduate Contact Dr. James R. Saker, Chair, Music Department, University of Nebraska at Omaha, Strauss Performing Arts Center, Omaha, Nebraska 68182-0245; 402-554-2251, fax: 402-554-2252.

Graduate Contact W. Kenton Bales, Graduate Program Committee Chair, Music Department, University of Nebraska at Omaha, Strauss Performing Arts Center, Omaha, Nebraska 68182-0245; 402-554-2251, fax: 402-554-2252.

University of Nebraska–Lincoln

Lincoln, Nebraska

State-supported, coed. Urban campus. Total enrollment: 23,854.

Degrees Bachelor of Music in the area of performance; Bachelor of Music Education in the area of music education. Majors: music education, performance. Graduate degrees offered: Master of Music in the areas of music theory, composition, performance, conducting, music education. Doctor of Musical Arts in the areas of performance, composition.

Music Student Profile Fall 1994: 300 total; 225 matriculated undergraduate, 75 matriculated graduate; 6% minorities, 50% females, 2% international.

Music Faculty Total: 45; 40 full-time, 5 part-time; 100% of full-time faculty have terminal degrees. Graduate students teach a few undergraduate courses. Undergraduate student–faculty ratio: 7:1.

Student Life Student groups include Sigma Alpha Iota, Music Educators National Conference, Mu Phi Epsilon.

Expenses for 1994–95 Application fee: $25. State resident tuition: $2415 full-time, $68.50 per credit hour part-time. Nonresident tuition: $5955 full-time, $186.50 per credit hour part-time. Part-time mandatory fees per semester range from $85 to $180. Full-time mandatory fees: $360. College room and board: $3145. College room only: $1375. Special program-related fees: $20 for applied fees, $5–$10 for instrument rental.

Application Procedures Deadline—freshmen and transfers: July 1. Required: high school transcript, college transcript(s) for transfer students, audition. Recommended: SAT I or ACT test scores. Auditions held 2 times on campus; recorded music is permissible as a substitute for live auditions for out-of-state applicants and videotaped performances are permissible as a substitute for live auditions for out-of-state applicants.

Undergraduate Contact Rosemary Petruconis, Administrative Assistant for Academic Affairs, School of Music, University of Nebraska–Lincoln, 120 Westbrook Music Building, Lincoln, Nebraska 68588-0100; 402-472-6845, fax: 402-472-8962, E-mail address: rgp@unlinfo.unl.edu.

Graduate Contact Colleen Nyhoff, Graduate Secretary, School of Music, University of Nebraska–Lincoln, 120 Westbrook Music Building, Lincoln, Nebraska 68588-0100; 402-472-2506, fax: 402-472-8962, E-mail address: mcdonald@unlinfo.unl.edu.

University of Nevada, Las Vegas

Las Vegas, Nevada

State-supported, coed. Urban campus. Total enrollment: 20,239.

Degrees Bachelor of Music in the areas of jazz, applied music, composition, music education. Majors: classical music, composition, jazz, music, music education, piano, stringed instruments, voice, wind and percussion instruments. Graduate degrees offered: Master of Music in the areas of performance, theory and composition, music education.

Music Student Profile Fall 1994: 263 total; 200 matriculated undergraduate, 28 matriculated graduate, 35 nondegree; 8% minorities, 55% females, 2% international.

Music Faculty Total: 49; 23 full-time, 26 part-time. Graduate students teach a few undergraduate courses. Undergraduate student–faculty ratio: 10:1.

Student Life Student groups include American Choral Directors Association, Music Educators National Conference. Special housing available for music students.

Estimated Expenses for 1995–96 Application fee: $40. State resident tuition: $1800 full-time, $60 per credit hour part-time. Nonresident tuition: $6800 full-time. Nonresident part-time tuition per semester ranges from $62 to $3400. Part-time mandatory fees: $25 per semester. Tuition for nonresidents who are eligible for the Western Undergraduate Exchange: $2700 full-time, $90 per credit hour part-time. Full-time mandatory fees: $50. College room and board: $5000. Special program-related fees: $75–$150 for private lessons, $35 for practice room fee.

Financial Aid Program-specific awards for Fall of 1994: 30 Department Scholarships for program majors ($500–$1000), 50 Band Scholarships for band members ($500–$2000), Orchestra Scholarships for orchestra members ($500–$2000).

Application Procedures Deadline—freshmen and transfers: June 15. Required: essay, audition, minimum 2.3 high school GPA. Auditions held 3 times in January and February on campus and off campus in various cities; recorded music is permissible as a substitute for live auditions for out-of-state applicants and videotaped performances are permissible as a substitute for live auditions for out-of-state applicants.

Undergraduate Contact Paul Kreider, Chair, Music Department, University of Nevada, Las Vegas, 4505 South Maryland Parkway, Las Vegas, Nevada 89154-5025; 702-895-3332, fax: 702-895-4194.

Graduate Contact Isabelle Emerson, Assistant Chair, Music Department, University of Nevada, Las Vegas, 4505 South Maryland Parkway, Las Vegas, Nevada 89154-5025; 702-895-3114, fax: 702-895-4194, E-mail address: emerson@cfpa.nevada.edu.

University of Nevada, Reno

Reno, Nevada

State-supported, coed. Urban campus. Total enrollment: 11,746.

Degrees Bachelor of Music in the areas of applied music, music education, jazz studies. Majors: applied music, jazz, music education. Graduate degrees offered: Master of Music in the areas of applied music, music education, orchestral career studies.

Music Student Profile Fall 1994: 842 total; 133 matriculated undergraduate, 19 matriculated graduate, 690 nondegree; 50% minorities, 50% females, 5% international.

Music Faculty Total: 29; 13 full-time, 16 part-time; 76% of full-time faculty have terminal degrees. Graduate students teach a few undergraduate courses.

Student Life Student groups include Sigma Alpha Iota, Collegiate Music Educators National Conference, Phi Mu Alpha.

Expenses for 1994–95 Application fee: $20. State resident tuition: $1740 full-time, $58 per credit part-time. Nonresident tuition: $6490 full-time. Nonresident part-time tuition per semester ranges from $58 to $3013. College room and board: $4635. College room only: $2685.

Financial Aid Program-specific awards for Fall of 1994: 144 Barringere Endowment Awards for undergraduates ($500).

Application Procedures Deadline—freshmen and transfers: March 1. Auditions held 1 time on campus and off campus in Las Vegas, NV; recorded music is permissible as a substitute for live auditions and videotaped performances are permissible as a substitute for live auditions. Portfolio reviews held on campus and off campus.

Undergraduate Contact Michael Cleveland, Chairman, Music Department (226), University of Nevada, Reno, Reno, Nevada 89557; 702-784-6145, fax: 702-784-6896.

Graduate Contact Michael Cleveland, Chairman, Department of Music (226), University of Nevada, Reno, Reno, Nevada 89557; 702-784-6145, fax: 702-784-6896.

University of New Hampshire

Durham, New Hampshire

State-supported, coed. Small-town campus. Total enrollment: 12,518.

Degrees Bachelor of Music in the areas of music education, organ, piano, strings, woodwind, brass, percussion, music theory/composition, voice. Majors: music education, music theory and composition, piano/organ, stringed instruments, voice, wind and percussion instruments.

Music Student Profile Fall 1994: 180 total; 150 matriculated undergraduate, 20 matriculated graduate, 10 nondegree; 5% minorities, 50% females, 3% international.

Music Faculty Total: 33; 21 full-time, 12 part-time; 100% of full-time faculty have terminal degrees. Graduate students teach a few undergraduate courses. Undergraduate student–faculty ratio: 7:1.

Student Life Student groups include Music Educators National Conference, Music Teachers National Association.

Expenses for 1994–95 State resident tuition: $3670 full-time, $157 per credit part-time. Nonresident tuition: $11,990 full-time, $500 per credit part-time. Part-time mandatory fees per semester (6 to 11 credits): $235.25. Full-time mandatory fees: $889. College room and board: $4038. College room only: $2326. Special program-related fees: $105 for applied music fee.

Financial Aid Program-specific awards for Fall of 1994: 50 University Music Scholarships for program students ($4600).

Application Procedures Deadline—freshmen: February 1; transfers: March 1. Notification date—freshmen: May 1. Required: essay, high school transcript, letter of recommendation, interview, audition, SAT I test score only. Recommended: portfolio. Auditions held 4 times and by appointment on campus; recorded music is permissible as a substitute for live auditions when distance is prohibitive and videotaped performances are permissible as a substitute for live auditions when

University of New Hampshire *(continued)*

distance is prohibitive. Portfolio reviews held continuously for composition applicants on campus.

Undergraduate Contact John E. Rogers, Chairperson, Music Department, University of New Hampshire, PCAC, Durham, New Hampshire 03824; 603-862-2404, fax: 603-862-3155, E-mail address: jer@christa.unh.edu.

University of New Mexico

Albuquerque, New Mexico

State-supported, coed. Urban campus. Total enrollment: 24,344.

Degrees Bachelor of Music in the areas of performance, music theory; Bachelor of Music Education in the area of music education. Majors: classical music, music, music education, opera, piano/organ, stringed instruments, voice, wind and percussion instruments. Graduate degrees offered: Master of Music in the areas of performance, music theory, conducting; Master of Music Education in the area of music education.

Music Student Profile Fall 1994: 200 total; 150 matriculated undergraduate, 48 matriculated graduate, 2 nondegree; 10% minorities, 60% females, 5% international.

Music Faculty Total: 41; 26 full-time, 15 part-time; 40% of full-time faculty have terminal degrees. Graduate students teach a few undergraduate courses. Undergraduate student–faculty ratio: 10:1.

Student Life Student groups include Music Educators National Conference, Collegiate Chorale.

Expenses for 1995–96 Application fee: $15. State resident tuition: $2080 full-time, $83.20 per semester hour part-time. Nonresident tuition: $7856 full-time, $314.25 per semester hour part-time. College room and board: $4176.

Financial Aid Program-specific awards for Fall of 1994: 20 Friends of Music Awards for freshmen ($1800).

Application Procedures Deadline—freshmen and transfers: July 24. Notification date—freshmen and transfers: August 24. Required: essay, high school transcript, minimum 2.0 high school GPA, 3 letters of recommendation, audition. Recommended: interview, video, portfolio. Auditions held by request on campus; recorded music is permissible as a substitute for live auditions and videotaped performances are permissible as a substitute for live auditions. Portfolio reviews held for composition majors on campus and off campus.

Undergraduate Contact Undergraduate Coordinator, Department of Music, University of New Mexico, Fine Arts Center, Room 1105, Albuquerque, New Mexico 87131-1411; 505-277-8923, fax: 505-277-0708.

Graduate Contact Dr. Karl Hinterbichler, Graduate Coordinator, Department of Music, University of New Mexico, Fine Arts Center, Room 1105, Albuquerque, New Mexico 87131-1411; 505-277-4331, fax: 505-277-0708.

University of North Alabama

Florence, Alabama

State-supported, coed. Urban campus. Total enrollment: 5,221.

Degrees Bachelor of Music in the area of performance; Bachelor of Music Education in the areas of instrumental music education, vocal/choral music education. Majors: music education, piano/organ, voice, wind and percussion instruments.

Music Student Profile Fall 1994: 112 total; all matriculated undergraduate; 5% minorities.

Music Faculty Total: 21; 9 full-time, 12 part-time; 78% of full-time faculty have terminal degrees. Graduate students do not teach undergraduate courses. Undergraduate student–faculty ratio: 13:1.

Student Life Student groups include Music Educators National Conference, Kappa Kappa Psi, Tau Beta Sigma.

Expenses for 1995–96 State resident tuition: $1800 full-time, $75 per semester hour part-time. Nonresident tuition: $3600 full-time, $150 per semester hour part-time. Part-time mandatory fees per year range from $23 to $86. Full-time mandatory fees: $92. College room and board: $3150. College room only: $1400. Special program-related fees: $60 for applied music lesson fee.

Financial Aid Program-specific awards for Fall of 1994: 135 Band Scholarships.

Application Procedures Deadline—freshmen and transfers: August 5. Notification date—freshmen and transfers: continuous. Required: high school transcript, minimum 2.0 high school GPA, audition. Auditions held as needed on campus and off campus in Panama City, FL; recorded music is permissible as a substitute for live auditions and videotaped performances are permissible as a substitute for live auditions.

Undergraduate Contact James Simpson, Chair, Music Department, University of North Alabama, Box 5040, Florence, Alabama 35632-0001; 205-760-4361, fax: 205-760-4329.

University of North Carolina at Chapel Hill

Chapel Hill, North Carolina

State-supported, coed. Small-town campus. Total enrollment: 24,463.

Degrees Bachelor of Music Education in the area of music education. Majors: classical music, music, music education, piano/organ, stringed instruments, voice, wind and percussion instruments. Graduate degrees offered: Master of Music in the areas of performance, composition.

Music Student Profile Fall 1994: 143 total; 98 matriculated undergraduate, 45 matriculated graduate; 3% minorities, 60% females, 7% international.

Music Faculty Total: 49; 28 full-time, 21 part-time; 97% of full-time faculty have terminal degrees. Graduate students teach a few undergraduate courses. Undergraduate student–faculty ratio: 20:1.

Student Life Student groups include Phi Mu Alpha, Sigma Alpha Iota.

Expenses for 1994–95 State resident tuition: $874 full-time. Nonresident tuition: $8400 full-time. Full-time mandatory fees: $695. College room and board: $4200. College room only: $2040. Special program-related fees: $260 for private lessons, $25 for practice fees.

Financial Aid Program-specific awards for Fall of 1994: 2 Richard and Christopher Edward Adler Scholarships for program majors ($750), 1 D. W. Woodward Scholarship for viola players ($1500), 1 J. M. Barham Scholarship for program majors ($500), 6 Sidney Dowd Scholarships for pianists ($1500), 1 Lisa Fields Scholarship for pianists ($500), 1 A. J. Fletcher Foundation Scholarship for program majors ($5000), 3 Janet and Newton Fischer Scholarships for vocalists ($1000), 1 Andy Griffith Fund Scholarship for program majors ($750), 2 Eric Schwarz Fund Scholarships for program majors ($600), 2 Lemuel Sedberry Scholarships for program majors ($800), 10 Music Scholarships for program majors ($500), 15 Wind, Brass and Percussion Scholarships for instrumentalists ($500), 1 Paisley Scott Scholarship for program majors ($1000).

Application Procedures Deadline—freshmen: January 15; transfers: March 1. Notification date—freshmen and transfers: April 15. Required: high school transcript, SAT I test score only.

Undergraduate Contact Michael Zenge, Professor, Music Department, University of North Carolina at Chapel Hill, CB# 3320 Hill Hall, Chapel Hill, North Carolina 27599-3320; 919-962-1039, fax: 919-962-3376.

Graduate Contact Evan Bonds, Director of Graduate Admissions, Music Department, University of North Carolina at Chapel Hill, CB# 3320 Hill Hall, Chapel Hill, North Carolina 27599-3320; 919-962-1039, fax: 919-962-3376.

University of North Carolina at Charlotte

Charlotte, North Carolina

State-supported, coed. Urban campus. Total enrollment: 15,513.

Degrees Bachelor of Music in the areas of performance, music education. Majors: classical music, composition, electronic music, jazz, music education, opera, piano/organ, stringed instruments, voice, wind and percussion instruments.

Music Student Profile Fall 1994: 50 total; all matriculated undergraduate.

Music Faculty Total: 24; 9 full-time, 15 part-time; 80% of full-time faculty have terminal degrees. Graduate students do not teach undergraduate courses. Undergraduate student–faculty ratio: 10:1.

Expenses for 1994–95 Application fee: $25. State resident tuition: $764 full-time. Nonresident tuition: $7248 full-time. Part-time tuition per semester ranges from $96 to $287 for state residents, $906 to $2718 for nonresidents. Part-time mandatory fees per semester range from $87 to $178.50. Full-time mandatory fees: $695. College room and board: $3260. College room only: $1670.

Application Procedures Deadline—freshmen and transfers: July 1. Required: high school transcript, minimum 2.0 high school GPA, letter of recommendation, audition, SAT I or ACT test scores, medical history. Auditions held 4 times on campus; recorded music is permissible as a substitute for live auditions and videotaped performances are permissible as a substitute for live auditions.

Undergraduate Contact Douglas E. Bish, Chair, Music Department, University of North Carolina at Charlotte, Charlotte, North Carolina 28223; 704-547-2472, fax: 704-547-3795.

University of North Carolina at Greensboro

Greensboro, North Carolina

State-supported, coed. Urban campus. Total enrollment: 12,094.

Degrees Bachelor of Music in the areas of performance, music education, composition, jazz performance. Majors: classical music, jazz, music education, piano/organ, stringed instruments, voice, wind and percussion instruments. Graduate degrees offered: Master of Music in the areas of performance, music education, composition, music theory. Doctor of Musical Arts in the area of performance. Cross-registration with Bennett College, Elon College, Greensboro College, Guilford College, High Point University, Guilford Technical Community College, North Carolina A and T University.

Music Student Profile Fall 1994: 420 total; 290 matriculated undergraduate, 130 matriculated graduate; 11% minorities, 53% females, 1% international.

Music Faculty Total: 50; 42 full-time, 8 part-time; 71% of full-time faculty have terminal degrees. Graduate students teach a few undergraduate courses. Undergraduate student–faculty ratio: 6:1.

Student Life Student groups include Collegiate Music Educators National Conference, Phi Mu Alpha Sinfonia, Mu Phi Epsilon.

Expenses for 1994–95 Application fee: $35. State resident tuition: $874 full-time. Nonresident tuition: $8400 full-time. Part-time tuition per semester ranges from $109 to $328 for state residents, $1050 to $3150 for nonresidents. Full-time mandatory fees: $891. College room and board: $3505. College room only: $1791.

Financial Aid Program-specific awards for Fall of 1994: 100–150 Music Scholarships for undergraduates ($200–$2000).

Application Procedures Deadline—freshmen and transfers: continuous. Required: audition. Auditions held 5

University of North Carolina at Greensboro
(continued)

times and by appointment on campus; recorded music is permissible as a substitute for live auditions when distance is prohibitive, for provisional acceptance and videotaped performances are permissible as a substitute for live auditions when distance is prohibitive, for provisional acceptance.

Undergraduate Contact James Prodan, Assistant Dean, School of Music, University of North Carolina at Greensboro, Corner of Tate and Walker Avenue, Greensboro, North Carolina 27412-5001; 910-334-5789, fax: 910-334-5497.

Graduate Contact James Sherbon, Director of Graduate Studies, School of Music, University of North Carolina at Greensboro, Corner of Tate and Walker Avenue, Greensboro, North Carolina 27412-5001; 910-334-5794, fax: 910-334-5497.

University of North Dakota

Grand Forks, North Dakota

State-supported, coed. Small-town campus. Total enrollment: 11,521.

Degrees Bachelor of Music in the areas of performance, music education. Majors: music education, piano/organ, stringed instruments, voice, wind and percussion instruments. Graduate degrees offered: Master of Music in the areas of music education, composition, vocal performance, vocal pedagogy, keyboard performance, keyboard pedagogy.

Music Student Profile Fall 1994: 107 total; 87 matriculated undergraduate, 20 matriculated graduate; 2% minorities, 50% females, 2% international.

Music Faculty Total: 24; 15 full-time, 9 part-time; 67% of full-time faculty have terminal degrees. Graduate students teach a few undergraduate courses. Undergraduate student–faculty ratio: 6:1.

Student Life Student groups include Music Educators National Conference, American Choral Directors Association.

Expenses for 1995–96 Application fee: $25. State resident tuition: $2878 full-time, $119.92 per credit hour part-time. Nonresident tuition: $6402 full-time, $266.75 per credit hour part-time. Full-time mandatory fees: $318. College room and board: $2816. Special program-related fees: $50 for applied music fees.

Financial Aid Program-specific awards for Fall of 1994: 45 Music Scholarships for program majors/minors ($500–$1000).

Application Procedures Deadline—freshmen and transfers: continuous. Required: high school transcript, audition. Auditions held 3 times on campus and off campus in various cities in North Dakota; recorded music is permissible as a substitute for live auditions when distance is prohibitive and videotaped performances are permissible as a substitute for live auditions when distance is prohibitive.

Contact E. John Miller, Chair, Music Department, University of North Dakota, Box 7125, Grand Forks, North Dakota 58202; 701-777-2644, fax: 701-777-3395, E-mail address: jmiller@rs1.cc.und.nodak.edu.

University of North Florida

Jacksonville, Florida

State-supported, coed. Urban campus. Total enrollment: 10,064.

Degrees Bachelor of Music in the area of jazz. Majors: jazz.

Estimated Expenses for 1995–96 Application fee: $20. State resident tuition: $1820 full-time, $55.01 per semester hour part-time. Nonresident tuition: $6390 full-time, $213.66 per semester hour part-time. College room and board: $3800.

Financial Aid Program-specific awards for Fall of 1994 available.

Undergraduate Contact Dr. Gerson Yessin, Chair, Department of Music, University of North Florida, 4567 St. Johns Bluff Road South, Jacksonville, Florida 32224-2645; 904-646-2960, fax: 904-646-2563.

University of North Texas

Denton, Texas

State-supported, coed. Urban campus. Total enrollment: 25,605.

Degrees Bachelor of Music in the areas of composition, theory, music history and literature, performance, jazz studies, music education. Majors: composition, jazz, music education, music history and literature, music theory, piano/organ, stringed instruments, voice, wind and percussion instruments. Graduate degrees offered: Master of Music in the areas of theory, composition, musicology, jazz studies, conducting, organ, piano, voice, performance, music education. Doctor of Musical Arts in the areas of performance, composition, conducting.

Music Student Profile Fall 1994: 1,500 total; 1,000 matriculated undergraduate, 500 matriculated graduate.

Music Faculty Total: 130; 100 full-time, 30 part-time; 100% of full-time faculty have terminal degrees. Graduate students teach a few undergraduate courses.

Student Life Student groups include Sigma Alpha Iota, Phi Mu Alpha Sinfonia, NT 40.

Expenses for 1995–96 Application fee: $25. State resident tuition: $900 full-time. Nonresident tuition: $6660 full-time, $222 per semester hour part-time. State resident part-time tuition per semester ranges from $120 to $330. Part-time mandatory fees per semester range from $92.30 to $332.30. Full-time mandatory fees: $813. College room and board: $3659. College room only:

$1877. Special program-related fees: $10–$40 for practice room fee, $10 for instrument rental, $30–$60 for applied lesson fee.

Financial Aid Program-specific awards for Fall of 1994: Music Scholarships for out-of-state students ($200–$2000).

Application Procedures Deadline—freshmen and transfers: June 15. Required: high school transcript, college transcript(s) for transfer students, 3 letters of recommendation, audition, SAT I or ACT test scores, minimum combined SAT I score of 800, minimum composite ACT score of 19. Auditions held 3 times on campus and off campus in Chicago, IL; Interlochen, MI; recorded music is permissible as a substitute for live auditions and videotaped performances are permissible as a substitute for live auditions.

Undergraduate Contact Judy Fisher, Undergraduate Advisor, College of Music, University of North Texas, P.O. Box 13887, Denton, Texas 76203-6887; 817-565-3734, fax: 817-565-2002, E-mail address: fisher@music.unt.edu.

Graduate Contact Dr. Edward Baird, Director of Graduate Studies, College of Music, University of North Texas, P.O. Box 13887, Denton, Texas 76203-6887; 817-565-3733, fax: 817-565-2002.

University of Northern Colorado

Greeley, Colorado

State-supported, coed. Suburban campus. Total enrollment: 10,426.

Degrees Bachelor of Music in the areas of instrumental performance, piano, music theory and composition, voice performance; Bachelor of Music Education in the areas of instrumental music education, piano/vocal music education, general music education. Majors: classical music, music, music education, music history, music theory and composition, opera, piano/organ, stringed instruments, voice, wind and percussion instruments. Graduate degrees offered: Master of Music in the areas of choral conducting, instrumental performance, music history and literature, music theory and composition, wind/orchestral conducting; Master of Music Education in the area of music education. Doctor of Arts in the area of music; Doctor of Music Education in the area of music education.

Music Student Profile Fall 1994: 418 total; 358 matriculated undergraduate, 50 matriculated graduate, 10 nondegree; 8% minorities, 58% females, 10% international.

Music Faculty Total: 45; 38 full-time, 7 part-time; 50% of full-time faculty have terminal degrees. Graduate students teach about a quarter undergraduate courses. Undergraduate student–faculty ratio: 9:1.

Student Life Student groups include Kappa Kappa Psi, National Association of Jazz Educators, Collegiate Music Educators National Conference.

Expenses for 1995–96 Application fee: $30. State resident tuition: $1872 full-time, $104 per credit hour part-time. Nonresident tuition: $8070 full-time, $448 per credit hour part-time. Part-time mandatory fees: $30 per credit hour. Full-time mandatory fees: $536. College room and board: $4270 (minimum). Special program-related fees: $3 for university technology fee, $20 for music major fee, $10 for music technology fee, $10 for private lesson fee for non-majors.

Financial Aid Program-specific awards for Fall of 1994: 200 Music Talent Awards for program majors ($500), 24 Academic Scholarships for program majors ($1000).

Application Procedures Deadline—freshmen and transfers: continuous. Required: high school transcript, college transcript(s) for transfer students, interview, audition, SAT I or ACT test scores, minimum combined SAT I score of 890, minimum composite ACT score of 22, minimum 2.8 high school GPA. Recommended: portfolio. Auditions held 5 times on campus; recorded music is permissible as a substitute for live auditions when distance is prohibitive and videotaped performances are permissible as a substitute for live auditions for conducting applicants. Portfolio reviews held 5 times for transfer students on campus and off campus.

Undergraduate Contact Dr. Shirley Howell, Director, School of Music, University of Northern Colorado, Frasier 108, Greeley, Colorado 80639; 303-351-2678, fax: 303-351-2679.

Graduate Contact Robert C. Ehle, Graduate Coordinator for Music, School of Music, University of Northern Colorado, Frasier 108, Greeley, Colorado 80639; 303-351-2678, fax: 303-351-2679.

University of Northern Iowa

Cedar Falls, Iowa

State-supported, coed. Small-town campus. Total enrollment: 12,572.

Degrees Bachelor of Music in the areas of performance, composition, music education. Majors: composition, music education, piano/organ, stringed instruments, voice, wind and percussion instruments. Graduate degrees offered: Master of Music in the areas of music education, performance, music history, conducting, jazz pedagogy, composition.

Music Student Profile Fall 1994: 199 total; 169 matriculated undergraduate, 30 matriculated graduate; 1% minorities, 55% females.

Music Faculty Total: 42; 39 full-time, 3 part-time; 56% of full-time faculty have terminal degrees. Graduate students teach a few undergraduate courses.

Student Life Student groups include Music Educators National Conference, American Choral Director's Association.

Expenses for 1995–96 Application fee: $20. State resident tuition: $2390 full-time, $100 per semester hour part-time. Nonresident tuition: $6462 full-time, $270 per semester hour part-time. Part-time mandatory fees per semester range from $11 to $32. Full-time mandatory fees: $172. College room and board: $3112. Special program-related fees: $78–$112 for applied music fee.

University of Northern Iowa *(continued)*

Financial Aid Program-specific awards for Fall of 1994: School of Music Awards for program majors ($200–$2500), Robert Dean Scholarship for music majors, Myron Russell Scholarships for music majors.

Application Procedures Deadline—freshmen: February 15. Required: high school transcript, college transcript(s) for transfer students, audition, SAT I or ACT test scores. Recommended: interview. Auditions held 2 times on campus and off campus; recorded music is permissible as a substitute for live auditions for out-of-state applicants and videotaped performances are permissible as a substitute for live auditions for out-of-state applicants. Portfolio reviews held on campus and off campus.

Undergraduate Contact Dr. Alan Schmitz, Associate Director, School of Music, University of Northern Iowa, Russell Hall Room 110, Cedar Falls, Iowa 50614-0246; 319-273-2024, fax: 319-273-2731.

Graduate Contact Graduate Coordinator, School of Music, University of Northern Iowa, Russell Hall Room 110, Cedar Falls, Iowa 50614-0246; 319-273-2024, fax: 319-273-2731.

University of Oklahoma

Norman, Oklahoma

State-supported, coed. Suburban campus. Total enrollment: 19,683.

Degrees Bachelor of Music in the areas of performance, composition, piano pedagogy; Bachelor of Music Education in the areas of instrumental music education, vocal music education, combined instrumental music education; Bachelor of Fine Arts in the areas of music, musical theater; Bachelor of Musical Arts in the area of music. Majors: composition, music, music education, music theater, piano/organ, stringed instruments, voice, wind and percussion instruments. Graduate degrees offered: Master of Music in the areas of performance, composition, conducting, music history, piano pedagogy; Master of Music Education in the areas of instrumental music, vocal music, Kodaly, conducting. Doctor of Musical Arts in the areas of performance, composition, conducting, piano pedagogy.

Music Student Profile Fall 1994: 391 total; 244 matriculated undergraduate, 147 matriculated graduate; 12% minorities, 52% females, 10% international.

Music Faculty Total: 51; 41 full-time, 10 part-time; 95% of full-time faculty have terminal degrees. Graduate students teach a few undergraduate courses. Undergraduate student–faculty ratio: 6:1.

Student Life Student groups include music fraternities and sororities, Music Educators National Conference, Percussive Arts Society.

Expenses for 1994–95 Application fee: $15. Part-time mandatory fees: $91 per semester. Full-time tuition ranges from $1688 to $1785 for state residents, $4928 to $5438 for nonresidents according to class level. Part-time tuition per credit hour ranges from $56.25 to $59.49 for state residents, $164.25 to $181.26 for nonresidents according to class level. Full-time mandatory fees: $182. College room and board: $3526. Special program-related fees: $40 for applied music fee, $5–$30 for special course fees.

Financial Aid Program-specific awards for Fall of 1994: 75–100 Fee/Tuition Waivers for program majors ($1000), 20–40 Scholarships for undergraduates ($500).

Application Procedures Deadline—freshmen and transfers: continuous. Required: high school transcript, college transcript(s) for transfer students, minimum 2.0 high school GPA, letter of recommendation, audition, SAT I or ACT test scores. Auditions held 3 times on campus; recorded music is permissible as a substitute for live auditions and videotaped performances are permissible as a substitute for live auditions.

Undergraduate Contact David Etheridge, Coordinator of Extended Programs and Recruiting, School of Music, University of Oklahoma, 560 Parrington Oval, Norman, Oklahoma 73019; 405-325-2081, fax: 405-325-7574.

Graduate Contact Jane Magrath, Associate Director, School of Music, University of Oklahoma, 560 Parrington Oval, Norman, Oklahoma 73019; 405-325-2081, fax: 405-325-7574, E-mail address: jmagrath@uoknor.edu.

University of Oregon

Eugene, Oregon

State-supported, coed. Urban campus. Total enrollment: 16,681.

Degrees Bachelor of Music in the areas of music composition, music education, music performance, music theory, jazz. Majors: composition, jazz, music, music education, music theory, piano/organ, stringed instruments, voice, wind and percussion instruments. Graduate degrees offered: Master of Music in the areas of composition, conducting, performance, piano pedagogy. Doctor of Musical Arts in the areas of music composition, music education, music performance.

Music Student Profile Fall 1994: 343 total; 197 matriculated undergraduate, 146 matriculated graduate; 3% minorities, 44% females.

Music Faculty Total: 47; 35 full-time, 12 part-time; 70% of full-time faculty have terminal degrees. Graduate students teach about a quarter undergraduate courses. Undergraduate student–faculty ratio: 15:1.

Student Life Student groups include Oregon Bach Festival, Martin Luther King Celebration events, Children's Concert Series. Special housing available for music students.

Estimated Expenses for 1995–96 Application fee: $50. State resident tuition: $2590 full-time. Nonresident tuition: $10,300 full-time. Part-time tuition per quarter ranges from $250 to $1112 for state residents, $481 to $3652 for nonresidents. Full-time mandatory fees: $790. College room and board: $3900. Special program-related fees: $50–$60 for non-majors private lessons, $25 for

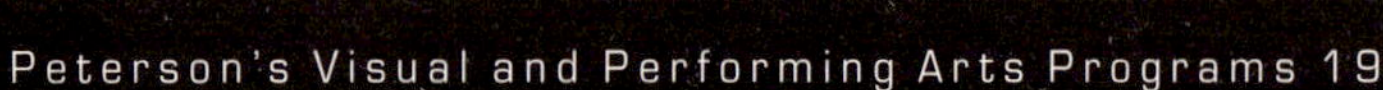

music major fee, $10 for music education class instrument fee, $80 for group lessons, $10 for ensemble fee, $25 for synthesizer lab fee, $10 for organ/harpsichord/ percussion fee, $10 for locked grand piano practice room fee, $30 for instrument rental, $5 for music locker rental, $50–$200 for accompanying fee, $65 for recital and recording fee.

Financial Aid Program-specific awards for Fall of 1994: 5 Phi Beta Patron Scholarships for program majors ($500), 1 Presser Scholarship for outstanding juniors and seniors ($2200), 1 Corbett Scholarship for Oregon students ($1200), 7 Stauffer Scholarships for male graduates of Oregon high schools ($1000), 3 Mu Phi Epsilon Patron Scholarships for program students ($1000), 1 Phi Beta Patrons (Saunders) Scholarship for pianists ($500), 2 Tuba Scholarships for tuba players ($375), 1 Moore Scholarship for vocalists ($800), 1 H.B. Densmore Scholarship for vocalists ($500), 1 Maude Densmore Scholarship for continuing vocalists ($500), 1 Dorian Scholarship for voice or piano majors ($1500), 1 Sandberg Scholarship for composition majors ($1500).

Application Procedures Deadline—freshmen: June 1; transfers: September 1. Notification date—freshmen and transfers: continuous. Required: high school transcript, college transcript(s) for transfer students, minimum 3.0 high school GPA, audition, SAT I or ACT test scores. Recommended: essay, 3 letters of recommendation. Auditions held 6 times and by appointment on campus and off campus in Seattle, WA; Portland, OR; recorded music is permissible as a substitute for live auditions when distance is prohibitive and videotaped performances are permissible as a substitute for live auditions when distance is prohibitive.

Undergraduate Contact Marilyn Bradetich, Undergraduate Secretary, School of Music, University of Oregon, 1225 University of Oregon, Eugene, Oregon 97403-1225; 503-346-1164, fax: 503-346-0723, E-mail address: mbradeti@oregon.uoregon.edu.

Graduate Contact Dana Martin, Graduate Secretary, School of Music, University of Oregon, 1225 University of Oregon, Eugene, Oregon 97403-1225; 503-346-5664, fax: 503-346-0723, E-mail address: dgmartin@oregon.uoregon.edu.

University of Portland

Portland, Oregon

Independent-religious, coed. Suburban campus. Total enrollment: 2,600.

Degrees Bachelor of Music Education in the area of music education. Majors: music education. Graduate degrees offered: Master of Fine Arts in the area of music education.

Music Student Profile Fall 1994: 65 total; 45 matriculated undergraduate, 20 matriculated graduate; 10% minorities, 60% females, 15% international.

Music Faculty Total: 19; 4 full-time, 15 part-time; 100% of full-time faculty have terminal degrees. Graduate students do not teach undergraduate courses. Undergraduate student–faculty ratio: 6:1.

Student Life Student groups include Collegiate Music Educators National Conference.

Expenses for 1995–96 Application fee: $30. Comprehensive fee of $17,490 includes full-time tuition ($13,200), mandatory fees ($50), and college room and board ($4240). College room only: $1750. Part-time tuition: $420 per semester hour. Special program-related fees: $30 for electronic music lab fees.

Financial Aid Program-specific awards for Fall of 1994: 1–3 Dean's Scholarships for performers ($1750), 1–3 Vance Scholarships for music education majors ($1750), 10–20 Talent Grants for program majors and minors ($1750).

Application Procedures Deadline—freshmen and transfers: continuous. Notification date—freshmen and transfers: continuous. Required: high school transcript, minimum 2.0 high school GPA. Recommended: essay, minimum 3.0 high school GPA, letter of recommendation, interview, audition. Auditions held 4 times on campus; recorded music is permissible as a substitute for live auditions if distance is prohibitive or scheduling is difficult and videotaped performances are permissible as a substitute for live auditions if distance is prohibitive or scheduling is difficult.

Undergraduate Contact Office of Admissions, University of Portland, 5000 North Willamette Boulevard, Portland, Oregon 97203; 503-283-7147, fax: 503-283-7399.

Graduate Contact Kenneth Kleszynski, Graduate Program Director/Music, Performing and Fine Arts Department, University of Portland, 5000 North Willamette Boulevard, Portland, Oregon 97203; 503-283-7294, fax: 503-283-7399.

University of Prince Edward Island

Charlottetown, Prince Edward Island

Province-supported, coed. Small-town campus. Total enrollment: 3,156.

Degrees Bachelor of Music in the areas of music education, general music. Majors: classical music, music, music education, music history, music theory and composition, piano/organ, voice, wind and percussion instruments.

Music Student Profile Fall 1994: 48 total; all matriculated undergraduate; 57% females.

Music Faculty Total: 9; 6 full-time, 3 part-time; 100% of full-time faculty have terminal degrees. Undergraduate student–faculty ratio: 8:1.

Student Life Special housing available for music students.

Expenses for 1994–95 Canadian resident tuition: $2620 full-time, $262 per course part-time. Nonresident tuition: $4320 full-time, $432 per course part-time. Part-time mandatory fees: $5 per course. (All figures are in Canadian dollars.). Full-time mandatory fees range from $300 to $550. College room and board: $4800. College room only: $2100. Special program-related fees: $60 for instrument rental, locker, telephone.

University of Prince Edward Island *(continued)*

Financial Aid Program-specific awards for Fall of 1994: 1 Tersteeg Music Scholarship for juniors ($250), 1 Bevan-MacRae Music Award for juniors ($250), 8 Music Alumni Scholarships for freshmen ($200–$750), 2 Music Society Scholarships for sophomores and seniors ($125), 2 Claude and Dr. Bernice Bell Awards for undergraduates ($1000), 1 Elsie Cuthbertson Memorial Music Scholarship for undergraduates ($250), 1 Frances Dindial Memorial Music Scholarship for freshmen ($600).

Application Procedures Deadline—freshmen and transfers: August 15. Notification date—freshmen and transfers: August 25. Required: high school transcript, college transcript(s) for transfer students, letter of recommendation, interview, audition. Auditions held 5 times on campus; recorded music is permissible as a substitute for live auditions when distance is prohibitive and videotaped performances are permissible as a substitute for live auditions when distance is prohibitive.

Undergraduate Contact Gloria J. Jay, Audition Coordinator, Music Department, University of Prince Edward Island, 550 University Avenue, Charlottetown, Prince Edward Island C1A 4P3, Canada; 902-566-0507, fax: 902-566-0420, E-mail address: gjay@upei.ca.

University of Puget Sound

Tacoma, Washington

Independent, coed. Suburban campus. Total enrollment: 3,163.

Degrees Bachelor of Music in the areas of performance, music education, and with elective studies in business. Majors: classical music, music, music business, music education, piano/organ, stringed instruments, voice, wind and percussion instruments.

Music Student Profile Fall 1994: 490 total; 90 matriculated undergraduate, 400 nondegree.

Music Faculty Total: 29; 12 full-time, 17 part-time; 90% of full-time faculty have terminal degrees. Graduate students do not teach undergraduate courses.

Student Life Special housing available for music students.

Expenses for 1995–96 Application fee: $35. Comprehensive fee of $22,170 includes full-time tuition ($17,310), mandatory fees ($140), and college room and board ($4720). Part-time tuition: $2180 per course.

Financial Aid Program-specific awards for Fall of 1994: Music Scholarships for incoming students.

Application Procedures Deadline—freshmen and transfers: February 1. Required: high school transcript, college transcript(s) for transfer students, 3 letters of recommendation, interview, audition, SAT I or ACT test scores. Recommended: minimum 3.0 high school GPA. Auditions held 1 time on campus; recorded music is permissible as a substitute for live auditions when distance is prohibitive and videotaped performances are permissible as a substitute for live auditions when distance is prohibitive.

Undergraduate Contact Office of Admission, University of Puget Sound, 1500 North Warner Street, Tacoma, Washington 98416.

University of Redlands

Redlands, California

Independent, coed. Small-town campus. Total enrollment: 3,950.

Degrees Bachelor of Music in the areas of performance, music education, composition, musical studies. Majors: classical music, composition, music, music education, piano/organ, stringed instruments, voice, wind and percussion instruments. Graduate degrees offered: Master of Music in the areas of performance, music education, composition.

Music Student Profile Fall 1994: 136 total; 92 matriculated undergraduate, 28 matriculated graduate, 16 nondegree; 9% minorities, 54% females, 23% international.

Music Faculty Total: 29; 12 full-time, 17 part-time; 100% of full-time faculty have terminal degrees. Graduate students teach about a quarter undergraduate courses. Undergraduate student–faculty ratio: 7:1.

Student Life Student groups include Sigma Alpha Iota, Phi Mu Alpha Sinfonia, Music Educators National Conference Student Chapter.

Expenses for 1995–96 Application fee: $40. Comprehensive fee of $23,850 includes full-time tuition ($17,110), mandatory fees ($225), and college room and board ($6515). College room only: $3620. Part-time tuition: $517 per unit.

Financial Aid Program-specific awards for Fall of 1994: 65 Music Merit Awards for incoming freshmen ($300–$4000), Area Specific Awards for program students.

Application Procedures Deadline—freshmen and transfers: May 1. Notification date—freshmen: September 1; transfers: August 1. Required: essay, high school transcript, college transcript(s) for transfer students, minimum 3.0 high school GPA, letter of recommendation, interview, audition, portfolio, SAT I or ACT test scores, minimum combined SAT I score of 950, minimum composite ACT score of 24. Auditions held 4 times on campus; recorded music is permissible as a substitute for live auditions when distance is prohibitive and videotaped performances are permissible as a substitute for live auditions when distance is prohibitive. Portfolio reviews held continuously for composition majors on campus.

Contact Pamela Stinson, Admissions Coordinator, School of Music, University of Redlands, 1200 East Colton Avenue, Box 3080, Redlands, California 92373; 909-335-4014, fax: 909-793-2029.

University of Regina

Regina, Saskatchewan

Province-supported, coed. Urban campus. Total enrollment: 11,537.

Degrees Bachelor of Music in the areas of performance, composition, music history; Bachelor of Music Education in the areas of music education, secondary music education. Majors: classical music, composition, music, music education, music history, opera, piano/organ, stringed instruments, voice, wind and percussion instruments. Graduate degrees offered: Master of Music in the areas of performance, composition, conducting.

Music Student Profile Fall 1994: 91 total; 86 matriculated undergraduate, 2 matriculated graduate, 3 nondegree; 1% minorities, 63% females, 3% international.

Music Faculty Total: 19; 10 full-time, 9 part-time; 27% of full-time faculty have terminal degrees. Graduate students teach a few undergraduate courses. Undergraduate student–faculty ratio: 8:1.

Student Life Student groups include Saskatchewan Music Educators Association, Music Students Association.

Expenses for 1994–95 Application fee: $25. Canadian resident tuition: $2490 full-time, $83 per credit hour part-time. Nonresident tuition: $4110 full-time, $137 per credit hour part-time. Full-time mandatory fees: $50. College room and board: $3759. College room only: $1542. Special program-related fees: $25 for instrument fee for techniques courses.

Financial Aid Program-specific awards for Fall of 1994: 2 Bachelor of Music Entrance Scholarships for Saskatchewan residents ($1300), 1 Entrance Scholarship for freshmen ($750), 1 Laubach Scholarship for strings majors ($1000), 5 Music Scholarships for piano or voice majors ($250–$1000).

Application Procedures Deadline—freshmen and transfers: July 31. Required: high school transcript, minimum 2.0 high school GPA, interview, audition. Auditions held 5 times on campus; recorded music is permissible as a substitute for live auditions when distance is prohibitive and videotaped performances are permissible as a substitute for live auditions when distance is prohibitive.

Undergraduate Contact Karen Shepherd, Administrative Assistant–Registration and Records, Office of the Registrar, University of Regina, 3737 Wascana Parkway, Regina, Saskatchewan S4S 0A2, Canada; 306-585-4176, fax: 306-585-5203.

Graduate Contact Dr. George Maslany, Associate Dean, Faculty of Graduate Studies and Research, University of Regina, Regina, Saskatchewan S4S 0A2, Canada; 306-585-4161, fax: 306-585-4893.

University of Rhode Island

Kingston, Rhode Island

State-supported, coed. Small-town campus. Total enrollment: 12,110.

Degrees Bachelor of Music in the areas of music education, music theory and composition, music history and literature, classical guitar, voice, piano or organ, orchestral instrument. Majors: classical guitar, music education, music history and literature, music theory and composition, piano/organ, voice. Graduate degrees offered: Master of Music in the areas of music education, performance.

Music Student Profile Fall 1994: 1,289 total; 67 matriculated undergraduate, 22 matriculated graduate, 1,200 nondegree; 8% minorities, 50% females, 5% international.

Music Faculty Total: 31; 13 full-time, 18 part-time; 90% of full-time faculty have terminal degrees. Graduate students do not teach undergraduate courses. Undergraduate student–faculty ratio: 8:1.

Student Life Student groups include Music Educators National Conference Student Chapter, Kappa Kappa Psi, Tau Beta Sigma.

Expenses for 1995–96 Application fee: $30. State resident tuition: $3154 full-time, $131 per credit part-time. Nonresident tuition: $10,846 full-time, $452 per credit part-time. Part-time mandatory fees: $70 per year. Tuition for nonresidents who are eligible for the New England Regional Student Program: $5744 full-time, $125 per credit part-time. Full-time mandatory fees: $1250. College room and board: $5564 (minimum). College room only: $3276. Special program-related fees: $190 for applied music lesson fee.

Financial Aid Program-specific awards for Fall of 1994: 35 Music Scholarships for program majors/minors ($250–$4000), 4 Honors String Quartet Scholarships for top string players ($4577–$11,603).

Application Procedures Deadline—freshmen and transfers: continuous. Notification date—freshmen and transfers: continuous. Required: high school transcript, audition, SAT I or ACT test scores, 2.5 college GPA for transfer students. Recommended: minimum 3.0 high school GPA, interview, video. Auditions held 7 times on campus; recorded music is permissible as a substitute for live auditions with approval from the department and videotaped performances are permissible as a substitute for live auditions with approval from the department.

Undergraduate Contact Music Office, Department of Music, University of Rhode Island, Fine Arts Center, Kingston, Rhode Island 02881; 401-792-2431, fax: 401-792-2772.

Graduate Contact Dr. Geoffrey Gibbs, Director, Graduate Studies in Music, Department of Music, University of Rhode Island, Fine Arts Center, Kingston, Rhode Island 02881; 401-792-2431, fax: 401-792-2772.

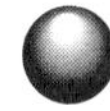

University of Richmond

Richmond, Virginia

Independent-religious, coed. Suburban campus. Total enrollment: 4,315.

Degrees Bachelor of Music in the areas of performance, music education, music theory. Majors: music education,

University of Richmond *(continued)*

music theory, performance, piano/organ, stringed instruments, voice, wind and percussion instruments.

Music Student Profile Fall 1994: 30 total; all matriculated undergraduate; 65% females.

Music Faculty Total: 28; 8 full-time, 20 part-time; 100% of full-time faculty have terminal degrees. Graduate students do not teach undergraduate courses. Undergraduate student–faculty ratio: 12:1.

Student Life Student groups include Music Educators National Conference.

Expenses for 1995–96 Application fee: $40. Comprehensive fee of $18,935 includes full-time tuition ($15,500) and college room and board ($3435). College room only: $1465. Part-time tuition: $775 per semester hour. Part-time tuition per semester hour for evening session: $152.

Financial Aid Program-specific awards for Fall of 1994: 6–8 Music Scholarships for program majors ($2500–$6000).

Application Procedures Deadline—freshmen and transfers: February 1. Notification date—freshmen and transfers: April 1. Required: essay, high school transcript, college transcript(s) for transfer students, SAT I or ACT test scores, SAT II. Recommended: 2 letters of recommendation, interview, audition. Auditions held 3 times on campus; recorded music is permissible as a substitute for live auditions when distance is prohibitive and videotaped performances are permissible as a substitute for live auditions when distance is prohibitive.

Undergraduate Contact Pam Spence, Dean of Admissions, University of Richmond, Sarah Brunet Hall, Richmond Way, Richmond, Virginia 23173; 804-289-8640.

Eastman School of Music

University of Rochester

Rochester, New York

Independent, coed. Suburban campus. Total enrollment: 8,336.

Degrees Bachelor of Music in the areas of composition, music education, music theory, performance, jazz studies. Majors: classical music, composition, guitar, harpsichord, music education, music theory, orchestral instruments, piano/organ, stringed instruments, voice, wind and percussion instruments. Graduate degrees offered: Master of Music in the areas of jazz, composition, conducting, music education, performance, accompanying, opera. Doctor of Musical Arts in the areas of composition, conducting, music education, performance, accompanying.

Music Student Profile Fall 1994: 813 total; 19% minorities, 52% females, 19% international.

Music Faculty Total: 105; 88 full-time, 17 part-time; 53% of full-time faculty have terminal degrees. Graduate students teach a few undergraduate courses. Undergraduate student–faculty ratio: 5:1.

Student Life Student groups include Music Educators National Conference, a variety of student ensembles, Composers' Forum.

Expenses for 1995–96 Application fee: $50. Comprehensive fee of $24,548 includes full-time tuition ($17,373), mandatory fees ($445), and college room and board ($6730). College room only: $4060. Part-time tuition: $586 per credit hour.

Financial Aid Program-specific awards for Fall of 1994: 330 Merit-based Scholarships for those demonstrating talent and academic achievement ($2000–$5000), 400 Financial Aid Awards for those demonstrating need ($2000–$17,000).

Application Procedures Deadline—freshmen and transfers: February 1. Notification date—freshmen and transfers: April 15. Required: high school transcript, 3 letters of recommendation, audition. Recommended: minimum 3.0 high school GPA, interview. Auditions held 18 times on campus and off campus in Atlanta, GA; Boston, MA; Chicago, IL; Cleveland, OH; Dallas, TX; Houston, TX; Los Angeles, CA; Minneapolis, MN; Seattle, WA; Washington, DC; New York, NY; Philadelphia, PA; San Francisco, CA; recorded music is permissible as a substitute for live auditions if a campus visit is impossible and videotaped performances are permissible as a substitute for live auditions if a campus visit is impossible.

Contact Charles Krusenstjerna, Director of Admissions, Eastman School of Music, University of Rochester, 26 Gibbs Street, Rochester, New York 14604; 716-274-1060, fax: 716-274-1088.

More about the School

Program Facilities Performance spaces include Eastman Theatre (3,094 seats), Kilbourn Hall (459 seats), Howard Hanson Recital Hall, Schmitt Organ Recital Hall, and Ciminelli Formal Lounge. The school has professional-quality recording studios. The Eastman Computer and Electronic Music Center features two studios (one software-based, the other MIDI-based). Several fine organs are available to Eastman students. The Sibley Music Library has holdings of over 500,000 items, including more than 50,000 recordings. The Student Living Center (opened in 1991) provides residence for 30 undergraduates as well as space for student services, including the Career Planning and Placement Office, Writing and Study Skills Center, and the Computing Room (IBM and MacIntosh computers with MIDI and electronic keyboards).

Faculty, Resident Artists, and Alumni Faculty members are performers, composers, and scholars. The Eastman Brass are members of the faculty. Alumni are active professionally as members of many leading American orchestras and as opera singers, composers, jazz artists, music critics, heads of music schools, managers of orchestras, school teachers, college professors, and arts administrators. Student Performance Opportunities Students present more than 400 recitals annually. Eastman ensembles include the Philharmonia, Wind Ensemble, Chorale, Opera Theatre, jazz Ensemble, Musica Nova, Collegium Musicum, InterMusica, Saxology, Trombone Choir, Percussion Ensemble, Marimba Ensemble, and Horn Choir. Each year, eight Composers' Forums allow composition students to hear their chamber works performed. Special Programs Eastman Philharmonia annual summer residency, Heidelberg, Germany; Eastman Wind Ensemble biennial Japan tour; Performer's Certificate and Artist's Diploma; Concerto Competition; Kneisel German Lied Competition; Early

Music Program. Career counseling is offered individually and in seminars. Volunteer and music outreach opportunities and professional performance opportunities are offered.

During its seventy-four-year history, the Eastman School of Music has become one of the world's most prestigious music schools. The School's stature is reflected in its seven Pulitzer Prize-winning composers, two of whom, Joseph Schwanter and Christopher Rouse, are current members of the composition faculty. Eastman students are guided by a renowned resident faculty. The impact of recordings, publications, compositions, performances, and research by Eastman faculty members is far-reaching.

The School is known for having fine programs in performance, scholarship, composition, and teaching and for its curricula in the liberal arts. The Humanities Department encourages students to refine their language and writing skills and to explore intellectual interests in fields as varied as visual arts and architecture, Western cultural history, ethics, educational psychology, and religion.

As Eastman is a professional school within the University of Rochester, its students may take advantage of diverse course offerings in other colleges of the University and may design personalized double-degree programs.

Nearly all Eastman students perform regularly in one of the School's more than twenty ensembles. Exceptional performance opportunities in Rochester and abroad are an Eastman hallmark. The Eastman Philharmonia has spent its summers at the Heidelberg Castle Festival since 1980. The Eastman Jazz Ensemble has played at the Montreux Jazz Festival, and the Eastman Wind Ensemble has made three major tours of Japan.

An Eastman School education is distinguished by the opportunity to work closely with some of the most influential musicians of our time. Recent guest conductors have included Sir Georg Solti, Karel Husa, Paul Sacher, Leonard Slatkin, and Robert Shaw. Yo-Yo- Ma, Marie-Claire Alain Murray Perahia, Heinz Hollinger, Leon Fleischer, Ani Kavafian, Dawn Upshaw, John Harbison, the Beaux Arts Trio, and the Kronos Quartet have recently taught master classes at Eastman.

The School's concert life includes faculty concerts, student recitals, fully staged opera, and Eastman ensemble performances. In addition, the Kilbourn Concert Series features guest artists in solo recitals and chamber music concerts. Malcolm Bilson, Anner Bylsma, Richard Goode, William Sharp, and the Saint Lawrence Quartet are among recent performers. Non-Western music is highlighted in the World Music Series.

In recent years, students have been able to attend presentations by conductor-composer Robert Kapilow, author Joseph Horowitz, and music critics Robert Commanday, Alan Rich, and Michael Walsh. In 1993, Eastman hosted "Federal Funding for the Arts: is the NEA the Best Approach?" bringing together authorities in arts and government to discuss the future of public support for the arts in America.

The distinctive combination of learning experiences that creates an Eastman School education has resulted in a tradition of student excellence. The School's composition students have regularly won the Prix de Rome, the Bearns Prize, and major awards from ASCAP and BML. Eastman graduates are consistently recognized at the American Guild of Organists competitions, and the School's jazz ensembles have repeatedly won honors in *Down Beat* magazine's annual recording competition. Winners of Eastman's Cleveland Quartet Competition have claimed top prizes in the Fischoff and Portsmouth International Quartet competitions and, most recently, the 1993 Naumburg Chamber Music Award.

University of South Alabama

Mobile, Alabama

State-supported, coed. Suburban campus. Total enrollment: 12,386.

Degrees Bachelor of Music in the area of performance; Bachelor of Music Education in the areas of choral music education, instrumental music education. Majors: classical music, music, music education, music technology, piano/organ, stringed instruments, voice, wind and percussion instruments.

Music Student Profile Fall 1994: 88 total; 80 matriculated undergraduate, 5 matriculated graduate, 3 nondegree; 10% minorities, 40% females, 1% international.

Music Faculty Total: 31; 11 full-time, 20 part-time; 91% of full-time faculty have terminal degrees. Graduate students do not teach undergraduate courses. Undergraduate student–faculty ratio: 7:1.

Student Life Student groups include Music Educators National Conference, Sigma Alpha Iota.

Expenses for 1995–96 Application fee: $20. State resident tuition: $2352 full-time, $49 per quarter hour part-time. Nonresident tuition: $3402 full-time. Nonresident part-time tuition per quarter ranges from $424 to $1214. Part-time mandatory fees per quarter range from $123 to $147. Full-time mandatory fees: $189. College room and board: $2940. College room only: $1440. Special program-related fees: $40–$75 for private lessons.

Financial Aid Program-specific awards for Fall of 1994: 85 Music Scholarships for ensemble performers ($600–$1500), 1 Theodore Presser Award for senior program majors ($2250), 2 Chester Piano Scholarships for enrolled piano students ($300–$500).

Application Procedures Deadline—freshmen and transfers: September 10. Required: high school transcript, college transcript(s) for transfer students, minimum 2.0 high school GPA, audition, SAT I or ACT test scores. Auditions held 3 times on campus; recorded music is permissible as a substitute for live auditions when distance is prohibitive and videotaped performances are permissible as a substitute for live auditions when distance is prohibitive.

Undergraduate Contact Dr. Andrew Harper, Chairman, Music Department, University of South Alabama, Faculty Court East, Room 10, Mobile, Alabama 36688; 205-460-6136, fax: 205-460-7928.

University of South Carolina

Columbia, South Carolina

State-supported, coed. Urban campus. Total enrollment: 26,754.

Degrees Bachelor of Music in the areas of piano pedagogy, performance, music education, music theory/composition, jazz studies. Majors: guitar, jazz, music education, music theory and composition, piano pedagogy, piano/organ, stringed instruments, voice, wind and percussion instruments. Graduate degrees offered: Master of Music in the areas of composition, performance, piano pedagogy, music history, music theory, conducting, jazz studies, opera theater; Master of Music Education in the area of music education. Doctor of Musical Arts in the areas of composition, performance, piano pedagogy.

Music Student Profile Fall 1994: 442 total; 290 matriculated undergraduate, 142 matriculated graduate, 10 nondegree; 1% minorities, 55% females, 3% international.

Music Faculty Total: 43; 41 full-time, 2 part-time; 90% of full-time faculty have terminal degrees. Graduate students teach a few undergraduate courses. Undergraduate student–faculty ratio: 10:1.

Expenses for 1995–96 Application fee: $35. State resident tuition: $3280 full-time, $148 per credit hour part-time. Nonresident tuition: $8324 full-time, $366 per credit hour part-time. College room and board: $3428 (minimum). College room only: $1646 (minimum).

Application Procedures Deadline—freshmen and transfers: continuous. Required: high school transcript, audition, SAT I test score only, minimum combined SAT I score of 900. Auditions held 1 time on campus; recorded music is permissible as a substitute for live auditions when distance is prohibitive and videotaped performances are permissible as a substitute for live auditions.

Contact Jean Smith, Administrative Assistant, School of Music, University of South Carolina, Columbia, South Carolina 29208; 803-777-4335, fax: 803-777-6508.

University of South Dakota

Vermillion, South Dakota

State-supported, coed. Small-town campus. Total enrollment: 7,739.

Degrees Bachelor of Music in the area of performance; Bachelor of Music Education in the area of music education. Majors: music education, piano/organ, stringed instruments, voice, wind and percussion instruments. Graduate degrees offered: Master of Music in the areas of music education, performance, music literature, history of musical instruments.

Music Student Profile Fall 1994: 135 total; 105 matriculated undergraduate, 30 matriculated graduate.

Music Faculty Total: 23; 15 full-time, 8 part-time.

Expenses for 1995–96 Application fee: $15. State resident tuition: $1648 full-time, $51.50 per credit hour part-time. Nonresident tuition: $4480 full-time, $140 per credit hour part-time. Part-time mandatory fees per semester range from $74.56 to $440.96. Minnesota residents pay state resident tuition. Tuition for nonresidents who are eligible for the Western Undergraduate Exchange: $2182 full-time, $68.18 per credit hour part-time. Full-time mandatory fees: $1105. College room and board: $2572. College room only: $1247.

Application Procedures Deadline—freshmen and transfers: continuous. Required: high school transcript, audition, SAT I or ACT test scores. Auditions held 4 times on campus; recorded music is permissible as a substitute for live auditions when distance is prohibitive.

Contact Lawrence Mitchell, Chair, Music Department, University of South Dakota, CFA 114a, 414 East Clark Street, 414 East Clark Street, Vermillion, South Dakota 57069; 605-677-5274.

University of South Florida

Tampa, Florida

State-supported, coed. Suburban campus. Total enrollment: 36,058.

Degrees Bachelor of Music in the areas of performance, composition, jazz studies. Majors: composition, jazz, performance, piano pedagogy. Graduate degrees offered: Master of Music in the areas of performance, theory, composition, piano pedagogy, jazz studies.

Music Faculty Total: 42; 32 full-time, 10 part-time; 94% of full-time faculty have terminal degrees. Graduate students teach a few undergraduate courses.

Student Life Student groups include College Music Education National Association.

Expenses for 1995–96 Application fee: $20. State resident tuition: $1877 full-time, $62.55 per credit hour part-time. Nonresident tuition: $6764 full-time, $225.96 per credit hour part-time. College room only: $1942.

Financial Aid Program-specific awards for Fall of 1994: Music Scholarships for music students.

Application Procedures Auditions held on campus and off campus. Portfolio reviews held on campus and off campus.

Undergraduate Contact Dr. Vance Jennings, Undergraduate Advisor, School of Music, University of South Florida, 4204 East Fowler Avenue, Tampa, Florida 33620-7350; 813-974-1753, fax: 813-974-2091.

Graduate Contact Don Owen, Graduate Advisor, School of Music, University of South Florida, 4204 East Fowler Avenue, Tampa, Florida 33620-7350; 813-974-3976, fax: 813-974-2091.

University of Southern California

Los Angeles, California

Independent, coed. Urban campus. Total enrollment: 27,864.

Degrees Bachelor of Music in the areas of performance, composition, music education, jazz, music industry. Majors: classical music, composition, film scoring, jazz, music, music education, piano/organ, stringed instruments, voice, wind and percussion instruments. Graduate degrees offered: Master of Music in the areas of choral music, church music, composition, jazz studies, music education, performance, composition; Master of Music Education in the area of music education. Doctor of Musical Arts in the areas of choral music, church music, composition, music education, performance.

Music Student Profile Fall 1994: 825 total; 379 matriculated undergraduate, 378 matriculated graduate, 68 nondegree; 28% minorities, 48% females, 20% international.

Music Faculty Total: 150; 52 full-time, 98 part-time; 55% of full-time faculty have terminal degrees. Graduate students teach a few undergraduate courses. Undergraduate student–faculty ratio: 8:1.

Expenses for 1995–96 Application fee: $50. Comprehensive fee of $25,988 includes full-time tuition ($19,198), mandatory fees ($352), and college room and board ($6438 minimum). College room only: $3502. Part-time tuition: $614 per unit. Part-time mandatory fees per year (6 to 11 units): $330. Special program-related fees: $980 for lessons for music majors.

Financial Aid Program-specific awards for Fall of 1994 available.

Application Procedures Deadline—freshmen: February 1; transfers: March 1. Notification date—freshmen and transfers: continuous. Required: essay, high school transcript, minimum 3.0 high school GPA, audition, SAT I or ACT test scores, resume. Recommended: letter of recommendation. Auditions held 12 times and by appointment on campus and off campus in regional locations; recorded music is permissible as a substitute for live auditions if a campus visit is impossible and videotaped performances are permissible as a substitute for live auditions if a campus visit is impossible.

Contact Carrie Tel-Oren, Director of Admissions, School of Music, University of Southern California, Los Angeles, California 90089-0851; 213-740-8986, fax: 213-740-8995.

More about the University

The USC School of Music provides a comprehensive academic base in virtually all professional and scholarly branches of music, including instrumental and vocal performance, opera, composition, film scoring, music history and literature, jazz, musicology, theory, electronic music, pedagogy, conducting, choral and church music, early music, music education, music industry, and recording arts.

Alumni include Herb Alpert, Bruce Broughton, Jerry Goldsmith, Lionel Hampton, James Horner, Martin Katz, Marilyn Horne, Marni Nixon, Christopher Parkening, Nathaniel Rosen, Tom Scott, and Michael Tilson Thomas.

Faculty are solo, chamber, jazz, and motion picture/television recording artists active in the international and local professional music arenas. USC faculty are members of the Los Angeles Philharmonic, Los Angeles Chamber Orchestra, Music Center Opera, and many other distinguished institutions. USC routinely hosts a lengthy roster of touring artists. Former faculty members include Jascha Heifetz, Gregor Piatigorsky, William Primrose, Arnold Schoenberg, and Ingolf Dahl.

Facilities include the 1,573-seat Bovard Auditorium main concert hall, the 336-seat Hancock Auditorium for recitals, the 553-seat Bing Theatre for opera, and three other smaller performance venues. Three principal structures comprise the main School of Music complex: the Virginia Ramo Hall of Music, Booth Ferris Memorial Hall, and the Raubenheimer Music Faculty Memorial Building. These buildings house the school's primary rehearsal and teaching studios dedicated to percussion, organ, harp, individual instruction, electronic music, and recording arts. Practice rooms are located in the Performing Arts Annex. The Music Library is housed in the University's Doheny Memorial Library and includes 18,000 books and periodical volumes; 47,000 scores, historical sets and collected editions; 14,000 recordings; 100 videotapes and laser discs; and 1,400 microforms. Facilities also include extensive computer and multimedia workstations.

Performance Opportunities include the USC Symphony, Chamber Orchestra, Wind Ensemble and Symphonic Winds, SC Jazz Ensembles, Percussion Ensemble, Chamber Singers, Concert Choir, Opera, Early Music Ensemble, Contemporary Music Ensemble, and the Trojan Marching Band. A full range of piano, string, woodwind, brass, percussion, and guitar ensembles comprise chamber music opportunities.

University of Southern Maine

Gorham, Maine

State-supported, coed. Urban campus. Total enrollment: 9,628.

Degrees Bachelor of Music in the areas of jazz, classical music; Bachelor of Music Education in the area of music education. Majors: classical music, jazz, music, music education.

Music Student Profile Fall 1994: 558 total; 133 matriculated undergraduate, 425 nondegree; 1% minorities, 56% females, 1% international.

Music Faculty Total: 40; 12 full-time, 28 part-time; 42% of full-time faculty have terminal degrees. Graduate students do not teach undergraduate courses. Undergraduate student–faculty ratio: 9:1.

Student Life Student groups include Music Educators National Conference, American String Teachers Association, National Association of Teachers of Singing.

Expenses for 1995–96 Application fee: $25. State resident tuition: $3180 full-time, $106 per credit hour part-time. Nonresident tuition: $9000 full-time, $300 per credit hour part-time. Part-time mandatory fees per

University of Southern Maine *(continued)*

semester range from $7 to $123. Tuition for nonresidents who are eligible for the New England Regional Student Program: $4545 full-time, $151 per credit hour part-time. Full-time mandatory fees: $290. College room and board: $4494. College room only: $2298. Special program-related fees: .

Financial Aid Program-specific awards for Fall of 1994: 5 Music Talent Scholarships for program majors ($600–$2400).

Application Procedures Deadline—freshmen and transfers: September 6. Notification date—freshmen and transfers: September 6. Required: essay, high school transcript, college transcript(s) for transfer students, letter of recommendation, audition, SAT I or ACT test scores. Auditions held 5 times on campus.

Undergraduate Contact John C. Boden, Chairman, Music Department, University of Southern Maine, 37 College Avenue, Gorham, Maine 04038-1032; 207-780-5269, fax: 207-780-5005.

University of Southern Mississippi

Hattiesburg, Mississippi

State-supported, coed. Suburban campus. Total enrollment: 11,587.

Degrees Bachelor of Music in the areas of performance, church music, music industry, jazz, music history and literature, composition; Bachelor of Music Education in the areas of instrumental music education, choral–vocal music education, choral–keyboard music education, choral–guitar music education. Majors: composition, jazz, music business, music education, music history and literature, piano/organ, sacred music, stringed instruments, voice, wind and percussion instruments. Graduate degrees offered: Master of Music in the areas of performance, church music, conducting, music history and literature, music theory/composition, woodwind performance/pedagogy; Master of Music Education in the area of music education. Doctor of Musical Arts in the areas of performance/pedagogy, conducting, composition.

Music Student Profile Fall 1994: 295 total; 246 matriculated undergraduate, 49 matriculated graduate; 13% minorities, 43% females, 4% international.

Music Faculty Total: 40; 39 full-time, 1 part-time; 63% of full-time faculty have terminal degrees. Graduate students teach a few undergraduate courses. Undergraduate student–faculty ratio: 7:1.

Student Life Student groups include Phi Mu Alpha Sinfonia, Mu Phi Epsilon.

Expenses for 1994–95 State resident tuition: $2428 full-time. Nonresident tuition: $4892 full-time. Part-time tuition per semester ranges from $100 to $970 for state residents, $202 to $2092 for nonresidents. College room and board: $2430. College room only: $1250 (minimum). Special program-related fees: $15 for instrument rental.

Financial Aid Program-specific awards for Fall of 1994: 450 Service Awards for program majors ($200–$1000), 30 Endowment Awards for program majors ($225–$1000).

Application Procedures Deadline—freshmen and transfers: August 2. Required: high school transcript, college transcript(s) for transfer students, minimum 2.0 high school GPA, SAT I or ACT test scores. Auditions held on campus.

Contact Rebecca J. Britain, Academic Advisor, School of Music, University of Southern Mississippi, Box 5081, Hattiesburg, Mississippi 39406-5081; 601-266-5369, fax: 601-266-4127.

The University of Southern Mississippi College of The Arts is one of the most respected in the South and consists of the School of Music, the Department of Art, and the Department of Theatre and Dance. All programs are fully accredited by the appropriate national accrediting association. The College has the faculty, facilities, curricula, and equipment to meet the needs of ambitious men and women seeking professional preparation for careers as artists, musicians, actors, dancers, directors, and certified teachers of art and music. The faculty of 57 full-time professional artists includes specialists in piano, harpsichord, organ, strings, all band and orchestral wind instruments, percussion, guitar, voice, conducting, music theory, music education, painting, drawing, graphic design, three-dimensional design, art education, acting, directing, scenery/lighting/costume design, dance, choreography, and the history and literature of all the arts.

Degree programs offered in music include the B.M., B.M.E., M.M., M.M.E., D.M.A., and Ph.D. in music education. Degree programs in art include the B.A., B.F.A., and the Master of Art Education. Degrees in theater are the B.A., B.F.A., and M.F.A. The B.F.A. degree is offered in dance.

Each year there are more than 300 public concerts and recitals, theater and dance productions, art exhibits, and musical theater productions presented on campus by faculty, students, and visiting artists. Many other performances are also presented annually throughout the South and other states in the Gulf South region.

Hattiesburg, Mississippi, one of America's most livable small cities, offers its residents a mild, pleasant climate; a friendly atmosphere; excellent medical facilities; large new shopping malls; and proximity to New Orleans, Louisiana; Natchez, Mississippi; and other well-known southern cities. The University of Southern Mississippi, a multipurpose university of some 13,000 students, is large enough to offer many diverse areas of study and activity but small enough to provide its students the personal attention they are seeking.

Scholarships, graduate assistantships, and other financial aid are available to qualified applicants in all areas of the College.

Please see the USM College of The Arts other programs listed under Art, Theater, and Dance.

University of Southwestern Louisiana

Lafayette, Louisiana

State-supported, coed. Urban campus. Total enrollment: 16,789.

Degrees Bachelor of Music in the areas of performance, music theory/composition, commercial music, jazz studies; Bachelor of Music Education in the area of music education. Majors: commercial music, jazz, music education, performance. Graduate degrees offered: Master of Music in the areas of performance, conducting, music theory/composition.

Music Student Profile Fall 1994: 155 total; 140 matriculated undergraduate, 15 matriculated graduate.

Music Faculty Total: 24; 22 full-time, 2 part-time. Graduate students teach a few undergraduate courses.

Student Life Student groups include Music Educators National Conference, Sigma Alpha Iota, Phi Mu Alpha.

Expenses for 1994–95 State resident tuition: $1898 full-time. Nonresident tuition: $4898 full-time. Part-time tuition per semester ranges from $274 to $845 for state residents, $274 to $2220 for nonresidents. College room and board: $2196.

Application Procedures Deadline—freshmen and transfers: continuous. Required: high school transcript, SAT I or ACT test scores.

Undergraduate Contact Dr. A. C. Himes, Director, School of Music, University of Southwestern Louisiana, Box 41207, Lafayette, Louisiana 70504-1207; 318-482-6016, fax: 318-231-6195.

Graduate Contact Graduate Coordinator, School of Music, University of Southwestern Louisiana, Box 41207, Lafayette, Louisiana 70504-1207; 318-482-6016, fax: 318-231-6195.

University of Tampa

Tampa, Florida

Independent, coed. Urban campus. Total enrollment: 2,388.

Degrees Bachelor of Music in the areas of music performance, music theory, music education. Majors: music education, music theory, performance.

Music Faculty Total: 15; 5 full-time, 10 part-time; 40% of full-time faculty have terminal degrees.

Expenses for 1995–96 Application fee: $25. Comprehensive fee of $18,182 includes full-time tuition ($12,900), mandatory fees ($712), and college room and board ($4570). College room only: $2210 (minimum). Part-time tuition per semester ranges from $275 to $5103.

Financial Aid Program-specific awards for Fall of 1994 available.

Application Procedures Deadline—freshmen and transfers: continuous. Notification date—freshmen and transfers: continuous. Required: essay, high school transcript, college transcript(s) for transfer students, 2 letters of recommendation, audition, SAT I or ACT test scores, music theory placement test, evidence of constructive extracurricular activities. Auditions held on campus and off campus. Portfolio reviews held on campus and off campus.

Undergraduate Contact Vice President for Enrollment Management, University of Tampa, 401 West Kennedy Boulevard, Tampa, Florida 33606-1480; 813-253-6228.

University of Tennessee at Chattanooga

Chattanooga, Tennessee

State-supported, coed. Urban campus. Total enrollment: 8,281.

Degrees Bachelor of Music in the areas of performance, sacred music, music theory/composition. Majors: music theory and composition, piano/organ, sacred music, stringed instruments, voice, wind and percussion instruments. Graduate degrees offered: Master of Music in the areas of music education, performance.

Music Student Profile Fall 1994: 29 total; 21 matriculated undergraduate, 8 matriculated graduate; 17% minorities, 49% females, 6% international.

Music Faculty Total: 21; 14 full-time, 7 part-time; 70% of full-time faculty have terminal degrees. Graduate students teach a few undergraduate courses.

Expenses for 1994–95 Application fee: $15. State resident tuition: $1850 full-time, $76 per semester hour part-time. Nonresident tuition: $5782 full-time, $208 per semester hour part-time. College room only: $1360 (minimum).

Application Procedures Deadline—freshmen and transfers: continuous. Required: high school transcript, college transcript(s) for transfer students, letter of recommenda-

Dawn Upshaw

**Manhattan School of Music—
Metropolitan Opera, Recordings
Elektra/Nonesuch**

For me, the Manhattan School of Music presented the best portion of two different worlds. On the one hand, it provided a stable, supportive environment in which to make my initial forays in the New York musical scene. I benefited from my exposure to the wealth of concerts and other cultural events in the city; from my contact with first-rate teachers and coaches; and from the kinds of connections that naturally arose in the course of everyday life in the halls of MSM and in the streets of New York. At the same time, perhaps partly as an extension of its uptown location, at MSM I didn't encounter the pressures and the weight of expectations that I might have found elsewhere. The more relaxed atmosphere made me feel like I had the liberty to do different things . . . the freedom to find out what kind of music interested me and what kind of musician *I* wanted to be.

University of Tennessee at Chattanooga *(continued)*

tion, SAT I or ACT test scores. Recommended: essay, audition. Auditions held 4 times on campus; recorded music is permissible as a substitute for live auditions when distance is prohibitive.

Undergraduate Contact Music Department, University of Tennessee at Chattanooga, 615 McCallie Avenue, Chattanooga, Tennessee 37403; 615-755-4601.

Graduate Contact Dr. James Stroud, Coordinator of Graduate Programs in Music, Music Department, University of Tennessee at Chattanooga, 615 McCallie Avenue, Chattanooga, Tennessee 37403; 615-755-4601.

University of Tennessee at Martin

Martin, Tennessee

State-supported, coed. Small-town campus. Total enrollment: 5,627.

Degrees Bachelor of Music in the area of performance; Bachelor of Music Education in the area of music education. Majors: music education, performance.

Music Student Profile Fall 1994: 66 total; all matriculated undergraduate; 5% minorities, 60% females, 2% international.

Music Faculty Total: 16; 12 full-time, 4 part-time; 80% of full-time faculty have terminal degrees. Graduate students do not teach undergraduate courses. Undergraduate student–faculty ratio: 4:1.

Student Life Student groups include Phi Mu Alpha Sinfonia, Sigma Alpha Iota, Music Educators National Conference.

Expenses for 1994–95 Application fee: $15. State resident tuition: $1900 full-time, $76 per semester hour part-time. Nonresident tuition: $5832 full-time, $240 per semester hour part-time. College room and board: $2890 (minimum). College room only: $1490 (minimum).

Financial Aid Program-specific awards for Fall of 1994: 25 Music Scholarships ($600).

Application Procedures Deadline—freshmen and transfers: continuous. Required: high school transcript, minimum 2.0 high school GPA, audition, SAT I or ACT test scores. Auditions held 1 time on campus and off campus; recorded music is permissible as a substitute for live auditions if a campus visit is impossible.

Undergraduate Contact Dr. Earl Norwood, Director, Division of Fine and Performing Arts, University of Tennessee at Martin, 102 Fine Arts Building, Martin, Tennessee 38238; 901-587-7400, fax: 901-587-7415, E-mail address: norwood@utm.edu.

University of Tennessee, Knoxville

Knoxville, Tennessee

State-supported, coed. Urban campus. Total enrollment: 25,890.

Degrees Bachelor of Music in the areas of music theory/composition, music history and literature, studio music and jazz, piano, organ, piano pedagogy and literature, sacred music, strings, voice, woodwind, brass, and percussion instruments; Bachelor of Music Education in the areas of instrumental music, voice. Majors: classical music, electronic music, jazz, music, music education, opera, piano/organ, sacred music, stringed instruments, voice, wind and percussion instruments. Graduate degrees offered: Master of Music in the areas of music education, music ensemble area, general music, music history, instrumental music, keyboard, theory, voice.

Music Student Profile Fall 1994: 244 total; 181 matriculated undergraduate, 63 matriculated graduate; 5% minorities, 26% females, 12% international.

Music Faculty Total: 48; 44 full-time, 4 part-time. Graduate students teach a few undergraduate courses.

Student Life Student groups include Sigma Alpha Iota, Phi Mu Alpha.

Expenses for 1994–95 Application fee: $15. State resident tuition: $2052 full-time, $87 per semester hour part-time. Nonresident tuition: $5986 full-time, $241 per semester hour part-time. College room and board: $3398. College room only: $1600. Special program-related fees: $60–$120 for private lessons.

Financial Aid Program-specific awards for Fall of 1994 available.

Application Procedures Deadline—freshmen and transfers: continuous. Required: audition. Auditions held 3 times on campus; recorded music is permissible as a substitute for live auditions when distance is prohibitive and videotaped performances are permissible as a substitute for live auditions when distance is prohibitive.

Undergraduate Contact Walter Hawthorne, Advising Coordinator, Music Department, University of Tennessee, Knoxville, Music Building, 1741 Volunteer Boulevard, Knoxville, Tennessee 37996-2600; 615-974-3241, fax: 615-974-1941.

Graduate Contact John Brock, Graduate Coordinator, Music Department, University of Tennessee, Knoxville, Music Building, 1741 Volunteer Boulevard, Knoxville, Tennessee 37996-2600; 615-974-3241, fax: 615-974-1941.

More about the University

Program Facilities Facilities include the main music building consisting of an auditorium (seating approximately 550) that is adaptable for use as a recital hall, a concert hall, large ensemble performances, and small operatic productions. Additional rehearsal spaces are available for band, orchestra, and chorus. There are classroom facilities, two computer labs, and a laboratory for electronic music and piano instruction, in addition to the studios for keyboard and voice-applied instruction. There are six annexes in addition to the main music building that are devoted to woodwinds, brass, strings, jazz, Suzuki instruction, and multiuse. The Music Library is situated on the third floor in the main music building.

Faculty The faculty consists of performing artists, conductors and composers of international reputation, and active scholars.

Student Performance Opportunities Cooperative arrangements between the department and the Knoxville Symphony Orchestra provide opportunities for advanced students to gain valuable performance experience as

orchestral players. Graduate students in voice often participate in the Knoxville Opera Apprentice Program, giving students more exposure on stage with professional singers while they pursue academic degrees. Students in the jazz program are actively involved in the local jazz scene around Knoxville and its environs. Many of them are recurrent performers at local clubs and restaurants.

University of Texas at Arlington

Arlington, Texas

State-supported, coed. Suburban campus. Total enrollment: 23,280.

Degrees Bachelor of Music in the areas of theory/composition, jazz studies, music/business, music/theater, music/media, performance. Majors: brass, stringed instruments, voice, wind and percussion instruments.

Music Student Profile Fall 1994: 270 total; all matriculated undergraduate.

Music Faculty Total: 37; 21 full-time, 16 part-time; 48% of full-time faculty have terminal degrees. Undergraduate student–faculty ratio: 7:1.

Student Life Student groups include Texas Music Educators National Conference, Kappa Kappa Phi, Phi Mu Alpha.

Expenses for 1995–96 State resident tuition: $930 full-time. Nonresident tuition: $5456 full-time, $176 per semester hour part-time. State resident part-time tuition per semester ranges from $100 to $330. Part-time mandatory fees per semester range from $89 to $289. Full-time mandatory fees: $706. College room and board: $2560. College room only: $1180 (minimum). Special program-related fees: $25 for instrument rental fee.

Financial Aid Program-specific awards for Fall of 1994: 200 various scholarships for music majors ($400).

Application Procedures Deadline—freshmen and transfers: August 4. Notification date—freshmen and transfers: continuous. Required: high school transcript, college transcript(s) for transfer students, SAT I or ACT test scores. Auditions held on campus and off campus. Portfolio reviews held on campus and off campus.

Undergraduate Contact Office of Admissions, University of Texas at Arlington, Box 19111, Arlington, Texas 76019-0111; 817-273-2118.

University of Texas at Austin

Austin, Texas

State-supported, coed. Urban campus. Total enrollment: 47,957.

Degrees Bachelor of Music in the areas of performance, keyboard, voice, music studies, theory, composition, literature and pedagogy, theory, composition, musicology, ethnomusicology. Majors: composition, harp, music theory, orchestral instruments, piano/organ, voice. Graduate degrees offered: Master of Music in the areas of performance, keyboard, voice, music education, opera, conducting, literature and pedagogy, theory, composition, musicology, ethnomusicology. Doctor of Musical Arts in the areas of performance, composition, music education.

Music Student Profile Fall 1994: 720 total; 348 matriculated undergraduate, 372 matriculated graduate.

Music Faculty Total: 87; 82 full-time, 5 part-time.

Expenses for 1995–96 Application fee: $35. State resident tuition: $900 full-time. Nonresident tuition: $6660 full-time, $222 per semester hour part-time. State resident part-time tuition per semester ranges from $120 to $330. Part-time mandatory fees per semester range from $169.85 to $570.14. Full-time mandatory fees: $1308. College room and board: $3632.

Application Procedures Deadline—freshmen and transfers: March 1. Required: high school transcript, audition, SAT I or ACT test scores. Auditions held 6 times on campus and off campus in Dallas, TX; Houston, TX; recorded music is permissible as a substitute for live auditions if a campus visit is impossible.

Undergraduate Contact Martha Hilley, Associate Director, Undergraduate Studies, School of Music, University of Texas at Austin, Austin, Texas 78712; 512-471-7764.

Graduate Contact Dr. Hunter C. Marsh, Director, School of Music, University of Texas at Austin, Austin, Texas 78712; 512-471-1502.

More about the University

At the highest level of excellence and with dynamic innovation, the UT-Austin School of Music prepares students for the practice, study, critiquing, and teaching of music; leads in research and the creation of new music; and provides performances and exchange forums to deepen the understanding of the art, expand audiences, and develop a better quality of life in the University, community, state, and nation.

The distinguished artists and scholars of the school's dedicated faculty prepare students and audiences for the twenty-first century by emphasizing cultural diversity and technological advancement and by exploring the interrelationships of all the arts. The school honors and preserves the past while striving to define the future.

Goals include preparing for life in the twenty-first century through expanding research, education, and public service in the arts; emphasizing the creation and performance of original works; expanding the use of advanced technology for research, instruction, communication, and administration; and the use of music to foster a global awareness and an understanding of cultural diversity.

The School of Music is located in the active and stimulating cultural environment of Austin, Texas. The atmosphere of a major institution of learning, with approximately 50,000 students and more than seventy academic departments and programs of study, combines with the resources and support of a large, artistically aware city to provide students with all the advantages of both modern educational facilities and rich and diverse cultural opportunities.

University of Texas at Austin *(continued)*

The School of Music has the friendly atmosphere of a small school. Much of the teaching in the school is by individual instruction; the student-faculty ratio is less than 12 to 1, and classes are small enough for each student to receive the individual attention that encourages learning.

The School of Music collaborates with the other components of the University in both academic and performance programs. Other academic units on campus, including the Department of Radio-Television-Film, the Folklore Program, the African and Afro-American Studies Center, the Institute of Latin American Studies, the Center for Asian Studies, and the Center for Middle Eastern Studies, also share faculty, course offerings, and special performance presentations.

The School of Music is housed in a superbly equipped six-story Music Building and Recital Hall, an integral part of the multimillion-dollar College of Fine Arts and Performing Arts Center (PAC). The PAC's performance and workshop areas are among the most technically advanced and best equipped in the world. Also housed in the facilities are the magnificent Bass Concert Hall (home to most major Austin performing arts organizations, including the Austin Symphony Orchestra, Austin Lyric Opera, and Ballet Austin), the Fine Arts Library, and the remarkable McCullough Theatre.

The Performance Library is the largest collection of performance materials in the Southwest and in special areas may rival some of the larger facilities in the nation. The collection includes more than 24,000 titles, and well over 1 million individual copies, which are primarily for the use of the School of Music's performing organizations.

Program Facilities The School of Music's performance facilities include Bass Concert Hall (3,000 seats), Bates Recital Hall (700 seats), McCullough Theatre (400 seats), Jessen Auditorium (325 seats), Recital Studio (185 seats), and the Organ Recital Room (60 seats). There are 133 practice rooms and over 300 pianos (110 Steinway grands). There are also over 1,000 other instruments, including every orchestra/band instrument; complete early music collection of sakbuts, recorders, viols, two clavichords, several harpsichords, a forte-piano, as well as a large ethnomusicology collection.

The school has specialized studios for chamber music, harp, organ (six pipe organs, three in practice rooms), percussion, electronic music (five studios, including MIDI), early music, education and instructional technology, student computer lab, three group piano labs, jazz improvisation, ethnomusicology. A state-of-the-art recording studio is available.

The school has the fifth-largest academic library in the United States: 6.8 million volumes, more than 4.9 million microfilms, 30 million pages of manuscripts, 347,000 maps, on-line access to hundreds of electronic databases. The Fine Arts Library has over 200,000 items, including 40,000 music books, over 30,000 records/CDs/cassettes, many videocassettes, and a 40-station computer lab. Also available are special collections about Asia, Latin America, and the Middle East, plus celebrated Ransom Humanities Research Center collections.

Faculty, Resident Artists, and Alumni A stellar faculty of artists and scholars is found at the University of Texas at Austin School of Music—plus residencies by Gunther Schuller, Mattiwilda Dobbs, Isaac Stern, Lukas Foss, Paul and Eva Badura-Skoda, Morton Subotnick, and Itzhak Perlman.

Student Performance/Exhibit Opportunities The UT-Austin School of Music has an award-winning symphony orchestra, a wind ensemble, bands, choirs, many chamber and ethnomusicology ensembles, and over 400 student and faculty performances annually. There are many community performance opportunities also, from Austin Symphony and Austin Lyric Opera to the legendary commercial music scene. Austin is considered the "Live Music Capital of the World."

University of Texas at El Paso

El Paso, Texas

State-supported, coed. Urban campus. Total enrollment: 17,188.

Degrees Bachelor of Music in the area of performance; Bachelor of Music Education in the area of music education. Majors: music education, music theory, voice, wind and percussion instruments. Graduate degrees offered: Master of Music in the area of performance; Master of Music Education in the area of music education. Cross-registration with El Paso Community College.

Music Student Profile Fall 1994: 170 total; 150 matriculated undergraduate, 20 matriculated graduate; 60% minorities, 55% females.

Music Faculty Total: 38; 21 full-time, 17 part-time; 90% of full-time faculty have terminal degrees. Graduate students teach a few undergraduate courses.

Expenses for 1995–96 State resident tuition: $840 full-time. Nonresident tuition: $5130 full-time, $171 per semester hour part-time. State resident part-time tuition per semester ranges from $100 to $308. Students who are Mexican nationals and able to demonstrate financial need pay state resident tuition. Full-time mandatory fees: $781. College room only: $1600 (minimum). Special program-related fees: $50 for applied lessons.

Application Procedures Deadline—freshmen and transfers: continuous. Required: high school transcript, audition. Recommended: minimum 2.0 high school GPA. Auditions held continuously for instrumental and vocal applicants on campus; recorded music is permissible as a substitute for live auditions and videotaped performances are permissible as a substitute for live auditions.

Undergraduate Contact Dr. Ron Hufstader, Chair, Music Department, University of Texas at El Paso, 500 West University Avenue, El Paso, Texas 79968-0552; 915-747-5606, fax: 915-747-5023.

Graduate Contact Dr. David Russ, Graduate Advisor, Music Department, University of Texas at El Paso, 500 West University Avenue, El Paso, Texas 79968-0552; 915-747-5606.

University of Texas at San Antonio

San Antonio, Texas

State-supported, coed. Suburban campus. Total enrollment: 17,579.

Degrees Bachelor of Music in the areas of performance, composition, music marketing, music education. Majors: classical music, music education, music marketing, piano/organ, stringed instruments, voice, wind and percussion instruments. Graduate degrees offered: Master of Music in the areas of performance, music education, conducting.

Music Student Profile Fall 1994: 245 total; 218 matriculated undergraduate, 27 matriculated graduate; 44% minorities, 46% females, 2% international.

Music Faculty Total: 38; 15 full-time, 23 part-time; 100% of full-time faculty have terminal degrees. Graduate students do not teach undergraduate courses. Undergraduate student–faculty ratio: 12:1.

Student Life Student groups include Music Educators National Conference Student Chapter, Sigma Alpha Iota.

Expenses for 1995–96 Application fee: $20. State resident tuition: $900 full-time. Nonresident tuition: $6660 full-time, $222 per semester part-time. State resident part-time tuition per semester ranges from $120 to $330. Part-time mandatory fees per semester range from $121 to $496. Full-time mandatory fees: $1168. College room only: $2724. Special program-related fees: $50 for music major fee.

Financial Aid Program-specific awards for Fall of 1994: 25 Division of Music Scholarships for program majors ($400–$2000).

Application Procedures Deadline—freshmen and transfers: July 1. Notification date—freshmen: August 1. Required: high school transcript, college transcript(s) for transfer students, SAT I or ACT test scores. Recommended: audition. Auditions held 2 times on campus; recorded music is permissible as a substitute for live auditions and videotaped performances are permissible as a substitute for live auditions.

Undergraduate Contact Brian Harris, Assistant Professor, Division of Music, University of Texas at San Antonio, 6900 North Loop 1604 West, San Antonio, Texas 78249-1130; 210-691-4354, fax: 210-691-4381.

Graduate Contact Rosemary Watkins, Associate Professor, Division of Music, University of Texas at San Antonio, 6900 North Loop 1604 West, San Antonio, Texas 78249-1130; 210-691-4354, fax: 210-691-4381.

University of the Arts

Philadelphia, Pennsylvania

Independent, coed. Urban campus. Total enrollment: 1,298.

Degrees Bachelor of Music in the areas of jazz performance, vocal performance, composition. Majors: composition, jazz, performance, voice. Graduate degrees offered: Master of Music in the area of performance.

Music Student Profile Fall 1994: 156 total; 142 matriculated undergraduate, 10 matriculated graduate, 4 nondegree; 9% minorities, 20% females, 10% international.

Music Faculty Total: 79; 7 full-time, 72 part-time; 70% of full-time faculty have terminal degrees. Graduate students do not teach undergraduate courses. Undergraduate student–faculty ratio: 2:1.

Student Life Student groups include Music Educators National Conference, Pennsylvania Music Educators Association, National Academy of Recording Arts and Sciences. Special housing available for music students.

Expenses for 1995–96 Application fee: $30. Tuition: $13,170 full-time, $570 per credit part-time. Full-time mandatory fees: $500. College room only: $3860.

Financial Aid Program-specific awards for Fall of 1994: 1 W. W. Smith Scholarship for program majors ($2000), 1 Edmund J. Parks Scholarship for international students ($2500), 1 Weil Scholarship for program majors ($2500), 50 Talent Scholarships for program majors ($2000), 1 Castaldo Scholarship for program majors ($2000).

Application Procedures Deadline—freshmen and transfers: continuous. Notification date—freshmen and transfers: September 1. Required: essay, high school transcript, college transcript(s) for transfer students, minimum 2.0 high school GPA, 3 letters of recommendation, audition, portfolio, SAT I or ACT test scores. Recommended: interview. Auditions held 8 times on campus and off campus in various cities; recorded music is permissible as a substitute for live auditions for international applicants and U.S. applicants for whom distance is prohibitive and videotaped performances are permissible as a substitute for live auditions for international applicants and U.S. applicants for whom distance is prohibitive. Portfolio reviews held 6 times on campus and off campus in various cities for composition applicants.

Undergraduate Contact Barbara Elliott, Director, Admissions Office, University of the Arts, 320 South Broad Street, Philadelphia, Pennsylvania 19102; 215-875-4808.

University of the Ozarks

Clarksville, Arkansas

Independent-religious, coed. Small-town campus. Total enrollment: 577.

Degrees Bachelor of Music Education in the areas of vocal music, instrumental music. Majors: music education.

Music Student Profile Fall 1994: 9 total; all matriculated undergraduate.

Music Faculty Total: 6; 2 full-time, 4 part-time; 100% of full-time faculty have terminal degrees. Graduate students do not teach undergraduate courses. Undergraduate student–faculty ratio: 7:1.

Expenses for 1995–96 Comprehensive fee of $9840 includes full-time tuition ($6400), mandatory fees ($140),

University of the Ozarks *(continued)*

and college room and board ($3300). College room only: $1350. Part-time tuition: $235 per semester hour. Special program-related fees: $100–$150 for private lessons.

Application Procedures Deadline—freshmen and transfers: continuous. Required: high school transcript, SAT I or ACT test scores, minimum 2.0 college GPA for transfer students.

Undergraduate Contact Dr. Michael Heater, Director of Admissions, Financial Aid Department, University of the Ozarks, 415 College Avenue, Clarksville, Arkansas 72830; 501-979-1209, fax: 501-979-1355.

University of the Pacific

Stockton, California

Independent, coed. Suburban campus. Total enrollment: 4,140.

Degrees Bachelor of Music in the areas of performance, music education, music therapy, music management/ business, composition, music history. Majors: classical music, composition, music business, music education, music history, music management, music therapy, piano/ organ, stringed instruments, voice, wind and percussion instruments. Graduate degrees offered: Master of Music in the areas of performance, music education, composition, music therapy.

Music Student Profile Fall 1994: 183 total; 161 matriculated undergraduate, 18 matriculated graduate, 4 nondegree; 22% minorities, 62% females, 8% international.

Music Faculty Total: 39; 23 full-time, 16 part-time; 96% of full-time faculty have terminal degrees. Graduate students do not teach undergraduate courses. Undergraduate student–faculty ratio: 6:1.

Student Life Student groups include Music Educators National Conference Student Chapter, Mu Phi Epsilon, Phi Mu Alpha Sinfonia.

Expenses for 1995–96 Application fee: $50. Comprehensive fee of $22,876 includes full-time tuition ($17,220), mandatory fees ($330), and college room and board ($5326). Part-time tuition per unit ranges from $530 to $673 according to course load. Full-time tuition for pharmacy program: $25,830. Special program-related fees: $35–$210 for applied music fee, $10–$15 for practice room fee.

Financial Aid Program-specific awards for Fall of 1994: 105 Music Scholarships for those demonstrating talent and need ($6700–$14,200), 32 Conservatory Performance Scholarships for those demonstrating musical achievement ($1000–$8600).

Application Procedures Deadline—freshmen and transfers: continuous. Required: essay, high school transcript, college transcript(s) for transfer students, letter of recommendation, audition, SAT I or ACT test scores. Recommended: minimum 3.0 high school GPA. Auditions held 14 times on campus and off campus in Seattle, WA; Los Angeles, CA; San Diego, CA; Anchorage, AK; Juneau, AK; Eugene, OR; Corvallis, OR; Salem, OR; Portland, OR; recorded music is permissible as a substitute for live auditions if a campus visit is impossible and videotaped performances are permissible as a substitute for live auditions if a campus visit is impossible.

Undergraduate Contact Joanne Paine, Secretary of Student Services, Conservatory of Music, University of the Pacific, 3601 Pacific Avenue, Stockton, California 95211; 209-946-2418, fax: 209-946-2770.

Graduate Contact George Nemeth, Chair of Music History and Composition, Conservatory of Music, University of the Pacific, 3601 Pacific Avenue, Stockton, California 95211-0197; 209-946-3294, fax: 209-946-2770.

University of Toledo

Toledo, Ohio

State-supported, coed. Suburban campus. Total enrollment: 23,107.

Degrees Bachelor of Music in the area of performance studies. Majors: jazz, music education, piano/organ, stringed instruments, voice, wind and percussion instruments. Graduate degrees offered: Master of Music in the area of performance studies; Master of Music Education in the area of music education. Cross-registration with Eastern Michigan University, Bowling Green State University.

Music Student Profile Fall 1994: 140 total; 100 matriculated undergraduate, 40 matriculated graduate; 5% minorities, 52% females, 1% international.

Music Faculty Total: 40; 18 full-time, 22 part-time; 67% of full-time faculty have terminal degrees. Graduate students teach about a quarter undergraduate courses.

Student Life Student groups include Mu Phi Epsilon, Music Educators National Conference, Ohio Music Teachers Association.

Expenses for 1994–95 Application fee: $30. State resident tuition: $3398 full-time, $94.40 per quarter hour part-time. Nonresident tuition: $8147 full-time, $226.30 per quarter hour part-time. College room and board: $3717. Special program-related fees: $35–$55 for applied music fees, $15 for ensemble and lab fees.

Financial Aid Program-specific awards for Fall of 1994: 10 Hassensall Awards for program majors ($300–$400), 3 Eckels Awards for upperclassmen ($200–$500), 2 Art Tatum Awards for African-Americans ($200–$300), 3 Baer Awards for pianists ($250–$500), 3 Key to the Sea Awards for brass/percussionists ($300–$400), Jacobson Awards for AGMA members, Band Scholarships for band members.

Application Procedures Deadline—freshmen and transfers: September 11. Notification date—freshmen and transfers: September 18. Required: high school transcript, college transcript(s) for transfer students, minimum 2.0 high school GPA, audition, SAT I or ACT test scores. Auditions held 4 times and by appointment on campus; recorded music is permissible as a substitute for live auditions for international applicants and on a case-by-case basis and videotaped performances are permissible as a substitute for live auditions for international applicants.

Undergraduate Contact Dr. Lee Heritage, Recruiting Office, Department of Music, University of Toledo, 2801 West Bancroft, Toledo, Ohio 43606-3398; 419-537-2447, fax: 419-537-8483.

Graduate Contact Dr. Robert DeYarman, Graduate Advisor, Department of Music, University of Toledo, 2801 West Bancroft, Toledo, Ohio 43606-3398; 419-537-2447, fax: 419-537-8483.

University of Tulsa

Tulsa, Oklahoma

Independent-religious, coed. Urban campus. Total enrollment: 4,573.

Degrees Bachelor of Music in the areas of performance, composition; Bachelor of Music Education in the areas of instrumental music education, vocal music education. Majors: composition, music education, piano, stringed instruments, voice, wind and percussion instruments. Graduate degrees offered: Master of Music in the areas of performance, composition, music theory; Master of Music Education in the areas of instrumental music education, vocal music education.

Music Faculty Total: 33; 17 full-time, 16 part-time.

Expenses for 1995–96 Application fee: $25. Comprehensive fee of $16,660 includes full-time tuition ($12,300) and college room and board ($4360). College room only: $2160. Part-time tuition: $440 per credit hour.

Application Procedures Deadline—freshmen and transfers: continuous. Required: high school transcript, minimum 2.0 high school GPA, letter of recommendation, audition, SAT I or ACT test scores. Auditions held 2 times and by appointment on campus and off campus in various cities; recorded music is permissible as a substitute for live auditions when distance is prohibitive.

Undergraduate Contact Ron Predl, Director, School of Music, University of Tulsa, 600 South College Avenue, Tulsa, Oklahoma 74104-3189; 918-631-2262.

Graduate Contact Dr. Joseph Rivers, Graduate Advisor, School of Music, University of Tulsa, 600 South College Avenue, Tulsa, Oklahoma 74104-3189; 918-631-2262.

University of Utah

Salt Lake City, Utah

State-supported, coed. Urban campus. Total enrollment: 25,226.

Degrees Bachelor of Music in the areas of performance, music education, theory, composition, piano pedagogy, history and literature; Bachelor of Music Education in the areas of instrumental music, choral music. Majors: brass, classical music, composition, electronic music, jazz, music education, music history and literature, music theory, piano, stringed instruments, voice, wind and percussion instruments. Graduate degrees offered: Master of Music in the areas of composition, history/literature, performance, music education, conducting; Master of Music Education in the area of music education.

Music Student Profile Fall 1994: 310 total; 260 matriculated undergraduate, 50 matriculated graduate; 2% minorities, 53% females, 10% international.

Music Faculty Total: 67; 22 full-time, 45 part-time; 80% of full-time faculty have terminal degrees. Graduate students teach a few undergraduate courses.

Student Life Student groups include Music Educators National Conference, world-wide competitions.

Expenses for 1994–95 Application fee: $30. State resident tuition: $2298 full-time. Nonresident tuition: $6795 full-time. Part-time tuition per quarter ranges from $206 to $766 for state residents, $597 to $2265 for nonresidents. College room and board: $4570. College room only: $1570. Special program-related fees: $60–$90 for practice rooms, $80–$270 for private lessons.

Financial Aid Program-specific awards for Fall of 1994: 20–30 Tracey Piano Awards for pianists ($2000–$5000), 20–30 Carmen Christianson Scholarships for program majors ($2000–$5000).

Application Procedures Deadline—freshmen and transfers: July 1. Required: high school transcript, college transcript(s) for transfer students, minimum 3.0 high school GPA, audition, SAT I or ACT test scores. Recommended: essay, 3 letters of recommendation, interview, video, portfolio. Auditions held 3–4 times on campus; recorded music is permissible as a substitute for live auditions when distance is prohibitive and videotaped performances are permissible as a substitute for live auditions when distance is prohibitive.

Undergraduate Contact Dr. Mark Ely, Undergraduate Counselor, Music Department, University of Utah, 204 DGH, Salt Lake City, Utah 84112; 801-581-7163, fax: 801-581-5683.

Graduate Contact Dr. Edward Asmus, Graduate Studies Director, Music Department, University of Utah, 204 DGH, Salt Lake City, Utah 84112; 801-581-7369, fax: 801-581-5683, E-mail address: ed.asmus@music.utah.edu.

University of Vermont

Burlington, Vermont

State-supported, coed. Small-town campus. Total enrollment: 9,072.

Degrees Bachelor of Music in the areas of performance, music theory/composition. Majors: classical guitar, classical music, harp, harpsichord, piano/organ, stringed instruments, voice, wind and percussion instruments.

Music Student Profile Fall 1994: 40 total; all matriculated undergraduate; 5% minorities, 50% females, 1% international.

University of Vermont *(continued)*

Music Faculty Total: 25; 10 full-time, 15 part-time; 100% of full-time faculty have terminal degrees. Graduate students do not teach undergraduate courses. Undergraduate student–faculty ratio: 10:1.

Student Life Student groups include Music Educators National Conference.

Expenses for 1995–96 State resident tuition: $6468 full-time, $269.50 per credit part-time. Nonresident tuition: $16,164 full-time, $673.50 per credit part-time. Full-time mandatory fees: $441. College room and board: $5032. Special program-related fees: $170 for private music lessons.

Application Procedures Deadline—freshmen: February 1; transfers: April 1. Recommended: interview, video, audition. Auditions held 15–20 times on campus; recorded music is permissible as a substitute for live auditions when distance is prohibitive and videotaped performances are permissible as a substitute for live auditions when distance is prohibitive.

Undergraduate Contact Admissions Office, University of Vermont, South Prospect Street, Burlington, Vermont 05405; 802-656-3370.

University of Washington

Seattle, Washington

State-supported, coed. Urban campus. Total enrollment: 33,719.

Degrees Bachelor of Music in the areas of performance, jazz studies, composition. Majors: jazz, music, music education, piano/organ, stringed instruments, voice, wind and percussion instruments. Graduate degrees offered: Master of Music in the area of music. Doctor of Musical Arts in the area of music.

Music Student Profile Fall 1994: 367 total; 193 matriculated undergraduate, 174 matriculated graduate; 14% minorities, 46% females, 6% international.

Music Faculty Total: 62; 47 full-time, 15 part-time; 80% of full-time faculty have terminal degrees. Graduate students teach a few undergraduate courses. Undergraduate student–faculty ratio: 3:1.

Student Life Student groups include Music Educators National Conference, Mu Phi Epsilon.

Expenses for 1995–96 Application fee: $35. State resident tuition: $3021 full-time. Nonresident tuition: $8523 full-time. Part-time tuition per 2 credit. College room and board: $4329. Special program-related fees: $80 for applied music lesson fee.

Application Procedures Deadline—freshmen: February 1; transfers: April 1. Required: high school transcript, college transcript(s) for transfer students, minimum 3.0 high school GPA, audition, SAT I test score only. Auditions held 4 times on campus; recorded music is permissible as a substitute for live auditions for provisional acceptance and videotaped performances are permissible as a substitute for live auditions for provisional acceptance.

Undergraduate Contact Linda Iltis, Undergraduate Advisor, School of Music, University of Washington, Box 352450, Seattle, Washington 98195-3450; 206-543-8273, fax: 206-685-9499.

Graduate Contact Elizabeth Westphal, Graduate Advisor, School of Music, University of Washington, Box 353450, Seattle, Washington 98195-3450; 206-543-2726, fax: 206-685-9499, E-mail address: westphal@u.washington.edu.

University of West Alabama

Livingston, Alabama

State-supported, coed. Small-town campus. Total enrollment: 2,320.

Degrees Bachelor of Music Education in the areas of instrumental music education, vocal/choral music education. Majors: music education.

Music Student Profile Fall 1994: 25 total; all matriculated undergraduate; 25% minorities, 50% females.

Music Faculty Total: 6; 5 full-time, 1 part-time; 20% of full-time faculty have terminal degrees. Graduate students do not teach undergraduate courses. Undergraduate student–faculty ratio: 10:1.

Student Life Student groups include Phi Mu Alpha Sinfonia, Omega Alpha Omicron, Music Educators National Conference.

Expenses for 1994–95 Application fee: $15. Comprehensive fee of $4328 includes full-time tuition ($1740), mandatory fees ($263), and college room and board ($2325 minimum). College room only: $1050 (minimum). Part-time tuition: $46 per quarter hour. Special program-related fees: $20–$30 for music fee, $10 for piano/organ rental.

Financial Aid Program-specific awards for Fall of 1994: 51 Band Scholarships for band players ($750), 8 Choir Scholarships for singers ($500).

Application Procedures Deadline—freshmen and transfers: continuous. Required: high school transcript, college transcript(s) for transfer students, SAT I or ACT test scores, minimum composite ACT score of 19. Recommended: essay, minimum 3.0 high school GPA, 3 letters of recommendation, interview, audition. Auditions held 1 time on campus; recorded music is permissible as a substitute for live auditions when distance is prohibitive and videotaped performances are permissible as a substitute for live auditions when distance is prohibitive. Portfolio reviews held 1 time on campus.

Undergraduate Contact Richard Hester, Recruiting Coordinator, Admissions Office, University of West Alabama, Station #4, Livingston, Alabama 35470; 205-652-9661 ext. 352, fax: 205-652-4065.

University of Wisconsin–Eau Claire

Eau Claire, Wisconsin

State-supported, coed. Urban campus. Total enrollment: 10,331.

Degrees Bachelor of Music in the areas of performance, theory/composition, music therapy; Bachelor of Music Education in the areas of choral music education, instrumental education. Majors: harpsichord, music education, music theory and composition, music therapy, piano/organ, stringed instruments, voice, wind and percussion instruments. Graduate degrees offered: Master of Music in the areas of performance, music theory/composition, music history and literature, conducting, music education, music theory.

Music Student Profile Fall 1994: 305 total; 270 matriculated undergraduate, 35 matriculated graduate.

Music Faculty Total: 35; 30 full-time, 5 part-time.

Expenses for 1994–95 Application fee: $25. State resident tuition: $2312 full-time, $96.25 per credit part-time. Nonresident tuition: $7100 full-time, $295.75 per credit part-time. Minnesota residents pay tuition at the rate they would pay if attending a comparable state-supported institution in Minnesota. College room and board: $2705 (minimum). College room only: $1565.

Application Procedures Deadline—freshmen and transfers: January 1. Required: high school transcript, audition, standing in top half of graduating class. Auditions held 3 times on campus; recorded music is permissible as a substitute for live auditions for international applicants.

Undergraduate Contact Timothy Lane, Admissions Coordinator, Department of Music and Theatre Arts, University of Wisconsin–Eau Claire, Room 156, Fine Arts Building, Eau Claire, Wisconsin 54702; 715-836-2284.

Graduate Contact School of Graduate Studies, University of Wisconsin–Eau Claire, 158 Human Sciences and Services Building, Eau Claire, Wisconsin 54702; 715-836-3400.

University of Wisconsin–Green Bay

Green Bay, Wisconsin

State-supported, coed. Suburban campus. Total enrollment: 5,630.

Degrees Bachelor of Music in the areas of music education, performance. Majors: music education, piano/organ, stringed instruments, voice, wind and percussion instruments.

Music Student Profile Fall 1994: 120 total; all matriculated undergraduate; 5% minorities, 55% females.

Music Faculty Total: 25; 10 full-time, 15 part-time; 55% of full-time faculty have terminal degrees. Graduate students do not teach undergraduate courses. Undergraduate student–faculty ratio: 12:1.

Student Life Student groups include Music Educators National Conference College Chapter, American Choral Directors Association College Chapter.

Expenses for 1994–95 Application fee: $25. State resident tuition: $2286 full-time. Nonresident tuition: $7074 full-time. Part-time tuition per semester ranges from $96.25 to $1049 for state residents, $295.75 to $3243 for nonresidents. Minnesota residents pay tuition at the rate they would pay if attending a comparable state-supported institution in Minnesota. College room and board: $2440 (minimum). College room only: $1540.

Financial Aid Program-specific awards for Fall of 1994: 20–25 Music Talent Scholarships for freshmen music majors ($400), 16 Show Choir Awards for choir singers ($400), 30 Pep Band Awards for program majors and non-majors ($400), 5 Continuing Music Awards for upperclass program majors ($500).

Application Procedures Deadline—freshmen: February 1; transfers: February 15. Required: high school transcript, college transcript(s) for transfer students, 2 letters of recommendation, interview, audition. Recommended: essay, minimum 3.0 high school GPA. Auditions held 4 times on campus.

Undergraduate Contact Kevin J. Collins, Chair of Music Scholarship and Recruitment Committee, Music Department–TH331, University of Wisconsin–Green Bay, 2420 Nicolet Drive, Green Bay, Wisconsin 54311-7001; 414-465-2635, fax: 414-465-2890, E-mail address: collinsk@uwgb.edu.

University of Wisconsin–Madison

Madison, Wisconsin

State-supported, coed. Urban campus. Total enrollment: 38,139.

Degrees Bachelor of Music in the areas of performance, music theory, music education. Majors: classical music, composition, jazz, music, music education, piano/organ, stringed instruments, voice, wind and percussion instruments. Graduate degrees offered: Master of Music Education in the area of music education; Master of Musical Arts in the areas of brass instruments, choral conducting, composition, music education, ethnomusicology, musicology, instrumental conducting–orchestra, instrumental conducting–wind ensemble, opera, organ, percussion, piano, piano–accompanying, piano pedagogy/performance,. Doctor of Musical Arts in the areas of brass instruments, choral conducting, composition, instrumental conducting–orchestra, instrumental conducting–wind ensemble, organ, piano, stringed instruments, voice, woodwind instruments.

Music Student Profile Fall 1994: 2,115 total; 280 matriculated undergraduate, 135 matriculated graduate, 1,700 nondegree.

Music Faculty Total: 55; 53 full-time, 2 part-time; 90% of full-time faculty have terminal degrees. Graduate students teach a few undergraduate courses. Undergraduate student–faculty ratio: 20:1.

Student Life Student groups include Sigma Alpha Iota, Music Educators National Conference Student Chapter.

Expenses for 1994–95 Application fee: $25. State resident tuition: $2737 full-time, $115 per semester hour

University of Wisconsin–Madison *(continued)*

part-time. Nonresident tuition: $9096 full-time, $379.75 per semester hour part-time. Minnesota residents pay tuition at the rate they would pay if attending University of Minnesota, Twin Cities Campus. College room and board: $2925.

Financial Aid Program-specific awards for Fall of 1994: 10 Evelyn Steenbock Scholarships for program majors ($1000–$2000), 15 Elsa Sawyer Scholarships for those demonstrating need, talent and academic achievement ($1000–$2000), 10–15 Margaret Rupp Cooper Scholarships for state residents ($1000–$2000), 1–2 Gertrude Meyne Bates Scholarships for talented program majors.

Application Procedures Deadline—freshmen: February 1; transfers: March 1. Notification date—freshmen: March 10; transfers: April 30. Required: high school transcript, minimum 3.0 high school GPA, 2 letters of recommendation, interview, audition. Auditions held 3 times on campus; recorded music is permissible as a substitute for live auditions when distance is prohibitive.

Undergraduate Contact Ellen Burmeister, Associate Director and Director of Undergraduate Programs, School of Music, University of Wisconsin–Madison, 1621 Humanities, Madison, Wisconsin 53706; 608-263-5986, fax: 608-262-8876.

Graduate Contact Deborah Lehmann, Graduate Coordinator, School of Music, University of Wisconsin–Madison, 3561 Humanities, Madison, Wisconsin 53706-1483; 608-263-5016, fax: 608-262-8876, E-mail address: dlehman@facstaff.wisc.edu.

More about the University

Program Facilities Activities occur in three areas on campus, which is nestled on the shores of Lake Mendota in the state capitol. The Humanities Building, where most classrooms and faculty studios are located, houses three performance spaces: newly refurbished 770-seat Mills Concert Hall, 200-seat Morphy Recital Hall, and 175-seat Eastman Organ Recital Hall. The building contains the Wisconsin Center for Music Technology, a sophisticated computer laboratory that positions the School as a national leader in computer-based education. Music Hall, built in 1879 and renovated in 1985, and its 385-seat auditorium are the opera program's home. Mills Music Library serves the School's research mission with 42,000 monographs and serials, 120,000 recordings, and over 1,000 microfilms.

Faculty, Resident Artists, and Alumni An international roster of 60 faculty artists and scholars strives to maintain a focus on individual student attention within the vast resources of the Madison campus. In 1939 the School gained distinction with the creation of the first musical artist-in-residence position at any American university. Today it has one of the nation's strongest chamber music programs with three faculty resident ensembles: Pro Arte String Quartet, Wingra Woodwind Quintet, and Wisconsin Brass Quintet. Master classes are taught by renowned musicians who visit Madison; recent guests include James Galway, Beaux Arts Trio, Max Roach, and Jeffrey Siegel. Living alumni number about 3,000 who perform and teach around the world.

Student Performances Three-hundred annual performances include those by seven choral groups; three orchestras; six bands; ensembles in jazz, early music, percussion, African-American music, and Javanese gamelan; and fully staged opera productions.

University of Wisconsin–Milwaukee

Milwaukee, Wisconsin

State-supported, coed. Urban campus. Total enrollment: 22,984.

Degrees Bachelor of Music in the areas of music, performance, music history and literature, music theory/composition, music education/general, music education/instrumental, music education/choral. Majors: brass, guitar, music, music education, piano/organ, stringed instruments, voice, wind and percussion instruments. Graduate degrees offered: Master of Music in the areas of performance, music theory/composition, conducting, accompanying, music education, music history and literature. Mandatory cross-registration with Wisconsin Conservatory of Music.

Music Student Profile Fall 1994: 260 total; 185 matriculated undergraduate, 55 matriculated graduate, 20 nondegree; 1% minorities, 55% females, 5% international.

Music Faculty Total: 50; 28 full-time, 22 part-time; 95% of full-time faculty have terminal degrees. Graduate students teach a few undergraduate courses. Undergraduate student–faculty ratio: 6:1.

Expenses for 1994–95 State resident tuition: $2772 full-time. Nonresident tuition: $8787 full-time. Part-time tuition per semester ranges from $212 to $1287 for state residents, $465.75 to $4046 for nonresidents. Minnesota residents pay tuition at the rate they would pay if attending a comparable state-supported institution in Minnesota. College room and board: $3000.

Financial Aid Program-specific awards for Fall of 1994: 50 Music Scholarships for undergraduates ($200–$2000).

Application Procedures Deadline—freshmen and transfers: continuous. Notification date—freshmen and transfers: continuous. Required: high school transcript, letter of recommendation, audition. Auditions held 4 times on campus; recorded music is permissible as a substitute for live auditions when distance is prohibitive and videotaped performances are permissible as a substitute for live auditions when distance is prohibitive.

Undergraduate Contact William Duvall, Undergraduate Director, Music Department, University of Wisconsin–Milwaukee, P.O. Box 413, Milwaukee, Wisconsin 53201; 414-229-4393, fax: 414-229-6154.

Graduate Contact Wayne E. Cook, Director, Graduate Studies, Fine Arts/Music Department, University of Wisconsin–Milwaukee, P.O. Box 413, Milwaukee, Wisconsin 53201; 414-229-4393, fax: 414-229-6154.

University of Wisconsin–Oshkosh

Oshkosh, Wisconsin

State-supported, coed. Suburban campus. Total enrollment: 10,567.

Degrees Bachelor of Music in the areas of performance, music therapy, music merchandising; Bachelor of Music Education in the areas of general music, choral music, instrumental music. Majors: brass, music education, music therapy, piano, retail music merchandising, sound recording technology, stringed instruments, voice, wind and percussion instruments.

Music Student Profile Fall 1994: 145 total; all matriculated undergraduate.

Music Faculty Total: 31; 20 full-time, 11 part-time; 75% of full-time faculty have terminal degrees. Graduate students do not teach undergraduate courses. Undergraduate student–faculty ratio: 12:1.

Student Life Student groups include Music Educators National Conference Student Chapter, National Association of Music Therapy Student Chapter, Oshkosh Recording Association.

Expenses for 1994–95 Application fee: $25. State resident tuition: $2162 full-time, $89.91 per credit part-time. Nonresident tuition: $6950 full-time, $289.41 per credit part-time. Minnesota residents pay tuition at the rate they would pay if attending a comparable state-supported institution in Minnesota. College room and board: $2256. College room only: $1396.

Financial Aid Program-specific awards for Fall of 1994: Willcockson Prizes in the Arts for incoming freshmen ($300–$400).

Application Procedures Deadline—freshmen and transfers: continuous. Required: high school transcript, audition. Auditions held 4 times on campus; recorded music is permissible as a substitute for live auditions when distance is prohibitive and videotaped performances are permissible as a substitute for live auditions when distance is prohibitive.

Undergraduate Contact Admissions Office, University of Wisconsin–Oshkosh, 800 Algoma Boulevard, Oshkosh, Wisconsin 54901; 414-424-0202.

University of Wisconsin–River Falls

River Falls, Wisconsin

State-supported, coed. Small-town campus. Total enrollment: 6,432.

Degrees Bachelor of Music Education in the areas of instrumental music, vocal music, piano/vocal music. Majors: music education. Cross-registration with University of Wisconsin, University of Minnesota.

Music Student Profile Fall 1994: 36 total; all matriculated undergraduate.

Music Faculty Total: 13; 11 full-time, 2 part-time; 27% of full-time faculty have terminal degrees.

Expenses for 1994–95 State resident tuition: $2304 full-time. Nonresident tuition: $7092 full-time. Part-time tuition per semester ranges from $121.74 to $1071 for state residents, $321.24 to $3266 for nonresidents. College room and board: $2214 (minimum). College room only: $1376.

Application Procedures Deadline—freshmen and transfers: January 1. Required: high school transcript, college transcript(s) for transfer students, SAT I or ACT test scores, minimum composite ACT score of 22. Auditions held on campus and off campus. Portfolio reviews held on campus and off campus.

Undergraduate Contact Admissions Office, University of Wisconsin–River Falls.

University of Wisconsin–Stevens Point

Stevens Point, Wisconsin

State-supported, coed. Small-town campus. Total enrollment: 8,424.

Degrees Bachelor of Music in the areas of music education, jazz studies, performance, music literature. Majors: jazz, music education, music literature, performance. Graduate degrees offered: Master of Music Education in the areas of instrumental music education, choral music education, Suzuki education, jazz pedagogy, studio pedagogy.

Music Student Profile Fall 1994: 200 total; all matriculated undergraduate.

Music Faculty Total: 25; 21 full-time, 4 part-time.

Estimated Expenses for 1995–96 Application fee: $25. State resident tuition: $2395 full-time. Nonresident tuition: $7422 full-time. Minnesota residents pay tuition at the rate they would pay if attending a comparable state-supported institution in Minnesota. College room and board: $3150. College room only: $1800.

Application Procedures Deadline—freshmen: January 15; transfers: February 15. Required: high school transcript, audition, ACT test score only. Auditions held 3 times and by appointment on campus; recorded music is permissible as a substitute for live auditions when distance is prohibitive.

Contact David Hastings, Chair, Music Department, University of Wisconsin–Stevens Point, Fine Arts Center, Stevens Point, Wisconsin 54481; 715-346-3107, fax: 715-346-2718.

University of Wisconsin–Superior

Superior, Wisconsin

State-supported, coed. Small-town campus. Total enrollment: 2,420.

Degrees Bachelor of Music in the area of performance; Bachelor of Music Education in the areas of choral music,

University of Wisconsin–Superior *(continued)*

instrumental music, general music. Majors: guitar, music education, piano/organ, stringed instruments, voice, wind and percussion instruments. Cross-registration with University of Minnesota&–Duluth, College of St. Scholastica.

Music Student Profile Fall 1994: 57 total; all matriculated undergraduate; 1% minorities, 50% females, 1% international.

Music Faculty Total: 19; 7 full-time, 12 part-time; 72% of full-time faculty have terminal degrees. Graduate students do not teach undergraduate courses. Undergraduate student–faculty ratio: 8:1.

Student Life Student groups include Music Educators National Conference Student Chapter.

Expenses for 1994–95 Application fee: $25. State resident tuition: $2182 full-time. Nonresident tuition: $6970 full-time. Part-time tuition per semester ranges from $102.55 to $1048 for state residents, $302.05 to $3342 for nonresidents. Minnesota residents pay tuition at the rate they would pay if attending a comparable state-supported institution in Minnesota. College room and board: $2716. College room only: $1408.

Financial Aid Program-specific awards for Fall of 1994: 1 NBC Keyboard Award for pianists and organists ($1000), 6 Foundation Awards for incoming freshmen ($500), 1 Rock Scholarship for junior and senior pianists ($1000).

Application Procedures Deadline—freshmen and transfers: May 1. Notification date—freshmen and transfers: August 1. Required: high school transcript, college transcript(s) for transfer students, interview, audition, standing in top half of graduating class. Recommended: letter of recommendation, SAT I or ACT test scores, minimum SAT I score of 900, minimum ACT score of 20. Auditions held 4 times on campus; recorded music is permissible as a substitute for live auditions when distance is prohibitive and videotaped performances are permissible as a substitute for live auditions when distance is prohibitive.

Undergraduate Contact T. A. Bumgardner, Chairman, Department of Music, University of Wisconsin–Superior, 1800 Grand Avenue, Superior, Wisconsin 54880-2898; 715-394-8255, fax: 715-394-8454, E-mail address: abumgard@wpo.uwsuper.edu.

University of Wisconsin–Whitewater

Whitewater, Wisconsin

State-supported, coed. Small-town campus. Total enrollment: 10,438.

Degrees Bachelor of Music in the areas of music education, performance, music history, music theory. Majors: music, music education, piano/organ, stringed instruments, voice, wind and percussion instruments. Graduate degrees offered: Master of Music Education in the area of music education.

Music Student Profile Fall 1994: 220 total; 200 matriculated undergraduate, 20 matriculated graduate.

Music Faculty Total: 27; 15 full-time, 12 part-time; 90% of full-time faculty have terminal degrees. Graduate students do not teach undergraduate courses. Undergraduate student–faculty ratio: 9:1.

Student Life Student groups include Music Educators National Conference Student Chapter, International Jazz Educators Association Student Chapter, music fraternities.

Expenses for 1994–95 State resident tuition: $2327 full-time, $96.90 per credit part-time. Nonresident tuition: $7115 full-time, $296.40 per credit part-time. Minnesota residents pay tuition at the rate they would pay if attending a comparable state-supported institution in Minnesota. College room and board: $2496. College room only: $1460.

Financial Aid Program-specific awards for Fall of 1994: 24 Music Scholarships for program majors ($400–$800).

Application Procedures Deadline—freshmen and transfers: continuous. Notification date—freshmen and transfers: continuous. Required: high school transcript, college transcript(s) for transfer students, letter of recommendation, audition, ACT test score only, standing in top half of graduating class. Auditions held 5 times on campus; recorded music is permissible as a substitute for live auditions if a campus visit is impossible and videotaped performances are permissible as a substitute for live auditions if a campus visit is impossible.

Undergraduate Contact Harry Johansen, Audition Coordinator, Department of Music, University of Wisconsin–Whitewater, 800 West Main Street, Whitewater, Wisconsin 53190; 414-472-1310, fax: 414-472-2808.

Graduate Contact Larry Davis, Dean, Graduate School, University of Wisconsin–Whitewater, Roseman 2031, Whitewater, Wisconsin 53190; 414-472-1006.

University of Wyoming

Laramie, Wyoming

State-supported, coed. Small-town campus. Total enrollment: 12,020.

Degrees Bachelor of Music in the area of music performance; Bachelor of Music Education in the area of music education. Majors: music, music education. Graduate degrees offered: Master of Music in the areas of music performance, music history, music theory; Master of Music Education in the area of music education. Cross-registration with Wyoming community colleges.

Music Student Profile Fall 1994: 152 total; 130 matriculated undergraduate, 12 matriculated graduate, 10 nondegree.

Music Faculty Total: 25; 15 full-time, 10 part-time; 85% of full-time faculty have terminal degrees. Graduate students do not teach undergraduate courses. Undergraduate student–faculty ratio: 12:1.

Student Life Student groups include Wyoming Music Educators Association, band fraternities.

Expenses for 1995–96 Application fee: $30. State resident tuition: $1686 full-time, $70.25 per semester hour

part-time. Nonresident tuition: $6084 full-time, $253.50 per semester hour part-time. Part-time mandatory fees: $5 per semester hour. Full-time mandatory fees: $319. College room and board: $3520. Special program-related fees: $5 for practice room fees.

Financial Aid Program-specific awards for Fall of 1994: 15 Private Awards ($300).

Application Procedures Deadline—freshmen and transfers: August 28. Notification date—freshmen and transfers: continuous. Required: high school transcript, college transcript(s) for transfer students, 3 letters of recommendation, audition, SAT I or ACT test scores, minimum 2.5 high school GPA. Recommended: interview, portfolio. Auditions held on campus and off campus. Portfolio reviews held 1 time on campus and off campus.

Undergraduate Contact Office of Admissions, University of Wyoming, Knight Hall, Laramie, Wyoming 82071; 307-766-5160, fax: 307-766-4042.

Graduate Contact Dr. Theodore Lapina, Director, Graduate Studies, Music Department, University of Wyoming, Laramie, Wyoming 82071-3037; 307-766-5242, fax: 307-766-5326, E-mail address: lapina@uwyo.edu.

Utah State University

Logan, Utah

State-supported, coed. Urban campus. Total enrollment: 20,371.

Degrees Bachelor of Music in the areas of music education, performance, piano pedagogy. Majors: guitar, music, music education, music therapy, piano pedagogy, piano/organ, stringed instruments, voice, wind and percussion instruments. Graduate degrees offered: Master of Music Education in the area of choral music education.

Music Student Profile Fall 1994: 226 total; 216 matriculated undergraduate, 5 matriculated graduate, 5 nondegree; 3% minorities, 70% females, 2% international.

Music Faculty Total: 21; 19 full-time, 2 part-time; 67% of full-time faculty have terminal degrees. Graduate students teach a few undergraduate courses. Undergraduate student–faculty ratio: 30:1.

Student Life Student groups include Music Therapy Student Association, Kappa Kappa Psi (band fraternity), Tau Beta Sigma (band sorority).

Expenses for 1995–96 Application fee: $35. State resident tuition: $1992 full-time. Nonresident tuition: $6042 full-time. Part-time tuition per quarter ranges from $146 to $625 for state residents, $418 to $1877 for nonresidents. Part-time mandatory fees per quarter range from $38 to $121. Full-time mandatory fees: $381. College room and board: $3069. Special program-related fees: $25 for piano/organ practice rooms, $5 for instrument locker rentals.

Application Procedures Deadline—freshmen and transfers: July 1. Required: high school transcript, college transcript(s) for transfer students, ACT test score only, minimum 2.5 high school GPA, interview for music therapy applicants. Recommended: minimum 3.0 high school GPA. Auditions held on campus and off campus in Salt Lake City, UT; recorded music is permissible as a substitute for live auditions when distance is prohibitive and videotaped performances are permissible as a substitute for live auditions when distance is prohibitive.

Undergraduate Contact Edie Despain, Music Department, Utah State University, Logan, Utah 84322-4015; 801-797-3000.

Graduate Contact Dr. Will Kesling, Music Department, Utah State University, Logan, Utah 84322-4015; 801-797-3000.

Valdosta State University

Valdosta, Georgia

State-supported, coed. Small-town campus. Total enrollment: 9,160.

Degrees Bachelor of Music in the areas of music performance, music education. Majors: jazz, music education, piano/organ, stringed instruments, voice, wind and percussion instruments. Graduate degrees offered: Master of Music Education in the area of music education.

Music Student Profile Fall 1994: 120 total; 102 matriculated undergraduate, 18 matriculated graduate; 15% minorities, 40% females, 1% international.

Music Faculty Total: 25; 24 full-time, 1 part-time; 90% of full-time faculty have terminal degrees. Graduate students do not teach undergraduate courses. Undergraduate student–faculty ratio: 5:1.

Student Life Student groups include Music Educators National Conference, Tau Beta Sigma, Sigma Alpha Iota.

Expenses for 1995–96 Application fee: $10. State resident tuition: $1887 full-time. Nonresident tuition: $5097 full-time. Part-time tuition per quarter ranges from $42 to $593 for state residents, $132 to $1583 for nonresidents. College room and board: $3165. College room only: $1440. Special program-related fees: $50 for applied music fee.

Financial Aid Program-specific awards for Fall of 1994: 2 Lucy Martin Stewart Scholarships for undergraduates ($1500), 2 Elene Dorminey Scholarships for undergraduates ($1500), 2 Robert F. Barr Scholarships for undergraduates ($1000), 20 Department Awards for freshmen ($500), 10 Valdosta Symphony Scholarships for undergraduates ($3000).

Application Procedures Deadline—freshmen and transfers: continuous. Required: high school transcript, minimum 2.0 high school GPA, audition. Auditions held continuously on campus; recorded music is permissible as a substitute for live auditions when distance is prohibitive and videotaped performances are permissible as a substitute for live auditions when distance is prohibitive.

Undergraduate Contact Walter Peacock, Director, Admissions Office, Valdosta State University, 1500 North Patterson Street, Valdosta, Georgia 31698-0170; 912-333-5791.

Valdosta State University *(continued)*

Graduate Contact Ernestine Clark, Dean, Graduate Studies, Valdosta State University, Valdosta, Georgia 31698-0004; 912-333-5694.

Valparaiso University

Valparaiso, Indiana

Independent-religious, coed. Small-town campus. Total enrollment: 3,480.

Degrees Bachelor of Music in the areas of church music, performance, composition; Bachelor of Music Education in the areas of vocal music, instrumental music, combined vocal and instrumental music. Majors: classical music, music, music education, piano/organ, sacred music, stringed instruments, voice, wind and percussion instruments. Graduate degrees offered: Master of Music in the areas of church music, music education.

Music Student Profile Fall 1994: 58 total; 50 matriculated undergraduate, 7 matriculated graduate, 1 nondegree.

Music Faculty Total: 31; 8 full-time, 23 part-time; 88% of full-time faculty have terminal degrees. Graduate students do not teach undergraduate courses. Undergraduate student–faculty ratio: 10:1.

Student Life Student groups include American Guild of Organists, Music Educators National Conference, Music Enterprises Student Association.

Expenses for 1995–96 Application fee: $30. Comprehensive fee of $16,310 includes full-time tuition ($12,390), mandatory fees ($470), and college room and board ($3450). College room only: $2100. Part-time tuition: $535 per credit hour. Tuition for engineering program: $12,760. Special program-related fees: $180 for studio instruction fee.

Financial Aid Program-specific awards for Fall of 1994: 35 Music Scholarships for performers ($800–$1500).

Application Procedures Deadline—freshmen and transfers: continuous. Notification date—freshmen and transfers: August 15. Required: high school transcript, SAT I or ACT test scores, video or audition. Recommended: essay, letter of recommendation, interview. Auditions held 3 times on campus; videotaped performances are permissible as a substitute for live auditions by request, with permission of the chair.

Contact Chair, Department of Music, Valparaiso University, Valparaiso, Indiana 46383-6493; 219-464-5454, fax: 219-464-5496, E-mail address: lferguson@exodus.valpo.edu.

VanderCook College of Music

Chicago, Illinois

Independent, coed. Urban campus. Total enrollment: 149.

Degrees Bachelor of Music Education in the areas of instrumental music education, vocal music education. Majors: music education. Graduate degrees offered: Master of Music Education in the areas of instrumental music education, vocal music education.

Music Student Profile Fall 1994: 789 total; 53 matriculated undergraduate, 86 matriculated graduate, 650 nondegree; 20% minorities, 35% females.

Music Faculty Total: 30; 6 full-time, 24 part-time; 4% of full-time faculty have terminal degrees. Graduate students do not teach undergraduate courses. Undergraduate student–faculty ratio: 4:1.

Student Life Student groups include Music Educators National Conference Student Chapter, International Association of Jazz Educators, Great Teachers Scholarship Fund Cabaret Benefit.

Estimated Expenses for 1995–96 Application fee: $25. Comprehensive fee of $14,120 includes full-time tuition ($9100), mandatory fees ($220), and college room and board ($4800). Part-time tuition: $305 per semester hour. Part-time mandatory fees per semester (6 to 11 credits): $110. Special program-related fees: $50 for techniques classes, $50 for computer lab use.

Financial Aid Program-specific awards for Fall of 1994: 15 Scholarships for voice and instrument majors ($2500), 4 Tuition Assistance Grants for program majors ($500), 8 VCM Work-Study Programs for program majors ($1000).

Application Procedures Deadline—freshmen and transfers: continuous. Notification date—freshmen and transfers: continuous. Required: essay, high school transcript, minimum 2.0 high school GPA, 3 letters of recommendation, audition. Auditions held by appointment on campus and off campus; recorded music is permissible as a substitute for live auditions when distance is prohibitive and videotaped performances are permissible as a substitute for live auditions when distance is prohibitive.

Contact Admissions Office, VanderCook College of Music, 3209 South Michigan Office, Chicago, Illinois 60616; 312-225-6288, fax: 312-225-5211.

Blair School of Music

Vanderbilt University

Nashville, Tennessee

Independent, coed. Urban campus. Total enrollment: 10,088.

Degrees Bachelor of Music in the areas of performance, musical arts, composition/music theory. Majors: classical guitar, piano/organ, stringed instruments, voice, wind and percussion instruments. Cross-registration with Fisk University.

Music Student Profile Fall 1994: 118 total; all matriculated undergraduate; 11% minorities, 61% females.

Music Faculty Total: 83; 23 full-time, 60 part-time; 84% of full-time faculty have terminal degrees. Graduate students do not teach undergraduate courses. Undergraduate student–faculty ratio: 8:1.

Student Life Student groups include Pi Kappa Lambda, Voice Major's Association.

Expenses for 1995–96 Application fee: $50. Comprehensive fee of $26,078 includes full-time tuition ($18,860), mandatory fees ($562), and college room and board ($6656 minimum). College room only: $4144 (minimum). Part-time tuition: $786 per semester hour.

Financial Aid Program-specific awards for Fall of 1994: 1 Harold Sterling Vanderbilt Scholarship for program majors ($18,860), Blair Dean's Honor Scholarships for program majors ($1000–$5000), Blair Help Loans for program majors ($500–$2400), 1 Frances Hampton Currey Music Scholarship for program majors ($18,860), 1 Laura Kemp Goad Honor Scholarship for program majors ($18,860), 1 Joel and Stella Hargrove Scholarship for program majors ($5000), 1 Rae S. Miller Piano Scholarship for piano majors ($5000), 1 Wilda and William Moennig Scholarship for program majors ($12,000), 1 Del Sawyer Trumpet Scholarship for trumpet majors ($18,860).

Application Procedures Deadline—freshmen and transfers: continuous. Notification date—freshmen and transfers: April 1. Required: essay, high school transcript, college transcript(s) for transfer students, 2 letters of recommendation, audition, portfolio, SAT I or ACT test scores, portfolio for composition/theory applicants. Recommended: minimum 3.0 high school GPA, video. Auditions held 3 times on campus; recorded music is permissible as a substitute for live auditions for musical arts or performance majors (except in percussion) when distance is prohibitive and videotaped performances are permissible as a substitute for live auditions for percussion majors when distance is prohibitive.

Undergraduate Contact Dwayne Sagen, Assistant Dean of Admissions, Blair School of Music, Vanderbilt University, 2400 Blakemore Avenue, Nashville, Tennessee 37212; 615-322-7651, fax: 615-343-2786.

More about the School

Program Facilities The Blair Recital Hall, a beautiful 300-seat facility, serves as the School's focal point and houses a new digital recording system. The Electronic Classroom provides cutting edge technology, and the music library has more than 30,000 books/scores, 15,500 sound recordings, and a substantial collection of videotapes.

Faculty, Resident Artists, and Alumni The Blair faculty is nationally known for composition, research, and performance. Resident ensembles perform throughout the United States, and the School has numerous faculty members with active solo careers, many principal players in the Nashville Symphony, and musicians in the city's thriving recording industry. Faculty members typically perform 1,000-plus concerts in the United States and abroad each year.

Student Performance Opportunities Students in a small music school (Blair's maximum is 150) have the advantage of frequent, varied performing experience, including participation in orchestral and vocal ensembles, student composition recitals, and solo and chamber music performances. The School's referral service allows students to perform for various functions in the Nashville area.

Special Programs The musical arts program, one of a handful in the country, facilitates a second major or minor outside of music. The BMI Composer-in-Residence Program offers an opportunity to learn from one of the world's leading composers every semester. Master classes by visiting artists are also frequent. Students are involved in internships in Nashville's music industry and in teaching at the W. O. Smith Community Music School for disadvantaged children.

Virginia Commonwealth University

Richmond, Virginia

State-supported, coed. Urban campus. Total enrollment: 21,523.

Degrees Bachelor of Music in the areas of music education, performance, composition, jazz studies. Majors: composition, jazz, music education, piano/organ, stringed instruments, voice, wind and percussion instruments. Graduate degrees offered: Master of Music in the areas of music education, performance, composition.

Music Student Profile Fall 1994: 272 total; 245 matriculated undergraduate, 27 matriculated graduate; 15% minorities, 50% females, 2% international.

Music Faculty Total: 59; 24 full-time, 35 part-time; 56% of full-time faculty have terminal degrees. Graduate students teach a few undergraduate courses. Undergraduate student–faculty ratio: 10:1.

Student Life Student groups include Music Educators National Conference Student Chapter, Pi Kappa Lambda.

Estimated Expenses for 1995–96 Application fee: $20. State resident tuition: $3034 full-time, $126 per credit part-time. Nonresident tuition: $10,217 full-time, $426 per credit part-time. Part-time mandatory fees: $30.50 per credit. Full-time mandatory fees: $880. College room and board: $4182. College room only: $2416 (minimum). Special program-related fees: $520 for private music lessons, $300 for school of art fee.

Financial Aid Program-specific awards for Fall of 1994: 15 Merit Scholarships for program majors ($1500), 15 Applied Music Scholarships for program majors ($520), 5 Endowed Scholarships for program majors ($400–$700).

Application Procedures Deadline—freshmen: February 1; transfers: June 1. Required: essay, high school transcript, college transcript(s) for transfer students, minimum 2.0 high school GPA, letter of recommendation, interview, audition, SAT I test score only, minimum combined SAT I score of 800. Auditions held 5 times on campus; recorded music is permissible as a substitute for live auditions when distance is prohibitive and videotaped performances are permissible as a substitute for live auditions when distance is prohibitive.

Contact Dr. Sandra Guerard, Assistant Chair, Department of Music, Virginia Commonwealth University, 922 Park Avenue, P.O. Box 842004, Richmond, Virginia 23284-2004; 804-828-1169.

Virginia Intermont College

Bristol, Virginia

Independent-religious, coed. Small-town campus. Total enrollment: 682.

Degrees Bachelor of Fine Arts in the area of performing arts (music). Majors: music education. Cross-registration with King College.

Music Student Profile Fall 1994: 3 total; all matriculated undergraduate.

Music Faculty Total: 3; 1 full-time, 2 part-time; 100% of full-time faculty have terminal degrees. Graduate students do not teach undergraduate courses.

Expenses for 1995–96 Application fee: $15. Comprehensive fee of $13,850 includes full-time tuition ($9500), mandatory fees ($100), and college room and board ($4250). Part-time mandatory fees: $25 per semester. Part-time tuition and fees per credit: $125 for the first 6 hours, $300 for the next 5 hours. Special program-related fees: $150 for private music lessons.

Financial Aid Program-specific awards for Fall of 1994: 15 Room Grants for program majors ($1800).

Application Procedures Deadline—freshmen and transfers: continuous. Notification date—freshmen and transfers: continuous. Required: high school transcript, minimum 2.0 high school GPA. Recommended: audition. Auditions held by appointment on campus.

Undergraduate Contact Robin Cozart, Acting Director of Admissions, Virginia Intermont College, Box D-460, Bristol, Virginia 24201; 703-669-6101 ext. 207, fax: 703-669-5763.

Virginia State University

Petersburg, Virginia

State-supported, coed. Suburban campus. Total enrollment: 4,007.

Degrees Bachelor of Music in the area of performance; Bachelor of Music Education in the areas of choral music education, instrumental music education. Majors: music education, piano/organ, stringed instruments, voice, wind and percussion instruments.

Music Student Profile Fall 1994: 65 total; all matriculated undergraduate.

Music Faculty Total: 16; 9 full-time, 7 part-time; 66% of full-time faculty have terminal degrees. Graduate students do not teach undergraduate courses. Undergraduate student–faculty ratio: 9:1.

Student Life Student groups include Music Educators National Conference.

Expenses for 1995–96 State resident tuition: $1951 full-time, $82 per credit hour part-time. Nonresident tuition: $5960 full-time, $252 per credit hour part-time. Part-time mandatory fees: $20 per credit hour. Full-time mandatory fees: $1305. College room and board: $4845. College room only: $2750.

Financial Aid Program-specific awards for Fall of 1994: 1 Theodore Presser Award for juniors ($3000), 4 Undine Smith Moore Awards for freshmen ($1000), 12 Aurelia Walford Awards for program majors ($500–$1000), 5 Provost Scholars for freshmen ($1500).

Application Procedures Deadline—freshmen and transfers: continuous. Required: high school transcript, audition. Recommended: 2 letters of recommendation. Auditions held 3 times and by appointment on campus and off campus in Hartford, CT; New York, NY; Trenton, NJ; Raleigh, NC; Durham, NC; Pittsburgh, PA; various cities in Virginia; recorded music is permissible as a substitute for live auditions when distance is prohibitive and videotaped performances are permissible as a substitute for live auditions when distance is prohibitive.

Undergraduate Contact Harold J. Haughton, Chair, Department of Music, Virginia State University, P.O. Box 9007, Petersburg, Virginia 23806; 804-524-5311, fax: 804-524-6862.

Viterbo College

La Crosse, Wisconsin

Independent-religious, coed. Urban campus. Total enrollment: 1,701.

Degrees Bachelor of Music in the areas of music education, applied music performance. Majors: applied music, music education.

Expenses for 1995–96 Application fee: $15. Comprehensive fee of $13,590 includes full-time tuition ($9780), mandatory fees ($70), and college room and board ($3740). College room only: $1610. Part-time tuition per semester ranges from $284 to $4,160 depending on course load. Special program-related fees: $180 for applied music fee.

Financial Aid Program-specific awards for Fall of 1994: Fine Arts Scholarships for program majors ($500–$1000).

Application Procedures Deadline—freshmen and transfers: August 1. Required: high school transcript, college transcript(s) for transfer students, interview, SAT I or ACT test scores. Auditions held on campus and off campus. Portfolio reviews held on campus and off campus.

Undergraduate Contact Dr. Roland Nelson, Director of Admissions, Admission Office, Viterbo College, 815 South 9th Street, LaCrosse, Wisconsin 54601; 608-791-0040, fax: 608-791-0367.

Walla Walla College

College Place, Washington

Independent-religious, coed. Small-town campus. Total enrollment: 1,725.

Degrees Bachelor of Music in the area of performance; Bachelor of Music Education in the area of music education. Majors: music education, piano/organ, stringed instruments, voice, wind instruments.

Music Student Profile Fall 1994: 30 total; all matriculated undergraduate; 17% minorities, 67% females, 23% international.

Music Faculty Total: 14; 7 full-time, 7 part-time; 57% of full-time faculty have terminal degrees. Graduate students do not teach undergraduate courses. Undergraduate student–faculty ratio: 4:1.

Student Life Special housing available for music students.

Expenses for 1995–96 Application fee: $30. Comprehensive fee of $14,673 includes full-time tuition ($11,193), mandatory fees ($282), and college room and board ($3198). College room only: $1698. Part-time tuition: $297 per quarter hour. Part-time mandatory fees: $35 per quarter hour.

Application Procedures Deadline—freshmen and transfers: August 15. Required: high school transcript, minimum 2.0 high school GPA, 3 letters of recommendation, audition, SAT I or ACT test scores. Auditions held 2 times on campus; videotaped performances are permissible as a substitute for live auditions when distance is prohibitive.

Undergraduate Contact Dan Shultz, Chair, Music Department, Walla Walla College, 204 South College Avenue, College Place, Washington 99324; 509-527-2562, fax: 509-527-2253.

Wartburg College

Waverly, Iowa

Independent-religious, coed. Small-town campus. Total enrollment: 1,405.

Degrees Bachelor of Music in the areas of voice, keyboard, instrumental music; Bachelor of Music Education in the areas of vocal music education, instrumental music education; Bachelor of Music Education/Music Therapy in the area of music therapy. Majors: guitar, piano/organ, stringed instruments, voice, wind and percussion instruments.

Expenses for 1995–96 Application fee: $20. Comprehensive fee of $16,100 includes full-time tuition ($12,240), mandatory fees ($130), and college room and board ($3730). College room only: $1730. Part-time mandatory fees per term range from $15 to $30. Part-time tuition: $550 per course up to 2.75 courses.

Application Procedures Deadline—freshmen and transfers: continuous. Notification date—freshmen and transfers: continuous. Auditions held on campus and off campus. Portfolio reviews held on campus and off campus.

Undergraduate Contact Director of Admissions, Wartburg College, Whitehouse Business Center 201, Waverly, Iowa 50677-0903; 319-352-8264, fax: 319-352-8579.

Washburn University of Topeka

Topeka, Kansas

City-supported, coed. Urban campus. Total enrollment: 6,439.

Degrees Bachelor of Music in the area of music performance; Bachelor of Music Education in the area of music education. Majors: music, music education, piano/organ, stringed instruments, voice, wind and percussion instruments.

Music Student Profile Fall 1994: 75 total; all matriculated undergraduate; 10% minorities, 2% international.

Music Faculty Total: 25; 10 full-time, 15 part-time; 80% of full-time faculty have terminal degrees. Graduate students do not teach undergraduate courses. Undergraduate student–faculty ratio: 10:1.

Expenses for 1995–96 State resident tuition: $2790 full-time, $93 per credit hour part-time. Nonresident tuition: $5730 full-time, $191 per credit hour part-time. Part-time mandatory fees: $8 per semester. Full-time mandatory fees: $32. College room and board: $3410.

Financial Aid Program-specific awards for Fall of 1994: 25–30 Music Endowments for program majors ($1000).

Application Procedures Deadline—freshmen and transfers: August 6. Notification date—freshmen and transfers: August 15. Required: high school transcript, college transcript(s) for transfer students. Recommended: interview, audition, SAT I or ACT test scores. Auditions held 3 times on campus; recorded music is permissible as a substitute for live auditions when distance is prohibitive and videotaped performances are permissible as a substitute for live auditions when distance is prohibitive.

Undergraduate Contact Rodney Boyd, Associate Chair, Music Department, Washburn University of Topeka, 1700 Southwest College, Topeka, Kansas 66621; 913-231-1010 ext. 1520, E-mail address: zzboyr@acc.wuacc.edu.

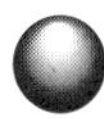

Washington State University

Pullman, Washington

State-supported, coed. Rural campus. Total enrollment: 19,314.

Degrees Bachelor of Music in the areas of voice, keyboard, instruments, composition; Bachelor of Music Education in the areas of choral music education, instrumental music education, general music education. Majors: composition, music, music education, piano/organ, stringed instruments, voice, wind and percussion instruments. Cross-registration with University of Idaho.

Music Student Profile Fall 1994: 1,610 total; 110 matriculated undergraduate, 1,500 nondegree; 5% minorities, 50% females.

Music Faculty Total: 27; 16 full-time, 11 part-time; 100% of full-time faculty have terminal degrees. Graduate students teach a few undergraduate courses. Undergraduate student–faculty ratio: 10:1.

Washington State University *(continued)*

Student Life Student groups include Music Educators National Conference Student Chapter, American Choral Directors Association Student Chapter, Music Teachers National Association Student Chapter.

Expenses for 1994–95 Application fee: $35. State resident tuition: $2908 full-time, $145 per credit part-time. Nonresident tuition: $8200 full-time, $410 per credit part-time. Full-time mandatory fees: $245. College room and board: $4050.

Financial Aid Program-specific awards for Fall of 1994: 20 Visual and Performing Arts Awards for undergraduates ($500).

Application Procedures Deadline—freshmen and transfers: May 1. Notification date—freshmen and transfers: August 22. Required: high school transcript, college transcript(s) for transfer students, minimum 2.0 high school GPA, audition, SAT I or ACT test scores. Auditions held by appointment on campus and off campus in various locations in Washington area; recorded music is permissible as a substitute for live auditions if a campus visit is impossible.

Undergraduate Contact Dr. Erich Lear, Director, School of Music and Theatre Arts, Washington State University, Kimbrough Building, Pullman, Washington 99164-5300; 509-335-8524, fax: 509-335-4245.

Wayland Baptist University

Plainview, Texas

Independent-religious, coed. Small-town campus. Total enrollment: 897.

Degrees Bachelor of Music in the areas of music education, church music. Majors: music education, sacred music.

Music Student Profile Fall 1994: 135 total; 35 matriculated undergraduate, 100 nondegree; 15% minorities, 60% females, 1% international.

Music Faculty Total: 12; 7 full-time, 5 part-time; 43% of full-time faculty have terminal degrees. Graduate students do not teach undergraduate courses. Undergraduate student–faculty ratio: 10:1.

Student Life Student groups include Phi Mu Alpha, Sigma Alpha Iota.

Expenses for 1995–96 Application fee: $35. Comprehensive fee of $8650 includes full-time tuition ($5400), mandatory fees ($350), and college room and board ($2900). College room only: $1213. Part-time tuition: $180 per semester hour. Part-time mandatory fees per semester: $40 for the first 6 semester hours, $175 for the next 5 semester hours. Special program-related fees: $25 for practice room fees, $50 for private study fee.

Application Procedures Deadline—freshmen and transfers: continuous. Required: high school transcript, college transcript(s) for transfer students, interview, audition, SAT I or ACT test scores, minimum combined SAT I score of 850, minimum composite ACT score of 18. Recommended: minimum 2.0 high school GPA. Auditions held 4 times on campus; recorded music is permissible as a substitute for live auditions when distance is prohibitive and videotaped performances are permissible as a substitute for live auditions.

Undergraduate Contact Dr. Carl C. Moman, Chair, Music Division, Wayland Baptist University, 1900 West Seventh Street, Plainview, Texas 79072-6998; 806-296-4741.

Wayne State University

Detroit, Michigan

State-supported, coed. Urban campus. Total enrollment: 32,906.

Degrees Bachelor of Music in the areas of church music, composition, jazz studies, music education, music technology, music management, performance, music theory, music theater. Majors: classical music, composition, jazz, music, music education, music management, music technology, music theater, music theory, piano/organ, sacred music, stringed instruments, voice, wind and percussion instruments. Graduate degrees offered: Master of Music in the areas of composition, choral conducting, music education, performance, music theory.

Music Student Profile Fall 1994: 273 total; 241 matriculated undergraduate, 32 matriculated graduate; 23% minorities, 40% females, 3% international.

Music Faculty Total: 87; 17 full-time, 70 part-time; 100% of full-time faculty have terminal degrees. Graduate students teach a few undergraduate courses. Undergraduate student–faculty ratio: 12:1.

Student Life Student groups include Delta Omicron, Phi Mu Alpha, Mu Phi Epsilon.

Expenses for 1994–95 Application fee: $20. State resident tuition: $3060 (minimum) full-time. Nonresident tuition: $6810 (minimum) full-time. Part-time mandatory fees: $70 per semester. Full-time tuition ranges up to $3705 for state residents, $8169 for nonresidents, according to class level. Part-time tuition per credit hour ranges from $98 to $115 for state residents, $218 to $259 for nonresidents, according to class level. Full-time mandatory fees: $70. Special program-related fees: $79–$157 for private lessons.

Financial Aid Program-specific awards for Fall of 1994: 66 Talent Scholarships for program majors ($700), 270 Activity Awards for ensemble participants ($50–$1000), 51 Awards for high academic and musical achievement ($150–$3750), 20–30 Full Scholarships for program majors ($2492–$2900).

Application Procedures Deadline—freshmen and transfers: continuous. Required: high school transcript, college transcript(s) for transfer students, minimum 2.0 high school GPA, SAT I or ACT test scores. Recommended: minimum 3.0 high school GPA, audition. Auditions held 2 times and by appointment on campus; recorded music is permissible as a substitute for live auditions when distance is prohibitive and videotaped performances are permissible as a substitute for live auditions when distance is prohibitive.

Contact Dennis J. Tini, Chair, Department of Music, Wayne State University, 105 Schaver Music Building, Detroit, Michigan 48202; 313-577-1795, fax: 313-577-5420.

Webster University

St. Louis, Missouri

Independent, coed. Suburban campus. Total enrollment: 10,834.

Degrees Bachelor of Music in the areas of jazz studies, vocal performance, composition, piano performance; Bachelor of Music Education in the area of choral music education; Bachelor of Fine Arts in the area of musical theater. Majors: classical music, composition, jazz, music, music education, piano/organ, voice, wind and percussion instruments. Graduate degrees offered: Master of Music in the areas of jazz pedagogy, piano, vocal performance, composition. Cross-registration with various colleges in St. Louis.

Music Student Profile Fall 1994: 96 total; 77 matriculated undergraduate, 19 matriculated graduate; 10% minorities, 60% females, 5% international.

Music Faculty Total: 36; 9 full-time, 27 part-time; 90% of full-time faculty have terminal degrees. Graduate students do not teach undergraduate courses. Undergraduate student–faculty ratio: 10:1.

Student Life Student groups include Sigma Alpha Iota.

Expenses for 1994–95 Application fee: $25. Comprehensive fee of $13,500 includes full-time tuition ($9160) and college room and board ($4340). Part-time tuition: $280 per credit hour. Special program-related fees: $175 for applied music fee.

Financial Aid Program-specific awards for Fall of 1994: 4 Buder Scholarships for incoming students ($1000).

Application Procedures Deadline—freshmen and transfers: continuous. Required: essay, high school transcript, college transcript(s) for transfer students, 2 letters of recommendation, audition, SAT I or ACT test scores. Auditions held 8 times on campus; recorded music is permissible as a substitute for live auditions when distance is prohibitive and videotaped performances are permissible as a substitute for live auditions when distance is prohibitive.

Undergraduate Contact Mary Walz, Auditions Coordinator, Office of Admissions, Webster University, 470 East Lockwood Avenue, St. Louis, Missouri 63119-3194; 314-968-7000, fax: 314-968-7115.

Graduate Contact John Schuster-Craig, Chair, Department of Music, Webster University, 470 East Lockwood Avenue, St. Louis, Missouri 63119-3194; 314-968-7032, fax: 314-963-6048, E-mail address: schustjo@webster2.websteruniv.edu.

West Chester University of Pennsylvania

West Chester, Pennsylvania

State-supported, coed. Small-town campus. Total enrollment: 11,168.

Degrees Bachelor of Music in the areas of piano/organ, voice, wind and percussion instruments, stringed instruments, composition, theory. Majors: classical music, composition, music education, music theory, piano/organ, stringed instruments, voice, wind and percussion instruments. Graduate degrees offered: Master of Music in the areas of music education, performance, theory, composition. Cross-registration with Cheyney University.

Music Student Profile Fall 1994: 370 total; 325 matriculated undergraduate, 45 matriculated graduate; 8% minorities, 47% females, 1% international.

Music Faculty Total: 59; 43 full-time, 16 part-time; 90% of full-time faculty have terminal degrees. Graduate students do not teach undergraduate courses. Undergraduate student–faculty ratio: 7:1.

Student Life Student groups include Music Educators National Conference Student Chapter, Music Teachers National Association Student Chapter, professional music fraternities.

Expenses for 1994–95 Application fee: $25. State resident tuition: $3086 full-time, $129 per credit part-time. Nonresident tuition: $7844 full-time, $327 per credit part-time. Part-time mandatory fees: $104 per semester. Full-time mandatory fees: $560. College room and board: $4080. College room only: $2580.

Application Procedures Deadline—freshmen and transfers: continuous. Required: essay, high school transcript, college transcript(s) for transfer students, minimum 2.0 high school GPA, audition, SAT I or ACT test scores, minimum combined SAT I score of 1000, minimum composite ACT score of 20. Recommended: minimum 3.0 high school GPA. Auditions held 10 times on campus and off campus; recorded music is permissible as a substitute for live auditions when distance is prohibitive and videotaped performances are permissible as a substitute for live auditions when distance is prohibitive. Portfolio reviews held on campus and off campus.

Undergraduate Contact Eugene Klein, Undergraduate Coordinator, School of Music, West Chester University of Pennsylvania, West Chester, Pennsylvania 19383; 610-436-2650, E-mail address: eklein@wcupa.edu.

Graduate Contact Timothy Blair, Graduate Coordinator, School of Music, West Chester University of Pennsylvania, West Chester, Pennsylvania 19383; 610-436-2536, E-mail address: tblair@wcupa.edu.

Potter College of Arts, Humanities, and Social Sciences

Western Kentucky University

Bowling Green, Kentucky

State-supported, coed. Suburban campus. Total enrollment: 14,765.

Degrees Bachelor of Music in the area of performance; Bachelor of Music Education in the areas of vocal music education, instrumental music education. Majors: guitar, music, music education, piano/organ, voice, wind and percussion instruments.

Music Student Profile Fall 1994: 146 total; all matriculated undergraduate; 10% minorities, 55% females, 1% international.

Music Faculty Total: 24; 16 full-time, 8 part-time; 100% of full-time faculty have terminal degrees. Graduate students do not teach undergraduate courses. Undergraduate student–faculty ratio: 12:1.

Student Life Student groups include music fraternities and sororities, musical production sponsored by Theater Department.

Expenses for 1995–96 Application fee: $15. State resident tuition: $1910 full-time, $78 per semester hour part-time. Nonresident tuition: $5270 full-time, $218 per semester hour part-time. Full-time mandatory fees: $125. College room and board: $2456 (minimum). College room only: $1316 (minimum). Special program-related fees: $50 for applied lessons.

Financial Aid Program-specific awards for Fall of 1994: 25–30 Talent Grants for program majors ($900–$1800).

Application Procedures Deadline—freshmen and transfers: August 1. Required: high school transcript, minimum 2.0 high school GPA, audition, ACT test score only, minimum composite ACT score of 17. Recommended: minimum 3.0 high school GPA. Auditions held 3 times and by appointment on campus; recorded music is permissible as a substitute for live auditions for out-of-state applicants and videotaped performances are permissible as a substitute for live auditions for out-of-state applicants.

Undergraduate Contact Office of Admissions, Western Kentucky University, 1 Big Red Way, Bowling Green, Kentucky 42101; 502-745-5422.

Western Michigan University

Kalamazoo, Michigan

State-supported, coed. Urban campus. Total enrollment: 25,673.

Degrees Bachelor of Music in the areas of performance, music education, jazz studies, music therapy, music history, music theory, music composition. Majors: classical music, composition, jazz, music, music education, music history, music theory, music therapy, piano/organ, stringed instruments, voice, wind and percussion instruments.

Music Student Profile Fall 1994: 396 total; all matriculated undergraduate; 6% minorities, 54% females, 3% international.

Music Faculty Total: 43; 34 full-time, 9 part-time; 88% of full-time faculty have terminal degrees. Graduate students teach a few undergraduate courses. Undergraduate student–faculty ratio: 11:1.

Student Life Student groups include Collegiate Music Educators National Conference, Music Therapy Club, music fraternities.

Expenses for 1994–95 Application fee: $25. Part-time mandatory fees: $85 per semester. Full-time tuition ranges from $2705 to $3046 for state residents, $6936 to $7804 for nonresidents, according to class level. Part-time tuition per credit hour ranges from $87.25 to $98.25 for state residents, $223.75 to $251.75 for nonresidents, according to class level. Full-time mandatory fees: $455. College room and board: $4097. Special program-related fees: $45 for music major fee, $7 for applied music fee.

Financial Aid Program-specific awards for Fall of 1994: 80 School of Music Scholarships for program majors ($500–$7000).

Application Procedures Deadline—freshmen and transfers: continuous. Required: high school transcript, college transcript(s) for transfer students, audition, ACT test score only. Auditions held 4 times on campus; recorded music is permissible as a substitute for live auditions when distance is prohibitive and videotaped performances are permissible as a substitute for live auditions when distance is prohibitive.

Undergraduate Contact Margaret J. Hamilton, Assistant Director, School of Music, Western Michigan University, Kalamazoo, Michigan 49008-3831; 616-387-4672, fax: 616-387-5809, E-mail address: margaret.hamilton@wmich.edu.

Western Washington University

Bellingham, Washington

State-supported, coed. Small-town campus. Total enrollment: 10,598.

Degrees Bachelor of Music in the areas of performance, composition, music history and literature, jazz studies, music education. Majors: composition, jazz, music, music education, performance. Graduate degrees offered: Master of Music in the areas of performance, composition, music history and literature, conducting, music education.

Music Student Profile Fall 1994: 500 total; 175 matriculated undergraduate, 25 matriculated graduate, 300 nondegree; 10% minorities, 50% females, 2% international.

Music Faculty Total: 27; 14 full-time, 13 part-time; 50% of full-time faculty have terminal degrees. Graduate students teach a few undergraduate courses.

Student Life Student groups include Music Educators National Conference Student Chapter.

Estimated Expenses for 1995–96 Application fee: $35. State resident tuition: $2406 full-time, $75 per quarter hour part-time. Nonresident tuition: $8124 full-time, $266 per quarter hour part-time. Full-time mandatory fees: $150. College room and board: $4144. Special program-related fees: $15 for piano practice fee, $5 for accompanying fee, $20 for instrument rental.

Application Procedures Deadline—freshmen: March 1; transfers: April 1. Notification date—freshmen and transfers: May 1. Required: high school transcript, college transcript(s) for transfer students, minimum 2.0 high school GPA, audition, SAT I or ACT test scores. Auditions held 1 time and continuously by appointment on campus; recorded music is permissible as a substitute for live auditions when distance is prohibitive.

Undergraduate Contact David Wallace, Chairman, Music Department, Western Washington University, MS-9107, Bellingham, Washington 98225-9107; 206-650-3130, fax: 206-650-3028.

Graduate Contact Edward Rutschman, Graduate Advisor, Music Department, Western Washington University, MS-9107, Bellingham, Washington 98225-9107; 206-650-3889, fax: 206-650-3028.

West Georgia College

Carrollton, Georgia

State-supported, coed. Small-town campus. Total enrollment: 8,310.

Degrees Bachelor of Music in the areas of music, jazz, theory–composition; Bachelor of Music Education in the area of classical music. Majors: jazz, music, music education, music theory and composition. Graduate degrees offered: Master of Music in the area of music; Master of Music Education in the area of music.

Music Student Profile Fall 1994: 91 total; 77 matriculated undergraduate, 14 matriculated graduate; 9% minorities, 37% females, 1% international.

Music Faculty Total: 17; 10 full-time, 7 part-time; 70% of full-time faculty have terminal degrees. Graduate students do not teach undergraduate courses. Undergraduate student–faculty ratio: 10:1.

Student Life Student groups include Music Educators National Conference Collegiate Chapter, Phi Mu Alpha Sinfonia, Sigma Alpha Iota.

Expenses for 1995–96 Application fee: $10. State resident tuition: $1884 full-time, $42 per quarter hour part-time. Nonresident tuition: $5094 full-time, $132 per quarter hour part-time. College room and board: $3093. College room only: $1545. Special program-related fees: $25 for applied music fee, $1 for practice room fee.

Financial Aid Program-specific awards for Fall of 1994: 34 Music Scholarships and Service Awards for music majors and non-major ensemble members ($1000).

Application Procedures Deadline—freshmen and transfers: continuous. Required: high school transcript, college transcript(s) for transfer students, audition, SAT I or ACT test scores, minimum combined SAT I score of 830, minimum composite ACT score of 17, minimum 2.5 high school GPA. Recommended: letter of recommendation, interview, portfolio. Auditions held 5 times on campus and off campus in Gainesville, GA; recorded music is permissible as a substitute for live auditions when distance is prohibitive and videotaped performances are permissible as a substitute for live auditions when distance is prohibitive. Portfolio reviews held 5 times on campus and off campus in Gainesville, GA.

Contact M. Scott McBride, Chair, Department of Music, West Georgia College, Carrollton, Georgia 30118-2210; 404-836-6516, fax: 404-836-6791, E-mail address: smcbride@sun.cc.westga.edu.

Westminster Choir College of Rider University

See Rider University, Westminster Choir College of Rider University

Westminster College

New Wilmington, Pennsylvania

Independent-religious, coed. Small-town campus. Total enrollment: 1,620.

Degrees Bachelor of Music in the areas of performance, music education, church music. Majors: classical music, music, music education, piano/organ, sacred music, stringed instruments, voice, wind and percussion instruments.

Music Student Profile Fall 1994: 215 total; 65 matriculated undergraduate, 150 nondegree; 5% minorities, 65% females, 1% international.

Music Faculty Total: 23; 5 full-time, 18 part-time; 80% of full-time faculty have terminal degrees. Graduate students do not teach undergraduate courses. Undergraduate student–faculty ratio: 10:1.

Student Life Student groups include Music Educators National Conference, Mu Phi Epsilon.

Expenses for 1995–96 Application fee: $20. Comprehensive fee of $17,495 includes full-time tuition ($13,245), mandatory fees ($270), and college room and board ($3980). College room only: $1910. Part-time tuition: $1310 per course. Part-time mandatory fees: $237.50 per term.

Financial Aid Program-specific awards for Fall of 1994: 20 Music Activity Grants for program majors ($800–$2000).

Application Procedures Deadline—freshmen and transfers: continuous. Required: essay, high school transcript, minimum 3.0 high school GPA, 3 letters of recommendation, audition. Recommended: interview. Auditions held 6 times on campus; recorded music is permissible as a substitute for live auditions when distance is prohibitive and videotaped performances are permissible as a substitute for live auditions when distance is prohibitive.

Westminster College *(continued)*

Undergraduate Contact Admissions, Westminster College, 319 South Market Street, New Wilmington, Pennsylvania 16172; 412-946-7100, fax: 412-946-7171.

Sybil B. Harrington College of Fine Arts and Humanities

West Texas A&M University

Canyon, Texas

State-supported, coed. Small-town campus. Total enrollment: 6,738.

Degrees Bachelor of Music in the area of applied music; Bachelor of Music Education. Majors: music, piano/organ, stringed instruments, voice, wind and percussion instruments. Graduate degrees offered: Master of Music in the area of performance.

Music Student Profile Fall 1994: 265 total; 225 matriculated undergraduate, 40 matriculated graduate; 10% minorities, 50% females, 5% international.

Music Faculty Total: 40; 30 full-time, 10 part-time; 50% of full-time faculty have terminal degrees. Graduate students teach a few undergraduate courses. Undergraduate student–faculty ratio: 20:1.

Student Life Student groups include National Association of Music Therapy Student Chapter, Kappa Kappa Psi, Mu Phi Epsilon.

Expenses for 1995–96 State resident tuition: $900 full-time. Nonresident tuition: $5280 full-time, $176 per semester hour part-time. State resident part-time tuition per semester ranges from $100 to $330. Full-time mandatory fees: $634. College room and board: $2900. College room only: $1400. Special program-related fees: $60 for applied music fee.

Application Procedures Deadline—freshmen and transfers: continuous. Required: high school transcript, audition. Auditions held 3 times on campus; recorded music is permissible as a substitute for live auditions if a campus visit is impossible and videotaped performances are permissible as a substitute for live auditions if a campus visit is impossible.

Contact Dr. Harry Haines, Head, Department of Music and Dance, West Texas A&M University, WTAMU Box 879, Canyon, Texas 79016; 806-656-2840, fax: 806-656-2779.

West Virginia University

Morgantown, West Virginia

State-supported, coed. Small-town campus. Total enrollment: 22,500.

Degrees Bachelor of Music in the areas of jazz, classical music, music theory, music history, composition; Bachelor of Music Education in the areas of instrumental music education, vocal music education. Majors: classical music, jazz, music, music education, music history, music theory, piano/organ, stringed instruments, voice, wind and percussion instruments. Graduate degrees offered: Master of Music in the areas of performance, composition, music theory, music history; Master of Music Education in the area of music education. Doctor of Musical Arts in the areas of piano, voice, organ, percussion/world music.

Music Student Profile Fall 1994: 291 total; 230 matriculated undergraduate, 50 matriculated graduate, 11 nondegree; 5% minorities, 55% females, 5% international.

Music Faculty Total: 40; 40 full-time; 90% of full-time faculty have terminal degrees. Graduate students teach a few undergraduate courses. Undergraduate student–faculty ratio: 18:1.

Student Life Student groups include Music Educators National Conference, Music Teachers National Association. Special housing available for music students.

Expenses for 1995–96 Application fee: $10. State resident tuition: $2192 full-time, $93 per credit hour part-time. Nonresident tuition: $6784 full-time, $284 per credit hour part-time. College room and board: $4434. Special program-related fees: $10 for practice room fee.

Financial Aid Program-specific awards for Fall of 1994 available.

Application Procedures Deadline—freshmen and transfers: continuous. Notification date—freshmen and transfers: August 1. Required: high school transcript, college transcript(s) for transfer students, minimum 2.0 high school GPA, audition, SAT I or ACT test scores. Recommended: letter of recommendation, interview. Auditions held 3 times and by appointment on campus; recorded music is permissible as a substitute for live auditions when distance is prohibitive and videotaped performances are permissible as a substitute for live auditions when distance is prohibitive.

Undergraduate Contact John Weigand, Director, Undergraduate Admissions, Music Department, West Virginia University, College of Creative Arts, P.O. Box 6111, Morgantown, West Virginia 26506-6111; 304-293-5511, fax: 304-293-3550.

Graduate Contact Barton Hudson, Director, Graduate Studies, Music Department, West Virginia University, College of Creative Arts, P.O. Box 6111, Morgantown, West Virginia 26506-6111; 304-293-5511, fax: 304-293-3550.

West Virginia Wesleyan College

Buckhannon, West Virginia

Independent-religious, coed. Small-town campus. Total enrollment: 1,680.

Degrees Bachelor of Music in the areas of voice, piano, orchestral instruments, guitar; Bachelor of Music Education in the areas of voice, piano, orchestral instruments, guitar. Majors: classical music, guitar, music, music education, piano, voice, wind and percussion instruments. Cross-registration with Alderson–Broaddus College, Davis & Elkins College.

Music Student Profile Fall 1994: 40 total; all matriculated undergraduate; 8% minorities, 50% females, 2% international.

Music Faculty Total: 11; 6 full-time, 5 part-time; 83% of full-time faculty have terminal degrees. Graduate students do not teach undergraduate courses. Undergraduate student–faculty ratio: 8:1.

Student Life Student groups include Music Educators National Conference Student Chapter, Sigma Alpha Iota.

Expenses for 1995–96 Application fee: $25. Comprehensive fee of $18,600 includes full-time tuition ($14,750) and college room and board ($3850). Part-time tuition: $615 per credit hour. Special program-related fees: $150 for applied music fees.

Financial Aid Program-specific awards for Fall of 1994: Music Scholarships for incoming students ($1000–$6000).

Application Procedures Deadline—freshmen and transfers: continuous. Required: high school transcript, minimum 2.0 high school GPA, audition. Recommended: minimum 3.0 high school GPA, interview, video, SAT I or ACT test scores. Auditions held on campus and off campus in Washington, DC; Portsmouth, NH; recorded music is permissible as a substitute for live auditions and videotaped performances are permissible as a substitute for live auditions.

Undergraduate Contact Robert N. Skinner, Director of Admission, West Virginia Wesleyan College, 59 College Avenue, Buckhannon, West Virginia 26201; 800-722-9933, fax: 304-473-8108.

More about the College

Program Facilities Music: The Loar Hall of Music has abundant performance and rehearsal accommodations, which include two pipe organs; fifty pianos, including a 9-foot Steinway-D; listening room with thousands of LP and CD recordings; music library with in-depth reference materials and periodical holdings; fourteen practice rooms; electronic recording studio with MIDI equipment; large collection of works of major composers in musical score; a 75-rank Casavant organ; computer labs; and two harpsichords. Senior music majors are featured in a solo recital as a capstone experience. Many are involved in internships in Washington, D.C., and New York City and also volunteer projects in the local community.

Art: Department highlights include recently renovated 7,000-square-foot art facility that includes the Sleeth Art Gallery; extended hours of use of studio space; weekend trips to major art centers like New York, Washington, D.C., Philadelphia, and Pittsburgh. Programs include regular visiting artists, workshops, and curated exhibitions. Study abroad is encouraged and is an actual requirement in the art history track of study. Experienced faculty includes the 1994 West Virginia Art Educator of the Year, a nationally recognized ceramic sculptor, a landscape painter, and an installation art specialist.

Drama: Department highlights include intensive program (requires more credit hours in major than most programs); internships that are widely available and that stress the department's commitment to finding employment for graduates; opportunity, especially with regard to student-directed productions; a very active Alpha Psi Omega chapter; and an experienced faculty that includes an award-winning children's playwright with a national reputation in children's theater.

The Wesleyan Music Program prepares students for professional positions in performing, teaching, conducting, music communications, and music business and offers numerous opportunities for practical musical experience on and off the campus.

Students study with professional instructors who guide them through their program, providing personalized attention. Opportunities to perform abound. Each year, the Wesleyan Concert Chorale, Concert Band, Jazz Ensemble, Wind Ensembles, and Concentus Vocum present public concerts. Wesleyan musicians regularly participate in concert tours of other states and often of other nations. There are also abundant opportunities for individual and ensemble performances through a series of recitals, oratorios, and music theater productions.

Wesleyan's Bachelor of Music Education plan prepares students for the teaching profession. The Bachelor of Arts program provides liberal arts study with an emphasis on performance or theory. There is also the option of designing a major in conjunction with other fields like business, Christian education, and radio/TV communications.

Applied music study is based on a system of proficiency levels. Entering freshmen are assigned a level on the basis of an audition and interview with the expectation that they advance one level per semester. Music majors normally earn credit in their chosen field of applied music at the rate of at least 2 semester hours each semester, until they achieve their required level.

The art program is designed to develop a knowledge of aesthetic elements and principals and provide the opportunity to develop creative potential. Emphasis is placed on the preparation of students for successful careers in art through study in such areas as painting, drawing, graphic design, ceramics, printmaking, art education, and art history. In addition, a general studio concentration prepares students for careers in areas such as art therapy.

The rigorous and challenging programs of study in art are capped with a required internship experience in the chosen field of study. Art majors are required to participate in a senior exhibition and assemble a portfolio of successful work.

The art faculty members are active professionals in their fields who have regional and national exhibition experience. All are dedicated to the idea of creative strength built on a foundation of basic skills and principals in an environment that encourages experimentation. Their teaching style is highly interactive and supportive, yet rigorous and challenging.

The degree in dramatic arts is designed to expose the student to all aspects of theater, including design, directing, literature, history, and acting. The Wesleyan faculty believes that it is important for the student to understand all the elements involved in the creation of a theatrical production in order to fully appreciate the complexity of each show. This is achieved by requiring all majors to be involved extensively in at least four full-length West Virginia Wesleyan Theatre productions. After graduation, students are qualified to pursue many different career avenues.

Wesleyan graduates are currently employed in radio, television, arts administration, the ministry, and educa-

West Virginia Wesleyan College *(continued)*

tion and in the professional theater as actors, designers, technicians, and administrators.

Wheaton Conservatory of Music

Wheaton College

Wheaton, Illinois

Independent-religious, coed. Suburban campus. Total enrollment: 2,642.

Degrees Bachelor of Music in the areas of performance, composition, music history/literature; Bachelor of Music Education in the areas of performance, composition, music history/literature. Majors: classical music, composition, music, music education, music history and literature, piano/organ, stringed instruments, voice, wind and percussion instruments.

Music Student Profile Fall 1994: 190 total; all matriculated undergraduate; 5% minorities, 55% females, 10% international.

Music Faculty Total: 30; 21 full-time, 9 part-time; 65% of full-time faculty have terminal degrees. Graduate students do not teach undergraduate courses. Undergraduate student–faculty ratio: 9:1.

Student Life Student groups include Music Educators National Conference, American Guild of Organists.

Expenses for 1995–96 Application fee: $30. Comprehensive fee of $16,670 includes full-time tuition ($12,300) and college room and board ($4370). College room only: $2540. Part-time tuition per hour ranges from $340 to $510. Special program-related fees: $16 for music fee, $170 for performance course, $35 for second instrument rental.

Financial Aid Program-specific awards for Fall of 1994: 3–4 Cording Awards for those demonstrating talent ($2000), 4 Presidential Honor Awards for those demonstrating talent ($1000), 4–5 Strickland Awards for those demonstrating need ($1000–$2000).

Application Procedures Deadline—freshmen and transfers: April 1. Notification date—freshmen and transfers: May 15. Required: essay, high school transcript, college transcript(s) for transfer students, minimum 2.0 high school GPA, 4 letters of recommendation, interview, audition, SAT I or ACT test scores. Auditions held 6–8 times on campus; recorded music is permissible as a substitute for live auditions when distance is prohibitive and videotaped performances are permissible as a substitute for live auditions when distance is prohibitive.

Undergraduate Contact Ray Zrinsky, Conservatory Admission Counselor, Wheaton Conservatory of Music, Wheaton College, Wheaton, Illinois 60187; 708-752-5098, fax: 708-752-5341, E-mail address: rzrinsky@david.wheaton.edu.

More about the Conservatory

Program Facilities Wheaton's main music facility is McAlister Hall, which houses most of the faculty offices and practice rooms. There are seventy-five pianos on campus, including six concert grands. Performances take place in Edman Memorial Chapel, with 2,400 seats; Pierce Chapel, with 900 seats; and Barrows Auditorium, with 500 seats. There are five pipe organs, including a 65-rank, 4-manual Schantz. The Music Library holds several thousand records, tapes, and compact discs, in addition to an extensive collection of scores and music reference books. The Technomusic Studio is available with a MacIntosh computer, Performer, Finale, and Studio Vision software, and several synthesizers, as well as digital recording capabilities.

Student Performance Opportunities There are nine performance ensembles directed by Wheaton Conservatory faculty members. Vocal and choral groups include Chapel Choir, Concert Choir, Men's Glee Club, Music Theatre Workshop, West Suburban Choral Union, and Women's Chorale. Instrumental ensembles include the Jazz Ensemble, Pep Band, Symphony Orchestra, and Wind Ensemble. In addition, chamber ensembles and soloists rehearse and perform regularly. Large ensembles join forces for the annual Christmas Festival and Festival of Faith, as well as for numerous other performances on and off campus. The ensembles maintain a touring ministry throughout the United States and occasionally overseas.

Special Programs The Bachelor of Music with elective study in an outside field offers students the opportunity to complement course work in music with a second subject area. Music with elective study degrees are available in biblical and theological studies, business, Christian education, communications, fine arts ministries, literature, mathematics/computer science, psychology, sociocultural studies, theater, and Third World studies.

Wichita State University

Wichita, Kansas

State-supported, coed. Urban campus. Total enrollment: 14,558.

Degrees Bachelor of Music in the areas of performance, musicology–music theory/composition; Bachelor of Music Education in the areas of choral music education, instrumental music education, general music education, special music education. Majors: classical music, conducting, jazz, music, music education, opera, piano/organ, stringed instruments, voice, wind and percussion instruments. Graduate degrees offered: Master of Music in the areas of performance, musicology–music theory/composition, piano pedagogy, instrumental conducting; Master of Music Education in the areas of choral music education, instrumental music education, general music education, special music education.

Music Student Profile Fall 1994: 429 total; 375 matriculated undergraduate, 54 matriculated graduate; 10% minorities, 52% females, 7% international.

Music Faculty Total: 51; 41 full-time, 10 part-time; 75% of full-time faculty have terminal degrees. Graduate students teach a few undergraduate courses. Undergraduate student–faculty ratio: 12:1.

Student Life Student groups include Music Educators National Conference Student Chapter, Tau Beta Sigma, Student Music Teachers National Association. Special housing available for music students.

Expenses for 1994–95 Application fee: $15. State resident tuition: $2090 full-time, $69.65 per credit hour part-time. Nonresident tuition: $7434 full-time, $247.80 per credit hour part-time. Part-time mandatory fees: $13 per semester. Full-time mandatory fees: $26. College room and board: $3121 (minimum).

Financial Aid Program-specific awards for Fall of 1994: 25 Scholarships for talented students.

Application Procedures Deadline—freshmen and transfers: continuous. Required: high school transcript, college transcript(s) for transfer students, minimum 2.0 high school GPA, audition. Recommended: minimum 3.0 high school GPA, letter of recommendation, interview. Auditions held 10 times on campus; recorded music is permissible as a substitute for live auditions if a campus visit is impossible and videotaped performances are permissible as a substitute for live auditions if a campus visit is impossible.

Contact Harold A. Popp, Director, School of Music, Wichita State University, Campus Box 53, Wichita, Kansas 67260-0053; 316-689-3500, fax: 316-689-3951, E-mail address: popp@uc.twsu.edu.

More about the University

Program Facilities Duerksen Fine Arts Center with Miller Concert Hall, Wiedemann Concert Hall, practice studios/rooms, electronic laboratory, classrooms, music library, rehearsal halls. Wiedemann Hall houses the Great Marcussen organ, considered the finest in North America. Audio Productions is a branch of the College of Fine Arts. Harpsichords, grand pianos, MIDI equipment, discklavier, multimedia centers.

Faculty and Alumni Forty-one full-time faculty members and 10 part-time artists/scholars. Performing faculty ensembles include Fairmount String Quartet, Lieurance Woodwind Quintet, Wichita Brass Quintet, Sotto Voce Trio, Faculty Vocal Quartet, Wiedemann Trio, and Hillside Blues. Ensembles active with tours, clinics, guest appearances, and recording tapes and CDs. Faculty hold all principal chairs of the Wichita Symphony Orchestra. Scholars publishing continually. Composers active with commissions. Educators, conductors, and master teachers commonly involved with guest appearances nationally and internationally. Alumni hold positions in public schools, higher education, world-renowned orchestras, opera companies, chamber ensembles, military ensembles, jazz ensembles, and the world of entertainment.

Student Performance Opportunities In addition to traditional ensembles of orchestras, band/wind ensembles, choirs, opera theater, and jazz ensembles, students participate in percussion ensemble, steel drum band, guitar ensemble, string chamber ensembles, woodwind chamber ensembles, brass chamber ensembles, vocal chamber ensembles, and jazz trio. Students appear in national finals of MTNA Collegiate Artist, Fishoff Chamber Music Competition, Spoleto Festival, Aspen, National Repertory Orchestra, and other prestigious competitions/festivals.

Special Events Students, faculty, and guest artists are involved in American Music Week, Contemporary Music Festival, Wichita Jazz Festival, Band Festival, and Madrigal Invitational. Major Fine Arts series include Connoisseur, Series, Opera Series, Organ Series, and Dance Series.

Wilfrid Laurier University

Waterloo, Ontario

Province-supported, coed. Urban campus. Total enrollment: 8,068.

Degrees Bachelor of Music in the areas of comprehensive, church music, composition, music history, performance, music theory, music education; Bachelor of Music Therapy in the area of music therapy. Majors: classical music, composition, music education, music history, music theory, music therapy, opera, piano/organ, sacred music, stringed instruments, voice, wind and percussion instruments. Cross-registration with University of Waterloo.

Music Student Profile Fall 1994: 283 total; 267 matriculated undergraduate, 16 nondegree; 3% minorities, 62% females, 1% international.

Music Faculty Total: 69; 19 full-time, 50 part-time; 37% of full-time faculty have terminal degrees. Graduate students do not teach undergraduate courses. Undergraduate student–faculty ratio: 4:1.

Student Life Student groups include Music Association, Music Therapy Association.

Expenses for 1994–95 Canadian resident tuition: $2228 full-time, $500 per course part-time. Nonresident tuition: $7620 full-time, $1524 per course part-time. (All figures are in Canadian dollars.). Full-time mandatory fees: $315. College room and board: $4643 (minimum). College room only: $2643 (minimum). Special program-related fees: $30–$60 for accompanying fees.

Financial Aid Program-specific awards for Fall of 1994: 21 Faculty of Music Awards for program majors ($750).

Application Procedures Deadline—freshmen and transfers: April 1. Notification date—freshmen and transfers: June 15. Required: high school transcript, minimum 3.0 high school GPA, letter of recommendation, interview, audition, music theory placement test. Auditions held 1 time on campus; recorded music is permissible as a substitute for live auditions when distance is prohibitive and videotaped performances are permissible as a substitute for live auditions when distance is prohibitive.

Undergraduate Contact Office of Admissions, Wilfrid Laurier University, 75 University Avenue West, Waterloo, Ontario N2L 3C5, Canada; 519-884-1970 ext. 3351, E-mail address: efehr@mach2.wlu.ca.

Willamette University

Salem, Oregon

Independent-religious, coed. Urban campus. Total enrollment: 2,519.

Willamette University *(continued)*

Degrees Bachelor of Music in the areas of music performance, music therapy, music education, composition. Majors: composition, music, music education, music therapy, piano/organ, voice, wind and percussion instruments.

Music Student Profile Fall 1994: 68 total; all matriculated undergraduate; 3% minorities, 65% females, 12% international.

Music Faculty Total: 29; 9 full-time, 20 part-time; 89% of full-time faculty have terminal degrees. Graduate students do not teach undergraduate courses. Undergraduate student–faculty ratio: 13:1.

Student Life Student groups include Music Educators National Conference Student Chapter, Music Therapy Chapter, Mu Phi Epsilon.

Expenses for 1995–96 Application fee: $35. Comprehensive fee of $21,290 includes full-time tuition ($16,400), mandatory fees ($90), and college room and board ($4800). Part-time tuition: $1700 per course. Tuition guaranteed not to increase for student's term of enrollment. Special program-related fees: $200 for applied music fee, $3 for locker rental fee.

Financial Aid Program-specific awards for Fall of 1994: 30 Music Scholarship Awards for talented performers ($1000–$2000).

Application Procedures Deadline—freshmen and transfers: February 1. Notification date—freshmen and transfers: April 1. Required: essay, high school transcript, college transcript(s) for transfer students, 2 letters of recommendation, SAT I or ACT test scores. Recommended: minimum 3.0 high school GPA, interview, audition. Auditions held 3 times and through miscellaneous ad hoc auditions on campus; recorded music is permissible as a substitute for live auditions and videotaped performances are permissible as a substitute for live auditions.

Undergraduate Contact James Sumner, Dean of Admissions, Willamette University, 900 State Street, Salem, Oregon 97301; 503-370-6303, fax: 503-375-5363.

Winters School of Music

William Carey College

Hattiesburg, Mississippi

Independent-religious, coed. Small-town campus. Total enrollment: 2,139.

Degrees Bachelor of Music in the areas of music education, church music, performance, music therapy. Majors: guitar, music education, music therapy, piano/organ, sacred music, voice, wind and percussion instruments.

Music Student Profile Fall 1994: 80 total; all matriculated undergraduate.

Music Faculty Total: 12; 10 full-time, 2 part-time.

Expenses for 1994–95 Application fee: $10. Comprehensive fee of $6810 includes full-time tuition ($4650) and college room and board ($2160 minimum). Part-time tuition: $155 per semester hour.

Application Procedures Deadline—freshmen and transfers: continuous. Required: high school transcript, audition. Recommended: minimum 2.0 high school GPA. Auditions held continuously on campus and off campus in various regional cities; recorded music is permissible as a substitute for live auditions when distance is prohibitive.

Undergraduate Contact Milfred Valentine, Dean, Winters School of Music, William Carey College, 498 Tuscan Avenue, Hattiesburg, Mississippi 39401; 601-582-6175, fax: 601-582-6454.

William Paterson College of New Jersey

Wayne, New Jersey

State-supported, coed. Small-town campus. Total enrollment: 9,669.

Degrees Bachelor of Music in the areas of performance, jazz studies, music management; Bachelor of Music Education in the area of music education. Majors: classical music, jazz, music, music education, music management, piano/organ, stringed instruments, voice, wind and percussion instruments.

Music Student Profile Fall 1994: 209 total; all matriculated undergraduate; 8% minorities, 50% females, 5% international.

Music Faculty Total: 62; 19 full-time, 43 part-time. Undergraduate student–faculty ratio: 6:1.

Student Life Student groups include Music Educators National Conference Student Chapter, Music Entertainment Industry Educators Student Association, Phi Mu Alpha.

Estimated Expenses for 1995–96 Application fee: $35. State resident tuition: $3072 full-time, $96 per credit part-time. Nonresident tuition: $4064 full-time, $127 per credit part-time. College room and board: $4500 (minimum). College room only: $2900. Special program-related fees: $100 for applied music fees, $30 for practice room fee, $30 for electronic music lab fee, .

Financial Aid Program-specific awards for Fall of 1994 available.

Application Procedures Deadline—freshmen and transfers: July 1. Required: audition. Auditions held 5 times on campus; recorded music is permissible as a substitute for live auditions for jazz and classical music applicants and videotaped performances are permissible as a substitute for live auditions for jazz applicants.

Undergraduate Contact Dr. William Woodworth, Director of Recruitment and Admissions, Music Department, William Paterson College of New Jersey, Shea Center for Performing Arts, Wayne, New Jersey 07470; 201-595-3199, fax: 201-595-2460.

Wingate University

Wingate, North Carolina

Independent-religious, coed. Small-town campus. Total enrollment: 1,383.

Degrees Bachelor of Music in the areas of church music, performance; Bachelor of Music Education in the area of music education. Majors: classical music, music, music education, piano/organ, sacred music, voice, wind and percussion instruments. Cross-registration with Charlotte Area Educational Consortium.

Music Student Profile Fall 1994: 36 total; all matriculated undergraduate; 8% minorities, 44% females, 6% international.

Music Faculty Total: 12; 6 full-time, 6 part-time; 100% of full-time faculty have terminal degrees. Graduate students do not teach undergraduate courses. Undergraduate student–faculty ratio: 6:1.

Student Life Student groups include Collegiate Music Educators National Conference.

Expenses for 1995–96 Application fee: $20. Comprehensive fee of $12,400 includes full-time tuition ($8400), mandatory fees ($400), and college room and board ($3600). College room only: $1800. Part-time tuition: $280 per credit hour. Part-time mandatory fees: $65 per semester. Special program-related fees: $75 for applied music fee.

Financial Aid Program-specific awards for Fall of 1994: 24 Music Scholarships for program majors ($2000).

Application Procedures Deadline—freshmen and transfers: continuous. Notification date—freshmen and transfers: August 15. Required: essay, high school transcript, college transcript(s) for transfer students, minimum 2.0 high school GPA, 2 letters of recommendation, interview, SAT I or ACT test scores. Recommended: minimum 3.0 high school GPA, audition. Auditions held 3 times on campus; recorded music is permissible as a substitute for live auditions when distance is prohibitive and videotaped performances are permissible as a substitute for live auditions when distance is prohibitive.

Undergraduate Contact Christopher Keller, Director of Admissions, Stegall Administration Building, Wingate University, Box 3059, Wingate, North Carolina 28174; 704-233-8201, fax: 704-233-8014.

Winters School of Music

See William Carey College, Winters School of Music

Winthrop University

Rock Hill, South Carolina

State-supported, coed. Small-town campus. Total enrollment: 5,164.

Degrees Bachelor of Music in the area of performance; Bachelor of Music Education in the areas of choral music education, instrumental music education. Majors: guitar, harpsichord, music education, piano/organ, voice, wind and percussion instruments. Graduate degrees offered: Master of Music in the area of performance; Master of Music Education in the areas of choral music education, instrumental music education.

Music Faculty Total: 33; 18 full-time, 15 part-time; 78% of full-time faculty have terminal degrees.

Student Life Student groups include Delta Omicron, Phi Mu Alpha.

Estimated Expenses for 1995–96 Application fee: $35. State resident tuition: $3801 full-time, $158 per credit hour part-time. Nonresident tuition: $6601 full-time, $274 per credit hour part-time. Part-time mandatory fees: $10 per semester. Full-time mandatory fees: $20. College room and board: $3780. College room only: $2058. Special program-related fees: $77–$100 for applied music fees.

Financial Aid Program-specific awards for Fall of 1994: Music Scholarships for above average freshmen and continuing students with exceptional artistic ability.

Application Procedures Deadline—freshmen: May 1; transfers: June 1. Required: high school transcript, letter of recommendation, audition, SAT I or ACT test scores. Recommended: essay. Auditions held 4 times on campus; recorded music is permissible as a substitute for live auditions when distance is prohibitive.

Contact Dr. Carol Quin, Chair, Music Department, Winthrop University, 129 Music Conservatory, Rock Hill, South Carolina 29733; 803-323-2255.

Wittenberg University

Springfield, Ohio

Independent-religious, coed. Suburban campus. Total enrollment: 2,160.

Degrees Bachelor of Music in the areas of performance, church music; Bachelor of Music Education in the areas of choral music education, instrumental music education. Majors: classical music, music, music education, piano/organ, sacred music, stringed instruments, voice, wind and percussion instruments. Cross-registration with Southwestern Consortium for Higher Education.

Music Student Profile Fall 1994: 652 total; 55 matriculated undergraduate, 597 nondegree; 11% minorities, 53% females, 5% international.

Music Faculty Total: 22; 8 full-time, 14 part-time; 63% of full-time faculty have terminal degrees. Graduate students do not teach undergraduate courses. Undergraduate student–faculty ratio: 14:1.

Student Life Student groups include Ohio Collegiate Music Education Association.

Expenses for 1995–96 Application fee: $40. Comprehensive fee of $22,232 includes full-time tuition ($16,854), mandatory fees ($842), and college room and board ($4536). College room only: $2256. Tuition guaranteed not to increase for student's term of enrollment. Special program-related fees: $15 for practice room rental.

Wittenberg University *(continued)*

Financial Aid Program-specific awards for Fall of 1994: 1–15 Music Alumni Scholarships for incoming students ($2500), 1–10 Alida Atwell Smith Scholarships for those demonstrating need ($2500).

Application Procedures Deadline—freshmen and transfers: continuous. Notification date—freshmen and transfers: August 1. Required: essay, high school transcript, college transcript(s) for transfer students, minimum 2.0 high school GPA, 2 letters of recommendation. Recommended: interview, audition. Auditions held 3 times and by appointment on campus; recorded music is permissible as a substitute for live auditions when distance is prohibitive and videotaped performances are permissible as a substitute for live auditions when distance is prohibitive.

Undergraduate Contact Ken Benne, Dean of Admission, Wittenberg University, P.O. Box 720, Springfield, Ohio 45501-0720; 513-327-6314, fax: 513-327-6340.

Wright State University

Fairborn, Ohio

State-supported, coed. Suburban campus. Total enrollment: 16,823.

Degrees Bachelor of Music in the areas of performance, music theory, composition, music history and literature, music education. Majors: classical music, music, music education, piano/organ, stringed instruments, voice, wind and percussion instruments. Graduate degrees offered: Master of Music Education in the area of music education. Cross-registration with Southern Ohio Consortium of Higher Education.

Music Student Profile Fall 1994: 161 total; 138 matriculated undergraduate, 23 matriculated graduate; 6% minorities, 55% females.

Music Faculty Total: 32; 14 full-time, 18 part-time; 71% of full-time faculty have terminal degrees. Graduate students teach a few undergraduate courses. Undergraduate student–faculty ratio: 10:1.

Student Life Student groups include Collegiate Music Educators National Conference, Phi Mu Alpha Sinfonia, Sigma Alpha Iota.

Expenses for 1995–96 Application fee: $30. State resident tuition: $3429 full-time, $107 per credit hour part-time. Nonresident tuition: $6858 full-time, $214 per credit hour part-time. College room and board: $4806. Special program-related fees: $5 for practice room key rental, $50 for junior, senior recital fee, $80–$240 for applied music lesson fee, $15 for instrumental rental fee.

Financial Aid Program-specific awards for Fall of 1994: 12–16 String Scholarships for string players ($3000), 50 Music Scholarships for program majors ($1500).

Application Procedures Deadline—freshmen and transfers: continuous. Required: high school transcript, minimum 2.0 high school GPA, 3 letters of recommendation, audition. Auditions held 7 times on campus.

Undergraduate Contact Kathie Barbour, Administrative Assistant, Music Department, Wright State University, Dayton, Ohio 45435; 513-873-2787, fax: 513-873-3787.

Graduate Contact Dr. Sharon Nelson, Director, Graduate Studies in Music, Music Department, Wright State University, Dayton, Ohio 45435; 513-873-2254.

Xavier University of Louisiana

New Orleans, Louisiana

Independent-religious, coed. Urban campus. Total enrollment: 3,486.

Degrees Bachelor of Music in the areas of performance, music education. Majors: music education, piano/organ, stringed instruments, voice, wind and percussion instruments. Cross-registration with Loyola University.

Music Student Profile Fall 1994: 25 total; all matriculated undergraduate.

Music Faculty Total: 15; 7 full-time, 8 part-time; 43% of full-time faculty have terminal degrees.

Expenses for 1994–95 Application fee: $25. Comprehensive fee of $11,015 includes full-time tuition ($6900), mandatory fees ($115), and college room and board ($4000). Part-time tuition: $300 per semester hour. Part-time mandatory fees: $5 per semester. Tuition for pharmacy degree program: $9,300 full-time, $400 per semester hour part-time. Special program-related fees: $175 for music fee.

Financial Aid Program-specific awards for Fall of 1994: 40 Music Talent Scholarships for program majors ($2000–$7000).

Application Procedures Deadline—freshmen: June 1. Required: high school transcript, college transcript(s) for transfer students, letter of recommendation, audition, SAT I or ACT test scores. Auditions held 3 times and by appointment on campus and off campus; recorded music is permissible as a substitute for live auditions when distance is prohibitive. Portfolio reviews held on campus and off campus.

Undergraduate Contact John E. Ware, Chairman, Department of Music, Xavier University of Louisiana, 7325 Palmetto Street, New Orleans, Louisiana 70125; 504-483-7597.

York University

North York, Ontario

Province-supported, coed. Urban campus. Total enrollment: 38,313.

Degrees Bachelor of Fine Arts in the area of music. Majors: classical performance, composition, jazz, performance, world music.

Music Student Profile Fall 1994: 270 total; all matriculated undergraduate.

Music Faculty Total: 17; 15 full-time, 2 part-time. Graduate students teach a few undergraduate courses. Undergraduate student–faculty ratio: 16:1.

Expenses for 1994–95 Application fee: $75. Canadian resident tuition: $2720 full-time, $90.67 per credit part-time. Nonresident tuition: $8894 full-time, $296.47 per credit part-time. (All figures are in Canadian dollars.). Full-time mandatory fees: $140. College room and board: $3796. College room only: $3201. Special program-related fees: $10–$40 for material fees.

Financial Aid Program-specific awards for Fall of 1994: 2 Talent Awards for students with outstanding auditions ($1000).

Application Procedures Deadline—freshmen and transfers: March 1. Notification date—freshmen: June 30; transfers: July 15. Required: high school transcript, college transcript(s) for transfer students, minimum 3.0 high school GPA, interview, audition, SAT, ACT or Canadian equivalent. Recommended: 2 letters of recommendation. Auditions held 1 time on campus; recorded music is permissible as a substitute for live auditions when distance is prohibitive. Portfolio reviews held on campus.

Undergraduate Contact Don Murdoch, Liaison Officer, Liaison and Advising, Faculty of Fine Arts, York University, 213 CFA, 4700 Keele Street, North York, Ontario M3J 1P3, Canada; 416-736-5135, fax: 416-736-5447, E-mail address: donm@vm2.yorku.ca..

Dana School of Music

Youngstown State University

Youngstown, Ohio

State-supported, coed. Urban campus. Total enrollment: 13,979.

Degrees Bachelor of Music in the areas of performance, music education, applied music, composition, accompanying, jazz studies. Majors: classical music, jazz, music education, piano/organ, stringed instruments, voice, wind and percussion instruments. Graduate degrees offered: Master of Music in the areas of performance, music education, music theory and composition, music history and literature.

Music Student Profile Fall 1994: 219 total; 174 matriculated undergraduate, 25 matriculated graduate, 20 nondegree; 4% minorities, 50% females, 1% international.

Music Faculty Total: 44; 24 full-time, 20 part-time; 40% of full-time faculty have terminal degrees. Graduate students teach a few undergraduate courses. Undergraduate student–faculty ratio: 8:1.

Expenses for 1994–95 Application fee: $25. State resident tuition: $2910 full-time, $81 per credit part-time. Tuition for nonresidents residing within a 100-mile radius: $4926 full-time, $137 per credit part-time. Tuition for nonresidents residing outside a 100-mile radius: $5430 full-time, $151 per credit part-time. College room and board: $3750. Special program-related fees: $18 for applied music fee.

Financial Aid Program-specific awards for Fall of 1994: 70 Youngstown State University Foundation Music Awards for program students ($800), 4 University Grants-in-Aid for program students ($1800), 2 Monday Musical Awards for program students ($1000), 10 Showcase Awards for program students ($600).

Application Procedures Deadline—freshmen and transfers: continuous. Required: high school transcript, letter of recommendation, audition. Auditions held 4 times on campus; recorded music is permissible as a substitute for live auditions when distance is prohibitive and videotaped performances are permissible as a substitute for live auditions when distance is prohibitive.

Undergraduate Contact Admissions Office, Youngstown State University, 410 Wick Avenue, Youngstown, Ohio 44555; 216-742-3150, fax: 216-742-1998.

Graduate Contact Dr. Darla Funk, Director of Graduate Studies, Graduate School, Youngstown State University, 410 Wick Avenue, Youngstown, Ohio 44555; 216-742-3091, fax: 216-742-1998.

THEATER PROGRAMS

THEATER PROGRAMS

There are degree-granting programs at universities, and there are nonuniversity programs that may or may not offer a certificate or degree of some kind. In most university programs, you have an opportunity to opt for the "conservatory" program or the "liberal arts" program. The conservatory program is a professional training program leading to a Bachelor of Fine Arts (B.F.A.) degree. You can pursue an emphasis in acting, directing, costume design, lighting design, scenic design, technical direction, stage management, theater management, and, in some cases, playwriting. Where you go from there depends on what specialization you choose. For example, if you choose the acting specialization, you can track either into a program that offers a particular method, such as Stanislavsky or Meisner or Strasberg, or into a program that offers a potpourri of all of them in addition to body movement and voice. There are also courses in theater history, theatrical production, make-up, directing, and so on. There are also certain university requirements, generally in the liberal arts, that you must meet.

Performance Opportunities: B.F.A. Programs

Conservatory programs *require* their students to be in productions. Some schools' performance requirements begin in the first year, others in the junior year. Students generally start performing in their junior year. Some universities have professional troupes attached to the university. You take course work at the university, but you perform with a professional theater company in the community.

Liberal Arts Theater Programs

In most universities, the liberal arts program combines theater arts with liberal

> ### Student Self-Evaluation
>
> #### Questions to Ask Yourself Before Applying to a Theater Program
>
> *How strongly am I committed to devoting my life to working in the theater?* It's an intensely competitive field, you don't always have steady employment, and it can be a difficult life—the whole notion of "rejection" is very real. There's a commitment involved in doing theater that I don't think you need to have in a lot of other programs. It's that desire to want to do theater as a part of your life, a part of who you are. You have to feel within yourself, 'this is something that I want to do.' You have to not only see it as a craft and a job but also derive enjoyment and pleasure from it.
>
> *Do I want the very focused professional training a B.F.A program or conservatory would give me, or do I want to study theater within a broader liberal arts context?* If you have any other interests besides one focal point, be that acting, directing, design, or whatever, you should choose a program that offers you the ability to explore and develop both. The B.A. will probably give you that opportunity.
>
> *What are my strengths and weaknesses?* What areas of my craft do I want and need to develop? What kind of social and intellectual setting do I want? A university program will offer more of a diverse "college experience, while a conservatory offers the company of like-minded and equally dedicated people.
>
> *What size school do I want?* Will I be most comfortable in a smaller, more intimate setting, or do I want the diversity of a large school?
>
> *In what geographic area do I want to be?* What particular section of the county? In a major cultural center? Near a theater in which I'd like to work? In a quiet rural area where I won't be distracted?

arts and leads to a Bachelor of Arts (B.A.) degree. The B.A. program is offered for students who have a passion for the theater but also have interests in other areas. Half of the courses are in theater, and the other half are taken from a selection of liberal arts courses. The Bachelor of Arts program is meant to give you a broad education—an overview in various areas of the theater—instead of focusing on one particular track, like acting or design, as in B.F.A. programs. A double major is common in a B.A. program. In some programs, there are also performance opportunities for B.A. students. Some schools even structure their B.A. program to mirror a B.F.A. program so that students can specialize in a particular area. Dramaturgy allows a student to focus on a more scholarly study of the theater, say as a critic or historian, however it's usually offered at the graduate level.

Advantages/Disadvantages: B.F.A./B.A.

Advantages of the B.A. are a well-rounded education in both theater and the liberal arts. A conservatory program gives students very focused professional training, but it's so specialized that it's difficult to pursue other interests because of the number of required courses. Of course, most students who go into B.F.A. programs probably don't want to pursue anything else! There are conservatory programs, like those at Juilliard in New York, that offer professional training. Different programs offer acting, directing, design—the whole gamut of the theater. Some, but not all, are four-year programs. They may offer a certificate, an associate degree, or a degree that's not recognized by an accrediting body for colleges. Thus, students can get an excellent education in acting or another discipline. However, they run the risk of attending a nonaccredited school. The courses are performance-oriented, and there are few outside liberal arts courses—perhaps less than a third.

The Nonuniversity Conservatory

The advantage would be the training—it's even more specialized and focused than a B.F.A. program. A student would be at a disadvantage if he or she wanted to go on for a master's degree. As a rule, your degree carries a lot more weight and credibility when it's from a major university. But if you want specialized training in a particular school that's known for that training—Juilliard, for example—then the school itself will carry the weight of a university.

Acting for Film or Video

A lot of students are looking for programs to teach acting for film; however, most

Program Evaluation

Questions to Ask About a Program to Determine if It's the Right One for You

What is the personality and mission of the program? Make sure that your personality fits the personality of the program. You also need to understand the mission and vision of the program to make sure they match your goals and desires; if not, there will be conflict.

What is the program's methodology? Some schools focus on teaching a specific track or a specific method, so you should know what you're getting into. For instance, if you know you want to study a particular acting technique, such as Strasberg or Meisner, make sure programs you're looking at focus on that type of training.

How large is the school or university? How many people are in the program in which you're interested? What's the student-faculty ratio in your area of study?

Does the school's location suit my needs and preferences?

Does the program feature guest artists, artists-in-residence, or industry visitors so I can meet practicing professionals and learn the latest theories and techniques? How long do they stay on campus? Do they give lectures, teach classes, or offer workshops? Do they work with all students or just with those at a certain level?

What opportunities are there for me to perform or practice my craft in the program? In the community? Does the program allow professional leave?

What kind of facilities are available to me to practice my craft? Is there adequate rehearsal space? Is the equipment state-of-the-art?

Who is on the faculty? Are faculty members practicing in their field? The strongest faculty members are those who currently work in the field and bring their expertise into the classroom on a day-to-day basis.

What are alumni of the program doing? Are they working in the field? Does the program arrange internship opportunities? What kind of placement help does the program or school offer? Does the program or school offer opportunities to study abroad?

programs teach theater and acting for the stage. Although those very same techniques can be used in front of a camera, there aren't any programs that offer a degree designed to teach you how to act for film. There may be courses on acting on film taught in the school of theater or in the school of cinema and television. Some schools offer students professional leave—allowing them to go out and work. In that case, you'd want to be in an area where there's a lot of work. Therefore, the advantage to being in New York or L.A. is important; you reap all the benefits of being in a culturally diverse metropolitan area that focuses on the entertainment industry.

The Application Process

In a B.A. program, students are usually required to complete a university application, and the admission decision is made on criteria such as standardized test scores and academic record. Some schools also require a supplementary application geared toward theater. It usually includes questions related to theater and an essay on why you're pursuing this degree.

For the B.F.A. program, some schools require a university application and a supplementary application. The supplementary application is the starting point of the audition process.

Auditions

The standard audition is a 5-minute audition consisting of one classical and one contemporary piece, usually about 2 minutes each. For musical theater programs, you have to prepare a song. Live auditions are usually held. There are so many individual requirements that it's best to contact the school to

find out exactly what you need to produce. For the most part, schools require the students to come to them. Some schools or consortiums of schools hold regional or national auditions. Audition judges are typically faculty and staff members directly from the school of theater—not admissions officers. There's usually a minimum of 2, sometimes up to 4. For a consortium audition, as many as 5 to 10 will judge auditions. Some auditions are very formal, very professional, and—unfortunately for the students—very intimidating. Others are very warm and informal. Some programs require call-backs, others don't. Some programs have an interview along with the audition; for some it's just the audition. Some are individual auditions, and others are "group auditions."

Potential and natural talent are what the adjudicators are looking for. A lot of students are very intimidated because they feel they should have some type of skill already inherent in their audition. But that's not a requirement. Adjudicators look for somebody they know they could work with and someone who has the potential to be great.

Potential and natural talent are what the adjudicators are looking for.

Auditions for B.F.A. Programs

Auditions are the deciding factor for most programs. Some consider the audition as well as the academic component, and some base their admissions on the auditions and don't really concern themselves with the academic component.

B.A. Programs That Don't Require Auditions

When applying to a B.A. program, your interest in theater will be paramount—the productions you've been in, what roles you've played, letters of recommendation, any type of outstanding achievement awards or theater awards—something to give an idea of who you are.

The Application Process

The earlier you file your application, the better, especially if you're interested in competitive scholarships, early notification of admissions, or scheduling an audition.

Study Abroad Programs

These important programs provide not only experience in theater but also experience with other cultures. Students learn different techniques and approaches that can only add to the experience. In fact, many students cite an overseas study program as the event that changed their life the most. If the theater school doesn't have an international study program, there are often other schools or departments in the university that offer overseas programs where you can study theater.

Guest Artists

Guest artists are very important. They connect students to what's going on outside, in the field, particularly in schools where students aren't allowed to do outside work. Such guest lecturers bring the industry in and give a very honest view of what's happening. Students get exposure to both acting and the technical side of theater, including the very latest in equipment and techniques.

Internships

Whether internships are offered depends on the school's location. Any school that has an active community theater or film and television or any type of performance arena would probably offer internships. Internship opportunities are most important for students who are in technical areas.

Competition for Performing Jobs

The competition is only increasing—students should be very aware of that as they choose theater as their major—so take the opportunity as undergraduates to do different things within the theater. For example, if you're taking an acting track, focusing on stage management can only enhance your job opportunities and make you more marketable. Some performance students who decide they don't want to perform go behind the scenes into production or casting or directing. Some go on for a graduate degree to teach. Some do a 180-degree change and go into a whole different field. Most schools conduct a personal management class to give students a range of opportunities to choose from. After all, a B.F.A. is a college degree, and most employers are looking for a person with a degree, whether it's theater, Slavic languages, or physics. Most companies now train their own employees, so it's not really a drawback if you have a degree in another field.

Jobs: The B.A. in Theater

This degree is based not only in theater but also in liberal arts; thus opportunities are probably more open. You could go into teaching, pursue a graduate degree, enter the entertainment market, or you could apply with various companies. A lot of students use the B.A. as a springboard to a law degree—that may be because they have the desire to be on stage, and there's something of that in lawyers as well. A lot of students go from acting into playwriting and directing. Others have gone into computer science, are in management, some have formed their own production companies, and are doing regional theater, film, and television. But students should have a very realistic perception of the possibilities of not being able to take this degree and make a living in theater. They should keep their options open to give themselves the broadest opportunities to be employed anywhere they choose.

Helping Graduates Get Jobs

Some schools stage a "showcase" at the end of the program where they invite industry people to see the students perform. Some schools open up their facilities for production companies to come in and actually hold auditions for film, television, and theater. Most schools do not have a traditional placement office that says, "We'll put your resume on file, and we'll get you a job." That's not very realistic, unless a school has a professional theater company associated with it and they can place students there.

Alumni can also provide good contacts. If your school's faculty members are working in the business, they'll also be able to open doors for you. In fact, most networking is done through faculty members.

Adelphi University

Garden City, New York

Independent, coed. Suburban campus. Total enrollment: 8,012.

Degrees Bachelor of Fine Arts in the area of theater. Majors: theater arts/drama.

Theater Student Profile Fall 1994: 55 total; all matriculated undergraduate; 18% minorities, 68% females, 2% international.

Theater Faculty Total: 11; 3 full-time, 8 part-time; 100% of full-time faculty have terminal degrees. Graduate students do not teach undergraduate courses. Undergraduate student–faculty ratio: 15:1.

Expenses for 1994–95 Application fee: $35. Comprehensive fee of $19,620 includes full-time tuition ($12,900), mandatory fees ($170), and college room and board ($6550). College room only: $3550. Part-time tuition: $380 per credit. Part-time mandatory fees: $184 per year.

Financial Aid Program-specific awards for Fall of 1994: 6–8 Barnes Scholarships for freshmen actors ($2000).

Application Procedures Deadline—freshmen and transfers: continuous. Required: essay, high school transcript, minimum 2.0 high school GPA, 2 letters of recommendation, interview, audition. Auditions held 10 times on campus; videotaped performances are permissible as a substitute for live auditions when distance is prohibitive.

Undergraduate Contact Nicholas Petron, Chair, Performing Arts, Adelphi University, Post Hall, Room 4, Garden City, New York 11530; 516-877-4930.

Adelphi University, the first liberal arts institution of higher education on Long Island, was chartered June 24, 1896, by the Board of Regents of the State of New York. The charter was one of the earliest granted by the Board of Regents to a coeducational college.

In keeping with its ninety-nine-year history, Adelphi University continues to make use of its rich resources to render significant service to Long Island, New York State, and the nation. The staging of cultural events in the University Center and the Olmsted Theatre, the strengthening of ties between the professional schools and the community, and, most essential to Adelphi's purpose, the education of a new generation of future leaders—all contribute to the University's mission to serve as a national center for liberal learning.

Today, Adelphi University reaffirms its commitment and dedication to providing excellence in education and to facing and surmounting the challenges of the twenty-first century with high standards and scholarship. In an era of increasing complexity in the nation's fundamental social fabric, society is changing and moving forward with momentum. In the face of the demands of rapid technological advances and worldwide social change, the University, with its faith in the rewards of individual merit, draws on a rich tradition of scholarly knowledge and human values to empower students for future leadership as learned and cultivated men and women.

The performing arts are concerned with supporting leadership in interpretive arts that gives living form to the performance of music, plays, and dance as well as to the production of original texts and dance pieces. The performing arts include acting, designing, directing, and producing choreography and dance theater. As a field of study, the performing arts involve the history and criticism of all forms of theater, dance, and playwriting.

The Department of Performing Arts offers programs leading to a B.A. degree in dance and a B.F.A. degree in theater arts, with specializations in acting and technical theater/design. The B.F.A. programs, designed to develop professional skills, craft, and attitudes, focus on professional training in the performing arts within a liberal learning context. The B.A. program offers a liberal arts and sciences education with a concentration in dance.

The proximity of New York City is a constant resource for observation and career opportunities for all performing arts programs.

Albertus Magnus College

New Haven, Connecticut

Independent-religious, coed. Urban campus. Total enrollment: 600.

Degrees Bachelor of Fine Arts in the area of performance/theater. Majors: performance, theater arts/drama. Cross-registration with University of New Haven, Southern Connecticut State University, Yale University.

Theater Student Profile Fall 1994: 12 total; 8 matriculated undergraduate, 4 nondegree; 25% females.

Theater Faculty Total: 1; 1 full-time; 100% of full-time faculty have terminal degrees. Graduate students do not teach undergraduate courses. Undergraduate student–faculty ratio: 8:1.

Student Life Student groups include Non-Equity Professional Theatre/Act 2 Theatre, student-directed projects.

Expenses for 1995–96 Application fee: $35. Comprehensive fee of $18,209 includes full-time tuition ($12,350), mandatory fees ($195), and college room and board ($5664). Part-time tuition: $412 per credit.

Application Procedures Deadline—freshmen and transfers: continuous. Notification date—freshmen and transfers: September 15. Recommended: essay, high school transcript, minimum 2.0 high school GPA, letter of recommendation, interview.

Undergraduate Contact Dick Lolatte, Director of Admissions, Albertus Magnus College, 700 Prospect Street, New Haven, Connecticut 06511; 203-773-8550.

More about the College

Program Facilities Theater facilities include a mainstage theater, a studio theater, and a cabaret theater. Library facilities include tapes of performances and an extensive profile of plays.

Faculty Members Alberto DeFabio—director, choreographer, and playwright. Susan Cole, Ph.D.—dramatist and professional theater artist. The College employs an impressive roster of part-time instructors and technicians.

Student Performance Opportunities The Theater Department at Albertus Magnus will guarantee that students will be offered five plays a year at its resident non-equity theater, Act Two Theater. Students are offered other opportunities to work in cabarets, at Yale Repertory Theater as an intern, and in various other theater works. Students will have at least twenty plays in which to perform during their four years of study. The College is large enough to have a wide variety of opportunities and small enough to give everyone the chances they need to fulfill their potential. Especially important is the chance to work closely with professionals at Act Two, a professional theater housed on campus.

Special Programs At Albertus students will be offered the opportunity to study abroad and to intern at local theaters. The College is located only one hour north of Manhattan. The College also houses an ELS Center and an intensive English language program. Students at Albertus also have the opportunity to enroll in the College's Tri-Session Plan, which enables them to earn a Bachelor of Arts or a Bachelor of Fine Arts degree in three years. During three years the academic calendar runs from September through the end of June. Students carry 15 credits each session. Students enrolled in the Tri-Session Plan not only save valuable time but also reduce tuition costs.

American Academy of Dramatic Arts

New York, New York

Independent, coed. Urban campus. Total enrollment: 224.

Degrees Majors: acting.

Theater Student Profile Fall 1994: 208 total; all matriculated undergraduate; 13% minorities, 56% females, 21% international.

Theater Faculty Total: 19; 11 full-time, 8 part-time; 20% of full-time faculty have terminal degrees. Graduate students do not teach undergraduate courses. Undergraduate student–faculty ratio: 14:1.

Expenses for 1995–96 Application fee: $35. Tuition: $8975 full-time. Full-time mandatory fees: $175. Special program-related fees: $175 for library and classroom materials.

Financial Aid Program-specific awards for Fall of 1994: 1–2 Cleavon Little Scholarships for minority students ($500–$1500), 2–3 Spencer Tracy Scholarships for sophomores ($1000–$3000), 1–2 Philip Loeb Scholarships for sophomores demonstrating need ($750–$1500), 1–2 Greta Nissen Scholarships for female sophomores demonstrating need ($750–$2000).

Application Procedures Deadline—freshmen and transfers: continuous. Required: high school transcript, 2 letters of recommendation, interview, audition, health certificate. Recommended: essay, minimum 2.0 high school GPA. Auditions held weekly on campus on campus and off campus in various cities in the U.S..

Undergraduate Contact Jeanne Gosselin, Director of Admissions, American Academy of Dramatic Arts, 120 Madison Avenue, New York, New York 10016-7004; 800-463-8990, fax: 212-545-7934.

More About the Academy

Facilities AADA in New York is housed in a six-story landmark building located in midtown Manhattan. AADA/West is located on a 5-acre campus in the Los Angeles suburb of Pasadena. Each site includes classrooms, rehearsal halls, movement studios, student lounge, production and costume departments, library/learning center, video studio, and theaters.

Faculty and Alumni Academy faculty are seasoned professionals, well trained within their own disciplines, and exemplars of the commitment to excellence that the Academy hopes to instill in its students. The soundness of the Academy's training is reflected in the achievements of its alumni, a diverse body of distinguished professionals. (Academy alumni have collectively received nominations for 93 Oscars, 67 Tonys, and 198 Emmys.)

Student Performances At each stage of development, the Academy student is tested in the disciplined arena of performance. In addition to classroom scene work, each student performs roles in four first-year performance projects and at least three second-year projects and full productions. The third-year Academy Company performs, on average, twelve fully mounted productions each year, including a showcase of scenes presented to casting directors and agents.

Danny DeVito
Actor

The Academy opened a new world to me. I had only seen one play in my life, and had never read one. But the Academy was exhilarating. All these men and women talking about "art, collaboration, and their craft." All of a sudden I'm taking fencing, and movement, and scene study; it was a curtain opening with light coming through. I got hooked.

American Academy of Dramatic Arts *(continued)*

Special Programs Seminars offered in the second year provide the practical information actors need to initiate professional careers. A limited number of graduates are offered a third-year program of advanced performance training as members of the Academy Company. A career counselor works closely with Company members, advising them on matters of career management and serving as a liaison with the professional community. Students invited to the second or third years may apply to transfer from New York to California, or from California to New York. The Academy also offers a six-week summer conservatory for those wishing to begin to study acting, to refresh basic acting skills, or to test their interest and ability in an environment of professional training.

An actor's talent, it's been said, begins in the soles of the feet and ends in a spirit than can vault beyond the stars. The American Academy of Dramatic Arts has been serving this talent for over a hundred years.

The Academy's one purpose has remained constant from the start: "To provide a broad and practical education to those desiring to make acting their profession." The love of acting, as an art and as a profession, is the motivating spirit of the school. Every course and every activity is related to the disciplined development of actors. While the Academy is accredited as a college, it is different from traditional colleges for its focus on a single educational objective.

Founded in New York in 1884, the Academy was the first conservatory for actors in the English-speaking world. It has served as a model for many other acting schools and drama departments, both in America and abroad. This experience contributes to the effectiveness of the Academy's training, programs, and teaching methods that show a clear vision of the knowledge, skills, and discipline needed by today's professional actor.

The Academy's approach to training stresses self-awareness, self-discipline, and practical experience. The study of acting leads to many areas of knowledge, including knowledge of self. Academy training demands such self-discovery and emphasizes the development of the actor as an individual, unique in his or her artistic potential and experience of life.

Academy training aims to develop the well-rounded actor, giving equal attention to such "internal" aspects of technique as relaxation, concentration, emotional involvement, and imagination and to the "external" disciplines of speech, voice, and movement.

When the Academy began, motion pictures and television were still years away. To work as an actor in those days could only mean performing on stage. Today, it is likely that much of an actor's working life will be spent before a camera rather than in a theater. To prepare for this, Academy students—once they have mastered the basic discipline of truthful behavior in imaginary circumstances—learn adjustments needed for camera work.

With facilities in New York and California, the Academy offers accredited training in both of America's centers of professional activity. Whether a student chooses to attend the Academy in New York or California, the training program will be essentially the same, and it will be enriched by the professional and cultural advantages of New York City or southern California.

Academy students come from all parts of the United States, from Canada, and from other countries as well. About half of the entering students are recent high school graduates. Others transfer to the Academy from traditional colleges to study acting in a more concentrated, professional environment. Still others have worked in non-theatrical fields before deciding to commit to the study of acting. Whatever their age or background, once at the Academy, they are united by the shared commitment to acting and the challenge of working to become the best actors they can be.

American Academy of Dramatic Arts/West

Pasadena, California

Independent, coed. Suburban campus. Total enrollment: 147.

Degrees Majors: acting.

Theater Student Profile Fall 1994: 237 total; all matriculated undergraduate; 11% minorities, 58% females, 13% international.

Theater Faculty Total: 24; 7 full-time, 17 part-time; 75% of full-time faculty have terminal degrees. Graduate students do not teach undergraduate courses. Undergraduate student–faculty ratio: 16:1.

Expenses for 1995–96 Application fee: $35. Tuition: $8700 full-time. Full-time mandatory fees: $175. Special program-related fees: $175 for library and classroom materials, $110 for books, scripts.

Financial Aid Program-specific awards for Fall of 1994: 1–2 Cleavon Little Scholarships for minority students ($500–$1500), 2–3 Spencer Tracy Scholarships for sophomores ($1000–$3000), 1–2 Philip Loeb Scholarships for sophomores demonstrating need ($750–$1500), 1–2 Greta Nissen Scholarships for female sophomores demonstrating need ($750–$2000), 1–3 Charles Jehlinger Scholarships for sophomores ($500–$1500).

Application Procedures Deadline—freshmen and transfers: continuous. Required: high school transcript, 2 letters of recommendation, interview, audition, health certificate. Recommended: essay, minimum 2.0 high school GPA. Auditions held weekly on campus on campus and off campus in various cities in the U.S..

Undergraduate Contact James Wickline, Director of Admissions, American Academy of Dramatic Arts/West, 2550 Paloma Street, Pasadena, California 91107-2697; 800-222-2867, fax: 818-798-5047.

Arizona State University

Tempe, Arizona

State-supported, coed. Suburban campus. Total enrollment: 42,189.

Degrees Bachelor of Fine Arts in the area of theater education. Majors: acting, directing, production and management specialities, theater design/technology, theater history. Graduate degrees offered: Master of Fine Arts in the area of theater. Cross-registration with Arizona State University West.

Theater Student Profile Fall 1994: 280 total; 230 matriculated undergraduate, 50 matriculated graduate; 12% minorities, 60% females, 1% international.

Theater Faculty Total: 29; 18 full-time, 11 part-time; 80% of full-time faculty have terminal degrees. Graduate students teach about a quarter undergraduate courses. Undergraduate student–faculty ratio: 18:1.

Student Life Student groups include Players Club.

Expenses for 1994–95 State resident tuition: $1894 full-time. Nonresident tuition: $7500 full-time, $310 per credit part-time. State resident part-time tuition per semester ranges from $96 to $576. Part-time mandatory fees: $32 per year. College room and board: $4690. College room only: $3090. Special program-related fees: $5–$10 for supplies.

Financial Aid Program-specific awards for Fall of 1994: 10 Regents Out of State Tuition ($6028), 8 Regents In-State Tuition ($1884).

Application Procedures Deadline—freshmen and transfers: continuous. Required: high school transcript, college transcript(s) for transfer students, minimum 2.0 high school GPA, SAT I or ACT test scores. Recommended: minimum 3.0 high school GPA. Auditions held 2 times on campus; videotaped performances are permissible as a substitute for live auditions by prior arrangement. Portfolio reviews held 2 times on campus; the submission of slides may be substituted for portfolios by prior arrangement.

Undergraduate Contact Marie Fay, Academic Advisor, Department of Theatre, Arizona State University, Box 872002, Tempe, Arizona 85287-2002; 602-965-9432, fax: 602-965-5351.

Graduate Contact Margaret Knapp, Graduate Advisor, Arizona State University, Box 872002, Tempe, Arizona 85287-2002; 602-965-2655, fax: 602-965-5351.

Arkansas State University

State University, Arkansas

State-supported, coed. Urban campus. Total enrollment: 9,631.

Degrees Bachelor of Fine Arts in the areas of theater arts: performance, theater arts: production. Majors: theater arts/drama.

Theater Student Profile Fall 1994: 34 total; all matriculated undergraduate; 6% minorities, 62% females.

Theater Faculty Total: 6; 5 full-time, 1 part-time; 83% of full-time faculty have terminal degrees. Graduate students teach a few undergraduate courses. Undergraduate student–faculty ratio: 18:1.

Expenses for 1995–96 Application fee: $25. State resident tuition: $1950 full-time, $82 per credit hour part-time. Nonresident tuition: $3600 full-time, $150 per credit hour part-time. College room and board: $2590.

Financial Aid Program-specific awards for Fall of 1994: Theater Arts Scholarships for program majors ($600).

Application Procedures Deadline—freshmen and transfers: continuous. Required: high school transcript, college transcript(s) for transfer students, minimum 2.0 high school GPA, SAT I or ACT test scores. Recommended: letter of recommendation, video, portfolio, interview for production applicants. Auditions held 2 times on campus; videotaped performances are permissible as a substitute for live auditions when distance is prohibitive. Portfolio reviews held on campus; the submission of slides may be substituted for portfolios when distance is prohibitive.

Undergraduate Contact Bobby W. Simpson, Director of Theater, Speech Communication and Theater Arts Department, Arkansas State University, P.O. Box 369, State University, Arkansas 72467; 501-972-2037.

Auburn University

Auburn University, Alabama

State-supported, coed. Small-town campus. Total enrollment: 21,226.

Degrees Bachelor of Fine Arts in the areas of performance, technology/design, management. Majors: design technology, performance, theater arts/drama, theater management.

Theater Student Profile Fall 1994: 75 total; all matriculated undergraduate; 60% females.

Theater Faculty Total: 9; 9 full-time; 100% of full-time faculty have terminal degrees. Graduate students do not teach undergraduate courses. Undergraduate student–faculty ratio: 3:1.

Student Life Student groups include Players Club, Alpha Psi Omega.

Expenses for 1994–95 Application fee: $25. State resident tuition: $2100 full-time. Nonresident tuition: $6300 full-time. Part-time tuition per quarter ranges from $178 to $758 for state residents, $534 to $2274 for nonresidents. College room only: $1410 (minimum).

Financial Aid Program-specific awards for Fall of 1994: 15 Malone Fund Scholarships for undergraduates ($400).

Application Procedures Deadline—freshmen and transfers: April 1. Required: high school transcript, college transcript(s) for transfer students, minimum 2.0 high school GPA, letter of recommendation, audition, portfolio. Auditions held 1 time for performance applicants on campus. Portfolio reviews held 1 time for design/technology and management majors on campus.

Undergraduate Contact Patricia D. McAdams, Head, Department of Theatre, Auburn University, 211 Telfair Peet Theatre, Auburn, Alabama 36849-5422, 5422; 205-844-4748, fax: 205-844-4743, E-mail address: mcadapd@mail.auburn.edu.

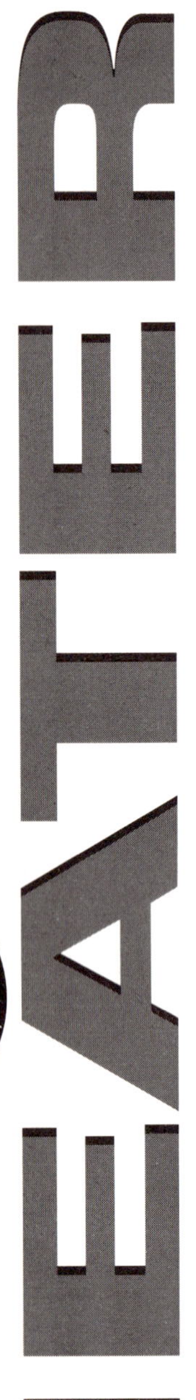

Avila College

Kansas City, Missouri

Independent-religious, coed. Suburban campus. Total enrollment: 1,429.

Degrees Bachelor of Fine Arts in the area of theater. Majors: acting, producing/directing, technical theater, theater arts/drama.

Theater Student Profile Fall 1994: 41 total; 37 matriculated undergraduate, 4 nondegree; 10% minorities, 60% females, 10% international.

Theater Faculty Total: 6; 2 full-time, 4 part-time; 100% of full-time faculty have terminal degrees. Graduate students do not teach undergraduate courses. Undergraduate student–faculty ratio: 12:1.

Student Life Student groups include Alpha Psi Omega.

Expenses for 1995–96 Comprehensive fee of $13,550 includes full-time tuition ($9500), mandatory fees ($100), and college room and board ($3950). Part-time tuition: $205 per credit hour. Part-time mandatory fees: $1 per credit hour. Tuition guaranteed not to increase for student's term of enrollment.

Financial Aid Program-specific awards for Fall of 1994: 50 Performance Grants for program majors and non-majors ($1200–$1500).

Application Procedures Deadline—freshmen and transfers: continuous. Notification date—freshmen and transfers: July 31. Required: essay, high school transcript, college transcript(s) for transfer students, 2 letters of recommendation, interview, audition, SAT I or ACT test scores, minimum composite ACT score of 20, minimum 2.5 high school GPA. Auditions held 4 times on campus; videotaped performances are permissible as a substitute for live auditions when distance is prohibitive. Portfolio reviews held on campus; the submission of slides may be substituted for portfolios when distance is prohibitive.

Undergraduate Contact Jim Millard, Director, Admissions Department, Avila College, 11901 Wornall Road, Kansas City, Missouri 64145; 816-942-8400 ext. 203, fax: 816-942-3362.

Baylor University

Waco, Texas

Independent-religious, coed. Urban campus. Total enrollment: 12,240.

Degrees Bachelor of Fine Arts in the areas of performance, design. Majors: design, performance. Graduate degrees offered: Master of Fine Arts in the area of directing.

Theater Student Profile Fall 1994: 56 total; 50 matriculated undergraduate, 6 matriculated graduate.

Theater Faculty Total: 9; 8 full-time, 1 part-time. Graduate students do not teach undergraduate courses.

Student Life Student groups include Student Theater Society.

Expenses for 1995–96 Application fee: $25. Comprehensive fee of $12,533 includes full-time tuition ($7740), mandatory fees ($654), and college room and board ($4139). College room only: $1790. Part-time tuition: $258 per semester hour. Part-time mandatory fees: $21 per semester hour. Special program-related fees: $25 for lab fee.

Financial Aid Program-specific awards for Fall of 1994: Theater Scholarships for upperclassmen.

Application Procedures Deadline—freshmen and transfers: continuous. Required: essay, high school transcript, SAT I or ACT test scores. Recommended: letter of recommendation, interview.

Contact Dr. Bill G. Cook, Chairman, Department of Theater Arts, Baylor University, BU Box 97262, Waco, Texas 76798; 817-755-1861.

Boston Conservatory

Boston, Massachusetts

Independent, coed. Urban campus. Total enrollment: 414.

Degrees Bachelor of Fine Arts in the area of musical theater. Majors: music theater. Graduate degrees offered: Master of Music in the area of musical theater. Cross-registration with ProArts Consortium.

Theater Student Profile Fall 1994: 134 total; 120 matriculated undergraduate, 14 matriculated graduate; 10% minorities, 60% females.

Theater Faculty Total: 16; 7 full-time, 9 part-time; 100% of full-time faculty have terminal degrees. Graduate students do not teach undergraduate courses. Undergraduate student–faculty ratio: 8:1.

Expenses for 1995–96 Comprehensive fee of $20,130 includes full-time tuition ($13,400), mandatory fees ($450), and college room and board ($6280). Part-time tuition: $555 per credit. Part-time mandatory fees per semester range from $56.25 to $168.75.

Financial Aid Program-specific awards for Fall of 1994: Conservatory Theater Scholarships for program majors ($5000–$8000).

Application Procedures Deadline—freshmen and transfers: continuous. Required: essay, high school transcript, audition. Recommended: SAT I or ACT test scores. Auditions held 4 times and by appointment on campus and off campus in Chicago, IL; St. Louis, MO; Minneapolis, MN; Seattle, WA; Houston, TX; Los Angeles, CA; Tampa/St. Petersburg, FL; Washington, DC; Pittsburgh, PA; videotaped performances are permissible as a substitute for live auditions if a campus visit is impossible.

Contact Neil Donohoe, Chairperson, Theater Division, Boston Conservatory, 8 The Fenway, Boston, Massachusetts 02215; 617-536-6340 ext. 44, fax: 617-536-3176.

More about the Conservatory

Program Facilities Mainstage Proscenium Arch Theater (400 seats), Studio Theater (Black Box—75 seats), two recital halls (400 and 75 seats), five dance studios, costume shop, theater/technical shop, twenty-five practice rooms, computer lab (Apple), library of over 60,000 volumes and scores and interlibrary loan availability with college network of Boston.

Faculty and Alumni Professional faculty members are active in all areas of acting, directing, voice, dance, and production. Alumni can be seen in major Broadway and Off-Broadway productions, national and international touring companies, television, and film.

Student Performance Opportunities Two mainstage musicals, one mainstage drama, Student Director Workshops (fifteen in 1993–94), opera scenes, mainstage opera, dance theater concerts, regional theater productions, industrial films, acting/vocal gigs.

Special Programs Gig office providing performance opportunities throughout the greater Boston area, career seminar series, counseling and health services, international student ESL classes/orientation program, academic year ESL course work, and tutorial assistance.

The Boston Conservatory, founded in 1867, is one of the oldest colleges offering training to serious students of the performing arts. The three divisions of the college—Music, Dance, and Theater—take full advantage of the wealth of cultural and academic offerings Boston has to offer. Guest artists, master classes, performance opportunities, and professional contacts and networking are provided to all students of the college. These experiences seek to ensure that each student receives a varied and professional level of education to augment the intensive study of the prescribed curriculum.

The Boston Conservatory was one of the first colleges to offer integrated training in theater encompassing acting, voice, and dance. Beginning as a full acting/drama program in the 1930s, the Theater Division now trains the "triple threat" actor/singer offering a complete acting curriculum coupled with music and voice study and a full range of dance (ballet, modern, tap, jazz, and styles).

The Musical Theater Division faculty comprises experienced performers and teachers committed to bringing out the best each student has to offer. Potential is acknowledged and developed within a strong interactive theater curriculum. Frequent in-class performance with appropriate coaching and critique give guidance and constant evaluation of the student's work. The music and dance aspects of the program are presented both in-class and one-on-one to ensure individual attention for each student.

Performance opportunities are available throughout the year, from in-class and studio work to mainstage productions. All major productions have an open, professional casting policy in order for the most qualified person to get the role regardless of class standing. Technical and stagecraft experience is provided, and production assistance is required by all students during major runs.

In addition to these opportunities, the studio theater offers small-scale productions throughout the year, most often with a senior student directing project pieces.

Boston Conservatory alumni can be seen in major productions on Broadway, in Europe, and in National Touring companies. In addition, many alumni find acting work in television and film. As many musical theater students are very advanced in both classical voice and dance, additional performance experience may be gained in the opera and dance productions offered by the other two divisions of the college.

The Boston area provides varied outside work in theater and dance as well as industrials. Regional theater productions often cast students in both lead and ensemble parts.

Boston is a major center of higher education in America, with over fifty major colleges and universities. The city provides a diverse student population and an endless array of courses, lectures, concerts, and social opportunities. The Conservatory is in the Pro-Arts Consortium with five area colleges (Emerson College, Berklee College of Music, Museum School, Massachusetts College of Art, and Boston Architectural Center), which offers extensive cross-registration course possibilities to all students.

On-campus housing is provided to all interested students, offering brownstone-style living accommodations just a few steps from the main training and rehearsal buildings. For those students interested in off-campus housing, Boston offers a wide range of architectural styles and rent prices in neighborhoods throughout the city, which are all within easy access to the school by public transportation.

The Boston Conservatory strives to meet each student's needs, musically and personally, and provides a nurturing, safe environment in which to study, learn, and grow. The supportive atmosphere of the college extends to student life areas as well. Over a dozen special interest groups and organizations exist on campus, with new ones developing constantly as the student population grows and needs change. As part of the student services, a number of career seminars are given each year ranging from résumé writing and audition anxiety to grant writing and tax laws for the performing artist. In addition, there is an active student government and a student-run newspaper.

Boston University

Boston, Massachusetts

Independent, coed. Urban campus. Total enrollment: 28,664.

Degrees Bachelor of Fine Arts in the areas of acting, design, stage management, independent theater study. Majors: acting, costume design, costume production, lighting design, set design, sound design, stage management, technical production, theater arts/drama, theater production. Graduate degrees offered: Master of Fine Arts in the areas of directing, design, theater education.

Theater Student Profile Fall 1994: 230 total; 190 matriculated undergraduate, 40 matriculated graduate; 5% minorities, 60% females.

Theater Faculty Total: 24; 22 full-time, 2 part-time; 80% of full-time faculty have terminal degrees. Graduate students do not teach undergraduate courses. Undergraduate student–faculty ratio: 10:1.

Student Life Special housing available for theater students.

Boston University *(continued)*

Expenses for 1995–96 Application fee: $50. Comprehensive fee of $26,800 includes full-time tuition ($19,420), mandatory fees ($280), and college room and board ($7100). College room only: $4110. Part-time tuition: $607 per credit. Part-time mandatory fees: $40 per semester.

Financial Aid Program-specific awards for Fall of 1994: 99 Grants–Need/Performance Scholarships for undergraduates ($9829), 55 Grants/Performance Scholarships for undergraduates ($4421).

Application Procedures Deadline—freshmen: January 15; transfers: May 1. Notification date—freshmen: April 15. Required: essay, high school transcript, minimum 2.0 high school GPA, 2 letters of recommendation, interview, audition, portfolio. Recommended: minimum 3.0 high school GPA. Auditions held 20 times on campus and off campus in New York, NY; Chicago, IL; Minneapolis, MN; San Francisco, CA; Houston, TX; Miami, FL; Los Angeles, CA. Portfolio reviews held 10 times on campus and off campus in New York, NY; Chicago, IL; Minneapolis, MN; San Francisco, CA; Houston, TX; Miami, FL; Los Angeles, CA; the submission of slides may be substituted for portfolios when distance is prohibitive.

Contact Eve B. Muson, Executive Assistant Director, Theatre Arts Department, Boston University, 855 Commonwealth Avenue, Room 470, Boston, Massachusetts 02215; 617-353-3390, fax: 617-353-4363.

More about the University

Program Facilities Performance spaces include the Boston University Theatre, an 850-seat proscenium house, and Studio 210, a 100-seat black box space, and a 100-seat proscenium studio. The Theatre is equipped with a computerized lighting system, shops for scenery and costume construction, and an electronic sound studio. There are three movement studios and six additional rehearsal studios.

Faculty, Guest Artists, and Alumni Faculty members are not only master teachers, but are also accomplished professionals who maintain vital careers in the theater. Distinguished faculty members include Peter Altman, Producing Director of the Huntington Theatre, and Jacques Cartier, founder of the Hartford Stage Company. Guest artists include director James Bohnen, actors Patricia Connolly and Katherine McGrath, and designers Ralph Funicello and Desmond Heeley. Alumni include actors Olympia Dukakis, Alfre Woodard, and Jason Alexander and designer Wynn Thomas.

Student Performance Opportunities The Theatre Arts Division produces six fully mounted productions each year, as well as forty to sixty workshop productions directed by faculty members and graduate and undergraduate students. An annual festival of plays provides a showcase for work by undergraduate playwrights.

Special Programs The Huntington Theatre Company, one of Boston's leading professional companies, is in residence at the Boston University Theatre. A variety of assistantships and internships are available for students in the areas of design, production, directing, stage management, and theater management. Advanced acting majors have the opportunity to audition for understudy assignments and supporting roles in Huntington productions. Master classes are conducted for student by artists associated with the professional shows.

Brenau University

Gainesville, Georgia

Independent, primarily women. Small-town campus. Total enrollment: 2,241.

Degrees Bachelor of Fine Arts in the areas of arts management, musical theater. Majors: arts management. Cross-registration with Gainesville College.

Theater Student Profile Fall 1994: 25 total; all matriculated undergraduate; 1% minorities, 94% females, 1% international.

Theater Faculty Total: 4; 3 full-time, 1 part-time; 100% of full-time faculty have terminal degrees. Graduate students do not teach undergraduate courses. Undergraduate student–faculty ratio: 10:1.

Student Life Student groups include Gainesville Theatre Alliance, Alpha Psi Omega, Gainesville Children's Theatre.

Estimated Expenses for 1995–96 Application fee: $30. Comprehensive fee of $16,040 includes full-time tuition ($9855) and college room and board ($6185). Part-time tuition: $205 per semester hour.

Financial Aid Program-specific awards for Fall of 1994: 20 Talent Scholarships for program majors ($2000–$3500).

Application Procedures Deadline—freshmen and transfers: continuous. Required: high school transcript, college transcript(s) for transfer students, minimum 2.0 high school GPA, audition, SAT I or ACT test scores, minimum combined SAT I score of 900, minimum composite ACT score of 16. Auditions held 8 times and by appointment on campus; videotaped performances are permissible as a substitute for live auditions when distance is prohibitive.

Undergraduate Contact Dr. Ann Demling, Director of Theatre, Brenau University, One Centennial Circle, Gainesville, Georgia 30501; 404-534-6264, fax: 404-534-6114, E-mail address: annd@lib.brenau.edu.

Brigham Young University

Provo, Utah

Independent-religious, coed. Suburban campus. Total enrollment: 30,413.

Degrees Bachelor of Fine Arts in the area of musical dance theater. Majors: music theater, theater arts/drama. Graduate degrees offered: Master of Fine Arts in the area of theater design and technology.

Theater Student Profile Fall 1994: 329 total; 301 matriculated undergraduate, 28 matriculated graduate.

Theater Faculty Total: 24; 20 full-time, 4 part-time; 70% of full-time faculty have terminal degrees. Graduate students teach a few undergraduate courses. Undergraduate student–faculty ratio: 15:1.

Expenses for 1995–96 Application fee: $25. Comprehensive fee of $6190 includes full-time tuition ($2450 minimum) and college room and board ($3740 minimum). Part-time tuition: $125 per credit (minimum). Tuition for non-church members: $3510 full-time, $180 per credit part-time.

Financial Aid Program-specific awards for Fall of 1994: 70 Performance Awards for program majors ($400).

Application Procedures Deadline—freshmen: February 15; transfers: March 15. Required: essay, high school transcript, college transcript(s) for transfer students, minimum 3.0 high school GPA, letter of recommendation, audition, SAT I or ACT test scores. Auditions held 1 time on campus; recorded music is permissible as a substitute for live auditions if a campus visit is impossible and videotaped performances are permissible as a substitute for live auditions if a campus visit is impossible.

Undergraduate Contact Academic Advisement Center, Brigham Young University, D-444 HFAC, Provo, Utah 84602; 801-378-3777.

Graduate Contact Marion Bentley, Theater and Film Department, Brigham Young University, F-455 HFAC, Provo, Utah 84602; 801-378-2122.

Brooklyn College of the City University of New York

Brooklyn, New York

State and locally supported, coed. Urban campus. Total enrollment: 13,045.

Degrees Bachelor of Fine Arts in the areas of acting, design and technical production. Majors: acting, theater arts/drama, theater design and production. Graduate degrees offered: Master of Fine Arts in the areas of acting, design and technical production, directing, dramaturgy, performing arts management.

Theater Faculty Total: 28; 15 full-time, 13 part-time; 100% of full-time faculty have terminal degrees. Graduate students teach a few undergraduate courses. Undergraduate student–faculty ratio: 2:1.

Student Life Student groups include Undergraduate Theater Organization.

Expenses for 1995–96 State resident tuition: $2450 full-time, $100 per credit part-time. Nonresident tuition: $5050 full-time, $210 per credit part-time. Part-time mandatory fees: $53.35 per semester. Full-time mandatory fees: $181.

Financial Aid Program-specific awards for Fall of 1994: 1 Brooklyn College Foundation Performing Arts Scholarship ($2450).

Application Procedures Deadline—freshmen and transfers: June 30. Required: high school transcript, audition. Recommended: SAT I or ACT test scores. Auditions held 1 time on campus; recorded music is permissible as a substitute for live auditions for international applicants and videotaped performances are permissible as a substitute for live auditions for international applicants.

Undergraduate Contact Karen Barracuda, Undergraduate Deputy Chair, Theater Department, Brooklyn College of the City University of New York, 317 Whitehead Hall, 2900 Bedford Avenue, Brooklyn, New York 11210; 718-951-5764.

Graduate Contact Stephen Langley, Graduate Deputy Chair, Theater Department, Brooklyn College of the City University of New York, 317 Whitehead Hall, 2900 Bedford Avenue, Brooklyn, New York 11210; 718-951-5764.

More about the College

Program Facilities Performance spaces include the Gershwin Theatre (550-seat, proscenium), the New Workshop Theatre (approximately 100-seat, black box), and Levinson Hall (160-seat, modern thrust). Classrooms include a directing studio, two acting studios, two movement studios, and fully equipped costume, carpentry, and design shops.

Faculty The 15 full-time faculty members of the department are all experienced professionals/scholars

Grace Kelly
Oscar-winning Actress

I am very grateful for the two years I spent at the American Academy of Dramatic Arts and the knowledge I gained there as an actor and as a person.

Brooklyn College of the City University of New York *(continued)*

who are known for the personal attention given to each student and for supportive but realistic evaluation of student progress.

Student Performances The department produces ten shows a year—four mainstage and six black box productions—directed by faculty and graduate directing majors, which provide the B.F.A. students plenty of hands-on experience in all phases of theatrical production. Casting for all departmental productions is by open call (undergraduate and graduate students), with a policy promoting multicultural and nontraditional casting. All B.F.A. acting majors are required to perform in a department production in their senior year. These are supplemented by Lunch-Time Theatre—informal presentation of monologues, class scenes, directing projects, etc.—and by scenes for directing classes. In addition, the College often collaborates with the Conservatory of Music on musicals, opera, and concert performances, and the departments of TV/Radio and Film often post calls for actors.

Special Programs The department maintains close ties with the Manhattan Theatre Club (a leading professional regional theater) and with CUNY, Brooklyn Technical College, which offers state-of-the-art computerized technology equipment. Independent study projects are encouraged, and some internships are available.

A senior college of the City University of New York, Brooklyn College is located just 45 minutes from the Great White Way, enabling students to take advantage of the rich offerings of Broadway, Off-Broadway, and Off-Off Broadway. The department offers a performance-based program balanced by substantial humanistic studies. Its threefold purpose is to instill an appreciation and respect for the collaborative nature of theater by providing both intellectual and experiential opportunities in all areas of theater, to provide a solid liberal arts foundation on which to base a specialized degree, and to provide the skills and experiences needed to prepare for a career in theater.

Many alumni continue to work in the profession. Among the best-known actors trained at Brooklyn College are recent Academy Award nominee Michael Lerner; Jimmy Smits, formerly of *L.A. Law*; and Ken Garito of the Fox series *Pacific Heights*.

While all faculty members are experienced professionals, special mention should be made of the following: David Garfield, Broadway actor and author of *The Actors Studio*; Mark Zeller, Broadway actor and voice specialist; Margaret Linney, professional film, television, and stage actor and specialist in improvisation and arts in education; Karen Barracuda, professional dancer and pioneer in ideokinectic acting techniques; Thomas Bullard, nationally known Obie-winning director and cofounder of the Manhattan Theater Club; John Scheffler, Obie award winner and professional scenic designer; Rebecca Cunningham, costume designer and author of *The Magic Garment*; Samuel L. Leiter, author of ten books and editor of the *Asian Theatre Journal*; Benito Ortolani, leading authority on Japanese theater and editor of the yearly *International Bibliography of Theatre*; Stephen Langley, renowned specialist on arts management and director of the department's M.F.A. program in performing arts management; Michael Turque, Broadway stage manager; designers Howard Becknell and Richard Kearney; Mona Heinze, head of the M.F.A. dramaturgy program; and Academy Award winner F. Murray Abraham, who provides acting majors with a bridge from the ivory tower to the professional world.

In addition, visiting professors, adjuncts, and guest lecturers have included some of the most important figures of the theater world, including Alan Schneider, Marshall W. Mason, and John Lee Beatty. The Sylvia Fine Kaye Chair in Musical Theatre has brought such distinguished guests as Betty Buckley, Betty Comden and Adolph Green, Joel Grey, Celeste Holm, and John Kander and Fred Ebb.

B.F.A. students benefit from close association with M.F.A. students from all over the world. They work together on productions, act in each others' classroom directing scenes, and are in daily contact with each other. Many professional opportunities have arisen from contacts made with former M.F.A. acting, directing, design, dramaturgy, and management students.

Another feature that gives alumni an edge in the profession is their solid liberal arts education. B.F.A. students are subject to the same core studies requirements as the rest of the College. Brooklyn offers an unusually large history curriculum, with courses in Western and American as well as Asian, black, and musical theater.

While Brooklyn College, CUNY, does not offer campus housing, many students share apartments in nearby areas.

California Institute of the Arts

Valencia, California

Independent, coed. Suburban campus. Total enrollment: 1,051.

Degrees Bachelor of Fine Arts in the areas of acting, directing, stage and production management, performing arts design and technology. Majors: acting, costume design, directing, lighting design, set design, sound design, stage management, technical direction. Graduate degrees offered: Master of Fine Arts in the areas of acting, directing, stage and production management, performing arts design and technology.

Theater Student Profile Fall 1994: 202 total; 135 matriculated undergraduate, 66 matriculated graduate, 1 nondegree; 19% minorities, 44% females, 4% international.

Theater Faculty Total: 39; 24 full-time, 15 part-time; 80% of full-time faculty have terminal degrees. Graduate students do not teach undergraduate courses. Undergraduate student–faculty ratio: 10:1.

Student Life Student groups include Community Arts Partnership, off-campus performances.

Expenses for 1995–96 Comprehensive fee of $21,225 includes full-time tuition ($15,450), mandatory fees ($75), and college room and board ($5700). College room only: $2550 (minimum).

Financial Aid Program-specific awards for Fall of 1994 available.

Application Procedures Deadline—freshmen and transfers: February 1. Required: essay, high school transcript, audition, portfolio. Recommended: interview. Auditions held 15 times on campus and off campus in New York, NY; Chicago, IL; San Francisco, CA. Portfolio reviews held continuously for design majors on campus.

Contact Kenneth Young, Director of Admissions, California Institute of the Arts, 24700 McBean Parkway, Valencia, California 91355; 805-253-7863, fax: 805-254-8352, E-mail address: kyoung@indy1.calarts.edu.

Carnegie Mellon University

Pittsburgh, Pennsylvania

Independent, coed. Urban campus. Total enrollment: 7,141.

Degrees Bachelor of Fine Arts in the area of drama. Majors: design production, music theater, theater arts/drama. Graduate degrees offered: Master of Fine Arts in the area of drama; Master of Arts Management in the area of arts management. Cross-registration with University of Pittsburgh, Pittsburgh Filmmakers, Moscow Art Theater School.

Theater Student Profile Fall 1994: 260 total; 200 matriculated undergraduate, 60 matriculated graduate; 5% minorities, 50% females, 5% international.

Theater Faculty Total: 41; 31 full-time, 10 part-time; 60% of full-time faculty have terminal degrees. Graduate students do not teach undergraduate courses.

Student Life Student groups include Scotch 'n Soda (student-run theater group). Special housing available for theater students.

Expenses for 1995–96 Application fee: $45. Comprehensive fee of $24,610 includes full-time tuition ($18,600), mandatory fees ($160), and college room and board ($5850). College room only: $3610.

Application Procedures Deadline—freshmen and transfers: January 1. Notification date—freshmen and transfers: April 1. Required: high school transcript, minimum 2.0 high school GPA, 3 letters of recommendation, interview, audition, portfolio. Recommended: minimum 3.0 high school GPA. Auditions held 1 time for acting, music theater, and directing applicants on campus and off campus in New York, NY; Chicago, IL; Seattle, WA; San Francisco, CA; Los Angeles, CA; Houston, TX; Miami, FL. Portfolio reviews held 1 time for design and production applicants on campus and off campus in New York, NY; Chicago, IL; Seattle, WA; San Francisco, CA; Los Angeles, CA; Houston, TX; Miami, FL; the submission of slides may be substituted for portfolios if a campus visit is impossible.

Undergraduate Contact Office of Admissions, Carnegie Mellon University, Warner Hall 100, Pittsburgh, Pennsylvania 15213; 412-268-2082, fax: 412-261-0281.

Graduate Contact Denise Pullen, Graduate Admissions Administrator, Drama Department, Carnegie Mellon University, College of Fine Arts 106, Pittsburgh, Pennsylvania 15213; 412-268-2392, fax: 412-621-0281.

Chapman University

Orange, California

Independent-religious, coed. Suburban campus. Total enrollment: 3,285.

Degrees Bachelor of Fine Arts in the areas of theater performance, dance and theater, technical theater, media performance. Majors: media performance, performance, technical theater, theater arts/drama.

Theater Student Profile Fall 1994: 100 total; all matriculated undergraduate; 36% minorities, 65% females, 4% international.

Theater Faculty Total: 10; 2 full-time, 8 part-time. Graduate students do not teach undergraduate courses. Undergraduate student–faculty ratio: 15:1.

Student Life Student groups include Shakespeare Orange County–Summer Professional Theaters, American Celebration, Performing Arts Society of Chapman.

Estimated Expenses for 1995–96 Application fee: $30. Comprehensive fee of $24,136 includes full-time tuition ($17,372), mandatory fees ($544), and college room and board ($6220). Part-time tuition: $538 per credit.

Financial Aid Program-specific awards for Fall of 1994: 20 Talent Awards for incoming students ($10,000).

Application Procedures Deadline—freshmen and transfers: continuous. Required: high school transcript, minimum 2.0 high school GPA, letter of recommendation. Recommended: essay, interview, video, audition.

Undergraduate Contact Michael Nehring, Theater Chair, Theatre and Dance Department, Chapman University, 333 North Glassell Street, Orange, California 92666; 714-997-6677.

Clarion University of Pennsylvania

Clarion, Pennsylvania

State-supported, coed. Rural campus. Total enrollment: 5,367.

Degrees Bachelor of Fine Arts in the areas of theater/acting, theater/technical direction and design. Majors: acting, theater design/technology.

Theater Faculty Total: 4; 4 full-time; 100% of full-time faculty have terminal degrees. Graduate students do not teach undergraduate courses. Undergraduate student–faculty ratio: 12:1.

Student Life Student groups include Alpha Psi Omega.

Expenses for 1994–95 State resident tuition: $3086 full-time, $129 per credit part-time. Nonresident tuition: $7844 full-time, $327 per credit part-time. Part-time mandatory fees: $46.45 per credit. Full-time mandatory fees: $792. College room and board: $2924. College room only: $1710.

Application Procedures Deadline—freshmen and transfers: continuous. Required: audition, portfolio. Auditions

Clarion University of Pennsylvania *(continued)*

held 2 times on campus. Portfolio reviews held 2 times on campus; the submission of slides may be substituted for portfolios.

Undergraduate Contact Dr. Myrna Kuehn, Chair, Speech, Communication and Theatre Department, Clarion University of Pennsylvania, 165-B Marwick-Boyd, Clarion, Pennsylvania 16214; 814-226-2284, E-mail address: kuehn@vaxa.clarion.edu.

College of Santa Fe

Santa Fe, New Mexico

Independent, coed. Small-town campus. Total enrollment: 1,365.

Degrees Bachelor of Fine Arts in the areas of acting, design/theater technology. Majors: acting, design, music theater, theater arts/drama, theater management.

Theater Student Profile Fall 1994: 120 total; all matriculated undergraduate; 15% minorities, 51% females.

Theater Faculty Total: 15; 7 full-time, 8 part-time; 100% of full-time faculty have terminal degrees. Graduate students do not teach undergraduate courses. Undergraduate student–faculty ratio: 12:1.

Student Life Student groups include Drama Club.

Expenses for 1995–96 Application fee: $25. Comprehensive fee of $16,006 includes full-time tuition ($11,796) and college room and board ($4210). College room only: $2036. Part-time tuition: $371 per semester hour. Part-time mandatory fees: $50 per year.

Financial Aid Program-specific awards for Fall of 1994: 12 Department Scholarships for freshmen ($1500).

Application Procedures Deadline—freshmen and transfers: March 1. Notification date—freshmen and transfers: August 1. Required: essay, high school transcript, 3 letters of recommendation, video, audition, minimum 2.5 high school GPA. Auditions held by appointment on campus and off campus in various cities in the U.S.; recorded music is permissible as a substitute for live auditions with approval from the department and videotaped performances are permissible as a substitute for live auditions with approval from the department.

Undergraduate Contact John Weckesser, Chair, Performing Arts Department, College of Santa Fe, 1600 St. Michael's Drive, Santa Fe, New Mexico 87505; 505-473-6439, fax: 505-473-6127.

More about the College

Facilities The Greer Garson Theatre Center is home to the College of Santa Fe Performing Arts Department. It includes a 500-seat mainstage theater named after the Academy Award–winning actress as well as the Weckesser Studio Theatre, a 100-seat black box performance space. Practice rooms, a dance studio and classrooms, and scenery and costume shops round out the facility.

Faculty, Guest Artists, Lecturers, and Alumni The Performing Arts Department faculty is composed of 9 full-time members specializing in acting, directing, costume design, music, voice, playwriting, dance, and technical theater. CSF has welcomed such guest artists as actress Greer Garson, the Joffrey Ballet Concert Group, actor Ben Kingsley, singer/songwriter Christine Lavin, members of the Royal Shakespeare Company, actress/director Kim Stanley, and actress Maureen Stapleton. Guest lecturers at CSF have included director Paul Baker, actress Carol Burnett, critic Martin Gottfried, actor Gregory Peck, singer Helen Vanni, and singer Harry Connick Jr. Alumni of the College of Santa Fe Performing Arts Department can be found in a wide variety of professional companies, regional theaters, and touring companies; on television; and in films. From New York's Carnegie Hall to *The Will Rogers Follies* on Broadway, CSF alumni are distinguishing themselves in the field.

Special Programs Semester in London: To increase the depth of the artistic training experience available through the College of Santa Fe, a semester in London has been established in conjunction with the British American Drama Academy. Acting majors will be eligible to study with leading actors, directors, and playwrights of the British stage one semester of the junior or senior year. New York Arts Program: CSF students are also eligible to participate in the New York Arts Program, a semester-long internship in the performing, visual, and media arts. Students spend the semester working as apprentices with artists or art organizations, as well as participating in seminars headed by professionals from various areas of the arts. Student Performances: Each theater season is packed with quality student productions ranging from dramas to musicals to comedy. CSF student performances continue to gain critical acclaim and mainstage productions have included *A Midsummer Night's Dream, Dancing at Lughnasa, Assassins, You Can Never Tell, The Skin of Our Teeth,* and *A Chorus Line.*

Cornish College of the Arts

Seattle, Washington

Independent, coed. Urban campus. Total enrollment: 623.

Degrees Bachelor of Fine Arts in the areas of acting, theater. Majors: acting, theater arts/drama.

Theater Student Profile Fall 1994: 94 total; all matriculated undergraduate; 7% minorities, 60% females, 2% international.

Theater Faculty Total: 16; 6 full-time, 10 part-time; 75% of full-time faculty have terminal degrees. Graduate students do not teach undergraduate courses. Undergraduate student–faculty ratio: 6:1.

Expenses for 1995–96 Application fee: $30. Tuition: $10,540 full-time, $405 per credit part-time. Special program-related fees: $155 for photographs.

Financial Aid Program-specific awards for Fall of 1994: Merit Awards for continuing students ($1500), Endowed/Restricted Awards for continuing students ($1000), 2 St. John Lodge Awards for talented students ($1500), 4

Conference Scholarship for new students ($1500), Trustee Grants for all students ($800–$1500), Cornish Scholarships for new students ($1000), 2–5 Kreielsheimer Scholarships for new students from Washington, Oregon, or Alaska ($15,000).

Application Procedures Deadline—freshmen and transfers: continuous. Required: essay, high school transcript, minimum 2.0 high school GPA, interview, audition. Recommended: minimum 3.0 high school GPA, letter of recommendation. Auditions held 5 times in the spring on campus and off campus in Los Angeles, CA and various other locations; videotaped performances are permissible as a substitute for live auditions when distance is prohibitive.

Undergraduate Contact Jane Buckman, Director, Admissions Office, Cornish College of the Arts, 710 East Roy Street, Seattle, Washington 98102; 206-323-1400, fax: 206-720-1011.

More about the College

Seattle's explosive arts community features a wealth of professional theater and dance companies that provide exciting opportunities for the next generation of actors, designers, directors, playwrights, and technicians. Cornish College's philosophy encourages artists to use a wide range of techniques in connecting their work to the world around them.

The Theater Department's training philosophy is to provide a variety of approaches to any particular acting problem rather than requiring adherence to any one method. The department presents up to eighteen productions each year in three campus theaters and at several off-campus locations. Students may perform in one-acts as freshmen, create an original show as sophomores, and play in two to four productions during each of the junior and senior years, including an outdoor Shakespeare show, and a guest-directed senior show. Students also have a chance to intern with many Equity theaters in Seattle.

The Performance Production Department offers studies in lighting, sound, set and costume design, technical direction, and stage management. Extensive hands-on experience and an intimate exploration of the aesthetics of performance comprise the core of the curriculum. Each year, students build, mount, and staff 125 productions for the Dance, Music, and Theater departments. A twelve-week internship with an arts organization is the final requirement of the B.F.A. degree.

Many Theater and Performance Production graduates have found work in Seattle, at organizations including the Seattle Repertory Theater, Intiman Theater, Empty Space Theater, Seattle Opera, and Seattle Children's Theater.

Culver-Stockton College

Canton, Missouri

Independent-religious, coed. Small-town campus. Total enrollment: 1,057.

Degrees Bachelor of Fine Arts in the area of theater. Majors: theater arts/drama, theater education.

Theater Student Profile Fall 1994: 24 total; all matriculated undergraduate; 8% minorities, 60% females.

Theater Faculty Total: 4; 3 full-time, 1 part-time; 100% of full-time faculty have terminal degrees. Graduate students do not teach undergraduate courses. Undergraduate student–faculty ratio: 10:1.

Student Life Student groups include Theta Alpha Phi.

Expenses for 1995–96 Comprehensive fee of $12,200 includes full-time tuition ($8400) and college room and board ($3800). College room only: $1700. Part-time tuition: $350 per hour.

Financial Aid Program-specific awards for Fall of 1994: 14 Theater Awards for program majors ($1500), 20 Interest Awards for program minors ($750).

Application Procedures Deadline—freshmen and transfers: August 31. Required: high school transcript. Recommended: interview, video, audition, portfolio, SAT I or ACT test scores. Auditions held as needed on campus; recorded music is permissible as a substitute for live auditions and videotaped performances are permissible as a substitute for live auditions. Portfolio reviews held as needed on campus; the submission of slides may be substituted for portfolios for applicants in technical areas.

Undergraduate Contact Betty Smith, Director of Admissions, Culver-Stockton College, College Hill, Canton, Missouri 63435-1299; 314-288-5221 ext. 461, fax: 314-288-3984.

DePaul University

Chicago, Illinois

Independent-religious, coed. Urban campus. Total enrollment: 16,747.

Degrees Bachelor of Fine Arts in the areas of acting, scene design, lighting design, costume design, production management, theater technology, playwriting, theater management, dramaturgy/criticism, theater studies, costume technology. Majors: acting, costume design, costume production, dramaturgy/criticism, lighting design, playwriting, production, set design, theater arts/drama, theater management, theater technology. Graduate degrees offered: Master of Fine Arts in the areas of acting, directing, scene design, lighting design, costume design.

Theater Student Profile Fall 1994: 281 total; 235 matriculated undergraduate, 45 matriculated graduate, 1 nondegree; 5% minorities, 60% females, 1% international.

Theater Faculty Total: 42; 20 full-time, 22 part-time; 98% of full-time faculty have terminal degrees. Graduate students do not teach undergraduate courses. Undergraduate student–faculty ratio: 10:1.

Expenses for 1995–96 Application fee: $25. Comprehensive fee of $16,575 includes full-time tuition ($11,856 minimum), mandatory fees ($30), and college room and board ($4689 minimum). College room only: $3489

DePaul University *(continued)*

(minimum). Part-time tuition: $247 per quarter hour (minimum). Part-time mandatory fees: $10 per quarter. Tuition for music program: $12,048 full-time, $302 per quarter hour part-time. Tuition for theater program: $13,077 full-time, $326 per quarter hour part-time.

Financial Aid Program-specific awards for Fall of 1994: 5 Talent Scholarships for incoming actors ($3000), 10 Dean's Scholarships for incoming program majors ($1000–$8000), 20–30 Merit Scholarships for upperclass program majors ($1500–$5000), 30 Academic Scholarships for freshmen ($1500–$8000).

Application Procedures Deadline—freshmen and transfers: February 1. Notification date—freshmen and transfers: April 15. Required: high school transcript, college transcript(s) for transfer students, 3 letters of recommendation, interview, audition, portfolio, SAT I or ACT test scores, minimum combined SAT I score of 1000, minimum composite ACT score of 23, minimum 2.5 high school GPA. Recommended: essay, photo/resume. Auditions held 10–15 times on campus and off campus in Los Angeles, CA; San Francisco, CA; New York, NY; Seattle, WA: New Orleans, LA; Houston, TX; Miami, FL. Portfolio reviews held continuously on campus and off campus in Los Angeles, CA; San Francisco, CA; New York, NY; Seattle, WA; New Orleans, LA; Houston, TX; Miami, FL; the submission of slides may be substituted for portfolios when campus visit is impossible or in special circumstances.

Contact Melissa Meltzer, Director of Admissions, The Theatre School, DePaul University, 2135 North Kenmore, Chicago, Illinois 60614; 312-325-7999, fax: 312-325-7920.

More about the University

The Theatre School, DePaul University, is a professional theater training conservatory located in Chicago. Founded as the Goodman School of Drama in 1925, The Theatre School's curricula prepare actors, designers, technicians, playwrights, dramaturges, theater managers, and other theater professionals for careers in theater and related fields. All applicants must audition or interview to be admitted.

Program Facilities Merle Reskin Theatre (formerly the Blackstone): 1,340 seats, proscenium, state-of-the-art technical equipment including fly space, trapped stage, computer and electronic lighting (240 dimmers), orchestra pit; The Theatre School Building and Annex: classrooms, rehearsal spaces, light lab, scene shop, costume shop, costume storage, script library, computer lab, makeup lab, design studios, faculty and staff offices, black box spaces.

Faculty, Resident Artists, and Alumni Distinguished faculty include Dr. Bella Itkin, master teacher and author, *Acting: Preparation, Practice, Performance* (HarperCollins), and Nan Cibula-Jenkins, costume designer for Broadway, regional theater, and film. Recent resident artists and guest speakers include Joan Plowright, William Petersen, Ted Wass, and Gillian Anderson. Alumni include Gillian Anderson, Lois Nettleton, Concetta Tomei, Melinda Dillon, Lee Richardson, Jose Quintero, Carrie Snodgress, Harvey Korman, David Beron, Heidi Kling, Joe Mantegna, Kevin Anderson, Elizabeth Perkins, Linda Hunt, Karl Malden, Michael Rooker, Adrian Zmed, Scott Ellis, Kelly Coffield, Jacqueline Williams, Tom Amandes, the late Geraldine Page, Eugene Lee, and Theoni V. Aldredge.

Student Performance/Exhibit Opportunities More than thirty productions each year.

Special Programs Senior Showcases in Chicago and New York or Los Angeles; special program for students with learning disabilities; internships for design, technical, and theater studies majors.

Drake University

Des Moines, Iowa

Independent, coed. Suburban campus. Total enrollment: 5,954.

Degrees Bachelor of Fine Arts in the area of theater. Majors: acting, music theater, theater arts/drama, theater design/technology, theater education. Cross-registration with National Theatre Institute, Eugene O'Neill Centre.

Theater Student Profile Fall 1994: 62 total; all matriculated undergraduate; 8% minorities, 65% females, 2% international.

Theater Faculty Total: 7; 7 full-time; 80% of full-time faculty have terminal degrees. Graduate students do not teach undergraduate courses. Undergraduate student–faculty ratio: 9:1.

Student Life Student groups include United States Institute of Theater Technology, American College of Theater Festival, Fiderlick Dramaturg.

Expenses for 1995–96 Application fee: $25. Comprehensive fee of $18,830 includes full-time tuition ($14,100) and college room and board ($4730 minimum). College room only: $2500. Part-time tuition per semester hour: $325 for daytime classes, $210 for evening classes.

Financial Aid Program-specific awards for Fall of 1994: 1 Fiderlick Award for junior program majors ($1000), 25 Fine Arts Awards for program majors ($1800–$3000).

Application Procedures Deadline—freshmen and transfers: continuous. Required: essay, high school transcript, college transcript(s) for transfer students, minimum 2.0 high school GPA, SAT I or ACT test scores. Recommended: minimum 3.0 high school GPA, 2 letters of recommendation, interview, video, audition, portfolio. Auditions held continuously on campus; recorded music is permissible as a substitute for live auditions if a campus visit is impossible and videotaped performances are permissible as a substitute for live auditions if a campus visit is impossible. Portfolio reviews held continuously on campus; the submission of slides may be substituted for portfolios.

Undergraduate Contact Mike A. Barton, Chair, Theatre Arts Department, Drake University, Harmon Fine Arts Center, Des Moines, Iowa 50311; 515-271-2867, fax: 515-271-2558, E-mail address: mb6531r@acad.drake.edu.

East Carolina University

Greenville, North Carolina

State-supported, coed. Urban campus. Total enrollment: 16,373.

Degrees Bachelor of Fine Arts in the areas of acting, musical theater, design, production. Majors: acting, design production, music theater, theater arts/drama.

Theater Faculty 95% of full-time faculty have terminal degrees. Graduate students do not teach undergraduate courses. Undergraduate student–faculty ratio: 5:1.

Student Life Student groups include East Carolina Playhouse, East Carolina Summer Theatre, studio theater workshops.

Expenses for 1994–95 Application fee: $35. State resident tuition: $764 full-time. Nonresident tuition: $7248 full-time. Part-time tuition per semester ranges from $96 to $287 for state residents, $906 to $2718 for nonresidents. Part-time mandatory fees per semester range from $99 to $298. Full-time mandatory fees: $793. College room and board: $3030. College room only: $1590 (minimum).

Application Procedures Deadline—freshmen: March 15; transfers: April 15. Required: high school transcript, SAT I test score only. Recommended: minimum 2.0 high school GPA, letter of recommendation.

Undergraduate Contact Undergraduate Admissions, East Carolina University, Wichard Building, Greenville, North Carolina 27858; 919-328-6640.

Eastern New Mexico University

Portales, New Mexico

State-supported, coed. Small-town campus. Total enrollment: 3,853.

Degrees Bachelor of Fine Arts in the areas of theater performance, music theater, technical theater/design. Majors: theater arts/drama, theater design/technology.

Theater Student Profile Fall 1994: 48 total; all matriculated undergraduate.

Theater Faculty Total: 5; 4 full-time, 1 part-time; 100% of full-time faculty have terminal degrees. Graduate students do not teach undergraduate courses. Undergraduate student–faculty ratio: 10:1.

Student Life Student groups include Alpha Phi Omega.

Expenses for 1995–96 Application fee: $15. State resident tuition: $2258 full-time, $94 per credit hour part-time. Nonresident tuition: $6500 full-time, $270.80 per credit hour part-time. College room and board: $2728. College room only: $1268.

Financial Aid Program-specific awards for Fall of 1994: University Theater Scholarships for program majors ($100–$300), 4 Talent Day Scholarships for program majors ($400), 15 Participation Grants for program majors ($200).

Application Procedures Deadline—freshmen and transfers: July 23. Required: high school transcript, minimum 2.0 high school GPA, audition. Auditions held continuously on campus; recorded music is permissible as a substitute for live auditions when distance is prohibitive and videotaped performances are permissible as a substitute for live auditions when distance is prohibitive.

Undergraduate Contact Dr. Patrick Rucker, Chair, Theatre/Dance Department, Eastern New Mexico University, Station #37, Portales, New Mexico 88130; 505-562-2711, fax: 505-562-2961.

Emporia State University

Emporia, Kansas

State-supported, coed. Small-town campus. Total enrollment: 6,075.

Degrees Bachelor of Fine Arts in the area of dramatic arts. Majors: theater arts/drama.

Theater Student Profile Fall 1994: 50 total; all matriculated undergraduate.

Theater Faculty Total: 7; 5 full-time, 2 part-time; 100% of full-time faculty have terminal degrees.

Expenses for 1995–96 Application fee: $15. State resident tuition: $1782 full-time, $65 per credit hour part-time. Nonresident tuition: $5764 full-time, $198 per credit hour part-time. College room and board: $3220.

Application Procedures Deadline—freshmen and transfers: continuous. Required: high school transcript. Recommended: audition. Auditions held 2 times on campus; recorded music is permissible as a substitute for live auditions if a campus visit is impossible.

Undergraduate Contact Dr. Harry B. Parker, Director of Theater, Emporia State University, Campus Box 4033, Emporia, Kansas 66801; 316-341-5256.

Schmidt College of Arts and Humanities

Florida Atlantic University

Boca Raton, Florida

State-supported, coed. Suburban campus. Total enrollment: 17,484.

Degrees Bachelor of Fine Arts in the area of theater. Majors: theater arts/drama. Graduate degrees offered: Master of Fine Arts in the area of theater.

Theater Student Profile Fall 1994: 73 total; 52 matriculated undergraduate, 21 matriculated graduate; 10% minorities, 57% females, 4% international.

Theater Faculty Total: 15; 12 full-time, 3 part-time; 75% of full-time faculty have terminal degrees. Graduate students teach about a quarter undergraduate courses. Undergraduate student–faculty ratio: 11:1.

Florida Atlantic University *(continued)*

Student Life Student groups include Coalition for the Advancement of Students in Theater.

Expenses for 1994–95 Application fee: $20. State resident tuition: $1791 full-time, $59.69 per semester hour part-time. Nonresident tuition: $6693 full-time, $223.10 per semester hour part-time. College room and board: $3930.

Financial Aid Program-specific awards for Fall of 1994: 1 Esther Griswold Award for program majors ($500).

Application Procedures Deadline—freshmen and transfers: continuous. Required: high school transcript, college transcript(s) for transfer students, minimum 2.0 high school GPA, 3 letters of recommendation, audition. Auditions held 2 times on campus.

Contact Joe Conaway, Chair, Theater Department, Florida Atlantic University, 777 Glades Road, Box 3091, Boca Raton, Florida 33431-6498; 407-367-3810, fax: 407-367-2752.

Florida State University

Tallahassee, Florida

State-supported, coed. Suburban campus. Total enrollment: 29,630.

Degrees Bachelor of Fine Arts in the areas of acting, music theater, design technology. Majors: theater arts/drama. Graduate degrees offered: Master of Fine Arts in the areas of acting, costume design, directing, lighting design, scenic design, theater management, scenic technology.

Theater Student Profile Fall 1994: 707 total; 259 matriculated undergraduate, 72 matriculated graduate, 376 nondegree; 15% minorities, 64% females, 1% international.

Theater Faculty Total: 29; 28 full-time, 1 part-time; 90% of full-time faculty have terminal degrees. Graduate students teach a few undergraduate courses. Undergraduate student–faculty ratio: 14:1.

Student Life Student groups include Florida Theatre Conference, Southeast Theatre Conference.

Expenses for 1995–96 Application fee: $20. State resident tuition: $1798 full-time, $59.93 per semester hour part-time. Nonresident tuition: $6700 full-time, $223.34 per semester hour part-time. College room and board: $4500. College room only: $2360.

Financial Aid Program-specific awards for Fall of 1994: 2 Presidential Scholarships for undergraduates ($1500), 5 Patron's Scholarships for undergraduates ($1000), 1 Hoffman Chair Scholarship for undergraduates ($1000), 3 Fallon Scholarships for undergraduates ($500), 1–9 School of Theatre Scholarships for undergraduates ($500–$1000).

Application Procedures Deadline—freshmen: March 1; transfers: June 20. Notification date—freshmen: April 1; transfers: July 15. Required: high school transcript, college transcript(s) for transfer students, letter of recommendation, SAT I or ACT test scores, interview for design technology applicants, audition for acting and music theater applicants. Auditions held 1 time for acting and music theater applicants on campus. Portfolio reviews held 1 time for design technology applicants on campus.

Undergraduate Contact Marie Behm, Undergraduate Coordinator, School of Theatre, Florida State University, 328 Fine Arts Building, Tallahassee, Florida 32306-2008; 904-644-5548, fax: 904-644-7246, E-mail address: mbehm@mailer.fsu.edu.

Graduate Contact Vinette Wilson, Graduate Coordinator, School of Theatre, Florida State University, 327 Fine Arts Building, Tallahassee, Florida 32306-2008; 904-644-7234, fax: 904-644-7246, E-mail address: vwilson@mailer.fsu.edu.

Hofstra University

Hempstead, New York

Independent, coed. Suburban campus. Total enrollment: 11,545.

Degrees Bachelor of Fine Arts in the areas of performance, production. Majors: acting, technical direction, theater arts/drama.

Theater Student Profile Fall 1994: 94 total; all matriculated undergraduate; 2% minorities, 65% females, 1% international.

Theater Faculty Total: 12; 7 full-time, 5 part-time; 100% of full-time faculty have terminal degrees. Graduate students do not teach undergraduate courses. Undergraduate student–faculty ratio: 10:1.

Student Life Student groups include Alpha Psi Omega, Spectrum, 101B (musical theater group).

Expenses for 1994–95 Application fee: $25. Comprehensive fee of $17,630 includes full-time tuition ($11,060), mandatory fees ($650), and college room and board ($5920 minimum). College room only: $3210 (minimum). Part-time tuition: $363 per semester hour. Part-time mandatory fees per term range from $89 to $149.

Financial Aid Program-specific awards for Fall of 1994: 8–10 Activity Grants for freshmen ($1000–$2500).

Application Procedures Deadline—freshmen and transfers: continuous. Required: high school transcript, minimum 3.0 high school GPA. Recommended: essay, interview, video. Auditions held on campus; videotaped performances are permissible as a substitute for live auditions when distance is prohibitive. Portfolio reviews held on campus; the submission of slides may be substituted for portfolios when distance is prohibitive.

Undergraduate Contact Admissions Counselor, Admissions Office, Hofstra University, Holland House, Hempstead, New York 11550-1090; 516-463-6697, fax: 516-560-7660.

Howard University

Washington, District of Columbia

Independent, coed. Urban campus. Total enrollment: 10,961.

Degrees Bachelor of Fine Arts in the areas of acting, musical theater, pre–directing, theater education, theater arts administration, theater technology. Majors: acting, music theater, theater education, theater management, theater technology.

Expenses for 1994–95 Comprehensive fee of $11,676 includes full-time tuition ($7130), mandatory fees ($401), and college room and board ($4145). Part-time tuition: $275 per credit hour. Part-time mandatory fees: $401 per year.

Application Procedures Deadline—freshmen and transfers: April 1. Required: high school transcript, 2 letters of recommendation, SAT I or ACT test scores, minimum combined SAT I score of 750, resume. Auditions held on campus and off campus. Portfolio reviews held on campus and off campus.

Undergraduate Contact Director, Office of Admissions, Howard University, Washington, District of Columbia 20059; 202-806-2700.

Illinois Wesleyan University

Bloomington, Illinois

Independent, coed. Suburban campus. Total enrollment: 1,855.

Degrees Bachelor of Arts/Bachelor of Fine Arts in the areas of theater arts, music theater. Majors: music theater, theater arts/drama.

Theater Student Profile Fall 1994: 95 total; all matriculated undergraduate; 1% minorities, 64% females.

Theater Faculty Total: 9; 6 full-time, 3 part-time; 100% of full-time faculty have terminal degrees. Graduate students do not teach undergraduate courses. Undergraduate student–faculty ratio: 12:1.

Expenses for 1995–96 Comprehensive fee of $19,800 includes full-time tuition ($15,410), mandatory fees ($100), and college room and board ($4290). College room only: $2450. Part-time tuition: $1925 per course.

Financial Aid Program-specific awards for Fall of 1994: Talent Awards for entering freshman ($2500–$6000).

Application Procedures Deadline—freshmen and transfers: April 1. Notification date—freshmen and transfers: May 1. Required: essay, high school transcript, minimum 3.0 high school GPA, interview, SAT I or ACT test scores, audition for performance applicants, portfolio for design applicants. Auditions held weekly on campus and off campus; videotaped performances are permissible as a substitute for live auditions if campus visit is impossible. Portfolio reviews held weekly on campus and off campus; the submission of slides may be substituted for portfolios if campus visit is impossible.

Undergraduate Contact Jared Brown, Director, School of Theatre Arts, Illinois Wesleyan University, Box 2900, Bloomington, Illinois 61702-2900; 309-566-3011, fax: 309-556-3411, E-mail address: jbrown@titan.iwu.edu.

School of Theatre Arts

Program Facilities Performance, rehearsal, and classroom spaces include the McPherson Theatre, supported by the scene shop, costume shop, and light lab, featuring seven productions each academic year; The E. Melba Johnson Kirkpatrick Laboratory Theatre, a flexible space, where most plays are student-directed and student-designed; The Phoenix Theatre, for experimental student productions; and The Dance Studio.

Faculty and Guest Artists The faculty is comprised of experienced and knowledgeable teachers of acting, directing, scene design, costume design, lighting design, dance, stage movement, theater history, and dramatic literature, many of whom have backgrounds in the professional theater. Guest speakers and artists (such as John Randolph, Stacy Keach, Sr., Kitty Carlisle, Jonathan Farwell) regularly visit with stays as brief as a single day or as long as one semester.

Student Performance Opportunities Since there is no graduate program in theater arts, undergraduates play all the roles in the varied production schedule. (Students audition for each role, so roles cannot be guaranteed.) Undergraduates have opportunities to direct and design mainstage and laboratory productions and to choreograph for a dance concert.

Special Programs Many students participate in pre-professional internship programs taken for academic credit. The faculty is eager to help create an internship that will be of value to each student. An annual Travel Seminar is offered during the unique May Term. Under the guidance of a faculty member, students attend as many as fifteen plays in New York City and (in alternate years) in London. Discussions with prominent theater professionals form an integral part of each Travel Seminar.

Ithaca College

Ithaca, New York

Independent, coed. Small-town campus. Total enrollment: 5,556.

Degrees Bachelor of Fine Arts in the areas of acting, musical theater, theatrical production arts. Majors: acting, music theater, theater arts/drama, theater production. Cross-registration with Cornell University.

Theater Student Profile Fall 1994: 194 total; all matriculated undergraduate; 6% minorities, 52% females, 2% international.

Theater Faculty Total: 25; 17 full-time, 8 part-time; 89% of full-time faculty have terminal degrees. Graduate students do not teach undergraduate courses. Undergraduate student–faculty ratio: 8:1.

Student Life Student groups include American College Theater Festival, Theatre Arts Student Organization, "IC Players" Drama Club. Special housing available for theater students.

Robert Redford
Actor and Director

You are only as good as you dare to be bad.

Ithaca College *(continued)*

Expenses for 1995–96 Application fee: $40. Comprehensive fee of $21,844 includes full-time tuition ($15,250) and college room and board ($6594). Part-time tuition: $477 per credit hour.

Financial Aid Program-specific awards for Fall of 1994: Peter Bergstrom Scholarship for acting or musical theater majors ($200–$500), Katherine B. "Toby" Clarey Memorial Scholarship for acting or musical theater arts majors ($500–$1500), Richard M. Clark Memorial Scholarship for talented program majors ($1000–$2000), George Hoerner Memorial Scholarship for technical theater and scenic design majors ($200–$500), Theater Arts Alumni Memorial Scholarship for junior or senior theater arts majors ($200–$500).

Application Procedures Deadline—freshmen: March 1; transfers: July 15. Notification date—freshmen: April 15. Required: essay, high school transcript, college transcript(s) for transfer students, minimum 2.0 high school GPA, letter of recommendation, audition, portfolio, SAT I or ACT test scores, interview for theatrical production arts applicants. Auditions held 15–20 times for acting and musical theater applicants on campus and off campus in New York, NY; Houston, TX; Dallas, TX; Miami, FL; Sarasota, FL; Washington, DC; Boston, MA; Chicago, IL; San Francisco, CA; Los Angeles, CA; Interlochen, MI; Las Vegas, NV; videotaped performances are permissible as a substitute for live auditions when distance is prohibitive. Portfolio reviews held continuously for theatrical production arts applicants on campus and off campus in various locations; the submission of slides may be substituted for portfolios when distance is prohibitive.

Undergraduate Contact Paula J. Mitchell, Director, Admissions, Ithaca College, 100 Job Hall, Ithaca, New York 14850-7020; 800-429-4274, fax: 607-274-1900.

More about the College

Program Facilities Performance facilities at Ithaca include a 535-seat proscenium theater, a 280-seat flexible theater, and a small studio theater, all featuring state-of-the-art equipment. Modern studios for acting, dance, and design combine with shops and workrooms for scenery, costumes, sound, electrics, and props to create a stimulating environment for artistic work. The School is a member of the National Association of Schools of Theatre.

Faculty, Resident Artists, and Alumni With 17 full-time theater faculty and an extensive professional staff, the Department of Theatre Arts offers small classes and individualized instruction. Since there are no graduate students, each opportunity in acting, directing, managing, technical direction, and design is specifically for the undergraduate student. Guest artists regularly visit campus, sharing their experience and insights and becoming valuable contacts for students. Ithaca alumni in the theater and entertainment world also actively provide career assistance.

Student Performance Opportunities The main stage season includes five to seven productions; the studio season, three to four productions. Other opportunities include an annual touring children's play and a student-directed season of eight to ten productions.

Special Programs One of the most popular options for theater students is a semester at Ithaca College's London Center. Students spend their time studying and seeing plays—as many as thirty-five productions in a semester. Senior theater majors have an opportunity to join department faculty for a week in New York City. Ithaca alumni discuss the theater and entertainment business, and acting and musical theater majors present their annual showcase for agents and casting directors at an off-Broadway theater during this week.

The Department of Theatre Arts offers a powerful combination of intensive classroom and performance experience that has made it one of the most effective and highly respected training programs in the nation. The goal is to prepare students for careers in the theater and entertainment business. It is a highly selective program, staffed by faculty members whose academic training and professional theater experience have prepared them for the focused, personalized instruction that is the key to successful theatrical training.

While the degree programs in acting and musical theater are performance-oriented, providing professional training and experience, the degrees in theatrical productions and theater management prepare students to enter other aspects of the theater world. As with other programs at Ithaca College, the emphasis is on learning by doing. Students pursuing the technology concentration in production, for example, will be involved in scenic carpentry, costume construction, drafting, electrics, sound, properties, stage management, and technical direction. The theatrical design concentration provides instruction in scenic design, costume design, lighting design, figure drawing, rendering, and art history, in addition to the technical areas. Theater management majors have the opportunity to develop skills in marketing, advertising, publicity, fund-raising, grant writing, accounting, stage management, personnel management, booking, and tour organization. For students who elect the liberal arts–based drama degree, courses include directing, acting, theater history, stagecraft, dramatic literature, dance, and playwriting.

In addition to the annual senior showcase for New York City agents and casting directors, students and faculty travel regularly into New York to see plays and participate in special theater events. Faculty assist students in securing summer stock employment, graduate program admission, and work after graduation. Extra time is taken with individual students to prepare them for auditions or interviews. Design and technical students have an outstanding record of acceptance at some of the finest graduate programs.

Students direct all No Bucks Theatre productions; seniors may also direct studio theater productions. Student playwrights are encouraged to submit their plays for production and receive individual guidance.

Theater students may take advantage of courses outside their major within the School of Humanities and Sciences or at any of Ithaca College's four other schools: Business, Communications, Health Sciences and Human Performance, and Music. A comprehensive college, Ithaca offers some 2,000 courses and 100 different academic majors. Theater students may be particularly interested in exploring communications courses in areas such as audio production or film directing.

The city of Ithaca is one of the country's premier college towns, with nearly 25,000 students at Ithaca College and Cornell University. Surrounded by magnificent gorges, lakes, and countryside in the Finger Lakes region of New York State, Ithaca is a thriving cultural center. The community supports an impressive array of concerts, gallery shows, and movies as well as theater productions mounted by four local theater companies.

The combination of excellent undergraduate theater programs, a vibrant community, and a beautiful location make Ithaca College an exceptional choice for the talented and motivated young artists who wish to make the theater and entertainment business their profession.

Jacksonville University

Jacksonville, Florida

Independent, coed. Suburban campus. Total enrollment: 2,480.

Degrees Bachelor of Fine Arts in the area of theater arts. Majors: acting, theater arts/drama, theater design/technology.

Theater Student Profile Fall 1994: 18 total; all matriculated undergraduate; 1% minorities, 90% females.

Theater Faculty Total: 6; 2 full-time, 4 part-time; 100% of full-time faculty have terminal degrees. Graduate students do not teach undergraduate courses. Undergraduate student–faculty ratio: 10:1.

Student Life Student groups include Alpha Psi Omega.

Expenses for 1995–96 Application fee: $25. Comprehensive fee of $15,178 includes full-time tuition ($10,080), mandatory fees ($500), and college room and board ($4598). Part-time tuition: $336 per semester hour. Part-time mandatory fees: $80 per semester. Special program-related fees: $15–$50 for materials.

Financial Aid Program-specific awards for Fall of 1994: 8 Theater Department Awards for program majors ($700).

Application Procedures Deadline—freshmen and transfers: continuous. Required: high school transcript, audition. Auditions held 2 times and by appointment on campus; videotaped performances are permissible as a substitute for live auditions if a campus visit is impossible.

Jacksonville University *(continued)*

Undergraduate Contact Director of Admissions, Jacksonville University, 2800 University Boulevard North, Jacksonville, Florida 32211; 904-744-3950, fax: 904-744-0101.

More about the University

Program Facilities Classes are held in the Swisher Auditorium and Phillips Fine Arts Building on the Jacksonville University campus. Built in 1955, the Auditorium offers acting and design classroom space and dressing rooms as well as a fully equipped auditorium with a seating capacity of 550 and a proscenium stage.

Faculty, Programs, and Alumni Faculty consists of 2 full-time and several adjunct faculty members. Students broaden their skills in acting and design technology in a diverse course curriculum that includes courses in acting, playwriting, directing, scene design, lighting design, costume history and design, theater history, acting styles, and speech theater. Alumni have been successful in the fields of both acting and design technology.

Student Performance Opportunities Performance opportunities are offered each semester, including two major productions directed by a faculty director and student-directed productions. There are also opportunities to perform in Jacksonville's First Coast *Nutcracker*. The Jacksonville metropolitan area offers a variety of opportunities for a career-minded actor/actress and designer.

Special Programs The curriculum at Jacksonville University is based on guidelines of the National Association of Schools of Theatre. Students may choose to pursue a B.A., or B.F.A. in theater. Independent study programs are offered for a one-on-one approach to a specific project or interest. Internships are also available within the Jacksonville community at many of the local community theaters.

Juilliard School

New York, New York

Independent, coed. Urban campus. Total enrollment: 825.

Degrees Bachelor of Fine Arts in the area of theater. Majors: theater arts/drama.

Theater Student Profile Fall 1994: 22 total; all matriculated undergraduate; 32% minorities, 33% females.

Theater Faculty Total: 38; 18 full-time, 20 part-time. Graduate students teach None undergraduate courses. Undergraduate student–faculty ratio: 4:1.

Student Life Special housing available for theater students.

Expenses for 1995–96 Application fee: $75. Comprehensive fee of $19,900 includes full-time tuition ($13,000), mandatory fees ($600), and college room and board ($6300).

Application Procedures Deadline—freshmen: December 15. Required: essay, high school transcript, audition. Auditions held on campus and off campus in Chicago, IL; San Francisco, CA.

Undergraduate Contact Admissions Office, Juilliard School, 60 Lincoln Center Plaza, New York, New York 10023-6590; 212-799-5000 ext. 223, fax: 212-724-0263.

Lake Erie College

Painesville, Ohio

Independent, coed. Small-town campus. Total enrollment: 732.

Degrees Bachelor of Fine Arts in the area of theater. Majors: acting, directing, lighting design, set design, theater history.

Expenses for 1995–96 Application fee: $20. Comprehensive fee of $17,226 includes full-time tuition ($11,840), mandatory fees ($480), and college room and board ($4906). Part-time tuition: $356 per semester hour. Part-time mandatory fees: $15 per semester.

Undergraduate Contact Paul Gothard, Director, Fine Arts Department, Lake Erie College, Box 354, 391 West Washington Street, Painesville, Ohio 44077; 216-639-7856.

Long Island University, C.W. Post Campus

Brookville, New York

Independent, coed. Small-town campus. Total enrollment: 7,919.

Degrees Bachelor of Fine Arts in the areas of acting, film. Majors: production, theater arts/drama.

Theater Student Profile Fall 1994: 50 total; 45 matriculated undergraduate, 5 nondegree; 30% minorities, 55% females, 25% international.

Theater Faculty Total: 11; 5 full-time, 6 part-time; 100% of full-time faculty have terminal degrees. Graduate students do not teach undergraduate courses. Undergraduate student–faculty ratio: 7:1.

Student Life Student groups include Jazz Ensemble, American College Dance Festival Association, American College Theater Festival.

Expenses for 1995–96 Application fee: $30. Comprehensive fee of $18,735 includes full-time tuition ($12,430), mandatory fees ($560), and college room and board ($5745). College room only: $3500. Part-time tuition: $387 per credit. Part-time mandatory fees: $130 per semester. Special program-related fees: $30 for accompanist fee, $35 for material fee.

Financial Aid Program-specific awards for Fall of 1994: 10–12 Theatre Department Awards for program majors ($1000–$2000).

Application Procedures Deadline—freshmen and transfers: continuous. Required: essay, high school transcript, 2 letters of recommendation, interview, SAT I or ACT test scores. Recommended: audition, minimum 2.5 high school GPA. Auditions held by appointment off campus in Southeastern Theater Conference, East Central Theater Conference, Theater Association of Pennsylvania, International Thespian Society; recorded music is permissible as a substitute for live auditions and videotaped performances are permissible as a substitute for live auditions if a campus visit is impossible.

Undergraduate Contact Dr. Cara Gargano, Chair, Department of Theatre, Film, Dance, Long Island University, C.W. Post Campus, 720 Northern Boulevard, Brookville, New York 11548; 516-299-2353, fax: 516-299-4180.

Longwood College

Farmville, Virginia

State-supported, coed. Small-town campus. Total enrollment: 3,277.

Degrees Bachelor of Fine Arts in the area of theater. Majors: music theater, performance, technical theater, theater management. Cross-registration with Hampden-Sydney College, Darby University (United Kingdom).

Theater Student Profile Fall 1994: 60 total; all matriculated undergraduate; 2% minorities, 56% females.

Theater Faculty Total: 11; 3 full-time, 8 part-time; 100% of full-time faculty have terminal degrees. Graduate students teach a few undergraduate courses. Undergraduate student–faculty ratio: 10:1.

Student Life Student groups include Alpha Psi Omega.

Expenses for 1995–96 Application fee: $25. State resident tuition: $2684 full-time, $112 per credit hour part-time. Nonresident tuition: $8156 full-time, $340 per credit hour part-time. Part-time mandatory fees: $25 per credit hour. Full-time mandatory fees: $1686. College room and board: $3934. College room only: $2352. Special program-related fees: $25 for lab fees, $100 for internship supervision.

Application Procedures Deadline—freshmen: March 1; transfers: continuous. Notification date—freshmen and transfers: June 1. Required: essay, high school transcript, college transcript(s) for transfer students, SAT I or ACT test scores, minimum combined SAT I score of 940, minimum composite ACT score of 20, minimum 2.5 high school GPA. Recommended: minimum 3.0 high school GPA. Auditions held as needed on campus; videotaped performances are permissible as a substitute for live auditions when distance is prohibitive. Portfolio reviews held 1 time on campus.

Undergraduate Contact Dr. Nancy Haga, Chair, Department of Speech and Theater, Longwood College, 201 High Street, Farmville, Virginia 23909-1899; 804-395-2643, fax: 804-395-2680.

Mars Hill College

Mars Hill, North Carolina

Independent-religious, coed. Small-town campus. Total enrollment: 1,056.

Degrees Bachelor of Fine Arts in the area of musical theater. Majors: music theater. Cross-registration with Warren Wilson College, University of North Carolina at Asheville.

Theater Student Profile Fall 1994: 8 total; all matriculated undergraduate; 80% females.

Theater Faculty Total: 7; 4 full-time, 3 part-time; 100% of full-time faculty have terminal degrees. Graduate students do not teach undergraduate courses. Undergraduate student–faculty ratio: 6:1.

Expenses for 1995–96 Application fee: $15. Comprehensive fee of $12,050 includes full-time tuition ($7850), mandatory fees ($550), and college room and board ($3650). College room only: $1650. Part-time tuition: $250 per credit.

Application Procedures Deadline—freshmen and transfers: continuous. Required: high school transcript, minimum 2.0 high school GPA, 2 letters of recommendation, interview, audition. Auditions held 4 times and by appointment on campus; recorded music is permissible as a substitute for live auditions when distance is prohibitive and videotaped performances are permissible as a substitute for live auditions when distance is prohibitive.

Undergraduate Contact Dr. Julie Fortney, Associate Director of Musical Theater, Music Department, Mars Hill College, Mars Hill, North Carolina 28754; 704-689-1222.

Marshall University

Huntington, West Virginia

State-supported, coed. Urban campus. Total enrollment: 12,659.

Degrees Bachelor of Fine Arts in the area of theater. Majors: acting and directing, theater arts/drama, theater design/technology.

Theater Student Profile Fall 1994: 125 total; 100 matriculated undergraduate, 25 nondegree; 2% minorities, 52% females.

Theater Faculty Total: 10; 6 full-time, 4 part-time; 80% of full-time faculty have terminal degrees. Graduate students do not teach undergraduate courses. Undergraduate student–faculty ratio: 15:1.

Student Life Student groups include Alpha Psi Omega, West Virginia Theater Conference–Southeast Theater Conference, Theta Theta Omicron.

Expenses for 1995–96 Application fee: $10. State resident tuition: $2050 full-time, $85.75 per semester hour part-time. Nonresident tuition: $5696 full-time, $237.50 per semester hour part-time. Tuition for Kentucky residents. College room and board: $4050.

Marshall University *(continued)*

Financial Aid Program-specific awards for Fall of 1994: 5 Tuition Waivers for program majors ($520–$1882), 4 Theater Scholarships for program majors ($1000).

Application Procedures Deadline—freshmen and transfers: continuous. Notification date—freshmen and transfers: continuous. Required: high school transcript, minimum 2.0 high school GPA. Recommended: interview.

Undergraduate Contact Maureen Milicia, Chairperson, Theatre Department, Marshall University, 400 Hal Greer Boulevard, Huntington, West Virginia 25755-2240; 304-696-6442, fax: 304-696-3333, E-mail address: dfa005@marshall.wvnet.edu.

Mason Gross School of the Arts

See Rutgers, The State University of New Jersey, Mason Gross School of the Arts

Meadows School of the Arts

See Southern Methodist University, Meadows School of the Arts

Midwestern State University

Wichita Falls, Texas

State-supported, coed. Small-town campus. Total enrollment: 5,819.

Degrees Bachelor of Fine Arts in the area of theater. Majors: theater arts/drama.

Theater Student Profile Fall 1994: 36 total; all matriculated undergraduate.

Theater Faculty Total: 4; 4 full-time; 100% of full-time faculty have terminal degrees. Graduate students do not teach undergraduate courses. Undergraduate student–faculty ratio: 9:1.

Expenses for 1995–96 State resident tuition: $1646 full-time. Nonresident tuition: $7406 full-time. Part-time tuition per semester ranges from $184.05 to $822.75 for state residents, $286.05 to $3703 for nonresidents. College room and board: $3430 (minimum). College room only: $1830.

Financial Aid Program-specific awards for Fall of 1994: 15–20 Theater Scholarships for program majors ($400–$1400).

Application Procedures Deadline—freshmen and transfers: April 1. Notification date—freshmen and transfers: May 1. Required: high school transcript, SAT I or ACT test scores. Auditions held on campus and off campus in theater conference locations; videotaped performances are permissible as a substitute for live auditions when distance is prohibitive.

Undergraduate Contact Laura N. Wilson, Coordinator, Theatre Department, Midwestern State University, 3410 Taft Boulevard, Wichita Falls, Texas 76308; 817-689-4395.

Millikin University

Decatur, Illinois

Independent-religious, coed. Suburban campus. Total enrollment: 1,863.

Degrees Bachelor of Fine Arts in the areas of music theater, acting, technical theater, directing. Majors: music theater, theater arts/drama.

Theater Student Profile Fall 1994: 133 total; all matriculated undergraduate; 5% minorities, 1% international.

Theater Faculty Total: 12; 10 full-time, 2 part-time; 100% of full-time faculty have terminal degrees. Graduate students do not teach undergraduate courses. Undergraduate student–faculty ratio: 16:1.

Student Life Student groups include Alpha Psi Omega, Children's Theater, Illinois High School Association.

Expenses for 1995–96 Application fee: $25. Comprehensive fee of $17,283 includes full-time tuition ($12,596), mandatory fees ($91), and college room and board ($4596). College room only: $2392. Part-time tuition: $364 per credit.

Financial Aid Program-specific awards for Fall of 1994: 110 Talent Awards for acting, directing majors ($1200–$2000), 20 Talent Awards for technology majors ($5500).

Application Procedures Deadline—freshmen and transfers: continuous. Required: high school transcript, video, audition, portfolio, SAT I or ACT test scores. Auditions held continuously on campus and off campus in Chicago, IL; Indianapolis, IN; St. Louis, MO; recorded music is permissible as a substitute for live auditions when distance is prohibitive and videotaped performances are permissible as a substitute for live auditions when distance is prohibitive. Portfolio reviews held continuously for technology applicants on campus and off campus in Chicago, IL; Indianapolis, IN; St. Louis, MO; the submission of slides may be substituted for portfolios.

Undergraduate Contact Dr. David A. Golden, Chair, Theatre and Dance Department, Millikin University, 1184 West Main Street, Decatur, Illinois 62522; 217-424-6282, fax: 217-424-3993, E-mail address: dgolden@mail.millikin.edu.

Montclair State University

Upper Montclair, New Jersey

State-supported, coed. Suburban campus. Total enrollment: 12,675.

Degrees Bachelor of Fine Arts in the areas of acting, production/design. Majors: acting, production/design.

Theater Student Profile Fall 1994: 75 total; all matriculated undergraduate; 8% minorities, 60% females.

Theater Faculty Total: 11; 7 full-time, 4 part-time; 80% of full-time faculty have terminal degrees. Graduate students do not teach undergraduate courses. Undergraduate student–faculty ratio: 12:1.

Student Life Student groups include Theatre Series–Mainstage, Studio, Experimental, Theta Alpha Phi.

Expenses for 1994–95 Application fee: $35. State resident tuition: $3000 full-time, $94.50 per semester hour part-time. Nonresident tuition: $4248 full-time, $133.50 per semester hour part-time. College room and board: $4834. College room only: $3160.

Application Procedures Deadline—freshmen: March 1; transfers: May 1. Notification date—freshmen and transfers: continuous. Required: high school transcript, 2 letters of recommendation, interview, audition, portfolio. Auditions held 4 times for acting applicants on campus. Portfolio reviews held continuously for production/design applicants on campus.

Undergraduate Contact Dr. Suzanne Trauth, Chair, Department of Broadcasting, Speech Communication, Dance, and Theatre, Montclair State University, Normal Avenue, Upper Montclair, New Jersey 07043; 201-655-4217.

Nebraska Wesleyan University

Lincoln, Nebraska

Independent-religious, coed. Suburban campus. Total enrollment: 1,610.

Degrees Bachelor of Fine Arts in the area of theater. Majors: theater arts/drama. Cross-registration with University of Nebraska–Lincoln.

Theater Student Profile Fall 1994: 5 total; all matriculated undergraduate; 40% females.

Theater Faculty Total: 5; 3 full-time, 2 part-time; 33% of full-time faculty have terminal degrees. Graduate students do not teach undergraduate courses. Undergraduate student–faculty ratio: 6:1.

Student Life Student groups include Theta Alpha Phi (theater honorary society), American College Theater Festival.

Expenses for 1995–96 Application fee: $20. Comprehensive fee of $13,736 includes full-time tuition ($9890), mandatory fees ($426), and college room and board ($3420 minimum). Part-time tuition: $400 per hour. Part-time mandatory fees: $48 per semester. Part-time tuition per hour for Wesleyan PM program: $125.

Financial Aid Program-specific awards for Fall of 1994: 7 Theater Scholarships for program majors ($750).

Application Procedures Deadline—freshmen and transfers: May 1. Notification date—freshmen and transfers: continuous. Required: high school transcript, college transcript(s) for transfer students, minimum 3.0 high school GPA, 2 letters of recommendation, interview, ACT test score only, minimum composite ACT score of 21. Auditions held on campus; videotaped performances are permissible as a substitute for live auditions when distance is prohibitive. Portfolio reviews held on campus; the submission of slides may be substituted for portfolios when distance is prohibitive.

Undergraduate Contact David M. Clark, Director of Theatre, Communication and Theatre Arts Department, Nebraska Wesleyan University, 5000 St. Paul Avenue, Lincoln, Nebraska 68504; 402-466-5693, fax: 402-456-2179.

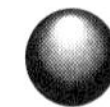

Tisch School of the Arts

New York University

New York, New York

Independent, coed. Urban campus. Total enrollment: 33,428.

Degrees Bachelor of Fine Arts in the area of dramatic writing. Graduate degrees offered: Master of Fine Arts in the area of dramatic writing.

Theater Student Profile Fall 1994: 250 total; 200 matriculated undergraduate, 50 matriculated graduate; 15% minorities, 47% females, 5% international.

Theater Faculty Total: 56; 11 full-time, 45 part-time; 100% of full-time faculty have terminal degrees. Graduate students do not teach undergraduate courses. Undergraduate student–faculty ratio: 5:1.

Student Life Student groups include Artists in the Community, Out Artists, United Artists of Color.

Expenses for 1994–95 Application fee: $45. Comprehensive fee of $26,001 includes full-time tuition ($18,739) and college room and board ($7262). Part-time tuition: $513 per credit. Part-time mandatory fees per semester range from $96 to $426.

Financial Aid Program-specific awards for Fall of 1994 available.

Application Procedures Deadline—freshmen: January 15; transfers: April 1. Notification date—freshmen: April 1; transfers: May 15. Required: essay, high school transcript, college transcript(s) for transfer students, letter of recommendation, portfolio. Recommended: minimum 3.0 high school GPA. Portfolio reviews held continuously from November through May on campus.

Undergraduate Contact Office of Undergraduate Admissions, New York University, 22 Washington Square North, 3rd floor, New York, New York 10011; 212-998-4500.

Graduate Contact Dan Sandford, Director of Graduate Admissions, New York University, 721 Broadway, 7th Floor, New York, New York 10003-6807; 212-998-1918.

North Carolina Agricultural and Technical State University

Greensboro, North Carolina

State-supported, coed. Urban campus. Total enrollment: 8,050.

Degrees Bachelor of Fine Arts in the areas of acting, directing. Majors: graphic arts, theater arts/drama, theater education, theater management, theater technology. Cross-registration with University of North Carolina System.

Theater Student Profile Fall 1994: 49 total; 34 matriculated undergraduate, 15 nondegree; 95% minorities, 65% females, 5% international.

Theater Faculty Total: 8; 6 full-time, 2 part-time; 100% of full-time faculty have terminal degrees. Graduate students do not teach undergraduate courses. Undergraduate student–faculty ratio: 15:1.

Student Life Student groups include American College Theater Festival, Regional Theatre Conferences, National Association of Dramatic and Speech Arts.

Expenses for 1994–95 Application fee: $25. State resident tuition: $764 full-time. Nonresident tuition: $7248 full-time. Part-time tuition per semester ranges from $96 to $287 for state residents, $906 to $2718 for nonresidents. Part-time mandatory fees per semester range from $59.13 to $333.50. Full-time mandatory fees: $667. College room and board: $3130.

Financial Aid Program-specific awards for Fall of 1994: 5 Chancellor's Awards for freshmen ($1000).

Application Procedures Deadline—freshmen and transfers: continuous. Required: high school transcript, minimum 2.0 high school GPA, letter of recommendation, interview, audition, portfolio. Auditions held 2 times on campus. Portfolio reviews held 2 times on campus.

Undergraduate Contact Miller Lucky Jr., Assistant Professor, Speech, Communication and Theatre Arts, North Carolina Agricultural and Technical State University, 1601 East Market Street, Greensboro, North Carolina 27411; 910-334-7221, fax: 910-334-7173.

North Carolina School of the Arts

Winston-Salem, North Carolina

State-supported, coed. Urban campus. Total enrollment: 613.

Degrees Bachelor of Fine Arts in the areas of drama/acting, design and production. Majors: acting, costume design, costume production, directing, lighting design, set design, stage management, technical production. Graduate degrees offered: Master of Fine Arts in the area of design and production.

Theater Student Profile Fall 1994: 172 total; 143 matriculated undergraduate, 29 matriculated graduate.

Theater Faculty Total: 11; 10 full-time, 1 part-time. Graduate students do not teach undergraduate courses. Undergraduate student–faculty ratio: 8:1.

Expenses for 1994–95 State resident tuition: $1233 full-time. Nonresident tuition: $8640 full-time. Full-time mandatory fees: $766. College room and board: $3600. College room only: $2376. Special program-related fees: $135 for instructional fees.

Financial Aid Program-specific awards for Fall of 1994: Talent Scholarships for artistically talented.

Application Procedures Deadline—freshmen and transfers: March 1. Required: high school transcript, 2 letters of recommendation, interview, audition. Auditions held by request on campus and off campus in New York, NY; Seattle, WA; Houston, TX; Chicago, IL; Miami, Fl; San Francisco, CA; Los Angeles, CA.

Undergraduate Contact Carol J. Palm, Director of Admissions, North Carolina School of the Arts, 200 Waughtown Street, Winston-Salem, North Carolina 27117; 910-770-3291, fax: 910-770-3370, E-mail address: palmc@ncsavx.ncart.edu.

Northern Illinois University

De Kalb, Illinois

State-supported, coed. Small-town campus. Total enrollment: 22,881.

Degrees Bachelor of Fine Arts in the areas of theater, dance performance. Majors: acting, dance, theater arts/drama, theater design/technology, theater education. Graduate degrees offered: Master of Fine Arts in the areas of theater, dance performance.

Theater Faculty Total: 27; 25 full-time, 2 part-time; 100% of full-time faculty have terminal degrees. Graduate students teach a few undergraduate courses. Undergraduate student–faculty ratio: 10:1.

Expenses for 1995–96 State resident tuition: $2930 full-time, $89.70 per credit hour part-time. Nonresident tuition: $8611 full-time, $269.10 per credit hour part-time. Part-time mandatory fees: $32 per credit hour. Full-time mandatory fees: $777. College room and board: $3416. Special program-related fees: $25 for applied fees.

Financial Aid Program-specific awards for Fall of 1994: 10 Tuition Waivers for program majors.

Application Procedures Deadline—freshmen and transfers: continuous. Notification date—freshmen and transfers: continuous. Required: high school transcript, college transcript(s) for transfer students, audition, ACT test score only. Auditions held 2 times on campus and off campus. Portfolio reviews held on campus and off campus.

Undergraduate Contact Coordinator of Undergraduate Admissions, Department of Theater Arts, Northern Illinois University, De Kalb, Illinois 60115; 815-753-1335.

Northern Kentucky University

Highland Heights, Kentucky

State-supported, coed. Suburban campus. Total enrollment: 11,978.

Degrees Bachelor of Fine Arts in the areas of acting/directing, musical theater, design/technology, generalist/management. Majors: theater arts/drama. Cross-registration with University of Cincinnati, Thomas More College.

Theater Student Profile Fall 1994: 121 total; 119 matriculated undergraduate, 2 nondegree; 5% minorities, 45% females, 2% international.

Theater Faculty Total: 18; 10 full-time, 8 part-time; 100% of full-time faculty have terminal degrees. Graduate students do not teach undergraduate courses. Undergraduate student–faculty ratio: 12:1.

Student Life Student groups include Student Theater, Stage One–Student Service Organization, Tour Troupes. Special housing available for theater students.

Expenses for 1995–96 Application fee: $25. State resident tuition: $1960 full-time, $83 per semester hour part-time. Nonresident tuition: $5320 full-time, $223 per semester hour part-time. College room and board: $3480 (minimum).

Financial Aid Program-specific awards for Fall of 1994: 13 Theater Department Scholarships for program majors ($1500).

Application Procedures Deadline—freshmen and transfers: continuous. Required: high school transcript, college transcript(s) for transfer students, minimum 2.0 high school GPA, ACT test score only. Recommended: minimum 3.0 high school GPA, 3 letters of recommendation, interview. Auditions held on campus; videotaped performances are permissible as a substitute for live auditions if a campus visit is impossible. Portfolio reviews held on campus.

Undergraduate Contact Office of Admissions, Administrative Centre, Northern Kentucky University, 4th Floor, Highland Heights, Kentucky 41099; 606-572-5220, fax: 606-572-5566.

Ohio Northern University

Ada, Ohio

Independent-religious, coed. Small-town campus. Total enrollment: 2,872.

Degrees Bachelor of Fine Arts in the area of musical theater. Majors: music theater, theater arts/drama. Cross-registration with Queen Margaret College, United Kingdom.

Theater Student Profile Fall 1994: 45 total; all matriculated undergraduate; 3% minorities, 65% females, 3% international.

Theater Faculty Total: 10; 4 full-time, 6 part-time; 100% of full-time faculty have terminal degrees. Graduate students do not teach undergraduate courses. Undergraduate student–faculty ratio: 13:1.

Student Life Student groups include Theta Alpha Phi, Touring Children's Company.

Expenses for 1995–96 Application fee: $30. Comprehensive fee of $21,240 includes full-time tuition ($16,950 minimum) and college room and board ($4290). College room only: $1875. Full-time tuition ranges up to $17,985 according to program. Part-time tuition per quarter hour ranges from $395 to $500 according to program.

Financial Aid Program-specific awards for Fall of 1994: 10–12 Talent Awards for program majors ($2000–$5000).

Application Procedures Deadline—freshmen and transfers: continuous. Notification date—freshmen and transfers: continuous. Required: high school transcript, minimum 2.0 high school GPA, interview, SAT I or ACT test scores. Recommended: essay, minimum 3.0 high school GPA, 2 letters of recommendation, video, audition, portfolio. Auditions held by appointment on campus; videotaped performances are permissible as a substitute for live auditions if a campus visit is impossible. Portfolio reviews held by appointment on campus.

Undergraduate Contact Karen Condeni, Office of Admissions, Ohio Northern University, 525 South Main Street, Ada, Ohio 45810; 419-772-2260, fax: 419-772-2313, E-mail address: kcondeni@henry.onu.edu.

More about the University

Program Facilities Music: Presser Hall, a recently renovated 200-seat recital hall; rehearsal hall; practice space, electronic music laboratory; library holdings. Art: Wilson Art Building (addition and renovation completed September 1995), including painting, ceramics, sculpture, computer graphics, and jewelry studios; gallery space; and computer labs. Theater/dance: Four-year-old Freed Center for the Performing Arts including 550-seat proscenium theatre, 125-seat laboratory theater, rehearsal spaces, dance studio, television/video studios, and the WONB-FM radio station and hosting more than sixty-five events per year.

Faculty The professionally active faculty is augmented by 18–20 nationally recognized professional guest artists annually.

Student Performance Opportunities Student works compose a major portion of all programs in gallery and production seasons.

Special Programs Touring; national, regional, and international touring of bands, choirs, children's theater, and musicals; new works; regular commissioning of dance, theater, music, and sculpture works; international opportunities; participation at the Edinburgh Festival, Eastern European guest artists, exchange programs; student directing; extensive undergraduate directing program and opportunities; art; commitment to culturally diverse programming; music; commitment to composition and jazz.

The Department of Art seeks to develop within the student an understanding of the fine arts and to provide the opportunity for the student to develop proficiency in various art media. The artist should be educated comprehensively through a program combining professional training and broad study in the liberal arts. It is on this premise that the student majoring in art receives as broad an understanding of art as possible, becomes

Ohio Northern University *(continued)*

acquainted with historical and cultural knowledge of the past and present, develops a working proficiency through mastery of the tools and skills of the profession, develops personal modes of expression in the media of the visual arts, and acquires an awareness of any competency in other academic disciplines.

The objectives of the Department of Communication Arts include emphasizing a strong liberal arts education for students entering the job market or graduate study and encouraging participation in and appreciation of the fine arts, thereby developing aesthetic standards. The course offerings of the department are structured around a series of core courses fundamental to an understanding of how humans communicate theoretically, practically, and aesthetically.

Ohio Northern University is an accredited institutional member of the National Association of Schools of Music. The Department of Music offers a full course of music and music education studies for the aspiring music educator, composer, or professional performer. The music student is given a variety of courses and experiences to help gain the knowledge and proficiency in breadth and depth that will help him or her achieve future success.

Otterbein College

Westerville, Ohio

Independent-religious, coed. Suburban campus. Total enrollment: 2,599.

Degrees Bachelor of Fine Arts in the areas of acting, design/technology, musical theater. Majors: design technology, music theater, performance. Cross-registration with American University.

Theater Student Profile Fall 1994: 129 total; all matriculated undergraduate; 8% minorities, 53% females.

Theater Faculty Total: 16; 9 full-time, 7 part-time; 90% of full-time faculty have terminal degrees. Graduate students do not teach undergraduate courses. Undergraduate student–faculty ratio: 14:1.

Student Life Student groups include Theta Alpha Phi (theater honorary society).

Expenses for 1995–96 Application fee: $15. Comprehensive fee of $18,180 includes full-time tuition ($13,611) and college room and board ($4569). College room only: $2019. Part-time tuition: $182 per credit hour.

Financial Aid Program-specific awards for Fall of 1994: 20 Theater Talent Grants for program majors ($300–$3000).

Application Procedures Deadline—freshmen and transfers: April 1. Notification date—freshmen and transfers: continuous. Required: high school transcript, college transcript(s) for transfer students, minimum 2.0 high school GPA, interview, audition, portfolio, SAT I or ACT test scores. Recommended: minimum 3.0 high school GPA. Auditions held continuously on campus; recorded music is permissible as a substitute for live auditions when distance is prohibitive and videotaped performances are permissible as a substitute for live auditions when distance is prohibitive. Portfolio reviews held 3 times a week for design/technology applicants on campus.

Undergraduate Contact Lavona See, Assistant Director of Admissions, Otterbein College, Administration Building, Westerville, Ohio 43081; 614-823-1500, fax: 614-823-1200.

More about the College

Program Facilities Theater dance: 1,100-seat proscenium theater, 260-seat thrust theater, acting studio space, 5,000-square-foot scene shop, costume shop, design studio and electronic lighting system, 3-D CAD system, dance studio. Music: 275-seat recital hall, individual practice rooms, electronic music studio, computer lab, teaching and practice studios. Visual art: Dunlap Gallery, John Fisher Gallery, individual painting areas, ceramic and sculpture studio equipped with gas/electric kilns, pottery wheels and raku pit, Macintosh computer lab, photography darkroom, large drawing studio.

Student Performance/Exhibit Opportunities Theater/dance: six mainstage productions, nine to twelve senior workshop productions, spring dance concert and workshops, Summer Theater, directing projects. Music: four bands, Westerville Civic Symphony, percussion ensemble, small ensembles, three principal choirs, musical theater and jazz ensembles, Opera Theater, early music ensemble. Visual art; receptions and annual exhibits for graduating seniors, interaction with visiting artists and exhibit installation opportunities.

Special Programs Theater/dance: professional guest artist program, ten-week internship program in New York, Los Angeles, London, and regional theaters nationwide. Music; internships, opportunities to student teach abroad. Visual art: monthly lectures and exhibits by professional artists, opportunities to cross-register for course work at Columbus College of Art and Design, study-abroad programs.

Alumni Hundreds of alumni in various fields, including Dee Hoty, Tony Award nominee; David Weller, *ABC News* scenic designer, Robert Woods, Grammy Award winner, and founder and president, Telarc, Inc.

The arts at Otterbein College have been thriving since 1847. A solid liberal arts core of study, combined with practical career-training programs, provides students with a broad education in diverse areas of study as well as concentrated professional preparation in their chosen field.

The Department of Theater and Dance, styled as a conservatory atmosphere in a liberal arts setting, is committed to helping create artists that have both "depth and breadth." Professors strive to develop artists who have experience and knowledge not only in theater but also in other disciplines. This collage of experience gives artists the raw material to create great work as well as the tools with which to work. Students are prepared for the professional world, not only through the classroom but also through numerous audition and performance experiences. Design technology students are provided with intensive hands-on work on all productions. Utilizing guest artists, directors, and designers gives students the opportunity to work directly with professionals who are in "the business." The internship program offers students the opportunity to work with casting agents and regional theaters nationwide.

The Department of Music is a member of the National Association of Schools of Music. Student performances are an academic requirement of the department as well as an integral medium of sharing by students, faculty, and guest artists. Excluding individual student recitals and cabarets, the department hosted over fifty performances for the 1994–95 school year. Performances range from Opera Theater to faculty recitals to joint concerts with the Westerville Civic Symphony and Otterbein College Choirs. Voice and/or instrumental study is a vital part of each student's curriculum. Seven full-time and 25 adjunct faculty members work with students individually, building technique and exploring repertory.

The Department of Visual Arts faculty members are working artists who are regularly involved in all aspects of the profession. A series of foundation courses in design, drawing, and art history is integral for all students. From this conceptual, technical, and theoretical base, students then choose to concentrate in one of several art areas. Monthly exhibits and lectures coupled with an extensive College collection of African, Japanese, and Columbian art provide hands-on learning and enrich the classroom experience.

Columbus, Ohio's capital city, is becoming one of the most exciting cities in the Midwest. Points of interest span the continuum from the Columbus Museum of Art to City Center Mall, with its 160 shops and restaurants. The Columbus Symphony Orchestra, Ballet Met, Jazz Arts Group, and numerous community theaters provide a wide range of performances. Corporations such as Wendy's International and The Limited as well as historic German Village and the Short North round out this great city.

The College, which has always recognized and supported creativity as an important part of individual growth and development, believes that the arts, as an area of creative endeavor, are central to the human experience.

Pace University

New York, New York

Independent, coed. Total enrollment: 12,312.

Degrees Bachelor of Fine Arts in the area of theater. Majors: acting, set design, technical theater.

Theater Student Profile Fall 1994: 31 total; all matriculated undergraduate; 23% minorities, 74% females, 3% international.

Theater Faculty Total: 6; 3 full-time, 3 part-time; 100% of full-time faculty have terminal degrees. Undergraduate student–faculty ratio: 20:1.

Student Life Student groups include Honors Program, Pace Players, Club Programs.

Expenses for 1994–95 Application fee: $30. Comprehensive fee of $16,400 includes full-time tuition ($11,100), mandatory fees ($300), and college room and board ($5000). College room only: $3600. Part-time tuition: $360 per credit. Part-time mandatory fees per semester range from $45 to $100.

Application Procedures Deadline—freshmen and transfers: continuous. Required: essay, high school transcript, college transcript(s) for transfer students, minimum 2.0 high school GPA, 2 letters of recommendation, interview, audition, portfolio. Recommended: video. Auditions held continuously for acting applicants on campus; videotaped performances are permissible as a substitute for live auditions when distance is prohibitive. Portfolio reviews held continuously for technical theater and scene design applicants on campus.

Undergraduate Contact Undergraduate Admissions Department, Pace University, Pace Plaza, New York, New York 10038; 212-346-1323, fax: 212-346-1821.

Pennsylvania State University University Park Campus

University Park, Pennsylvania

State-related, coed. Small-town campus. Total enrollment: 38,294.

Degrees Bachelor of Fine Arts in the areas of production, music theater, stage management. Majors: music theater, production, stage management, theater arts/drama. Graduate degrees offered: Master of Fine Arts in the areas of acting, directing, costume, lighting, scene design, technical direction.

Theater Student Profile Fall 1994: 211 total; 174 matriculated undergraduate, 37 matriculated graduate; 9% minorities, 59% females.

Theater Faculty Total: 20; 19 full-time, 1 part-time; 98% of full-time faculty have terminal degrees. Graduate students teach a few undergraduate courses. Undergraduate student–faculty ratio: 15:1.

Student Life Student groups include University Park Ensemble, Minority Theatre Workshop, Drama Duo. Special housing available for theater students.

Expenses for 1994–95 Application fee: $35. State resident tuition: $4966 full-time, $208 per credit part-time. Nonresident tuition: $10,654 full-time, $445 per credit part-time. Part-time mandatory fees per semester range from $12 to $25. Full-time mandatory fees: $70. College room and board: $3920.

Financial Aid Program-specific awards for Fall of 1994: 1 Mona Shibley Bird Scholarship for above-average students ($500), 1 Golumbic Scholarship for upperclassmen ($1000), 2 Gallu Scholarships for freshmen ($1000), 2 Lethbridge-Jackson Awards for outstanding achievement ($300).

Application Procedures Deadline—freshmen and transfers: continuous. Required: essay, high school transcript, college transcript(s) for transfer students, minimum 2.0 high school GPA, 2 letters of recommendation, interview, audition, portfolio, SAT I or ACT test scores. Auditions held 7–8 times on campus and off campus in Chicago, IL; Long Beach, CA; New York, NY; videotaped performances are permissible as a substitute for live auditions if distance is prohibitive or scheduling is difficult. Portfolio reviews held 7–8 times on campus and off campus in Chicago, IL; Long Beach, CA; New York, NY; the submission of slides may be substituted for portfolios only if accompanied by interview.

Pennsylvania State University University Park Campus *(continued)*

Undergraduate Contact Margaret French, Professor, Department of Theatre Arts, Pennsylvania State University University Park Campus, 103 Arts Building, University Park, Pennsylvania 16802; 814-865-7586, fax: 814-865-7140.

Graduate Contact Richard Nichols, Professor, Department of Theatre Arts, Pennsylvania State University University Park Campus, 103 Arts Building, University Park, Pennsylvania 16802; 814-865-7586, fax: 814-865-7140.

Point Park College

Pittsburgh, Pennsylvania

Independent, coed. Urban campus. Total enrollment: 2,397.

Degrees Bachelor of Fine Arts in the areas of acting, musical theater, technical theater/design, arts management. Majors: arts management, music theater, theater arts/drama, theater design/technology. Cross-registration with Carnegie Mellon University, University of Pittsburgh, Chatham College, Robert Morris College, Duquesne University, Carlow College.

Theater Student Profile Fall 1994: 141 total; all matriculated undergraduate; 15% minorities, 70% females, 1% international.

Theater Faculty Total: 36; 9 full-time, 27 part-time; 80% of full-time faculty have terminal degrees. Graduate students do not teach undergraduate courses. Undergraduate student–faculty ratio: 14:1.

Student Life Student groups include Theater Association of Pennsylvania, American College Theater Foundation, University Resident Theater Association.

Expenses for 1995–96 Application fee: $20. Comprehensive fee of $15,624 includes full-time tuition ($10,552) and college room and board ($5072). Part-time tuition: $275 per credit. Special program-related fees: $265 for voice/piano private lessons, $20–$60 for music course fees, $335 for lab fees.

Financial Aid Program-specific awards for Fall of 1994: 8–26 Golden Key and Academic Scholarships for those demonstrating academic achievement and talent ($2500–$9000), 24–35 Apprenticeships for those demonstrating academic achievement and talent ($500–$2000), 39–49 Talent Scholarships for those demonstrating academic achievement and talent ($500–$3500).

Application Procedures Deadline—freshmen and transfers: June 1. Required: high school transcript, college transcript(s) for transfer students, minimum 2.0 high school GPA, letter of recommendation, interview, audition, portfolio, SAT I or ACT test scores. Recommended: resume. Auditions held 9 times on campus and off campus in Louisville, KY; San Juan, PR; Lincoln, NE; Colorado; recorded music is permissible as a substitute for live auditions on a case-by-case basis with permission of the chair and videotaped performances are permissible as a substitute for live auditions if distance is prohibitive or in special circumstances. Portfolio reviews held 9 times on campus.

Undergraduate Contact Joseph McGoldrick, Assistant to the Chair, Department of Fine, Applied and Performing Arts, Point Park College, 201 Wood Street, Pittsburgh, Pennsylvania 15222-1984; 800-321-0129.

More about the Program

The program of Fine, Applied, and Performing Arts (FAPA) at Point Park College is conservatory-oriented within a liberal arts context. Students receive intense grounding in their specialty and a well-rounded education. Because the faculty of PAPA believes that performing arts majors develop best in front of a live audience, the program offers many performing opportunities for students at The Playhouse of Point Park College.

Nationally renowned, The Playhouse (formerly called "The Pittsburgh Playhouse") is the performance facility for the Department of Fine, Applied, and Performing Arts. Here, students participate in live theater experiences before a subscription audience. Containing three working theaters, this sixty-year-old facility is fully staffed by a production team of designers and artisans who train and supervise student apprentices in building, designing, lighting, and managing shows. The front-of-house staff, box office, and public relations personnel engage all students in the full range of theater operations. The season, which features student actors, dancers, designers and stage managers, consists of five Playhouse Junior Shows for children; four College Theater Company dramas and musicals; and two Playhouse Theater Company presentations for professional faculty, alumni, visiting artists, and selected undergraduates, who perform in them.

The dance students are featured in three Playhouse Dance Theater productions, plus a Playhouse Junior Children's Ballet, as well as public school outreach program in cooperation with the Gateway to Music organization.

Arts management majors receive practical on-stage experience as well as training in business, public relations, and budgeting, which culminate in two major internships with arts groups outside the College.

The newly formed stage management concentration similarly requires outside internships.

The innovative children's theater degree provides opportunities for majors to plan, teach, and direct creative drama activities. Venues for these opportunities exist within the Children's School of the Education Department, Playhouse Junior, and classes offered by the Community Conservatories of Dance, Music, and Theater.

Pittsburgh is a vibrant arts and education center. FAPA students can reach the Pittsburgh Symphony, Opera, Ballet, Dance Council, and public theaters, as well as eight other institutions of higher learning, within a 15-minute drive. The whole city is, in a sense, a performance laboratory.

FAPA has over 150 graduates performing in touring companies, on Broadway, in dance groups, in movies, on television, and in other theaters, as well as many more teaching in schools, on faculties, choreographing, writing, directing, and stage managing across the world. Within the last eighteen months, graduates of the program have had roles in New York and national touring productions of *Carousel, Cats, Gentleman Prefer Blondes, Joseph and the Technicolor Dreamcoat, Tommy, Damn Yankees, The Rink, and Kiss of the Spider Women.* Others have also appeared on screen in *Pulp Fiction* and *NYPD Blue.*

Faculty members are working professionals in acting, singing, dancing, choreographing, writing, composing, painting, designing, and other specialties. Guest and master teachers in musical theater, voice and speech, and dance are regularly featured. Guest artists have included Cicely Berry, Paul Gavert, Albert Poland, Barbara Pontecorvo, Edward Villella, Maxine Sherman, and Claire Bataille.

The program offers eight dance studios; three theater complexes at The Playhouse of Point Park College; performance opportunities for students in front of subscription audiences; on-site costume/set construction apprenticeships; nine private signing and piano instructors; college choir; and art and design classes.

During the summer, there is an International Summer Dance program (open by audition and special registration only) featuring renowned performers in the world of dance. The six-week session offers jazz, ballet, and modern dance from a distinguished faculty including Laura Alonso, Roberto Muniz, Miguel Canpaneira, Alexander Filipov, Michael Uthoff, and Whilheim Burman.

Prospective students must apply and be accepted by the College. An audition or an interview by faculty members is required of all majors. Training scholarships and apprenticeships ranging from $750 to $2,500 are available. Additional scholarship support may be available to students with distinguished academic credentials.

Potter College of Arts, Humanities, and Social Sciences

See Western Kentucky University, Potter College of Arts, Humanities, and Social Sciences

Purchase College, State University of New York

Purchase, New York

State-supported, coed. Small-town campus. Total enrollment: 2,498.

Degrees Bachelor of Fine Arts in the areas of acting, design technology. Majors: acting, design technology, theater arts/drama. Graduate degrees offered: Master of Fine Arts in the areas of theater design, theater technology.

Theater Student Profile Fall 1994: 166 total; 158 matriculated undergraduate, 8 matriculated graduate; 14% minorities, 37% females, 4% international.

Theater Faculty Total: 59; 12 full-time, 47 part-time; 75% of full-time faculty have terminal degrees. Graduate students do not teach undergraduate courses. Undergraduate student–faculty ratio: 4:1.

Expenses for 1995–96 Application fee: $25. State resident tuition: $3400 full-time, $137 per credit part-time. Nonresident tuition: $8300 full-time, $346 per credit part-time. Part-time mandatory fees: $13.30 per credit. Full-time mandatory fees: $399. College room and board: $4872. College room only: $3130.

Application Procedures Deadline—freshmen and transfers: May 15. Notification date—freshmen and transfers: July 1. Required: essay, high school transcript, interview, audition. Auditions held at various times for acting students on campus and off campus in Seattle, WA; New York, NY; San Francisco, CA; Chicago, IL; Houston, TX; Miami, FL; Los Angeles; CA; videotaped performances are permissible as a substitute for live auditions for international applicants.

Undergraduate Contact Janice Hamm, Assistant Director, Admissions Office, Purchase College, State University of New York, 735 Anderson Hill Road, Purchase, New York 10577; 914-251-6300, fax: 914-251-6314.

Graduate Contact Michael Cesario, Director, Design Technology Department, Purchase College, State University of New York, 735 Anderson Hill Road, Purchase, New York 10577; 914-251-6850, fax: 914-251-6839.

Professional training for a working career in acting, design technology, and film is the dominant goal of the program. Young artists are selected for both the intensity of their interest in becoming professionals and their professional potential. The program offers focused and in-depth training in theater and film with a faculty that is working, creating, and succeeding in New York's professional world.

The community of students and professional faculty are constantly enriched by the creative bustle and aesthetic influence of New York City, just 30 minutes away. They work and strive together on the modern Purchase campus and Performing Arts Center located in Westchester County, a beautiful and elegant suburb of New York City.

Practical learning and practical experience is the daily life for the student artist at Purchase. State-of-the-art equipment, theaters, and work spaces for every aspect of training abound in this woods-surrounded center of contemporary art and learning.

All classes, rehearsals, productions, and filming are taught and supervised by men and women who are contributing participants in the professional artistic life of New York City. These artist-teachers have a common goal: to thoroughly train young artists so that the individual creativity of each student is preserved and augmented by the most strenuous and critical practice and performance standards possible.

In an intense and joyful collaboration, the student and teacher discover not only what art is, but how to make it happen. In addition to this serious concentration in the arts, each student is offered one class a semester in letters and/or sciences so that a grounding in our cultural heritage is part of his or her development. Life at Purchase consists of a rich social intermix of the performing and visual arts with the more traditional academic life of the College of Letters and Sciences.

The student's life after graduation is a powerfully active concern of the training program. Therefore, as the student gains proficiency, his or her work has gradually been presented to the professional community, and, by

Purchase College, State University of New York
(continued)

the time of graduation, when the work is formally introduced to that professional community using New York City presentations of actors; internships, portfolio reviews, and faculty personal contacts for designers; and completed student films (for filmmakers), Purchase students find that an extraordinary number of doors open for them: agents, producers, theaters, film companies, and television producers are available for the next creative and working step of the Purchase graduate.

The Division of Theatre Arts and Film is now graduating some of the most exciting and successful young actors, designers, and filmmakers in America. It is not only the flagship program of the State University of New York but also among the finest and most prestigious of the conservatory programs offered in the disciplines of theatre and film.

Roosevelt University

Chicago, Illinois

Independent, coed. Urban campus. Total enrollment: 6,709.

Degrees Bachelor of Fine Arts in the areas of theater, musical theater. Majors: directing, music theater, performance. Graduate degrees offered: Master of Fine Arts in the areas of theater, musical theater.

Theater Student Profile Fall 1994: 150 total; 90 matriculated undergraduate, 60 matriculated graduate.

Theater Faculty Total: 23; 3 full-time, 20 part-time; 50% of full-time faculty have terminal degrees. Graduate students teach about a quarter undergraduate courses. Undergraduate student–faculty ratio: 10:1.

Expenses for 1995–96 Application fee: $25. Comprehensive fee of $14,485 includes full-time tuition ($9450), mandatory fees ($85), and college room and board ($4950). College room only: $3850. Part-time tuition: $315 per semester hour. Part-time mandatory fees: $85 per year.

Financial Aid Program-specific awards for Fall of 1994 available.

Application Procedures Deadline—freshmen and transfers: continuous. Required: high school transcript, minimum 2.0 high school GPA, audition, SAT I or ACT test scores, minimum 2.0 college GPA for transfer students. Auditions held continuously on campus and off campus in Muncie, IN; videotaped performances are permissible as a substitute for live auditions.

Contact Yolanda Lyon-Miller, Head, Faculty of Theater Arts, Roosevelt University, 430 South Michigan Avenue, Chicago, Illinois 60605; 312-341-3719, fax: 312-341-3680.

Mason Gross School of the Arts

Rutgers, The State University of New Jersey

New Brunswick, New Jersey

State-supported, coed. Small-town campus. Total enrollment: 647.

Degrees Bachelor of Fine Arts in the area of theater arts. Majors: acting, design, production and management specialities. Graduate degrees offered: Master of Fine Arts in the area of theater arts.

Theater Student Profile Fall 1994: 146 total; 72 matriculated undergraduate, 74 matriculated graduate; 21% minorities, 36% females, 1% international.

Theater Faculty Total: 48; 12 full-time, 36 part-time; 50% of full-time faculty have terminal degrees. Graduate students teach a few undergraduate courses.

Expenses for 1995–96 Application fee: $50. State resident tuition: $3786 full-time, $122.50 per credit hour part-time. Nonresident tuition: $7707 full-time, $249.75 per credit hour part-time. Mandatory fees range from $105 to $1045 full-time, $155 to $187 per year part-time, according to college of affiliation. College room and board: $4253. Special program-related fees: $30–$100 for class supplies, models, transportation to museums, salon costumes.

Application Procedures Deadline—freshmen: February 15; transfers: March 15. Notification date—freshmen and transfers: July 1. Required: high school transcript, college transcript(s) for transfer students, interview, SAT I or ACT test scores, audition for acting majors, portfolio for design majors. Recommended: essay, 2 letters of recommendation. Auditions held on campus and off campus; videotaped performances are permissible as a substitute for live auditions when distance if prohibitive. Portfolio reviews held on campus and off campus.

Undergraduate Contact Dr. Elizabeth Mitchell, Assistant Vice President for University Undergraduate Admissions, Rutgers, The State University of New Jersey, P.O. Box 2101, New Brunswick, New Jersey 08903-2101; 908-445-3770, fax: 908-932-0237.

Graduate Contact Dr. Donald Taylor, Director of Graduate Admissions, Rutgers, The State University of New Jersey, Van Nest Hall, New Brunswick, New Jersey 08903; 908-932-7711, fax: 908-932-8231.

Samford University

Birmingham, Alabama

Independent-religious, coed. Suburban campus. Total enrollment: 4,571.

Degrees Bachelor of Fine Arts in the area of performance/technical theater. Majors: theater arts/drama. Cross-registration with University of Alabama at Birmingham.

Theater Student Profile Fall 1994: 25 total; all matriculated undergraduate; 65% females.

Theater Faculty Total: 4; 2 full-time, 2 part-time; 100% of full-time faculty have terminal degrees. Graduate students do not teach undergraduate courses.

Student Life Student groups include Alpha Psi Omega.

Expenses for 1995–96 Application fee: $25. Comprehensive fee of $12,492 includes full-time tuition ($8648) and college room and board ($3844). Part-time tuition: $284 per semester hour.

Financial Aid Program-specific awards for Fall of 1994: 6–8 Bonnie Bolding Swearingen Scholarships for program majors ($7500), 2–3 Bates-Norris Scholarships for program majors ($1500), 2–4 Gail Patrick Scholarships for program majors ($2000).

Application Procedures Deadline—freshmen: April 1; transfers: continuous. Auditions held 1 time on campus.

Undergraduate Contact Harold L. Hunt, Chair, Speech Communication and Theatre Department, Samford University, 800 Lakeshore Drive, Birmingham, Alabama 35229; 205-870-2952.

Schmidt College of Arts and Humanities

See Florida Atlantic University, Schmidt College of Arts and Humanities

Shenandoah University

Winchester, Virginia

Independent-religious, coed. Small-town campus. Total enrollment: 1,652.

Degrees Bachelor of Fine Arts in the area of music theater. Majors: music theater.

Theater Student Profile Fall 1994: 90 total; all matriculated undergraduate; 7% minorities, 59% females, 1% international.

Theater Faculty Total: 8; 6 full-time, 2 part-time; 67% of full-time faculty have terminal degrees. Graduate students do not teach undergraduate courses. Undergraduate student–faculty ratio: 11:1.

Student Life Student groups include Alpha Psi Omega Fraternity Shows, Special Workshops, Children's Theater.

Expenses for 1995–96 Application fee: $30. Comprehensive fee of $16,270 includes full-time tuition ($11,470) and college room and board ($4800). Part-time tuition: $360 per semester hour.

Financial Aid Program-specific awards for Fall of 1994: 25 Talent Scholarships for program students ($500).

Application Procedures Deadline—freshmen and transfers: continuous. Required: high school transcript, college transcript(s) for transfer students, minimum 2.0 high school GPA, interview, video, audition, SAT I or ACT test scores. Recommended: letter of recommendation, portfolio. Auditions held 10 times on campus and off campus in various cities; recorded music is permissible as a substitute for live auditions if a campus visit is impossible and videotaped performances are permissible as a substitute for live auditions if a campus visit is impossible. Portfolio reviews held throughout the year for design students on campus and off campus in various cities.

Undergraduate Contact Michael Carpenter, Director, Admissions Office, Shenandoah University, 1460 University Drive, Winchester, Virginia 22601-5195; 540-665-4581, fax: 540-665-4627, E-mail address: admit@su.edu.

Simon Fraser University

Burnaby, British Columbia

Province-supported, coed. Suburban campus. Total enrollment: 18,252.

Degrees Bachelor of Fine Arts in the area of theater. Majors: theater arts/drama. Graduate degrees offered: Master of Fine Arts in the area of interdisciplinary studies.

Theater Student Profile Fall 1994: 214 total; all matriculated undergraduate.

Theater Faculty Total: 2; 2 full-time; 50% of full-time faculty have terminal degrees. Graduate students teach a few undergraduate courses. Undergraduate student–faculty ratio: 70:1.

Student Life Student groups include Black Box Theater Company.

Expenses for 1994–95 Application fee: $20. Canadian resident tuition: $2190 full-time, $73 per credit hour part-time. Nonresident tuition: $6570 full-time, $219 per credit hour part-time. Part-time mandatory fees: $50 per trimester. (All figures are in Canadian dollars.). Full-time mandatory fees: $178. College room only: $2120.

Financial Aid Program-specific awards for Fall of 1994: 1 Murray Farr Award for program majors ($500), 5 Adaline May Clark Scholarships for program majors ($100–$500).

Application Procedures Deadline—freshmen and transfers: May 1. Required: high school transcript, college transcript(s) for transfer students, minimum 3.0 high school GPA, audition. Auditions held 2 times on campus and off campus. Portfolio reviews held on campus and off campus.

Meadows School of the Arts

Southern Methodist University

Dallas, Texas

Independent-religious, coed. Suburban campus. Total enrollment: 9,014.

Southern Methodist University *(continued)*

Degrees Bachelor of Fine Arts in the area of theater. Majors: acting, theater arts/drama. Graduate degrees offered: Master of Fine Arts in the area of theater.

Theater Student Profile Fall 1994: 148 total; 121 matriculated undergraduate, 27 matriculated graduate.

Theater Faculty Total: 17; 17 full-time.

Student Life Special housing available for theater students.

Expenses for 1994–95 Application fee: $40. Comprehensive fee of $19,474 includes full-time tuition ($12,772), mandatory fees ($1624), and college room and board ($5078). College room only: $2426. Part-time tuition: $532 per credit hour. Part-time mandatory fees: $68 per semester.

Financial Aid Program-specific awards for Fall of 1994: 20 Meadows Artistic Scholarships for talented program majors ($1000–$5000).

Application Procedures Deadline—freshmen and transfers: March 1. Required: essay, high school transcript, college transcript(s) for transfer students, letter of recommendation, audition, SAT I or ACT test scores. Recommended: interview. Auditions held 20 times on campus and off campus in various locations.

Undergraduate Contact Charles J. Helfert, Associate Dean, Meadows School of the Arts, Southern Methodist University, P.O. Box 750356, Dallas, Texas 75275-0356; 214-768-3217, fax: 214-768-3272.

Graduate Contact Jeannette Garnsey, Director, Graduate Admissions and Records, Meadows School of the Arts, Southern Methodist University, P.O. Box 750356, Dallas, Texas 75275-0356; 214-768-3765, fax: 214-768-3272.

Southern Oregon State College

Ashland, Oregon

State-supported, coed. Small-town campus. Total enrollment: 4,554.

Degrees Bachelor of Fine Arts in the area of theater arts. Majors: theater arts/drama.

Theater Student Profile Fall 1994: 110 total; all matriculated undergraduate; 8% minorities, 53% females, 3% international.

Theater Faculty Total: 9; 5 full-time, 4 part-time; 100% of full-time faculty have terminal degrees. Graduate students do not teach undergraduate courses. Undergraduate student–faculty ratio: 20:1.

Expenses for 1994–95 Application fee: $50. State resident tuition: $2835 full-time. Nonresident tuition: $7824 full-time. Part-time tuition per quarter ranges from $114 to $875 for state residents, $114 to $2399 for nonresidents. College room and board: $3562.

Financial Aid Program-specific awards for Fall of 1994: 1 Angus Bowmer Award for performers ($1000), 1 Harry Bartell Award for actors ($1500), 1 Leon Mulling Award for program majors ($1500), 10 Departmental Awards for program majors ($500).

Application Procedures Deadline—freshmen and transfers: continuous. Required: high school transcript, college transcript(s) for transfer students, minimum 3.0 high school GPA, 3 letters of recommendation, interview, audition, portfolio, SAT I or ACT test scores, minimum combined SAT I score of 1,010, minimum composite ACT score of 21. Auditions held 2 times on campus. Portfolio reviews held 2 times on campus; the submission of slides may be substituted for portfolios.

Undergraduate Contact Allen H. Blaszak, Director of Admissions, Southern Oregon State College, 1250 Siskiyou Boulevard, Ashland, Oregon 97520; 503-552-6411, fax: 503-552-6329.

Southwest Missouri State University

Springfield, Missouri

State-supported, coed. Suburban campus. Total enrollment: 17,310.

Degrees Bachelor of Fine Arts in the area of theater. Majors: theater arts/drama.

Theater Student Profile Fall 1994: 156 total; 145 matriculated undergraduate, 11 matriculated graduate; 4% minorities, 58% females.

Theater Faculty Total: 12; 12 full-time; 80% of full-time faculty have terminal degrees. Graduate students do not teach undergraduate courses. Undergraduate student–faculty ratio: 18:1.

Student Life Student groups include In-School Players, Footnotes Entertainment Troupe, Peer Education Troupe.

Expenses for 1995–96 Application fee: $15. State resident tuition: $2370 full-time, $79 per credit hour part-time. Nonresident tuition: $4898 full-time. Part-time mandatory fees per semester range from $41 to $88. Part-time tuition per credit hour for nonresidents: $79 for the first 3 credits, $158 for the next 8 credits. Full-time mandatory fees: $176. College room and board: $2722 (minimum). College room only: $1755 (minimum).

Financial Aid Program-specific awards for Fall of 1994: 10 Theatre Activity Awards for program majors ($1700), 6 In-School Players for program majors ($1700), 10 Out-of-State Waivers for program majors ($2550), 8 Footnotes Entertainment Troupe Awards for program majors ($1700).

Application Procedures Deadline—freshmen and transfers: August 1. Required: high school transcript, college transcript(s) for transfer students, minimum 2.0 high school GPA, ACT test score only, minimum composite ACT score of 18, standing in top 67% of graduating class.

Undergraduate Contact Robert H. Bradley, Head, Department of Theatre and Dance, Southwest Missouri State University, 901 South National, Springfield, Missouri 65804; 417-836-5268, fax: 417-836-6940.

Graduate Contact Robert H. Bradley, Head, Department of Theatre and Dance, Southwest Missouri State University, 901 South National, Springfield, Missouri 65804; 417-836-5268, fax: 417-836-6940.

Southwestern University

Georgetown, Texas

Independent-religious, coed. Suburban campus. Total enrollment: 1,238.

Degrees Bachelor of Fine Arts in the area of theater. Majors: theater arts/drama. Cross-registration with Ohio Wesleyan University.

Theater Student Profile Fall 1994: 52 total; all matriculated undergraduate; 5% minorities, 65% females.

Theater Faculty Total: 6; 4 full-time, 2 part-time; 100% of full-time faculty have terminal degrees. Graduate students do not teach undergraduate courses. Undergraduate student–faculty ratio: 10:1.

Student Life Student groups include Alpha Psi Omega, Mask and Wig Players.

Expenses for 1995–96 Application fee: $25. Comprehensive fee of $17,570 includes full-time tuition ($12,700) and college room and board ($4870). Part-time tuition: $530 per semester hour.

Financial Aid Program-specific awards for Fall of 1994: 15 Departmental Scholarships for undergraduates ($1500).

Application Procedures Deadline—freshmen and transfers: April 1. Required: essay, high school transcript, minimum 3.0 high school GPA, letter of recommendation, interview, audition. Auditions held by appointment on campus and off campus in the Texas Educational Theatre Association; videotaped performances are permissible as a substitute for live auditions when distance is prohibitive.

Undergraduate Contact Richard J. Hossalla, Chair, Theater and Communications Department, Southwestern University, 1001 East University Avenue, Georgetown, Texas 78626; 512-863-1365, fax: 512-863-5788.

State University of New York College at Fredonia

Fredonia, New York

State-supported, coed. Small-town campus. Total enrollment: 4,892.

Degrees Bachelor of Fine Arts in the areas of acting, musical theater, production design. Majors: theater arts/drama.

Theater Student Profile Fall 1994: 130 total; all matriculated undergraduate; 65% females.

Theater Faculty Total: 7; 7 full-time; 100% of full-time faculty have terminal degrees. Graduate students do not teach undergraduate courses. Undergraduate student–faculty ratio: 12:1.

Student Life Student groups include Performing Arts Company, Opera Theatre, Orchesis Dance.

Expenses for 1995–96 Application fee: $25. State resident tuition: $3400 full-time, $137 per credit hour part-time. Nonresident tuition: $8300 full-time, $346 per credit hour part-time. Part-time mandatory fees: $17.35 per credit hour. Full-time mandatory fees: $519. College room and board: $4670. College room only: $2750. Special program-related fees: $12 for visiting artist program.

Financial Aid Program-specific awards for Fall of 1994: 1–2 Jack Cogdill Scholarships for incoming freshmen ($1000–$2000).

Application Procedures Deadline—freshmen and transfers: continuous. Required: high school transcript, college transcript(s) for transfer students, 2 letters of recommendation, audition, portfolio, SAT I or ACT test scores. Recommended: minimum 3.0 high school GPA. Auditions held 8 times on campus and off campus in Selden, NY; Troy, NY; recorded music is permissible as a substitute for live auditions and videotaped performances are permissible as a substitute for live auditions. Portfolio reviews held on campus; the submission of slides may be substituted for portfolios.

Undergraduate Contact Chairperson, Theater Arts Department, State University of New York College at Fredonia, Rockefeller Arts Center, Fredonia, New York 14063; 716-673-3596, fax: 716-673-3338.

State University of New York College at Purchase

See Purchase College, State University of New York

State University of New York at New Paltz

New Paltz, New York

State-supported, coed. Rural campus. Total enrollment: 7,897.

Degrees Bachelor of Fine Arts in the area of scenography. Majors: music theater.

Theater Faculty Total: 3; 3 full-time; 66% of full-time faculty have terminal degrees. Graduate students do not teach undergraduate courses.

Expenses for 1995–96 Application fee: $25. State resident tuition: $3400 full-time, $142 per credit part-time. Nonresident tuition: $8300 full-time, $346 per credit part-time. Part-time mandatory fees per semester range from $40.60 to $148.60. Full-time mandatory fees: $351. College room and board: $4918. College room only: $2920.

Application Procedures Deadline—freshmen: May 1; transfers: June 1. Required: high school transcript, interview, portfolio, SAT I or ACT test scores. Portfolio reviews held 2 times on campus; the submission of slides may be substituted for portfolios.

Undergraduate Contact Katherine Ingram, Chair, Theatre Arts Department, State University of New York

State University of New York at New Paltz
(continued)

at New Paltz, 75 South Manheim Boulevard, New Paltz, New York 12561-2449; 914-257-3865.

Stephen F. Austin State University

Nacogdoches, Texas

State-supported, coed. Small-town campus. Total enrollment: 12,206.

Degrees Bachelor of Fine Arts in the area of theater. Majors: performance, technical theater. Cross-registration with Rose Bruford College, United Kingdom.

Theater Student Profile Fall 1994: 105 total; all matriculated undergraduate; 2% minorities, 65% females.

Theater Faculty Total: 10; 7 full-time, 3 part-time; 85% of full-time faculty have terminal degrees. Graduate students teach a few undergraduate courses. Undergraduate student–faculty ratio: 18:1.

Student Life Student groups include Beta Phi Chapter of Alpha Psi Omega.

Expenses for 1994–95 State resident tuition: $896 full-time. Nonresident tuition: $5472 full-time, $171 per semester hour part-time. State resident part-time tuition per semester ranges from $100 to $308. Part-time mandatory fees per semester range from $32.25 to $166.50. Full-time mandatory fees: $832. College room and board: $3542. Special program-related fees: $7 for supplies, $8 for theater admission.

Financial Aid Program-specific awards for Fall of 1994: 8–10 Department Scholarships for incoming students passing audition evaluations ($750–$1000), 1 Gray Scholarship for Nacogdoches County, TX residents ($250), 5–8 Stokes Foundation Scholarships for enrolled students ($600–$1000), 1 Cochran Scholarship for enrolled students ($350), 1 Alumni Scholarship for enrolled students ($200).

Application Procedures Deadline—freshmen and transfers: continuous. Required: high school transcript, college transcript(s) for transfer students, minimum 2.0 high school GPA, portfolio, SAT I or ACT test scores, evaluation interview at end of sophomore year for entrance into BFA program. Auditions held on campus and off campus in conjunction with Texas Educational Theatre Association Convention and Junior College Theatre Festival. Portfolio reviews held 4 times for design and technology applicants on campus and off campus; the submission of slides may be substituted for portfolios if a campus visit is impossible.

Undergraduate Contact Dr. Clarence W. Bahs, Chairman, Theatre Department, Stephen F. Austin State University, P.O. Box 9090 SFA Station, Nacogdoches, Texas 75962-9090; 409-568-4003, fax: 409-568-1168.

Stephens College

Columbia, Missouri

Independent, women only. Urban campus. Total enrollment: 600.

Degrees Bachelor of Fine Arts in the area of theater arts. Majors: theater arts/drama. Cross-registration with University of Missouri&–Columbia.

Theater Student Profile Fall 1994: 70 total; all matriculated undergraduate; 100% females.

Theater Faculty Total: 11; 8 full-time, 3 part-time; 80% of full-time faculty have terminal degrees. Graduate students do not teach undergraduate courses. Undergraduate student–faculty ratio: 11:1.

Student Life Student groups include Warehouse Theatre.

Expenses for 1995–96 Application fee: $25. Comprehensive fee of $19,770 includes full-time tuition ($14,400) and college room and board ($5370). College room only: $2900. Part-time tuition: $1140 per course.

Financial Aid Program-specific awards for Fall of 1994: 2 Musical Theater Awards for vocalists ($3000), 1 Annie Potts Award for actors ($3000), 1 Patricia Barry Award for actors ($1500), 1 Maude Adams Award for actors ($1000).

Application Procedures Deadline—freshmen and transfers: April 1. Notification date—freshmen: continuous; transfers: August 1. Required: essay, high school transcript, minimum 2.0 high school GPA, 2 letters of recommendation, interview. Recommended: portfolio. Portfolio reviews held as needed for design/technical applicants on campus and off campus.

Undergraduate Contact Office of Admission, Stephens College, Box 2121, Columbia, Missouri 65215; 800-876-7207, fax: 314-876-7248.

More about the College

Stephens owes its reputation as a fine theater program to its imaginative programs and its faculty made up of teacher-performers/artists. Whether it's a question about stage presence or stage lighting, a professional is there to help. Actor/teachers work with students in the classroom as well as act opposite them on stage. No other undergraduate program offers this apprentice-like environment. The B.F.A. at Stephens is earned in 3 years and 2 summers. Stephens offers intensive training in acting, musical theater, design, directing and stage management, with a schedule of eleven productions yearly plus two summer programs.

Special Programs Summer Theatre Institute: Students work 5½ days for seven weeks, beginning with dance movement, followed by acting, technical, management, and audition classes. In the evening, students are rehearsing and doing production work. The principal aim of STI is to give students the chance to take the theatrical knowledge out of the classroom and apply it to a grinding schedule. Okoboji Summer Theatre: Stephens has operated this stock theater since 1958. Nine plays in ten weeks are presented in a 450-seat proscenium stage on a weekly stock schedule, with performances running Tuesday through Sunday. Four children's plays are presented in the Boji Bantam Theatre. The value of a summer stock experience transcends the acquisition of knowledge and skill in theater. Learning to live and work closely with a group under the pressure of producing a new show every week is a valuable experience for any career.

Scholarships Annie Potts Designing Women Scholarship in Acting ($3000), Musical Theatre Scholarships ($3000), Full Technical and Design Scholarships (full tuition). All scholarships require a 2.5 GPA, one letter of recommendation, and an interview. Students must be working toward a B.F.A. in theater that is earned in 3 years and 2 summers. Videotapes or audiotapes are required for acting scholarships and a portfolio for design and technical scholarships. Please call or write the program for specific application guidelines.

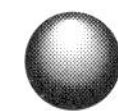

Syracuse University

Syracuse, New York

Independent, coed. Urban campus. Total enrollment: 14,550.

Degrees Bachelor of Fine Arts in the areas of drama, musical theater, design/technical theater. Majors: apparel design, design/technical theater, theater arts/drama. Graduate degrees offered: Master of Fine Arts in the areas of drama, design/technical theater.

Theater Student Profile Fall 1994: 430 total; 200 matriculated undergraduate, 15 matriculated graduate, 215 nondegree; 11% minorities, 63% females, 1% international.

Theater Faculty Total: 23; 13 full-time, 10 part-time; 69% of full-time faculty have terminal degrees. Graduate students teach a few undergraduate courses. Undergraduate student–faculty ratio: 12:1.

Student Life Student groups include Syracuse University Musical Stage, First Year Players, Black Box Players.

Expenses for 1995–96 Application fee: $40. Comprehensive fee of $23,190 includes full-time tuition ($15,910), mandatory fees ($370), and college room and board ($6910). College room only: $3760. Special program-related fees: $145 for private music lessons, $10 for piano maintenance.

Financial Aid Program-specific awards for Fall of 1994: 17 Chancellor's Awards for those demonstrating academic achievement ($6000), 40 Dean's Awards for those demonstrating academic achievement ($4000).

Application Procedures Deadline—freshmen: February 1; transfers: July 1. Notification date—freshmen: March 15; transfers: August 15. Required: essay, high school transcript, college transcript(s) for transfer students, minimum 2.0 high school GPA, audition, portfolio, SAT I or ACT test scores, high school counselor evaluation. Recommended: minimum 3.0 high school GPA, interview. Auditions held 10 times on campus and off campus in New York, NY; Washington, DC; videotaped performances are permissible as a substitute for live auditions. Portfolio reviews held 7 times for design/technical theater applicants on campus; the submission of slides may be substituted for portfolios.

Undergraduate Contact Coordinator of Recruiting, College of Visual and Performing Arts, Syracuse University, 202P Crouse College, Syracuse, New York 13244-1010; 315-443-2769, fax: 315-443-1935, E-mail address: admissu@vpa.syr.edu.

Graduate Contact Graduate School, Syracuse University, Suite 303 Bowne Hall, Syracuse, New York 13244; 315-443-4492.

More about the University

Program Facilities Regent Theatre Complex: John D. Archbold Theatre (500 seats), Arthur Storch Theatre (200 seats), Black Box Theatre 960 seats), Sutton Pavilion (75-seat cabaret space). New studio and classroom building: dance studios, seminar rooms, design labs with a state-of-the-art CAD lab, lecture rooms, performance/rehearsal studios, music practice rooms, and shower and locker rooms.

Faculty, Resident Artists, and Alumni Many faculty members are members of the Actors' Equity Association; all are working artists as well as teachers. Several Syracuse Stage professionals, including artistic director

Ingrid Rogers

Actor, *All My Children, Carlito's Way*

My father wanted me to go to business school—something professional. *Acting wasn't professional!* I was a business major, but I wasn't happy, so I followed my heart and changed to drama without telling Dad. I then gained practical acting experience at the American Academy of Dramatic Arts, and was invited into the elite third-year performance program—the Academy Company. That led to my contact with and my contract for *All My Children.*

Syracuse University *(continued)*

Tazewell Thompson, teach in the drama program. Among the ranks of alumni are Tony award winners; New York City talent and casting agents; actors on Broadway, television, and in movies; screenplay and movie writers; and artistic and managing directors of theater companies.

Student Theater Opportunities Department of Drama productions, Syracuse Stage, Black Box Players student group, After Ours cabaret theater series.

Special Programs The Department of Drama's partnership with Syracuse Stage allows undergraduates to experience professional theater while in school. Study abroad in London is offered through SU's Division of International Programs Abroad (DIPA). Internships at Syracuse Stage, in New York City, or in Los Angeles, for credit or in a volunteer capacity, are available. Each Wednesday, Drama Lab brings students together with visiting artists, alumni, agents, union representatives, or to perform scenes from class. Qualified senior travel to New York City in the Spring for "Scene Night," a presentation of scenes and songs for New York agents and casting directors. All University activities are available to students in the Department of Drama. Honors program is available for students who desire a rigorous academic challenge.

The Department of Drama at Syracuse University offers students the chance to nurture their creative abilities through a unique combination of active faculty, diverse performance and staging opportunities, excellent facilities, and a liberal education. Students prepare for a professional career in theater beginning with the first semester; four years are spent in intensive work in a student's major field of study in tandem with academic course work taken in other areas of the University.

The first year is a nonperformance year that allows young actors to focus on developing their basic acting and musical theater skills. From the second year on, drama students compete for roles in the twenty to thirty productions produced each year by the Department of Drama, Syracuse Stage, Black Box Players, and the After Ours cabaret series. Considered an extension of classroom work, mainstage Drama Department productions are reserved for drama majors only. In addition, drama majors may earn Equity points by working in Syracuse Stage productions.

Design/technical theater majors at SU have a particular advantage: they can work as assistants to professional designers on Syracuse Stage productions and as assistants to faculty designers on mainstage Drama Department productions. They may also create their own designs in the Black Box and After Ours shows. Junior and senior design majors can create their own designs for the department mainstage shows. In addition, a unique partnership with the School of Art and Design provides opportunities for design/technical theater freshmen to develop their drawing and sketching skills.

The Regent Theatre Complex, shared by the Department of Drama and Syracuse Stage, houses four performance spaces that provide a broad range of possibilities.

The department's affiliation with Syracuse Stage, one of the country's outstanding Equity theater companies, opens the world of professional theater to students. Faculty members are not only outstanding teachers and mentors but also successful theater professionals. All performance and studio classes in acting, design, and musical theater, including freshman courses, are taught by full-time faculty.

Graduates of the Department of Drama are involved in every aspect of professional theater, from lead roles in Broadway plays and musicals and television dramas to casting directors and Actors' Equity Association staff members. The Department maintains close ties to active alumni associations in New York, Chicago, and Los Angeles.

Through the University's Division of International Programs (DIPA), students can study drama for a semester in London. Internships with one of London's Fringe theaters are also available for qualified students.

The activities of the Department of Drama are an integral part of the College of Visual and Performing Arts, which also governs programs in art and design, music, and speech communication. The College serves as the center of SU's cultural life, on a campus whose diverse schedule of events could only be found at a large university.

The city of Syracuse itself offers rich culture; it is a regular stop for touring companies of popular Broadway musicals and experimental theater troupes and is home to the Syracuse Symphony Orchestra, the Syracuse Opera, and the Society for New Music.

Texas Christian University

Fort Worth, Texas

Independent-religious, coed. Suburban campus. Total enrollment: 6,706.

Degrees Bachelor of Fine Arts in the area of theater. Majors: design technology, performance.

Theater Student Profile Fall 1994: 48 total; all matriculated undergraduate; 16% minorities, 66% females.

Theater Faculty Total: 8; 7 full-time, 1 part-time; 100% of full-time faculty have terminal degrees. Graduate students do not teach undergraduate courses. Undergraduate student–faculty ratio: 6:1.

Expenses for 1995–96 Application fee: $30. Comprehensive fee of $13,840 includes full-time tuition ($9000), mandatory fees ($1000), and college room and board ($3840). Part-time tuition: $300 per semester hour. Part-time mandatory fees: $25 per semester hour.

Financial Aid Program-specific awards for Fall of 1994: 12 Activity Grants for incoming students ($2000), 8 Nordan Grants for incoming students ($3000), 2 Stokes Grants for incoming students ($2000).

Application Procedures Deadline—freshmen: February 15; transfers: August 1. Notification date—freshmen: May 1; transfers: August 1. Required: essay, high school transcript, college transcript(s) for transfer students, 2 letters of recommendation, SAT I or ACT test scores, minimum 2.0 college GPA for transfer students. Recommended: minimum 3.0 high school GPA, interview, audition, portfolio. Auditions held 1 time at end of sophomore year on campus; videotaped performances are permissible as a substitute for live auditions for transfer applicants. Portfolio reviews held on campus; the submission of slides may be substituted for portfolios.

Undergraduate Contact Forrest Newlin, Chair, Theater Department, Texas Christian University, P.O. Box 32928, Fort Worth, Texas 76129; 817-921-7625, fax: 817-921-7344, E-mail address: f.newlin@tcu.edu.

Tisch School of the Arts

See New York University, Tisch School of the Arts

University of Arizona

Tucson, Arizona

State-supported, coed. Urban campus. Total enrollment: 35,306.

Degrees Bachelor of Fine Arts in the areas of theater production, theater education, musical theater. Majors: acting, design technology, music theater, theater education, theater production. Graduate degrees offered: Master of Fine Arts in the areas of theater arts, acting, design technology.

Theater Student Profile Fall 1994: 290 total; 250 matriculated undergraduate, 40 matriculated graduate; 5% minorities, 60% females, 1% international.

Theater Faculty Total: 22; 21 full-time, 1 part-time; 100% of full-time faculty have terminal degrees. Graduate students teach about a quarter undergraduate courses. Undergraduate student–faculty ratio: 20:1.

Student Life Student groups include Theta Alpha Phi.

Expenses for 1995–96 State resident tuition: $1950 full-time. Nonresident tuition: $7978 full-time. Part-time tuition per semester ranges from $103 to $975 for state residents, $334 to $3989 for nonresidents. College room and board: $4400. College room only: $2400. Special program-related fees: $10–$40 for material fees for design/technology courses.

Application Procedures Deadline—freshmen and transfers: May 1. Notification date—freshmen and transfers: continuous. Required: high school transcript, college transcript(s) for transfer students, minimum 3.0 high school GPA, audition. Recommended: 3 letters of recommendation, interview, portfolio. Auditions held 1 time for musical theater applicants on campus and off campus in Irvine, CA; Evanston, IL; New York, NY; videotaped performances are permissible as a substitute for live auditions for out-of-state applicants. Portfolio reviews held 1 time on campus and off campus in Irvine, CA; Evanston, IL; the submission of slides may be substituted for portfolios for applicants in technical areas.

Undergraduate Contact Undergraduate Secretary, Department of Theatre Arts, University of Arizona, Tucson, Arizona 85721; 520-621-7008, fax: 520-621-2412.

Graduate Contact Graduate Secretary, Department of Theatre Arts, University of Arizona, Tucson, Arizona 85721; 520-621-7007, fax: 520-621-2412.

University of California, Santa Barbara

Santa Barbara, California

State-supported, coed. Suburban campus. Total enrollment: 17,834.

Degrees Bachelor of Fine Arts in the area of acting. Majors: acting.

Theater Student Profile Fall 1994: 45 total; all matriculated undergraduate.

Theater Faculty Total: 6; 6 full-time; 67% of full-time faculty have terminal degrees. Graduate students teach a few undergraduate courses. Undergraduate student–faculty ratio: 6:1.

Student Life Student groups include American College Theater Festival, Intercampus Arts Festival.

Expenses for 1995–96 Application fee: $40. State resident tuition: $0 full-time. Nonresident tuition: $7699 full-time. Full-time mandatory fees: $4098. College room and board: $5990.

Financial Aid Program-specific awards for Fall of 1994: 4 Drama and Dance Affiliate Scholarships for seniors ($200–$400).

Application Procedures Deadline—freshmen and transfers: November 30. Notification date—freshmen: March 15; transfers: April 1. Required: essay, high school transcript, minimum 3.0 high school GPA, audition. Auditions held 2 times on campus.

Undergraduate Contact Marilyn Romine, Undergraduate Advisor, Department of Dramatic Art, University of California, Santa Barbara, Snidecor 2645, Santa Barbara, California 93106; 805-893-3241, fax: 805-893-3242, E-mail address: romine@humanitas.ucsb.edu.

University of Central Florida

Orlando, Florida

State-supported, coed. Suburban campus. Total enrollment: 25,363.

Degrees Bachelor of Fine Arts in the areas of theater performance, technical theater/design, stage management. Majors: theater arts/drama.

Theater Student Profile Fall 1994: 412 total; 112 matriculated undergraduate, 300 nondegree; 10% minorities, 65% females.

Theater Faculty Total: 6; 6 full-time. Graduate students do not teach undergraduate courses.

Student Life Student groups include Alpha Psi Omega, Florida Theatre Association.

University of Central Florida *(continued)*

Expenses for 1995–96 Application fee: $20. State resident tuition: $1842 full-time, $58.19 per credit hour part-time. Nonresident tuition: $6743 full-time, $221.60 per credit hour part-time. Part-time mandatory fees: $47.30 per semester. Full-time mandatory fees: $95. College room and board: $4310. College room only: $2500.

Financial Aid Program-specific awards for Fall of 1994: 20 Talent Grants for program majors ($500).

Application Procedures Deadline—freshmen and transfers: August 1. Notification date—freshmen and transfers: August 15. Required: high school transcript, minimum 3.0 high school GPA, 3 letters of recommendation, interview, audition, portfolio, SAT I or ACT test scores. Auditions held 6 times on campus; videotaped performances are permissible as a substitute for live auditions when distance is prohibitive. Portfolio reviews held 6 times on campus; the submission of slides may be substituted for portfolios when distance is prohibitive.

Undergraduate Contact Office of Admissions, University of Central Florida, P.O. Box 160111, Orlando, Florida 32816; 407-823-3180.

University of Cincinnati

Cincinnati, Ohio

State-supported, coed. Urban campus. Total enrollment: 18,473.

Degrees Bachelor of Fine Arts in the areas of musical theater, dramatic performance, theater design and production. Majors: dramatic performance, music theater, theater design and production. Graduate degrees offered: Master of Fine Arts in the areas of theater performance, directing, theater design and production. Cross-registration with Greater Cincinnati Consortium of Colleges and Universities.

Theater Student Profile Fall 1994: 171 total; 136 matriculated undergraduate, 35 matriculated graduate; 11% minorities, 53% females.

Theater Faculty Total: 16; 16 full-time; 95% of full-time faculty have terminal degrees. Graduate students teach a few undergraduate courses. Undergraduate student–faculty ratio: 6:1.

Expenses for 1994–95 Application fee: $30. State resident tuition: $3732 full-time, $104 per credit hour part-time. Nonresident tuition: $9405 full-time, $261 per credit hour part-time. Full-time mandatory fees: $166. College room and board: $4698.

Financial Aid Program-specific awards for Fall of 1994: 12–50 Honors Awards for program majors ($800–$3200).

Application Procedures Deadline—freshmen and transfers: February 1. Notification date—freshmen and transfers: continuous. Required: high school transcript, letter of recommendation, audition, portfolio, essay, interview for design and production applicants, 2 letters of recommendation for design and production applicants. Recommended: minimum 3.0 high school GPA. Auditions held 8 times on campus and off campus in New York, NY; Chicago, IL; Los Angeles, CA; San Francisco, CA. Portfolio reviews held 8 times for design and production applicants on campus and off campus in New York, NY; Chicago, IL: Los Angeles, CA; San Francisco, CA; the submission of slides may be substituted for portfolios with approval from the department.

Contact Paul R. Hillner, Assistant Dean, University of Cincinnati, College–Conservatory of Music, P.O. Box 210003, Cincinnati, Ohio 45221-0003; 513-556-5462, fax: 513-556-1028.

University of Colorado at Boulder

Boulder, Colorado

State-supported, coed. Urban campus. Total enrollment: 24,548.

Degrees Bachelor of Fine Arts in the area of theater. Majors: acting, design technology, music theater, theater arts/drama.

Theater Student Profile Fall 1994: 140 total; all matriculated undergraduate; 1% minorities, 50% females, 1% international.

Theater Faculty Total: 16; 13 full-time, 3 part-time; 100% of full-time faculty have terminal degrees. Graduate students teach a few undergraduate courses. Undergraduate student–faculty ratio: 12:1.

Expenses for 1995–96 Application fee: $40. Part-time tuition per credit hour ranges from $138 to $165 for state residents, $741 to $776 for nonresidents. Part-time mandatory fees per semester range from $55.99 to $243.70. Full-time tuition ranges from $2216 to $2672 for state residents, $12,780 to $13,374 for nonresidents according to program. Full-time mandatory fees: $487. College room and board: $4162.

Financial Aid Program-specific awards for Fall of 1994: 12 Technical Assistant Awards for undergraduates ($2000).

Application Procedures Deadline—freshmen and transfers: continuous. Required: essay, high school transcript, 3 letters of recommendation, audition. Recommended: minimum 3.0 high school GPA, interview. Auditions held by appointment on campus; videotaped performances are permissible as a substitute for live auditions.

Undergraduate Contact Undergraduate Advisor, Theatre and Dance Department, University of Colorado at Boulder, CB 261, Boulder, Colorado 80309-0261; 303-492-7355, fax: 303-492-7722.

University of Connecticut

Storrs, Connecticut

State-supported, coed. Rural campus. Total enrollment: 15,626.

Degrees Bachelor of Fine Arts in the areas of acting, design/technical theater, puppetry. Majors: acting, design/technical theater, puppetry. Graduate degrees offered: Master of Fine Arts in the areas of acting, design (lighting, costume, scenery), puppetry, technical direction.

Theater Student Profile Fall 1994: 106 total; 74 matriculated undergraduate, 29 matriculated graduate, 3 nondegree; 52% females.

Theater Faculty Total: 23; 15 full-time, 8 part-time; 73% of full-time faculty have terminal degrees. Graduate students teach a few undergraduate courses. Undergraduate student–faculty ratio: 5:1.

Student Life Student groups include Connecticut Repertory Theatre.

Expenses for 1995–96 Application fee: $40. State resident tuition: $3900 full-time. Nonresident tuition: $11,890 full-time. Part-time tuition per semester ranges from $163 to $1950 for state residents, $495 to $5945 for nonresidents. Part-time mandatory fees per semester range from $104 to $414. Full-time mandatory fees: $949. College room and board: $5124.

Financial Aid Program-specific awards for Fall of 1994: 10 University Drama Scholarships for incoming students ($750).

Application Procedures Deadline—freshmen: April 1; transfers: May 1. Notification date—freshmen and transfers: continuous. Required: essay, high school transcript, college transcript(s) for transfer students, audition, SAT I or ACT test scores. Recommended: letter of recommendation, portfolio for design/technical theater applicants. Auditions held by appointment for acting and puppetry majors on campus; videotaped performances are permissible as a substitute for live auditions for acting applicants when distance is prohibitive. Portfolio reviews held by appointment for design/technical applicants on campus; the submission of slides may be substituted for portfolios.

Contact Admissions Assistant, Department of Dramatic Arts, University of Connecticut, U-127, 802 Bolton Road, Storrs, Connecticut 06269-1127; 203-486-4025, fax: 203-486-3110.

University of Evansville

Evansville, Indiana

Independent-religious, coed. Suburban campus. Total enrollment: 3,162.

Degrees Bachelor of Fine Arts in the areas of performance, design and technology. Majors: design, performance, theater technology.

Theater Student Profile Fall 1994: 95 total; all matriculated undergraduate; 7% minorities, 65% females, 2% international.

Theater Faculty Total: 10; 6 full-time, 4 part-time; 92% of full-time faculty have terminal degrees. Graduate students do not teach undergraduate courses. Undergraduate student–faculty ratio: 7:1.

Student Life Student groups include United States Institute of Theater Technology.

Expenses for 1995–96 Application fee: $30. Comprehensive fee of $16,570 includes full-time tuition ($12,400) and college room and board ($4170 minimum). Part-time tuition: $365 per semester hour.

Financial Aid Program-specific awards for Fall of 1994: 28 Academic/Department Scholarships for program students ($2000–$6000).

Application Procedures Deadline—freshmen: March 1; transfers: June 1. Notification date—freshmen: May 1; transfers: continuous. Required: essay, high school transcript, college transcript(s) for transfer students, minimum 2.0 high school GPA, interview, audition, portfolio, SAT I or ACT test scores. Recommended: minimum 3.0 high school GPA, letter of recommendation. Auditions held 17 times for performance applicants on campus and off campus in Denver, CO; Indianapolis, IN; Austin, TX; New York, NY; Chicago, IL; Los Angeles, CA; San Francisco, CA; Las Vegas, NV; Louisville, KY; Atlanta, GA; videotaped performances are permissible as a substitute for live auditions if a campus visit is impossible, with permission. Portfolio reviews held on campus and off campus in Denver, CO; Indianapolis, IN; Austin, TX; New York, NY; Chicago, IL; Los Angeles, CA; San Francisco, CA; Las Vegas, NV; Louisville, KY; Atlanta, GA.

Undergraduate Contact John David Lutz, Director, Theatre Department, University of Evansville, 1800 Lincoln Avenue, Evansville, Indiana 47722; 812-479-2744, fax: 812-471-6995.

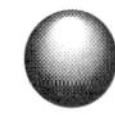

University of Florida

Gainesville, Florida

State-supported, coed. Suburban campus. Total enrollment: 38,277.

Degrees Bachelor of Fine Arts in the areas of theater, performance, theater production. Majors: acting, music theater, performance, theater production. Graduate degrees offered: Master of Fine Arts in the area of theater. Cross-registration with State University System of Florida.

Theater Student Profile Fall 1994: 118 total; 93 matriculated undergraduate, 25 matriculated graduate.

Theater Faculty Total: 18; 15 full-time, 3 part-time; 100% of full-time faculty have terminal degrees. Graduate students teach a few undergraduate courses. Undergraduate student–faculty ratio: 7:1.

Student Life Student groups include Alpha Psi Omega.

Expenses for 1995–96 Application fee: $20. State resident tuition: $1820 full-time, $56.83 per semester hour part-time. Nonresident tuition: $7090 full-time, $220.24 per semester hour part-time. College room and board: $4310. College room only: $2050. Special program-related fees.

Financial Aid Program-specific awards for Fall of 1994: Theater Scholarships for program majors.

Application Procedures Deadline—freshmen: February 1; transfers: June 9. Notification date—freshmen and

University of Florida *(continued)*

transfers: continuous. Required: high school transcript, minimum 2.0 high school GPA, audition, portfolio, SAT I or ACT test scores. Auditions held on campus; videotaped performances are permissible as a substitute for live auditions with approval from the department. Portfolio reviews held on campus; the submission of slides may be substituted for portfolios with approval from the department.

Undergraduate Contact Dr. Ralph Remshardt, Undergraduate Coordinator, Department of Theatre, University of Florida, McCarty C/Hume Library, 4th Floor, Gainesville, Florida 32611-2039; 904-392-2038, fax: 904-392-5114.

Graduate Contact Dr. David Shelton, Graduate Coordinator, Department of Theatre, University of Florida, McCarty C/Hume Library, 4th Floor, Gainesville, Florida 32611-2039; 904-392-2038, fax: 904-392-5114.

University of Illinois at Urbana-Champaign

Champaign, Illinois

State-supported, coed. Small-town campus. Total enrollment: 36,191.

Degrees Bachelor of Fine Arts in the areas of acting, design, technology and management, performance studies. Majors: acting, costume design, design technology, lighting design, performance, set design, stage management, theater technology. Graduate degrees offered: Master of Fine Arts in the areas of acting, design, technology and management. Cross-registration with Parkland College.

Theater Student Profile Fall 1994: 186 total; 116 matriculated undergraduate, 70 matriculated graduate; 3% minorities, 54% females, 5% international.

Theater Faculty Total: 32; 17 full-time, 15 part-time; 100% of full-time faculty have terminal degrees. Graduate students teach a few undergraduate courses. Undergraduate student–faculty ratio: 3:1.

Student Life Student groups include American College Theater Festival.

Expenses for 1994–95 Application fee: $30. Part-time mandatory fees per semester range from $201 to $474. Full-time tuition ranges from $2760 to $2900 for state residents, $7560 to $7980 for nonresidents, according to class level. Part-time tuition per semester ranges from $480 to $977 for state residents, $1300 to $2607 for nonresidents, according to class level and course load. Full-time mandatory fees: $920. College room and board: $4260. Special program-related fees: $5–$15 for CAD lab fee.

Financial Aid Program-specific awards for Fall of 1994: 50 Talented Undergraduate Student Tuition Waivers for undergraduates ($1200).

Application Procedures Deadline—freshmen and transfers: continuous. Notification date—freshmen and transfers: May 15. Required: high school transcript, college transcript(s) for transfer students, interview, audition, portfolio, SAT I or ACT test scores. Recommended: essay, letter of recommendation. Auditions held 9 times for acting applicants on campus and off campus in Chicago, IL; New York, NY; San Francisco, CA; Los Angeles, CA; videotaped performances are permissible as a substitute for live auditions if a campus visit is impossible. Portfolio reviews held 5 times for design, technology, management, or performance studies applicants on campus; the submission of slides may be substituted for portfolios for international applicants.

Undergraduate Contact Office of Admissions and Records, University of Illinois at Urbana-Champaign, 10 Henry Administration Building, 506 South Wright, Urbana, Illinois 61801; 217-333-0302.

Graduate Contact Department of Theatre, University of Illinois at Urbana-Champaign, 4-122 Krannert Center for the Performing Arts, 500 South Goodwin Avenue, Urbana, Illinois 61801; 217-333-2371, fax: 217-244-1861.

More about the University

Facilities Krannert Center for the Performing Arts is "arguably the best performing arts facility in the nation" (*Time* magazine). It consists of four major theaters seating 200 to 2,000, eight rehearsal and teaching studios, a fully equipped color television studio, a computer design laboratory, three professional design and technical ateliers, and five production shops. More than 320 performances are presented annually, including productions of the I.R.T. and others such as the Guthrie Theatre, the National Theatre of the Deaf, The Chicago and Royal Philharmonic Symphonies.

Student Performances The Illinois Repertory Theatre presents eight plays per academic year from the classical to the most contemporary. Summerfest, a rotating summer repertory of three plays, is presented each summer with a paid company of actors, designers, and technicians drawn from students of the department and professionals. Chicago Showcase: Each Spring graduating students in acting, design, and management present Chicago Showcase. Agents, casting directors, producers, and alumni from the wider Chicago area and throughout the Midwest attend, resulting in contacts, auditions, and engagements.

Guest Artists Directors and designers visit the department each year, such as Robert Falls (alumnus, 1992 Tony Award Winner), Artistic Director, the Goodman Theatre, Chicago; Lawrence Wilker (alumnus, 1992 Tony Award Winner), Chief Operating Officer, the Kennedy Center; Richard Hornung (alumnus), costume designer, Hollywood; Niel Galen (alumnus), lighting designer, Hollywood; John Lee Beatty, scenic designer, Broadway; Ron Himes, artistic director, The Black Rep of St. Louis; Michael Filerman (alumnus), producer, Hollywood; Robert Greenblatt (alumnus), senior Vice President for Drama Development, Fox Television, Hollywood.

University of Kentucky

Lexington, Kentucky

State-supported, coed. Urban campus. Total enrollment: 23,622.

Degrees Bachelor of Fine Arts. Majors: acting, design technology.

Expenses for 1995–96 Application fee: $15. State resident tuition: $2260 full-time, $95 per semester hour part-time. Nonresident tuition: $6780 full-time, $283 per semester hour part-time. Part-time mandatory fees: $6 per semester hour. Full-time mandatory fees: $330. College room and board: $3226.

Undergraduate Contact Russ Jones, Chair, Theater Department, University of Kentucky, 114 Fine Arts Building, Lexington, Kentucky 40506; 606-257-3297.

University of Memphis

Memphis, Tennessee

State-supported, coed. Urban campus. Total enrollment: 19,848.

Degrees Bachelor of Fine Arts in the area of theater. Majors: theater arts/drama. Graduate degrees offered: Master of Fine Arts in the area of theater. Cross-registration with Middlesex University (UK).

Theater Student Profile Fall 1994: 94 total; 70 matriculated undergraduate, 24 matriculated graduate; 14% minorities, 50% females, 3% international.

Theater Faculty Total: 20; 15 full-time, 5 part-time. Graduate students teach a few undergraduate courses.

Student Life Student groups include Fred Mertz Student Activity Group, University Dance Company, Memphis Moving Line.

Expenses for 1995–96 Application fee: $5. State resident tuition: $2094 full-time. Nonresident tuition: $6224 full-time. Part-time tuition per semester ranges from $92 to $989 for state residents, $273 to $2980 for nonresidents. College room and board: $2200 (minimum).

Financial Aid Program-specific awards for Fall of 1994: 3 Talent Scholarships for program majors ($2200–$4400).

Application Procedures Deadline—freshmen and transfers: August 15. Required: high school transcript, college transcript(s) for transfer students, interview, SAT I or ACT test scores.

Contact Dr. Lesley Ferris, Artistic Director, Department of Theatre and Dance, University of Memphis, Memphis, Tennessee 38152; 901-678-2523, fax: 901-678-4331.

University of Miami

Coral Gables, Florida

Independent, coed. Suburban campus. Total enrollment: 13,410.

Degrees Bachelor of Fine Arts in the area of theater arts. Majors: design production, music theater, performance, stage management, theater arts/drama, theater management.

Theater Student Profile Fall 1994: 85 total; all matriculated undergraduate; 17% minorities, 60% females.

Theater Faculty Total: 17; 15 full-time, 2 part-time; 100% of full-time faculty have terminal degrees. Graduate students do not teach undergraduate courses. Undergraduate student–faculty ratio: 6:1.

Estimated Expenses for 1995–96 Application fee: $35. Comprehensive fee of $24,552 includes full-time tuition ($17,340), mandatory fees ($360), and college room and board ($6852). College room only: $3830. Part-time tuition: $672 per credit.

Financial Aid Program-specific awards for Fall of 1994 available.

Application Procedures Deadline—freshmen and transfers: March 1. Notification date—freshmen and transfers: April 1. Required: essay, high school transcript, letter of recommendation, interview, audition, SAT I or ACT test scores. Recommended: minimum 3.0 high school GPA, portfolio. Auditions held by appointment on campus and off campus in New York, NY; Washington, DC; Chicago, IL; Louisville, KY; Houston, TX; Philadelphia, PA; Boston, MA; Dallas, TX; New Orleans, LA; videotaped performances are permissible as a substitute for live auditions if a campus visit is impossible. Portfolio reviews held on campus and off campus in New York, NY; Chicago, IL; Louisville, KY; Houston, TX; Boston, MA; New Orleans, LA.

Undergraduate Contact Chairman, Theatre Arts Department, University of Miami, P.O. Box 248273, Coral Gables, Florida 33124; 305-284-6439, fax: 305-284-5702.

More about the University

Programs Bachelor of Fine Arts Conservatory programs: B.F.A. degrees are offered in the areas of performance, musical theater, stage management, theater management, and design/production. Auditions: Two contrasting monologues, 2 minutes each (performance majors), two contrasting songs, 16 bars each (performance majors) and two complete songs (musical theater majors). The department also offers a B.A. degree.

Program Facilities The facilities are housed in the newly renovated Jerry Herman Theatre and the Hecht Rehearsal and Studio Complex. The Ring Stage in the Jerry Herman Theatre is a 300-seat thrust stage or a 600-seat arena stage with a state-of-the-art sound and lighting system, including computer lightboard with 96 dimmers and a 24-channel audio mixer.

Faculty, Guest Artists, and Alumni Full-time faculty are chosen not only for excellent teaching skills but also for professional expertise. Each year guest directors and designers work with students on at least two mainstage productions. Graduates include: Jerry Herman (*Hello Dolly, La Cage Aux Folles, Mame*); Ray Liotta (*Goodfellas, Field of Dreams, Unlawful Entry*); Saundra Santiago (*Miami Vice, A View from the Bridge*—on Broadway); Ernie Sabella (*Perfect Strangers, Guys and Dolls*—Broadway revival, *Robber Bridegroom, Little Johnny Jones*); Susan Elrod (Company Manager for Circle in the Square, Broadway).

University of Miami *(continued)*

Student Performances B.F.A. students are guaranteed a performance or technical experience every semester and do not compete against graduate students for stage roles or design or stage management opportunities as there is no M.F.A. program and all energies are focused on the undergraduate programs.

Special Programs The theater management and stage management programs culminate in a one-semester internship in a professional theater.

University of Michigan

Ann Arbor, Michigan

State-supported, coed. Suburban campus. Total enrollment: 36,543.

Degrees Bachelor of Fine Arts in the areas of performance, design and production. Majors: theater arts/drama. Graduate degrees offered: Master of Fine Arts in the area of design.

Theater Student Profile Fall 1994: 124 total; 86 matriculated undergraduate, 37 matriculated graduate, 1 nondegree; 10% minorities, 53% females, 6% international.

Theater Faculty Total: 24; 16 full-time, 8 part-time; 100% of full-time faculty have terminal degrees. Graduate students do not teach undergraduate courses. Undergraduate student–faculty ratio: 5:1.

Student Life Student groups include Basement Arts, Musket Theatre Productions, Gilbert and Sullivan Society.

Expenses for 1994–95 Application fee: $40. Full-time tuition ranges from $5040 to $6698 for state residents, $15,732 to $17,850 for nonresidents according to class level and program. Part-time tuition and fees per term (1 to 11 credits) range from $525 to $3204 for state residents, $970 to $8530 for nonresidents according to course load, class level, and program. Full-time mandatory fees: $175. College room and board: $4659.

Financial Aid Program-specific awards for Fall of 1994: 15 Merit Awards for continuing students ($800–$3000), 20 Scholarships for continuing students ($500–$4000).

Application Procedures Deadline—freshmen and transfers: continuous. Required: essay, high school transcript, college transcript(s) for transfer students, minimum 3.0 high school GPA, letter of recommendation, audition, SAT I or ACT test scores, minimum combined SAT I score of 1000, minimum composite ACT score of 24, portfolio for design applicants. Recommended: production photos for design and production applicants. Auditions held 8 times on campus and off campus in Chicago, IL; Las Vegas, NV; New York, NY; San Francisco, CA; Los Angeles, CA; videotaped performances are permissible as a substitute for live auditions when distance is prohibitive. Portfolio reviews held 4 times and by appointment on campus and off campus in Chicago, IL, and at Southeast Theater Conference and United States Institute for Theater Technology conferences; the submission of slides may be substituted for portfolios when distance is prohibitive.

Contact Laura Strozeski, Senior Admissions Counselor, School of Music, Department of Theatre and Drama, University of Michigan, Moore Building, Ann Arbor, Michigan 48109-2085; 313-764-0593, fax: 313-763-5097, E-mail address: music.admissions@umich.edu.

More about the University

Program Facilities Performance spaces: Power Center (1,400 seats), with a thrust stage of flexible size and shape; Lydia Mendelssohn Theatre (700 seats), a lovely intimate theater built in 1928; Trueblood Theatre (open-space seating for 175), with flexibility of thrust, three-quarter, and arena staging; Arena Theatre (100 seats), a black box space suitable for workshops, studios, and student-produced works. Spacious, newly renovated design studios are fully equipped and include a Macintosh workstation, printer, and a variety of state-of-the-art design software.

Faculty, Guest Artists, and Alumni Faculty are all theater professionals with experience on the Broadway, London, and regional stage. Michigan is dedicated to maintaining ties with the professional theater community; actors, designers, and directors frequently visit campus to teach master classes and direct or design productions. Recent guests have included artistic director Libby Appel, actress Christine Lahti (alumna), film and stage director Robert Altman, actor James Earl Jones (alumnus), producer Hal Cooper (alumnus), actor Jeff Daniels, director Lloyd Richards, and designers Susan Benson and Dawn Chiang.

Performance Opportunities The department mounts five mainstage productions each year. Recent productions include the works of Shakespeare, Molière, Euripides, Coward, Shaw, Wilder, Gogol, and Brecht, as well as many contemporary works. The School of Music produces operas, dance concerts, and musical theater, and resident student groups also mount full productions. Local theater groups, from the nontraditional to the Civic Theater, all are in need of a constant supply of performers, designers, and technicians. The department also has professional ties with Purple Rose Theater, founded by actor Jeff Daniels.

University of Minnesota, Duluth

Duluth, Minnesota

State-supported, coed. Suburban campus. Total enrollment: 7,497.

Degrees Bachelor of Fine Arts in the area of theater. Majors: design/technical theater, performance, theater arts/drama. Cross-registration with University of Minnesota–Twin Cities, University of Minnesota –Morris.

Theater Student Profile Fall 1994: 75 total; all matriculated undergraduate; 1% minorities, 60% females.

Theater Faculty Total: 9; 8 full-time, 1 part-time; 100% of full-time faculty have terminal degrees. Undergraduate student–faculty ratio: 10:1.

Student Life Student groups include Stage 2, American College Theater Festival, United States Institute of Theatre Technology.

Expenses for 1994–95 Application fee: $25. State resident tuition: $2995 full-time, $71.30 per credit part-time. Nonresident tuition: $8828 full-time, $210.20 per credit part-time. Part-time mandatory fees (6 to 11 credits): $103.45 per quarter. Full-time mandatory fees: $310. College room and board: $3474.

Financial Aid Program-specific awards for Fall of 1994: 6 Marshall Center Awards for program majors ($500–$1000), 1 Earl Jensen Award for technical/design majors ($500), 1 Ann Upgren Award for program majors ($400), 2 Gersghol Awards for program majors ($750).

Application Procedures Deadline—freshmen and transfers: continuous. Required: high school transcript, college transcript(s) for transfer students, ACT test score only, minimum composite ACT score of 19.

Undergraduate Contact Chair, Department of Theatre, University of Minnesota, Duluth, 141 MPAC, 10 University Drive, Duluth, Minnesota 55812; 218-726-8778.

University of Montana–Missoula

Missoula, Montana

State-supported, coed. Urban campus. Total enrollment: 11,067.

Degrees Bachelor of Fine Arts in the areas of acting, design/technical theater. Majors: acting, design/technical theater, theater arts/drama. Graduate degrees offered: Master of Fine Arts in the areas of directing, acting, design/technical theater.

Theater Student Profile Fall 1994: 148 total; 130 matriculated undergraduate, 18 matriculated graduate; 1% minorities, 65% females.

Theater Faculty Total: 17; 13 full-time, 4 part-time; 100% of full-time faculty have terminal degrees. Graduate students teach a few undergraduate courses. Undergraduate student–faculty ratio: 16:1.

Student Life Student groups include Montana Repertory Theatre, The Young Rep.

Expenses for 1994–95 Application fee: $30. State resident tuition: $2251 full-time. Nonresident tuition: $6311 full-time. Part-time tuition per semester ranges from $99.10 to $943.10 for state residents, $244.10 to $2538 for nonresidents. College room and board: $3667.

Financial Aid Program-specific awards for Fall of 1994: 2 Wallace Scholarships for incoming freshmen ($500), 1 Gordon Scholarship for state resident acting students ($350), 6 Dean Scholarships for upperclassmen ($600), 1 Carol Scholarship for those demonstrating need ($450).

Application Procedures Deadline—freshmen and transfers: March 15. Notification date—freshmen and transfers: continuous. Required: high school transcript, audition. Auditions held 1 time for acting applicants on campus.

Contact Co-Chairs, Drama/Dance Department, University of Montana–Missoula, Missoula, Montana 59812-1058; 406-243-4481, fax: 406-243-5726.

University of Nebraska–Lincoln

Lincoln, Nebraska

State-supported, coed. Urban campus. Total enrollment: 23,854.

Degrees Bachelor of Fine Arts in the area of technical theater. Majors: technical theater, theater arts/drama. Graduate degrees offered: Master of Fine Arts in the areas of acting, directing, design. Doctor of Arts in the area of communication studies.

Theater Student Profile Fall 1994: 116 total; 82 matriculated undergraduate, 34 matriculated graduate; 1% minorities, 60% females.

Theater Faculty Total: 14; 12 full-time, 2 part-time; 100% of full-time faculty have terminal degrees. Graduate students teach a few undergraduate courses. Undergraduate student–faculty ratio: 7:1.

Student Life Student groups include American College Theater Festival, Musical Arts Theatre Conference, National Association for Schools of Theatre/University Resident Theatre Association.

Expenses for 1994–95 Application fee: $25. State resident tuition: $2415 full-time, $68.50 per credit hour part-time. Nonresident tuition: $5955 full-time, $186.50 per credit hour part-time. Part-time mandatory fees per semester range from $85 to $180. Full-time mandatory fees: $360. College room and board: $3145. College room only: $1375.

Financial Aid Program-specific awards for Fall of 1994: 4 Hal Floyd Scholarships for freshmen ($500).

Application Procedures Deadline—freshmen and transfers: continuous. Required: high school transcript, minimum 3.0 high school GPA.

Undergraduate Contact Shirley Carr Mason, Assistant Professor, Department of Theatre Arts and Dance, University of Nebraska–Lincoln, P.O. Box 880201, 215 Temple Building, Lincoln, Nebraska 68588-0201; 402-472-1603, fax: 402-472-9055.

Graduate Contact Tice L. Miller, Chair, Department of Theatre Arts and Dance, University of Nebraska–Lincoln, P.O. Box 880201, 215 Temple Building, Lincoln, Nebraska 68588-0201; 402-472-2072, fax: 402-472-9055.

University of New Mexico

Albuquerque, New Mexico

State-supported, coed. Urban campus. Total enrollment: 24,344.

Degrees Bachelor of Fine Arts in the areas of theater, acting, technical theater/design. Majors: acting, theater design/technology.

Theater Student Profile Fall 1994: 33 total; all matriculated undergraduate; 9% minorities, 58% females.

Theater Faculty Total: 11; 11 full-time; 100% of full-time faculty have terminal degrees. Graduate stu-

University of New Mexico *(continued)*

dents do not teach undergraduate courses. Undergraduate student–faculty ratio: 8:1.

Student Life Student groups include Associated Students of Theater Arts.

Expenses for 1995–96 Application fee: $15. State resident tuition: $2080 full-time, $83.20 per semester hour part-time. Nonresident tuition: $7856 full-time, $314.25 per semester hour part-time. College room and board: $4176.

Financial Aid Program-specific awards for Fall of 1994: 2–3 Theater Scholarships for program majors ($2000).

Application Procedures Deadline—freshmen and transfers: July 21. Required: essay, high school transcript, college transcript(s) for transfer students, SAT I or ACT test scores, minimum 2.5 high school GPA. Auditions held on campus and off campus. Portfolio reviews held on campus and off campus.

Undergraduate Contact Office of Admissions and Outreach Services, University of New Mexico, Albuquerque, New Mexico 87131; 505-277-2446.

Jason Alexander

Boston University—Tony Award Winning Actor, "George" on *Seinfeld*, and Director

Jason Alexander landed his first film (*The Burning*) while studying acting at Boston University. Born and raised in New Jersey, Alexander first found an audience with his classmates, entertaining them in an effort to distract from his chubbiness. He memorized comedy albums, movie dialogue, and did impressions so well that he never gave his peers a chance to laugh at him, only with him. He progressed to win the 1989 Tony for Best Actor in a Musical in *Jerome Robbins' Broadway*.

University of North Carolina at Greensboro

Greensboro, North Carolina

State-supported, coed. Urban campus. Total enrollment: 12,094.

Degrees Bachelor of Fine Arts in the areas of acting, design and technical theater. Majors: theater arts/drama. Graduate degrees offered: Master of Fine Arts in the areas of acting, design, directing, film and video production, theater for youth.

Theater Student Profile Fall 1994: 193 total; 145 matriculated undergraduate, 48 matriculated graduate; 5% minorities.

Theater Faculty Total: 24; 20 full-time, 4 part-time; 100% of full-time faculty have terminal degrees. Graduate students teach a few undergraduate courses. Undergraduate student–faculty ratio: 15:1.

Student Life Student groups include Alpha Psi Omega, North Carolina Theatre for Young People, North Carolina Theatre Conference.

Expenses for 1994–95 Application fee: $35. State resident tuition: $874 full-time. Nonresident tuition: $8400 full-time. Part-time tuition per semester ranges from $109 to $328 for state residents, $1050 to $3150 for nonresidents. Full-time mandatory fees: $891. College room and board: $3505. College room only: $1791.

Financial Aid Program-specific awards for Fall of 1994: 1 W. Raymond Taylor Scholarship for drama majors ($500).

Application Procedures Deadline—freshmen and transfers: August 1. Notification date—freshmen and transfers: continuous. Required: high school transcript, college transcript(s) for transfer students, minimum 2.0 high school GPA, SAT I test score only, minimum combined SAT I score of 900. Recommended: 3 letters of recommendation. Auditions held 2 times on campus and off campus; videotaped performances are permissible as a substitute for live auditions if a campus visit is impossible. Portfolio reviews held on campus and off campus; the submission of slides may be substituted for portfolios.

Contact Robert C. Hansen, Head, Broadcasting/Cinema and Theatre Department, University of North Carolina at Greensboro, 201 Taylor, Greensboro, North Carolina 27412; 910-334-5576, fax: 910-334-5039.

University of North Dakota

Grand Forks, North Dakota

State-supported, coed. Small-town campus. Total enrollment: 11,521.

Degrees Bachelor of Fine Arts in the areas of performance, design/technology. Majors: theater arts/drama.

Theater Student Profile Fall 1994: 50 total; all matriculated undergraduate; 5% minorities, 60% females, 2% international.

Theater Faculty Total: 10; 7 full-time, 3 part-time; 100% of full-time faculty have terminal degrees. Graduate students teach a few undergraduate courses. Undergraduate student–faculty ratio: 5:1.

Expenses for 1995–96 Application fee: $25. State resident tuition: $2878 full-time, $119.92 per credit hour part-time. Nonresident tuition: $6402 full-time, $266.75 per credit hour part-time. Full-time mandatory fees: $318. College room and board: $2816.

Financial Aid Program-specific awards for Fall of 1994: 2–3 Various Donors Awards for program majors ($1200), 10–15 Department Awards for program majors ($600).

Application Procedures Deadline—freshmen and transfers: continuous. Required: high school transcript, minimum 2.0 high school GPA. Recommended: 2 letters of recommendation, interview, video, audition, portfolio. Auditions held 1 time for performance applicants on campus; videotaped performances are permissible as a substitute for live auditions. Portfolio reviews held 1 time for design/technology applicants on campus.

Undergraduate Contact Dan Plato, Chair, Theatre Arts Department, University of North Dakota, Box 8136, Grand Forks, North Dakota 58202; 701-777-3446, fax: 701-777-3522, E-mail address: plato@badlands.nodak.edu.

University of South Carolina

Columbia, South Carolina

State-supported, coed. Urban campus. Total enrollment: 26,754.

Degrees Bachelor of Arts/Bachelor of Fine Arts in the area of theater. Majors: acting, design/technical theater, theater arts/drama. Graduate degrees offered: Master of Fine Arts in the area of theater.

Theater Student Profile Fall 1994: 115 total; 80 matriculated undergraduate, 35 matriculated graduate.

Theater Faculty Total: 18; 18 full-time. Graduate students teach a few undergraduate courses.

Expenses for 1995–96 Application fee: $35. State resident tuition: $3280 full-time, $148 per credit hour part-time. Nonresident tuition: $8324 full-time, $366 per credit hour part-time. College room and board: $3428 (minimum). College room only: $1646 (minimum).

Application Procedures Required: high school transcript, college transcript(s) for transfer students, letter of recommendation, interview, audition, portfolio, SAT I or ACT test scores. Auditions held 2 times on campus and off campus; videotaped performances are permissible as a substitute for live auditions. Portfolio reviews held on campus and off campus.

Undergraduate Contact Office of Admissions, University of South Carolina, Columbia, South Carolina 29208; 800-868-5USC, E-mail address: admissions-ugrad@scarolina.edu.

Graduate Contact Dennis Maulden, Graduate Director, Department of Theater, Speech, and Dance, University of South Carolina, Columbia, South Carolina 29208; 803-777-4288, fax: 803-777-6669.

University of South Dakota

Vermillion, South Dakota

State-supported, coed. Small-town campus. Total enrollment: 7,739.

Degrees Bachelor of Fine Arts in the areas of acting, theater and drama, design and theater technology. Majors: acting, technical theater, theater arts/drama. Graduate degrees offered: Master of Fine Arts in the areas of directing, design and theater technology.

Theater Student Profile Fall 1994: 63 total; 42 matriculated undergraduate, 21 matriculated graduate; 1% minorities, 50% females.

Theater Faculty Total: 9; 9 full-time; 100% of full-time faculty have terminal degrees. Graduate students teach a few undergraduate courses. Undergraduate student–faculty ratio: 4:1.

Student Life Student groups include Student Theatre Cooperative, Strollers, Coyote Capers.

Expenses for 1995–96 Application fee: $15. State resident tuition: $1648 full-time, $51.50 per credit hour part-time. Nonresident tuition: $4480 full-time, $140 per credit hour part-time. Part-time mandatory fees per semester range from $74.56 to $440.96. Minnesota residents pay state resident tuition. Tuition for nonresidents who are eligible for the Western Undergraduate Exchange: $2182 full-time, $68.18 per credit hour part-time. Full-time mandatory fees: $1105. College room and board: $2572. College room only: $1247.

Financial Aid Program-specific awards for Fall of 1994: 1–10 Theatre Scholarships for program majors ($400–$1000).

Application Procedures Deadline—freshmen and transfers: continuous. Required: high school transcript, college transcript(s) for transfer students, SAT I or ACT test scores. Auditions held for acting applicants during February and March by appointment on campus and off campus; videotaped performances are permissible as a substitute for live auditions when distance is prohibitive. Portfolio reviews held on campus; the submission of slides may be substituted for portfolios when distance is prohibitive.

Undergraduate Contact Roberta N. Rude, Chair, Department of Theatre, University of South Dakota, CFA 179, 414 East Clark Street, Vermillion, South Dakota

University of South Dakota *(continued)*

57069-2390; 605-677-5418, fax: 605-677-5988, E-mail address: rrude@charlie.usd.edu.

Graduate Contact Ronald L. Moyer, Director of Graduate Studies, Department of Theatre, University of South Dakota, 414 East Clark Street, Vermillion, South Dakota 57069-2390; 605-677-5735, fax: 605-677-5988, E-mail address: rmoyer@charlie.usd.edu.

University of Southern California

Los Angeles, California

Independent, coed. Urban campus. Total enrollment: 27,864.

Degrees Bachelor of Fine Arts in the areas of acting, stage management, technical direction, design. Majors: acting, design, technical direction, theater arts/drama. Graduate degrees offered: Master of Fine Arts in the areas of acting, playwriting, design, directing.

Theater Student Profile Fall 1994: 392 total; 367 matriculated undergraduate, 25 matriculated graduate; 16% minorities, 57% females, 2% international.

Theater Faculty Total: 41; 19 full-time, 22 part-time; 100% of full-time faculty have terminal degrees. Graduate students teach a few undergraduate courses. Undergraduate student–faculty ratio: 16:1.

Student Life Student groups include community-based theater lab, Theatre for Youth, Theater Representative Council.

Expenses for 1995–96 Application fee: $50. Comprehensive fee of $25,988 includes full-time tuition ($19,198), mandatory fees ($352), and college room and board ($6438 minimum). College room only: $3502. Part-time tuition: $614 per unit. Part-time mandatory fees per year (6 to 11 units): $330.

Financial Aid Program-specific awards for Fall of 1994: 4 Trustee Scholarships for program majors demonstrating talent and academic achievement ($16,000), 16 Dean's Scholarships for program majors demonstrating talent and academic achievement ($6000), 2 Jack Nicholson Awards for performers demonstrating talent and academic achievement ($8000), 2 Stanley Musgrove Awards for undergraduates demonstrating talent and academic achievement ($2500), 2 John Blankenship/William C. White Awards for undergraduates demonstrating talent and academic achievement ($2000), 1 James Pendleton Award for program majors demonstrating talent and academic achievement ($2500).

Application Procedures Deadline—freshmen and transfers: January 2. Notification date—freshmen: March 1; transfers: April 1. Required: essay, high school transcript, minimum 3.0 high school GPA, letter of recommendation, interview, audition, portfolio. Auditions held 14 times for acting applicants on campus and off campus in Chicago, IL; New York, NY; Los Angeles, CA; videotaped performances are permissible as a substitute for live auditions for international students and U.S. students from great distances. Portfolio reviews held 14 times for stage management, technical direction, and design applicants on campus and off campus in Chicago, IL; New York, NY; Los Angeles, CA.

Contact Director, Academic Services, University of Southern California, School of Theatre, Los Angeles, California 90089-0791; 813-740-1285, fax: 813-740-8888.

More about the University

Program of Study The B.A. combines a theater and liberal arts education. This program is ideal for students with a passion for theater and a desire to explore one of the other 500 major/minor combinations at USC. The B.F.A. in acting is a rigorous four-year professional training program comprising an integrated four-year sequence of training in acting, voice, and body movement. The B.F.A. production program incorporates study in scenic, lighting, and costume design; management; technical direction; stage; and theater management.

Program Facilities Bing Theatre, a modern proscenium 589-seat house; Massman Theatre, an intimate studio that seats 60; and Greenroom Theatre, a second studio with flexible seating for 60 people.

Faculty/Visiting Artists The faculty members are award-winners in their fields and maintain active professional lives in theater, film, and television while teaching. Each year the School invites leading international artists to interact with students as directors, lecturers, and teachers of specialized workshops.

Program Supplements The Theatre Council, an elected body of students, represents their peers in meetings with the School's administration and faculty; The Peacock Player Children's Theatre provides an excellent opportunity for the School to actively participate in the greater Los Angeles community; the Casting Office maintains students' résumés and headshots on file for use by student filmmakers and outside agencies. Students are encouraged to seek professional recognition while continuing their studies through professional leave and internship opportunities. Overseas study programs are available. The School of Cinema and Television also offers theater students a unique opportunity to gain experience in these media.

University of Southern Mississippi

Hattiesburg, Mississippi

State-supported, coed. Suburban campus. Total enrollment: 11,587.

Degrees Bachelor of Fine Arts in the areas of acting, design and technical theater; Bachelor of Arts/Bachelor of Fine Arts in the area of theater. Majors: acting, design/technical theater, theater arts/drama. Graduate degrees offered: Master of Fine Arts in the areas of performance (acting and directing), design and technical theater.

Theater Student Profile Fall 1994: 69 total; 52 matriculated undergraduate, 17 matriculated graduate; 10% minorities, 50% females, 3% international.

Theater Faculty Total: 6; 6 full-time; 66% of full-time faculty have terminal degrees. Graduate students teach a few undergraduate courses. Undergraduate student–faculty ratio: 9:1.

Expenses for 1994–95 State resident tuition: $2428 full-time. Nonresident tuition: $4892 full-time. Part-time tuition per semester ranges from $100 to $970 for state residents, $202 to $2092 for nonresidents. College room and board: $2430. College room only: $1250 (minimum).

Financial Aid Program-specific awards for Fall of 1994: 10–20 Service Awards for talented students with high test scores ($500).

Application Procedures Deadline—freshmen and transfers: August 1. Notification date—freshmen and transfers: August 8. Required: high school transcript, college transcript(s) for transfer students, minimum 2.0 high school GPA, SAT I or ACT test scores, minimum composite ACT score of 18. Recommended: 2 letters of recommendation. Auditions held 4 times and by arrangement on campus and off campus; recorded music is permissible as a substitute for live auditions and videotaped performances are permissible as a substitute for live auditions. Portfolio reviews held 2 times and by arrangement on campus and off campus.

University of Tennessee at Martin

Martin, Tennessee

State-supported, coed. Small-town campus. Total enrollment: 5,627.

Degrees Bachelor of Fine Arts in the area of fine and performing arts. Majors: theater arts/drama.

Theater Student Profile Fall 1994: 16 total; all matriculated undergraduate; 5% minorities, 60% females, 2% international.

Theater Faculty Total: 2; 2 full-time; 100% of full-time faculty have terminal degrees. Graduate students do not teach undergraduate courses. Undergraduate student–faculty ratio: 9:1.

Student Life Student groups include Vanguard Theatre.

Expenses for 1994–95 Application fee: $15. State resident tuition: $1900 full-time, $76 per semester hour part-time. Nonresident tuition: $5832 full-time, $240 per semester hour part-time. College room and board: $2890 (minimum). College room only: $1490 (minimum). Special program-related fees.

Application Procedures Deadline—freshmen and transfers: continuous. Required: high school transcript, minimum 2.0 high school GPA, audition, SAT I or ACT test scores. Auditions held 1 time on campus; videotaped performances are permissible as a substitute for live auditions.

Undergraduate Contact Dr. Earl Norwood, Director, Division of Fine and Performing Arts, University of Tennessee at Martin, 102 Fine Arts Building, Martin, Tennessee 38238; 901-587-7400, fax: 901-587-7415, E-mail address: norwood@utm.edu.

University of Texas at Austin

Austin, Texas

State-supported, coed. Urban campus. Total enrollment: 47,957.

Degrees Bachelor of Fine Arts in the areas of acting, theater design and technology, theater education. Majors: acting, theater design/technology, theater education. Graduate degrees offered: Master of Fine Arts in the areas of acting, creative drama, directing, playwriting, theater technology, design.

Theater Student Profile Fall 1994: 421 total; 293 matriculated undergraduate, 128 matriculated graduate; 36% minorities, 55% females, 1% international.

Theater Faculty Total: 35; 35 full-time; 99% of full-time faculty have terminal degrees. Graduate students teach a few undergraduate courses. Undergraduate student–faculty ratio: 12:1.

Student Life Student groups include Drama Education Organization.

Expenses for 1995–96 Application fee: $35. State resident tuition: $900 full-time. Nonresident tuition: $6660 full-time, $222 per semester hour part-time. State resident part-time tuition per semester ranges from $120 to $330. Part-time mandatory fees per semester range from $169.85 to $570.14. Full-time mandatory fees: $1308. College room and board: $3632. Special program-related fees: $45 for production and performance fee.

Financial Aid Program-specific awards for Fall of 1994 available.

Application Procedures Deadline—freshmen: March 1; transfers: February 1. Notification date—freshmen and transfers: continuous. Required: essay, high school transcript, SAT I or ACT test scores. Recommended: 3 letters of recommendation.

Undergraduate Contact Sharon Vasquez, Chair, Department of Theatre and Dance, University of Texas at Austin, WIN 1.144, Austin, Texas 78712; 512-471-5793, fax: 512-471-0824.

Graduate Contact David Nancarrow, Graduate Advisor, Department of Theatre and Dance, University of Texas at Austin, WIN 2.160, Austin, Texas 78712; 512-471-5793, fax: 512-471-0824.

University of the Arts

Philadelphia, Pennsylvania

Independent, coed. Urban campus. Total enrollment: 1,298.

Degrees Bachelor of Fine Arts in the area of theater arts. Majors: acting, music theater, theater arts/drama.

Theater Student Profile Fall 1994: 164 total; all matriculated undergraduate; 18% minorities, 55% females, 1% international.

Theater Faculty Total: 29; 4 full-time, 25 part-time; 60% of full-time faculty have terminal degrees. Graduate

University of the Arts *(continued)*

students do not teach undergraduate courses. Undergraduate student–faculty ratio: 8:1.

Student Life Student groups include Students for Environmental Education, Student Government. Special housing available for theater students.

Expenses for 1995–96 Application fee: $30. Tuition: $13,170 full-time, $570 per credit part-time. Full-time mandatory fees: $500. College room only: $3860.

Financial Aid Program-specific awards for Fall of 1994: 30 Merit Scholarships for incoming students ($500–$5000).

Application Procedures Deadline—freshmen and transfers: continuous. Required: essay, high school transcript, college transcript(s) for transfer students, minimum 2.0 high school GPA, letter of recommendation, interview, audition, SAT I or ACT test scores, resume and photograph. Recommended: minimum 3.0 high school GPA. Auditions held 8 times on campus; videotaped performances are permissible as a substitute for live auditions when distance is prohibitive.

Undergraduate Contact Barbara Elliott, Director of Admissions, University of the Arts, 320 South Broad Street, Philadelphia, Pennsylvania 19102; 800-616-ARTS, fax: 215-875-5458.

University of Utah

Salt Lake City, Utah

State-supported, coed. Urban campus. Total enrollment: 25,226.

Degrees Bachelor of Fine Arts in the areas of actor training, teaching, design, stage management. Majors: theater arts/drama. Graduate degrees offered: Master of Fine Arts in the areas of directing, design.

Theater Student Profile Fall 1994: 266 total; 241 matriculated undergraduate, 25 matriculated graduate; 45% females.

Theater Faculty Total: 36; 15 full-time, 21 part-time; 100% of full-time faculty have terminal degrees. Graduate students teach a few undergraduate courses. Undergraduate student–faculty ratio: 12:1.

Student Life Student groups include Kingsbury Hall Young Persons Drama Season, National Student Film and Video Festival.

Expenses for 1994–95 Application fee: $30. State resident tuition: $2298 full-time. Nonresident tuition: $6795 full-time. Part-time tuition per quarter ranges from $206 to $766 for state residents, $597 to $2265 for nonresidents. College room and board: $4570. College room only: $1570.

Financial Aid Program-specific awards for Fall of 1994: 3 Special Departmental Scholarships for resident incoming freshmen ($2000), 2 Continuing Studies Scholarships for continuing students ($2000).

Application Procedures Deadline—freshmen and transfers: continuous. Notification date—freshmen and transfers: continuous. Required: college transcript(s) for transfer students, minimum 2.0 high school GPA, letter of recommendation, SAT I or ACT test scores. Recommended: essay, high school transcript, minimum 3.0 high school GPA, interview, video. Auditions held 2 times on campus; videotaped performances are permissible as a substitute for live auditions for out-of-state applicants. Portfolio reviews held 2 times on campus; the submission of slides may be substituted for portfolios for design applicants.

Undergraduate Contact Undergraduate Advisor, Theatre and Film Department, University of Utah, 206 PAB, Salt Lake City, Utah 84112; 801-581-6448, fax: 801-585-6154.

Graduate Contact Thomas B. Sobchack, Graduate Advisor, Theatre and Film Department, University of Utah, 206 PAB, Salt Lake City, Utah 84112; 801-581-5761.

University of Wisconsin–Milwaukee

Milwaukee, Wisconsin

State-supported, coed. Urban campus. Total enrollment: 22,984.

Degrees Bachelor of Fine Arts in the area of theater. Majors: acting, costume production, stage management, technical production. Graduate degrees offered: Master of Fine Arts in the area of performing arts.

Theater Student Profile Fall 1994: 30 total; 12 matriculated undergraduate, 18 matriculated graduate; 3% minorities, 50% females.

Theater Faculty Total: 16; 14 full-time, 2 part-time; 57% of full-time faculty have terminal degrees. Graduate students teach a few undergraduate courses. Undergraduate student–faculty ratio: 1:1.

Expenses for 1994–95 State resident tuition: $2772 full-time. Nonresident tuition: $8787 full-time. Part-time tuition per semester ranges from $212 to $1287 for state residents, $465.75 to $4046 for nonresidents. Minnesota residents pay tuition at the rate they would pay if attending a comparable state-supported institution in Minnesota. College room and board: $3000. Special program-related fees: $25 for audition/interview fee.

Financial Aid Program-specific awards for Fall of 1994: 10–15 Professional Theater Training Program Scholarships for undergraduates ($1000–$3000).

Application Procedures Required: high school transcript, college transcript(s) for transfer students, minimum 2.0 high school GPA, 3 letters of recommendation, interview, audition, SAT I or ACT test scores. Recommended: portfolio. Auditions held 1 time on campus and off campus in Chicago, IL; New York, NY; San Francisco, CA. Portfolio reviews held 1 time on campus and off campus in various locations.

Undergraduate Contact Undergraduate Admissions Office, University of Wisconsin–Milwaukee, P.O. Box 729, Milwaukee, Wisconsin 53201; 414-229-3800.

Graduate Contact Graduate Admissions Office, University of Wisconsin–Milwaukee, P.O. Box 340, Milwaukee, Wisconsin 53201; 414-229-4982, fax: 414-229-6967.

University of Wisconsin–Stevens Point

Stevens Point, Wisconsin

State-supported, coed. Small-town campus. Total enrollment: 8,424.

Degrees Bachelor of Fine Arts in the areas of acting, design/technology, musical theater. Majors: acting, design technology, music theater, theater arts/drama.

Theater Student Profile Fall 1994: 110 total; all matriculated undergraduate; 1% minorities, 50% females.

Theater Faculty Total: 9; 8 full-time, 1 part-time; 100% of full-time faculty have terminal degrees. Graduate students do not teach undergraduate courses. Undergraduate student–faculty ratio: 10:1.

Estimated Expenses for 1995–96 Application fee: $25. State resident tuition: $2395 full-time. Nonresident tuition: $7422 full-time. Minnesota residents pay tuition at the rate they would pay if attending a comparable state-supported institution in Minnesota. College room and board: $3150. College room only: $1800.

Financial Aid Program-specific awards for Fall of 1994: 6 Theater Scholarships for incoming students ($500–$800).

Application Procedures Deadline—freshmen and transfers: January 20. Required: high school transcript, audition, standing in top half of graduating class or ACT minimum score of 23. Auditions held continuously on campus.

Undergraduate Contact Arthur B. Hopper, Chair, Department of Theatre and Dance, University of Wisconsin–Stevens Point, COFAC, Stevens Point, Wisconsin 54481; 715-346-4429, fax: 715-346-2718.

University of Wisconsin–Superior

Superior, Wisconsin

State-supported, coed. Small-town campus. Total enrollment: 2,420.

Degrees Bachelor of Fine Arts in the area of theater. Majors: theater arts/drama. Cross-registration with University of Minnesota&–Duluth.

Theater Student Profile Fall 1994: 30 total; all matriculated undergraduate; 10% minorities, 60% females, 5% international.

Theater Faculty Total: 8; 8 full-time; 80% of full-time faculty have terminal degrees. Graduate students do not teach undergraduate courses. Undergraduate student–faculty ratio: 12:1.

Expenses for 1994–95 Application fee: $25. State resident tuition: $2182 full-time. Nonresident tuition: $6970 full-time. Part-time tuition per semester ranges from $102.55 to $1048 for state residents, $302.05 to $3342 for nonresidents. Minnesota residents pay tuition at the rate they would pay if attending a comparable state-supported institution in Minnesota. College room and board: $2716. College room only: $1408.

Financial Aid Program-specific awards for Fall of 1994: Scholarships for undergraduates ($100–$500).

Application Procedures Deadline—freshmen and transfers: continuous. Notification date—freshmen and transfers: continuous. Required: high school transcript, college transcript(s) for transfer students, minimum 2.0 high school GPA, SAT I or ACT test scores. Auditions held 3 times on campus.

Undergraduate Contact Jon Wojciechowski, Director, Admissions Office, University of Wisconsin–Superior, 1800 Grand Avenue, Superior, Wisconsin 54880-2898; 715-394-8396.

Valdosta State University

Valdosta, Georgia

State-supported, coed. Small-town campus. Total enrollment: 9,160.

Degrees Bachelor of Fine Arts in the area of theater arts. Majors: theater arts/drama.

Theater Student Profile Fall 1994: 65 total; all matriculated undergraduate; 5% minorities, 60% females.

Theater Faculty Total: 9; 8 full-time, 1 part-time; 100% of full-time faculty have terminal degrees. Undergraduate student–faculty ratio: 15:1.

Student Life Student groups include College Theater, Georgia Theatre Conference.

Expenses for 1995–96 Application fee: $10. State resident tuition: $1887 full-time. Nonresident tuition: $5097 full-time. Part-time tuition per quarter ranges from $42 to $593 for state residents, $132 to $1583 for nonresidents. College room and board: $3165. College room only: $1440.

Financial Aid Program-specific awards for Fall of 1994: 14 Theater Scholarships for undergraduates ($600–$1500).

Application Procedures Deadline—freshmen and transfers: continuous. Required: high school transcript. Recommended: minimum 2.0 high school GPA, interview. Auditions held 2 times on campus and off campus in Atlanta, GA; recorded music is permissible as a substitute for live auditions and videotaped performances are permissible as a substitute for live auditions. Portfolio reviews held 2 times on campus and off campus in Atlanta, GA; the submission of slides may be substituted for portfolios.

Undergraduate Contact Walter Peacock, Director, Admissions Office, Valdosta State University, 1500 North Patterson Street, Valdosta, Georgia 31698; 912-333-5791.

Virginia Commonwealth University

Richmond, Virginia

State-supported, coed. Urban campus. Total enrollment: 21,523.

Degrees Bachelor of Fine Arts in the areas of theater, theater education. Majors: design, performance, theater education. Graduate degrees offered: Master of Fine Arts in the area of theater.

Theater Student Profile Fall 1994: 217 total; 178 matriculated undergraduate, 39 matriculated graduate; 10% minorities, 57% females.

Theater Faculty Total: 17; 11 full-time, 6 part-time; 90% of full-time faculty have terminal degrees. Graduate students teach a few undergraduate courses. Undergraduate student–faculty ratio: 16:1.

Estimated Expenses for 1995–96 Application fee: $20. State resident tuition: $3034 full-time, $126 per credit part-time. Nonresident tuition: $10,217 full-time, $426 per credit part-time. Part-time mandatory fees: $30.50 per credit. Full-time mandatory fees: $880. College room and board: $4182. College room only: $2416 (minimum). Special program-related fees: $150 for materials.

Application Procedures Deadline—freshmen and transfers: continuous. Notification date—freshmen and transfers: continuous. Required: high school transcript, college transcript(s) for transfer students, minimum 2.0 high school GPA, letter of recommendation, interview, audition, portfolio, SAT I test score only. Recommended: essay. Auditions held 6 times on campus and off campus in Southeastern Theatre Conference; videotaped performances are permissible as a substitute for live auditions when distance is prohibitive. Portfolio reviews held 6 times on campus and off campus in Southeastern Theatre Conference.

Undergraduate Contact Richard Newdick, Chair, Theatre Department, Virginia Commonwealth University, Box 842524, Richmond, Virginia 23284-2524; 804-828-1514.

Graduate Contact Dr. James Parker, Director of Graduate Studies, Theatre Department, Virginia Commonwealth University, Box 842524, Richmond, Virginia 23284-2524; 804-828-2697.

Virginia Intermont College

Bristol, Virginia

Independent-religious, coed. Small-town campus. Total enrollment: 682.

Degrees Bachelor of Fine Arts in the area of performing arts (theater and musical theater). Majors: performance, theater arts/drama. Cross-registration with King College.

Theater Student Profile Fall 1994: 7 total; all matriculated undergraduate.

Theater Faculty Total: 4; 2 full-time, 2 part-time; 100% of full-time faculty have terminal degrees. Graduate students do not teach undergraduate courses.

Student Life Student groups include Technical Crew Club.

Expenses for 1995–96 Application fee: $15. Comprehensive fee of $13,850 includes full-time tuition ($9500), mandatory fees ($100), and college room and board ($4250). Part-time mandatory fees: $25 per semester. Part-time tuition and fees per credit: $125 for the first 6 hours, $300 for the next 5 hours.

Financial Aid Program-specific awards for Fall of 1994: 15 Room Grants for program majors ($1800).

Application Procedures Deadline—freshmen and transfers: continuous. Notification date—freshmen and transfers: continuous. Required: high school transcript, minimum 2.0 high school GPA. Recommended: audition. Auditions held by appointment on campus.

Undergraduate Contact Robin Cozart, Acting Director of Admissions, Virginia Intermont College, Box D-460, Bristol, Virginia 24201; 703-669-6101 ext. 207, fax: 703-669-5763.

Wayne State University

Detroit, Michigan

State-supported, coed. Urban campus. Total enrollment: 32,906.

Degrees Bachelor of Fine Arts in the area of theater. Majors: theater arts/drama. Graduate degrees offered: Master of Fine Arts in the areas of acting, lighting, costuming, management, scenography, stage management. Doctor of Arts in the areas of theater history, criticism.

Theater Student Profile Fall 1994: 280 total; 198 matriculated undergraduate, 82 matriculated graduate; 10% minorities, 42% females, 1% international.

Theater Faculty Total: 17; 14 full-time, 3 part-time; 100% of full-time faculty have terminal degrees. Graduate students teach a few undergraduate courses. Undergraduate student–faculty ratio: 16:1.

Expenses for 1994–95 Application fee: $20. State resident tuition: $3060 (minimum) full-time. Nonresident tuition: $6810 (minimum) full-time. Part-time mandatory fees: $70 per semester. Full-time tuition ranges up to $3705 for state residents, $8169 for nonresidents, according to class level. Part-time tuition per credit hour ranges from $98 to $115 for state residents, $218 to $259 for nonresidents, according to class level. Full-time mandatory fees: $70.

Financial Aid Program-specific awards for Fall of 1994: 10 Freshman Incentive Awards for incoming freshmen ($1500).

Application Procedures Deadline—freshmen and transfers: August 1. Notification date—freshmen and transfers: continuous. Required: minimum 2.0 high school GPA.

Undergraduate Contact Undergraduate Admissions, Wayne State University, 3 East, Joy Student Services Building, Detroit, Michigan 48202; 313-577-3577, fax: 313-577-7536.

Graduate Contact Dr. James Thomas, Chair, Theatre Department, Wayne State University, 95 West Hancock, Detroit, Michigan 48202; 313-577-3508, fax: 313-577-0935.

More about the University

Program Facilities In late 1996, the Department of Music will move to greatly expanded facilities in historic Old Main, now undergoing a $42-million renovation. Present facilities: Schaver Music Building, with administrative and faculty offices, rehearsal halls, classrooms, piano labs with twenty-seven Kawai and Korg MIDI keyboards, Macintosh-equipped listen lab/library, practice modules; The Community Arts Auditorium, with 550 seats, 50 rank organ; Music North Building, housing jazz, theory, composition, music technology programs: applied faculty studios, practice modules, up-to-date multitrack recording studio using Macintosh-based programs; The Music Annex, with offices and studios for vocal and choral faculty, rehearsal hall, practice rooms, and up to forty-five new pianos each year for student and faculty use.

Faculty, Resident Artists, and Alumni Honorary Adjunct Professors: Neemi Jarvi, Music Director, Detroit Symphony Orchestra; David DiChiera, Director, Michigan Opera Theatre; Brazeal Dennard, Director/Founder, Brazeal Dennard Chorale.

Applied music faculty: Twenty-six current or retired members of the Detroit Symphony Orchestra, some of Detroit's most respected and active music professionals in jazz, guitar, piano, and voice.

Distinguished alumni include: Metropolitan Opera stars George Shirley, Shirley Love; jazz guitarist Kenny Birrell; conductors Harry Begian, Robert Harris, Brazal Dennard, saxophonist Donald Sinta; violinists Daniel Majeske, Isidor Saslav; organist Robert Bates; composer John Rea.

Student Performance Opportunities Department of Music: Thirty regular ensemble performances annually, invitational performances with the Detroit Symphony and at festivals, corporate and government events, national and international ensemble tours, outreach performances for elementary through secondary students, extensive freelance opportunities in the Detroit metro area.

Special Programs Extensive outreach programs, internships with WSU, arts institutions, businesses.

Webster University

St. Louis, Missouri

Independent, coed. Suburban campus. Total enrollment: 10,834.

Degrees Bachelor of Fine Arts in the areas of theater, musical theater. Majors: costume design, costume management, lighting design, music theater, performance, set design, sound design, stage management, technical production. Cross-registration with various colleges in St. Louis.

Theater Student Profile Fall 1994: 147 total; all matriculated undergraduate; 10% minorities, 50% females, 1% international.

Theater Faculty Total: 32; 12 full-time, 20 part-time; 100% of full-time faculty have terminal degrees. Graduate students do not teach undergraduate courses. Undergraduate student–faculty ratio: 12:1.

Student Life Student groups include United States Institute of Theater Technology.

Expenses for 1994–95 Application fee: $25. Comprehensive fee of $13,500 includes full-time tuition ($9160) and college room and board ($4340). Part-time tuition: $280 per credit hour.

Application Procedures Deadline—freshmen and transfers: continuous. Required: essay, high school transcript, college transcript(s) for transfer students, minimum 2.0 high school GPA, 2 letters of recommendation, audition, portfolio, SAT I or ACT test scores. Recommended: minimum 3.0 high school GPA. Auditions held 8 times on campus and off campus in New York, NY; San Francisco, CA; Los Angeles, CA; Dallas, TX; Houston, TX; Atlanta, GA; Cincinnati, OH. Portfolio reviews held 8 times on campus and off campus in New York, NY; San Francisco, CA; Los Angeles, CA; Dallas, TX; Houston, TX; Atlanta, GA; Cincinnati, OH; the submission of slides may be substituted for portfolios when distance is prohibitive.

Undergraduate Contact Mary Walz, Auditions Coordinator, Office of Admissions, Webster University, 470 East Lockwood Avenue, St. Louis, Missouri 63119-3194; 314-968-7000, fax: 314-968-7115.

More about the University

The Conservatory of Theatre Arts is a four-year, sequential professional training program located within a strong liberal arts teaching university. The Conservatory is among the few undergraduate programs in the country that utilize on-campus performing organizations: The Repertory Theatre of Saint Louis and the Opera Theatre of Saint Louis. They present their seasons in Webster's Loretto-Hilton Center for the Performing Arts, which is also the home for the Conservatory's six-play season of student-performed and -designed productions.

Students are selected through a national audition/interview process for their academic strengths and perceived professional potential. It is important that potential participants in the program exhibit a positive interest in combining study in the liberal arts with the discipline that a significant professional program demands.

The graduating class presents an annual showcase in New York. Webster hosts the annual Mid-West Theatre Auditions that presents opportunities for employment in the summer and year-round professional theaters. A regularly updated list of alumni activities is available upon request.

The Conservatory's goal is to present to its students the best possible opportunities to be challenged and to excel in all of the disciplines of theater. Because the program demands hard work in an intense situation, students tend to be goal-oriented.

Western Carolina University

Cullowhee, North Carolina

State-supported, coed. Rural campus. Total enrollment: 6,619.

Degrees Bachelor of Fine Arts in the area of theater arts. Majors: theater arts/drama.

Theater Student Profile Fall 1994: 32 total; all matriculated undergraduate; 1% minorities, 65% females.

Theater Faculty Total: 5; 4 full-time, 1 part-time; 100% of full-time faculty have terminal degrees. Graduate students do not teach undergraduate courses. Undergraduate student–faculty ratio: 12:1.

Student Life Student groups include Alpha Psi Omega, University Players.

Expenses for 1994–95 Application fee: $20. State resident tuition: $764 full-time. Nonresident tuition: $7248 full-time. Part-time tuition per semester ranges from $96 to $287 for state residents, $906 to $2718 for nonresidents. Full-time mandatory fees: $787. College room and board: $2454.

Financial Aid Program-specific awards for Fall of 1994: 8 Fine and Performing Arts Awards for those demonstrating talent and academic achievement ($500).

Application Procedures Deadline—freshmen and transfers: continuous. Required: essay, high school transcript, 3 letters of recommendation, interview, SAT I or ACT test scores. Recommended: audition. Auditions held 3–4 times on campus. Portfolio reviews held 3–4 times on campus.

Undergraduate Contact Lawrence J. Hill, Head, Communication/Theatre Arts Department, Western Carolina University, 123 Stillwell, Cullowhee, North Carolina 28723; 704-227-7491, fax: 704-227-7647.

Potter College of Arts, Humanities, and Social Sciences

Western Kentucky University

Bowling Green, Kentucky

State-supported, coed. Suburban campus. Total enrollment: 14,765.

Degrees Bachelor of Fine Arts in the area of theater. Majors: theater arts/drama.

Theater Student Profile Fall 1994: 22 total; all matriculated undergraduate; 15% minorities, 40% females, 5% international.

Theater Faculty Total: 7; 6 full-time, 1 part-time; 100% of full-time faculty have terminal degrees. Graduate students do not teach undergraduate courses. Undergraduate student–faculty ratio: 17:1.

Student Life Student groups include Alpha Psi Omega.

Expenses for 1995–96 Application fee: $15. State resident tuition: $1910 full-time, $78 per semester hour part-time. Nonresident tuition: $5270 full-time, $218 per semester hour part-time. Full-time mandatory fees: $125. College room and board: $2456 (minimum). College room only: $1316 (minimum).

Application Procedures Deadline—freshmen and transfers: June 1. Required: high school transcript, minimum 2.0 high school GPA. Recommended: portfolio. Portfolio reviews held by request for scene majors on campus.

Undergraduate Contact Office of Admissions, Western Kentucky University, 101 Cravens Center, One Big Red Way, Bowling Green, Kentucky 42101-3576; 502-745-5422.

Western Michigan University

Kalamazoo, Michigan

State-supported, coed. Urban campus. Total enrollment: 25,673.

Degrees Bachelor of Fine Arts in the area of music theater performance. Majors: music theater, theater arts/drama. Cross-registration with Kalamazoo Valley Community College.

Theater Student Profile Fall 1994: 154 total; all matriculated undergraduate; 9% minorities, 50% females, 1% international.

Theater Faculty Total: 14; 11 full-time, 3 part-time; 100% of full-time faculty have terminal degrees. Undergraduate student–faculty ratio: 13:1.

Student Life Special housing available for theater students.

Expenses for 1994–95 Application fee: $25. Part-time mandatory fees: $85 per semester. Full-time tuition ranges from $2705 to $3046 for state residents, $6936 to $7804 for nonresidents, according to class level. Part-time tuition per credit hour ranges from $87.25 to $98.25 for state residents, $223.75 to $251.75 for nonresidents, according to class level. Full-time mandatory fees: $455. College room and board: $4097. Special program-related fees: $20 for practicum lab fee, $20 for stagecraft fee.

Application Procedures Deadline—freshmen and transfers: March 1. Notification date—freshmen and transfers: April 1. Required: high school transcript, college transcript(s) for transfer students, minimum 3.0 high school GPA, letter of recommendation, interview, audition, SAT I or ACT test scores. Recommended: portfolio. Auditions held 3 times on campus and off campus; videotaped performances are permissible as a substitute for live auditions when the video is of adequate quality. Portfolio reviews held 3 times on campus and off campus; the submission of slides may be substituted for portfolios when the slides are of adequate quality.

Undergraduate Contact Dr. D. Terry Williams, Chairman, Department of Theatre, Western Michigan University, Kalamazoo, Michigan 49008; 616-387-3224, fax: 616-387-3222, E-mail address: williamst@wmich.edu.

West Virginia University

Morgantown, West Virginia

State-supported, coed. Small-town campus. Total enrollment: 22,500.

Degrees Bachelor of Fine Arts in the area of theater. Majors: theater arts/drama. Graduate degrees offered: Master of Fine Arts in the area of theater.

Theater Student Profile Fall 1994: 133 total; 116 matriculated undergraduate, 17 matriculated graduate; 5% minorities, 50% females.

Theater Faculty Total: 18; 17 full-time, 1 part-time; 90% of full-time faculty have terminal degrees. Graduate students teach a few undergraduate courses. Undergraduate student–faculty ratio: 12:1.

Student Life Student groups include Alpha Psi Omega, Puppetry Touring Program.

Expenses for 1995–96 Application fee: $10. State resident tuition: $2192 full-time, $93 per credit hour part-time. Nonresident tuition: $6784 full-time, $284 per credit hour part-time. College room and board: $4434.

Financial Aid Program-specific awards for Fall of 1994: 20 Performance Grants for incoming freshmen ($850–$2000), 1 Tanner Scholarship for state residents ($500–$1000), 1–2 Boyd Scholarships for program majors ($500), 1–4 Tate-Ensley Scholarships for undergraduates ($500–$1000).

Application Procedures Deadline—freshmen and transfers: continuous. Notification date—freshmen and transfers: continuous. Required: high school transcript, college transcript(s) for transfer students, minimum 2.0 high school GPA, 2 letters of recommendation, interview, audition, portfolio, SAT I test score only. Auditions held 2 times on campus and off campus; videotaped performances are permissible as a substitute for live auditions when distance is prohibitive. Portfolio reviews held on campus and off campus; the submission of slides may be substituted for portfolios when distance is prohibitive.

Contact Registrar, Admissions and Records, West Virginia University, P.O. Box 6009, Morgantown, West Virginia 26506-6009; 304-293-2124 ext. 510.

Wichita State University

Wichita, Kansas

State-supported, coed. Urban campus. Total enrollment: 14,558.

Degrees Bachelor of Fine Arts in the area of performing arts/theater. Majors: design/technical theater, performance.

Theater Student Profile Fall 1994: 445 total; 62 matriculated undergraduate, 383 nondegree; 8% minorities, 51% females, 12% international.

Theater Faculty Total: 10; 7 full-time, 3 part-time; 100% of full-time faculty have terminal degrees. Graduate students teach a few undergraduate courses. Undergraduate student–faculty ratio: 7:1.

Student Life Student groups include American College Theater Festival, Alpha Psi Omega, Theatre in Public Schools Project.

Expenses for 1994–95 Application fee: $15. State resident tuition: $2090 full-time, $69.65 per credit hour part-time. Nonresident tuition: $7434 full-time, $247.80 per credit hour part-time. Part-time mandatory fees: $13 per semester. Full-time mandatory fees: $26. College room and board: $3121 (minimum).

Financial Aid Program-specific awards for Fall of 1994: 34 Miller Theatre Scholarships for incoming students ($650–$1500).

Application Procedures Deadline—freshmen and transfers: continuous. Required: high school transcript, college transcript(s) for transfer students, minimum 2.0 high school GPA, SAT I or ACT test scores. Recommended: interview, audition. Auditions held 2 times and by arrangement on campus.

Undergraduate Contact Christine Schneikart-Luebbe, Director of Admissions, Wichita State University, 1845 Fairmount, Wichita, Kansas 67260-0124; 316-689-3085.

William Carey College

Hattiesburg, Mississippi

Independent-religious, coed. Small-town campus. Total enrollment: 2,139.

Degrees Bachelor of Fine Arts in the area of theater. Majors: theater arts/drama.

Theater Student Profile Fall 1994: 15 total; all matriculated undergraduate; 8% minorities, 53% females.

Theater Faculty Total: 5; 3 full-time, 2 part-time; 67% of full-time faculty have terminal degrees. Graduate students teach a few undergraduate courses. Undergraduate student–faculty ratio: 6:1.

Student Life Student groups include Alpha Psi Omega, Serampore Players.

Expenses for 1994–95 Application fee: $10. Comprehensive fee of $6810 includes full-time tuition ($4650) and college room and board ($2160 minimum). Part-time tuition: $155 per semester hour.

Financial Aid Program-specific awards for Fall of 1994: 3 Named Scholarships for enrolled students ($500–$5000), 12 Theater Talent Awards for program majors ($500–$5000).

Application Procedures Deadline—freshmen and transfers: July 1. Notification date—freshmen and transfers: August 1. Required: high school transcript, college transcript(s) for transfer students, minimum 2.0 high school GPA, letter of recommendation, SAT I or ACT test scores. Recommended: interview, audition, portfolio. Auditions held at various times on campus; videotaped performances are permissible as a substitute for live auditions. Portfolio reviews held at various times on campus; the submission of slides may be substituted for portfolios.

Undergraduate Contact O. L. Quave, Chair, Theatre and Communication Department, William Carey College, 498 Tuscan Avenue, Hattiesburg, Mississippi 39401-5499; 601-582-6218, fax: 601-582-6454.

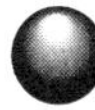

Wright State University

Fairborn, Ohio

State-supported, coed. Suburban campus. Total enrollment: 16,823.

Degrees Bachelor of Fine Arts in the areas of acting, directing/stage management, design/technology. Majors: design technology, directing/stage management, theater arts/drama.

Theater Student Profile Fall 1994: 150 total; all matriculated undergraduate.

Theater Faculty Total: 11; 11 full-time; 75% of full-time faculty have terminal degrees. Graduate students do not teach undergraduate courses.

Expenses for 1995–96 Application fee: $30. State resident tuition: $3429 full-time, $107 per credit hour part-time. Nonresident tuition: $6858 full-time, $214 per credit hour part-time. College room and board: $4806. Special program-related fees: $125 for private voice lessons.

Financial Aid Program-specific awards for Fall of 1994: Theatre Arts Talent Awards for incoming students ($500–$2500).

Application Procedures Deadline—freshmen and transfers: March 14. Required: high school transcript, interview, audition, SAT I or ACT test scores, photograph, video if unavailable to audition in person. Auditions held 2–3 times for acting, directing/stage management applicants on campus; videotaped performances are permissible as a substitute for live auditions if a campus visit is impossible.

Undergraduate Contact Victoria Oleen, Administrative Coordinator, Department of Theatre Arts, Wright State University, 3640 Colonel Glenn Highway, T148 CAC, Dayton, Ohio 45435; 513-873-3072, fax: 513-873-3787.

More about the University

Program Facilities The Department of Theatre Arts is housed in a newly constructed, state-of-the-art facility that includes acting studios, a 95-seat directing lab, design labs, dance studios, movement studio, lighting lab, and motion picture production facilities. Mainstage theater productions are held in the Festival Playhouse, a 376-seat proscenium theatre. Studio productions are in a 100-seat black box theater. The department has access to a comprehensive collection of playscripts, musical theater scores and soundtracks, and videotape library.

Faculty, Resident Artists, and Alumni Chair W. Stuart McDowell is the founder and former artistic director of the Riverside Shakespeare Company in New York City and stage director of numerous professional productions in New York and across the country. Other faculty have worked professionally at the Alabama Shakespeare Festival, Milwaukee Repertory Theatre, Cincinnati Playhouse in the Park, Dayton Ballet, Dayton Contemporary Dance Company, and the Human Race Theatre Company. Motion picture professors James Klein and Julia Reichert have been nominated for the Academy Award.

Student Performance Opportunities Students may work on six mainstage and three studio productions as actors, designers, dancers, or technicians. Students are also offered directing, design, choreography, acting, and dance opportunities in student productions in the directing lab and studio theater. Motion picture production majors are required to complete two fully realized films prior to graduation. Performance opportunities are also offered with the Human Race Theatre Company, Dayton's professional Equity theater, and with Dayton Ballet and Dayton Contemporary Dance Company.

York University

North York, Ontario

Province-supported, coed. Urban campus. Total enrollment: 38,313.

Degrees Bachelor of Fine Arts in the area of theater. Majors: acting, production. Graduate degrees offered: Master of Fine Arts in the area of theater.

Theater Student Profile Fall 1994: 368 total; 350 matriculated undergraduate, 18 matriculated graduate.

Theater Faculty Total: 20; 15 full-time, 5 part-time. Graduate students teach a few undergraduate courses. Undergraduate student–faculty ratio: 17:1.

Expenses for 1994–95 Application fee: $75. Canadian resident tuition: $2720 full-time, $90.67 per credit part-time. Nonresident tuition: $8894 full-time, $296.47 per credit part-time. (All figures are in Canadian dollars.). Full-time mandatory fees: $140. College room and board: $3796. College room only: $3201. Special program-related fees: $10–$40 for materials and supplies.

Financial Aid Program-specific awards for Fall of 1994: 2 Talent Awards for students with outstanding auditions ($1000).

Application Procedures Deadline—freshmen and transfers: March 1. Notification date—freshmen: June 30; transfers: July 15. Required: essay, high school transcript, college transcript(s) for transfer students, minimum 3.0 high school GPA, 2 letters of recommendation, interview, audition. Auditions held 1 time on campus and off campus; videotaped performances are permissible as a substitute for live auditions when distance is prohibitive. Portfolio reviews held on campus and off campus.

Undergraduate Contact Don Murdoch, Liaison Officer, Liaison and Advising, Faculty of Fine Arts, York University, 213 CFA, 4700 Keele Street, North York, Ontario M3J 1P3; 416-736-5135, fax: 416-736-5447, E-mail address: donm@vm2.yorku.ca.

Graduate Contact David Smukler, Graduate Program Director, Theatre Department, York University, 306 CFT, 4700 Keele Street, North York, Ontario M3J 1P3; 416-736-5172, fax: 416-736-5785.

APPENDIX

BACHELOR'S-LEVEL ARTS DEGREE PROGRAMS

This Appendix lists all U.S. and Canadian four-year colleges and universities that offer the Bachelor of Arts or Bachelor of Science degree in the visual and performing arts.

A

Abilene Christian University
Abilene, TX
Art/fine arts, music, theater arts/drama. Contact Mr. Don King, Director of University Outreach, ACU Box 8483, Abilene, TX 79699, 915-674-2650.

Adams State College
Alamosa, CO
Art/fine arts, music, theater arts/drama. Contact Mr. Mark Manzanares, Director of Admissions, Alamosa, CO 81102, 719-589-7712.

Adelphi University
Garden City, NY
Art/fine arts, dance, music, theater arts/drama. Contact Mr. Kenneth Stevenson, Dean of Admissions, South Avenue, Garden City, NY 11530, 516-877-3050.

Adrian College
Adrian, MI
Art/fine arts, music, theater arts/drama. Contact Mr. George Wolf, Director of Admissions and Enrollment Management, 110 South Madison Street, Adrian, MI 49221-2575, 517-265-5161 Ext. 4326.

Agnes Scott College
Decatur, GA
Art/fine arts, music, theater arts/drama. Contact Ms. Stephanie Balmer, Acting Director of Admission, 141 East College Avenue, Decatur, GA 30030-3797, 404-638-6285.

Alabama Agricultural and Mechanical University
Normal, AL
Art/fine arts, music. Contact Mr. James Heyward, Director of Admissions, PO Box 908, Normal, AL 35762-1357, 205-851-5245.

Alabama State University
Montgomery, AL
Art/fine arts, music, theater arts/drama. Contact Mr. Samuel Leon Mitchell, Interim Director of Admissions and Recruitment, 915 South Jackson Street, Montgomery, AL 36101-0271, 334-293-4291.

Albany State College
Albany, GA
Art/fine arts, music. Contact Mrs. Kathleen Caldwell, Director of Admissions and Financial Aid, 504 College Drive, Albany, GA 31705-2717, 912-430-4650.

Albertson College of Idaho
Caldwell, ID
Art/fine arts, music, theater arts/drama. Contact Mr. Dennis P. Bergvall, Dean of Admissions, 2112 Cleveland Boulevard, Caldwell, ID 83605-4494, 208-459-5305.

Albertus Magnus College
New Haven, CT
Art/fine arts, theater arts/drama. Contact Mr. Richard Lolatte, Dean of Admissions and Enrollment Management, 700 Prospect Street, New Haven, CT 06511-1189, 203-773-8501.

Albion College
Albion, MI
Art/fine arts, music, theater arts/drama. Contact Dr. Frank Bonta, Dean of Admissions, 611 East Porter Street, Albion, MI 49224-1831, 517-629-0321.

Albright College
Reading, PA
Theater arts/drama. Contact Ms. S. Elizabeth VanVelsor, Director of Admissions, PO Box 15234, Reading, PA 19612-5234, 610-921-7512.

Alcorn State University
Lorman, MS
Music. Contact Mr. Emmanuel Barnes, Director of Admissions, Lorman, MS 39096, 601-877-6147.

Alderson-Broaddus College
Philippi, WV
Music, theater arts/drama. Contact Mr. Craig W. Gould, Director of Admissions, Philippi, WV 26416, 304-457-1700 Ext. 310.

Alfred University
Alfred, NY
Art/fine arts, theater arts/drama. Contact Ms. Laurie Richer, Director of Admissions, Alumni Hall, Alfred, NY 14802-1232, 607-871-2115.

Allegheny College
Meadville, PA
Art/fine arts, music, theater arts/drama. Contact Ms. Gayle Pollock, Director of Admissions, North Main Street, Meadville, PA 16335, 814-332-4351.

Allentown College of St. Francis de Sales
Center Valley, PA
Dance, theater arts/drama. Contact Mr. James McCarthy, Director of Admissions, 2755 Station Avenue, Center Valley, PA 18034-9568, 610-282-1100 Ext. 1205.

Allen University
Columbia, SC
Music. Contact Ms. Lisa Mills, Director of Admission, 1530 Harden Street, Columbia, SC 29204-1085, 803-376-5716.

Alma College
Alma, MI
Art/fine arts, dance, music, theater arts/drama. Contact Mr. John Seveland, Vice President for Enrollment and Student Affairs, 614 West Superior, Alma, MI 48801-1599, 517-463-7139.

Alverno College
Milwaukee, WI
Art/fine arts, music. Contact Ms. Colleen Hayes, Director of Admissions, 3401 South 39th St, PO Box 343922, Milwaukee, WI 53234-3922, 414-382-6100.

The American College
Los Angeles, CA
Art/fine arts. Contact Ms. Maryclair Pulver, Director of Admissions, 1651 Westwood Boulevard, Los Angeles, CA 90024-5603, 310-470-2000 Ext. 32.

The American College
Atlanta, GA
Art/fine arts. Contact Ms. Suzanne McBride, Vice President and Director of Admissions, 3330 Peachtree Road, NE, Atlanta, GA 30326-1019, 404-231-9000.

American Conservatory of Music
Chicago, IL
Music. Contact Ms. Theodora Schulze, President, 16 North Wabash Avenue, Suite 1850, Chicago, IL 60602-4792, 312-263-4161.

American University
Washington, DC
Art/fine arts, music, theater arts/drama. Contact Ms. Marcelle D. Heerschap, Director of Admissions, 4400 Massachusetts Avenue, NW, Washington, DC 20016-8001, 202-885-6000.

Amherst College
Amherst, MA
Art/fine arts, dance, music, theater arts/drama. Contact Ms. Jane E. Reynolds, Dean of Admission, Amherst, MA 01002, 413-542-2328.

Anderson College
Anderson, SC
Art/fine arts, music, theater arts/drama. Contact Mr. Carl D. Lockman, Director of Admissions, 316 Boulevard, Anderson, SC 29621-4035, 803-231-2030.

Anderson University
Anderson, IN
Art/fine arts, music, theater arts/drama. Contact Mr. James A. King, Director of Admissions, 1100 East Fifth Street, Anderson, IN 46012-3495, 317-641-4080.

Andrews University
Berrien Springs, MI
Art/fine arts, music. Contact Dr. Kermit Netteburg, Executive Director of Enrollment Management, Berrien Springs, MI 49104, 616-471-3203.

Angelo State University
San Angelo, TX
Art/fine arts, music, theater arts/drama. Contact Mr. Manuel R. Lujan, Dean of Admissions/Registrar, 2601 West Avenue N, San Angelo, TX 76909, 915-942-2042.

Anna Maria College
Paxton, MA
Art/fine arts, music. Contact Mr. David M. Pirani, Director of Admissions, Box 78, Paxton, MA 01612, 508-849-3360.

Antioch College
Yellow Springs, OH
Art/fine arts, dance, music, theater arts/drama. Contact Mr. James H. Williams Jr., Dean of Admissions, 795 Livermore Street, Yellow Springs, OH 45387-1697, 513-767-6400.

Appalachian State University
Boone, NC
Art/fine arts, music, theater arts/drama. Contact Mr. Joe Watts, Director of Admissions/Enrollment Services, Boone, NC 28608, 704-262-2120.

Aquinas College
Grand Rapids, MI
Art/fine arts, music. Contact Mrs. Paula Meehan, Dean of Admissions, 1607 Robinson Road, SE, Grand Rapids, MI 49506-1799, 616-459-8281 Ext. 5205.

Arizona College of the Bible
Phoenix, AZ
Music. Contact Mrs. Robin Dunn, Director of Enrollment Management, 2045 West Northern Avenue, Phoenix, AZ 85021-5197, 602-995-2670 Ext. 312.

Arizona State University
Tempe, AZ
Art/fine arts, dance, music, theater arts/drama. Contact Ms. Susan R. Dolbert, Director of Undergraduate Admissions, Tempe, AZ 85287, 602-965-7788.

Arizona State University West
Phoenix, AZ
Art/fine arts. Contact Mr. Tom Cabot, Coordinator, 4701 West Thunderbird Road, PO Box 37100, Phoenix, AZ 85069-7100, 602-543-8123.

Arkansas State University
Jonesboro, AR
Art/fine arts, music, theater arts/drama. Contact Ms. Paula James, Director of Admissions, State University, AR 72467, 501-972-3024.

Arkansas Tech University
Russellville, AR
Art/fine arts, music, theater arts/drama. Contact Dr. Dix Stallings, Vice President for Public Affairs, Russellville, AR 72801-2222, 501-968-0400.

Arlington Baptist College
Arlington, TX
Music. Contact Mrs. Helen Sullivan, Registrar, 3001 West Division, Arlington, TX 76012-3425, 817-461-8741.

Armstrong State College
Savannah, GA
Art/fine arts, music, theater arts/drama. Contact Mr. Kim West, Registrar/Director of Admissions, 11935 Abercorn Street, Savannah, GA 31419-1997, 912-927-5275.

Asbury College
Wilmore, KY
Art/fine arts, music. Contact Mr. Stan F. Wiggam, Dean of Admissions, 1 Macklem Drive, Wilmore, KY 40390, 606-858-3511 Ext. 2142.

Ashland University
Ashland, OH
Art/fine arts, music, theater arts/drama. Contact Mr. Carl A. Gerbasi Jr., Vice President of Enrollment Management, 401 College Avenue, Ashland, OH 44805-3702, 419-289-5054.

Assumption College
Worcester, MA
Music. Contact Mr. Thomas E. Dunn, Vice President for Enrollment Management, 500 Salisbury Street, PO Box 15005, Worcester, MA 01615-0005, 508-767-7285.

Athens State College
Athens, AL
Art/fine arts. Contact Ms. Necedah Henderson, Coordinator of Admissions, 300 North Beaty Street, Athens, AL 35611-1902, 205-233-8217.

Atlanta Christian College
East Point, GA
Music. Contact Ms. Sheryl Turner, Director of Admissions and Financial Aid, 2605 Ben Hill Road, East Point, GA 30344-1999, 404-761-8861.

Atlanta College of Art
Atlanta, GA
Art/fine arts. Contact Mr. John A. Farkas, Director of Enrollment Management, 1280 Peachtree Street, NE, Atlanta, GA 30309-3582, 404-733-5100.

Atlantic Union College
South Lancaster, MA
Art/fine arts, music. Contact Ms. Osa Canto, Enrollment Manager, PO Box 1000, South Lancaster, MA 01561-1000, 508-368-2255.

Auburn University
Auburn, AL
Art/fine arts, music, theater arts/drama. Contact Dr. Charles F. Reeder, Director of Admissions, 202 Mary Martin Hall, Auburn University, AL 36849-0001, 334-844-4080.

Auburn University at Montgomery
Montgomery, AL
Art/fine arts, theater arts/drama. Contact Mr. Lee Davis, Director of Admissions, 7300 University Drive, Montgomery, AL 36117-3596, 334-244-3611.

Augsburg College
Minneapolis, MN
Art/fine arts, music, theater arts/drama. Contact Ms. Sally Daniels, Director of Admissions, 2211 Riverside Avenue South, Minneapolis, MN 55454-1351, 612-330-1001.

Augusta College
Augusta, GA
Art/fine arts, music. Contact Mr. Lee Young, Director of Admissions/Assistant Dean for Enrollment Service, 2500 Walton Way, Augusta, GA 30904-2200, 706-737-1632.

Augustana College
Rock Island, IL
Art/fine arts, music, theater arts/drama. Contact Mr. Martin Sauer, Director of Admissions, 639 38th Street, Rock Island, IL 61201-2296, 309-794-7341.

Augustana College
Sioux Falls, SD
Music, theater arts/drama. Contact Mr. Robert A. Preloger, Assistant to the President/Dean of Enrollment, 29th and Summit, Sioux Falls, SD 57197, 605-336-5516.

Austin College
Sherman, TX
Art/fine arts, music. Contact Mr. Jay Evans, Senior Associate Director of Admissions, 900 North Grand Avenue, Sherman, TX 75090-4440, 903-813-3000.

Austin Peay State University
Clarksville, TN
Art/fine arts, music, theater arts/drama. Contact Mr. Charles McCorkle, Director of Admissions, PO Box 4548, Clarksville, TN 37044-0001, 615-648-7661.

Averett College
Danville, VA
Art/fine arts, music, theater arts/drama. Contact Mr. Gary Sherman, Dean of Enrollment and Management, 420 West Main Street, Danville, VA 24541-3692, 804-791-5660.

Avila College
Kansas City, MO
Art/fine arts, music, theater arts/drama. Contact Mr. James E. Millard, Director of Admissions, 11901 Wornall Road, Kansas City, MO 64145-1698, 816-942-8400 Ext. 3500.

Azusa Pacific University
Azusa, CA
Art/fine arts, music. Contact Mrs. Deana Porterfield, Director of Undergraduate Admissions, 901 East Alosta Avenue, PO Box APU, Azusa, CA 91702-2701, 818-812-3016.

B

Baker College of Flint
Flint, MI
Art/fine arts. Contact Mr. Mark Heaton, Vice President for Admissions, 1050 West Bristol Road, Flint, MI 48507-5508, 810-766-4015.

Baker College of Owosso
Owosso, MI
Art/fine arts. Contact Mr. Bruce A. Lundeen, Director of Admissions, 1020 South Washington Street, Owosso, MI 48867-4400, 517-723-5251 Ext. 454.

Baker University
Baldwin City, KS
Art/fine arts, music, theater arts/drama. Contact Mr. John Haynes, Director of Admissions, Box 65, Baldwin City, KS 66006-0065, 913-594-6451 Ext. 328.

Baldwin-Wallace College
Berea, OH
Art/fine arts, dance, music, theater arts/drama. Contact Mr. J. Edward Warner, Dean of Enrollment Services, 275 Eastland Road, Berea, OH 44017-2088, 216-826-2222.

Ball State University
Muncie, IN
Art/fine arts, dance, music, theater arts/drama. Contact Mrs. Ruth Vedvik, Director of Admissions, 2000 University Avenue, Muncie, IN 47306-1099, 317-285-8300.

Baptist Bible College
Springfield, MO
Music. Contact Dr. Joseph Gleason, Director of Admissions, 628 East Kearney, Springfield, MO 65803-3498, 417-869-6000 Ext. 2219.

Baptist Bible College of Pennsylvania
Clarks Summit, PA
Music. Contact Mr. Glenn Amos, Director of Enrollment Management, PO Box 800, Clarks Summit, PA 18411-1297, 717-586-2400 Ext. 380.

Barat College
Lake Forest, IL
Art/fine arts, dance, music, theater arts/drama. Contact Mr. Douglas Schacke, Director of Admissions, 700 East Westleigh Road, Lake Forest, IL 60045-3297, 708-295-4260 Ext. 675.

Barclay College
Haviland, KS
Music. Contact Ms. Anita Fitzh, Director of Admissions, PO Box 288, Haviland, KS 67059-0288, 316-862-5252.

Bard College
Annandale-on-Hudson, NY
Art/fine arts, dance, music, theater arts/drama. Contact Ms. Mary Backlund, Director of Admissions, Annandale-on-Hudson, NY 12504, 914-758-7472.

Barnard College
New York, NY
Dance, music, theater arts/drama. Contact Ms. Doris Davis, Director of Admissions, 3009 Broadway, New York, NY 10027-6598, 212-854-2014.

Barry University
Miami Shores, FL
Art/fine arts, theater arts/drama. Contact Mr. Michael Backes, Dean of Admissions and Enrollment Services, 11300 Northeast Second Avenue, Miami Shores, FL 33161-6695, 305-899-3100.

Barton College
Wilson, NC
Art/fine arts, music, theater arts/drama. Contact Mr. Anthony Britt, Director of Admissions, College Station, Wilson, NC 27893, 919-399-6314.

Baruch College of the City University of New York
New York, NY
Music. Contact Ms. Ellen Washington, Director of Admissions, Box H-0720, New York, NY 10010-5585, 212-802-2300.

Bates College
Lewiston, ME
Art/fine arts, music, theater arts/drama. Contact Mr. Wylie L. Mitchell, Dean of Admissions, 23 Campus Avenue, Lewiston, ME 04240-6028, 207-786-6000.

Baylor University
Waco, TX
Art/fine arts, music, theater arts/drama. Contact Mrs. Diana M. Ramey, Director of Admissions, PO Box 97056, Waco, TX 76798, 817-755-1811.

Beaver College
Glenside, PA
Art/fine arts, theater arts/drama. Contact Mr. Dennis Nostrand, Vice President for Enrollment Management, 450 South Easton Road, Glenside, PA 19038-3295, 215-572-2179.

Belhaven College
Jackson, MS
Art/fine arts, music, theater arts/drama. Contact Mrs. Mary I. Word, Director of Admissions, 1500 Peachtree Street, Jackson, MS 39202-1789, 601-968-5940.

Bellarmine College
Louisville, KY
Art/fine arts, music. Contact Mr. R. Edwin Wilkes, Dean of Admissions and Financial Aid, 2001 Newburg Road, Louisville, KY 40205-0671, 502-452-8131.

Bellevue University
Bellevue, NE
Art/fine arts. Contact Ms. Christel Vanmeter, Director of Marketing and Enrollment, 1000 Galvin Road South, Bellevue, NE 68005-3098, 402-293-3711.

Belmont University
Nashville, TN
Art/fine arts, music, theater arts/drama. Contact Dr. Kathryn Baugher, Dean of Admissions, 1900 Belmont Boulevard, Nashville, TN 37212-3757, 615-385-6785.

Beloit College
Beloit, WI
Art/fine arts, music, theater arts/drama. Contact Mr. Alan G. McIvor, Vice President of Enrollment Services, 700 College Street, Beloit, WI 53511-5596, 608-363-2500.

Bemidji State University
Bemidji, MN
Art/fine arts, music, theater arts/drama. Contact Mr. Paul Muller, Associate Director of Admissions, 1500 Birchmont Drive, NE, Bemidji, MN 56601-2699, 218-755-2040.

Benedict College
Columbia, SC
Art/fine arts. Contact Dr. LeRoy R. Brown, Director of Enrollment Management, Harden and Blanding Streets, Columbia, SC 29204, 803-253-5143.

Benedictine College
Atchison, KS
Music, theater arts/drama. Contact Mr. James J. Hoffman, Dean of Enrollment Management, 1020 North 2nd Street, Atchison, KS 66002-1499, 913-367-5340 Ext. 2475.

Bennett College
Greensboro, NC
Art/fine arts, music. Contact Ms. Helene Cameron, Dean of Enrollment Management, 900 East Washington Street, Greensboro, NC 27401-3239, 910-370-8624.

Bennington College
Bennington, VT
Art/fine arts, dance, music, theater arts/drama. Contact Ms. Elena Ruocco Bachrach, Dean of Admissions, Bennington, VT 05201-9993, 802-442-6349.

Berea College
Berea, KY
Art/fine arts, music, theater arts/drama. Contact Mr. John S. Cook, Director of Admissions, CPO 2344, KY 40404, 606-986-9341 Ext. 5083.

Berklee College of Music
Boston, MA
Music. Contact Mr. Steven Lipman, Assistant Dean of Students/Director of Admissions, 1140 Boylston Street, Boston, MA 02215-3693, 617-266-1400.

Berry College
Mount Berry, GA
Art/fine arts, music, theater arts/drama. Contact Mr. George Gaddie, Dean of Admissions, 159 Mount Berry Station, Mount Berry, GA 30149-0159, 706-236-2215.

Bethany College
Lindsborg, KS
Art/fine arts, music. Contact Mrs. Louise Cummings-Simmons, Dean of Admissions and Financial Aid, 421 North First Street, Lindsborg, KS 67456-1897, 913-227-3311 Ext. 111.

Bethany College
Bethany, WV
Art/fine arts. Contact Mr. Gary R. Forney, Vice President for Enrollment Management, Bethany, WV 26032, 304-829-7611.

Bethany College of the Assemblies of God
Scotts Valley, CA
Music, theater arts/drama. Contact Miss Carmine H. Wilson, Registrar, 800 Bethany Drive, Scotts Valley, CA 95066-2820, 408-438-3800 Ext. 1405.

Bethel College
Mishawaka, IN
Art/fine arts, music. Contact Mr. Steve Matteson, Dean of Admissions, 1001 West McKinley Avenue, Mishawaka, IN 46545-5591, 219-257-3339 Ext. 319.

Bethel College
North Newton, KS
Art/fine arts, music, theater arts/drama. Contact Mr. Michael Lamb, Director of Admissions, 300 East 27th Street, North Newton, KS 67117, 316-283-2500 Ext. 230.

Bethel College
St. Paul, MN
Art/fine arts, music, theater arts/drama. Contact Dr. Tom Johnson, Executive Vice President for Enrollment, 3900 Bethel Drive, St. Paul, MN 55112-6999, 612-638-6187.

Bethel College
McKenzie, TN
Music. Contact Mr. Joe Rigell, Assistant to the President for Admissions and Financial Aid, 325 Cherry Street, McKenzie, TN 38201, 901-352-1000.

Bethune-Cookman College
Daytona Beach, FL
Music. Contact Dr. Catherine Cook, Interim Director of Admissions and Recruitment, 640 Dr. Mary McLeod Bethune Blvd, Daytona Beach, FL 32114-3099, 904-255-1401 Ext. 333.

Biola University
La Mirada, CA
Art/fine arts, music, theater arts/drama. Contact Mr. Greg Vaughan, Director of Admissions, 13800 Biola Avenue, La Mirada, CA 90639-0001, 310-903-4727.

Birmingham-Southern College
Birmingham, AL
Art/fine arts, dance, music, theater arts/drama. Contact Mr. Robert Dortch, Vice President of Admissions Services, 900 Arkadelphia Road, Birmingham, AL 35254, 205-226-4686.

Blackburn College
Carlinville, IL
Art/fine arts, music. Contact Mr. John Malin, Director of Admissions, 700 College Avenue, Carlinville, IL 62626-1498, 217-854-3231 Ext. 4252.

Black Hills State University
Spearfish, SD
Art/fine arts, music, theater arts/drama. Contact Mrs. April Meeker, Director of Admissions and Records, College Station Box 9501, Spearfish, SD 57799-9501, 605-642-6343.

Bloomfield College
Bloomfield, NJ
Art/fine arts, theater arts/drama. Contact Mr. George P. Lynes II, Dean of Admissions, Park Place, Bloomfield, NJ 07003-9981, 201-748-9000 Ext. 230.

Bloomsburg University of Pennsylvania
Bloomsburg, PA
Art/fine arts, music, theater arts/drama. Contact Mr. James Christy, Interim Director of Admissions, Ben Franklin Building, Room 10, Bloomsburg, PA 17815-1905, 717-389-4316.

Bluefield College
Bluefield, VA
Art/fine arts, music, theater arts/drama. Contact Mrs. Nina Wilburn, Vice President of Enrollment Management, 3000 College Drive, Bluefield, VA 24605-1799, 703-326-4213.

Bluefield State College
Bluefield, WV
Art/fine arts. Contact Mr. John C. Cardwell, Director of Admissions and Enrollment Management, 219 Rock Street, Bluefield, WV 24701-2198, 304-327-4065.

Blue Mountain College
Blue Mountain, MS
Music, theater arts/drama. Contact Ms. Rhonda Cockrell, Director of Admissions, PO Box 126, Blue Mountain, MS 38610-9509, 601-685-4161.

Bluffton College
Bluffton, OH
Art/fine arts, music. Contact Mr. Michael Hieronimus, Dean of Admissions, 280 West College Avenue, Bluffton, OH 45817-1196, 419-358-3254.

Boise State University
Boise, ID
Art/fine arts, music, theater arts/drama. Contact Mr. Stephen Spafford, Dean of Admissions, 1910 University Drive, Boise, ID 83725-0399, 208-385-1177.

Boston College
Chestnut Hill, MA
Art/fine arts, music, theater arts/drama. Contact Mr. John L. Mahoney Jr., Director of Undergraduate Admission, 140 Commonwealth Avenue, Chestnut Hill, MA 02167-9991, 617-552-3100.

Boston Conservatory
Boston, MA
Dance, music, theater arts/drama. Contact Mr. Richard Wallace, Director of Enrollment, 8 The Fenway, Boston, MA 02215, 617-536-6340 Ext. 16.

Boston University
Boston, MA
Art/fine arts, music, theater arts/drama. Contact Mr. Thomas Rajala, Director of Admissions, 121 Bay State Road, Boston, MA 02215, 617-353-2300.

Bowdoin College
Brunswick, ME
Art/fine arts, dance, music, theater arts/drama. Contact Dr. Richard E. Steele, Dean of Admissions, Brunswick, ME 04011-2546, 207-725-3190.

Bowie State University
Bowie, MD
Art/fine arts, music, theater arts/drama. Contact Ms. Margery Cook, Director of Admissions, Records, and Registration, 14000 Jericho Park Road, Bowie, MD 20715-3318, 301-464-6570.

Bowling Green State University
Bowling Green, OH
Art/fine arts, dance, music, theater arts/drama. Contact Mr. Michael D. Walsh, Director of Admissions, Bowling Green, OH 43403, 419-372-2086.

Bradford College
Bradford, MA
Art/fine arts, dance, music, theater arts/drama. Contact Mr. William Dunfey, Dean of Admissions, South Main Street, Bradford, MA 01835, 508-372-7161 Ext. 271.

Bradley University
Peoria, IL
Art/fine arts, music, theater arts/drama. Contact Mr. Gary Bergman, Executive Director of Enrollment Management, 1501 West Bradley Avenue, Peoria, IL 61625-0002, 309-677-1000.

Brandeis University
Waltham, MA
Art/fine arts, music, theater arts/drama. Contact Mr. David L. Gould, Dean of Admissions, 415 South Street, Waltham, MA 02254-9110, 617-736-3500.

Brenau University
Gainesville, GA
Art/fine arts, dance, music, theater arts/drama. Contact Dr. John D. Upchurch, Director of Admissions, One Centennial Circle, Gainesville, GA 30501-3697, 404-534-6100.

Brescia College
Owensboro, KY
Art/fine arts. Contact Mr. Thomas G. Green, Director of Admissions, 717 Frederica Street, Owensboro, KY 42301-3023, 502-686-4241.

Brewton-Parker College
Mt. Vernon, GA
Music. Contact Mrs. Jill O'Neal, Director of Admissions, Highway 280, Mt. Vernon, GA 30445, 912-583-2241 Ext. 268.

Briar Cliff College
Sioux City, IA
Art/fine arts, music, theater arts/drama. Contact Mrs. Sharisue Wilcoxon, Executive Director of Admissions and Marketing, 3303 Rebecca Street, Sioux City, IA 51104-2100, 712-279-5200.

Bridgewater College
Bridgewater, VA
Art/fine arts, music. Contact Mr. Brian C. Hildebrand, Dean for Enrollment Management, Bridgewater, VA 22812, 703-828-2501 Ext. 400.

Bridgewater State College
Bridgewater, MA
Art/fine arts, music, theater arts/drama. Contact Mr. James F. Plotner Jr., Associate Dean of Academic Admissions, Bridgewater, MA 02325-0001, 508-697-1237.

Brigham Young University
Provo, UT
Art/fine arts, dance, music, theater arts/drama. Contact Mr. Erlend D. Peterson, Dean of Admissions and Records, Provo, UT 84602-1001, 801-378-2539.

Brigham Young University–Hawaii Campus
Laie, Oahu, HI
Art/fine arts, music. Contact Dr. David Settle, Assistant Dean for Admissions and Records, 55-220 Kulanui Street, Laie, Oahu, HI 96762-1294, 808-293-3738.

Brooklyn College of the City University of New York
Brooklyn, NY
Art/fine arts, dance, music, theater arts/drama. Contact Mr. John Fraire, Director of Admissions, 1602 James Hall, Brooklyn, NY 11210-2889, 718-951-5921.

Brown University
Providence, RI
Art/fine arts, dance, music, theater arts/drama. Contact Mr. Michael Goldberger, Director of Admission, Box 1876, Providence, RI 02912, 401-863-2378.

Bryan College
Dayton, TN
Music. Contact Mr. Thomas Shaw, Director of Admissions, PO Box 7000, Dayton, TN 37321-7000, 615-775-2041 Ext. 205.

Bryn Mawr College
Bryn Mawr, PA
Art/fine arts, music. Contact Ms. Elizabeth G. Vermey, Director of Admissions, 101 North Merion Avenue, Bryn Mawr, PA 19010-2899, 610-526-5152.

Bucknell University
Lewisburg, PA
Art/fine arts, music, theater arts/drama. Contact Mr. Mark D. Davies, Dean of Admissions, Lewisburg, PA 17837, 717-524-1101.

Buena Vista University
Storm Lake, IA
Art/fine arts, music, theater arts/drama. Contact Mr. Mike Frantz, Director of Admissions, 610 West Fourth Street, Storm Lake, IA 50588, 712-749-2235.

Burlington College
Burlington, VT
Art/fine arts. Contact Ms. Nancy Wilson, Director of Admissions, 95 North Avenue, Burlington, VT 05401-2998, 802-862-9616 Ext. 32.

Butler University
Indianapolis, IN
Dance, music, theater arts/drama. Contact Ms. Carroll Davis, Dean of Admission, 4600 Sunset Avenue, Indianapolis, IN 46208-3485, 317-283-9255.

C

Cabrini College
Radnor, PA
Art/fine arts. Contact Ms. Nancy Gardner, Executive Director of Admissions and Financial Aid, 610 King of Prussia Road, Radnor, PA 19087-3698, 610-902-8552.

Caldwell College
Caldwell, NJ
Art/fine arts, music. Contact Mr. Raymond Sheenan, Director of Admissions, 9 Ryerson Avenue, Caldwell, NJ 07006-6195, 201-228-4424 Ext. 220.

California Baptist College
Riverside, CA
Art/fine arts, music, theater arts/drama. Contact Mr. Kent Dacus, Director of Admissions, 8432 Magnolia Avenue, Riverside, CA 92504-3206, 909-689-5771.

California College of Arts and Crafts
Oakland, CA
Art/fine arts. Contact Ms. Sheri Sivin McKenzie, Director of Enrollment Services, 5212 Broadway at College Avenue, Oakland, CA 94618, 510-653-8118 Ext. 312.

California Institute of the Arts
Valencia, CA
Art/fine arts, dance, music, theater arts/drama. Contact Mr. Kenneth Young, Director of Admissions, 24700 McBean Parkway, Valencia, CA 91355-2340, 805-255-1050 Ext. 7863.

California Lutheran University
Thousand Oaks, CA
Art/fine arts, music, theater arts/drama. Contact Mr. Ernie Sandlin, Director of Admissions, 60 West Olsen Road, Thousand Oaks, CA 91360-2700, 805-493-3135.

California Polytechnic State University, San Luis Obispo
San Luis Obispo, CA
Art/fine arts, music. Contact Mr. James Maraviglia, Director of Admissions and Evaluations, San Luis Obispo, CA 93407, 805-756-2311.

California State Polytechnic University, Pomona
Pomona, CA
Art/fine arts, music, theater arts/drama. Contact Ms. Laraine D. Turk, Acting Director of Enrollment Services, 3801 West Temple Avenue, Pomona, CA 91768-2557, 909-869-2989.

California State University, Bakersfield
Bakersfield, CA
Art/fine arts, music, theater arts/drama. Contact Dr. Homer S. Montalvo, Associate Dean of Admissions and Records, 9001 Stockdale Highway, Bakersfield, CA 93311-1022, 805-664-2160.

California State University, Chico
Chico, CA
Art/fine arts, music, theater arts/drama. Contact Dr. Kenneth Edson, Director of Admissions and Records, Chico, CA 95929-0150, 916-898-6321.

California State University, Dominguez Hills
Carson, CA
Art/fine arts, music, theater arts/drama. Contact Ms. Anita Gash, Director of Admissions, 1000 East Victoria Street, Carson, CA 90747-0001, 310-516-3600.

California State University, Fresno
Fresno, CA
Art/fine arts, dance, music, theater arts/drama. Contact Mr. Joseph Marshall, Associate Vice President of Enrollment Services, 5241 North Maple Avenue, Fresno, CA 93740, 209-278-2287.

California State University, Fullerton
Fullerton, CA
Art/fine arts, dance, music, theater arts/drama. Contact Dr. James Blackburn, Director of Admissions and Records, PO Box 34080, Fullerton, CA 92634-9480, 714-773-2300.

California State University, Hayward
Hayward, CA
Art/fine arts, dance, music, theater arts/drama. Contact Dr. Leigh W. Mintz, Associate Vice President of Curriculum and Academic Programs, 25800 Carlos Bee Boulevard, Hayward, CA 94542-3000, 510-885-3716.

California State University, Long Beach
Long Beach, CA
Art/fine arts, dance, music, theater arts/drama. Contact Dr. Gloria Kapp, Director of Admissions and Financial Aid, 1250 Bellflower Boulevard, Long Beach, CA 90840-0119, 310-985-4641.

California State University, Los Angeles
Los Angeles, CA
Art/fine arts, dance, music, theater arts/drama. Contact Mr. David Godoy, Director of Admissions, 5151 State University Drive, Los Angeles, CA 90032-4221, 213-343-3762.

California State University, Northridge
Northridge, CA
Art/fine arts, dance, music, theater arts/drama. Contact Ms. Lorraine Newlon, Director of Admissions, 18111 Nordhoff Street, Northridge, CA 91330-0001, 818-885-3773.

California State University, Sacramento
Sacramento, CA
Art/fine arts, music, theater arts/drama. Contact Mr. Larry Glasmire, Director of Admissions and Records, 6000 J Street, Sacramento, CA 95819-6048, 916-278-3901.

California State University, San Bernardino
San Bernardino, CA
Art/fine arts, music, theater arts/drama. Contact Mrs. Cheryl Smith, Associate Vice President for Enrollment Services, 5500 University Parkway, San Bernardino, CA 92407-2318, 909-880-5214.

California State University, San Marcos
San Marcos, CA
Theater arts/drama. Contact Ms. Betty Huff, Director of Enrollment Services, San Marcos, CA 92096, 619-750-4809.

California State University, Stanislaus
Turlock, CA
Art/fine arts, music, theater arts/drama. Contact Mr. Jaime Alcaraz, Director of University Outreach Services, 801 West Monte Vista Avenue, Turlock, CA 95382, 209-667-3070.

California University of Pennsylvania
California, PA
Art/fine arts, theater arts/drama. Contact Mr. Norman Hasbrouck, Dean of Enrollment Management and Academic Services, Third Street, California, PA 15419-1394, 412-938-4404.

Calumet College of Saint Joseph
Whiting, IN
Art/fine arts. Contact Mrs. Cynthia Hillman, Director of Enrollment Management, 2400 New York Avenue, Whiting, IN 46394-2195, 219-473-4216.

Calvary Bible College and Theological Seminary
Kansas City, MO
Music. Contact Mr. Brian Krause, Director of Admissions, 15800 Calvary Road, Kansas City, MO 64147-1341, 816-322-0110 Ext. 1326.

Calvin College
Grand Rapids, MI
Art/fine arts, music, theater arts/drama. Contact Mr. Thomas E. McWhertor, Director of Admissions, 3201 Burton Street, SE, Grand Rapids, MI 49546-4388, 616-957-6106.

Cameron University
Lawton, OK
Art/fine arts, music, theater arts/drama. Contact Ms. Zoe Du Rant, Director of Admissions, 2800 West Gore Boulevard, Lawton, OK 73505-6377, 405-581-2288.

Campbellsville College
Campbellsville, KY
Art/fine arts, music. Contact Mr. R. Trent Argo, Director of Admissions, 200 West College Street, Campbellsville, KY 42718-2799, 502-789-5220.

Campbell University
Buies Creek, NC
Art/fine arts, music, theater arts/drama. Contact Mr. Herbert V. Kerner Jr., Dean of Admissions, Financial Aid, and Veterans Affairs, Buies Creek, NC 27506, 910-893-1291.

Capital University
Columbus, OH
Art/fine arts, music. Contact Ms. Beth Heiser, Director of Admission, 2199 East Main Street, Columbus, OH 43209-2394, 614-236-6101.

Cardinal Stritch College
Milwaukee, WI
Art/fine arts, theater arts/drama. Contact Mr. David Wegener, Director of Admissions, 6801 North Yates Road, Milwaukee, WI 53217-3985, 414-352-5400 Ext. 444.

Carleton College
Northfield, MN
Art/fine arts, music. Contact Mr. Paul Thiboutot, Dean of Admissions, One North College Street, Northfield, MN 55057-4001, 507-663-4190.

Carlow College
Pittsburgh, PA
Art/fine arts. Contact Ms. Carol Descak, Director of Admissions, 3333 Fifth Avenue, Pittsburgh, PA 15213-3165, 412-578-6059.

Carnegie Mellon University
Pittsburgh, PA
Art/fine arts, music, theater arts/drama. Contact Mr. Michael Steidel, Director of Admissions, 5000 Forbes Avenue, Pittsburgh, PA 15213-3891, 412-268-2082.

Carroll College
Helena, MT
Theater arts/drama. Contact Ms. Candace A. Cain, Director of Admission, 1601 North Benton Avenue, Helena, MT 59625-0002, 406-447-4384.

Carroll College
Waukesha, WI
Art/fine arts, music, theater arts/drama. Contact Mr. James V. Wiseman III, Dean of Admission, 100 North East Avenue, Waukesha, WI 53186-5593, 414-524-7221.

Carson-Newman College
Jefferson City, TN
Art/fine arts, music, theater arts/drama. Contact Mrs. Sheryl M. Gray, Director of Undergraduate Admissions, PO Box 72025, Jefferson City, TN 37760, 615-471-3223.

Carthage College
Kenosha, WI
Art/fine arts, music, theater arts/drama. Contact Ms. Brenda P. Poggendorf, Vice President for Enrollment, 2001 Alford Park Drive, Kenosha, WI 53140-1994, 414-551-6000.

Case Western Reserve University
Cleveland, OH
Music, theater arts/drama. Contact Mr. William T. Conley, Dean of Undergraduate Admissions, 10900 Euclid Avenue, Cleveland, OH 44106, 216-368-4450.

Castleton State College
Castleton, VT
Art/fine arts, music, theater arts/drama. Contact Ms. Candace A. Thierry, Dean of College Relations/ Acting Director of Admissions, Castleton, VT 05735, 802-468-5611.

Catawba College
Salisbury, NC
Music, theater arts/drama. Contact Mr. Robert W. Bennett, Dean of Admissions, 2300 West Innes Street, Salisbury, NC 28144-2488, 704-637-4402.

Catholic University of America
Washington, DC
Art/fine arts, music, theater arts/drama. Contact Mr. David R. Gibson, Dean of Admissions and Financial Aid, Cardinal Station, Washington, DC 20064, 202-319-5305.

Cedar Crest College
Allentown, PA
Art/fine arts, music, theater arts/drama. Contact Ms. Cynthia Phillips, Director of Admissions, 100 College Drive, Allentown, PA 18104-6196, 610-740-3780.

Cedarville College
Cedarville, OH
Music, theater arts/drama. Contact Mr. David Ormsbee, Director of Admissions, PO Box 601, Cedarville, OH 45314-0601, 513-766-7700.

Centenary College
Hackettstown, NJ
Art/fine arts. Contact Mr. Dennis Kelly, Dean of Admissions, 400 Jefferson Street, Hackettstown, NJ 07840-2100, 908-852-4696.

Centenary College of Louisiana
Shreveport, LA
Art/fine arts, dance, music, theater arts/drama. Contact Dr. Dorothy Bird Gwin, Dean of Enrollment Management, 2911 Centenary Boulevard, PO Box 41188, Shreveport, LA 71134-1188, 318-869-5131.

Central Bible College
Springfield, MO
Music. Contact Mrs. Eunice A. Bruegman, Director of Admissions and Records, 3000 North Grant, Springfield, MO 65803-1096, 417-833-2551 Ext. 1184.

Central Christian College of the Bible
Moberly, MO
Music. Contact Mr. Russell Cobb, Director of Admissions, 911 Urbandale Drive East, Moberly, MO 65270-1997, 816-263-3900.

Central College
Pella, IA
Art/fine arts, music, theater arts/drama. Contact Mr. Eric Sickler, Vice President of Admission and Marketing, 812 University Street, Pella, IA 50219-1999, 515-628-5285.

Central Connecticut State University
New Britain, CT
Art/fine arts, music, theater arts/drama. Contact Ms. Charlotte Bisson, Director of Admissions, 1615 Stanley Street, New Britain, CT 06050-4010, 203-832-2278.

Central Methodist College
Fayette, MO
Music, theater arts/drama. Contact Mr. Anthony J. Boes, Vice President for Student Affairs, 411 Central Methodist Square, Fayette, MO 65248-1198, 816-248-3391 Ext. 251.

Central Michigan University
Mount Pleasant, MI
Art/fine arts, music, theater arts/drama. Contact Mr. Michael A. Owens, Director of Admissions and Minority Enrollment, Mount Pleasant, MI 48859, 517-774-3076.

Central Missouri State University
Warrensburg, MO
Art/fine arts, music, theater arts/drama. Contact Mrs. Delores Hudson, Director of Admissions, Warrensburg, MO 64093, 816-543-4811.

Central State University
Wilberforce, OH
Art/fine arts, music, theater arts/drama. Contact Mr. Robert E. Johnson III, Director of Admissions and Enrollment Management, Wilberforce, OH 45384, 513-376-6348.

Central Washington University
Ellensburg, WA
Art/fine arts, music, theater arts/drama. Contact Dr. James G. Pappas, Dean of Academic Services, Mitchell Hall, Ellensburg, WA 98926-7567, 509-963-3001.

Centre College
Danville, KY
Art/fine arts, music, theater arts/drama. Contact Mr. Thomas B. Martin, Executive Director of Enrollment Management, 600 West Walnut Street, Danville, KY 40422-1394, 606-238-5350.

Chadron State College
Chadron, NE
Art/fine arts, music, theater arts/drama. Contact Mr. Dale Williamson, Director of Admissions and Records, 10th and Main Streets, Chadron, NE 69337, 308-432-6221.

Chapman University
Orange, CA
Art/fine arts, dance, music, theater arts/drama. Contact Mr. Michael Drummy, Director of Admissions, 333 North Glassell Street, Orange, CA 92666-1011, 714-997-6711.

Charleston Southern University
Charleston, SC
Music. Contact Ms. Melinda Mitchum, Director of Admissions, PO Box 118087, Charleston, SC 29423-8087, 803-863-7050.

Chatham College
Pittsburgh, PA
Art/fine arts, dance, music, theater arts/drama. Contact Dr. Annette Giovengo, Acting Vice President for Admissions, Woodland Road, Pittsburgh, PA 15232-2826, 412-365-1290.

Chestnut Hill College
Philadelphia, PA
Art/fine arts, music. Contact Sr. Margaret Anne Birtwistle SSJ, Director of Admissions, 9601 Germantown Avenue, Philadelphia, PA 19118-2695, 215-248-7001.

Cheyney University of Pennsylvania
Cheyney, PA
Art/fine arts, music, theater arts/drama. Contact Ms. Sharon Cannon, Director of Admissions, Cheyney, PA 19319, 610-399-2099.

Chicago State University
Chicago, IL
Art/fine arts, music. Contact Ms. Romi Lowe, Director of Admissions, 95th Street at King Drive, Chicago, IL 60628, 312-995-2516.

Chowan College
Murfreesboro, NC
Art/fine arts, music. Contact Mrs. Austine O. Evans, Vice President for Student Enrollment, PO Box 1848, Murfreesboro, NC 27855, 919-398-4101 Ext. 238.

Christian Brothers University
Memphis, TN
Theater arts/drama. Contact Mr. Michael Dausch, Dean of Admissions, 650 East Parkway South, Memphis, TN 38104-5581, 901-722-0205 Ext. 210.

Christian Heritage College
El Cajon, CA
Music. Contact Mr. Paul Berry, Director of Enrollment Management/Registrar, 2100 Greenfield Drive, El Cajon, CA 92019-1157, 619-441-2200.

Christopher Newport University
Newport News, VA
Art/fine arts, music, theater arts/drama. Contact Mr. Keith F. McLoughland, Dean of Admissions, 50 Shoe Lane, Newport News, VA 23606-2998, 804-594-7015.

Cincinnati Bible College and Seminary
Cincinnati, OH
Music. Contact Mr. Philip G. Coleman, Director of Admissions, 2700 Glenway Avenue, Cincinnati, OH 45204-1799, 513-244-8141.

Circleville Bible College
Circleville, OH
Music. Contact Rev. Michael Adkins, Director of Enrollment Services, 1476 Lancaster Pike, PO Box 458, Circleville, OH 43113-9487, 614-474-8896 Ext. 701.

City College of the City University of New York
New York, NY
Art/fine arts, dance, music, theater arts/drama. Contact Ms. Nancy P. Campbell, Director of Enrollment Management, Convent Avenue at 138th Street, New York, NY 10031, 212-650-6419.

Claflin College
Orangeburg, SC
Art/fine arts, music. Contact Mr. George Lee, Director of Admission and Records, 700 College Avenue, NE, Orangeburg, SC 29115, 803-534-2710 Ext. 339.

Claremont McKenna College
Claremont, CA
Art/fine arts, music, theater arts/drama. Contact Mr. Richard C. Vos, Vice President/Dean of Admission and Financial Aid, 890 Columbia Avenue, Claremont, CA 91711-3901, 909-621-8088.

Clarion University of Pennsylvania
Clarion, PA
Art/fine arts, music, theater arts/drama. Contact Mr. John S. Shropshire, Dean of Enrollment Management and Academic Records, Clarion, PA 16214, 814-226-2306.

Clark Atlanta University
Atlanta, GA
Art/fine arts, music, theater arts/drama. Contact Mr. Clifton Rawels, Director of Admissions, James P Brawley Drive at Fair Street, SW, Atlanta, GA 30314, 404-880-8000 Ext. 8784.

Clarke College
Dubuque, IA
Art/fine arts, music, theater arts/drama. Contact Ms. Bobbe Ames, Vice President for Marketing/Recruitment, 1550 Clarke Drive, Dubuque, IA 52001-3198, 319-588-6316.

Clark University
Worcester, MA
Art/fine arts, music, theater arts/drama. Contact Mr. Richard W. Pierson, Dean of Admissions, 950 Main Street, Worcester, MA 01610-1477, 508-793-7431.

Clayton State College
Morrow, GA
Music. Contact Mrs. Tonya R. Hobson, Director of Admissions and Registrar, PO Box 285, Morrow, GA 30260-0285, 404-961-3500.

Clearwater Christian College
Clearwater, FL
Music. Contact Mr. Benjamin J. Puckett, Director of Admissions and Placement Services, 3400 Gulf-to-Bay Boulevard, Clearwater, FL 34619-4595, 813-726-1153 Ext. 228.

Clemson University
Clemson, SC
Art/fine arts. Contact Dr. Michael Heintze, Director of Admissions, 105 Sikes Hall, PO Box 345124, Clemson, SC 29634, 803-656-2287.

Cleveland State University
Cleveland, OH
Art/fine arts, music, theater arts/drama. Contact Mr. David Norris, Director of Admissions, East 24th and Euclid Avenue, Cleveland, OH 44115, 216-687-3763.

Coastal Carolina University
Myrtle Beach, SC
Art/fine arts, music, theater arts/drama. Contact Mr. Timothy J. McCormick, Director of Admissions, PO Box 1954, Myrtle Beach, SC 29578-1954, 803-349-2026.

Coe College
Cedar Rapids, IA
Art/fine arts, music, theater arts/drama. Contact Mr. Michael White, Dean of Admissions and Financial Aid, 1220 1st Avenue, NE, Cedar Rapids, IA 52402-5070, 319-399-8500.

Cogswell Polytechnical College
Sunnyvale, CA
Art/fine arts. Contact Mr. Paul A. Schreivogel, Dean of Student Services, 1175 Bordeaux Drive, Sunnyvale, CA 94089-1299, 408-541-0100 Ext. 112.

Coker College
Hartsville, SC
Art/fine arts, dance, music, theater arts/drama. Contact Dr. Stephen B. Terry, Vice President for Enrollment Management, College Avenue, Hartsville, SC 29550, 803-383-8050.

Colby College
Waterville, ME
Art/fine arts, music, theater arts/drama. Contact Mr. Parker J. Beverage, Dean of Admissions and Financial Aid, Mayflower Hill, Waterville, ME 04901, 207-872-3168.

Colby-Sawyer College
New London, NH
Art/fine arts. Contact Dr. Stephen Cloniger, Vice President for Enrollment Management, 100 Main Street, New London, NH 03257-4648, 603-526-3700.

Colgate University
Hamilton, NY
Art/fine arts, music. Contact Mr. Gary L. Ross, Director of Admission, 13 Oak Drive, Hamilton, NY 13346-1386, 315-824-7401.

College of Charleston
Charleston, SC
Art/fine arts, music, theater arts/drama. Contact Mr. Donald Burkard, Dean of Admissions, 66 George Street, Charleston, SC 29424-0002, 803-953-5670.

College of Mount St. Joseph
Cincinnati, OH
Art/fine arts, music. Contact Mr. Edward Eckel, Director of Admission, 5701 Delhi Road, Cincinnati, OH 45233 1670, 513-244-4302.

College of New Rochelle
New Rochelle, NY
Art/fine arts. Contact Mr. John P. Hine Jr., Director of Admission, 29 Castle Place, New Rochelle, NY 10805-2308, 914-654-5262.

College of Notre Dame
Belmont, CA
Art/fine arts, music, theater arts/drama. Contact Dr. Gregory Smith, Director of Admissions, 1500 Ralston Avenue, Belmont, CA 94002-1997, 415-508-3607.

College of Notre Dame of Maryland
Baltimore, MD
Art/fine arts, music. Contact Ms. Theresa C. Boer, Director of Admissions and Enrollment Management, 4701 North Charles Street, Baltimore, MD 21210-2476, 410-532-5330.

College of Saint Benedict
Saint Joseph, MN
Art/fine arts, music, theater arts/drama. Contact Mr. Rick J. Smith, Dean of Admissions/Vice President of Enrollment Management, 37 South College Avenue, Saint Joseph, MN 56374, 612-363-5308.

College of St. Catherine
St. Paul, MN
Art/fine arts, music, theater arts/drama. Contact Ms. Mary Docken, Associate Dean of Admissions, 2004 Randolph Avenue, St. Paul, MN 55105-1789, 612-690-6505.

College of Saint Elizabeth
Morristown, NJ
Art/fine arts, music. Contact Ms. Donna Yamanis, Dean of Admission and Financial Aid, 2 Convent Road, Morristown, NJ 07960-6989, 201-292-6351.

College of St. Francis
Joliet, IL
Art/fine arts. Contact Mr. Charles Beutel, Director of Admissions, 500 North Wilcox Street, Joliet, IL 60435-6188, 815-740-3400.

College of Saint Mary
Omaha, NE
Art/fine arts. Contact Ms. Sheila K. Haggas, Vice President of Enrollment Services, 1901 South 72nd Street, Omaha, NE 68124-2377, 402-399-2407.

College of Saint Rose
Albany, NY
Art/fine arts, music. Contact Ms. Mary O'Donnell, Director of Admissions, 432 Western Avenue, Albany, NY 12203-1419, 518-454-5150.

College of St. Scholastica
Duluth, MN
Music. Contact Ms. Rebecca Urbanski-Junkert, Vice President for Admissions and Student Financial Planning, 1200 Kenwood Avenue, Duluth, MN 55811-4199, 218-723-6046.

College of Santa Fe
Santa Fe, NM
Art/fine arts, music, theater arts/drama. Contact Mr. Dale Reinhart, Director of Admissions, 1600 Saint Michael's Drive, Santa Fe, NM 87505, 505-473-6133.

College of Staten Island of the City University of New York
Staten Island, NY
Art/fine arts, music, theater arts/drama. Contact Mr. Ramon Hulsey, Director of Admissions, 715 Ocean Terrace, Staten Island, NY 10314-6600, 718-982-2011.

College of the Atlantic
Bar Harbor, ME
Art/fine arts. Contact Mr. Steve Thomas, Director of Admission and Student Services, 105 Eden Street, Bar Harbor, ME 04609-1198, 207-288-5015 Ext. 233.

College of the Holy Cross
Worcester, MA
Art/fine arts, music, theater arts/drama. Contact Ms. Ann Bowe McDermott, Director of Admissions, Worcester, MA 01610, 508-793-2443.

College of the Ozarks
Point Lookout, MO
Art/fine arts, music, theater arts/drama. Contact Dr. M. Glen Cameron, Dean of Admissions, Point Lookout, MO 65726, 417-334-6411 Ext. 4218.

College of William and Mary
Williamsburg, VA
Art/fine arts, music, theater arts/drama. Contact Ms. Virginia Carey, Dean of Admission, PO Box 8795, Williamsburg, VA 23187-8795, 804-221-4223.

The College of Wooster
Wooster, OH
Art/fine arts, music, theater arts/drama. Contact Dr. W. A. Hayden Schilling, Dean of Admissions, Wooster, OH 44691, 216-263-2270.

Colorado Christian University
Lakewood, CO
Music, theater arts/drama. Contact Miss Anna DiTorrice, Director of Admissions, 180 South Garrison Street, Lakewood, CO 80226-1053, 303-202-0100 Ext. 165.

The Colorado College
Colorado Springs, CO
Art/fine arts, dance, music, theater arts/drama. Contact Mr. Terrance K. Swenson, Dean of Admission and Financial Aid, 14 East Cache La Poudre, Colorado Springs, CO 80903-3294, 719-389-6344.

Colorado State University
Fort Collins, CO
Art/fine arts, dance, music, theater arts/drama. Contact Ms. Mary Ontiveros, Director of Admissions, Fort Collins, CO 80523, 970-491-6909.

Columbia College
Chicago, IL
Art/fine arts, dance, music, theater arts/drama. Contact Mr. Terry Miller, Director of Admissions and Recruitment, 600 South Michigan Avenue, Chicago, IL 60605-1997, 312-663-1600 Ext. 133.

Columbia College
Columbia, MO
Art/fine arts. Contact Mr. Ron Cronacher, Director of Admissions, 1001 Rogers Street, Columbia, MO 65216-0002, 314-875-7352.

Columbia College
New York, NY
Art/fine arts, dance, music, theater arts/drama. Contact Ms. Drusilla Blackman, Dean of Undergraduate Admissions and Financial Aid, 212 Hamilton Hall, New York, NY 10027, 212-854-2522.

Columbia College
Columbia, SC
Art/fine arts, dance, music. Contact Dr. J. Joseph Mitchell, Dean of Enrollment Management, 1301 Columbia College Drive, Columbia, SC 29203-5998, 803-786-3871.

Columbia International University
Columbia, SC
Music. Contact Mr. Edward B. Germann, Dean of Students, PO Box 3122, Columbia, SC 29230-3122, 803-754-4100 Ext. 3234.

Columbia Union College
Takoma Park, MD
Music. Contact Mrs. Sheila Burnette, Director of Admissions, 7600 Flower Avenue, Takoma Park, MD 20912-7794, 301-891-4503.

Columbia University, School of General Studies
New York, NY
Art/fine arts, music, theater arts/drama. Contact Dr. Barbara L. Tischler, Director of Admissions and Financial Aid, 303 Lewisohn Hall, New York, NY 10027, 212-854-3331.

Columbus College
Columbus, GA
Art/fine arts, music, theater arts/drama. Contact Ms. Patty L. Ross, Director of Admissions, 4225 University Avenue, Columbus, GA 31907-5645, 706-568-2035.

Concord College
Athens, WV
Art/fine arts, music. Contact Mr. Dale Dickens, Director of Admissions, Vermillion Street, PO Box 1000, Athens, WV 24712-1000, 304-384-5248.

Concordia College
Ann Arbor, MI
Art/fine arts, music. Contact Mr. Don Vogt, Director of Admission, 4090 Geddes Road, Ann Arbor, MI 48105-2797, 313-995-7322.

Concordia College
Moorhead, MN
Art/fine arts, music, theater arts/drama. Contact Mr. James L. Hausmann, Vice President for Admissions and Financial Aid, 901 8th Street South, Moorhead, MN 56562, 218-299-3004.

Concordia College
St. Paul, MN
Art/fine arts, music, theater arts/drama. Contact Mr. Tim Utter, Director of Admissions, 275 Syndicate Street North, St. Paul, MN 55104-5494, 612-641-8230.

Concordia College
Seward, NE
Art/fine arts, music, theater arts/drama. Contact Mr. Don Vos, Dircetor of Admission, Seward, NE 68434-1599, 402-643-7233 .

Concordia College
Bronxville, NY
Music. Contact Mr. John Bahr, Director of Admission, 171 White Plains Road, Bronxville, NY 10708-1998, 914-337-9300 Ext. 2150.

Concordia University
Portland, OR
Art/fine arts, music. Contact Mr. William H. Balke, Vice President of Student Services and Admissions, 2811 Northeast Holman, Portland, OR 97211-6099, 503-280-8501.

Concordia University
Irvine, CA
Art/fine arts, music, theater arts/drama. Contact Mr. W. Stanley Meyer, Vice President of Enrollment Services, 1530 Concordia West, Irvine, CA 92715-3299, 714-854-8002 Ext. 108.

Concordia University
River Forest, IL
Art/fine arts, music, theater arts/drama. Contact Mrs. Sara Dahms, Director of Admission, 7400 Augusta Street, River Forest, IL 60305-1499, 708-209-3100.

Concordia University at Austin
Austin, TX
Music. Contact Mr. Jay Krause, Dean of Enrollment Management, 3400 Interstate 35 North, Austin, TX 78705, 512-452-7661.

Connecticut College
New London, CT
Art/fine arts, dance, music, theater arts/drama. Contact Ms. Claire K. Matthews, Dean of Admissions and Planning, 270 Mohegan Avenue, New London, CT 06320-4196, 203-439-2200.

Converse College
Spartanburg, SC
Art/fine arts, music, theater arts/drama. Contact Mr. John F. Fluke, Vice President for Enrollment, 580 East Main, Spartanburg, SC 29302-0006, 803-596-9040.

Cooper Union for the Advancement of Science and Art
New York, NY
Art/fine arts. Contact Mr. Richard Bory, Dean of Admissions and Records, 30 Cooper Square, New York, NY 10003-7120, 212-353-4120.

The Corcoran School of Art
Washington, DC
Art/fine arts. Contact Mr. Mark Sistek, Director of Admissions, 500 17th Street, NW, Washington, DC 20006-4899, 202-628-9484 Ext. 700.

Cornell College
Mount Vernon, IA
Art/fine arts, music, theater arts/drama. Contact Mr. Kevin Crockett, Dean of Admissions and Enrollment Management, 600 First Street West, Mount Vernon, IA 52314-1098, 319-895-4477.

Cornell University
Ithaca, NY
Art/fine arts, dance, music, theater arts/drama. Contact Mr. Donald Saleh, Acting Dean of Admissions and Financial Aid, 410 Thurston Avenue, Ithaca, NY 14850, 607-255-5241.

Cornerstone College
Grand Rapids, MI
Music. Contact Mr. Rick Newberry, Director of Admissions, 1001 East Beltline Avenue, NE, Grand Rapids, MI 49505-5897, 616-949-5300 Ext. 426.

Covenant College
Lookout Mountain, GA
Music. Contact Dr. Richard Allen, Director of Admissions, Lookout Mountain, GA 30750, 706-820-1560 Ext. 1132.

Creighton University
Omaha, NE
Art/fine arts, music, theater arts/drama. Contact Mr. Howard J. Bachman, Assistant Vice President for Enrollment Management, 2500 California Plaza, Omaha, NE 68178-0001, 402-280-2703.

Crichton College
Memphis, TN
Music. Contact Mr. Barry Mooney, Director of Admissions, 6655 Winchester Road, PO Box 757830, Memphis, TN 38175-7830, 901-367-3888.

Crown College
St. Bonifacius, MN
Music. Contact Ms. Lynn M. Hauger, Vice President of Enrollment Services, 6425 County Road 30, St. Bonifacius, MN 55375-9001, 612-446-4141.

Culver-Stockton College
Canton, MO
Art/fine arts, music, theater arts/drama. Contact Ms. Betty A. Smith, Dean of Admissions, One College Hill, Canton, MO 63435-1299, 314-288-5221 Ext. 331.

Cumberland College
Williamsburg, KY
Art/fine arts, music, theater arts/drama. Contact Mrs. Erica Harris, Senior Admissions Counselor, 6178 College Station Drive, Williamsburg, KY 40769-1372, 606-539-4241.

Curry College
Milton, MA
Art/fine arts. Contact Ms. Janet Cromie Kelly, Dean of Admissions and Financial Aid, 1071 Blue Hill Avenue, Milton, MA 02186-9984, 617-333-2210.

The Curtis Institute of Music
Philadelphia, PA
Music. Contact Ms. Judi Lynn Gattone, Admissions and Financial Aid Officer, 1726 Locust Street, Philadelphia, PA 19103-6107, 215-893-5262.

D

Daemen College
Amherst, NY
Art/fine arts. Contact Ms. Maria P. Dillard, Director of Enrollment Management, 4380 Main Street, Amherst, NY 14226-3592, 716-839-8225.

Dakota State University
Madison, SD
Music. Contact Ms. Kathy Engbrecht, Acting Director of Admissions, 820 North Washington, Madison, SD 57042-1799, 605-256-5139.

Dakota Wesleyan University
Mitchell, SD
Art/fine arts, theater arts/drama. Contact Ms. Melinda S. Larson, Director of Admissions, Office of Admissions, Mitchell, SD 57301-4398, 605-995-2650.

Dallas Baptist University
Dallas, TX
Art/fine arts, music. Contact Mr. Aaron T. Vann, Director of Admissions, 3000 Mountain Creek Parkway, Dallas, TX 75211-9299, 214-333-5360.

Dana College
Blair, NE
Art/fine arts, music, theater arts/drama. Contact Mr. John Schueth, Director of Admissions, 2848 College Drive, Blair, NE 68008-1099, 402-426-7222.

Dartmouth College
Hanover, NH
Art/fine arts, music, theater arts/drama. Contact Mr. Karl M. Furstenberg, Dean of Admissions and Financial Aid, 6016 McNutt Hall, Hanover, NH 03755, 603-646-2875.

David Lipscomb University
Nashville, TN
Art/fine arts, music. Contact Mrs. Cyndi Butler, Director of Admissions, 3901 Granny White Pike, Nashville, TN 37204-3951, 615-269-1000 Ext. 1776.

Davidson College
Davidson, NC
Art/fine arts, music, theater arts/drama. Contact Dr. Nancy Cable Wells, Dean of Admission and Financial Aid, PO Box 1719, Davidson, NC 28036-1719, 704-892-2231.

Davis & Elkins College
Elkins, WV
Art/fine arts, music, theater arts/drama. Contact Mr. Kevin Chenoweth, Director of Admissions, 100 Campus Drive, Elkins, WV 26241-3996, 304-636-1900 Ext. 301.

The Defiance College
Defiance, OH
Art/fine arts. Contact Mr. Randy Tumblin, Director of Enrollment Management, 701 North Clinton Street, Defiance, OH 43512-1610, 419-784-4010.

Delaware State University
Dover, DE
Art/fine arts, music, theater arts/drama. Contact Mr. Jethro C. Williams, Director of Admissions, 1200 North DuPont Highway, Dover, DE 19901-2277, 302-739-4917.

Delta State University
Cleveland, MS
Art/fine arts, music. Contact Mr. James Donald Cooper, Director of Admissions, Kethley 107, Cleveland, MS 38733-0001, 601-846-4040.

Denison University
Granville, OH
Art/fine arts, dance, music, theater arts/drama. Contact Ms. Stuart Oremus, Director of Admissions, Box H, Granville, OH 43023, 614-587-6627.

DePaul University
Chicago, IL
Art/fine arts, music, theater arts/drama. Contact Ms. Lucy Leusch, Dean of Admission and Records, 1 East Jackson Boulevard, Chicago, IL 60604-2287, 312-362-8712.

DePauw University
Greencastle, IN
Art/fine arts, music. Contact Mr. David Murray, Dean of Admissions and Associate Provost, 313 South Locust Street, Greencastle, IN 46135-1772, 317-658-4006.

Dickinson College
Carlisle, PA
Art/fine arts, music, theater arts/drama. Contact Mr. R. Russell Shunk, Dean of Admissions, PO Box 1773, Carlisle, PA 17013-2896, 717-245-1231.

Dickinson State University
Dickinson, ND
Art/fine arts, music, theater arts/drama. Contact Mr. Marshall Melbye, Director of Admissions and Registrar, 291 Campus Drive, Dickinson, ND 58601-4896, 701-227-2331.

Dillard University
New Orleans, LA
Music, theater arts/drama. Contact Mrs. Vernese B. O'Neal, Director of Admissions, 2601 Gentilly Boulevard, New Orleans, LA 70122-3097, 504-283-8822 Ext. 4670.

Doane College
Crete, NE
Art/fine arts, music, theater arts/drama. Contact Mr. Dan Kunzman, Dean of Admissions, 1014 Boswell Avenue, Crete, NE 68333-2430, 402-826-8242.

Dominican College of San Rafael
San Rafael, CA
Art/fine arts, music. Contact Mr. Robert Gleeson, Director of Admissions, 50 Acacia Avenue, San Rafael, CA 94901-8008, 415-485-3204.

Dordt College
Sioux Center, IA
Art/fine arts, music, theater arts/drama. Contact Mr. Quentin Van Essen, Director of Admissions, 498 4th Avenue, NE, Sioux Center, IA 51250-1697, 712-722-6081.

Dowling College
Oakdale, NY
Art/fine arts, music, theater arts/drama. Contact Ms. Kate Rowe, Director of Admissions, Idle Hour Boulevard, Oakdale, NY 11769-1999, 516-244-3030.

Drake University
Des Moines, IA
Art/fine arts, music, theater arts/drama. Contact Mr. Thomas F. Willoughby, Director of Admission, 2507 University Avenue, Des Moines, IA 50311-4516, 515-271-3181.

Drew University
Madison, NJ
Art/fine arts, music, theater arts/drama. Contact Mr. Roberto Noya, Dean of Admissions for the College of Liberal Arts, 36 Madison Avenue, Madison, NJ 07940-1493, 201-408-3739.

Drexel University
Philadelphia, PA
Art/fine arts, music. Contact Mr. Donald Dickason, Vice Provost for Enrollment Management, Room 220, Philadelphia, PA 19104-2875, 215-895-2400.

Drury College
Springfield, MO
Art/fine arts, music, theater arts/drama. Contact Mr. Michael Thomas, Director of Admissions, 900 North Benton Avenue, Springfield, MO 65802-3791, 417-873-7879.

Duke University
Durham, NC
Art/fine arts, music, theater arts/drama. Contact Mr. Christoph Guttentag, Director of Admissions, Durham, NC 27708-0586, 919-684-3214.

Duquesne University
Pittsburgh, PA
Art/fine arts, music, theater arts/drama. Contact Fr. Thomas Schaefer, Dean of Admissions, 600 Forbes Avenue, Pittsburgh, PA 15282-0001, 412-396-6220.

E

Earlham College
Richmond, IN
Art/fine arts, music, theater arts/drama. Contact Mr. Robert L. deVeer, Dean of Admissions, Richmond, IN 47374, 317-983-1600.

East Carolina University
Greenville, NC
Art/fine arts, dance, music, theater arts/drama. Contact Dr. Thomas Powell Jr., Director of Admissions, East Fifth Street, Greenville, NC 27858-4353, 919-328-6640.

East Central University
Ada, OK
Art/fine arts, music. Contact Ms. Pamla Armstrong, Registrar, Ada, OK 74820-6899, 405-332-8000 Ext. 234.

East Coast Bible College
Charlotte, NC
Music. Contact Dr. Sammy Oxendine, Dean of Academic Affairs, 6900 Wilkinson Boulevard, Charlotte, NC 28214, 704-394-2307 Ext. 23.

Eastern College
St. Davids, PA
Art/fine arts, music. Contact Dr. Ronald L. Keller, Vice President for Enrollment Management, 10 Fairview Drive, St. Davids, PA 19087-3696, 610-341-5970.

Eastern Connecticut State University
Willimantic, CT
Art/fine arts, music. Contact Mr. Antonio Marrero Jr., Interim Director of Admissions and Enrollment Management, 83 Windham Street, Willimantic, CT 06226-2295, 203-465-5286.

Eastern Illinois University
Charleston, IL
Art/fine arts, music, theater arts/drama. Contact Mr. Dale W. Wolf, Director of Admissions, 600 Lincoln Avenue, Charleston, IL 61920-3099, 217-581-2223.

Eastern Kentucky University
Richmond, KY
Art/fine arts, dance, music, theater arts/drama. Contact Mr. Les Grigsby, Director of Admissions, Richmond, KY 40475-3102, 606-622-2106.

Eastern Mennonite University
Harrisonburg, VA
Art/fine arts, music. Contact Mrs. Ellen B. Miller, Director of Admissions, 1200 Park Road, Harrisonburg, VA 22801-2462, 703-732-4118.

Eastern Michigan University
Ypsilanti, MI
Art/fine arts, dance, music, theater arts/drama. Contact Mr. M. Dolan Evanovich, Director of Admissions, Ypsilanti, MI 48197, 313-487-0193.

Eastern Nazarene College
Quincy, MA
Music. Contact Mr. D. William Nichols, Executive Director of Enrollment Management, 23 East Elm Avenue, Quincy, MA 02170-2999, 617-773-2373.

Eastern New Mexico University
Portales, NM
Art/fine arts, music, theater arts/drama. Contact Mr. Larry Fuqua, Director of Admissions, Station #5 ENMU, Portales, NM 88130, 505-562-2178.

Eastern Oregon State College
La Grande, OR
Art/fine arts, music, theater arts/drama. Contact Ms. Terral Schut, Director of Admissions and New Student Programs, 1410 L Avenue, La Grande, OR 97850-2899, 503-962-3393.

Eastern Washington University
Cheney, WA
Art/fine arts, dance, music, theater arts/drama. Contact Mr. Roger Pugh, Assistant Vice Provost for Enrollment Management, EWU MS-148, Cheney, WA 99004-2431, 509-359-6319.

East Stroudsburg University of Pennsylvania
East Stroudsburg, PA
Art/fine arts, music, theater arts/drama. Contact Mr. Alan T. Chesterton, Director of Admission, 200 Prospect Street, East Stroudsburg, PA 18301-2999, 717-424-3542.

East Tennessee State University
Johnson City, TN
Art/fine arts, music, theater arts/drama. Contact Dr. Nancy Dishner, Dean of Admissions, PO Box 70731, ETSU, Johnson City, TN 37614-0734, 615-929-4213.

East Texas Baptist University
Marshall, TX
Music, theater arts/drama. Contact Mr. Mike Davis, Director of Admissions, 1209 North Grove, Marshall, TX 75670-1498, 903-935-7963 Ext. 225.

East Texas State University
Commerce, TX
Art/fine arts, music, theater arts/drama. Contact Ms. Suzanne Woodley, Assistant Director of Admissions and School Relations, East Texas Station, Commerce, TX 75429-3011, 903-886-5101.

East Texas State University at Texarkana
Texarkana, TX
Art/fine arts. Contact Mrs. Sandra Rogers, Director of Academic and Student Services, PO Box 5518, Texarkana, TX 75505-5518, 903-838-6514 Ext. 227.

Eckerd College
St. Petersburg, FL
Art/fine arts, music, theater arts/drama. Contact Dr. Richard R. Hallin, Dean of Admissions, 4200 54th Avenue South, St. Petersburg, FL 33711, 813-864-8331.

Edgewood College
Madison, WI
Art/fine arts, music, theater arts/drama. Contact Mr. Kevin C. Kucera, Dean of Admissions and Financial Aid, 855 Woodrow Street, Madison, WI 53711-1998, 608-257-4861 Ext. 2294.

Edinboro University of Pennsylvania
Edinboro, PA
Art/fine arts, music, theater arts/drama. Contact Mr. Terrence Carlin, Assistant Vice President for Admissions, Edinboro, PA 16444, 814-732-2761.

Elizabeth City State University
Elizabeth City, NC
Art/fine arts, music. Contact Mr. Erthel Hines, Coordinator of Admissions, PO Box 901 ECSU, Elizabeth City, NC 27909-7806, 919-335-3305.

Elizabethtown College
Elizabethtown, PA
Art/fine arts, music, theater arts/drama. Contact Mr. Ronald D. Potier, Director of Admissions, 1 Alpha Drive, Elizabethtown, PA 17022-2298, 717-361-1400.

Elmhurst College
Elmhurst, IL
Art/fine arts, music, theater arts/drama. Contact Mr. John Hopkins, Director of Enrollment Development, 190 Prospect, Elmhurst, IL 60126-3296, 708-617-3400.

Elmira College
Elmira, NY
Art/fine arts, music, theater arts/drama. Contact Mr. William S. Neal, Dean of Admissions, Park Place, Elmira, NY 14901, 607-735-1724.

Elms College
Chicopee, MA
Art/fine arts. Contact Sr. Betty Broughan, Dean of Admissions and Financial Aid, 291 Springfield Street, Chicopee, MA 01013-2839, 413-592-3189.

Elon College
Elon College, NC
Art/fine arts, music, theater arts/drama. Contact Mrs. Nan P. Perkins, Dean of Admissions and Financial Planning, 2700 Campus Box, Elon College, NC 27244, 910-584-2370.

Emerson College
Boston, MA
Dance, theater arts/drama. Contact Ms. Jane Brown, Vice President and Dean of Admissions, 100 Beacon Street, Boston, MA 02116-1511, 617-578-8600.

Emmanuel College
Boston, MA
Art/fine arts. Contact Ms. Kathleen K. Manning, Director of Admissions, 400 The Fenway, Boston, MA 02115, 617-735-9715.

Emory & Henry College
Emory, VA
Art/fine arts, music, theater arts/drama. Contact Dr. Jean-Marie Luce, Dean of Admissions and Financial Aid, PO Box 947, Emory, VA 24327-0947, 703-944-4121 Ext. 3133.

Emory University
Atlanta, GA
Music, theater arts/drama. Contact Mr. Daniel C. Walls, Dean of Admissions, Boisfeuillet Jones Center–Office of Admissions, Atlanta, GA 30322-1100, 404-727-6036.

Emporia State University
Emporia, KS
Art/fine arts, music, theater arts/drama. Contact Dr. Barbara Tarter, Director of Admissions, 1200 Commercial Street, Emporia, KS 66801-5087, 316-341-5465.

Erskine College
Due West, SC
Music. Contact Mrs. Dot Carter, Director of Admissions and Financial Aid, PO Box 176, Due West, SC 29639-0176, 803-379-8830.

Eugene Bible College
Eugene, OR
Music. Contact Mr. Trent Combs, Director of Admissions, 2155 Bailey Hill Road, Eugene, OR 97405-1194, 503-485-1780 Ext. 35.

Eugene Lang College, New School for Social Research
New York, NY
Theater arts/drama. Contact Ms. Jennifer Fondiller, Director of Admissions, 65 West 11th Street, New York, NY 10011-8601, 212-229-5665.

Eureka College
Eureka, IL
Art/fine arts, music, theater arts/drama. Contact Ms. Susan R. Jordan, Dean of Admissions and Financial Aid, 300 East College Avenue, Eureka, IL 61530-0128, 309-467-6350.

Evangel College
Springfield, MO
Art/fine arts, music. Contact Mr. David I. Schoolfield, Executive Director of Enrollment, 1111 North Glenstone Avenue, Springfield, MO 65802-2191, 417-865-2811 Ext. 7202.

The Evergreen State College
Olympia, WA
Art/fine arts, dance, music, theater arts/drama. Contact Ms. Wanda E. Curtis, Acting Assistant to the Dean for Admissions, Olympia, WA 98505, 360-866-6000 Ext. 6170.

F

Fairfield University
Fairfield, CT
Art/fine arts. Contact Mr. David Flynn, Dean of Admission, Fairfield, CT 06430-7524, 203-254-4100.

Fairleigh Dickinson University, Florham-Madison Campus
Madison, NJ
Art/fine arts, theater arts/drama. Contact Dr. Philomena Mantella, Associate Vice President for Enrollment Management, 270 Montross Avenue, Rutherford, NJ 07070, 201-692-2607.

Fairleigh Dickinson University, Teaneck-Hackensack Campus
Teaneck, NJ
Art/fine arts, theater arts/drama. Contact Dr. Philomena Mantella, Associate Vice President for Enrollment Management, 1000 River Road, Teaneck, NJ 07666-1914, 201-692-7300.

Fairmont State College
Fairmont, WV
Art/fine arts, music, theater arts/drama. Contact Dr. John G. Conaway, Director of Admissions, Locust Avenue, Fairmont, WV 26554, 304-367-4141.

Faith Baptist Bible College and Theological Seminary
Ankeny, IA
Music. Contact Mr. Jeff Newman, Director of Admissions, 1900 Northwest 4th Street, Ankeny, IA 50021-2198, 515-964-0601 Ext. 216.

Fashion Institute of Technology
New York, NY
Art/fine arts. Contact Mr. Jim Pidgeon, Director of Admissions, Seventh Avenue at 27th Street, New York, NY 10001-5992, 212-760-7675.

Fayetteville State University
Fayetteville, NC
Art/fine arts, music, theater arts/drama. Contact Mr. James Scurry, Director of Enrollment Management, Newbold Station, Fayetteville, NC 28301, 910-486-1371.

Felician College
Lodi, NJ
Art/fine arts. Contact Sr. Mary Austin, Director of Admissions, 262 South Main Street, Lodi, NJ 07644-2198, 201-778-1029.

Ferrum College
Ferrum, VA
Art/fine arts, theater arts/drama. Contact Mr. Robert H. Bailey, Director of Admissions, Ferrum, VA 24088-9001, 703-365-4290.

Fisk University
Nashville, TN
Art/fine arts, music, theater arts/drama. Contact Mr. Harrison F. DeShields Jr., Director of Admissions and Records, 1000 17th Avenue North, Nashville, TN 37208-3051, 615-329-8665.

Fitchburg State College
Fitchburg, MA
Art/fine arts. Contact Mrs. Marke Vickers, Director of Admissions, 160 Pearl Street, Fitchburg, MA 01420-2697, 508-665-3144.

Five Towns College
Dix Hills, NY
Music. Contact Ms. Jennifer Roemer, Director of Admissions, 305 North Service Road, Dix Hills, NY 11746-6055, 516-424-7000 Ext. 110.

Flagler College
St. Augustine, FL
Art/fine arts, theater arts/drama. Contact Mr. Marc G. Williar, Director of Admissions, PO Box 1027, St. Augustine, FL 32085-1027, 904-829-6481 Ext. 220.

Florida Agricultural and Mechanical University
Tallahassee, FL
Art/fine arts, music, theater arts/drama. Contact Mr. Roland Gaines, Director of Admissions, Office of the University Registrar, Tallahassee, FL 32307, 904-599-3115.

Florida Atlantic University
Boca Raton, FL
Art/fine arts, music, theater arts/drama. Contact Mr. Richard Griffin, Acting Director of Admissions, 777 Glades Road, PO Box 3091, Boca Raton, FL 33431-0991, 407-367-3040 Ext. 3031.

Florida Baptist Theological College
Graceville, FL
Music. Contact Rev. O. Lavan Wilson, Director of Student Affairs/Admissions, PO Box 1306, Graceville, FL 32440-3306, 904-263-3261 Ext. 62.

Florida International University
Miami, FL
Art/fine arts, dance, music, theater arts/drama. Contact Ms. Carmen Brown, Director of Admissions, University Park, Miami, FL 33199, 305-348-2363.

Florida Memorial College
Miami, FL
Music. Contact Mrs. Peggy Kelley, Director of Admissions and International Student Advisor, 15800 NW 42nd Avenue, Miami, FL 33054, 305-626-3750.

Florida Southern College
Lakeland, FL
Art/fine arts, music, theater arts/drama. Contact Mr. William B. Stephens Jr., Director of Admissions, 111 Lake Hollingsworth Drive, Lakeland, FL 33801-5698, 941-680-4131.

Florida State University
Tallahassee, FL
Art/fine arts, dance, music, theater arts/drama. Contact Mr. John Barnhill, Director of Admissions, Tallahassee, FL 32306-1009, 904-644-6200 Ext. 16.

Fontbonne College
St. Louis, MO
Art/fine arts, theater arts/drama. Contact Ms. Peggy Musen, Director of Admission, 6800 Wydown Boulevard, St. Louis, MO 63105-3098, 314-889-1400.

Fordham University
New York, NY
Art/fine arts, theater arts/drama. Contact Mr. John W. Buckley, Director of Admissions, East Fordham Road, New York, NY 10458, 718-817-4000.

Fort Hays State University
Hays, KS
Art/fine arts, music, theater arts/drama. Contact Mrs. Pat Mahon, Director of Admissions, 600 Park Street, Hays, KS 67601-4009, 913-628-5666.

Fort Lewis College
Durango, CO
Art/fine arts, music, theater arts/drama. Contact Mr. Harlan Steinle, Dean of Admission and Development, 1000 Rim Drive, Durango, CO 81301-3999, 303-247-7184.

Framingham State College
Framingham, MA
Art/fine arts. Contact Dr. Philip M. Dooher, Dean of Admissions, 100 State Street, Framingham, MA 01701-9101, 508-626-4500.

Franciscan University of Steubenville
Steubenville, OH
Theater arts/drama. Contact Mrs. Margaret Weber, Director of Admissions, University Boulevard, Steubenville, OH 43952-6701, 614-283-6226.

Francis Marion University
Florence, SC
Art/fine arts, theater arts/drama. Contact Mr. Marvin W. Lynch, Director of Admissions, Box 100547, Florence, SC 29501-0547, 803-661-1231.

Franklin and Marshall College
Lancaster, PA
Art/fine arts, music, theater arts/drama. Contact Mr. Peter W. VanBuskirk, Dean of Admissions, PO Box 3003, Lancaster, PA 17604-3003, 717-291-3953.

Franklin College of Indiana
Franklin, IN
Art/fine arts, theater arts/drama. Contact Mr. Bruce Stephen Richards, Dean of Enrollment Management, 501 East Monroe Street, Franklin, IN 46131-2598, 317-738-8062.

Franklin Pierce College
Rindge, NH
Art/fine arts, music, theater arts/drama. Contact Mr. Thomas E. Desrosiers, Director of Admissions, College Road, PO Box 60, Rindge, NH 03461-0060, 603-899-4050.

Freed-Hardeman University
Henderson, TN
Art/fine arts, music, theater arts/drama. Contact Mr. Paul E. Pinckley Sr., Director of Admissions, 158 East Main Street, Henderson, TN 38340-2399, 901-989-6651.

Free Will Baptist Bible College
Nashville, TN
Music. Contact Dr. Charles E. Hampton, Registrar and Chairman of Department of General Education, 3606 West End Avenue, Nashville, TN 37205-2498, 615-383-1340 Ext. 2233.

Fresno Pacific College
Fresno, CA
Music. Contact Mr. Cary Templeton, Director of Admissions, 1717 South Chestnut Avenue, Fresno, CA 93702-4709, 209-453-2030.

Friends University
Wichita, KS
Art/fine arts, dance, music. Contact Ms. Cynthia Bergman, Director of Admissions, 2100 University, Wichita, KS 67213, 316-261-5842.

Frostburg State University
Frostburg, MD
Art/fine arts, music, theater arts/drama. Contact Mr. Edgerton Devel II, Dean of Admissions, Midlothian Road, Frostburg, MD 21532-2302, 301-689-4201.

Furman University
Greenville, SC
Art/fine arts, music, theater arts/drama. Contact Mr. J. Carey Thompson, Director of Admissions, 3300 Poinsett Highway, Greenville, SC 29613, 803-294-2034.

G

Gallaudet University
Washington, DC
Art/fine arts, theater arts/drama. Contact Ms. Deborah E. DeStefano, Director of Admissions, 800 Florida Avenue, NE, Washington, DC 20002-3625, 202-651-5114.

Gannon University
Erie, PA
Art/fine arts, theater arts/drama. Contact Ms. Joyce Scheid-Gilman, Director of Freshman and Transfer Admissions, University Square, Erie, PA 16541, 814-871-7240.

Gardner-Webb University
Boiling Springs, NC
Art/fine arts, music. Contact Mr. Ray McKay Hardee, Dean of Admissions, PO Box 817, Boiling Springs, NC 28017, 704-434-2361 Ext. 220.

Geneva College
Beaver Falls, PA
Music. Contact Dr. William Katip, Vice President for Enrollment Management, 3200 College Avenue, Beaver Falls, PA 15010-3599, 412-847-6513.

George Fox College
Newberg, OR
Art/fine arts, music. Contact Mr. Randall C. Comfort, Director of Admissions, 414 North Meridian, Newberg, OR 97132-2697, 503-538-8383 Ext. 2240.

George Mason University
Fairfax, VA
Art/fine arts, dance, music, theater arts/drama. Contact Dr. Patricia M. Riordan, Dean of Admissions, Mason Hall Room D205, Fairfax, VA 22030-4445, 703-993-2400.

Georgetown College
Georgetown, KY
Art/fine arts, music, theater arts/drama. Contact Mr. Garvel Kindrick, Director of Admissions, 400 East College Street, Georgetown, KY 40324-1696, 502-863-8009.

Georgetown University
Washington, DC
Art/fine arts. Contact Mr. Charles A. Deacon, Dean of Undergraduate Admissions, 37th and O Street, NW, Washington, DC 20057, 202-687-3600.

The George Washington University
Washington, DC
Art/fine arts, dance, music, theater arts/drama. Contact Mr. Frederic A. Siegel, Director of Undergraduate Admissions, Office of Undergraduate Admissions, Washington, DC 20052, 202-994-6054.

Georgia College
Milledgeville, GA
Art/fine arts, music, theater arts/drama. Contact Mr. Larry A. Peevy, Associate Vice President for Admissions and Records, CPO Box 023, Milledgeville, GA 31061, 912-453-5004.

Georgian Court College
Lakewood, NJ
Art/fine arts, music. Contact Ms. Sandra Zerby, Director of Admissions, 900 Lakewood Avenue, Lakewood, NJ 08701-2697, 908-367-4440.

Georgia Southern University
Statesboro, GA
Art/fine arts, music. Contact Dr. Dale Wasson, Director of Admissions, Landrum Box 8033, Statesboro, GA 30460-8100, 912-681-5531.

Georgia Southwestern College
Americus, GA
Art/fine arts, music, theater arts/drama. Contact Mr. Gary Fallis, Director of Admissions, 800 Wheatley Street, Americus, GA 31709-4693, 912-928-1273.

Georgia State University
Atlanta, GA
Art/fine arts, dance, music, theater arts/drama. Contact Dr. Ernest W. Beals, Dean of Admissions and Acting Dean for Enrollment Services, University Plaza, Atlanta, GA 30303-3083, 404-651-3010.

Gettysburg College
Gettysburg, PA
Art/fine arts, music, theater arts/drama. Contact Mr. Delwin K. Gustafson, Dean of Admissions, Gettysburg, PA 17325-1411, 717-337-6100.

Glenville State College
Glenville, WV
Music. Contact Dr. Nancy McClure, Registrar/Director of Enrollment Management, 200 High Street, Glenville, WV 26351-1200, 304-462-7361 Ext. 152.

Goddard College
Plainfield, VT
Art/fine arts, music, theater arts/drama. Contact Mr. Peter Burns, Director of Admissions, Plainfield, VT 05667, 802-454-8311 Ext. 257.

God's Bible School and College
Cincinnati, OH
Music. Contact Mr. Fred Wingham, Director of Admissions, 1810 Young Street, Cincinnati, OH 45210-1599, 513-721-7944 Ext. 205.

Gonzaga University
Spokane, WA
Art/fine arts, music, theater arts/drama. Contact Mr. Philip Ballinger, Dean of Admissions, Spokane, WA 99258, 509-328-4220 Ext. 3172.

Gordon College
Wenham, MA
Art/fine arts, music. Contact Mrs. Pamela B. Lazarakis, Dean of Admissions, 255 Grapevine Road, Wenham, MA 01984-1899, 508-927-2300 Ext. 4217.

Goshen College
Goshen, IN
Art/fine arts, music, theater arts/drama. Contact Ms. Martha Lehman, Director of Admissions, 1700 South Main Street, Goshen, IN 46526-4794, 219-535-7535.

Goucher College
Baltimore, MD
Art/fine arts, dance, music, theater arts/drama. Contact Ms. Elise Seraydarian, Director of Admissions, 1021 Dulaney Valley Road, Baltimore, MD 21204-2794, 410-337-6100.

Governors State University
University Park, IL
Art/fine arts. Contact Mr. William T. Craig, Admissions Officer, University Parkway, University Park, IL 60466, 708-534-4490.

Grace Bible College
Grand Rapids, MI
Music. Contact Miss Linda K. Siler, Registrar, 1011 Aldon Street SW, PO Box 910, Grand Rapids, MI 49509-1921, 616-538-2330.

Grace College
Winona Lake, IN
Art/fine arts, music. Contact Mr. Ron Henry, Dean of Enrollment, 200 Seminary Drive, Winona Lake, IN 46590-1294, 219-372-5128.

Graceland College
Lamoni, IA
Art/fine arts, music, theater arts/drama. Contact Ms. Bonita A. Booth, Dean of Admissions, 700 College Avenue, Lamoni, IA 50140, 515-784-5118.

Grace University
Omaha, NE
Music. Contact Mr. Jeff Edgar, Director of Admissions, Ninth and William Streets, Omaha, NE 68108, 402-449-2831.

Grambling State University
Grambling, LA
Art/fine arts, music, theater arts/drama. Contact Ms. Nora D. Bingaman, Director of Admissions and Recruitment, Grambling, LA 71245, 318-274-2435.

Grand Canyon University
Phoenix, AZ
Art/fine arts, music, theater arts/drama. Contact Mr. Carl Tichenor, Director of Admissions, 3300 W Camelback Road, PO Box 11097, Phoenix, AZ 85017-3030, 602-589-2855.

Grand Valley State University
Allendale, MI
Art/fine arts, music, theater arts/drama. Contact Mr. Robert Fletcher, Associate Provost, 1 Campus Drive, Allendale, MI 49401-9403, 616-895-2025.

Grand View College
Des Moines, IA
Art/fine arts, theater arts/drama. Contact Ms. Lori Hanson, Director of Admissions, 1200 Grandview Avenue, Des Moines, IA 50316-1599, 515-263-2810.

Great Lakes Christian College
Lansing, MI
Music. Contact Mr. Ray Maurer, Director of Admissions, 6211 West Willow Highway, Lansing, MI 48917-1299, 517-321-0242.

Green Mountain College
Poultney, VT
Art/fine arts. Contact Mr. Steven D. Klein, Dean of Admissions and Financial Aid, 16 College Street, Poultney, VT 05764-1199, 802-287-9313 Ext. 208.

Greensboro College
Greensboro, NC
Art/fine arts, music, theater arts/drama. Contact Mr. Randy Doss, Dean of Admissions, 815 West Market Street, Greensboro, NC 27401-1875, 910-272-7102.

Greenville College
Greenville, IL
Art/fine arts, music, theater arts/drama. Contact Mr. Kent Krober, Director of Admissions, 315 East College, Greenville, IL 62246-1199, 618-664-1840 Ext. 218.

Grinnell College
Grinnell, IA
Art/fine arts, music, theater arts/drama. Contact Mr. Vincent Cuseo, Director of Admission, PO Box 805, Grinnell, IA 50112-0807, 515-269-3600.

Grove City College
Grove City, PA
Music. Contact Mr. Jeffrey C. Mincey, Director of Admissions, 100 Campus Drive, Grove City, PA 16127-2104, 412-458-2100.

Guilford College
Greensboro, NC
Art/fine arts, music, theater arts/drama. Contact Mr. Alton Newell, Dean of Admission, 5800 West Friendly Avenue, Greensboro, NC 27410-4173, 910-316-2124.

Gustavus Adolphus College
St. Peter, MN
Art/fine arts, dance, music, theater arts/drama. Contact Mr. Mark Anderson, Director of Admissions, 800 West College Avenue, St. Peter, MN 56082-1498, 507-933-7676.

H

Hamilton College
Clinton, NY
Art/fine arts, dance, music, theater arts/drama. Contact Mr. Douglas C. Thompson, Dean of Admission, 198 College Hill Road, Clinton, NY 13323-1218, 315-859-4421.

Hamline University
St. Paul, MN
Art/fine arts, music, theater arts/drama. Contact Dr. W. Scott Friedhoff, Dean of Undergraduate Admissions, 1536 Hewitt Avenue, St. Paul, MN 55104-1284, 612-641-2207.

Hampshire College
Amherst, MA
Art/fine arts, dance, music, theater arts/drama. Contact Ms. Audrey Smith, Director of Admissions, Amherst, MA 01002, 413-582-5471.

Hampton University
Hampton, VA
Art/fine arts, music, theater arts/drama. Contact Dr. Ollie M. Bowman, Dean of Admissions, Hampton, VA 23668, 804-727-5328.

Hannibal-LaGrange College
Hannibal, MO
Art/fine arts, music. Contact Mr. Raymond Carty, Acting Dean of Admissions, 2800 Palmyra Road, Hannibal, MO 63401-1940, 314-221-3675 Ext. 264.

Hanover College
Hanover, IN
Art/fine arts, music. Contact Mr. John W. Rogers Jr., Director of Admissions, Box 108, Hanover, IN 47243, 812-866-7021.

Harding University
Searcy, AR
Art/fine arts, music, theater arts/drama. Contact Mr. Mike Williams, Director of Admissions, 900 East Center, Searcy, AR 72149-0001, 501-279-4407.

Hardin-Simmons University
Abilene, TX
Art/fine arts, music, theater arts/drama. Contact Mrs. Laura Moore, Director of Admissions, Drawer M, HSU Station, Abilene, TX 79698-0001, 915-670-1206.

Hartwick College
Oneonta, NY
Art/fine arts, music, theater arts/drama. Contact Mrs. Karyl B. Clemens, Dean of Admissions, Oneonta, NY 13820-4020, 607-431-4150.

Harvard University
Cambridge, MA
Art/fine arts, music. Contact Dr. William R. Fitzsimmons, Dean of Admissions and Financial Aid, Byerly Hall, 8 Garden Street, Cambridge, MA 02138, 617-495-1551.

Hastings College
Hastings, NE
Art/fine arts, music, theater arts/drama. Contact Mr. Michael Karloff, Director of Admissions, Box 269, Hastings, NE 68902-0269, 402-461-7316.

Haverford College
Haverford, PA
Art/fine arts, music. Contact Ms. Delsie Phillips, Director of Admissions, 370 Lancaster Avenue, Haverford, PA 19041-1392, 610-896-1350.

Heidelberg College
Tiffin, OH
Music, theater arts/drama. Contact Mr. Richard J. DeLoof, Dean of Admission, 310 East Market Street, Tiffin, OH 44883-2462, 419-448-2330.

Henderson State University
Arkadelphia, AR
Art/fine arts, music, theater arts/drama. Contact Mr. Tom Gattin, Registrar, 1100 Henderson Street, Arkadelphia, AR 71999-0001, 501-230-5135.

Hendrix College
Conway, AR
Art/fine arts, music, theater arts/drama. Contact Ms. Caroline Kelsey, Vice President of Enrollment, 1601 Harkrider Street, Conway, AR 72032, 501-450-1362.

Heritage College
Toppenish, WA
Art/fine arts. Contact Ms. Winona Zack, Director of Admissions, 3240 Fort Road, Toppenish, WA 98948-9599, 509-865-2244 Ext. 2002.

High Point University
High Point, NC
Art/fine arts, theater arts/drama. Contact Mr. James L. Schlimmer, Dean of Admissions, University Station, Montlieu Avenue, High Point, NC 27262-3598, 910-841-9216.

Hillsdale College
Hillsdale, MI
Art/fine arts, music, theater arts/drama. Contact Mr. Jeffrey S. Lantis, Director of Admissions, 33 East College, Hillsdale, MI 49242-1298, 517-437-7341 Ext. 2327.

Hiram College
Hiram, OH
Art/fine arts, music, theater arts/drama. Contact Mr. Gary G. Craig, Dean of Admissions, Box 96, Hiram, OH 44234-0096, 216-569-5169.

Hobart College
Geneva, NY
Art/fine arts, dance, music, theater arts/drama. Contact Ms. Mara O'Laughlin, Director of Admission, 639 South Main Street, Geneva, NY 14456-3397, 315-781-3622.

Hobe Sound Bible College
Hobe Sound, FL
Music. Contact Mrs. Ann French, Director of Admissions, PO Box 1065, Hobe Sound, FL 33475-1065, 407-546-5534 Ext. 415.

Hofstra University
Hempstead, NY
Art/fine arts, dance, music, theater arts/drama. Contact Ms. Mary Beth Carey, Dean of Admissions, Hempstead, NY 11550-1090, 516-463-6700.

Hollins College
Roanoke, VA
Art/fine arts, music, theater arts/drama. Contact Mrs. Stuart Trinkle, Director of Admissions, PO Box 9657, Roanoke, VA 24020-1657, 703-362-6401.

Holy Family College
Philadelphia, PA
Art/fine arts. Contact Dr. Mott R. Linn, Director of Admissions, Grant and Frankford Avenues, Philadelphia, PA 19114-2094, 215-637-3050.

Holy Names College
Oakland, CA
Art/fine arts, music. Contact Sr. Carol Sellman SNJM, Vice President for Institutional Research, 3500 Mountain Boulevard, Oakland, CA 94619-1699, 510-436-1195.

Hood College
Frederick, MD
Art/fine arts. Contact Ms. Nancy Gillece, Director of Admissions, 401 Rosemont Avenue, Frederick, MD 21701-8575, 301-696-3400.

Hope College
Holland, MI
Art/fine arts, dance, music, theater arts/drama. Contact Dr. James R. Bekkering, Vice President for Admissions and Student Life, 69 East 10th Street, Holland, MI 49422-9000, 616-395-7955.

Houghton College
Houghton, NY
Art/fine arts, music. Contact Mr. Timothy R. Fuller, Vice President for Alumni and Admissions, PO Box 128, Houghton, NY 14744, 716-567-9353.

Houston Baptist University
Houston, TX
Art/fine arts, music. Contact Ms. Estelle S. Jeu, Director of Admissions, 7502 Fondren Road, Houston, TX 77074-3298, 713-995-3210.

Howard Payne University
Brownwood, TX
Art/fine arts, music, theater arts/drama. Contact Mrs. Marsha Larremore, Director of Admissions, 1000 Fisk Street, Brownwood, TX 76801-2715, 915-643-7689.

Howard University
Washington, DC
Art/fine arts, music, theater arts/drama. Contact Mr. Emmett R. Griffin Jr., Director of Admissions, 2400 Sixth Street, NW, Washington, DC 20059-0002, 202-806-2750.

Humboldt State University
Arcata, CA
Art/fine arts, music, theater arts/drama. Contact Mr. Robert L. Hannigan, Dean of Admissions, Records, and School Relations, Arcata, CA 95521-8299, 707-826-4402.

Hunter College of the City University of New York
New York, NY
Art/fine arts, dance, music, theater arts/drama. Contact Mr. William Zlata, Director of Admissions, 695 Park Avenue, New York, NY 10021-5085, 212-772-4490.

Huntingdon College
Montgomery, AL
Art/fine arts, dance, music, theater arts/drama. Contact Ms. Suellen Ofe, Vice President of Enrollment Management, 1500 East Fairview Avenue, Montgomery, AL 36106-2148, 334-834-3300.

Huntington College
Huntington, IN
Art/fine arts, music, theater arts/drama. Contact Mr. Jeff Berggren, Executive Director of Admissions and Financial Aid, 2303 College Avenue, Huntington, IN 46750-1299, 219-356-6000 Ext. 1016.

Huron University
Huron, SD
Art/fine arts. Contact Mr. David Herringer, Vice President of Enrollment Management, 333 9th Street SW, Huron, SD 57350-2798, 605-352-8721.

Huston-Tillotson College
Austin, TX
Music. Contact Mr. Donnie J. Scott, Director of Admissions, 900 Chicon Street, Austin, TX 78702-2753, 512-505-3027 Ext. 217.

I

Idaho State University
Pocatello, ID
Art/fine arts, music, theater arts/drama. Contact Ms. Jennifer Fisher, Executive Director of Enrollment Planning/Academic Services, PO Box 8054, Pocatello, ID 83209, 208-236-2121.

Illinois Benedictine College
Lisle, IL
Music. Contact Ms. Jane L. Smith, Associate Dean of Admissions, 5700 College Road, Lisle, IL 60532-0900, 708-960-1500 Ext. 4008.

Illinois College
Jacksonville, IL
Art/fine arts, music, theater arts/drama. Contact Mr. Gale Vaughn, Director of Enrollment, 1101 West College Avenue, Jacksonville, IL 62650-2299, 217-245-3030.

Illinois State University
Normal, IL
Art/fine arts, music, theater arts/drama. Contact Mr. Steve Adams, Director of Admissions, Normal, IL 61790-2200, 309-438-2181.

Illinois Wesleyan University
Bloomington, IL
Art/fine arts, music, theater arts/drama. Contact Mr. James R. Ruoti, Dean of Admissions, PO Box 2900, Bloomington, IL 61702-2900, 309-556-3031.

Immaculata College
Immaculata, PA
Music. Contact Mr. James P. Sullivan, Director of Admission, Immaculata, PA 19345-0900, 610-647-4400 Ext. 3015.

Incarnate Word College
San Antonio, TX
Art/fine arts, music, theater arts/drama. Contact Mr. Brian F. Dalton OSF, Dean of Enrollment, 4301 Broadway, San Antonio, TX 78209-6397, 210-829-6005.

Indiana State University
Terre Haute, IN
Art/fine arts, music, theater arts/drama. Contact Mr. Richard Riel, Assistant V.P. for Academic Affairs/Director of Admissions, Terre Haute, IN 47809-1401, 812-237-2121.

Indiana University Bloomington
Bloomington, IN
Art/fine arts, dance, music, theater arts/drama. Contact Mr. Robert Magee, Director of Admissions, 300 North Jordan Avenue, Bloomington, IN 47405, 812-855-0661.

Indiana University Northwest
Gary, IN
Art/fine arts, theater arts/drama. Contact Mr. William D. Lee, Director of Admissions, 3400 Broadway, Gary, IN 46408-1197, 219-980-6991.

Indiana University of Pennsylvania
Indiana, PA
Art/fine arts, music, theater arts/drama. Contact Mr. William Nunn, Dean of Admissions, 216 Pratt Hall, Indiana, PA 15705, 412-357-2230.

Indiana University–Purdue University Fort Wayne
Fort Wayne, IN
Art/fine arts, music, theater arts/drama. Contact Mr. Karl F. Zimmerman, Director of Admissions, 2101 Coliseum Boulevard East, Fort Wayne, IN 46805-1499, 219-481-6812.

Indiana University–Purdue University Indianapolis
Indianapolis, IN
Art/fine arts, theater arts/drama. Contact Dr. Alan Crist, Director of Admissions, Cavanaugh Hall Room 129, Indianapolis, IN 46202-5143, 317-274-4591.

Indiana University South Bend
South Bend, IN
Art/fine arts, music, theater arts/drama. Contact Mr. Esker E. Ligon, Director of Admissions, 1700 Mishawaka Avenue, PO Box 7111, South Bend, IN 46634-7111, 219-237-IUSB.

Indiana University Southeast
New Albany, IN
Art/fine arts, music. Contact Mr. David B. Campbell, Director of Admissions, 4201 Grant Line Road, New Albany, IN 47150-6405, 812-941-2212.

Indiana Wesleyan University
Marion, IN
Art/fine arts, music. Contact Ms. Gaytha Holloway, Director of Admissions, 4201 South Washington Street, Marion, IN 46953-4999, 317-674-6901 Ext. 138.

Iona College
New Rochelle, NY
Art/fine arts, theater arts/drama. Contact Ms. Laurie Austin, Director of Undergraduate Admissions, 715 North Avenue, New Rochelle, NY 10801-1890, 914-633-2502.

Iowa State University of Science and Technology
Ames, IA
Art/fine arts, music, theater arts/drama. Contact Mr. Karsten Smedal, Director of Admissions, Ames, IA 50011-2010, 515-294-0815.

Iowa Wesleyan College
Mount Pleasant, IA
Art/fine arts, music. Contact Mr. Tony Damewood, Director of Admissions, 601 North Main Street, Mount Pleasant, IA 52641-1398, 319-385-6231.

Ithaca College
Ithaca, NY
Art/fine arts, dance, music, theater arts/drama. Contact Ms. Paula Mitchell, Director of Admissions, 953 Danby Road, Ithaca, NY 14850-7020, 607-274-3124.

J

Jackson State University
Jackson, MS
Art/fine arts, music. Contact Mrs. Stephanie Chatman, Director of Admissions and Recruitment, PO Box 17330, 1400 John R. Lynch Street, Jackson, MS 39217, 601-968-2100.

Jacksonville State University
Jacksonville, AL
Art/fine arts, music, theater arts/drama. Contact Dr. Jerry D. Smith, Dean of Admissions and Records, 700 Pelham Road North, Jacksonville, AL 36265-9982, 205-782-5400.

Jacksonville University
Jacksonville, FL
Art/fine arts, dance, music, theater arts/drama. Contact Mr. Frank J. Vastola, Director of Admission, 2800 University Boulevard North, Jacksonville, FL 32211-3394, 904-745-7000.

James Madison University
Harrisonburg, VA
Art/fine arts, dance, music, theater arts/drama. Contact Mrs. Roxie Shabazz, Director of Admissions, Office of Admissions, Harrisonburg, VA 22807, 540-568-6147.

Jamestown College
Jamestown, ND
Art/fine arts, music, theater arts/drama. Contact Mrs. Carol Schmeichel, Dean of Students, 6080 Jamestown College, Jamestown, ND 58405, 701-252-3467 Ext. 2562.

Jarvis Christian College
Hawkins, TX
Music. Contact Ms. Anetha D. Francis, Director of Admissions, PO Drawer G, Hawkins, TX 75765-9989, 903-769-5700 Ext. 736.

Jersey City State College
Jersey City, NJ
Art/fine arts, music, theater arts/drama. Contact Mr. Samuel T. McGhee, Director of Admissions, 2039 Kennedy Boulevard, Jersey City, NJ 07305, 201-200-3234.

Jewish Theological Seminary of America
New York, NY
Music. Contact Ms. Marci Harris Blumenthal, Director of Admissions, Room 614 Schiff, 3080 Broadway, New York, NY 10027-4649, 212-678-8832.

John Brown University
Siloam Springs, AR
Art/fine arts, music. Contact Mr. Don Crandall, Vice President for Enrollment Management, 2000 West University Street, Siloam Springs, AR 72761-2121, 501-524-3131.

Johns Hopkins University
Baltimore, MD
Music. Contact Mr. Paul White, Director of Undergraduate Admissions, 3400 North Charles Street, Baltimore, MD 21218-2699, 410-516-8171.

Johnson C. Smith University
Charlotte, NC
Music. Contact Mr. Michael Jackson, Director of Admissions, 100-300 Beatties Ford Road, Charlotte, NC 28216, 704-378-1010.

Johnson State College
Johnson, VT
Art/fine arts, dance, music, theater arts/drama. Contact Ms. Penny Howrigan, Director of Admissions, Johnson, VT 05656-9405, 802-635-2356 Ext. 219.

Judson College
Marion, AL
Art/fine arts, music. Contact Mrs. Charlotte Clements, Director of Admissions, PO Box 120, Marion, AL 36756, 334-683-5110.

Judson College
Elgin, IL
Art/fine arts, music, theater arts/drama. Contact Mr. Matthew Osborne, Director of Enrollment Services, 1151 North State Street, Elgin, IL 60123-1498, 708-695-2500 Ext. 2310.

Juilliard School
New York, NY
Dance, music, theater arts/drama. Contact Ms. Mary K. Gray, Director of Admissions, 60 Lincoln Center Plaza, New York, NY 10023-6588, 212-799-5000 Ext. 223.

Juniata College
Huntingdon, PA
Art/fine arts, music. Contact Mr. Carlton E. Surbeck III, Director of Admissions, 1700 Moore Street, Huntingdon, PA 16652-2119, 814-643-4310 Ext. 420.

K

Kalamazoo College
Kalamazoo, MI
Art/fine arts, music, theater arts/drama. Contact Ms. Teresa M. Lahti, Dean of Admission, Mandelle Hall, Kalamazoo, MI 49006-3295, 616-337-7166.

Kansas City Art Institute
Kansas City, MO
Art/fine arts. Contact Mr. Charles Van Gilder, Director of Admissions, 4415 Warwick Boulevard, Kansas City, MO 64111-1820, 816-561-4852 Ext. 281.

Kansas Newman College
Wichita, KS
Art/fine arts. Contact Mr. Kenneth Rasp, Dean of Admissions, 3100 McCormick Avenue, Wichita, KS 67213-2084, 316-942-4291 Ext. 145.

Kansas State University
Manhattan, KS
Art/fine arts, music, theater arts/drama. Contact Mr. Richard N. Elkins, Director of Admissions, Anderson Hall, Room 1, Manhattan, KS 66506, 913-532-6250.

Kansas Wesleyan University
Salina, KS
Art/fine arts, theater arts/drama. Contact Ms. Valerie D. Robinson, Director of Admissions, 100 East Claflin, Salina, KS 67401-6196, 913-827-5541 Ext. 307.

Kean College of New Jersey
Union, NJ
Art/fine arts, music, theater arts/drama. Contact Mr. Audley Bridges, Director of Admissions, 1000 Morris Avenue, Union, NJ 07083, 908-527-2195.

Keene State College
Keene, NH
Art/fine arts, music, theater arts/drama. Contact Mrs. Kathryn Dodge, Director of Admissions, 229 Main Street, Keene, NH 03435-1701, 603-358-2276.

Kendall College of Art and Design
Grand Rapids, MI
Art/fine arts. Contact Mr. Geoff Kehoe, Director of Enrollment Management, 111 Division Avenue North, Grand Rapids, MI 49503, 616-451-2787 Ext. 111.

Kennesaw State College
Marietta, GA
Art/fine arts, music. Contact Mr. Joe F. Head, Director of Admissions, PO Box 444, Marietta, GA 30061-0444, 404-423-6300.

Kent State University
Kent, OH
Art/fine arts, dance, music, theater arts/drama. Contact Mr. Charles Rickard, Director of Admissions, 161 Michael Schwartz Center, Kent, OH 44240, 216-672-2444.

Kentucky Christian College
Grayson, KY
Music. Contact Mrs. Sandra Deakins, Director of Admissions, 1000 Academic Parkway, Grayson, KY 41143-1123, 606-474-3266.

Kentucky State University
Frankfort, KY
Art/fine arts, music. Contact Mr. Lyman Dale, Director of Records, Registration, and Admission, East Main Street, Dept. PG-92, Frankfort, KY 40601, 502-227-6340.

Kentucky Wesleyan College
Owensboro, KY
Art/fine arts, music, theater arts/drama. Contact Ms. Gloria Smith Kunik, Director of Enrollment Services, 3000 Frederica Street, PO Box 1039, Owensboro, KY 42302-1039, 502-926-3111 Ext. 143.

Kenyon College
Gambier, OH
Art/fine arts, dance, music, theater arts/drama. Contact Mr. John W. Anderson, Dean of Admissions, Gambier, OH 43022-9623, 614-427-5776.

King College
Bristol, TN
Art/fine arts, music, theater arts/drama. Contact Mr. Roger Kieffer, Vice President for Enrollment, 1350 King College Road, Bristol, TN 37620-2699, 615-652-4861.

King's College
Wilkes-Barre, PA
Theater arts/drama. Contact Mr. Daniel P. Conry, Dean of Admissions, 133 North River Street, Wilkes-Barre, PA 18711-0801, 717-826-5858.

Knox College
Galesburg, IL
Art/fine arts, music, theater arts/drama. Contact Mr. Paul Steenis, Director of Admissions, Admissions Office, Box K-148, Galesburg, IL 61401, 309-343-0112 Ext. 123.

Knoxville College
Knoxville, TN
Music. Contact Ms. Carol Scott, Director of Admissions, 901 College Street, NW, Knoxville, TN 37921-4799, 615-524-6525.

Kutztown University of Pennsylvania
Kutztown, PA
Art/fine arts, dance, music, theater arts/drama. Contact Mr. George McKinley, Director of Admissions, Kutztown, PA 19530, 610-683-4060.

L

Lafayette College
Easton, PA
Art/fine arts, music. Contact Dr. Gary Ripple, Director of Admissions, Easton, PA 18042-1798, 610-250-5100.

LaGrange College
LaGrange, GA
Art/fine arts, music, theater arts/drama. Contact Mr. Philip T. Dodson, Dean of Admissions, 601 Broad Street, LaGrange, GA 30240-2999, 706-812-7260.

Lake Erie College
Painesville, OH
Art/fine arts, dance, music, theater arts/drama. Contact Ms. Mary Ann Kalbaugh, Director of Admissions, 391 West Washington Street, Painesville, OH 44077-3389, 216-639-7879.

Lake Forest College
Lake Forest, IL
Art/fine arts, music. Contact Mr. William G. Motzer Jr., Director of Admissions, 555 North Sheridan Road, Lake Forest, IL 60045-2399, 708-735-5000.

Lakeland College
Sheboygan, WI
Art/fine arts, music, theater arts/drama. Contact Mr. Lyle Krueger, Vice President, PO Box 359, Sheboygan, WI 53082-0359, 414-565-1498.

Lamar University–Beaumont
Beaumont, TX
Art/fine arts, dance, music, theater arts/drama. Contact Mr. James Rush, Director of Academic

Services, 4400 Martin Luther King Parkway, Beaumont, TX 77710, 409-880-8354.

Lambuth University
Jackson, TN
Art/fine arts, music, theater arts/drama. Contact Mrs. Nancy M. Callis, Director of Admissions, 705 Lambuth Boulevard, Jackson, TN 38301, 901-425-3223.

Lander University
Greenwood, SC
Art/fine arts, music, theater arts/drama. Contact Ms. Jacquelyn C. DeVore Roark, Director of Admissions, 320 Stanley Avenue, Greenwood, SC 29649-2099, 803-229-8307.

Lane College
Jackson, TN
Music. Contact Ms. E. R. Maddox, Director of Admissions, 545 Lane Avenue, Jackson, TN 38301-4598, 901-426-7532.

Langston University
Langston, OK
Art/fine arts, music, theater arts/drama. Contact Mr. Ronald Smith, Director of Admissions and Records, PO Box 728, Langston, OK 73050-0907, 405-466-2980.

La Roche College
Pittsburgh, PA
Art/fine arts. Contact Mr. Barry Duerr, Director of Admissions, 9000 Babcock Boulevard, Pittsburgh, PA 15237-5898, 412-367-9300 Ext. 185.

La Salle University
Philadelphia, PA
Art/fine arts, music. Contact Mr. Christopher P. Lydon, Director of Undergraduate Admissions, 20th Street at Olney Avenue, Philadelphia, PA 19141-1199, 215-951-1500.

La Sierra University
Riverside, CA
Art/fine arts, music. Contact Mrs. Myrna Costa-Casado, Director of Admissions, 4700 Pierce Street, Riverside, CA 92515, 909-785-2939.

Lawrence University
Appleton, WI
Art/fine arts, music, theater arts/drama. Contact Mr. Steven T. Syverson, Dean of Admissions and Financial Aid, PO Box 599, Appleton, WI 54912-0599, 414-832-6500.

Lebanon Valley College
Annville, PA
Music. Contact Mr. William J. Brown, Director of Admissions, PO Box R, Annville, PA 17003-0501, 717-867-6181.

Lee College
Cleveland, TN
Music. Contact Mr. Gary T. Ray, Director of Admissions, 1120 North Ocoee Street, Cleveland, TN 37311-4475, 615-478-7875.

Lees-McRae College
Banner Elk, NC
Dance, theater arts/drama. Contact Dr. Tim C. Bailey, Dean of Admissions and Financial Aid, PO Box 128, Banner Elk, NC 28604-0128, 704-898-8723.

Lehigh University
Bethlehem, PA
Art/fine arts, music, theater arts/drama. Contact Mrs. Patricia G. Boig, Director of Admissions, 27 Memorial Drive West, Bethlehem, PA 18015-3094, 610-758-3100.

Lehman College of the City University of New York
Bronx, NY
Art/fine arts, dance, music, theater arts/drama. Contact Mr. Clarence Wilkes, Director of Admissions, 250 Bedford Park Boulevard West, Bronx, NY 10468-1589, 718-960-8131.

LeMoyne-Owen College
Memphis, TN
Art/fine arts. Contact Dr. David Valentine, Director of Admissions, 807 Walker Avenue, Memphis, TN 38126-6595, 901-942-7303.

Lenoir-Rhyne College
Hickory, NC
Music, theater arts/drama. Contact Mr. Tim Jackson, Director of Admissions, Hickory, NC 28603, 704-328-7300 Ext. 300.

Lewis & Clark College
Portland, OR
Art/fine arts, music, theater arts/drama. Contact Mr. Michael Sexton, Dean of Admissions and Student Financial Services, 0615 Southwest Palatine Hill Road, Portland, OR 97219-7879, 503-768-7040.

Lewis-Clark State College
Lewiston, ID
Theater arts/drama. Contact Mr. Steve Bussolini, Director of Admissions, 500 Eighth Avenue, Lewiston, ID 83501-2698, 208-799-2210.

Lewis University
Romeoville, IL
Art/fine arts, music, theater arts/drama. Contact Mr. Irish O'Reilly, Director of Admissions, Route 53, Romeoville, IL 60441, 815-838-0500 Ext. 470.

Liberty University
Lynchburg, VA
Art/fine arts, music, theater arts/drama. Contact Mr. Jay Spener, Associate Vice President of Recruitment and Admissions, Box 20000, Lynchburg, VA 24506-8001, 804-582-2158.

Limestone College
Gaffney, SC
Art/fine arts, music. Contact Ms. Sherri R. Horton, Vice President for Admissions and Student Services, 1115 College Drive, Gaffney, SC 29340, 803-489-7151 Ext. 548.

Lincoln Christian College
Lincoln, IL
Music. Contact Mr. Lynn Laughlin, Director of Enrollment Management, 100 Campus View Drive, Lincoln, IL 62656-2167, 217-732-3168 Ext. 219.

Lincoln Memorial University
Harrogate, TN
Art/fine arts. Contact Mr. Conrad Daniels, Dean of Admissions and Recruitment, Cumberland Gap Parkway, Harrogate, TN 37752, 615-869-6281.

Lincoln University
Jefferson City, MO
Art/fine arts, music. Contact Mr. Stanford Baddley, Executive Director of Enrollment Services, 820 Chestnut, Jefferson City, MO 65102, 314-681-5599.

Lincoln University
Lincoln University, PA
Music. Contact Mr. Carlton Clark, Acting Director of Admissions, PO Box 179, Lincoln University, PA 19352, 610-932-8300 Ext. 205.

Lindenwood College
St. Charles, MO
Art/fine arts, dance, music, theater arts/drama. Contact Dr. David R. Williams, Dean of Admissions and Financial Aid, 209 South Kingshighway, St. Charles, MO 63301-1695, 314-949-4944.

Lindsey Wilson College
Columbia, KY
Art/fine arts. Contact Mr. Kevin A. Thompson, Director of Admissions, 210 Lindsey Wilson Street, Columbia, KY 42728-1298, 502-384-2126 Ext. 8100.

Linfield College
McMinnville, OR
Art/fine arts, music, theater arts/drama. Contact Mr. John W. Reed, Dean of Enrollment Services, 900 South Baker Street, McMinnville, OR 97128-6894, 503-434-2213.

Livingstone College
Salisbury, NC
Music. Contact Ms. Marsha Pruitt, Assistant Director of Admissions, 701 West Monroe Street, Salisbury, NC 28144-5298, 704-638-5502.

Lock Haven University of Pennsylvania
Lock Haven, PA
Art/fine arts, music, theater arts/drama. Contact Mr. Joseph A. Coldren, Director of Admissions, Lock Haven, PA 17745-2390, 717-893-2352.

Long Island University, Brooklyn Campus
Brooklyn, NY
Art/fine arts, dance, music. Contact Mr. Alan B. Chaves, Dean of Admissions, University Plaza, Brooklyn, NY 11201, 718-488-1011.

Long Island University, C.W. Post Campus
Brookville, NY
Art/fine arts, music, theater arts/drama. Contact Ms. Christine Natali, Director of Admissions, Northern Boulevard, Brookville, NY 11548, 516-299-2413.

Long Island University, Southampton Campus
Southampton, NY
Art/fine arts. Contact Ms. Carol Gilbert, Director of Admissions, 239 Montauk Highway, Southampton, NY 11968, 516-283-4000 Ext. 200.

Longwood College
Farmville, VA
Art/fine arts, dance, music, theater arts/drama. Contact Mr. Robert J. Chonko, Director of Admissions, 201 High Street, Farmville, VA 23909-1800, 804-395-2060.

Loras College
Dubuque, IA
Art/fine arts, music. Contact Mr. Kelly Myers, Director of Admissions, 1450 Alta Vista, Dubuque, IA 52004-0178, 319-588-7236.

Louisiana College
Pineville, LA
Art/fine arts, music, theater arts/drama. Contact Ms. Karin Gregorczyk, Acting Director of Admissions, Box 560, Pineville, LA 71359-0001, 318-487-7259.

Louisiana State University and Agricultural and Mechanical College
Baton Rouge, LA
Art/fine arts, music, theater arts/drama. Contact Ms. Lisa Harris, Director of Admissions, Baton Rouge, LA 70803-3103, 504-388-1175.

Louisiana State University in Shreveport
Shreveport, LA
Art/fine arts. Contact Ms. Kathy Plante, Registrar/Director of Admissions, One University Place, Shreveport, LA 71115-2399, 318-797-5249.

Louisiana Tech University
Ruston, LA
Art/fine arts, music. Contact Mrs. Karen Akin, Dean of Admissions, PO Box 3186, Tech Station, Ruston, LA 71272, 318-257-3036.

Lourdes College
Sylvania, OH
Art/fine arts. Contact Mrs. Mary Ellen Briggs, Director of Admissions, 6832 Convent Boulevard, Sylvania, OH 43560-2898, 419-885-5291 Ext. 299.

Loyola College
Baltimore, MD
Art/fine arts, music, theater arts/drama. Contact Mr. William Bossemeyer, Director of Admissions, 4501 North Charles Street, Baltimore, MD 21210-2699, 410-617-2000 Ext. 2252.

Loyola Marymount University
Los Angeles, CA
Art/fine arts, dance, music, theater arts/drama. Contact Mr. Matthew X. Fissinger, Director of Admissions, 7101 West 80th Street, Los Angeles, CA 90045-2699, 310-338-2750.

Loyola University Chicago
Chicago, IL
Art/fine arts, music, theater arts/drama. Contact Mr. Robert Blust, Director of Admissions, 820 North Michigan Avenue, Chicago, IL 60611-2196, 312-915-6500.

Loyola University, New Orleans
New Orleans, LA
Art/fine arts, music, theater arts/drama. Contact Ms. Nan Massingill, Director of Admissions, 6363 Saint Charles Avenue, New Orleans, LA 70118-6195, 504-865-3240.

Lubbock Christian University
Lubbock, TX
Art/fine arts, music. Contact Mr. Jerry Shelton, Director of Admissions, 5601 19th Street, Lubbock, TX 79407-2099, 806-796-8800 Ext. 262.

Luther College
Decorah, IA
Art/fine arts, dance, music, theater arts/drama. Contact Dr. David Sallee, Dean for Enrollment Management, 700 College Drive, Decorah, IA 52101-1045, 319-387-1287.

Lycoming College
Williamsport, PA
Art/fine arts, music, theater arts/drama. Contact Mr. James Spencer, Dean of Admissions and Financial Aid, 700 College Place, Williamsport, PA 17701-5192, 717-321-4026.

Lynchburg College
Lynchburg, VA
Art/fine arts, music, theater arts/drama. Contact, Lynchburg, VA 24501-3199, 804-522-8100 .

Lyndon State College
Lyndonville, VT
Art/fine arts. Contact Mr. Joseph Bellavance Jr., Director of College Recruitment, Lyndonville, VT 05851, 802-626-9371 Ext. 113.

Lynn University
Boca Raton, FL
Art/fine arts. ContactDirector of Admissions, 3601 North Military Trail, Boca Raton, FL 33431-5598, 407-994-0770.

Lyon College
Batesville, AR
Art/fine arts, music, theater arts/drama. Contact Mr. Jonathan Stroud, Dean of Admissions and Financial Aid, PO Box 2317, Batesville, AR 72503-2317, 501-698-4250.

M

Macalester College
St. Paul, MN
Art/fine arts, music, theater arts/drama. Contact Mr. William M. Shain, Dean of Admissions, 1600 Grand Avenue, St. Paul, MN 55105-1899, 612-696-6357.

MacMurray College
Jacksonville, IL
Art/fine arts, music. Contact Dr. Edwin R. Hockett, Dean of Admissions, East College Avenue, Jacksonville, IL 62650, 217-479-7056.

Madonna University
Livonia, MI
Art/fine arts, music. Contact Mr. Louis E. Brohl III, Director of Admissions and Marketing, 36600 Schoolcraft Road, Livonia, MI 48150-1173, 313-591-5052.

Maharishi International University
Fairfield, IA
Art/fine arts. Contact Mr. Brad Mylett, Director of Admissions, 1000 North 4th Street, DB 1155, Fairfield, IA 53557-1155, 515-472-7000 Ext. 1110.

Maine College of Art
Portland, ME
Art/fine arts. Contact Ms. Beth Shea, Director of Admissions, 75 Spring Street, Portland, ME 04101-3987, 207-775-3052.

Malone College
Canton, OH
Art/fine arts, music, theater arts/drama. Contact Mr. Leland J. Sommers, Dean of Admissions, 515 25th Street, NW, Canton, OH 44709-3897, 216-471-8145.

Manchester College
North Manchester, IN
Art/fine arts, music, theater arts/drama. Contact Mr. David McFadden, Vice President for Enrollment Management, 604 College Avenue, North Manchester, IN 46962-1225, 219-982-5055.

Manhattan Christian College
Manhattan, KS
Music. Contact Mr. John Poulson, Vice President for Admissions, 1415 Anderson, Manhattan, KS 66502-4081, 913-539-3571 Ext. 30.

Manhattan College
Riverdale, NY
Art/fine arts. Contact Mr. John J. Brennan Jr., Dean of Admissions, Manhattan College Parkway, Riverdale, NY 10471, 718-920-0200.

Manhattan School of Music
New York, NY
Music. Contact Mr. James Gandre, Dean of Enrollment and Alumni, 120 Claremont Avenue, New York, NY 10027-4698, 212-749-2802 Ext. 501.

Manhattanville College
Purchase, NY
Art/fine arts, dance, music, theater arts/drama. Contact Mr. David Harvey, Director of Admissions, 2900 Purchase Street, Purchase, NY 10577-2132, 914-694-2200 Ext. 464.

Mankato State University
Mankato, MN
Art/fine arts, music, theater arts/drama. Contact Mr. Malcolm O'Sullivan, Director of Admissions, South Rd and Ellis Ave, PO Box 8400, Mankato, MN 56002-8400, 507-389-1822.

Mannes College of Music, New School for Social Research
New York, NY
Music. Contact Ms. Marilyn Groves, Director of Admissions and Registration, 150 West 85th Street, New York, NY 10024-4402, 212-580-0210 Ext. 46.

Mansfield University of Pennsylvania
Mansfield, PA
Art/fine arts, music, theater arts/drama. Contact Mr. John J. Abplanalp, Director of Enrollment Services, Beecher House, Mansfield, PA 16933, 717-662-4243.

Maranatha Baptist Bible College
Watertown, WI
Music. Contact Mr. David Hershberger, Registrar, 745 West Main Street, Watertown, WI 53094, 414-261-9300 Ext. 363.

Marian College
Indianapolis, IN
Art/fine arts, music, theater arts/drama. Contact Dr. Brent Smith, Dean for Enrollment Management and Admissions, 3200 Cold Spring Road, Indianapolis, IN 46222-1997, 317-929-0321.

Marian College of Fond du Lac
Fond du Lac, WI
Art/fine arts, music. Contact Ms. Carol A. Reichenberger, Vice President for Enrollment Services, 45 South National Avenue, Fond du Lac, WI 54935-4699, 414-923-7650.

Marietta College
Marietta, OH
Art/fine arts, music, theater arts/drama. Contact Mr. Dennis DePerro, Dean of Admission and Financial Aid, 215 Fifth Street, Marietta, OH 45750-4000, 614-374-4600.

Marist College
Poughkeepsie, NY
Art/fine arts. Contact Mr. Harry W. Wood, Vice President for Admissions and Enrollment Planning, 290 North Road, Poughkeepsie, NY 12601-1387, 914-575-3000 Ext. 2227.

Marlboro College
Marlboro, VT
Art/fine arts, dance, music, theater arts/drama. Contact Mr. Wayne R. Wood, Director of Admissions, Box A, Marlboro, VT 05344, 802-257-4333 Ext. 237.

Marquette University
Milwaukee, WI
Theater arts/drama. Contact Mr. David Buckholdt, Director of Enrollment Management, PO Box 1881, Milwaukee, WI 53201-1881, 414-288-7302.

Marshall University
Huntington, WV
Art/fine arts, music, theater arts/drama. Contact Dr. James W. Harless, Admissions Director, 400 Hal Greer Boulevard, Huntington, WV 25755-2020, 304-696-3160.

Mars Hill College
Mars Hill, NC
Art/fine arts, music, theater arts/drama. Contact Mr. Rick Hinshaw, Dean of Admissions and Financial Aid, Mars Hill, NC 28754, 704-689-1201.

Martin University
Indianapolis, IN
Art/fine arts, music. Contact Ms. Bobbye Craig, Director of Enrollment Management, 2171 Avondale Place, PO Box 18567, Indianapolis, IN 46218-3867, 317-543-3238.

Mary Baldwin College
Staunton, VA
Art/fine arts, theater arts/drama. Contact Mr. Doug Clark, Executive Director of Admissions, Staunton, VA 24401, 703-887-7019.

Marygrove College
Detroit, MI
Art/fine arts, dance, music. Contact Ms. Carla R. Stepp, Director of Admissions, 8425 West McNichols Road, Detroit, MI 48221-2599, 313-862-5200 Ext. 570.

Marylhurst College
Marylhurst, OR
Art/fine arts, music. Contact Mr. John Rolston, Registrar, PO Box 261, Marylhurst, OR 97036-0261, 503-636-8141 Ext. 324.

Marymount College
Tarrytown, NY
Art/fine arts, theater arts/drama. Contact Ms. Christine Richard, Director of Admissions, 100 Marymount Avenue, Tarrytown, NY 10591-3796, 914-332-8295.

Marymount Manhattan College
New York, NY
Art/fine arts, dance, theater arts/drama. Contact Ms. Suzanne Murphy, Dean & Director of Admissions & Enrollment Management, 221 East 71st Street, New York, NY 10021, 212-517-0555.

Marymount University
Arlington, VA
Art/fine arts. Contact Mr. Charles Coe, Director of Admissions, 2807 North Glebe Road, Arlington, VA 22207-4299, 703-284-1500.

Maryville College
Maryville, TN
Art/fine arts, music, theater arts/drama. Contact Ms. Donna Davis, Vice President of Admissions and Enrollment, 502 East Lamar Alexander Parkway, Maryville, TN 37804-5907, 615-981-8092.

Maryville University of Saint Louis
St. Louis, MO
Art/fine arts, music. Contact Dr. Martha Wade, Dean of Admissions and Enrollment Management, 13550 Conway Road, St. Louis, MO 63141-7299, 314-529-9350.

Mary Washington College
Fredericksburg, VA
Art/fine arts, dance, music, theater arts/drama. Contact Dr. Martin A. Wilder Jr., Vice President for Admissions and Financial Aid, 1301 College Avenue, Fredericksburg, VA 22401-5358, 703-899-4681.

Marywood College
Scranton, PA
Art/fine arts, music, theater arts/drama. Contact Mr. Fred R. Brooks Jr., Director of Admissions, 2300 Adams Avenue, Scranton, PA 18509-1598, 717-348-6234.

Massachusetts Institute of Technology
Cambridge, MA
Art/fine arts, music, theater arts/drama. Contact Mr. Michael C. Behnke, Director of Admissions, 77 Massachusetts Avenue, Cambridge, MA 02139-4307, 617-253-4791.

Master's College and Seminary
Santa Clarita, CA
Music. Contact Mr. Todd Brooks, Director of Admissions, 21726 West Placerita Canyon Road, Santa Clarita, CA 91321-1200, 805-259-3540 Ext. 347.

McKendree College
Lebanon, IL
Art/fine arts. Contact Mrs. Sue Cordon, Dean of Admissions, 701 College Road, Lebanon, IL 62254-1299, 618-537-4481 Ext. 124.

McMurry University
Abilene, TX
Art/fine arts, music, theater arts/drama. Contact Dr. L. Russell Watjen, Vice President, Enrollment Management and Student Relations, Box 716, Abilene, TX 79697, 915-691-6370.

McNeese State University
Lake Charles, LA
Art/fine arts, music, theater arts/drama. Contact Ms. Kathy Bond, Admissions Counselor, PO Box 92495, Lake Charles, LA 70609-2495, 318-475-5148.

McPherson College
McPherson, KS
Art/fine arts, music, theater arts/drama. Contact Mrs. Karlene Tyler, Registrar, 1600 East Euclid, McPherson, KS 67460-3899, 316-241-0731.

Medaille College
Buffalo, NY
Art/fine arts. Contact Mrs. Jacqueline S. Matheny, Director of Enrollment Management, 18 Agassiz Circle, Buffalo, NY 14214-2695, 716-884-3281 Ext. 204.

Mercer University
Macon, GA
Art/fine arts, music, theater arts/drama. Contact Dr. J. Thompson Biggers, Vice President for Enrollment Management, 1400 Coleman Avenue, Macon, GA 31207-0003, 912-752-2021.

Mercy College
Dobbs Ferry, NY
Art/fine arts, music. Contact Ms. Joy Colelli, Director of Admissions, 555 Broadway, Dobbs Ferry, NY 10522-9988, 914-674-7434.

Mercyhurst College
Erie, PA
Art/fine arts, dance, music. Contact Mr. Andrew Roth, Dean of Enrollment Services, Glenwood Hills, Erie, PA 16546, 814-824-2241.

Meredith College
Raleigh, NC
Art/fine arts, dance, music, theater arts/drama. Contact Mrs. Sue E. Kearney, Director of Admissions, 3800 Hillsborough Street, Raleigh, NC 27607-5298, 919-829-8581.

Mesa State College
Grand Junction, CO
Art/fine arts, music, theater arts/drama. Contact Mr. Paul Jones, Acting Director of Admissions, PO Box 2647, Grand Junction, CO 81502-2647, 970-248-1376.

Messiah College
Grantham, PA
Art/fine arts, music, theater arts/drama. Contact Mr. Ron E. Long, Vice President for Communications, Grantham, PA 17027, 717-691-6000.

Methodist College
Fayetteville, NC
Art/fine arts, music, theater arts/drama. Contact Mr. J. Alan Coheley, Vice President of Enrollment Services, 5400 Ramsey Street, Fayetteville, NC 28311-1420, 910-630-7027.

Metropolitan State College of Denver
Denver, CO
Art/fine arts, music. Contact Mr. Thomas R. Gray, Assistant Dean of Admissions and Records, PO Box 173362, Denver, CO 80217-3362, 303-556-3977.

Miami University
Oxford, OH
Art/fine arts, music, theater arts/drama. Contact Dr. James S. McCoy, Assistant Vice President for Enrollment Services, Oxford, OH 45056, 513-529-2531.

Michigan State University
East Lansing, MI
Art/fine arts, music, theater arts/drama. Contact Dr. William H. Turner, Director of Admissions, East Lansing, MI 48824-1020, 517-355-8332.

Mid-America Bible College
Oklahoma City, OK
Music. Contact Mr. Derry Ebert, Director of Student Recruitment, 3500 Southwest 119th Street, Oklahoma City, OK 73170-4504, 405-691-3800 Ext. 107.

MidAmerica Nazarene College
Olathe, KS
Music. Contact Dr. Bob Drummond, Director of Admission, 2030 East College Way, Olathe, KS 66062-1899, 913-782-3750 Ext. 140.

Middlebury College
Middlebury, VT
Art/fine arts, dance, music, theater arts/drama. Contact Mr. Geoffrey Smith, Director of Admissions, Middlebury, VT 05753-6000, 802-388-3711 Ext. 2222.

Middle Tennessee State University
Murfreesboro, TN
Art/fine arts, dance, music, theater arts/drama. Contact Ms. Lynn Palmer, Director of Admissions, Murfreesboro, TN 37132, 615-898-2111.

Midland Lutheran College
Fremont, NE
Art/fine arts, music, theater arts/drama. Contact Mr. Roland R. Kahnk, Vice President for Enrollment Services, 900 North Clarkson Street, Fremont, NE 68025-4200, 402-721-5480 Ext. 6500.

Midwestern State University
Wichita Falls, TX
Art/fine arts, music, theater arts/drama. Contact Ms. Billye Tims, Registrar, 3410 Taft Boulevard, Wichita Falls, TX 76308-2096, 817-689-4321.

Miles College
Birmingham, AL
Music. Contact Ms. Brenda Grant Smith, Director of Recruitment and Admissions, PO Box 3800, Birmingham, AL 35208, 205-923-2771 Ext. 226.

Millersville University of Pennsylvania
Millersville, PA
Art/fine arts, music, theater arts/drama. Contact Mr. Darrell Davis, Director of Admissions, PO Box 1002, Millersville, PA 17551-0302, 717-872-3371.

Milligan College
Milligan College, TN
Art/fine arts, music, theater arts/drama. Contact Mr. Michael A. Johnson, Director of Admissions, PO Box 210, Milligan College, TN 37682, 615-461-8730.

Millikin University
Decatur, IL
Art/fine arts, music, theater arts/drama. Contact Mr. Lin Stoner, Dean of Admission, 1184 West Main Street, Decatur, IL 62522, 217-424-6210.

Millsaps College
Jackson, MS
Art/fine arts, music, theater arts/drama. Contact Mr. Gary L. Fretwell, Vice President of Enrollment and Student Services, 1701 North State Street, Jackson, MS 39210-0001, 601-974-1050.

Mills College
Oakland, CA
Art/fine arts, dance, music, theater arts/drama. Contact Ms. Genevieve Ann Flaherty, Dean of Admission and Financial Aid, 5000 MacArthur Boulevard, Oakland, CA 94613-1000, 510-430-2135.

Minot State University
Minot, ND
Art/fine arts, music, theater arts/drama. Contact Mr. Brad Mahnke, Director of Admissions, 500 University Avenue West, Minot, ND 58707-0002, 701-857-3350.

Mississippi College
Clinton, MS
Art/fine arts, music. Contact Mr. Jim Turcotte, Director of Admissions, PO Box 4203, Clinton, MS 39058, 601-925-3240.

Mississippi State University
Mississippi State, MS
Art/fine arts, music. Contact Mr. Jerry Inmon, Director of Admissions, PO Box 5268, Mississippi State, MS 39762, 601-325-2224.

Mississippi University for Women
Columbus, MS
Art/fine arts, music, theater arts/drama. Contact Ms. Teresa Thompson, Director of Enrollment Management and Legislative Liaison, PO Box 1613, Columbus, MS 39701-9998, 601-329-7106.

Mississippi Valley State University
Itta Bena, MS
Art/fine arts, music. Contact Mrs. Maxine B. Rush, Director of Admissions and Recruitment, 14000 Highway 82 West, Itta Bena, MS 38941-1400, 601-254-3344.

Missouri Baptist College
St. Louis, MO
Music. Contact Mrs. Gloria Vertrees, Director of Admissions, 12542 Conway Road, St. Louis, MO 63141-8698, 314-434-1115 Ext. 242.

Missouri Southern State College
Joplin, MO
Art/fine arts, music, theater arts/drama. Contact Mr. Richard D. Humphrey, Director of Admission, 3950 East Newman Road, Joplin, MO 64801-1595, 417-625-9537.

Missouri Valley College
Marshall, MO
Art/fine arts, theater arts/drama. Contact Mr. Chadwick B. Freeman, Director of Admissions and Financial Aid, 500 East College, Marshall, MO 65340-3197, 816-886-6924 Ext. 168.

Missouri Western State College
St. Joseph, MO
Art/fine arts, music. Contact Mr. Howard McCauley, Director of Admissions, 4525 Downs Drive, St. Joseph, MO 64507-2294, 816-271-4267.

Molloy College
Rockville Centre, NY
Art/fine arts, music, theater arts/drama. Contact Mr. Wayne F. James, Director of Admissions and Freshman Transfer Aid, 1000 Hempstead Avenue, Rockville Centre, NY 11570-1199, 516-678-5000 Ext. 233.

Monmouth College
Monmouth, IL
Art/fine arts, music, theater arts/drama. Contact Mr. Richard Valentine, Dean of Admissions, 700 East Broadway, Monmouth, IL 61462-1998, 309-457-2131.

Monmouth University
West Long Branch, NJ
Art/fine arts, music, theater arts/drama. Contact Mr. David Waggoner, Director of Undergraduate Admissions, West Long Branch, NJ 07764-1898, 908-571-3456.

Montana State University–Billings
Billings, MT
Art/fine arts, music, theater arts/drama. Contact Mrs. Karen Everett, Director of Admissions and Records, 1500 North 30th Street, Billings, MT 59101-0298, 406-657-2158.

Montana State University–Bozeman
Bozeman, MT
Art/fine arts, music, theater arts/drama. Contact Mr. Charles Nelson, Registrar and Director of Admissions, 120 Hamilton Hall, Bozeman, MT 59717, 406-994-2601.

Montana State University–Northern
Havre, MT
Theater arts/drama. Contact Mr. Kelly Palmer, Director of Admissions, PO Box 7751, Havre, MT 59501-7751, 406-265-3704.

Montclair State University
Upper Montclair, NJ
Art/fine arts, dance, music, theater arts/drama. Contact Dr. Alan L. Buechler, Director of Admissions, Valley Road and Normal Avenue, Upper Montclair, NJ 07043-1624, 201-655-5116.

Moody Bible Institute
Chicago, IL
Music. Contact Mr. Philip Van Wynen, Dean of Enrollment Management/Registrar, 820 North LaSalle Boulevard, Chicago, IL 60610, 312-329-4261.

Moorhead State University
Moorhead, MN
Art/fine arts, music, theater arts/drama. Contact Ms. Jean Lange, Director of Admissions, Owens Hall, Moorhead, MN 56563-0002, 218-236-2548.

Moravian College
Bethlehem, PA
Art/fine arts, music. Contact Mr. Bernard Story, Director of Admissions, 1200 Main Street, Bethlehem, PA 18018-6650, 610-861-1320.

Morehead State University
Morehead, KY
Art/fine arts, music, theater arts/drama. Contact Mr. Charles Myers, Director of Admissions, University Boulevard, Morehead, KY 40351, 606-783-2000.

Morehouse College
Atlanta, GA
Art/fine arts, music, theater arts/drama. Contact Mr. Milford Green, Director of Admissions, 830 Westview Drive, SW, Atlanta, GA 30314, 404-215-2632.

Morgan State University
Baltimore, MD
Art/fine arts, music, theater arts/drama. Contact Ms. Chelseia Harold-Miller, Director of Admission and Recruitment, Cold Spring Lane and Hillen Road, Baltimore, MD 21239, 410-319-3000.

Morningside College
Sioux City, IA
Art/fine arts, music, theater arts/drama. Contact Ms. Lora Vander Zwaag, Director of Admissions, 1501 Morningside Avenue, Sioux City, IA 51106-1751, 712-274-5111.

Morris Brown College
Atlanta, GA
Art/fine arts, music, theater arts/drama. Contact Rev. Deborah Grant, Director of Enrollment Management, 643 Martin Luther King Jr Drive, NW, Atlanta, GA 30314-4195, 404-220-0145.

Morris College
Sumter, SC
Art/fine arts, music. Contact Mrs. Queen W. Spann, Director of Admissions and Records, 100 West College Street, Sumter, SC 29150-3599, 803-775-9371 Ext. 225.

Mount Holyoke College
South Hadley, MA
Art/fine arts, dance, music, theater arts/drama. Contact Ms. Anita Smith, Director of Admissions, 50 College Street, South Hadley, MA 01075-1414, 413-538-2023.

Mount Marty College
Yankton, SD
Music. Contact Mrs. Paula Tacke, Director of Admissions, 1105 West 8th Street, Yankton, SD 57078-3724, 605-668-1545.

Mount Mary College
Milwaukee, WI
Art/fine arts, music. Contact Mrs. Mary Jane Reilly, Director of Admission, 2900 North Menomonee River Parkway, Milwaukee, WI 53222-4597, 414-258-4810 Ext. 360.

Mount Mercy College
Cedar Rapids, IA
Art/fine arts, music, theater arts/drama. Contact Mr. Larry Erenberger, Vice President for Enroll-

ment Management, 1330 Elmhurst Drive, NE, Cedar Rapids, IA 52402-4797, 319-363-8213 Ext. 221.

Mount Olive College
Mount Olive, NC
Art/fine arts. Contact Mrs. Dianne B. Riley, Director of Admissions, 634 Henderson Street, Mount Olive, NC 28365, 919-658-2502 Ext. 3009.

Mount Saint Mary College
Newburgh, NY
Theater arts/drama. Contact Mr. J. Randall Ognibene, Director of Admissions, 330 Powell Avenue, Newburgh, NY 12550-3494, 914-569-3248.

Mount St. Mary's College
Los Angeles, CA
Art/fine arts, music. Contact Ms. Katy Murphy, Executive Director of Admissions and Financial Aid, 12001 Chalon Road, Los Angeles, CA 90049-1597, 310-476-2237 Ext. 516.

Mount Saint Mary's College
Emmitsburg, MD
Art/fine arts, music, theater arts/drama. Contact Mr. Michael D. Kennedy, Director of Admissions, Emmitsburg, MD 21727-7799, 301-447-5214.

Mount Senario College
Ladysmith, WI
Art/fine arts, music. Contact Mr. Dewey Floberg, Dean of Admissions and Student Life, 1500 College Avenue West, Ladysmith, WI 54848-2128, 715-532-5511 Ext. 107.

Mount Union College
Alliance, OH
Art/fine arts, music, theater arts/drama. Contact Mr. Greg King, Director of Admissions and Enrollment Management, 1972 Clark Avenue, Alliance, OH 44601-3929, 216-823-2590.

Mount Vernon College
Washington, DC
Art/fine arts. Contact Mrs. Dreama Skorupski, Director of Admissions, 2100 Foxhall Road, NW, Washington, DC 20007-1199, 202-625-4682.

Mount Vernon Nazarene College
Mount Vernon, OH
Art/fine arts, music, theater arts/drama. Contact Rev. Bruce Oldham, Director of Admissions and Student Recruitment, 800 Martinsburg Road, Mount Vernon, OH 43050-9509, 614-397-1244 Ext. 4510.

Muhlenberg College
Allentown, PA
Art/fine arts, dance, music, theater arts/drama. Contact Mr. Christopher Hooker-Haring, Dean of Admissions, 2400 Chew Street, Allentown, PA 18104-5586, 610-821-3200.

Multnomah Bible College and Biblical Seminary
Portland, OR
Music. Contact Miss Joyce L. Kehoe, Director of Admissions and Registrar, 8435 Northeast Glisan Street, Portland, OR 97220-5898, 503-255-0332 Ext. 371.

Murray State University
Murray, KY
Art/fine arts, music, theater arts/drama. Contact Mr. Phil Bryan, Dean of Admission and Registrar, PO Box 9, Murray, KY 42071-0009, 502-762-3380.

Muskingum College
New Concord, OH
Art/fine arts, music, theater arts/drama. Contact Mr. Jeff Zellers, Dean of Enrollment, New Concord, OH 43762, 614-826-8137.

N

Naropa Institute
Boulder, CO
Art/fine arts, dance, music, theater arts/drama. Contact Ms. Marta Shoman, Director of Admissions, 2130 Arapahoe Avenue, Boulder, CO 80302-6697, 303-444-0202 Ext. 514.

National–Louis University
Evanston, IL
Art/fine arts, theater arts/drama. Contact Mr. Randall Berd, Director of Student Enrollment, 1000 Capitol Drive, Wheeling, IL 60090, 708-465-0575 Ext. 5151.

Nazarene Bible College
Colorado Springs, CO
Music. Contact Rev. J. Fred Shepard, Director of Admissions/Public Relations, PO Box 15749, Colorado Springs, CO 80916, 719-596-5110 Ext. 167.

Nazareth College of Rochester
Rochester, NY
Art/fine arts, music, theater arts/drama. Contact Mr. Thomas K. DaRin, Director of Admissions, 4245 East Avenue, Rochester, NY 14618-3790, 716-586-2525 Ext. 265.

Nebraska Christian College
Norfolk, NE
Music. Contact Mr. Jerry Hopkins, Director of Admissions, 1800 Syracuse Avenue, Norfolk, NE 68701-2458, 402-371-5960.

Nebraska Wesleyan University
Lincoln, NE
Art/fine arts, music, theater arts/drama. Contact Mr. Ken Sieg, Director of Admissions, 5000 Saint Paul Avenue, Lincoln, NE 68504-2796, 402-465-2218.

Newberry College
Newberry, SC
Art/fine arts, music, theater arts/drama. Contact Mr. John Ryder, Director of Admissions, 2100 College Street, Newberry, SC 29108-2197, 803-321-5127.

New College of the University of South Florida
Sarasota, FL
Art/fine arts, music. Contact Mr. David L. Anderson, Director of Admissions, 5700 North Tamiami Trail, Sarasota, FL 34243-2197, 813-359-4269.

New England College
Henniker, NH
Art/fine arts, theater arts/drama. Contact Mr. Donald Parker, Director of Admission, 7 Main Street, Henniker, NH 03242-3293, 603-428-2223.

New England School of Art and Design
Boston, MA
Art/fine arts. Contact Ms. Anne Blevins, Director of Admissions and Placement, 28 Newbury Street, Boston, MA 02116, 617-536-0383 Ext. 11.

New Mexico Highlands University
Las Vegas, NM
Art/fine arts, music. Contact Mr. John Coca, Director of Admissions, Las Vegas, NM 87701, 505-454-3424.

New Mexico State University
Las Cruces, NM
Art/fine arts, music, theater arts/drama. Contact Ms. Angela Mora, Interim Director of Admissions, Box 30001, Department 3A, Las Cruces, NM 88003-8001, 505-646-3121.

New York Institute of Technology
Old Westbury, NY
Art/fine arts. Contact Mr. Arthur Lambert, Executive Director of Enrollment Services, PO Box 8000, Old Westbury, NY 11568-8000, 516-686-7520.

New York University
New York, NY
Art/fine arts, dance, music, theater arts/drama. Contact Mr. Richard Avitabile, Director of Admissions, 22 Washington Square North, New York, NY 10012-1019, 212-998-4500.

Niagara University
Niagara Falls, NY
Theater arts/drama. Contact Mr. George C. Pachter Jr., Dean of Admissions and Records, Niagara University, NY 14109, 716-286-8700 Ext. 208.

Nicholls State University
Thibodaux, LA
Art/fine arts, music. Contact Mr. John A. Williamson, Director of Admissions, University Station, Thibodaux, LA 70310, 504-448-4145.

Norfolk State University
Norfolk, VA
Art/fine arts, music. Contact Dr. Frank W. Cool, Director of Admissions, 2401 Corprew Avenue, Norfolk, VA 23504-3907, 804-683-8391.

North Adams State College
North Adams, MA
Art/fine arts, music, theater arts/drama. Contact Ms. Denise Richardello, Director of Admissions, Church Street, North Adams, MA 01247-4100, 413-662-5410 Ext. 5416.

North Carolina Agricultural and Technical State University
Greensboro, NC
Music, theater arts/drama. Contact Mr. John Smith, Director of Admissions, 1601 East Market Street, Greensboro, NC 27411, 910-334-7946.

North Carolina Central University
Durham, NC
Art/fine arts, music, theater arts/drama. Contact Mrs. Nancy R. Rowland, Director of Admissions, 1801 Fayetteville Street, Durham, NC 27707-3129, 919-560-6326.

North Carolina School of the Arts
Winston-Salem, NC
Dance, music, theater arts/drama. Contact Ms. Carol J. Palm, Director of Admissions, 200 Waughtown Street, PO Box 12189, Winston-Salem, NC 27117-2189, 910-770-3290.

North Carolina Wesleyan College
Rocky Mount, NC
Theater arts/drama. Contact Mr. Brett Freshour, Director of Admissions, 3400 North Wesleyan Boulevard, Rocky Mount, NC 27804-8677, 919-985-5200.

North Central Bible College
Minneapolis, MN
Music. Contact Mr. Dan Neary, Director of Admissions, 910 Elliot Avenue South, Minneapolis, MN 55404-1322, 612-343-4480.

North Central College
Naperville, IL
Art/fine arts, music, theater arts/drama. Contact Mr. Fred Schebor, Dean of Admission, 30 North Brainard Street, PO Box 3063, Naperville, IL 60566-7063, 708-420-3414.

North Dakota State University
Fargo, ND
Art/fine arts, music, theater arts/drama. Contact Dr. Kate Haugen, Director of Admission, University Station, Fargo, ND 58105, 701-231-8643.

Northeastern Illinois University
Chicago, IL
Art/fine arts, music. Contact Ms. Miriam Rivera, Director of Admissions and Records, 5500 North St. Louis Avenue, Chicago, IL 60625-4699, 312-794-2853.

Northeastern State University
Tahlequah, OK
Art/fine arts, music, theater arts/drama. ContactDirector of Admissions and Registrar, 600 North Grand, Tahlequah, OK 74464-2399, 918-456-5511 Ext. 2200.

Northeastern University
Boston, MA
Art/fine arts, music, theater arts/drama. Contact Mr. Kevin Kelly, Dean of Admissions, 360 Huntington Avenue, Boston, MA 02115-5096, 617-373-2200.

Northeast Louisiana University
Monroe, LA
Art/fine arts, music. Contact Dr. James Robertson, Registrar, 700 University Avenue, Monroe, LA 71209-0001, 318-342-5252.

Northeast Missouri State University
Kirksville, MO
Art/fine arts, music, theater arts/drama. Contact Ms. Kathy Rieck, Dean of Admission and Records, 205 McClain Hall, Kirksville, MO 63501, 816-785-4114.

Northern Arizona University
Flagstaff, AZ
Art/fine arts, music, theater arts/drama. Contact Ms. Molly Carder, Director of Admissions, PO Box 4084, Flagstaff, AZ 86011, 602-523-5511.

Northern Illinois University
De Kalb, IL
Art/fine arts, dance, music, theater arts/drama. Contact Dr. Daniel S. Oborn, Director of Admissions, De Kalb, IL 60115-2864, 815-753-0446.

Northern Kentucky University
Highland Heights, KY
Art/fine arts, music, theater arts/drama. Contact Mrs. Margaret Winchell, Director of Admissions, Administrative Center 400, Highland Heights, KY 41099-7010, 606-572-5755.

Northern Michigan University
Marquette, MI
Art/fine arts, music, theater arts/drama. Contact Ms. Nancy Rehling, Director of Admissions, 1401 Presque Isle Avenue, Marquette, MI 49855-5301, 906-227-2650.

Northern State University
Aberdeen, SD
Art/fine arts, music, theater arts/drama. Contact Mr. Steve Ochsner, Director, Admissions, 1200 South Jay Street, Aberdeen, SD 57401-7198, 605-626-2544.

North Georgia College
Dahlonega, GA
Art/fine arts, music. Contact Mr. Gary R. Steffey, Director of Admissions and Enrollment Management, Admissions Center, Dahlonega, GA 30533, 706-864-1750.

Northland College
Ashland, WI
Music. Contact Mr. James L. Miller, Dean of Student Development and Enrollment, 1411 Ellis Avenue, Ashland, WI 54806-3925, 715-682-1224.

North Park College
Chicago, IL
Art/fine arts, music, theater arts/drama. Contact Mr. John Schafer, Dean of Admissions and Financial Aid, 3225 West Foster Avenue, Chicago, IL 60625-4895, 312-244-5504.

Northwest Christian College
Eugene, OR
Music. Contact Dr. Randolph P. Jones, Director of Admissions, 828 East 11th Avenue, Eugene, OR 97401-3727, 503-343-1641 Ext. 20.

Northwest College of Art
Poulsbo, WA
Art/fine arts. Contact Mr. Craig Freeman, President, 16464 State Highway 305, Poulsbo, WA 98370, 360-779-9993.

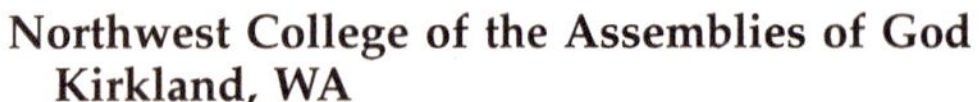

Northwest College of the Assemblies of God
Kirkland, WA
Music. Contact Dr. Calvin L. White, Director of Enrollment Services, PO Box 579, Kirkland, WA 98083-0579, 206-889-5231.

Northwestern College
Orange City, IA
Art/fine arts, music, theater arts/drama. Contact Mr. Ronald K. DeJong, Director of Admissions, 101 College Lane, Orange City, IA 51041-1996, 712-737-7000.

Northwestern College
St. Paul, MN
Art/fine arts, music, theater arts/drama. Contact Mr. Ralph D. Anderson, Dean of Admissions, 3003 Snelling Avenue North, St. Paul, MN 55113-1598, 612-631-5111.

Northwestern Oklahoma State University
Alva, OK
Music, theater arts/drama. Contact Mr. S. L. White, Director of Pre-Admissions, 709 Oklahoma Boulevard, Alva, OK 73717-2799, 405-327-1700 Ext. 213.

Northwestern State University of Louisiana
Natchitoches, LA
Art/fine arts, music. Contact Mr. Chris Maggio, Director of Recruiting and Admissions, Natchitoches, LA 71497, 318-357-4503.

Northwestern University
Evanston, IL
Art/fine arts, dance, music, theater arts/drama. Contact Ms. Carol Lunkenheimer, Director of Admissions, 1801 Hinman Avenue, Evanston, IL 60208, 708-491-7271.

Northwest Missouri State University
Maryville, MO
Art/fine arts, music, theater arts/drama. Contact Mr. Roger Pugh, Executive Director of Enrollment Management, 800 University Drive, Maryville, MO 64468-6001, 816-562-1562.

Northwest Nazarene College
Nampa, ID
Art/fine arts, music. Contact Mr. Terry Blom, Director of Enrollment Management, 623 Holly Street, Nampa, ID 83686-5897, 208-467-8773.

Notre Dame College
Manchester, NH
Art/fine arts. Contact Mr. Joseph P. Wagner, Dean of Admissions, 2321 Elm Street, Manchester, NH 03104-2299, 603-669-4298 Ext. 169.

Notre Dame College of Ohio
South Euclid, OH
Art/fine arts. Contact Mrs. Karen Poelking, Dean of Admission and Records, 4545 College Road, South Euclid, OH 44121-4293, 216-381-1680 Ext. 239.

Nyack College
Nyack, NY
Music. Contact Mr. Miguel O. Sanchez, Director of Admissions, Nyack, NY 10960, 914-358-1710 Ext. 350.

O

Oak Hills Bible College
Bemidji, MN
Music. Contact Mrs. Monica Bush, Admissions Director, 1600 Oak Hills Road, SW, Bemidji, MN 56601-8832, 218-751-8670 Ext. 230.

Oakland City University
Oakland City, IN
Art/fine arts, music. Contact Mrs. Faye Camp, Director of Admissions, 143 North Lucretia Street, Oakland City, IN 47660-1099, 812-749-1222.

Oakland University
Rochester, MI
Dance, music, theater arts/drama. Contact Ms. Anne M. Sandoval, Acting Director of Admissions and Scholarships, 101 North Foundation Hall, Rochester, MI 48309-4401, 810-370-3360.

Oakwood College
Huntsville, AL
Music. Contact Mr. Robert Edwards, Director of Enrollment Management, PO Box 107, Huntsville, AL 35896, 205-726-7354.

Oberlin College
Oberlin, OH
Art/fine arts, dance, music, theater arts/drama. Contact Mr. Thomas C. Hayden, Vice President of Admissions and Financial Aid, Oberlin, OH 44074, 216-775-8919.

Occidental College
Los Angeles, CA
Art/fine arts, music, theater arts/drama. Contact Mr. David P. Morgan, Interim Dean of Admissions, 1600 Campus Road, Los Angeles, CA 90041-3392, 213-259-2700.

Oglethorpe University
Atlanta, GA
Art/fine arts. Contact Mr. Dennis T. Matthews, Director of Admissions, 4484 Peachtree Road, NE, Atlanta, GA 30319-2797, 404-364-8307.

Ohio Dominican College
Columbus, OH
Art/fine arts. Contact Mr. James Sagona, Vice President of Student Services and Admissions, 1216 Sunbury Road, Columbus, OH 43219-2099, 614-251-4595.

Ohio Northern University
Ada, OH
Art/fine arts, music, theater arts/drama. Contact Ms. Karen Condeni, Dean of Admissions and Financial Aid, Ada, OH 45810, 419-772-2260.

The Ohio State University
Columbus, OH
Art/fine arts, dance, music, theater arts/drama. Contact Dr. James J. Mager, Director of Admissions and Financial Aid, 3rd Floor, Lincoln Tower, Columbus, OH 43210, 614-292-3980.

Ohio University
Athens, OH
Art/fine arts, dance, music, theater arts/drama. Contact Mr. N. Kip Howard, Director of Admissions, Athens, OH 45701, 614-593-4100.

Ohio Wesleyan University
Delaware, OH
Art/fine arts, music, theater arts/drama. Contact Mr. Douglas C. Thompson, Dean of Admission, 61 South Sandusky Street, Delaware, OH 43015, 614-368-3020.

Oklahoma Baptist University
Shawnee, OK
Art/fine arts, music, theater arts/drama. Contact Mr. Jody Johnson, Dean of Admissions, 500 West University, Shawnee, OK 74801-2558, 405-878-2033.

Oklahoma Christian University of Science and Arts
Oklahoma City, OK
Art/fine arts, music, theater arts/drama. Contact Mr. Tom Clark, Vice President for Admissions and Marketing, Box 11000, Oklahoma City, OK 73136-1100, 405-425-5051.

Oklahoma City University
Oklahoma City, OK
Art/fine arts, dance, music, theater arts/drama. Contact Mr. Keith Hackett, Director of Admissions, 2501 North Blackwelder, Oklahoma City, OK 73106-1402, 405-521-5050.

Oklahoma Panhandle State University
Goodwell, OK
Music. Contact Mr. Jim Gourley, Interim Registrar and Director of Student Support, PO Box 430, Goodwell, OK 73939-0430, 405-349-2611 Ext. 212.

Oklahoma State University
Stillwater, OK
Art/fine arts, music, theater arts/drama. Contact Mr. Gordon Reese, Associate Director of Admissions, Stillwater, OK 74078, 405-744-6861.

Old Dominion University
Norfolk, VA
Art/fine arts, dance, music, theater arts/drama. Contact Ms. Patty Cavender, Director of Admissions, 5215 Hampton Boulevard, Norfolk, VA 23529, 804-683-3637.

Olivet College
Olivet, MI
Art/fine arts, music. Contact Mr. Tim Nelson, Vice President of Enrollment Management, Olivet, MI 49076-9701, 616-749-7635.

Olivet Nazarene University
Kankakee, IL
Art/fine arts, music. Contact Rev. John Mongerson, Director of Admissions, PO Box 592, Kankakee, IL 60901-0592, 815-939-5203.

O'More College of Design
Franklin, TN
Art/fine arts. Contact Mr. Thomas L. Campbell, Registrar and Director of Admissions, 423 South Margin Street, PO Box 908, Franklin, TN 37065-0908, 615-794-4254 Ext. 81.

Oral Roberts University
Tulsa, OK
Art/fine arts, music, theater arts/drama. Contact Mr. Shawn Nichols, Director of Admissions, 7777 South Lewis Avenue, Tulsa, OK 74171-0001, 918-495-6518.

Oregon School of Arts and Crafts
Portland, OR
Art/fine arts. Contact Ms. Penelope Hunter, Director of Admissions, 8245 Southwest Barnes Road, Portland, OR 97225, 503-297-5544.

Oregon State University
Corvallis, OR
Art/fine arts, music, theater arts/drama. Contact Ms. Kay Conrad, Director of Admissions, Corvallis, OR 97331, 503-737-4411.

Ottawa University
Ottawa, KS
Art/fine arts, music, theater arts/drama. Contact Mr. Steve Koberlein, Director of Admissions, 1001 South Cedar, Ottawa, KS 66067-3399, 913-242-5200 Ext. 5558.

Otterbein College
Westerville, OH
Art/fine arts, dance, music, theater arts/drama. Contact Ms. Cass Johnson, Director of Admissions, Westerville, OH 43081, 614-823-1500.

Ouachita Baptist University
Arkadelphia, AR
Art/fine arts, music, theater arts/drama. Contact Mr. Michael Kolb, Registrar, 410 Ouachita Street, Arkadelphia, AR 71998-0001, 501-245-5578.

Our Lady of the Lake University of San Antonio
San Antonio, TX
Art/fine arts, music, theater arts/drama. Contact Ms. Loretta Schlegel, Dean of Enrollment Management, 411 Southwest 24th Street, San Antonio, TX 78207-4689, 210-434-6711 Ext. 316.

Ozark Christian College
Joplin, MO
Music. Contact Mr. James Marcum, Director of Enrollment Growth, 1111 North Main Street, Joplin, MO 64801-4804, 417-624-2518 Ext. 260.

P

Pace University
New York, NY
Art/fine arts, theater arts/drama. Contact Ms. Desiree Cilmi, Director of Enrollment Management, Pace Plaza, New York, NY 10038, 212-346-1781.

Pacific Christian College
Fullerton, CA
Art/fine arts, music. Contact Mrs. Diane LeJeune, Director of Admissions, 2500 East Nutwood Avenue, Fullerton, CA 92631-3138, 714-879-3901 Ext. 215.

Pacific Lutheran University
Tacoma, WA
Art/fine arts, music, theater arts/drama. Contact Mr. David Hawsey, Dean of Admissions and Enrollment Management, Tacoma, WA 98447, 206-535-7151.

Pacific Union College
Angwin, CA
Art/fine arts, music. Contact Mrs. H. Susi Mundy, Registrar, Angwin, CA 94508, 707-965-6673.

Pacific University
Forest Grove, OR
Art/fine arts, music, theater arts/drama. Contact Mr. Bart Howard, Dean of Admission and Financial Aid, 2043 College Way, Forest Grove, OR 97116-1797, 503-359-2267.

Paine College
Augusta, GA
Music. Contact Mrs. Ellen C. King, Acting Director of Admission, 1235 15th Street, Augusta, GA 30901-3182, 706-821-8320.

Palm Beach Atlantic College
West Palm Beach, FL
Art/fine arts, music. Contact Mr. Buck James, Dean of Admissions, 901 South Flagler Drive, PO Box 24708, West Palm Beach, FL 33416-4708, 407-835-4309.

Park College
Parkville, MO
Art/fine arts. Contact Mr. Randy Condit, Director of Admissions, 8700 River Park Drive, Parkville, MO 64152-4358, 816-741-2000 Ext. 215.

Patten College
Oakland, CA
Music. Contact Mrs. Sharon Barta, Director of Admissions, 2433 Coolidge Avenue, Oakland, CA 94601-2699, 510-533-8306 Ext. 265.

Pembroke State University
Pembroke, NC
Art/fine arts, music, theater arts/drama. Contact Dr. Deborah Basket, Director of Admissions, PO Box 1510, Pembroke, NC 28372-1510, 910-521-6262.

Pennsylvania State University at Erie, The Behrend College
Erie, PA
Music. Contact Ms. Mary-Ellen Madigan, Admissions Director, Station Road, Erie, PA 16563, 814-898-6100.

Pennsylvania State University University Park Campus
State College, PA
Art/fine arts, music, theater arts/drama. Contact Dr. John J. Romano, Vice Provost for Enrollment Management and Administration, 201 Old Main, University Park, PA 16802-1503, 814-865-5471.

Pepperdine University
Malibu, CA
Art/fine arts, music, theater arts/drama. Contact Mr. Paul Long, Dean of Admission, 24255 Pacific Coast Highway, Malibu, CA 90263-0001, 310-456-4392.

Peru State College
Peru, NE
Art/fine arts, music, theater arts/drama. Contact Mr. Curt E. Luttrell, Director of Admissions and School Relations, PO Box 10, Peru, NE 68421, 402-872-3815 Ext. 2221.

Pfeiffer College
Misenheimer, NC
Music, theater arts/drama. Contact Mr. David Maltby, Dean of Admission and Financial Aid, PO Box 960, Misenheimer, NC 28109-0960, 704-463-1360 Ext. 2065.

Philadelphia College of Bible
Langhorne, PA
Music. Contact Mrs. Fran Emmons, Director of Admissions and Financial Aid, 200 Manor Avenue, Langhorne, PA 19047-2990, 215-752-5800 Ext. 239.

Philadelphia College of Textiles and Science
Philadelphia, PA
Art/fine arts. Contact Ms. Sue Chalfin, Director of Admissions, School House Lane and Henry Avenue, Philadelphia, PA 19144-5497, 215-951-2800.

Philander Smith College
Little Rock, AR
Music. Contact Ms. Beverly Richardson, Dean of Enrollment Management and Records, 812 West 13th Street, Little Rock, AR 72202-3799, 501-375-5215.

Phillips University
Enid, OK
Art/fine arts, music, theater arts/drama. Contact Ms. Linn Cole, Vice President for Enrollment Management, 100 South University Avenue, Enid, OK 73701-6439, 405-548-2303.

Piedmont Bible College
Winston-Salem, NC
Music. Contact Mr. Brian Cockram, Director of Institutional Advancement, 716 Franklin Street, Winston-Salem, NC 27101-5197, 910-725-8344 Ext. 231.

Piedmont College
Demorest, GA
Art/fine arts, music, theater arts/drama. Contact Dr. Ronnie Booth, Vice President of Enrollment, PO Box 10, Demorest, GA 30535-0010, 706-778-3000 Ext. 189.

Pikeville College
Pikeville, KY
Art/fine arts. Contact Dr. John Sanders, Associate Dean of Admissions and Financial Aid, Sycamore Street, Pikeville, KY 41501, 606-432-9325.

Pillsbury Baptist Bible College
Owatonna, MN
Music. Contact Mr. Larry Tindall, Director of Admissions, 315 South Grove, Owatonna, MN 55060-3097, 507-451-2710 Ext. 275.

Pine Manor College
Chestnut Hill, MA
Art/fine arts. Contact Mr. Mark P. Gonthier, Director of Admissions and Financial Aid, 400 Heath Street, Chestnut Hill, MA 02167-2332, 617-731-7011.

Pittsburg State University
Pittsburg, KS
Art/fine arts, music, theater arts/drama. Contact Dr. James S. Taylor, Director of Enrollment Services, 1701 South Broadway, Pittsburg, KS 66762-5880, 316-235-4137.

Pitzer College
Claremont, CA
Art/fine arts, music, theater arts/drama. Contact Dr. Paul B. Ranslow, Dean of Admission and College Relations, 1050 North Mills Avenue, Claremont, CA 91711-6110, 909-621-8129.

Plymouth State College of the University System of New Hampshire
Plymouth, NH
Art/fine arts, dance, music, theater arts/drama. Contact Mr. Eugene Fahey, Director of Admissions, 15 Holderness Road, Plymouth, NH 03264-1600, 603-535-2237.

Point Loma Nazarene College
San Diego, CA
Art/fine arts, music, theater arts/drama. Contact Mr. Bill Young, Executive Director for Enrollment Services, 3900 Lomaland Drive, San Diego, CA 92106-2899, 619-221-2225.

Point Park College
Pittsburgh, PA
Art/fine arts, dance, theater arts/drama. Contact Mr. Brian C. Kesse, Dean of Admissions and Financial Aid, 201 Wood Street, Pittsburgh, PA 15222-1984, 412-392-3430.

Pomona College
Claremont, CA
Art/fine arts, dance, music, theater arts/drama. Contact Mr. Bruce Poch, Dean of Admissions, 550 North College Avenue, Claremont, CA 91711-6301, 909-621-8134.

Portland State University
Portland, OR
Art/fine arts, music, theater arts/drama. Contact Mr. Jesse R. Welch, Director of Admissions, PO Box 751, Portland, OR 97207-0751, 503-725-3511.

Prairie View A&M University
Prairie View, TX
Art/fine arts, music, theater arts/drama. Contact Mr. Robert Ford, Director of Admissions and Records, PO Box 3089, Prairie View, TX 77446-2610, 409-857-2626.

Presbyterian College
Clinton, SC
Art/fine arts, music, theater arts/drama. Contact Ms. Margaret Williamson, Vice President of Enrollment and Dean of Admissions, South Broad Street, Clinton, SC 29325, 803-833-8229.

Prescott College, Adult Degree Program
Prescott, AZ
Art/fine arts, dance, music, theater arts/drama. Contact Ms. Lydia Mitchell, Director of Admissions, 220 Grove Avenue, Prescott, AZ 86301-2990, 602-776-7116 Ext. 106.

Prescott College Center for Indian Bilingual Teacher Education
Prescott, AZ
Music. Contact Ms. Karen Winings, Admissions Counselor, 220 Grove Avenue, Prescott, AZ 86301-2990, 602-776-5189.

Prescott College, Resident Degree Program
Prescott, AZ
Art/fine arts. Contact Ms. Shari Sterling, Director of RDP Admissions, 220 Grove Avenue, Prescott, AZ 86301-2990, 520-776-5180.

Princeton University
Princeton, NJ
Art/fine arts, music, theater arts/drama. Contact Mr. Fred A. Hargadon, Dean of Admission, Princeton, NJ 08544-1019, 609-258-3060.

Principia College
Elsah, IL
Art/fine arts, music, theater arts/drama. Contact Ms. Martha Green Quirk, Director of Admissions and Enrollment, Elsah, IL 62028-9799, 618-374-5176.

Providence College
Providence, RI
Art/fine arts, music, theater arts/drama. Contact Mr. William DiBrienza, Dean of Admissions and Financial Aid, River Avenue and Eaton Street, Providence, RI 02918, 401-865-2535.

Puget Sound Christian College
Edmonds, WA
Music. Contact Ms. Delores Scarbrough, Registrar, 410 4th Avenue North, Edmonds, WA 98020-3171, 206-775-8686 Ext. 231.

Purchase College, State University of New York
Purchase, NY
Art/fine arts, dance, music, theater arts/drama. Contact Ms. Betsy Immergut, Director of Admissions, 735 Anderson Hill Road, Purchase, NY 10577-1400, 914-251-6300.

Purdue University
West Lafayette, IN
Art/fine arts, theater arts/drama. Contact Dr. Douglas L. Christiansen, Director of Admissions, Schleman Hall, West Lafayette, IN 47907-1080, 317-494-1776.

Q

Queens College
Charlotte, NC
Art/fine arts, music, theater arts/drama. Contact Ms. Jennifer Garner, Director of Admissions, 1900 Selwyn Avenue, Charlotte, NC 28274-0002, 704-337-2367.

Queens College of the City University of New York
Flushing, NY
Art/fine arts, dance, music, theater arts/drama. Contact Ms. Susan Reantillo, Executive Director of Admissions, Marketing, and Scholarship, 65-30 Kissena Boulevard, Flushing, NY 11367-1597, 718-997-5600.

Quincy University
Quincy, IL
Art/fine arts, music. Contact Mr. Frank Bevec, Director of Admissions, 1800 College Avenue, Quincy, IL 62301-2699, 217-222-8020 Ext. 5215.

R

Radford University
Radford, VA
Art/fine arts, dance, music, theater arts/drama. Contact Mr. Chris B. Knauer, Director of Admissions and Records, PO Box 6903, Radford, VA 24142, 703-831-5371.

Ramapo College of New Jersey
Mahwah, NJ
Art/fine arts, theater arts/drama. Contact Ms. Nancy Jaeger, Director of Admissions, 505 Ramapo Valley Road, Mahwah, NJ 07430-1681, 201-529-7600.

Randolph-Macon College
Ashland, VA
Art/fine arts, music, theater arts/drama. Contact Mr. John C. Conkright, Dean of Admissions and Financial Aid, PO Box 5005, Ashland, VA 23005-5505, 804-752-7305.

Randolph-Macon Woman's College
Lynchburg, VA
Art/fine arts, dance, music, theater arts/drama. Contact Ms. Jean H. Stewart, Director of Admissions, 2500 Rivermont Avenue, Lynchburg, VA 24503-1526, 804-947-8100.

Ray College of Design
Chicago, IL
Art/fine arts. Contact Ms. Mindy Spritz, Director of Admissions, 350 North Orleans, 136, Chicago, IL 60654, 312-280-3500.

Reed College
Portland, OR
Art/fine arts, dance, music, theater arts/drama. Contact Mr. Robert Mansueto, Dean of Admission, 3203 Southeast Woodstock Boulevard, Portland, OR 97202-8199, 503-777-7511.

Regis College
Weston, MA
Art/fine arts. Contact Ms. Valerie L. Brown, Associate Director of Admissions, 235 Wellesley Street, Weston, MA 02193-1571, 617-893-1820 Ext. 2050.

Rensselaer Polytechnic Institute
Troy, NY
Music. Contact Ms. Teresa Duffy, Acting Dean of Admissions, 110 8th Street, Troy, NY 12180-3590, 518-276-6216.

Rhode Island College
Providence, RI
Art/fine arts, music, theater arts/drama. Contact Mr. William H. Hurry Jr., Dean of Admissions and Financial Aid, 600 Mount Pleasant Avenue, Providence, RI 02908-1924, 401-456-8234.

Rhodes College
Memphis, TN
Art/fine arts, music, theater arts/drama. Contact Mr. David J. Wottle, Dean of Admissions and Financial Aid, 2000 North Parkway, Memphis, TN 38112-1690, 901-726-3700.

Rice University
Houston, TX
Art/fine arts, music. Contact Mr. Richard N. Stabell, Dean of Admissions and Records, MS 17, Houston, TX 77005, 713-527-4038.

The Richard Stockton College of New Jersey
Pomona, NJ
Art/fine arts, dance, music. Contact Mr. Salvatore Catalfamo, Dean of Enrollment Management, Pomona, NJ 08240-9988, 609-652-4261.

Rider University
Lawrenceville, NJ
Art/fine arts, music, theater arts/drama. Contact Mr. Thomas Kelly, Dean of Admissions and Financial Aid, 2083 Lawrenceville Road, Lawrenceville, NJ 08648-3001, 609-896-5042.

Ripon College
Ripon, WI
Art/fine arts, music, theater arts/drama. Contact Mr. Paul J. Weeks, Vice President and Dean of Admission, 300 Seward Street, PO Box 248, Ripon, WI 54971, 414-748-8102.

Rivier College
Nashua, NH
Art/fine arts. Contact Mr. James Slattery, Director of Admissions, 420 Main Street, Nashua, NH 03060-5086, 603-888-1311 Ext. 8507.

Roanoke College
Salem, VA
Art/fine arts, music, theater arts/drama. Contact Mr. Michael C. Maxey, Vice President of Admissions, 221 College Lane, Salem, VA 24153-3794, 703-375-2270.

Roberts Wesleyan College
Rochester, NY
Art/fine arts, music. Contact Miss Linda Kurtz, Director of Admissions, 2301 Westside Drive, Rochester, NY 14624-1997, 716-594-6400.

Rochester Institute of Technology
Rochester, NY
Art/fine arts. Contact Mr. Daniel Shelley, Director of Admissions, One Lomb Memorial Drive, Rochester, NY 14623-5604, 716-475-6631.

Rockford College
Rockford, IL
Art/fine arts, music, theater arts/drama. Contact Mr. Christopher Moderson, Acting Vice President for Enrollment Management, 5050 East State Street, Rockford, IL 61108-2393, 815-226-4050.

Rockhurst College
Kansas City, MO
Theater arts/drama. Contact Ms. Barbara O'Connell, Director of Enrollment Services, 1100 Rockhurst Road, Kansas City, MO 64110-2561, 816-926-4100.

Rocky Mountain College
Billings, MT
Art/fine arts, music, theater arts/drama. Contact Ms. Cari Karns, Director of Admissions, 1511 Poly Drive, Billings, MT 59102-1796, 406-657-1026.

Rocky Mountain College of Art & Design
Denver, CO
Art/fine arts. Contact Mr. Rex Whisman, Admissions Director, 6875 East Evans Avenue, Denver, CO 80224-2329, 303-753-6046.

Roger Williams University
Bristol, RI
Art/fine arts, dance, theater arts/drama. Contact Mr. William R. Galloway, Dean of Admissions, Old Ferry Road, Bristol, RI 02809, 401-254-3145.

Rollins College
Winter Park, FL
Art/fine arts, music, theater arts/drama. Contact Mr. David Erdmann, Dean of Admissions and Student Financial Planning, 1000 Holt Avenue, Winter Park, FL 32789-4499, 407-646-2161.

Roosevelt University
Chicago, IL
Music, theater arts/drama. Contact Ms. Barbara Gianneschi, Dean of Admissions, Office of Admissions, Chicago, IL 60605-1394, 312-341-3515.

Rosary College
River Forest, IL
Art/fine arts. Contact Ms. Hildegarde Schmidt, Dean of Admissions and Financial Aid, 7900 West Division Street, River Forest, IL 60305-1099, 708-524-6800.

Rosemont College
Rosemont, PA
Art/fine arts, theater arts/drama. Contact Dr. Linda DeSimone, Director of Enrollment Management, 1400 Montgomery Avenue, Rosemont, PA 19010-1699, 610-527-0200 Ext. 2210.

Rowan College of New Jersey
Glassboro, NJ
Art/fine arts, music, theater arts/drama. Contact Mr. Marvin G. Sills, Director of Admissions, 201 Mullica Hill Road, Glassboro, NJ 08028-1702, 609-256-4200.

Russell Sage College
Troy, NY
Theater arts/drama. Contact Mrs. Patrice M. Tate, Director of Admissions, 45 Ferry Street, Troy, NY 12180-4115, 518-270-2217.

Rust College
Holly Springs, MS
Music. Contact Miss Joann Scott, Director of Admissions, 150 East Rust Avenue, Holly Springs, MS 38635-2328, 601-252-8000 Ext. 4068.

Rutgers, The State University of New Jersey, Camden College of Arts and Sciences
Camden, NJ
Art/fine arts, music, theater arts/drama. Contact Dr. Elizabeth Mitchell, Asst. Vice President for University Undergraduate Admissions, PO Box 2101, New Brunswick, NJ 08903-2101, 908-445-3770.

Rutgers, The State University of New Jersey, Douglass College
New Brunswick, NJ
Art/fine arts, dance, music, theater arts/drama. Contact Dr. Elizabeth Mitchell, Asst. Vice President for University Undergraduate Admissions, PO Box 2101, New Brunswick, NJ 08903-2101, 908-445-3770.

Rutgers, The State University of New Jersey, Livingston College
New Brunswick, NJ
Art/fine arts, dance, music, theater arts/drama. Contact Dr. Elizabeth Mitchell, Asst. Vice President for University Undergraduate Admissions, PO Box 2101, New Brunswick, NJ 08903-2101, 908-445-3770.

Rutgers, The State University of New Jersey, Mason Gross School of the Arts
New Brunswick, NJ
Art/fine arts, dance, music, theater arts/drama. Contact Dr. Elizabeth Mitchell, Asst. Vice President for University Undergraduate Admissions, PO Box 270, New Brunswick, NJ 08903-0270, 908-445-3770.

Rutgers, The State University of New Jersey, Newark College of Arts and Sciences
Newark, NJ
Art/fine arts, music, theater arts/drama. Contact Dr. Elizabeth Mitchell, Asst. Vice President for University Undergraduate Admissions, PO Box 2101, New Brunswick, NJ 08903-2101, 908-445-3770.

Rutgers, The State University of New Jersey, Rutgers College
New Brunswick, NJ
Art/fine arts, dance, music, theater arts/drama. Contact Dr. Elizabeth Mitchell, Asst. Vice President for University Undergraduate Admissions, PO Box 2101, New Brunswick, NJ 08903-2101, 908-445-3770.

Rutgers, The State University of New Jersey, University College–Camden
Camden, NJ
Art/fine arts, music, theater arts/drama. Contact Dr. Elizabeth Mitchell, Asst. Vice President for University Undergraduate Admissions, PO Box 2101, New Brunswick, NJ 08903-2101, 908-445-3770.

Rutgers, The State University of New Jersey, University College–New Brunswick
New Brunswick, NJ
Art/fine arts, dance, music, theater arts/drama. Contact Ms. Loretta Daniel, Director of Admissions, 14 College Avenue, New Brunswick, NJ 08903, 908-932-7276.

S

Sacred Heart University
Fairfield, CT
Art/fine arts, music, theater arts/drama. Contact Mr. James Barquinero, Vice President of Enrollment Planning and Student Affairs, 5151 Park Avenue, Fairfield, CT 06432-1000, 203-371-7880.

Saginaw Valley State University
University Center, MI
Art/fine arts, music, theater arts/drama. Contact Mr. James P. Dwyer, Director of Admissions, 7400 Bay Road, University Center, MI 48710, 517-790-4200.

St. Ambrose University
Davenport, IA
Art/fine arts, music, theater arts/drama. Contact Mr. Patrick O'Connor, Dean of Admissions, 518 West Locust Street, Davenport, IA 52803-2898, 319-383-8888.

St. Andrews Presbyterian College
Laurinburg, NC
Art/fine arts, music. Contact Mr. Dale B. Montague, Dean of Admissions and Financial Aid, 1700 Dogwood Mile, Laurinburg, NC 28352-5598, 910-277-5000.

Saint Anselm College
Manchester, NH
Art/fine arts. Contact Mr. Donald E. Healy, Director of Admissions, 100 Saint Anselm Drive, Manchester, NH 03102-1310, 603-641-7500.

Saint Augustine's College
Raleigh, NC
Music. Contact Mr. Wanzo Hendrix, Director of Admissions, 1315 Oakwood Avenue, Raleigh, NC 27610-2298, 919-516-4000 Ext. 207.

St. Cloud State University
St. Cloud, MN
Art/fine arts, dance, music, theater arts/drama. Contact Mr. Sherwood Reid, Director of Admissions, 720 4th Avenue South, St. Cloud, MN 56301-4498, 612-255-2244.

St. Edward's University
Austin, TX
Art/fine arts, theater arts/drama. Contact Ms. Megan Murphy, Director of Admissions, 3001 South Congress Avenue, Austin, TX 78704-6489, 512-448-8500.

Saint Francis College
Fort Wayne, IN
Art/fine arts. Contact Mr. Scott Flanagan, Director of Admissions, 2701 Spring Street, Fort Wayne, IN 46808-3994, 219-434-3244.

Saint John's University
Collegeville, MN
Art/fine arts, music, theater arts/drama. Contact Ms. Mary Milbert, Director of Admissions, Collegeville, MN 56321, 612-363-2196.

St. John's University
Jamaica, NY
Art/fine arts. Contact Ms. Jeanne Umland, Assoc. Vice President and Executive Director of Admissions, 8000 Utopia Parkway, Jamaica, NY 11439, 718-990-6240.

Saint Joseph College
West Hartford, CT
Music. Contact Ms. Mary C. Demo, Director of Admissions, 1678 Asylum Avenue, West Hartford, CT 06117-2700, 203-232-4571 Ext. 360.

Saint Joseph's College
Rensselaer, IN
Music, theater arts/drama. Contact Mr. Louis Levy, Dean of Admissions, PO Box 890, Rensselaer, IN 47978-0850, 219-866-6170.

Saint Joseph's University
Philadelphia, PA
Art/fine arts. Contact Mr. David Conway, Dean of Enrollment Management, 5600 City Avenue, Philadelphia, PA 19131-1376, 610-660-1300.

St. Lawrence University
Canton, NY
Art/fine arts, music, theater arts/drama. Contact Mr. Joel Wincowski, Dean of Admissions and Financial Aid, Canton, NY 13617-1455, 315-379-5261.

Saint Leo College
Saint Leo, FL
Art/fine arts, music. Contact Ms. Bonnie Black, Director of Admissions, PO Box 2008, Saint Leo, FL 33574-2008, 904-588-8283.

St. Louis Christian College
Florissant, MO
Music. Contact Ms. Christine Cable, Registrar/Dean of Students, 1360 Grandview Drive, Florissant, MO 63033-6499, 314-837-6777.

Saint Louis University
St. Louis, MO
Art/fine arts. Contact Director of Undergraduate Admissions, 221 North Grand Boulevard, St. Louis, MO 63103-2097, 314-977-2500.

Saint Mary College
Leavenworth, KS
Art/fine arts, music, theater arts/drama. Contact Mr. Domenic Teti, Director of Admissions, 4100 South Fourth Street Trafficway, Leavenworth, KS 66048-5082, 913-682-5151 Ext. 6118.

Saint Mary-of-the-Woods College
Saint Mary-of-the-Woods, IN
Art/fine arts, music. Contact Ms. Lynn R. Doran, Director of Admissions, Guerin Hall, Saint Mary-of-the-Woods, IN 47876, 812-535-5106.

Saint Mary's College
Notre Dame, IN
Art/fine arts, music, theater arts/drama. Contact Ms. Mary Pat Nolan, Director of Admission, Notre Dame, IN 46556, 219-284-4587.

Saint Mary's College of California
Moraga, CA
Art/fine arts, dance, music, theater arts/drama. Contact Mr. Michael Tressel, Director of Admissions, PO Box 4800, Moraga, CA 94575, 510-631-4224.

St. Mary's College of Maryland
St. Mary's City, MD
Art/fine arts, music, theater arts/drama. Contact Mr. Richard Edgar, Director of Admissions, Admissions Office, St. Mary's City, MD 20686, 301-862-0292.

Saint Mary's University of Minnesota
Winona, MN
Art/fine arts, music, theater arts/drama. Contact Mr. Anthony M. Piscitiello, Vice President for Admission, 700 Terrace Heights, Winona, MN 55987-1399, 507-457-1700.

St. Mary's University of San Antonio
San Antonio, TX
Music. Contact Mr. Richard Castillo, Director of Admissions, 1 Camino Santa Maria, San Antonio, TX 78228-8503, 210-436-3126.

Saint Michael's College
Colchester, VT
Art/fine arts, music, theater arts/drama. Contact Mr. Jerry E. Flanagan, Dean of Admissions, Winooski Park, Colchester, VT 05439, 802-654-3000.

St. Norbert College
De Pere, WI
Art/fine arts, music, theater arts/drama. Contact Mr. Craig Wesley, Dean of Admission, 100 Grant Street, Office of Admission, De Pere, WI 54115-2099, 414-337-3005.

St. Olaf College
Northfield, MN
Art/fine arts, dance, music, theater arts/drama. Contact, Northfield, MN 55057-1098, 507-646-2222 .

St. Thomas Aquinas College
Sparkill, NY
Art/fine arts. Contact Mr. Joseph L. Chillo, Director of Admissions, 125 Route 340, Sparkill, NY 10976, 914-398-4100.

Saint Vincent College
Latrobe, PA
Art/fine arts, music, theater arts/drama. Contact Rev. Earl J. Henry OSB, Dean of Admission and Financial Aid, Latrobe, PA 15650, 412-537-4540.

Saint Xavier University
Chicago, IL
Art/fine arts, music, theater arts/drama. Contact Sr. Evelyn McKenna, Director of Admissions, 3700 West 103rd Street, Chicago, IL 60655-3105, 312-298-3050.

Salem College
Winston-Salem, NC
Art/fine arts, music. Contact Ms. Katherine Knapp Watts, Director of Admissions, PO Box 10548, Winston-Salem, NC 27108-0548, 910-721-2621.

Salem State College
Salem, MA
Art/fine arts, theater arts/drama. Contact Dr. David Sartwell, Director of Admissions, 352 Lafayette Street, Salem, MA 01970-5353, 508-741-6200.

Salisbury State University
Salisbury, MD
Art/fine arts, music, theater arts/drama. Contact Mrs. Jane H. Dané, Dean of Admissions and

Financial Aid, 1101 Camden Avenue, Salisbury, MD 21801-6837, 410-543-6161.

Salve Regina University
Newport, RI
Art/fine arts, music, theater arts/drama. Contact Mr. David Pedro RSM, Associate Dean of Admissions, 100 Ochre Point Avenue, Newport, RI 02840-4192, 401-847-6650.

Samford University
Birmingham, AL
Art/fine arts, music, theater arts/drama. Contact Dr. Don Belcher, Dean of Admissions and Financial Aid, 800 Lakeshore Drive, Birmingham, AL 35229-0002, 205-870-2901.

Sam Houston State University
Huntsville, TX
Art/fine arts, dance, music, theater arts/drama. Contact Ms. Joey Chandler, Director of Admissions and Recruitment, PO Box 2448, Huntsville, TX 77341-2448, 409-294-1056.

San Diego State University
San Diego, CA
Art/fine arts, dance, music, theater arts/drama. Contact Dr. Nancy C. Sprotte, Director of Admissions and Records, 5500 Campanile Drive, San Diego, CA 92182-0771, 619-594-5384.

San Francisco State University
San Francisco, CA
Art/fine arts, dance, music, theater arts/drama. Contact Mr. Edward Apodaca, Associate Vice President for Enrollment Services, 1600 Holloway Avenue, San Francisco, CA 94132-1722, 415-338-2163.

San Jose State University
San Jose, CA
Art/fine arts, dance, music, theater arts/drama. Contact Mr. Edgar Chambers, Associate Executive Vice President of Admissions and Records, One Washington Square, San Jose, CA 95192-0009, 408-924-2009.

Santa Clara University
Santa Clara, CA
Art/fine arts, music, theater arts/drama. Contact Mr. Daniel J. Saracino, Dean of Admissions, Santa Clara, CA 95053-0001, 408-554-4700.

Sarah Lawrence College
Bronxville, NY
Art/fine arts, dance, music, theater arts/drama. Contact Mr. Robert M. Kinnally, Dean of Admissions, Bronxville, NY 10708, 914-395-2510.

Savannah State College
Savannah, GA
Music. Contact Dr. Roy A. Jackson, Director of Admissions, PO Box 20209, Savannah, GA 31404, 912-356-2181.

Schreiner College
Kerrville, TX
Art/fine arts. Contact Ms. Sandy Speed, Director of Admission, 2100 Memorial Boulevard, Kerrville, TX 78028-5697, 210-896-5411 Ext. 225.

Scripps College
Claremont, CA
Art/fine arts, dance, music, theater arts/drama. Contact Ms. Mimi Tung, Director of Admission, 1030 Columbia Avenue, Claremont, CA 91711-3948, 909-621-8149.

Seattle Pacific University
Seattle, WA
Art/fine arts, music, theater arts/drama. Contact Ms. Janet Ward, Registrar, 3307 Third Avenue West, Seattle, WA 98119-1997, 206-281-2021.

Seattle University
Seattle, WA
Art/fine arts, theater arts/drama. Contact Mr. Lee Gerig, Dean of Admission, Broadway and Madison, Seattle, WA 98122, 206-296-5800.

Seton Hall University
South Orange, NJ
Art/fine arts, music. Contact Ms. Patricia Burgh, Assistant Provost for Enrollment Management, 400 South Orange Avenue, South Orange, NJ 07079-2697, 201-761-9330.

Seton Hill College
Greensburg, PA
Art/fine arts, music, theater arts/drama. Contact Mr. Peter Egan, Director of Admissions, Greensburg, PA 15601, 412-838-4255.

Shawnee State University
Portsmouth, OH
Art/fine arts. Contact Ms. Rosemary K. Poston, Director of Admission, 940 Second Street, Portsmouth, OH 45662-4344, 614-355-2228.

Shaw University
Raleigh, NC
Music, theater arts/drama. Contact Mr. Alfonzo L. Carter, Director of Admissions and Recruitment, 118 East South Street, Raleigh, NC 27601-2399, 919-546-8275.

Shenandoah University
Winchester, VA
Dance, music, theater arts/drama. Contact Mr. Michael Carpentar, Director of Admissions, 1460 University Drive, Winchester, VA 22601-5195, 703-665-4581.

Shepherd College
Shepherdstown, WV
Art/fine arts, music, theater arts/drama. Contact Mr. Karl L. Wolf, Director of Admissions, Shepherdstown, WV 25443, 304-876-5212.

Shippensburg University of Pennsylvania
Shippensburg, PA
Art/fine arts. Contact Mr. Joseph Cretella, Dean of Admissions, 1871 Old Main Drive, Shippensburg, PA 17257, 717-532-1231.

Shorter College
Rome, GA
Art/fine arts, music, theater arts/drama. Contact Mr. John McElveen, Director of Admissions, 315 Shorter Avenue, Rome, GA 30165-4298, 706-291-2121 Ext. 222.

Siena Heights College
Adrian, MI
Art/fine arts, music, theater arts/drama. Contact Mr. Charles Gregory, Dean of Admissions and Financial Aid, 1247 East Siena Heights Drive, Adrian, MI 49221-1796, 517-263-0731 Ext. 214.

Sierra Nevada College
Incline Village, NV
Art/fine arts, music. Contact Ms. Lane H. Murray, Director of Admissions, PO Box 4269, Incline Village, NV 89450-4269, 702-831-1314 Ext. 29.

Silver Lake College
Manitowoc, WI
Art/fine arts, music. Contact Ms. Allyn French, Vice President of Program Outreach and Enrollment Management, 2406 South Alverno Road, Manitowoc, WI 54220-9319, 414-684-5955 Ext. 175.

Simmons College
Boston, MA
Art/fine arts, music. Contact Ms. Deborah Wright, Dean of Admissions, 300 The Fenway, Boston, MA 02115, 617-521-2051.

Simon's Rock College of Bard
Great Barrington, MA
Art/fine arts. Contact Mr. Brian R. Hopewell, Director of Admissions, 84 Alford Road, Great Barrington, MA 01230-9702, 413-528-0771 Ext. 313.

Simpson College
Redding, CA
Music. Contact Mrs. Marion Brown, Director of Admissions, 2211 College View Drive, Redding, CA 96003-8606, 916-224-5606 Ext. 2609.

Simpson College
Indianola, IA
Art/fine arts, music, theater arts/drama. Contact Mr. John Kellogg, Vice President of Enrollment and Planning, 701 North C Street, Indianola, IA 50125-1297, 515-961-1624.

Skidmore College
Saratoga Springs, NY
Art/fine arts, dance, music, theater arts/drama. Contact Ms. Mary Lou Bates, Director of Admissions, 815 North Broadway, Saratoga Springs, NY 12866-1632, 518-584-5000 Ext. 2213.

Slippery Rock University of Pennsylvania
Slippery Rock, PA
Art/fine arts, dance, music, theater arts/drama. Contact Mr. David Collins, Director of Admissions, Slippery Rock, PA 16057, 412-738-2015.

Smith College
Northampton, MA
Art/fine arts, dance, music, theater arts/drama. Contact Ms. Nanci Tessier, Director of Admissions, 7 College Lane, Northampton, MA 01063, 413-585-2500.

Sonoma State University
Rohnert Park, CA
Art/fine arts, music, theater arts/drama. Contact Dr. Frank Tansey, Dean of Admissions, 1801 East Cotati Avenue, Rohnert Park, CA 94928-3609, 707-664-2778.

South Carolina State University
Orangeburg, SC
Music, theater arts/drama. Contact Mr. Benny Mayfield, Dean of Enrollment Management, 300 College Street Northeast, Orangeburg, SC 29117-0001, 803-536-7185.

South Dakota State University
Brookings, SD
Art/fine arts, music, theater arts/drama. Contact Mr. Dean Hofland, Director of Admissions, PO Box 2201, Brookings, SD 57007, 605-688-4121.

Southeastern Bible College
Birmingham, AL
Music. Contact Dr. F. David Farnell, Academic Dean, 3001 Highway 280 East, Birmingham, AL 35243-4181, 205-969-0880 Ext. 210.

Southeastern College of the Assemblies of God
Lakeland, FL
Music. Contact Rev. Royce M. Shelton, Director of Admissions and Records, 1000 Longfellow Boulevard, Lakeland, FL 33801-6099, 813-665-4404 Ext. 209.

Southeastern Louisiana University
Hammond, LA
Art/fine arts, dance, music, theater arts/drama. Contact Mr. Stephen C. Soutullo, Director of Enrollment Services, PO Drawer 752, University Station, Hammond, LA 70402, 504-549-2066.

Southeastern Oklahoma State University
Durant, OK
Art/fine arts, music, theater arts/drama. Contact Dr. Fred Stroup, Director of Admissions and Records, Fifth and University, Durant, OK 74701-0609, 405-924-0121 Ext. 2502.

Southeast Missouri State University
Cape Girardeau, MO
Art/fine arts, music, theater arts/drama. Contact Ms. Juan Crites, Director of Admissions, One University Plaza, Cape Girardeau, MO 63701-4799, 314-651-2590.

Southern Arkansas University– Magnolia
Magnolia, AR
Art/fine arts, music, theater arts/drama. Contact Mr. James E. Whittington, Director of Admissions, Magnolia, AR 71753, 501-235-4040.

Southern California College
Costa Mesa, CA
Music, theater arts/drama. Contact Mr. Rick Hardy, Dean for Enrollment Management, 55 Fair Drive, Costa Mesa, CA 92626-6597, 714-556-3610 Ext. 223.

Southern College of Seventh-day Adventists
Collegedale, TN
Music. Contact Dr. Ronald M. Barrow, Vice President for Admissions and College Relations, PO Box 370, Collegedale, TN 37315-0370, 615-238-2843.

Southern Connecticut State University
New Haven, CT
Art/fine arts, theater arts/drama. Contact Ms. Sharon Brennan, Director of Admissions, 501 Crescent Street, New Haven, CT 06515-1355, 203-397-4450.

Southern Illinois University at Carbondale
Carbondale, IL
Art/fine arts, music, theater arts/drama. Contact Dr. Roland Keim, Director of Admissions, Carbondale, IL 62901-6806, 618-453-4381.

Southern Illinois University at Edwardsville
Edwardsville, IL
Art/fine arts, dance, music, theater arts/drama. Contact Ms. Christa Oxford, Director of Admissions and Registrar, Edwardsville, IL 62026-0001, 618-692-2010.

Southern Methodist University
Dallas, TX
Art/fine arts, dance, music, theater arts/drama. Contact Mr. Ron W. Moss, Director of Admission and Enrollment Management, Dallas, TX 75275, 214-768-2058.

Southern Nazarene University
Bethany, OK
Art/fine arts, music, theater arts/drama. Contact Ms. Tollya Spindle, Director of Admissions, 6729 Northwest 39th Expressway, Bethany, OK 73008-2694, 405-491-6324.

Southern Oregon State College
Ashland, OR
Art/fine arts, music, theater arts/drama. Contact Mr. Allen H. Blaszak, Director of Admissions and Records, Siskiyou Boulevard, Ashland, OR 97520, 503-552-6411.

Southern University and Agricultural and Mechanical College
Baton Rouge, LA
Art/fine arts, music, theater arts/drama. Contact Ms. Velva Johnson Thomas, Acting Director, Baton Rouge, LA 70813, 504-771-2430.

Southern University at New Orleans
New Orleans, LA
Art/fine arts. Contact Dr. Melvin Hodges, Registrar/Director of Admissions, 6400 Press Drive, New Orleans, LA 70126-1009, 504-286-5314.

Southern Utah University
Cedar City, UT
Art/fine arts, dance, music, theater arts/drama. Contact Mr. Dale S. Orton, Director of Admissions, 351 West Center Street, Cedar City, UT 84720-2498, 801-586-7744.

Southern Wesleyan University
Central, SC
Music. Contact Mr. Charles Mealy, Dean of Enrollment Management, 907 Wesleyan Drive, PO Box 1020, Central, SC 29630-1020, 803-639-2453 Ext. 327.

Southwest Baptist University
Bolivar, MO
Art/fine arts, music, theater arts/drama. Contact Vice President for Admissions and Student Life, 1600 University Avenue, Bolivar, MO 65613-2597, 417-326-1801.

Southwestern Assemblies of God University
Waxahachie, TX
Music. Contact Mr. Greg Dufrene, Registrar, 1200 Sycamore Street, Waxahachie, TX 75165-2342, 214-937-4010 Ext. 114.

Southwestern College
Phoenix, AZ
Music. Contact Mr. Randy Williams, Dean of Admissions, 2625 East Cactus Road, Phoenix, AZ 85032-7097, 602-992-6101 Ext. 27.

Southwestern College
Winfield, KS
Music, theater arts/drama. Contact Mr. Douglas M. Mason, Director of Admissions, 100 College Street, Winfield, KS 67156-2499, 316-221-8236.

Southwestern College of Christian Ministries
Bethany, OK
Music. Contact Mr. Tim Moore, Director of Admissions, PO Box 340, Bethany, OK 73008-0340, 405-789-7661.

Southwestern Oklahoma State University
Weatherford, OK
Art/fine arts, music, theater arts/drama. Contact Mr. Bob Klaassen, Registrar/Director of Admissions, 100 Campus Drive, Weatherford, OK 73096-3098, 405-774-3777.

Southwestern University
Georgetown, TX
Art/fine arts, music, theater arts/drama. Contact Mr. John W. Lind, Vice President for Enrollment Management, University Avenue, Georgetown, TX 78626, 512-863-1202.

Southwest Missouri State University
Springfield, MO
Art/fine arts, dance, music, theater arts/drama. Contact Dr. Richard A. Davis, Director of Admissions, 901 South National, Springfield, MO 65804-0094, 417-836-5517.

Southwest State University
Marshall, MN
Art/fine arts, music, theater arts/drama. Contact Mr. Richard Shearer, Director of Admissions, 1501 State Street, Marshall, MN 56258-3306, 507-537-6286.

Southwest Texas State University
San Marcos, TX
Art/fine arts, music, theater arts/drama. Contact Mr. Fernando Yarrito, Director of Admissions, Admissions and Visitors Center, San Marcos, TX 78666, 512-245-2364 Ext. 2803.

Spalding University
Louisville, KY
Art/fine arts, theater arts/drama. Contact Ms. Dorothy Allen, Director of Admissions, 851 South Fourth Street, Louisville, KY 40203-2188, 502-585-7111 Ext. 225.

Spelman College
Atlanta, GA
Art/fine arts, music, theater arts/drama. Contact Ms. Victoria Valle, Director of Admissions and Orientation Services, 350 Spelman Lane, SW, Atlanta, GA 30314-4399, 404-681-3643 Ext. 2188.

Spring Arbor College
Spring Arbor, MI
Art/fine arts, music. Contact Mr. Steve Schippers, Director of Enrollment Services, 106 Main Street, Spring Arbor, MI 49283-9799, 517-750-1200 Ext. 1470.

Springfield College
Springfield, MA
Art/fine arts. Contact Mr. Frederick Bartlett, Director of Admissions, 263 Alden Street, Springfield, MA 01109-3797, 413-748-3136.

Spring Hill College
Mobile, AL
Art/fine arts, theater arts/drama. Contact Mr. Timothy Williams, Director of Undergraduate Admissions, 4000 Dauphin Street, Mobile, AL 36608-1791, 334-380-3030.

Stanford University
Stanford, CA
Art/fine arts, music, theater arts/drama. Contact Mr. James Montoya, Dean of Undergraduate Admissions, Stanford, CA 94305-9991, 415-723-2091.

State University of New York at Binghamton
Binghamton, NY
Art/fine arts, music, theater arts/drama. Contact Mr. Geoffrey D. Gould, Director of Admissions, PO Box 6001, Binghamton, NY 13902-6001, 607-777-2171.

State University of New York at Buffalo
Buffalo, NY
Art/fine arts, dance, music, theater arts/drama. Contact Mr. Kevin M. Durkin, Director of Admis-

sions, Capen Hall, Room 17, North Campus, Buffalo, NY 14260-1660, 716-645-6900.

State University of New York at New Paltz
New Paltz, NY
Art/fine arts, music, theater arts/drama. Contact Mr. Robert J. Seaman, Dean of Admissions, 75 South Manheim Boulevard, New Paltz, NY 12561-2449, 914-257-3200.

State University of New York at Oswego
Oswego, NY
Art/fine arts, music, theater arts/drama. Contact Dr. Joseph F. Grant Jr., Vice President for Development, Enrollment, and Marketing, Oswego, NY 13126, 315-341-2250.

State University of New York at Stony Brook
Stony Brook, NY
Art/fine arts, music, theater arts/drama. Contact Ms. Theresa La Rocca-Meyer, Dean of Enrollment Planning and Management, Stony Brook, NY 11794, 516-632-6868.

State University of New York College at Brockport
Brockport, NY
Art/fine arts, dance, theater arts/drama. Contact Mr. James R. Cook, Director of Admissions, 350 New Campus Drive, Brockport, NY 14420-2997, 716-395-2751.

State University of New York College at Buffalo
Buffalo, NY
Art/fine arts, music, theater arts/drama. Contact Ms. Deborah Renzi, Director of Admissions, 1300 Elmwood Avenue, Buffalo, NY 14222-1095, 716-878-5519.

State University of New York College at Cortland
Cortland, NY
Art/fine arts, music, theater arts/drama. Contact Mr. Michael K. McKeon, Director of Admission, PO Box 2000, Cortland, NY 13045, 607-753-4711.

State University of New York College at Fredonia
Fredonia, NY
Art/fine arts, music, theater arts/drama. Contact Mr. William S. Clark, Director of Admissions, Fredonia, NY 14063, 716-673-3251.

State University of New York College at Geneseo
Geneseo, NY
Art/fine arts, music, theater arts/drama. Contact Ms. Jill Conlon, Director of Admissions, 1 College Circle, Geneseo, NY 14454-1401, 716-245-5571.

State University of New York College at Old Westbury
Old Westbury, NY
Art/fine arts, dance, music, theater arts/drama. Contact Mr. Michael Sheehy, Director of Admissions, PO Box 307, Old Westbury, NY 11568-0210, 516-876-3073.

State University of New York College at Oneonta
Oneonta, NY
Art/fine arts, music, theater arts/drama. Contact Mr. Richard Burr, Director of Admissions, Alumni Hall 116, Oneonta, NY 13820-4016, 607-436-2524.

State University of New York College at Plattsburgh
Plattsburgh, NY
Art/fine arts, theater arts/drama. Contact Mr. Richard Higgins, Director of Admissions, Plattsburgh, NY 12901, 518-564-2040.

State University of New York College at Potsdam
Potsdam, NY
Art/fine arts, dance, music, theater arts/drama. Contact Ms. Karen O'Brien, Director of Admissions and Financial Aid, Pierrepont Avenue, Potsdam, NY 13676, 315-267-2180.

State University of New York Empire State College
Saratoga Springs, NY
Art/fine arts. Contact Dr. Martin Thorsland, Director of Admissions and Assessment, 1 Union Avenue, Saratoga Springs, NY 12866-4391, 518-587-2100 Ext. 223.

Stephen F. Austin State University
Nacogdoches, TX
Art/fine arts, music, theater arts/drama. Contact Mr. Dennis Jones, Senior Associate of Admission and Records, 1936 North Street, Nacogdoches, TX 75962, 409-468-2504.

Stephens College
Columbia, MO
Art/fine arts, dance, theater arts/drama. Contact Mr. Richard Blomgren, Director of Admissions, Box 2121, Columbia, MO 65215-0002, 314-442-2211 Ext. 207.

Sterling College
Sterling, KS
Art/fine arts, music, theater arts/drama. Contact Mr. Dennis W. Dutton, Director of Admissions, North Broadway, Sterling, KS 67579, 316-278-4364.

Stetson University
DeLand, FL
Art/fine arts, music, theater arts/drama. Contact Ms. Linda Glover, Dean of Admissions, 421 North Woodland Boulevard, DeLand, FL 32720-3781, 904-822-7100.

Stillman College
Tuscaloosa, AL
Music. Contact Mrs. Barbara Smith, Director of Admissions, PO Drawer 1430, Tuscaloosa, AL 35403-9990, 205-349-4240 Ext. 347.

Suffolk University
Boston, MA
Art/fine arts, theater arts/drama. Contact Ms. Barbara K. Ericson, Associate Dean of Enrollment and Retention Management, 8 Ashburton Place, Boston, MA 02108-2770, 617-573-8460.

Sul Ross State University
Alpine, TX
Art/fine arts, music, theater arts/drama. Contact Mr. Robert Cullins, Dean of Admissions and Records, Box C-2, Alpine, TX 79832, 915-837-8052.

Susquehanna University
Selinsgrove, PA
Art/fine arts, music, theater arts/drama. Contact Mr. Richard Ziegler, Director of Admissions, University Avenue, Selinsgrove, PA 17870-1001, 717-372-4260.

Swarthmore College
Swarthmore, PA
Art/fine arts, music, theater arts/drama. Contact Dean of Admissions, 500 College Avenue, Swarthmore, PA 19081-1397, 610-328-8308.

Sweet Briar College
Sweet Briar, VA
Art/fine arts, dance, music, theater arts/drama. Contact Ms. Nancy E. Church, Executive Director of Admissions and Financial Aid, PO Box B, Sweet Briar, VA 24595, 804-381-6142.

Syracuse University
Syracuse, NY
Art/fine arts, music, theater arts/drama. Contact Mr. David Smith, Dean of Admissions and Financial Aid, 201 Tolley Administration Building, Syracuse, NY 13244-0003, 315-443-2300.

T

Tabor College
Hillsboro, KS
Music. Contact Mr. Glenn Lygrisse, Vice President of Enrollment Management, Hillsboro, KS 67063, 316-947-3121 Ext. 275.

Talladega College
Talladega, AL
Music. Contact Mr. Monroe Thornton, Director of Admissions, 627 West Battle Street, Talladega, AL 35160, 205-761-6253 Ext. 253.

Tarleton State University
Stephenville, TX
Art/fine arts, music, theater arts/drama. Contact Ms. Gail Mayfield, Director of Admissions, Box T-2003 Tarleton Station, Stephenville, TX 76402, 817-968-9125.

Taylor University
Upland, IN
Art/fine arts, music, theater arts/drama. Contact Mr. Stephen R. Mortland, Director of Admissions, 500 West Reade Avenue, Upland, IN 46989-1001, 317-998-5134.

Taylor University, Fort Wayne Campus
Fort Wayne, IN
Music. Contact Mr. D. Nathan Phinney, Director of Admissions, 1025 West Rudisill Boulevard, Fort Wayne, IN 46807-2197, 219-456-2111 Ext. 2274.

Teikyo Marycrest University
Davenport, IA
Art/fine arts, theater arts/drama. Contact Mr. Tim McDonough, Assistant Vice President for Enrollment Management, 1607 West 12th Street, Davenport, IA 52804-4096, 319-326-9225.

Teikyo Westmar University
Le Mars, IA
Art/fine arts, dance, music. Contact Mr. Terrance Kizina, Dean for Enrollment Management, 1002 3rd Avenue, SE, Le Mars, IA 51031-2697, 712-546-2070 Ext. 2617.

Temple University
Philadelphia, PA
Art/fine arts, dance, music, theater arts/drama. Contact Mr. Randy H. Miller, Director of Admissions, Broad Street and Montgomery Avenue, Philadelphia, PA 19122, 215-204-8556.

Tennessee State University
Nashville, TN
Art/fine arts, music. Contact Mr. John Cade, Dean of Admissions and Records, 3500 John A Merritt Boulevard, Nashville, TN 37209-1561, 615-963-5101.

Tennessee Technological University
Cookeville, TN
Art/fine arts, music. Contact Mr. Jim Rose, Director of Admissions, TTU Box 5006, Cookeville, TN 38505, 615-372-3888.

Tennessee Temple University
Chattanooga, TN
Music. Contact Mr. Dick Costner, Registrar, 1815 Union Avenue, Chattanooga, TN 37404-3587, 615-493-4373.

Tennessee Wesleyan College
Athens, TN
Music. Contact Mr. James G. Harrison, Dean of Enrollment, PO Box 40, Athens, TN 37303, 615-745-7504 Ext. 211.

Texas A&M University
College Station, TX
Theater arts/drama. Contact Mr. Gary R. Engelgau, Office of Admissions and Records, 217 John J. Koldus Building, College Station, TX 77843-1265, 409-845-3741.

Texas A&M University–Corpus Christi
Corpus Christi, TX
Art/fine arts, music. Contact Ms. Margaret Dechant, Director of Admissions, 6300 Ocean Drive, Corpus Christi, TX 78412-5503, 512-994-2414.

Texas A&M University–Kingsville
Kingsville, TX
Art/fine arts, music, theater arts/drama. Contact Mr. Joe Estrada, Registrar/Admissions Director, West Santa Gertrudis, Kingsville, TX 78363, 512-595-2811.

Texas Christian University
Fort Worth, TX
Art/fine arts, dance, music, theater arts/drama. Contact Mr. Leo Munson, Dean of Admissions, 2800 South University Drive, Fort Worth, TX 76129-0002, 817-921-7490.

Texas College
Tyler, TX
Art/fine arts, music. Contact Mrs. Veretta Rider, Director for Admissions and Recruitment, 2404 North Grand Ave, PO Box 4500, Tyler, TX 75712-4500, 903-593-8311 Ext. 236.

Texas Lutheran College
Seguin, TX
Art/fine arts, music. Contact Mrs. Jennifer Ehlers, Director of Admissions, 1000 West Court Street, Seguin, TX 78155-5999, 210-372-8051.

Texas Southern University
Houston, TX
Art/fine arts, music, theater arts/drama. Contact Mrs. Audrey Pearsall, Director of Admissions, 3100 Cleburne, Houston, TX 77004-4598, 713-527-7472.

Texas Tech University
Lubbock, TX
Art/fine arts, music, theater arts/drama. Contact Mr. Dale Grusing, Director of Admissions, Box 45005, Lubbock, TX 79409-5005, 806-742-1493.

Texas Wesleyan University
Fort Worth, TX
Art/fine arts, music, theater arts/drama. Contact Ms. Kim Campbell, Director of Admissions, 1201 Wesleyan, Fort Worth, TX 76105-1536, 817-531-4422.

Texas Woman's University
Denton, TX
Art/fine arts, dance, music, theater arts/drama. Contact Dr. Paul Travis, Dean of Enrollment Management, PO Box 22909, Denton, TX 76204-0909, 817-898-3000.

Thomas College
Thomasville, GA
Music. Contact Ms. Darla Glass, Registrar, 1501 Millpond Road, Thomasville, GA 31792-7499, 912-226-1621 Ext. 20.

Thomas Edison State College
Trenton, NJ
Art/fine arts, dance, music, theater arts/drama. Contact Ms. Janice Toliver, Director of Admissions Services, 101 West State Street, Trenton, NJ 08608-1176, 609-984-1150.

Thomas More College
Crestview Hills, KY
Art/fine arts, theater arts/drama. Contact Ms. Victoria Thompson-Campbell, Director of Admissions, 333 Thomas More Parkway, Crestview Hills, KY 41017-3495, 606-344-3332.

Toccoa Falls College
Toccoa Falls, GA
Music. Contact Mr. Matthew L. King, Director of Admissions, Toccoa Falls, GA 30598-5201, 706-886-6831 Ext. 5380.

Tougaloo College
Tougaloo, MS
Art/fine arts, music. Contact Mr. Washington Cole, Director of Admissions and Recruitment, 500 County Line Road, Tougaloo, MS 39174, 601-977-7764.

Towson State University
Towson, MD
Art/fine arts, dance, music, theater arts/drama. Contact Ms. Angel Jackson, Director of Admissions, Towson, MD 21204-7097, 410-830-3333.

Transylvania University
Lexington, KY
Art/fine arts, music, theater arts/drama. Contact Mr. Michael J. Suzo, Director of Admissions, 300 North Broadway, Lexington, KY 40508-1797, 606-233-8242.

Trenton State College
Trenton, NJ
Art/fine arts, music. Contact Mr. Frank Cooper, Director of Admissions, Hillwood Lakes, CN 4700, Trenton, NJ 08650-4700, 609-771-2131.

Trevecca Nazarene College
Nashville, TN
Music, theater arts/drama. Contact Mr. Jan R. Forman, Dean of Enrollment Services, 333 Murfreesboro Road, Nashville, TN 37210-2834, 615-248-1782.

Trinity Bible College
Ellendale, ND
Music, theater arts/drama. Contact Mrs. Janet A. Johnson, Director of Academic Records, 50 South 6th Avenue, Ellendale, ND 58436-7150, 701-349-3621 Ext. 2039.

Trinity Christian College
Palos Heights, IL
Art/fine arts, music. Contact Mr. David Lageveen, Director of Admissions, 6601 West College Drive, Palos Heights, IL 60463-0929, 708-239-4709.

Trinity College
Hartford, CT
Art/fine arts, dance, music, theater arts/drama. Contact Dr. David M. Borus, Dean of Admissions and Financial Aid, 300 Summit Street, Hartford, CT 06106-3100, 203-297-2180.

Trinity College
Deerfield, IL
Music. Contact Mrs. Sherri Sandberg, Director of Admissions, 2077 Half Day Road, Deerfield, IL 60015-1284, 708-317-7000.

Trinity College of Florida
New Port Richey, FL
Music. Contact Mr. Joel Riley, Director of Admissions, 2430 Trinity Oaks Boulevard, New Port Richey, FL 34655, 813-376-6911 Ext. 1216.

Trinity College of Vermont
Burlington, VT
Art/fine arts. Contact Dr. Patricia Connelly, Vice President for Enrollment, 208 Colchester Avenue, Burlington, VT 05401-1470, 802-658-0337 Ext. 216.

Trinity University
San Antonio, TX
Art/fine arts, music, theater arts/drama. Contact Dr. George Boyd, Director of Admissions, 715 Stadium Drive, San Antonio, TX 78212-7200, 210-736-7207.

Troy State University
Troy, AL
Art/fine arts, music, theater arts/drama. Contact Mr. Jim Hutto, Dean of Enrollment Services, University Avenue, Troy, AL 36082, 334-670-3179.

Tufts University
Medford, MA
Art/fine arts, music, theater arts/drama. Contact Mr. David D. Cuttino, Dean of Undergraduate Admissions, Medford, MA 02155, 617-627-3170.

Tulane University
New Orleans, LA
Art/fine arts, music, theater arts/drama. Contact Mr. Richard Whiteside, Dean of Admission and Enrollment Management, 6823 St Charles Avenue, New Orleans, LA 70118-5669, 504-865-5731.

Tusculum College
Greeneville, TN
Art/fine arts. Contact Mr. Mark A. Stokes, Vice President for Student and Auxiliary Services, 2299 Tusculum Boulevard, Greeneville, TN 37743-9997, 615-636-7312.

U

Union College
Barbourville, KY
Music, theater arts/drama. Contact Mr. Donald Hapward, Dean of Admissions, 310 College Street, Barbourville, KY 40906-1499, 606-546-1220 Ext. 220.

Union College
Lincoln, NE
Art/fine arts, music. Contact Mr. Timothy J. Simon, Director of Enrollment Services, 3800 South 48th Street, Lincoln, NE 68506-4300, 402-486-2504.

Union College
Schenectady, NY
Art/fine arts. Contact Mr. Daniel Lundquist, Vice President for Admissions and Financial Aid, Schenectady, NY 12308-2311, 518-388-6112.

Union University
Jackson, TN
Art/fine arts, music. Contact Mr. Carroll Griffin, Director of Admissions, Highway 45 Bypass North, Jackson, TN 38305, 901-661-5000.

University at Albany, State University of New York
Albany, NY
Art/fine arts, music, theater arts/drama. Contact Dr. Michelleen Treadwell, Director of Admissions, 1400 Washington Avenue, Albany, NY 12222-0001, 518-442-5435.

University of Akron
Akron, OH
Art/fine arts, dance, music, theater arts/drama. Contact Dr. Greg Stewart, Director of Admissions, 381 Buchtel Common, Akron, OH 44325-2001, 216-972-7100.

University of Alabama
Tuscaloosa, AL
Art/fine arts, dance, music, theater arts/drama. Contact Dr. Randall W. Dahl, Director of Admissions, Records and Testing, Box 870166, Tuscaloosa, AL 35487-0166, 205-348-5666.

University of Alabama at Birmingham
Birmingham, AL
Art/fine arts, dance, music, theater arts/drama. Contact Ms. Stella Cocoris, Director of Enrollment Management, UAB Station, Birmingham, AL 35294, 205-934-8221.

The University of Alabama in Huntsville
Huntsville, AL
Art/fine arts, music. Contact Dr. Ron R. Koger, Assistant Vice President for Enrollment Management, University Center 119, Huntsville, AL 35899, 205-895-6750.

University of Alaska Anchorage
Anchorage, AK
Art/fine arts, music, theater arts/drama. Contact Ms. Linda Berg Smith, Associate Vice Chancellor, Administration Building, Room 176, Anchorage, AK 99508-8060, 907-786-1480.

University of Alaska Fairbanks
Fairbanks, AK
Art/fine arts, music, theater arts/drama. Contact Ms. Ann Tremarello, Director of Admissions and Records, PO Box 757480, Fairbanks, AK 99775-7480, 907-474-7521.

University of Alaska Southeast
Juneau, AK
Art/fine arts. Contact Mr. Greg Wagner, Coordinator of Admissions and Placement, 11120 Glacier Highway, Juneau, AK 99801-8625, 907-465-6239.

University of Arizona
Tucson, AZ
Art/fine arts, dance, music, theater arts/drama. Contact Mr. Loyd Bell, Director of Admissions, Tucson, AZ 85721, 602-621-3237.

University of Arkansas
Fayetteville, AR
Art/fine arts, music, theater arts/drama. Contact Mr. Steven J. Henderson, Assistant Vice Chancellor for Enrollment Management, 200 Silas H. Hunt Hall, Fayetteville, AR 72701-1201, 501-575-5346.

University of Arkansas at Little Rock
Little Rock, AR
Art/fine arts, music, theater arts/drama. Contact Mr. David Peat, Director of Admissions and Records, 2801 South University Avenue, Little Rock, AR 72204-1000, 501-569-3127.

University of Arkansas at Monticello
Monticello, AR
Music. Contact Mrs. JoBeth Johnson, Director of Admissions, Monticello, AR 71656, 501-460-1026.

University of Arkansas at Pine Bluff
Pine Bluff, AR
Art/fine arts, music, theater arts/drama. Contact Ms. Kwurly M. Floyd, Director of Admissions and Academic Records, UAPB Box 17, 1200 University Drive, Pine Bluff, AR 71601-2799, 501-543-8487.

University of Bridgeport
Bridgeport, CT
Art/fine arts, music. Contact Ms. Suzanne Dale Wilcox, Dean of Admissions and Financial Aid, 380 University Avenue, Bridgeport, CT 06601, 203-576-4552.

University of California, Berkeley
Berkeley, CA
Art/fine arts, dance, music, theater arts/drama. Contact Mr. Bob Laird, Director, Undergraduate Admission and Relations with Schools, Berkeley, CA 94720, 510-642-2316.

University of California, Davis
Davis, CA
Art/fine arts, music, theater arts/drama. Contact Dr. Gary Tudor, Director of Undergraduate Admissions, Davis, CA 95616, 916-752-2971.

University of California, Irvine
Irvine, CA
Art/fine arts, dance, music, theater arts/drama. Contact Ms. Susan Wilbur, Director of Admissions, Irvine, CA 92717-1425, 714-824-6703.

University of California, Los Angeles
Los Angeles, CA
Art/fine arts, dance, music, theater arts/drama. Contact Dr. Rae Lee Siporin, Director of Undergraduate Admissions, 405 Hilgard Avenue, Los Angeles, CA 90024-1301, 310-825-3101.

University of California, Riverside
Riverside, CA
Art/fine arts, dance, music, theater arts/drama. Contact, Riverside, CA 92521-0102, 909-787-1012 .

University of California, San Diego
La Jolla, CA
Art/fine arts, music, theater arts/drama. Contact Dr. Richard L. Backer, Assistant Vice Chancellor of Enrollment Management/Registrar, Student Outreach and Recruitment (SOAR), Box 0337, La Jolla, CA 92093-5003, 619-534-3156.

University of California, Santa Barbara
Santa Barbara, CA
Art/fine arts, dance, music, theater arts/drama. Contact Mr. William Villa, Director of Admissions/ Relations with Schools, Santa Barbara, CA 93106, 805-893-2485.

University of California, Santa Cruz
Santa Cruz, CA
Art/fine arts, dance, music, theater arts/drama. Contact Mr. C. James Quann, Associate Vice Chancellor of Enrollment Management, Admissions Office, Cook House, Santa Cruz, CA 95064, 408-459-4008.

University of Central Arkansas
Conway, AR
Art/fine arts, music, theater arts/drama. Contact Mr. Joe F. Darling, Director of Admissions, Conway, AR 72035-0001, 501-450-5145.

University of Central Florida
Orlando, FL
Art/fine arts, music, theater arts/drama. Contact Ms. Susan J. McKinnon, Acting Director of Admissions, 4000 Central Florida Boulevard, Orlando, FL 32816, 407-823-2511.

University of Central Oklahoma
Edmond, OK
Art/fine arts, music, theater arts/drama. Contact Ms. Evelyn Wilson, Director of Admissions, 100 North University Drive, Edmond, OK 73034-0172, 405-341-2980 Ext. 3366.

University of Charleston
Charleston, WV
Art/fine arts, music. Contact Mr. Alan Liebrecht, Director of Admissions, 2300 MacCorkle Avenue, SE, Charleston, WV 25304-1099, 304-357-4800.

University of Chicago
Chicago, IL
Art/fine arts, music. Contact Mr. Theodore O'Neill, Dean of Admissions, 1116 East 59th Street, Chicago, IL 60637-1513, 312-702-8650.

University of Cincinnati
Cincinnati, OH
Art/fine arts, dance, music, theater arts/drama. Contact Mr. James Williams, Director of Admissions, Mail Location 91, 100 Edwards Center, Cincinnati, OH 45221-0091, 513-556-1100.

University of Colorado at Boulder
Boulder, CO
Art/fine arts, dance, music, theater arts/drama. Contact Mr. Gary M. Kelsey, Director of Admissions, Campus Box 30, Boulder, CO 80309-0030, 303-492-6694.

University of Colorado at Colorado Springs
Colorado Springs, CO
Art/fine arts. Contact Mr. Randall E. Kouba, Director of Admissions and Records, PO Box 7150, Colorado Springs, CO 80933-7150, 719-593-3116.

University of Colorado at Denver
Denver, CO
Art/fine arts, music, theater arts/drama. Contact Ms. Barbra Edwards, Director of Admissions, PO Box 173364, Denver, CO 80217-3364, 303-556-2704.

University of Connecticut
Storrs, CT
Art/fine arts, music, theater arts/drama. Contact Dr. Ann L. Huckenbeck, Director of Admissions, Storrs, CT 06269, 203-486-3137.

University of Connecticut at Hartford
West Hartford, CT
Art/fine arts. Contact Dr. Ann Huckenbeck, Director of Admissions, 2131 Hillside Road, Storrs, CT 06269, 203-486-3137.

University of Dallas
Irving, TX
Art/fine arts, theater arts/drama. Contact Ms. Darbie Ann Dallman, Director of Admissions and Financial Aid, 1845 East Northgate Drive, Irving, TX 75062-4799, 214-721-5266.

University of Dayton
Dayton, OH
Art/fine arts, music, theater arts/drama. Contact Mr. Myron H. Achbach, Director of Admissions, 300 College Park, Dayton, OH 45469-1611, 513-229-4411.

University of Delaware
Newark, DE
Art/fine arts, music, theater arts/drama. Contact Dr. Bruce Walker, Associate Provost for Admissions and Student Financial Aid, Newark, DE 19716, 302-831-8123.

University of Denver
Denver, CO
Art/fine arts, music, theater arts/drama. Contact Mr. Roger Campbell, Dean of Admissions, University Park, Denver, CO 80208, 303-871-2043.

University of Detroit Mercy
Detroit, MI
Theater arts/drama. Contact Dr. Robert Johnson, Dean of Enrollment Management, PO Box 19900, Detroit, MI 48219-0900, 313-993-1245.

University of Dubuque
Dubuque, IA
Music. Contact Mr. Cliff Bunting, Dean of Admissions and Records, 2000 University Avenue, Dubuque, IA 52001-5099, 319-589-3200.

University of Evansville
Evansville, IN
Art/fine arts, music, theater arts/drama. Contact Ms. Elizabeth Lyon, Director of Undergraduate Admission, 1800 Lincoln Avenue, Evansville, IN 47722-0002, 812-479-2468.

The University of Findlay
Findlay, OH
Art/fine arts, theater arts/drama. Contact Dr. Mary Ellen Klein, Dean of Enrollment Management, 1000 North Main Street, Findlay, OH 45840-3653, 419-424-4540.

University of Florida
Gainesville, FL
Art/fine arts, music, theater arts/drama. Contact Mr. Stirling W. Kolb, Director of Admissions, PO Box 118140, 302 Little Hall, Gainesville, FL 32611-8140, 904-392-1365.

University of Georgia
Athens, GA
Art/fine arts, dance, music, theater arts/drama. Contact Dr. Claire Swann, Director of Admissions, Athens, GA 30602, 706-542-2112.

University of Great Falls
Great Falls, MT
Art/fine arts, music. Contact Ms. Audrey Thompson, Director of Admissions and Records, 1301 Twentieth Street South, Great Falls, MT 59405, 406-761-8210 Ext. 260.

University of Hawaii at Hilo
Hilo, HI
Art/fine arts, music. Contact Mr. James West, UH Student Services Specialist III, 200 West Kawili Street, Hilo, HI 96720-4091, 808-933-3315.

University of Hawaii at Manoa
Honolulu, HI
Art/fine arts, dance, music, theater arts/drama. Contact Dr. David Robb, Director of Admissions, 2444 Dole Street, Honolulu, HI 96822, 808-956-8975.

University of Houston
Houston, TX
Art/fine arts, dance, music, theater arts/drama. Contact Mr. Rob Sheinkopf, Director of Admissions, 4800 Calhoun, Houston, TX 77204-2161, 713-743-9570.

University of Houston–Clear Lake
Houston, TX
Art/fine arts. Contact Ms. Darella L. Banks, Executive Director of Enrollment Services, 2700 Bay Area Boulevard, Box 13, Houston, TX 77058-1098, 713-283-2517.

University of Idaho
Moscow, ID
Art/fine arts, dance, music, theater arts/drama. Contact Mr. Dan Davenport, Director of Admissions, Moscow, ID 83844, 208-885-6326.

University of Illinois at Chicago
Chicago, IL
Art/fine arts, music, theater arts/drama. Contact Dr. Marilyn Fiduccia, Executive Director of Admissions, PO Box 5220, Chicago, IL 60680-5220, 312-996-4350.

University of Illinois at Urbana-Champaign
Champaign, IL
Art/fine arts, dance, music, theater arts/drama. Contact Ms. Patricia E. Askew, Director of Admissions and Records, 10 Henry Administration Building, Urbana, IL 61820-5711, 217-333-0302.

University of Illinois at Springfield
Springfield, IL
Art/fine arts. Contact Dr. Steven R. Neiheisel, Director of Enrollment Services, Springfield, IL 62794-9243, 217-786-6626.

University of Indianapolis
Indianapolis, IN
Art/fine arts, music, theater arts/drama. Contact Mr. Mark T. Weigand, Director of Admissions, 1400 East Hanna Avenue, Indianapolis, IN 46227-3697, 317-788-3216.

The University of Iowa
Iowa City, IA
Art/fine arts, dance, music, theater arts/drama. Contact Mr. Michael Barron, Director of Admissions, Iowa City, IA 52242, 319-335-3847.

University of Kansas
Lawrence, KS
Art/fine arts, dance, music, theater arts/drama. Contact Ms. Deborah Castrop, Director of Admissions, 126 Strong Hall, Lawrence, KS 66045-1910, 913-864-3911.

University of Kentucky
Lexington, KY
Art/fine arts, music, theater arts/drama. Contact Dr. Joseph L. Fink, Associate Vice Chancellor for Academic Affairs, Lexington, KY 40506-0032, 606-257-2722.

University of La Verne
La Verne, CA
Art/fine arts, music, theater arts/drama. Contact Mr. Douglas Wible, Director of Admissions, 1950 Third Street, La Verne, CA 91750-4443, 909-593-3511 Ext. 4026.

University of Louisville
Louisville, KY
Art/fine arts, music, theater arts/drama. Contact Ms. Lynn Bacon, Director of Admissions for School Relations, 2301 South Third Street, Louisville, KY 40292-0001, 502-852-6531.

University of Maine
Orono, ME
Art/fine arts, music, theater arts/drama. Contact Ms. Joyce Henckler, Assistant Vice President for Enrollment Management, Orono, ME 04469-5713, 207-581-1572.

University of Maine at Farmington
Farmington, ME
Art/fine arts, music, theater arts/drama. Contact Mr. J. Anthony McLaughlin, Director of Admissions, 86 Main Street, Farmington, ME 04938-1911, 207-778-7050.

University of Maine at Presque Isle
Presque Isle, ME
Art/fine arts. Contact Dr. Gerald K. Wuori, Director of Admissions, 181 Main Street, Presque Isle, ME 04769-2888, 207-768-9523.

University of Mary
Bismarck, ND
Music. Contact Mrs. Steph Storey, Director of Admissions, 7500 University Drive, Bismarck, ND 58504-9652, 701-255-7500 Ext. 429.

University of Mary Hardin-Baylor
Belton, TX
Art/fine arts, music. Contact Mr. Bobby Johnson, Director of Admissions, UMBH Station Box 8004, Belton, TX 76513, 817-939-4520.

University of Maryland Baltimore County
Baltimore, MD
Art/fine arts, dance, music, theater arts/drama. Contact Ms. Mindy Hand, Director of Admissions, 5401 Wildens Avenue, Baltimore, MD 21228-5398, 410-455-2291.

University of Maryland College Park
College Park, MD
Art/fine arts, dance, music, theater arts/drama. Contact Dr. Linda Clement, Director of Admissions, College Park, MD 20742, 301-314-8385.

University of Maryland Eastern Shore
Princess Anne, MD
Music. Contact Dr. Rochell Peoples, Assistant Vice President of Student Affairs, Princess Anne, MD 21853, 410-651-6410.

University of Maryland University College
College Park, MD
Art/fine arts. Contact Mr. Gary Thornhill, Director of Undergraduate Enrollment Service, University Boulevard at Adelphi Rd, College Park, MD 20742-1600, 301-985-7265.

University of Massachusetts Amherst
Amherst, MA
Art/fine arts, dance, music, theater arts/drama. Contact Ms. Arlene Cash, Director of Undergraduate Admissions, Amherst, MA 01003-0120, 413-545-0222.

University of Massachusetts Boston
Boston, MA
Art/fine arts, music, theater arts/drama. Contact Ms. Mary Mahoney, Director of Undergraduate Admissions, 100 Morrissey Boulevard, Boston, MA 02125-3393, 617-287-6000.

University of Massachusetts Dartmouth
North Dartmouth, MA
Art/fine arts, music. Contact Mr. Raymond M. Barrows, Director of Admissions, 285 Old Westport Road, North Dartmouth, MA 02747-2512, 508-999-8605.

University of Massachusetts Lowell
Lowell, MA
Art/fine arts, music. Contact Mr. Lawrence R. Martin, Director of Admissions, 1 University Avenue, Lowell, MA 01854-2881, 508-934-3939.

The University of Memphis
Memphis, TN
Art/fine arts, music, theater arts/drama. Contact Mr. David Wallace, Director of Admissions, Memphis, TN 38152, 901-678-2101.

University of Miami
Coral Gables, FL
Art/fine arts, music, theater arts/drama. Contact Mr. Edward Gillis, Director of Admissions and Associate Dean of Enrollment, PO Box 248025, Coral Gables, FL 33124, 305-284-4323.

University of Michigan
Ann Arbor, MI
Art/fine arts, dance, music, theater arts/drama. Contact Mr. Ted Spencer, Director of Undergraduate Admissions, Ann Arbor, MI 48109-1316, 313-764-7433.

University of Michigan–Dearborn
Dearborn, MI
Music. Contact Ms. Carol S. Mack, Director of Admissions, 4901 Evergreen Road, Dearborn, MI 48128-1491, 313-593-5100.

University of Michigan–Flint
Flint, MI
Art/fine arts, music, theater arts/drama. Contact Mr. David L. James, Director of Admissions, Flint, MI 48502-2186, 810-762-3300.

University of Minnesota, Duluth
Duluth, MN
Art/fine arts, music, theater arts/drama. Contact Mr. Gerald R. Allen, Director of Admissions, 10 University Drive, Duluth, MN 55812-2496, 218-726-7500.

University of Minnesota, Morris
Morris, MN
Art/fine arts, music, theater arts/drama. Contact Mr. Robert J. Vikander, Director of Admissions and Financial Aid, 600 East 4th Street, Morris, MN 56267, 612-589-6035.

University of Minnesota, Twin Cities Campus
Minneapolis, MN
Art/fine arts, dance, music, theater arts/drama. Contact Dr. Wayne Sigler, Director of Admissions, 240 Williamson, Minneapolis, MN 55455-0213, 612-625-2006.

University of Mississippi
Oxford, MS
Art/fine arts, music, theater arts/drama. Contact Mr. Beckett Howorth, Director of Admissions and Records, University, MS 38677, 601-232-7226.

University of Missouri–Columbia
Columbia, MO
Art/fine arts, music, theater arts/drama. Contact Dr. Gary L. Smith, Director of Admissions/Registrar, 305 Jesse Hall, Columbia, MO 65211, 314-882-7651.

University of Missouri–Kansas City
Kansas City, MO
Art/fine arts, dance, music, theater arts/drama. Contact Mr. Mel Tyer, Director of Admissions, 5100 Rockhill Road, Kansas City, MO 64110-2499, 816-235-1111.

University of Missouri–St. Louis
St. Louis, MO
Music. Contact Mrs. Mimi La Marca, Director of Admissions/Registrar, Woods Hall, St. Louis, MO 63121-4499, 314-516-5460.

University of Mobile
Mobile, AL
Art/fine arts, music, theater arts/drama. Contact Mrs. Kim Leousis, Director of Admissions, PO Box 13220, Mobile, AL 36663-0220, 334-675-5990 Ext. 290.

The University of Montana–Missoula
Missoula, MT
Art/fine arts, dance, music, theater arts/drama. Contact Dr. Frank L. Matule, Director of Admissions, Missoula, MT 59812-0002, 406-243-6266.

University of Montevallo
Montevallo, AL
Art/fine arts, music, theater arts/drama. Contact Mr. Robert A. Doyle, Director of Admissions, Station 6001, Montevallo, AL 35115, 205-665-6030.

University of Nebraska at Kearney
Kearney, NE
Art/fine arts, music, theater arts/drama. Contact Dr. Wayne Samuelson, Director of Admissions, 905 West 26th Street, Kearney, NE 68849-0001, 308-865-8526.

University of Nebraska at Omaha
Omaha, NE
Art/fine arts, music. Contact Mr. John Flemming, Director of Admissions, 60th and Dodge Streets, Omaha, NE 68182, 402-554-2709.

University of Nebraska–Lincoln
Lincoln, NE
Art/fine arts, dance, music, theater arts/drama. Contact Ms. Lisa Schmidt, Director of Admissions, 14th and R Streets, Lincoln, NE 68588-0417, 402-472-2030.

University of Nevada, Las Vegas
Las Vegas, NV
Art/fine arts, dance, music, theater arts/drama. Contact Mr. Larry Mason, Director of Admissions, 4505 Maryland Parkway, Las Vegas, NV 89154-9900, 702-895-3443.

University of Nevada, Reno
Reno, NV
Art/fine arts, music, theater arts/drama. Contact Dr. Melisa N. Choroszy, Associate Dean of Records and Enrollment Services, Reno, NV 89557, 702-784-6865.

University of New Hampshire
Durham, NH
Art/fine arts, dance, music, theater arts/drama. Contact Mr. David Kraus, Director of Admissions, Grant House, Durham, NH 03824, 603-862-1360.

University of New Haven
West Haven, CT
Art/fine arts. Contact Mr. Steve Briggs, Dean of Admissions and Financial Aid, 300 Orange Avenue, West Haven, CT 06516-1916, 203-932-7088.

University of New Mexico
Albuquerque, NM
Art/fine arts, dance, music, theater arts/drama. Contact Ms. Cynthia Stuart, Director of Admissions, Albuquerque, NM 87131-2039, 505-277-2446.

University of New Orleans
New Orleans, LA
Art/fine arts, music, theater arts/drama. Contact Ms. Roslyn Sheley, Director of Admissions, Lake Front, New Orleans, LA 70148, 504-286-6595.

University of North Alabama
Florence, AL
Art/fine arts, music, theater arts/drama. Contact Dr. G. Daniel Howard, Dean of Enrollment Management, University Station, Florence, AL 35632-0001, 205-760-4221.

University of North Carolina at Asheville
Asheville, NC
Art/fine arts, music, theater arts/drama. Contact Mr. John White, Director of Admissions, University Heights, Asheville, NC 28804-3299, 704-251-6481.

University of North Carolina at Chapel Hill
Chapel Hill, NC
Art/fine arts, music, theater arts/drama. Contact Dr. James Walters, Associate Provost/Director of Undergraduate Admissions, Chapel Hill, NC 27599, 919-966-3621.

University of North Carolina at Charlotte
Charlotte, NC
Art/fine arts, dance, music, theater arts/drama. Contact Ms. Kathi M. Baucom, Director of Admissions, University City Boulevard, Charlotte, NC 28223, 704-547-2213.

University of North Carolina at Greensboro
Greensboro, NC
Art/fine arts, dance, music, theater arts/drama. Contact Ms. Rachel M. Hendrickson, Director of Admissions, 1000 Spring Garden Street, Greensboro, NC 27412-0001, 910-334-5243.

University of North Carolina at Wilmington
Wilmington, NC
Art/fine arts, music, theater arts/drama. Contact Mr. Ronald E. Whittaker, Director of Admissions and Registrar, 601 South College Road, Wilmington, NC 28403-3201, 910-395-3243.

University of North Dakota
Grand Forks, ND
Art/fine arts, music, theater arts/drama. Contact Dr. Dean Schieve, Director of Enrollment Services, Box 8382, Grand Forks, ND 58202, 701-777-4463.

University of Northern Colorado
Greeley, CO
Art/fine arts, dance, music, theater arts/drama. Contact Mr. Gary O. Gullickson, Director of Admissions, Greeley, CO 80639, 970-351-2881.

University of Northern Iowa
Cedar Falls, IA
Art/fine arts, music, theater arts/drama. Contact Mr. Clark Elmer, Director of Enrollment Management and Admissions, 1222 West 27th Street, Cedar Falls, IA 50614, 319-273-2281.

University of North Florida
Jacksonville, FL
Art/fine arts, music. Contact Ms. Mary Bolla, Director of Admissions, 4567 St John's Bluff Road South, Jacksonville, FL 32224-2645, 904-646-2624.

University of North Texas
Denton, TX
Art/fine arts, dance, music, theater arts/drama. Contact Ms. Marcilla Collinsworth, Director of Admissions, Box 13797, Denton, TX 76203-6737, 817-565-3921.

University of Notre Dame
Notre Dame, IN
Art/fine arts, music, theater arts/drama. Contact Mr. Kevin M. Rooney, Director of Admissions, Notre Dame, IN 46556, 219-631-7505.

University of Oklahoma
Norman, OK
Art/fine arts, dance, music, theater arts/drama. Contact Mr. Marc S. Borish, Director of Admissions, 407 West Boyd, Norman, OK 73019, 405-325-2251.

University of Oregon
Eugene, OR
Art/fine arts, dance, music, theater arts/drama. Contact Mr. James R. Buch, Director of Admissions, Eugene, OR 97403, 503-346-3201.

University of Pennsylvania
Philadelphia, PA
Art/fine arts, music, theater arts/drama. Contact Mr. Willis J. Stetson Jr., Dean of Admissions, 1 College Hall, Levy Park, Philadelphia, PA 19104, 215-898-7507.

University of Pittsburgh
Pittsburgh, PA
Art/fine arts, music, theater arts/drama. Contact Dr. Betsy A. Porter, Director of Admissions and Financial Aid, Bruce Hall, Second Floor, Pittsburgh, PA 15260-0001, 412-624-7488.

University of Pittsburgh at Johnstown
Johnstown, PA
Theater arts/drama. Contact Mr. James F. Gyure, Director of Admissions, 133 Biddle Hall, Johnstown, PA 15904-2990, 814-269-7050.

University of Portland
Portland, OR
Music, theater arts/drama. Contact Mr. Daniel B. Reilly, Director of Admissions, 5000 North Willamette Boulevard, Portland, OR 97203-5798, 503-283-7147.

University of Puget Sound
Tacoma, WA
Art/fine arts, music, theater arts/drama. Contact Dr. George H. Mills, Dean of Admission, 1500 North Warner Street, Tacoma, WA 98416-0005, 206-756-3211.

University of Redlands
Redlands, CA
Art/fine arts, music. Contact Mr. Paul Driscoll, Dean of Admissions, PO Box 3080, Redlands, CA 92373-0999, 909-335-4074.

University of Rhode Island
Kingston, RI
Art/fine arts, music, theater arts/drama. Contact Mr. David Taggart, Dean of Admissions and Financial Aid, Kingston, RI 02881, 401-792-9800.

University of Richmond
Richmond, VA
Art/fine arts, music, theater arts/drama. Contact Ms. Pamela Spence, Dean of Admissions, Richmond, VA 23173, 804-289-8640.

University of Rio Grande
Rio Grande, OH
Art/fine arts, music, theater arts/drama. Contact Mr. Mark F. Abell, Executive Director of Admissions, Rio Grande, OH 45674, 614-245-5353 Ext. 207.

University of Rochester
Rochester, NY
Art/fine arts, music. Contact Mr. Wayne A. Locust, Director of Admissions, Wilson Boulevard, Rochester, NY 14627-0001, 716-275-3221.

University of St. Thomas
St. Paul, MN
Music, theater arts/drama. Contact Ms. Marla Friederichs, Director of Admissions, 2115 Summit Avenue, St. Paul, MN 55105-1089, 612-962-6150.

University of St. Thomas
Houston, TX
Art/fine arts, music, theater arts/drama. Contact Mrs. Elsie Biron, Director of Admissions, 3800 Montrose Boulevard, Houston, TX 77006-4694, 713-525-3500.

University of San Diego
San Diego, CA
Art/fine arts, music. Contact Mr. Warren Muller, Director of Undergraduate Admissions, 5998 Alcala Park, San Diego, CA 92110-2492, 619-260-4506.

University of San Francisco
San Francisco, CA
Art/fine arts. Contact Dr. Elizabeth Johnson, Dean of Academic Services, 2130 Fulton Street, San Francisco, CA 94117-1080, 415-666-6534.

University of Science and Arts of Oklahoma
Chickasha, OK
Art/fine arts, music, theater arts/drama. Contact Dr. Tim McElroy, Registrar and Director of

Admissions and Records, PO Box 82345, Chickasha, OK 73018-0001, 405-224-3140 Ext. 205.

University of Sioux Falls
Sioux Falls, SD
Art/fine arts, music, theater arts/drama. Contact Ms. Susan Reese, Director of Admissions, 1101 West 22nd Street, Sioux Falls, SD 57105-1699, 605-331-6600.

University of South Alabama
Mobile, AL
Art/fine arts, music, theater arts/drama. Contact Ms. Catherine P. King, Director of Admissions, 307 University Boulevard, Mobile, AL 36688-0002, 205-460-6141.

University of South Carolina
Columbia, SC
Art/fine arts, music, theater arts/drama. Contact Ms. Terry L. Davis, Director of Admissions, Columbia, SC 29208, 803-777-7700.

University of South Dakota
Vermillion, SD
Art/fine arts, music, theater arts/drama. Contact Mr. David Lorenz, Associate Dean of Students and Director of Admissions, 414 East Clark Street, Vermillion, SD 57069-2390, 605-677-5434.

University of Southern California
Los Angeles, CA
Art/fine arts, music, theater arts/drama. Contact Mr. Joseph Allen, Vice Provost for Enrollment, University Park Campus, Los Angeles, CA 90089-0911, 213-740-6753.

University of Southern Colorado
Pueblo, CO
Art/fine arts, music, theater arts/drama. Contact Mr. Frederick Kidd, Dean of Admissions and Enrollment Services, 2200 Bonforte Boulevard, Pueblo, CO 81001-4990, 719-549-2261.

University of Southern Indiana
Evansville, IN
Art/fine arts, theater arts/drama. Contact Mr. Timothy K. Buecher, Dean of Enrollment Services, 8600 University Boulevard, Evansville, IN 47712-3590, 812-464-1765.

University of Southern Maine
Portland, ME
Art/fine arts, music, theater arts/drama. Contact Dr. Susan Roberts Campbell, Director of Admissions, 37 College Avenue, Gorham, ME 04038, 207-780-5670.

University of Southern Mississippi
Hattiesburg, MS
Art/fine arts, dance, music, theater arts/drama. Contact Mr. Danny W. Montgomery, Registrar and Director of Admissions, Box 5001, Hattiesburg, MS 39406-5001, 601-266-5006.

University of South Florida
Tampa, FL
Art/fine arts, dance, music, theater arts/drama. Contact Ms. Pam Lapan, Interim Director of Admissions, 4202 East Fowler Avenue, Tampa, FL 33620-6900, 813-974-3350.

University of Southwestern Louisiana
Lafayette, LA
Art/fine arts, dance, music, theater arts/drama. Contact Mr. Leroy Broussard Jr., Director of Admissions, PO Box 41770, Lafayette, LA 70504-1770, 318-482-6473.

The University of Tampa
Tampa, FL
Art/fine arts, music. Contact Mr. Robert W. Cook, Dean of Admission, 401 West Kennedy Boulevard, Tampa, FL 33606-1480, 813-253-6211.

University of Tennessee at Chattanooga
Chattanooga, TN
Art/fine arts, music, theater arts/drama. Contact Dr. Bill Aiken, Associate Provost for Academic Administration, 615 McCallie Avenue, Chattanooga, TN 37403-2504, 615-755-4541.

University of Tennessee at Martin
Martin, TN
Music. Contact Dr. Nick Dunagan, Executive Vice Chancellor/Vice Chancellor for Development, Martin, TN 38238-1000, 901-587-7626.

University of Tennessee, Knoxville
Knoxville, TN
Art/fine arts, dance, music, theater arts/drama. Contact Dr. Gordon Stanley, Director of Admissions, Knoxville, TN 37996, 615-974-2184.

University of Texas at Arlington
Arlington, TX
Art/fine arts, music, theater arts/drama. Contact Mr. Paul Hermesmeyer, Director of Admissions, Arlington, TX 76019, 817-273-2225.

University of Texas at Austin
Austin, TX
Art/fine arts, dance, music, theater arts/drama. Contact Ms. Shirley F. Binder, Director of Admissions, Austin, TX 78712, 512-475-7399.

The University of Texas at Brownsville
Brownsville, TX
Art/fine arts. Contact Mr. Ernesto Garcia, Director of Enrollment, 80 Fort Brown, Brownsville, TX 78520-4991, 210-544-8254.

University of Texas at Dallas
Richardson, TX
Art/fine arts. Contact Mr. Barry Samsula, Director of Admissions, PO Box 830688 Mail Station MC18, Richardson, TX 75083-0688, 214-883-2294.

University of Texas at El Paso
El Paso, TX
Art/fine arts, music, theater arts/drama. Contact Ms. Diana Guerrero, Director of Admission, 500 West University Avenue, El Paso, TX 79968-0001, 915-747-5588.

University of Texas at San Antonio
San Antonio, TX
Art/fine arts, music. Contact Dr. John H. Brown, Director of Admissions and Registrar, 6900 North Loop 1604 West, San Antonio, TX 78249-1130, 210-691-4547.

University of Texas at Tyler
Tyler, TX
Art/fine arts, music, theater arts/drama. Contact Ms. Martha Wheat, Director of Admissions and Student Records, 3900 University Boulevard, Tyler, TX 75799-0001, 903-566-7201.

University of Texas of the Permian Basin
Odessa, TX
Art/fine arts, music. Contact Ms. Vicki Gomez, Director of Admissions, 4901 East University, Odessa, TX 79762-0001, 915-552-2605.

University of Texas–Pan American
Edinburg, TX
Art/fine arts, music. Contact Mr. David Zuniga, Director of Admissions, 1201 West University Drive, Edinburg, TX 78539-2999, 210-381-2209.

University of the District of Columbia
Washington, DC
Art/fine arts, music, theater arts/drama. Contact Ms. Sandra Dolphin, Director of Recruitment and Admissions, 4200 Connecticut Avenue, NW, Washington, DC 20008-1175, 202-274-6071.

University of the Ozarks
Clarksville, AR
Art/fine arts, music, theater arts/drama. Contact Mr. Michael Heator, Director of Admissions, 415 North College Avenue, Clarksville, AR 72830-2880, 501-979-1227.

University of the Pacific
Stockton, CA
Art/fine arts, music, theater arts/drama. Contact Mr. Edward Schoenberg, Dean of Admissions, 3601 Pacific Avenue, Stockton, CA 95211-0197, 209-946-2211.

University of the South
Sewanee, TN
Art/fine arts, music, theater arts/drama. Contact Mr. Robert M. Hedrick, Director of Admission, 735 University Avenue, Sewanee, TN 37383-1000, 615-598-1238.

University of the State of New York, Regents College
Albany, NY
Music. Contact Dean of Enrollment Management, 7 Columbia Circle, Albany, NY 12203-5159, 518-464-8500.

University of Toledo
Toledo, OH
Art/fine arts, music, theater arts/drama. Contact Mr. Richard J. Eastop, Dean of Admission Services, 2801 West Bancroft, Toledo, OH 43606-3398, 419-537-2696.

University of Tulsa
Tulsa, OK
Art/fine arts, music, theater arts/drama. Contact Mr. John C. Corso, Assoc. Vice President for Administration/Dean of Admission, 600 South College Avenue, Tulsa, OK 74104-3126, 918-631-2307.

University of Utah
Salt Lake City, UT
Art/fine arts, dance, music, theater arts/drama. Contact Dr. J. Stayner Landward, Director of Admissions, 250 South Student Services Building, Salt Lake City, UT 84112, 801-581-7281.

University of Vermont
Burlington, VT
Art/fine arts, music, theater arts/drama. Contact Ms. Carol Hogan, Director of Admissions, Burlington, VT 05401-3596, 802-656-3370.

University of Virginia
Charlottesville, VA
Art/fine arts, music, theater arts/drama. Contact Mr. John A. Blackburn, Dean of Admission, Charlottesville, VA 22906, 804-982-3200.

University of Washington
Seattle, WA
Art/fine arts, dance, music, theater arts/drama. Contact Mr. Wilbur W. Washburn IV, Executive Director of Admissions and Records, Seattle, WA 98195, 206-543-4000.

University of West Alabama
Livingston, AL
Music. Contact Dr. Ervin L. Wood, Dean of Students, Livingston, AL 35470, 205-652-9661 Ext. 352.

University of Wisconsin–Eau Claire
Eau Claire, WI
Art/fine arts, music, theater arts/drama. Contact Mr. Roger GroeneWold, Director of Admissions, PO Box 4004, Eau Claire, WI 54702-4004, 715-836-5415.

University of Wisconsin–Green Bay
Green Bay, WI
Art/fine arts, dance, music, theater arts/drama. Contact Mr. Myron Van de Ven, Director of Admissions, 2420 Nicolet Drive, Green Bay, WI 54311-7001, 414-465-2111.

University of Wisconsin–La Crosse
La Crosse, WI
Art/fine arts, music, theater arts/drama. Contact Mr. Gale Grimslid, Director of Admissions and Records, 1725 State Street, La Crosse, WI 54601-3742, 608-785-8576.

University of Wisconsin–Madison
Madison, WI
Art/fine arts, music, theater arts/drama. Contact Mr. Millard Storey, Director of Admissions, 140 Peterson Office Building, 750 University Avenue, Madison, WI 53706-1490, 608-262-3961.

University of Wisconsin–Milwaukee
Milwaukee, WI
Art/fine arts, dance, music, theater arts/drama. Contact Ms. Beth Weckmueller, Director of Admissions, PO Box 413, Milwaukee, WI 53201-0413, 414-229-6164.

University of Wisconsin–Oshkosh
Oshkosh, WI
Art/fine arts, music, theater arts/drama. Contact Mr. Roger Herold, Director of Admissions, 800 Algoma Boulevard, Oshkosh, WI 54901-3551, 414-424-0202.

University of Wisconsin–Parkside
Kenosha, WI
Art/fine arts, music, theater arts/drama. Contact Mr. Charles Murphy, Director of Admissions, 900 Wood Road, Box 2000, Kenosha, WI 53141-2000, 414-595-2355.

University of Wisconsin– Platteville
Platteville, WI
Art/fine arts, music. Contact Dr. Richard Schumacher, Dean of Admissions and Enrollment Management, 1 University Plaza, Platteville, WI 53818-3099, 608-342-1125.

University of Wisconsin–River Falls
River Falls, WI
Art/fine arts, music, theater arts/drama. Contact Mr. Alan Tuchtenhagen, Director of Admissions, 410 South Third Street, River Falls, WI 54022-5013, 715-425-3500.

University of Wisconsin–Stevens Point
Stevens Point, WI
Art/fine arts, dance, music, theater arts/drama. Contact Dr. John A. Larsen, Director of Admissions, Stevens Point, WI 54481-3897, 715-346-2441.

University of Wisconsin–Stout
Menomonie, WI
Art/fine arts. Contact Mr. Charles Kell, Director of Admissions, Menomonie, WI 54751, 715-232-1293.

University of Wisconsin–Superior
Superior, WI
Art/fine arts, music, theater arts/drama. Contact Mr. Jon Wojciechowski, Director of Admissions, 1800 Grand Avenue, Superior, WI 54880-2873, 715-394-8396.

University of Wisconsin–Whitewater
Whitewater, WI
Art/fine arts, music, theater arts/drama. Contact Mr. Irv Madsen, Executive Director of Admissions, 800 West Main Street, Whitewater, WI 53190-1790, 414-472-1440.

University of Wyoming
Laramie, WY
Art/fine arts, dance, music, theater arts/drama. Contact Mr. James T Mansfield, Director of Admissions, Box 3435, Laramie, WY 82071, 307-766-5160.

Upper Iowa University
Fayette, IA
Art/fine arts, music. Contact Mr. Kent McElvania, Vice President for Enrollment Management, Box 1859, Fayette, IA 52142-1857, 319-425-5281.

Ursinus College
Collegeville, PA
Art/fine arts, music. Contact Mr. Richard G. Di Feliciantonio, Director of Admissions and Enrollment, Box 1000, Main Street, Collegeville, PA 19426-1000, 610-409-3200 Ext. 2224.

Ursuline College
Pepper Pike, OH
Art/fine arts. Contact Mr. Dennis L. Giacomino, Director of Admissions, 2550 Lander Road, Pepper Pike, OH 44124-4398, 216-449-4203.

Utah State University
Logan, UT
Art/fine arts, dance, music, theater arts/drama. Contact Mr. Rodney Clark, Director of Admissions, University Hill, Logan, UT 84322, 801-797-1107.

Utica College of Syracuse University
Utica, NY
Art/fine arts, theater arts/drama. Contact Ms. Leslie North, Director of Admissions, 1600 Burrstone Road, Utica, NY 13502-4892, 315-792-3006.

V

Valdosta State University
Valdosta, GA
Art/fine arts, music, theater arts/drama. Contact Mr. Walter Peacock, Director of Admissions, Valdosta, GA 31698, 912-333-5791.

Valley City State University
Valley City, ND
Art/fine arts, music. Contact Mr. LaMonte Johnson, Director of Admissions, Valley City, ND 58072, 701-845-7101.

Valley Forge Christian College
Phoenixville, PA
Music. Contact Mr. James Barco, Executive Director of Enrollment Management, Charlestown Road, Phoenixville, PA 19460-2917, 610-935-0450.

Valparaiso University
Valparaiso, IN
Art/fine arts, music, theater arts/drama. Contact Ms. Katharine E. Wehling, Vice President of Admissions and Financial Aid, Valparaiso, IN 46383-6493, 219-464-5011.

Vanderbilt University
Nashville, TN
Art/fine arts, music, theater arts/drama. Contact Dr. Neill Sanders, Dean of Undergraduate Admissions, Nashville, TN 37240-1001, 615-322-2561.

Vassar College
Poughkeepsie, NY
Art/fine arts, music, theater arts/drama. Contact Mr. Thomas Matos, Director of Admissions, Poughkeepsie, NY 12601, 914-437-7300.

Vennard College
University Park, IA
Music. Contact Mrs. Lori Hyndman, Director of Admissions, PO Box 29, University Park, IA 52595, 515-673-8391 Ext. 218.

Virginia Commonwealth University
Richmond, VA
Art/fine arts, dance, music, theater arts/drama. Contact Mr. Horace W. Wooldridge, Director of Undergraduate Admissions, 821 West Franklin Street, Box 842526, Richmond, VA 23284-9005, 804-828-6125.

Virginia Intermont College
Bristol, VA
Art/fine arts, dance, music, theater arts/drama. Contact Dr. Bruce Storey Jr., Dean of Students and Admissions, 1013 Moore Street, Bristol, VA 24201-4298, 703-669-6101 Ext. 207.

Virginia Polytechnic Institute and State University
Blacksburg, VA
Art/fine arts, music, theater arts/drama. Contact Mr. David R. Bousquet, Director of Admissions, 104 Burruss Hall, Blacksburg, VA 24061-0202, 703-231-6267.

Virginia State University
Petersburg, VA
Art/fine arts, music. Contact Mr. Garoy Knight, Director of Admissions, Petersburg, VA 23806, 804-524-5902.

Virginia Union University
Richmond, VA
Music. Contact Mr. Gil Powell, Director of Admissions, 1500 North Lombardy Street, Richmond, VA 23220-1170, 804-257-5881.

Virginia Wesleyan College
Norfolk, VA
Art/fine arts, music, theater arts/drama. Contact Dr. Martha E. Rogers, Vice President for Enrollment Management, Dean of Admissions, 1584 Wesleyan Drive, Norfolk, VA 23502-5599, 804-455-3208.

Viterbo College
La Crosse, WI
Art/fine arts, music, theater arts/drama. Contact Dr. Roland Nelson, Director of Admissions, 815 South Ninth Street, La Crosse, WI 54601-4797, 608-791-0421.

W

Wabash College
Crawfordsville, IN
Art/fine arts, music, theater arts/drama. Contact Mr. Gregory Birk, Director of Admissions, PO Box 352, Crawfordsville, IN 47933-0352, 317-364-4253.

Wagner College
Staten Island, NY
Art/fine arts, music, theater arts/drama. Contact Mr. Angelo Araimo, Director of Admissions, 631 Howard Avenue, Staten Island, NY 10301, 718-390-3411.

Wake Forest University
Winston-Salem, NC
Art/fine arts, music, theater arts/drama. Contact Mr. William G. Starling, Director of Admissions, PO Box 7305, Winston-Salem, NC 27109, 910-759-5201.

Walla Walla College
College Place, WA
Art/fine arts, music. Contact Mr. Stephen Payne, Vice President for Admissions and Marketing, 204 South College Avenue, College Place, WA 99324-3000, 509-527-2327.

Warner Pacific College
Portland, OR
Music. Contact Mr. William D. Stenberg, Dean of Admissions, 2219 Southeast 68th Avenue, Portland, OR 97215-4099, 503-775-4366 Ext. 518.

Warner Southern College
Lake Wales, FL
Music. Contact Mr. Todd Miller, Associate Director of Admissions, 5301 US Highway 27 South, Lake Wales, FL 33853-8725, 813-638-1426 Ext. 7213.

Wartburg College
Waverly, IA
Art/fine arts, music. Contact Mr. John Olsen, Director of Admissions, 222 Ninth Street, NW, PO Box 1003, Waverly, IA 50677-1033, 319-352-8264.

Washburn University of Topeka
Topeka, KS
Art/fine arts, music, theater arts/drama. Contact Dr. Greg Greider, Dean of Students, Topeka, KS 66621, 913-231-1010 Ext. 1625.

Washington and Lee University
Lexington, VA
Art/fine arts, music, theater arts/drama. Contact Mr. William M. Hartog, Dean of Admissions and Financial Aid, Lexington, VA 24450, 703-463-8710.

Washington Bible College
Lanham, MD
Music. Contact Mr. Jon Evans, Director of Recruitment, 6511 Princess Garden Parkway, Lanham, MD 20706-3599, 301-552-1400 Ext. 213.

Washington College
Chestertown, MD
Art/fine arts, music, theater arts/drama. Contact Mr. Kevin Coveney, Vice President for Admissions, 300 Washington Avenue, Chestertown, MD 21620-1197, 410-778-7700.

Washington State University
Pullman, WA
Art/fine arts, music, theater arts/drama. Contact Ms. Terese M. Flynn, Director of Admissions, Office of Admissions, 342 French Administration Building, Pullman, WA 99164-1036, 509-335-5586.

Washington University
St. Louis, MO
Art/fine arts, music, theater arts/drama. Contact Mr. Harold Wingood, Dean of Admissions, Campus Box 1089, 1 Brookings Drive, St. Louis, MO 63130-4899, 314-935-6000.

Wayland Baptist University
Plainview, TX
Art/fine arts, music, theater arts/drama. Contact Mr. Claude Lusk, Director of Student Admissions, 1900 West Seventh Street, Plainview, TX 79072-6998, 806-296-4709.

Waynesburg College
Waynesburg, PA
Art/fine arts. Contact Mrs. Robin L. Moore, Director of Admissions, 51 West College Street, Waynesburg, PA 15370-1222, 412-627-8191 Ext. 333.

Wayne State College
Wayne, NE
Art/fine arts, music, theater arts/drama. Contact Mr. Robert Zetocha, Director of Admissions, 1111 Main Street, Wayne, NE 68787, 402-375-7234.

Wayne State University
Detroit, MI
Art/fine arts, dance, music, theater arts/drama. Contact Mr. Ronald C. Hughes, Director of University Admissions, Detroit, MI 48202, 313-577-3581.

Weber State University
Ogden, UT
Art/fine arts, music, theater arts/drama. Contact Mr. Christopher Rivera, Director of Admissions, 3750 Harrison Boulevard, Ogden, UT 84408-0002, 801-626-6046.

Webster University
St. Louis, MO
Art/fine arts, dance, music, theater arts/drama. Contact Mr. Niel DeVasto, Director of Admission, 470 East Lockwood Avenue, St. Louis, MO 63119-3194, 314-968-7000.

Wellesley College
Wellesley, MA
Art/fine arts, music, theater arts/drama. Contact Ms. Janet Lavin, Dean of Admission, 240 Green Hall, Wellesley, MA 02181, 617-283-2270.

Wells College
Aurora, NY
Art/fine arts, dance, music, theater arts/drama. Contact, Aurora, NY 13026, 315-364-3440 .

Wesleyan College
Macon, GA
Art/fine arts, music. Contact Mr. John A. Thompson, Dean of Admissions, 4760 Forsyth Road, Macon, GA 31297-4299, 912-757-5206.

Wesleyan University
Middletown, CT
Art/fine arts, dance, music, theater arts/drama. Contact Ms. Barbara-Jan Wilson, Dean of Admissions and Financial Aid, Middletown, CT 06459-0260, 203-685-3000.

West Chester University of Pennsylvania
West Chester, PA
Art/fine arts, music, theater arts/drama. Contact Ms. Marsha Haug, Director of Admissions, 100 West Rosedale Avenue, West Chester, PA 19383, 610-436-3411.

Western Baptist College
Salem, OR
Music. Contact Dr. Reno Hoff, Vice President for Administration, 5000 Deer Park Drive, SE, Salem, OR 97301-9392, 503-375-7003 Ext. 2510.

Western Carolina University
Cullowhee, NC
Art/fine arts, music, theater arts/drama. Contact Mr. Drumont Bowman, Director of Admissions, Cullowhee, NC 28723, 704-227-7317.

Western Connecticut State University
Danbury, CT
Art/fine arts, music, theater arts/drama. Contact Mr. Delmore Kinney Jr., Director of Admissions, 181 White Street, Danbury, CT 06810-6885, 203-837-9000.

Western Illinois University
Macomb, IL
Art/fine arts, music, theater arts/drama. Contact Dr. Robert Caruso, Director of Admissions, 1 University Circle, Macomb, IL 61455-1396, 309-298-3157.

Western Kentucky University
Bowling Green, KY
Art/fine arts, music, theater arts/drama. Contact Dr. Cheryl C. Chambless, Director of Admissions, One Big Red Way, Bowling Green, KY 42101-3576, 502-745-5422.

Western Maryland College
Westminster, MD
Art/fine arts, music, theater arts/drama. Contact Ms. M. Martha O'Connell, Director of Admissions, 2 College Hill, Westminster, MD 21157-4390, 410-857-2230.

Western Michigan University
Kalamazoo, MI
Art/fine arts, dance, music, theater arts/drama. Contact Mr. Stanley Henderson, Director of Admissions, West Michigan Avenue, Kalamazoo, MI 49008, 616-387-2000.

Western Montana College of the University of Montana
Dillon, MT
Art/fine arts, music. Contact Ms. Michele O'Neill, Director of Admissions, 710 South Atlantic, Dillon, MT 59725-3598, 406-683-7452.

Western New Mexico University
Silver City, NM
Art/fine arts, music. Contact Mr. Michael Alecksen, Director of Admissions, College Avenue, Silver City, NM 88062-0680, 505-538-6106.

Western Oregon State College
Monmouth, OR
Art/fine arts, music, theater arts/drama. Contact Mr. Craig Kolins, Director of Admissions, 345 North Monmouth Avenue, Monmouth, OR 97361, 503-838-8211.

Western State College of Colorado
Gunnison, CO
Art/fine arts, music, theater arts/drama. Contact Ms. Sara Axelson, Director of Admissions, Gunnison, CO 81231, 303-943-2119.

Western Washington University
Bellingham, WA
Art/fine arts, music, theater arts/drama. Contact Ms. Karen Copetas, Director of Admissions, 516 High Street, Bellingham, WA 98225-9009, 360-650-3440 Ext. 3443.

Westfield State College
Westfield, MA
Art/fine arts, music. Contact Ms. Michelle Mattie, Director of Admission and Financial Aid, Western Avenue, Westfield, MA 01086, 413-572-5218 Ext. 218.

West Georgia College
Carrollton, GA
Art/fine arts, music, theater arts/drama. Contact Ms. Catherine Lawrence, Acting Director of Admissions, 1600 Maple Street, Carrollton, GA 30118, 404-836-6416.

West Liberty State College
West Liberty, WV
Art/fine arts, music. Contact Mr. Paul Milam, Director of Admissions, West Liberty, WV 26074, 304-336-8076.

Westminster Choir College of Rider University
Princeton, NJ
Music. Contact Ms. Anne Farmer Meservey, Director of Admissions, 101 Walnut Lane, Princeton, NJ 08540-3899, 609-921-7100 Ext. 211.

Westminster College
Fulton, MO
Art/fine arts. Contact Mr. E. Norman Jones, Dean of Admissions, 501 Westminster Avenue, Fulton, MO 65251-1299, 314-592-1251.

Westminster College
New Wilmington, PA
Art/fine arts, music, theater arts/drama. Contact Mr. R. Dana Paul, Director of Admissions, South Market Street, New Wilmington, PA 16172-0001, 412-946-7100.

Westminster College of Salt Lake City
Salt Lake City, UT
Art/fine arts, theater arts/drama. Contact Ms. Beverly K. Levy, Associate Director of Admissions, 1840 South 1300 East, Salt Lake City, UT 84105-3697, 801-488-4200.

Westmont College
Santa Barbara, CA
Art/fine arts, music, theater arts/drama. Contact Mr. David Morley, Director of Admissions, 955 La Paz Road, Santa Barbara, CA 93108-1099, 805-565-6200.

West Texas A&M University
Canyon, TX
Art/fine arts, dance, music, theater arts/drama. Contact Ms. Lila Vars, Director of Admissions, WT Box 907, Canyon, TX 79016-0001, 806-656-2020.

West Virginia State College
Institute, WV
Art/fine arts, music. Contact Mr. John L. Fuller, Director of Admissions and Registration, Post Office Box 1000, Institute, WV 25112-1000, 304-766-3144.

West Virginia University
Morgantown, WV
Art/fine arts, music, theater arts/drama. Contact Dr. Glenn G. Carter, Director of Admissions and Records, Box 6009, Morgantown, WV 26506-6009, 304-293-2121 Ext. 511.

West Virginia Wesleyan College
Buckhannon, WV
Art/fine arts, music, theater arts/drama. Contact Mr. Robert N. Skinner II, Director of Admission, Buckhannon, WV 26201, 304-473-8510.

Wheaton College
Wheaton, IL
Art/fine arts, music, theater arts/drama. Contact Mr. Dan Crabtree, Director of Admissions, 501 East College Avenue, Wheaton, IL 60187-5571, 708-752-5011.

Wheaton College
Norton, MA
Art/fine arts, music, theater arts/drama. Contact Ms. Gail Berson, Dean of Admission and Student Aid, East Main Street, Norton, MA 02766, 508-285-8251.

Whitman College
Walla Walla, WA
Art/fine arts, music, theater arts/drama. Contact Mr. Chris Ellertson, Acting Director of Admission, 345 Boyer Avenue, Walla Walla, WA 99362-2083, 509-527-5176.

Whittier College
Whittier, CA
Art/fine arts, music, theater arts/drama. Contact Mr. Thomas Enders, Dean of Enrollment, 13406 E Philadelphia Street, PO Box 634, Whittier, CA 90608-0634, 310-907-4229.

Whitworth College
Spokane, WA
Art/fine arts, music, theater arts/drama. Contact Mr. Fred Pfursich, Dean of Enrollment Services, West 300 Hawthorne Road, Spokane, WA 99251-0001, 509-466-3212.

Wichita State University
Wichita, KS
Art/fine arts, dance, music, theater arts/drama. Contact Ms. Rita Abent, Director of Admissions, 1845 North Fairmount, Wichita, KS 67260, 316-689-3085.

Wilberforce University
Wilberforce, OH
Art/fine arts, music. Contact Dr. Ella M. Wilson, Vice President for Student Affairs, Wilberforce, OH 45384, 513-376-2911 Ext. 611.

Wiley College
Marshall, TX
Music. Contact Mr. Van B. McLellan Jr., Director of Admissions, 711 Wiley Avenue, Marshall, TX 75670-5199, 903-927-3311.

Wilkes University
Wilkes-Barre, PA
Art/fine arts, music, theater arts/drama. Contact Mr. Emory Guffrovich, Dean of Admissions, 170 South Franklin Street, PO Box 111, Wilkes-Barre, PA 18766-0002, 717-831-4400.

Willamette University
Salem, OR
Art/fine arts, music, theater arts/drama. Contact Mr. James M. Sumner, Dean of Admissions, 900 State Street, Salem, OR 97301-3931, 503-370-6303.

William Carey College
Hattiesburg, MS
Art/fine arts, music, theater arts/drama. Contact Dr. William Curry, Acting Director of Admissions, 498 Tuscan Avenue, Hattiesburg, MS 39401-5499, 601-582-5051.

William Jewell College
Liberty, MO
Art/fine arts, music. Contact Mr. Vic Davolt, Interim Director of Admission, 500 College Hill, Liberty, MO 64068-1843, 816-781-7700 Ext. 5137.

William Paterson College of New Jersey
Wayne, NJ
Art/fine arts, music, theater arts/drama. Contact Mr. Leo DeBartolo, Director of Admissions, 300 Pompton Road, Wayne, NJ 07470-8420, 201-595-2906.

William Penn College
Oskaloosa, IA
Music. Contact Mr. Eric Otto, Director of Admissions, 201 Trueblood Avenue, Oskaloosa, IA 52577-1799, 515-673-1012.

Williams Baptist College
Walnut Ridge, AR
Art/fine arts, music. Contact Mr. Scott Wright, Director of Admissions, Box 3668, Walnut Ridge, AR 72476, 501-886-6741 Ext. 127.

Williams College
Williamstown, MA
Art/fine arts, music, theater arts/drama. Contact Mr. Philip F. Smith, Dean of Admission, Williamstown, MA 01267, 413-597-2211.

William Smith College
Geneva, NY
Art/fine arts, dance, music, theater arts/drama. Contact Ms. Mara O'Laughlin, Director of Admissions, Geneva, NY 14456, 315-781-3472.

William Tyndale College
Farmington Hills, MI
Music. Contact, Farmington Hills, MI 48331, 810-553-7200 .

William Woods University
Fulton, MO
Art/fine arts, music, theater arts/drama. Contact Dr. Eric Staley, Vice President of Enrollment Management, 200 West Twelfth Street, Fulton, MO 65251-1098, 314-592-4221.

Wilmington College
New Castle, DE
Theater arts/drama. Contact Mr. Michael Lee, Dean of Admissions, Financial Aid and Marketing, 320 DuPont Highway, New Castle, DE 19720-6491, 302-328-9407 Ext. 105.

Wilmington College
Wilmington, OH
Music, theater arts/drama. Contact Dr. Lawrence T. Lesick, Dean of Admission and Financial Aid, Pyle Center Box 1185, Wilmington, OH 45177, 513-382-6661 Ext. 265.

Wilson College
Chambersburg, PA
Art/fine arts. Contact Ms. Karen L. Jewell, Director of Admissions, 1015 Philadelphia Avenue, Chambersburg, PA 17201-1285, 717-264-4141 Ext. 223.

Wingate University
Wingate, NC
Art/fine arts, music. Contact Mr. Christopher J. Keller, Director of Admissions, Wingate, NC 28174, 704-233-8201.

Winona State University
Winona, MN
Art/fine arts, music, theater arts/drama. Contact Dr. J. A. Mootz, Director of Admissions, PO Box 5838, Winona, MN 55987-5838, 507-457-5100.

Winston-Salem State University
Winston-Salem, NC
Art/fine arts, music. Contact Mr. Van C. Wilson, Director of Admissions, 601 Martin Luther King Jr Drive, Winston-Salem, NC 27110-0003, 910-750-2070.

Winthrop University
Rock Hill, SC
Art/fine arts, dance, music, theater arts/drama. Contact Mr. James Black, Dean of Enrollment Management, 701 Oakland Avenue, Rock Hill, SC 29733, 803-323-2191.

Wisconsin Lutheran College
Milwaukee, WI
Music. Contact Mr. Joel Mischke, Director of Admissions, 8800 West Bluemound Road, Milwaukee, WI 53226-4699, 414-774-8620 Ext. 12.

Wittenberg University
Springfield, OH
Art/fine arts, music, theater arts/drama. Contact Mr. Kenneth G. Benne, Dean of Admissions, PO Box 720, Springfield, OH 45501-0720, 513-327-6314.

Woodbury University
Burbank, CA
Art/fine arts. Contact Mr. Pat Contrades, Director of Admission, 7500 Glenoaks Boulevard, Burbank, CA 91510-7846, 818-767-0888.

Worcester Polytechnic Institute
Worcester, MA
Music. Contact Mr. Robert G. Voss, Executive Director of Admissions and Financial Aid, 100 Institute Road, Worcester, MA 01609-2247, 508-831-5286.

Wright State University
Dayton, OH
Art/fine arts, dance, music, theater arts/drama. Contact Mr. Ken Davenport, Director of Undergraduate Admissions, Colonel Glenn Highway, Dayton, OH 45435, 513-873-2211.

X

Xavier University
Cincinnati, OH
Art/fine arts, music. Contact Director of Admissions, 3800 Victory Parkway, Cincinnati, OH 45207-5311, 513-745-3301.

Xavier University of Louisiana
New Orleans, LA
Art/fine arts, music. Contact Mr. Winston D. Brown, Dean of Admissions, 7325 Palmetto Street, New Orleans, LA 70125, 504-483-7388.

Y

Yale University
New Haven, CT
Art/fine arts, music, theater arts/drama. Contact Mr. Richard H. Shaw Jr., Dean of Undergraduate Admissions and Financial Aid, PO Box 208234, New Haven, CT 06520, 203-432-9316.

Yeshiva University
New York, NY
Music, theater arts/drama. Contact Mr. Michael Kranzler, Associate Director of Admissions, 500 West 185th Street, New York, NY 10033-3201, 212-960-5400 Ext. 277.

York College
York, NE
Art/fine arts, music. Contact Mr. Steddon Sikes, Admissions Director, 912 Kiplinger Avenue, York, NE 68467-2699, 402-363-5628.

York College of Pennsylvania
York, PA
Art/fine arts, music, theater arts/drama. Contact Mrs. Nancy L. Spataro, Director of Admissions, York, PA 17405-7199, 717-846-7788.

York College of the City University of New York
Jamaica, NY
Art/fine arts, music, theater arts/drama. Contact Ms. Sally Nelson, Director of Admissions, 94-20 Guy R Brewer Boulevard, Jamaica, NY 11451-0001, 718-262-2165.

Youngstown State University
Youngstown, OH
Art/fine arts, music, theater arts/drama. Contact Dr. Harold Yiannaki, Director of Admissions, 410 Wick Avenue, Youngstown, OH 44555-0002, 216-742-3150.

Canada

Acadia University
Wolfville, NS
Art/fine arts, music, theater arts/drama. Contact Mr. Robert Stead, Director of Admissions and Student Aid, Wolfville, NS B0P 1X0, 902-542-2201 Ext. 536.

Athabasca University
Athabasca, AB
Art/fine arts. Contact Mr. R. Alex Reed, Registrar, Box 10000, Athabasca, AB T0G 2R0, 403-675-6168.

Bethany Bible College
Sussex, NB
Music. Contact Rev. Dana Lamos, Director of Enrollment Services, 26 Western Street, Sussex, NB E0E 1P0, 506-432-4402.

Bishop's University
Lennoxville, PQ
Art/fine arts, music, theater arts/drama. Contact Mrs. Jane Wilson, Director of Admissions, Lennoxville, PQ J1M 1Z7, 819-822-9680.

Brandon University
Brandon, MB
Music. Contact Ms. Faye Douglas, Director of Admissions, 270 18th Street, Brandon, MB R7A 6A9, 204-727-7352.

Briercrest Bible College
Caronport, SK
Music. Contact Mr. Michael Penner, Director of Enrollment Management, 510 College Drive, Caronport, SK S0H 0S0, 306-756-3200 Ext. 309.

Brock University
St. Catharines, ON
Art/fine arts, music, theater arts/drama. Contact Mr. Keith Rae, Associate Registrar/Admissions, St. Catharines, ON L2S 3A1, 905-688-5550 Ext. 3566.

Canadian Bible College
Regina, SK
Music. Contact Mrs. Pat Webb, Head of Division of Enrollment Management, 4400 Fourth Avenue, Regina, SK S4T 0H8, 306-545-1515 Ext. 272.

Carleton University
Ottawa, ON
Music, theater arts/drama. Contact Mr. Victor Chapman, Director of Admissions and Academic Records, 1125 Colonel By Drive, Ottawa, ON K1S 5B6, 613-788-3663.

Concord College
Winnipeg, MB
Music. Contact Mrs. Morna C. Christian, Director of Admissions and Student Records, 169 Riverton Avenue, Winnipeg, MB R2L 2E5, 204-669-6583 Ext. 234.

Concordia University
Montreal, PQ
Art/fine arts, dance, music, theater arts/drama. Contact Mr. T. Swift, Director of Admissions, 1455 de Maisonneuve Boulevard West, Montreal, PQ H3G 1M8, 514-848-2658.

Dalhousie University
Halifax, NS
Music, theater arts/drama. Contact Ms. Elizabeth Yeo, Associate Registrar/Admissions, Halifax, NS B3H 3J5, 902-494-2450.

Emmanuel Bible College
Kitchener, ON
Music. Contact Mrs. Chureb Kowtecky, Admissions Officer, 100 Fergus Avenue, Kitchener, ON N2A 2H2, 519-894-8900 Ext. 27.

The King's University College
Edmonton, AB
Music. Contact Mr. Tom Dolhanty, Registrar/Director of Admissions, 9125-50 Street, Edmonton, AB T6B 2H3, 403-465-3500.

Lakehead University
Thunder Bay, ON
Art/fine arts, music. Contact Ms. Sarena Knapik, Assistant Registrar, Thunder Bay, ON P7B 5E1, 807-343-8500.

Laurentian University
Sudbury, ON
Music, theater arts/drama. Contact Mr. Steve Junkin, Assistant Registrar, Ramsey Lake Road, Sudbury, ON P3E 2C6, 705-675-1151 Ext. 3915.

McGill University
Montreal, PQ
Music. Contact Mrs. Mariela Johansen, Director of Admissions Office, 845 Sherbrooke Street West, Montreal, PQ H3A 2T5, 514-398-3910.

McMaster University
Hamilton, ON
Art/fine arts, music, theater arts/drama. Contact Ms. Ann McLaughlin, Associate Registrar, Admissions and Liaison, 1280 Main Street West, Hamilton, ON L8S 4L8, 905-525-4600.

Memorial University of Newfoundland
St. John's, NF
Art/fine arts, music, theater arts/drama. Contact Mr. I. Joseph Byrne, Admissions Manager, Elizabeth Avenue, St. John's, NF A1C 5S7, 709-737-3200.

Mount Allison University
Sackville, NB
Art/fine arts, music, theater arts/drama. Contact Mr. J. Hollett, Director of Admissions and Academic Awards, Sackville, NB E0A 3C0, 506-364-2270.

Mount Saint Vincent University
Halifax, NS
Art/fine arts. Contact Ms. Susan Tanner, Assistant Registrar, Halifax, NS B3M 2J6, 902-457-6128.

North American Baptist College and Edmonton Baptist Seminary
Edmonton, AB
Music. Contact Mr. Greg Charyna, Director of Admissions, 11525 Twenty-third Avenue, Edmonton, AB T6J 4T3, 403-437-1960.

Nova Scotia College of Art and Design
Halifax, NS
Art/fine arts. Contact Mrs. Jane Harmon, Director of Student Affairs and Admissions, 5163 Duke Street, Halifax, NS B3J 3J6, 902-422-7381 Ext. 188.

Ontario Bible College
North York, ON
Music. Contact Rev. Stephen Thomson, Registrar and Director of Admissions, 25 Ballyconnor Court, North York, ON M2M 4B3, 416-226-6380 Ext. 2150.

Providence College and Theological Seminary
Otterburne, MB
Music. Contact Mr. Dewey Thiele, Director of Enrollment Management, Otterburne, MB R0A 1G0, 204-433-7488.

Queen's University at Kingston
Kingston, ON
Art/fine arts, music, theater arts/drama. Contact Mrs. Shelagh McDonald, Assistant Registrar for Admissions, Victoria School Building, 110 Alfred Street, Kingston, ON K7L 3N6, 613-545-2218.

Redeemer College
Ancaster, ON
Art/fine arts, music, theater arts/drama. Contact Ms. Marian Ryks-Szelekovszky, Registrar, 777 Highway 53 East, Ancaster, ON L9K 1J4, 905-648-2131 Ext. 224.

Rocky Mountain College
Calgary, AB
Music. Contact, Calgary, AB T2L 1L1, 403-284-5100.

Ryerson Polytechnic University
Toronto, ON
Art/fine arts, dance, theater arts/drama. Contact Mr. Gene Logel, Program Director of Admissions and Liaison Services, 350 Victoria Street, Toronto, ON M5B 2K3, 416-979-5028.

St. Francis Xavier University
Antigonish, NS
Music. Contact Ms. Rose Ann Richards, Director of Admissions, Box 5000, Antigonish, NS B2G 2W5, 902-867-2219.

Simon Fraser University
Burnaby, BC
Art/fine arts, dance, music, theater arts/drama. Contact Mr. Nick Heath, Director of Admissions, Burnaby, BC V5A 1S6, 604-291-3224.

Trent University
Peterborough, ON
Art/fine arts. Contact Mr. P. Alan Saxby, Registrar, Office of the Registrar, Peterborough, ON K9J 7B8, 705-748-1215.

Trinity Western University
Langley, BC
Art/fine arts, music, theater arts/drama. Contact Mr. Kirk Kauffeldt, Director of Admissions, 7600 Glover Road, Langley, BC V3A 6H4, 604-888-7008 Ext. 2015.

Université de Moncton
Moncton, NB
Art/fine arts, music, theater arts/drama. Contact Mr. Luc Levesque, Director of Admissions, Moncton, NB E1A 3E9, 506-858-4113.

Université de Montréal
Montréal, PQ
Art/fine arts, music. Contact Mr. Fernand Boucher, Director of Admissions, Case Postale 6205, Succursale, Montréal, PQ H3C 3T5, 514-343-7076.

Université de Sherbrooke
Sherbrooke, PQ
Music. Contact Mr. Jacques Carbonneau, Registrar, 2500, Boulevard de l'Université, Sherbrooke, PQ J1K 2R1, 819-821-7685.

Université du Québec à Chicoutimi
Chicoutimi, PQ
Art/fine arts. Contact Mrs. Renee Gagnon, Registrar, 555, boulevard de L'Université, Chicoutimi, PQ G7H 2B1, 418-545-5005.

Université du Québec à Hull
Hull, PQ
Art/fine arts. Contact Mr. Richard Berube, Registraire, Case Postale 1250, Succursale "B", Hull, PQ J8X 3X7, 819-595-3900.

Université du Québec à Montréal
Montreal, PQ
Art/fine arts, dance, music, theater arts/drama. Contact Mr. Ygal Leibu, Registrar, CP 8888, Succursale Centre-ville, Montreal, PQ H3C 3P8, 514-987-7740.

Université du Québec à Trois-Rivières
Trois-Rivières, PQ
Art/fine arts, music. Contact Mr. Michel Côté, Registrar, 3351 boulevard des Forges, Case post 500, Trois-Rivières, PQ G9A 5H7, 819-376-5045.

Université Laval
Sainte-Foy, PQ
Art/fine arts, music, theater arts/drama. Contact Mr. Pierre Allard, Registrar, Cité Universitaire, Sainte-Foy, PQ G1K 7P4, 418-656-3080 Ext. 7170.

University of Alberta
Edmonton, AB
Art/fine arts, dance, music, theater arts/drama. Contact Mr. B. J. Silzer, Registrar/Associate Vice President, 89 Avenue and 114 Street, Edmonton, AB T6G 2M7, 403-492-3111.

University of British Columbia
Vancouver, BC
Art/fine arts, music, theater arts/drama. Contact Dr. Richard Spencer, Registrar, 1874 East Mall, Vancouver, BC V6T 1Z1, 604-822-2844.

University of Calgary
Calgary, AB
Art/fine arts, music, theater arts/drama. Contact Mr. David Hinton, Director of Admissions, Office of Admissions, Calgary, AB T2N 1N4, 403-220-6640.

University of Guelph
Guelph, ON
Art/fine arts, music, theater arts/drama. Contact Ms. Starr Ellis, Assistant Registrar/Admissions, Guelph, ON N1G 2W1, 519-824-4120 Ext. 8714.

University of King's College
Halifax, NS
Theater arts/drama. Contact Dr. Patricia M. Robertson, Registrar, 6350 Coburg Road, Halifax, NS B3H 2A1, 902-422-1271 Ext. 122.

University of Lethbridge
Lethbridge, AB
Art/fine arts, music, theater arts/drama. Contact Mr. Peter Haney, Assistant Registrar/Admissions, 4401 University Drive, Lethbridge, AB T1K 3M4, 403-382-7134.

University of Manitoba
Winnipeg, MB
Art/fine arts, music, theater arts/drama. Contact Mr. D. H. Halstead, Director of Admissions, Winnipeg, MB R3T 2N2, 204-474-8810.

University of New Brunswick
Fredericton, NB
Theater arts/drama. Contact Mr. Michael Shanks, Associate Registrar/Admission and Enrollment, PO Box 4400, Fredericton, NB E3B 5A3, 506-453-4864.

University of Ottawa
Ottawa, ON
Art/fine arts, music, theater arts/drama. Contact Mr. André Pierre Lepage, Director of Admissions, PO Box 450, Station A, Ottawa, ON K1N 6N5, 613-564-3288.

University of Prince Edward Island
Charlottetown, PE
Music. Contact Mr. G. Urbain Gaudin, Assistant Registrar, 550 University Avenue, Charlottetown, PE C1A 4P3, 902-566-0439.

University of Regina
Regina, SK
Art/fine arts, music, theater arts/drama. Contact Ms. Gail Meehan, Registrar, Regina, SK S4S 0A2, 306-585-4743.

University of Saskatchewan
Saskatoon, SK
Art/fine arts, music, theater arts/drama. Contact Dr. K. M. Smith, Registrar, Saskatoon, SK S7N 5A2, 306-966-6723.

University of Toronto
Toronto, ON
Art/fine arts, music, theater arts/drama. Contact Ms. Karel Swift, Associate University Registrar (Admissions and Awards), Toronto, ON M5S 1A1, 416-978-2190.

University of Victoria
Victoria, BC
Art/fine arts, music, theater arts/drama. Contact Mr. Kevin Paul, Director of Admissions, PO Box 1700, Victoria, BC V8W 2Y2, 604-721-8111.

University of Waterloo
Waterloo, ON
Art/fine arts, music, theater arts/drama. Contact Mr. K. A. Lavigne, Associate Registrar/Admissions, Waterloo, ON N2L 3G1, 519-885-1211 Ext. 2265.

The University of Western Ontario
London, ON
Art/fine arts, music, theater arts/drama. Contact Mr. R. J. Tiffin, Director, Office of the Registrar, London, ON N6A 5B8, 519-661-2120.

University of Windsor
Windsor, ON
Art/fine arts, music, theater arts/drama. Contact Mr. Frank L. Smith, Registrar, 401 Sunset Avenue, Windsor, ON N9B 3P4, 519-253-4232 Ext. 3315.

The University of Winnipeg
Winnipeg, MB
Music, theater arts/drama. Contact Ms. Nancy LaTocki, Director of Admissions, 515 Portage Avenue, Winnipeg, MB R3B 2E9, 204-786-9740.

Western Pentecostal Bible College
Abbotsford, BC
Music. Contact Mrs. Laurel Archer, Registrar, Box 1700, Abbotsford, BC V2S 7E7, 604-853-7491.

Wilfrid Laurier University
Waterloo, ON
Art/fine arts, music, theater arts/drama. Contact Mr. B. George Granger, Associate Registrar and Director of Admissions, 75 University Avenue West, Waterloo, ON N2L 3C5, 519-884-1970 Ext. 3351.

York University
North York, ON
Art/fine arts, dance, music, theater arts/drama. Contact Mr. Tom Myers, Director of Admissions, 150 Atkinson Building, North York, ON M3J 1P3, 416-736-5100.

INDEX

INDEX
610

Carol Walker of Purchase College, State University of New York helped with the preparation of the introduction to dance programs, page 199–203.

Essential Guides for Today's College-Bound Student!

Paying Less for College 1996

"One of the best guidebooks around for families who want to compare the financial aid alternatives."
—Smart Money

A one-stop information resource and financial aid adviser featuring in-depth financial aid data and money-saving options at more than 1,600 U.S. four-year colleges and universities. Includes **Financial Aid Planner, IBM-compatible software for estimating college costs and planning family finances.**

ISBN 1-56079-520-4, 696 pp., 81/2 x 11, $26.95 pb, 13th edition

The Ultimate College Survival Guide

Janet Farrar Worthington and Ronald Farrar

". . . easy-to-read, factual, personal . . . tells you everything to expect." —Christina Shuren, Senior, Lawrence High School, Lawrenceville, NJ

Covers everything a college-bound student wants—and needs—to know about college life. It's a "get real" guide to campus life, written in lively, conversational language that hits just the right note with students.

ISBN 1-56079-396-1, 256 pp., 7 x 9, $11.95 pb

USA TODAY Getting into College

A Quick Guide to Everything You Need to Know

Pat Ordovensky

Provides parents and students with a concise overview of the entire selection, application, and admissions process. Includes the most commonly asked questions—and answers—from *USA TODAY*'s annual "Financial Aid and Admissions Hotline."

ISBN 1-56079-463-1, 160 pp., 6 x 9, $8.95 pb

USA TODAY Financial Aid for College

A Quick Guide to Everything You Need to Know, with the New 1996 Forms

Pat Ordovensky

Explains the types of aid available, tells how to qualify for aid, and answers commonly asked questions from *USA TODAY*'s annual "Financial Aid and Admissions Hotline."

ISBN 1-56079-568-9, 160 pp., 6 x 9, $8.95 pb, revised edition

To Order Call:
800-338-3282
or
Fax: 609-243-9150

New on the Internet
Peterson's Education Center
A World of Information and News About College and M
http://www.petersons.com

Peterson's Princeton, NJ